Acclaim for RON CHERNOW's

TITAN

A *New York Times Book Review* Editors' Choice

A *Business Week* Best Business Book of the Year

A *Time* Magazine Book of the Year

An *Economist* Best Biography of the Year

"Splendid . . . a blue chip biography." —*Newsweek*

"Ron Chernow's portrait of Rockefeller, an eccentric on a heroic scale as well as a genius, is convincing. . . . This is the best biography of the man so far." —*The Washington Post Book World*

"What a story! An outstanding business biography." —*The New York Observer*

"A triumph of research, understanding and elegant writing." —*Houston Chronicle*

"With uncanny timing, Ron Chernow has written a captivating biography of one of the most famous men in American business history. . . . Business needs more books like *Titan.* —*Newsday*

"Good biographies are hard to find and great ones even rarer. . . . A thoughtful and balanced approach to one of the most significant and controversial lives of the past century . . . spellbinding." —*The Seattle Times*

"A masterful synthesis of research and writing . . . an extraordinary achievement in biography." —*The New Republic*

"Chernow's detailed picture of this 'implausible blend of sin and sanctity' is a scrupulously balanced, frequently fascinating and humanizing portrait of a figure of seemingly superhuman energy and ambition."   —*People*

"Altogether splendid."   —*American Heritage*

"Sweeping. . . . Chernow lays out the [Rockefeller] conundrum superbly, delineating the forces that shaped this man and the ways he responded to them."   —*USA Today*

"[Ron Chernow is] America's best business biographer."   —*Fortune*

"Ron Chernow's splendid biography of John D. Rockefeller Sr. will stand out as one of the best books of the year. He again proves himself remarkably facile with a huge amount of information. . . . I'd be hard pressed to find a page that isn't interesting. . . . Chernow succeeds brilliantly."   —*Detroit Free Press*

"Powerful, meticulously researched. . . . Chernow encompasses better than any writer before him the powerful contradictions and polarities in Rockefeller's character. *Titan* . . . is one of the richest and most rewarding biographies of an American magnate."
                                        —*St. Petersburg Times*

"[No biographer] has been as skilled, or as exhaustive, as Ron Chernow."   —*The Philadelphia Inquirer*

RON CHERNOW

TITAN

Ron Chernow's first book, *The House of Morgan*, won the National Book Award, the Ambassador Award for the year's best study of American culture, and was named one of the 100 best nonfiction books of the century by the Modern Library. His second book, *The Warburgs*, won the Eccles Prize as the Best Business Book of 1993 and was also selected by the American Library Association as one of that year's best nonfiction books. In reviewing his recent collection of essays, *The Death of the Banker*, *The New York Times* called the author "as elegant an architect of monumental histories as we've seen in decades" and chose the paperback original as one of the year's Notable Books.

TITAN

TITAN

THE LIFE OF
John D. Rockefeller, Sr.

RON CHERNOW

VINTAGE BOOKS

A DIVISION OF RANDOM HOUSE, INC.

NEW YORK

FIRST VINTAGE BOOKS EDITION, SEPTEMBER 1999

The Library of Congress has cataloged the Random House edition as follows:
Chernow, Ron.
Titan : the life of John D. Rockefeller, Sr. / Ron Chernow.
p. cm.
Includes bibliographical references and index.
ISBN 0-679-43808-4
1. Rockefeller, John D. (John Davison), 1839–1937.   2. Capitalists and
financiers—United States—Biography.   3. Industrialists—United States—
Biography.   4. Philanthropists—United States—Biography.
I.   Title.
CT275.R75C47   1997   338.7'622382'092—dc21
[B]   97-33117

Vintage ISBN: 0-679-75703-1

Author photograph © Bill Zules
Book design by J. K. Lambert

www.vintagebooks.com

To my brother, Dr. Bart Chernow,

who pulled me back, at the last moment, from the brink,

and to the lovely Valerie

CONTENTS

TITAN

*The earliest known photographs of William Avery
and Eliza Davison Rockefeller.*
(Courtesy of the Rockefeller Archive Center)

CHAPTER 1

The Flimflam Man

I n the early 1900s, as Rockefeller vied with Andrew Carnegie for the title of the world's richest man, a spirited rivalry arose between France and Germany, with each claiming to be Rockefeller's ancestral land. Assorted genealogists stood ready, for a sizable fee, to manufacture a splendid royal lineage for the oilman. "I have no desire to trace myself back to the nobility," he said honestly. "I am satisfied with my good old American stock."[1] The most ambitious search for Rockefeller's roots traced them back to a ninth-century French family, the Roquefeuilles, who supposedly inhabited a Languedoc château—a charming story that unfortunately has been refuted by recent findings. In contrast, the Rockefellers' German lineage has been clearly established in the Rhine valley dating back to at least the early 1600s.

Around 1723, Johann Peter Rockefeller, a miller, gathered up his wife and five children, set sail for Philadelphia, and settled on a farm in Somerville and then Amwell, New Jersey, where he evidently flourished and acquired large landholdings. More than a decade later, his cousin Diell Rockefeller left southwest Germany and moved to Germantown, New York. Diell's granddaughter Christina married her distant relative William, one of Johann's grandsons. (Never particularly sentimental about his European forebears, John D. Rockefeller did erect a monument to the patriarch, Johann Peter, at his burial site in Flemington, New Jersey.) The marriage of William and Christina produced a son named Godfrey Rockefeller, who was the grandfather of the oil titan and a most unlikely progenitor of the clan. In 1806,

Godfrey married Lucy Avery in Great Barrington, Massachusetts, despite the grave qualms of her family.

Establishing a pattern that would be replicated by Rockefeller's own mother, Lucy had, in her family's disparaging view, married down. Her ancestors had emigrated from Devon, England, to Salem, Massachusetts, around 1630, forming part of the Puritan tide. As they became settled and gentrified, the versatile Averys spawned ministers, soldiers, civic leaders, explorers, and traders, not to mention a bold clutch of Indian fighters. During the American Revolution, eleven Averys perished gloriously in the battle of Groton. While the Rockefellers' "noble" roots required some poetic license and liberal embellishment, Lucy could justly claim descent from Edmund Ironside, the English king, who was crowned in 1016.

Godfrey Rockefeller was sadly mismatched with his enterprising wife. He had a stunted, impoverished look and a hangdog air of perpetual defeat. Taller than her husband, a fiery Baptist of commanding presence, Lucy was rawboned and confident, with a vigorous step and alert blue eyes. A former schoolteacher, she was better educated than Godfrey. Even John D., never given to invidious comments about relatives, tactfully conceded, "My grandmother was a brave woman. Her husband was not so brave as she."[2] If Godfrey contributed the Rockefeller coloring—bluish gray eyes, light brown hair—Lucy introduced the rangy frame later notable among the men. Enjoying robust energy and buoyant health, Lucy had ten children, with the third, William Avery Rockefeller, born in Granger, New York, in 1810. While it is easy enough to date the birth of Rockefeller's father, teams of frazzled reporters would one day exhaust themselves trying to establish the date of his death.

As a farmer and businessman, Godfrey enjoyed checkered success, and his aborted business ventures exposed his family to an insecure, peripatetic life. They were forced to move to Granger and Ancram, New York, then to Great Barrington, before doubling back to Livingston, New York. John D. Rockefeller's upbringing would be fertile with cautionary figures of weak men gone astray. Godfrey must have been invoked frequently as a model to be avoided. By all accounts, Grandpa was a jovial, good-natured man but feckless and addicted to drink, producing in Lucy an everlasting hatred of liquor that she must have drummed into her grandson. Grandpa Godfrey was the first to establish in John D.'s mind an enduring equation between bonhomie and lax character, making the latter prefer the society of sober, tight-lipped men in full command of their emotions.

The Rockefeller records offer various scenarios of why Godfrey and Lucy packed their belongings into an overloaded Conestoga wagon and headed west between 1832 and 1834. By one account, the Rockefellers, along with several neighbors, were dispossessed of their land in a heated title dispute with some English investors. Another account has an unscrupulous businessman gulling

This seems an auspicious time to resurrect Rockefeller's ghost. With the fall of trade barriers and the vogue for free-market economics, the world is now united by a global marketplace that touches five billion souls, with many countries just emerging from Marxist or mercantilist systems and having their first taste of capitalism. The story of John D. Rockefeller transports us back to a time when industrial capitalism was raw and new in America, and the rules of the game were unwritten. More than anyone else, Rockefeller incarnated the capitalist revolution that followed the Civil War and transformed American life. He embodied all its virtues of thrift, self-reliance, hard work, and unflagging enterprise. Yet as someone who flouted government and rode roughshod over competitors, he also personified many of its most egregious vices. As a result, his career became the focal point for a debate about the proper role of government in the economy that has lasted until the present day.

they brought me the transcript of an interview privately conducted with Rockefeller between 1917 and 1920. It was done by William O. Inglis, a New York newspaperman who questioned Rockefeller for an authorized biography that was never published. As I pored over this seventeen-hundred-page verbatim transcript, I was astonished: Rockefeller, stereotyped as taciturn and empty, turned out to be analytic, articulate, even fiery; he was also quite funny, with a dry midwestern wit. This wasn't someone I had encountered in any biography. When I returned home, I told Ann Godoff, my editor at Random House, that I was now eager to do the book.

To delve into the voluminous Rockefeller papers is to excavate a lost continent. Yet even with such massive documentation, I had the frustrating sense, early in my research, that I was confronting a sphinx. Rockefeller trained himself to reveal as little as possible, even in private letters, which he wrote as if they might someday fall into the hands of a prosecuting attorney. With his instinctive secrecy, he excelled at employing strange euphemisms and elliptical phrasing. For this reason, the twenty thousand pages of letters that Rockefeller received from his more outspoken business associates proved a windfall of historic proportions. Written as early as 1877, seven years after Standard Oil's formation, they provide a vivid portrait of the company's byzantine dealings with oil producers, refiners, transporters, and marketers, as well as railroad chieftains, bank directors, and political bosses. This panorama of greed and guile should startle even the most jaundiced students of the Gilded Age. I was also extremely fortunate to have access to the papers of five distinguished predecessors, all of whom left behind complete research files. I combed through the abundant papers of Ida Tarbell at the Drake Well Museum in Titusville, Pennsylvania, Henry Demarest Lloyd at the State Historical Society of Wisconsin, and Allan Nevins at Columbia University, in addition to those of William O. Inglis and Raymond B. Fosdick (the author of the official biography of John D. Rockefeller, Jr.) at the Rockefeller Archive Center. These collections contain a vast number of contemporary interviews and other materials that were only partly used by their authors.

Like many moguls of the Gilded Age, Rockefeller was either glorified by partisan biographers, who could see no wrong, or vilified by vitriolic critics, who could see no right. This one-sidedness has been especially harmful in the case of Rockefeller, who was such an implausible blend of sin and sanctity. I have tried to operate in the large space between polemics and apologetics, motivated by the belief that Rockefeller's life was of a piece and that the pious, Bible-thumping Rockefeller wasn't simply a cunning façade for the corporate pirate. The religious and acquisitive sides of his nature were intimately related. For this reason, I have stressed his evangelical Baptism as the passkey that unlocks many mysteries of his life. Those who would like to see Rockefeller either demonized or canonized in these pages will be disappointed.

count of our foremost nineteenth-century industrialist that explores his inner and outer worlds and synthesizes them into a fully rounded portrait.

For all the ink provoked by Rockefeller, his biographies have been marred by a numbing repetition. Whatever their political slant, they have, on the whole, followed the same chronology, raked over the same disputes about his business methods, rehashed the same stale anecdotes. One has the impression of sitting through the same play over and over again, albeit from slightly different seats in the theater. Some of this derives from our shifting conception of biography. With the exception of *John D.*, a slender volume by David Freeman Hawke published in 1980, the Rockefeller biographies were all published before mid-century and betray a Victorian reticence about private matters. Whatever their merits as business reportage, they betray minimal post-Freudian curiosity. They touch only glancingly, for instance, on the story of Rockefeller's father, a bigamist and snake-oil salesman, who so indelibly shaped his son's life. Even the exhaustive Nevins showed scant interest in Rockefeller's marriage or his three daughters. The feminist concerns of our own day have recently produced two books—Bernice Kert's *Abby Aldrich Rockefeller* and Clarice Stasz's *The Rockefeller Women*—that have begun to pry open this hermetically sealed family world. Rockefeller's social life beyond the office—his friendships, hobbies, sports, et cetera—has suffered from equally conspicuous neglect. Other matters that warrant investigation include Rockefeller's political views and theory of trusts, his attitude toward public relations, his stewardship of his investments beyond Standard Oil, his transfer of money to his children and his dynastic ambitions, his persistent fascination with medicine, and the imprint he left upon the many philanthropies he endowed. There has also been a remarkable lack of curiosity about the forty-odd years that he spent in retirement, with some biographers omitting those decades altogether. Yet it was during those decades that John D. Rockefeller, Jr., both perpetuated and radically modified his father's legacy, a subject to which I devote considerable attention.

When Random House proposed that I write the first full-length biography of Rockefeller since Allan Nevins's in the 1950s, I frankly balked, convinced that the subject had been exhausted by writers too eager to capitalize on his fame. How could one write about a man who made such a fetish of secrecy? In the existing literature, he came across as a gifted automaton at best, a malevolent machine at worst. I couldn't tell whether he was a hollow man, deadened by the pursuit of money, or someone of great depth and force but with eerie self-control. If the former was true, I would respectfully decline; in the unlikely case that the latter proved true—well, then I was intrigued.

To settle the matter, I spent a day at the Rockefeller Archive Center in Sleepy Hollow, New York, the repository of millions of family documents. When I told the curators of my misgivings and explained that I couldn't write about Rockefeller unless I heard his inner voice—the "music of his mind," as I phrased it—

FOREWORD

The life of John Davison Rockefeller, Sr., was marked to an exceptional degree by silence, mystery, and evasion. Even though he presided over the largest business and philanthropic enterprises of his day, he has remained an elusive figure. A master of disguises, he spent his life camouflaged behind multiple personae and shrouded beneath layers of mythology. Hence, he lingers in our national psyche as a series of disconnected images, ranging from the rapacious creator of Standard Oil, brilliant but bloodless, to the wizened old codger dispensing dimes and canned speeches for newsreel cameras. It is often hard to piece together the varied images into a coherent picture.

This has not been for lack of trying. Earlier in the century, Rockefeller inspired more prose than any other private citizen in America, with books about him tumbling forth at a rate of nearly one per year. As he was the most famous American of his day, his statements and actions were reported and analyzed minutely in the press. Yet even in his heyday of popular interest, he could seem maddeningly opaque, with much of his life unfolding behind the walls of his estates and the frosted-glass doors of his office.

Rockefeller often seems to be missing from his own biographies, flitting through them like a ghostly, disembodied figure. For the principal muckrakers, such as Henry Demarest Lloyd and Ida Tarbell, he served as shorthand for the Standard Oil trust, his personality submerged in its machinations. Even in the two-volume biography by Allan Nevins, who strove to vindicate Rockefeller's reputation, Rockefeller vanishes for pages at a time amid a swirl of charges and countercharges. The attention paid to the depredations of Standard Oil has tended to overshadow everything else about Rockefeller's life. H. G. Wells defended this biographical approach: "The life history of Rockefeller is the history of the trust; he made it, and equally it made him . . . so that apart from its story it seems hardly necessary to detail his personal life in chronological order."[1] So steadfastly have biographers clung to this dated view that we still lack an ac-

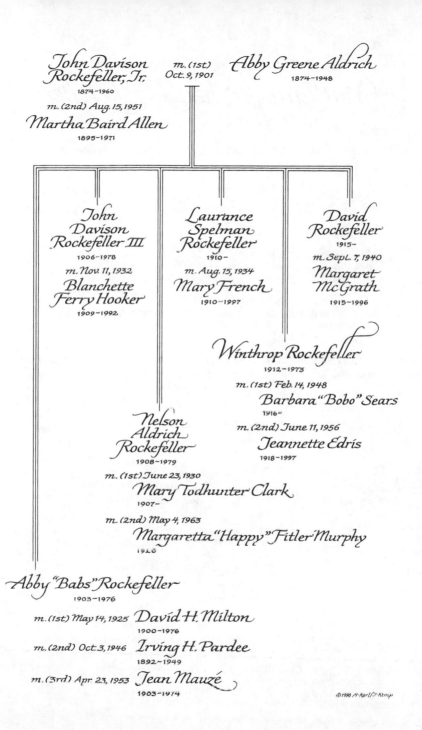

John Davison Rockefeller, Jr.
1874–1960

m. (1st) Oct. 9, 1901

Abby Greene Aldrich
1874–1948

m. (2nd) Aug. 15, 1951
Martha Baird Allen
1895–1971

John Davison Rockefeller III
1906–1978
m. Nov. 11, 1932
Blanchette Ferry Hooker
1909–1992

Laurance Spelman Rockefeller
1910–
m. Aug. 15, 1934
Mary French
1910–1997

David Rockefeller
1915–
m. Sept. 7, 1940
Margaret McGrath
1915–1996

Winthrop Rockefeller
1912–1973
m. (1st) Feb. 14, 1948
Barbara "Bobo" Sears
1916–
m. (2nd) June 11, 1956
Jeannette Edris
1918–1997

Nelson Aldrich Rockefeller
1908–1979
m. (1st) June 23, 1930
Mary Todhunter Clark
1907–
m. (2nd) May 4, 1963
Margaretta "Happy" Fitler Murphy
1926

Abby "Babs" Rockefeller
1903–1976
m. (1st) May 14, 1925 David H. Milton
1900–1976
m. (2nd) Oct. 3, 1946 Irving H. Pardee
1892–1949
m. (3rd) Apr. 23, 1953 Jean Mauzé
1903–1974

©1998 A. Karl/J. Kemp

DESCENDANTS OF
William & Eliza Rockefeller

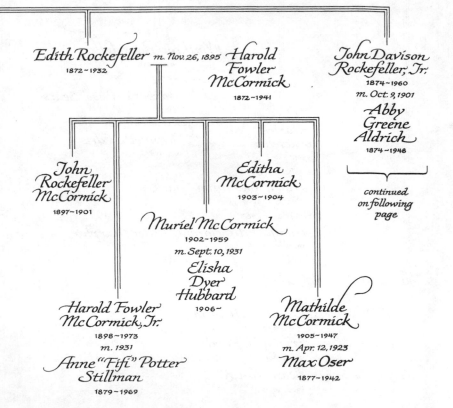

Mary Ann Rockefeller
1843–1925
m. Oct. 17, 1872
William Cullen Rudd
1845–1915

Franklin Rockefeller
1845–1917
m. Oct. 12, 1870
Helen Elizabeth Scofield
1848–1932

Francis Rockefeller
1845–1847

Edith Rockefeller m. Nov. 26, 1895 **Harold Fowler McCormick**
1872–1932
1872–1941

John Davison Rockefeller, Jr.
1874–1960
m. Oct. 9, 1901
Abby Greene Aldrich
1874–1948

continued
on following
page

John Rockefeller McCormick
1897–1901

Editha McCormick
1903–1904

Muriel McCormick
1902–1959
m. Sept. 10, 1931
Elisha Dyer Hubbard
1906–

Harold Fowler McCormick, Jr.
1898–1973
m. 1931
Anne "Fifi" Potter Stillman
1879–1969

Mathilde McCormick
1905–1947
m. Apr. 12, 1923
Max Oser
1877–1942

Two men have been supreme in creating the modern world: Rockefeller and Bismarck. One in economics, the other in politics, refuted the liberal dream of universal happiness through individual competition, substituting monopoly and the corporate state, or at least movements toward them.

—BERTRAND RUSSELL
Freedom Versus Organization, 1814 to 1914

Something in the nature of J. D. Rockefeller had to occur in America, and it is all to the good of the world that he was tight-lipped, consistent and amazingly free from vulgar vanity, sensuality and quarrelsomeness. His cold persistence and ruthlessness may arouse something like horror, but for all that he was a forward-moving force, a constructive power.

—H. G. WELLS
The Work, Wealth and Happiness of Mankind

When history passes its final verdict on John D. Rockefeller, it may well be that his endowment of research will be recognized as a milestone in the progress of the race. . . . Science today owes as much to the rich men of generosity and discernment as the art of the Renaissance owes to the patronage of Popes and Princes. Of these rich men, John D. Rockefeller is the supreme type.

—WINSTON CHURCHILL
St. Louis Post-Dispatch, July 8, 1936

Rockefeller, you know, is reputed the richest man in the world, and he certainly is the most powerfully suggestive personality I have ever seen. A man 10 stories deep, and to me quite unfathomable. Physionomie de Pierrot (not a spear of hair on head or face) flexible, cunning, quakerish, superficially suggestive of naught but goodness and conscientiousness, yet accused of being the greatest villain in business whom our country has produced.

—WILLIAM JAMES in a letter to Henry James
January 29, 1904

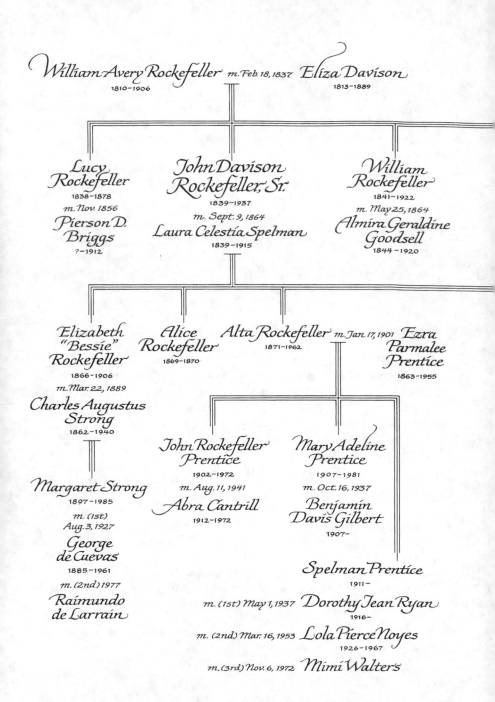

William Avery Rockefeller m. Feb. 18, 1837 Eliza Davison
1810–1906   1813–1889

Lucy
Rockefeller
1838–1878
m. Nov. 1856
Pierson D.
Briggs
?–1912

John Davison
Rockefeller, Sr.
1839–1937
m. Sept. 9, 1864
Laura Celestia Spelman
1839–1915

William
Rockefeller
1841–1922
m. May 25, 1864
Almira Geraldine
Goodsell
1844–1920

Elizabeth
"Bessie"
Rockefeller
1866–1906
m. Mar. 22, 1889
Charles Augustus
Strong
1862–1940

Alice
Rockefeller
1869–1870

Alta Rockefeller m. Jan. 17, 1901 Ezra
1871–1962   Parmalee
                                                  Prentice
                                                  1863–1955

Margaret Strong
1897–1985
m. (1st)
Aug. 3, 1927
George
de Cuevas
1885–1961
m. (2nd) 1977
Raimundo
de Larrain

John Rockefeller
Prentice
1902–1972
m. Aug. 11, 1941
Abra Cantrill
1912–1972

Mary Adeline
Prentice
1907–1981
m. Oct. 16, 1937
Benjamin
Davis Gilbert
1907–

Spelman Prentice
1911–

m. (1st) May 1, 1937 Dorothy Jean Ryan
1916–

m. (2nd) Mar. 16, 1953 Lola Pierce Noyes
1926–1967

m. (3rd) Nov. 6, 1972 Mimi Walters

PRELUDE:
POISON TONGUE

"Reading this book brings back to my mind facts and situations that I had forgotten for years," John D. Rockefeller mused. "It digs up things long past and dead, so that they stand before me once more alive. I am glad of it, very glad of it."[1]

For months, Rockefeller had listened to his authorized biographer read aloud from Henry Demarest Lloyd's *Wealth Against Commonwealth*, a savage account of his career published in 1894. Now retired and in his late seventies, the world's richest man had reluctantly agreed to reminisce behind closed doors. Starting in 1917, for an hour each morning, Rockefeller fielded questions while slumped in an easy chair or reclining on a lounge in his bedroom at Kykuit, a Georgian mansion set amid the woodland beauty of Westchester County's Pocantico Hills. Serene in his conscience, convinced that God had blessed his career and that the court of history would acquit him, Rockefeller had submitted to this exercise only to please his son, who wanted to cleanse the family name of all controversy. As Rockefeller reminded his appointed Boswell, the affable William O. Inglis, a newspaperman recruited from Rockefeller's old nemesis, the *World*, but "for the urgent request of my son, who is not familiar with this history . . . I would never have taken the time and the trouble to make any refutation to these questions."[2]

Despite his initial hesitation, Rockefeller couldn't resist the invitation to relive his turbulent early years in the petroleum industry, and he warmed to the giant task of remembrance. During hundreds of hours of interviews, spanning a three-year period, he revisited the past and spoke his mind freely. At times, he evoked his life in the dulcet tones of a preacher addressing a brotherhood of kindred souls. At other moments, he was dryly sardonic or brutally funny about his critics—though all the while, as a good Christian, he tried to suppress vengeful feelings toward them.

Before Inglis's wondering eyes, the old man was rejuvenated by the flood tide of memory, and his voice deepened from the high, breathy pitch of age to the mellow baritone of early adulthood. His step grew springy and lithe as he paced the floor, recounting the glorious struggles of his career. Far from dodging controversy, Rockefeller suggested a novel structure for this retrospective talk: Inglis would read passages from Rockefeller's two chief antagonists, Henry Lloyd and Ida Tarbell (whose influential broadside had been published in the early 1900s), and Rockefeller would refute them, paragraph by paragraph. Having dismissed their indictments as beneath his dignity, he hadn't deigned to read them when they first appeared. Now, in a measure of his feisty self-confidence, he decided to tackle the toughest charges point-blank. "I was averse for eight months to say anything in response to these foolish writers," he noted, "but now that I've gotten into it I find it interesting."[3] And once John D. Rockefeller, Sr., set his mind to something, he brought awesome powers of concentration to bear.

As Rockefeller undertook this extended defense, he clearly believed that he had been vindicated in the time since these journalists had blackened his reputation in the early 1900s and made him America's most hated businessman. "All of those in the business today are doing business along the modern lines, following the plans which we were the first to propose," he said with pride.[4] Public bitterness toward him had waned, he believed, and opposition to his petroleum empire was "practically nil and has been for many years, and it has ceased to be popular to raid the Standard Oil Company."[5] Indeed, the American public during World War I appreciated the industrial strength conferred by the Standard Oil companies, and Rockefeller imagined, with some justice, that his compatriots now viewed him as a public benefactor, not as a corporate buccaneer. The huge philanthropies he had endowed in recent years had also mitigated public animosity toward him.

As always with Rockefeller, the pregnant silences in the interview spoke as eloquently as the words. Coached by his publicist, Ivy Lee, Rockefeller eschewed such loaded terms as *trust, monopoly, oligopoly,* or *cartel* when referring to Standard Oil and preferred to speak of "cooperation." He expressed scorn for the textbook world of free markets evoked by Adam Smith: "What a blessing it was that the idea of cooperation, with railroads, with telegraph lines, with steel companies, with oil companies, came in and prevailed, to take the place of this chaotic condition in which the virtuous academic Know-Nothings about business were doing what they construed to be God's service in eating each other up."[6] During the three-year interview, Rockefeller never once alluded to his most stinging setback: the federal government's 1911 dismemberment of Standard Oil into dozens of constituent companies. Annulling the Supreme Court verdict by a trick of memory, Rockefeller talked of Standard Oil as if the old monolith still stood unscathed.

Of all the poses he assumed, perhaps the hardest to maintain was that he bore no grudges against his detractors. He peppered his talk with references to his forgiving nature. "The representatives of the Standard Oil Company cherish most kindly and brotherly feelings even toward those who abused them most, and are ready to lay it to their weakness and ignorance and whatever else was controlling them."[7] Furthermore: "And to those who have uttered against them harsh words, we cherish no resentment. 'To err is human, to forgive divine.' "[8] And, even more conciliatory: "And I rejoice also that we are charitable and sweet-spirited to these jealous, small men who made it the business of their lives to try to pull us down because their vision did not extend beyond the ends of their noses."

Over time, however, the sacerdotal tone began to falter. Rockefeller couldn't conceive of a genuinely principled objection to his career and increasingly resorted to ad hominem attacks, deriding his critics as croakers, howlers, grumblers, complainers, blackmailers, pirates, spoiled children, whiners, adventurers, wolves, and freebooters. Clearly, the allegations rankled, especially those of Ida Minerva Tarbell, whose cool, clear-eyed investigative prose had turned his name into a byword for corporate greed. With golf cronies, Rockefeller had poked fun at her, calling her "Miss Tarbarrel," but this was a transparent attempt to draw the sting from her words.

During the marathon interview, Inglis saw Rockefeller's iron poise and self-mastery crumble only twice and both times, significantly, in responding to Tarbell. The first time came when he read aloud her charge that in 1872 the thirty-two-year-old Rockefeller had taken over the Cleveland refineries by threatening to crush rivals who refused to join his cartel. Now, 1872 had been the starting point of his relentless march toward supremacy in oil. If that year was tainted, then everything was. Inglis recorded a graphic account of Rockefeller's reaction to Tarbell's allegation:

> "That is absolutely false!" exclaimed Mr. Rockefeller so loudly that I looked up from the notes. As he spoke he jumped up from the big chair in which he was reclining and walked over to my table. His face was flushed and his eyes were burning. It was the first time I had ever seen him show any but pleasant feeling, and there could be no doubt that he was aflame with anger and resentment. His voice rang out loud and clear. He did not beat the desk with his fist, but stood there with his hands clenched, controlling himself with evident effort. He could not immediately regain his balance. "This is absolutely false!" he cried, "and no man was told that by me or by any of our representatives. You may put that down once and for all. That statement is an absolute lie!"[9]

After this outburst, Rockefeller's emotions subsided, but the insinuation stung. Later, he and Inglis roamed over the hills and golf fairways of his vast estate; "How ridiculous all that talk is!" he exclaimed, "It's twaddle, poisonous twaddle, put out for a purpose. As a matter of fact, we were all in a sinking ship, if existing cut-throat competition continued, and we were trying to build a lifeboat to carry us all to the shore. You don't have to threaten men to get them to leave a sinking ship in a lifeboat."[10] The purchase of his competitors' firms had not been the benevolent act that Rockefeller suggested, but he had a powerfully selective memory.

Rockefeller reserved his most bitter epithets for another passage, where Tarbell dealt with the touchiest matter in his personal life: the character of his colorful, raffish father, William Avery Rockefeller. In July 1905, she had capped off her serial history of Standard Oil with a two-part "Character Study" of Rockefeller filled with venomous portrayals of his father, an itinerant peddler of patent medicines who had led a shadowy, vagabond life. William Avery Rockefeller had been the sort of fast-talking huckster who thrived in frontier communities of early-nineteenth-century America, and Tarbell amply reported his misdemeanors. At one point in her blistering portrait, she said, "Indeed he had all the vices save one—he never drank."[11]

This thrust against his dead father probed some buried pain, some still-festering wound inside Rockefeller, and he suddenly erupted with explosive fury. "What a wretched utterance from one calling herself a historian," he jeered, speculating, quite incorrectly, that Tarbell had been embittered by the failure of her series to dent the Standard Oil empire. "So she turned to this miserable fabrication, with all the sneers, all the malice, all the sly hintings and perversions of which she is master, and with more bitterness than ever attacked my father."[12] Momentarily, Rockefeller couldn't regain his self-control: His famous granite composure had utterly broken down. And for one of the few times in his life, he let forth a torrent of intemperate abuse. Spluttering with rage, he railed against "the poison tongue of this poison woman who seeks to poison the public with every endeavor . . . to cast suspicion on everything good, bad, or indifferent appertaining to a name which has thus far not been ruined by her shafts." Aware that he had, uncharacteristically, let down his guard, Rockefeller soon checked himself and restored the old pose of philosophic calm, reassuring Inglis in soothing tones, "After all, though, I am grateful that I do not cherish bitterness even against this 'historian,' but pity."[13] The titan had regained his dignity, and he made sure that his tightly fitted mask never slipped again in front of his authorized biographer.

Godfrey into swapping his farm for allegedly richer turf in Tioga County. (If this claim was in fact made, it proved a cruel hoax.) Some relatives later said that Michigan was Godfrey's real destination but that Lucy vetoed such a drastic relocation, preferring the New England culture of upstate New York to the wilds of Michigan.

Whatever the reason, the Rockefellers reenacted the primordial American rite of setting out in search of fresh opportunity. In the 1830s, many settlers from Massachusetts and Connecticut were swarming excitedly into wilderness areas of western New York, a migration that Alexis de Tocqueville described as "a game of chance" pursued for "the emotions it excites, as much as for the gain it procures."[3] The construction of the Erie Canal in the 1820s had lured many settlers to the area. Godfrey and Lucy heaped up their worldly possessions in a canvas-topped prairie schooner, drawn by oxen, and headed toward the sparsely settled territory. For two weeks, they traveled along the dusty Albany-Catskill turnpike, creeping through forests as darkly forbidding as the setting of a Grimms' fairy tale. With much baggage and little passenger space, the Rockefellers had to walk for much of the journey, with Lucy and the children (except William, who did not accompany them) taking turns sitting in the wagon whenever they grew weary. As they finally reached their destination, Richford, New York, the last three and a half miles were especially arduous, and the oxen negotiated the stony, rutted path with difficulty. At the end, they had to lash their exhausted team up a nearly vertical hillside to possess their virgin sixty acres. As family legend has it, Godfrey got out, tramped to the property's peak, inspected the vista, and said mournfully, "This is as close as we shall ever get to Michigan." So, in a memorial to dashed hopes, the spot would forever bear the melancholy name of Michigan Hill.

Even today scarcely more than a crossroads, Richford was then a stagecoach stop in the wooded country southeast of Ithaca and northwest of Binghamton. The area's original inhabitants, the Iroquois, had been chased out after the American Revolution and replaced by revolutionary army veterans. Still an uncouth frontier when the Rockefellers arrived, this backwater had recently attained township status, its village square dating from 1821. Civilization had taken only a tenuous hold. The dense forests on all sides teemed with game—bear, deer, panther, wild turkey, and cottontail rabbit—and people carried flaring torches at night to frighten away the roaming packs of wolves.

By the time that John D. Rockefeller was born in 1839, Richford was acquiring the amenities of a small town. It had some nascent industries—sawmills, gristmills, and a whiskey distillery—plus a schoolhouse and a church. Most inhabitants scratched out a living from hardscrabble farming, yet these newcomers were hopeful and enterprising. Notwithstanding their frontier trappings, they had carried with them the frugal culture of Puritan New England, which John D. Rockefeller would come to exemplify.

The Rockfellers' steep property provided a sweeping panorama of a fertile valley. The vernal slopes were spattered with wildflowers, and chestnuts and berries abounded in the fall. Amid this sylvan beauty, the Rockfellers had to struggle with a spartan life. They occupied a small, plain house, twenty-two feet deep and sixteen feet across, fashioned with hand-hewn beams and timbers. The thin soil was so rocky that it required heroic exertions just to hack a clearing through the underbrush and across thickly forested slopes of pine, hemlock, oak, and maple.

As best we can gauge from a handful of surviving anecdotes, Lucy ably managed both family and farm and never shirked heavy toil. Assisted by a pair of steers, she laid an entire stone wall by herself and had the quick-witted cunning and cool resourcefulness that would reappear in her grandson. John D. delighted in telling how she pounced upon a grain thief in their dark barn one night. Unable to discern the intruder's face, she had the mental composure to snip a piece of fabric from his coat sleeve. When she later spotted the man's frayed coat, she confronted the flabbergasted thief with the missing swatch; having silently made her point, she never pressed charges. One last item about Lucy deserves mention: She had great interest in herbal medicines and home-brewed remedies prepared from a "physic bush" in the backyard. Many years later, her curious grandson sent specimens of this bush to a laboratory to see whether they possessed genuine medicinal value. Perhaps it was from Lucy that he inherited the fascination with medicine that ran through his life, right up to his creation of the world's preeminent medical-research institute.

By the time he was in his twenties, William Avery Rockefeller was already a sworn foe of conventional morality who had opted for a vagabond existence. Even as an adolescent, he disappeared on long trips in midwinter, providing no clues as to his whereabouts. Throughout his life, he expended considerable energy on tricks and schemes to avoid plain hard work. But he possessed such brash charm and rugged good looks—he was nearly six feet tall, with a broad chest, high forehead, and thick auburn beard covering a pugnacious jaw— that people were instantly beguiled by him. This appealing façade, at least for a while, lulled skeptics and disarmed critics. It wasn't surprising that this nomad did not accompany his parents on their westward trek to Richford but instead drifted into the area around 1835 in his own inimitable fashion. When he first appeared in a neighboring hamlet, he quickly impressed the locals with his unorthodox style. Posing as a deaf-mute peddler selling cheap novelties, he kept a small slate with the words "I am deaf and dumb" chalked across it tied by a string to his buttonhole. On this slate, he conversed with the locals and later boasted how he exploited this ruse to flush out all the town secrets. To win the confidence of strangers and soften them up for the hard sell, he toted along a kaleidoscope, inviting people to peer into it.[4] During his long career as a confidence man, Big Bill always risked reprisals from people who might suddenly among the Richford townspeople, who tended to spy guile on Bill's part. Compared to the Davisons, the Rockefellers were poor country folk, and it is very likely that Bill was entranced by reports of John Davison's modest wealth. As early as 1801, the frugal Davison had acquired 150 acres in Cayuga County. In John D.'s words, "My grandfather was a rich man—that is, for his time he was counted rich. In those days one who had his farm paid for and had a little money beside was counted rich. Four or five or six thousand was counted rich. My grandfather had perhaps three or four times that. He had money to lend."[9]

Most Richford residents believed that Big Bill's meeting with Eliza was less a random encounter than a premeditated bid to snare her father's money. A notorious cad who regarded every pretty young woman as a potential conquest, Bill had at least one serious romance that antedated his wooing of Eliza. As Ralph P. Smith, a longtime Richford resident, recalled, "Billy was unmarried when he came here, and it was supposed that he would marry Nancy Brown, who was his housekeeper, but he broke with her, settling a sum said to have been about $400 on her when he concluded to win the daughter of the rich John Davison, over at Niles, on the outskirts of Moravia."[10] The story is corroborated by John D.'s cousin, Mrs. John Wilcox, who said, "Nancy Brown, of Harford Mills, was a beautiful girl, remarkably beautiful. William fell in love with her. She was poor. William would have money. Eliza Davison's father was to give her $500 when she married; so William married her."[11]

This marriage, consummated under false pretenses, fused the lives of two highly dissimilar personalities, setting the stage for all the future heartache, marital discord, and chronic instability that would so powerfully mold the contradictory personality of John D. Rockefeller.

When Bill brought his bride back to the Richford house he'd built half a mile from his parents' place, Eliza must have pondered the wisdom of her father's disapproval: Life promised to be hard and flinty in this rough-hewn homestead. Surviving photos of John D. Rockefeller's birthplace show a plain clapboard house set on a treeless slope, outlined bleakly against the sky. The rude dwelling looked like two attached boxcars, the austere simplicity broken only by a small awning over one door. However primitive the exterior, the snug house was solidly built out of timber from local forests. The main floor had two bedrooms and a living room, topped by a low sleeping loft and attic storage room; the little attached building served as a barn and woodshed. (This bucolic birth site of the future kerosene king was probably lit by sperm oil or tallow candles.) The grounds were much more ample than the house, as the fifty-acre lot included an apple orchard and a trout-filled stretch of Owego Creek, which bubbled along the bottom of the property.

Before long, Big Bill roughly disabused Eliza of any high-flown romantic notions she might have had about matrimony. Far from renouncing his girlfriend, Nancy Brown, he brought her into the cramped house as a "housekeeper" and

unmask his deceptions, and he narrowly escaped detection at the ho
Deacon Wells. The deacon and his daughter, a Mrs. Smith, pitied the po
dler who knocked on their door one Saturday and sheltered him in thei
that night. The next morning, when they invited him to church, Big Bill
resort to some fancy footwork, for he always shied away from crowds
somebody might recognize him and expose his imposture. "Billy told [th
con] in writing that he liked to go to church, but that his infirmity caused
to be stared at, so that he was abashed and would not go," recalled a to
man. "He really feared that he might be exposed by someone."[5] Seven mo
later, after the deacon and Big Bill had both moved to Richford, Mrs. Sm
spotted the erstwhile deaf-mute at a social gathering and marveled at
miraculous recovery of speech. "I see that you can talk better than when I s
you last," she said. Big Bill smiled, unfazed, his bravado intact. "Yes, I'm son
what improved."[6] When he arrived in Richford, the local citizens immediat
got a taste of his fakery, for he wordlessly flashed a slate with the scribbl
query, "Where is the house of Godfrey Rockefeller?"[7]

Since he usually presented false claims about himself and his products, B
worked a large territory to elude the law. He was roving more than thirty mile
northwest of Richford, in the vicinity of Niles and Moravia, when he first me
his future wife, Eliza Davison, at her father's farmhouse. With a flair for show
manship and self-promotion, he always wore brocaded vests or other brightly
colored duds that must have dazzled a sheltered farm girl like Eliza. Like many
itinerant vendors in rural places, he was a smooth-talking purveyor of dreams
along with tawdry trinkets, and Eliza responded to this romantic wanderer. She
was sufficiently taken in by his deaf-and-dumb humbug that she involuntarily
exclaimed in his presence, "I'd marry that man if he were not deaf and dumb."[8]
Whatever tacit doubts she might have harbored when she discovered his deceit, she soon succumbed, as did other women, to his mesmerizing charm.

A prudent, straitlaced Baptist of Scotch-Irish descent, deeply attached to hi
daughter, John Davison must have sensed the world of trouble that awaite
Eliza if she got mixed up with Big Bill Rockefeller, and he strongly discourage
the match. In later years, Eliza Rockefeller would seem to be a dried-up, witl
ered spinster, but in late 1836 she was a slim, spirited young woman with flan
ing red hair and blue eyes. Pious and self-contained, she was the antithesis
Bill and probably found him so hypnotic for just that reason. Who knows wh
gloom hung around her doorstep that was dispelled by Bill's glib patter? H
mother had died when Eliza was only twelve—she had dropped dead after ta
ing a pill dispensed by a traveling doctor—and Eliza was raised by her older s
ter, Mary Ann, leaving Eliza deprived of maternal counsel.

On February 18, 1837, despite the express opposition of John Davison, t
most improbable couple—Bill was twenty-seven, Eliza twenty-four—were
at the home of one of Eliza's friends. The marriage was a favorite gossip i

began having children, alternately, by wife and mistress. In 1838, Eliza gave birth to their first child, Lucy, followed a few months later by Nancy's first illegitimate daughter, Clorinda. On the night of July 8, 1839, Bill and Eliza again summoned the midwife, this time to deliver a boy, who came into the world in a bare front bedroom measuring eight by ten feet. This child, born during Martin Van Buren's presidency and destined to become the country's foremost capitalist, would survive into the second term of Franklin D. Roosevelt's New Deal. Like many other future magnates—Andrew Carnegie (born in 1835), Jay Gould (1836), and J. Pierpont Morgan (1837)—he was born in the late 1830s and would therefore come to maturity on the eve of the post–Civil War industrial boom. Several months after John's birth, Nancy Brown gave birth to a second daughter, Cornelia, which meant that Bill, lord of his own harem, managed to sire four children under one roof in just two years. Thus, the fiercely moralistic John Davison Rockefeller (appropriately named after Eliza's sober father) was sandwiched tightly between two illegitimate sisters, born into a situation steeped in sin.

Eliza couldn't have felt very comfortable with her in-laws. In general, the Rockefellers were a hard-drinking hillbilly clan, sociable and funny, fond of music, liquor, and uproarious good times, and adhering to a coarse frontier morality. As the strong matriarch, Lucy was the conspicuous exception, and Eliza drew close to her while frowning upon many of her more dissipated in-laws. During the Richford period, Bill's younger brother, Miles Avery Rockefeller, deserted his wife and decamped to South Dakota with Ella Brussee, a young woman who had done domestic work for Eliza. In a move that prefigured a future stratagem for Bill, Miles entered into a bigamous marriage with Ella and adopted his middle name as his new surname. Such re-created lives were common at a time when America had a vast, unmapped frontier and numerous sanctuaries from the law.

For a callow farm girl fresh from home, Eliza proved unexpectedly tolerant of Nancy Brown. Contrary to what one might expect, she pitied this intruder, perhaps considering the cramped ménage à trois fit punishment for having flouted her father's advice. As her niece observed, "Aunt Eliza loved her husband and she liked poor Nancy. But Aunt Eliza's brothers came down and made William put Nancy away."[12] In this period of Eliza's marriage, Mr. Davison is conspicuous by his absence, leaving one to wonder whether he had temporarily washed his hands of his disobedient daughter or whether, cowed by guilt and embarrassment, she had hidden her troubles from him. By one account, when Nancy grew quarrelsome after Bill's marriage, he seized the chance to expel his shrewish mistress from the packed household. Heeding the pleas from the Davisons, he posted Nancy and the two daughters to live with her parents in nearby Harford Mills. Family legend claims that Bill, who had a weak but not entirely dormant conscience, secretly deposited clothing bundles on her doorstep. Fortunately, the years with Bill didn't blight Nancy's life, for she married a man named Burlingame, bore other children, and furnished her first two daughters with a respectable upbringing.[13] From the skimpy documentary evidence, we know that Clorinda died young while Cornelia grew up into a tall, smart, attractive schoolteacher with a telling resemblance to Big Bill. Sometimes he acceded to her demands for money, but there were strict limits to Bill's generosity, and he would rebuff her when she became too clamorous. Cornelia married a man named Sexton and remained in the Richford area, but only a few local residents and Rockefeller relatives knew that she was John D.'s half-sister.[14] To her credit, Cornelia never tried to cash in on her kinship with the world's richest man, perhaps because it would unavoidably have advertised her illegitimacy. It is impossible to determine whether Rockefeller ever knew of the existence of his two illegitimate half-sisters.

The Nancy Brown affair wasn't the only indignity visited upon Eliza, for she was often abandoned by Bill during her three cheerless years in Richford. He remained a restless and defiant individualist who preferred life beyond the pale of society. Early in the marriage, he stayed put for a while, operating a small sawmill on Michigan Hill and dealing in salt, fur, horses, and timber, but he soon resumed the footloose life of a peddler, his trips cloaked in unfathomable mystery. Like a fugitive, he would depart furtively under cover of night and return after dark, weeks or months later, flinging pebbles at the window to signal his return. To tide over his family in his absence, he arranged for credit at the general store. "Give my family anything they want while I'm away," he instructed Chauncey Rich, whose father, Ezekiel, had founded Richford, "and when I come back I'll settle."[15] Never knowing when this credit might be canceled, Eliza became extremely frugal and drilled her children in thrifty maxims such as "Willful waste makes woeful want."

When Bill returned home, a sudden, smiling apparition, he would be riding new horses, wearing fine clothes, and brandishing a thick wad of crisp bills. Before going to see Eliza, he would pay off Chauncey Rich so that he could confidently tell her everything was now squared away at the store. His seductive charm melted away whatever hostility his absence had aroused; it took time before his extended absences and repeated betrayals burned the romance out of her system, leaving a residue of stoic resignation. For the moment, whatever her anxieties or loneliness, she seemed girlishly lovelorn during his trips, still smitten with her flimflam man. "Just look at that moon!" she once sighed to a cousin when Bill was on the road. "Is William, miles and miles away, perhaps looking at it, too, at this moment? I do hope he is."[16]

On the road, Bill improvised ever more fanciful ways to make money. A crack shot, he made the circuit of shooting contests, often bringing home prize money. A glad-handing huckster, he sold rings and other knickknacks at fantastic markups. Mostly, though, he styled himself a "botanic physician" or "herbal doctor"—euphemisms faithfully parroted by some Rockefeller descendants. At a time when physicians still resorted to bleeding, blistering, and violent purgatives, and many rustic areas lacked access to medical care, such traveling salesmen filled a vacuum. Nevertheless, in William Avery Rockefeller one clearly detects the blarney and easy conviviality of the mountebank. Sometimes he peddled bottles of home-brewed elixir or patent medicines bought from druggists, but he scored his greatest success with natural medicines culled from Lucy's physic bush. Though his mother had a sincere interest in herbal remedies, Bill would grossly distort or exaggerate their properties. For instance, he harvested small, purplish berries from her garden that resembled small pills and would hawk them to farmers' wives as a sovereign remedy for stomach troubles. His sales pitch went even further, for, as a Richford neighbor reported many years later, "he would warn them solemnly that they must not be given to a woman in a delicate condition, for they would surely cause abortion. Thereupon he would sell his pills at a high price. They were perfectly harmless, and he broke no law in selling them. He had remarkable imagination."[17]

The midnight rambles and peculiar commerce of William Rockefeller mystified the Richford citizenry. He both fired and troubled the imagination, generating so much gossip and speculation that they christened him Devil Bill. Rumors raced periodically through town that he was a gambler, a horse thief, a desperado. Though he seemed to operate on the edge of the law, people were delighted by his bluff humor and tall tales, if dismayed by his treatment of his family. "When he finally succeeded as a peddler he would dress up like a prince and kept everyone wondering," said one town resident who participated in the guessing game about Bill's manifold sources of income. "He laughed a great deal and enjoyed the speculation he caused. He was not a drinking man and treated his family well when he was home, but everyone knew that he neglected the family by leaving them to shift for themselves for long months at a time."[18] He frustrated those neighbors who ached for his comeuppance. After one prolonged absence of several months, when Eliza's bill at Chauncey Rich's topped a thousand dollars, the scuttlebutt said that Devil Bill had been arrested. Instead, like a country squire, he came trotting into town in a magnificent carriage, seated behind a team of splendid horses, diamonds glittering in his shirtfront. At the general store, he made a point of settling the tab with large bills. After such trips, Bill gathered friends and family around the dinner table and, while wolfing down heaps of food, would regale them with picaresque tales of his adventures among the western settlers and Indians. Devil Bill had a knack for weaving his experiences into spellbinding narratives, making Eliza and the children vicarious partners in his travels. As the chief casualty of Bill's peregrinations, Eliza received sympathy from her neighbors, who felt she was being abused by her husband. Yet she remained loyal to him, declined many opportunities to denigrate him, and carried herself with considerable dignity.[19]

However overblown the frequent biographical claims about John D. Rockefeller's impoverished childhood have been, several people testified to the family's squalor in Richford. "I do not remember ever to have seen more pitiably neglected children," one neighbor observed. "Their clothing was old and tattered, and they looked dirty and hungry."[20] It was a measure of Eliza's desperation that she sought relief in the home of her brother-in-law, Jacob Rockefeller, a bawdy, jolly, not infrequently besotted man. An oft-told tale about Jacob recounted how he won a five-dollar bet by staying sober during an entire trip to town.[21] Jacob's kindly wife became a second mother to the two toddlers, Lucy and John, darning their clothes and knitting them mittens from woolen homespun.

In this nightmarish situation, Eliza seemed to draw strength from adversity. One Richford native praised her as "a most excellent woman, but one who bore too heavy a burden at that time properly to look after her children. Her husband was away for long periods, and she had to look after their farm of sixty acres and try to make it pay their expenses. She did not know at what time the shopkeepers of the village might shut down on her credit, and she worked very hard."[22]

When John D. later evoked his idyllic, sunlit boyhood in upstate New York, he blotted out Richford from these reveries. Just three when he left there, he retained only a few hazy memories of the place. "I remember very clearly the brook that ran near the front of the house and how careful I had to be to keep far away from it. I remember my mother vaguely at Richford and my grandmother, who lived half a mile or so up the hill."[23] One notes that Rockefeller's earliest memory was associated with caution and that he edited out the absentee father and inebriated grandfather while retaining the strong, enduring mother and grandmother. He always possessed an unusual, self-protective capacity to suppress unpleasant memories and keep alive those things that fortified his resolve.

As best we can tell, Rockefeller knew nothing of Nancy Brown and the seamy side of Richford existence, yet he carried through life a vague sense of an infernal place. "I shudder to think of what I should have been if I had remained in Richford all my life," he later confided. "There were many men who hunt a little, fish a little, and drink whiskey a little, and only attain a little success in life, and all for the lack of a little religion."[24] Of his family's decision to leave Richford, Rockefeller offered an economic explanation that probably served as the standard cover story of his childhood: stingy soil. "The country there is beautiful," Rockefeller would say, "but the settlers wasted their energy in trying to get the stumps out of the ground, and trying to make crops grow in the poor soil."[25] The true reason, of course, was Eliza's horror at the town's low moral tone, as reflected by its single church; she was probably also eager to remove the children from the influence of her boisterous, drunken Rockefeller in-laws and expose them to the steadier Davisons. By no coincidence, the Rockefellers moved to Moravia, three miles from the Davison farm, where Eliza could enjoy her father's presence during her husband's habitual absences.

John D. Rockefeller, right, at age thirteen,
with brother William, eleven, and sister Mary Ann, nine.
(Courtesy of the Rockefeller Archive Center)

CHAPTER 2

Fires of Revival

hen the Rockefellers moved thirty miles north from Richford to Moravia, they progressed from a backward, frontier settlement to a more sedate community with neat frame houses in the town center. Settled by the United Brethren in Christ—an evangelical denomination that later merged with the United Methodist Church—Moravia was already a stronghold of temperance and antislavery sentiment and boasted a hotel, general store, cotton mill, and Congregational church. Even today, Moravia is a quaintly authentic piece of Americana, with graceful, shady streets that have a companionable feel and houses with wide, friendly verandas.

The Rockefellers lived on the rural outskirts north of town. Around 1843, Bill put down a thousand dollars for a ninety-two-acre parcel of grassy upland that gently sloped down to Owasco Lake, one of the most picturesque of the Finger Lakes. He enlarged an existing house until it contained seven or eight rooms favored with superb views, framed by tall pines, of the bright blue lake set against a backdrop of wooded hills on the far shore. Barns stood across the road, and a smokehouse out back enabled the family to cure ham and bacon. For John D., this two-story clapboard house was a scene of enchantment and became his enduring emblem of pastoral beauty. In the summertime, he loved to pull yellow perch from the cold, clear lake, and even winters captivated him in spite of the bitter cold. The Rockefeller children slept in an unplastered upstairs room that was heated only by a stovepipe rising from the kitchen; snow flurries and sharp winter squalls pressed through cracks in the walls. "How the wind used to roar among the hemlocks by the shore of the lake!" Rockefeller remembered dreamily in his late seventies.[1] In the predawn dark, the children were often awakened by the sharp chopping of woodcutters or the squeal of sleds on hard-packed snow. Eliza would stand at the foot of the stairs and call up to her eldest son, "Come, my son; time to get up and milk your cow!"[2] To warm his feet in the dim, cold barn, John always stood on the steaming earth just vacated by the cow he was milking.

The first three Rockefeller children—Lucy, John, and William—had been born in Richford. Now, in 1843, with Big Bill again on the road during months of her pregnancy, Eliza gave birth to a second daughter, Mary Ann; two years later, twins arrived. The boy, Frank, was healthy, but Frances was sickly from birth and received some seventy visits from a local doctor before she died just short of her second birthday. Eliza tried to protect the seven-year-old John D. from this first lacerating brush with death, but it remained engraved on his memory. When he visited Moravia as an old man in his eighties, he pointed to a field and explained that "when Frances was buried I was sent over to that field to pick stones, so that I should not know."[3] He later exhibited an unacknowledged dread of death, and Eliza was perhaps the first to intuit it.

In Moravia, William Avery Rockefeller acted like a strange amalgam of solid citizen and engaging ne'er-do-well. As in Richford, the townsfolk goggled as he sped by on swift horses, decked out in smart clothes, and his prodigal spending sometimes fostered the impression that he was the town's richest man. Mary Ann later dismissed the "ridiculous" stories of their childhood poverty. "We always had plenty to eat and wear, and every reasonable kind of comfort. We were not rich, of course—far from it; but we had enough to eat and use and save—always."[4] Moravia was the golden period of John's boyhood when his father briefly aspired to gentility. One neighbor even labeled Bill "about the most notable man in the community."[5] Since the region was rich in pristine pine forests, he organized a legitimate and quite successful logging business. Before dawn, guided only by starlight and lanterns, he and his work gangs carted logs to the lakeside by bobsled, then floated them up to Auburn, situated at the lake's northern tip. In a sudden burst of civic spirit, Bill helped to select the site for the town school by counting the revolutions of his buggy wheels as he drove through town, then placing the school at the exact middle of the community; he persuaded local taxpayers to pay for it at a time when many people still thought families should educate their children at home. With the resourceful, go-getter attitude later transmitted to his son, Bill also stocked Owasco Lake with pickerel and even headed the local temperance committee. "That's the kind of man he was," boasted John D. "He'd get a thing done while his neighbors were beginning to talk about it."[6] The Moravia period revealed an important truth about Bill: He had an underlying craving for respectability and probably didn't plan to spend his whole life as a floating charlatan, preying on the gullible.

Bill never deigned to dirty his hands with farmwork, of course, which he considered beneath his dignity. He hired a railroad worker named Hiram Odell to work the farm and look after his family during his still-frequent wanderings. As Bill instructed him, "Their mother ain't strong enough to manage 'em and they need some managing. Do just what you think is right for 'em."[7] While Odell cultivated the garden in his spare time, Eliza assigned chores to the children. Drawing a string across the garden one day, she told the two oldest boys, "John, you take care of this side of the string, and, Will, this side is yours."[8] In contrast to his father's disdain for manual labor, John—always a self-styled son of the common people—gloried in the rigors of country life, which, he came to believe, toughened him for later industrial struggle. His frugal boyhood hardened an already stoic nature and made him proof against later adversity.

There was enough economic activity in the America of the 1840s to stimulate the fancy of any future mogul. Banks sprang up everywhere, canals crosshatched the countryside, steamboats plied the rivers, railroads and telegraphs welded together the first national markets. Territorial expansion was in the air: Texas was annexed in 1845, and war with Mexico seemed inevitable. Though only dimly aware of such distant developments, John D. Rockefeller already seemed a perfect specimen of *homo economicus*. Even as a boy, he bought candy by the pound, divided it into small portions, then sold it at a tidy profit to his siblings. By age seven, encouraged by his mother, he was dropping gold, silver, and copper coins that he earned into a blue china bowl on the mantel. John's first business coup came at age seven when he shadowed a turkey hen as it waddled off into the woods, raided its nest, and raised the chicks for sale. To spur his enterprise, Eliza gave him milk curds to feed the turkeys, and the next year he raised an even larger brood. As an old man, Rockefeller said, "To this day, I enjoy the sight of a flock of turkeys, and never miss an opportunity of studying them."[9]

Despite Rockefeller's roseate memories, early photos of him tell a much more somber tale. His face was grim, expressionless, lacking boyish joy and animation; the skin is drawn, the eyes blank and devoid of luster. To other people, he often seemed abstracted, and they remembered him with a deadpan face trudging along country roads, lost in thought, as if unraveling deep problems. "He was a quiet boy," said one Moravia resident. "He seemed always to be thinking."[10] In many respects, John was forgettable and indistinguishable from many other boys. When he later dazzled the world, many former neighbors and classmates struggled to summon up even a fuzzy image of him. He was a slow learner but patient and persistent and, like J. P. Morgan and Jay Gould, exhibited a terrific head for math. "I was not an easy student, and I had to apply myself diligently to prepare my lessons," said Rockefeller, who described himself accurately as "reliable" but not "brilliant."[11] For thirty weeks per year (rural children needed time off for farm chores), he attended the one-room schoolhouse established by his father, a spare white building with a pitched roof and windows adorned with dark shutters. Discipline was harsh and exacting: When students misbehaved, the teacher menacingly held a slate over their heads. If Rockefeller didn't excel in class, it might have been in part because he lacked the bright boy's exhibitionism, the yearning for gold stars; always inner-directed and indifferent to the approval of others, he was therefore free of a certain boyish vanity.

With the benefit of hindsight, we can see that there *was* something extraordinary about the way this stolid boy pinpointed goals and doggedly pursued them without any trace of childish impulsiveness. When playing checkers or chess, he showed exceptional caution, studying each move at length, working out every possible countermove in his head. "I'll move just as soon as I get it figured out," he told opponents who tried to rush him. "You don't think I'm playing to get beaten, do you?"[12] To ensure that he won, he submitted to games only where he could dictate the rules. Despite his slow, ponderous style, once he had thoroughly mulled over his plan of action, he had the power of quick decision.

Although he was generally grave and devoted much time to books, music, and church, he had a sly wit, the sort that curled up unexpectedly around the edges of a sentence. As his sister-in-law said, "He had a quick sense of humor, though one might say he was soberly mirthful. His appreciation was keen, but I do not recall him as ever laughing loudly. But I do remember the quick lighting up of his eyes, and the dimples that showed in his cheek when he heard or saw anything amusing."[13] His sister Mary Ann remembered him as an inveterate tease. "He would plague us all with his jokes, always with a straight, solemn face."[14] Rockefeller always had a droll sense of fun, but it was often obscured behind a mask of gravity.

=

John D. Rockefeller was drawn to the church, not as some nagging duty or obligation but as something deeply refreshing to the soul. The Baptist church of his boyhood provides many clues to the secrets of his character. As a young man, he was raised on a steady diet of maxims, grounded in evangelical Protestantism, that guided his conduct. Many of his puritanical attitudes, which may seem antiquated to a later generation, were merely the religious commonplaces of his boyhood. Indeed, the saga of his monumental business feats is inseparable from the fire-and-brimstone atmosphere that engulfed upstate New York in his childhood. Even his father, wont to flirt with the devil's company, knew many hymns by heart and urged his children to go to church; he once offered John five dollars to read the Bible cover to cover, thus creating an early, unintentional association between God and money. Always an iconoclastic, outlaw spirit, Bill never actually joined a church—that would have been going too far—so John identified religion with his beloved mother, who found in the Bible a balm for her troubled spirit.

John attended a Sunday school a short distance from their hilltop house and remembered the teacher as a formerly profane man who had repented and become an earnest Christian. The boy saw religion less as a system of other-worldly rewards than as a means for moral reformation on earth. Since Bill was often away, Eliza coaxed a Presbyterian neighbor into dropping off her and the children at the Baptist church on Sunday mornings. As the family huddled together in a pew, Eliza encouraged the children to drop pennies into the collection plate; Rockefeller later cited his mother's altruism as the genesis of his philanthropy. Early in life, he learned that God wanted his flock to earn money and then donate money in a never-ending process. "I was trained from the beginning to work and to save," Rockefeller explained. "I have always regarded it as a religious duty to get all I could honorably and to give all I could. I was taught that way by the minister when I was a boy."[15] The low-church Baptists didn't prohibit the accumulation of wealth but did oppose its vain, ostentatious display, setting up a tension that would be threaded throughout Rockefeller's life.

While the first Baptist church had been founded by Roger Williams in Rhode Island in 1639, the denomination didn't flourish until the so-called Great Awakening that began around 1739. This upsurge of religious fervor gathered force following the tour of the eastern seaboard by the charismatic English Methodist evangelist George Whitefield. In open fields, amid much weeping, shrieking, fainting, and guilty writhing on the ground, masses of people were converted to Christianity or had their sagging faith restored. This period of rabid emotion spurred fantastic growth among Baptists, who believed in voluntary immersion and a public confession of faith from adherents. More than one hundred new Baptist churches sprang up in New England alone. With their lay leaders and autonomous congregations, the Baptists were ideally suited to frontier areas and the democratic ethos of the colonists. Recruited from the common people, often unpaid and poorly educated, Baptist ministers ventured into the hinterlands where other clergymen feared to tread. Because they opposed religious establishments and owed no allegiance to supervisory bishops or a central church hierarchy, they could start up a church in any creek or hollow. They emerged as a major religious force by the close of the eighteenth century.

A Second Great Awakening aroused New England and the mid-Atlantic states to a new pitch of religious fever from 1800 to the late 1830s. This protracted movement peaked around 1830, when the revival fires blazed so hotly that Rochester and other sections of upstate New York and Ohio were dubbed the Burned-Over District. When revivalists—of whom Charles Grandison

Finney was the most celebrated—arrived in a town, they held prayer meetings that often lasted through the night. These theatrical spectacles, marked by dramatic outpourings of emotion, featured hardened sinners who sat on the "anxious bench" as townspeople publicly urged them to repent. When they saw the light, the guilty parties often burst into tears and knelt in prayer. Preachers tried to reach people through vivid appeals to hope and fear, invoking heavenly bliss and burning lakes of hellfire. One popular evangelist, Jacob Knapp, described tormented sinners crawling up the sides of burning pits while devils with pitchforks, perched on the rim, sadistically prodded them back down into the flames. The revival movement was self-perpetuating, for the saved were expected to rescue others from Satan's clutches. They would go door-to-door, trying to flush sinners from their homes until the entire town was caught up in passionate, hysterical emotion.

Several aspects of this revival movement are worth noting because they are so strikingly reflected in Rockefeller's life. In the late 1820s, militant evangelicals in Rochester agitated against smoking, dancing, card playing, billiards, and the theater, while boycotting stores that opened on the Sabbath. As Rockefeller said, "Going back . . . to my early business days and boyhood, the Baptists I knew listened to their consciences and their religious instructions, not only did not dance in public places but did not dance anywhere and did not even concede the reputability of dancing. . . . The theater was considered a source of depravity, to be shunned by conscientious Christians."[16] Because liquor was considered a satanic brew, a believer couldn't make it, sell it, or offer it to guests, and a temperance pledge became a standard component of accepting Christ into one's life. In his boyhood, Rockefeller internalized an abiding sense that the professing Christian had to be a soldier armed against all secular temptation and must never stray far from godly circles.

Departing from strict Calvinism, Baptist evangelicals clung to the egalitarian view that *all* errant souls could be saved, not just a small, predestined elect, and they actively engaged in evangelism and missionary work. Rockefeller was brought up to believe that nobody was ever irretrievably lost, that people were free agents who could be redeemed by an act of will—a self-reliant outlook that stamped his conservative political views. His Baptist upbringing also predisposed him to follow the cult of perpetual self-improvement that played so prominent a role in nineteenth-century American culture. Finney, for instance, was a Presbyterian who exhorted his listeners to pursue perfection in their earthly lives.

Rockefeller entered the Baptist Church at a fateful moment. In May 1845, in a schism over the issue of slaveholders serving as missionaries, Baptist delegates from nine southern states seceded from the national body to create the Southern Baptist Convention. Northern Baptists fervently believed that abolitionism was consistent with their opposition to ecclesiastical hierarchy, their populist spirit, and their broad-based campaign to purge sin from society. The Second Great Awakening had explicitly linked personal conversion with community reform, spawning political activism. During the colonial period, Americans had liberally consumed demon rum, but the new evangelical emphasis on social uplift helped to foster a national temperance movement in the 1820s and 1830s. For Rockefeller, an apolitical man, the church narrowed his social life but widened his vision, providing a bridge to larger social concerns and ultimately preparing him for the world of philanthropy.

If John D. believed, despite the flamboyant antics of Devil Bill, that he had enjoyed a homespun boyhood out of a Currier & Ives print, it was largely due to the compensating influence of Eliza and the church. Her hardships tapped some deep reserve of strength and wisdom in the simple country woman with the spare face, quiet ways, and steady blue-gray eyes. "Mother was wonderful," said Mary Ann. "She managed the family and the house and did it all so easily."[17] Though Eliza dutifully read the Bible, her few surviving missives reveal an extremely rudimentary education; she misspelled the most elementary words, writing *herd* for *heard*, *plesant* for *pleasant*, and *ben* for *been*. (John was a faultless speller and grammarian.) All but a stranger to grammar, she sometimes wrote letters that consisted of a single run-on sentence.

It is hard not to be stirred by Eliza's uncomplaining bravery in steadily tending five children in the face of her husband's erratic, irresponsible ways. When Bill was on the road, she never knew where he was, what he was doing, or when he might surface again. Though she had Hiram Odell, and her father lived just across Owasco Lake, Eliza was often alone with the children at night in a town on the fringe of a wilderness. As she thumbed her Bible and puffed on a corncob pipe, she must have worried about roving thieves. One of Rockefeller's favorite stories reveals her coolheaded response to danger:

> Mother had whooping cough and was staying in her room so that we should not catch it. When she heard thieves trying to get at the back of the house and remembered that there was no man to protect us, she softly opened the window and began to sing some old Negro melody, just as if the family were up and about. The robbers turned away from the house, crossed the road to the carriage house, stole a set of harness and went down the hill to their boat at the shore.[18]

From such early experiences, John D. took away a deep, abiding respect for women; unlike other moguls of the Gilded Age, he never saw them in purely ornamental terms.

Born in 1813, Eliza had grown up in the shadow of the Second Great Awakening and was never lax about discipline. While Devil Bill dispensed gifts to the children, Eliza, by default, meted out punishment and tried to subdue the wild

Rockefeller streak in her children. A kindred spirit, John accepted her stern country justice when she drew out the birch switch, strapped him to the apple tree, and "laid on Macduff," as she styled it. "On those occasions I made my protests, which she heard sympathetically and accepted sweetly—but [she] still laid on, explaining that I had earned the punishment and must have it," Rockefeller recalled. "She would say, 'I'm doing this in love.' "[19] She typically erred on the side of severity. Once, while punishing John for misbehavior at school, he started to plead his innocence. "Never mind," she interrupted, "we have started in on this whipping, and it will do for the next time."[20] Rockefeller told a tale of his adolescence that highlighted his mother's grim discipline. They then lived in Owego, and she had forbidden him to ice-skate on the Susquehanna River, but the lure of a moonlit night overwhelmed the better judgment of John and his brother William. They were gliding along the river when they heard the desperate cries of a young boy who had fallen through the ice. Pushing a pole to the flailing boy, John and William fished him from the water and saved his life. When they returned home, Eliza hailed their courage, then promptly got down to business. "We thought we should be left off without punishment," said Rockefeller, "but mother gave us a good tanning, nevertheless."[21]

Where William and Frank had their father's broad face and high forehead, John had Eliza's narrow face, piercing eyes, and sharp chin and a personality that conformed more to the Davison pattern. He also had his mother's slow metabolism and ability to bear a large burden for long periods in an unruffled way. Many neighbors testified that the unflappable Eliza never lost her temper, never raised her voice, never scolded anyone—a style of understated authority that John inherited. From his mother he learned economy, order, thrift, and other bourgeois virtues that figured so largely in his success at Standard Oil. Forced to pay a heavy penalty for her impetuous decision to marry Devil Bill, Eliza trained her children to reflect coolly before making decisions; her frequent admonition "We will let it simmer" was a saying John employed throughout his business career.

For a woman of Eliza's intense pride and religiosity, it must have been hard to endure the unaccountable absences of her gallivanting husband, and she drew closer, of necessity, to her oldest son, who struck her as precocious and prematurely wise. She saw qualities in him still invisible to the world at large. Because she confided in him and gave him adult responsibilities, he matured rapidly and acquired unusual confidence; it must have flattered his pride that he served as a surrogate father and was so vital to the family's survival. His relations with his siblings seemed more paternal than fraternal, and he often instructed them. As he put it, "I know that in my own case I have been greatly helped by the confidence imposed in me since early boyhood."[22] Of course, this boyhood responsibility took its toll on John D., who experienced little of the spontaneous joy or levity of youth. Growing up as a miniature adult, burdened with duties, he developed an exaggerated sense of responsibility that would be evident throughout his life. He learned to see himself as a reluctant savior, taking charge of troubled situations that needed to be remedied.

Until he came to appraise him through more mature eyes, John idolized his father. A man capable of Paul Bunyan–esque feats, William Avery Rockefeller possessed the dash and virility that every young boy dreams of in a father. "I come of a strong family, men of unusual strength, a family of giants," Rockefeller stated later in life.[23] "What a bright smile my father had. Everybody liked him. 'Uncle Billy,' they called him."[24] By all accounts, Bill was a man of abundant talents. He was such a superb athlete that he could stand beside a fence and jump over it backward; such an amazing ventriloquist that he could create half a dozen characters talking at once; such a legendary animal trainer that he once taught tricks to a pet bear he had won in a shooting competition; and such a skillful hypnotist that he was darkly rumored to "throw a mist" around person and beast alike.[25]

If the children associated Eliza with discipline, they identified Bill with laughter, plenty, and good times. He was the ideal hunting and fishing buddy, a crack shot who could bring down small birds in flight. Mesmerized by guns, he kept a splendid set of clean, well oiled rifles (including one with a telescopic sight) in the Moravia house. Taking aim at a pine tree while standing in a meadow, he would toss off rapid shots until the bark was shredded by bullets. When selling patent medicines, his marksmanship served him extremely well, for he would use it to draw a crowd in strange towns. Setting up a manikin with a clay pipe in its mouth, he retreated to a distance of two hundred paces, shot the pipe to smithereens, then offered a ten-dollar bill to anybody in the crowd who could match his prowess.

Lively and fun-loving, Bill created infectious merriment wherever he went. As his son noted, "He always wanted something going on in the house, singing or music of some sort."[26] He was nothing if not shrewd and used his talents to further his enjoyment. One day, he heard of a violin virtuoso who had been clapped in the town jail for drunkenness. The offender was given a choice: Either he could pay a hundred-dollar fine or serve a hundred days in jail, with each day served reducing the fine by a dollar. Unable to muster the hundred dollars, Bill let the musician stew for thirty-five days, then bailed him out for sixty-five dollars, taking his violin in exchange. For decades, Bill cherished this rich-toned, concert-quality instrument, which he would bow at waist level, like a country fiddler. It was undoubtedly from the Rockefeller side of the family that John inherited his lasting love of music.

With Owasco Lake always shimmering through the window, many of John D.'s dearest memories of Moravia centered upon fishing with Bill, who was prone to do outrageous things in the boat. During one lake outing, the middle brother, William, then a fat little boy unable to swim, made the mistake of grumbling about the heat. "Then cool off," said his father, who plucked up the flabbergasted boy by the waistband and pitched him headlong into the water. When William sank straight to the bottom, Big Bill dived overboard, retrieved him, then tried to teach him to swim. As John said of the incident, looking on the bright side, "He was always training us to meet responsibilities and take care of ourselves."[27]

It would be wrong (if highly tempting) to see William Avery Rockefeller as simply some blithe, hedonistic spirit, for he was moralistic in his own way. He was a militant temperance advocate—alcohol having ruined his father, Godfrey—and he fiercely reproached John and William when he caught them smoking in the barn. "When, after my brother had reached the age of 40 years my father learned that he smoked, tears came into his eyes," said John, who liked to focus on his father's virtuous side as a convenient way to sidestep his vices.[28]

In no area did Bill impress his eldest son more—or did his eldest son prove more impressionable—than in the magical realm of money. Big Bill had an almost sensual love of cash and enjoyed flashing plump rolls of bills. "John D. Rockefeller inherited his shrewdness and love of money from his father," remarked one of Bill's companions. "The old man had a passion for money that amounted almost to a craze. I never met a man who had such a love of money."[29] Exhibiting a small-town, populist mistrust of banks—a mistrust he would pass along to John, who later kept Standard Oil free from the talons of Wall Street financiers—Bill stashed away his money at home. As one neighbor recalled, "He had money, lots of it. He kept it in a bureau drawer. There I've seen it, ones, twos, threes (we had three-dollar bills then), fives, tens, twenties, and fifties, all corded like wood and the bundles tied with twine, the stacks filling the drawer."[30] According to legend, he also had a four-gallon pail brimming with gold pieces, though it probably concealed base metal beneath the glittering surface. Once, at a family gathering, Bill disappeared for a time, then suddenly burst forth from his room with a patchwork tablecloth crafted from banknotes of varying denominations. This was part of his obsessive need to project a big-shot image to conceal the pettiness of his accomplishments. Neither as a boy nor a man did John find anything pathological about his father's money madness, suggesting that he shared the same blind spot. After he had made his gargantuan fortune, he said admiringly of his father, "He made a practice of never carrying less than $1,000, and he kept it in his pocket. He was able to take care of himself, and was not afraid to carry his money."[31]

The bane of John's boyhood wasn't poverty so much as chronic worry about money, and it is easy to see how cash came to seem like God's bounty, the blessed stuff that relieved all of life's cares. After the family spent anxious weeks or months running up credit bills and waiting for Father's return, Bill would abruptly materialize, a jolly Santa Claus, swimming in lucre. He would compensate for his long absence by extravagant shows of generosity with his children. For John, money became associated with these brief but pleasurable interludes when the mercurial father was at home and the Rockefellers functioned as a true family.

During the early Moravia years, Big Bill began to train his eldest son in business matters, dispatching him at age eight or nine to evaluate and buy cordwood for the house. "I knew what a cord of good solid beech and maple wood was," said Rockefeller. "My father told me to select only the solid wood and the straight wood and not to put any limbs in it or any punky wood."[32] Of all the lessons John absorbed from his father, perhaps none surpassed in importance that of keeping meticulous accounts. This was a matter of necessity, for Bill's wayward life forced his family to husband their credit and closely monitor their often precarious financial situation.

When it came to business ethics, Bill was a most curious compound, extremely honorable one moment, a sharpster the next. To his son, he tacitly conveyed the message that commerce was a tough, competitive struggle and that you were entitled to outwit the other fellow by any means, fair or foul. He tutored John in a sharp, relentless bargaining style that the latter made famous. (A most unorthodox bargainer, Bill once bid a thousand dollars less for a farm than the owner was asking; to settle matters, he suggested they shoot at a target. Bill won and got his thousand-dollar discount.) As a traveling mountebank, selling dubious cures to credulous rural folk, Bill took a dim view of people's intelligence and didn't hesitate to exploit their naive trust.

As a boss, Bill patented his own queer style of managing people. During his respectable time in the lumber business, he paid his men well and promptly and was said by his son to be very popular. Yet he had a habit of hiring workers for a spell, informing them politely, "I don't need you any longer," then hiring them again a few days later—what he proudly dubbed his "policy of firing and hiring over." If this made him sound like a less-than-lovable boss, his son applauded the unsettling tactic. "It kept the men up on tip-toe; no stagnation among them."[33] Oddly enough, John described his father as "most liberal and kindly with his employees, yet eminently practical and keen and wide-awake and resourceful."[34] This was one of many areas where he seemed to embroider the truth about Big Bill. Would the people he fired and hired again have described Bill as "liberal and kindly"?

John D. Rockefeller portrayed his father as a paragon of business virtue, and if this was mostly an effort to cover up the shady side of Bill's life, it had a grain of truth. Bill paid his debts punctually and believed implicitly in the sacredness of contracts, taking great pains in writing them up. As John observed, "He was very scrupulous to carry out his contracts, particular[ly] that they were clearly understood and carefully drawn, that is, committed to writing. And the training he gave me along those lines was very valuable, has proven so in all my life."³⁵ In his business career, John D. Rockefeller was accused of many sins, but he took pride in paying his debts promptly and abiding strictly by contracts. He was also accused of mixing the lawless and the honorable, of ignoring ethical niceties, in a manner reminiscent of his father.

Whether John D. Rockefeller ultimately followed his father's unscrupulous craft or his mother's stern respectability in steering Standard Oil is the question that weighs most heavily on his historical reputation. Bertrand Russell once said of Rockefeller, "What he said, what he thought, and what he felt, came from his mother, but what he did came from his father, with the addition of a great caution generated by early unpleasantness."³⁶ The issue is much more complicated than that, but there's no doubt that Rockefeller's achievement arose from the often tense interplay between the two opposing, deeply ingrained tendencies of his nature—his father's daring and his mother's prudence—yoked together under great pressure.

Given the paucity of hard evidence about Bill's affairs in Moravia, one is led to rake over the rich folklore he left behind. In 1927, a carpenter turned author named Charles Brutcher published a book entitled *Joshua: A Man of the Finger Lakes Region*, a thinly disguised roman à clef about William Avery Rockefeller. The privately printed 130-page book has become something of a collector's item, with copies sometimes fetching hundreds of dollars. The protagonist is one William Rockwell, a.k.a. Big Bill, and the author brazenly mingles fact and fiction by reproducing an actual photo of Rockefeller's father in the front. *Joshua* professes, redundantly, to be a "true story taken from life" and gathers lore about Devil Bill that was still titillating the town gossips in the 1920s. Much of its store of legend came from Melvin Rosekrans, whose father, Joshua, had locked horns with Big Bill in the 1840s. The book presents a slanted, hyperbolic portrait of Bill's career, a compendium of his presumed misdeeds, yet enough details tally with documentary material from other sources that it merits review.

According to this potboiler, the "masterful and self-confident" Big Bill became "the terror of the Finger Lakes region," whose "evil influence would be felt in every household for miles around." Eliza makes a cameo appearance as "a sad-faced little woman" kept ignorant of the true reasons for her husband's mysterious trips: "She was always opposed to 'Big Bill's' roving disposition and his evil minded tendencies."³⁷ If she suspected wrongdoing, she kept it to herself to spare the children. That the fictional Eliza earned the sympathy of the community jibes with what we know of the real Eliza's Moravia life.

The book narrates how Rockwell fell in with a bunch of desperadoes who stole horses and delivered them to the notorious Loomis Brothers gang. (This grave, unsubstantiated charge shadowed Bill in all three New York towns he lived in.) Another equally grave charge in the book concerns Dr. William Cooper, a cousin of the novelist James Fenimore Cooper. Dr. Cooper disliked Bill and refused to deal with him. The book asserts that Rockwell once coerced at gunpoint a reluctant Dr. Cooper to treat Eliza and that somebody afterward took potshots at the doctor through the blinds of his living-room window, narrowly missing him. Rockwell is further portrayed as an unconscionable philanderer, who lures pretty girls with a secret love potion and tries to seduce a young woman working in his house. He openly squires his girlfriends around Moravia in his carriage and takes them rowing on the lake, notwithstanding Eliza's dismay. "The poor, long suffering little woman knew the failings of her dashing mate. She was overpowered by his master mind and had long since become resigned to her fate."[38] The diabolical Bill is even accused of palming off counterfeit bills.

At first, the locals were so petrified of the rough-and-tumble Rockwell that they didn't dare to confront him. Yet *Joshua* ends as a tale of justice triumphant as Bill's gang is disbanded by an irate citizenry. In a climactic courtroom scene, it is proved that Rockwell had paid a black man ten dollars to steal rafting chains in order to smuggle logs across Owasco Lake. His luck having run out, Bill flees the courtroom, though another gang member serves time in Auburn prison for horse theft. When last seen in the book, Big Bill has shifted operations to Owego, where horses again begin to disappear suspiciously. In a shameless bit of press agentry that Bill himself would have savored, Brutcher ends by promising a sequel, adding, "Negotiations are pending for the filming of this gripping story and its early appearance on the silver screen is assured."[39]

In the early 1900s, when Ida Tarbell dispatched a research assistant to upstate New York, he picked up the same allegations of horse theft that flavor the pages of *Joshua*. Horses were said to have begun vanishing after Big Bill moved first to Richford and later to Moravia. "It became noised about the neighborhood that 'Old Bill's gang' were the horse thieves," reported Tarbell's assistant.[40] In 1850, three of Bill's cronies—Caleb Palmer, Charles Tidd, and a man named Bates—were arrested for stealing mares. After Tidd turned state's evidence, he provided the testimony that was used to incarcerate Palmer and Bates. It must be stressed that no court records actually connect Bill with the crime and that biographer Allan Nevins, after much examination, branded the horse-thieving charges "ridiculous."[41] Yet the anecdotal evidence can't be so easily dismissed. Tarbell's assistant noted, "Everyone I talked with in Moravia declares that 'Old Bill' was the head of the gang." John Monroe Palmer, son of one of the jailed culprits, fingered Bill as the mastermind of the "underground horse railroad." "Rockefeller was too smart to be caught," he griped. "He ruined my father, and then left him in the lurch."[42]

Another tale circulating in upstate New York at the turn of the century contended that Bill had corrupted the village youth by teaching them how to gamble. One ancient resident, Hiram Alley, recalled that the village boys would pay Bill five dollars to instruct them in card tricks so they could then fleece other boys. John D. never commented on allegations against his father but, having never touched cards in his life, scoffed at this particular libel. "If my father had been a gambler, I would have known something about cards, wouldn't I?"[43]

Clearly, Devil Bill had a suggestive personality that made imaginations run riot, and some of the stories about him were likely embellished. Yet one charge left behind a more convincing paper trail. Beginning with Nancy Brown in Richford, Eliza had always employed a young woman to assist with the housework, and in Moravia she had a tall, pretty young woman helper named Anne Vanderbeak. On July 26, 1849, according to papers filed at the Auburn Court House, William Avery Rockefeller was indicted for assaulting Anne Vanderbeak on May 1, 1848, and "then and there violently against her will feloniously did ravish and carnally know" her.[44] The rape indictment deepens suspicions that Bill was more than just a charming, flirtatious rogue.

The aftermath of the indictment was inconclusive, and the whole affair has been obscured by a heavy fog of speculation. Bill never appeared in court, never went to trial, and was never arrested. Everybody who has examined the case has tripped over the same set of questions. Why was the indictment handed down more than a year after the supposed rape? (One feminist scholar has helpfully noted the formidable obstacles placed in the way of women pressing rape charges in those days.)[45] Why did the prosecuting attorney never endorse the indictment? Why didn't anybody set off in hot pursuit of Bill when he fled from Cayuga County? And why did Anne Vanderbeak let the matter lapse? Once again, a handful of oral histories suggest a tangled skein of local intrigue. Bill had seduced a young woman named Charlotte Hewitt, whose brothers, Earl and Lew, loathed him for it. One Hewitt brother sat on the jury that indicted Big Bill, leading some to see it as a trumped-up charge, a vendetta by the brothers. Ida Tarbell's assistant devised another theory: "I believe the indictment was quashed, possibly on the understanding that he was to leave the county. This was not unusual procedure in those days."[46]

The scandal ended whatever tentative truce Bill had struck with John Davison, who had long rued the day when Bill Rockefeller first bewitched his sensible daughter. During the Moravia period, Davison had patched up relations with Bill and lent him almost $1,000 in two installments, one in August 1845, the other in October 1846. Now the rape indictment shattered their still tenuous relationship—lending greater credence to the charge. When Bill informed Davison of the accusation and asked him to post bail, Davison gruffly replied that he was "too old a man to go bail for anyone." Taken aback, Bill replied bitterly that he would leave the county and never see him again. Worried about his two outstanding loans, Davison went straight to court, claimed his son-in-law planned to defraud his creditors, and sued him for $1,210.75.[47] For Eliza and her offspring, it must have been a thoroughly humiliating moment when the sheriff and two neighbors came to appraise their property and attached all their movable goods in the name of John Davison. Davison also modified his will, placing Eliza's inheritance in the hands of trustees, in all likelihood to keep it safely beyond the eager grasp of his son-in-law.

During the second half of 1849, Bill abandoned his family and gadded about the countryside to reconnoiter new towns. In the spring of 1850, the same year Nathaniel Hawthorne published *The Scarlet Letter,* Bill resettled his family in Owego, near the Pennsylvania border. As a fugitive from justice, he might have wanted to be near the state line whenever trouble loomed. Though only ten at the time and probably ignorant of what had happened—it's hard to imagine Eliza confiding such scandalous things to a young boy—John later ridiculed the rape charge and mocked the idea of his father fleeing justice. "If [my father] left 'under compulsion' . . . I should have known something about it. There was nothing of the sort. We moved over to Owego, and if he were fleeing from justice that wasn't very far away."[48] John's later tendency to minimize the disgrace probably had several causes, ranging from filial piety to shrewd public relations; he knew people bent upon proving his own immorality wanted to buttress their case by first tarnishing his father. One must also note his penchant for denial, his potent capacity to filter out uncomfortable thoughts, especially about his father, just as he later deflected criticism of his questionable business behavior. John D. Rockefeller drew strength by simplifying reality and strongly believed that excessive reflection upon unpleasant but unalterable events only weakened one's resolve in the face of enemies.

At some point in his boyhood, however, possibly after the flight from Moravia, John's reverence for his father did begin to be intermingled with more hostile, unexpressed feelings. (One writer of a wildly psychoanalytic bent has even suggested that Rockefeller's icy self-control was a reaction to repressed fantasies of murdering his father.)[49] In later years, scores of John D.'s friends and associates noted that Big Bill was a taboo topic that they broached at their peril, one on which John maintained a thoroughgoing silence. As one early biographer remarked, "From the beginning to the end of his career, he has made secrecy respecting his father and stealth respecting paternal visits a matter of religious observance."[50]

We cannot tell when Rockefeller first felt shame about his father, but this emotion was so consequential for his entire development that we must pause briefly to consider it. In the towns of John's boyhood, Bill was an engaging but notorious character who prompted interminable speculation about his travels and sources of income. A boy with such a father needed to screen out malicious gossip and cultivate a brazen indifference to community opinion. This bred in him a reflexive habit of secrecy, a fear of the crowd, a deep contempt for idle chatter and loose tongues that lasted a lifetime. He learned to cultivate a secretive style and a defiant attitude toward strangers. Perhaps out of a self-protective instinct, Bill taught his children to be wary of strangers and even of himself. When John was a child, Bill would urge him to leap from his high chair into his waiting arms. One day, he dropped his arms, letting his astonished son crash to the floor. "Remember," Bill lectured him, "never trust anyone completely, not even me." Somewhat later, walking with his boys through Cleveland, he warned them to ignore the pell-mell rush of people to fires and parades. "Never mind the crowd," he told them. "Keep away from it. Attend to your own business."[51] Eliza also must have inoculated the children's minds against talebearers and told them not to discuss family matters with other people. The boy who faced down the vicious talk of neighbors would be extremely well prepared to walk unscathed and even defiant through the turbulent controversies that later surrounded his life.

=====

For all the uncertainty of their lives, the Rockefellers, in their restless, driven odyssey across the southern tier of New York, enjoyed a sense of upward mobility as they journeyed from Richford to Moravia to Owego, with each town larger, more prosperous, and more hopeful than its predecessor. The county seat of Tioga County, located south of Richford and west of Binghamton, Owego sits astride a broad, beautiful bend of the Susquehanna River. Decidedly more cosmopolitan than anything young John D. had experienced before, it was a refined village with genteel homes along Front Street that vouchsafed glimpses of a finer life. The incorporated village of Owego had an imposing courthouse, a well-stocked library, a renowned school, and other nascent hints of culture. For a country town of seventy-two hundred people, it also boasted a disproportionate number of resident writers and artists.

Perhaps because his sojourn there was shorter, Rockefeller never developed quite the same fond attachment to Owego as to Moravia, but he retained pleasing associations with it. "What a beautiful place Owego is!" he once exclaimed. "How fortunate we were to grow up there, in a beautiful country, with good neighbors, people of culture and refinement, kind friends."[52] With amusement, he recalled how Owego had exploded his provincial boyhood. "Down at the railroad station one day I saw a Frenchman! Think of that—a real, live Frenchman. And he wore a mustache—the first I ever saw."[53] On June 1, 1849, shortly before the Rockefellers arrived, the Erie Railroad had first puffed into Owego, thousands of spectators packing the hillsides to cheer the train as it slid into the station amid a burst of ceremonial cannonades and pealing church bells. "Railroad trains were known even when I was a boy but they were few, short and sooty," Rockefeller said of the conveyances that would figure so largely in his own exploits.[54] In small towns like Owego, the railroad ended isolated, self-contained economies, absorbing them into regional and national markets while also sharpening their inhabitants' appetites for material goods and inviting them to seek their fortunes in distant cities.

The Rockefellers lived three miles east of town in an area of soft, bucolic meadows and riverine groves. Of the two frame houses they occupied during their time in Owego, the second was smaller, suggesting that Bill and Eliza needed to retrench as they grappled with financial problems. The second house—more a cottage than a farm—had a fine view of the winding, muddy Susquehanna, with the wooded silhouette of Big Island (later Hiawatha Island) in the foreground, ringed by a curtain of blue hills in the distance. In these snug quarters, John shared a bed with brother William. "It was a small house," John reminisced years later, "but a dear good house."[55]

Bill might have chosen Owego because it had signal business advantages for someone who dabbled in the lumber business. During freshets, log rafts were easily floated down the Susquehanna River, and several lumber mills, in consequence, had sprung up in the town. It might also be significant that on September 27, 1849, right before the Rockefellers moved to Owego, an appalling conflagration had consumed 104 downtown buildings, the blaze sparing only three stores, a disaster that presaged a booming lumber business as the town was rebuilt. Finally, the town had a reputation as a mecca for self-styled doctors. As one Owego resident recalled, "After the Civil War, there were a dozen of them living here."[56]

During the three Owego years, Bill's escapades seemed even more bizarrely unpredictable than before. His appearances in town were brief and infrequent, however memorable to the gaping natives. "He was the best-dressed man for miles around," said a close neighbor. "You never saw him without his fine silk hat."[57] Now in her late thirties, Eliza was losing her youthful bloom and developing the hard, thin face that told of her many trials. Many townsfolk recalled her as a sweet, fine, dignified lady who called on neighbors in the afternoon, always clad in a black silk dress that looked like widow's weeds. Everybody commended her unsparing discipline, neat appearance, and commanding presence. For all her travails, she didn't seem as forlorn as she had in Richford and Moravia, as if growing more accustomed to the burden that she bore and more reconciled to Bill's absences.

Once the swaggering, autocratic husband, Bill had now been irredeemably exposed as a scoundrel and was demoted in Eliza's esteem. Her disillusionment with her handsome husband might have simplified matters in the household. "It was she who brought up the family," said one observer, "for even when he was at home the father did not interfere with her discipline. And it was discipline."[58] Another neighbor termed her "an unusually clear-minded and capable Christian mother. Perhaps her discipline might seem very strict or even severe today, but, although she made them obey her and kept them all busily employed, the children all loved her as she loved them."[59] She wasn't a mother to be trifled with. Once, while sick in bed, she discovered that John had neglected to perform a task for her, and judgment was swift: She sent him to the Susquehanna to select a willow switch. With the quiet cunning that would become a pronounced trait of his nature, he nicked the switch in several places with his knife, so it would bend and crack after the initial blows. Eliza wasn't deceived. "Go and get another switch," she instructed him, "and see that it is not slashed this time."[60]

Eliza must have found the religious atmosphere in Owego suitably wholesome. One of John's imperishable images of Owego was of standing behind the house and hearing the dutiful Eliza praying aloud in an upstairs bedroom. The local Baptists were enterprising evangelists, and every winter they marched scores of reformed sinners down to the frozen Susquehanna, carved out openings in the ice, and baptized them. Every Sunday, neighbors picked up Eliza and the children and drove them to a Baptist church in the village. Inspired by a Sunday-school class on forgiveness, the children initiated a custom that suggests how religion permeated their lives. Each night, when they got into bed, they turned to their siblings and said, "Do you forgive me all I have done to you today?"[61] By the time they fell asleep, the air had been cleared of all recriminations or festering anger.

In Owego, Eliza increased her dependence on John, as if training him to be everything Bill wasn't. Like his mother, John seemed stronger without Bill, able to escape his shadow and forge a separate identity. His manifold duties habituated him to a heavy workload. When not attending school, he cut wood, milked the cow, drew well water, tended the garden, and went on shopping expeditions while also supervising his younger siblings in their mother's absence. "I was taught to do as much business at the age of ten or eleven as it was possible for me to do," he later noted.[62]

As the stand-in for Bill, he kept a tight rein on the family budget and learned to appraise the world shrewdly. Once he spent three days helping a local farmer dig potatoes for 37½ cents per day. This set up an instructive contrast for the frugal boy when, soon afterward, he loaned one farmer $50 at 7 percent interest and collected $3.50 at year's end—without a stitch of work. He was thunderstruck by the happy math, which hit him with the force of a revelation. "The impression was gaining ground with me that it was a good thing to let the money be my slave and not make myself a slave to money."[63] Brother William—a good-natured boy who pitched in with gusto and never asked too many questions—was far more popular with the local farmers, whereas the more rational John analyzed work, broke it down into component parts, and figured out how to perform it most economically.

Throughout his life, John D. Rockefeller, Sr., reacted in a vitriolic manner to accusations that he had lusted after money as a child and yearned to be fabulously rich. Doubtless embarrassed, he contested insinuations that he was motivated by greed instead of a humble desire to serve God or humanity. He preferred to portray his fortune as a pleasant accident, the unsought by-product of hard work. Yet stories surface of Rockefeller daydreaming about money in Owego when he was only in his early teens. One day, strolling by the Susquehanna with a friend, he blurted out: "Some day, sometime, when I am a man, I want to be worth a-hundred-thousand-dollars. And I'm going to be, too—some day."[64] Nearly identical accounts come from so many sources that one is forced to conclude he had conveniently expunged such memories. Given his father's panting ardor for money, it would have been strange had he *not* been bewitched by gold.

There was nothing unusual about Rockefeller's boyhood dreams, for the times were feeding avaricious fantasies in millions of susceptible schoolboys. Antebellum America was a place of high adventure and unbounded opportunity for industrious young men. Following the war with Mexico, huge chunks of land—Texas, New Mexico, and upper California—were annexed to the country in early 1848. That same year, gold was discovered at John Sutter's sawmill in California, triggering a mad westward rush of ninety thousand prospectors. Just as the Rockefellers were moving from Moravia to Owego, hordes of frantic men swarmed across the continent, sailed around South America, or slogged across the Isthmus of Panama, hell-bent to reach California. The pandemonium foreshadowed the petroleum craze in western Pennsylvania a decade later. Though the gold rush proved a snare and a delusion for most miners, the occasional success stories nonetheless inflamed the popular imagination. Mark Twain singled out the California gold rush as the watershed event that sanctified a new money worship and debased the country's founding ideals.

Before he left Owego, John secured a first-rate education, then a rarity in rural America, where few children attended secondary school. At first, the Rockefeller children went to a schoolhouse a short walk from their house; due to the family's straitened circumstances, a friendly neighbor purchased their textbooks. In August 1852, John and William entered Owego Academy, which had been founded in 1827 and was unquestionably the finest secondary school in that part of New York. Topped by a tall steeple, fenced in by lovely parkland, the three-story brick school building must have awed the still-rustic Rockefeller boys. Presiding over the academy was an able Scot, Dr. William Smythe, who made the students hone their verbal skills by writing fortnightly essays and delivering speeches on assigned themes; the linguistic skills mastered at Owego became evident in Rockefeller's concise business letters. The school produced many eminent graduates, including Thomas C. Platt, later the "Easy Boss" who ran the New York Republican machine, and Washington Gladden, the preacher who issued some of the most scorching screeds directed against Standard Oil.

Many of the 350 pupils came from affluent urban families, and John later lauded this exposure to city boys, saying it was "bound to benefit country boys."[65] The school charged a steep tuition of three dollars per term, suggesting that Bill's medical road show was finally prospering after two years in Owego. John never expressed resentment at being, by academy standards, a poor boy. When a photographer came to shoot class pictures, John and William were excluded because their suits were too shabby. Other boys might have smarted, but John always prized his daguerreotypes of his fellow scholars, later insisting, "I would not part with this collection for any money."[66] In Eliza Rockefeller's household, one didn't morbidly dwell on slights but kept one's sights fixed on the practical goals ahead. John never aspired to popularity at the school. It was as if, after the inordinate attention that his father attracted, John wanted to be quiet and inconspicuous and blend into the crowd.

While many well-to-do students boarded at the school, the Rockefeller boys undertook a three-mile hike to school every morning and, like many students, wandered barefoot down the dusty lanes in warm weather. This long trek led John past fine, imposing homes with well-trimmed lawns facing the Susquehanna River. With his slow, deliberate pace, he often set out early and reflected in an unhurried manner as he walked, his eyes always fixed on the ground ahead. Not averse to taking shortcuts, however, he sometimes sat by the roadside and asked passing teamsters for a lift.

John was a plodding, lackluster student, with no discernible trace of brilliance, and only one aspect of school life truly seemed to intrigue him. Every Saturday, the principal demonstrated the newfangled devices then revolutionizing American business, and John was riveted by displays of a telegraph instrument (invented by Samuel F. B. Morse in 1837), galvanic batteries, and other modern contrivances. Such things captured his mind more than the rousing social issues raised by Harriet Beecher Stowe in *Uncle Tom's Cabin*, which was published in 1852 in horrified response to the Fugitive Slave Law of 1850.

To the extent that the Rockefeller children had difficulties with schoolwork, it stemmed from the chaotic situation at home. For five growing, energetic children, their small cottage was noisy and cramped. Each evening, Eliza packed her brood off to a teenage neighbor named Susan La Monte, who tutored them and ensured that they completed their homework. She remembered William and Frank as typically mischievous boys, kicking and teasing each other, while John was oddly self-possessed, already a boy-man, a model of adult decorum. "I have no recollection of John excelling at anything. I do remember he worked hard at everything; not talking much, and studying with great industry. . . . There was nothing about him to make anybody pay especial attention to him or speculate about his future."[67]

An 1852 photo of the Rockefeller children shows John, age thirteen, William, eleven, and Mary Ann, nine, sitting in the inky gloom of a photo studio. They are a cheerless trio as they stare blankly into the camera. Wearing a plaid suit, and with his hair neatly brushed back from a wide forehead, John has a long, impassive face, and his expression is inscrutable. William has a softer, rounder face, and his garments—including a polka-dotted vest and a watch chain—suggest his father's more outgoing personality. Mary Ann wears the plain dress of a farm girl, her hair in pigtails and parted down the middle. Although the group portrait suggests middle-class respectability, its somber mood—which also must owe something to the slower photography of the day—discloses something less than the idyllic boyhood John liked to evoke.

The drudgery of daily life was often leavened by play as John had his first chances to flirt with young ladies, and he exhibited flashes of droll wit. One afternoon, at a Sunday picnic—he was perhaps twelve—he passed a group of young ladies seated before heaps of food and observed, "Remember, girls, if you eat slowly, you can eat more!"[68] Rockefeller was intensely aware of the opposite sex yet, knowing of his father's history, kept his impulses under tight control. Susan La Monte saw a sensitivity in the boy that escaped casual observers; she was struck by "his great admiration of beauty. There was a little girl going to school near our home, a pretty little thing named Freer, with red cheeks and bright eyes and a sweet face. In after years Mr. Rockefeller would ask for her, and when she was left a widow in distress he aided her with a modest pension."[69] Susan La Monte saw that the boy's eerie self-discipline concealed a deep fund of emotion, and she remembered the ceremony of grief he went through when one of her sisters died. "On the day she died John came to our house and stretched out on the ground and would not go away. He was so sorry that he would not go away, but lay there all day."[70] Such stories reveal a sensitivity in Rockefeller that would always be there but that would later be studiously concealed behind the polished façade of the hard-driving businessman.

Margaret Allen, who first met William Avery Rockefeller
in the early 1850s, while she was still in her teens.
(Courtesy of the Rockefeller Archive Center)

CHAPTER 3

Bound to Be Rich

s a roving salesman, William Avery Rockefeller was fast becoming a relic of an earlier America when markets were extended not by new methods of communication or transportation but by the salesman simply covering more ground. A magnetic pull lured Big Bill even farther west, away from the burgeoning cities and industries of the eastern seaboard and toward remote hamlets on the American frontier. In early 1853, the Rockefellers were again uprooted and swept along in the whirlwind of Bill's life when he took them by train to a prairie town in Ohio called Strongsville, about a dozen miles southwest of Cleveland. At this juncture, Bill quietly began to distance himself from his dazed family, having formed a new romantic attachment that proved far deeper than earlier infidelities and that finally severed his familial ties.

Where Eliza and the children had at least enjoyed their own homes in Richford, Moravia, and Owego, retaining some modicum of dignity, Bill now dumped them at the home of his sister and brother-in-law, Sara Ann and William Humiston, paying his relatives three hundred dollars a year to board his clan. To his hapless family, this must have seemed, after all their wanderings, terribly unfair. Their lives had always been uncommonly restless, but now they were castoffs, pariahs in a strange new Ohio town, tumbling back down the social ladder they had so arduously climbed.

The six Rockefellers were squashed into a small house with six or seven Humistons, even though Bill seems to have been flush with cash at the time. Years later, Billy Humiston insisted that Devil Bill was considered rich, that he gave out loans at hefty rates, kept three or four fine guns, stocked a rich wardrobe, and sported diamond rings and a gold watch—all of which suggested that the abrupt move to Ohio was less a matter of financial stringency than of personal convenience.[1] The Humistons greatly admired Eliza for her excellent business head and thrifty money management, but enormous tension was bottled up in the overcrowded Humiston household. Billy junior later portrayed his cousins William and Frank as very rowdy and John as a prig. "John was just such a boy as he is a man—sanctimonious and precise."[2] Fortunately for all concerned, the Rockefellers soon moved out and took up residence on a small farm at the edge of Strongsville.

By now Big Bill had relinquished all interest in lumber and other settled trades and had permanently assumed the persona of the rambling doctor or "botanic physician," as he was soon listed in the Cleveland directory. In the first year after he deposited his family in Strongsville, Bill returned only three or four times, but, by a curious fluke, the townspeople learned a good deal about his fraudulent activities on the road. One day, a Strongsville resident, Joe Webster, checked into a hotel in Richfield, Ohio, and was stunned to see a sign in the lobby trumpeting the news, "Dr. William A. Rockefeller, the Celebrated Cancer Specialist, Here for One Day Only. All cases of cancer cured unless too far gone and then can be greatly benefited." Soon after, with the smooth vaudevillian patter employed by so many patent-medicine vendors, Bill collected a crowd outside the hotel. Standing up in his buggy, his sign propped against the wheels, a showman in a silk hat, black frock coat, and dark red beard, he presented himself as Doc Rockefeller and offered full-fledged cancer cures for the extremely steep price of twenty-five dollars; those strapped for cash could purchase cheaper bottles of medicine. When Webster approached him afterward, Bill wasn't abashed and bragged that he had lately been "doctoring" as far afield as Iowa and was buying up land there. After Webster returned to Strongsville and told of his startling discovery, word quickly got around town and everybody thereafter referred to their shadowy, footloose neighbor as Doc Rockefeller—doubtless with some mirth. The moniker stuck.

In the fall of 1853, after eight months in Strongsville, Big Bill decided that the time had come for John and William to resume their educations, so he drove them into Cleveland and settled them as boarders with a Mrs. Woodin on Erie Street, where they paid a dollar a week for room and board. John was penalized by the Cleveland schools because his family had moved around so much. In the sole extant reference to the matter, he wrote in 1923, "I had just come from New York State and recall my humiliation in being obliged to remain one term in the old Clinton Street School—I had been for several years in the Owego Academy . . . and supposed I should go at once into the High School instead of the Grammar School."[3] For this proud boy, the demotion must have been one of many small but wounding indignities suffered during these anxious years.

When John finally entered high school (later called Central High School) in 1854 at the age of fifteen, it was still a modest, one-story affair, shaded by trees and standing behind a clean white picket fence; it would receive a much fancier new building in 1856. Operating on the progressive theory of free education for boys and girls, the school enjoyed a superb reputation. Since it stressed composition, John had to submit essays on four topics to advance to the next grade: "Education," "Freedom," "The Character of St. Patrick," and "Recollections of the Past." At a time when America was deeply split over the question of extending slavery to new territories—the Kansas-Nebraska Act was passed in May 1854—these writings exhibit Rockefeller as a young democrat and confirmed abolitionist. In "Freedom," he branded it a "violation of the laws of our country and the laws of our God that man should hold his fellow man in bondage." Unless slavery was curbed speedily, he prophesied, it "will end in the ruin of our country."[4] America would only progress, he believed, with an educated citizenry. "In former times when learning was confined to the monks and priests, then it was that the world stood still, and it was not until the people were educated and began to think for themselves that it progressed."[5] Such views on abolitionism and universal literacy echoed those of northern Baptist evangelicals who scorned political no less than ecclesiastical despotism. As a self-made man, Rockefeller would always deplore aristocracies and priesthoods as effete, reactionary foes of true progress, defenders of privilege against enterprising commoners.

Rockefeller expressed himself with great clarity and precision. (Schoolmates called him "John D." because he signed his essays this way.) He also excelled as a debater, demonstrating that beneath his reserved manner he could articulate his thoughts forcefully. He began one speech with the line "I'm pleased although I'm sad," and this gambit so tickled his fellow students that they nicknamed him "Old Pleased-Although-I'm-Sad."[6] He bore another, equally doleful nickname, "the Deacon," and it says much about his preferences that he actually *liked* this sobriquet. As his future sister-in-law, Lucy Spelman, said, "He was a studious boy, grave, reserved, never noisy or given to boisterous play."[7] Rockefeller frequently hugged his slate to his chest, a pose that hinted at his guarded nature.

However private or solitary, John D. always had his quota of friends. One close chum was Mark Hanna, the descendant of well-to-do grocers and commodity brokers and later a U.S. senator and Republican Party boss. Another friend, Darwin Jones, who formed a boyhood triumvirate with them, recalled the sharply etched contrast between Hanna and Rockefeller. "Mark was of the virile type, always active and took part in almost all forms of athletics, while John Rockefeller was reserved, studious, though always pleasant. No matter what the excitement, John retained his quietude and smiled on all occasions."[8] In future years, Rockefeller cringed when Mark Hanna was quoted posthumously as describing him as "sane in every respect save one—he is money mad!"[9] As at Owego Academy, classmates in Cleveland remembered Rockefeller voicing the fervent wish to be worth a hundred thousand dollars someday.

John's boyhood gravity pleased many adults but unsettled others, who found something queer and unnatural about him. One high-school teacher described him, with patent distaste, as "the coldest blooded, the quietest and most deliberate chap."[10] Even as a teenager, Rockefeller demanded to be treated with adult dignity. In recollecting the school principal, Dr. Emerson E. White, Rockefeller mentioned only his behavior toward him: "Mr. White was a gentleman. He treated me like a gentleman—and treated all the boys so."[11] Rockefeller was sensitive about adults who behaved in a high-handed fashion toward him. Having assumed so much responsibility at home, he now thought of himself as a mature person. Bill had set him up with his own bank account, and his life was far more independent than those of his classmates.

This tough, self-possessed boy had no tincture of rebellion in his makeup. Seeing his education solely in utilitarian terms, he studied hard but showed no intellectual playfulness. "I was very sedate and earnest," he said, "preparing to meet the responsibilities of life."[12] Once again, he displayed a fantastic mind for numbers. "Arithmetical problems most attracted him," said Lucy Spelman, "for he had been taught at home to keep accurate account of his gains and losses."[13]

Perhaps the most surprising dimension of John D.'s early adolescence was his deep absorption in music. He even briefly aspired to be a musician and practiced the piano for up to six hours a day, driving Eliza mad with the racket while they still lived in Owego. The piano was then the symbol of a decorous middle-class home and his playing might have hinted at his genteel aspirations. For a man who would distrust other art forms as vaguely subversive, encouraging ungovernable emotions and pagan sensuality, music provided him with an artistic medium that he could wholeheartedly enjoy with church approval.

For the teenage boy, Mrs. Woodin's boardinghouse was an education in itself. Her daughter, Martha, was several years older than John and William, and they engaged in lively, heated discussions on many topics, with the bright, outspoken Mrs. Woodin often joining in. The most controversial topic was lending money at interest. In an extremely peculiar arrangement, John, age fifteen, was already lending small sums to his father at interest; never sentimental when it came to business, he simply charged his father what the traffic would bear—a practice Bill probably applauded enthusiastically. According to Rockefeller, Mrs. Woodin was "violently opposed to loaners obtaining high rates of interest, and we had frequent and earnest arguments on the subject."[14] It was typical of Rockefeller that this question of business method and morality occupied his attention far more than the esoteric matters found in schoolbooks.

As if embarrassed by his peripatetic family life, Rockefeller tended to over-simplify the chronology of his early years, especially when speaking of his ado-lescence. After a year in Strongsville, John claimed, his family moved to Parma, about seven miles south of Cleveland, then into their own house in Cleveland proper. In fact, he omitted a critical two-step Cleveland detour before the shift to Parma, as can be gleaned from a revealing anecdote told by his school prin-cipal, Dr. White: "One day in 1854 a tall, angular boy came to me and said that his widowed mother and two sisters were coming to Cleveland to live and he wished my help in finding a temporary home for them." The good-natured White invited the Rockefellers to move in with him and his new bride, and John "liked the idea and always insisted that it was a happy time for his mother."[15]

Two words leap from the story—*widowed mother.* It seems of some psycho-logical significance that the first recorded instance of Rockefeller's capacity to lie came in an effort to hush up his father's existence—in fact, to bury him alive. Since Bill popped up in Cleveland three or four times a year, it took a cer-tain cheek for his son to invent this story. The small episode acquires added in-terest when one notes that more than thirty years later, when Eliza died before Bill did, John instructed the preacher to describe her as a widow at the funeral. Further, despite the principal's gracious response, it must have been perfectly dreadful for John, as a teenager, to go on a begging mission to find temporary lodgings for his family.

When Bill reappeared, he moved his family to a house on Perry Street in downtown Cleveland, rented from a Mr. O. J. Hodge, who remembered John as "an unassuming youth who showed none of the hilarity often seen in boys of that age. Usually he sat quietly in his chair listening to what was being said."[16] As had been true since the Richford days, Bill was scrupulous about making timely rent payments. "Never was rent—$200 for a year—paid more promptly, nor did I have in all respects a better tenant," said the landlord.[17] Before the year was out, Bill had resettled his family on a ten-acre, creek-side farm in Parma while John returned to Mrs. Woodin, who had relocated first to Saint Clair Street and then to Hamilton Street.

A contemporary photo of John with his two sisters and two brothers, all of them unsmiling, is again drenched in a mortuary gloom. Now a tall, thin boy who weighed about 140 pounds, John had tidily brushed light brown hair and clothes that were always clean and presentable. He later laughed at his solemn boyhood demeanor: "From fourteen years of age to twenty-five I was much more dignified than I am now," he said with truth in his seventies.[18] In Strongsville and Parma, Eliza fretted about the ubiquitous taverns in town and worked hard to shield her children from illicit entertainments. She must have been especially alarmed as her eldest son approached that perilous rite of passage, first love. Interestingly, John D. reenacted his father's penchant for dal-liances with the domestic help. In Strongsville, Eliza hired a household assis-

tant, a pretty young farmer's daughter named Melinda Miller, who did chores
for the family and shared their meals. When the Rockefellers moved to Parma,
Melinda resumed working for them, and John, a year younger than she, often
came out from Cleveland to take walks with her. Rumors soon drifted about
town that John had taken away the girl's virginity. Whatever the truth, the
Millers raised an unholy ruckus about the romance. In one of the less
prophetic judgments in parental history, they argued that they didn't want
their daughter to throw herself away on a young man with such poor
prospects. According to legend, one of Melinda's parents came to fetch her by
buggy to break up the liaison. Eventually, she married young Joe Webster,
whose father had discovered Big Bill's doctor act.[19] From the standpoint of
Rockefeller's career, the failure of this relationship was fortunate, for he ended
up with a woman of much greater social standing and intellectual attainment,
who would provide him with the strong, stable home life and religious certitude that he craved.

=

At this point, we need to sketch in some events in William Avery Rockefeller's
life in the early 1850s, for his behavior began to shade over from the eccentric
to the quasi-pathological. A man of multiple disguises, he had always been
fond of assuming names; even when he first arrived in Richford, he had told
some people that his name was Rockafellow. During the Owego years, Bill occasionally appeared in surrounding towns and presented himself as an eye-
and-ear specialist named Dr. William Levingston. We know now that by the
time he transplanted his family to Ohio, he was leading a full-blown double life
as both Dr. William A. Rockefeller and Dr. William Levingston, the latter name
appropriated from the town of his father's birth, Livingston, New York. While
this second name probably began as a simple alias to shield his family from his
shady practices, it hardened in the early 1850s into a separate identity away
from home. Bill's traveling partner in his later years attributed Bill's use of the
pseudonym to the fact that he was practicing medicine without a license or
diploma and always feared retribution from indignant local doctors, who instigated legal proceedings against him on several occasions.[20]

In the last gasp of his lumber career, Bill had ventured north into Canada in
the early 1850s, buying up fine walnut and ash and selling it at a handsome
profit to timber mills. After he moved to the town of Niagara, Ontario (almost
certainly without his family's knowledge), he began to canvass the surrounding countryside as a traveling doctor. "Dr. Levingston" was a blatant quack,
but he partially believed his own bombast and had enough success stories to
deceive his patients and perhaps even himself. As his future partner said, "He
had not studied medicine in any college. But he was a natural healer and had
great skill. He had great fame in Canada and northern New York."[21]

Devil Bill had an unerring instinct for spotting those pretty, docile, long-suffering women who would patiently endure his escapades. Around 1852, with his oblivious family still in Owego, he met a lovely, gentle teenage girl in Norwich, Ontario, named Margaret Allen. Bill was then forty-two and Margaret about seventeen, or only four years older than John D. By a small oversight, Dr. Levingston neglected to mention his other life as Doc Rockefeller, to say nothing of his wife and five children, and he wooed Margaret like a lusty bachelor. Bill was an expert confidence man, and Margaret's trusting family was totally fooled. "He was a steady, temperate man of good habits, kind hearted, sociable and well liked by everybody," said Margaret's sister of this jolly wooer. "He was a famous marksman and loved to hunt. He was fond of a good story."[22] Doc Levingston was clearly more popular with the Allens than Doc Rockefeller had been with the Davisons, and Bill was tempted to start afresh with an adoring, innocent young woman, supported by a friendly family. On June 12, 1855, he married Margaret Allen in Nichols, New York, just south of Owego, and started a clandestine life as a bigamist that would persist for the rest of his days.

One can plausibly argue that every time Bill moved his family to another town, it related to his secret philandering, and that he probably relocated his family in Cleveland because Ontario lay just across Lake Erie. True to his earlier behavior, Bill didn't take up permanent residence with Margaret at first. To initiate her into his capricious ways, he started out by visiting her in Ontario once a year and staying with her credulous family. He didn't plan, at the outset, to desert his original family, and for a time in the 1850s Bill continued to tread a tightrope between his old and new wives, neither of whom knew of the existence of the other.

It seems likely that Bill's second marriage had immediate repercussions in the life of his oldest son. All along John had planned to attend college, with Eliza fortifying his resolve in the hope that he would someday become a Baptist minister. Then he received a letter from his father that dispelled his dreams. As he recalled, "My father . . . conveyed an intimation that I was not to go [to college]. I felt at once that I must get to work, find a situation somewhere."[23] Rockefeller never clarified why he dropped out of high school around May 1855, just two months shy of commencement exercises on July 16, but Bill's second marriage on June 12 supplies the missing piece of the puzzle. About to enter into his second marriage, Bill must have been drastically scaling back on first-family expenditures, albeit without disclosing the reason for the sudden urgency. As John said, "There were younger brothers and sisters to educate and it seemed wise for me to go into business."[24] Bill was eager to groom his eldest son as the surrogate father who would care for Eliza during his longer absences.

Never a great believer in book learning, Bill probably derided a college degree as a costly indulgence at a time when people didn't equate it with enhanced income. Young men on the make were more likely to attend so-called business colleges or to take correspondence courses to supplement their education. Following his father's suggestion, John paid forty dollars for a three-month course of study at E. G. Folsom's Commercial College, a chain college with branches in seven cities. The Cleveland branch occupied the top floor of the Rouse Building, the town's premier office building, which overlooked the Public Square. It taught double-entry bookkeeping, clear penmanship, and the essentials of banking, exchange, and commercial law—the sort of purposeful courses that appealed to John. By the time his studies ended in the summer of 1855, he had turned sixteen and was ready to flee the traumas of his family life by focusing his energies on a promising business situation.

<hr/>

Perhaps no job search in American history has been so mythologized as that begun by sixteen-year-old John D. Rockefeller in the sweltering Cleveland of August 1855. Although he was a rural boy, his family hadn't been full-time farmers, and this must have made it easier for him to escape from his small-town, agricultural past and enter the new market economy. Though times were tough, the boy set out with no modest ambition as he pored over the city directory, identifying those establishments with high credit ratings. Already endowed with instinctive respect for big business, he knew exactly what he wanted. "I went to the railroads, to the banks, to the wholesale merchants," he later said. "I did not go to any small establishments. I did not guess what it would be, but I was after something big."[25] Most of the businesses he visited lay in a bustling area known as the Flats, where the Cuyahoga River twisted through a clanging, roaring landscape of lumber mills, iron foundries, warehouses, and shipyards before emptying into Lake Erie, which was crowded with side-wheel steamboats and schooners. His quest had a touch of callow grandiosity. At each firm, he asked to speak to the top man—who was usually unavailable—then got straight to the point with an assistant: "I understand bookkeeping, and I'd like to get work."[26]

Despite incessant disappointment, he doggedly pursued a position. Each morning, he left his boardinghouse at eight o'clock, clothed in a dark suit with a high collar and black tie, to make his rounds of appointed firms. This grimly determined trek went on each day—six days a week for six consecutive weeks—until late in the afternoon. The streets were so hot and hard that he grew footsore from pacing them. His perseverance surely owed something to his desire to end his reliance upon his fickle father. At one point, Bill suggested that if John didn't find work he might have to return to the country; the thought of such dependence upon his father made "a cold chill" run down his spine, Rockefeller later said.[27] Because he approached his job hunt devoid of any doubt or self-pity, he could stare down all discouragement. "I was working every day at my business—the business of looking for work. I put in my full time at this every day."[28] He was a confirmed exponent of positive thinking.

With almost thirty thousand inhabitants, Cleveland was a boomtown that would have thrilled any young man avid for business experience. It had drawn many transplants from New England who had brought along the Puritan mores and Yankee trading culture of their old hometowns. While the streets were largely unpaved and the town lacked a sewage system, Cleveland was expanding rapidly, with immigrants pouring in from Germany and England as well as the eastern seaboard. The plenty of the Midwest passed through this commercial crossroads of the Western Reserve: coal from Pennsylvania and West Virginia, iron ore from around Lake Superior, salt from Michigan, grain and corn from the plains states. As a port on Lake Erie and the Ohio Canal, Cleveland was a natural hub for transportation networks. When the Cleveland, Columbus and Cincinnati Railroad arrived in 1851, it created excellent opportunities for transport by both water and rail, and nobody would more brilliantly exploit these options than John D. Rockefeller.

For all the thriving waterfront commerce, the job prospects were momentarily bleak. "No one wanted a boy, and very few showed any overwhelming anxiety to talk with me on the subject," said Rockefeller.[29] When he exhausted his list, he simply started over from the top and visited several firms two or three times. Another boy might have been crestfallen, but Rockefeller was the sort of stubborn person who only grew more determined with rejection.

Then, on the morning of September 26, 1855, he walked into the offices of Hewitt and Tuttle, commission merchants and produce shippers on Merwin Street. He was interviewed by Henry B. Tuttle, the junior partner, who needed help with the books and asked him to return after lunch. Ecstatic, Rockefeller walked with restraint from the office, but when he got downstairs and rounded the corner, he skipped down the street with pure joy. Even as an elderly man, he saw the moment as endowed with high drama: "All my future seemed to hinge on that day; and I often tremble when I ask myself the question: 'What if I had not got the job?' "[30] In a "fever of anxiety," Rockefeller waited until the noonday meal was over, then returned to the office, where he was interviewed by senior partner Isaac L. Hewitt. Owner of a good deal of Cleveland real estate and a founder of the Cleveland Iron Mining Company, Hewitt must have seemed a mighty capitalist indeed. After scrutinizing the boy's penmanship, he declared, "We'll give you a chance."[31] They were evidently in urgent need of an assistant bookkeeper, since they told Rockefeller to hang up his coat and go straight to work, without any mention of wages. In those days, it wasn't unusual for an adolescent to serve an unpaid apprenticeship, and it was three months before John received his first humble, retroactive pay. For the rest of his life, he would honor September 26 as "Job Day" and celebrate it with more genuine brio than his birthday. One is tempted to say that his real life began on that day, that he was born again in business as he would be in the Erie Street Baptist Mission Church. All the latent dynamism that had been dormant during his country youth would now quicken into robust, startling life in the business world. He was finally liberated from Big Bill, the endless flight from town to town, the whole crazy upside-down world of his boyhood.

=

Poised on a high stool, bent over musty ledger books at Hewitt and Tuttle, the new clerk could gaze from the window and watch the busy wharves or canal barges drifting by on the Cuyahoga River a block away. Though his day began at dawn, in an office lit dimly by whale-oil lamps, this mercantile world never struck him as arid or boring but "was delightful to me—all the method and system of the office."[32] Work enchanted him, work liberated him, work supplied him with a new identity. "My duties were vastly more interesting than those of an office boy in a large house today," he later said.[33] The mature Rockefeller liked to dub himself "just a man of figures," and he found nothing dry or soporific about the tall ledgers.[34] Having helped Eliza keep the books, he enjoyed a head start. "As I began my life as a bookkeeper, I learned to have great respect for figures and facts, no matter how small they were. . . . I had a passion for detail which afterward I was forced to strive to modify."[35]

Business historians and sociologists have stressed the centrality of accounting to capitalist enterprise. In *The Protestant Ethic and the Spirit of Capitalism*, Max Weber identified "rational bookkeeping" as integral to capitalism's spirit and organization.[36] For Joseph Schumpeter, capitalism "turns the unit of money into a tool of rational cost-profit calculations, of which the towering monument is double-entry bookkeeping."[37] It thus seems fitting that John D. Rockefeller, the archetypal capitalist, betrayed a special affinity for accounting and an almost mystic faith in numbers. For Rockefeller, ledgers were sacred books that guided decisions and saved one from fallible emotion. They gauged performance, exposed fraud, and ferreted out hidden inefficiencies. In an imprecise world, they rooted things in a solid empirical reality. As he chided slipshod rivals, "Many of the brightest kept their books in such a way that they did not actually know when they were making money on a certain operation and when they were losing."

When Hewitt and Tuttle assigned Rockefeller to pay the bills, he went at this task with an undisguised zeal, a precocious virtuosity, and "attended [to it] with more responsibility than the spending of my own funds."[38] He closely reviewed the bills, confirming the validity of each item and carefully adding up the totals. He pounced on errors of even a few cents and reacted with scornful amazement when the boss next door handed his clerk a lengthy, unexamined plumbing bill and blithely said, "Please pay this bill."[39] Rockefeller was appalled by such cavalier indifference, having just caught the same firm in an overcharge of several cents. One suspects that this stickler for detail taught Hewitt and Tuttle a thing or two about economy. "I recall that there was one captain who was always putting in claims for damages to shipments and I decided to investigate. I examined all the invoices, bills of lading and other documents and found this captain had presented entirely unwarranted claims. He never did it again."[40] In all probability, the boy's orderly nature reflected a need to govern potentially unruly emotions, an exaggerated reaction to his disorderly father and helter-skelter childhood.

Besides writing letters, keeping books, and paying bills, young Rockefeller also served as a one-man collection agency for Hewitt's rental properties. Although patient and polite, he displayed a bulldog tenacity that took people by surprise. Sitting outside in his buggy, pale and patient as an undertaker, he would wait until the debtor capitulated. He dunned people as if his life depended upon it, an experience apparently laced with considerable anxiety. "How many times I have dreamed now and then up to recent years that I was trying to collect those bills!" he marveled fifty years later. "I would wake up exclaiming: 'I can't collect So-and-So's account!' "[41] One explanation for his anxiety is that his flight from his distressing family life was still tenuous, and failure at work would mean reverting to reliance on his father. Another explanation is that while he was persistent, he was also extremely slow, as at school, some people thought him a rather dim-witted dolt who would never rise in the world, and he had to prove himself to naysayers.

However modest an operation, Hewitt and Tuttle was an excellent training ground for an aspiring young businessman, for it exposed Rockefeller to a broad commercial universe. Before the Civil War, most businesses still confined themselves to a single service or product. Hewitt and Tuttle, in contrast, traded a wide array of commodities on commission. Though it had started out dealing in foodstuffs, it had pioneered in importing iron ore from Lake Superior three years before Rockefeller was hired. The firm relied upon the railroad and the telegraph, the two technologies then revolutionizing the American economy. As Rockefeller remarked, "My eyes were opened to the business of transportation"—no small thing, given Standard Oil's subsequent controversial relations with the railroads.[42] Even a simple consignment of Vermont marble to Cleveland required complex calculations of the relative costs of railroad, canal, and lake transportation. "The cost of losses or damage had to be somehow fixed between these three different carriers, and it taxed all the ingenuity of a boy of 17 to work out this problem to the satisfaction of all concerned, including my employers."[43] No business experience was ever wasted upon Rockefeller.

On the last day of 1855, Hewitt handed Rockefeller $50 for three months of work, or slightly more than 50 cents a day. Effective immediately, Hewitt announced, the assistant bookkeeper would have his wages boosted sharply to $25 a month or $300 per year. Oddly, Rockefeller felt guilty about the raise: "I felt like a criminal."[44] Again, one has a hunch that he was jubilant but feared, out of religious scruples, his own greed. Accumulating money was one thing, Rockefeller knew, but outwardly coveting it was another.

===

In many ways, John D. Rockefeller exemplified the enterprising young businessman of his era. Thrifty, punctual, industrious, he was a fervent adherent of the gospel of success. He could have been the hero of any of the 119 inspirational tracts soon to be penned by Horatio Alger, Jr., books that bore such sonorous titles as *Strive and Succeed, Luck and Pluck, Brave and Bold,* and *Bound to Rise.* This last title, in fact, echoed Rockefeller's ecstatic boast to an older businessman one day: "I am bound to be rich—bound to be rich—BOUND TO BE RICH!" He was said to have punctuated this refrain by several smart, emphatic whacks on his companion's knee.[45] And John D. didn't become demonstrative about too many topics.

Though Rockefeller steadfastly denied these stories of his boyhood obsession with money, he related the following story of his time at Hewitt and Tuttle:

> I was a young man when I got my first look at a banknote of any size. I was clerking at the time down on the Flats here. One day my employer received a note from a down-State bank for $4,000. He showed it to me in the course of the day's business, and then put it in the safe. As soon as he was gone I unlocked the safe, and taking out that note, stared at it with open eyes and mouth, and then replaced it and double-locked the safe. It seemed like an awfully large sum to me, an unheard of amount, and many times during the day did I open that safe to gaze longingly at the note.[46]

In this story, one can almost feel the erotic charge that the banknote aroused in the boy, the way it cast a hypnotic trance over him. One is reminded of how Big Bill bundled his bills, stored them away, then enjoyed peeking at his hidden treasure. This lusting after money is the more striking in a phlegmatic young man who claimed never to struggle with disruptive impulses. "I never had a craving for tobacco, or tea and coffee," he once stated flatly. "I never had a craving for anything."[47]

If motivated by greed more than he ever cared to admit, Rockefeller also derived a glandular pleasure from work and never found it cheerless drudgery. In fact, the business world entranced him as a fount of inexhaustible wonders. "It is by no means for money alone that these active-minded men labor—they are engaged in a fascinating occupation," he wrote in his memoirs, published in 1908–1909. "The zest of the work is maintained by something better than the mere accumulation of money."[48]

Because American culture encouraged—nay, glorified—acquisitive behavior, there was always the possibility that it might be taken to extremes and people would end up enslaved by their greed. As a result, children were taught to monitor and supervise their behavior. In his posthumously published *Autobiography*, Benjamin Franklin describes how he drew up a little moral ledger that allowed him, at a glance, to track his virtues and vices every day. Many people in the mid–nineteenth century kept such journals to enforce thrift and also objectify their moral performance. Adolescents kept diaries larded with pep talks, exhortations, inspirations, and warnings. Andrew Carnegie wrote hortatory memos to himself, while William C. Whitney kept a small notebook of little homilies. A contradictory impulse was at work: People were spurring themselves to excel but also trying to curb their insatiable appetites in the new competitive economy.

John D. Rockefeller took such internal monitoring to an advanced stage. Like a good Puritan, he scrutinized his daily activities and regulated his desires, hoping to banish spontaneity and unpredictability from his life. Whenever his ambition was about to devour him, his conscience urged restraint. Since he worked a long day at Hewitt and Tuttle, business threatened to become an overwhelming compulsion. Starting work each day at 6:30 A.M., he brought a box lunch to the office and often returned after dinner, staying late. One day he decided to throttle this obsession. "I have this day covenanted with myself not to be seen in [the office] after 10 o'clock P.M. within 30 days," he wrote to himself.[49] It is telling that the young man made such a pledge to himself and equally revealing that he found it impossible to obey.

No less than his business life, Rockefeller's private life was ruled by bookkeeping entries. Since he found numbers so clean and soothing in their simplicity, he applied the business principles of Hewitt and Tuttle to his own personal economy. When he started working in September 1855, he paid a dime for a small red book, anointed Ledger A, in which he minutely recorded his receipts and expenditures. Many of his young contemporaries kept such record books but seldom with such exacting care. For the remainder of his life, Rockefeller treated Ledger A as his most sacred relic. Producing it before Bible classes more than fifty years later, he became almost tearful and trembled as he thumbed its pages, so potent were the emotions it evoked. At a Bible class of the Fifth Avenue Baptist Church in 1897, a deeply moved Rockefeller held the book aloft and intoned, "I haven't seen this book for twenty-five years. You couldn't get it from me for all the modern ledgers in New York and what they all would bring in."[50] The book rested in a safety-deposit vault, like some priceless heirloom.

As Ledger A confirms, Rockefeller was now self-supporting and entirely free of his father, spending half his income for his lodging with Mrs. Woodin and for a washerwoman. He took pride in memories of this threadbare adolescence. "I could not secure the most fashionable cut of clothing. I remember I bought mine then from a cheap clothier. He sold me clothing cheap such as I could pay for and it was a great deal better than buying clothes I could not pay for."[51] He was long puzzled by one lapse from strict economy: He bought a pair of fur gloves for $2.50 to replace his customary woolen mittens and, at age ninety, was still clucking his tongue over this shocking extravagance. "No, I can't say to this day what caused me to waste that $2.50 on regular gloves."[52] Another expense pregnant with interest for the mature Rockefeller was his purchase of an illuminant called camphene for eighty-eight cents per gallon. Thanks to massive economies of scale, Standard Oil eventually sold a superior illuminant, kerosene, for five cents a gallon—something Rockefeller was wont to recall when people later accused him of gouging the populace.

In one critical respect, Rockefeller didn't exaggerate the value of Ledger A, for it spoke authoritatively to the question of whether he was a rapacious man who later misused charity to cleanse a "tainted" fortune. Here Ledger A speaks with a firm and unequivocal voice: Rockefeller was fantastically charitable from boyhood. During his first year on the job, the young clerk donated about 6 percent of his wages to charity, some weeks much more. "I have my earliest ledger and when I was only making a dollar a day I was giving five, ten, or twenty-five cents to all these objects," he observed.[53] He gave to the Five Points Mission in a notorious lower Manhattan slum, as well as to "a poor man in church" and "a poor woman in church."[54] By 1859, when he was twenty, his charitable giving surpassed the 10 percent mark. Despite a pronounced tilt toward Baptist causes, he gave early hints of an ecumenical bent, contributing money to a black man in Cincinnati in 1859 so he could buy his wife out of slavery. The next year, he gave to a black church, a Methodist church, and a Catholic orphanage.

The clerk's philanthropic gifts were as salient as his business talents. It testifies to Rockefeller's deeply paradoxical nature that he was smitten by a $4,000 banknote but equally entranced by an 1855 book entitled *Extracts from the Diary and Correspondence of the Late Amos Lawrence.* A wealthy New England textile manufacturer, Lawrence gave away more than $100,000 in a planned, thoughtful fashion. "I remember how fascinated I was with his letters," said Rockefeller, who might have gotten from Lawrence his later habit of handing out freshly minted money to people. "Crisp bills! I could see and hear them. I made up my mind that, if I could manage it, some day I would give away crisp bills, too."[55] However rare and admirable such thoughts are in a teenage boy, we must note that it was again a case of money exerting a magical effect upon his mind. He saw that money could bring majesty in the moral as well as secular sphere, which excited him more than fancy estates or clothes.

As if he knew he would someday be rich and had to prepare for the appointed hour, the assistant bookkeeper became a perceptive observer of the businessmen around the port and noted their avoidance of ostentation. For instance, he tremendously admired a shipping merchant named L. R. Morris and was struck "by the way he walked, the way he looked, quite unaffected by his great riches. I saw other wealthy men, and I was glad to see that they went about their business without any display of power or money. Later I saw some who wore rich jewels and luxurious clothes. It seemed unfortunate that they were led into such lavish style." If Rockefeller kept to a Quakerish sobriety of dress and later resisted the vulgar display of the Vanderbilts and other Gilded Age moguls, with their elaborate mansions and yachts, it had something to do with his Baptist beliefs, but also with the plain, understated style of the wealthy Cleveland businessmen he studied so attentively at a formative stage of his life.

Like innumerable young people before him, Rockefeller turned to the church for all-encompassing answers to intractable family problems. He possessed a sense of calling in both religion and business, with Christianity and capitalism forming the twin pillars of his life. While Charles Darwin's *Origin of Species* began to chip away at many people's faith after it was published in 1859, Rockefeller's religion remained of the simple, undeviating sort. When challenges to orthodoxy arose in later decades, he stuck by the spiritual certainties of his boyhood. Because of his father's often unscrupulous behavior, the young clerk was ripe for fiery denunciations of sin and the talk of personal salvation and moral reformation that were then staples of Baptist discourse. From the beginning, his Baptist faith served as a powerful instrument to control forbidden feelings and check his father's unruly nature within him. After the constant flux of his childhood, he yearned to be rooted in a church that would act as his substitute family but without the shameful aspects of his real one.

While John and William boarded with Mrs. Woodin and her daughter, Martha, the four of them began to attend a poor, struggling church nearby called the Erie Street Baptist Mission Church. Organized three years earlier by the well-heeled First Baptist Church, the mission church was a spare white building with a belfry and tall narrow windows, standing in a flat, treeless space. Several religious revivals had rolled through Cleveland in the 1850s, and the Erie Street Baptist Mission Church was created in the aftermath of a revival meeting that lasted 150 consecutive nights.

The church gave Rockefeller the community of friends he craved and the respect and affection he needed. Having studied in Deacon Alexander Sked's Bible class, Rockefeller was recruited to the church by Sked, a florist by trade, a poetical Scot who loved to spout psalms and prophecies and seemed to know the whole Bible by heart. Born in Scotland in 1780, Sked arrived in America in 1831 and moved to Cleveland four years later. During services, he would lift his hands in supplication to God, his face shining with fervor. This pious, elderly man served as a mentor to Rockefeller, who sought him out to report the good news when he got his job at Hewitt and Tuttle, an encounter that produced an unexpected snub that Rockefeller never forgot. "Before I went away, he remarked that he liked me pretty well, but that he had always liked my brother William better. I could never think why he said that. I did not hold it against him, but it puzzled me."[56]

In the fall of 1854, after making a personal confession of faith, John was immersed in the baptismal basin by Deacon Sked and became a full-fledged church member. Never a snob, Rockefeller was proud of being "brought up in a mission church."[57] Notwithstanding his worldly ambition, he didn't seek social shortcuts to success by joining a prosperous congregation or a high-church denomination. As a loner and outsider, he was drawn by the warm fellowship of the faithful and liked the egalitarian atmosphere of the Erie Street church, which gave him the opportunity to associate, as he put it, with "people in the most humble of circumstances."[58] A central tenet of Baptism is the autonomy of individual congregations, and the mission churches, which weren't dominated by established families, were the most democratic of all. The Erie Street church was populated by salesmen, shop assistants, railroad conductors, factory workers, clerks, artisans, and others of extremely modest means. Even in its later, fancier incarnation as the Euclid Avenue Baptist Church, the membership remained more plebeian than patrician. In his later years, Rockefeller declared, with heartfelt warmth, "How grateful I am that these associations were given to me in my early boyhood, that I was contented and happy with . . . the work in the church, with the work in the Sunday school, with the work with good people—that was my environment, and I thank God for it!"[59]

Instead of merely attending services, Rockefeller performed numberless tasks in the church. While still in his teens, he became a Sunday-school teacher, a trustee, and an unpaid clerk who kept the board minutes in his own hand. Free of false pride, he delighted even in menial chores, and one woman in the congregation left this vivid vignette of his ubiquitous presence:

In those years . . . Rockefeller might have been found there any Sunday sweeping out the halls, building a fire, lighting the lamps, cleaning the walks, ushering the people to their seats, studying the bible, praying, singing, performing all the duties of an unselfish and thorough going church member. . . . He was nothing but a clerk, and had little money, and yet he gave something to every organization in the little, old church. He was always very precise about it. If he said that he would give fifteen cents, not a living soul could move him to give a penny more, or a penny less. . . . He studied his Bible regularly and diligently, and he knew what was in it.[60]

One notes his proprietary feeling about the church, how lovingly he tended it. In some respects, he acted as a volunteer janitor, sweeping the austere chapel, washing the windows, replenishing the candles in wall sconces or stoking the corner base burner with wood. On Sundays, he rang the bell to summon people to prayer and kindled the fire and then, to economize, snuffed out all the candles save one as people filed from the service. "Save when you can and not when you have to," he instructed others and urged them to wear their good Sunday clothing to work as a sign of their Christian pride.[61] Besides Friday evening prayer meetings, he went to services twice on Sunday and was always a conspicuous figure in a straight-backed pew, kneeling and leading the congregation in prayer. He prized the special intensity of feeling that Baptists brought to their faith, which provided an emotional release lacking elsewhere in his life. With a ripe baritone voice, refined by singing lessons at church, he boomed out hymns with deep joy. His favorite, "I've Found a Friend," portrayed Jesus in tenderly familiar terms: "I've found a Friend; oh, such a Friend! / He bled, he died to save me."[62]

In a world full of snares to entrap the unsuspecting pilgrim, Rockefeller tried hard to insulate himself from all temptation. As he later saw it, "a boy must ever be careful to avoid the temptations which beset him, to select carefully his associates and give attention as well to his spiritual and . . . mental and material interests."[63] Since evangelicals abstained from dancing, cards, and theater, Rockefeller restricted his private life to church socials and picnics, where he could play blindman's buff and engage in other innocent pastimes. As a model Baptist, he was sought after by the young ladies. "The girls all liked John immensely," said one congregant. "Some of them came dangerously near to being in love with him. He was not especially attractive in his person and his clothes were strenuously plain and well worn. He was thought much of by these spiritual minded young women because of his goodness, his religious fervor, his earnestness and willingness in the church, and his apparent sincerity and honesty of purpose."[64]

Over lemonade and cake at church socials, Rockefeller developed a close attachment to a pretty young woman named Emma Saunders, who chafed that John wouldn't broaden his social activities and insisted upon confining their dating to the church. For Rockefeller, the church was more than a set of theological positions: It was a fellowship of virtuous, like-minded people, and he always hesitated to stray too far from its protective embrace.

Though generally reserved, Rockefeller developed convivial habits in church that lingered for life, and it bothered him when people marched off right after the Sunday service. "There ought to be something that makes the church homelike," he insisted. "Friends should be glad to see each other and to greet strangers."[65] Even in later years, when huge swarms of people congregated at the church door to glimpse the world's richest man, he would still clasp people's hands and bask in the glow of familial warmth. The handshake acquired symbolic meaning for him, for it was "the friendly hand extended to the man who doesn't know that he is wanted [that] brings many a one into the church. This early feeling about handshaking has stayed with me. All my life, I have enjoyed this thing that says: 'I am your friend.' "[66]

Just as Rockefeller was sensitive to condescending treatment in the business world, he couldn't stand it in the religious realm either. Since mission churches weren't self-financing, Rockefeller and other trustees had to submit to patronizing advice from the mother church. "This strengthened our resolve to show them that we could paddle our own canoe."[67] While Rockefeller's religious faith ran strong, he was most involved in the temporal affairs of the church, which he thought should be run like a tidy business. He soon had a chance to defend the church's solvency when it fell behind on interest payments on a $2,000 mortgage held by a deacon. One Sunday, the pastor announced from the pulpit that this creditor threatened to foreclose on the church and that they had to raise $2,000 very fast to survive. As the stunned congregation filed out, they found Rockefeller stationed at the door, buttonholing people and asking them to pledge specific amounts. "I pleaded, urged, and almost threatened. As each one promised, I put his name and the amount down in my little book, and continued to solicit from every possible subscriber."[68] Perhaps nothing in his early life so foreshadowed his unswerving pursuit of business goals. "The plan absorbed me," he admitted. "I contributed what I could, and my first ambition to earn money was aroused by this and similar undertakings in which I was constantly engaged."[69] In a matter of months, he had raised $2,000 and saved the church. By age twenty, he had emerged as the second most important member of the congregation, surpassed only by the preacher.

With a mostly spartan country education and scant exposure to big-city culture, John D. Rockefeller's mind was largely furnished with precepts and phrases from his Baptist fundamentalist church. Throughout his life, he extracted from Christianity practical lessons for living and emphasized the utility of religion as a guide in mundane affairs. Over time, the American public would wonder how he squared his predatory bent with his religion, yet much that was preached in the church of his youth—at least as Rockefeller saw it— encouraged his moneymaking predilections. Far from placing obstacles in his path, the religion he encountered seemed to applaud him in his course, and he very much embodied the sometimes uneasy symbiosis between church and business that defined the emerging ethos of the post–Civil War American economy.

Rockefeller never wavered in his belief that his career was divinely favored and asserted bluntly, "God gave me my money."[70] During the decades that he taught Sunday-school classes, he found plenty of scriptural evidence to buttress this claim. (Of course, his critics would cite many contrary quotations, warning of the pernicious influence of wealth.) When Benjamin Franklin was a boy, his father had pounded into his head the proverb "Seest thou a man diligent in his business? He shall stand before kings," and Rockefeller often presented this text to his class. Martin Luther had exhorted his congregation, "Even though [your work] seems very trivial and contemptible, make sure you regard it as great and precious, not on account of your worthiness, but because it has its place within that jewel and holy treasure, the Word and Commandment of God."[71] Many eminent nineteenth-century theologians took the Calvinist view that wealth was a sign of God's grace and poverty a telltale sign of heavenly disfavor. Henry Ward Beecher, calling poverty the fault of the poor, proclaimed in a sermon that "generally the proposition is true, that where you find the most religion you find the most worldly prosperity."[72]

As to why God had singled out John D. Rockefeller for such spectacular bounty, Rockefeller always adverted to his own adherence to the doctrine of stewardship—the notion of the wealthy man as a mere instrument of God, a temporary trustee of his money, who devoted it to good causes. "It has seemed as if I was favored and got increase because the Lord knew that I was going to turn around and give it back."[73] Rockefeller said this in his late seventies, and one wonders whether the equation between moneymaking and money giving only entered his mind later. Yet even as a teenager, he took palpable pleasure in distributing money for charitable purposes, and he insisted that from an early date he discerned the intimate spiritual link between earning and dispensing money. "I remember clearly when the financial plan—if I may call it so—of my life was formed. It was out in Ohio, under the ministration of a dear old minister, who preached, 'Get money; get it honestly and then give it wisely.' I wrote that down in a little book."[74] This echoed John Wesley's dictum, "If those who 'gain all they can' and 'save all they can,' will likewise 'give all they can,' then the more they will grow in grace."[75] Rockefeller operated by such spiritual double-entry bookkeeping, with his charity serving, in time, as incontestable proof of his fortune's purity. It might well be that his early commitment to charity gave him some inner license needed to pursue wealth with unparalleled—and at times unprincipled—vigor.

As Max Weber observed, ascetic Christianity was a matchless breeding ground for would-be businessmen. The practice of tithing, for instance, instilled habits of thrift, self-denial, and careful budgeting that were invaluable assets for any aspiring capitalist. John D. Rockefeller was the Protestant work ethic in its purest form, leading a life so consistent with Weber's classic essay that it reads like his spiritual biography. It might be useful to note some of Weber's aperçus that apply with especial force to Rockefeller. Weber argued that the Puritans had produced a religion that validated worldly activity, with "the making of money by acquisition as the ultimate purpose" of life.[76] They approached business in a rational, methodical manner, banishing magic from the marketplace and reducing everything to method. Because prosperity was a sign of future salvation, the elect worked with special diligence to reassure themselves of God's favor. Even those who amassed great wealth continued to labor, since they worked, ostensibly, for God's glory, not for their own aggrandizement. The church didn't want to be in the position of promoting greed, so it circumvented this problem by legitimating the pursuit of money if channeled into a calling—that is, the steady dedication to a productive task. Once a person discovered his calling, he was supposed to apply himself with all-consuming devotion, the money thus acquired being deemed a sign of God's blessing.

One by-product of the emphasis on a calling was that Puritans relegated activities outside the religious and economic sphere to a lesser order of importance. The believer wasn't supposed to search for pleasure beyond the sheltered confines of family, church, and business, and the gravest sins were wasting time, indulging in idle chatter, and wallowing in luxurious diversions. Bent on making money, the good Puritan had to restrain his impulses instead of gratifying them. As Weber remarked, "Unlimited greed for gain is not in the least identical with capitalism, and is still less in spirit. Capitalism *may* even be identical with the restraint, or at least a rational tempering, of this irrational impulse."[77] That is, the man who would be rich must be thrifty. People had to regulate their lives, Weber argued, so that self-abnegation could bring forth plenty. A fateful contradiction lay at the heart of this Puritan culture, for the virtues of godly people made them rich, and these riches, in turn, threatened to undermine that godliness. As Cotton Mather declared of the Plymouth colony in the 1690s, "Religion begot prosperity, and the daughters devoured the mother."[78] This contradiction posed a central dilemma for John D. Rockefeller and his descendants, who would struggle tirelessly against the baneful effects of wealth.

Of the four principal groups of ascetic Protestants analyzed by Weber, we should note, the Baptists alone rejected predestination and therefore couldn't construe wealth as an infallible sign of God's favor. On the other hand, as Weber pointed out, certain Baptist tenets prepared its adherents to prosper in the marketplace. Abhorring religious idolatry, demoting sacraments as a means to salvation, Baptism fostered a rational outlook that was well suited to advancement in capitalist society. Rockefeller was convinced that he had a God-given talent for making money, was obligated to develop it, and was liberally rewarded by God—all compatible with Baptist doctrine. For this reason, he found religion far more of a spur than a hindrance to his ambitions. Where others saw him as an anomaly in a denomination that always welcomed working people and harbored a faint distrust of the rich, he never saw any such contradiction.

Before leaving Rockefeller's early Baptist indoctrination, we should note that the economic climate of his adolescence must have deepened his religious convictions. In 1857, while he was still at Hewitt and Tuttle, America fell into an economic slump. The proximate cause was the end of the Crimean War in 1856, which dealt a blow to American farmers who had profited from the war. On a more profound level, the crisis capped a decade of frantic speculation in railroad securities and land, stoked by heavy borrowing. As five thousand businesses failed and hundreds of thousands of workers were idled, the exuberant boosterism of the 1850s was suddenly and dramatically quelled.

As happened in the Great Depression of the 1930s, people were shocked that an effervescent economy could stall so woefully. As one contemporary observer put it, "It seems indeed strange that in the very midst of apparent health and strength . . . the whole country . . . should suddenly come to a dead stop and be unable to move forward—and that we should suddenly wake up from our dreams of wealth and happiness, and find ourselves poor and bankrupt."[79] A wave of hysterical breast-beating ensued, with President James Buchanan insisting that the crisis came "solely from our extravagant and vicious system of paper currency and bank credits, exciting the people to wild speculations and gambling in stocks."[80]

Rather than blaming the business cycle, many evangelical Christians interpreted the downturn as divine punishment for a society grown lax, worldly, and dissolute. One Boston reformer descried redeeming features in the slump, hoping it would "teach good and much needed lessons . . . and will reduce all things here to a more sober, sound, and healthy condition."[81] The mood of national self-flagellation prompted a religious upsurge known as the Businessmen's Revival. In 1857, businessmen gathered in many cities for lunchtime prayer meetings where they publicly swore off drink and other indulgences. During this massive outpouring of repentance, evangelical churches recruited tens of thousands of new members. The shift from euphoria to depression in the business sphere—mirrored by a shift from sin to salvation in the religious sphere—probably strengthened Rockefeller's innate conservatism as a fledgling businessman while bolstering his already deep-seated Baptist inclinations. As he said, "What a school—the school of adversity and stress—to train a boy in!"[82]

=

Whatever the general misery caused by the 1857 panic, William Avery Rockefeller's medical road show thrived that year, and he briefly managed to support and juggle two marriages. In the spring of 1856, Bill had surfaced again in Cleveland, rooming with John and William at Mrs. Woodin's while scouting out a permanent home for his family. He was residing intermittently with Margaret Allen's family in Ontario, posing as Dr. William Levingston, and now had to make some final disposition before he deserted his first wife and children for good. When he found a roomy brick house for rent at 35 Cedar Street, equipped with such luxuries as indoor toilet and bathroom, he brought Eliza and the children in from Parma. John and William moved out of Mrs. Woodin's place and were reunited with their family. At this point, Bill decided that John should contribute to the family upkeep and pay him the same rent he had given to Mrs. Woodin.

In 1857, Bill decided to build for his family a substantial brick house on Cheshire Street in downtown Cleveland, a farewell gift that would enable him to abscond with a clear conscience. "In 1857 my father told me to build a house," said John D., giving the story a positive gloss. "It was a lesson in self-reliance. He handed me the money, told me the sort of house he wanted and left all the details of the business to me. I drew plans, got the material, found a builder, and built the house."[83] Did Bill regard this as some final test, a crash course in business for John, before he abandoned his family to the tender mercies of chance? As he warned his son, "I shall be away and must rely on your judgment."[84] Or perhaps Bill just wanted to be spared the inconvenience of doing it himself.

Rockefeller was justifiably proud of his feat of superintending this house, a bravura performance for a boy of eighteen with an already demanding schedule at Hewitt and Tuttle. As if he had been doing nothing but construction work all his life, he solicited estimates from eight contractors and selected the lowest bidder. He reviewed the plans, negotiated the contracts, and settled the bills with implicit confidence in his judgment. In fact, so closely did he supervise the contractors, so zealously did he outbargain them, that they lost money on the project. If Bill was testing his son's ability, he passed with flying colors.

By one account, a dispute arose as to whether John would pay rent at the new house. He presumably felt that, having built the structure, he had earned the right to occupy it free of rent, but Devil Bill laid down his own arbitrary rules and overrode Eliza's protests. "You bought your time, didn't you?" he told John. "What you're getting now is your own, ain't it? Well, you have to pay me board."[85] Once again, one marvels at Bill's barefaced cheek no less than his son's fortitude in the face of repeated provocations.

Now that the Rockefellers were reconstituted in Cleveland, John was deputized as the new paterfamilias, as Bill again exited from the scene, setting up house in Philadelphia with Margaret Allen sometime in the late 1850s. For several more years, Bill was weirdly enmeshed in John's affairs and for five decades continued to materialize, like a burly, smiling genie, at odd intervals. But from this point forward, the gap between Bill's two lives and two wives began to widen into an unbridgeable chasm. By an exquisite (and, for Bill, surely excruciating) irony, this scheming, selfish, money-mad charlatan turned his back on his family just as his eldest son began to amass the largest fortune in history. John D. Rockefeller inhabited a stoic universe in which it was considered a sign of strength and mental health to banish your cares and forge ahead instead of morbidly dwelling on your parents' failings. But if John nursed vengeful feelings toward Bill, it must have been secretly gratifying to him that his father left at the very dawn of his triumph and forfeited any claim to his wealth.

Eliza probably never knew that after she'd raised his five children, Bill had traded her in for a much younger woman, but she was now better equipped to withstand his loss than she had been a few years earlier. When John Davison died on June 1, 1858, he left her an annuity that lasted through 1865, when she inherited the principal. With two sons drawing income—William was now working under John as a bookkeeper at Hewitt and Tuttle—and with occasional assistance from Bill, Eliza could muddle through on her own. She especially relied upon her eldest son, the wunderkind who seemed capable of anything and who was as steady and trustworthy as her husband had been feckless and mercurial. Eliza was now in her mid-forties, and photos show a prim, sad, gaunt woman. Divorce wasn't an option for a devout nineteenth-century woman, and her giddy fling with the handsome young peddler had left her imprisoned in a premature widowhood. Bill had been her sole chance, her crazily squandered bid to escape from rural tedium, and the misbegotten marriage left both her and her eldest son with a lifelong suspicion of volatile people and rash actions.

In his trilogy of Frank Cowperwood novels, his fictionalized version of the life of the Chicago traction magnate Charles Yerkes, Theodore Dreiser described the uncanny perspicacity about his bosses that distinguished the adolescent Cowperwood in his first job as a clerk in a grain-commission business. "He could see their weaknesses and their shortcomings as a much older man might have viewed a boy's."[86] The remark aptly captures the coolly critical eye with which Rockefeller sized up his elders at Hewitt and Tuttle. He was respectful toward his superiors but never awed by them and was always aware of their shortcomings. For the record, he professed great respect for Isaac Hewitt, twenty-five years his senior, but he was much more caustic in private, referring to him as a "disgruntled" man, forever entangled in litigation.

Despite his youth, Rockefeller soon came to feel that he was being underpaid. When Tuttle quit in January 1857, Rockefeller was elevated to chief bookkeeper, performing, at the age of seventeen, all the tasks formerly discharged by the departed partner. Where Tuttle had earned $2,000 a year as partner, Rockefeller was given only $500, and this vexing inequity was only slightly mitigated when Hewitt raised him to $600 a year by 1858. With the same preternatural confidence evident in his campaign to pay off the church mortgage or oversee the Cheshire Street house, the boy began to trade for his own account, making small but successful forays into flour, ham, and pork. Soon, this adolescent businessman was cutting something of a figure on the Cleveland docks, where he was always addressed as Mr. Rockefeller.

A variety of factors conspired to bring about his departure from Hewitt's firm. Though his salary grated on him, he waited until the economy snapped back from the 1857 downturn before making his move. In charge of the books, he could see that the firm had nearly been bankrupted by the slump and faced a bleak future—a suspicion confirmed by the fact that Hewitt shrewdly kept his extensive real-estate holdings segregated from his stake in the commission house. Big Bill, who always liked to play the freelance banker, had given a thousand-dollar loan to Hewitt, and when John informed him of the concern's precarious state, he barged into the office and demanded (and got) immediate repayment from Hewitt.

John D. Rockefeller wasn't one to dawdle in an unprofitable concern. His career had few wasted steps, and he never vacillated when the moment ripened for advancement. When he asked Hewitt for an $800 salary, his cash-strapped boss dithered for weeks before deciding he could go no higher than $700. Later, Rockefeller claimed he would have stayed if Hewitt had matched his demand, but added, "even then I was preparing, getting ready for something big."[87] While he and Hewitt were bickering in early 1858, an attractive opportunity arose that settled the issue. Rockefeller had befriended a young Englishman, twenty-eight-year-old Maurice B. Clark, who worked down the street at a produce house called Otis, Brownell. They had been classmates at E. G. Folsom's Commercial College and were also neighbors on Cheshire Street. According to Clark, Rockefeller already had "the reputation of being a young bookkeeper of more than ordinary ability and reliability," and Clark proposed that they form a new partnership for buying and selling produce, with each partner investing an initial $2,000—an amount equal to $36,000 in 1996 dollars.[88] Amazingly enough, Rockefeller had saved $800, equivalent to a year's salary, in less than three years on the job, but he still fell considerably short of Clark's figure.

As he brooded over how to raise the money, he was informed by his father that he had always intended to give each of his children $1,000 at age twenty-one, and he now offered to advance John the money. "But, John," he added, lest his son expect miracles, "the rate is ten."[89] Having just retrieved a thousand dollars from Hewitt, Bill might have been looking for a high return on these idle funds. John knew his father far too well to plead for a gift and accepted the 10 percent loan, which was higher than the prevailing rate. So on April 1, 1858, backed up by this borrowed money, John D. Rockefeller left Isaac Hewitt and joined the new partnership of Clark and Rockefeller at 32 River Street. At eighteen, he was catapulted to a partner's rank in a commission house. "It was a great thing to be my own employer," said Rockefeller. "Mentally I swelled with pride—a partner in a firm with $4,000 capital!"[90] The moment was fraught with meaning for him, and after his first day at work he went back to the Cheshire Street house, fell to his knees, and implored the Lord to bless his new enterprise.

Rockefeller never regretted his apprenticeship at Hewitt and Tuttle and, like many self-made men, lavished a retrospective tenderness on his early years. If anything, he drenched the whole experience in a sentimental syrup that only grew thicker and sweeter with time. Even in 1934, at age ninety-five, Rockefeller tried to rally one grandson with tales of his heroic initiation at Hewitt and Tuttle, his stirring baptism in business. "Oh how blessed the young men are who have to struggle for a foundation and a beginning in life. I shall never cease to be grateful for the three and a half years of apprenticeship and the difficulties to be overcome, all the way along."

John D. Rockefeller in his early twenties.
(Courtesy of the Rockefeller Archive Center)

Baptism in Business

hen the sign reading "Clark and Rockefeller" was hoisted atop the warehouse at 32 River Street, the local business community warmly greeted the new arrivals. The *Cleveland Leader* wrote, "As experienced, responsible and prompt businessmen, we recommend their house to the favorable consideration of our readers."[1] In this first partnership, success seemed to come quickly and easily to Rockefeller. With a booming traffic in meat, grain, and other foodstuffs circulating through the Great Lakes, he and Clark nimbly bought and sold carloads of produce. As the firm's ambitious circular stated, they were prepared to deal in "grain, fish, water, lime, plaster, coarse fine solar and dairy salt."[2] The fledgling firm weathered just enough perils to lend, retrospectively, nostalgic charm to this maiden period. Two months after opening for business, the partners had to cope with a severe frost that damaged midwestern crops. Having contracted to buy a large shipment of beans, they wound up with a big, semispoiled batch, strewn with dirt and rubbish. "When we were not needed in the office we used to go out to the warehouse, my partner and I, and sort out those beans."[3] This setback didn't detract from the firm's overall performance, for by year's end it had netted a highly respectable $4,400, tripling the income that John had made during his last year at Hewitt and Tuttle.

But because of the bean fiasco, John had to turn again, however grudgingly, to Big Bill for a rescue loan. To excel in commodities, it was imperative to offer generous financing, and Clark and Rockefeller advertisements trumpeted to prospective clients that they were "prepared to make liberal advances and consignments of produce, etc."[4] With his son, Bill often liked to play sadistic money games and then defended his knavish behavior by citing some warped, peda-gogical purpose. As he bragged to a Strongsville neighbor, "I trade with the boys and skin 'em and I just beat 'em every time I can. I want to make 'em sharp."[5] John was by now resigned to the bizarrely commercial character of his dealings with his father, and in his memoirs he even idealized Bill's lending ma-neuvers as teaching him valuable lessons. "To my father I owe a great debt in that he himself trained me to practical ways. He was engaged in different en-terprises; he used to tell me about these things, explaining their significance; and he taught me the principles and methods of business."[6]

As John knew, his father's style as a banker followed a grimly manic pattern of conviviality giving way to Scrooge-like severity. "Our relations on finances were a source of some anxiety to me, and were not quite so humorous as they seem now as I look back on them," Rockefeller allowed, permitting a smidgen of anger to show.[7] When Bill offered a 10 percent loan, the real motive was something other than altruism, for he had an infuriating habit of calling in loans at the least opportune time. "Just at the moment when I required the money most he was apt to say, 'My son, I find I have got to have that money,' " John D. recalled in his memoirs. " 'Of course, you shall have it at once,' I would answer, but I knew that he was testing me, and that when I paid him, he would hold the money without its earning anything for a little time and then offer it back later."[8] About this continuing psychodrama, Rockefeller later said, in an-other fleeting moment of candor, "he would never know how angry I felt be-neath the surface."[9]

An intimate, critical perspective on the perverse relations between Rocke-feller and his father comes from George W. Gardner, who joined Clark and Rockefeller as a partner on April 1, 1859. Having worked with Clark at Otis, Brownell, he was evidently invited into the firm to shore up its capital. Scion of an elite Cleveland family, cut from a different cloth than the self-made men of Rockefeller's early years, Gardner later served as mayor of Cleveland and com-modore of the Cleveland Yacht Club. With Gardner's arrival, Rockefeller's name was dropped from the firm's title, and the new partnership was styled Clark, Gardner and Company, the ostensible and quite cogent reason being that Gardner's name would entice more clients. Rockefeller always felt uneasy about venting anger or making an egotistical show of protest, and he pre-tended to accept this demotion with equanimity. "Maurice Clark was very pleasant about it," he later insisted. "And he said, 'Never mind. It won't be very long—before many years you'll be doing better than any of us.' Yes, he was very nice about it. I made no objection."[10] Yet this stinging blow rankled, as he later admitted. "I considered this a great injustice to me as I was an equal part-ner and Gardner brought in only his share of the capital, but I thought it best to submit."[11] It says much about Rockefeller that he thought it unseemly and unchristian to confess to such understandable feelings of injured pride.

Rockefeller was bound to clash with Gardner and Clark, for he was a Round-head among Cavaliers and approached his work with unflagging, humorless energy. "Your future hangs on every day that passes," he admonished himself.[12] "Long before I was twenty-one men called me, 'Mr Rockefeller,' " he recalled. "Life was a serious business to me when I was young."[13] The only time he showed any youthful gaiety was when sealing a lucrative deal. Like the resident moral overseer, he felt contempt for Clark and Gardner's easygoing ways and irreverent spirit, and they found this young killjoy both a welcome and grating presence in the office.

Afraid that any levity would diminish their chances of getting loans, the twenty-year-old sought to stifle the excesses of his older partners. When Gardner and three friends purchased a $2,000 yacht, Rockefeller roundly condemned this extravagance. One Saturday afternoon, Gardner was about to escape from the office for an afternoon sail when he saw Rockefeller hunched glumly over his ledgers. "John," he said agreeably, "a little crowd of us are going to take a sail over to Put-in-Bay and I'd like to have you go along. I think it would do you good to get away from the office and get your mind off business for a while." Gardner had touched an exposed nerve and, as he recounted years later to a reporter, his young partner wheeled on him savagely. "George Gardner," he sputtered, "you're the most extravagant young man I ever knew! The idea of a young man like you, just getting a start in life, owning an interest in a yacht! You're injuring your credit at the banks—your credit and mine. . . . No, I won't go on your yacht. I don't even want to see it!" With that, Rockefeller leaned back over his account books. "John," said Gardner, "I see that there are certain things on which you and I probably will never agree. I think you like money better than anything else in the whole world, and I do not. I like to have a little fun along with business as I go through life."[14]

Later on, Rockefeller learned to camouflage his business anxiety behind a studied calm, but during these years it was often graphically displayed. Clark remembered one daring venture when the firm wagered its entire capital on a large grain shipment to Buffalo. With foolish, atypical imprudence, Rockefeller suggested that they skip the insurance and pocket the $150 premium; Gardner and Clark reluctantly acquiesced. That night, a terrible storm blew across Lake Erie, and when Gardner came to the office the next morning, a frightfully pale Rockefeller paced the floor in agitation. "Let's take out insurance right away," he said. "We still have time—if the boat hasn't been wrecked by now." Gardner ran off to pay the premium. By the time he got back, Rockefeller was waving a telegram announcing the ship's safe arrival in Buffalo. Whether unnerved by the episode or upset at having paid the unnecessary premium, Rockefeller went home ill that afternoon.[15]

One suspects that Rockefeller associated the bon vivant Gardner with his father, much to Gardner's detriment. Indeed, Gardner felt an affinity with Bill, relishing his bonhomie and outlandish humor and calling him "one of the most companionable and most likeable old men I ever knew. He would crack jokes and have more to say in one conversation than John would utter in a week."[16] Gardner was the first of many Rockefeller associates to note the unanswered questions about Bill, who returned to Cleveland at irregular intervals, invariably depositing or withdrawing huge amounts of cash from Clark, Gardner. "I wondered what business a man could be in that he would have $1,000 to spare one month and need it the next," said Gardner.[17]

Thanks to Gardner, we can date the earliest moment at which we can say with some certainty that John knew of his father's scandalous relationship, if not of his bigamy. The firm was starting to cultivate business contacts in Philadelphia, and it occurred to Gardner that on his next trip there, he might solicit information from Bill. "So I asked John for his father's address. He hesitated and finally said he couldn't remember." This immediately puzzled Gardner, who knew Rockefeller had a phenomenal memory, and he asked if he could secure the address from Eliza at lunchtime. After lunch, John never alluded to the matter, and as they prepared to leave that evening, Gardner again inquired after the address. "He flushed up and said he'd forgotten to ask for it when he went home. I pressed him no further, and never found out where his father lived."[18] When John began to fathom the depth of his father's duplicity toward his mother, he must have inwardly reeled, and he reacted with the same repressed emotion and steadfast evasion that had served him as a boy. Already Rockefeller was treating his father as the supreme taboo subject, setting a pattern for the unremitting secrecy that would pervade Standard Oil.

Photos of Rockefeller from the Clark, Gardner period show a tall young man with a vigorous air and alert, penetrating eyes. His tightly compressed lips expressed a fierce determination and a guarded nature. Big and broad-shouldered, he had an incipient stoop that gave him a wary air. Despite his occasional, priggish blowups with Gardner, he had that sublime self-confidence that speaks with quiet authority. Neatly dressed and well groomed, Rockefeller was the first to arrive at and the last to leave work each day. In a natural division of labor, Clark took charge of buying and selling while Rockefeller tended the books. Rockefeller seemed destined to succeed as much from his fastidious work habits as from innate intelligence. With the avidity of a zealous auditor, he liked to smoke out wrongdoing and uncover errors. Maurice Clark thought John congenial but "too exact. He was methodical to an extreme, careful as to details and exacting to a fraction. If there was a cent due us, he wanted it. If there was a cent due a customer, he wanted the customer to have it."[19] The portrait, if slightly chilling, also underscores Rockefeller's prudish honesty during this phase of his career.

From the outset, Rockefeller had to wrestle with the demons of pride and greed. When rebuffed by a bank officer for a loan, he shot back in anger, "Some day I'll be the richest man in the world."[20] He went through the week cautioning himself with proverbs taught by Eliza, such as "Pride goeth before a fall," and this spiritual self-scrutiny intensified with his growing wealth.[21] When he rested his head on the pillow at night, he warned himself, "Because you have got a start, you think you are quite a merchant; look out, or you will lose your head—go steady. Are you going to let this money puff you up? Keep your eyes open. Don't lose your balance."[22] Had Rockefeller not feared his own capacity for excess, he wouldn't have engaged in such strenuous introspection. As he said, "These intimate conversations with myself, I'm sure, had a great influence on my life. I was afraid I could not stand my prosperity, and tried to teach myself not to get puffed up with any foolish notions."[23] It's easy to suppose that Rockefeller's typically sententious style was borrowed from church and first polished by these nightly sermons that he preached to himself.

That Rockefeller led an unblemished Christian life played no small role in his business accomplishments, for he appealed to the older citizens in town. During his first year with Clark, he hired someone to look after the books while he took to the open road to drum up business, traveling widely in Ohio and Indiana. Contrary to what one might expect, Rockefeller was a smoothly persuasive salesman. Instead of brashly trying to poach clients from rivals, he modestly outlined his firm's services. "I would go into an office and present my card and say to the man that I supposed his business connections were satisfactory, and that I did not wish to intrude upon him, but that I had a proposition that I myself believed in and believed it would be to his advantage, that I did not expect him to decide off hand but asked him to think it over and I would see him again about it."[24] Orders to handle commodity trades poured in almost faster than he could handle them. "I found that old men had confidence in me right away, and after I stayed a few weeks in the country, I returned home and the consignments came in and our business was increased and it opened up a new world for me."[25]

Rockefeller handled people adroitly and wasn't the cold curmudgeon of later myth. However, he *was* persistent, which pleased or displeased people according to taste. Previewing a problem that bedeviled the oil business, the commodity business was chronically short of railroad cars to transport flour, grain, and pork, and Rockefeller badgered one railroad official so much that the older man finally wagged a finger at him and snapped, "Young man, I want you to understand you can't make a shuttlecock of me."[26] Rockefeller often related how the firm's best customer once pressed him to violate conservative business practice and advance him money before the produce or bill of lading was in hand. Though Rockefeller refused him, he still tried to keep the customer. "But he stormed about, and in the end I had the further humiliation of confessing to my partner that I had failed."[27] Only afterward did Rockefeller learn that the customer's intransigence was a cunning trap set by a local banker to see whether these young men could withstand temptation and hew to their conservative principles.

For all his populist mistrust of bankers, Rockefeller owed much of his incandescent rise to their assistance. "The hardest problem all through my business career was to obtain enough capital to do all the business I wanted to do and could do, given the necessary amount of money."[28] The banking system was then weak and atomized. Many Main Street banks were thinly capitalized, and they inspired so little trust that Rockefeller's firm kept spare cash in the safe. Rockefeller got his first extrafamilial loan from a kindly, benevolent old banker named Truman P. Handy, who agreed to take warehouse receipts as collateral. After getting this $2,000 loan, John almost floated down the sidewalk. "Just think of it," he mused, "a bank had trusted me for $2,000! I felt that I was now a man of importance in the community."[29] Handy made Rockefeller swear that he would never speculate with the $2,000, and the young man must have sensed that he had won the first of many influential mentors in Cleveland's financial community. Besides being a bank president, the gravely proper Handy was a Sunday-school superintendent and had sounded out Isaac Hewitt on the young man's character and habits. As Rockefeller realized, his credit rating depended upon reports of his sterling character—just as he had lectured George Gardner—and his status as a mainstay of the Erie Street Baptist Mission Church guaranteed him a friendly reception at banks. Thus, Rockefeller's initial loan shows the close mesh of Christianity and capitalism in his early career.

Famously averse to borrowing in later years, Rockefeller was extraordinarily adept at it when he needed the capital. As Clark said, "Oh, John was the greatest borrower you ever saw!"[30] In bargaining with banks, Rockefeller gave evidence of his father's wiliness and mastery of crowd psychology. If he wanted to borrow $5,000, he let it be bruited about town that he wished to invest $10,000. This rumor would certify his firm's rock-solid credit while also giving bankers an added incentive to extend him a loan. Rockefeller's need for money only grew during the Civil War, which was a bonanza for the commodity business. As a partner in a Cleveland produce house, John D. Rockefeller was strategically positioned to profit from the war, and for the rest of the century his career seemed to march in perfect lockstep with the progress of American business history.

═══

For Rockefeller, the Civil War was principally an opportunity to pile up riches, yet he betrayed intense sympathy for the Union cause and fervently advocated abolishing slavery. As early as his 1854 high-school essay on freedom, he had railed against "cruel masters" who worked their slaves "beneath the scorching suns of the South. How under such circumstances can America call herself free?"[31] As a teenager, he had contributed to several charities that aided blacks. At the time, his antislavery views were representative of the prevailing views in

Cleveland, which had many relocated New Englanders and was a hotbed of abolitionist sentiment. With its favorable political climate and position as a big Lake Erie port, Cleveland was a stop on the Underground Railroad that transported fugitive slaves to freedom in Canada, and many of them surreptitiously boarded ships just blocks from Rockefeller's office. When slave hunters invaded the town, abolitionist sympathizers rushed to the Stone Church on the Public Square and tolled the bell to alert the populace. In 1860, Rockefeller cast his first presidential vote for Abraham Lincoln, and on the eve of the war he attended meetings that resounded with thunderous denunciations of slavery. Abolitionist fervor was especially widespread among evangelical Christians who deplored slavery and Catholicism as twin tyrannies, and northern Baptist congregations warmly received black preachers and lecturers who spoke for the abolitionist cause.

So why didn't Rockefeller act on his keenly felt sympathies when Lincoln appealed for 75,000 volunteers after Fort Sumter's fall in April 1861? Why did he turn a deaf ear to the torchlight rallies and street-corner recruiters swarming through Cleveland that spring? "I wanted to go in the army and do my part," Rockefeller said. "But it was simply out of the question. We were in a new business, and if I had not stayed it must have stopped—and with so many dependent on it."[32] This last sentence hinted gingerly at what must have been the main reason behind his failure to serve: his father's desertion of the family and his own need to sustain it. Though the Union government offered no occupational exemptions from the draft, men were excused if they were the sole means of support for siblings, children, or parents. Though only twenty-one at the outbreak of the war, John D. was effectively in the position of a middle-aged father responsible for a family of six.

Like J. P. Morgan, Grover Cleveland, Theodore Roosevelt, Sr., and other well-heeled young men, Rockefeller hired a substitute for $300 and ended up outfitting a small army. One morning, Levi Scofield, a captain in the Union army and a friend of Rockefeller's, marched thirty raw recruits into his River Street office. They evidently passed muster, for Rockefeller dug into his safe and handed a ten dollar bill to each of them. "God, but he must be rich," gasped one young man, causing another to reply, "Yes, they say he is a rich man—that he is worth as much as $10,000!"[33] For the first time, Rockefeller had triggered fantasies of riches. Allan Nevins has suggested that Rockefeller exaggerated when he claimed to have financed between twenty and thirty soldiers, noting that Rockefeller's ledger itemizes only $138.09 for war purposes. Yet a historian of Rockefeller's Cleveland years, Grace Goulder, pointed out that by 1864, Rockefeller was giving about $300 per year to substitutes and their families besides his general donations to wartime charities.

Since Rockefeller's commodity business depended upon market intelligence and a rapid flow of telegrams from various sections of the country, his office became a clubhouse for the latest battlefield bulletins. He and Maurice Clark tacked up two large, detailed maps and tracked the war's progress with rapt attention. "Our office became a great rallying-place," said Rockefeller. "We were all deeply interested. Men used to drop in often, and we followed the war keenly, reading the latest dispatches and studying the maps."

While Rockefeller's brother William also managed to duck service and keep on working, the youngest brother, Frank, was both physically and psychologically wounded during the war. Not yet sixteen when the war started, Frank was hot-blooded and temperamental. With a wide face, broad forehead, and handlebar mustache, he was very much in his father's mold. Where John had a tidy, inner-directed nature, Frank was quick to yield to impulses both base and noble. A much better mixer than John, an outgoing backslapper, he could be kindhearted and generous toward friends.

Frank had an adolescent yearning for battlefield glory but was initially thwarted in this storybook aspiration by his family. George Gardner, who always took a jaundiced view of John, claimed that John had coldly declined his brother's request for $75 to enlist in the Union army. In Gardner's telling, John gave his brother a tongue-lashing: "You would be a wild, foolish boy to go away and waste youthful years that you might utilize in getting a start and making money."[34] When John remained adamant, Gardner advanced Frank the $75—the first of innumerable loans that Frank, professing good intentions all the while, incurred but never repaid. This altercation was the first of many rancorous feuds that poisoned relations between John and Frank through the years.

While Gardner might have accurately reported John's words, he omitted some important mitigating circumstances. Frank had already tried to slip off and furtively enlist and had been reprimanded by his father for his secrecy. "Young man," said Bill, "when you go to war you will say goodbye to the family and go out the front door in broad daylight."[35] (It took a certain gall for Bill to get on his high horse on the subject of secrecy and family responsibility.) Another factor probably swaying John was that Frank had already been rejected as underage and would need to resort to deception to join the army. To aid his memory, Frank now chalked the number eighteen on his soles, and when the recruiting station sergeant asked for his age, he piped up, "I'm over eighteen, sir."[36] In the end, John relented and paid for his brother's clothing, rifle, and accessories during his three years of military service.

As a private in the Seventh Ohio Volunteer Infantry, Frank was wounded twice during the war, at Chancellorsville and Cedar Mountain, which didn't help his already strained relations with John. It must have seemed terribly unjust to Frank that while he waded through bloody battlefields, his eldest brother was raking in the money at home. He always felt that he had paid a severe price for heroism while John was rewarded for his self-aggrandizement.

Ineffectual and full of self-pity, feeling cursed by bad luck, Frank envied his remarkable older brother, who seemed to succeed at every assignment and moved through his charmed business life with icily inexorable efficiency.

The Civil War accelerated the North's economic development, setting the stage for its postwar industrial prowess. It greatly enlarged its industrial capacity, broadening the infrastructure of railroads and telegraphs, coal mines and iron mills as the economy became more mechanized to meet the unprecedented demand for materials. Sewing machines stitched uniforms for soldiers while reapers harvested grain to feed them. As both sides swiftly conveyed huge armies from one theater of battle to the next, the railroad network had to be modernized and expanded accordingly. To encourage further development, the federal government began to provide land grants, with a dozen railroads ultimately taking title to a staggering 158 million acres. This pell-mell growth played a pivotal role in Rockefeller's career, for the proliferation of railroads enabled him to extract discounts from them by playing one off against the other.

The war's psychological impact was equally consequential as it afforded opportunities for commercial gain on a scale never seen before. The outsize profits garnered from government contracts contributed to a money delirium that long outlasted the war. The Civil War not only generated new fortunes but bred in countless people an insatiable appetite for riches. As farm boys in uniform were exposed to cities and given titillating glimpses of luxury goods and urban sophistication, consumerism received a huge impetus. Even many men who didn't enter the army abandoned farms and villages during the war and flocked to populated areas with flourishing munition plants.

The war enhanced Cleveland's strategic importance for a simple logistical reason: As North-South fighting severed freight routes on the Mississippi River, the east-west routes through the rivers and Great Lakes gained a corresponding amount of traffic. Though Rockefeller and his associates secured no lucrative government contracts, they profited from the enormous inflation in commodity prices and the general business surge. Selling mostly on commission, they dealt in numerous foodstuffs and farm implements. By 1862, their annual profits had soared to $17,000, or almost four times what they had earned during their only prewar year. One of their 1863 advertisements listed the bountiful produce now heaped in their bulging warehouse: 1,300 barrels of salt, 500 bushels of clover seed, 800 bushels of timothy seed, and 200 barrels of pork.

At the end of 1862, Rockefeller eliminated a major irritant when he banished George Gardner from the firm. He later obliterated all traces of Gardner from the oral and written accounts of his life, burying him forever with silence. On December 1, 1862, the *Cleveland Herald* ran the following item: "M. B. Clark and John D. Rockefeller, late of Clark, Gardner and Company, will continue the produce business under style and firm of Clark and Rockefeller, at warehouse recently occupied by Clark, Gardner and Company, Nos. 39, 41, 43, and 45 River Street." That the firm had now swelled to occupy four separate numbers on River Street attests to its runaway success. While he was still in his twenties, the Civil War had converted Rockefeller into a wealthy man, giving him the funds to capitalize on a new industry then flowering in the northwest corner of Pennsylvania. For all the substantial profits booked by Rockefeller during the war, they would prove mere pocket change compared to the profits flowing from the rivers of black gold now gushing from wells around Titusville.

CHAPTER 5

The Auction

Long before oil was struck in western Pennsylvania by Colonel Edwin Drake, it had oozed from subterranean springs into Oil Creek (the name dated from the eighteenth century), mantling the surface with an iridescent scum. The slimy liquid was so ubiquitous that it tainted well water and plagued local contractors drilling for salt. Already in the eighteenth century, the Seneca and Cornplanter Indians devised manifold uses for it, employing it for soothing skin liniment, medicine, and even war paint. To extract oil from the creek, they floated blankets or flannel rags on the water, then wrung the oil from the saturated material. Even before Drake's find, Seneca Oil had become known as a sovereign remedy for stiff joints, headaches, and other ailments. Around 1850, Samuel Kier gathered unwanted oil from his father's salt wells, bottled it in little half-pint bottles, and marketed it as Kier's Rock Oil. With a touch of the charlatan, Kier touted the all-purpose medicinal properties of this elixir, contending it would cure liver complaints, bronchitis, and consumption—and that was just for starters. One wonders whether Doc Rockefeller flogged Kier's Rock Oil from the back of his buggy.

In the 1850s, the whale fisheries had failed to keep pace with the mounting need for illuminating oil, forcing up the price of whale oil and making illumination costly for ordinary Americans. Only the affluent could afford to light their parlors every evening. There were many other lighting options—including lard oil, tallow oil, cottonseed oil, coal oil refined from shale, and wicks dipped in fat—but no cheap illuminant that burned in a bright, clean, safe manner. Both urbanization and industrialization sped the search for an illuminant that would extend day into night, breaking the timeless rhythm of rural hours that still governed the lives of farmers and city folk alike.

The petroleum industry was hatched in a very modern symbiosis of business acumen and scientific ingenuity. In the 1850s, George Bissell, a Dartmouth College graduate in his early thirties who had enjoyed a checkered career as a reporter, Greek professor, school principal, and lawyer, had the inspired intuition that the rock oil plentiful in western Pennsylvania was more likely than coal oil to yield a first-rate illuminant. To test this novel proposition, he organized the Pennsylvania Rock-Oil Company, leasing land along Oil Creek, a tributary of the Allegheny River, and sending a specimen of local oil to be analyzed by one of the most renowned chemists of the day, Professor Benjamin Silliman, Jr., of Yale. In his landmark 1855 report, Silliman vindicated Bissell's hunch that this oil could be distilled to produce a fine illuminant, plus a host of other useful products. Now the Pennsylvania Rock-Oil Company faced a single, seemingly insurmountable obstacle: how to find sizable quantities of petroleum to turn Professor Silliman's findings into spendable cash.

It took nearly three years for Bissell's company (which soon evolved into the Seneca Oil Company) to dispatch someone to Pennsylvania to hunt for large, marketable pools of oil. To this end, an investor in the project, a New Haven banker named Townsend, enlisted a boarder in his rooming house, Edwin Drake, to travel to Titusville in December 1857. A former conductor on the New Haven Railroad, Drake was a thirty-eight-year-old widower who was solemn, rather courtly, and disabled by neuralgia of the spine. Photos present a dashing figure with a full beard, broad forehead, and bright, heavy-lidded eyes. Though he made only a nominal investment in the venture, he was dressed up with the fancy title of president to dazzle the gullible yokels and was conveniently endowed (and permanently entered the history books) with the honorific title of colonel.

When Drake arrived in Titusville, Oil Creek Valley was still an idyllic place of dense pine and hemlock forest, rich in game. In his stovepipe hat and somber black clothes, the pallid Drake formed a picturesque contrast with this wilderness setting. Despite the enticing traces of oil that stained the creek's surface, the search for significant oil deposits, without geological knowledge of underground oil structures, proved a long and frustrating one. While the locals found Drake charming and sociable and supplied with a good repertoire of stories, they also mocked him as a harebrained dreamer, seized by a wild obsession. When he tried to dig for oil, the walls caved in. Then, borrowing a method used for salt wells, he started to drill for oil. In this inhospitable setting, choked with underbrush, it was a feat just to assemble the necessary machinery and erect a strange, tall, wooden structure known as a derrick. On Sunday, August 28, 1859, Drake's folly was rewarded when oil bubbled up from a well drilled a day earlier. It was less a matter of Drake discovering oil—its existence was

Laura Celestia Spelman, always known to friends as "Cettie."
(Courtesy of the Rockefeller Archive Center)

scarcely a secret—than of his figuring out a way to tap commercial quantities in a controlled process so that it could be pumped from the earth in systematic fashion.

Drake's feat touched off pandemonium as bands of fortune seekers streamed into Titusville and its pastoral surroundings. Speculators scrambled over the greasy slopes of the creek, leasing acreage from unsophisticated, often unlettered, owners; one farmer turned down an offer of a one-quarter royalty and stubbornly held out for a one-eighth share. Pretty soon derricks sprouted everywhere along the dark, narrow valley, the drilling scarring and denuding the once lush forest slopes. Drilling was the first step in an extended production chain. Within a year of Drake's discovery, a dozen ramshackle refineries sprang up along the creek's steep, secluded banks. Inevitably, this tumultuous activity attracted notice in Cleveland, which had the advantage of proximity to northwest Pennsylvania. Even in those days of slow transport, one could travel from Titusville to Cleveland in a day. Several Cleveland businessmen were already refining illuminating oil from bituminous coal and were naturally interested in a rival method. On November 18, 1859, nearly three months after Drake's find, the *Cleveland Leader* reported on the mad hubbub around Titusville, saying that "the oil springs of northern Pennsylvania were attracting considerable speculation" and that there was "quite a rush to the oleaginous locations." Among the first Clevelanders descending upon the area was a produce merchant named James G. Hussey, who was a former boss of Rockefeller's partner, Maurice B. Clark, and he came home with ecstatic stories about the riches to be made.

We don't know what Rockefeller thought of Drake's breakthrough at the time, but years later, having harvested his unparalleled fortune from oil, John D. Rockefeller saw a large and providential design in the discovery of Pennsylvania oil, stating that "these vast stores of wealth were the gifts of the great Creator, the bountiful gifts of the great Creator." He expressed his gratitude that "Colonel Drake and the Standard Oil Company and all others connected with this industry had the opportunity for useful work in preparing and distributing this valuable product to supply the wants of the world."[1] As we shall see, Rockefeller always viewed the industry through this rose-tinted spiritual lens, and it materially aided his success, for his conviction that God had given kerosene to suffering mankind gave him unswerving faith in the industry's future, enabling him to persist where less confident men stumbled and faltered.

For all his later evangelical fervor about oil, John D. Rockefeller didn't behold its potential in a sudden revelatory flash but made an incremental transition from produce to oil. Clark and Rockefeller might have taken on consignment some of the first crude-oil shipments that reached Cleveland in early 1860, but it was the friendship between Maurice Clark and Samuel Andrews, an Englishman from Clark's hometown in Wiltshire, that drew Rockefeller into the business. A hearty, rubicund man with a broad face and genial manner, Andrews was a self-taught chemist, a born tinkerer, and an enterprising mechanic. Arriving in Cleveland in the 1850s, he worked in a lard-oil refinery owned by yet another Englishman, C. A. Dean, and acquired extensive experience in making tallow, candles, and coal oil. Then, in 1860, Dean got a ten-barrel shipment of Pennsylvania crude from which Andrews distilled the first oil-based kerosene manufactured in Cleveland. The secret of "cleansing" oil with sulfuric acid—what we now term refining—was then a high mystery, zealously guarded by a local priesthood of practical chemists, and many curious businessmen beat a path to Andrews's door.

An expert on illuminants enthralled by the unique properties of kerosene, Andrews was convinced it would outshine and outsell other sources of light. Finances were tight in the Andrews household—his wife took in sewing to supplement his income—but by 1862, Sam was plotting to leave Dean and strike out on his own. On the lookout for backers, he frequently dropped by the offices of Clark and Rockefeller. In another instance of the worldly advantages of his religious affiliations, Rockefeller knew Andrews and his wife from the Erie Street Baptist Mission Church. When Andrews started talking about oil refining, the dubious Clark cut short his perfervid talk: "I told him there was no chance, that John and I together did not have more than $250 we could spare out of our business; we simply had enough working capital, together with our credit at the banks, to enable us to make advances to consignors, paying insurance and rent."[2] Stymied by one partner, Andrews barged into Rockefeller's office and resumed his sales pitch. Already so flush that he had invested in his first railroad stock, with cash to spare for the firm, Rockefeller was far more receptive. After one chat with Rockefeller, Andrews went back into the warehouse to badger Clark. "I started to shut him off," recalled Clark, "but when he said, 'Mr. Rockefeller thinks well of it,' I impulsively replied, 'Well, if John will go in I will.' "[3] With becoming modesty, Rockefeller later interpreted his own role as more passive, even skeptical toward the fateful oil venture and said that Maurice Clark's two brothers, James and Richard, were such oil enthusiasts that he had been railroaded into refining by the combined pressure of the three Clarks and Sam Andrews.

Whatever the truth, Rockefeller and Maurice Clark pledged $4,000 for half the working capital of the new refining venture, Andrews, Clark and Co., placing the twenty-four-year-old Rockefeller squarely in the oil business in 1863, the year of the Emancipation Proclamation and the stunning Union victories at Gettysburg and Vicksburg. Of the initial $4,000 investment, he said dryly, "It seemed very large to us, *very large*."[4] Scarcely dreaming that oil would ever supersede their main commodity business, they considered it "a little side issue, we retaining our interest in our business as produce commission merchants."[5] As a commission agent distant from the oil wells, stationed at the commercial crossroads of Cleveland, Rockefeller naturally entered the industry as a refiner.

As a middleman, he belonged to a new breed of people in the emerging industrial economy who traded, refined, or distributed products in the widening chasm that separated raw-material producers in the countryside from their urban consumers.

The spot chosen for the new refinery tells much in miniature about Rockefeller's approach to business. He exercised an option on a three-acre parcel on the sloping, red-clay banks of a narrow waterway called Kingsbury Run, which flowed into the Cuyahoga River and thus provided passage to Lake Erie. A mile and a half from downtown Cleveland, it seemed at first glance an inauspicious site for the new refinery, christened the Excelsior Works. In these bucolic outskirts beyond the city limits, cows browsed peacefully, and trees still shaded the waterway. But for Rockefeller, the inconvenience was outweighed by the fact that it would soon adjoin new railroad tracks. On November 3, 1863, proudly flying the Union colors, a gleaming locomotive of the Atlantic and Great Western Railroad pulled into a Cleveland station decked with bunting and launched a new era, giving the town access to New York City via the Erie Railroad and to a valuable direct route to the Pennsylvania oil fields. Able to ship by water or over land, Rockefeller gained the critical leverage he needed to secure preferential rates on transportation—which was why he agonized over plant locations throughout his career.

Before long, a string of other refineries had sprouted along Kingsbury Run. With a population of about 44,000, Cleveland was full of dynamic young men struggling to get ahead, and oil refining presented a rare chance to parlay a small investment into a huge fortune. It cost a pittance—as little as $1,000, or less than the cost of opening a well-stocked store—to construct a small refinery and hire hands to run it. By mid-1863, twenty refineries operated in the Cleveland area and shipped a quarter of their kerosene abroad. At first, the profits came in so thick and fast that everybody—big and small, clever and inept—made handsome profits without the fierce winnowing of adversity, the stern lash of marketplace discipline. Rockefeller sarcastically alluded to these palmy days as "the harvest time in which such large profits were reaped by the saloon-keepers and preachers and tailors and men from all the walks of life who were fortunate enough to find an oil still."[6] Oil was put to myriad uses during the Civil War, treating the wounds of Union soldiers and serving as a substitute for turpentine formerly supplied by the South. Even on the battlefield, the use of kerosene refined from crude oil spread, and Ulysses S. Grant often sat in his tent, drafting dispatches by the flicker of a kerosene lamp.

Later on, Rockefeller became so embittered toward Sam Andrews that he denigrated him, quite unjustly, as the expendable figure in the Standard Oil saga. "Samuel Andrews was taken into the business as a poor workingman with little or nothing in the early stages when it was difficult to find men to cleanse the oil. . . . He had too much conceit, too much bull-headed English obstinacy and so little self-control. Was his own worst enemy."[7] This verdict, rendered much later, was darkly tinged by intervening events, but in the beginning Andrews enjoyed cordial relations with Rockefeller. Andrews knew nothing of business but was content to let Maurice Clark and Rockefeller mind the office while he acted as refinery boss. Reversing Rockefeller's harsh judgment, Ida Tarbell went so far as to label Andrews "a mechanical genius" who had improved the quality of the kerosene and the percentage of it yielded by each barrel of crude oil.[8]

In the early days, Rockefeller wasn't so detached from the practical side of refining as when his empire later grew and he withdrew into the impregnable fortress of his office. Devoid of superior airs, he was often seen at Kingsbury Run at 6:30 A.M., going into the cooper shop to roll out barrels, stack hoops, or cart out shavings, reflecting the thrift inculcated by his mother and his puritanical religious upbringing. Since a residue of sulfuric acid remained after refining, Rockefeller drew up plans to convert it to fertilizer—the first of many worthwhile and extremely profitable attempts to create by-products from waste materials. Shaped by a childhood of uncertainty, he aspired to be self-sufficient in business no less than in life and reacted to a perpetual shortage of barrels by deciding to build his own. Disgusted by a suspicious error in a plumber's bill, he told Sam Andrews, "Hire a plumber by the month. Let us buy our own pipes, joints, and all other plumbing material."[9] The refinery also did its own hauling and loading. Such was Rockefeller's ingenuity, his ceaseless search for even minor improvements, that within a year refining had overtaken produce as the most profitable side of the business. Despite the unceasing vicissitudes of the oil industry, prone to cataclysmic booms and busts, he would never experience a single year of loss.

If Rockefeller entered the refining business with some reservations, he soon embraced it as the big, bold opportunity he had craved. Never one to do things halfway, he plunged headlong into the business, and his enthusiasm overflowed into his home life. Sharing a room with brother William, he often nudged him awake in the dead of night. "I've been thinking out a plan to do so and so," he would ask. "Now, what do you think of this scheme?"[10] "Keep your ideas till morning," Will would sleepily protest. "I want to sleep."[11] In the predawn dark, John usually chatted with Maurice Clark and Sam Andrews at Cheshire Street, where they talked interminably of oil. As John's sister Mary Ann observed, the older men deferred to him instinctively. "They did not seem to want to go without him. They would . . . walk in and visit in the dining room while John was at breakfast." She found the infatuation with oil repugnant, screening out the dreadful carnage of the Civil War. "I got sick of it and wished morning after morning that they would talk of something else."[12]

Rockefeller leaped into oil with a zest reminiscent of his absorption in the Baptist Church. He lovingly tended his refinery much as he had swept the chapel floor, a parallel not lost on contemporaries. Said Maurice Clark: "John had abiding faith in two things—the Baptist creed and oil."[13] This very old, very young man found boyish pleasure in doing business, and when he captured a large contract, he strutted and whooped with a buoyant step or cut a small comic caper. As one early associate remarked, "The only time I ever saw John Rockefeller enthusiastic was when a report came in from the creek that his buyer had secured a cargo of oil at a figure much below the market price. He bounded from his chair with a shout of joy, danced up and down, hugged me, threw up his hat, acted so like a madman that I have never forgotten it."[14] These isolated joyful outbursts only underscored the usual constriction of his personality.

Rockefeller's overwhelming influence on the oil industry stemmed from the conflict between his overmastering need for order and the turbulent, unruly nature of the infant industry. In the overheated memories of his enemies, Rockefeller became an omnipresent bogeyman who first appeared in the Oil Regions—the name given to the area along Oil Creek that encompassed Titusville, Oil City, and Franklin—not long after Drake's discovery. One legend, rehashed by several early biographers, was that Rockefeller went to Titusville in 1860 to represent a group of Cleveland capitalists and advised them to refrain from the business, citing the uncertain flow of oil. In truth, Rockefeller testified, "I was engaged in the business when I took the trip; that was why I took the trip, to see about a supply of oil for my refinery."[15]

To reach his destination, he had to travel first by rail and then by stagecoach to penetrate the dark forests and wooded hills along Oil Creek. Despite the spot's isolation—news of Fort Sumter's fall took four days to arrive—so many adventurers descended upon the area that train aisles were jammed with newcomers while others squatted on the roof. It was no place for the squeamish. To reach the railroad, oil had to be carted in barrels across more than twenty miles of rough backcountry, a trade serviced by thousands of brawling, swearing teamsters with shaggy beards and slouch hats who charged extortionate rates. (The Pennsylvania barrel, equal to forty-two gallons, remains the industry standard to this day.) Sometimes oil-laden wagons stretched in interminable caravans along the rutted roads. Many barrels tipped over and smashed, making the hills treacherous. During wet seasons, the mud grew so thick that teamsters often took two horses, one to pull the other out when it invariably got stuck. Horses were routinely lashed to death with heavy black whips as they pulled enormous loads through the black muck. Left to die by the roadside, their hides and hair were eaten away by petroleum chemicals, leaving ghastly, corroded carcasses strewn across the landscape. Transport by water was no less revolting. Oil Creek flowed into the Allegheny River, where hundreds of flatboats and steamers handled the cargo traffic. Sometimes oil barrels were loaded on barges and floated down to Pittsburgh on man-made freshets produced by suddenly releasing water stored behind floodgates. "Lots of oil was lost by the capsizing of barges and smashing of barrels in the confusion and crush of the rafts," said Rockefeller.[16] By 1863, the Allegheny, befouled with oil, actually caught fire and burned a bridge in Franklin.

Tramping the banks, Rockefeller beheld the satanic new world bequeathed by the oil boom, an idyllic valley blackened with derricks and tanks, engine houses and ramshackle huts, thickly crowded together in a crazy-quilt pattern. Boomtowns appeared briefly, witnessed frantic activity, then vanished as abruptly as they had appeared. Rockefeller saw something slapdash about the industry. "You will remember that the business in its early years was a sort of gold-field rush," he reminisced. "Great fortunes were made by some of the first adventurers, and everything was carried on in a sort of helter-skelter way."[17] Rockefeller represented the second, more rational stage of capitalist development, when the colorful daredevils and pioneering speculators give way, as Max Weber wrote, to the "men who had grown up in the hard school of life, calculating and daring at the same time, above all temperate and reliable, shrewd and completely devoted to their business, with strictly bourgeois opinions and principles."[18]

By the time Rockefeller arrived in the Oil Regions, it looked as if the oil would be more than a transient phenomenon. In September 1861, two Clevelanders brought in the Empire Well, the first mighty gusher, which rose "higher than steeples," in the evocative words of one observer, yielding three thousand barrels of oil per day.[19] To onlookers, there was something uncanny about this towering jet of oil. So fast did the Empire Well flow that its owners could scarcely find barrels to carry it off, and people came running with pails, dippers, cups, and buckets to scoop up the black gold. A sudden oil glut sent prices skidding to ten cents a barrel even as teamsters continued to charge $3 or $4 per barrel to ship it to the railroads. From its first days, the industry tended to oscillate between extremes: gluts so dire that prices plummeted below production costs, or shortages that sent prices skyward but raised the even more troubling specter of the oil running dry.

Among the many tales of Rockefeller's first trip to the oil fields, one told by Franklin Breed, a Titusville producer, has a ring of authenticity. He and Rockefeller rode on horseback through the valley to reach Breed's well, then negotiated the final half mile on foot. As Breed later wrote:

> It was necessary to cross a bayou of five or six feet in width and probably four feet deep. This bayou contained sediment which the oil men took from the bottom of the tanks. This, with mud in the bayou, resembled tar. Spanning the bayou was a six inch log. . . . I was used to crossing on it but Rockefeller de-

clared he could not walk on it. He did, however, and he fell off. . . . He looked up at me with a smile and said, "Well, Breed, you have got me into the oil business head and ears."[20]

In talking to the hard-bitten wildcatters, Rockefeller must have seemed standoffish and self-possessed, but he professed to enjoy their company, calling them "pleasant fellows, the same type we meet in the mining regions, jolly, good-natured, happy-go-lucky."[21] The description is not without a note of condescension. But he listened closely to what people said and filed away as much information as he could, repeating valuable information to himself until it was memorized. There was humility in this eagerness to learn. As he said, "It is very important to remember what other people tell you, not so much what you yourself already know."[22]

However stimulated by the money to be made, Rockefeller was appalled by the loose morals of a place infested with cardsharpers and prostitutes and already dubbed "Sodden Gomorrah."[23] The wildcatters were so rowdy, said a visitor, that throughout the area you could hear "the slap of cards on whiskey-stained tables of groggeries."[24] Another visitor marveled at the universal dissipation and reported, "The orgies in Petroleum Centre sometimes eclipsed Monte Carlo and the Latin Quarter combined."[25] For a sober, pious Christian such as Rockefeller, this world of brawny men addicted to vice must have seemed infernal. The oilmen walked around in tall boots, leaving black footprints in the brothels, taverns, and gambling houses of Titusville and Oil City. Many flaunted their nouveau-riche excesses, wearing high silk hats, diamond stickpins, and gold watch chains. In travelers' reports, it is striking how frequently people resorted to hellish imagery to capture the mood. Rockefeller's trips to the Oil Regions must have strengthened his belief that he stood foursquare for virtue in a godforsaken place. As an ardent temperance advocate, he was extremely uncomfortable around drinkers—perhaps one reason why he seldom visited the oil fields.

Two stories, both of uncertain authenticity, convey Rockefeller's disdain for the morals prevalent among many producers. One night in Rouseville, a local committee of vigilantes crept up to a flatboat moored to a bank and filled with ladies of easy virtue and whiskey salesmen; at the height of a bacchanal, they cut the boat loose and sent the sinners twenty miles downriver. It is said that Rockefeller "thoroughly approved" of the action.[26] Another story tells of the time he stayed in Franklin, where he boarded at the Exchange Hotel and liked to have bread and milk for supper. Occasionally, he donned a dingy old suit to help his men load barrels. One Sunday, an employee came rushing in to tell Rockefeller that the river was rising dangerously and might sweep away their barrels. Rockefeller, preparing for church, put on his hat with aplomb, said he had to go to prayer, and refused to attend to business. Perhaps Rockefeller really did have God on his side, for his barrels survived the flooding intact.[27]

Drilling for oil often seemed less an industry than a lottery: Nobody knew if oil would prove a lasting benefit to mankind or an evanescent wonder. If the Oil Regions created many millionaires, they left many more paupers. Instead of building up an industry, most producers preferred to drain their wells as quickly as possible in this harum-scarum atmosphere. Under the so-called rule of capture, people could drill diagonally and siphon off a neighbor's oil, adding to their haste to pump. Rockefeller succeeded because he believed in the long-term prospects of the business and never treated it as a mirage that would soon fade. Rockefeller's first visit to Pennsylvania must also have persuaded him that he had picked the right entry point to the business. Searching for oil was wildly unpredictable, whereas refining seemed safe and methodical by comparison. Before too long, he realized that refining was the critical point where he could exert maximum leverage over the industry.

John D. Rockefeller had an unfailing knack for knowing who would help or hinder him in his career, an instinct only sharpened by time. Sensitive to patronizing behavior, he bridled when anyone tried to lord it over him, and he wanted to be dealt with as a peer even by senior men. Recoiling at what he saw as the Clark brothers' pomposity, he eventually grew as censorious of them as he had been of George Gardner. The Clarks were the first of many business partners to underrate the audacity of the quietly calculating Rockefeller, who bided his time as he figured out how to get rid of them.

All along, crosscurrents had ruffled his relationship with Maurice B. Clark, whom he dismissed as "an ignorant, conceited Englishman."[28] A tall, bluff man with a fiery temper and shadowy past, Clark had started out as a gardener in his native Wiltshire, chafing under a tyrannical boss. One day in 1847, he reared up and flattened the man. Fearing arrest, he fled to Boston as a penniless, uneducated fugitive from justice. He migrated west to Cleveland and worked as a woodchopper and teamster before entering the produce business. More of a free spirit than Rockefeller, Clark smoked, drank, and swore freely in the warehouse and showed scant religious interest. The personality profile didn't appeal to Rockefeller, who bristled at Clark's profanity, but he praised him as a smart, hustling businessman.

Because Rockefeller had such respect for ledgers, Clark, nearly ten years older, looked down on him as a mere clerk, a rigid, blinkered man without vision. "He did not think I could do anything but keep accounts and look after the finances," said Rockefeller.[29] "You see, it took him a long time to feel that I was no longer a boy."[30] He thought Clark envious of his success in soliciting business on the road, perhaps because this undercut Clark's image of him as an expendable clerk. At first, Rockefeller swallowed his anger and stoically endured

this injustice. "He tried almost from the beginning of our partnership to dominate and override me," he said of Clark. "A question he asked several times in
our discussion of business matters was, 'What in the world would you have
done without *me?*' I bore it in silence. It does no good to dispute with such a
man."[31] Rockefeller had no doubt who was contributing the lion's share of
business. "I was the one who made the firm's success. I kept the books, looked
out for the money."[32] As part of Rockefeller's silent craft and habit of extended
premeditation, he never tipped off his adversaries to his plans for revenge, preferring to spring his reprisals on them.

The investment in oil refining had brought Maurice's brother James into the
office, and Rockefeller came to detest him. An ex-prizefighter, James Clark was
a powerful, bullying young man, and he tried to intimidate Rockefeller, who responded with great sangfroid and courage. One morning, James burst into his
office and started swearing violently at Rockefeller, who put his feet up on the
desk with imperturbable poise and showed no sign of upset; a fine actor, he always had masterful control of his facial muscles. When James finished, Rockefeller said evenly, "Now James, you can knock my head off but you might as
well understand that you can't scare me."[33] This fearless young man couldn't
be intimidated. After that confrontation, James Clark didn't rant and bluster as
much around Rockefeller, but it was clear that they were incompatible colleagues.

As with Maurice, Rockefeller quarreled with James about business methods
and was dismayed by his devious side deals in oil. When James boasted about
swindling a former boss or cheating people on buying trips to Pennsylvania, it
must have aroused Rockefeller's innermost suspicions, for he closely audited
his partner's expenses. Like Maurice, James smarted at Rockefeller's self-
righteousness and branded him the "Sunday-school superintendent."[34] Already contemplating the future, Rockefeller wanted to be surrounded by
trustworthy people who could inspire confidence in customers and bankers
alike. He drew a characteristic conclusion: The weak, immoral man was also
destined to be a poor businessman. "We were beginning to prosper and I felt
very uneasy at my name being linked up with these speculators."[35] Later on,
the Clarks fully reciprocated this contempt, with James describing Rockefeller's
sole contribution to Andrews, Clark as that of a "financial manipulator" and
claiming that in 1863 Rockefeller had cheated him of several thousand dollars.[36]

If their differences had been chiefly a clash of personalities, Rockefeller's
partnership with Maurice Clark might have lasted years, but they had sharply
divergent views about oil's future and the desirable pace of expansion. Despite
the Civil War, the drills never stopped in Pennsylvania, except when General
Lee invaded the state and producers had to defend it. As the export business in
kerosene widened, Andrews, Clark banked solid profits in refining during every

year of the war. Yet prices remained as volatile as the war itself, with the supply-demand equation shifting radically each time a single spouter or gusher came in. Amid the ruthlessly competitive conditions, it was never clear where prices would settle or what constituted a normal price. The price fluctuations in a single year were staggering, veering between 10¢ and $10 a barrel in 1861 and $4 and $12 in 1864. Undeterred by these extreme gyrations, both Rockefeller and Andrews wanted to borrow heavily and expand, while Clark favored a more circumspect approach.

What likely clinched Rockefeller's decision to break from the three Clarks was that they had the votes to override him and Andrews and didn't hesitate to use their majority in a high-handed way. In later reminiscences, Rockefeller disclosed an incident that casts light on his relations with the Clarks: "[Maurice Clark] was very angry when I borrowed money to extend our business of refining oil. 'Why, you have borrowed $100,000,' he exclaimed, as if that were some sort of offense."[37] Rockefeller's amazement seems somewhat disingenuous: It was a stupendous sum, but all Rockefeller could see was that Maurice Clark lacked his audacity. "Clark was an old grandmother and was scared to death because we owed money at the banks."[38] One can forgive the Clarks if they found something overbearing about this bumptious young man who would risk all their capital, evidently without notifying them. Significantly, the Clarks were irked by both Rockefeller's frugality *and* his prodigality—his tight-fisted control of details and advocacy of unbridled expansion. Daring in design, cautious in execution—it was a formula he made his own throughout his career.

By 1865, Rockefeller, age twenty-five, decided it was time for a showdown with the Clarks. He wasn't the sort to persist in a flawed situation, and he was now prepared to clear away the encumbrances that had thwarted his early career.

=

For Rockefeller, success in the oil business required a bullish, nearly glandular faith in its future. Before deciding to enter the business on a large scale, he needed one last God-given proof that the oil wouldn't disappear—decisive evidence that came in January 1865 at a place called Pithole Creek. The nearby rocks and chasms had always emitted sulfur gas and attracted the notice of oilmen. One day, a group of eccentric producers, waving a witch-hazel twig serving as a divining rod, drilled on the spot where the twig dipped down. When a tremendous gusher spouted up days later, another madcap chapter in the oil industry commenced, with speculators, drillers, and business agents converging on the spot. Within a few months, the sleepy frontier settlement with four log cabins was transformed into a hectic little metropolis of twelve thousand people. Overnight, fifty hotels sprang up, along with a theater that seated one hundred and was lit by crystal chandeliers. So improbable was Pithole's rise that it seemed a phantom city, a conjurer's trick. "It was more than a city," says one chronicler, "it was a state of postwar euphoria."[39] Even by the sordid standards of the Oil Regions, it was a disreputable place. "Every other shop is a liquor saloon," said one journalist. "It is safe to assert that there is more vile liquor drunk in this town than in any other of its size in the world."[40]

One eyewitness to the whole Pithole lunacy was an observant eight-year-old girl named Ida Minerva Tarbell, who lived ten miles away in Rouseville and saw hordes of eager men streaking to the boomtown. When her father built an oil-tank shop there, he made the fastest money of his life. Unfortunately, Pithole's ebullient heyday was short-lived, and within a few years its wells were exhausted from fire and overproduction. Before the town reverted back to sylvan peace, people began to scavenge for scrap. For $600, Ida Tarbell's father bought the fancy Bonta House hotel, constructed a few years earlier for $60,000, and carried off its lumber, doors, and windows to erect a home for the Tarbell family in Titusville. By 1874, the moment of its greatness having flickered, Pithole counted just six voters.

In hindsight, Pithole was a cautionary fable of blasted hopes and counterfeit dreams, renewing fears of the industry's short life span. But in January 1865, it suggested that there were many undiscovered pockets of oil, and it probably acted as a catalyst that hastened Rockefeller's break with the Clarks. This parting was vintage Rockefeller: He slowly and secretly laid the groundwork, then moved with electrifying speed to throw his adversaries off balance. That January, Maurice Clark had openly fumed when Rockefeller asked him to sign yet another note. "We have been asking too many loans in order to extend this oil business," Clark said. Undaunted, Rockefeller shot back: "We should borrow whenever we can safely extend the business by doing so."[41] Trying to intimidate Rockefeller, the Clark brothers threatened to dissolve the partnership, which required the unanimous consent of all the partners.

Determined to break loose from the Clarks and the commission business, Rockefeller sounded out Sam Andrews privately and told him:

Sam, we are prospering. We have a future before us, a big future. But I don't like Jim Clark and his habits. He is an immoral man in more ways than one. He gambles in oil. I don't want this business to be associated with a gambler. Suppose I take them up the next time they threaten a dissolution. Suppose I succeed in buying them out. Will you come in with me?[42]

When Andrews agreed, they shook hands on the deal.

A few weeks later, just as Rockefeller expected, he quarreled with Maurice Clark, and the latter threatened to dissolve the partnership. "If that's the way you want to do business we'd better dissolve, and let you run your own affairs to suit yourself," Clark warned.[43] Moving swiftly to implement his scenario, Rockefeller invited the partners to his home on February 1, 1865, and vigorously expounded a policy of rapid refinery expansion—a policy he knew was anathema to the Clarks. Playing right into Rockefeller's hands, James Clark tried to browbeat him. "We'd better split up," he declared.[44] In conformity with the partnership agreement, Rockefeller got everyone to state publicly that he favored dissolution, and the Clarks left imagining they had cowed Rockefeller. In fact, he raced to the office of the *Cleveland Leader* and placed a notice in the morning paper dissolving the partnership. The next morning, when the Clarks saw it, they were stunned. "Do you really mean it?" an incredulous Maurice Clark asked Rockefeller. He hadn't realized before that Rockefeller had lined up Andrews on his side. "You really want to break it up?" "I really want to break it up," replied Rockefeller, who had sounded out sympathetic bankers in the preceding weeks.[45] It was agreed that the firm would be auctioned to the highest bidder.

Even as a young man, Rockefeller was extremely composed in a crisis. In this respect, he was a natural leader: The more agitated others became, the calmer he grew. It was an index of his matchless confidence that when the auction occurred, the Clarks brought a lawyer while Rockefeller represented himself. "I thought that I could take care of so simple a transaction," he boasted.[46] With the Clarks' lawyer acting as auctioneer, the bidding began at $500 and quickly rose to a few thousand dollars, then inched up slowly to about $50,000—already more than Rockefeller thought the refining business worth. Since this auction was a turning point on his road to industrial supremacy, let us quote his account of the historic moment as he related it in his memoirs:

> Finally it advanced to $60,000, and by slow stages to $70,000, and I almost feared for my ability to buy the business and have the money to pay for it. At last the other side bid $72,000. Without hesitation I said $72,500. Mr. Clark then said: "I'll go no higher, John; the business is yours." "Shall I give you a check for it now?" I suggested. "No," Mr. Clark said, "I'm glad to trust you for it; settle at your convenience."[47]

Rockefeller knew the moment was fraught with consequences. "It was the day that determined my career. I felt the bigness of it, but I was as calm as I am talking to you now," he told William O. Inglis.[48] He paid a lofty price for his freedom, surrendering to Clark his half interest in the commission business along with the $72,500. (The purchase price would be equivalent to $652,000 today.) Yet he had captured a tremendous prize. At age twenty-five, he had won control of Cleveland's largest refinery, which could treat five hundred barrels of crude oil daily—twice the capacity of its nearest local rival—and ranked as one of the world's largest facilities. On February 15, 1865, the *Cleveland Leader* printed the following item: "Copartnership Notice—The undersigned, having purchased the entire interest of Andrews, Clark & Co. in the 'Excelsior Oil Works,' and all the stock of barrels, oil, etc., will continue the business of the late firm under the name of Rockefeller & Andrews."[49] Rockefeller savored his revenge against the Clarks, who were shocked that their junior partner had lined up, on the sly, financing for such a large deal, and Rockefeller gloated at the older men's complacent naïveté. "Then [the Clark brothers] woke up and saw for the first time that my mind had not been idle while they were talking so big and loud."[50] All of Rockefeller's Baptist contempt for vanity, show, and loose talk is condensed in that single observation. On March 2, 1865, Clark and Rockefeller was also dissolved, and Rockefeller eliminated the three fractious Clark brothers from his life forever.

For Rockefeller, the harrowing memory of the Clarks stayed with him, and he talked as if he had survived a nightmare. "The sufferings I went through in those years, the humiliation and the anguish, I have not words to describe. And I ever point to the day when I separated myself from them by paying this large bonus as the beginning of the success I have made in my life."[51] It's hard to know whether Rockefeller exaggerated the Clarks' haughtiness, but the important points are that he was proud and sensitive and that their barbed words reverberated deeply in his mind. Having emerged as his own boss, he would never again feel his advancement blocked by shortsighted, mediocre men.

The demise of Clark and Rockefeller unfolded against the waning days of the Civil War. By December 1864, General Sherman had reached Savannah and swung north through the Carolinas. About two months after Rockefeller won the refining business, Robert E. Lee surrendered to Ulysses S. Grant at Appomattox Courthouse. As a town that had sheltered many runaway slaves before the war, Cleveland was especially grieved by the subsequent news of Lincoln's assassination. On April 27, the funeral train brought his body to lie in state for several hours in a special mortuary pavilion, with women in spotless white robes gathering by the railroad tracks to sing choral dirges to the slain president.

By this point, the new firm of Rockefeller and Andrews had been installed on the second floor of a brick building on Superior Street, several blocks from the Cuyahoga River, in an office complex known as the Sexton Block. From his new command post, the young entrepreneur could stare out the window and follow the progress of barges drifting by laden with oil barrels from his refinery. Already a mature businessman, he relied on Andrews only as a technician and assumed control of all other aspects of the business. Having discarded several older partners, the young man had no real business mentors, heroes, or role models and was beholden to no one. John D. Rockefeller was not only self-made but self-invented and already had unyielding faith in his own judgment.

For all his resoluteness as a young businessman, Rockefeller tarried in settling his private life. Yet he had already fathomed his own needs and sought a woman who would be pious and loving, dedicated to the church, and strongly supportive of his career. Because of his easy, affectionate way with his mother, Rockefeller felt comfortable with women, took genuine pleasure in their company, and, unlike the caddish Bill, treated them with respect.

During his brief period at Central High School, Rockefeller had befriended two bright, literate sisters, Lucy and Laura Celestia Spelman, and taken a special fancy to Laura, or "Cettie," as she was called. Though he still had an awkward manner with girls, the sisters saw a warm, likable side to him. Unlike most other girls at the school, the practical-minded Cettie was taking commercial courses to master business principles, and she applauded John in his storied 1855 job search. As a friend of Cettie's later noted, "She saw that he was ambitious, and she thought that he was honest, which probably appealed to her more than anything else."[52] Clearly, she transmitted to John the message that his chances of winning her would be materially enhanced if his economic prospects improved.

There seems little doubt that in courting Cettie, John was held back by the disparity in their socioeconomic status, which accounts for the nine-year hiatus between their first meeting in high school and their 1864 marriage. The Spelmans were high-toned people, a blue-ribbon family living in a fine house. A friend of Laura's recalled, "Perhaps Cettie wasn't exactly rich and beautiful, but her father was as well off as any of the girls in our class, a member of the Ohio legislature, and somewhat known for his philanthropic work, so—you know how those things are among children—we thought that it was strange for her to rather show a leaning toward Johnny."[53] It's easy to see what drew John to Laura aside from patent compatibility, for the Spelmans signified the respectability that had so frustratingly eluded his own family.

Civic-minded, stirred to action by social injustice, the Spelmans offered more than entrée into the local gentry and were a family of genuine substance. Born in Massachusetts, Harvey Buel Spelman, a direct descendant of the Puritans, and Lucy Henry met in Ohio and were married in 1835, giving birth to Laura Celestia on September 9, 1839. When they moved to Akron in 1841, they lived humbly at first, with Mrs. Spelman taking in washing to extend their income; Cettie, as a little girl, sometimes yanked a small red wagon around town to deliver laundry. Even when Harvey Spelman opened a dry-goods store and amassed considerable wealth, he and Lucy didn't retreat into private pleasures but redoubled their militant reform efforts. As a member of the local board of education, Harvey Spelman spearheaded the creation of a progressive public-school system, a crusade that propelled him into the Ohio state legislature in 1849. Also busy in church causes, the Spelmans helped to found a Congregational church in Akron. Their religious beliefs buttressed their secular activism, and they were pledged to root out evil as part of both their religious and political agendas.

With his broad forehead, tufty brows, and pugnacious beard, Harvey Buel Spelman was a man of burning fundamentalist convictions and apocalyptic musings. He frequently discerned God's hand smiting the American people for their wicked extravagance, and he issued flaming diatribes against demon rum: "The widespread and excessive use of rum is the tinder which inflames the worst passions in human nature, fosters riots, Communism and strikes, promotes ignorance, vice and crime, and more than any other cause, threatens the stability of our free institutions," he said in 1879.[54] Lucy Henry, his dignified, industrious wife, enjoyed singing hymns and had little time for small talk, though she could be jolly with her daughters. "At any reference to the Bible, to temperance, to education, to the widening sphere of women, her eyes flashed with old-time fire, and her face was aglow with conviction," a preacher said, with pardonable hyperbole, at her funeral.[55]

As an outgrowth of their church involvement—and this was true of many evangelicals after the Second Great Awakening—Harvey and Lucy were uncompromising abolitionists and temperance activists. With their home serving as a station on the Underground Railroad, they shepherded many slaves from Tennessee and Kentucky to freedom, and Sojourner Truth, the former slave, abolitionist, and itinerant preacher, spent several days with them. According to Cettie, the only time she ever saw her mother cooking on the Sabbath was to prepare hot meals for slaves in flight to Canada. The Spelmans felt no less ardently about drink. The crusading Mrs. Spelman not only marched in the streets but stormed the saloons, dropped to her knees in prayer, and pleaded with sinners at the bar stools to mend their ways, while Mr. Spelman carried on a parallel campaign to shut down rum shops.

The Spelmans' prosperous life in Akron ended in 1851 when Mr. Spelman's business went bankrupt, the casualty of a bank panic. The family then moved to Cleveland, where Mr. Spelman's fortunes revived, but a dark edge of economic uncertainty always shadowed the family. So while the Spelmans occupied a higher social rung than young Rockefeller, they were haunted by the prospect of economic misfortune and inclined to look favorably upon an up-and-coming suitor with a proper Christian pedigree. Cettie needed to find a husband who could safeguard her family's security, so it is not surprising that she championed John's career and eagerly coached him to succeed from the start.

It is hard to picture a young woman more perfectly suited to John D. Rockefeller's values than the sensible, cheerful Laura Celestia Spelman, who shared his devotion to duty and thrift. They ratified each other's views about the fundamentals of life. Two months younger than John, Cettie was short and slender, with a round face, dark brown eyes, and a wealth of chestnut hair parted down the middle and smoothly pulled back from her forehead. Rockefeller would never have tolerated a noisy woman, and Cettie was soft in voice and manner. Like John, though, her mild surface belied an adamantine determination. She was "gentle and lovely, but resolute with indomitable will," noted her sister Lucy, better known in the family as Lute.[56] "There was a persuasion in her touch as she laid her fingers ever so gently on your arm."[57] Again like John, her geniality covered a hard core of sustained willpower. "She was full of mirth and cheer, yet . . . rather inclined to be grave and reserved," Lute recalled.[58] A paragon of self-control, she never lost her temper and lacked the skittish frivolity of youth.

Early on, John and Laura must have spotted each other as kindred souls, especially when it came to religion. Cettie so unswervingly performed her duties at church and Sunday school that even her loving sister tactfully suggested that she went to extremes. "She was a *religieuse.* God and church came first with her. She cared little for the 'social life,' so called; and together she and her husband deepened and expanded their religion to cover and include every phase of life."[59] Even in photos, one notes a Quakerish simplicity to her appearance, her black dress and lace collar evoking her Puritan ancestors. Despite her evangelical beliefs, she never imposed her views on others and preferred to instruct by example. As one high-school classmate remembered, "She exerted a strong influence upon the rest of us. For one thing she didn't believe in dancing and theatregoing, because she did not think it was proper for church people to engage in pursuits that she considered worldly."[60] For all that, Laura was no shallow philistine and had a wide range of interests in art, culture, and society. She played the piano for three hours daily and often accompanied John in duets, but she also had a taste for literature and poetry and could be an entertaining conversationalist.

An assiduous student, she was the valedictorian of her high-school class and her commencement speech, "I Can Paddle My Own Canoe," was a ringing manifesto of female emancipation. (She graduated seven years after the first historic attempt by Elizabeth Cady Stanton and Lucretia Mott to organize women in Seneca Falls, New York.) From this speech, we can infer something of her adolescent values. "We may not tamely submit, and suffer ourselves to be led by any person or party, but have a mind of our own, and having once formed a decision ever abide by it."[61] This credo augured well for a woman destined to be embroiled in her future husband's controversial career. In an outspoken statement of feminist belief, she chided men for depriving women of culture then hypocritically blaming them for their dependency. "But give woman culture—let her thread the many paths of science—allow mathematics and exact thought on all subjects to exert their influence on her mind and conventions need not trouble about her 'proper sphere.' "[62]

In 1856, Harvey and Lucy Spelman left Cleveland for Burlington, Iowa; the move evidently reflected renewed business hardships for Mr. Spelman, and they stayed away from Cleveland for three years. To alleviate the financial stress, Cettie and Lute stayed behind and jointly applied for teaching posts in the Cleveland public schools. Two years later, as the economic pinch eased, the two sisters spent a year at the Oread Collegiate Institute in Worcester, Massachusetts. Established in 1849, this junior college was among the first institutions of higher learning open to women. Founded by abolitionist Eli Thayer, Oread stressed Christianity and the reading of the classics. Drawings show a picturesque, medieval-looking building on a hill, festooned with turrets, towers, and crenellations and surrounded by a stone wall. The cultural atmosphere, with its impassioned support for women's rights and black welfare, must have been highly congenial to the sisters. Among other speakers, they heard inspirational lectures given by Ralph Waldo Emerson, Wendell Phillips, Henry Ward Beecher, and John Brown. A devotee of the Protestant work ethic, Cettie even approved of the school's daily regimen, which was minutely budgeted from wake-up at 5:30 A.M. until the lights went out at 9:45 P.M. "I do not call the rules strict but am pleased with all of them," she informed her former music teacher.[63] At Oread, she dropped an occasional friendly note to Rockefeller, though the relationship was at this point less one of romance than of close camaraderie.

Over the years, Laura's growing commitment to religion smothered her literary bent, but at Oread she was a veritable bluestocking, writing poetry, running the literary society, and editing the campus literary magazine. In a revealing article in the *Oread Euphemia*, she wrote about three aristocracies then ruling America—an aristocracy of intellect in New England, wealth in the mid-Atlantic states, and blood in the South. In view of later events, her descriptions of Boston's intellectual preeminence or southern social decadence are less noteworthy than the vitriol she poured on the New York nouveaux riches. "In this specified portion of our glorious republic, the 'parvenu' lady, with a brain all guiltless of ever having developed an idea, attires her self in habiliments, whose *cast* (but not *style*) would admit of their being worn in the presence of royalty." After lambasting the dominion of the "almighty dollar" in the mid-Atlantic aristocracy, she concluded mordantly, "The gigantic intellect of Boston must bow to *Wall St. Stocks and Bonds*."[64] Such midwestern scorn for Wall Street's monied upstarts was certainly consonant with Rockefeller's beliefs. Little did the two know they would one day become synonymous with the "almighty dollar" and reside in the heart of Manhattan's swankest, most sinful precincts.

In the spring of 1859, the Spelman sisters returned to Cleveland and began to take French, Latin, piano, and voice lessons at the Cleveland Institute. That autumn, Cettie and Lute, who always moved in tandem, began to teach in the public schools, Cettie serving as a teacher and principal's assistant while Lute taught boys in the same building. Later on, Laura left no doubt of her family's straitened circumstances at the time. "I had to do [work], which was a good thing," she later told her son, "and I loved to do it, which was another good thing."[65] Despite a well-merited reputation as a disciplinarian, she was a popular teacher, and on her last day on the job "all the girls in her class remained after dismissal to say good-bye to her and to cry over losing her," said one pupil. "My! how they cried."[66]

In the early 1860s, Laura was sufficiently pleased with work that she felt in no special rush to get married. All the while, John Rockefeller, with the dogged patience that would defeat scores of embattled competitors, waited determinedly in the wings. In April 1860, Laura wrote her former music teacher, "I seem to have no anxiety about leading a life of single-blessedness," but she mentioned Rockefeller and said that "a gentleman told me not long ago, that he was in no particular rush to have me get married, but he hoped that in the multitude of my thoughts I would not forget the subject."[67] She must have been torn when contemplating a match with Rockefeller, for teachers had to remain single, and marriage would end her career.

In 1862, Rockefeller, buoyed by his rising wealth in the produce business, began to woo Cettie in earnest, often appearing at her school at day's end to take her home. The Spelmans then lived in a lovely area of apple groves and greenery called The Heights, and on weekends John and brother William often rode out there under the guise of watching Civil War recruits drill nearby. After the Spelmans moved to a new home in downtown Cleveland, John, often wearing boots spattered with oil from his new refinery, stopped by and took Cettie out for drives in his buckboard, and she heard with delight the details of his business. "Her judgment was always better than mine," Rockefeller said. "She was a woman of great sagacity. Without her keen advice, I would be a poor man."[68] There was loving exaggeration here, but in the early days of their marriage, he did bring home the books and review them with her.

Despite her constant reluctance, Rockefeller pursued her with quiet persistence; in love as in business, he had a longer time frame, a more settled will, than other people. By early 1864, with the first profits rolling in from refining, he had become a substantial person in Cleveland, cutting an impressive figure in his frock coat, silk hat, and striped trousers. He was a handsome young man, with a fine, straight nose, rather humorless mouth, and vaguely mournful visage. His mustache flowed into fluffy side-whiskers, but his hair was already receding at the temples. His eyes were steady and lucid, as if confidently scanning the horizon for business opportunities.

Later on, Rockefeller was peculiarly reluctant to divulge to his children details of his courtship, referring to the delicacy of the situation. One gathers that another man, more practiced in the arts of love, was after Laura and that by March 1864 John feared his rival might best him. The time had come to force the situation. As one person who heard the story secondhand remembered, "John D. wanted to marry her, so he went to her one day and proposed in a business-like way, just like he would make a business proposition. She accepted him in the same business-like way."[69] One imagines the two of them smiling shyly with relief. Shortly afterward, the ascetic Rockefeller did something wholly out of character, spending a shocking $118 for a diamond engagement ring. The splurge, one suspects, had a point: He wished to telegraph to the Spelmans that he was no longer a callow country boy but a rising young businessman who could support them in a style to which they were accustomed.

After a discreet, six-month engagement, on September 8, 1864, hard on the heels of Sherman's march into Atlanta, John D. Rockefeller, twenty-five, married Laura Celestia Spelman, twenty-four, in the living room of the Spelman home on Huron Street. It was a small, private affair attended only by the two families. Like many things in Rockefeller's life, it was carried out in secrecy, and the Cleveland papers printed no notice of it—very odd given the Spelmans' prominence. It is unlikely that Big Bill attended, and John might have worried that his absence would spark curiosity about him. Having established his financial wherewithal, Rockefeller now reverted to type and spent just $15.75 on the wedding ring, which was duly recorded in Ledger B under the rubric "Sundry Expenses."[70] In a denominational compromise, the pastors from Laura's Plymouth Congregational Church and John's Erie Street Baptist Mission Church jointly officiated, though Laura henceforth switched her allegiance to the Baptists.

Refusing to deviate from routine, John worked the morning of his wedding day, visiting both his downtown office and the cooperage at the refinery. He had arranged a special luncheon for twenty-six employees, without disclosing at first the reason for the celebration. When the jovial bridegroom left for the wedding, he told the foreman facetiously, "Treat them well, but see that they work."[71] With the Swiss precision that governed his life, Rockefeller allotted exactly one month—September 8 to October 8, 1864—for a honeymoon that traced a conventional itinerary. The newlyweds started off at Niagara Falls, followed by a stay at the Saint Lawrence Hall Hotel in Montreal and the Summit House in Mount Washington, New Hampshire. On the way home, they stopped off at Oread Collegiate Institute and met two new teachers, Sophia B. Packard and Harriet E. Giles, who would play important roles in their future.

Prior to his honeymoon, Rockefeller's travels had been limited, and the provincial young man in the tall silk hat exhibited voracious curiosity throughout the trip. While touring Niagara Falls, he peppered the guide with so many questions that the man grew distracted, ran the buggy into a ditch, and smashed a wheel. At another point, they met an old man in the roadway whom

John so sedulously drained of local lore that the latter finally pleaded with weary resignation, "For God's sake if you will go with me over to that barn yonder, I will start and tell you everything I ever knew."[72] This was the same monotonously inquisitive young man who was known as "the Sponge" in the Oil Regions.

For the first six months of their marriage, John and Laura lived with Eliza at 33 Cheshire Street; then they moved into a dignified, two-story brick house at 29 Cheshire Street. Surrounded by a white picket fence, the house had tall, graceful windows but was disfigured by an ugly portico. Even though Rockefeller now operated and partially owned the largest refinery in Cleveland, he and Laura lived frugally without house servants. Rockefeller always cherished the chaste simplicity of this early period and preserved their first set of dishes, which stirred him to wistful reflections in later years. Thus, by the end of the Civil War, John D. Rockefeller had established the foundations of his personal and professional life and was set to capitalize on the extraordinary opportunities beckoning him in postwar America. From this point forward, there would be no zigzags or squandered energy, only a single-minded focus on objectives that would make him both the wonder and terror of American business.

The rakish young Henry Morrison Flagler.
(Courtesy of the Henry Morrison Flagler Museum)

CHAPTER 6

The Poetry of the Age

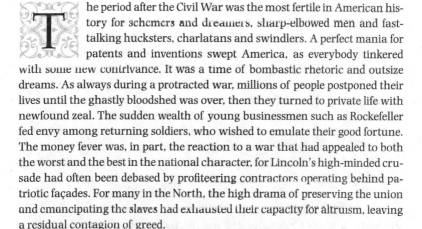

he period after the Civil War was the most fertile in American history for schemers and dreamers, sharp-elbowed men and fast-talking hucksters, charlatans and swindlers. A perfect mania for patents and inventions swept America, as everybody tinkered with some new contrivance. It was a time of bombastic rhetoric and outsize dreams. As always during a protracted war, millions of people postponed their lives until the ghastly bloodshed was over, then they turned to private life with newfound zeal. The sudden wealth of young businessmen such as Rockefeller fed envy among returning soldiers, who wished to emulate their good fortune. The money fever was, in part, the reaction to a war that had appealed to both the worst and the best in the national character, for Lincoln's high-minded crusade had often been debased by profiteering contractors operating behind patriotic façades. For many in the North, the high drama of preserving the union and emancipating the slaves had exhausted their capacity for altruism, leaving a residual contagion of greed.

As the banker Thomas Mellon observed of these years of unfettered growth,

It was such a period as seldom occurs, and hardly ever more than once in anyone's lifetime. The period between 1863 and 1873 was one in which it was easy to grow rich. There was a steady increase in the value of property and commodities, and an active market all the time. One had only to buy anything and wait, to sell at a profit; sometimes, as in real estate for instance, at a very large profit in a short time.[1]

A new cult of opportunity sprang up, producing a generation of business leaders for whom work was the greatest adventure life afforded. As Mark Twain and Charles Dudley Warner wrote in *The Gilded Age*, "To the young American . . . the paths to fortune are innumerable and all open; there is invitation in the air and success in all his wide horizon."[2] Or as one character in William Dean Howells's novel *The Rise of Silas Lapham* phrased it, "There's no doubt but money is to the fore now. It is the romance, the poetry of our age."[3] Self-made businessmen were the new demigods, and a copious self-help literature sermonized that young men who worked hard and saved could enter the millionaires' pantheon. This new industrial boom downgraded the power of the old gentry and rural elites, substituting a new species of self-made men: economic marauders too busy making money to be overly concerned with tradition. The era of the Great Barbecue—the felicitous name coined by literary historian Vernon Parrington—was dominated by arrogant, enterprising men in railroads, shipping, and stock manipulation: Jay Cooke, Commodore Vanderbilt, Jay Gould, Daniel Drew, Jim Fisk, and many others. The age was presided over by an inept president, General Ulysses S. Grant, a small-town businessman before the war, who was enamored of the rich, no matter how frequently they tried to fleece him.

The public was divided about these colossal developments. The appetite for gain fostered new fortunes and built up the industrial infrastructure, setting the stage for American industrial preeminence, but it also unsettled people with a sense of something frightening, gigantic, and poorly understood that was drastically transforming their innocent country. The Civil War invited people to repudiate their pasts as they staked out new lives. As Grant phrased it in his memoirs, "The war begot a spirit of independence and enterprise. The feeling now is, that a youth must cut loose from his old surroundings to enable him to get up in the world."[4] As people took unethical shortcuts to success, the universal race for riches threatened to overthrow existing moral systems and subvert the authority of church and state.

The triumph of the North meant the ascendancy of urbanization, immigration, industrial capitalism, and wage labor over an agrarian southern economy doomed to stagnate for decades. The war markedly accelerated the timetable of economic development, promoting the growth of factories, mills, and railroads. By stimulating technological innovation and standardized products, it ushered in a more regimented economy. The world of small farmers and businessmen began to fade, upstaged by a gargantuan new world of mass consumption and production. As railroad expansion gained momentum, populating the West and culminating in completion of the first transcontinental railroad in 1869, it spawned an accompanying mania in land deals, stock promotions, and mining developments. People rushed to exploit millions of acres of natural resources that could be economically brought to market for the first time.

In short, by the end of the Civil War, the preconditions existed for an industrial economy of spectacular new proportions. Before the war, the federal government had only twenty thousand employees and shied away from attempts to regulate business. Unlike Europe, America had no tradition of political absolutism or ecclesiastic privilege to quench entrepreneurial spirits, and the weak, fragmented political system gave businessmen room to flourish. At the same time, America had the legal and administrative apparatus necessary to support modern industry. There was respect for private property and contracts; people could get limited corporate charters or file for bankruptcy; and bank credit, while not yet plentiful, was everywhere available in a highly fragmented banking system. In time, the government redefined the rules of the capitalist game to tame trusts and preserve competition, but as John D. Rockefeller set about building his fortune, the absence of clear-cut rules probably aided, at first, the creative vigor of the new industrial economy.

Perhaps no industry so beguiled the Civil War veterans with promises of overnight wealth than the oil industry. In astonishing numbers, a ragtag group of demobilized soldiers, many still in uniform and carrying knapsacks and rifles, migrated to northwest Pennsylvania. The potential money to be made was irresistible, whether in drilling or in auxiliary services; people could charge two or three times as much as they dared to ask in the city. Ida Tarbell speculated that "this little corner of Pennsylvania absorbed a larger portion of men probably than any other spot in the United States. There were lieutenants and captains and majors—even generals—scattered all over the field."[5] They brought with them a military sense of organization and a bellicose competitive spirit, but they were eager for quick killings and betrayed little sense of how to fashion a stable, lasting business, providing an opening for the organization-minded Rockefeller.

The war had stimulated growth in the use of kerosene by cutting off the supply of southern turpentine, which had yielded a rival illuminant called camphene. The war had also disrupted the whaling industry and led to a doubling of whale-oil prices. Moving into the vacuum, kerosene emerged as an economic staple and was primed for a furious postwar boom. This burning fluid extended the day in cities and removed much of the lonely darkness from rural life. The petroleum industry also furnished lubricants to grease the wheels of heavy industry. Though the world oil industry was squeezed into western Pennsylvania, the repercussions were felt everywhere. In 1865, Congressman James Garfield alluded to the oil craze in a letter to a former staff officer: "I have conversed on the general question of oil with a number of members who are in the business, for you know the fever has assailed Congress in no mild form. . . .

Oil, not cotton, is King now, in the world of commerce."[6] Soon, John D. Rockefeller would reign as the undisputed king of that world.

In many ways, Rockefeller seemed a finely tuned instrument of the zeitgeist, the purest embodiment of the dynamic, acquisitive spirit of the postwar era. Like other Gilded Age moguls, he was shaped by his faith in economic progress, the beneficial application of science to industry, and America's destiny as an economic leader. He steeled himself to persevere, subordinating his every impulse to the profit motive, working to master unruly emotions and striving for an almost Buddhist detachment from his own appetites and passions. "I had a bad temper," Rockefeller said. "I think it might be called an ugly temper when too far provoked."[7] So he trained himself to control this temper and tried never to be guided by ego or pique.

By the end of the Civil War, the pale, trim twenty-six-year-old with the reddish gold hair and side-whiskers carried himself like a man of importance. No sooner had he formed a new firm with Sam Andrews than he was bent on expanding it. In December 1865, he and Andrews inaugurated a second refinery, the Standard Works, with brother William appointed its nominal head. The combined Excelsior and Standard Works confirmed Rockefeller as the leading Cleveland refiner at a time when the city ranked among the top refining centers. Photos of his first refineries show an unprepossessing cluster of buildings, scarcely bigger than sheds, spaced irregularly across a hillside. With hands clasped behind his back, Rockefeller paced these works, poking his head in everywhere, a perfectionist alert to the tiniest details. When he saw somebody attending to a neglected, unswept corner, he smiled and said, "That's right, eternal vigilance!"[8] For foreman, he recruited a man named Ambrose McGregor who was, in Rockefeller's description, "a precise, exacting man, honest as the day but perhaps not given to cultivating people."[9] An imposing, bewhiskered figure, McGregor won Rockefeller's absolute trust on all technical matters. Since the refineries stood some distance from downtown, Rockefeller and McGregor often lunched at the boardinghouse of a Mrs. Jones; the two men in their oil-soaked boots regularly offended the nostrils of other diners and were exiled to the porch.

As a self-made man in a new industry, Rockefeller wasn't stultified by precedent or tradition, which made it easier for him to innovate. He continued to value autonomy from outside suppliers. At first, he had paid small coopers up to $2.50 for white oak barrels before he showed, in an early demonstration of economies of scale, that he could manufacture dry, tight casks more cheaply himself; soon his firm made thousands of blue-painted barrels daily for less than a dollar per barrel. Other Cleveland coopers bought and shipped green timber to their shops, whereas Rockefeller had the oak sawed in the woods then dried in kilns, reducing its weight and slicing transportation costs in half. And he continually extended the market for petroleum by-products, selling benzine, paraffin, and petroleum jelly in addition to kerosene.

In this early period, Rockefeller was a chronic worrier who labored under a great deal of self-imposed stress. Though not versed in the scientific side of refining, he often exercised a direct managerial role in the plant. With fluctuating market conditions, he sometimes needed to send shipments to New York with great dispatch and personally rushed down to the railroad tracks to motivate his freight handlers. "I shall never forget how hungry I was in those days. I stayed out of doors day and night; I ran up and down the tops of freight cars when necessary; I hurried up the boys."[10]

At the time, refiners were tormented by fears that the vapors might catch fire, sparking an uncontrollable conflagration. Fire had already taken many lives in the industry—Edwin Drake's well, for example, was destroyed by fire in the autumn of 1859. During the Civil War, there were so many spectacularly destructive blazes along Oil Creek that producers posted signs warning, "Smokers Will Be Shot."[11] Mark Hanna, who later managed President McKinley's campaign, recalled how one morning in 1867 he woke up and discovered that his Cleveland refinery had burned to the ground, wiping out his investment, and such fears kept refiners on tenterhooks around the clock. "I was always ready, night and day, for a fire alarm from the direction of our works," said Rockefeller. "Then proceeded a dark cloud of smoke from the area, and then we dashed madly to the scene of the action. So we kept ourselves like the firemen, with their horses and hose carts always ready for immediate action."[12]

Such was the perpetual fire menace posed by the new industry that refineries were soon banned within the Cleveland city limits, hastening the growth of Kingsbury Run. In those years, oil tanks weren't hemmed in earthen banks as they later were, so if a fire started it quickly engulfed all neighboring tanks in a flaming inferno. Before the automobile, nobody knew what to do with the light fraction of crude oil known as gasoline, and many refiners, under cover of dark, let this waste product run into the river. "We used to burn it for fuel in distilling the oil," said Rockefeller, "and thousands and hundreds of thousands of barrels of it floated down the creeks and rivers, and the ground was saturated with it, in the constant effort to get rid of it."[13] The noxious runoff made the Cuyahoga River so flammable that if steamboat captains shoveled glowing coals overboard, the water erupted in flames. Each time a black cloud billowed up in the sky, people assumed another refinery had exploded, and kerosene prices soared. At least in retrospect, Rockefeller sounded philosophic about this omnipresent danger. "In those days, when the fire bell rang, we would all go to the refinery and help put it out. When the fire was burning I would have my pencil out, making plans for the rebuilding of our works."[14]

Even the dread of fire paled beside recurrent worries that the Pennsylvania oil wells would dry up, with no substitute in sight. As Rockefeller noted, "It was here today and there tomorrow, and none of us knew with any certainty about the continuance of the supply, without which these investments were valueless."[15] Already by the late 1860s, stern prophecies were issued about the industry's impending demise. There were two types of oilmen: those who thought the sudden boom an insubstantial mirage and who cashed in their profits as soon as possible; and those, like Rockefeller, who saw petroleum as the basis of an enduring economic revolution. During the salutary nightly sermons he gave himself in bed, Rockefeller often meditated on the transience of earthly wealth, especially oil, and admonished himself, "You've got a fair fortune. You have a good property—now. But suppose the oil fields gave out!"[16] Yet the future of the oil business became an article of religious faith for him, as did the feeling that the Lord had blessed him and his enterprise. In late 1867, several days before Christmas, he just missed a train that ended up in a terrible wreck, killing many passengers, and Rockefeller at once wrote to Cettie, "I do (and did when I learned that the first train left) regard the thing as the *Providence of God*."[17]

Not yet the bête noire of oil producers, Rockefeller frequently donned his shabby oil suit and traveled to Franklin, Pennsylvania, where he kept an office that purchased oil, saving on the cost of middlemen. The oil fever was so infectious in the Oil Regions that these trips always silenced any fugitive doubts he might have entertained about the industry's survival. As one traveler reported after visiting Oil Creek in 1866, "Men think of oil, talk of oil, dream of oil, the smell and taste of oil predominate in all they eat and drink."[18] These trips energized Rockefeller, who returned to Cleveland with renewed faith. As a friend recalled, "When he came back he would always have great tales to tell, and his eyes would snap as he would speak of his desires to succeed."[19]

In the 1860s, nobody knew if significant oil deposits existed outside the rugged terrain of northwest Pennsylvania, so the industry had immediately taken on global proportions. Within a year of Drake's discovery, his backers were marketing oil in London and Paris, and Europe emerged rapidly as the foremost market for American kerosene, importing hundreds of thousands of barrels yearly during the Civil War. Perhaps no other American industry had such an export outlook from its inception. By 1866, fully two-thirds of Cleveland kerosene was flowing overseas, most of it routed through New York, which became the export entrepôt for oil. At once, Rockefeller saw that he had to look beyond American shores to soak up excess production: "It seemed absolutely necessary to extend the market for oil by exporting to foreign countries, which required a large and most difficult development."[20] To accomplish this, he dispatched brother William to New York City in 1866 to launch the firm of Rockefeller and Company, which would oversee the exports of their Cleveland refineries.

If William wasn't much younger than John—"My brother is one year, one month and eight days younger than I am," John specified with comic exactitude—he certainly had a younger brother's deference and mentality.[21] Already settled by this time, William had gotten married in May 1864 to Almira ("Mira") Geraldine Goodsell, who came from a well-heeled Cleveland family with Yankee antecedents. The photos of William in his early twenties reveal a young man with thick muttonchop whiskers, clear eyes, and a broad, smooth forehead who looks more placid and less driven than his elder brother. Throughout their lives, despite their antithetical temperaments—William was bluff and friendly and freer than John in morals and manners—the brothers remained warm companions and close colleagues. William was a natural salesman who easily charmed people. Even in Pennsylvania, he was a popular figure who swapped tales with oil producers while John held himself aloof. "William always judges everything by intuition and instinct," said John, tacitly contrasting his brother with himself. "He doesn't act on analysis."[22] But those instincts were sound, and, while William took things seriously, he didn't puff them up into grand moral crusades the way his brother did.

As a novice businessman, William had been precocious like his brother. After joining John as a bookkeeper at Hewitt and Tuttle, he was spirited away by a local miller and ended up at a produce-commission house, making partner after just one year. By age twenty, he was already earning $1,000 a year— "much more than I got," noted John wryly—and winning his older brother's confidence.[23] "My brother was a young, active and efficient, and successful, businessman."[24] The quality that most endeared William to John was sheer dependability. In later years, John repeated the anecdote of how his brother, as a young bookkeeper, awoke in the night and realized that he had made an error in a bill of lading. He was so disturbed that he couldn't wait till morning to correct it and marched down to the lakefront warehouse during the night so that the ship could sail on time with proper paperwork. In September 1865, William left the produce house of Hughes, Davis and Rockefeller to join his brother's oil-refining business, and, when the Standard Works was organized that December, it bore the name of William Rockefeller and Company.

Before long, John D. Rockefeller was cast by critics as the omnipotent wizard of the oil market, setting prices as the whim seized him, but by sending William to New York he acknowledged that the export market decisively influenced oil prices. Whenever news of a Pennsylvania gusher reached New York, the French and German buyers, anticipating lower prices, simply stopped buying, and this made them the ultimate arbiters of price. "They sat there like a lot of vultures," said Rockefeller. "They wouldn't buy until the price of refined had fallen very low on account of the flood of crude oil in the market."[25] One of William's tasks in New York was to apprise the firm's buyers in the Oil Regions of sudden drops in export prices so that they could temporarily curtail crude-oil purchases.

When William arrived in New York, he set up unadorned offices at 181 Pearl Street, and the proximity to Wall Street was critical. To implement their audacious schemes, the Rockefellers needed massive capital but encountered two problems that seemed insuperable. The elite Wall Street bankers preferred to finance railroads and government and regarded oil refining as a risky, untested business, nothing short of outright gambling. Mindful of the extreme fire hazards and the specter of the oil running dry, only a few intrepid souls dared to wager on it. At the same time, John D.'s insatiable need for money outstripped the meager resources of Cleveland banks, forcing him to widen his search to New York, where he could secure credit at more advantageous rates. "And my dear brother, William, being located in the metropolis, where the opportunities were better for securing money, had upon him this financial burden, and he showed marked ability in keeping a steady nerve and presenting our case very well to the bankers."[26] As a result of John's foresight in assigning him to New York, William's career became closely intertwined with that of Wall Street—to an uncomfortable extent, from John's later perspective.

As a gray eminence of the business world in his retirement, John D. betrayed a deep suspicion of financiers, boasted that he never borrowed, and was celebrated for his financial conservatism. Yet at this stage of his career, he turned inescapably to bankers. "One can hardly recognize how difficult it was to get capital for active business enterprises at that time," he admitted.[27] If Rockefeller ever came close to groveling, it was in his eternal appeals to bankers. "In the beginning we had to go to the banks—almost on our knees—to get money and credit."[28] When dealing with the banks, he vacillated between caution and daring: He often went to bed worrying how he would repay his large volume of loans, then awoke in the morning, refreshed by a night's sleep and determined to borrow even more.[29]

The Civil War introduced a new greenback currency and national banking system that generously stoked the postwar economy with credit. Many people grew rich with borrowed funds, creating a false flush of prosperity. Rockefeller was very much a product of this new credit-based society and owed a great deal to Truman Handy and other Cleveland bankers who identified him as a young businessman of exceptional promise. He cleverly projected the image of a rising star whom bankers spurned at their peril. One day, he ran into a banker, William Otis, who had allowed Rockefeller to borrow up to his credit limit; some directors were now expressing misgivings. Could Rockefeller stop by to discuss the loans? "I shall be very glad to demonstrate the strength of my credit at any time," replied Rockefeller. "Next week I shall need more money. I would like to give my business to your bank. Soon I shall have a great deal of money to invest."[30]

Obliging but never fawning, he knew how to soothe jittery creditors, and one of his cardinal rules was never to seem too eager to borrow. With amusement, he recalled how one day he was walking down the street, trying to figure out how to find an urgently needed $15,000 loan, when a local banker pulled up in a buggy and serendipitously asked, "Do you think you could use $50,000, Mr. Rockefeller?" Rockefeller, gifted with more than a touch of his father's showmanship, studied the man's face for a long time then drawled, "Well-l-l, can you give me twenty-four hours to think it over?" By stalling, Rockefeller believed, he pinned down the deal on the most favorable terms.[31]

Aside from his reputation for exemplary character, especially among Baptist business executives, Rockefeller had several other traits that inspired passionate allegiance from bankers. He was a stickler for the truth in presenting facts, never fudged or equivocated in discussing problems, and promptly repaid loans. At numerous points in his early career, he was rescued by bankers from crises that might have capsized his business. At one bank, the directors balked at extending him further credit after he suffered a refinery fire and hadn't yet been compensated by insurers. Stepping into the breach, director Stillman Witt asked a clerk to fetch his own strongbox and announced with a flourish, "Here, gentlemen, these young men are all O.K., and if they want to borrow more money I want to see this bank advance it without hesitation, and if you want more security, here it is; take what you want."[32]

It is impossible to comprehend Rockefeller's breathtaking ascent without realizing that he always moved into battle backed by abundant cash. Whether riding out downturns or coasting on booms, he kept plentiful reserves and won many bidding contests simply because his war chest was deeper. Rockefeller vividly described the way that he had hastily enlisted the aid of bankers to snap up one refinery:

> It required many hundreds of thousands of dollars—and in cash; securities would not answer. I received the message at about noon, and had to get off on the 3 o'clock train. I drove from bank to bank, asking each president or cashier, whomever I could find first, to get ready for me all the funds he could possibly lay hands on. I told them I would be back to get the money later. I rounded up all of our banks in the city, and made a second journey to get the money, and kept going until I secured the necessary amount. With this I was off on the 3 o'clock train, and closed the transaction.[33]

To have orchestrated such a rapid campaign required a long relationship of trust with the banks.

So adroitly did Rockefeller manage his unending quest for money that he became a director of a fire-insurance company in 1866 and a director of the Ohio National Bank in 1868. By that point, he must have felt very sure of himself, even cocky, because he didn't bother to attend bank meetings and was ejected posthaste from one board. One is again impressed by the fantastic forward motion of his career, how quickly he evolved from humble supplicant to impatient businessman. Now in his late twenties, he had little time for fuddy-duddy directors and often dispensed with the niceties. As he said of the bank's board meetings: "I used to go at first, and there were some nice old gentlemen sitting stolidly about a table discussing earnestly the problem offered by new departures in vault locks. It was all right in its way, but I was a busy man even then and I really didn't have the time for it. So they got rid of me speedily."

For all his self-assurance, Rockefeller needed one associate who would share his daydreams, endorse his plans, and stiffen his resolve, and that indispensable alter ego was Henry Morrison Flagler. Nine years older than Rockefeller, with roguish good looks, Flagler was a dashing figure with luminous blue eyes, smooth black hair, and a handlebar mustache. "His clothes were of the most recent cut," an office messenger said admiringly. "He carried himself with a confidence that was regal. He had a heavy black moustache and the most beautiful hair I had ever seen."[34] Funny and voluble, brisk and energetic, Flagler was nevertheless reticent about his motives and background and in time surpassed his tight-lipped younger partner in fending off public inquiries.

Flagler's upbringing had some noticeable parallels to Rockefeller's. Born in Hopewell, New York, in 1830, the son of an impecunious Presbyterian pastor, he grew up in the Finger Lakes region of upstate New York before moving to Toledo, Ohio. In a previous marriage, his mother had been married to a Bellevue, Ohio, doctor named David Harkness, who already had a son, Stephen, from his first marriage. They had a second son, Dan, before David Harkness died. Flagler's mother, Elizabeth, then married the Reverend Isaac Flagler. Evidently a man of courage and principle, Reverend Flagler created an uproar when he officiated over the marriage in Toledo of a young mulatto man to a white woman.

Dropping out of school at fourteen, Henry made his way to Republic, Ohio, and worked in the small country store of Lamon Harkness, Dr. Harkness's younger brother. He later spun romantic tales of this first job, where he sold molasses and dry goods by day and slept in the drafty rear of the store at night. For special customers, Flagler would dip into a keg of brandy hidden upstairs. Becoming further entangled with his Harkness relatives, Henry married Lamon's daughter, the dark-eyed, demure Mary, in 1853.

Before the Civil War, Henry earned good money in Lamon's grain business in Bellevue, in the corn and wheat belt of Sandusky County, where he shipped much produce through Cleveland. "John D. Rockefeller was a commission merchant in Cleveland, and I sent him a good many carloads of wheat, which he sold as my agent," he recalled.[35] In a lucrative sideline, Flagler and his Harkness relatives took an interest in a whiskey distillery, which also provided an outlet for surplus grain. Like Rockefeller, Flagler was a prudish young man who never swore an oath stronger than "Thunder!" As a teetotaler, Sunday-school teacher, and minister's son, Flagler's liquor venture didn't square with his principles—though the profits evidently provided balm to his conscience. "I had scruples about the business and gave it up," he confided, "but not before I made $50,000 in Bellevue."[36] Awash with cash, he built a stately Victorian mansion, the Gingerbread House, that was brightly illuminated with coal-oil lamps. Among the visitors was John D. Rockefeller, then canvassing accounts for his partnership with Maurice Clark. "He was a bright and active young fellow full of vim and push," said Rockefeller, as if Flagler were the younger of the two.[37]

During the Civil War, Flagler, like Rockefeller, hired a substitute. His firm was a major contractor for grain purchases by the Union army and in 1862, brimful of wartime profits, he cast about for a fresh opportunity. At this point, Flagler stumbled into the sole business blunder of his career when he took a sizable stake in a salt company in Saginaw, Michigan, and moved his family there. When the war ended, slashing demand for salt, his firm went bankrupt, the victim of a classic boom-and-bust cycle. Losing everything, he had to be bailed out by a giant loan from the Harkness family. "At the end of three years, I had lost my little fortune and owed $50,000 to about 50,000 Irishmen who had been working in the salt factory," said Flagler.[38] He had much occasion to ponder the contradictions of a market economy in which dynamic industries swiftly expand during prosperity only to find themselves overextended during downturns. To cope with excess production, many Saginaw salt companies opted for cooperation over competition and joined a cartel arrangement to try to prop up salt prices, providing a precedent for Standard Oil.

After his sobering reversal of fortune, Flagler entered a despondent period in which he sometimes skipped lunch to save money. Returning to Bellevue, he tried to market felt wool as well as a machine he had invented that would supposedly produce the perfect horseshoe. Deciding to try his luck in Cleveland (where Stephen V. Harkness had moved in 1866), he took a job selling grain with Rockefeller's ex-partner, Maurice Clark, and by coincidence filled the post recently vacated by Rockefeller. Perhaps to tweak Clark, Rockefeller invited Flagler to rent desk space in his office suite in the Sexton Block. As Flagler prospered, he settled his debts, bought a fine house on Euclid Avenue, and joined the First Presbyterian Church.

As they strolled to and from work together, Flagler and Rockefeller must have soon discovered their remarkable affinity as businessmen. Chafing at his dependence on loans and wondering when he might deplete the capital of local banks, Rockefeller now scouted out large individual investors and was probably acutely aware of the wealth of Flagler's relatives. Through Flagler's introduction, Rockefeller solicited money from Stephen V. Harkness, by now one of Cleveland's richest men. A bearish man with thick, slightly unkempt hair, fluffy sideburns, and a walrus mustache, Harkness had capitalized on inside political information to make a fortune during the war. As an ally of U.S. senator John Sherman of Ohio, he had received timely word in 1862 of an upcoming government move to levy a two-dollar tax on every gallon of malt and distilled liquor. Before the tax took effect, he busily stockpiled wine and whiskey and even raided the deposits of a local bank he owned to pour more money into this operation.[39] When the tax was enacted in July 1862, he sold his enormous cache of spirits for a fast $300,000 profit. It is deeply ironic that Rockefeller, a staunch temperance advocate, got one of his most significant cash infusions from questionable gains in liquor.

While Rockefeller was negotiating a large loan from Stephen V. Harkness during an hour-long talk in 1867, the latter saw an excellent opportunity to set up Henry in business and instead of extending a loan asked for a large block of stock in the company. Investing $100,000—a third of the new firm's capital—Harkness made it a precondition of his investment that Henry become treasurer and his personal deputy in the firm. As Harkness said to Rockefeller, "Young man, you can have all the money you want. You are on the right track and I am with you." As to Henry's part, he added, "I'll make Henry my watchdog."[40] Since Harkness was also a director of banks, railroads, mining, real estate, and manufacturing companies, the tie ushered Rockefeller into a new universe of business connections.

On March 4, 1867, the *Cleveland Leader* announced the formation of a new partnership, Rockefeller, Andrews and Flagler, with offices in the Case Building, a solid masonry structure with rounded, Romanesque windows and a prestigious address on the Public Square. "This firm is one of the oldest in the refining business and their trade already a mammoth one. . . . Their establishment is one of the largest in the United States. Among the many oil refining enterprises, this seems to be one of the most successful; its heavy capital and consummate management having kept it clear of the many shoals upon which oil refining . . . houses have so often [been] stranded."[41] From reading this description, one would have thought the firm was run by gray, reverend men, whereas Rockefeller, the boy wonder of Cleveland business, was just twenty-seven.

Starting with Flagler's recruitment, Rockefeller began to assemble the team of capable, congenial executives who would transform the Cleveland refiner into the world's strongest industrial company. Both Rockefeller and Flagler had nimble minds for numbers and infinite dexterity with balance sheets. Neither was interested in a modest success, and they were both prepared to go as far and as fast as the marketplace allowed. As Flagler boasted, "I have always been contented, but I have never been satisfied."[42] Rockefeller found his partner's enthusiasm a tonic, noting that Flagler "was always on the active side of every question, and to his wonderful energy is due much of the rapid progress of the company in the early days."[43] Given their exalted goals, it probably helped that Flagler had been chastened by failure and was acquainted with the perils of complacency.[44]

Rockefeller loved Flagler's dictum that a friendship founded on business was superior to a business founded on friendship, and for several decades they worked together in an almost seamless fashion. In the early years, the two men were bound by a common dream, lived near each other, and seemed virtually inseparable. As Rockefeller said in his memoirs, "We met and walked to the office together, walked home to luncheon, back again after luncheon, and home again at night. On these walks, when we were away from the office interruptions, we did our thinking, talking, and planning together." For a man as reserved as Rockefeller, this picture suggests an unbuttoned exchange of ideas of a sort he permitted with few people.

In the office, their intimacy was patent to visitors, for they had back-to-back desks and shared many duties. They even developed a collective letter-writing style, passing drafts back and forth with each making minor improvements until they expressed what was wanted but not one syllable more. At this point, the letters were ready to be vetted by the severest judge, Mrs. Rockefeller, who was, said one office worker, "known to be the most valued adviser."[45] Endowed with considerable verbal skill, Flagler had such a gift for drawing up legal documents or sniffing out hidden pitfalls in contracts that Rockefeller insisted he could have taught the fine points of contract law to lawyers—no small edge for a firm that would be engaged in running legal battles.

In his later years, Flagler developed into a grandee of such rich tastes that it is instructive to note his austere early style. Not only did he labor six days a week, but he shunned bars and theaters as the devil's playgrounds and became superintendent of the First Presybterian Church. Like Rockefeller, he advocated self-discipline and deferred gratification. As he said of his first threadbare days in Cleveland: "I wore a thin overcoat and thought how comfortable I should be when I could afford a long, thick Ulster. I carried a lunch in my pocket until I was a rich man. I trained myself in the school of self-control and self-denial. It was hard on [me], but I would rather be my own tyrant than have some one else tyrannize me."[46] After his wife, Mary, gave birth to a son, Henry Harkness Flagler, in 1870, she never regained her health and turned into an invalid. For the next seventeen years, Flagler stayed home at night so he could read to her for hours on end, with John and Laura Rockefeller often stopping by to mitigate the gloom.

That Flagler was his most valuable partner was always unquestioned dogma for Rockefeller, yet one wonders whether the influence was altogether benign. An ebullient man, Flagler wouldn't stop to quibble over legal niceties when taken by a powerful idea, and even Rockefeller hinted obliquely at the dangers posed by Flagler's headstrong nature. "He was a man of great force and determination," said Rockefeller, "though perhaps he needed a restraining influence at times when his enthusiasm was roused."[47] On his desk, Flagler kept a quote from a popular novel, *David Harum*, which said, "Do unto others as they would do unto you—and do it first."[48] What makes Flagler's ethics consequential for Rockefeller's career was that he was the mastermind of many negotiations with the railroads—the single most controversial aspect of Standard Oil history. It's not clear that anyone could have tempered the fiercely irrepressible drive of John D. Rockefeller, but the swashbuckling Flagler had especially little interest in transposing the lessons of his Sunday-school classes to the profane, turbulent world of oil refining. As far as Rockefeller was concerned, however, Flagler's arrival was providential, for the oil industry was about to be thrown into unprecedented turmoil, making relations with the railroads all-important.

Transportation assumed a pivotal place in the petroleum business for an elementary reason: Drake had discovered oil in a distant, inaccessible spot that was, at first, poorly served by the railroads. For several years, teamsters—the wagoners who hauled out the barrels—exercised a brutal tyranny and charged exorbitant sums. Since oil was a relatively cheap, standardized commodity, transportation costs inevitably figured as a critical factor in the competitive struggle. The logical and elegant solution—to construct a comprehensive pipeline network—encountered harsh resistance from the threatened teamsters. During the 1865 Pithole frenzy, Samuel Van Syckel laid a two-inch iron pipeline from Oil Creek to railroad tracks six miles away. Defying armed guards, roaming gangs of teamsters descended each night and tore up sections of the pipeline. When Henry Harley launched a second pipeline, they again dug up pipes and set storage tanks ablaze, forcing Harley to field a small army of Pinkerton detectives to squash the revolt. The teamsters must have known they were fighting a rearguard action, but for a time they managed to delay the installation of a pipeline system.

Between the benighted rule of the teamsters and the future domination by efficient pipelines, there arose an interregnum in which the railroads exercised pervasive influence over everything that happened in the industry. At first, they tried to ship barrels on open flatcars, but the swaying, jolting ride splintered the containers and spilled their contents. After the Civil War, this hazardous method was superseded by primitive tank cars—twin pine tubs mounted on flatcars—that were soon replaced, in turn, by single iron tanks that became the industry norm. Such technical advances allowed the railroads to speed oil across the continent and vastly expanded the market for petroleum products.

During the first few years, the oil business was so effortlessly profitable that refineries sprang up in six competing centers. The inland centers (the Oil Regions, Pittsburgh, and Cleveland) and the seaboard centers (New York, Philadelphia, and Baltimore) engaged in pitched battles to control the business. Favored by proximity to the wells, the western Pennsylvania refiners seemed to possess an incalculable edge, but they had to import chemicals, barrels, machinery, and labor and therefore labored under distinct handicaps. Nonetheless, these refiners saved so much on transportation that they fancied they would emerge supreme in the oil business. Later, Rockefeller admitted that he'd been tempted to switch operations to Pennsylvania, yet he and his partners didn't wish to uproot their families or write off their considerable investment in Cleveland. They also feared that the glory of the Oil Regions might soon fade into history, as Rockefeller later noted in a statement reminiscent of Percy Bysshe Shelley's poem "Ozymandias":

> You have seen Pithole and Petroleum Center—the places where once stood big, prosperous cities in which men made millions of dollars out of oil. Now they are bits of wilderness, overgrown with weeds, and with nothing left to tell of their greatness but a few scattered parts of old houses and the memory of a few aged men. Prudent men did not want to place all their capital into business in such places.[49]

Even late in life, Rockefeller was loath to confess, for political reasons, the overriding reason for his attachment to Cleveland: It was the hub of so many transportation networks that he had tremendous room to maneuver in freight negotiations. During the summer months, he could send oil by water, greatly enhancing his bargaining power with the railroads. His firm "could load their oil in the season of lake navigation and canal navigation, upon vessels at Cleveland and from Buffalo by the Erie Canal [and] could deliver the oil to their warehouses in New York at a cost lower than the current rates at which the railway companies had been seeking the business."[50] Armed with this potent weapon, Rockefeller obtained such excellent railroad rates that it compensated for having to ship the crude oil to Cleveland before sending refined oil to the Atlantic coast—a far more circuitous route than shipping from Titusville straight to New York. Fed by rail links to Chicago, Saint Louis, and Cincinnati, Cleveland also served as a natural gateway to western markets. Other Cleveland refiners evidently made the same calculation, and by late 1866 the city supported fifty refineries, ranking second only to Pittsburgh. Cleveland's refineries were so numerous that their foul, acrid atmosphere enveloped the outskirts, tainting the beer from local breweries and souring the milk.

Besides access to the Erie Canal and Lake Erie, Cleveland was serviced by three main railroad lines that gave its inland refineries direct access to eastern ports: the New York Central, which ran north from New York City to Albany and then west to Buffalo, where its Lake Shore line ran along Lake Erie to Cleveland; the Erie Railroad, which also sped across New York State to a point south of Buffalo, where its Atlantic and Great Western subsidiary headed down into

Cleveland and the Oil Regions; and the august Pennsylvania Railroad, which went from New York and Philadelphia to Harrisburg and Pittsburgh. With virtuosic brilliance, Rockefeller and Flagler played these three railroads against each other in seemingly endless permutations. They even managed to manipulate such redoubtable figures as the notorious Jay Gould, who had wrested the Erie Railroad from Commodore Vanderbilt in 1868. Flagler singled out Gould as the fairest and squarest of the railroad chieftains in his dealings, and Rockefeller, when asked to name the greatest businessman he had ever met, instantly cited Gould.[51] Gould himself later asserted that John D. Rockefeller had possessed "the highest genius for constructive organization" in American economic history.[52]

Before long, the various oil-refining centers were rushing to form tactical alliances with these railroad networks. As a natural outgrowth of their route structure, the New York Central and the Erie wanted to promote Cleveland as a refining center and regarded Rockefeller as a critical ally in efforts to boost their oil-freight business. With easy access to the oil fields via the Allegheny River, Pittsburgh might have seemed the optimal location, but its refiners were always held hostage to the freight monopoly of the Pennsylvania Railroad. Following a myopic and ultimately destructive policy toward Pittsburgh, the Pennsylvania Railroad decided it was more profitable to carry crude oil from Oil Creek all the way to Philadelphia or New York refineries rather than to have it refined in Pittsburgh. By penalizing Pittsburgh refiners with crushing rates, the railroad fattened its short-term profits but sacrificed the city's future as a refining center and paved the way for the hegemony of the city the Pennsylvania wanted most to eradicate: Cleveland. As Rockefeller later said, the Pennsylvania Railroad's attitude made it easy for him to find common cause with its archrivals, and he forged a cabal with the New York Central and the Erie that the Pennsylvania was hard-pressed to stop.

By the late 1860s, the press was rife with reports that the Pennsylvania Railroad had decreed that Cleveland would be "wiped out as a refining center as with a sponge"—a statement forever engraved on Rockefeller's unforgiving memory. Taking this as a declaration of war, he was emboldened to respond with the most robust countermeasures at his command. He was a man who always acted on Flagler's business motto of favoring "sharp, vigorous and decisive measures."[53] The Pennsylvania statement set off a panic-stricken reaction in Cleveland as local refiners prepared to transfer their operations to Oil Creek. Coolheaded in the face of such hysteria, Rockefeller saw that he could convert this chaos to advantage. By threatening to strip the others of their oil traffic, the Pennsylvania had placed the Erie and New York Central in a vulnerable position, and Rockefeller and Flagler decided to use this leverage to wring extreme concessions from them.

In the spring of 1868, Jay Gould hatched a secret deal with Rockefeller and Flagler that gave them shares in a subsidiary company called the Allegheny Transportation Company, which was the first major pipeline network serving Oil Creek. Through this deal, the Cleveland refiners received a staggering 75 percent rebate on oil shipped through the Erie system. As part of this extraordinary bonanza, Flagler also cut a deal with the Atlantic and Great Western, an Erie subsidiary, that gave Rockefeller, Andrews and Flagler highly advantageous rates on rail shipments between Cleveland and the Oil Regions.

In this season of bountiful concessions, Flagler also approached General J. H. Devereux, the newly installed vice president of the Lake Shore Railroad, which formed part of the New York Central system. Trained as a civil engineer, Devereux had revamped the railroad system in northern Virginia to assist the Union army and was commended by Lincoln for his work. In negotiating a new framework with him, Rockefeller and Flagler argued for preferential rates that would more than match discounts extended by the Pennsylvania Railroad to its customers in the Oil Regions. In other words, the young Cleveland refiners cannily converted their geographic disadvantage into a powerful bargaining tool and secured covert rates that allowed them to ship crude oil to Cleveland and then refined oil to New York for only $1.65 per barrel compared to an officially listed rate of $2.40.

In exchange for this extraordinary concession, Rockefeller and Flagler didn't simply try to squeeze the railroads—they were much too shrewd and subtle for that—but offered compelling incentives. For instance, they agreed to assume legal liability for fire or other accidents and stop using water transport during the summer months. The biggest plum they dangled before Devereux was a promise to supply the Lake Shore with an astonishing sixty carloads of refined oil daily. Since Rockefeller lacked the refining capacity to fulfill this ambitious pledge, he was evidently prepared to coordinate shipments with other Cleveland refiners. For any railroad, the prospect of steady shipments was irresistible, for they could dispatch trains composed solely of oil-tank cars instead of a motley assortment of freight cars picking up different products at different places. By consolidating many small shippers into one big shipper making regular, uniform shipments in massive quantities, the railroads could reduce the average round-trip time of their trains to New York from thirty days to ten and operate a fleet of 600 cars instead of 1,800.

Never shy about his accomplishments, Rockefeller knew that he had broached a revolutionary deal: "It was a large, regular volume of business, such as had not hitherto been given to the roads in question."[54] From that moment, the railroads acquired a vested interest in the creation of a gigantic oil monopoly that would lower their costs, boost their profits, and generally simplify their lives. As in other industries, the railroads developed a stake in the growth of big businesses whose economies of scale permitted them to operate more efficiently—an ominous fact for small, struggling refiners who were gradually weeded out in the savage competitive strife.

Without doubt, the Lake Shore deal marked a turning point for Rockefeller, the oil industry, and the entire American economy. Decades later, Ida Tarbell condemned it as Rockefeller's original sin from which all others sprang. "Mr. Rockefeller certainly saw by 1868 that he had no *legitimate* superiority over those competing with him in Cleveland which would ever enable him to be anything more than one of the big men in his line."[55] Only Rockefeller's willingness to cheat and cut corners, Tarbell contended, had enabled him to outdistance the pack. This claim, echoed by Rockefeller's most virulent critics, overstates the case, for even before Rockefeller accepted his first rebate, he was the world's largest refiner, equal in size to the next three largest Cleveland refineries combined. In fact, it was the unparalleled scope of his operation that had enabled him to cut this exceptional deal in the first place. Tarbell perceived correctly, however, that the principal advantage of Rockefeller's commanding position was that it meant special power to compel railroad-freight concessions.

In closing their historic deal, Rockefeller and Flagler suffered no twinges of conscience and were frankly elated by their triumph. "I remember when the Standard received its first rebate," said Flagler. "I went home in great delight. I had won a great victory, I thought."[56] But they knew they had dabbled in a dark and controversial practice, for the rebates were predicated on great secrecy. Many years later, Rockefeller explained to one railroad negotiator that their dealings with the Lake Shore rested on oral agreements that were never committed to paper. "Our people do not think it would be best for the Lake Shore Road, or us, to have a contract, but with the good faith between us and desire to promote each other's interest, we can serve each other better by being able to say we have no contracts."[57] Because many railroad deals ended with a handshake, not a signature, Rockefeller could breezily deny their existence without fear of embarrassing refutations later on.

As the chief transportation deal maker, Flagler had overseen the landmark pact, and Rockefeller always credited him for it. Some of this derived from Rockefeller's humility, but it also betrayed a lifelong habit of covering his tracks and pretending to be elsewhere when critical decisions were made. Although Rockefeller didn't lead the Lake Shore negotiations, he was smack in the thick of them. On August 19, 1868, he sent a fascinating letter to Cettie from New York that shows his toughness vis-à-vis the Vanderbilts, who controlled the New York Central, the Lake Shore's parent. "We were sent for by Mr. Vanderbilt yesterday, at twelve o'c & did not go, he is anxious to get our business and said that he could meet us on the terms. We sent our card by the messenger, that Vanderbilt might know where to find our office later."[58] The point is worth underscoring: Twenty-nine-year-old John D. Rockefeller demanded that seventy-four-year-old Commodore Vanderbilt, the emperor of the railroad world, *come to him*. This refusal to truckle, bend, or bow to others, this insistence on dealing with other people on his own terms, time, and turf, distinguished Rockefeller throughout his career.

Bolstered by the Lake Shore deal, Cleveland soon surpassed Pittsburgh as the leading refining center, and for the first time journalists began to track Rockefeller's ascendancy. In 1869, one writer marveled at the power that this laconic young man, in his understated manner, had already attained in Cleveland. "He occupies a position in our business circles second to but few. Close application to one kind of business, an avoidance of all positions of honorary character that cost time, keeping everything pertaining to his business in so methodical a manner that he knows every night how he stands with the world."[59]

Today an arcane, forgotten subject, the issue of railroad rebates generated heated debate in post–Civil War America since they directly affected the shape of the economy and the distribution of wealth. Railroads had obtained the power to produce either a concentrated economy, with progressively larger business units, or to perpetuate the small-scale economy of antebellum America. The proliferation of rebates hastened the shift toward an integrated national economy, top-heavy with giant companies enjoying preferential freight rates.

Rockefeller justly argued that he hadn't invented the rebate and that the Pennsylvania Railroad had granted thousands of them in the six years before his seminal Lake Shore deal. "It was a common practice in all descriptions of freighting, not peculiar to oil; in merchandise, grain, everything."[60] Rebates had inevitably accompanied railroad expansion. As the total railroad trackage doubled to 70,000 miles within eight years after the Civil War, the roads were saddled with high fixed costs and heavy bonded debt. This forced them to maintain a high, steady freight volume to stay alive and waylaid them into vicious rate wars. Rebates weren't just solicited by shippers but were sedulously pushed by railway freight agents eager to win over new business. Rebates enabled them to maintain the fiction of listed rates while secretly giving discounts to favored shippers. Over time, relations grew ever closer and more incestuous between the railroads and large shippers. For decades, Rockefeller and his colleagues enjoyed free passes on all major railroads, which they regarded not as payoffs but as natural perquisites of their business.

Rockefeller never saw rebates as criminal or illegitimate or as favors secured only by bullying monopolies. He was correct in stating that listed rates were always a farce, a starting point for haggling. Many refiners received rebates, not just the leading firms, and some tiny rivals actually got superior discounts, especially from the Pennsylvania Railroad. Rockefeller's business papers display much internal grumbling about this presumed inequity, for which he and his colleagues regularly chastised railroad officials at critical moments in negotiations. But in spite of numerous scattered cases of rival refiners getting comparable rebates, no other firm received so many rebates so consistently over so many years or on such a colossal scale as Rockefeller's. It was therefore disingenuous of him to suggest that rebates played only an incidental role in his success.

So were Ida Tarbell and other detractors justified in tarring Rockefeller's whole career based on railroad rebates? Unfortunately, the controversy was played out in a gray area of ethics and the law that makes a definitive answer impossible. From a strictly economic standpoint, Rockefeller rested on solid ground when he insisted that bulk shippers deserved a discount. "Who can buy beef the cheapest—the housewife for her family, the steward for a club or hotel, or the commissary for an army? Who is entitled to better rebates from a railroad, those who give it 5000 barrels a day, or those who give 500 barrels—or 50 barrels?"[61] Besides providing a steady flow of oil shipments, Rockefeller's firm invested heavily in warehouses, terminals, loading platforms, and other railroad facilities so that the roads probably derived more profit from his shipments than from those of rivals who paid higher rates. Small, irregular shippers were the bane of railroads for the simple, mechanical reason that they forced the trains to stop repeatedly to pick up single carloads of oil. To meet the terms of his deal with the Lake Shore, Rockefeller had to run his refineries at full capacity even when kerosene demand slackened. He therefore paid a price for his rebates and felt that equal rates for all shippers would have unfairly penalized his firm.

Perhaps because Ida Tarbell trained a glaring spotlight on the rebate issue, Rockefeller insisted vehemently in later interviews that the real profitability of his firm lay elsewhere. In an intriguing aside in later years, he even hinted that the clamor over rebates conveniently deflected public attention away from other, more profitable aspects of his operation: "Along this line much was said about rebates and drawbacks for long years, and the Standard Oil Company knew full well that the public were not on the right scent. They knew where their profits came from, but they did not deem it wise to inform the public, and especially their competitors, of the real secret sources of their strength."[62] Indeed, one can argue that the obsession among reformers with the rebate issue might have blinded them to a multitude of other sins.

Not until the Interstate Commerce Act in 1887 did it become an illegal, punishable offense for railroads to give rebates, and the practice didn't cease entirely until the 1903 Elkins Act. Nevertheless, by the end of the Civil War, a widespread belief had begun to take hold that railroads were common carriers and should shun favoritism. Ida Tarbell cited provisions in the Pennsylvania state constitution that, as she interpreted them, compelled railroads to serve as common carriers and avoid discrimination. Yet in the last analysis, she based her withering critique of Rockefeller less on specific laws than on her belief that he had violated a sense of fair play. "That is," she wrote in *McClure's Magazine* in July 1905, "rebate giving then as now, was regarded as one of those lower business practices which characterizes commerce at all periods, and against which men of honor struggle, and of which men of greed take advantage."[63] In the privacy of his study in 1917, an unrepentant Rockefeller disputed her view of the prevailing business ethics. "I deny that it was regarded as a dishonorable practice for a merchant or manufacturer to obtain the best rates possible for his goods."[64] As to Tarbell's charge that the secrecy of rebates proved their immorality, Rockefeller countered that railroads didn't wish to advertise discounts that might then be demanded by other shippers. "For these arrangements were not except by the academic expected to be published, any more than the general of an army's plans are published to enable the enemy to defeat him."[65]

The most compelling argument against rebates was that railroads received state charters and therefore had the right of eminent domain—that is, the right to claim private property in order to lay down tracks—investing their activities with a public character. In 1867, a committee of the Ohio senate declared that railroads, as common carriers, should charge equal rates, but a bill incorporating these ideas was defeated. The following year, just as Rockefeller implemented his Lake Shore deal, a Pennsylvania senate committee reported that railroads were common carriers and had "no right to show partiality among their customers"; but, again, no regulatory changes ensued.[66] Almost twenty years passed before reformers succeeded in introducing public regulation that forced an end to the railroad favoritism that so incensed farmers and other small shippers across America. In the meantime, Rockefeller profited enormously from the failure of public authorities to rectify the inequities of the transportation system, and his firm understandably kept up vigorous lobbying efforts to perpetuate the status quo.

John D. Rockefeller, Jr., forced to wear his sisters' hand-me-downs.
(Courtesy of the Rockefeller Archive Center)

CHAPTER 7

Millionaires' Row

Rockefeller had speedily acquired a level of respectability that would have seemed unthinkable fifteen years before when he and his demoralized family were crowded into the Humiston house in Strongsville. In August 1868, after his rebate deal with the Lake Shore Railroad, he certified his enhanced status in Cleveland when he and Cettie moved from Cheshire Street to a solid brick home at 424 Euclid Avenue. This move dramatized the immense distance he had traveled after a few years in the oil business. Local boosters had already tagged Euclid Avenue "the most beautiful street in the world," with homes that lavishly mirrored the local fortunes in oil, iron, banking, timber, railroads, and real estate. All of the town's new opulence was reflected in this street of massive houses. The residential address for such local luminaries as Henry B. Payne, Amasa Stone, and John Hay, Euclid Avenue claimed so many mansions that it had richly earned its sobriquet of "millionaires' row."

With the spacious grandeur of a fine Victorian street, always busy with fashionable horses and carriages, the wide avenue had a double row of elms that created a tall, shady canopy overhead. The imposing homes were deeply recessed from the street, their trimmed lawns and shapely shrubbery providing buffer zones between the houses and their distant front gates. Since few houses were separated from adjoining houses by fences, the street sometimes gave the impression of being a single, flowing park, with elegant homes standing in an unbroken expanse of greenery.

While Rockefeller's home looked small and cramped beside Amasa Stone's towering manse and other gaudy monstrosities, it was a substantial two-story structure with a mansard roof, a portico, and arched windows, shielded from the street by an iron picket fence that spanned its entire 116-foot frontage. Rockefeller could have afforded something showier than this $40,000 house, and pedestrians might have thought its owner a lesser light in business, yet this was exactly the misimpression that he wanted to convey. Far from trying to parade his wealth, he wanted to blend into the scenery. Even at home, Rockefeller was discreet and behaved as if he was concealing some secret from prying eyes. Beyond that, he had the Puritan's discomfort with possessions, a nagging Baptist anxiety that decoration might appear idolatrous. Again, like Weber's ideal capitalist, "he avoids ostentation and unnecessary expenditure, as well as conscious enjoyment of his power, and is embarrassed by the outward signs of the social recognition which he receives."[1]

Fond of roomy, ungainly houses that he could remodel ceaselessly, Rockefeller would have been stymied by a house that required no improvement. Utilitarian by nature, he was more concerned with the grounds and interiors of homes than with the subtleties of architectural ornamentation. "I hate frills," he once said. "Useful things, beautiful things, are admirable; but frills, affectations, mere pretenses of being something very fine, bore me very much."[2] With a country boy's love of open spaces, he hated anything confined or cluttered and probably chose the Euclid Avenue house for its large, high-ceilinged rooms, which included a parlor, a sitting room, and a dining room downstairs plus four bedrooms upstairs.

Rockefeller devoted more time and expense to the trees and shrubbery than to the house itself. To expand his gardens, he bought an adjoining lot but was disturbed by the house that came with it and obstructed his view. Since he detested waste, he donated the house to a new girls' school being built a block away. In what was hailed as an engineering wonder at the time, the brick house was jacked up by a windlass and rolled down the block on greased logs—a spectacle that was covered by local papers and drew spectators. "Mr. Rockefeller . . . set [the house] on new foundations where it was as good as ever," Lucy Spelman said of her brother-in-law's feat. "This was a marvelous undertaking, but then he was always undertaking marvelous things."[3]

Behind the house, he built a stone stable and coach house more magnificent than the residence itself. Over one hundred feet long, it had stout beams, pine panels, and elaborate chandeliers. An expert driver with either a pair of horses or a four-in-hand, Rockefeller had a passion for trotters, and Euclid Avenue provided a perfect straightaway for races. If anybody tried to pass him, the hypercompetitive Rockefeller automatically turned it into a trial of speed. John, William, and Frank were stockholders in a racing club called the Cleveland Driving Park Company, the first amateur club of its sort in America. Unable to do anything in a casual manner, Rockefeller became obsessive about his hobbies, which he could sometimes indulge in extravagant fashion. In the 1870s, his records show, he paid stupendous sums—from $10,000 to $12,500—for thoroughbred trotters with such evocative names as Midnight, Flash, Jesse, Baron, and Trifle.

In his early days in business, Rockefeller often suffered from severe neck pains that might have indicated stress on the job, and he turned to horses as a therapeutic diversion. "I would leave my office in the afternoon and drive a pair of fast horses as hard as they could go: trot, break, gallop—everything."[4] Since Cettie was also fond of horses, they often rode together. His style of racing was also revealing: He never applied cruel, coercive measures to recalcitrant horses but studied them closely and tried to coax them along gently and with great patience. "I remember when my brother William and I used to go riding," he said. "I would invariably come in first. He would be covered with perspiration, as was his horse. My horse would be too—but I would be as cool as I am now. I always would talk to my horses—quietly, steadily—never get excited."[5] This unflappable style and conservation of energy also characterized his approach to the management of his vast oil empire.

Unlike his philandering father, John D. Rockefeller remained firmly, almost prudishly, anchored in domestic life. Much like Jay Gould—who didn't drink, smoke, or gallivant with women—Rockefeller's harsh business tactics were counterbalanced by exemplary behavior at home where he was a sweet, respectful Victorian husband. To borrow a line from Flaubert, to be fiercely revolutionary in business, he needed to be utterly conventional at home. Eternally at war with the devil, John and Cettie allowed their religious beliefs to define their entire cultural agenda. They subscribed to seats at the philharmonic, for instance, but theater and opera were too racy for these professing Christians. Shying away from social situations that weren't safely predictable, they socialized only within a small circle of family members, business associates, and church friends and never went to clubs or dinner parties. "Club life did not appeal to me," said Rockefeller. "I was meeting all the people I needed to meet in my day's work. . . . My family would rather have me at home—even if I were snoring in an easy chair—than going out for the evening, and certainly I preferred to stay at home."[6] He especially enjoyed the company of ministers whose genial, homiletic style matched his own. Thus walled off from temptation, Rockefeller was virtually untouched by the decadence of the Gilded Age.

Much of Rockefeller's preference for home life stemmed from his strict temperance views. Even late in life, he accepted an invitation to a hotel barbecue, then went to investigate the site beforehand. When he spotted empty beer bottles on the premises, he promptly withdrew his acceptance. Since he and Cettie were deeply involved in temperance work—they did everything from sponsoring lecture tours to lobbying to have temperance principles inserted in school textbooks—they avoided the very presence of liquor, and this severely cramped their social activities. Yet within their circumscribed world, they had a happy home life.

Rockefeller bridled at the notion that he was a business-obsessed drudge, a slave to the office. "I know of nothing more despicable and pathetic than a man who devotes all the waking hours of the day to making money for money's sake," he recorded in his memoirs.[7] He worked at a more leisurely pace than many other executives, napping daily after lunch and often dozing in a lounge chair after dinner. To explain his extraordinary longevity, he later said, doubtless overstating the matter, "I'm here because I shirked: did less work, lived more in the open air, enjoyed the open air, sunshine and exercise."[8] By his mid-thirties, he had installed a telegraph wire between home and office so that he could spend three or four afternoons each week at home, planting trees, gardening, and enjoying the sunshine. Rockefeller didn't do this in a purely recreational spirit but mingled work and rest to pace himself and improve his productivity. In time, he became something of an evangelist on health-related issues. "It is remarkable how much we all could do if we avoid hustling, and go along at an even pace and keep from attempting too much."[9]

There was a clockwork regularity about Rockefeller's life that made it seem mechanical to outsiders but that he found soothing. He didn't seem to require time to indulge normal human idleness, much less illicit passion. In his rigidly compartmentalized life, each hour was tightly budgeted, whether for business, religion, family, or exercise. Perhaps these daily rituals helped him to deal with underlying tensions that might otherwise have become ungovernable, for although he tried to project an air of unhurried calm, he was under terrific strain in creating his oil empire. He fretted endlessly about his company and, below the surface, was constantly on edge. In one of his few admissions of weakness, he recalled that "for years on end I never had a solid night's sleep, worrying about how it was to come out. . . . I tossed about in bed night after night worrying over the outcome. . . . All the fortune that I have made has not served to compensate for the anxiety of that period."[10]

By the time they moved to Euclid Avenue, the Rockefellers already had one child, Elizabeth (always called Bessie), who was born in the Cheshire Street house in 1866. (When Cettie was confined during childbirth and couldn't attend church, John jotted down notes on the sermon and read them back to her afterward.) All of the remaining children were born in an upstairs bedroom at Euclid Avenue. Their second child, Alice, was born in July 1869 but died a year later; then came Alta (1871), Edith (1872), and John Jr. (1874). They were delivered by a pioneering physician, Dr. Myra Herrick, Cleveland's first woman doctor, who organized a short-lived homeopathic college to train women in the field. When she set up a free medical dispensary, staffed exclusively by female doctors, to assist low-income women, Cettie and Mary Flagler were prominent contributors.

A surprisingly flexible, egalitarian father, Rockefeller never shrank from child care. His sister-in-law, Lute, who gave up teaching and went to live with them, told how John eased the burden from Cettie's shoulders when he was at home: "He would get up from his nap the moment he heard a baby cry and carry the little one up and down the room until she was quieted."[11] Rockefeller was always patient with his children and seldom lost his temper or uttered a harsh word. As the son of a self-absorbed absentee father, he made a point of being an affectionate parent and something of a homebody.

Like Big Bill, however, Rockefeller could be a sprightly companion for his children. He would get down on all fours and bear them on his back, recapturing a boyish glee that was seldom evident at the office. When they played blindman's buff, he electrified them with daring feints, sudden thrusts, and unexpected, wheeling turns, followed by whoops of delight when he won. Attuned to their fantasy world, he liked to gather the children around him and tell fairy tales. Also like his father, he had an inexhaustible supply of stunts. At dinner, he dazzled the children by balancing fine china plates on the tip of his nose; he also balanced crackers on his nose, then gave them a sudden flip and caught them in his mouth. He taught the children to swim, row, skate, and ride, and he had a talent for devising imaginative outings. On moonlit nights at Forest Hill—the Cleveland estate Rockefeller bought in the 1870s—they ventured forth on bicycle trips, with Rockefeller pinning a large white handkerchief to the back of his coat and leading the children through winding, mysterious forest roads. John Jr. never forgot skating with his father: "The lake was deep, so we took under each arm long narrow boards, which would hold us up in case we broke through the ice. That was characteristic of Father. He always took the utmost care to examine any project thoroughly; then when convinced it was safe, put it through without further question."[12]

Perhaps to create a substitute for theater and other entertainments proscribed by their religion, John and Cettie encouraged the children's musical talents, and each one took up an instrument. They formed their own quartet with Bessie on violin, Alta on piano, Edith on cello, and John Jr. on violin—so that the house echoed with the works of Mozart, Beethoven, and Handel. The children approached music as serious art, not frivolous amusement, and performed frequently at church events. They weren't barred from playing contemporary popular music.

If there was more merriment in Rockefeller's household than we might have suspected, there was also an underlying sobriety. His children remembered the playful moments, but outsiders were struck by the somber, stuffy atmosphere and found something almost spooky about the Rockefeller home, with one disgruntled tutor leaving this ghastly description: "The elastic step, the laughter of youth, the light heartedness, the romping about, the playfulness, which one is supposed to meet among the young and happy were entirely lacking, lacking almost to dejection. It was a gloomy horizon, with a heaviness that pervaded the entire household. Silence and gloom everywhere."[13]

Rockefeller kept his children hermetically cut off from the world and hired governesses to educate them at home. Aside from church, they never engaged in outside social or civic functions and betrayed a very Baptist fear of worldly entertainments. In the summertime, the children's friends might come to visit for a week or two at a time, but *never* the reverse, and even these playmates were the cautiously screened offspring of John and Cettie's church companions. As John Jr. remembered, "Our interests centered in the house; our friends came there almost wholly. We went rarely, practically none at all, to neighbors' houses."[14] John Jr. hinted that the children brought to visit weren't real companions and were mostly window dressing to gratify his parents. "We had no childhood friends, no school friends."[15] It was a far cry from Thorstein Veblen's image of the spoiled leisure class.

Convinced that struggle was the crucible of character, Rockefeller faced a delicate task in raising his children. He wanted to accumulate wealth while inculcating in them the values of his threadbare boyhood. The first step in saving them from extravagance was keeping them ignorant of their father's affluence. Until they were adults, Rockefeller's children never visited his office or refineries, and even then they were accompanied by company officials, never Father. At home, Rockefeller created a make-believe market economy, calling Cettie the "general manager" and requiring the children to keep careful account books.[16] They earned pocket money by performing chores and received two cents for killing flies, ten cents for sharpening pencils, five cents per hour for practicing their musical instruments, and a dollar for repairing vases. They were given two cents per day for abstaining from candy and a dime bonus for each consecutive day of abstinence. Each toiled in a separate patch of the vegetable garden, earning a penny for every ten weeds they pulled up. John Jr. got fifteen cents an hour for chopping wood and ten cents per day for superintending paths. Rockefeller took pride in training his children as miniature household workers. Years later, riding on a train with his thirteen-year-old daughter, he told a traveling companion, "This little girl is earning money already. You never could imagine how she does it. I have learned what my gas bills should average when the gas is managed with care, and I have told her that she can have for pin money all that she will save every month on this amount, so she goes around every night and keeps the gas turned down where it is not needed."[17] Rockefeller never tired of preaching economy and whenever a package arrived at home, he made a point of saving the paper and string.

Cettie was equally vigilant. When the children clamored for bicycles, John suggested buying one for each child. "No," said Cettie, "we will buy just one for all of them." "But, my dear," John protested, "tricycles do not cost much." "That is true," she replied. "It is not the cost. But if they have just one they will learn to give up to one another."[18] So the children shared a single bicycle. Amazingly enough, the four children probably grew up with a level of creature comforts not that far above what Rockefeller had known as a boy. Except on Sundays, the girls wore simple gingham dresses and hand-me-downs. In later life, John Jr. confessed sheepishly that until the age of eight he wore only dresses, because he was the youngest child and the three older siblings were girls.[19]

Rockefeller's home secretary saw much of the children because they liked to sit quietly and observe the mysterious clicking of the telegraph wires in her office. She described Rockefeller as extremely gentle with the children but attached to certain fixed principles that he expounded with didactic, wearying repetition. The children were told so often that cards were sinful that they couldn't distinguish one card suit from another. To teach self-restraint, Rockefeller limited them to one piece of cheese daily. One afternoon, little Alta tattled on her younger sister Edith for having eaten *two* pieces of cheese, and Rockefeller professed shock at this epicurean indulgence. As the secretary recalled: "All that afternoon whenever Edith came within hearing her father would say, slowly and impressively, 'Edith was greedy.' At another time both little John and Alta called out, 'Edith took the biggest.' Repeatedly that afternoon, Mr. Rockefeller said in his impressive manner, 'Edith was selfish.' "[20]

Yet the thing to be husbanded most jealously was time. One could neither be too early nor too late. In fact, there was such a fetish about punctuality that it occasioned discernible anxiety among the children. Rockefeller's home secretary said that John Jr. had computed, down to the second, how long it took to get from her telegraph office to the schoolroom upstairs. "After that, whenever I read to the children near school time, John would sit with watch in hand, and his rising was signal for the reading to stop and for the girls to follow him."[21]

Each morning before breakfast, Rockefeller led the family in prayer, meting out a penny fine to latecomers. Everyone took turns reciting from scripture, and John or Cettie elucidated difficult portions and prayed for guidance. Before bed, Cettie listened to the children recite their prayers, and nothing could divert her from this sacred duty. They were encouraged to be active in prayer, especially at Friday night prayer meetings. As John Jr. recalled, at an early age they were encouraged "to take part like the older people, either in a brief word of prayer or a word of personal experience."[22]

Sunday was a heavily regimented day, starting with morning prayers and Sunday school then proceeding through afternoon prayer meetings and culminating with evening hymns. If the children had spare time, they couldn't read novels or worldly literature but had to restrict themselves to the Bible and Sunday-school literature. Strangely enough, the children didn't remember this as oppressive. As John Jr. observed, "A day with such limitations as this would simply appall the modern child. And yet I have only the happiest recollections of the Sundays of my childhood."[23] Cettie turned Sunday into a day for serious reflection, asking the children to reflect upon such weighty maxims as "He who conquers self is the greatest victor" or "The secret of sensible living is simplicity."[24] Leading the children in an hour-long "home talk," she asked each child to select a "besetting sin" and then prayed with the child, asking for God's help in combating the sin. The implicit Baptist message was that people were inherently flawed but—with prayer, willpower, and God's grace—infinitely capable of improvement.

In business, John D. Rockefeller operated in a rough, virile world, whereas at home he was surrounded by a harem of doting women that included, at various times, his wife, sister-in-law, mother, mother-in-law, and three daughters. He seemed equally comfortable in these masculine and feminine spheres of existence. When they first got married, John and Cettie lived with his mother Eliza, but she remained behind on Cheshire Street when they moved to Euclid Avenue. For the rest of her life, Eliza rotated among the homes of her five children, who provided her with more security than she had ever known with her prodigal husband. Evidently, she had some idea of where Bill lived, for she had a mailing address and forwarded letters to him from their grandchildren. In a confused manner, the grandchildren knew that their jolly grandfather lived an odd life somewhere out West, but the picture was left deliberately cloudy.

It is hard to retrace Bill's movements with precision, for John D. seldom referred to him in either his business or private papers; his father's banishment was no less psychological than geographic. As best one can piece the story together in these middle years, Bill and his second wife, Margaret, moved to Illinois in 1867 and bought a 160-acre farm in Maroa, with John secretly sending money to help complete the purchase. As the area grew too settled for Bill, the couple moved again in 1875 to Freeport, Illinois, and here Margaret's wanderings, at least, ended. According to stories told later by their Freeport neighbors, Bill—known to them as Dr. William Levingston—was regarded as a profane braggart and con man, a notorious quack doctor who claimed to specialize in cancer and kidney treatments and bought jugs of diuretic from a local druggist that he then resold on the road. Just as the long-suffering Eliza had endured long separations, it was now Margaret's turn to wait as Bill disappeared for months before returning home with thick wads of money, always careful to fold a $100 bill on the outside. Yet Big Bill never entirely lost touch with his Rockefeller family. From out of the blue, he would materialize in Cleveland, jovial and carefree, and spend several days shooting at targets and playing his fiddle before disappearing for another year. John maintained a frosty civility toward his father, and their meetings tended to be both brief and infrequent. Later on, we shall have more to say about Bill's queer odyssey, for as his son grew famous, the whereabouts of Doc Rockefeller turned into a national obsession as reporters tried to reconstruct his renegade career.

===

In marrying Laura "Cettie" Spelman, Rockefeller had found a woman with his mother's gentle tenacity and religiosity. An 1872 photo shows a short, fragile, dark-haired woman with a wide face, high cheekbones, and deep, earnest eyes. Steeped in religious sentiment, she was more likely to be found meditating on a sermon than gossiping about a shopping expedition. Her marriage to John was harmonious, formal, and devoid of quarrels. Like her husband, Cettie was fiercely democratic, disdaining conspicuous consumption and the snobbery of the rich. "She was no respecter of persons," said her son. "To her all men were brothers."[25] She scorned frippery and dismissed fashion plates as vain, silly people. Though always supportive of her husband in his ambitions, she inveighed against "the desperate struggle to obtain the 'almighty dollar.' "[26] Even more of a pinchpenny than John, she wore patches on her clothes and shocked one acquaintance by stating that a young woman needed just two dresses in her wardrobe. Even as her husband grew rich, she continued to perform much of the housework herself, employing two maids and a coachman when they could have afforded many more.

Since he left the house each day and trafficked in a sinful world, John was a broader person than his wife, whose interests contracted sharply after she married. Despite her early bluestocking bent, she lost much of her intellectual brightness as she made the transition from teacher to pedagogical mother, relentlessly molding her children. She liked to quote the maxim, "To be a good wife and mother is the highest and hardest privilege of woman."[27] Where John derived escapist pleasure from the children, Laura took her maternal duties too seriously and was a firm, if loving, martinet. As her son said, she "talked to us constantly about *duty*—and displeasing the Lord and pleasing your parents. She instilled a personal consciousness of right and wrong, training our wills and getting us to want to do the things we ought to do."[28] No less than her husband, she believed in the economical use of time. As one observer said, "She realized her responsibilities, subjecting herself to a fixed daily regimen of duties, dividing her day off methodically into hours and minutes for each, that no moment might be misspent, and no duty neglected."[29]

There was danger in the very congruence of values between John and Cettie, for it made their intellectual life rather airless, allowing no room for disagreement. Had their opinions clashed, John might have been exposed to critical perspectives that could have saved him from his business excesses. Instead, his marriage strengthened his virtuous sense that he was one of God's soldiers and therefore bound to be vilified by sinners. Cettie was similarly braced for the terrible ostracism that came with Rockefeller's wealth. "She was always like the Spartan mothers," said her daughter Edith. "Everything which came to her she accepted, and she bore her frailty of body with uncomplaining patience. . . . She had faith and trust in those she loved and never questioned or criticized."[30]

Cettie's sister Lucy—Aunt Lute, as the children called her—acted as something of a leavening influence in this arid setting. The close relationship of the two sisters was touching since Lute, two years older, was an adopted child. By a strange coincidence, they looked so much alike that everybody assumed they were biological sisters. Lute was bright and cultivated, read contemporary literature, and gave John and Laura a window on secular culture when she read aloud after dinner. Though he was extremely fond of his sister-in-law, Rockefeller found her comically prim and spinsterish and delighted in mimicking the way she lifted her skirts as she mounted the staircase; she would often turn and find him stealthily climbing the steps behind her, aping her in his cutaway coat, much to the family's amusement. In time, Lute developed the prissy manner of the proverbial old maid, and the children, for all their love, found her a little trying. But she was a beloved figure and an integral part of the family, and she introduced some needed cultural enrichment into a household that conformed rigidly to Christian doctrine.

CHAPTER 8

Conspirators

T he great industrial revolution that transformed America after the Civil War triggered an inflationary boom that swamped the country with goods. When this expanded supply led to lower prices and a deflationary bust, it set the pattern for the rest of the nineteenth century, which experienced huge economic advances, punctuated by treacherous slumps. Lured by easy profits, legions of investors rushed into a promising new field and, when big gluts developed from overproduction, they found it impossible to recoup their investment. This was especially true in new industries where people lacked the caution bred by experience and thus expanded with reckless abandon. As a result, many businessmen began to distrust unfettered competition and flirted with newfangled notions of cooperation—pools, monopolies, and other marketing arrangements that might curb production and artificially buoy prices.

While all commodity prices fluctuated, crude-oil prices were especially volatile. Based on locating deep, unseen pools, the industry was an unpredictable, nerve-racking affair. Every time some lucky devil hit a gusher, this bonanza drove prices down. In 1865, producers began to torpedo wells by exploding gunpowder (later nitroglycerine) deep inside them to shake loose more oil, swelling the surplus. Within a year or two after the Civil War, the oil flood caused prices to skid to as low as $2.40 a barrel—they had traded as high as $12 in 1864—leading producers to contemplate forming a cartel to boost prices. The same predicament roiled refining, which had generated astronomical profits at first. As Rockefeller said tartly, the spoiled refiners "were disappointed if they did not make one hundred percent profit in a year—sometimes in six months."[1] With sky-high profits and ridiculously low start-up costs, the field had soon grown overcrowded. "In came the tinkers and the tailors and the boys who followed the plow, all eager for this large profit," said Rockefeller.[2]

By the late 1860s, this dynamic produced a pervasive slump in the oil industry, keeping it depressed for the next five years. Low kerosene prices, a boon to consumers, were catastrophic for refiners, who saw the profit margin between crude- and refined-oil prices shrink to a vanishing point. Rampant speculation had so overbuilt the industry that total refining capacity in 1870 was triple the amount of crude oil being pumped. By then, Rockefeller estimated, 90 percent of all refineries were operating in the red. At this bleak impasse, a leading Cleveland rival, John H. Alexander, offered to sell his interest to William Rockefeller at ten cents on the dollar, as the entire industry faced ruin. Worse, the oil market wasn't correcting itself according to the self-regulating mechanism dear to neoclassical economists. Producers and refiners didn't shut down operations in the expected numbers, causing Rockefeller to doubt the workings of Adam Smith's theoretical invisible hand: "So many wells were flowing that the price of oil kept falling, yet they went right on drilling."[3] The industry was trapped in a full-blown crisis of overproduction with no relief in sight.

Thus, in 1869, one year after his stellar railroad coup, Rockefeller feared that his wealth might be snatched away from him. As someone who tended toward optimism, "seeing opportunity in every disaster," he studied the situation exhaustively instead of bemoaning his bad luck.[4] He saw that his individual success as a refiner was now menaced by industrywide failure and that it therefore demanded a systemic solution. This was a momentous insight, pregnant with consequences. Instead of just tending to his own business, he began to conceive of the industry as a gigantic, interrelated mechanism and thought in terms of strategic alliances and long-term planning.

Rockefeller cited the years 1869 and 1870 as the start of his campaign to replace competition with cooperation in the industry. The culprit, he decided, was "the over-development of the refining industry," which had created "ruinous competition."[5] If this fractious industry was to be made profitable and enduring, he would have to tame and discipline it. A trailblazer who improvised solutions without any guidance from economic texts, he began to envision a giant cartel that would reduce overcapacity, stabilize prices, and rationalize the industry. If Rockefeller first expounded this idea among refiners, he was anticipated by the very drillers who later railed at his machinations. During the Civil War, they had formed an Oil Creek Association to curtail production and lift prices, and on February 1, 1869, they again met in Oil City to create the Petroleum Producers' Association to protect their interests.

To devise a comprehensive solution for the industry, Rockefeller again needed money: money to create economies of scale, money to build cash re-

The chaotic, derrick-covered slopes of Oil Creek,
Pennsylvania, in 1865.
(Courtesy of the Drake Well Museum)

serves to endure downturns, money to heighten efficiency. "And to buy in the many refineries that were a source of overproduction and confusion we needed a great deal of money."[6] The tricky part for Rockefeller and Flagler was how to supplement their capital without relinquishing control; the solution was to incorporate, which would enable them to sell shares to select outside investors. "I wish I'd had the brains to think of it," said Rockefeller. "It was Henry M. Flagler."[7]

Luckily, many states had now passed laws permitting companies to incorporate. The one hitch—and it was a formidable one for Rockefeller—was that these firms couldn't own property outside their state of incorporation; to finesse this restriction would require endless legal legerdemain. On January 10, 1870, the partnership of Rockefeller, Andrews and Flagler was abolished and replaced by a joint-stock firm called the Standard Oil Company (Ohio), with John D. Rockefeller as president, William Rockefeller as vice president, and Henry M. Flagler as secretary and treasurer. Besides echoing their Standard Works refinery, the name advertised the uniform quality of their kerosene at a time when consumers feared explosions from impurities. With $1 million in capital—$11 million in contemporary money—the new company became an instant landmark in business history, for "there was no other concern in the country organized with such a capital," Rockefeller said.[8] Already a mini-empire, Standard Oil controlled 10 percent of American petroleum refining, as well as a barrel-making plant, warehouses, shipping facilities, and a fleet of tank cars. From the outset, Rockefeller's plans had a wide streak of megalomania. As he told Cleveland businessman John Prindle, "The Standard Oil Company will some day refine all the oil and make all the barrels."[9]

Despite his lack of legal training, Henry M. Flagler drew up the act of incorporation. Nearly sixty years later, when this document was dredged up in a legal dispute, people were stunned by its simplicity. Instead of a fancy embossed paper, dripping with seals, one reporter described it as "a cheap looking legal paper, faded yellow and of evident poor material, granting the Standard Oil Company the right to engage in business."[10] This economical, no-nonsense approach appealed to investors, as did Rockefeller's decision that the leading men would receive no salary but would profit solely from the appreciation of their shares and rising dividends—which Rockefeller thought a more potent stimulus to work.

Standard Oil started out in a modest suite of offices in a four-story building known as the Cushing Block on the Public Square. The office shared by Rockefeller and Flagler was somber and austere. Furnished with funereal dignity, it had a black leather couch and four black walnut chairs with elaborately carved backs and arms, plus a fireplace to provide warmth in winter. Rockefeller never allowed his office decor to flaunt the prosperity of his business, lest it arouse unwanted curiosity.

From the start, he owned more shares of Standard Oil than anybody else and exploited every opportunity to augment his stake. Of the original 10,000 shares, he took 2,667, while Flagler, Andrews, and William Rockefeller each took 1,333; Stephen Harkness took 1,334; and the former partners of Rockefeller, Andrews and Flagler divided another 1,000. The final 1,000 shares went to Oliver B. Jennings, William Rockefeller's brother-in-law and the first outside investor. An adventurous figure, Jennings had gone to California during the gold rush and profited from selling supplies to prospectors.

Rich investors did not line up to invest in Standard Oil, among other reasons because it was an inauspicious time for new ventures. On September 24, 1869—the infamous Black Friday—Jay Gould and Jim Fisk's scheme to corner the gold market by manipulating President Grant's monetary policy collapsed, fomenting financial panic and ruining more than a dozen Wall Street houses. Beyond that, the speculative aura of the oil industry still deterred many reputable businessmen. Rockefeller never forgot how his scheme was savagely derided as a "rope of sand" or how sage businessmen told him that similar attempts to create a Great Lakes shipping cartel had misfired. "Either this experiment will result in a great success or a dismal failure," one aging financier warned him.[11] As Rockefeller recalled, it was "a course which older and more conservative business men shrank back from and regarded as reckless, almost to the point of insanity."[12] Embittered by these skeptics and set to prove them wrong, Rockefeller managed to pay dividends of 105 percent on Standard Oil stock during the first year of operations despite one of the worst financial bloodbaths in the industry's early history.

The man with the hypertrophied craving for order was about to impose his iron rule on this lawless, godless business. As Ida Tarbell described Rockefeller in 1870, he was "a brooding, cautious, secretive man, seeing all the possible dangers as well as all the possible opportunities in things, and he studied, as a player at chess, all the possible combinations, which might imperil his supremacy."[13] As he scanned the field of battle, the first target of opportunity lay close to home: the twenty-six rival Cleveland refiners. His strategy would be to subjugate one part of the battlefield, consolidate his forces, then move briskly on to the next conquest. His victory over the Cleveland refiners would be the first but also the most controversial campaign of his career.

═══

For his admirers, 1872 was the annus mirabilis of John D. Rockefeller's life, while for his critics it constituted the darkest chapter. The year revealed both his finest and most problematic qualities as a businessman: his visionary leadership, his courageous persistence, his capacity to think in strategic terms, but also his lust for domination, his messianic self-righteousness, and his contempt for those shortsighted mortals who made the mistake of standing in his way.

What rivals saw as a naked power grab, Rockefeller regarded as a heroic act of salvation, nothing less than the rescue of the oil business.

The state of the kerosene trade had further deteriorated in 1871 as prices sagged another 25 percent. As competitors skidded into bankruptcy, Standard Oil declared a 40 percent dividend, with a small surplus to spare. Despite this, John D. Rockefeller sold off a small block of Standard Oil shares—the only time he ever lost heart momentarily—prompting brother William to lament, "Your anxiety to sell makes me feel uneasy."[14] This discouragement was short-lived. In late 1871, Rockefeller engineered the covert acquisition of Bostwick and Tilford, New York's premier oil buyers, who owned barges, lighters, and a large refinery at Hunter's Point on the East River. A former Kentucky banker who had also dealt in cotton and grain and peddled Bibles, Jabez Abel Bostwick was a devout Baptist in the Rockefeller mold: "strict almost to sternness in his business dealings, preferring justice to sentiment," as one contemporary said.[15] The purchase of Bostwick's firm gave Rockefeller a sophisticated purchasing agency at a critical moment. Oil prices were now being set on exchanges in western Pennsylvania, with powerful syndicates pushing aside the lone speculators who had once dominated trading. The move set a pattern of stealth that shadowed Rockefeller's career: Renamed J. A. Bostwick and Company, the newly acquired firm brazenly feigned independence of Standard Oil while acting as its cat's-paw.

On January 1, 1872, the Standard Oil executive committee, bracing for the tumultuous events ahead, boosted the firm's capital from $1 million to $2.5 million and then to $3.5 million the next day.[16] Among the new shareholders were several luminaries of Cleveland banking, including Truman P. Handy, Amasa Stone, and Stillman Witt. An intriguing new investor was Benjamin Brewster, a direct descendant of Elder Brewster of the Plymouth colony, who had made a fortune with Oliver Jennings during the California gold rush. It was a sign of Rockefeller's exceptional self-confidence that he gathered strong executives and investors at this abysmal time, as if the depressed atmosphere only strengthened his resolve. "We were gathering information which confirmed us in the idea that to enlarge our own Standard Oil of Ohio and actually take into partners with us the refining interest would accomplish the protection of the oil industry as a whole."[17] On January 1, 1872, the executive committee made its historic decision to purchase "certain refining properties in Cleveland and elsewhere."[18] This seemingly innocuous resolution was the opening shot of a bloody skirmish that historians came to label the Cleveland Massacre.

The mayhem in Cleveland began when Rockefeller struck a clandestine and richly ironic deal with Tom Scott, the overlord of the Pennsylvania Railroad. As noted, the Pennsylvania had threatened to blot out Cleveland as a refining center, prompting Rockefeller to solidify his ties with the Erie and New York Central systems. Rockefeller had no personal love of Scott and later branded him "perhaps the most dominant, autocratic power that ever existed, before or since, in the railroad business of our country."[19] Like many railroad executives, Scott had made his reputation during the Civil War by keeping railroad lines open between Washington and the North and winning appointment as an assistant secretary of war. A shrewd, dashing man with long, curling side-whiskers, he wore an enormous felt hat and exuded an aura of power. Of this master political manipulator, Wendell Phillips observed that "as he trailed his garments across the country the members of 20 legislatures rustled like dry leaves in a winter's wind."[20] Though Andrew Carnegie was a protégé of Scott before going into the iron and steel business, the railroad executive didn't appeal to the sanctimonious Rockefeller.

In business matters, however, Rockefeller stood ready to strike a deal with the devil himself. Since he dreaded an alliance between the Pennsylvania Railroad and Pittsburgh and Philadelphia refiners, he wanted to drive a wedge between them. "They went on their knees to [Scott] for rates," Rockefeller said disparagingly of his rivals. "They reverenced the Pennsylvania Railroad administration; would do anything at their beck; would do anything to get in return help in the transportation of oil."[21] So Rockefeller was receptive to an overture from Scott, which came unexpectedly from Peter H. Watson, an official of the rival Lake Shore Railroad and an intimate ally of Commodore Vanderbilt. As president of a Lake Shore branch that joined Cleveland to Oil Creek, Watson had a personal stake in advancing the fortunes of his largest customer, Standard Oil. When Standard Oil expanded its capital in January 1872, Watson quietly pocketed five hundred shares in another example of the growing back-scratching between Rockefeller and the railroads. It was probably through Watson that Commodore Vanderbilt discreetly invested $50,000 in Standard Oil that year.

On November 30, 1871, Watson met Rockefeller and Flagler at the Saint Nicholas Hotel in New York and presented an audacious scheme devised by Tom Scott, who proposed an alliance between the three most powerful railroads—the Pennsylvania, the New York Central, and the Erie—and a handful of refiners, notably Standard Oil. To implement this, Scott had obtained a special charter for a shell organization bearing the blandly misleading name of the South Improvement Company (SIC). After the Civil War, the venal Pennsylvania legislature had created dozens of such charters by special enactment. These improvement companies possessed such broad, vague powers—including the right to hold stock in companies outside Pennsylvania—that some economic historians have christened them the first real holding companies. The Pennsylvania Railroad had a special purchase on these instruments of corporate power and sometimes traded them for favors.

Under the terms of the proposed pact, the railroads would sharply raise freight rates for all refiners, but refiners in the SIC would receive such substantial rebates—up to 50 percent off crude- and refined-oil shipments—that their competitive edge over rivals would widen dramatically. In the most deadly innovation, the SIC members would also receive "drawbacks" on shipments made by rival refiners—that is, the railroads would give the SIC members rebates for every barrel shipped by *other* refiners. On shipments from western Pennsylvania to Cleveland, for instance, Standard Oil would receive a forty-cent rebate on every barrel it shipped, plus another forty cents for every barrel shipped to Cleveland by competitors! One Rockefeller biographer has called the drawback "an instrument of competitive cruelty unparalleled in industry."[22] Through another provision, Standard Oil and other SIC refiners would receive comprehensive information about all oil shipped by their competitors—invaluable in underpricing them. The SIC members were naturally sworn to secrecy about the inner workings of this alarming scheme. All in all, it was an astonishing piece of knavery, grand-scale collusion such as American industry had never witnessed.

Though Rockefeller and his coconspirators contended that all refiners were impartially invited to join the SIC, the group excluded refiners from Oil Creek and New York, and Standard Oil was indisputably the driving force. Of the 2,000 shares issued, over one-fourth were held by John and William Rockefeller and Henry Flagler; counting Jabez Bostwick and Oliver H. Payne (soon to be a leader of Standard Oil), the Rockefeller group controlled 900 of 2,000 shares. The SIC president was Peter H. Watson, who held 100 shares and was also now a Standard Oil shareholder, thus ensuring the supremacy of Cleveland refiners over the Pittsburgh and Philadelphia members of the group.

Why did the nation's leading railroads offer Rockefeller and his confederates terms so generous as to render them all but omnipotent in oil refining? How did they benefit from this association? First, the railroads had engaged in such fierce, internecine price wars that freight rates had fallen sharply. No less than the oil producers, they needed somebody to arbitrate their disputes and save them from their own cutthroat tactics. The cornerstone of the SIC was a provision that Standard Oil would act as "evener" for the three railroads and ensure that each received a predetermined share of the oil traffic: Forty-five percent of the oil shipped by SIC members would travel over the Pennsylvania Railroad, 27.5 percent on the Erie, and 27.5 percent on the New York Central. Unless the railroads had greater control over the oil business, Rockefeller knew, they "could not make the divisions of business necessary so as to prevent rate-cutting."[23] Rockefeller would become their official umpire and try to govern their pool in a fair, disinterested fashion. As mentioned, the railroads also had an economic interest in greater consolidation among refiners to streamline their own operations. One other factor tempted the railroads to come to terms with Rockefeller: In a farsighted tactical maneuver, he had begun to accumulate hundreds of tank cars, which would be in perpetually short supply.

The SIC—soon exposed as an infamous conspiracy—was a masterful move in Rockefeller's quest for industrial domination. Both refiners and railroads were struggling with excess capacity and suicidal price wars. Rockefeller's supreme insight was that he could solve the oil industry's problems by solving the railroads' problems at the same time, creating a double cartel in oil and rails. One of Rockefeller's strengths in bargaining situations was that he figured out what he wanted *and* what the other party wanted and then crafted mutually advantageous terms. Instead of ruining the railroads, Rockefeller tried to help them prosper, albeit in a way that fortified his own position.

Later on, trying to distance himself from the SIC fiasco, Rockefeller scoffed at charges that he had been the ringleader. All along, he insisted, he knew it would fail and had gone along simply as a tactical maneuver. "We acceded to it because [Tom Scott] and the Philadelphia and Pittsburgh men, we hoped, would be helpful to us ultimately. We were willing to go with them as far as the plan could be used; so that when it failed, we would be in a position to say, 'Now try our plan.' "[24] Rockefeller's plan was to unify the industry under Standard Oil. By his own admission, he had not opposed the SIC on ethical grounds but solely as a practical matter, convinced it wouldn't apply the needed discipline to member refiners. The scheme never bothered his conscience. "It was right," an unreconstructed Rockefeller said in later years. "I knew it as a matter of conscience. It was right before me and my God. If I had to do it tomorrow I would do it again the same way—do it a hundred times."[25] Even in hindsight, he couldn't tolerate doubts about his career but had to present it as one long, triumphal march, sanctified by his religion.

Rockefeller's assertion that he reluctantly followed the railroads' lead conveniently distorted the truth. Far from coyly stepping aside and waiting for a misbegotten scheme to founder, he took a leading role and promoted it zealously. We know this because of several remarkable letters he wrote to Cettie from New York, where for several agitated weeks he remained closeted with railroad officials. He knew the negotiations were controversial, since he advised Cettie on November 30, 1871, "A man who succeeds in life must sometimes go against the current."[26] While these letters confirm that he didn't originate the scheme, they show that he soon warmed to the project, declaring on December 1, "indeed the project *grows on me.*"[27] When Watson secured Commodore Vanderbilt's blessing, Rockefeller was positively jubilant, and he emerged as natural leader of the group, particularly as others grew skittish. In late January 1872, trapped in New York, he wanted to return to Cleveland but told Cettie that "our men *would not hear to it,* they are nervous, and lean on me. . . . I feel like a caged lion and would roar if it would do any good."[28] Obviously, had Rockefeller wished the SIC to collapse, he would have renounced a leadership position and returned to Cleveland sooner.

The small batch of letters he wrote to Cettie at this time—among his few early, surviving letters to her—betray a surprisingly romantic sensibility, as if seven years of marriage hadn't dimmed his ardor. Amid negotiations, he told her, "I dreamed last night of the girl Celestia Spelman and awoke to realize she was my 'Laura.' "[29] Repeatedly, Rockefeller complained about how lonely he felt in New York—"like a wandering Jew"—and reiterated his yearning to be at home. Far from being beguiled by the money, fashion, and power of New York, his Baptist soul recoiled from it. "The world is full of Sham, Flattery, and Deceptions," he wrote, "and *home* is a haven of rest and freedom."[30] At this stage, Rockefeller still found his wealth wonderful and slightly unreal, telling Cettie that "we have been so prospered and placed in *independent* circumstances, it seems a fabulous dream but I assure you it is a solid and comforting fact—how different our condition from the multitudes, let us be thankful."[31] Perhaps this financial independence emboldened Rockefeller to undertake the risky SIC scheme, confident that it wouldn't endanger his family's security. And lest Cettie worry about his risky new venture, he reminded her, "You know we are independently rich outside investments in oil—but I believe my oil stock the very best."[32]

By late January 1872, as the conspirators drew up and signed the last contracts while trying to preserve total secrecy, rumors of an impending jump in freight rates began to filter through western Pennsylvania. On February 22, the *Petroleum Centre Record* alluded darkly to a "rumored scheme of gigantic combination among certain railroads and refiners to control the purchase and shipment of crude and refined oil from this region."[33] Definite word of the plot didn't leak out until days later, when the local freight agent for the Lake Shore Railroad rushed off to visit a dying son and left in charge a subordinate who didn't realize that the new freight rates hadn't yet been enacted. Oblivious to the historic impact he would have, this minor functionary promulgated the staggering rates for outside refiners decreed by the SIC. On February 26, the stunned residents of Oil Creek read in the morning papers that freight rates had doubled overnight for everyone—everyone, that is, except a privileged group of refiners in Cleveland, Pittsburgh, and Philadelphia who belonged to a shadowy entity called the South Improvement Company.

For the horror-struck refiners in Titusville or Oil City, this wasn't simply a new competitive threat: It was a death warrant, and they stopped work and poured into the streets, denouncing the action in strident tones. "The oil region was afire with all sorts of wild stories," recalled Rockefeller. "There were meetings of protest, of bitter denunciation."[34] On the night of February 27, three thousand people stormed into the Titusville Opera House, waving banners that stated, "Down with the conspirators," "No compromise," and "Don't give up the ship!" while Rockefeller and his cabal were denounced as "the Monster" and "the Forty Thieves."[35] Perhaps the most impassioned speaker was a short young refiner named John D. Archbold, the hard-drinking, poker-playing son of a circuit preacher. Though Peter Watson had tried to inveigle him into the SIC, Archbold had indignantly refused and now told the crowd, "We have been approached by the great anaconda, but do not desire to yield."[36] The Oil Creek refiners believed they had a God-given right to market the oil drilled in their backyards and Archbold—destined, ironically, to succeed Rockefeller at the Standard Oil helm—endorsed this view. "We believe this is the natural point for the business," he told the cheering audience. "This is the last desperate struggle of desperate men."[37] After he was elected secretary of a new Petroleum Producers' Union, the group agreed to retaliate by starving out the SIC conspirators, selling crude oil only to refiners along Oil Creek.

Amid this frenzied hue and cry, the local citizenry created a small army of roving protesters who moved from town to town, organizing torchlight rallies and picking up new adherents. On the night of March 1, refiners and producers jammed another tumultuous meeting at the opera house in Oil City. One featured speaker was a young producer, Lewis Emery, Jr., who supported a proposal by Archbold to cut existing production by 30 percent and suspend new drilling for thirty days. With this speech, the indefatigable Emery launched a crusade against Standard Oil that would persist for decades. By the end of the meeting, a thousand men stood ready to besiege the state capitol in Harrisburg and demand relief from the SIC.

In this warlike atmosphere, the *Oil City Derrick* printed a daily blacklist of the conspirators—Peter Watson, followed by Rockefeller and six other directors—in a black-bordered box on the front page. Each day, a new inflammatory caption was supplied, such as "Behold 'The Anaconda' in all his hideous deformity."[38] It was in the context of such hysterical emotion that the world first learned the name of John D. Rockefeller. As if his foes already intuited his special power, he was singled out for abuse, one newspaper crowning him "the Mephistopheles of Cleveland."[39] As people learned of his central place in the SIC, vandals defaced the blue Standard Oil barrels with skulls and crossbones. Two Standard employees on Oil Creek, Joseph Seep and Daniel O'Day, barricaded themselves in their offices and fended off marauding mobs. "It was a tense situation," said Seep. "Some of my friends were actually afraid to be seen talking with me in the street. There were threats of violence. Captain John W. Jones, a big producer, wanted the people to burn the Standard Oil Company's tanks."[40] Saboteurs attacked the railroads, raiding oil cars and spilling their contents on the ground or tearing tracks apart. A local lawyer, Samuel C. T.

Dodd, said that if the protests had continued indefinitely, "there would not have been one mile of railroad track left in the County of Venango. The people had come to that pitch of desperation."[41] Few residents of Oil Creek imagined that their dread adversary was a clean-cut, churchgoing young man. This nightmarish period left an especially deep imprint upon a flabbergasted fourteen-year-old schoolgirl named Ida Tarbell. "I remember a night when my father came home with a grim look on his face and told how he with scores of other producers had signed a pledge not to sell to the Cleveland ogre that also had profited from the scheme—a new name, that of the Standard Oil Company, replacing the name South Improvement Company in popular contempt."[42]

Far from giving Rockefeller pause, the vandalism only confirmed his view of Oil Creek as a netherworld of rogues and adventurers who needed to be ruled by stronger men. He was always quick to impugn the motives of enemies while regarding his own as somehow beyond reproach. "The Standard Oil Company were a very orderly body, and these producers were a rabble of wild, excitable men, waiting for a war-cry to rush into the arena with a suitable noise."[43] Clad in the armor of self-righteousness, Rockefeller felt no need to explain his actions and turned away reporters at his door. After Flagler told reporters that Standard Oil's opponents were "a few soreheads," Rockefeller advised silence, and Flagler desisted from further comment. With threats being made on his life, Rockefeller posted a special detail of policemen outside both office and home and kept a revolver by his bed for good measure.

Only in the twilight of life did Rockefeller realize how poorly his taciturnity had served him in business battles. This was especially true during the SIC furor, which evolved into a political and public-relations battle. By remaining silent in the face of criticism, he thought he would seem confident and secure in his integrity—in fact, he seemed guilty and arrogantly evasive. Throughout his career, Rockefeller endured abuse with so much equanimity that Flagler once shook his head and said, "John, you have a hide like a rhinoceros!"[44] He had an early Christian's fierce defiance of critics, his boyhood with Big Bill having also taught him to disregard the malicious gossip of neighbors. He had a great general's ability to focus on his goals and brush aside obstacles as petty distractions. "You can abuse me, you can strike me," Rockefeller said, "so long as you let me have my own way."[45]

As always, the greater the tumult, the cooler Rockefeller became, and a strange calm settled over him when his colleagues were most disconcerted. When pushed, he always stood his ground. The SIC episode showed that Rockefeller was now developing exalted faith in his own judgment. Like all revolutionaries, he saw himself as an instrument of higher purpose, endowed with a visionary faith. He knew that his actions would at first be resisted and misunderstood by the myopic crowd, but he believed that the force and truth of his ideas would triumph in the end.

When the petroleum producers embargoed the sale of crude oil to members of the SIC, Rockefeller professed a lack of concern. Yet this impromptu coalition, welded together by the overwhelming threat, responded with impressive unity, creating sixteen districts, each with a separate committee, that blocked oil sales to the cabal. By moonlight, the producers patrolled Oil Creek on horseback to guard against any clandestine drilling that would subvert their cause. Ida Tarbell recalled how her father had proudly spurned a lucrative contract to ship oil to the conspirators for a tempting $4.50 a barrel. In the meantime, the producers busied themselves on the legislative front, lobbying in Harrisburg to annul the SIC charter and submitting to the U.S. Congress a scroll-like, ninety-three-foot petition, demanding an industrywide investigation. While Rockefeller dodged the press, producers handed out thirty thousand copies of a polemical tract about the SIC so that "enemies of freedom of trade may be known and shunned by the honest men."[46]

The uproar didn't weaken Rockefeller's resolve, yet for all his bravado the boycott exacted a grave toll on his operations. Ninety percent of his employees had to be temporarily laid off, leaving a skeletal staff at his refineries. In letters to Cettie in March 1872, he tried to reconcile his actions with his conscience as he became the bugbear of Oil Creek. As he wrote from New York on March 15,

> It is easy to write newspaper articles but we have other business. We will do right and not be troubled about what the papers say. By and by when all are through possibly we may briefly respond (though it is not our policy) and leave future events in the business to demonstrate our intentions and plans were just & warranted—I want to act perfectly conscientiously and fearlessly in the matter and feel confident of good results. . . . I am hopeful [we] can get at least a good fraction of the N.Y. Refiners to join at an early day.[47]

Further, he wrote on March 21, "I am still persevering and hopeful, remember *our* side have not yet been in the papers. We know a *few* things the people generally may not, at all events we know our own intentions, and they are *right* and *only so*—but please say *nothing* only you know your husband will stand by and *stick* to the right."[48]

The conspirators committed a major strategic gaffe by omitting the New York refiners, who therefore sided with the Oil Creek refiners to pressure the railroads. To head their liaison committee, the New York refiners appointed a suave thirty-two-year-old named Henry H. Rogers, who had the flashing eyes and confident air of a young buccaneer. When Rogers met Tom Scott at a Philadelphia hotel on March 18, the railroad chief struck a conciliatory note, admitting that the SIC contract was unfair and offering a similar deal to the excluded New York and Pennsylvania refiners. While Scott was backpedaling and angling for peace, Rockefeller remained uncompromising, telling his wife on

March 22, "I assure you it is not my pleasure to remain all this time but a stern sense of duty to this cause—I haven't any idea giving up ship or letting go my hold."[49]

On March 25, the Rogers group held a climactic meeting with wavering railroad officials at the Erie Railroad's offices in the ornate Grand Opera House in New York. While they conferred, an edgy Rockefeller and Peter Watson tapped at the door and asked to enter. While Watson was admitted, Rockefeller was barred and so anxiously paced the corridor. For the first time, Rockefeller appeared in *The New York Times*—his name was misspelled as "Rockafellow"— with the reporter noting that, excluded from the talks, Rockefeller had finally gone off looking "pretty blue."[50] The meeting dealt a blow to Rockefeller and Watson, for the railroads agreed to abrogate the SIC contract, end rebates and drawbacks, and institute uniform rates for all shippers. The serpent had been killed in the egg.

Far sooner than Rockefeller, the railroads had foreseen the political reaction and inevitable defeat. In this era before railroad regulation and antitrust legislation, the SIC contract didn't violate any obvious laws, only a universal sense of fair play. In early April, the Pennsylvania legislature canceled the SIC charter, while a congressional committee, a month later, branded the scheme the "most gigantic and daring conspiracy" ever to confront a free nation.[51] On April 8, 1872, Rockefeller capitulated and wired the oil producers that all contracts between the SIC and the railroads were now void. In his own defense, he added: "I state unqualifiedly that reports circulated in the Oil Region and elsewhere, that this company, or any member of it, threatened to depress oil, are false."[52] On this last count, Rockefeller was probably sincere, for what he envisioned was less a conspiracy against producers than against consumers, a united effort to ensure steady prices and adequate returns on investment. Till the very end, he saw the producers' outrage against him as shot through with envy and hypocrisy. "The producers . . . held to the view that rebates were wrong unless the rebates were given to them."[53]

=

It always mystified Rockefeller that people made such a fuss about a phantom company. "There never was a shipment made or a rebate or drawback collected under the South Improvement plan."[54] Though only a latent threat, the scheme acquired lasting infamy for two reasons. First, Rockefeller's fiercest critics regarded it as a dress rehearsal for the grand pageant, the place where he first revealed his master plan, to be implemented in a thousand secret, disguised, and indirect ways. The second reason for all the later attention was that during the brief interval while the SIC was alive, Rockefeller engineered his most important coup: the swift, relentless consolidation of Cleveland's refineries, which gave him irresistible momentum. The threat of the SIC, critics alleged, was the invisible club that he had waved over Cleveland refiners, forcing them to submit to his domination. Between February 17 and March 28, 1872—between the first rumors of the SIC and the time it was scuttled—Rockefeller swallowed up twenty-two of his twenty-six Cleveland competitors. During one forty-eight-hour period alone in early March, he bought six refineries. As one refiner, John H. Alexander, recalled:

> There was a pressure brought to bear upon my mind, and upon almost all citizens of Cleveland engaged in the oil business, to the effect that unless we went into the South Improvement Company we were virtually killed as refiners; that if we did not sell out we should be crushed out. . . . It was said that they had a contract with railroads by which they could run us into the ground if they pleased.[55]

Since petroleum output promised to shatter records in 1872 and keep prices depressed, Rockefeller increasingly sought to own as large a portion of the industry as possible and didn't think he could afford to wait for the marketplace to prune out weak refiners by attrition. "We had to do it in self-defense," he said of the Cleveland takeovers. "The oil business was in confusion and daily growing worse."[56]

Another businessman might have started with small, vulnerable firms, building on easy victories, but Rockefeller started at the top, believing that if he could crack his strongest competitor first, it would have a tremendous psychological impact. His major rival was Clark, Payne and Company, and conquering it would give Rockefeller special satisfaction, since he had already tangled with one partner, James Clark, early in his career and now coveted his Star Works refinery. The firm also had social cachet in Cleveland: Colonel Oliver H. Payne—a Yale graduate, honored Civil War colonel, and son of politician Henry B. Payne—was extremely wealthy, lived in a Euclid Avenue mansion, and was descended from one of Cleveland's founding families. (Commodore Matthew Perry, who opened Japan to commerce in 1854, came from a collateral branch of the family.) With an erect, military bearing and coolly formal manner, many people found the young bachelor pompous—Flagler dubbed him the "kin of God"—but Rockefeller always paid tribute to Payne as a stalwart and capable ally.[57]

One afternoon in December 1871, Rockefeller asked Payne, an old high-school friend, to meet in the parlor of a downtown Cleveland bank, where Rockefeller outlined his plan for a vast, efficient industry under Standard Oil control. Telling Payne about the impending capital increase at Standard Oil, he asked point-blank: "If we can agree upon values and terms do you want to come in?"[58] As Clark, Payne's largest shareholder, Colonel Payne gave his qualified approval, but he first wanted to examine Rockefeller's books before selling his company. That afternoon, when he surveyed Standard Oil's ledgers, he was thunderstruck by the profits. Whether he was impressed by the railroad rebates or operating efficiencies is unclear, but he eagerly told Rockefeller, "Let us get the appraisers in and see what the plant is worth."[59] After conferring with his partners, Payne consented to a $400,000 price for his refinery. Rockefeller knew that he was overpaying but couldn't resist a deal that would certify his position as the world's largest oil refiner at age thirty-one. Though Rockefeller stipulated that James Clark wasn't welcome at Standard Oil, he wanted to enlist Payne's services, and the latter soon shared a private office with Rockefeller and Flagler. James Clark later told Ida Tarbell that he sold out only from fear of the SIC contract. As Tarbell's assistant reported, "He stated positively that Clark, Payne & Co. did *not* sell out before the organization of the SIC, and that it *never* considered selling out to the Standard before the SIC was formed."[60]

According to later lawsuits, whenever Rockefeller suggested that rivals sell out to him, the SIC formed the burden of his appeal. Some old Cleveland refiners told Ida Tarbell that his menacing pitch ran as follows:

> You see, this scheme is bound to work. It means an absolute control by us of the oil business. There is no chance for anyone outside. But we are going to give everybody a chance to come in. You are to turn over your refinery to my appraisers, and I will give you Standard Oil Company stock or cash, as you prefer, for the value we put upon it. I advise you to take the stock. It will be for your good.[61]

Stung by charges that he had used coercion, Rockefeller retorted that he had been unfailingly friendly and courteous and never mentioned the SIC in negotiations. Strictly speaking, this was probably true, yet the timing of his twenty-two takeovers suggests strongly that the SIC was a prime factor and that the deals were done amid an atmosphere of well-timed intimidation. Several rivals alleged that Rockefeller orchestrated a chorus of terrifying rumors about his secret pact with the railroads. Even without direct threats, he knew his opponents' imaginations would embellish these stories and conjure up a conspiracy of unfathomable scope. "In 1872 reports were purposely circulated to the effect that the Standard Oil Company had entered into agreement with the railroads, whereby no outside refiner could bring crude oil to Cleveland and manufacture it without a loss," rival refiner J. W. Fawcett of Fawcett and Critchley told Ida Tarbell in the early 1900s.[62] "The refiners became prematurely alarmed at the reports of destructive competition and inability to secure crude oil, and they 'fell over each other' in their haste to sell out. Had they refused to be coerced, and had they held together, there never would have been a Standard Oil Company."[63] When Fawcett received word that he should see the

Standard people and dispose of his refinery, he was told "that they had the railroads in a position where they would control the rates, that Fawcett and Critchley would *not* ever ship *any* oil."[64] Like many vanquished refiners, Fawcett surrendered his independence and went to work for Rockefeller, but he never quite overcame his anger at what he perceived as clever manipulation.

Rockefeller dismissed as "an absolute lie" the idea that he had stampeded the Cleveland refiners and added that the vast majority of those refiners "were already crushed by the competition which had been steadily increasing up to this time" and were staring at ruin. For these concerns, he insisted, the opportunity to sell to Standard Oil and receive stock instead "was a godsend to them all."[65] Had Standard Oil not existed, he asserted, these refiners would simply have gone bust—which would have been true for many of them. Even Fawcett conceded that "at that time some of the refineries were not making money, and they were the first to 'run to cover' and sell out. Eventually all sold out."[66]

Several Cleveland refiners claimed that Rockefeller had directly threatened them. John H. Heisel of Bishop and Heisel remembered telling Rockefeller that he wasn't afraid of him, to which Rockefeller supposedly replied, "You may not be afraid to have your hand cut off, but your body will suffer."[67] Yet it seems unlikely that Rockefeller menaced refiners quite so blatantly, for it didn't serve his purpose. Gifted with persuasive powers, he preferred to talk earnestly to his rivals, tapping them on the knee or gesturing with his hands, reasoning with them in richly cadenced, evangelical tones. As one refiner said of Rockefeller, "He knew that he and his associates had a better knowledge of the business and a better command of the business than anyone else. You never saw anyone so confident as he was."[68] He liked to make Standard Oil sound like a philanthropic agency or an angel of mercy, come to succor downtrodden refiners. "We will take your burdens," he remembered telling his weaker brethren in 1872. "We will utilize your ability; we will give you representation; we will unite together and build a substantial structure on the basis of cooperation."[69] Similarly, he said, "We here at Cleveland are at a disadvantage. Something should be done for our mutual protection. We think this plan of ours is a good scheme. Think it over. We would be glad to consider it with you if you are so inclined."[70] Sure of his mission, Rockefeller castigated those who resisted Standard Oil as foolish and shortsighted. "Take Standard Oil stock," he urged them, "and your family will never know want."[71]

If these refiners had surrendered faith in oil's future, as Rockefeller insisted, then why did they so bitterly resent him after he bought them out? Why didn't they regard him as their savior, as he preferred to depict himself? The answer lies partly in the way their plants were appraised. Since so many refiners were losing money, Rockefeller paid them a pittance, typically a quarter of their original construction costs, or what the plants might have fetched if auctioned off for scrap; he paid little or nothing for goodwill—that is, the intangible value in a thriving business, such as its reputation or client list. If this was hard policy, it wasn't necessarily unscrupulous. "No, the good will of a business which is losing money is not worth much," said Rockefeller.[72] "If there isn't work for an oil refinery to do, it has less value than ships or railroad property, which can be used on other lines."[73] One must also remember that Rockefeller was in the anomalous position of taking over many plants not to operate them but to shut them down and eliminate excess capacity. He ridiculed many of the refineries he bought as "old junk, fit only for the scrap heap."[74] Rockefeller probably paid a fair price for many antiquated plants, but it was a bitter pill for the ruined owners to swallow. And he operated in a climate of fear that gave his rivals little choice in the matter.

Whether by chance or design, Rockefeller's 1872 business papers have vanished, and we aren't privy to his thoughts during these crucial negotiations. But in later years, he was a fair-minded bargainer who often paid too much for properties that served a strategic purpose. Indeed, his papers are chock-full of lamentations about how he overpaid for properties. When it came to mergers, he didn't fight for the last dollar and tried to conclude matters cordially. Since he aimed to convert competitors into members of his cartel and often retained the original owners, he preferred not to resort to naked intimidation. As Rockefeller said, he and his colleagues weren't "so short-sighted as to antagonize these very men whom they were eager to have come into a close and profitable relationship with them."[75] He wasn't a sadistic man, but he had a hard, unyielding sense of purpose that brooked no opposition. If Rockefeller expressed elation, it was behind closed doors. According to one legend, after taking over a new refinery, he would rush into the office, perform a little dance, and shout joyously to Sam Andrews, "We've got another refinery, Sam. One more in the fold!"[76]

During the Cleveland Massacre, Rockefeller savored a feeling of sweet revenge against some of the older men who had patronized him when he started in business. This was especially true of his negotiations with Alexander, Scofield and Company, whose partners included his original boss, Isaac L. Hewitt. After Hewitt came to Rockefeller's Euclid Avenue home to plead for mercy, they strolled down Euclid Avenue together, and Rockefeller told him his firm would never survive if it didn't sell out to Standard Oil. He made a cryptic statement to Hewitt that entered into Rockefeller folklore: "I have ways of making money you know nothing about."[77] Disconcerted by such assertions, Hewitt and his partners finally sold out for $65,000, though they believed their business was worth $150,000. Rockefeller felt merciful toward Hewitt and loaned him money to buy Standard stock, but he despised Hewitt's partner, John H. Alexander, who still viewed him, he thought, as Hewitt's former clerk. As Rockefeller put it, "How could this conceited Englishman ever conceive it possible that a young man who had been a bookkeeper, and especially at a time when he had been employed in an oil refinery, be qualified to lead in a movement of this kind?"[78]

Rockefeller's most controversial purchase—and one that resulted in a bitter lawsuit—was the takeover of Hanna, Baslington and Company. When Robert Hanna, the uncle of Mark Hanna, was summoned to Standard Oil's offices, he bluntly told Rockefeller that he wouldn't sell. In response, Rockefeller sighed and wearily shrugged his shoulders, as if expressing regret that this benighted sinner hadn't seen the light. "You will stand alone," he warned Hanna. "Your firm can never make any more money in Cleveland. No use trying to do business in competition with the Standard Oil Company. If you do it will end in your being wiped out."[79] What seemed a barefaced threat to Hanna was later interpreted by Rockefeller as a timely warning and sincere advice.

Irate over the rebates enjoyed by Standard Oil, Hanna pleaded with executives of the Lake Shore Railroad to grant his refinery equal treatment. They defended Standard Oil's freight rates as the privilege due to a big bulk shipper and promised to give Hanna the same rates if he delivered the same volume of oil— which he couldn't. The railroads employed this as an all-purpose defensive tactic, since nobody could ever match Standard Oil's voluminous shipments. In the end, Hanna accepted $45,000 for a refinery that he believed was worth $75,000.

It is interesting to note that Rockefeller perjured himself in an affidavit he submitted for the lawsuit brought jointly by William S. Scofield and Hanna, Baslington. Not only did he state that "but few persons who were stockholders in the Standard Oil Co. of Cleveland, Ohio were subscribers to stock in the South Improvement Company," but he added that "P. H. Watson, Pres. of the South Improvement Co. . . . was not a stockholder in nor was he in any way connected with the Standard Oil Company."[80] As mentioned, Standard Oil executives controlled almost 50 percent of the SIC shares and issued five hundred shares of Standard to Watson sub rosa in the January 1872 recapitalization. Although Rockefeller professed that he never lied under oath, the claim doesn't bear up under close examination.

The oil wars of 1872 turned Cleveland society upside down. Many who had made easy fortunes in oil refining and built splendid mansions on Euclid Avenue found themselves bankrupt and forced to sell. Whether it was Rockefeller or the slumping oil market that forced them to sell their refineries at distress-sale prices, they chose to see Rockefeller as the author of their woes. It is likely that in many cases the marketplace would eventually have closed their unprofitable firms, but Rockefeller certainly speeded up the winnowing. Though several independent refiners held on for a few years, in most cases this merely postponed the day of reckoning. Ella Grant Wilson, a social chronicler of nineteenth-century Cleveland, recalled how her father, a partner in the refinery of Grant, Foote and Company, had befriended Rockefeller in various Baptist causes but refused to join Standard Oil, convinced it would fail. When it became impossible to compete with this leviathan, his refinery went bankrupt, and he surrendered his life savings. "Father went almost insane over this terrible upset to his business. He walked the house night and day. . . . [He] left his church and never entered a church afterward. His whole life was embittered by this experience."[81] With so many losers in the struggle—and one shrewd, gigantic winner—it comes as no surprise to learn that John D. Rockefeller had made his first group of implacable enemies.

=

Nowadays, most people imagine that American businessmen have always favored free competition, at least in the abstract. But in the industrial boom after the Civil War, the most significant revolt against free-market capitalism came not from reformers or zealous ideologues but from businessmen who couldn't control the maddening fluctuations in the marketplace. In an unregulated economy, they had to improvise the rules of the game as they went along. Pestered by overproduction in the early oil industry, Rockefeller tirelessly mocked those "academic enthusiasts" and "sentimentalists" who expected business to conform to their tidy competitive models. Like some of his contemporaries, he didn't see how they could build vast, enduring industries in a volatile economy disrupted by recessions, deflation, and explosive boom-and-bust cycles, and he decided to subjugate markets instead of responding endlessly to their changing price signals. Thus, Rockefeller and other industrial captains conspired to kill competitive capitalism in favor of a new monopoly capitalism.

Economic historians often cite the exuberance of Gilded Age businessmen, their red-blooded faith in America's future, without noting the constant uncertainty that lurked underneath. As Rockefeller's story shows, many of the age's most controversial business practices were forged in a desperate spirit of self-preservation. "It was forced upon us," Rockefeller said of Standard Oil's genesis. "We had to do it in self-defence. The oil business was in confusion and daily growing worse. Someone had to make a stand." Though he foresaw the triumph of cooperation, its far-ranging ramifications weren't yet clear to him. "This movement was the origin of the whole system of economic administration. It has revolutionized the way of doing business all over the world. The time was ripe for it. It had to come, though all we saw at the moment was the need to save ourselves from wasteful conditions." Then he added, as if enunciating his economic credo: "The day of combination is here to stay. Individualism has gone, never to return"[82]

Of course, companies had colluded to restrain the open play of market forces before. In Europe, guilds and state monopolies were of ancient provenance, and even Adam Smith had noted the alacrity with which businessmen hatched conspiracies against consumers. In 1872, Standard Oil was just one of many companies whose leaders had daydreams of controlling prices and production throughout their industry. When the SIC scheme surfaced, one newspaper observed, "This great monopoly is one of many now forming to control the commercial products of this great nation," and it referred to the western grain and livestock trades as analogous situations.[83] As his own inspiration, Rockefeller cited Western Union, then busily buying up small telegraph lines, and the New York Central Railroad, which had consolidated its trunk line from the Atlantic seaboard to Chicago. During the 1870s, pools and rings flourished among salt, rope, and whiskey concerns.

It was only fitting that someone with Rockefeller's personality and values should have questioned the canons of free-for-all capitalism. If the most creative and dynamic of economic systems, capitalism can also seem wasteful and inefficient to those who endure its rocky transitions and violent dislocations. By bringing forth superior methods, capitalism renders existing skills and equipment outmoded and thus fosters unceasing turmoil and change. Such a mutable system violated Rockefeller's need for stability, order, and predictability. Indeed, the sober, thrifty Puritan identified by Max Weber as the prototypical capitalist was almost certain to feel distressed by this unstable economy, which forced him to steer his orderly business through a maelstrom of incessant change.

From the three-year interview he gave privately to William O. Inglis in the late 1910s, it is clear that Rockefeller brooded for many years on a theoretical defense of monopoly. His comments are fragmentary and do not cohere into a full-blown system, yet they show that he gave the subject a great deal of intelligent thought, much more than one might have expected. He knew that he had latched on to a mighty new principle, and arose as the prophet of a new dispensation in economic history. As he said, "It was the battle of the new idea of cooperation against competition, and perhaps in no department of business was there a greater necessity for this cooperation than in the oil business."[84]

Rockefeller's logic deserves some scrutiny. If, as he asserted, Standard Oil was the efficient, low-cost producer in Cleveland, why didn't he just sit back and wait for competitors to go bankrupt? Why did he resort to the tremendous expense of taking over rivals and dismembering their refineries to slash capacity? According to the standard textbook models of competition, as oil prices fell below production costs, refiners should have retrenched and padlocked plants. But the oil market didn't correct itself in this manner because refiners carried heavy bank debt and other fixed costs, and they discovered that, by operating at a loss, they could still service some debt. Obviously, they couldn't lose money indefinitely, but as they soldiered on to postpone bankruptcy, their output dragged oil prices down to unprofitable levels for everybody.

Hence, a perverse effect of the invisible hand: Each refiner, pursuing his own self-interest, generated collective misery. As Rockefeller phrased it, "Every man assumed to struggle hard to get all of the business . . . even though in so doing he brought to himself and the competitors in the business nothing but disaster."[85] In a day of primitive accounting systems, many refiners had only the haziest notion of their profitability or lack thereof. As Rockefeller noted, "oftentimes the most difficult competition comes, not from the strong, the intelligent, the conservative competitor, but from the man who is holding on by the eyelids and is ignorant of his costs, and anyway he's got to keep running or bust!"[86]

What made an expeditious shutdown of outmoded rivals vital to Rockefeller was that he had borrowed heavily to build gigantic plants so that he could drastically slash his unit costs. Even his first partner, Maurice Clark, remembered that "the volume of trade was what he always regarded as of paramount importance."[87] Early on, Rockefeller realized that in the capital-intensive refining business, sheer size mattered greatly because it translated into economies of scale. Once, describing the "foundation principle" of Standard Oil, he said it was the "theory of the originators . . . that the larger the volume the better the opportunities for the economies, and consequently the better the opportunities for giving the public a cheaper product without . . . the dreadful competition of the late '60's ruining the business."[88] During his career, Rockefeller cut the unit costs of refined oil almost in half, and he never deviated from this gospel of industrial efficiency.

To service the outsize debt that made this possible, Rockefeller needed to smooth out the inordinate price fluctuations that made the oil business so hazardous. Realizing that the higher the economic peaks the deeper the subsequent troughs, Rockefeller feared booms no less than busts. "Neither the depressions nor the advances were profitable. The depressions gave occasion to the advances; so that the conditions of the depressions had to be offset by the advances. I concede that so far as the oil industry was concerned we were successful in preventing to an extent these extremes so trying and unprofitable."[89] Rockefeller preferred moderate growth purely as a matter of self-interest. His goal was to forestall potential competitors through low prices and thus minimize risk and chance disruptions. By this approach, Rockefeller believed, he could beneficently spare Standard Oil employees the plight of other industrial workers who "find themselves in each period of ten or fifteen years in destitute circumstances, with bankrupt employers, owing to the foolish and universal competitive methods accompanying the excessive production of any and all products."[90]

At times, when he railed against cutthroat competition and the vagaries of the business cycle, Rockefeller sounded more like Karl Marx than our classical image of the capitalist. Like the Marxists, he believed that the competitive free-for-all eventually gave way to monopoly and that large industrial-planning units were the most sensible way to manage an economy. But while Rockefeller had faith in such private monopolies, the Marxists saw them as merely halfway houses on the road to socialism.

The most tantalizing question in Rockefeller's story—and one that allows no final answer—is whether Standard Oil stimulated or retarded the oil industry's growth. Rockefeller's foremost academic supporter, Allan Nevins, believed that after the Civil War it was so cheap and easy to enter oil refining that only a monopoly could have curbed surplus capacity and brought order to the industry. Without Standard Oil, he argued, the business would have fragmented into small, antiquated units, and oil gluts, with their accompanying low prices, would have persisted indefinitely. Rockefeller believed that only a firm with the strength of Standard Oil could have attained the necessary economies of scale at that stage of the industry's development.

Long after Rockefeller had exited the industrial scene, various economists, while espousing the general superiority of competition, conceded the economic wisdom of trusts under certain conditions. The conservative, Austrian-born economist Joseph A. Schumpeter, for example, contended that monopolies might prove beneficial during depressions or in new, rapidly shifting industries. By replacing turmoil with stability, a monopoly "may make fortresses out of what otherwise might be centers of devastation" and "in the end produce not only steadier but also greater expansion of total output than could be secured by an entirely uncontrolled onward rush that cannot fail to be studded with catastrophes."[91] Schumpeter imagined that entrepreneurs wouldn't commit large sums to risky ventures if the future seemed cloudy and new competitors could easily spoil their plans. "On the one hand, largest-scale plans could in many cases not materialize at all if it were not known from the outset that competition will be discouraged by heavy capital requirements or lack of experience, or that means are available to discourage or checkmate it so as to gain the time and space for further developments."[92] As we shall see, Rockefeller keenly felt a need to freeze the industry's size, stymie new entrants, and create an island of stability in which expansion and innovation could then occur unimpeded.

When Rockefeller took over competing refiners, he retained plants with up-to-date facilities and shuttered obsolete ones. It would have been impossible to shrink the industry and steady prices, however, if those who sold their outmoded plants took the money only to open new refineries. Unencumbered by antitrust laws, Rockefeller forced these refiners to sign restrictive contracts that prohibited them from sneaking back into the oil business. Rockefeller regarded these agreements—which would today be outlawed as in restraint of trade—as sacred obligations. For the most part, they were faithfully honored, though on several occasions Rockefeller hauled violators into court.

For all the uproar about Rockefeller's predatory tactics, many refiners continued to defy him, and dozens of small independents survived outside of Standard Oil. Rockefeller lured many of them into his tent with an intermediate step that he called "running arrangements," in which Standard Oil guaranteed them a certain level of profits if they accepted a ceiling on their output. This allowed Standard Oil to restrict the output of rivals and made Rockefeller, a hundred years before the Organization of Petroleum Exporting Countries (OPEC), the chief administrator of a sweeping oil cartel. Much like OPEC leaders, Rockefeller had to arbitrate demands for increased quotas among restive members and cope with the immemorial problem of cartels: how to prevent cheaters. Whenever refiners with running arrangements exceeded their assigned allotment, Standard Oil, as the swing producer, curtailed its own output to maintain prices—exactly the dilemma faced by Saudi Arabia as the world's largest oil exporter in the 1970s. This situation steeled Rockefeller in his determination to own his competitors instead of just presiding over a confederation of perennially warring members.

Where Rockefeller differed most from his fellow moguls was that he wanted to be both rich *and* virtuous and claim divine sanction for his actions. Perhaps no other businessman in American history has felt so firmly on the side of the angels. Critics were quick to spy an oily sanctimony in this servant of God and Mammon and wonder why his religious beliefs didn't trammel his acquisitive nature. They converted him into a wily Machiavellian or a stock figure from a Balzac novel—the pious, cunning hypocrite who showily attends church on Sunday then spends the rest of the week trampling rivals underfoot. More generous critics argued that he simply led parallel lives, with a complete separation of his public and private selves. Rockefeller himself felt no such discontinuity and always insisted that his private and commercial activities should be judged by the same exacting standards. Many years later, William O. Inglis read to him John Milton's stern denunciation of King Charles I: "For his private virtues they are beside the question. If he oppress and extort all day, shall he be held blameless because he prayeth night and morn?" In response, Rockefeller exclaimed, "That's well put! And the oil men have got to stand the test of that."[93] Clearly, he felt that his business conduct could withstand the most rigorous scrutiny.

It is too glib to say that Rockefeller was a hypocrite who used his piety as a cloak for greed. The voice that reverberated in his ears was one of burning zeal, not low, devious cunning. He was a sincere if highly self-serving churchgoer and, however deluded, extremely devout. From an early age, he had learned both to use and to abuse religion, to interpret and to misinterpret Christian doctrine to suit his purposes. The church provided him with a stock of images and ideas that, instead of checking him, enabled him to proceed with a clear conscience. Religion validated his business misdeeds no less than his charitable bequests, buttressing his strongest impulses. If religion made him great, it also armed him with theological justification for his actions and may have blinded him to their brutal consequences.

To reiterate an earlier point, John D. regarded God as an ally, a sort of honorary shareholder of Standard Oil who had richly blessed his fortunes. Consider this impassioned outburst he made to a reporter:

> I believe the power to make money is a gift from God—just as are the instincts for art, music, literature, the doctor's talent, the nurse's, yours—to be developed and used to the best of our ability for the good of mankind. Having been endowed with the gift I possess, I believe it is my duty to make money and still more money, and to use the money I make for the good of my fellow man according to the dictates of my conscience.[94]

For Rockefeller, there was a perfect fusion of Christianity and capitalism and, given his extensive church involvement, it would have been odd if his career hadn't been saturated with his own version of evangelical Protestantism. Even the business of drilling and refining oil was wrapped for him in religious mystery. "The whole process seems a miracle," he once said. "What a blessing the oil has been to mankind!"[95] In pleading for his oil monopoly, Rockefeller always exhibited many qualities of the Baptist missionary. He needed to endow his aggressive business tactics with transcendent purpose and elevate his material designs into holy crusades. When faced with the squalid disorder of the oil business in the early 1870s, he converted Standard Oil, in his own mind, into the moral equivalent of the Baptist Church. His career as a trust king would be for him a Christian saga, a pilgrim's progress, where he was the exemplary man, rescuing sinful refiners from their errant ways.

What's most striking, both in the extensive Inglis interview and elsewhere, is that every time Rockefeller explained the rationale for Standard Oil, he resorted to patently religious imagery. "The Standard was an angel of mercy, reaching down from the sky, and saying, 'Get into the ark. Put in your old junk. We'll take all the risks!' "[96] He referred to Standard Oil as "the Moses who delivered them [the refiners] from their folly which had wrought such havoc in their fortunes."[97] Charged with destroying competition, Rockefeller was indignant: "I repeat again, it was not a process of destruction and waste; it was a process of upbuilding and conservation of all the interests . . . in our efforts most heroic, well meant—and I would almost say, reverently, Godlike—to pull this broken-down industry out of the Slough of Despond [for which] we are charged with criminal proceedings."[98] Far from being an outlaw band, Standard Oil had "rendered a missionary service to the whole world. Strong as this statement is, it is the Gospel truth."[99] Further, "Faith and work were the rocks upon which Standard Oil was built."[100] He credited Standard Oil with "the salvation of the oil business and making it a reputable pursuit instead of a disgraceful, gambling, mining scheme."[101] While he and his partners were "missionaries of light" and tried to treat weaker competitors with compassion, there were limits to their tolerance since they could not "stop the car of salvation in their great enterprise which meant so much to the consuming public the world over."[102] If his stewardship of Standard Oil exposed him to vitriolic persecution, it was exactly the martyrdom he expected.

Rockefeller has often been described as a social Darwinist who viewed the harsh struggle of capitalism as a salutary process that rewarded the industrious and punished the lazy. And it is true that he adamantly opposed any government program or private charity that sapped the frontier spirit of self-reliance. Yet Rockefeller could hold contradictory views on essential matters, and his philosophic justification of cooperation rested heavily upon a direct refutation of social Darwinism:

> The struggle for the survival of the fittest, in the sea and on the land the world over, as well as the law of supply and demand, were observed in all the ages past until the Standard Oil Company preached the doctrines of cooperation, and it did cooperate so successfully and so fairly that its most bitter opponents were won over to its views and made to realize that rational, sane, modern, progressive administration was necessary to success.[103]

Standard Oil was thus presented as the *antidote* to social Darwinism, a way to bring universal brotherhood to a fractious industry. Without Standard Oil, said Rockefeller, "there would have been the survival of the fittest—and we had proved ourselves to be the fittest, and we could have picked up the wrecks as the less fortunate brethren went down. This we did not do, but tried to call a halt and avert the impending disaster."[104] Standard Oil would be a cooperative commonwealth, open to refiners who renounced their selfish ways to join the faithful. It would be for Rockefeller a unique case of the strong showing mercy to their weaker brethren by inviting them to participate in a common effort to save the industry.

In a critical distinction, he viewed competitive capitalism—and not capitalism per se—as producing a vulgar materialism and rapacious business practices that dissolved the bonds of human brotherhood. In a state of ungoverned competition, selfish individuals tried to maximize their profits and thereby impoverished the entire industry. What the American economy needed instead were new cooperative forms (trusts, pools, monopolies) that would restrain grasping individuals for the general good. Rockefeller thus tried to reconcile trusts with Christianity, claiming that cooperation would end the egotism and materialism abhorrent to Christian values. It was an ingenious rationalization. While religion did not lead him to the concept of trusts, it did enable him to invest his vision of cooperation with a powerful moral imperative.

From the outset, Standard Oil was permeated by an us-versus-them attitude that emanated from the top. At moments, Rockefeller made it sound as if he and his colleagues were a band of early Christians, misunderstood by the pagans. In this moralistic frame of mind, he was bound to see his opponents as benighted, misguided people, "governed by their narrow jealousies and unwarranted prejudices" and unaware that the old gods were now obsolete.[105] Rockefeller developed an inverted worldview, accusing his critics of exactly the same sins of which they accused him. Far from seeing himself as a rascal or bully, the Standard Oil chieftain presented himself as a respectable gentleman who attempted in vain to reason with wicked independents. In his correspondence, Rockefeller betrayed a characteristic manner of referring to his rivals: They were selfish people forever stirring up trouble or creating annoyances, like so many mischievous children who needed a good stiff spanking from father. Never conceding any legitimacy to dissent, Rockefeller denigrated his critics as blackmailers, sharpsters, and crooks. He was now dangerously impervious to criticism.

Charles Pratt, Sr., Rockefeller's colleague and frequent adversary.
(Courtesy of the Rockefeller Archive Center)

CHAPTER 9

The New Monarch

resh from the South Improvement Company brouhaha and the bruising struggle over the Cleveland refineries, Rockefeller didn't pause to catch breath. Anybody else might have consolidated his gains and proceeded cautiously, but Rockefeller, a man in a hurry, launched a new offensive instead. The SIC contretemps had stranded him in an untenable spot. Since Cleveland refiners paid the same freight rates as other refining centers, they labored under a huge competitive handicap, paying fifty cents a barrel just to ship crude oil to Cleveland before sending on the refined oil to New York; by contrast, a Titusville refiner shipped straight to the seaboard. In April 1872, Henry Flagler again extracted concessions from the Lake Shore Railroad but not enough to appease Rockefeller. Because the Pittsburgh refiners shared a similar cost disadvantage, Rockefeller decided to make common cause with them and press the railroads for new discounts.

With unmitigated cheek, Rockefeller decided that if the Oil Regions couldn't tolerate a small, secret consortium such as the SIC, he would confront them with a giant public consortium of refiners. In mid-May 1872—scarcely more than a month after the railroads scrapped the SIC—Rockefeller and Flagler journeyed to Pittsburgh to meet with the city's three foremost refiners, William G. Warden, William Frew, and O. T. Waring. The group then went by train to Titusville, bearing a plan for a new National Refiners' Association, which would be popularly dubbed the Pittsburgh Plan. This venture envisioned a new refiners' cartel, headed by a central board that would negotiate advantageous terms with the railroads and maintain prices by assigning refining quotas to members. Eschewing subterfuge, the confederation was thrown open to all refiners, but with John D. Rockefeller serving as president.

Before long, Rockefeller was so detested in the Oil Regions that he ceased to visit and retreated to the status of a dim, shadowy legend; no authenticated photo shows him in the rural backwater to which he owed his fortune. Though the National Refiners' Association theoretically embraced all comers, the Titusville refiners saw the group as the old SIC in disguise, and local newspapers admonished oilmen to beware of the slippery, smooth-talking men from Cleveland. On the Titusville streets, Rockefeller was greeted with the somber respect accorded a new monarch. As always, he presented a cordial façade that disarmed people and in one office after another reassured wary refiners, "You misunderstand our intention. It is to save the business, not to destroy it that we are come."[1] At two turbulent public meetings, Flagler was hooted and jeered while Rockefeller stared impassively at the audience. One refiner left an indelible portrait of Rockefeller's aloof, cryptic manner at a private meeting:

> One day several of us met at the office of one of the refiners, who, I felt pretty sure, was being persuaded to go into the scheme which they were talking up. Everybody talked except Mr. Rockefeller. He sat in a rocking chair, softly swinging back and forth, his hands over his face. I got pretty excited when I saw how those South Improvement men were pulling the wool over our men's eyes, and making them believe we were all going to the dogs if there wasn't an immediate combination to put up the price of refined and prevent new people coming into the business, and I made a speech which, I guess, was pretty warlike. Well, right in the middle of it John Rockefeller stopped rocking and took down his hands and looked at me. You never saw such eyes. He took me all in, saw just how much fight he could expect from me, and I knew it, and then up went his hands and back and forth went his chair.[2]

At a second big public meeting, the Pittsburgh Plan was defeated resoundingly by local refiners, yet Rockefeller still gained ground, having enlisted influential local defectors, especially his erstwhile foe, young John D. Archbold. During the following months, in a divide-and-conquer policy, Rockefeller tried to isolate the Oil Creek refiners by successfully recruiting into his Pittsburgh Plan refiners from the other major centers.

But before long, this cartel was bedeviled by cheaters exceeding their quotas. It also grappled with what economists call the "free rider" problem—that is, opportunistic refiners stayed outside the plan and enjoyed the higher prices it produced without being bound by its production limits. As Rockefeller later said in a comparable situation, "These men who claimed that they had been 'crushed' and 'ruined' by the Standard Oil Company were existing under its shelter and protection."[3] And he was besieged by problems closer to home.

After Standard Oil bought decrepit old refineries in Cleveland to cut back on capacity, many sellers violated their covenants and started up new plants with improved equipment. They were drawn back, Rockefeller argued, only because he had markedly improved conditions and boosted prices. To complicate matters, new refiners now entered the business expressly to blackmail him into buying them out.

In the end, frustrated by rampant cheating and freeloaders, Rockefeller gathered refiners in Saratoga Springs, New York, on June 24, 1873, and dissolved the short-lived Pittsburgh Plan. He was momentarily disheartened by this failure, which again confirmed his preference for outright fusion rather than an unwieldy federation of firms. "There are some people whom the Lord Almighty cannot save," he later said wearily of the Oil Creek refiners. "They don't want to be saved. They want to go on and serve the devil and keep on in their wicked ways."[4]

In her influential polemic, Ida Tarbell evoked a paradise of free, independent producers in western Pennsylvania, "ruddy and joyous" men, enamored of competition, who were snuffed out by the sinister Standard Oil. In her morality play, Rockefeller was the venomous toad in this garden of earthly delights. In fact, the producers didn't respond to Rockefeller by advocating freer competition but by forming their own counterconspiracy. In the summer of 1872, under the aegis of the Petroleum Producers' Association, they approved a moratorium on new drilling to steady prices and briefly called for a complete halt to production. The producers terrorized each other, meting out nocturnal punishment to noncooperators by setting their wells ablaze or smashing their pumping engines with sledgehammers. The producing end of the industry was populated by thousands of freebooting, high-spirited speculators who were far harder to organize than the more sober refiners, concentrated in a few urban centers—something that gave Rockefeller a decided edge.

So long as he could maintain ample spreads between crude and refined prices, Rockefeller blessed the producers' efforts to impose higher prices and control output. It was a common misconception along Oil Creek—and one that fed anti-Rockefeller demonology—that he was trying to drive drillers to the wall to keep prices low. In reality, he was fully prepared to deal with a strong producers' cartel so long as they capped production. On December 19, 1872, Rockefeller met with producers at the Fifth Avenue Hotel in New York and signed the so-called Treaty of Titusville. Under this agreement, the refiners' association pledged to buy oil from the producers' association at five dollars a barrel—nearly *twice* the spot market rate—in exchange for tightly enforced production limits. The agreement crumbled not because of Rockefeller but because producers couldn't enforce discipline in their ranks. Instead of throttling the oil flow, they scrambled to pump more, with wholesale cheating driving the price as low as two dollars a barrel on the crude-oil market. Many small drillers outside the producers' association took advantage of the pact to undersell their bigger competitors.

This behavior ratified Rockefeller's low opinion of the producers as dissolute, unreliable men who couldn't contain a "wild and uncontrollable element" that "would sneak out at midnight and start the pumps going so that the oil might flow before the songs of the birds were heard."[5] With the the oil industry drowning in another glut, Rockefeller terminated the agreement in January 1873, chiding the recalcitrant producers: "You have not kept your part of the contract—you have not limited the supply of oil—there is more being pumped today then ever before in the history of the region."[6] While uncontrollable drilling was to blame, the producers found it easier to scapegoat Standard Oil. After the agreement fell apart, the disorganized producers lost all incentive to curtail production, feeding another downward spiral in oil prices.

By 1873, Standard Oil was shipping about a million barrels of refined oil per year and earning about a dollar a barrel, yet the business remained on an unsure footing. Rockefeller had clarified one thing in his own mind, however: Voluntary associations couldn't move with the speed, unity, and efficiency he wanted. "We proved that the producers' and refiners' associations were ropes of sand," he said.[7] He was now through with ineffectual alliances and ready to bring the industry to heel under Standard Oil control. "The idea was mine. The idea was persisted in, too, in spite of the opposition of some who became fainthearted at the magnitude of the undertaking, as it constantly assumed larger proportions."[8] By early 1873, he had crossed his own Rubicon and never looked back. Once embarked on a course of action, he wasn't a man to be hobbled by doubts.

In 1873, the mad dash for riches that followed the Civil War ended in a prolonged slump that ground on for six interminable years. On Black Thursday—September 18, 1873—the august banking house of Jay Cooke and Company failed because of problems in financing the Northern Pacific Railway. This event ignited a panic, leading to a stock-exchange shutdown, a string of bank failures, and widespread railroad bankruptcies. During the next few years, deflated by massive unemployment, daily wages plunged 25 percent, exposing many Americans to the horror of downward mobility. The six lean years accelerated the process of consolidation that had gathered force in many economic sectors.

This depression especially exacerbated the problems of the oil industry. Soon after Black Thursday, crude prices touched a shocking low of eighty cents a barrel; within a year, prices had tumbled to forty-eight cents—cheaper than the cost of hauling water in some towns. Just as Carnegie expanded his steel operations after the 1873 panic, so Rockefeller saw the slump as a chance to translate his master blueprint into reality. To capitalize on rival companies selling at distress-sale prices, he slashed Standard Oil's dividend to increase its cash reserves. Standard Oil weathered the six-year depression magnificently, a fact Rockefeller attributed to its conservative financial policy and unparalleled access to bank credit and investor cash.

The oil-refining industry staggered under so much surplus capacity that even Standard Oil, comprising a quarter of the industry, operated only two of its six main Cleveland plants. For all that, it managed to post such creditable profits that it sometimes wooed competitors simply by giving them a privileged peek at its books. Rockefeller was acquiring unstoppable momentum and, having subdued Cleveland, he soon began his march from city to city in an unrelenting campaign of national consolidation.

As his operations grew, Rockefeller made a fetish of secrecy, flavored with paranoia, a legacy of his self-conscious boyhood. One day, he saw an office employee talking to a stranger and later inquired after the man's identity. Although the subordinate said the man was a friend, Rockefeller lectured him, "Well, be very careful what you say. What does he want here? Don't let him find out anything." "But he is just a friend," the employee replied. "He doesn't want to know anything. He has just come to see me." "Quite so," said Rockefeller, "but you can never tell. Be careful, be very careful."[9]

In absorbing competitors, Rockefeller was equally secretive and asked them to continue operating under their original names and not divulge their Standard Oil ownership. They were instructed to retain their original stationery, keep secret accounts, and not allude on paper to their Cleveland connection; internal correspondence with Standard Oil was often conducted in code or with fictitious names. Rockefeller also did this as a necessary legal expedient, for under existing law Standard Oil of Ohio couldn't own property outside the state, a situation that invited deception by companies that operated nationally.

Rockefeller warned refiners joining Standard Oil not to parade their sudden wealth, lest people wonder where they got the cash. After striking a deal with one Cleveland refiner, he invited him to his Euclid Avenue home one night and said: "But you must keep this contract secret even from your wife. When you begin to make more money, don't let anybody know it. Don't put on any more style. You have no ambition to drive fast horses, have you?"[10] With such thoroughgoing stealth, Standard Oil executives worried that if some newly acquired refiner died, his heirs might mistakenly claim ownership of the refinery.

Rockefeller was similarly suspicious of any boasting or ostentation among associates. One day, he was riding on a train in Cleveland with Pittsburgh refiner O. T. Waring when Waring asked him who owned a handsome, dark green hillside house in the distance. "You wish to know who owns that house?" asked Rockefeller, suddenly very upset. "It's our Mr. Hopper, who makes barrels for us. Whew! It's an expensive house, isn't it? I wonder if Hopper isn't making altogether *too much* money? Let's look into it."[11] Back in the office, he pored over the accounts, decided that Hopper's profits were excessive, and terminated the contracts with him. In a similar vein, Rockefeller was concerned that if he advertised his own wealth through fancy houses, he might attract investors into the refining business and only worsen the excess capacity problem.

As will be seen, Rockefeller was capable of extraordinary ferocity in compelling submission from competitors. He might starve out obdurate firms by buying all available barrels on the market or monopolize local tank cars to paralyze their operations. Yet Rockefeller didn't apply this pressure lightly and preferred patience and reason—if possible—to terror. He was not only purchasing refineries but assembling a managerial team. The creation of Standard Oil was often less a matter of stamping out competitors than of seducing them into cooperation. In general, Rockefeller was so eager to retain original management that he accumulated expensive deadwood on the payroll and, for the sake of intraempire harmony, preferred to be conciliatory. Several years later, one colleague wrote to him that almost the entire executive committee "have made up their minds that the policy of buying out our competitors has had its day and that to pay men salaries for doing nothing is poor business, though these men have been all their active business lives in the Oil business."[12] This policy, which kept colleagues from defecting and forming competing companies, was one of many expensive extravagances that accompanied the creation of the monopoly.

With access to Oil Creek via the Allegheny River, Pittsburgh was an optimal crossroads for oil traffic, and it was inevitably targeted by Rockefeller for his second great wave of consolidation. After the failed Pittsburgh Plan, Rockefeller hoped to prod, wheedle, and cajole both Pittsburgh and Philadelphia refiners into Standard Oil.

During the autumn of 1874, Rockefeller and Flagler attended a secret summit meeting in Saratoga Springs with their Pittsburgh and Philadelphia counterparts, Charles Lockhart and William G. Warden. By snapping up the strongest refiners in these two towns, Standard Oil hoped that it would then easily corral the smaller refiners in their wake. With its racetrack and gambling casino, Saratoga Springs was a fashionable resort for wealthy sportsmen and, as Commodore Vanderbilt's summer home, a popular gathering spot for confidential business talks. After breakfast, the four refiners retreated to a pleasant pavilion by a spring, where they talked for six hours. Only by banding together in one firm, Rockefeller argued in his most soothing manner, could they avert destructive price-cutting. When Lockhart and Warden hesitated, Rockefeller played his trump card: He invited Warden to come to Cleveland and inspect the Standard Oil books. When Warden later examined them, he was taken aback: Rockefeller could manufacture kerosene so inexpensively that he could sell below Warden's production costs and earn a profit. After several weeks of appraising Standard Oil and being assured of a voice in its management, Warden and Lockhart joined forces with Rockefeller. In the clandestine sale of their plants, they had the foresight to take payment in Standard Oil stock. Since Rockefeller's papers from this period are sparse, we don't know precisely why these powerful rivals yielded to him, but they were probably attracted by the access to railroad rebates, lower interest rates, scarce tank cars, and technical expertise that went along with the partnership.

With this decisive stroke, Rockefeller absorbed more than half of the Pittsburgh refining capacity, with the leading Philadelphia refinery tossed in for good measure. In this way, he activated a self-sustaining movement as his new allies agreed to consolidate business in their localities and supervise the purchase of the remaining independent refineries. A massive chain reaction was thus set in motion that rippled through both refining centers, with local businessmen now acting as Rockefeller's agents. Of twenty-two Pittsburgh refiners in existence when Rockefeller struck his Saratoga Springs deal, only one was still in existence independently two years later.

Rockefeller was especially delighted to snare Charles Lockhart, a bearded Scot with a frosty, taciturn manner who was, in Rockefeller's words, "one of the most experienced, self-contained, and self-controlled men in business."[13] During the Saratoga meeting, he impressed the Standard men because he listened attentively but hardly breathed a syllable, which elicited Rockefeller's highest praise: "That's the kind of man I'd like to have go fishing with me."[14] Though the oil business was comparatively young, Lockhart was already a veteran, having sold Seneca Oil along with William Frew in a Pittsburgh store in the 1850s. Soon after Edwin Drake's discovery, Lockhart had carried the first samples of Pennsylvania kerosene to London. Besides creating the top Pittsburgh refiner, Lockhart, Frew and Company, the two men had also joined forces with William Warden to establish a Philadelphia affiliate, Warden, Frew and Company, which later evolved into the Atlantic Refining Company. This innovative trio of refiners shipped oil to Liverpool aboard steamers lined with iron tanks, reducing both the risk of fire and the noisome smells. The antithesis of the penurious Lockhart, Warden was an effusive, bighearted man with a broad face and muttonchop whiskers. With wider ranging interests than the average Standard Oil man, he was a former abolitionist who had donated money to black causes after the war, a conscientious Presbyterian, and an active reformer in Philadelphia politics.

While stepping up his Pittsburgh and Philadelphia campaigns, Rockefeller also established a critical foothold in New York, where he had already bought the Devoe Manufacturing Company, specialists in case oil, and the Long Island Company, operator of a large refinery. Through the efforts of brother William, Rockefeller now took over Charles Pratt and Company. A short man with a sandy beard, Charles Pratt was a self-made Baptist with the habitual reticence that Rockefeller prized. He had manufactured paints before the Civil War and this had led him into oil refining. With a flair for merchandising, he had made his high-quality kerosene, Astral Oil, a common fixture in American households and so adroitly managed exports to Europe and Asia that the brand acquired international fame.

In time, Charles Pratt felt slighted and pushed aside by Rockefeller, who sometimes admired his conservative style but generally mocked him as an old fogy lacking in vision. Quite unlike Warden and Lockhart, Pratt ended up on the losing side of many policy disputes with Rockefeller and took to writing him querulous letters laced with self-pity. During one squabble with Rockefeller in 1881, Pratt wrote petulantly, "I cannot see good in any effort of mine to influence you or others by any arguments."[15]

The undisclosed purchase of Charles Pratt's firm brought into the Standard fold one of the most energetic, swaggering figures in its history: Henry H. Rogers, who had led the committee of New York refiners that indignantly contested the SIC. He was now one of the first turncoats who defected to the Standard camp, and Rockefeller gloated over such conquests. "I'm happy to state that in most cases the very men who were desperately opposed to anything the Standard Oil Company might suggest . . . when they met us face to face, when they came to know from us rather than from those maligners, they readily joined us and never had occasion to regret."[16] Though he later clashed with Rockefeller, Rogers was a versatile executive who directed, in turn, Standard's crude-oil purchases, pipelines, and manufacturing operations. As petroleum by-products grew in importance, Rogers, with a technical grasp that exceeded Rockefeller's, patented a landmark process for separating naphtha from crude oil.

No sooner had Standard Oil enlisted Charles Pratt than New York independents began to experience unaccountable shortages of vital supplies. John Ellis and Company, which manufactured petroleum jelly, suddenly found it couldn't book the requisite railroad cars for crude-oil shipments. Some invisible force was working against them. As the firm tried to unravel this mystery, a Standard Oil representative took the opportunity to drop by for a friendly chat with John Ellis and warned him, "You are helpless. You will have to sell out." Appalled by this heavy-handed treatment, Ellis retorted, "I will never sell out to any company as crooked as the Standard Oil."[17] Ellis stayed independent, but few firms had the resources or fortitude to withstand the unceasing pressure exerted by the growing legions of Standard Oil minions.

In his lightning offensives in Pittsburgh, Philadelphia, and New York, Rockefeller was buying refineries in strategic railroad and shipping hubs, where he could negotiate excellent transportation rates. But despite its proximity to the wells, he never considered Oil Creek an economical place for refineries—which didn't enhance his popularity in western Pennsylvania. Many ingredients used in refining—from sulfuric acid to glue to barrel hoops—cost more in that secluded area than in urban centers. By demoting the Oil Regions as a refining center, Rockefeller threatened the livelihood of thousands of people in Titusville, Franklin, and Oil City and offended their sense of justice. The locals were taught to believe, in Rockefeller's words, that "the place where the oil was produced, gave certain rights and privileges that persons seeking to engage in other localities had no right to presume to share."[18] Rockefeller struck them as an evil interloper, a usurper of their birthright, when he was merely exercising his right to practice business where he pleased.

Nonetheless, to enforce an airtight monopoly, he needed to capture the Oil Creek refineries, if only to dismantle the least efficient ones. On January 22, 1874, he stunned local refiners by buying the Imperial Refining Company and its vast facility near Oil City. For local anti-Standard firebrands, it was a move laden with ominous symbolism. One of the consenting sellers was Captain Jacob J. Vandergrift, a husky little man with a Santa Claus beard. A former skipper on the Ohio River, Vandergrift was a wealthy, God-fearing temperance advocate who commanded universal power and respect. Along Oil Creek, his desertion to Standard Oil was considered treasonous betrayal, and it demoralized local independents—precisely what Rockefeller had wanted. In early 1875, Rockefeller captured the second largest Titusville refiner, Porter, Moreland and Company, which brought twenty-seven-year-old John D. Archbold—the diminutive homilist who had electrified the crowd at the Titusville Opera House with his blazing oratory against the SIC—into the Standard Oil fold. Now, convinced that competition was a dated concept, Archbold suddenly enlisted under the banner of industrial consolidation.

Aside from Henry Flagler, Archbold was the most significant figure recruited by Rockefeller. Even before he set eyes on him, Rockefeller was intrigued. Registering at a Titusville hotel one day, he noted the signature above his own name: "John D. Archbold, $4 a barrel." This cocky self-promotion impressed Rockefeller, for crude oil was selling at substantially below that price.[19] Nine years younger than Rockefeller, the boyish Archbold was a short spark plug of a man, weighing about 130 pounds. The son of a Baptist circuit preacher who abandoned his family when John was ten (the prevalence of ministers' sons at Standard Oil is striking), he had come to Titusville as a teenager and grown up with the industry. Quick-witted and optimistic, a jovial raconteur, he "laughed his way to a great fortune," as one contemporary said.[20] Though not easily charmed, Rockefeller was enchanted by Archbold's high spirits, his inexhaustible fountain of jokes and stories; his short stature aside, he was the man at Standard Oil who most resembled Big Bill. Archbold became Rockefeller's proxy, picked successor, surrogate son, and court jester. Before long, Rockefeller learned that this preacher's son was overly fond of worldly pleasure and spent his nights drinking and playing poker. In time, Rockefeller forced him to repudiate alcohol, but even this only seemed to draw them closer together.

When Archbold went over to Standard Oil, he was denounced bitterly as a "renegade" and "deserter" and incurred special resentment from former admirers.[21] He was such a deft, good-natured diplomat, however, that Rockefeller assigned him to absorb the Oil Creek refiners. In no other place did Rockefeller so sorely need an attractive substitute. Around Titusville, Standard Oil was reviled as the "octopus," and Rockefeller was regarded as a monster. Mothers scolded their children by saying, "Run, children, or Rockefeller'll get you!"[22] As a result, the original Standard Oil officials never conducted buyout talks directly but operated through "acquaintances, competitors, and friends of the competitive refiners, best calculated to explain to them the situation, best fitted to succeed in the negotiations because of their intimate acquaintance, kindly relations and the mutual confidence of neighbors and friends."[23] Archbold was the smiling face who mollified enemies and restored peace, and with his advent Rockefeller no longer needed to go to Oil Creek.

In September 1875, Standard Oil formed the Acme Oil Company, a front organization to take over local refiners under Archbold's guidance. Within months, he had bought or leased twenty-seven refineries, moving at such a hectic pace that he nearly drove himself to collapse. Over the next three or four years, Archbold herded the remaining independents into Standard Oil. Several letters from Archbold to Rockefeller confirm the latter's contention that he paid fairly for refiners. After grudgingly paying an exorbitant $12,000 for one refinery, Archbold told Rockefeller, "We have the feeling that it is a large price for the property and do not doubt but that if we could hold out for a time on the present low basis we might do better, but whether the difference is worth the ammunition is a question."[24] Once the purchase was settled, he added, "I found it a very difficult trade to make, & was compelled to make some concessions to the parties that I disliked very much to make regarding which I will explain to you more fully when I see you."[25] Though independent refiners often felt squeezed by Rockefeller, he didn't always exploit their vulnerability to the maximum possible extent and sometimes even showed leniency.

At least one prominent refiner contended that he was subjected to coercion by Standard Oil when he tried to build a new refinery. Samuel Van Syckel, the pipeline pioneer, said a Standard Oil representative had offered him a good salary to abandon the project. "He then said that I could make no money if I did refine oil. He also said if I did I could not ship it. He said he would say to me confidentially that they had made such arrangements with the railroads in reference to freight—in reference to getting cars—he knew I could make no money if I did make oil."[26] Van Syckel bowed to superior force.

In May 1875, Rockefeller completed his grand design of controlling all the major refining centers when he covertly bought J. N. Camden and Company of Parkersburg, West Virginia, and rechristened it the Camden Consolidated Oil Company. Camden's correspondence documents the stealth involved in this sort of takeover. Before consummating the sale, Standard Oil requested a minute inventory of his properties and was ready to send its expert superintendent, Ambrose McGregor, to investigate. Yet Johnson Newlon Camden himself, a well-known Democratic politician, feared that the superintendent of his barrel factory might recognize McGregor and warned Standard Oil, "We would prefer having him to come here, but don't see how he could do it without exposing the whole thing. I find the Superintendent of the Barrel Factory is a little curious about what is going on."[27] That even a superintendent was kept in the dark about the new owners underscores the priority that Standard Oil placed on confidentiality.

The Camden deal remedied a flagrant weakness for Rockefeller, who dominated refineries in the areas served by the New York Central, the Erie, and the Pennsylvania Railroads. There was only one gaping hole left in the map: the territory controlled by the maverick Baltimore and Ohio (B&O) Railroad, whose tracks spanned southern Pennsylvania, connecting a cluster of refineries in Parkersburg and Wheeling, West Virginia, with an oil-export center in Baltimore. Even more intolerable for Rockefeller, the upstart B&O dared to handle crude oil shipped to Pittsburgh through a pipeline called the Columbia Conduit Company, which had defied Standard Oil at every turn. In short, the B&O was providing comfort to the last independent refiners still holding out in open rebellion against his imperial rule.

The president of the B&O, John W. Garrett, had long exhorted Camden to fight the Standard Goliath and offered him marked-down freight rates to do so. Now that he had—unbeknownst to Garrett—defected to Rockefeller, Camden wanted to retain the rates expressly designed to shore up Standard Oil opponents. On May 12, 1875, scarcely able to suppress his mischievous glee, Camden informed his new owners in Cleveland, "Mr. Garrett . . . is coming out to see us tomorrow. I suppose he will encourage us to keep up our oil business and fight the 'combination' "—that is, Standard Oil.[28] And he negotiated excellent rates with Garrett. In exchange for shipping fifty thousand barrels of oil monthly, he would receive a ten-cent-a-barrel drawback on *all* refined oil sent via the B&O—whether shipped by Camden or by his competitors. That Garrett revived the infamous drawback when he thought he was *fighting* Standard Oil shows that nobody could claim exclusive virtue in this business.

That spring, Rockefeller gave Camden wide leeway to buy up refiners serviced by the B&O, and he quickly snatched up three Parkersburg refiners. At several points, Camden, like Archbold, bristled at the excessive prices he paid.

"It almost makes me weepy to pay out good money for this kind of junk," he told Rockefeller, "but as it is a part of our duty to mankind, I suppose it is necessary to carry it through without flinching."[29] The completion of the Baltimore campaign left John D. Rockefeller, still in his thirties, the sole master of American oil refining. Since no major crude-oil deposits had been unearthed beyond western Pennsylvania—Russia, perhaps, being the lone exception—it also meant that he monopolized the world kerosene market. He was now living a fantasy of extravagant wealth that would have dwarfed the most febrile daydreams of William Avery Rockefeller. And few people beyond the oil business had ever even heard of him.

The swift raids on the principal refining centers cost such a king's ransom that Rockefeller's most ticklish problem was how to bankroll this marathon buying spree. To entice refiners, he offered them the option of taking payment either in cash or stock, and he always dreaded the choice of cash. "I would whip out our check book with rather a lordly air and remark, as if it were a matter of entire indifference to us, 'Will I write a check or would you prefer payment in Standard Oil shares?' "[30] If they chose cash, he often had to scramble among banks to scrounge up money. By encouraging opponents to take stock, he conserved funds and also enlisted the allegiance of quondam foes in his burgeoning enterprise. But few companies followed the lead of Clark, Payne and invested in Standard Oil instead of taking payment.

It mortified Rockefeller that so few trusting souls took Standard Oil stock. Mostly, they doubted that Rockefeller and his Young Turks could realize their experimental plan. As he recalled, "So when I offered them either spot cash outright for their property or stock in the new company, they took my money and laughed in their sleeves at my folly."[31] Rockefeller knew, with his customary certitude, that the people who took shares would be enriched. Indeed, American high society in the twentieth century would be loaded with descendants of those refiners who opted for stock. At every opportunity, Rockefeller sounded a prophetic note about the future appreciation of these shares. One Cleveland refiner who took stock later ran into Rockefeller, who asked, "Do you still hold your stock?" When told that was the case, Rockefeller entreated him, "Sell everything you've got even to the shirt on your back, but hold on to the stock."[32] Not all of them did, and Rockefeller always fancied that much of the venom turned against him came from disgruntled refiners who regretted having declined the stock.

Despite his stupendous borrowing needs, Rockefeller no longer needed to truckle to bankers and defied the most fearsome of them all: Amasa Stone. Cold, stern, and unapproachable, Stone amassed a fortune building bridges and railroads and became managing director of the Lake Shore Railroad at the personal behest of Commodore Vanderbilt. Twenty years older than Rockefeller, he expected the refiner to defer to him, and this irked the younger man. To ensure a steady flow of credit, Rockefeller put Stone on Standard's board, but when the latter grew arbitrary and domineering, Rockefeller plotted to banish him. He soon had his chance when Stone inadvertently let an option expire for buying more Standard Oil stock. Several weeks later, recognizing his error, Stone showed up at the Standard office and induced Flagler to extend the expiration date. Itching for a showdown, Rockefeller overrode Flagler and refused to sell Stone any more shares, prompting the irate banker to liquidate his stake in the company. Rockefeller now considered himself the equal of any Cleveland businessman and wouldn't grovel to anyone.

Just as he dreamed of emancipation from his bankers, Rockefeller hoped to escape the clutches of Vanderbilt, Gould, Scott, and other railroad barons. Early on, he had demonstrated the edge possessed by large-scale shippers in haggling with railroads. Now, he went a critical step further, figuring out how to insinuate himself into the very infrastructure of the industry.

Still uneasy at the specter of the oil fields drying up, the railroads shrank from investments in custom-made facilities for handling oil, worried that this specialized equipment might someday be rendered worthless. Exploiting this fear, Rockefeller worked out a clever bargain with the Erie Railroad in April 1874. The railroad would transfer control of its Weehawken, New Jersey, terminal to Standard Oil if Standard met two conditions: First, it would have to outfit the rail yards with modern apparatuses that would help to expedite oil shipments to New England and the South; second, it would have to ship 50 percent of its western refinery output over Erie tracks. For Rockefeller, the arrangement promised multiple advantages, for he not only received preferential rates from Erie but could also chart the oil movements of competitors across the country. He could even block the export of rivals' oil—an option that, having made this huge investment, he freely exercised. As he argued, "I know of no parallel case in other branches of business where the competitor felt injured because he could not use his rival's capital and facilities for his own advantage and the disadvantage of the owner of the capital and facilities."[33] Rockefeller's logic was unimpeachable—unless one accepted the still controversial proposition that railroads were common carriers and should deal with all shippers impartially.

Rockefeller was embraced no less warmly by the New York Central, which was controlled by the Vanderbilt family. Commodore Vanderbilt reportedly said that Rockefeller was the one man in America who could dictate terms to him; meanwhile, his son, William H. Vanderbilt, discreetly purchased Standard Oil stock for his own account.[34] It was the younger Vanderbilt who said presciently of Rockefeller in the 1870s: "He will become the richest man in the country," thus inheriting the title from his father.[35] Standard Oil eventually became so enmeshed in the railroad business that it controlled virtually all the oil traffic that traveled over the Erie and the New York Central tracks.

Standard Oil also profited immeasurably from the revolution in oil transport as barrels gave way to tank cars. As Rockefeller later testified, "We soon discovered as the business grew that the primary method of transporting oil in barrels could not last. The package often cost more than the contents, and the forests of the country were not sufficient to supply the necessary material for an extended length of time."[36] Once again, the railroads balked at investing in rolling stock that couldn't also transport general freight, so Rockefeller stepped boldly into the breach. In 1874, Standard Oil—with that kindly solicitude for the railroads' welfare that artfully tied them up with myriad strings—began to raise tens of thousands of dollars to build oil-tank cars, which they would then lease to the roads for a special mileage allowance. Decades later, Armour and Company, the Chicago butcher, mimicked the same strategy by buying up refrigerator cars.

As the owner of almost all the Erie and New York Central tank cars, Standard Oil's position grew unassailable: At a moment's notice, it could crush either railroad by threatening to withdraw its tank cars. It also prodded the railroads into granting favors for tank cars not enjoyed by the small refiners who shipped by barrel. For instance, railroads levied a charge for the return of empty barrels, while tank cars traveled free on the return route from the East Coast to the Midwest refineries. Tank-car clients also received the exact same leakage allowance received by barrel shippers, even though the tank cars didn't leak—which effectively allowed Standard Oil to carry sixty-two gallons gratis in every tank car.

In this impregnable position, Rockefeller fulfilled a longtime wish and abolished forever the freight advantage of the Oil Creek refiners. In high-level talks with railway officials at Long Branch, New Jersey, and Saratoga Springs in the summer of 1874, he made them equalize rates for all refiners shipping to the East Coast. Crude oil would now effectively travel free on the 150-mile stretch between Oil Creek and Cleveland, destroying the advantage of owning a refinery in the oil fields and creating parity for Cleveland. When this shocking news surfaced in the so-called Rutter Circular of September 9, 1874, it sparked mass meetings and howls of protest along Oil Creek, where Rockefeller was universally execrated. Unlike the situation with the SIC, the railroads didn't tremble at the uproar but reacted with cool intransigence, knowing the independent refiners were now doomed. Three weeks passed before A. J. Cassatt of the Pennsylvania Railroad issued a curt, unrepentant letter in defense of the new uniform rates. For a long time, the independents had fought a valiantly unequal contest with Standard Oil, but now that the railroads had fallen under Standard's spell, the contest was over.

Had oil been found in scattered places after the Civil War, it's unlikely that even Standard Oil could have mustered the resources to control it so thoroughly. It was the confinement of oil to a desolate corner of northwest Pennsylvania that made it susceptible to monopoly control, especially with the emergence of pipelines. Pipelines unified the Pennsylvania wells into a single network and ultimately permitted Standard Oil to start or stop the flow of oil with the turn of a spigot. In time, they relegated collaboration with the railroads into something of a sideshow for Rockefeller.

Only belatedly did Rockefeller discern the full potential of pipelines, and his entry into the business seemed somewhat of a defensive, rearguard action. He knew that the railroads felt threatened by the pipelines, and for a time he thought it worthwhile to help them safeguard their interests by delaying the introduction of this new technology. Then, one of the railroads forced him to modify his plans. During the summer of 1873, he was taken aback when the Pennsylvania Railroad expanded into pipelines through an aggressive, fast-freight subsidiary known as the Empire Transportation Company, which integrated two of the largest Oil Creek pipelines into its railroad network. Thus far, pipelines had only pumped oil short distances from the wellhead to the railroads, but this move presaged a time when pipelines would span great distances and supplant railroads altogether. Even worse from Rockefeller's viewpoint, Empire seemed the harbinger of a pipeline monopoly under the thumb of his rival and sometime coconspirator Tom Scott of the Pennsylvania Railroad. Rockefeller's paranoia was fully justified. In the perpetual game of shifting alliances, Tom Scott had made his tactical compromises with Rockefeller, but he generally feared Standard Oil and sought to shatter its refining monopoly, presumably to replace it with his own.

In a deft countermove, Rockefeller called upon Daniel O'Day, one of the most colorful figures in Standard history, to lay down a pipeline system. Born in County Clare, O'Day was a profane, two-fisted Irishman who tempered ruthless tactics with wit and charm. He inspired loyalty among subordinates and raw terror among adversaries. On his forehead O'Day bore a scar from an old Oil Creek brawl that was a constant reminder of his bare-knuckled approach to business. In 1874, under O'Day's tutelage, Standard launched the American Transfer Company to construct a pipeline network. Jockeying for position, Rockefeller also acquired a one-third interest in Vandergrift and Forman, controlled by Jacob J. Vandergrift, the steamboat captain who had merged his refining interests with Standard Oil. The Vandergrift pipelines formed the core of a new venture, the United Pipe Lines, that pretended to be free of Standard Oil control. By giving small stakes in United to William H. Vanderbilt of the New York Central and Amasa Stone of the Lake Shore, Rockefeller tightened his grip over friendly railroads. This set him up to extract maximum advantage from both the railroads and pipelines so long as these two means of transport coexisted in the oil business. When the owners of the first pipeline systems established a pool to set rates and allocate quotas among putatively competing networks in the summer of 1874, Rockefeller's pipelines gained an impressive 36 percent market share.

Between American Transfer and United Pipe Lines, Rockefeller now sat astride nearly a third of the crude oil flowing from Oil Creek wells. Henceforth, Standard's influence in petroleum transport would be no less pervasive and even more profitable than its unmatched position in refining. This power offered many temptations for abuse. An oilman could make a tremendous strike and suddenly feel fabulously rich, but if he couldn't hook up the gushing black liquid to a pipeline, it was worthless. The drillers had always credited Rockefeller with a life-and-death hold over them, and as the Standard Oil pipelines encroached upon the oil fields, snaking across the slopes of Oil Creek, that power took on a frighteningly tangible form.

CHAPTER 10

Sphinx

I n April 1874, as befitted the status of this new oil colossus, Standard Oil moved into a new four-story building that Rockefeller and Harkness had erected at 43 Euclid Avenue, east of the Public Square. Behind a heavy stone façade, the two Standard Oil floors were roomy and airy, drawing extra light from a skylight above the central stairway. Every morning at 9:15 sharp, Rockefeller arrived, elegantly attired, with the letter R neatly incised in his black onyx cuff links; for someone from a frugal, rural background, he was unexpectedly fastidious. "Mr. Rockefeller came in with an air of calm dignity," recalled one clerk. "He was immaculately dressed—he looked as if he had been turned out of a bandbox. He carried an umbrella and his gloves, and wore a high silk hat."[1] He placed such faith in polished shoes that he provided, free of charge, a shoe-shining kit for each office unit. Tall and pale, with neatly trimmed reddish gold side-whiskers, he had a barber shave him each morning at the same hour. Extremely punctual for all appointments, he said, "A man has no right to occupy another man's time unnecessarily."[2]

In his imperturbable style, Rockefeller quietly bid his colleagues good morning, inquired after their health, then vanished into his modest office. Even within the Standard Oil kingdom, his employees found his movements as wraithlike as his most paranoid Titusville antagonists did. As one secretary remarked, "He is sly. I never have seen him enter the building or leave it."[3] "He's never there, and yet he's always there," echoed an associate.[4] Rockefeller seldom granted appointments to strangers and preferred to be approached in writing. Ever alert against industrial espionage, he never wanted people to know more than was required and warned one colleague, "I would be very careful about putting [someone] into a position where he could learn about our business and be troublesome to us."[5] Even close associates found him inscrutable and loath to reveal his thoughts. As one wrote, "His long silences, so that we could not locate even his objections, were sometimes baffling."[6] Schooled in secrecy, he trained his face to be a stony mask so that when underlings brought him telegrams, they couldn't tell from his expression whether the news was favorable or not.

Rockefeller equated silence with strength: Weak men had loose tongues and blabbed to reporters, while prudent businessmen kept their own counsel. Two of his most cherished maxims were "Success comes from keeping the ears open and the mouth closed" and "A man of words and not of deeds is like a garden full of weeds."[7] Big Bill's deaf-and-dumb routine curiously prefigured his son's habit of hearing as much as possible and saying as little as possible to gain a tactical edge. When bargaining, he employed his Midwest taciturnity to effect, throwing people off stride and keeping them guessing. When angry, he tended to grow eerily quiet. He liked to tell how a blustering contractor stormed into his office and launched into a snarling tirade against him while he sat hunched over his writing desk and didn't look up until the man had exhausted himself. Then, spinning about in his swivel chair, he looked up and coolly asked, "I didn't catch what you were saying. Would you mind repeating that?"[8]

Much of the time, he was closeted in his office, where he had oil prices chalked on a blackboard. He paced this spartan office, hands laced behind his back. Periodically, he emerged from his lair, mounted a high stool, and studied ledgers, scribbling calculations on pad and paper. (During meetings, he was a restless doodler and note taker.) Frequently, he stared out the window, motionless as an idol, gazing at the sky for fifteen minutes at a stretch. He once asked rhetorically, "Do not many of us who fail to achieve big things . . . fail because we lack concentration—the art of concentrating the mind on the thing to be done at the proper time and to the exclusion of everything else?"[9]

Rockefeller adhered to a fixed schedule, moving through the day in a frictionless manner. He never wasted time on frivolities. Even his daily breaks—the midmorning snack of crackers and milk and the postprandial nap—were designed to conserve energy and help him to strike an ideal balance between his physical and mental forces. As he remarked, "It is not good to keep all the forces at tension all the time."[10]

In the early days, Rockefeller knew the name and face of each employee and occasionally perambulated about the office. He walked with a measured gait, steady as a metronome, always covering the same distance in the exact same time. He had the soundless movements and modulated voice of an undertaker. Gliding about with silent footfalls, he startled people by materializing at their desks and politely asking, in a mellow voice, to inspect their work. Since he was

A photograph of John D. Rockefeller that clearly shows his keen determination as a young businessman.
(Courtesy of the Rockefeller Archive Center)

seldom seen, people often wondered about his whereabouts. "His was the least known face in the offices," one employee recalled fifty years later, still perplexed about Rockefeller's daily schedule. "He was reported to inhabit them three hours a day, but his appearances and disappearances were curtained, suggested private approaches, withdrawn stairways and corridors."[11]

As a former bookkeeper, Rockefeller devoted special attention to ledgers. One accountant recalled him stopping by his desk and saying courteously, "Permit me," then flipping quickly through his books. "Very well kept," he said, "very, indeed." Then his eye leaped to a tiny error. "A little error here; will you correct it?" The accountant was flabbergasted by the speed with which Rockefeller had scanned so many dense columns of figures. "And I will take my oath," he reported, "that it was the only error in the book!"[12]

Everybody noted the man's preternatural calm. Though he had honed his will into a perfect instrument, he was even-tempered by nature. As he remarked, "You could do or say the most outrageous thing at this moment and I would not show the least sign of excitement."[13] He was always proud of the fact that he had an abnormally low pulse of fifty-two. Many employees said he never lost his temper, raised his voice, uttered a profane or slang word, or acted discourteously. He defied many stereotypes of the overbearing tycoon and generally received excellent reviews from employees who regarded him as fair and benevolent, free of petty temper and dictatorial airs. This was nicely illustrated by an anecdote. As a fitness buff, Rockefeller placed in the accounting department a wood-and-rubber contrivance that he pushed and pulled for exercise. When he showed up one morning for exercise, a junior accountant didn't recognize him, called the gadget a damned nuisance, and demanded that it be carted off. "All right," said Rockefeller and had the contraption removed. Somewhat later, to his horror, the young man realized that he had berated the chief executive, yet he never endured one word of reprimand. Rockefeller even hesitated to punish serious offenses and instead of prosecuting the occasional embezzler simply dismissed him.

Throughout his life, Rockefeller was wounded deeply by accusations that he was a cold, malignant personality. In truth, like many retiring personalities, he provoked varied reactions in people. One cooper who sold him barrels in the early days told Ida Tarbell that "Rockefeller was never a great talker; that he was not liked by his fellows; that everybody was afraid of him; and that he was solitary."[14] But Rockefeller never turned the ferocity that he trained against rivals against his own employees and people who worked for him usually found him a model of propriety and paternalistic concern. As one refinery worker remembered him, "He always had a nod and a kind word for everybody. He never forgot anyone. We had some trying times in the business in those early years, but I've never seen Mr. Rockefeller when he was not friendly and kind and unruffled. Nothing excited him."[15] Rockefeller's sister Mary Ann dismissed as an absurd canard the idea that he was a curmudgeon. "John could always get along so easily with anyone," she declared.[16] Indeed, had he not possessed some charm, or at least cordiality, he could never have accomplished so much in the business world.

So highly did Rockefeller value personnel that during the first years of Standard Oil he personally attended to routine hiring matters. (After conquering the other refining centers, the payroll ballooned to 3,000 people, and this became impossible.) Taking for granted the growth of his empire, he hired talented people as found, not as needed.

Far more than a technocrat, Rockefeller was an inspirational leader who exerted a magnetic power over workers and especially prized executives with social skills. "The ability to deal with people is as purchasable a commodity as sugar or coffee," he once said, "and I pay more for that ability than for any other under the sun."[17]

Employees were invited to send complaints or suggestions directly to him, and he always took an interest in their affairs. His correspondence is replete with inquiries about sick or retired employees. Reasonably generous in wages, salaries, and pensions, he paid somewhat above the industry average. Forty years later, a former subordinate wrote of the firm, with some exaggeration, "It has never had a strike or a dissatisfied workman; and today no business organization cares for its veterans in their old age as does the Standard Oil Company."[18] It is important to point out that oil refining was a capital-intensive industry without the seething discontents that afflicted the coal mines or steel mills. Even in lean years, Standard Oil was flush with profits, permitting it the luxury of good intentions. One biographer has gone so far as to say of Rockefeller, "He was the best employer of his time, instituting hospitalization and retirement pensions."[19]

He was a fine boss if workers abided by his rules, but if they did something foolish, like show interest in a union, they promptly forfeited his sympathy. Rockefeller never acknowledged the legitimacy of organized labor, nor did he tolerate union organizers on the premises. He also reserved the right to pass judgment on the private lives of employees. Imposing his own prudish standards on his staff, he penalized any executive implicated in an adulterous affair and frowned on divorce. Sabbath observance was de rigueur, and if colleagues wrote to him when they should have been in church, they tended not to put the real dates on their letters.

The most remarkable instance of Rockefeller participating in an associate's moral reformation occurred with John D. Archbold, the jovial young protégé whose pranks and infectious laughter so delighted Rockefeller. When Rockefeller initially entreated him to stop drinking, Archbold pretended to abide by the temperance pledge while keeping cloves in his vest pocket to mask telltale smells. By 1881, his drinking binges were too palpable and self-destructive to conceal, and he wrote a contrite letter to Rockefeller, renewing his pledge: "My Dear Mr. Rockefeller—Any words from me seem like a mockery. I give you the promise appreciating its solemnity and importance as I never did before. I will write you the letter every Sunday as long as our relation gives me the privilege, or until you ask me to stop."[20] Thereafter, every Sunday for eight months, Archbold sent Rockefeller a letter confirming his sobriety that week, writing for instance, "Please let this bear witness to the completion of the 5th period."[21] Archbold made a sincere effort, but he had at least one violent relapse four years later and felt mortified at having let his mentor down. "I have never before known him to be so thoroughly cast down and in such abject mental misery," one Standard Oil executive told Rockefeller. "I do not think any one can fully realize the fight he must make against this unfortunate habit, nor the really heartbroken condition he is in after it has come over him."[22] Aware of Rockefeller's dismay, other executives tried to make it seem that Archbold had unwittingly swallowed some alcoholic medicine.

His employees tended to revere Rockefeller and vied to please him. As one said, "I have never heard of his equal in getting together a lot of the very best men in one team and inspiring each man to do his best for the enterprise. . . . He was so big, so broad, so patient; I don't believe a man like him comes to this world oftener than once in five or six hundred years."[23] Rockefeller worked by subtle hints, doling out praise sparingly to employees and nudging them along. At first, he tested them exhaustively, yet once he trusted them, he bestowed enormous power upon them and didn't intrude unless something radically misfired. "Often the best way to develop workers—when you are sure they have character and think they have ability—is to take them to a deep place, throw them in and make them sink or swim," he observed, recalling a method that Big Bill had used with his sons on Owasco Lake. "They will not fail."[24] To orchestrate such a gigantic operation, he had to delegate authority, and part of the Standard Oil gospel was to train your subordinate to do your job. As Rockefeller instructed a recruit, "Has anyone given you the law of these offices? No? It is this: nobody does anything if he can get anybody else to do it. . . . As soon as you can, get some one whom you can rely on, train him in the work, sit down, cock up your heels, and think out some way for the Standard Oil to make some money."[25] True to this policy, Rockefeller tried to extricate himself from the intricate web of administrative details and dedicate more of his time to broad policy decisions.

Most of all, Rockefeller inspired subordinates with his fanatic perfectionism. He never did anything haphazardly and wrote hundreds of thousands of business letters that were models of concision and balanced phrasing, the products of painstaking revision. Dictating letters to his secretary, he went through five or six drafts until he had eliminated every superfluous word and produced precisely the impression desired before affixing his signature with the best penmanship at his command. As one top aide recalled: "I have seen him sign his name to hundreds of papers at a sitting. He did each signature carefully as if this particular one was to be the only one by which he was to be remembered for all time. Each signature became in his mind a work of art."[26] This passion for excellence originated with Rockefeller and radiated throughout the organization. The ethos of Standard Oil's operations around the world was John D. Rockefeller's personality writ large.

While Rockefeller was responsible for policy questions and formulated the theoretical underpinnings of the trust, he didn't introduce many technical innovations associated with Standard Oil. Rather, he was a matchless executive, an unerring monitor of the stream of proposals channeled to him daily. He had an extraordinary reactive ability, a first-rate power of judgment when presented with options. Perhaps for this reason, he resembles modern chief executives more than he does his domineering industrial contemporaries.

Given the primitive communications and record keeping of the late nineteenth century, Rockefeller couldn't have managed his decentralized empire without masterfully coordinating a vast array of data. The ledger book enabled him to play the puppeteer and manipulate his empire by invisible strings. By mastering numbers, he reduced the most varied systems to a common standard, and he accepted their harsh verdicts without hesitation. "I charted my course by figures, nothing but figures," he once said.[27] Mark Hanna disparaged Rockefeller as "a kind of economic super-clerk, the personification of ledger-keeping."[28] This comment not only overlooks the farsighted nature of Rockefeller's leadership but discounts the importance of ledger keeping in modern corporations. Numbers gave Rockefeller an objective yardstick to compare his far-flung operations, enabling him to cut through the false claims of subordinates. It was the way that he extended rationality from the top of his organization down to the lowest rung: Every cost in the Standard Oil universe was computed to several decimal places.

Having always shown an aptitude for math, Rockefeller valued this quality in underlings. When he hired his young secretary, George D. Rogers, Rockefeller drew forth a watch to see how fast Rogers could total up a sheet of figures. At the end, Rockefeller said, "Well, you have completed it in the required time," and then promptly hired the young man, who served him ably for many years. Rogers left some interesting recollections of his boss's attention to detail and punctilious regard for money. When leaving the office one day, Rockefeller fished in his pockets and realized that he had forgotten his change purse. When he asked to borrow a nickel from Rogers, his assistant volunteered to make a gift of it, but Rockefeller protested. "No, Rogers," he said, "don't forget this transaction. This is a whole year's interest on a dollar."[29]

Rockefeller attributed much of his success to his quick head for figures. While he was negotiating to buy the long-sought million-dollar Columbia Conduit Company from Dr. David Hostetter, he purposely kept his interlocutor talking for half an hour as he computed the ways the interest could be paid. "When we ended the talk," Rockefeller said, "he agreed to the terms I offered—and I had saved $30,000 on the interest by my mental calculations that had never ceased while we were talking."[30] This episode brought out a subtle vein of anti-Semitism that is intermittently threaded through Rockefeller's papers. Of his mathematical prowess in outwitting Dr. Hostetter, he boasted, "How well I remember when it helped me to beat a Jew!"[31]

As time went on, Rockefeller had little physical contact with the actual refining, transportation, or marketing of oil—activities that unfolded in dusty outposts of the Standard Oil kingdom—but stayed sequestered in the executive suite, concentrating on finance, personnel, administration, and general policy matters. He downplayed the significance of technical knowledge in business. "I never felt the need of scientific knowledge, have never felt it. A young man who wants to succeed in business does not require chemistry or physics. He can always hire scientists."[32]

Nevertheless, in the first years of Standard Oil, Rockefeller regularly toured his facilities and was extremely inquisitive and observant, soaking up information and assiduously quizzing plant superintendents. In his pocket, he carried a little red notebook in which he jotted suggestions for improvements and always followed up on them. He knew the terror inspired by that red book. "More than once I have gone to luncheon with a number of our heads of departments and have seen the sweat start out on the foreheads of some of them when that little red notebook was pulled out," Rockefeller admitted with relish.[33]

With a talent for seeing things anew, Rockefeller could study an operation, break it down into component parts, and devise ways to improve it. In many ways, he anticipated the efficiency studies of engineer Frederick Winslow Taylor. Regarding each plant as infinitely perfectible, he created an atmosphere of ceaseless improvement. Paradoxically, the mammoth scale of operations encouraged close attention to minute detail, for a penny saved in one place might then be multiplied a thousandfold throughout the empire. In the early 1870s, Rockefeller inspected a Standard plant in New York City that filled and sealed five-gallon tin cans of kerosene for export. After watching a machine solder caps to the cans, he asked the resident expert: "How many drops of solder do you use on each can?" "Forty," the man replied. "Have you ever tried thirty-eight?" Rockefeller asked. "No? Would you mind having some sealed with thirty-eight and let me know?"[34] When thirty-eight drops were applied, a small percentage of cans leaked—but none at thirty-nine. Hence, thirty-nine drops of solder became the new standard instituted at all Standard Oil refineries. "That one drop of solder," said Rockefeller, still smiling in retirement, "saved $2,500 the first year; but the export business kept on increasing after that and doubled, quadrupled—became immensely greater than it was then; and the saving has gone steadily along, one drop on each can, and has amounted since to many hundreds of thousands of dollars."[35]

Rockefeller performed many similar feats, fractionally reducing the length of staves or the width of iron hoops without weakening a barrel's strength. He was never a foolish penny-pincher, however; for example, he saved on repairs by insisting that Standard build only solid, substantial plants, even if that meant higher start up costs. He also tried to use all of the fractions refined from the crude oil. During its first two years, Standard Oil had dealt largely in kerosene and naphtha. Then, in 1874, the company branched out into petroleum by-products, selling paraffin wax for chewing gum and residual oil tar and asphalt for road building. Before long, the company was manufacturing lubricants for railroads and machine shops, as well as candles, dyes, paints, and industrial acids. In 1880, Standard Oil took over the Chesebrough Manufacturing Company in New Jersey in order to strengthen its sales of petroleum jelly.

Ever since his first foray into refining, Rockefeller had relied for technical advice on the ruddy Sam Andrews, who first transmitted to him the technique for cleansing crude oil with sulfuric acid. In 1874, a stiff new competitor to Andrews emerged when Ambrose McGregor was named superintendent of the Standard Oil refineries in Cleveland. Rockefeller was beginning to think Andrews a mediocre man who couldn't keep up with new developments in the field and felt threatened by the more able McGregor.

A man of blinkered vision, Andrews was distressed by Rockefeller's soaring ambition, his constant borrowing and spending. The split between them worsened in August 1878 when Standard declared a 50 percent dividend on its stock. As Andrews later grumbled, "There was plenty of money made to throw that dividend out twice over and make a profit."[36] Though Rockefeller tried to avert clashes with colleagues, nothing nettled him more than directors who preferred fatter dividends to earnings plowed back into the business. One day, Andrews snapped at Rockefeller, "I wish I was out of this business." Calling his bluff, Rockefeller replied, "Sam, you don't seem to have faith in the way this company is operating. What will you take for your holdings?" "I will take one million dollars," Andrews shot back. "Let me have an option on it for twenty-four hours," said Rockefeller, "and we will discuss it tomorrow." When Andrews stopped by the next morning, Rockefeller had a check made out for one million dollars.[37] In truth, Rockefeller was petrified at the thought of Andrews's large stake being sold on the open market, which might have depressed the share price and harmed Standard Oil's credit at a time when he was borrowing heavily against those shares.

At first, Andrews exulted over the sale and was convinced that he had unloaded the stock at a premium. Then Rockefeller turned around and sold the same shares to William H. Vanderbilt for a quick $300,000 profit.[38] When Andrews loudly cried foul, Rockefeller sent an emissary to tell Andrews that he could buy back his stock at the original sale price. Embittered, Andrews spurned this fair offer and opted to keep the money. Had he kept the stock, it would have been worth $900 million by the early 1930s, by one estimate.[39] This rash decision, motivated by pure pique and a bruised ego, kept him from becoming one of America's richest men.

Irate at Andrews's behavior, Rockefeller lost whatever residual gratitude he felt for his founding partner and ridiculed his business abilities. Whenever he feuded with someone, he tended to turn that person into a reprobate, and he later said of Andrews, "He was ignorant, conceited, lost his head . . . governed by the same wicked sort of prejudice accompanying the egotism so characteristic of that type of ignorant Englishman."[40] It was one of many times that Rockefeller singled out the English for special abuse. As for Andrews, he not only squandered a chance to make a colossal fortune but later poured the money into an ugly, ornate house on Euclid Avenue where he dreamed of someday entertaining Queen Victoria. Once described as "the most pretentious residence ever built in Cleveland," this five-story monstrosity, with one hundred rooms and as many servants, won the well-deserved nickname of "Andrews's Folly."[41] For the rest of his life, Andrews lambasted Rockefeller in long-winded diatribes to anyone who would listen. Maurice Clark probably caught the truth about Sam Andrews when he said, "Before selling he was sore at John. After selling he was sore at himself."[42] Standard Oil was never kind to skeptics who doubted its bright future.

CHAPTER 11

The Holy Family

At a time when America's brand-new millionaires reveled in garish houses that paid queer homage to everything from medieval romance to the *Arabian Nights*, Rockefeller preferred to own raw land. In 1873, he invested in seventy-nine scenic acres at Forest Hill, a lovely, thickly wooded spot, crisscrossed by steep ravines and gulleys, just four miles east of his Euclid Avenue home. Two years later, he assembled a team of investors who bought the land from him to construct a sanatorium that would specialize in homeopathic medicine and water cures. As part of the deal, Rockefeller and Stephen Harkness set up a short railroad to whisk people out to this suburban resort. When both ventures fell victim to the depression of the 1870s, Rockefeller repurchased the land, now crowned with an enormous rambling building. Starting in 1877, he began to use it as a summer home, perhaps with some therapeutic intention in mind, for the previous year doctors had diagnosed Cettie as consumptive. At the doctors' urging, Rockefeller and his family vacationed in the dry, fresh air of Colorado in the summer of 1876. Perhaps he believed his wife would find relief from the lake breezes at Forest Hill.

Eager to expose Rockefeller as a tasteless vulgarian, Ida Tarbell mocked the Forest Hill house as "a monument of cheap ugliness," and other satirical critics rushed to pile on equally insulting epithets.[1] This much-maligned house was, in fact, John D.'s favorite hideaway. "Oh, I like Forest Hill much better than any other home!" he proclaimed.[2] It enjoyed an excellent location, standing on the brow of a sharply sloping hill, with wonderful views of Lake Erie; it reminded Rockefeller of his boyhood home in Moravia, poised above Owasco

Lake. This ungainly Victorian confection was a wilderness of porches and gables, turrets and bay windows, covered with gingerbread detail. Rockefeller loved the large, spacious rooms with their unobstructed views. Fond of light and air, he stripped away the curtains and wall hangings and flooded the house with sunshine, adding a glassed-in porch. He even had a huge pipe organ installed in one parlor.

Those who accurately faulted Rockefeller's taste missed a deeper point, however: At a time when moguls vied to impress people with their possessions, Rockefeller preferred comfort to refinement. His house was bare of hunting trophies, shelves of richly bound but unread books, or other signs of conspicuous consumption. Rockefeller molded his house for his own use, not to awe strangers. As he wrote of the Forest Hill fireplaces in 1877: "I have seen a good many fireplaces here [and] don't think the character of our rooms will warrant going into the expenditures for fancy tiling and all that sort of thing that we find in some of the extravagant houses here. What we want is a sensible, plain arrangement in keeping with our rooms."[3]

It took time for the family to adjust to Forest Hill. The house had been built as a hotel, and it showed: It had an office to the left of the front door, a dining room with small tables straight ahead, upstairs corridors lined with cubicle-sized rooms, and porches wrapped around each floor. The verandas, also decorated in resort style, were cluttered with bamboo furniture. It was perhaps this arrangement that tempted John and Cettie to run Forest Hill as a paying club for friends, and they got a dozen to come and stay during the summer of 1877. This venture proved no less of a debacle than the proposed sanatorium. As "club guests," many visitors expected Cettie to function as their unlikely hostess. Some didn't know they were in a commercial establishment and were shocked upon returning home to receive bills for their stay. The Rockefeller children were no less bemused and disoriented as they found themselves eating in a big dining room, attended by a troop of gentlemanly black waiters. After a year, Rockefeller scrapped this misbegotten venture, fired the waiters, and began to convert the large warren of tiny upstairs rooms into suites and master bedrooms.

From 1877 to 1883, the Rockefellers retained the Euclid Avenue house as their primary residence while spending summers at Forest Hill. Gradually, the stays at Forest Hill lengthened, the estate itself expanding to more than seven hundred acres and the number of employees eventually rising to as high as 136. After a time, the family spent only brief spring and autumn stints at Euclid Avenue. They still went there every Sunday, however, bringing in a cold lunch from Forest Hill when they attended the Euclid Avenue Baptist Church. After late 1883, when the Rockefellers moved to New York, they turned Forest Hill into their exclusive Cleveland residence but never renounced a sentimental attachment to 424 Euclid Avenue. They kept the old house in constant repair,

*Laura Spelman Rockefeller, who seldom wore
anything fancier than this dress.*
(Courtesy of the Rockefeller Archive Center)

always ready to receive family members, even though they never went there and it slowly lapsed into an honored, deserted monument to bygone days. Plans to turn it into a convalescent home for crippled children or aged couples never materialized. "It seemed too sacred for common use, we all loved it so," Cettie later said.[4]

Despite its considerable distance from his office, Rockefeller, clad in goggles and duster, drove downtown each morning from Forest Hill, seated in a little two-seat surrey behind a pair of fast-trotting horses. He was still passionate about trotting horses and now had a dozen of them. He constructed his own half-mile racetrack at Forest Hill, shaded by maples planted by his son, and bought Welsh and Shetland ponies for each child. By the mid-1870s, he often returned home from the office for lunch then spent the rest of the afternoon *en famille* in a constant flurry of outdoor activity. He dammed a stream to make two artificial lakes, one for boating, the other for swimming, and on sultry days often swam the mile-long circuit, a straw hat perched on his head to guard his fair skin from the sun. After becoming a biking enthusiast, he smoothed out many dangerously curving paths and rewarded visitors who learned to ride with free bikes. He took unusual delight in ice skating and frequently as many as fifty people—many of them strangers from the neighborhood—skated on the Rockefeller pond on a frosty day. Since he wouldn't allow the pond to be flooded on the Sabbath, Rockefeller sometimes rose after midnight on a freezing Sunday night to direct the workmen in preparing for the next day's skating.

Though he lacked interest in the homely interior of Forest Hill, Rockefeller spent hours daily out on the grounds. A tall, angular figure striding about and surveying the property, he planned new vistas, gravel paths, gardens, barns, and carriage houses. He created a fair-sized farm with sixteen cows and thousands of chickens. Serving as his own engineer and following the natural grades, Rockefeller laid out twenty miles of roadway for horse and buggy rides through stands of aspen, beech, oak, and maple trees. Supervising fifty or sixty workmen, he developed a limestone quarry on the property to service his grandiose projects and adorned the roads with picturesque bridges over streams. To secure striking vistas, he also began to relocate large trees and did this so expertly that they weren't damaged in transition. This constant re-arrangement of his domain was more than just a matter of framing pretty views or beautifying a patch of garden. It was Rockefeller's typical way of re-making his own miniature universe and working out some vast, never-ending design.

For the Rockefeller children, life at Forest Hill could seem melancholy as they drifted alone about the huge estate, cut off from worldly temptation by their parents. This mood of solitary yearning especially afflicted John Jr., who was tutored at home until age ten and later described his boyhood self as "shy, ill-adjusted and frail."[5]

From the start he wasn't made of his father's indestructible stuff. On January 29, 1874, in an unusual moment of tearful joy, Rockefeller arrived at the Standard Oil office and informed Henry Flagler and Oliver Payne that Cettie had given birth to their first son. Dr. Myra Herrick delivered the infant in an upstairs bedroom at Euclid Avenue while Rockefeller waited expectantly across the hall. "How glad all were that the baby was a boy—for there had been four girls—and that he was perfectly formed," Cettie wrote.[6] She always associated the birth of Junior—as he was known to distinguish him from John Senior—with the launch of the Women's Christian Temperance Union in Ohio. As a founding member, she had planned to aid her evangelical sisters with rousing prayers and biblical hymns in local saloons, and, as she later told Junior, "I might have joined them, if a wee baby boy had not claimed me."[7] She fired him with that same crusading, Christian spirit and horror of liquor.

The baby boy was small and sickly, lacking his father's robust energy and reflecting his mother's more delicate constitution; for three years, his parents worried about his health. He had a cloistered childhood, insulated from a world that might contaminate his values. In later years, he could recall only a single male playmate from these early years, Harry Moore, the son of the Forest Hill housekeeper. "I had a camera and he and I took pictures and played together constantly."[8] Nevertheless, Junior found oases of enchantment on the estate and later cherished idyllic memories of summer afternoons spent rowing, swimming, and hiking. As they read aloud to one another, Junior and his sisters often lolled on a great beech tree whose limbs dipped over a creek. Even if his recollections sound highly idealized, with the shadows expunged, his boyhood letters are suffused with the warm glow of a protected childhood, secure in the love of his doting parents. Perhaps Junior's boyhood wasn't quite as lonesome as it seems from afar. Many decades later, his childhood friend Kate Strong reminisced to him, "You were quite the nicest boy that ever was in those days, so all your friends thought . . . affectionate, considerate, thoughtful and full of fun as well as wise almost beyond your years."[9] Junior was always bathed in female love, almost suffocated by it.

Just as Standard Oil workers never remembered a cross word from John Senior, so Junior couldn't cite a single instance of paternal anger. His father was patient and encouraging, if notably stingy with praise. As Junior said, his father was a "beloved companion. He had a genius with children. He never told us what to do or not to do. He was one with us."[10] In contrast to Big Bill's narcissism, John D. had an overdeveloped sense of family responsibility. John and Cettie never administered corporal punishment, and they inculcated moral principles by instruction and example. Each child was taught to listen to his or her conscience as a severely infallible guide.

For this boy destined to be the world's greatest heir, money was so omnipresent as to be invisible—something "there, like air or food or any other element," he later said—yet it was never easily attainable.[11] As if he were a poor, rural boy, he earned pocket change by mending vases and broken fountain pens or by sharpening pencils. Aware of the rich children spoiled by their parents, Senior seized every opportunity to teach his son the value of money. Once, while Rockefeller was being shaved at Forest Hill, Junior entered with a plan to give away his Sunday-school money in one lump sum, for a fixed period, and be done with it. "Let's figure it out first," Rockefeller advised and made Junior run through calculations that showed he would lose eleven cents interest while the Sunday school gained nothing in return. Afterward, Rockefeller told his barber, "I don't care about the boy giving his money in that way. I want him to give it. But I also want him to learn the lesson of being careful of the little things."[12]

When Rockefeller was complimented upon his son, he protested truthfully, "It was his mother who developed him."[13] Cettie brought up her children in her own ascetic style and tutored them in the rites of self-abnegation. She imagined that she presided with a light touch and had no idea that she could be quite overbearing. As she remarked, "I never like to interfere with the children so long as they make happy noises."[14] A sweet, good-natured woman, Cettie nevertheless had a strong didactic side that could verge on fanaticism. As she once confessed to a neighbor, "I am so glad my son has told me what he wants for Christmas, so now it can be denied him."[15] Dutiful, eager to please his mother, Junior absorbed the full force of her piety. "How good God is to have added to our lovely daughters our only son," Cettie later wrote. "Though the youngest, he is the strongest in courage, independence and Christian character."[16] She hemmed him in with numerous prohibitions. He was told that square dancing was promiscuous and immoral, and by age ten this little paragon had to sign a solemn oath that he would abstain from "tobacco, profanity, and the drinking of any intoxicating beverages."[17] Mother wasn't the only earnest female drumming him full of morality; Grandma Spelman also badgered him to attend children's temperance meetings. Thus, an extraordinary contradiction lay at the core of Junior's life: While his father was being rebuked publicly as a corporate criminal, his mother was pumping him brimful of morality and religion. Like his father, Junior developed an upside-down worldview in which the righteous Rockefeller household was always under attack by a godless, uncomprehending world.

With three older sisters, John grew up in largely female surroundings as a delicate boy spared the rough play and teasing of brothers. He was feminized by the experience, wearing his sisters' cast-off dresses, learning to sew and knit, and even attending cooking classes, as if he might someday have to keep house and prepare his own sandwiches. Eight years older than Junior, Bessie was warmly attentive to her brother but inhabited a different world, and he grew up with the wilder and more willful Alta and Edith. One visitor remembered Alta as "mischievous, impulsive, the ringleader of the trio," while Edith was "scrutinizing, calculating," if high-spirited.[18] Because the girls got less attention than their brother did, they probably had more freedom to rebel and explore. As Alta once teased him, "We girls often thought John should have been a girl and we the boys of the family."[19] Despite his sex, Junior ended up as his mother's favorite because he was surely the most like her—obedient, crucified by duty, and almost too eager to please. The model child would struggle to become the model adult, with often painful consequences.

=

Soon after the Rockefellers had moved to 424 Euclid Avenue, they were followed by the Erie Street Baptist Mission Church—soon renamed the Euclid Avenue Baptist Church—the struggling church that had exerted such a formative influence upon Rockefeller's life. As far as fashion or convenience went, it would have behooved the Rockefellers to attend the nearby Saint Paul's Episcopal Church, where elegant couples stepped from tony carriages each Sunday morning. Instead, they drove back down Euclid Avenue to a plain brownstone church with a tall, narrow steeple and a lower-middle-class congregation. As Junior said, "There weren't half a dozen families that were not of limited means."[20] Rockefeller felt no discomfort at being surrounded by humble people and valued this continuity with his roots. He needed the spiritual refreshment of the plain but emotional Baptist style of prayer and probably also wanted to show that he wasn't being spoiled by wealth.

The Euclid Avenue Baptist Church was celebrated as the Rockefeller church and with good reason: By the early 1880s, he was covering half its annual budget, even pledging weekly money from his children and stipulating that "the 20 cents from each child will be earned by the sweat of their brows, pulling weeds, etc."[21] Avoiding clubs, theaters, and other such wicked haunts, Rockefeller was seen publicly only at church, a fixture in his ninth-row pew, his presence generating a growing army of oglers: curiosity seekers, feature writers, panhandlers, and idlers. He loved the bold, joyous, militant spirit of the Baptists and contributed openhandedly to their local charities. His foremost beneficiaries included the celebrated one-armed "Brother" J. D. Jones, who proselytized from a derelict barge moored to a Cleveland dock; the Ragged School, which taught the Bible and trade skills to vagabond teenagers; and the Cleveland Bethel Union, which preached temperance and Christianity to hard-drinking sailors and where Rockefeller himself often stopped by at lunchtime to mingle anonymously with the seamen.

Religion was a form of sustenance for Rockefeller, a necessary complement to his buttoned-up business life. Praising the ministry's role, he once said he needed "good preaching to wind me up, like an old clock, once or twice every week."[22] His life records no crises of faith, no agonizing skepticism toward the inherited orthodoxy of his youth. He believed that good works had to accompany faith, and even during the service his eyes darted around the room as he selected needy recipients of his charity. Taking small envelopes from his pocket, he slipped in some money, wrote the congregants' names on top, then unobtrusively pressed these gifts into their palms as they shook hands and said goodbye. He and Cettie also faithfully attended Friday night prayer meetings and were said to have seldom missed a gathering when in Cleveland over a forty-year period.

From 1872 until 1905, Rockefeller served as superintendent of the Sunday school—for a small portion of time he was seconded to a poor mission school—while Cettie headed the infant department. She liked to audit his classes and stare admiringly at him as he talked. He arrived early to kindle a fire then dimmed the gas lights at the close. In autumn, in an oddly poetic touch, he gathered up bushels of leaves and distributed them to the children. Many of his talks rang variations on the commonplaces of the temperance movement. "Boys, do you know why I never became a drunkard?" Rockefeller asked, scanning the room. "Because I never took the *first* drink."[23] To drive home his message, he told them not to be too free or easy or drink just to please the crowd. "Now I can't be a good fellow," he said sarcastically. "I haven't taken my first drink yet."[24] Each summer, he invited the Sunday-school teachers to a nonalcoholic picnic at Forest Hill, which was probably the most festive day on his annual calendar.

As word circulated that Rockefeller sometimes recruited Standard Oil employees from his Bible class, its size swelled enormously. He made any talk of business taboo, a lesson that one assistant superintendent, to his chagrin, belatedly learned. The man had bought oil at $1.09 a barrel and tried to solicit Rockefeller's advice about whether to sell. The reaction, recalled by one member of the class, was swift and eloquent:

> Mr. Rockefeller immediately changed the expression of his face. He crossed his knees and then uncrossed them. He bent his body forward and proceeded to cross his knees again. But he never said a word. The assistant superintendent grew restless and a little embarrassed. . . . Finally the assistant superintendent asked: "If you were me, what would you do?" Rockefeller replied: "I would do what I thought best."[25]

A fidgety silence was always Rockefeller's harshest expression of scorn.

While Rockefeller resented being pumped for advice, he himself mingled business and religion and converted the church into a powerful platform for espousing capitalism. He had no interest in theological disputation or in discussing otherworldly matters. To Sunday-school classes, he frequently reiterated his motto, "I believe it is a religious duty to get all the money you can, fairly and honestly; to keep all you can, and to give away all you can."[26] When he met his secretary out riding one Sunday, he advised her to save for a rainy day. "By way of apology for talking business on a Sunday," the secretary reported, "he said that there was a great deal of religion in good business."[27] The widening income inequality that accompanied industrialization didn't faze him because it formed part of the divine plan. By this stage of his career, Rockefeller's material success must have undergirded his faith. That he had earned so much surely signaled divine favor, a grace so awesome as to suggest that God had chosen him for some special mission—or else why had He favored him with such bounty? The usual picture of the Gilded Age is that greed eroded religious values, whereas for Rockefeller, his golden heaps seemed like so many tokens of heavenly support.

For John and Cettie, the temperance movement gratified their puritan itch to save the world, and their children joined a prohibition group called the Loyal Legion, which scared them with evil visions of demon rum. As a charter member of the Women's Christian Temperance Union, Cettie and other well-bred ladies periodically descended on a Cleveland slum known as Whiskey Hill, which was mostly populated by immigrant mill hands. Around 11 A.M., they surged into the saloons, falling on their knees and praying for the sodden sinners. These militant ladies rented storefronts and set up a series of "friendly inns" that dispensed "wholesome foods and sarsaparilla" to thirsty "souls drowning in drink."[28] John was the principal donor of the main temperance outpost, Central Friendly Inn, making him an early pioneer in the settlement-house movement. Sometimes he joined Cettie on raids into the grogshops and never forgot how in one saloon he came upon a former classmate from E. G. Folsom's Commercial College who sat there, bloated and red-faced, doomed shortly to die from drink.

Cettie's parents had transferred their abolitionist ardor to the temperance cause after the Civil War. By 1870, they were living in Brooklyn, New York, where they exhibited the same fiery moralism that had distinguished their civic and religious activism in Ohio. In a division of labor, Mr. Spelman agitated to shut down the 2,500 rum shops he counted in Brooklyn, while Mrs. Spelman acted directly on drinkers through prayer and persuasion in taverns. During the post-1873 depression, Mr. Spelman foresaw an impending Armageddon pitting rum against temperance, Satan against Christ. He viewed hard times as the Lord's punishment for avarice manifested by the grasping demands of both workmen and employers. As he sternly concluded, "God's method for punishing man's folly and extravagance are silent, but resistless."[29] Mr. Spelman, who now drew a paycheck from Standard Oil in New York, couched his economic views in terms that suited his son-in-law. "The great trouble arises from extravagant management and reckless and ruinous competition on freights," he declared, tacitly endorsing monopoly. After Harvey Spelman died in 1881, his wife returned to Cleveland to live with John and her two daughters, Cettie and Lute, and the combined influence of the three Spelman women added to the militant, Christian spirit that informed the Rockefeller household.

The man who was now infuriating his rivals with the devilish cunning of his business methods was a tender son to his aging mother. Eliza retained the old Cheshire Street house, where John's portrait held pride of place above the parlor mantel. Though she spent most of her time with Frank and Mary Ann, she reserved summers for Forest Hill. She was still profoundly attached to her eldest son. She confided in John, felt a peaceful glow in his presence, and he responded with deep compassion. As Junior recalled, "She always sat next to Father at the table and how well I can remember often seeing him hold her hand lovingly at the table. Grandmother trusted Father absolutely and loved him devotedly. 'John's judgment' on any question was to her always right and the last word."[30] Rockefeller wrote often to "his dear mother" and struck a note of fond banter not evident elsewhere in his letters. "Your rooms at Forest Hill seem very lonesome and we hope you will not permit them to remain vacant all the summer," he wrote her one June. "The robins already begin to inquire for you and we can have the whole lawn full if you will only come back to greet them."[31]

By the late 1870s, Eliza's health began to fail—she was now in her late sixties—and John pleaded with her to stop smoking her pipe. In a preview of her son's later alopecia, all her hair fell out and she sometimes wore a gray toupee. As Eliza's strength declined, John grew more solicitous. "When she was feeling ill and confined to her room, Father would go to her in his quiet, cheery, reassuring way and tell her she was doing nicely and would soon be well," said Junior, "whereupon she never failed to take new courage and improve in health."[32] Her maladies took precedence over Standard Oil business, and if she had a nervous attack while John was at a meeting, he rushed back to Forest Hill, went straight to her bedside, took her hand, and said, "There, there, Mother. It's all right."[33]

To explain his father's disappearance, John D. often told people that Bill had asthma—which was true as far as it went—and needed a dry, warm western climate. Once or twice a year, Devil Bill—or Dr. William Levingston—popped up in Cleveland in his typically idiosyncratic fashion. Without any warning, he telephoned Forest Hill from the last stop of the Cleveland trolley line and asked to have a carriage sent to fetch him. Or he appeared in an impressive rig, behind a fine team of horses, and rode grandly up Euclid Avenue. Or, pulling up in front of the Standard Oil building, he bolted up the steps like a much younger man. A blithe spirit, he wandered about and always did as he pleased. As one

Standard Oil attorney said, "If you didn't like it, you could go hang!"[34] He still looked impressive, with a bald head, massive forehead, and a full red beard now speckled with gray. In many respects, he was the same carefree, ebullient spirit of yesteryear, sporting snappy clothes and a diamond stickpin in his shirtfront, playing his fiddle, cracking jokes, and telling tall tales.

As they got older, the Rockefeller children were enchanted by Grandfather Rockefeller, whom they regarded as a colorful, folksy relic of the family's rustic past. Innocent of his darker side, they loved his rough country ways, lusty fiddling, and bawdy humor. His antics must have relieved the bottled-up tensions in this straitlaced household. Junior, who found him "jolly and entertaining," said, "My Grandfather Rockefeller was a most lovable person. . . . All the family loved him. He was a very entertaining man, coming and going when he felt like it."[35] Much as he once had with his own children, Bill gave his grandchildren rifles and taught them to shoot, nailing a bull's-eye to a distant tree and regaling them with tales of his wild-duck hunting. The sassy Edith pleased him most, and when she hit the target, he executed a dance (much like John) and hollered, "Bet you she hits it eight times out of ten!"[36] After a few days of such uproarious times, Grandpa would abruptly disappear, giving no sense of where he went.

John resented his father and never wrote to him, but he didn't poison the children's minds against him, and he behaved civilly in his presence, even if he kept studiously aloof. To strangers and the press, he never spoke of his father as anything but a fine, upstanding figure. Bill's visits provoked similarly ambivalent sentiments in Eliza. When he visited Forest Hill in 1885, she refused, at first, to see him, blaming a stitch in her side, then agreed to spend the day with him. By this point, she was surely glad to be rid of him.

In many respects, Bill's life as Doc Levingston resembled his former life with Eliza. He spent winters with Margaret in Freeport, Illinois, then took to the open road for the rest of the year, leaving her alone. A renegade individualist, he felt that footloose American urge to eke out a living on the fringes of civilization, and he penetrated ever farther into the wilderness. As a flimflam man, he had to practice his wiles on country bumpkins and other credulous folks and stay away from skeptical city slickers. Either because suckers had grown scarce or sheriffs more vigilant, he now traversed entire states to peddle his wares.

In his incarnation as Dr. Levingston, Bill had to not only endure the silent lash of John's indignation, but forgo any claims to his money. Could God have devised a more excruciating curse for his sins? Faced with his son's dizzying wealth, he must have sometimes pondered whether to throw off his disguise and resume his Rockefeller identity. Yet this was not a feasible option, since he could not do so without shocking Margaret and betraying his own shameful bigamy. So the father of the leading figure in the oil industry went on practicing his petty scams on the road under an assumed name.

＝

Rockefeller's sisters played a limited role in his adult life. His favorite sister, Lucy, was sweet and placid, arguably the best-adjusted sibling, but she was chronically sick and died in 1878 at age forty—the event that probably triggered the deterioration of Eliza's health. Her husband, Pierson Briggs, spent nearly fifteen years as a purchasing agent for Standard Oil of Ohio. He was a kindly, jolly man and very popular with John's children. After Lucy's death, Briggs remarried into a wealthy Cleveland family while his musical daughter, Florence, spent a great deal of time at Forest Hill under the watchful care of John and Cettie.

The younger sister, Mary Ann, married a genial man named William Rudd, the president of Chandler and Rudd, a Cleveland grocery concern, and they had two sons and two daughters. Quiet and withdrawn, Mary Ann turned into a queerly reclusive personality. Always clad in funereal black clothes that covered a deformed body—some people thought she was a hunchback—she laid down arbitrary social rules at her Euclid Avenue house. For example, visitors had to arrive punctually and could only stay briefly. Despite her husband's wealth, Mary Ann insisted on a crackpot frugality and behaved as if they were always strapped for cash. In a morbid caricature of the Protestant work ethic, she scrubbed the front porch of their plain white house, performed her own housework, and refused to have any servants. She never went to church and seldom visited John and Cettie, even though they lived a short distance away. The antithesis of his hermit wife, William Rudd was a frequent visitor at Forest Hill, where he found a refuge from the lugubrious atmosphere at home. One of John D.'s favorite people, Rudd overflowed with gags and pranks, and his pockets always bulged with nuts and candy for the children. One day, he lugged a sack of dirty old potatoes to Forest Hill; the Rockefeller children were mystified until they found a gold piece artfully tucked into each potato.

Of the three brothers, John remained the most like Eliza, while William mixed qualities of both parents. Frank aped Bill's swaggering ways. He was an avid hunter and rollicking storyteller who loved to drink, smoke cigars, make boisterous jokes, and hobnob in Cleveland clubs. Yet increasingly, a disagreeable side surfaced in Frank: Choleric, paranoid, and suspicious, he constantly clashed with John. As one of Frank's friends said, "You never saw two men from one family that were more unlike."[37] Though they went through periods of reconciliation, their mutual dislike soon ripened into a hatred that split the family, with William lining up with John and Big Bill siding with Frank. Although he liked William—who often tried to make peace between his brothers—Frank felt William was too much under John's thumb, and it irked him that he, too, didn't rebel openly against John's leadership.

After being wounded in the Union army, Frank attended business school and, like John and William, got a bookkeeping job in a small commission house. But unlike his brothers, he didn't prosper, foreshadowing things to come. Trying to emulate his brothers, Frank entered oil refining as a competitor to Standard Oil after he married the tall, handsome Helen E. Scofield in 1870. The Scofields were a relatively old Cleveland family, and Helen's father, William Scofield, was a partner in Alexander, Scofield and Company, one of the major refiners that John absorbed during the 1872 Cleveland Massacre. That Frank married the daughter of one of John's chief competitors could only have been interpreted by John as a provocation.

In 1876, the antipathy between the two brothers flared into open conflict when Frank testified before a congressional committee probing the South Improvement Company and charged John with heavy-handed tactics in buying out Alexander, Scofield. Already sensing the press's insatiable desire for incendiary statements about his brother, Frank electrified reporters with John's warning, "We have a combination with the railroads. We are going to buy out all the refiners in Cleveland. We will give every one a chance to come in. We will give you a chance. Those who refuse will be crushed. If you don't sell your property to us it will be valueless."[38] According to Frank, the experience of Alexander, Scofield wasn't unique. "There are some twenty men in Cleveland who sold out under the fright, and almost any of them would tell you that story."[39] Confronted with this indictment years later, John shook his head sadly and moaned, "Poor Frank!"[40] Indeed, after these public outbursts, Frank often came to John and apologized profusely. "John, can you forgive me? I have been an ass."[41] One possible reason for this contrition was that Frank was chronically in debt to his brother.

Every time the brothers tried to call a truce, it ended abysmally. After allegedly being squeezed out in 1872, Frank took the money for his Alexander, Scofield interest and invested in a fleet of Lake Erie boats. In a conciliatory gesture, John gave him a contract for Standard Oil shipments, but Frank botched the opportunity. While Frank was away hunting, Standard Oil urgently needed more lake shipments, and his poorly maintained fleet couldn't cope with the increased volume. When Frank returned to Cleveland, John reprimanded him sharply. "Frank, this will have to stop. If you are going to attend to business, very well. If not, we shall have to make other arrangements." When Frank grew belligerent, John replied, "What do you think your interest in those boats is worth? State your figure!" The following day, John wrote a check and bought up Frank's interest in the boats.[42] Frank incessantly gambled in stocks and commodities, further alienating his more prudent brother.

Also aggravating fraternal tensions was the fact that John despised Frank's father-in-law, William Scofield, a relationship so acrimonious that John supposedly told Sam Andrews on one occasion, "There, Sam, is Scofield. I'll knife that fellow under the ribs some day. You'll see."[43] The story was told to Ida Tarbell by Cleveland refiner J. W. Fawcett and might be apocryphal—Rockefeller almost never spoke so viciously—but he did bear a special grudge against Scofield. When Standard Oil bought out Alexander, Scofield in 1872, the selling partners pledged to steer clear of refining. Nevertheless, a year later—in what Rockefeller considered an unforgivable breach of faith—Scofield organized a new refining company, Scofield, Shurmer and Teagle. "They were a lot of pirates," Rockefeller said later. "You may call them that with justice."[44] After fuming for three years, he cut a secret deal with his nemesis in 1876. Investing $10,000 in Scofield, Shurmer, he forged a joint venture, agreed to purchase crude oil for them, market their refined oil, and negotiate their railroad rebates, while also assigning them a refining quota. In thrashing out this deal, Rockefeller and his new secret partners agreed to communicate by a special post-office box, prompting Ida Tarbell to write, "In fact, smugglers and housebreakers never surrounded their operations with more mystery."[45] If Rockefeller imagined he had neutralized a rival, he was soon disabused. When Scofield, Shurmer produced far beyond their quotas, Standard Oil was forced to sue them. In a significant decision—but one that didn't inhibit Rockefeller in future—a Cleveland judge ruled against Standard Oil in 1880, saying that by assigning production limits to a competitor, it had executed a contract in restraint of trade.

In 1878, in yet another affront to his brother, Frank joined with C. W. Scofield and J. W. Fawcett to start a Cleveland refinery known as the Pioneer Oil Works. Often operating through William as an intermediary, John began a determined campaign to bring Frank's company into Standard Oil, telling him that Standard could refine oil at half the cost. At first, this campaign seemed to backfire. In the spring of 1879, Frank began to plot strategy with some independent refiners from Marietta, Ohio, who had accused Standard Oil of colluding with the railroads and wanted to take the company to court. John D. was mortified when subordinates informed him that his youngest brother was holed up at a drugstore down the block along with men who were trying to buttonhole Standard Oil executives and serve them with subpoenas. Things grew only more lunatic with the passage of time.

CHAPTER 12

Insurrection in the Oil Fields

I n 1875, Henry E. Wrigley, the head of the Pennsylvania Geological Survey, issued a doomsday warning that the state—and hence the world—production of oil had peaked and would soon experience a precipitous decline, aggravating fears that had overshadowed the oil industry since its inception. Within months, his forecast was refuted when a new field was discovered in Bradford, Pennsylvania, northeast of the old Oil Creek fields. As thousands of wild-eyed drillers besieged the area, oil production soared, and prices sank from $4 a barrel in 1876 to 70 cents two years later. Once again, the industry's salvation proved its undoing, with the boom-and-bust cycle unleashing volatile emotions among producers who found themselves rich one moment and then desperate the next.

As the master of storage tanks and pipelines, refineries and by-product plants, *Rockefeller* had become a byword in the oil fields, a phantom of vast, indeterminate proportions who operated entirely through agents. His remoteness frustrated opponents, who felt they were boxing with a ghost. In the crisis provoked by the new Bradford production, he was blamed for price manipulation even when he simply reflected the law of supply and demand. With the immediate-shipment controversy of 1878, the running warfare between Standard Oil and the producers expanded from minor skirmishes into a large, violent engagement reminiscent of the South Improvement Company furor.

The roots of the controversy were as follows. As oil wells sprang up around Bradford, Standard Oil wanted to retain its pipeline monopoly and worked overtime to connect new wells to its system free of charge. In a bravura performance, Daniel O'Day's scrappy, hustling teams hooked up five wells a day to the

United Pipe Lines network and threw up huge tank farms to store the surplus oil. They moved at a breathtaking tempo: Between April and November 1878, the Bradford tankage swelled from a little more than 1 million barrels to 4.5 million. Nonetheless, the producers, repeating past errors, exercised no discipline and drilled far beyond the system's capacity. When their oil ran into the ground for lack of storage space, they didn't praise Standard's efforts to accommodate them but detected a malevolent conspiracy. O'Day's letters to Rockefeller reflect exasperation at the misperception. No matter how fast they went, he moaned, "There will be at least ten thousand barrels a day that I don't know how we can move, no matter how good our disposition to do it might be."[1]

Nevertheless, if he didn't create the crisis, as many producers believed, Rockefeller never passed up a chance to exploit a legitimate advantage against his beleaguered rivals. With its tanks overflowing, Standard Oil issued a sweeping edict that it would no longer accept oil for temporary storage but only for immediate shipment to refineries. Standard Oil quoted a purchase price for crude oil a full 20 percent below prevailing prices, then stalled on payments to desperate producers. One market letter caustically described this policy as a "bull issued by his infallible holiness Rockefeller." It was a terribly high-handed and insensitive way to respond to the crisis.[2] But even by oil-industry standards, the producers reacted with exceptional fury. Every day, sullen mobs lined up at the Standard Oil office and grudgingly negotiated their oil shipments. With wide room for partiality, Standard Oil favored shipments to its own refiners—a fact that struck Rockefeller as eminently fair—while producers argued that the pipeline network was a common carrier and obligated to treat everyone equally. Producers felt that their fortunes, their very lives, hung in the balance. As one Standard Oil lawyer recalled, "Arson and murder were threatened by the producers, who marched in masked bands at midnight uttering their threats."[3] One of O'Day's men reminisced, "They paraded at night in big gangs, covered with sheets from head to foot in regular ku-klux fashion, groaning and booing the Standard."[4] Orators urged the burning of Standard pumping stations, the skulls and crossbones appeared on Standard buildings, and vandalism spread.

To mollify producers, the state of Pennsylvania deputed William McCandless, its commissioner of internal affairs, to study the petroleum industry. Officials of the Standard pipelines, who now arrogantly behaved as if they owned the oil industry, ignored his subpoenas and boycotted testimony. Nevertheless, when McCandless issued a report in October 1878 that exonerated Standard Oil, the producers erupted in hysterical protest. It was widely rumored that McCandless had been bribed, and on the Bradford streets he was hung in effigy with a big, bogus $20,000 check, signed by Rockefeller and endorsed by the Pennsylvania Railroad, protruding from his pocket. Newspapers told how one Bradford man invited Rockefeller to the region but then, remembering the im-

*William Rockefeller, brother of John D. and
a leading Standard Oil executive.*
(Courtesy of the Rockefeller Archive Center)

broglio, warned him instead, "Don't you do it, for if you do, you will never come back alive."[5]

The immediate-shipment controversy engendered mutual enmity, for Rockefeller saw the producers as so many ingrates and malcontents whose oil was worthless without his superefficient United Pipe Lines system, which would soon be connected to twenty thousand wells. He mockingly described his foes' attitude as follows: "We have disregarded all advice, and produced oil in excess of the means of storing and shipping it. We have not built storage of our own. How dare you refuse to take all we produce? Why do you not pay us the high prices of 1876, without regard to the fact that the glut has depressed every market?"[6] The episode convinced Rockefeller that the producers nursed an unreasonable hostility against him, and this inoculated him against even valid criticism. But unlike the producers, Standard Oil paid no real penalty for the Bradford crisis and in 1878 declared an impressive $60 dividend on shares with a $100 par value. Rockefeller had positioned himself exactly where he wished to be—poised to profit from either surplus or scarcity and all but immune to the vagaries of the marketplace.

As masses of drillers descended upon Bradford, this major shift in the geography of oil awakened dormant ambitions in Rockefeller's foe, Tom Scott of the Pennsylvania Railroad. As Standard Oil erased the surviving independent refiners, competing pipeline and railroad officials were petrified that Standard might soon be in a position to eliminate their oil traffic at whim. Since it had tracks near the Bradford wells, the Pennsylvania spotted a chance to loosen Standard Oil's grip and win new business. Its vehicle for this challenge was its assertive subsidiary, the Empire Transportation Company, which owned five hundred miles of pipeline and one thousand tank cars. Empire had had the temerity to threaten Standard Oil in its refining strongholds, buying up rivals in New York, Philadelphia, and Pittsburgh and trying to win over new refining customers with bargain transportation rates. Now, as if spoiling for a fight, the Empire began to lay pipes for pumping crude oil from Bradford to the seaboard refineries—a direct challenge to Standard Oil dominance.

The driving force behind this incursion was a man who was *almost* a match for Rockefeller but who fancied that, had Rockefeller only played fair, he would have been much *more* than a match: Colonel Joseph D. Potts, president of Empire Transportation. A civil engineer descended from a family of Quaker ironmasters, Potts was a capable man who had attained a colonel's rank in the Civil War. He had a prominent nose and a long preacher's face, fringed by a white beard. Gravely earnest, no less conversant with the Bible than with the oil industry, Potts aspired to be Rockefeller's equal. If Rockefeller respected Potts's "indomitable will," he also patronized him as "a shrewd oily man, as smooth as oil."[7] Potts repaid the compliment, castigating Rockefeller as a merciless predator. Of Rockefeller's current refiners' cartel, the Central Refiners' Association,

Potts said memorably, "It resembled the gentle fanning of the vampire's wing, and it had the same end in view—the undisturbed abstraction of the victim's blood."[8]

When Potts poached on his territory, Rockefeller demanded a meeting with Tom Scott and A. J. Cassatt of the Pennsylvania Railroad. As his private reminiscences attest, Rockefeller was cynical about Empire, which he thought a transparent front for corrupt Pennsylvania officials to line their pockets with profits that belonged rightly to shareholders; it was also, he saw, a handy vehicle for the railroad to cheat on pooling agreements while escaping detection. In confronting the railroad officials, Rockefeller struck a characteristic tone of injured innocence: "Here, I have gone out of my way to be friendly to the Pennsylvania in the allotment of oil shipments and now you gentlemen are permitting your associate, Colonel Potts, actually to invade the Central Association's field. Why, it is nothing less than piracy! You must call off this poacher, Potts."[9] Although nearly two-thirds of the oil carried by the Pennsylvania Railroad now originated with Standard Oil, Scott decided to flout his biggest customer and, if not annihilate Rockefeller, chop him down to size.

Rockefeller interpreted Scott's intransigence as a declaration of war. In taking on the Pennsylvania Railroad, he was battling America's most powerful corporation, yet he proceeded with unwavering confidence. In spring 1877, Rockefeller told railroad officials point-blank that if Empire didn't retreat from refining, Standard Oil would divert its shipments to other railroads. When they didn't flinch, Rockefeller launched an all-out attack. To starve out the railroad, he idled all his Pittsburgh refineries and ordered corresponding increases in output in his Cleveland refineries. He sent out word that Standard Oil refineries should fiercely undersell Empire refineries in every market where they vied for kerosene sales. Turning to the two railroads long solidly in his corner, the Erie and the New York Central, Rockefeller had them trim rates to ratchet up the pressure on the Pennsylvania Railroad. To handle the extra volume expected on these two railroads, Flagler negotiated a deal with William Vanderbilt to build another six hundred tank cars. With blazing speed, Rockefeller was on his way to humbling the world's largest freight carrier, a company long thought invincible in the business and political world. Afterward, A. J. Cassatt admitted that the railroad had to grant such large rebates to keep up with Standard Oil that it ended up literally paying shippers to transport their oil.

In the end, providence itself conspired in the railroad's comeuppance. As he slashed rates to withstand the Standard onslaught, Tom Scott fired hundreds of workers and reduced wages 20 percent. When he doubled the length of trains without expanding their crews, trainmen walked off the job in protest. After the Baltimore and Ohio Railroad announced comparable wage cuts in 1877, the protest flamed up into a general railroad strike, one of the bloodiest battles in American labor history, resulting in dozens of fatalities. In Pittsburgh alone,

500 tank cars, 120 locomotives, and 27 buildings were torched by union vandals, sabotage so costly that Pennsylvania officials tapped Wall Street for a large emergency loan from Drexel, Morgan and Company. As state governors ordered out their militias and President Rutherford B. Hayes supplemented them with federal troops, the country watched the insurrection in horror. However pleased by the railroad's travails, Rockefeller must have felt a dreadful chill as rumors circulated that two thousand pistol-packing radicals would march down Euclid Avenue. After the riots ended, one Titusville reporter disclosed that the Oil Creek citizenry had nearly exploited the upheavals to take revenge against Standard Oil: "Had certain men given the word there would have been an outbreak that contemplated the seizure of the railroads and running them, the capture and control of the United Pipe Line's property, and in all probability the burning of all the property of the Standard Oil Company in the region."[10] Though after burning more than two thousand freight cars the strikers capitulated, their revolt inaugurated a new age of labor militance in American industry.

Reeling from these blows, the Pennsylvania Railroad skipped its dividend, sending its share price tumbling on the stock exchange. Though Potts wished to fight on, Scott was inclined to relent. Although the railroad didn't wholly own Empire, it had an option to buy the remaining shares, and, faced with Potts's recalcitrance, Scott did just that. It amused Rockefeller how agilely Scott switched direction when it served his interest and how—without notifying Potts, who would resent his treachery—he dispatched A. J. Cassatt to Cleveland to tell Rockefeller and Flagler that he was "anxious for a settlement."[11] Rockefeller gloated over Potts's crushing defeat: "The effort of Colonel Potts to make it appear that he was the great Moses failed, utterly failed."[12]

Empire's capitulation represented a greater boon than Rockefeller had envisaged, for the spoils were bountiful. The cash-strapped Scott didn't simply agree to stop refining oil but offered Standard Oil a huge fire sale of assets—refineries, storage tanks, pipelines, a fleet of steamships, tugboats, barges, loading docks—in fact, far more than Standard could afford. During negotiations with Rockefeller at a Philadelphia hotel in October 1877, Scott swept in with a self-confident panache that thinly camouflaged his defeat. As Rockefeller recalled, "I can see [Scott] now with his big soft hat, marching into the room in that little hotel to meet us; not to sweep us away as he had always done, but coming in with a smile, walking right up to the cannon's mouth. 'Well, boys, what will we do?' " In the ensuing talks, Scott drove a tough bargain and refused to budge on two conditions: that Standard Oil buy *all* of Empire's assets, including its antiquated lake vessels; and that within twenty-four hours it pay $2.5 million of the $3.4 million offering price by certified check.

This last demand taxed even Standard Oil, which had only about half the necessary cash in its coffers. Rockefeller raced back to Cleveland and flew through local banks in a hectic tour such as he hadn't made in years. Climbing into his buggy, he approached one bank president after another and told them breathlessly, "I must have all you've got! I need it all! It's all right! Give me what you have! I must catch the noon train."[13] Unable to persuade his Standard Oil confrères to buy the steamships—Rockefeller always operated by consensus—he had the nerve to borrow several hundred thousand dollars on his own account and buy the ships himself. Although these money-losing ships drained him for years, their purchase was dictated by the larger interest of Standard Oil, and he never regretted his snap decision.

In dueling with Scott, Rockefeller didn't try to demolish him—as Scott might have done to him—but called a truce to strengthen their alliance. His constant aim was to be conciliatory whenever possible and extend his range of influence. In a new pooling arrangement, Standard Oil agreed to ship at least two million barrels yearly over the Pennsylvania Railroad and restore its faded luster in the oil trade; in exchange, Standard would pocket a 10 percent commission (read: rebate) on its shipments over the road. More important, Standard was designated as the evener—that is, the enforcer—of a new master plan brokered by the railroads whereby the railroad would receive 47 percent of all oil traffic; the Erie and the New York Central 21 percent apiece; and the B&O 11 percent. Tightening the vise, Rockefeller's pipeline chieftain, Daniel O'Day, informed the Pennsylvania Railroad in February 1878 that Standard would henceforth want at least twenty cents for *every* barrel of crude oil the railroad shipped—an arrangement Standard Oil had foisted upon the Erie and the New York Central. Having outsmarted the largest railroad, Rockefeller had acquired a stranglehold on the three major roads, and his taming of the imperious Tom Scott guaranteed that no railroad president would ever dare to tangle with him again.

The defeat left Colonel Potts a broken, humiliated man. As his son recalled, "He always believed some of the Pennsylvania directors had been approached by the Standard and bought out. Others talked of bribery; of course nothing could be proved."[14] In all likelihood, Potts didn't want to admit that he had been outwitted by Rockefeller. Ida Tarbell, in her romanticized view of some of Rockefeller's foes, converted Colonel Potts into an incorruptible martyr, the Abraham Lincoln of the oil industry, crucified by Standard Oil, when he was just an able, aggressive businessman who lost out in a power struggle to a shrewder, bolder opponent. In the early 1880s, Potts renounced his principled opposition to Standard Oil and became an active director of the National Transit Company, a Standard Oil pipeline subsidiary.

The Grand Guignol of the Empire battle diverted attention from another momentous drama that unfolded at about the same time: the purchase of the Columbia Conduit Company from Dr. David Hostetter. For Rockefeller, the Columbia purchase had far-reaching strategic implications, for the pipeline functioned as the B&O's crude-oil lifeline. Columbia pumped western Pennsylvania crude to the B&O's Pittsburgh terminal, whence it traveled by rail to Baltimore refineries. Thus, if he could smother Columbia, Rockefeller would be able to conquer the fourth and last major railroad system while also gaining uncontested control of *all* major pipeline systems connecting oil wells to railroad trunk lines. He would have extended his reach, in short, into every nook and cranny of the oil industry. As Ida Tarbell noted, after the Columbia Conduit fell into Rockefeller's lap, "Practically not a barrel of oil could get to a railroad without [Rockefeller's] consent."[15]

By this point, Standard Oil had effectively stamped out competing refiners in Cleveland, Philadelphia, and Pittsburgh and faced only a smattering of weak New York holdouts. The last major pockets of resistance lay in West Virginia and Baltimore, whose refiners relied upon the B&O. Thus, by controlling the Columbia Conduit Company, Rockefeller would be able to snuff out the last independent refiners. Conversely, if he controlled the West Virginia and Baltimore refiners, he could pressure the railroad into submission.

The man assigned to carry out this convoluted campaign was Johnson Newlon Camden, the Parkersburg, West Virginia, refiner whose company had secretly joined Standard some years earlier. Elected to Congress several times, Camden later served as a U.S. senator, but his civic involvement didn't translate into superior business ethics. On the contrary, Camden dealt with rivals in an especially coercive manner, as he showed in early 1876 when absorbing Pittsburgh refiners. To snuff out the last competitors, he peremptorily informed Alexander McDonald, the leading supplier of barrel staves to the city's independent refiners, "that no staves must be sold to Pittsburgh, that it was our policy to control the oil business of Pittsburgh by controlling the supply of staves and barrels at that point," as he told Standard headquarters. Further, McDonald was under strict instructions, he said, "that he must ship no staves to Pittsburgh without [Standard Oil's] consent."[16] Whenever competition flared up in Pittsburgh, Rockefeller dispatched Camden to douse the flames, once telling him, "At this particular moment it is especially important that outside Pittsburgh refineries should have no chance whatever in any market for local trade oil. . . . Our feeling of anxiety to accomplish the object of centralization is so strong we want you to yield to it for a few days longer when we hope you will be forever relieved."[17]

Like Rockefeller, Camden had a devious talent for concocting anticompetitive practices and paralyzing the trade. To soften up local competitors, he cornered the supply of West Virginia crude, leaving independent refiners high and dry. When confronted with such shameless manipulation, Rockefeller sighed, disclaimed any knowledge, and blamed overly zealous subordinates—a recurring pose in his career. But Camden, like other subordinates, kept Rockefeller thoroughly posted about his actions and told him apropos of early negotiations with independents, "I am having interviews with all the little refinery men here [Parkersburg] and at Marietta. . . . We will either get them or starve them."[18]

Camden was thwarted by the same problems that had confronted Rockefeller in forming cartels in other cities. Aware that Standard would buy ramshackle plants to shut them down, many blackmailers entered the business in order to sell out. The harried Camden groused that small refineries were "multiplying like rats" and concluded despairingly that they would be "as hard to keep down as weeds in a garden."[19] As Standard Oil succeeded in steadying kerosene prices, it drew people back into the business. At this point, Rockefeller took a tougher line with blackmailers who wanted to be bought out. In responding to several Baltimore refiners who had previously rejected fair prices from Standard Oil but now wished to sell, Rockefeller sounded like the voice of divine retribution, telling Camden that "they will be sick unto death now having failed in their wicked scheme. A good sweating will be healthy for them. If . . . these people could wait and sell out their works at a loss, thereby making a poor speculation of blackmailing, it would probably cure this batch and save you endless trouble in future."[20] Camden's files support Rockefeller's contention that he bought loads of worthless junk and enriched men who knew little about refining oil but everything about extortion.

Applying a formula that Rockefeller had perfected in New York, New Jersey, and Philadelphia, Camden bought waterfront property in Baltimore, where he erected wharves and warehouses for a B&O oil-export terminal. With Standard Oil now embedded in the local transportation infrastructure, it became impossible for Baltimore refiners to operate autonomously. Standard Oil had become virtually indistinguishable from the railroad industry. On December 21, 1877, Camden triumphantly told Rockefeller that they had completed their conquest of the last independent refining center. "We have cleared up every seed in which a refining interest could spring up in Baltimore, so far as we can at present determine."[21]

Thus, only five years after the Cleveland Massacre, the thirty-eight-year-old Rockefeller, with piratical flair and tactical brilliance, had come to control nearly 90 percent of the oil refined in the United States. Perhaps a hundred tiny refineries still eked out a meager living in the interstices of the industry, but they were mostly tolerated as minor nuisances and scarcely threatened Standard Oil. As Rockefeller himself acknowledged, these isolated cases served a useful political purpose, providing a mirage of competition when it had ceased to exist altogether. He liked to point to these doughty survivors as proof that all the stories about the strong-arm tactics of Standard Oil were grossly exaggerated and that the oil industry was a scene of vibrant competition.

In his implacable quest to rule the oil business, Rockefeller shifted focus in the late 1870s from the railroads to outright ownership of the superior alternative: pipelines. Undeterred by prophecies of exhausted oil fields, Standard Oil had both the capital and the incentive to blanket western Pennsylvania with a gigantic maze of pipelines. By 1879, the combine controlled almost the entire pipeline system, siphoning crude oil from thousands of wells and pumping it to storage tanks or railroad depots. When a driller struck oil, Standard Oil swooped down in a flash to connect his well, assuring both his livelihood and irrevocable reliance on the combine.

Standard's rough, brawling pipeline boss, Daniel O'Day, made sure that his construction gangs kept pace with the new fields, laying pipe at a furious pace of up to one and a half miles per day. O'Day stood forth as the agent of wealth or ruin for producers. If he wanted to punish a producer, he might hint that the producer's backcountry well was too inaccessible for Standard to run a line through the woods. And if the producer lacked money to erect storage tanks, he might watch his fortune seep into the ground as he bickered impotently with Standard Oil.

That O'Day exploited his power to silence dissent and cripple refractory competitors is amply documented in Rockefeller's papers. It is important to recall that O'Day, like other Standard Oil lieutenants in the field, was the executor of Rockefeller's will, whatever the latter's disclaimers. When O'Day discovered that a producer named Murphy held a small stake in a competing pipeline, he dispatched to the scene John D. Archbold, who pointedly reminded this upstart that he had expected Standard "to take care of his production that might be located far back in the interior, as we have always done for him, and where such companies as the Pittsburgh line would not care to go."[22] O'Day scared the daylights out of railroads, too. When one railway official complained that Standard was hogging crude-oil shipments between Olean, New York, and Buffalo, O'Day retorted that Standard Oil might just decide to ship all the *refined* oil by pipeline as well. As O'Day reported with glee to Rockefeller—who again professed ignorance of such machinations—"This seemed to stagger him a little and we may be able to hold it over him (as a club) successfully."[23] While Rockefeller communicated with his subordinates in genteel fashion, discussing muscular tactics with unctuous euphemisms, his colleagues were less restrained and gloried in their brutal shenanigans.

As Rockefeller consolidated his virtual monopoly over the pipeline network, it provoked pandemonium along Oil Creek, where he was now dubbed the Lord of the Oil Regions. In late 1877, desperate independents thronged a "Petroleum Parliament" in Titusville, hoping to plot their escape from Standard Oil servitude. These extended, crowded sessions generated a host of resolutions, including enactment of a free-pipeline bill and another to prohibit railroad-freight discrimination. But Standard Oil spiked all such reform efforts through the liberal application of backdoor payments to legislators.

In a historic departure, the independents endorsed plans for two long-distance pipelines that would bypass the whole Standard-rigged web of pipelines and railroads and open a path to the sea. The less ambitious project was the Equitable Petroleum Company, formed by Lewis Emery, Jr., to pipe oil from the Bradford fields to a railroad that would then carry the oil to Buffalo, where it would travel east over the Erie Canal. This roundabout route posed only a modest threat to Standard Oil, yet Rockefeller wired Daniel O'Day, "Don't let them get a pipe to Buffalo."[24] To sabotage the effort, Standard Oil unleashed its full arsenal of obstructive tactics. It bought up the connecting railroad to Buffalo; threatened to yank orders from pipe manufacturers who sold to Equitable; and disconnected pipelines from all Bradford refiners who dealt with it. Despite this intimidation, the pipeline commenced operations in August 1878, exposing the first small chink in Standard Oil's armor.

The second, far more threatening project, led by Byron Benson, envisaged a pipeline to the seaboard, a revolutionary development in long-distance transport. Before this time, pipelines had never covered more than thirty miles. This seaboard pipeline would eclipse the railroads and shatter the whole complex structure of secret rebates and drawbacks that Rockefeller had cobbled together. Before the seaboard-pipeline battle, one could argue that Standard Oil had been an innovative force, modernizing the industry through up-to-date plants, superior management, and smoother coordination of the oil flow from wellhead to consumer. Now, it became a benighted custodian of the status quo, squelching progress to safeguard its own interests.

At first, the independents (acting through the Tidewater Pipe Line Company) contemplated running a line from Oil Creek to Baltimore, but J. N. Camden quickly dealt a mortal blow to this plan: He bought an exclusive pipeline charter in the Maryland legislature that carried an ironclad guarantee that no other company would receive a charter that session. The Standard Oil hierarchy in Cleveland was kept closely apprised of his underhanded activities. Of the substantial money needed to grease this shady deal, Camden told Flagler: "The price is nominally $40,000."[25]

Foiled in crossing Maryland, the Tidewater Pipe Line Company then opted for a 110-mile pipeline from Bradford to Williamsport in central Pennsylvania, where the oil would then journey east by the Philadelphia and Reading Railroad. On November 22, 1878, it began its great race to the sea, laying down a ribbon of pipe at a rapid rate of two miles a day. Since the whole concept was experimental—nobody knew if oil could be pumped over 2,600-foot mountains—the Standard Oil cognoscenti reacted with cynical snickers. Writing to Rockefeller, a smug John D. Archbold professed himself "greatly amused" by the "seaboard scheme."[26] Rockefeller was dubious yet circumspect, predicting at one point, "They are quite likely to have some disappointments yet, before consummating all their plans in that direction."[27] The Tidewater people mobilized powerful financial interests, and two Wall Street tycoons, George F. Baker and Harris C. Fahnestock of First National Bank, aided them financially.

The fierceness of Standard Oil's response was previewed in one of O'Day's first letters to Rockefeller about the mavericks. "I would have no mercy on them that don't deserve nor appreciate it."[28] In combating this challenge, Rockefeller again showed himself a virtuoso of industrial warfare. He sent his underlings to tank manufacturers, warning them not to deal with Tidewater, and deluged tank-car manufacturers with orders that kept them busy, depriving the pipeline of rolling stock needed to transport construction materials. Refiners who used Tidewater were lured away with concessionary rates on Standard Oil pipelines, and Rockefeller swiftly bought up any remaining independent refineries that might be prospective Tidewater customers.

Standard Oil also embarked on a real-estate spree of monumental proportions, buying up strips of land or "dead lines" that ran in a straight line from the northern to the southern border of Pennsylvania, to block the Tidewater's advance. Overnight, bewildered farmers became rich by selling parcels for extravagant sums to Standard Oil agents who invaded their sleepy towns. In another tack, Standard Oil placed stories in local papers, warning farmers who sold to Tidewater that their crops would be spoiled by pipeline leaks. And Standard Oil conspired with the railroads to withhold permission from any pipeline wishing to cross their tracks. Quick to exploit this, O'Day told Rockefeller, "The Penna R.R. should be informed of the efforts that are being made towards laying pipe lines from the Bradford District and they should see to it that the right of way secured some time since in their interest 'across the country' is well guarded and watched."[29]

Still, Tidewater pushed relentlessly ahead. When Standard Oil bought an entire valley at one point, the unstoppable Tidewater changed course and climbed up over the surrounding hills. It began to look as if it might actually outflank Rockefeller and his resolute henchmen. Right on the eve of Tidewater's success, Rockefeller decided that he might recoup in the political arena what he was on the verge of losing in the economic sphere. It was in the last-minute effort to halt Tidewater that Standard Oil first resorted to the wholesale bribery of state legislators.

Before wading into the muck of Standard Oil's political operations, we should note the general squalor of business-government dealings in the Gilded Age. Rockefeller had emerged in a fluid business world, with little government regulation to check entrepreneurs. At the same time, the government was heavily involved in the economy as it awarded land grants, railway franchises, and bank charters. After the Civil War, Washington hotels were crammed with businessmen jockeying for government contracts and toting suitcases full of cash to obtain them. President Grant admired the industrial captains, aspired to their society, and assembled a cabinet full of cronies and mediocrities eager to do their bidding. Government degenerated into a sink of iniquity, reflected in Mark Twain's witticism at a contemporary banquet, "There is a Congressman—I mean a son of a bitch—But why do I repeat myself?"[30] In 1876, politics touched a new nadir when Rutherford B. Hayes defeated Samuel J. Tilden for the presidency in what is now commonly regarded to have been a stolen election. A tremendous amount of money changed hands as businessmen and legislators trafficked in mutual manipulation. Businessmen such as Rockefeller preferred to think of themselves as victims of political extortion, not as initiators of bribes. Yet despite decades of categorical denials, Rockefeller's papers reveal that he and Standard Oil entered willingly into a staggering amount of corruption. (We should remark in passing that Allan Nevins, who had access to Rockefeller's papers, somehow managed to document only a single instance of Standard Oil bribery—in the Pennsylvania state legislature in 1887.) Standard Oil officials betrayed no qualms about paying bribes, and there is no recorded instance of Rockefeller rebuking a subordinate for engaging in graft.

During the Tidewater battle, Standard lobbied hard to perpetuate the system that allowed state legislatures to grant exclusive pipeline charters. Representing independent producers, reformers in the late 1870s introduced measures in several states to enact free-pipe bills, which would enable Standard Oil foes to lay competing lines and enjoy the right of eminent domain; under the existing system, Tidewater had to buy costly rights-of-way along its 110-mile east-west route. Standard Oil regarded these bills with such apprehension that Henry Flagler returned from Florida, where he was recuperating from poor health, to spearhead the lobbying campaign. To foster the impression of a popular groundswell against the bill, he hired lawyers to pose as incensed farmers and landowners in favor of the status quo. Flagler and A. J. Cassatt secretly exchanged drafts of the Pennsylvania bill and killed it with crippling amendments.

To stifle a similar pipeline bill in New York, Flagler coordinated efforts with Hugh J. Hewett of the Erie Railroad. Payoffs were an expensive business, and even Standard Oil welcomed rich partners to ease the burden. At one point, Flagler grumbled to a railroad leader, "We have spent a large sum of money to squelch Seaboard Pipe Line Charters," and he sourly asked that the railroads pick up the tab for these "lobbying" efforts in the future.[31] When Flagler recruited an Albany lobbyist, aptly named Smith M. Weed, he was ready to distribute $60,000 to legislators, but Hewett demurred and insisted that $15,000 would suffice.[32] "I send $10,000 currency," Flagler agreed, adding, "if you need the other $5000 or any part of it, send word by bearer and (we or he) can get it for you."[33] That $15,000 would today be worth $220,000.

As always, Rockefeller floated serenely above the bustle, pretending to be oblivious to any wrongdoing, but his correspondence implicates him directly in this skulduggery. On March 4, 1878, A. N. Cole, a New York state senator, wrote to Rockefeller on New York State Senate stationery and presented himself as an "attorney" to be hired by Standard Oil to manage the campaign against the free-pipe bill. Evidently, Rockefeller responded favorably to this overture, for Cole then mapped out an extensive campaign of pressure and subornation, complete with precise money-laundering instructions:

> Two or three good attorneys will be wanted in the Senate, and five or six in the Assembly, and these I have no hesitation in undertaking to employ, if authorized to do so. . . . Government bonds are better to deal in than money, since, were "attorneys" to be paid in cash, it *might* be construed into *corruption*, but then one can sell bonds, you know, in fact, dealing in them is an eminently becoming business. . . . In Heaven's name, don't make this letter public, since, were you to do so, I fear my brethren of the Methodist Church might fear I had so far fallen from grace as to leave no hope of recovery.[34]

While Standard Oil conducted statehouse offensives against free pipelines, it also put out brushfires in Washington as public sentiment began to lean toward railroad reform. The electorate was beginning to realize that big-business domination of the transportation network was incompatible with a competitive economy. In 1876, a bill was introduced in Congress "to regulate Commerce and prohibit unjust discriminations by Common Carriers."[35] By this point, J. N. Camden was a West Virginia congressman. Since he also headed the Camden Consolidated Oil Company, covertly owned by Standard Oil, he kept Rockefeller and Flagler minutely informed of legislative developments and swapped messages with them in Standard Oil code. Regarding the railroad bill, Camden assured Flagler, "I have the ear of some half dozen Senators that I will see. I can't think there is the least probable danger of such a bill getting through the Senate."[36] True to Camden's words, the railroad bill passed the House of Representatives then faltered in the Senate.

By the late 1870s, as news of his wealth spread, Rockefeller was badgered for campaign contributions, sometimes by the same politicians who lambasted Standard Oil. When Ohio representative James A. Garfield ran for president in 1880, he sounded out a Cleveland source, Amos Townsend, as to whether "Mr. Rockafeller" might be sympathetic. When Garfield asked, "Do you know his state of feeling toward me?" Townsend advised extreme caution. "It would not do for him to visit us, as it would be reported and *cut* like a *knife* in Pennsylvania."[37] A more subtle approach was another matter, and Rockefeller, along with Jay Gould, Chauncey Depew, and Levi Morton, ended up a top contributor to Garfield's victorious campaign. Garfield was the first of many presidential contenders who grappled with the quandary of whether it made better sense to court Rockefeller's money or capitalize on public animosity against him.

For all his success in bottling up pipeline bills, Rockefeller couldn't scotch the Tidewater. As the project neared completion, he executed a flurry of last-minute maneuvers and even tried to buy an interest in the operation for $300,000—all to no avail. On May 28, 1879, the Tidewater people held their breath as the great pumps whirred into motion near Bradford and the oil began to slide eastward through the pipeline. Nobody knew if the crude oil would actually scale the intervening mountains, and for days people expectantly tracked its slow progress. After seven days of suspense, the first oil drops sputtered out the Williamsport end and led to jubilation in western Pennsylvania, where Tidewater promised deliverance from the Standard Oil monopoly. Construction of the pipeline rated as one of the supreme engineering feats of its day, and its impresario, Byron Benson, achieved heroic status.

Faced with a rare defeat, Standard Oil did not react with equanimity. Daniel O'Day wanted to resort to thuggery to smash the pipeline. "I feel extremely satisfied that the Tidewater Pipe Line can be stopped and torn up if it is thought best to do it," he told Rockefeller. "I also think that the sooner the Tidewater knows this the better, as it might have a healthy effect upon them."[38] Rockefeller vetoed such crude reprisals and conceived a more elegant solution to the Tidewater menace. He had to bide his time, though, because he first had to dispose of two legal challenges that dogged his footsteps throughout 1879.

Some of Rockefeller's critics weren't content to expose him but wanted to put this pious churchgoer and Sunday-school superintendent behind bars. The producers were still seething from the immediate-shipment controversy and Standard Oil's refusal to store their surplus oil. One upshot was that on April 29, 1879, a grand jury in Clarion County, Pennsylvania, indicted nine Standard Oil officials—including Rockefeller, Flagler, O'Day, and Archbold—and charged them with conspiracy to monopolize the oil business, extort railroad rebates, and manipulate prices to cripple rivals. Those who resided in Pennsylvania, such as Warden, Lockhart, and Vandergrift, were arrested and released on bail while those, such as Rockefeller, who lived outside the state were able to evade prosecution. Reformers who stalked the Standard knew they had to get Rockefeller or Flagler on the stand, for many top executives were kept in the dark about the organization's intricate inner workings. When Captain Jacob J. Vandergrift testified at an Ohio hearing that spring, for instance, Flagler was able to reassure Rockefeller: "If it is a question of railroad freights, and discrimination in them, my judgment is [Vandergrift] knows nothing, or if knowing will not be compelled to answer."[39]

In spring 1879, Rockefeller began a thirty-year career as a fugitive from justice, learning to stay nimbly ahead of the law. For all his scoffing about the Clarion County indictments—"This case will never be brought to trial"—he took no chances.[40] Afraid of being extradited from New York, Rockefeller asked Chauncey Depew, the attorney for the New York Central, to approach New York governor Lucius Robinson, who agreed to deny any such requests from Pennsylvania. At the same time, Rockefeller had A. J. Cassatt approach Pennsylvania governor Henry M. Hoyt with a request that he cease further efforts to haul him into court. To make sure that the Pennsylvania Railroad didn't double-cross him, Rockefeller boosted production at his Philadelphia refineries serviced by the railroad—a generous bonus that could be canceled at any moment for misbehavior. Meticulous in such maneuvers, Rockefeller made sure to leave no fingerprints and told Captain Vandergrift that it was "of utmost importance that nobody knows of [Standard Oil's] thought of doing something about [the suit] outside the [Clarion] County."[41]

From the outset, Standard Oil defendants saw an advantage in the Clarion County affair, which enabled them to refuse to testify at many civil proceedings by claiming it might harm them in the criminal case. Nevertheless, Rockefeller feared that the Clarion suit might set a precedent and adopted a combative approach. "We are disposed to fight the thing and not be subject to this blackmailing process always," he insisted.[42]

At bottom, Rockefeller must have been genuinely alarmed by the impending criminal prosecution, for he decided to placate the producers and cut a political deal. On the day before Christmas 1879, Standard Oil rescinded the immediate-shipment policy and agreed to meet with producers at the Fifth Avenue Hotel in New York. In a historic agreement, Standard Oil renounced—or *seemed* to renounce—the use of secret rebates and drawbacks and consented to publicly posted freight rates; its United Pipe Lines would no longer discriminate among shippers and would transport all oil within reasonable limits. In return, the criminal and civil cases against Standard Oil in Pennsylvania were scuttled. In time, it emerged that Standard's pledge to repudiate rebates was largely a rhetorical flourish to settle the cases.

Aware that Standard Oil's fate was now being thrashed out in the political arena, Rockefeller reversed a long-standing prejudice and took shares in two Cleveland newspapers, investing $5,000 in the *Herald* and $10,000 in the *Leader,* explaining to Colonel Oliver Payne that since "Mr. Flagler felt perhaps we had given too little heed to influences of this kind, I decided best to do it."[43] While Rockefeller's official policy remained one of obdurate silence, he now had more avenues of press access than he admitted. Payne, meanwhile, believed that Standard Oil should move from bribing politicians to controlling them directly, telling Rockefeller, apropos of the Ohio legislature, "I wish to say that I have got through with sentiment in politics. . . . We must see hereafter that there is one man in the Legislature from this County that has brains, influence and is *our man.*"[44] Rockefeller told Payne to do "all that is necessary."[45]

Around this time, Rockefeller recruited to the Standard legal staff Roger Sherman, who had masterminded the producers' case against him. For years a champion of Oil Creek, Sherman had fought valiantly to imprison Rockefeller. Now Rockefeller was wily enough to offer him a job, and Sherman was naive enough—or original enough—to accept it. Always proud of his persuasive powers, Rockefeller took special pleasure in wooing opponents whom he had learned to appreciate by tracking their ploys against him. When a lawyer named Virgil Kline won two lawsuits against him in the 1880s, Rockefeller invited him to his office. "Mr. Kline," he said, "you have given us a good licking. Now I would like to have you come and work for me."[46] Kline agreed and became a long-standing member of the Standard Oil legal staff.

Things worked out differently for Roger Sherman, who realized after a strangely inactive year on the payroll that Rockefeller had given him a five-year contract expressly to neutralize him. When he tried to wriggle free of the contract, he was able only to strike a compromise that allowed him to resume his general practice in western Pennsylvania while remaining on retainer to Standard Oil. When he later returned to the crusade against Rockefeller, the independents were too disenchanted by his flirtation with Standard to deal with him. True to his wishes, Rockefeller had tarnished Sherman, separating him from his onetime admirers.

Ever since his boyhood as the son of the town pariah, Rockefeller had evinced more than a trace of paranoia. Now, embattled in courts and legislative chambers, he was convinced that evildoers were plotting against him and complained to one colleague about "this iniquitous proceeding of getting the United States out with a drag-net for the Standard Oil Co."[47] As chief instigator of his misery, he cited George Rice, an independent refiner, who would pursue him with the tenacity of a harpy for decades.

Rockefeller's movements in 1879 were governed largely by the need to duck subpoenas. In July, the New York State Assembly held hearings, chaired by Alonzo Barton Hepburn, to probe clandestine relations between the railroads and various industries. While the panel examined flour millers, meatpackers, and salt makers, it zeroed in on Standard Oil as the most notorious beneficiary of back-scratching with the railroads. That summer, Rockefeller stayed at Forest Hill, safely beyond the committee's reach.

As was true of many exposés of Rockefeller, the Hepburn hearings fueled public indignation against him while it also inadvertently enhanced his mystique as an invulnerable genius. The committee trotted out William H. Vanderbilt, who paid resounding tribute to the disciplined craft of the Standard Oil executives. "Long ago I said if the thing kept on the oil people would own the roads. . . . These men are smarter than I am a great deal. They are very enterprising and smart men. I never came into contact with any class of men so smart and able as they are in their business."[48]

John D. Archbold's testimony previewed the manner—flippant, arrogant, glib, and high-handed—in which he disposed of future legal challenges to Standard Oil's authority. Asked about his functions as a director, Archbold retorted, "I am a clamorer for dividends. That is the only function I have in connection with the Standard Oil Company."[49] He blatantly perjured himself when he said that Standard didn't control Acme Oil Company. When chairman Hepburn asked him to return for further questioning the next day, Archbold dismissed the committee, instead of the other way around. "I have given today to the matter," he told them. "It will be impossible for me to be with you again."[50] For the most part, Standard officers dodged questions with the ritual evasion, "I refuse to answer on the advice of counsel."[51]

When the Hepburn report was issued, it lent credence to what might otherwise have seemed fantastic conjecture, documenting a pattern of pervasive railroad favoritism toward large shippers. The New York Central alone enforced six thousand secret contracts, while the Erie's business was equally honeycombed with privileged arrangements. The committee assailed Standard Oil as "a mysterious organization whose business and transactions are of such a character that its members decline giving a history or description of it lest this testimony be used to convict them of a crime."[52]

For years, refiners had debated whether railroads were unregulated enterprises, free to strike what bargains they pleased, or common carriers, committed to treat all alike. The Hepburn report buttressed the latter view, saying that railroad bias toward Standard Oil was "the most shameless perversion of the duties of a common carrier to private ends . . . in the history of the world."[53] To remedy this, the New York legislature set up a railroad commission to regulate rates in a fair, uniform manner. The Hepburn report, however, was both belated and insufficient in hobbling Rockefeller's triumphant march, for by this time he had parlayed his secret railroad contracts into preeminence in oil. More important, his firm had now advanced far beyond the railroads to more efficient pipelines. In fact, a cynic might argue that the advent of the Hepburn hearings was incontestable proof that the railroads no longer mattered.

The growing agitation over railway reform hardened Rockefeller's determination to bring the Tidewater pipeline to bay, and he began to harass his competitor with a bewildering array of challenges. He tried to throttle the pipeline's access to crude oil and explored the purchase of several New York refineries before they could become Tidewater clients. At one point, he reduced rates on Standard Oil pipelines while the railroads dropped prices to such risible levels that one freight agent said that they scarcely covered the wheel grease. This relentless price war forced Tidewater to operate at half capacity.

It turned out that Rockefeller's adversary, Byron Benson, was no more en-amored of free markets than Rockefeller was and had created the pipeline to join in the feast. In March 1880, Daniel O'Day chanced to meet Benson on a train traveling from Oil City to Bradford and was shocked by his rival's words. As O'Day reported to Rockefeller, "[Benson] told me that he wanted to 'let the bars down,' as he expressed it, for any overtures that might be made to his company, with a view of an adjustment of the pipe line questions. He said that he felt that the time had about come when the companies should work together with a view of preventing other companies from engaging in the business."[54] Benson's solution suited Rockefeller just fine: Tidewater, instead of cutting rates to compete with the railroads, would collude with them to raise rates. Thus, within a year of its completion, the pipeline that was supposed to eman-cipate independents from Standard Oil bondage was drawn into a railroad pool supervised by John D. Rockefeller. In 1882, when Byron Benson decided to bor-row two million dollars to expand Tidewater, it prompted vigorous opposition from a group of minority shareholders. Exploiting this dissension, parties friendly to Standard Oil bought the minority stake, enabling Rockefeller to strike a bargain with Tidewater the following year. Under this pact, Standard Oil divided the pipeline business in Pennsylvania, taking 88.5 percent of the trade and leaving just 11.5 percent to Tidewater.

It was now abundantly clear to Rockefeller that the railroads represented a fading order. For a long time, he had resisted an irreversible shift to pipes for fear of antagonizing the railroads, but this concern had lost its force. When Standard Oil constructed four pipelines from western Pennsylvania to Cleve-land, New York, Philadelphia, and Buffalo, he pressured the railroads to grant it right-of-way concessions, even though the pipelines signaled their doom.

When Standard Oil subdued Tidewater, it again demoralized the indepen-dents and suggested that all opposition to the behemoth was a foolish, chimeri-cal dream. While a band of intrepid reformers continued to joust with Standard Oil in courthouses and legislatures, most producers now surrendered hope of any improvement in their plight. They knew they would either have to quit the business or swallow their pride and make peace with the oil giant. With the passing of Tidewater's complete independence, they could no longer ship oil from Pennsylvania without paying tribute to the all-powerful Mr. Rockefeller.

*Harriet E. Giles (left) and Sophia B. Packard, the founders of
Spelman Seminary, later Spelman College, who recruited Rockefeller
as the school's major donor in the early 1880s.*
(Courtesy of the Spelman College Archives)

CHAPTER 13

Seat of Empire

W hen John D. Rockefeller turned forty on July 8, 1879, he was already numbered among America's twenty richest men, yet he was likely the most obscure of the pantheon. While this resulted largely from his aversion to publicity, it also stemmed from his residing in Cleveland. As one chronicler said of the town, "Its rich folk were not scandalous or showy; its politics had not the violent quality essential to American fame."[1] In other words, it was an ideal place for a reclusive magnate. Throughout his career, Rockefeller pooh-poohed "exaggerated" press estimates of his wealth, yet they often understated his true worth. In the late 1870s, one newspaper pegged his wealth at more than $5 million, when his Standard Oil stock alone was by then worth $18 million, or $265 million in 1996 dollars. By comparison, when America's richest citizen, Commodore Vanderbilt, died in 1877, he left an estate valued at nearly $100 million.

Photos of Rockefeller from this period show two contrasting faces. In his serious mode, his expression seemed grim and unsmiling, with tremendous force in his gaze but no softness or joy. Yet when photographed in leisure hours in the sanctuary of Forest Hill, he looked trim and whimsical, surprisingly boyish for such a powerful man. Gone were the old side-whiskers, but he still had a full red mustache and sandy brown hair. In a period when moguls prided themselves on their embonpoint, Rockefeller was as lean as a greyhound. And at a time when top hats and watch chains were de rigueur for any self-respecting plutocrat, Rockefeller generally conformed to the requisite style, but his family constantly had to remind him to buy a new suit when his current one got too shiny.

If Rockefeller generally enjoyed excellent health, there were early warning symptoms of the toll taken by the excruciating pressures of Standard Oil. In 1878, he wrote to Eliza, "I am eating celery which I understand to be very good for nervous difficulty."[2] Colleagues plied him with advice to take more vacations and spend more time away from business, even though Rockefeller later said he was almost semiretired at this point. He tried to spend as many afternoons as possible at Forest Hill in "the bracing air of Lake Erie."[3] He displayed a strong interest in herbal medicines and other folk remedies, advising one associate that he could dispense more easily with tobacco if he had an orange peel before breakfast every day. Big Bill's interest in medicine, conventional and otherwise, began to surface in his son and became more pronounced with time.

Now that Rockefeller headed almost all of America's oil refineries and pipelines, the press belatedly awakened to his existence, acknowledging him as a new deity in the industrial firmament. In November 1878, he sat for his first full-length newspaper profile in the *New York Sun*. The article disclosed the scope of an ambition that Rockefeller took pains to deny: "The people of Cleveland say that it is his ambition to become the richest man in Ohio and one of the ten richest men in the United States. . . . He is in a fair way of being able to count on his fingers the men in the country who are richer than he is."[4] This first sketch, which portrayed him as quiet, reserved, and methodical, was shot through with ambivalence. Of Rockefeller's business ability, the reporter rhapsodized: "Business men in Cleveland, in the oil regions and in New York who know him or know of him, regard him as one of the great commercial intellects of the country."[5] Yet the article concluded that his Olympian success arose from a strange, unsavory bargain with the railroads—a pact that people surmised but could never quite prove. Within a year, the Hepburn hearings began to document what had long been mooted about Rockefeller's dealings with the railroads, and by the early 1880s he had moved a considerable distance from his former anonymity to something closer to universal notoriety.

In late 1883, Rockefeller's life assumed a marginally higher profile when he moved to New York. Eighteen eighty-four would prove to be a pivotal year for the country, marked by bank failures and panics and the demise of General Grant's brokerage firm, Grant and Ward. The Democratic reformer Grover Cleveland triumphed in the presidential election over the corrupt Republican candidate, James G. Blaine, installing a Democrat in the White House for the first time in many years.

Rockefeller had long felt the gravitational pull of New York, with its lively export trade in kerosene, and routinely spent part of each winter there. Haunted by his father's wanderings, he was loath to abandon Cettie and the children, and for two winters in the mid-1870s he lodged them at the Windsor Hotel on Fifth Avenue, where Jay Gould often plotted his corporate raids. From 1877 to 1884, Rockefeller and his family stayed at the Buckingham Hotel, a residential hotel on Fifth Avenue on the present site of the Saks department store. They had a large suite of rooms in the shadow of Saint Patrick's Cathedral, whose huge stained-glass windows loomed up dreamily outside their windows at night. (One of Junior's early memories was of being reprimanded sharply by his mother for failing to thank a hotel waiter for bringing him food.) After Harvey Spelman's death in 1881, Grandmother Spelman and Aunt Lute took a suite on the same floor and shared meals with them. From late spring through early fall, the entourage returned to Forest Hill, where Rockefeller stayed in touch with the New York office by sophisticated telegraphy.

Business now dictated Rockefeller's move to the East Coast. In an age of long-distance pipelines, huge volumes of crude oil were flowing to seaboard refineries where they fed a flourishing export traffic, relegating Cleveland and other inland centers to an inferior status. Responding to the export boom, Standard Oil established sprawling refineries in Brooklyn, Bayonne, Philadelphia, and Baltimore. A latent tension now strained relations between the Cleveland headquarters and its burgeoning New York branch. One day, Benjamin Brewster, a Standard director, told Rockefeller that a two-headed calf belonged only in the circus and that the combine needed a single head. "You can't have one head in Cleveland and another in New York," he told Rockefeller. "And therefore either you have got to quit Cleveland and come on here or we have got to pack up and leave New York and go out to Cleveland."[6]

By the time Rockefeller and Oliver Payne transferred to New York in late 1883 and early 1884, Henry Flagler had preceded them by two years. Though now immensely rich, John and Cettie possessed the low-key style and resolute sense of privacy of old money and searched for a house on a peaceful side street. They swapped nine parcels of Manhattan real estate, appraised at $600,000, for a four-story brownstone mansion at 4 West Fifty-fourth Street. Garlanded with ivy, flanked by lawns, the residence stood on a site that would later house the Museum of Modern Art sculpture garden. If roomy and comfortable, it was extremely modest for someone of Rockefeller's wealth and, like his Cleveland residence, subtly masked the size of his fortune. For all its social cachet, Fifth Avenue was now a busy, nerve-jangling thoroughfare, as Junior remembered with dismay: "It was paved with cobblestones and I can still hear the noise of the steel tires rumbling along the street. It was fearfully noisy."[7] By contrast, West Fifty-fourth Street was a shady retreat, situated north of the Elgin Botanical Gardens, which later formed part of Rockefeller Center. Opposite the Rockefeller home stood Saint Luke's Hospital, with lawns and gardens that spread a fragrant tranquillity over the street.

The home that the Rockefellers bought was the opulent boudoir of the beautiful Arabella Worsham, who had tried to pass herself off as a niece of railroad mogul Collis Huntington when she was actually his mistress. When Huntington's wife died in late 1883, he decided to marry Arabella and make an honest woman of her. The sober brownstone that had sheltered their assignations went on the market, and it is amusing to think of the Rockefellers snapping up their love nest. A frugal man, John D. followed his accustomed practice of keeping the furnishings, even if the style in this case diverged ludicrously from his own. The interior contained touches of voluptuous sensuality, such as Arabella's exotic Moorish salon on the ground floor and the Turkish bath upstairs. The sumptuous master bedroom was artistically designed in Anglo-Japanese style, with dark ebonized woodwork, a queen-size canopied sleigh bed, and a magnificent silver and gilt chandelier. The bay window provided an intimate Turkish corner, tantalizingly glimpsed through a stained-glass screen. Doubtless as a legacy of Arabella Worsham—one can't picture the prudish Rockefellers shopping for such things—4 West Fifty-fourth Street had paintings by Corot, Meissonier, Daubigny, and other French painters then in vogue among local parvenus. The house also had the latest conveniences, including one of the city's first elevators in a private residence. The only thing removed by Rockefeller were the worn carpets, which he donated to the needy through a local church.

Though West Fifty-fourth Street was a tree-lined oasis, the Rockefellers had chosen the most sybaritic precinct of New York society in the Gilded Age. Much of the wealth amassed in what Mark Twain called the "raging, tearing, booming nineteenth century" had now settled in Manhattan. The old New York aristocracy, huddled around Washington Square and Gramercy Park, shuddered at the pretentious uptown mansions, which paid tribute to postwar fortunes in railroads, steel, and oil. Along Fifth Avenue near the Rockefeller home, the palaces of the rich—notably the fantastic, turreted confections of William K. Vanderbilt at Fifty-first Street and Cornelius Vanderbilt II at Fifty-eighth Street—stretched uptown in gaudy profusion.

With Standard Oil moving its headquarters to New York, the neighborhood was becoming a colony of company directors. At one point in this corporate relocation, twenty-eight Standard Oil executives arrived in a single Pullman car from Cleveland and were taken straight to the Saint James Hotel, where William presided over their first breakfast and John their first dinner. The latter liked to greet new arrivals at the train station and help them to find houses. Soon, the Fifth Avenue strip near Rockefeller's home was thickly populated with Standard Oil men, Henry Flagler occupying the southeast corner of Fifty-fourth Street and William Rockefeller the northeast corner, with Benjamin Brewster next door to William. William departed from his brother's ascetic style and raised his children in a looser, freer atmosphere, causing envious pangs among John's children. As Junior said, "We children didn't have what those children had and we used to notice the difference. They had a gay kind of social life, with many parties which we used to wish we could have."[8] Since William refused to take on debt to build his house, he sold $50,000 of Standard

Oil stock to John despite his brother's heartfelt plea to retain the stock. William's imprudent decision figured importantly in the enormous disparity in wealth that developed between the two brothers.

In New York, John D. did not acquire cosmopolitan interests but stuck with his old Cleveland pastimes, creating a large ice-skating rink every winter in a space adjoining his house. Each morning, curious pedestrians could glimpse the chief of the American oil industry, dressed in overcoat and top hat, ice skates strapped to his patent-leather boots, as he glided placidly around the horseshoe-shaped area. A great enthusiast for the sport, he created rows of shelves in his house on which dozens of guests could store their skates.

Though Rockefeller resisted the yacht-owning fad that swept New York society in the 1880s and owned neither a boat nor private railroad car, he spared no expense for fast-trotting horses in his large, heated stable at 21 West Fifty-fifth Street. Every afternoon after work, he took out his black gelding trotters and mingled with the pageant of fashionable carriages thronging Central Park, often racing against his brother William, with an excited Junior seated at his side. So keenly did Rockefeller relish trotting that at one point he told his son, "I drove four times yesterday making an aggregate in the two days of about eighty miles. Don't you think I am an enthusiastic youth?"[9] Junior left a description of his father's racing style that seems a metaphor for his assertive but careful stewardship of Standard Oil:

> Other drivers would often lose their tempers when a horse broke gait or pulled hard; Father never. If a horse was excitable or difficult he always kept his temper, and patiently, quietly worked with the animal until he steadied it. Frequently I have seen him driving at a very rapid pace through Central Park; in the middle of the roadway through two streams of traffic, pushing always a little to the left, as he explained to me, so as to open his way through, but keeping margin enough on the right so that if the approaching traffic did not swing over in time, he would still have room enough to pass.[10]

Never dazzled by New York, Rockefeller was insulated from the beau monde that threw costly dinners and costume balls and frequented the theater, opera, and clubs. He had no interest in debauchery, and it is hard to picture him milling about with portly men smoking cigars or women wearing expensive furs and jewels. The newspapers noted his total boycott of social functions. As one periodical said, "He never entertains notables, his home is never given to entertainment, and he follows the policy of self-effacement at all times and in all places."[11] Although he joined the Union League Club, Rockefeller did not feel comfortable with the splendor of the Astors and Vanderbilts. When Cettie asked for a new four-wheeled carriage in 1882, John stared at her, aghast, and said they could scarcely afford it unless they traded in the old one. Abiding by his daily rituals, he still enjoyed bread and milk in the morning and a paper bag of apples in the evening. Each morning before work, a barber shaved him in his dressing room before he trotted down the brownstone stoop at exactly the same hour and for a nickel took the Sixth Avenue elevated train downtown. The wheels of his mind already turning, he jotted penciled notes on his shirt cuff as the train jolted toward Wall Street. Moving with spectral stealth, as if tiptoeing on a cushion of air, he slipped into the Standard Oil building at the stroke of nine. "I never knew anyone to enter an office as quietly as Mr. Rockefeller," said his private secretary, George Rogers. "He seemed almost to have a coat of invisibility."[12]

In late 1883, Standard Oil began to assemble real estate at the southern tip of Manhattan for new headquarters, destined to soar above Broadway at Bowling Green on the onetime site of Alexander Hamilton's home. Having long outgrown William's old offices at two different locations on Pearl Street, the firm had operated for three years from modest, unprepossessing quarters at 44 Broadway. Now, on May 1, 1885, after spending nearly one million dollars on it, Standard Oil moved into its impregnable new fortress, a massive, granite, nine-story building. The combine's name didn't appear outside, just the building number. Twenty-six Broadway soon became the world's most famous business address, shorthand for the oil trust itself, evoking its mystery, power, and efficiency. Standard Oil was now America's premier business, with a reach that ramified into a labyrinth of railroads, banks, and other businesses. The purple prose aroused by the new building perhaps owed less to its imposing neoclassical architecture than to its symbolic heft. Said one reporter: "Many worthy men are convinced that No. 26 Broadway is the most perilous shelter on earth—a cave for pirates, a den for the cutthroats of commerce."[13] Otherwise sober writers seemed to swoon before the saturnine grandeur of Rockefeller's seat of power:

At the lower end of the greatest thoroughfare in the greatest city of the New World is a huge structure of plain gray-stone. Solid as a prison, towering as a steeple, its cold and forbidding facade seems to rebuke the heedless levity of the passing crowd, and frown on the frivolity of the stray sunbeams which in the late afternoon play around its impassive cornices. Men point to its stern portals, glance quickly up at the rows of unwinking windows, nudge each other, and hurry onward, as the Spaniards used to do when going by the offices of the Inquisition. The building is No. 26 Broadway.[14]

Reporters who managed to slip past the watchful guards found a world at odds with the grim exterior, a dignified place with mahogany rolltop desks and mustard-colored carpets. The subdued atmosphere—people instinctively conferred in hushed tones—mirrored Rockefeller's own personality. Rockefeller's office faced south and east, with a spectacular view of New York harbor. As one reporter commented, "There is an absence of bustle and noise. While transactions involving millions may be involved, the negotiations are conducted in a quiet methodical manner, apparently free from excitement."[15] The offices had some unusual security features, including ground-glass partitions that reached to the ceiling and obscured the proceedings within. In a quintessential Rockefeller touch, the doors were equipped with special secret rim locks: One had to know how to twist the rim with thumb and forefinger before turning the knob, so that an intruder could find himself suddenly trapped in a maze of ostensibly locked doors.

In these new quarters, the Standard Oil mandarins preserved a tradition launched years before. Each day at noon, the executive committee gathered for lunch in a top-floor room decorated with hunting and fishing trophies and with a port view that suited their global empire. There was no surer proof of favor in the Standard Oil empyrean than to receive an invitation to dine at the long table. Arriving in silk hats, frock coats, and gloves, the directors always took the same assigned seats. In his deceptively self-effacing style, Rockefeller yielded the head of the table to his most frequent adversary, Charles Pratt, who was the group's oldest member; Flagler sat to Pratt's right, then Rockefeller, then Archbold. It says much about his managerial approach that Rockefeller sat indistinguishably among his colleagues, though the leveling arrangement scarcely disguised his unique status. As philosopher Herbert Spencer once said, "A business partnership, balanced as the authorities of its members may theoretically be, presently becomes a union in which the authority of one partner is tacitly recognized as greater than that of the other or others."[16]

Few outsiders knew that one of Rockefeller's greatest talents was to manage and motivate his diverse associates. As he said, "It is chiefly to my confidence in men and my ability to inspire their confidence in me that I owe my success in life."[17] He liked to note that Napoleon could not have succeeded without his marshals.[18] Free of an autocratic temperament, Rockefeller was quick to delegate authority and presided lightly, genially, over his empire, exerting his will in unseen ways. At meetings, Rockefeller had a negative capability: The quieter he was, the more forceful his presence seemed, and he played on his mystique as the resident genius immune to petty concerns. As one director recalled, "I have seen board meetings, when excited men shouted profanity and made menacing gestures, but Mr. Rockefeller, maintaining the utmost courtesy, continued to dominate the room."[19] Sometimes, he dozed on a couch after lunch. "I can see him now," one executive recalled, "lying back on a lounge at a directors' meeting, eyes closed taking it all in. Now and then he'd open his eyes and make a suggestion."[20]

Rockefeller placed a premium on internal harmony and tried to reconcile his contending chieftains. A laconic man, he liked to canvass everyone's opinion before expressing his own and then often crafted a compromise to maintain cohesion. He was always careful to couch his decisions as suggestions or questions. Even in the early days, he had lunched daily with brother William, Harkness, Flagler, and Payne to thrash out problems. As the organization grew, he continued to operate by consensus, taking no major initiative opposed by board members. Because all ideas had to meet the supreme test of unanimous approval among strong-minded men, Standard Oil made few major missteps. As Rockefeller said, "We made sure that we were right and had planned for every contingency before we went ahead."[21]

Even though Rockefeller feuded sporadically with Charles Pratt, Henry Rogers, and others, the firm was free of the petulant bickering and bureaucratic jealousy that usually accompany vast power. At least to hear Rockefeller tell it, the directors—former foes who had banded together in corporate brotherhood—were bound by an almost mystic faith. For him, their belief in each other explained their cohesion and certified their virtue. "Crooked men cannot be held as these Standard Oil Company men were held for all this long term."[22] The continuity of leadership made the firm all but impervious to snooping reporters and government investigators, who could never penetrate the tight-knit phalanx of like-minded men who ran the oil empire for four consecutive decades.

The unity of the Standard Oil partners was especially impressive given the organization's byzantine structure, a far-flung patchwork of firms, each nominally independent but in reality taking orders from 26 Broadway. In the absence of a federal incorporation law, Rockefeller, like other contemporary businessmen, had to cope with a tangle of restrictive laws that made it fiendishly difficult to run an interstate company. As he said, "Our federal form of government, making every corporation created by a state foreign to every other state, renders it necessary for persons doing business through corporate agency to organize corporations in some or many of the different states in which their business is located."[23] This handicap forced business leaders to devise cunning ways to circumvent laws and led them to corrupt politicians and legislatures; much of Rockefeller's political cynicism issued from this source. For Standard Oil, a national operation from the start, the antiquated legal framework lured it into myriad legal adaptations. But if Rockefeller correctly considered the legal system an unfair impediment, it was also a spur to his ingenuity.

His first major improvisation came with an ingenious trust agreement that was executed privately in 1879. Under its charter, Standard Oil of Ohio couldn't own companies outside the state, so it assigned three midlevel employees—Myron R. Keith, George F. Chester, and George H. Vilas—to serve as trustees who held stock in a score of subsidiaries outside the state. When they received dividends, they distributed them to the thirty-seven investors of

Standard of Ohio *as individuals*, in amounts proportionate to their stakes in the parent company. (Of the 35,000 Standard shares, Rockefeller held nearly 9,000, or three times the amount of Flagler, Harkness, Pratt, or Payne.)[24] This jerry-built structure enabled Rockefeller to swear under oath that Standard Oil of Ohio didn't own property outside of Ohio, even though it controlled most of the pipelines and refineries in Pennsylvania, New York, New Jersey, and Maryland; technically speaking, the trustees owned these properties.

The 1879 agreement, a makeshift arrangement, lasted only three years. When the state of Pennsylvania tried in 1881 to tax the property of Standard of Ohio within its borders, Rockefeller feared that other states might copy this precedent and hold him hostage. At the same time, he had absorbed so many new pipelines and refineries that he was struggling to coordinate policy among many scattered units. The time had come to streamline operations, impose guidance, and attain new efficiencies. The brains behind this next stage of development was an affable, roly-poly lawyer and Presbyterian elder named Samuel C. T. Dodd, a man so fat that one wag claimed he was the same size in every direction. As general solicitor of Standard Oil from 1881 to 1905, he was its leading theoretician and publicist, as much ideologist as lawyer. A carpenter's son from Franklin, Pennsylvania, and an amateur poet passionate about classical literature, he had been a vocal, high-minded resident of Titusville. Ironically, as a Democratic member of Pennsylvania's constitutional convention in 1872, Dodd had won attention as a scourge of the railroads, excoriating Rockefeller and the South Improvement Company for taking advantage of rebates.

The way Dodd entered Standard Oil should have tipped him off to the depth of Rockefeller's guile. In 1878, two refiners named Taylor and Satterfield hired him in a dispute against United Pipe Lines, which was ostensibly owned by Vandergrift and Forman. Since Dodd was also a lawyer for Captain Jacob J. Vandergrift, he found himself representing both sides in the case. At one point, Vandergrift made a shocking confession to him: United Pipe Lines actually belonged lock, stock, and barrel to Standard Oil. At the behest of his clients, Dodd journeyed to Cleveland to draw up a mutually satisfactory settlement. As he recalled:

Here, for the first time, I met John D. Rockefeller, a very pleasant, gentlemanly, unassuming man, but slow in his deliberations and particular as possible at every point of negotiation. Being a little vexed one day at my objection to some clause he desired in the contract which was being drawn, he said in a sarcastic tone: "Mr. Dodd, do you often act for both sides in a case?" I said, "Not often, Mr. Rockefeller, but I am always ready to do so when both sides want an honest lawyer." This seemed to amuse him and we soon brought the matter to a settlement.[25]

When Rockefeller hired him in 1879, Dodd held out, not for more money or titles but for assurances of his integrity. Taking a relatively small salary (it would never exceed $25,000 a year), he resisted Rockefeller's plea that he take Standard Oil stock, arguing that this might compromise his legal judgment, and he never became a Standard director for that reason. He also emphasized that he would never alter his settled views on the injustice of railroad rebates. To all these conditions, Rockefeller assented breezily—perhaps too breezily. As will be seen, he spent years fooling Dodd about Standard Oil's relations with the railroads, to the point that one must conclude that Dodd fairly asked to be duped and suspended all skepticism. After being hired by Rockefeller, Dodd was ostracized by many former clients along Oil Creek. To these critics, he shrugged and said, "Well, as the ministers say when they get a call to a higher salary, it seems to be the Lord's will."[26] Rockefeller bestowed this encomium on Dodd: "A more just man never lived. . . . He was a lovable, loyal man."[27] In many antitrust hearings, Rockefeller looked to the redoubtable Dodd and awaited his nod of approval before answering questions.

Dodd was a wizard at contriving forms that obeyed the letter but circumvented the spirit of the law. As the Keith-Chester-Vilas travesty became known, Dodd studied new organizational structures that might allow Standard to expand business while maintaining centralized control. That the major directors lived in separate cities—mostly Cleveland, New York, Pittsburgh, Philadelphia, and Baltimore—was impeding finely meshed coordination. Dodd came up with a sudden brainstorm as to how to meld intrastate firms into an interstate giant. The first step was to set up a separate Standard Oil company in each state in which it had major interests. As a result, Standard Oil of New York was formed on August 1, 1882, with William Rockefeller as president; four days later, John became president of the new Standard Oil of New Jersey. This stratagem was designed to prevent each state from taxing Standard Oil property located outside the state. Dodd realized that separate companies required separate boards of directors and considered how to prevent a fragmentation of power. The answer, he explained, was that "you could have a common name, a common office, and a common management by means of a common executive committee. The stock could in effect be made common by placing the corporate stock in the hands of Trustees who shall issue certificates of interest in the Trust estate, which certificates will be entitled to their due proportions of the various stock dividends."[28] As Dodd noted, this elaborate stock swap would create a union not of corporations but of stockholders, ensuring that the companies could behave in concert without running afoul of the law.

Dodd and Flagler drafted the new Standard Oil trust agreement, which was dated January 2, 1882. The public knew nothing of this contrivance that spawned a $70 million enterprise and controlled 90 percent of American refineries and pipelines until it emerged, accidentally, in antitrust hearings six years later. The agreement created a board of nine New York–based trustees— the group that assembled daily for lunch at 26 Broadway. Today, we would term it a holding company, but at the time it seemed an imaginary entity, lacking any real legal existence. It couldn't make deals, sign contracts, or keep books, though it wielded infinite power. It received the stock of Standard of Ohio and forty other companies—twenty-six of them partially, fourteen fully owned—with the power to name their officers and directors. Among the shareholders, the distribution of power and wealth remained lopsided, with Rockefeller holding more than one-third of the trust certificates, a block worth $19 million. The five members of the Cleveland wing—John and William Rockefeller, Flagler, Payne, and Harkness—retained a commanding majority of shares and formed a pool within the top echelon to buy and sell jointly interests in other companies.

For the first time, the trust's formation created negotiable securities, and this profoundly affected the Standard Oil culture. Not only did Rockefeller urge underlings to take stock but made money abundantly available to do so. As such shareholding became widespread, it welded the organization more tightly together, creating an esprit de corps that helped in steamrolling over competitors and government investigators alike. With employees receiving huge capital gains and dividends, they converted Standard Oil into a holy crusade. Rockefeller hoped the trust would serve as a model for a new populist capitalism, marked by employee share ownership. "I would have every man a capitalist, every man, woman and child," he said. "I would have everyone save his earnings, not squander it; own the industries, own the railroads, own the telegraph lines."[29]

In many ways, Standard Oil's metamorphosis previewed the trajectory of other major American business organizations in the late nineteenth century as they moved from freewheeling competition to loosely knit cartels to airtight trusts. The 1882 agreement introduced the concept of the trust as something synonymous with industrial monopoly. During the 1880s, industrywide pools sprouted in many industries in America, England, and Germany, but their leaders found it difficult to prevent cheating and secret price-cutting among members. Now, Standard Oil came up with a way to introduce centralized control, backed by enforcement powers and managerial direction. So many companies duplicated the pattern over the years that one can say, with pardonable exaggeration, that the 1882 trust agreement executed by Standard Oil led straight to the Sherman Antitrust Act eight years later.

Rockefeller was a unique hybrid in American business: both the instinctive, first-generation entrepreneur who founds a company and the analytic second-generation manager who extends and develops it. He wasn't the sort of rugged, self-made mogul who quickly becomes irrelevant to his own organization. For that reason, his career anticipates the managerial capitalism of the twentieth century.

Since he never owned more than a third of his company, he needed the co-operation of other people. Having created an empire of unfathomable complexity, he was smart enough to see that he had to submerge his identity in the organization. Many people noted that Rockefeller seldom said "I," except when telling a joke, preferring the first-person plural when discussing Standard Oil. "Don't say that I ought to do this or that," he preached to colleagues. "We ought to do it. Never forget that we are partners; whatever is done is for the general good of us all."[30] He preferred outspoken colleagues to weak-kneed sycophants and welcomed differences of opinion so long as they weren't personalized. In their private deliberations, the Standard executives, for all their swashbuckling reputation, tended to be cordial and formal. As Cleveland Amory said of them, "No group of American tycoons were ever more forbidding or high and mighty publicly or more gentle and shy and retiring privately."[31]

By creating new industrial forms, Rockefeller left his stamp on an age that lauded inventors, not administrators. That he created one of the first multinational corporations, selling kerosene around the world and setting a business pattern for the next century, was arguably his greatest feat. As he said, "Our nation was in a state of transition from agriculture to wholesale manufacture and commerce, and we had to invent methods and machinery as we went along."[32] Whatever the debates about his ethics, economists and historians have unanimously extolled his role as a pioneer of the modern corporation. Despite the legal impediments, he was able to fuse together dozens of disparate firms into a seamless whole. What might have been a cumbersome apparatus developed into an efficient instrument in Rockefeller's hands. Standard Oil led the way in industrial planning and large-volume production, exploiting economies of scale that might otherwise have been hard to achieve at this stage in a purely competitive state. Under Rockefeller's tutelage, the trust made notable strides in improving kerosene, developing by-products, and reducing the cost of packaging, transporting, and distributing petroleum products worldwide. As one biographer has remarked, "Rockefeller must be accepted as the greatest business administrator America has produced."[33] An oil historian echoes this verdict: "Rockefeller was the single most important figure in shaping the oil industry. The same might arguably be said for his place in the history of America's industrial development and the rise of the modern corporation."[34]

The secret to unifying the dozens of affiliated concerns proved to be the committee system patented by Standard Oil. The inner sanctum was the executive committee. Though they recommended actions to field supervisors, they held considerable power in reserve, for they had to approve all expenditures above $5,000 and salary increases above $50 a month, enabling them to retard the growth of any unit. Below the executive committee came a battery of specialized committees dedicated to transportation, pipelines, domestic trade, export trade, manufacturing, purchasing, and so on. These committees standardized the quality of subsidiaries engaged in similar work, enabling managers to swap insights and align their operations. As Rockefeller said of this innovation: "A company of men, for example, were specialists in manufacture. These were chosen experts, who had daily sessions and study of the problems, new as well as old, constantly arising. The benefit of their research, their study, was available for each of the different concerns whose shares were held by these trustees."[35] Under the committee system, Standard Oil created a self-sufficient universe, overseeing plants that made acid, chemicals, staves, barrels, wicks, pumps, and even tank cars. It shut down more than thirty obsolete refineries, concentrating more than a quarter of world kerosene production in three monster plants in Cleveland, Bayonne, and Philadelphia.

The committee system was an ingenious adaptation, integrating the policy of constituent companies without stripping them of all autonomy. We must recall that Standard Oil remained a confederation and most of its subsidiaries were only partially owned. A top-down hierarchical structure might have hampered local owners whom Rockefeller had promised a measure of autonomy in running their plants. The committee system galvanized their energies while providing them with general guidance. The committees encouraged rivalry among local units by circulating performance figures and encouraging them to compete for records and prizes. The point is vitally important, for monopolies, spared the rod of competition, can easily lapse into sluggish giants. At Standard Oil, in contrast, as Rockefeller stated, "the stimulus to make the best showing, each concern for itself, led to active and aggressive work in competition."[36]

For many years, Rockefeller had tried to free himself from details and applauded the committee system as relegating him to a fifth wheel. He never attended individual committee meetings but sometimes, in his odd way, dropped by when committee heads conferred. As one member said:

I have seen Mr. Rockefeller often at a meeting of the heads of the different departments of the Company, listening carefully to each one and not saying a word. Perhaps he would stretch out on a lounge and say: "I am a little tired, but go right on gentlemen, for I know you want to reach a decision." He might close his eyes now and then; but he never missed a point. He would go away without saying a word but good-bye. But next day when he came down he had digested the whole proposition and worked out the answer—and he always worked out the right answer.[37]

Although Standard Oil encouraged cooperation and allowed strong executives to flourish, Rockefeller retained unrivaled influence. While colleagues embarked on shopping binges to buy palatial homes and European art, Rockefeller husbanded his money. He believed in Standard Oil and gladly purchased all available stock from other directors. "Oh, I was the dumping ground for them all in those days," he once laughed, and his unequaled shareholding gave his opinions extra weight.[38]

Beyond the size of his stake, Rockefeller also possessed an unlikely charisma. He never backslapped, roughhoused, or skylarked with his colleagues, and his statesmanlike calm evoked feelings of awe. As one reporter said in 1905, "No man, however unimpressionable he may be, can stand in the presence of Mr. Rockefeller without feeling the repressed power of the man."[39] He seemed to possess oracular powers. As Archbold conceded, "Rockefeller always sees a little further than the rest of us—and then he sees around the corner."[40] Another Standard executive, Edward T. Bedford, paid him this high tribute: "Mr. Rockefeller was really a superman. He not only envisaged a new system of business upon a grand scale but he also had the patience, the courage and the audacity to put it into effect in the face of almost insuperable difficulties, sticking to his purpose with a tenacity and confidence [that were] simply amazing."[41]

He also had a tactful, easy manner with less exalted employees and never reacted angrily when presented with grievances. Once a year, each employee had the right to appear before the executive committee and argue for a higher salary, and Rockefeller always reacted pleasantly. As one employee recalled, "When H. H. Rogers would say gruffly that he had had enough and we had no right to ask for an increase of salary, Mr. Rockefeller would say, 'Oh, give him a chance.' "[42] But the mildness was deceiving, for while Rockefeller might sometimes be prepared to pay wages 10 or even 20 percent above the prevailing levels, he would never countenance unions or organized employee protest.

In the last analysis, Rockefeller prevailed at Standard Oil because he had mastered a method for solving problems that carried him far beyond his native endowment. He believed there was a time to think and then a time to act. He brooded over problems and quietly matured plans over extended periods. Once he had made up his mind, however, he was no longer troubled by doubts and pursued his vision with undeviating faith. Unfortunately, once in that state of mind, he was all but deaf to criticism. He was like a projectile that, once launched, could never be stopped, never recalled, never diverted.

=

Amid the murky temptations of Manhattan, the Rockefeller home was a tranquil island of missionary work, temperance meetings, and prayer vigils. Beset by fears of big-city vice and determined to avoid exposure to liquor, cards, tobacco, and dancing, the Rockefellers still socialized only with kindred spirits.

The greater the controversy surrounding Standard Oil, the more decorous their home life.

The family belied John Wesley's dictum that "wherever riches have increased, the essence of religion has decreased in the same proportion."[43] The Rockefellers had also figured out how to solve the riddle that John Adams posed to Thomas Jefferson in 1819: "Will you tell me how to prevent riches from producing luxury? Will you tell me how to prevent luxury from producing effeminacy, intoxication, extravagance, Vice and folly?"[44] The fear that wealth would adulterate their values only pushed John and Cettie deeper into church activism and the temperance movement. In 1883, John sat on an advisory committee of the Women's Christian Temperance Union, which was campaigning for an amendment to the Ohio constitution to outlaw the manufacture and sale of liquor. Though the initiative petered out, he later became a major benefactor of the Ohio Anti-Saloon League and grew steadily more militant in the cause. "I fear unless a great temperance reform sweeps over our whole land, the Republic itself may be imperilled," he thundered.[45] Among other pet causes of this period, he gave substantial sums to the revivalist Dwight L. Moody and urged Henry Flagler to follow suit.

Right before the Rockefellers left Cleveland, some friends asked Cettie why her children hadn't been baptized, and she was haunted by the question. She began intensive prayer meetings with her children, which led three of the four—Alta (twelve), Edith (eleven), and John (nine)—to be baptized jointly on October 28, 1883, the last Sunday before their move to New York. Afterward, Cettie recorded her impressions: "It was a beautiful and impressive sight, after the morning service—there were plants and flowers around the baptistry, and a dove suspended over it."[46] Since the Rockefellers returned to Cleveland each summer, John and Cettie retained their positions at the Euclid Avenue Baptist Church. Upon arriving in Manhattan, they joined the Fifth Avenue Baptist Church and imported the Reverend William H. P. Faunce from Springfield, Massachusetts, to head it. It never occurred to the Rockefellers to trade up to a more socially prestigious denomination. "Most Americans when they accumulate money climb the golden spires of the nearest Episcopal Church," H. L. Mencken later observed. "But the Rockefellers cling to the primeval rain-god of the American hinterland and show no signs of being ashamed of him."[47] They would not have felt comfortable with the splendor and formality of a high-church denomination.

After having been taught at home for many years, the Rockefeller children began to venture forth tentatively from their often-stifling family cocoon. Rockefeller said he educated his children at home because he had divided his time between Cleveland and New York for several years, but he also might have wanted to sequester them from forbidden contacts. Bessie, Alta, and Edith now attended the Rye Female Seminary in Westchester County, directed by a Mrs.

Life, the former Susan La Monte, who had tutored Rockefeller in his early adolescence in Owego. Though the progeny of one of America's richest men, the three young heiresses seemed to drift about in a state of perpetual longing. As one intimate companion recollected,

> The allowances given to the children were small. Edith confided to me one day while we were shopping that it was the dearest wish of her heart to have some silk underwear, but that "*Mother* wouldn't hear of it." Alta yearned for a high hat to wear with her riding costume, and when after months of cajoling she finally got it, she had [a] picture taken. . . . Then the dream of her life became riding boots.[48]

Edith became positively clothes crazy, displaying a craving for fashionable outfits and jewelry in defiance of her parents' values.

By avoiding talk of money as unbecoming, Rockefeller concealed from his children the magnitude of his fortune. When Bessie enrolled at Vassar in the mid-1880s—she was the only daughter to attend college—she went on a shopping expedition with some classmates to purchase a Christmas present for a favorite teacher. At a Manhattan store, they found the perfect gift: a $100 desk. Since Bessie and her companions had only $75, they asked the merchant if he could wait a few days for the remaining $25. He agreed to do so if a New York businessman would vouch for them. "My father is in business," Bessie offered meekly. "He will vouch for us." Who is your father? asked the man. "His name is Mr. Rockefeller," she said. "John D. Rockefeller; he is in the oil business." The merchant gasped. "John D. Rockefeller your father!" When he agreed to ship the furniture, Bessie imagined he had merely changed his mind to please them.[49]

When it came time for Junior to dispense with private tutors, he went to the New York School of Languages, followed by a school run by C. N. Douglass, and then the tony Cutler School, whose student body included Albert Milbank, Cornelius N. Bliss, and Cornelius Vanderbilt. Junior trudged the pavement to school each morning while he watched poorer classmates rolling by in fine carriages. Though he belittled his own intelligence, this bright, dutiful boy always scored high grades and led a purposeful life that allowed small time for leisure. When not doing homework, he often practiced his violin, and for eight years he took lessons from Richard Arnold, first violinist of the Philharmonic Orchestra. Though never spanked or punished, Junior had to put up with unremitting religious indoctrination from Cettie.[50] By comparison, Father was almost playful. Eager to please his parents and other adult authority figures, Junior took things too seriously and was petrified of making a mistake.

It is a small miracle that, with so much duty so regularly dinned into their heads, the Rockefeller children didn't go batty. They did, however, erupt in a mass of psychosomatic symptoms. During his first year at Cutler, at age thirteen, Junior racked up a 98.1 grade average only to succumb to some sort of nervous collapse from overwork.[51] Too much expectation had been heaped on this frail vessel, and he buckled beneath the weight. His father ordered the staple Victorian cure of hard outdoors work. In late 1887, Junior and his mother wintered at Forest Hill, where he furiously chopped wood (fifteen cents a cord), broke stones, burned brush, and raked leaves, working the nervous tension from his system. Junior enjoyed this fleeting monopoly on his mother's affections and the respite from his regimented New York life. His letters to his father evoke the melancholy beauty of a snowbound winter, with moonlit sleigh rides and afternoons skating on the frozen lake as he pushed Cettie before him in a wooden chair.

Reinvigorated by his stay, Junior completed a second year at Cutler before being transferred to a school custom-made for him. John and William Rockefeller conferred with a talented instructor, John A. Browning, who created the tiny Browning School with just two classes: one built around Junior, the other around William's son Percy. A Rockefeller operation from the outset, it was set up in a family-owned brownstone on West Fifty-fifth Street, with John and William paying Browning's salary and reserving the right to screen applicants. From the beginning, the school emphasized manual crafts as well as classical studies and was animated by an egalitarian spirit. Nettie Fowler McCormick of the Chicago reaper clan sent her two sons, Harold and Stanley, and the student body of twenty-five also included two sons of William's estate superintendent in Greenwich, Connecticut. The Browning School was yet another attempt by John D. to prevent his children from putting on airs or slipping into idle dissipation.

The letters Junior sent his father from Forest Hill during the winter of 1887–1888 make clear that his mother was also recuperating from a bout of ill health. He told a friend, "Although it would be pleasant to be with the rest of the family, when we think how much good it is doing mother—and she really is getting much better, she sleeps so well and feels so much better—we are perfectly happy to be separated."[52] Always weak, Cettie was beginning to betray signs of the frailty that would convert her into an invalid. She enjoyed driving with her husband and shared his love of skating but took these activities only in small doses. "She was not strong . . . and could not endure much exercise," said her son.[53]

For the biographer of John D. Rockefeller, the most exasperating lacuna in his story is Cettie's transformation from a bright, witty girl into a rather humorless woman, prone to a nunlike religiosity. One wonders what happened to the high-spirited, vivacious young woman who was the high-school valedictorian and literary editor at Oread Collegiate Institute. By the 1880s, when she was in her forties, her letters were suffocated by a treacly piety and endless platitudes as she grew righteous and slightly unreal. As one magazine noted, "It would be hard to find anyone who has anything to say against Mrs. John D. Rockefeller, for the reason that Mrs. Rockefeller's life is almost wholly devoted to religious and benevolent work."[54] She uttered only noble and uplifting thoughts, constantly thanked the Lord, and never stooped to gossip or flip remarks.

Was this the case of another smart Victorian woman who felt trapped by the few options open to her and took to bed and religion from boredom or self-defense? The social conventions of her day clearly approved of her decision to confine herself to church and home. But one also wonders whether her cloistered religiosity wasn't a reaction to the mounting controversy surrounding Standard Oil. This gentle, brown-eyed woman adored her husband and believed implicitly in his goodness, but she was bothered by the charges hurled against him. We know from two of Rockefeller's colleagues that Cettie sometimes wanted him to respond to attacks that he preferred to slough off and ignore. In the 1860s and early 1870s, Rockefeller wrote her confidential, highly informative letters about his business dealings, including the SIC. Starting in the 1880s, however, his letters suddenly became bland and empty, full of banalities about the weather and barren of business news.

In general, Rockefeller kept his family apart from Standard Oil matters, with one curious exception. At the breakfast table, he sometimes read aloud samples from the reams of abusive crank mail that swamped his office. Perhaps he did this to make light of the threats or take the sting from controversy. Aside from this, he steered clear of anything even faintly controversial. Did Cettie's religion become her impenetrable shield against the venomous criticism of her husband? And did John become more self-righteous about temperance and other social issues to assert his own virtue and assuage his conscience? These are intriguing questions, but ones avoided so sedulously by Rockefeller and his family that they left no comments that might shed any light on them. Certain aspects of Rockefeller's married life—those critical things whispered about Standard Oil in the privacy of the bedroom at night—will likely remain a mystery forever.

=

Rockefeller always took umbrage at the accusation that he was a narrow workaholic, yet he didn't begin to travel abroad until after he had moved to New York and was well into his forties. A stubborn provincial, he didn't hanker after the exotic, and he shunned Asia, Africa, Latin America, and other distant outposts serviced by Standard Oil. For him, the aim of travel wasn't to submit to the charms of an alien place but to transport his culture there intact. He never traveled without a clergyman (typically Edward Judson or Augustus Strong) and a doctor (usually Hamilton Biggar) in tow to cater to his spiritual

Lucy Avery Rockefeller, the doughty grandmother of John D. Rockefeller. (Courtesy of the Rockefeller Archive Center)

John D. Rockefeller's humble birthplace in Richford, New York. (Courtesy of the Rockefeller Archive Center)

The five children of William and Eliza Rockefeller. Seated, from left: John, twenty, Mary Ann, sixteen, and William, eighteen. Standing: Lucy, twenty-one, and Frank, fourteen. (Courtesy of the Rockefeller Archive Center)

Lucy Henry Spelman, Rockefeller's mother-in-law, and Harvey Buel Spelman, his father-in-law. The Spelmans were staunch temperance advocates and abolitionists. (Courtesy of the Rockefeller Archive Center)

The inseparable Spelman sisters: Lucy, also known as "Lute" (left), and Laura. (Courtesy of the Rockefeller Archive Center)

A top-hatted "Colonel" Edwin Drake stands before the landmark well he drilled in Titusville, Pennsylvania, in 1859. (Courtesy of the Drake Well Museum)

After the Civil War, Rockefeller & Andrews occupied second-floor offices in the Sexton Block in Cleveland. (Courtesy of the Rockefeller Archive Center)

The storied oil boomtown of Pithole, which sprang up miraculously in 1865 and vanished within a decade. (Courtesy of the Rockefeller Archive Center)

The stately Rockefeller home at 424 Euclid Avenue in Cleveland. (Courtesy of the Rockefeller Archive Center)

Rockefeller's rambling retreat at Forest Hill, which was briefly run by the family as a hotel. (Courtesy of the Rockefeller Archive Center)

A studio portrait of a polished John D. Rockefeller in 1884. (Courtesy of the Rockefeller Archive Center)

A family picnic at Forest Hill, circa 1880. Rockefeller stands at far left. Daughters Bessie, left, and Edith, right, sit directly behind the table, while Alta lounges impishly below. Cettie sits at far left and Grandmother Spelman at far right.(Courtesy of the Rockefeller Archive Center)

Rockefeller dines on sardines al fresco during an 1899 camping trip in the American West. (Courtesy of the Rockefeller Archive Center)

Rockefeller sits erect on the steps of brother William's estate, Rockwood Hall, flanked to the rear by daughter Alta, left, and William's daughter Emma; in the foreground, from left, sit William's children Percy and Ethel and John D. Rockefeller, Jr. (Courtesy of the Rockefeller Archive Center)

The first graduating class of Spelman Seminary, 1887, which was founded to educate freed women slaves and their daughters. (Courtesy of the Spelman College Archives)

John D. Rockefeller, Jr., sits astride his first pony, which was hand-picked by his father. (Courtesy of the Rockefeller Archive Center)

John D. Rockefeller, Jr., circa 1880, with his sole childhood friend, Harry Moore, son of the Forest Hill housekeeper. (Courtesy of the Rockefeller Archive Center)

Alta Rockefeller on the day of her wedding to Ezra Parmalee Prentice. (Courtesy of the Rockefeller Archive Center)

Harold Fowler McCormick, dreamer and businessman. (Courtesy of the Rockefeller Archive Center)

Edith Rockefeller McCormick holds aloft John Rockefeller McCormick, whose early death from scarlet fever led to the founding of an institute for infectious diseases in Chicago. (Courtesy of the Rockefeller Archive Center)

Senior's massive house at 4 West Fifty-fourth Street, foreground, and Junior's still grander adjoining house at 10 West Fifty-fourth, on the site now occupied by the Museum of Modern Art. Their carriage house is visible in the foreground. (Courtesy of the Rockefeller Archive Center)

For their bedroom at 4 West Fifty-fourth Street, John and Cettie Rockefeller retained the richly exotic furnishings of their predecessor, Arabella Worsham, the mistress of Collis P. Huntington. Such luxury was not their usual style. (Courtesy of the Rockefeller Archive Center)

Senator Nelson W. Aldrich of Rhode Island, whom Lincoln Steffens dubbed "the political boss of the United States." (Courtesy of the Rockefeller Archive Center)

The Aldrich sisters in 1910. From left: Abby Aldrich Rockefeller, Elsie Aldrich, and Lucy Aldrich. (Courtesy of the Rockefeller Archive Center)

The Aldrich family. From left: Abby, Lucy, Senator Aldrich, Winthrop (?), and Mrs. Aldrich. (Courtesy of the Rockefeller Archive Center)

William Rockefeller.
(Courtesy of the Rockefeller
Archive Center)

Frank Rockefeller. (Courtesy of the Rockefeller
Archive Center)

**Frederick T. Gates in his
later years.** (Courtesy of the
Rockefeller Archive Center)

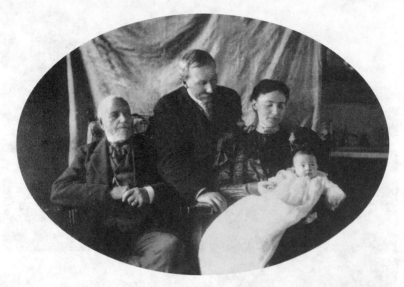

The only existing photo that shows John D. with his father, William Avery Rockefeller, who sits rather awkwardly to the left, while Edith holds John Rockefeller McCormick on her lap, circa 1897. (Courtesy of the Rockefeller Archive Center)

The tombstone of William Avery Rockefeller—a.k.a. Dr. William Levingston—in Freeport, Illinois. (Courtesy of Heather Brownfield)

The aging Eliza Davison Rockefeller bore a comical resemblance to her famous son in his later years. (Courtesy of the Rockefeller Archive Center) and physical needs. Although Rockefeller never owned a private railroad car, the railroads hooked one up for him, as needed, to a transcontinental train for domestic trips. These plush carriages were divided into six compartments, including a kitchen, pantry, observatory room, private room, and staterooms. Streaking across the Great Plains, the family exuberantly sang hymns, or the children practiced their musical instruments. For an hour each morning, the clergyman led a Bible session, expounding another beatitude. In mapping his itinerary, Rockefeller ensured access to a Baptist church each Sunday, and he especially liked to drop in on black churches, often leaving a substantial donation in his wake. Most of all, he rejoiced to find a good, rousing tent meeting on the road—that was a real vacation treat for a man who always found religion an uplifting experience.

In 1883, Rockefeller and Henry Flagler toured Jacksonville and Saint Augustine, Florida, and reviewed the state's economic prospects with Dr. Andrew Anderson and tobacco mogul George P. Lorillard. The next year, the Rockefellers headed down to Atlanta, swung west to New Orleans, and wound up in Los Angeles and San Francisco. Two years later, they made an extended trip to Yellowstone Park and returned by way of Chicago. By this point, even Rockefeller wondered whether he would ever escape the continental United States, telling Benjamin Brewster, "I may never get to Europe with my family although we have been expecting we might go in a year or two, but I am very desirous to know more of this dear land in which we live."[55]

Deliverance came on June 1, 1887, when Rockefeller and his family set sail for a three-month European vacation, the Standard Oil executives trailing after them on a tugboat to wave good-bye. They must have been relieved because they feared that his indefatigable exertions at Standard Oil might injure his health. It took Rockefeller time to shed his obsessive concern for Standard Oil and allow himself to be lulled by the restful sea spirit. While still 460 miles from Southampton, unable to stop wondering about oil, he broke down and wired George Rogers, "I find I already *thirst* for knowledge about the business."[56] A month later, he pleaded from Berlin, "Can't you glean more of interest from Ex[ecutive] Com[mittee] for me about current business. Am anxious for every scrap of information."[57]

After the Civil War, so many Americans flocked to Europe for vacations, presenting a cavalcade of innocents abroad, that their showy vulgarity and bumptious patriotism were frequently parodied by contemporary writers. The Rockefellers must have struck the Europeans as a dry, antiseptic family, somewhat awkward and ill at ease with foreign languages. Rockefeller made no concessions to the European milieu, which only accentuated his homespun style. In London, he booked a hotel room in Piccadilly that gave his family a front-row seat for Queen Victoria's jubilee, and they stared agog as she whisked by in a magnificent golden carriage.

As the party crossed to France, John D. was alert for sharp characters out to swindle him and prey upon his American innocence. Because he didn't speak French, he knew he looked like a vulnerable rube. At one point, he suspected, correctly, that their tour guide was fleecing them. Politely firing the man, he took charge of financial matters and pored over stacks of incomprehensible bills. Junior left a splendid vignette of his father trying to decipher a French check:

> I can see him now, going over the long French bills, studying each item, many of them being unintelligible to him. "Poulets!" he would exclaim. "What are poulets, John?" Or again, "Bougies, bougies—what in the world is a bougie?" And so on down the bill. Father was never willing to pay a bill which he did not know to be correct in all its items. Such care in small things might seem penurious to some people, yet to him it was the working out of a life principle.[58]

Another traveling companion remembered the Rockefellers sitting at a private dining room in a Roman hotel as the paterfamilias dissected the weekly bill, trying to ascertain whether they had really consumed two whole chickens, as these slippery foreigners alleged:

> Mr. Rockefeller listened for a while to the discussion, and then said quietly: "I can settle that very easily. John, did you have a chicken leg?" "Yes." "Alta, did you have a chicken leg?" "Yes." "Well, Mother, I think I remember that you had one. Is that right?" "Yes," said the mother. "I know that I had one, and no chicken has 3 legs. The bill is correct." I can still see the faces of that family group and hear the tone of Mr. Rockefeller's voice as he so quietly and so uniquely settled that dispute.[59]

As he grew older, Junior was deputized to handle tips and bills, which he later cited as excellent business training.

Needless to say, Rockefeller spurned the European music halls and spent most of the trip making pilgrimages to churches or touring pretty scenery. At first, he declined an audience with the pope and yielded only when advised that it might please the Catholic workmen at Standard Oil. Still a man of exceptional fortitude, he and Junior went off for a vigorous mountain climb in Zermatt, Switzerland, and his stamina amazed his son. On this European trip, Rockefeller even found time to read and grew enraptured in Paris by Lew Wallace's *Ben-Hur* and by Edward Bulwer-Lytton's *Last Days of Pompeii* on a visit to Vesuvius. Yet he couldn't disappear into a reverie for long. He was now so famous that as he went from city to city, his arrival was celebrated in the local papers and crank mail and begging letters began to follow him. So many letters piled up at hotels along the way that he finally had to purchase a big trunk just to carry them back. It was testimony to Rockefeller's thoroughgoing sense of responsibility that he preserved each letter for review at home. For a man who had fled to Europe for a peaceful interlude, it must have been startling to realize that his fame and notoriety were now so widespread in a world dominated by Standard Oil that he could no longer find refuge anywhere from his own reputation.

—

Beleaguered by supplicants, Rockefeller tried to expand his disbursements to keep pace with his mounting income, and his donations nearly doubled from $61,000 in 1881 to $119,000 three years later. Notwithstanding his somewhat frigid image, he took a close interest in the recipients of his charity and directly monitored their progress. Even as he was being reviled as a corporate malefactor in the press, this contradictory man agonized over the judicious application of his money and found it harder to exercise scrutiny over charities than over business. In this seminal phase of Rockefeller philanthropy, the entire family judged the merits of applications, and the children sometimes audited important meetings. Once grace was said at breakfast, Rockefeller pulled out a folder stuffed with appeals from around the globe and assigned them to the children for further study. At this point, he drew no invidious distinctions among the children and involved all four equally in disposing of his fortune.

Rockefeller's benevolent innovations have often been credited to his extraordinary philanthropic chief, Frederick T. Gates, who arrived on the scene in the 1890s. Yet by the 1880s, Rockefeller had already formulated certain core principles for his bequests, many of them stemming from beliefs he had long entertained as a businessman. For instance, like other industrialists, he worried that charity fostered dependence and pauperized recipients. After he had escorted his family to the notorious Five Points slum of lower Manhattan on their first Thanksgiving Day in New York, he lauded a shelter for homeless men but carped at the "policy of feeding all the tramps that came. My impression is they only do it once a year. I would give them work and make them earn their food."[60]

Again, contrary to his stereotype, Rockefeller was acutely concerned about the poverty that accompanied industrialization, urbanization, and immigration in the late nineteenth century. Far from taking refuge in the world to come, he also stressed salvation in this world, prodding one clergyman to go into "the midst of the multitudes thronging up and down the Bowery or thereabouts, and settle and stay right there with them, establish a church."[61] Starting in 1882, he underwrote the ministry of Edward Judson, who exemplified his belief that a shepherd should abide with his flock. He was the youngest son of Adoniram Judson, a saintly figure among nineteenth-century Baptists for converting the Burmese and translating the Bible into their tongue. Abandoning an affluent congregation in New Jersey, Edward Judson took over the Berea Baptist Church on Manhattan's West Fifteenth Street to evangelize among poor Italian immigrants. As an exponent of the social gospel, which blended social work with spiritual comfort, he convinced Rockefeller to contribute to a fresh-air and cool-water fund offering poor immigrants a refreshing two-week retreat in the country each summer.

As a regular dinner guest on Fifty-fourth Street, Judson won over Rockefeller to his vision of a comprehensive religious center that would unite elements of both an urban church and settlement house, ministering to both the worldly and spiritual needs of congregants, a vision spectacularly realized with construction of the Judson Memorial Church on Washington Square in 1892. For this imposing edifice, designed in Greco-Romanesque style by McKim, Mead and White with stained-glass windows by John La Farge, Rockefeller contributed $40,000 of the original $256,000. Both a community center and house of worship, it offered a broad spectrum of services from day nurseries to sewing classes for the poor. By this point, Rockefeller was indisputably the most powerful Baptist layman, and his largesse was already stirring fierce dissension in the ranks—not at all surprising in a denomination filled with working people. In the late 1880s, Judson told him about a convention of Baptist ministers in Philadelphia at which "some very shallow and ill-advised . . . vehement insinuations were made against the Standard Oil," prompting another clergyman to deliver a "brave, ringing speech" in Rockefeller's defense.[62] During the next two decades, this controversy grew more obstreperous as the Baptists tried to figure out whether the munificent oil mogul had been sent to them from heaven or hell.

The most important concept Rockefeller bequeathed to philanthropy was that of wholesale giving, as opposed to small, scattershot contributions. As Cleveland's wealthiest philanthropist in the early 1880s, Rockefeller already felt oppressed by the appeals cascading in on him. In 1881, he apologized to Reverend George O. King of the Willson Avenue Baptist Church in Cleveland, saying, "I have been holding back [an] answer in part from the fact that I had so many obligations for benevolent objects that I was almost overwhelmed."[63] Since for Rockefeller the imperative to make money and donate money emanated from a common religious impulse—"I am more and more satisfied no member of a church can afford not to contribute as the Lord prosper him," he told a friend—he approached his donations with extreme gravity.[64]

In 1882, two of Rockefeller's interests dovetailed memorably in a commitment to a black women's school at a time when higher education for both blacks and women was held suspect. He had had a long-standing interest in education, having contributed for years to Denison University, a Baptist college in Ohio. In the 1880s and 1890s, he gave so openhandedly to A. C. Bacone's Indian University (today Bacone College) in present-day Oklahoma that its first major building was named Rockefeller Hall. During the Civil War, Rockefeller gave to black ministers, churches, orphanages, and a deaf and mute society. He never relinquished a special solicitude for black welfare—quite atypical for a businessman at that time. Imbued with Baptist egalitarianism, he was ripe for conversion to a new cause when Sophia B. Packard and Harriet E. Giles reentered his life.

The Rockefellers had first met Packard and Giles on their honeymoon stopover at Oread Collegiate Institute, where the two women were newly recruited teachers. They were absorbed in the dismal plight of poor blacks, partly as an extension of their Baptist evangelism. After the Civil War, Baptists had been in the vanguard of forming churches for freed slaves and teaching them to read the Bible and had enjoyed the strongest growth in the black community of any denomination. So when Packard was named corresponding secretary of the new Woman's American Baptist Home Mission Society in 1878, she had a serviceable vehicle for advancing black education. When she and Giles toured southern black schools two years later, they were appalled by the educational facilities for black women and found one especially glaring omission: Georgia, with the largest black population, lacked a single institution of higher learning for black women. To rectify this, in 1881 they opened a school for young black women—many of them born under slavery and still illiterate—in the dank, dilapidated basement of the Friendship Baptist Church in Atlanta, christening it the Atlanta Baptist Female Seminary. The first class had eleven students, mostly mothers. For two sedate, decorous New England ladies to venture into the troubled area of southern race relations represented a courageous act.

In June 1882, Packard and Giles visited Cleveland to make an appeal to potential donors at the Willson Avenue Baptist Church. For forty years, the Spelmans had passionately backed abolitionism and sundry black causes. The recently deceased Harvey B. Spelman had sat on the executive committee of the American Freedmen's Union Commission. In consequence, Reverend King had a powerful hunch that the Rockefellers would respond enthusiastically to the pleas of Packard and Giles and promised the two women that if they came to his church, he would deliver John and Cettie Rockefeller in the audience.

Packard and Giles dressed with the same spinsterish simplicity, but the similarities ended there. Tall and blue-eyed, Packard was a brisk woman with a ready wit and great managerial gifts, while the younger Giles seemed timorous, gentle, and retiring in manner. That evening they made an affecting presentation, summoning up images of the 150 students, many unlettered but eager, who crowded the drab church basement to learn. As rain dripped down the walls and gathered in stagnant pools on the muddy floor, Packard and Giles sometimes stood in puddles as they taught eleven or twelve classes apiece each day; some classes were tightly wedged into a dusty area formerly used for coal storage. Breathing air thick with smoke and dust and ducking overhead heat-ing pipes, the students had to kneel and write on wooden benches. To teach math, Packard and Giles laid sticks across the planks and had the students count them. At first, most of the women were provided with little more than a Bible, pad, and pencil, and the lighting was so poor that they couldn't read on rainy days.

This poignant presentation would have wrung tears from a stone, and the Rockefellers were transfixed. As Harriet Giles recalled, "It was at that meeting that Mr. John D. Rockefeller first became interested in the school. After having emptied his pockets when the box was passed, he asked [us] the characteristic question, 'Are you going to stick?' and added, 'If so, I will do more for you.' "[65] On the spot, he pledged $250 more for their building fund. Much to the amazement of the teachers, he returned the next afternoon with three carriages and took them off to Forest Hill, where they drove about as honored guests.

Inspired by these women, Rockefeller, though socially conservative, became unalterably committed to black education. As one chronicler of Rockefeller philanthropy has noted, "The Rockefeller files are more extensive on this subject of the welfare of the Negro race than on almost any other."[66] More than any benevolent project, the black women's college in Atlanta became a Rockefeller family affair, as John was joined in his interest by his Spelman wife, sister-in-law, and mother-in-law. When it came to black education and welfare, Rockefeller displayed unwonted ardor. "Kindly assure the colored people of my sympathy for and interest in them and tell them, I hope they will in addition to securing knowledge from books, strive to learn to do all kinds of work, and better than any other class of men," he wrote to one minister friend in the late 1880s.[67] Reciprocating the personal tone of his correspondence, Sophia Packard always saluted him as "Dear Brother" or "Dear Friend." Amid the hectic rounds of his life, Rockefeller always found time to send letters and small, thoughtful gifts to Packard and Giles to buck up their morale.

Rockefeller's involvement in the Atlanta school was at first cautious but gradually acquired irresistible momentum. In late 1882, the Atlanta school bought nine acres and five buildings that had housed Union occupation troops. By late 1883, the fast-growing school had enrolled 450 students, the mortgage on the barracks property was coming due, and the school wavered on the edge of fiscal crisis. At this point, Packard and Giles entreated Rockefeller for a donation to secure the school on a permanent footing: "Give it a name; let it if you please be called Rockefeller College, or if you prefer let it take your good wife's Maiden name or any other which suits you."[68] Although Rockefeller retired the $5,000 debt, he humbly declined to use his own name. Instead, in a fitting tribute to his in-laws, he opted for the Spelman name, thus giving birth to Spelman Seminary, renamed Spelman College in 1924. It developed into one of America's most respected schools for black women, counting Martin Luther King, Jr.'s mother and grandmother among its many prominent alumnae.

On April 11, 1884, Rockefeller and his family went by train to Atlanta to celebrate the school's third anniversary, and 450 students packed the chapel to glimpse their patrons. Rockefeller adored Negro hymns and spirituals and now heard them in abundance. After the opening hymn, Sophia Packard exclaimed, "I bless the Lord that I have lived to see this day."[69] In a string of brief speeches, Cettie Rockefeller paid tribute to the liberating power of song, sister Lute memorialized their father's abolitionist work, and their mother told how the Spelman home had been a stop on the Underground Railroad. Though Rockefeller virtually never spoke in public, he delivered a talk of unaffected eloquence: "It is in your hearts to make the school one that people will believe in. God will take these small beginnings to do a great work. I am thankful to be here."[70] When Rockefeller sat down, it was announced, amid sustained cheers and hosannas, that the school had been renamed Spelman Seminary.

As a paradigm of future Rockefeller philanthropy, several things about Spelman should be flagged for attention. In a delicate balancing act, Rockefeller gave enough to get projects under way, yet not so much as to obviate future fund-raising. In 1886, Rockefeller Hall was dedicated, which included dormitory rooms and a beautiful chapel. During the coming years, he gave another eleven acres plus the money for additional dormitories, a laundry, a dining hall, and numerous other buildings, creating a lovely, elegant campus. Presented with architectural plans for one new building, he commented, "My suggestion is to err in getting what seems at present too much room rather than not enough. I judge the crop of colored folks will be large."[71] In the 1890s, Rockefeller sent his own landscape architects to redesign the campus, and he himself selected the trees and shrubbery.

Yet for all this fervent support, Packard and Giles had to struggle for years to keep the school afloat. With one check, Rockefeller might have relieved their anxiety forever, but he wanted to avert excessive dependence and keep alive a creative ambiguity about his intentions. While briefly serving on the Spelman board of trustees, he preferred to remain slightly detached and subtly enigmatic, never telegraphing his plans too far in advance.

Another cardinal principle of Rockefeller philanthropy was to rely upon expert opinion. Many of his gifts to Spelman Seminary were channeled through Dr. Henry L. Morehouse, the field secretary of the American Baptist Home Mission Society, which increasingly functioned as a conduit for Rockefeller's wholesale philanthropy in education. Taxed by too many pleas for money, Rockefeller wrote to Morehouse on December 24, 1883, and inquired whether "to avoid having all these people from every part of the country calling" on him it might not be "much better for the cause" for him "to give all through the Home Mission Society."[72] Frederick T. Gates later took credit for this sane, efficient method of giving through umbrella groups that would then allocate money locally, but the idea had already taken root in Rockefeller's mind. In these early years, one also sees Rockefeller using contributions to stimulate collaboration from others as he inched toward the concept of matching grants. For instance, in 1886, he pledged $30,000 to Morehouse, hoping that it would prove the catalyst for a $150,000 fund drive.

Since Rockefeller believed in meritocracy, not aristocracy, he favored educational opportunities for minorities. Spelman Seminary taught nursing, teaching, printing, and other useful trades, but the focal point was training young black women for a good Christian life. Some of the first graduates went to the Congo as missionaries. As Packard and Giles told Rockefeller several years later, "God is blessing the school spiritually as well as temporally; a number [of students] have entered upon the Christian life since the term commenced. We believe the salvation of the race and our country depends upon the Christian training of these girls who are to be future mothers and educators."[73] In the early years, Spelman Seminary encouraged a Victorian gentility among the students, turning out well-bred young ladies in hats and gloves. At the same time, it evinced much of the practical, enterprising spirit espoused by Booker T. Washington, the principal of Tuskegee Institute in Alabama, who stressed vocational training for blacks. Before long, this approach to black education would be anathematized as futile and condescending by W.E.B. Du Bois and other critics who thought blacks capable of the same higher education as whites and felt they were doomed to mediocrity by vocational training. But whatever its early imperfections, Spelman College ultimately evolved into one of the most highly regarded institutions for black women in America.

CHAPTER 14

The Puppeteer

Because Standard Oil had long exercised a global monopoly, Rockefeller's name was already known abroad. Foreign markets were larger and more lucrative than domestic markets—some 70 percent of American oil went abroad in the mid-1880s—while some feeble competition managed to sputter on at home in the face of daunting odds. In the early 1870s, kerosene penetrated China, Japan, and other far-off spots, and one American traveler in 1874 saw Standard kerosene flickering in the ancient quarters of Babylon and Nineveh. In the early 1880s, 85 percent of world crude-oil production was still extracted from Pennsylvania soil, making it America's fourth-largest export, and only Russian oil constituted a serious competitive threat. Since it made no sense to clamp down excess capacity at home only to see it expand abroad, Rockefeller could never tolerate foreign rivals, telling one colleague, "We have the capacity to do all the home trade as well as the export, and I hope we can devise ways and means to accomplish it later on; at all events we must continue to strive for it."[1]

Standard Oil studied foreign markets and posted a cultivated oil merchant, William Herbert Libby, to the Far East in 1882 to make a two-year survey. Observing that oil had "found its way into more nooks and corners of the civilized and uncivilized countries than any other product in business history emanating from a single source," Libby proselytized for kerosene in Japan, China, and India.[2] After translating into Chinese a pamphlet touting the safety of kerosene lamps, Libby had the satisfaction of seeing sampans laden with Standard Oil products floating up rivers deep in China's interior. To inflate demand, the combine sold hundreds of thousands of cheap lamps and wicks and sometimes distributed them gratis along with the first kerosene purchase. "In many countries," said Rockefeller, "we had to teach the people . . . to burn oil by making lamps for them; we packed the oil to be carried by camels or on the backs of runners in the most remote portions of the world; we adapted the trade to the needs of strange folk."[3]

For a time, Standard ruled foreign markets no less dictatorially than domestic ones, and with crude oil found in large quantities only in western Pennsylvania, it seemed this idyll might last forever. Then this fool's paradise was roughly shattered in the early 1870s by a giant scramble for oil at the Russian port of Baku on the Caspian Sea. For more than a century, the natives had scooped up crude oil from huge pits, selling it mostly to Persians to lubricate their cart wheels, grease leather harnesses, and alleviate rheumatic pains. In the early 1870s, this primitive industry was suddenly thrust into the modern world when drillers struck wells of unprecedented force. Amid deafening roars, black geysers shot into the air with such staggering power that some of them couldn't be capped for months; one raging gusher spouted 2,400 tons of oil within its first twenty-four hours.

In 1873, Robert Nobel, a member of the illustrious Swedish family, arrived in the Caucasus on a mission unrelated to oil. His brother had a contract to produce rifles for the Russian government, and Robert was scouting walnut trees for use as rifle stocks. Instead, he stumbled upon the bedlam of Baku, a frantic scene of such ghastly beauty that Maxim Gorky later limned it as "a dark hell painted by an artist of genius."[4] A crossroads as exotic as it was hellish, a Moslem enclave bristling with minarets, mosques, and palaces, Baku presented two faces to the traveler. In the bazaars, vendors hawked everything from Russian sugar to Persian silks, while outside of town a thick canopy of black smoke enveloped the refineries.

Robert Nobel took his 25,000 rubles of walnut money and plumped it down to buy a refinery. Where local kerosene had hitherto been mocked as Baku sludge, the Nobel refineries produced kerosene equal to that of Standard Oil, which monopolized the Russian marketplace in the early 1870s. Bringing sophisticated management and ample funds to the industry, Nobel and his brothers had created by decade's end an eight-mile pipeline to the Caspian Sea, where they floated the world's first oil tanker, the *Zoroaster.* They pioneered a continuous refining method that was superior to Standard's batch system for sorting out distillates. In 1879, the Nobels organized the Nobel Brothers Petroleum Producing Company and soon cobbled together an impressive distribution system, complete with flatcars, tank cars, and storage depots, ejecting Standard Oil from Russia. That year, a roving Standard operative, William Brough, sent Rockefeller samples of Russian crude and refined oil along with prophecies that in a few years the Nobels would build a pipeline or railroad

*Rockefeller's first influential critic, Henry
Demarest Lloyd, in Boston in 1903.*
(Courtesy of the State Historical Society of Wisconsin)

from the Caspian to the Black Sea, setting the stage for Russian oil to challenge Standard Oil in European markets.

By the early 1880s, two hundred refineries cluttered Baku's oil-stained slopes, and in 1883—true to Brough's forecast—a railroad connected Baku on the Caspian Sea to Batumi on the Black Sea. The potent Russian wells flowed with such fierce abundance that it was cheaper to produce oil in Russia than at Titusville, and cut-rate kerosene soon flooded European markets, undercutting Standard's prices. The American consul in Batumi, J. C. Chambers, who had been dispatched by Standard Oil to harvest intelligence, kept Rockefeller apprised of these developments and sounded an alarm about the Russians' "quixotic ambition to drive the American oil from the markets of the world."[5] Whatever the coolness between Rockefeller and American officialdom at home, they cooperated overseas to stop tariffs against American oil. Paying tribute to the State Department, Rockefeller later said, "Our ambassadors and ministers and consuls have aided to push our way into new markets to the utmost corners of the world."[6]

Rockefeller seems to have been caught napping by the Russian incursion just as he had snuffed out all his major domestic rivals. When his Hamburg agent, Charles F. L. Meissner, reported in 1885 on extensive Russian penetration of European markets, Rockefeller, taken aback, fired off an indignant blast at his executive committee: "I am at a loss to understand how the bulk transportation could have been carried on to the extent referred to in Switzerland and elsewhere, without our having received more information about it."[7] To retaliate, Rockefeller resorted to the usual high-powered weaponry, cutting prices across Europe and starting an insidious whispering campaign to question the safety of Russian kerosene. His files also reveal numberless secret contacts in Paris and London hotels with shadowy, self-appointed intermediaries inquiring whether Standard wished to buy a stake in Nobel Brothers or join with them in slicing up European markets. In 1885, Standard's peripatetic emissary, W. H. Libby, held talks with the Nobels in Saint Petersburg, but these overtures faltered. The Nobels' power in Russia hinged on their relationship with the despotic czarist government, and they didn't intend to admit Standard Oil into their preserve.

By the mid-1880s, another powerful force appeared on the world oil scene. The Paris Rothschilds, led by Baron Alphonse de Rothschild, had built refineries at Rijeka and Trieste on the Adriatic Sea. In organizing the Caspian and Black Sea Petroleum Company—better known by its Russian initials, Bnito—they stood to reap a fortune from inexpensive Russian oil. No sooner had the Rothschilds entered the business than reports filtered back to Rockefeller that the Nobels, who were heavily in debt to the Rothschilds, could not meet their payments and might be forced to make common cause with the French bankers. For many years, the Rothschilds, the Nobels, and Standard Oil circled around each other, each trying to forge links with a second party to isolate the third.

This vigorous competition abroad aroused Rockefeller's fighting spirit, and he even took to lecturing his colleagues in verse: "We are neither old nor sleepy and must 'Be up and doing, with a heart for any fate; Still achieving, still pursuing, learn to labor and to wait.' "[8] Both Rockefeller and Archbold favored scrapping their former system of operating through European brokers and instead launching their own marketing subsidiaries. For a time, they were held back by Benjamin Brewster, and Rockefeller, unwilling to move without a consensus, yielded against his better judgment. When the Rothschilds set up a British oil-marketing firm in 1888, Brewster's logic suddenly crumbled, and twenty-four days later Standard Oil set up its first overseas affiliate, the Anglo-American Oil Company, which soon monopolized the British oil trade. Two years later, Standard started the Deutsche-Amerikanische Petroleum Gesellschaft in Bremen to handle the north German market. Neither old nor sleepy, Rockefeller set up an oil terminal at Rotterdam, struck a deal to supply all of France's crude oil, took stakes in oil firms in Holland, Italy, and Scandinavia, and orchestrated heated price wars in India. Taking a cue from the Nobels, Standard launched its first oil-tank steamer to Europe, a mammoth vessel that transported a million gallons of oil, the first of what would shortly be an entire ocean fleet piloted from 26 Broadway.

Despite the low price of Russian oil, Standard barred it from America and retained nearly 80 percent of world markets in the late 1880s. For all the complaints about adulterated kerosene that Rockefeller heard on his European travels, the Nobels and Rothschilds never matched the quality of Standard's products or surpassed its integrated operation. For Archbold, it was the Russians' failure to consolidate their domestic industry—that is, to suppress competition and establish a trust—that consigned them to secondary status. "If there had been as prompt and energetic action on the part of the Russian oil industry as was taken by the Standard Oil Company, the Russians would have dominated many of the world's markets which have been made to inure so largely to the benefit of the American oil industry."[9]

If the Nobels and the Rothschilds weren't mortal threats, neither did they capitulate tamely to Standard Oil, as so many American rivals had. These contending forces clashed repeatedly in the oil wars of the 1890s, a protracted battle that saw periods of blistering competition followed by cozy deals to divvy up markets. When competition forced price-cutting in the early 1890s, Rockefeller advocated a tactical rapprochement with his erstwhile foes and induced Baron Alphonse de Rothschild to visit 26 Broadway in secret. Archbold's report to Rockefeller about the July 1892 meeting revealed that, beneath the competitive veneer, the Rothschilds were eager to come to terms with Standard Oil:

> We reached a tentative agreement with them. . . . I need hardly report again that it seems desirable on all sides that this matter be kept exceedingly confidential. It was thought best that we should not see the Nobel people, but that the approach be made to them on the subject by the Rothschilds. We were treated with great courtesy by Baron Rothschild, and we [were] much delighted that he spoke English fluently, which greatly facilitated our intercourse.[10]

In the end, Count Sergei Witte, the Russian finance minister, spiked the scheme for a grand alliance of Standard Oil with the Nobels and Rothschilds—to the dismay of countless European newspaper cartoonists who had made sport evoking the clumsy embrace of the octopus and the bear. All the while, Russia kept pumping crude oil and by the late 1890s briefly overtook the United States in oil production, even though Standard Oil handily eclipsed it in refining.

By 1890, it was self-evident that oil existed throughout the earth's crust and that only a freak accident (plus some timely Yankee ingenuity) had led to the business being founded in Titusville. In 1884, Dutch drillers began prospecting for oil in Sumatra and six years later received a royal charter to exploit Dutch East Indian reserves, christening their company Royal Dutch. Meanwhile, another aggressive contender waited in the wings. In 1891, the enterprising London merchant Marcus Samuel signed a contract with the Rothschilds to market their kerosene in the Far East. Samuel used the Suez Canal to speed the export of Russian kerosene to Asian markets. Oil had taken four months to travel from New York to the Far East but now reached it from Batumi in a month. Even though Samuel designed a custom-made bulk tanker, the *Murex*, to conform to the canal's strict requirements, Standard Oil hired London solicitors to sow doubts about the project, spreading nasty rumors about a "powerful group of financiers and merchants" under "Hebrew influence" who planned to take tankers through the canal.[11] Rockefeller later ranted against "our Asiatic competitors controlled by Jewish men who cry 'Wolf! Wolf! Standard Oil Company!' and keep moving in and getting control of markets."[12] (He once compared Standard Oil's supposedly "fair-minded" methods with "the old, old Jew method of treating one customer one way and another in another [way].")[13] Warding off this verbal sabotage, Samuel managed to defeat Standard Oil decisively, and his trademark red oilcans—in contrast to Standard's blue cans—soon became known throughout Asia.

By 1892, with oil production booming in Burma and Java, Standard Oil belatedly recognized the need for concerted action in Asian markets. It tried in vain to buy the business of both Royal Dutch and Marcus Samuel, who renamed his company Shell Transport and Trading Company in 1897 to honor his family's old seashell-box business. Standard even stooped to trading for Russian kerosene in order to serve better its Asian customers. It finally set up a series of Asian stations and assigned a small army of agents to Shanghai, Calcutta, Bombay, Yokohama, Kobe, Nagasaki, and Singapore. These operatives sold Standard kerosene in tin cans with wooden frames because Asian customers recycled the tin as roofing and turned the wooden cases into household objects. For all these smart marketing ploys, Standard Oil was forced to coexist with Royal Dutch and Shell, which merged to create a rival empire in the early 1900s. Henceforth, competition was enshrined as a permanent fact of the international oil business—despite a multitude of secret, market-sharing deals—and it was only a matter of time before the deadly contagion of competition infected North America.

═

Even as it was menaced by new competitors abroad, Standard Oil seemed omnipotent in American oil. Everything about its operation was colossal: Twenty thousand wells poured their output into 4,000 miles of Standard Oil pipelines, carrying the crude to seaboard or to 5,000 Standard Oil tank cars. The combine now employed 100,000 people and superintended the export of 50,000 barrels of oil to Europe daily. Rockefeller's creation could be discussed only in superlatives: It was the biggest and richest, the most feared and admired business organization in the world. Earning steady, reliable profits, year in and year out, Rockefeller could be forgiven for believing he had outwitted the business cycle. For a man who craved order, he had reached his apogee. No longer at the mercy of unpredictable economic forces, he thrived even in recessions.

Rockefeller was exceedingly pleased by the harmonious workings of his fantastic machinery and the neat, orderly unfolding of his days. When he arrived at work each morning, he sat at his rolltop desk and examined two stacks of paper, one representing decisions made, the other matters to be thought over, and he slowly burrowed his way through both piles. Starting in the 1880s, he adopted a policy of never doing business with strangers or even meeting them, avoiding unwanted solicitations and controversy. If this simplified his life, it also strengthened the unsettling image of an untouchable tycoon, hidden behind the scenes.

Many of Rockefeller's critics alleged that he divided his life into compartments and kept two separate sets of moral ledger books: one governing his exemplary private life, another sanctioning his reprehensible business behavior. But he saw his entire life guided by the same lofty ideals. In retirement, he wrote to Harvard president Charles Eliot, apropos of Standard Oil, "I can say without hesitation that no business organization with which I have ever been connected has been controlled by higher ideals."[14] One way that he upheld this belief was to become self-righteous about his opponents, whom he reviled as undisguised rascals. "The other people were up to all sorts of tricks, mixing benzine with the oil, and so forth," he said of rival refiners.[15] Nobody was more vigilant about being cheated than Rockefeller nor quicker to seize the moral high ground. To convince himself that he was a highly ethical businessman, he redefined exactly what that meant. For instance, he always made much of the fact that he honored contracts, paid bills and debt promptly, treated small shareholders fairly, and never watered stock. To confirm his clean, sanctimonious image of himself, he reiterated these ideals with a kind of incantatory relish, and the more naysayers dwelled on his railroad dealings or secret subsidiaries, the more he affirmed his own compensating code of business honor. This was as much to preserve his own self-image as to persuade a skeptical public that he was honorable, for Rockefeller desperately needed to have a good opinion of himself.

What further blinded Rockefeller to his misdeeds was that by the 1880s he always stood at several removes from any mayhem. He was now a master puppeteer, adroitly manipulating his marionettes, with the strings artfully concealed. As Standard Oil's leading figure, he was the only person who didn't have any direct operational responsibility. Instead, statesmanlike, he applied himself to general policy and monitored the performance of lieutenants, who sent him copious reports about their activities and often boasted shamelessly of their unsavory deeds. In contrast, Rockefeller replied in brief, opaque letters. He never assumed total confidentiality, even in internal memorandums, and cultivated a spare, elliptical style, devoid of names or specifics, that would have baffled any prosecuting attorney. In creating this self-protective structure, Rockefeller could run Standard Oil while simultaneously sidestepping responsibility, erasing incriminating evidence, and avoiding contact with his victims. It enabled him to distance himself from the dirty work down below and feign ignorance of what was happening. When confronted with well-documented cases of terror tactics used by subordinates, he blandly conceded some few indiscretions by overly zealous employees and cast himself as a helpless spectator. But if one examines the reams of letters sent to him by his associates, his pose of innocence crumbles. He knew everything that was going on and now, for the first time, we can document it. For that reason, we will digress occasionally in this chapter from the linear narrative of Rockefeller's life to examine reports he received from the field. They leave no doubt that he was the brains of the operation, directing activities he professed to deplore and setting the tone for his subordinates. This, of course, only complicates the mystery of how he integrated the various facets of his life—of how the enlightened patron of Spelman Seminary could also be the brutal overlord of Standard Oil. In the end, we can only explain how he rationalized his behavior to himself and others; given the absence of revelatory letters or diaries, we can say little about the unconscious drives that led him to do this or the mental strains it might have caused.

In his memoirs, Rockefeller implied that Standard took no rebates after 1880, whereas his files disclose that collusion with the railroads became even more brazen after that date. By the early 1880s, the railroads had ceded supremacy in oil transport to the Standard-dominated pipelines, which now carried more than three-fourths of the crude oil from the Pennsylvania wells to coastal cities, charging Standard Oil's own refineries half the posted price. Not surprisingly, as the railroads weakened, Standard Oil only browbeat them more. The combine owned a subsidiary, the Galena-Signal Oil Company, which monopolized the manufacture of high-grade railroad lubricants. Simply by stalling on shipments of this indispensable grease, it could bring any railroad to a halt. If Standard wished to extract a railroad rebate, it merely tacked on a surcharge to the price of Galena cylinder or engine oils. And Rockefeller continued to play his favorite trump card: the tank-car fleet. By the late 1880s, Standard Oil was leasing its tank cars to 196 railroads, forcing most of them to pay a double-mileage tribute to 26 Broadway—that is, a mileage royalty on outward-bound trips, when the cars were topful of oil, and also on inward-bound trips, when they returned empty.

One reason for Rockefeller's continuing solicitude toward the roads after the pipeline revolution was that he himself had a significant investment in them. He conceded as much when he stated that Standard Oil stockholders "as the years had gone by were becoming more and more a factor in railway problems and other enterprises."[16] At the time, railroad shares were among the few blue-chip securities available to rich investors, which meant that Rockefeller invested heavily in the Erie, the New York Central, and other oil-carrying roads. In March 1881, Rockefeller wrote A. J. Cassatt of the Pennsylvania Railroad about rumors that his railroad would soon issue $400,000 worth of stock. He suggested they set up a joint private account of Pennsylvania stock—with Rockefeller making the payment.[17] Whether this deal was executed is unclear, but it was a blatant bid to connive with a major railroad executive.

In later years, when Ida Tarbell made railroad manipulation the focal point of her Standard Oil indictment, Rockefeller pleaded ignorance of such dealings, claiming they were handled by his colleagues while he magisterially confined himself to broader matters. In fact, his papers document that he either met directly with railroad presidents or else was given graphic, blow-by-blow accounts of negotiations by Flagler, Archbold, O'Day, Payne, Warden, and a formerly little-noticed figure, Colonel W. P. Thompson, who had headed a Virginia cavalry unit for the Confederacy. The secretary of Standard Oil of Ohio and a brother-in-law of Standard power broker Johnson N. Camden, Colonel Thompson shared a Cleveland office with Rockefeller and Payne, and his letters furnish explosive proof of extensive railroad collusion in the 1880s. While Rockefeller made it seem as if such shenanigans occurred far from his sphere, he was fully briefed by Thompson, who liked to boast of his maneuvers.

Rockefeller's files are chock-full of examples of rebates well into the 1880s. In March 1886, William G. Warden reported from Philadelphia that the Pennsylvania Railroad had agreed to the following discounts: Fifty-two cents per barrel to ship oil from Oil Creek to New York (versus a listed rate of 78 cents) and 39 cents to Philadelphia (versus 65 cents for other refiners). Rockefeller was always insistent that Standard's competitive advantage had nothing to do with preferential transport rates, but his correspondence reveals that rebates could single-handedly transform an unprofitable plant into a profitable one. In 1886, Colonel Thompson told him that it made sense to proceed with a new naphtha plant at Oil City (naphtha was a crude-oil fraction used to make gas or solvents) only if the Lake Shore hauled the finished product to Cleveland for ten cents instead of seventeen.[18] During these negotiations, Colonel Thompson also reported that low freight rates would enable them to rehabilitate an otherwise insolvent Oil City refinery. Wherever possible, Thompson preferred oral agreements, once telling Rockefeller of his talks with two railroads, "I think they will concede the undesirability of a regular written contract."[19]

The backdoor deals with the railroads necessarily generated more speculation than proof at the time. But it was the trust's marketing operation that ultimately proved its undoing, for it directly touched consumers and tens of thousands of small businessmen located in every congressional district. In the 1870s, Rockefeller began to assemble a marketing organization to eliminate the middlemen, independent agents who had earned three to five cents per gallon of kerosene. Since they handled Standard kerosene *and* competing products—an intolerable situation for Rockefeller—and often cared more about gouging consumers than expanding markets, he decided to get rid of them.

Furthermore, Standard's refinery flow was now too huge to depend upon this fragmented, obsolete distribution system. Kerosene demand was booming as it illuminated mills, factories, hotels, and office buildings in the growing cities. To exploit economies of scale, Rockefeller noted, "we had to create selling methods far in advance of what then existed; we had to dispose of two, or three, or four gallons of oil where one had been sold before, and we could not rely upon the usual trade channels then existing to accomplish this."[20] To have high-volume, low-cost production, the Standard needed huge guaranteed sales. This forced Rockefeller to integrate vertically the entire industry, controlling everything from the wellhead to the consumer.

Around 1882, in a revolutionary development, the trust began to sweep away the old distribution system, with its horse-drawn carts full of swaying barrels, and disburse millions of dollars to build thousands of tank wagons to service every American town. Rockefeller hailed the efficient new system: "I believe it one of our best means for getting and holding the trade."[21] It worked thus: Standard's tank cars or pipelines delivered refined oil to storage tanks, where the tank wagons were filled up. From here, the wagons set out for local groceries and hardware stores—the principal retail outlets—where they replenished special canisters that the trust provided. Sometimes, over the furious opposition of storekeepers, tank wagons even went door-to-door, selling directly to households and putting Standard smack in the retail trade. (In some places, the trust manipulated local retailers by saying that they would refrain from this practice *if* storekeepers dealt exclusively in Standard kerosene.) The combine also sold, almost at cost, heaters, stoves, lamps, and lanterns to widen the market; in the manner of a modern corporation, Standard Oil created demand as well as satisfied it, and its obliging agents helped consumers clean lamps and burners to enhance their use.

Grocers and hardware merchants resented the demand to stock only Standard Oil kerosene or be starved out of the business. Along with wholesalers rendered obsolete by the Standard marketing effort, they emerged as Rockefeller's most potent enemies. Conveniently, Rockefeller never set eyes on these men, had no sympthy for them, and chided them for standing in the way of progress. "Of course it is natural that the man who drove the stage coach should be antagonistic to the railroad and that the man who used to keep the small inn should look with disfavor upon the big, magnificent hotels."[22]

Since jobbers often adulterated Standard Oil kerosene with poor-quality product from independent refiners, Rockefeller hoped that his marketing operation would ensure a uniform quality of Standard Oil products. The 1870s witnessed five thousand to six thousand deaths annually from accidents caused by faulty kerosene.[23] Far from being immune to complaints, however, Standard Oil was bedeviled by reports that its kerosene emitted an offensive odor, crusted wicks, and smoked lamps. One day in Cleveland, an angry woman pushed her way into Rockefeller's office and demanded to know what he planned to do about his poor kerosene. Indignantly, he marched off to the lab and had the woman's sample analyzed, the results unknown. At 26 Broadway, he tracked the activities of the manufacturing committee, which burned kerosene lamps for six hours at a time to test oil quality. Always touchy about complaints, Rockefeller often blamed poor wicks and developed the Acme wick to eliminate those complaints. To his consternation, customers still grumbled even after they switched to this allegedly foolproof article.

Standard's marketing subsidiaries were conducted with such controlled ferocity that they became the most hated part of the entire organization. One must recall that Standard Oil was a federation of companies, not a single firm, and held only a partial interest in many affiliated companies. This invited trouble, for Standard often retained the original managers and allowed them a fair degree of autonomy. When the combine absorbed established marketing concerns, it brought into the organization several rogue proprietors who tarnished the Standard Oil name. Later on, Rockefeller feigned ignorance of their actions and disclaimed responsibility when, as we shall see, he received elaborate warnings about their methods.

In 1873, Standard secretly bought half of Chess, Carley and Company, which had a Louisville refinery and a lucrative marketing operation in the Southeast. The owner, F. D. Carley, was a lapsed Methodist minister who set a new standard for pitiless methods in oil marketing. Confidential reports informed Rockefeller that Carley was a charming scoundrel, an inveterate gambler who went straight from board meetings to his bookie's office; even the circumspect Rockefeller referred euphemistically to Carley's "want of balance."[24] Although Rockefeller planned to pack Chess, Carley's board with a majority of Standard directors, Carley blocked outright control from 26 Broadway until 1881, and another five years elapsed before Standard swallowed the firm whole and renamed it Standard Oil of Kentucky.

By then, Chess, Carley had become a byword for vicious tactics. When F. D. Carley learned that Standard Oil's nemesis George Rice had shipped a scant seventy barrels of kerosene to a Louisville merchant, he reacted furiously. As a director of the Louisville, Nashville and Great Southern Railroad, which had granted Rice low freight rates, Carley had an underling dash off a peremptory letter to the railroad's freight agent, telling him exactly how to treat Rice: "Please turn the screw."[25] When this quotation was revealed by investigators years later, it was emblazoned in newspaper headlines across America.

Carley went to extravagant lengths to stop competitors. When he learned that Rice planned to sell kerosene in Columbus, Mississippi, he sent local grocers an unambiguous letter: "If you do not buy our oil we will start a grocery store and sell goods at cost and put you all out of business."[26] No bluffer, Carley set up a store that sold Standard Oil kerosene at cut-rate prices, as well as oats, meat, sugar, coffee, and other household items at or below cost. In many localities, grocers gladly took a 5 percent discount offered on foodstuffs by Carley in exchange for an agreement to carry only Standard kerosene, one of many anticompetitive practices perfected by Standard Oil that shaped future antitrust legislation. Notwithstanding the public uproar, Rockefeller claimed to be unaware of Carley's practices. Yet at one point, Colonel Thompson confidentially told Rockefeller that Carley was a "secret, surreptitious" man with "mysterious, dishonest secrets" who even cheated on his agreements with Standard Oil.[27]

In 1878, Standard Oil boldly expanded its marketing territory by acquiring a 40 percent stake in the Waters-Pierce Company, which was based in Saint Louis and dominated a wide swatch of territory from Arkansas to Texas. It was decided that Chess, Carley would monopolize the oil trade east of the Mississippi, while Waters-Pierce would control the area southwest of the river. The

Waters-Pierce deal brought another patent scoundrel into the trust, Henry Clay Pierce, who made F. D. Carley look like a cherub in comparison. By age nineteen, this country doctor's son monopolized the kerosene trade in Saint Louis, and then he mounted a pony and branched out into Arkansas and Texas. Even Standard Oil people never defended Henry Clay Pierce. One executive recalled him as a gifted businessman but added, "He couldn't do a thing straight if it could be done crooked. He was cordial and polite enough, and it was only when he got into a jam with people that he became nasty. Then they knew they were fighting someone. He was the greatest fighter you ever saw."[28]

Once again, Rockefeller self-servingly disclaimed knowledge of the rough-house tactics used by the Waters-Pierce salesmen and portrayed Pierce as a loose cannon who operated on his own initiative. He said that he never gave "a minute in a month to this local trade" and that any marketing excesses, when exposed, were condemned by the executive committee, but his files show that he received a full accounting of Pierce's high crimes and misdemeanors.[29] When Pierce made a highly profitable foray into the Mexican market in 1880, Colonel Thompson reported to Rockefeller that this had been accomplished "largely by evasion of the enormous duty placed upon Refined oil by Mexico."[30] Enriched by this operation, Pierce declared a 100 percent dividend on capital the next year. Thompson repeatedly warned Rockefeller about Pierce, branding him "a man not without designs" and relaying a letter "showing great duplicity on the part of Mr. Pierce."[31] Far from rebuking Pierce, in 1892 Rockefeller extended him a personal loan for $200,000—a king's ransom—and patiently carried him for eight years. Clearly, he had no qualms about the buccaneering spirit of the Waters-Pierce business.

The Standard Oil marketing subsidiaries fanned out across the remaining sections of the continent. In 1878, the Consolidated Tank Line Company took over the territory north of the Missouri River, spread across Michigan and Minnesota, then expanded westward into the Dakotas. Formed in 1884, the Continental Oil Company covered the Rocky Mountain states. In the mid-1870s, the trust sent a young executive to California, Wesley H. Tilford, who foresaw the state's potential as both an oil producer and consumer; a decade later, Standard Oil of Iowa developed this West Coast trade. Many frustrated customers of Waters-Pierce turned, in revenge, to Republic Oil, a New York–based company that specialized in cultivating retailers who loathed the trust. Of course, Republic was secretly owned by Standard Oil.

Around 1886, 26 Broadway divided the continent into eleven marketing districts, with boundary disputes to be resolved by a domestic-trade committee. As subsidiaries raided each other's territories, their clashes were arbitrated by headquarters. Nothing so clearly reveals the trust's imperial character than its deliberations about marketing territories, where exclusive rights to entire states and countries were dispensed like so many royal charters. At one point, when Chess, Carley; Waters-Pierce; and Consolidated Tank Line tangled over the virgin southwestern territory, Colonel Thompson explained to Rockefeller, "I have, for a long time, waited for the opportunity of defining the western limits of all these connections and take the liberty of saying on behalf of Standard Oil Co. that we had never conceded to any one the right to go and occupy Colorado, New Mexico, Arizona or Mexico."[32] In the end, Standard Oil ceded Mexico to Henry Pierce in a swap for the state of New Mexico.

Once Rockefeller controlled a marketing territory, he protected it fiercely and quickly dispatched troops to fend off the smallest incursion. If Standard Oil spotted even one carload of outside oil entering its territory, it traced its source through railroad agents and moved swiftly to halt it. Standard Oil marketing men were known to trail competitors' wagons and undersell them if necessary. This unceasing drive, this implacable need to win, emanated from Rockefeller himself. When told that competitors had appeared in Saint Louis, he exhorted Oliver Payne, "Regret to hear that those parties have established an agency in St. Louis. We must not let them get the business. Why not make a good, hard, vigorous fight with the view of taking it all back again and not let them retain a foothold there, and the same in St. Paul."[33]

As the capstone of this system, Rockefeller fostered an extensive intelligence network, assembling thick card catalogs with monthly reports from field agents, showing every barrel of oil sold by independent marketers in their territory. From 26 Broadway, the titan could peer into the most distant corners of his realm. Standard Oil spies collected much of this information from grocers and railway-freight agents. One Cleveland refiner discovered that Standard paid his bookkeeper twenty-five dollars a month to provide information on his shipments, mailing these trade secrets to Box 164 at the Cleveland post office. Standard's reputation as a pervasive, all-seeing presence was richly deserved.

The manic vigor of Standard's salesmen becomes understandable in light of a secret policy that Archbold enunciated to Rockefeller in an 1891 letter. Station managers were expected to command at least 85 percent—and, if possible, much more—of the oil trade in their district, a punishing standard that goaded them into aggressive tactics.[34] Because they had carte blanche to reduce prices and use any other means necessary to hold the trade, they created pitched battles in many cities. One repentant Standard Oil marketer named Charles Woodbury recalled a favorite scare tactic. "Substantial rumors that the few independents surviving might not much longer be able to supply oil at all continually alarmed their customers."[35]

Rockefeller found nothing reprehensible about this intelligence network and could never understand the eternal fuss. "The practice of the Standard Oil Company in this regard brings no credit or discredit to the Standard Oil Company," he later told William O. Inglis. "It was following out a method in universal use by the largest and most intelligent distributors of goods the country over."[36] Some Standard Oil people, however, refused to stoop to these methods. When Charles Woodbury protested eavesdropping on competitors, his superior gruffly insisted, "We do not intend merely to grasp the situation—we must control it." Woodbury replied, "But this is espionage. I cannot stand over these men and make them go after these details."[37] After being censured for such squeamishness, he quit in protest. Recounting this in 1911, Woodbury left some tart comments about Rockefeller's assumed innocence. "Results were what the master asked for," he explained. "Details [Rockefeller] need not know. He could be left to his own self-effacement. He had selected his staff."[38] In short, Rockefeller posted the sales targets, whipped up the fervor, then foreswore any knowledge of the inevitable consequences.

To square his actions with his conscience—always a necessity for Rockefeller—he needed to invoke an overarching theme: vouchsafing cheap light to humanity. Touring a well drilled on Oil Creek in the early days, he stared at it silently and then intoned, "This is the poor man's light."[39] Such remarks weren't just for public consumption but were commonplaces in his correspondence. In 1885, he instructed a young colleague, Henry C. Folger, "Let the good work go on. We must ever remember we are refining oil for the poor man and he must have it cheap and good."[40] Having grown up in secluded farmhouses, reading by candlelight, he understood the revolutionary impact of cheap kerosene.

Rockefeller never had a single motive for any action and was surely motivated by more than altruism in championing cheap kerosene. He was obsessed with high-volume, low-cost production to maintain market share, even if he temporarily sacrificed profit margins. As he noted, "This fact the Standard Oil Company always kept in mind: that they must render the best service and be content with a largely increasing volume of business, rather than increase the profit so as to tempt others to compete with them."[41] When discussing prices with subordinates, he frequently reminded them, "We want to continue, in reason, that policy which will give us the largest percentage of the business."[42]

The public tolerated the trust's brawny tactics for a long time because it believed that it had, over the long run, cheapened kerosene and exercised a relatively benevolent dictatorship. As journalist Henry Demarest Lloyd wrote scornfully to George Rice in 1891, "Thus the public—dear fools—believe, and it entirely reconciles them—knavish fools—to the piracies, treasons and murders by which the fabled cheapness has been brought to them."[43] Befuddled reformers assailed the trust for selling both too high and too low, for fleecing consumers and underselling rivals. As John Archbold summed up the paradox, "It is usually alleged that whenever the Standard, for whatever reason, advances its prices, it is oppressing the consumer, and when if, on the other hand, it lowers its prices, it is then oppressing its competitors."[44] Of course, both things were often true, since Standard Oil kept prices high where it faced no competition and low where it had to keep rivals at bay. On balance, the trust wielded its monopolistic power to keep prices artificially low to forestall competition.

In general, Standard Oil did an excellent job at providing kerosene at affordable prices. It boasted far lower unit costs than competitors and relentlessly drove down costs over the years. Between 1880 and 1885, its average cost of processing a gallon of crude oil went from 2.5 to 1.5 cents. In a rare 1890 newspaper interview, a supremely confident Rockefeller said that since Standard's birth twenty years before, the retail price of kerosene had plunged from 23.5 to 7.5 cents per gallon. Only half that drop, he contended, had resulted from the steep fall in crude-oil prices, and he credited the tank-wagon system for much of the savings. In the early 1900s, the Bureau of Corporations attributed most of the drop in kerosene prices to a sharp dip in crude-oil prices, not to Standard's superefficient management. Whatever the truth, the resulting low prices inoculated the public for a long time against the anti-Standard venom.

Many of Rockefeller's foes contended that routine underselling was his most lethal weapon, even more destructive than railroad rebates. As the industry's low-cost producer, Standard merely had to dump oil at cost to stamp out competitors. The practice of selling at or below cost, which started in the 1870s, intensified with the tank-wagon system, which permitted the trust to set retail prices. Hesitant to initiate price wars, which smacked of the old, Darwinian competition, Rockefeller said that he cut prices only defensively—that is, when forced to retaliate against price-cutting independents. When he did so, he showed no mercy against these reprobates and said with righteous indignation, "These people did not want cooperation. They wanted competition. And when they got it they didn't like it."[45]

Allan Nevins cited a federal study of predatory pricing that found that Standard Oil practiced it in only 37 of 37,000 towns serviced by its tank wagons and then only in response to cuts by competitors. Yet Rockefeller's files are so rife with references to this practice as to refute Nevins's verdict. In an 1886 letter, Colonel Thompson told Rockefeller that Standard sold at cost wherever competition appeared and compensated for the lost profits by raising prices in less competitive locales: "We find the outsiders mainly from Pittsburgh and the Oil Region had 2,000 barrels of oil in Cincinnati. . . . We have lowered the Cincinnati market an additional half cent temporarily to meet that competition and forced them to sell their oil without a profit." In contrast, he noted that with independents now banished from Chicago, "we jacked that price up a quarter or so, without multiplying instances, we are doing all around. The system is working well, better than any other we can devise and our feeling is to hold along on this basis—I beg you and the other gentlemen will keep in mind the fact that we are selling ¼ of all the oil we handle without a farthing of profit to this department."[46]

If Standard Oil sold one-quarter of all its oil at cost, as Thompson alleged, that would have meant anticompetitive price cuts in more than 9,000 towns—quite different from the 37 cited by Nevins. The trust used such infinite sleight of hand in setting prices, obscuring the real price through secret discounts, that a definitive accounting is impossible. Though many states had already outlawed predatory pricing, they found such a ban difficult to enforce. On this issue, Rockefeller remained an unreconstructed monopolist, defending Standard Oil's price-cutting years later by commenting, "If in doing so they were losing money, which they made up on some of the specialties—they made up the difference—would it be a crime?"[47] Eventually, a national ban on such predatory pricing formed an integral component of antitrust legislation.

Standard's policy of differential pricing also proved expedient in the global marketplace. During the 1880s and 1890s, trying to stem the tide of Russian and East Indian oil, the organization charged lower prices in Europe and compensated with higher American prices. Its tight control of the home market enabled it to prosecute savage price wars against the Nobels, Rothschilds, Royal Dutch, and Shell. For this reason, Standard Oil always considered its domestic monopoly a necessary precondition for its overseas conquests.

But Standard Oil never sought a perfect monopoly because Rockefeller realized that it was politically prudent to allow some feeble competition. As he admitted, "We realized that public sentiment would be against us if we actually refined all the oil."[48] The combine ceded about 10 percent of the refining and marketing business to a tiny group of fringe rivals. Even in the mid-1880s, ninety-three mostly marginal refineries were allowed to operate. A very smart monopolist, Rockefeller kept prices low enough to retain control of the market but not so low as to wipe out all lingering competitors.

We must retire one common canard about Rockefeller: He didn't set crude-oil prices through blanket edicts. In his correspondence, one sees the oil king trying to guess the trend of crude prices and bemoaning speculation. As he told one of his personal financial advisers in 1882, crude oil "is about the worst commodity in the world to speculate in. . . . It is about as uncertain as railroad stocks."[49] Perhaps the chief way that Standard Oil influenced crude prices was by elevating or dropping storage charges at its pipelines, which the firm sometimes used to break speculative raids. By issuing certificates against oil stored by its pipelines, it stimulated a free market in crude oil, and hundreds of thousands of people speculated in or borrowed against these certificates, creating the first oil-futures market and setting the trend for spot prices. After the National Petroleum Exchange opened in Manhattan in late 1882, the speculators far outweighed the trust in importance in pegging prices.

As Rockefeller boasted, Standard Oil was an infallible moneymaker. In the late 1880s, Henry M. Flagler testified it had average earnings of 13 percent a year on net assets, which considerably understated its performance. When

Teddy Roosevelt's Bureau of Corporations later examined the matter, it computed a more handsome 19 percent return from 1882 to 1896. Rockefeller defended these high returns as justified by the fear that the oil might run dry and render the trust's vast investment worthless. He knew public opinion was inflamed by the exorbitant dividends declared on Standard Oil shares, which sometimes ran as high as 200 percent. These figures were misleading, Rockefeller argued, since Standard Oil's actual capital was typically ten times its official capitalization. In terms of real capital, the 200 percent dividend declared in January 1885 was more like 20 percent—extremely high but not astronomical. Such a rich but not altogether outrageous return was just what the politic Rockefeller wanted.

Rockefeller knew that if he got greedy, other products could be substituted for kerosene, and this, too, curbed his appetite for excess profits. Oil was just one of many fossil fuels and kerosene one of many potential illuminants. In the fall of 1878, America's wunderkind, Thomas Alva Edison, boasted to reporters at Menlo Park, New Jersey, that he had dreamed up a practical electric lightbulb; within a year, he had created a miraculous bulb that glowed brightly for one hundred straight hours and directly threatened Rockefeller's kerosene business. The new Edison Electric Light Company enlisted affluent bankers, including the august Drexel, Morgan and Company. On September 4, 1882, Edison stood in J. P. Morgan's offices at 23 Wall Street and threw a switch that brightened Morgan's office with electric lighting, inaugurating a generating plant in lower Manhattan. Luckily for Rockefeller, the lightbulb didn't instantly drive out kerosene: It took time for Edison to cover the country with power stations, and by 1885 only 250,000 lightbulbs shone across America.

Instead of electric light, the soft, shimmering glow of gaslight began illuminating many American cities in the 1880s. For a long time, natural gas had been discarded by oilmen as a waste product until a business group led by J. N. Pew piped natural gas to Pittsburgh in 1883. Quick to perceive that natural gas complemented the oil business, Rockefeller advised Daniel O'Day that Standard Oil should develop its own strength in this area rather than turning to outsiders. O'Day and his ebullient team assured Rockefeller that they could pipe explosive gas long distances without mishaps. Within two years, they were piping gas from western Pennsylvania to cities in Ohio and New York, and by the late 1890s Rockefeller secretly oversaw natural-gas companies in Titusville, Oil City, Buffalo, and thirteen other localities. As one newspaper said, "Consumers in some of these places would be surprised to learn that they are burning Standard Oil gas."[50]

To counter competition from gaslight, Edison based his promotional scheme upon a moral and aesthetic contrast between good electric light and evil gaslight. Of the flickering gaslight that later generations found so enchantingly poetic, he sneered, "It is a nasty, yellow light, too, and far removed from the color of the lovely natural light," while he touted the "soft radiance" of electric lights as "singularly powerful and even . . . perfectly steady."[51] With a persistence worthy of Standard Oil's crusaders, Edison sales agents approached customers using "outmoded" gas jets and urged them to switch to advanced electric lamps.

The promotion of natural gas involved Rockefeller in sanguinary battles, for the major customers were municipalities, and the decisions were always highly political. The natural-gas business fed rampant corruption, a veritable cornucopia of graft, as companies manipulated urban officials to get these franchises. Though Rockefeller regularly denied knowledge of such machinations, his papers tell a different story: He exercised a supervisory role and knew all about the money funneled to politicians. In securing the Detroit franchise, Standard Oil furnished an emissary, G. A. Shelby, with $15,000 in cash and $10,000 in gas stock to sway politicians. When payment came tardily, Shelby groused to Rockefeller: "Will you guarantee the amount stated if Ordinance passes and is approved by the Mayor. . . . I have been to considerable expense and want to be sure of prompt settlement when work is completed."[52]

In the natural-gas battles, the porous boundaries between politics and business began to crumble and disappear. In 1886, Daniel O'Day met behind closed doors in Philadelphia with the rival Columbia Natural Gas Company and fairly gasped at the political luminaries who were represented. As he told Rockefeller, "I was astonished to learn the people who are in it. All of the Republican local politicians of Philadelphia are stockholders. They are very much afraid of their investment, and feel now that unless they make some alliance with us that they will in all probability lose all their money, or a great share of it." From pure expediency, O'Day favored a deal with their rivals, telling Rockefeller, "The feeling generally was to push the co. to the wall, a feeling in which I would fully share, were it not for the fact that the stockholders of the company might be very bad enemies to have in the Penna. legislature next winter."[53] Unconvinced by such pragmatic reasoning, the executive committee overruled Day.

The most bitter natural-gas fracas erupted in Toledo, Ohio, where the former governor, Charles Foster, was an old boyhood friend of Flagler and a recipient of Standard Oil campaign largesse. In July 1886, O'Day reported to Flagler that the ex-governor had agreed to merge his Fostoria Illuminating Gas Company with the Standard's Toledo gas start-up to form the Northwestern Ohio Natural Gas Company. O'Day relayed the secret terms of this arrangement: "That Gov. Foster be President of the Co. But that we would have full control of management."[54] Toledo citizens were delighted when the Eastern Ohio Natural Gas Company decided to vie with Northwestern for a gas franchise; in a compromise settlement, both companies received franchises. Then it surfaced that *both* rival companies were controlled by Standard Oil, and in the ensuing brouhaha city officials decided, in retaliation, to erect their own municipal gasworks.

Politicians in the Gilded Age tended to dispense with euphemisms, preferring cash on the barrelhead. Having done Standard Oil's bidding in the gas business, Foster demanded his payoff from Rockefeller in January 1888, saying his campaign committee had a debt of almost $1,200. "My suggestion to you," he told Rockefeller bluntly, "is that you send me a cheque for this amount. . . . I have refused to ask you or your people for contributions for several years past. In this case I did it because I know that you feel an interest with us, and for the further reason that I thought it would be helpful in warding off the blows made at you, and at our Gas Co."[55] In reply, Rockefeller sent Foster a thousand dollars, though he couldn't resist appending some barbed comments on his past performance. "Our friends do feel that we have not received fair treatment from the Republican Party, but we expect better things in the future."[56]

In 1886, Standard Oil set up the Natural Gas Trust, with Rockefeller as its largest shareholder. As such, he presided over these sordid municipal skirmishes, albeit keeping a sanitary distance. He followed matters closely but never soiled his hands, so that he could profess ignorance of the whole matter.

=

If Rockefeller tried to deny responsibility for his more deplorable actions, he had legions of critics who loudly proclaimed that he had maliciously ruined them. As Ida Tarbell noted, his foes endowed him with superhuman powers. "Strange as the statement may appear, there is no disputing that by 1884 the Oil Regions as a whole looked on Mr. Rockefeller with superstitious awe."[57] Each day's mailbag brought more invective from total strangers who cursed him and pleaded for relief. The most bile flowed from western Pennsylvania oilmen who believed that he capriciously decreed crude-oil prices each morning. As one Bradford producer told him, "The situation here is truly alarming and hundreds of families are in actual distress that need not be if the price of oil was what thousands believe *you could make it*."[58] Another correspondent warned him, "There are thousands here on the verge of financial ruin on account of the low price obtained for their product, and *if it is within your power* to give them a better price you would bestow a boon inestimable in its value to this entire country."[59] Sometimes these malcontents seemed torn over whether Rockefeller was Satan or Santa Claus, as shown by this muddled query from P. O. Laughner:

I am a poor devil of a pyker on the oil market and have been in the business for eight years. During all this time I have been cursing the Standard Oil Company with the rest of the boys—curses loud and deep. But with all the anathemas hurled at it the S.O.C. is still in existence and continues to pile up enormous wealth. Now as the market is completely dead and my occupation gone, I have come to the conclusion that it would be wisdom to stop cursing the Standard and strike it for a good fat position.[60]

After his scandal-ridden childhood with Big Bill, Rockefeller had a fine instinct for enemies and was sensitive to this crescendo of criticism. When out for a walk, he was vigilant and preternaturally aware of anyone following him; it was impossible to sneak up behind him. Yet he lent no credence to his critics and regarded their putative idealism as a flimsy cover for selfish motives. Rockefeller saw himself stoically suffering the fate of all revolutionary figures. "The ideas on which we worked were new . . . ," he explained. "But knowing that we were right, we went steadily about our business, founded on ideas that were an irresistible force."[61] He identified many critics as competing refiners who had foolishly taken cash instead of Standard Oil stock for their plants. His melodramatic rendition of it was this: "We think about Hades. What more can punish a man than to sit and groan as he contemplates what might have been!"[62]

Despite being the target of so much public obloquy, Rockefeller seemed fearless. "The word 'fear' is not found in my father's vocabulary," his son once said, "nor does he know what the sensation is."[63] Junior recalled being driven to a train station in Manhattan by his father at a time when he was swamped by anarchist threats. Though Junior begged him to hire bodyguards, his father scoffed:

"Why John," he said, "I can protect myself. If any man should be foolish enough to attack me—well." . . . He did not boast. I have never heard him boast. But he stood up full height with his fists clenched. What he said was to the effect that if anyone should attack him he was feeling sturdy—and he hoped he wouldn't hurt the poor fellow too much.[64]

Junior remembered the evening in Cleveland years earlier when a maid shrieked that a burglar was upstairs. Rockefeller unhesitatingly seized a pistol and strode to the back door, hoping to nab the burglar, who had already slipped down a post and escaped.

Rockefeller professed that he bore no malice toward critics and approached them in a spirit of Christian tolerance—so long as they conceded their error. To those "who repented their attacks and abuse we freely extended forgiveness, as we ourselves might hope for mercy and forgiveness from a higher source," he said.[65] As his private life and philanthropy attest, he was not a cruel man and did not have sadistic impulses. Yet he countered critics with ad hominem attacks and frequently referred to their actions as schemes, implying something devious and illegitimate. Whenever he was about to commit some particularly heinous act, he first found a character flaw in the victim then proceeded with a serene conscience.

Proof against criticism, Rockefeller nonetheless provoked a small army of gadflies. Perhaps the most picturesque was Lewis Emery, Jr., the rich Bradford producer and pipeline owner and a Pennsylvania legislator, who served as a major source for Ida Tarbell. If only Rockefeller had played fair, Emery insisted, *he* would have ended up the more powerful oilman. "I had and have as much brains as John D. Rockefeller, but I have never had his cunning nor his ability to use unscrupulous means or unscrupulous men to carry out a programme," he maintained.[66] Though he spent much of his life stalking the titan, he never actually met Rockefeller, who was, he explained, "too much in the background, too cunning."[67]

Standard Oil applied merciless measures to stop Emery's pipelines from linking up with railroads, as shown with his Equitable pipeline to Buffalo. In 1892, Emery was about to complete a major pipeline to Hancock, New York, where he expected the Ontario and Western Railroad to pick up his oil and transport it to New York City. When Archbold got wind of this, he demanded a showdown with the railroad. His report to Rockefeller shows the lengths that Standard Oil would go to cripple a competitor:

We have had further interviews with the Ontario & Western people, and feel that we have made some progress toward a possible understanding with them. It is now entirely sure that there has been no definite engagement entered into by them with the Emery party, and we think they are now convinced that the rates they had been talking about with the Emery party are absurdly low, and that business on any such basis would be undesirable and unprofitable. We have made them a proposition of business covering a period of five years, and expect an answer from them this week. Our proposition is that we put over their lines 400,000 barrels of oil yearly, or, in default of any part of the amount, pay a penalty of 10 per cent of the existing rates. We think it a very liberal proposition to them.[68]

Standard Oil was not content to advance its own interest; it worked actively to damage the business interests of its adversaries. Rockefeller's papers also reveal that Emery was prepared, at one point, to sell his oil properties to Standard Oil, asking for $750,000 in shares of the trust—hypocrisy that only validated Rockefeller's dim opinion of his critics.

Another embittered foe was George Rice, a Vermont native and independent refiner from Marietta, Ohio. A vigorous man with a bulldog face, Rice thrived on crossing swords with the oil trust. More than anyone else, Rice was driven mad by Standard Oil's unjust methods and became a professional Rockefeller hater. He instigated many legislative probes of Standard Oil and in 1881 published a pamphlet entitled *Black Death*, an anthology of scathing newspaper exposés. For Rockefeller, Rice was nothing but a blackmailer. "He liked to harass, embarrass, annoy the Standard Oil interests with a view of enabling him to sell his quite unimportant refinery interest. . . . This is the whole story of George Rice."[69] In fairness to Rockefeller, Rice tried repeatedly to extort money from him, asking an outrageous $250,000 for a refinery Rockefeller valued at only $25,000. To banish this pest, Rockefeller and his colleagues alternated between trying to buy him out and trying to bludgeon him to death. As Colonel Thompson reported to Rockefeller, "[Rice] admitted that it could be better to occupy friendly relations with us and assumed to be willing to make some arrangement, but extortion was written in every lineament of his countenance and burdened every syllable that fell from his lips."[70] At the time, Rice was lobbying for a federal investigation of Standard Oil's railroad rebates.

Though Rice insisted that Standard Oil laid deep plots against him, Rockefeller mocked his criticism as the ravings of an overactive mind. "We might as well assume that the Standard Oil Company would get a 21-inch cannon to shoot mosquitoes."[71] Yet his files show that such a cannonade was fired at Rice. In 1885, Daniel O'Day struck a deal with the Cleveland and Marietta Railroad, which was the lifeline of Rice's refinery. The railroad agreed to charge Standard Oil 10 cents a barrel versus 35 cents for Rice and his fellow independents. Resurrecting the infamous drawback, Standard would also be paid 25 cents for every barrel that Rice shipped. In dictating this deal, O'Day bluntly warned the railroad that if it didn't comply, he would build a competing pipeline and drive them out of business. In a rare successful suit against the trust, Rice forced Standard Oil to repudiate the nefarious contract and refund him $250.

With his own brand of courage, Rice tried to market oil against the two roughest Standard Oil subsidiaries, Chess, Carley and Waters-Pierce. As soon as Rockefeller got reports of even minuscule shipments made by Rice, Standard Oil agents in the affected states were told to thwart him by any means necessary. In 1885, W. H. Tilford told Rockefeller, "As far as Chess, Carley Co.'s territory is concerned, every effort is being made to dislodge Rice. Travelling men are being put upon the road, who go from station to station selling oil in competition with any oil which Rice may have in the various towns."[72] Every time Rice was ejected from another hamlet, Rockefeller was informed. "We have recently driven Rice entirely out of Anniston, Alabama, and feel that we shall soon have him also out of Birmingham," the Chess, Carley treasurer reported to Tilford. "Wherever this result is accomplished, however, it has only been by our making very low prices, frequently at a loss to this company, and such loss continued through a long period."[73] No threat to his empire was too small for Rockefeller to overlook.

If Emery, Rice, and other anti-Rockefeller mavericks made little headway in the oil industry itself, they were destined to have a powerful impact in the court of public opinion as they coalesced into an influential lobbying group. They formed a ready source of information for journalists, of whom their first polemical champion was a rich, elegant newspaperman named Henry Demarest Lloyd. The son of a Dutch Reformed minister, Lloyd attended Columbia College, passed the New York bar, then married into the wealthy Bross family, co-owners of the *Chicago Tribune*. Starting in 1878, Lloyd wrote withering editorials about Standard Oil in a florid style that captured the public's imagination. He profited from the flood of revelations produced by the Hepburn hearings in New York and the Pennsylvania lawsuits against Rockefeller. In the March 1881 issue of the *Atlantic Monthly*, editor William Dean Howells published Lloyd's mordant account of Standard Oil entitled "Story of a Great Monopoly." The first serious exposé of the trust in a prestigious, mass-circulation magazine, Lloyd's seminal article was a sensation, and the issue went through six printings.

For Lloyd, the essence of Standard Oil power resided in its secret alliances with the railroads, which had fostered the growth of many trusts. While conceding the "legitimate greatness" of Standard Oil, he said that it only made its ethical shortcuts the more reprehensible. "Their great business capacity would have insured the managers of the Standard success, but the means by which they achieved monopoly were by conspiracy with the railroads."[74] A vociferous critic of William H. Vanderbilt, Jay Gould, Tom Scott, and Collis Huntington, Lloyd incorporated his critique of Standard Oil into a comprehensive crusade for railroad reform. He also fastened public attention on John D. Rockefeller as the trust's embodiment, speculating that only William H. Vanderbilt had earned more money the previous year.

Lloyd was a slipshod reporter, and his account is marred by many inaccuracies. At one point, he says that Rockefeller had owned a Cleveland flour store. Yet he wrote lapidary prose and showed a keen political and cultural understanding. In a cunning stroke, he converted the piece into a consumer story, stating at the outset, "Very few of the forty millions of people who burn kerosene know that its production, manufacture, and export, its price at home and abroad, have been controlled for years by a single corporation—the Standard Oil Company."[75] For Lloyd, the octopus—he helped to popularize the nickname—did more than threaten free competition and fair play; it jeopardized American democracy itself. He charged that Standard Oil controlled two U.S. senators and had engaged in so much corruption in Harrisburg that it had "done everything with the Pennsylvania legislature except to refine it."[76] A superb phrasemaker, Lloyd declared in a rousing finale that "America has the proud satisfaction of having furnished the world with the greatest, wisest, and meanest monopoly known to history."[77]

The article introduced Rockefeller to a national audience and fixed antitrust legislation high on the reform agenda. In proposing a federal agency to ensure uniform railroad rates, Lloyd anticipated the Interstate Commerce Act by six years. If his attack was a harbinger of things to come, so was Rockefeller's total silence. Confident that posterity would vindicate him, the latter would later explain, "I was concentrated upon extending and developing and perfecting our business, rather than on stopping by the wayside to squabble with slanderers."[78]

In common with many contemporary moguls—including J. P. Morgan, Andrew Mellon, James Stillman, Henry Clay Frick, and George F. Baker— Rockefeller resented the press, and his ferocious allegiance to his concern transcended other claims on his conscience. One of his favorite refrains was "The Standard Oil Company's business was that of saying nothing and sawing wood."[79] During the antitrust furor of 1888, he told one minister, "We have gone upon the principle it were better to attend to our business and pay no attention to the newspapers, with the idea that if we were right they could not permanently injure us, and if we were wrong all their comments, though favorable, would not make it right."[80] Rockefeller asserted that he was less afraid of exposing misbehavior by talking to the press than of inadvertently spilling trade secrets. "What could we say," he asked rhetorically, "without telling the world just how we were making our success?"[81]

Those few intrepid reporters who tried to penetrate Standard Oil often gave up in despair. When the *New York Sun* dispatched a reporter to Cleveland in 1882 to investigate Rockefeller, he could not get near the mogul and was stunned by the layers of secrecy that surrounded him. He was further impressed by the silence of hundreds of Standard Oil employees he buttonholed, all schooled in Rockefeller's philosophy. Even with friendly journalists, Rockefeller would not supply a photo of himself in an oil field or refinery and banned photographers from his home for even the most innocuous magazine spreads. Of course, this invisibility only piqued the public's interest. That silence came so easily to Rockefeller should not surprise us. As an inner-directed man, he required no approbation from others and was much too circumspect to toss out opinions in a newspaper interview.

By the mid-1880s, facing severe political assaults, Standard Oil could no longer decline all press contact. In 1885, the *Oil City Derrick*—long a heated critic of the trust—was bought by an intimate of Captain Vandergrift, who installed Patrick Boyle, a Standard Oil adherent, as its editor. Around 1887, Standard Oil hired a press bureau called the Jennings Publishing Company to place favorable ads, disguised as independent articles, in Ohio newspapers. Soon the Standard cooperated selectively with other periodicals. When *Harper's Weekly* profiled Rockefeller in 1889, the article was first thoroughly vetted by Archbold. On those odd occasions where Rockefeller sat for interviews, he came across as unfailingly dignified and courteous. In 1890, a reporter for the *World* described him as a man "with an intelligent and pleasant countenance, fair complexion, sandy hair and mustache intermixed with gray, a somewhat prominent nose, mild gray eyes, and an agreeably expressive mouth."[82] The next year, another reporter, braced for a bloody ogre, said of Rockefeller, "He is modest, retiring, gentle-mannered, and without the human vanities which we associate with great millionaires."[83] This favorable coverage should have alerted Rockefeller to two critical facts: that even hostile reporters could be swayed and that he had a flair for public relations no less pronounced than his gift for making money.

Some of the most pungent criticism came from within Standard Oil's own ranks, from isolated subordinates who thought that the trust's muscular tactics offended Christian principle. In the 1870s, Rockefeller recruited a stout, bewhiskered young man, William Jay Cooke, a grandnephew of Jay Cooke, whom he had befriended at the Cleveland YMCA. A former wholesale milliner, Cooke prospered at Standard and was soon elevated to a manager's post in Toledo. After three years, he suddenly quit, unable to reconcile the trust's sales tactics with his Christian faith. As a history of Standard of Ohio notes tactfully, "He didn't see eye to eye with Mr. Rockefeller in the manner of eliminating competitors."[84] Unfortunately, we don't know how Rockefeller reacted to this defection by a devout protégé.

Perhaps the most extraordinary act of contrition in Standard history came in an eloquent appeal to Rockefeller written by William G. Warden on May 24, 1887. One of the trust's most senior figures, Warden sent Rockefeller a haunting letter regretting the revulsion that the firm inspired in the popular imagination:

> We have met with a success unparalleled in commercial history, our name is known all over the world, and our public character is not one to be envied. We are quoted as the representative of all that is evil, hard hearted, oppressive, cruel (we think unjustly), but men look askance at us, we are pointed at with contempt, and while some good men flatter us, it's only for our money and we scorn them for it and it leads to a further hardness of heart. This is not pleasant to write, for I had longed for an honored position in commercial life. None of us would choose such a reputation; we all desire a place in the good will, honor & affection of honorable men.[85]

After advancing a profit-sharing plan that might assuage the hostility of the oil producers, Warden urged Rockefeller to ponder his letter:

> Don't put this down or throw it to one side, think over it, talk with Mrs. Rockefeller about it—She is the salt of the earth. How happy she would be to see a change in public opinion & see her husband honored & blessed. May he who's [*sic*] wisdom alone can put it in our hearts to love our fellow men, guide and direct you at this time. . . . The whole world will rejoice to see such an effort made for the people, the working people.[86]

The Warden letter is an exceptional statement, as dramatic in its way as a deathbed confession. It also confirms that Cettie Rockefeller was extremely upset by the opprobrium heaped upon her husband. And how did Rockefeller respond to this brave, thoughtful letter? About to sail to Europe with his family, he employed his departure as an excuse to send a short, platitudinous reply: "I have not been able to write you sooner," he wrote the following week, "nor to give a careful consideration but be assured its content will not escape me."[87] To cool off a tense situation with a bland note was vintage Rockefeller, and there is no evidence that he ever again communicated with Warden on the subject.

A dignified but slightly careworn John D. Rockefeller,
probably then in his fifties.
(Courtesy of the Rockefeller Archive Center)

CHAPTER 15

Widow's Funeral

s John D. Rockefeller was busy consolidating America's largest industrial empire, his father, William Avery Rockefeller—a.k.a Dr. William Levingston—was showing his old wanderlust, peddling panaceas under his assumed name. A frontiersman in a nation where the frontier was vanishing, he gravitated to wilderness areas that provided asylum from the modern, industrial world epitomized by his son.

Huge patches of Bill's life remained a mystery to earlier Rockefeller biographers, but a rough portrait of his later years can now be sketched from Rockefeller's papers and some previously overlooked newspaper and magazine accounts. Bill had relatively little contact with his rich sons, John and William, but was extremely close to the envious Frank, who shared his love of fishing and hunting. (Perhaps associating these sports with his prodigal father, John never hunted or fished in later years.) After Frank bought an immense ranch in Kansas in the 1880s, his father was a frequent guest, and they hunted quail and prairie chickens together.

Much of what we know about Bill's later years derives from his remarkable friendship with a surrogate son, Dr. Charles H. Johnston. When Charles was a baby in 1853, Dr. Levingston visited his Ontario home and cured his mother of an illness. In 1874, Charles, now a young man, encountered Bill in Wisconsin, where Bill cured him of a fever and promised to tutor him in the "art of healing." In Freeport, Illinois, Johnston met Mrs. Margaret Allen Levingston and later called her "one of the sweetest women I ever knew."[1]

It might have been Charles Johnston's appearance that suggested to Bill a scam tailor-made for the Indian reservations. Before meeting Johnston, Bill had fallen back on his old deaf-and-dumb peddler routine. Native Americans believed that when the gods deprived people of one sense, they granted them supernatural healing powers in return, and this made them easy targets for Bill's act. Now he spotted a new opportunity. Charles Johnston had high cheekbones, nut-brown skin, and flowing black hair and could easily be mistaken for a Native American. Bill hired him as his assistant, decked him out in splendid feathers and war paint, and featured him as his adopted Indian son. From the back of his wagon, Bill told his spellbound audience that Johnston, an Indian prince, had learned secret medicinal formulas from his father, a great chieftain. It was testimony to Bill's gall that Johnston had to pay him for this apprenticeship in fraud. "In spite of his friendship and liking for me," Johnston said, "he made me pay him $1,000 for my tuition, which illustrates his shrewdness as a bargain driver and his love of money."[2] As he had once done with John, Big Bill toughened Johnston by goading and cheating him at every turn. One is left to wonder whether Bill saw in Johnston a substitute son who might fill the large emotional void left by his formerly adoring eldest son.

As he traveled with Johnston across Illinois, Minnesota, Iowa, and the Dakotas, Bill's business methods deviated little from the methods he had honed in upstate New York. As Johnston recounted after Bill's death: "He would drive into a town, scatter handbills in which the great Dr. Levingston asserted that he could cure all diseases and we would have a suite of rooms at the best hotel and to the doctor there would come the sick and the halt and the lame. In all cases of common ailments he could detect the cause almost at a glance."[3] To impress yokels, Bill wore a glittering diamond in his shirtfront, although when negotiating hotel rates he covered it up to get the cheapest deal. According to Johnston, he pulled in hefty profits, sometimes $200 a day, and gave the false impression that he was worth several hundred thousand dollars. As in earlier years, Bill dabbled in commodity speculations. At one point, he bought fifty thousand bushels of corn and stored them in bins, selling the lot for a steep markup when grasshoppers devoured crops the following summer. Johnston always admired this colorful, rough-hewn character with his bottomless bag of tricks. "He was all business and his mind was centered on the almighty dollar."[4]

At first, Johnston did not know that Dr. Levingston was related to the Rockefellers, though he noticed a recurring obsession with John D. Rockefeller, whom Levingston claimed to visit in Cleveland once or twice a year. "He told me he went there to look after his money invested with John D. Rockefeller, and he would tell me wonderful stories of John, his shrewdness and great wealth." One time, a skeptical Johnston asked Bill how he knew this famous personage. "I started John D. Rockefeller in the oil business," Bill said flatly. "I loaned him the first money he invested in it and I helped him all along." Bill boasted that his Standard Oil investment was now worth $375,000. "He used to say that he made John D. rich and he told me if I would stay with him and do as he said he would make me rich, too."[5] At first, it never dawned on Johnston that Bill was Rockefeller's father, for the braggadocio seemed part of his carnival-barker blarney, but when Bill began to chatter about old man Davison, Johnston recognized the name of Rockefeller's maternal grandfather and began to wonder. He remained suspicious for several years, while Bill resolutely denied the truth, scattering hints all the while.

In 1881, John D. agreed to buy his father a 160-acre ranch in Park River, North Dakota, on a simple condition: that he never take Margaret Allen there. (Bill spent winters with her in Freeport.) Never resigned to his father's desertion and always fearing press exposure of his bigamy, John was still trying to lure his seventy-one-year-old father back to Eliza and away from the sinful second marriage. Johnston later explained how Dr. Levingston had told him "that John D. Rockefeller early had learned that his father was a bigamist, and that the ranch in North Dakota had been taken by [him] upon the advice of John D., who, in the later years of his father's life, wished to wean him away from his second wife and have him live alone in a secluded place. Thus, if the old man should be discovered on his ranch, there would be no second wife with him."[6]

When Bill bought his first parcel of land in Park River, John allowed him to hold it under the name of Levingston. But when he purchased additional acreage in 1884, the deed was conveyed to Pierson Briggs, John's brother-in-law and a Standard Oil purchasing agent. In all likelihood, John paid for the property, using Briggs as a blind. When the land was conveyed back to Bill in 1886, he had to sign the transfer document "William Avery Rockefeller," though he was known locally as Levingston, and one suspects that John insisted upon this step to strip Margaret Allen of any legal claim to the property. It was this legal maneuver that later established incontrovertibly that William Levingston and William Rockefeller were the same person.

For a long time, Bill and Charles Johnston occupied adjoining properties in Park River and spent lazy summers hunting and fishing. Their secluded town, thirty miles from the nearest railroad, gave Bill exactly the protective distance from sheriffs and medical societies that he required. During the sixteen summers he spent there, Bill shunned the main roads of town and carved out paths through the wheat fields. The townsfolk found him a queer, solitary old buzzard. Now and then, unaccountably, he cashed a Standard Oil check at the local bank. If the check was for $3,000, he might throw up his hands in mock surprise and pretend he had thought it was for only $300, as if someone of his wealth could afford to be negligent with money.

Later on, when he became a physician of distinction and president of the College of Medicine and Surgery in Chicago, Charles Johnston feared legal repercussions for his earlier gypsy wanderings with Bill and sought to portray him as a genuine folk healer instead of as a bald-faced quack. But neighbors had little doubt that Doc Levingston and Johnston were first-class bunco artists. "They had a big jug full of medicine and they treated all diseases from the same jug," one acquaintance recalled. "I have often heard them joking together about the cure-all properties of the mixture in that jug. Dr. Levingston would say, 'Yes, sir, that medicine will cure anything, providing the patient has got $5 to pay for a bottle of it.' "[7] In this distant hamlet, Bill functioned as a medical factotum, rigging up a funny gadget that pulled an aching tooth for a buck, and he even did some horse doctoring.

Johnston might never have unearthed the startling truth about Doc Levingston had it not been for a freak accident soon after they moved to Park River. They were constructing a cattle shed together when Bill injured himself lifting a heavy bar. Gasping in agony, he feared that he had a ruptured intestine and that death might be imminent. When Johnston asked if he should notify Margaret, Bill snapped, "I don't want the Allens to get any more of my money than I can help."[8] (Relations with the Allens were apparently no more cordial than with John Davison.) Instead, Bill blurted out a shocking confession: He was the father of John D. Rockefeller, who should be informed in case he died. "No, you notify John D. Rockefeller, but be very careful and let no one else know it."[9]

When the injury wasn't fatal and Bill recovered, he tried to resume the tired old charade that he was unrelated to Rockefeller, but Johnston's hunch had now ripened into certainty, and Bill eventually gave up the game. Bill began to speak freely and often quite emotionally about his estranged son. When Johnston asked why he had concealed this relationship for so long, "he told me that the reason he kept it secret was that he found it necessary in his younger days to assume a name because he was practicing medicine without a license, he might be arrested any time, and he did not wish to disgrace the name of Rockefeller because of his children. He stuck to the name later, he said, because it was then too late to honorably take the right name."[10] This overlooks the awkward truth that he also assumed a new name to enter into a bigamous marriage with Margaret Allen and conceal the truth from Eliza.

The stories about John D. suddenly came tumbling forth. Bill bragged about his career, always reserving a good deal of credit for himself. "He never tired of boasting to me of John D.'s cleverness and how he was too smart for any of his competitors in the business. . . . He seemed to just dote on John D. Rockefeller. He told me hundreds of anecdotes of John D.'s boyhood, of fishing and hunting with him and of his cleverness and shrewdness as a boy."[11] For all of Bill's glaring faults, there is something touching about a father admiring his extraordinary son from afar and taking vicarious pleasure in his achievements while being pointedly excluded from his affections. John's success provided its own tacit commentary on Bill's employment. Where Bill had squandered his considerable talents, John had succeeded on a scale that made Bill look cheap and tawdry. Like many pathological liars, Bill's achievements were too meager to satisfy his exaggerated need to feel important. He had never arrived at a larger vision of his own potentiality, remaining mired in the petty arts of a small-time con man.

Charles Johnston finally wearied of his escapades with Bill and opted for a legitimate career. Like any Pied Piper, Bill was upset when one of his followers no longer hearkened to his beguiling tune. As Johnston remembered: "We parted when I decided to go to college and get a medical education and a diploma. He was very indignant at that. He declared that a college education would spoil me and that his was the only method of curing diseases."[12] Bill later recanted and helped to put his young protégé through medical school. When Johnston began practicing medicine in Chicago, Bill visited and showered him with gifts, including his gold-headed cane and his violin. In the interest of protecting his newfound respectability, Johnston kept his frontier liaison with Bill a deeply buried secret until the press forced him to come clean in 1908. By this point, the search for Doc Rockefeller had developed into a national obsession.

=

In March 1889, the ailing Eliza was at William's mansion at 689 Fifth Avenue when she suffered a stroke that paralyzed her right side. As she hung on for another ten days, both John and William skipped work to maintain a bedside vigil. "She knew us all," John D. wrote of the deathbed scene to a cousin, "and did all her strength would permit to show her affection, appreciation, and Christian resignation."[13] She died quietly on March 28, age seventy-six, never having known that her husband had taken a second wife, twenty years his junior, and adopted a brand-new identity. John, William, and Frank buried their differences long enough to accompany the casket by train to Cleveland.

Whatever solace John derived from Eliza's peaceful death was soon shattered by the events surrounding her funeral. Never accepting Bill's double life, John had sold his father's lot in Woodland Cemetery in 1882 so that he could be buried in "the portion for him and Mother" in the Rockefeller family plot at Lake View Cemetery. This transaction required Bill's signature, but John's relations with his father were so uneasy that he had to ask brother Frank and Pierson Briggs to act as intermediaries. When Doc Rockefeller predictably bridled at this slap at his second marriage, John threw up his hands in frustration. "Guess *you* will have to manage this matter with him," he told Frank.[14] John succeeded in making the transfer, for, as Eliza's condition deteriorated in February 1889, he wrote to Frank and referred to "the arrangement for father and mother to be buried in that portion which we have designated as theirs."[15] Perhaps Bill pretended to submit to this arrangement only to placate John, for he had no real intention of being buried beside Eliza or abandoning Margaret.

When Eliza's death seemed imminent, Frank alerted John that their father was suffering from asthma and would not attend the funeral service, to be held at John's old Euclid Avenue house. Something snapped in John when his father thus offended his mother's memory, and he decided to kill him off, at least symbolically. The day before the funeral, he paid a visit to the Reverend George T. Dowling of the Euclid Avenue Baptist Church, who would officiate at Eliza's burial and deliver the oration. As someone who later discussed this meeting with Dowling recalled, "The most interesting fact I got from him was the pains John D. Rockefeller took to have it announced that his mother died a widow. Among other things he told of the years of widowhood and her faithfulness to the memory of her departed husband."[16] That this story was gathered by Rockefeller's official biographer, William O. Inglis, only adds to its credibility.

Eliza's sons and grandsons served as pallbearers at the funeral, and John read the final chapter of Proverbs, while Bill was conspicuously absent among the mourners. Eliza's death certificate kept up the fiction that she was a widow. After the funeral, John was still fuming over his father's absence and for weeks insisted that Bill should come to Cleveland to pay his last respects at the gravesite. On April 18, 1889, he told Bill's brother Egbert, in an unaccustomed show of open wrath, that "if he does not soon come, we shall go for him."[17] Eliza's death, far from putting the whole situation to rest, only inflamed John's feelings anew, complicating his stormy relationship with his father.

That October, in apparent reprisal for his father's failure to attend, John made him sell his Park River ranch, which had now outlived its usefulness as a possible path to rehabilitation. On these transfer documents, John again forced his father to write his real name, "William Avery Rockefeller, widower of Cleveland," so as to keep the money from Margaret.[18] Determined to mete out further punishment, John pushed his father to sell all his western property, move back east, and abandon Margaret Allen altogether, but Bill would not leave Park River. He bought new property nearby and until 1897 continued to spend summers there and winters with Margaret in Freeport.

Six months after Eliza's funeral, Bill had the cheek to arrive in Cleveland, unannounced, his health suddenly and miraculously restored. It was probably this visit that sealed John's decision to sell the ranch in North Dakota. Apparently bent upon patching up relations with John and William, Bill prevailed upon Egbert, an upstate New York farmer, to accompany him on a trip to Manhattan in October 1890. The image of these two hillbillies in the big city measures the extraordinary distance that John and William had traveled from their small-town origins. Maintaining his civility, John gave them a tour of 26 Broadway and took them to Saint Patrick's Cathedral. The sixteen-year-old Junior whimsically narrated these events to a girlfriend in a letter; emerging from the cavernous church, Egbert turned to his hosts and said, "Well, that do beat all I ever see."[19] Even though Egbert was extremely close to Bill, John's children had never met this folksy old character before and were entranced by him. As Junior wrote,

Uncle is a farmer from Oswego, New York, and has only been to the city once, and then on business, so that he knew nothing about the life that is led here and he has been most interested to ride in the park and see all the fine carriages and horses besides the many other sights of interest to one only accustomed to country life. He is such a dear, simple minded old man and is so appreciative of anything done for him that it is a great pleasure to make his visit as enjoyable as possible. Grandfather said to me the other day when we were driving together, "Uncle Bert is so happily disappointed in your family and Uncle Will's." I said why how do you mean. "Well," said he, "he told me that he supposed you would be stiff and high minded and hardly pay any attention to an old country man like him, and he is so delighted to find you all so social and entertaining." And, he said, "he does enjoy everything he sees here so much, why he talks to me until nearly eleven o'clock every night, telling me all about it."[20]

John suspected that this would be his aging father's last East Coast visit, though Bill continued to show up in Cleveland, often escorted by Uncle Egbert. In the acrimonious style that marked all their business dealings, John continued to wrangle with his father about money matters. In 1881, he had advanced him money to enlarge Eliza's Cheshire Street house, the one John had built as an adolescent under Bill's intermittent supervision. Even though Bill had decamped, John had allowed him to retain a share in the house, leaving open the possibility of the penitent's eventual return. For this loan, John had charged—but never collected—6 percent interest. Around 1900, John told his ninety-year-old father that he would cancel his claim to the accumulated interest if Bill signed over his interest in the property to his granddaughters. It was yet another round in his never-ending quest to prevent Margaret Allen from inheriting a penny of Rockefeller money.

Communications between John and his father were routinely routed through Frank or William. As John wrote to Frank in a typical letter in 1898, "I enclose a letter to Father, as I have not his address."[21] Despite the chronic friction between them, Big Bill continued to borrow money from his son and by the end of the century still had a $64,000 loan outstanding—more than $1 million in today's money. This dependency grated on Bill, as was evident in September 1902, when John and Frank hosted a daylong party for their father at Forest Hill, gathering up his cronies from Strongsville days. Though he put on his finest duds—a broadcloth coat with silk lapels, a silk hat tilted at a jaunty angle, and a blazing diamond in his shirtfront—Bill was now a bloated 250 pounds. At ninety-two, he was gouty, rheumatic, asthmatic, hard of hearing, nearly blind, cantankerous, and unsteady on his feet. For all that, when they held a turkey shoot in his honor, Bill won hands down. The guests spent much time reminiscing and were doubled over with laughter as Bill told his salty tales. Later, when asked where he lived, he grew extremely coy; pressed, he raised his hand, saying, "No, no, boys; that's one thing I shall not tell."[22] He did drop two hints, however: that he lived somewhere out west and that he shot "shirt-tail swans" on a nearby lake—trivial details that sparked one of the great wild-goose chases in journalism history.

What makes the Forest Hill reunion so fascinating is that outsiders had an unusual chance to observe relations between John and his father. From his constant trips to Kansas, it was clear that Bill felt warmly toward Frank, but the tension between Bill and John was palpable. The old man seemed to delight in embarrassing his son before their guests. At one point, Bill was sitting on the lawn, holding court, when John approached quietly. "Here comes Johnnie," Bill taunted him. "I suppose he is a good Baptist, but look out how you trade with him."[23] Later, he told John that if he didn't pay him fifty cents for every squirrel on the place, he would "shoot every damn one of them."[24] Everybody but John seemed to enjoy the humor. To John's extreme discomfort, Bill launched into a long string of bawdy stories, narrated with all the brio he could muster. In a revealing moment, John tried to slip away so that he would not have to hear his father's remarks, but Bill grabbed his son and made him stand and listen to these ribald jokes. At the end of the day, while John tried to recover from this public humiliation, Frank and Bill took a long, sentimental drive through the Cleveland streets.

The tense relations between John and his father were paralleled by increasing rancor between John and his malcontent brother Frank, who was always maddened by his success. As a vast discrepancy in wealth arose between him and his two brothers, Frank tried to redress the imbalance by gambling, only to stumble into fresh fiascoes and exacerbate his reliance on them. Whenever he attempted to emulate John's business flair, he acted in a dangerously capricious fashion, and his subsequent failures further infuriated him against his brother. As he waded into commercial blunders and rash speculations, his dark side acquired a pathological intensity, with one observer depicting Frank as "hot-tempered and vindictive. . . . Sometimes I have thought that he was insane. He was a very violent man. Perhaps brooding over some wrong, real or imaginary, had upset his mind."[25]

Aware of the problems his legendary stature caused Frank, John felt acutely the difference in their fortunes and wanted to find a place in business for Frank, but he couldn't countenance his methods and was offended by his public tirades against him. In the late 1870s, Frank was a partner in the rival Cleveland refinery Pioneer Oil Works, and John classified his brother among the blackmailers who tried to unload their antiquated refineries on him at extortionate prices. "He and others were up to such schemes all the time till they got their property sold out at the price they wanted—schemes of blackmail!"[26] John labored tirelessly to win control of Pioneer Oil Works and, instead of snuffing it out, favored its discreet absorption by Standard Oil. Using William as an intermediary—there were times when John and Frank did not speak—he offered Frank lucrative deals in which the trust would refine Pioneer's oil. While Frank thought he was negotiating only with William, John secretly monitored their exchanges and dictated letters sent under William's signature. The genial William was also the front man for large loans that Frank might have spurned if offered directly by John. In the end, Frank negotiated an advantageous deal in which Standard Oil would market Pioneer's surplus oil whenever Pioneer lacked enough customers—a one-sided deal John would have approved only out of fraternal sentiment. Instead of showing gratitude, Frank rewarded John by trying to steal away Standard Oil customers and raiding territories it controlled.

An incorrigible ingrate, Frank wanted to have it both ways: to be heavily indebted to his brothers yet operate free of their control. He asked John to become his banker then expected leniency from him. He took several gigantic loans from John and William—some as large as $80,000—with all too predictable results. When Frank piled up staggering losses in private oil speculations, Colonel Payne reported to John in 1882: "*Confidentially*—it is reported that Frank has lost very largely in his operations at Chicago—it is put as high as $1,000,000."[27] When Frank's health broke under the strain, John tried, to no avail, to wean him away from gambling.

Trying to equalize his status with his brothers, Frank lived on a lavish scale that far outstripped his income. He later bought a beautiful country home in Wickliffe, Ohio, seven miles from Forest Hill, complete with 160 acres of barns, paddocks, and a racetrack. He trained fine racehorses, raised Shetland ponies and prize cattle, and stocked a hunting preserve with deer, bear, foxes, and squirrels. Nothing pleased Frank more than to dust off his Civil War uniform on patriotic holidays and strut around his property with fellow veterans, perhaps to remind John and William that they hadn't flocked to the Union banner.

On his travels, Big Bill had spotted a large tract of cheap land in Belvidere, Kansas, west of Wichita, which Frank turned into an 8,000-acre ranch. When he first bought the property, it was remote from railroads, and he could graze his buffalo herd, pedigreed horses, and shorthorn cattle on vast, unfenced plains. Not surprisingly, John and William carried the ranch mortgage and financed additional land purchases. Then the Atchison, Topeka and Santa Fe Railroad inaugurated service to the area, fresh settlers swarmed in, and the free range shrank for cattlemen. Where Frank's livestock had been able to forage for ten miles to the east and twenty-eight miles to the north, now they could go just two miles to the east and four miles to the north. This ruined the ranch for breeding beef, and Frank tried futilely to sell the depreciated property.

Striking a familiar whining note, Frank told John, "I can't understand why this vein of ill luck & misfortune holds to me in every piece of property I have."[28] At such moments, he dropped the bravado and showed almost abject gratitude to his brothers, now signing a written agreement to end his speculations. As he reassured John, "I take this opportunity of thanking you & Will for your great kindness to me, & agree not to enter any new business of *any kind*, without first conferring with you."[29] Instead of chiding him, John steadily advanced more money in 1884, retired his debts, provided income for his family, and rallied his bruised spirits, saying, "Keep a stiff upper lip, clean up as you go, and the skies will brighten by and bye."[30]

That year, Frank rewarded John's generosity by again testifying against Standard Oil in congressional testimony, charging it with accepting huge railroad rebates. With Frank, John tried to show a preacher's patience, yet he was caught on the horns of a dilemma: If he showed generosity toward Frank, it deepened his brother's dependence and bred anger; if he didn't give him money, Frank threw a tantrum. His brother's two-faced behavior rankled, causing John to exclaim in later life: "My poor brother! He has had his day. I pulled him up four times out of bankruptcy."[31]

Oppressed by debts from oil speculation and ranching, Frank could no longer contribute capital to Pioneer Oil Works, and the firm shut down. His partner, J. W. Fawcett, pleaded with John D. to buy the firm, but Standard already had excess Cleveland refining capacity. After a brief fling as a stockbroker, in 1886 Frank was appointed a second vice president of Standard Oil of Ohio, a post created for him by his brother. For all his sermonizing about John, Frank gladly took advantage of nepotism and, once on the trust's payroll, had no scruples about enforcing policies he had recently excoriated. When competition loomed up in Michigan, he reveled in stamping it out and proudly wired John that "our idea . . . to wipe out all M[ichigan] companies completed—doing the business in the name of the Standard Oil Company of Ohio."[32] He bullied Cleveland refiners who requested higher refining allotments from Standard Oil—much as he had tried to do for Pioneer Oil Works. And he wasn't above milking his position for personal gain. After visiting the new oil boomtown of Lima in 1886, he wrote to John, "Lima, Ohio, is a very pretty town of 12,000 inhabitants and it seems very natural that the oil interest there and the building of a refinery would create quite a boom in real-estate."[33] He had the effrontery to ask John for money for his real-estate speculation in the city—which would only drive up the price of land Standard Oil was trying to buy.

Frank Rockefeller never fared well in the business world and spread dissension in the Standard ranks. He was jealous of the power wielded by the office head, Colonel Thompson, the former Confederate colonel. (That Frank had been wounded on the Union side couldn't have helped.) For one tumultuous year, Frank and Thompson waged their own civil war, Frank steaming at duties Thompson assigned to him. In confidential letters to John D., Frank tried to smear Thompson as a power-mad executive, feathering his nest at the company's expense. As Standard Oil angled for a natural-gas charter in Cleveland, Frank wrote privately that Thompson "is intending to so pull wires and spend money . . . in such a way as if possible, to wield such an influence as would result in his own personal aggrandizement politically."[34] Thompson, a tough, wily customer, could have outmaneuvered Frank, but he wisely sensed the perils of beating the president's brother and withdrew from the field of battle. Instead, he moved to New York and chaired the domestic-trade committee at 26 Broadway, leaving Frank outwardly in charge in Cleveland.

In February 1887, the trust further downgraded Cleveland in the Standard Oil hierarchy, reducing it to a shipping and manufacturing center, with actual business decisions taken in New York. In other words, high-level orders would now emanate from Thompson's committee. As Frank wrote John from Cleveland, "When I returned to the city Monday morning I found the people throughout the entire building in a fearfully demoralized state of mind, and was besieged more or less for several days by different ones—all anxious to know what their fate was to be—the general impression prevailing that a majority of them would lose their situations, business going to *New York*."[35]

Irritated by Frank's griping, John was soon coldly writing "Dear Sir" letters to him and signing them, "John D. Rockefeller, President." Gradually, Frank was shunted aside by Feargus Squire, nominally secretary of Standard of Ohio and lower than Frank on the organization chart, but the real boss of the office. It seems that Frank alienated virtually everyone in the building and was increasingly ostracized. An official history of Standard of Ohio describes the denouement: "The vice-president's interest in what was going on, seldom noticeable, diminished as time went by, and there were those who came to regard him as a millstone around the neck of a more talented man. Many thought he was being retained because his name was Rockefeller—an opinion which a hundred contrary pronouncements from 26 Broadway would not have altered."[36]

The four Rockefeller children strike a pose in 1885.
Left to right: Alta, Bessie, Edith, and John, Jr.
(Courtesy of the Rockefeller Archive Center)

CHAPTER 16

A Matter of Trust

F or twenty-five years after Drake's discovery, no major oil field was discovered in America beyond the Pennsylvania borders, so that it was never clear whether Rockefeller's empire rested on terra firma or quicksand. When somebody told John D. Archbold in 1885 that traces of oil had been found in what later became Oklahoma, he reacted with incredulity. "Are you crazy, man?" he scoffed. "Why, I'll *drink* every gallon of oil produced west of the Mississippi!"[1] Though small amounts of crude were being pumped in California and Kentucky, one expert solemnly assured Archbold that the chances of finding another bonanza on the scale of the Bradford field were one in a hundred; in alarm, Archbold liquidated some of his Standard Oil shares. Writing to Rockefeller that September, he mused gloomily that "we have opened nothing of importance in the way of production this summer, and next winter must see a great reduction in the old Bradford and Allegheny fields, from which the bulk of the production is yet obtained."[2] The American oil business seemed headed toward premature extinction.

Rockefeller and his associates had long been haunted by two antithetical nightmares: Either the oil would dry up, starving their network of pipelines and refineries, or they would drown in a sea of cheap oil that would drag prices below their overhead costs. At one panicky executive-committee meeting in the early 1880s, it was even suggested that Standard Oil should exit the business and enter something more stable. After listening quietly to such defeatist talk, Rockefeller stood up, pointed skyward, and intoned, "The Lord will provide."[3] Rockefeller tended to see a heavenly design in all things and was convinced that the Almighty had buried the oil in the earth for a purpose.

In retrospect, it seems peculiar that Standard Oil—omnipotent in refining, transportation, and distribution—owned just four producing properties in the early 1880s. Thousands of Standard Oil employees had never seen a well. Why had Rockefeller not taken over the oil fields and completed his mastery of the industry? One must recall that in its formative years, the business suffered more gluts than shortages, giving Rockefeller the option of sitting back and watching producers slash prices in chaotic competition. He had long profited from the juxtaposition of cooperation in refining and competition in production. Political tact also dictated that he tread warily. As late as 1884, Archbold vigorously opposed any move into production as overly provocative: "I think if the name of the Standard Oil Co. were to go forth coupled with the movement, it would make new food for demagogues, politicians, papers, and howlers of all descriptions."[4]

Why, then, did a radical policy shift occur within a year or two? Partly, this derived from the trust's entry into natural gas, which put it, willy-nilly, in the drilling business, but the more compelling reason was that Standard Oil had built up a huge global machinery with a ravenous thirst for crude oil. As the Pennsylvania fields were depleted, Rockefeller feared that he might have to turn to Russian crude, and it seemed certain that the Russians would exploit their control of the oil fields to weaken or even eradicate Standard Oil. Already by 1884, an anxious Rockefeller was badgering associates to create a crude-oil reserve beyond their immediate needs, and he invested in some West Virginia producing properties. As he warned a skeptical colleague, "We must keep in sight always a large volume of the raw material, and better that this stock be somewhat excessive than run the risk of Russian competition shutting us out."[5]

Then came a turning point almost as momentous as Drake's discovery. In May 1885, a group of small operators, searching for natural gas in northwest Ohio, tapped a pocket of oil instead. This threw the industry into a wild uproar, providing incontestable proof that substantial deposits existed in the United States outside of Pennsylvania. By year's end, more than 250 derricks had sprouted around the town of Lima, spilling across the border into Indiana. Yet the cheering was restrained, for the chemical content of Lima crude had intractable quality problems that threatened to destroy its value. For one thing, it contained less kerosene than Pennsylvania petroleum and that kerosene spread a film over lamps. Even more troublesome, its high sulfur content corroded machinery and gave off a deadly smell. (Pennsylvania crude had a paraffin base.) As one newspaper put it, "The chief fault found with Ohio stuff is the fact that it smells like a stack of polecats and is only worth forty cents a barrel."[6] For a household item, this stench was a fatal drawback, and the standard practice of cleansing crude with sulfuric acid was not enough to disinfect it.

It was, arguably, Rockefeller's supreme inspiration that he believed in the Ohio-Indiana fields—one of those flashes of vatic power that made him a business legend. As he said, "It seemed to us impossible that this great product had come to the surface to be wasted and thrown away; so we went on experimenting with every process to utilize it."[7] To solve the problem, in July 1886 Rockefeller imported a distinguished, German-born chemist named Herman Frasch and gave him simple marching orders: Banish the odor from Lima crude and turn it into a marketable commodity. While Frasch burrowed away at this problem, the Standard Oil board faced an excruciating dilemma: Should they assume Frasch would succeed and buy up huge leases along the Ohio-Indiana border; or should they wait until Frasch had finished and risk losing the choicest properties?

Despite his prudent style, Rockefeller could exhibit visionary daring and undertake colossal gambles. He was now prepared to wager an enormous amount on Lima oil, a decision that tested his belief in management by consensus, for a conservative board clique headed by Charles Pratt obstinately resisted him. Rockefeller had always derided Pratt as weak-kneed and fainthearted, a "small man" who contributed little beyond the marketing area.[8] Yet far from imposing his will, Rockefeller tolerated prolonged debate about Lima crude, producing "a continual wrangle in the Board of the Standard Oil Company, day by day, month by month, year after year."[9]

A thin man with a Vandyke, active in his Baptist church, Pratt shared Rockefeller's puritanical style. "Waste neither time nor money" was his favorite motto.[10] A donor to many causes, Pratt was the first president and principal donor of the Adelphia Academy in Brooklyn and later bequeathed several million dollars to found the Pratt Institute, which offered classes in manual trades, the arts, and domestic economy. Despite their similarities, Pratt was a timid executive who lacked Rockefeller's audacity and often felt slighted by him. He now turned the Lima debate into a referendum on his own business acumen. At every meeting, when Rockefeller proposed purchasing Ohio leases, Pratt and his faction objected. As Rockefeller said in mockery, they "held up their hands in holy horror."[11] Finally, to break the deadlock, Rockefeller took an incalculable gamble. At one board meeting, after Rockefeller made his standard pitch for a Lima investment, Pratt lost his temper, threw back his head in agitation, and shouted "No!" Whereupon Rockefeller replied coolly, "I will build this improvement out of my own funds and underwrite it for two years." He astonished his colleagues by pledging $3 million—about $47 million in 1996 dollars. "At the end of that time if it is a success the company can reimburse me. If it is a failure, I will take the loss."[12] Whether impressed by Rockefeller's unflinching resolve or realizing that he had lost, Pratt capitulated. "If that's the way you feel about it, we'll go it together," he replied. "I guess I can take the risk if you can."[13]

Standard Oil spent millions of dollars to buy oil properties, build tank cars, and construct pipelines in Lima. Daniel O'Day had never seen an oil field that he didn't want to crosshatch with pipes, and when the trust started the Buckeye Pipe Lines Company to gather Lima crude in March 1886, he informed producers with more force than subtlety that they had to give Buckeye all their crude. Any driller who struck oil was accosted on the spot by one of O'Day's determined agents. As he told Rockefeller, "I believe it is for the best interest of our company that as soon as we learn of any new development either oil or gas that we have a man there at once and have him stay there ready to take hold of anything that may turn up."[14] An irresistible force, O'Day soon cornered 85 percent of the Lima oil. Even though no market yet existed for the "skunk oil," the trust bought every single barrel offered by producers and by 1888 had over forty million barrels in storage tanks. By that point, the foul-smelling fluid sold for fifteen cents per barrel.

In taking his gamble, Rockefeller hadn't *entirely* trusted to the Lord and the Standard Oil chemists and was casting about for a new application for the malodorous oil. He found the answer in fuel oil. The trust sent out teams of salesmen and technicians to persuade railroads to burn oil instead of coal in their locomotives and to suggest to hotels, factories, and warehouses that they switch from coal furnaces to oil burners. Although this effort flourished, the resulting business still didn't equal the scale of the kerosene industry and only marginally diminished the fierce pressure weighing on Herman Frasch in his laboratory.

Nicknamed the Wild Dutchman, the vainglorious Frasch conformed to the stereotype of the eccentric scientist. A short man of explosive temper, he had immigrated to the United States after the Civil War. In the mid-1870s, Rockefeller brought him to Cleveland, where he did splendid work with paraffin, producing a new wax for British candle makers and a new ingredient for Cleveland's chewing-gum magnate, William J. White. Afterward, Frasch set up shop in Canada and patented a process for eliminating sulfur from sour Ontario oils. Since the Ontario fields lay across Lake Erie from northwest Ohio, Rockefeller must have assumed a high likelihood of success when he hired Frasch to work on a kindred problem. By February 1887, Frasch had achieved partial success with Lima crude, introducing copper oxides to remove the sulfur. Then came the big breakthrough of October 13, 1888, when Feargus Squire wired Rockefeller with the historic news he had eagerly awaited for two years: "We are pleased to advise you that by experimenting with the Frasch process we have succeeded in producing a merchantable oil."[15]

Frasch's feat did more than vindicate Rockefeller's reputation as an uncanny prophet of industry trends. Had Frasch not figured out how to use Lima crude, a critical shortage of American oil would have arisen between the depletion of western Pennsylvania crude and the Texas and Kansas booms of the early 1900s. For fifteen years, Frasch's patents furnished dazzling profits for Rockefeller and Standard Oil and boosted the status of research scientists throughout the industry. The original oilmen were self-made roughnecks, biased against science and prone to operate by intuition, whereas Rockefeller brought a rational spirit to the business, and this counted among his greatest contributions. As the philosopher Alfred North Whitehead said, "The greatest invention of the nineteenth century was the invention of the *method* of invention."[16] When Frasch cracked the riddle of Lima crude, he was probably the only trained petroleum chemist in the United States. By the time Rockefeller retired, he had a test laboratory in every refinery and even one on the top floor of 26 Broadway. This was yet another way in which he converted Standard Oil into a prototype of the modern industrial organization, its progress assured by the steady application of science.

Once Rockefeller had an insight, it often gripped him with the irresistible force of an epiphany, and he now decided that Standard Oil must guarantee its crude-oil supply. After Frasch certified the worth of Lima crude, the trust moved into oil production with all the formidable resources within its reach. In 1889, a production committee was formed under the aegis of John D. Archbold, and it spent money at such a torrid pace that within two years it had disbursed $22 million—a figure that strained even Standard Oil's budget, prompting more anguished howls from Charles Pratt. Rockefeller's faith was vindicated, however, as the Ohio-Indiana field overtook the waning Pennsylvania industry and became the country's crude-oil leader in the 1890s.

Rejuvenated by Lima, Rockefeller embarked on a buying binge such as the industry had never seen. Swallowing up Union Oil and three other big producing firms in 1890, he took over three hundred thousand acres of Pennsylvania and West Virginia—huge chunks of acreage that encompassed whole counties. The most feared man in the Oil Regions now became their dominant landlord and producer. "Hitherto the attention of the big Octopus has been largely directed toward crushing out all opposition in the refining of oil," noted one agitated newspaper. "This latest deal shows that it has started to crush out the producers of the crude oil and obtain control of their property."[17] By 1891, Rockefeller had gained control of a majority of the Lima fields and a quarter of American oil production. (The trust's share of American crude production peaked at 33 percent in 1898.) By narrowing the range of competition in oil production, the move hastened the day of political reckoning for Standard Oil.

In future years, the discovery of new fields both at home and abroad provided openings for upstart competitors, but the trust's swift, complete control of the Lima field gave it unchallenged control of American oil in the 1890s. The only major competitor spawned by the new territory was the Sun Oil Company, started by J. N. Pew in 1886. In spring 1891, Archbold visited Lima, cast a proprietary eye over oil fields stretching more than one hundred miles, and gloated in a letter to Rockefeller, "We undoubtedly have, as the case stands, well in reserve the greater part of the defined territory, and we will certainly be able to produce oil in the Ohio field more cheaply than anybody else, owning, as we do, great bodies of territories which we can drill judiciously."[18] Now that Rockefeller had scored such a gratifying triumph in production, he instructed Archbold to grab anything that could still turn a profit with crude at fifty cents a barrel. "If so would buy all we can get," he wired.[19] In this rush into exploration and production, Rockefeller created the model for the vertically integrated oil giants that would straddle the globe in the twentieth century.

The discovery of oil in Ohio radically redrew the map of the Standard universe, for it was senseless to ship crude oil to eastern refineries only to ship kerosene back to markets in the Midwest and Far West. In 1886, even before Frasch had completed his work, O'Day scouted northwest Ohio for an appropriate refinery site and chose the charming town of Lima itself, which was served by four railroads. The emergence of the giant Lima refinery accelerated the demise of Cleveland and Pittsburgh as refining centers, and by 1896 Standard Oil phased out its largest Cleveland refinery.

The Lima refinery was a mere preamble to the main event in the Midwest. In June 1889, the trust organized Standard Oil of Indiana, which would build America's premier oil refinery at Whiting, Indiana, seventeen miles from downtown Chicago. During his 1891 tour, Archbold, trembling at the magnitude of this undertaking, told Rockefeller that the plant's ability to process 36,000 barrels of crude oil daily struck him as "almost impossible to comprehend."[20] The refinery remained a wonder of world oil for many years. At Whiting, Dr. William M. Burton produced his revolutionary discovery of how to "crack" petroleum, vastly increasing its yield of gasoline—an essential precondition of the auto age.

It took time for Standard Oil to wipe away the stigma of Lima crude, for just enough sulfur remained in the kerosene to clog chimneys and lamps in damp weather. In a confidential letter to Rockefeller, Archbold confessed that for the first time their competitors could justly claim a superior product. The trust was now a victim of its own dirty tricks. After the Ohio oil was discovered but before Rockefeller had won over Pratt, Standard had engineered a propaganda campaign to convince consumers that Lima oil was inferior to Pennsylvania oil. This strategy had now boomeranged on them, Archbold told Rockefeller, "so that it is necessary, until this prejudice is gotten out of the way, that the greatest possible care must be taken to have every shipment from both Lima and Whiting absolutely beyond the possibility of legitimate complaint."[21] The original slander was refuted with difficulty.

⸻

As Standard Oil secured complete control of the oil industry, many ordinary citizens were frightened by its gargantuan size, rapacious methods, and inexorable growth, and it came to symbolize all the disquieting forces reshaping America. It was the "parent of the great monopolies which at present masquerade under the new-found name of 'Trusts,' " said one newspaper, and it served as shorthand for the new agglomerations of economic power. A business system based on individual enterprise was creating combinations of monstrous size that seemed to threaten that individualism. And modern industry not only menaced small-scale commerce but appeared to constitute a sinister despotism that endangered democracy itself as giant corporations overshadowed government as the most dynamic force in American society.

As the leading figure in this consolidation, Rockefeller was the emblematic figure of the Gilded Age and hence a lightning rod for criticism. He closely followed political developments and was keenly alert to any potential threats to his business interests. In his personal campaign contributions, though, he won a well-earned reputation as a stingy giver, and some politicians even felt miffed at his paltry gifts. The clandestine payoffs made by Standard Oil were a different matter, and Rockefeller never stinted in making payments to get the job done.

At the turn of the century, reporters spilled a great deal of ink over charges that Standard Oil had bought Henry B. Payne's election to the U.S. Senate in 1884. This putative case of political corruption received more attention from critics than any other, although little evidence was ever adduced to substantiate it. With his white hair and wire-rimmed glasses, Henry B. Payne—father of Standard Oil's treasurer, Oliver Payne—was an affable man with a distinguished air. A Cleveland lawyer and perpetual candidate for public office, he lobbied for mandatory education in Cleveland, worked ardently for the Union cause, and helped to found the Case School of Applied Sciences, while also serving as part owner of two railroads. Unlike his wealthy Euclid Avenue neighbors, Payne was a Democrat who had campaigned for Stephen Douglas in his 1860 presidential bid against Abraham Lincoln. Ironically, in light of later allegations, when he first ran for Congress, Standard Oil supported his opponent and helped to defeat him. Ambitious for his father, the cold, haughty Oliver Payne acted as his perennial campaign manager, starting with his congressional victory in 1874. Two years later, Oliver tried unsuccessfully to capture the Democratic presidential nomination for his father—a presumptuous bid for an elderly freshman congressman. This lost cause earned Oliver a somewhat Machiavellian reputation, and one newspaper observed acidly: "He's got a purse that is inexhaustible, a silent tongue, and a capacity for the organization and manipulation of men."[22]

In the late 1870s, Henry Payne lost his congressional seat. Approaching seventy, he might have retired gracefully from politics, but he could not seem to shed his daydreams of higher office. When he sought the Democratic presidential nomination in 1880, his opponents cruelly baited him about his age, and one stooped to calling him "an attenuated, dried-up old fossil."[23] To retire these charges, Payne gave a nimble spring to his step, a youthful vigor to his gestures. Possibly more harmful was Payne's association with Standard Oil, which blemished his reputation among many Democrats. Payne received only eighty-one votes on the first ballot as General Winfield Hancock walked off with the nomination.

At the time, U.S. senators were elected by state legislatures, creating an open season for graft and influence peddling by business interests. When the Ohio legislature elected Henry B. Payne to the Senate in 1884—the legislature would go down in history as the infamous "Coal-oil Legislature" for its obeisance to Standard Oil—it was widely rumored that Oliver had sat behind a desk in a Columbus hotel room and doled out bills to legislators, the final tab reaching $100,000. These bribery allegations, though never proved, shadowed Senator Payne and provoked a firestorm of abuse against Standard Oil. Whether Oliver Payne bought the election is uncertain, but it seems far-fetched that Rockefeller or Standard Oil conspired with him. Henry Payne was a staunch Democrat, and Standard Oil was a Republican stronghold. Rockefeller likely spoke the literal truth when he said, "I was opposed to the election of Senator Payne, as a Republican and never anything else but a Republican. And not one farthing of the money of the Standard Oil Company went to his election; nor were the Standard Oil Company favorable to his election, as a company."[24]

Aside from his father, Oliver Payne gave Standard Oil a second important link to the Democratic Party through his brother-in-law, William C. Whitney. Even though Oliver had been two years older and infinitely richer than Whitney at the time, the two were fast friends at Yale. To an extent that some observers found unhealthy, Oliver doted on his lovely, gregarious sister Flora; when he arranged for her to meet Whitney in 1868, he already "knew that if they met, they would fall in love with each other," he later admitted.[25] When they married a year later, he became their self-appointed benefactor, buying them a five-story Park Avenue brownstone. This was a mere curtain-raiser to his next gift, a showy $700,000 mansion, glistening with gorgeous paintings and Gobelin tapestries, at the corner of Fifth Avenue and Fifty-seventh Street, across from Cornelius Vanderbilt's residence. One historian said that Oliver insouciantly "presented it to the Whitneys as one might present a poodle," and with his sublime self-assurance, this lifelong bachelor moved into one of its sumptuous second-floor apartments.[26]

William C. Whitney was a dashing man with a matchless talent for attracting monied patrons. Though he stayed only one year at Harvard Law School, he became a rich Wall Street lawyer, representing Commodore Vanderbilt and other railroad clients. Active in the Democratic Party, he won the patronage of Samuel J. Tilden, who, as governor, had him named New York City's corporation counsel. In 1884, Whitney shrewdly supported Grover Cleveland, the mayor of Buffalo, for president and brokered a truce between the reform-minded Cleveland and Tammany Hall. When Whitney emerged as an influential insider in Cleveland's presidential campaign, some critics thought him a Standard Oil tool. In reality, Rockefeller voted for James G. Blaine, a paladin of business interests, and predicted the election would be "a great calamity" if Cleveland won.[27] In an unprecedented step, Rockefeller allowed his name to be listed as vice president for a Republican fund-raising effort in the city of Cleveland.

To further Grover Cleveland's candidacy, Whitney persuaded Henry B. Payne that the growing furor over Standard Oil made it an inauspicious time for him to vie for the Democratic nomination. Instead, Henry and Oliver Payne poured $170,000 into Cleveland's war chest. After Cleveland's victory, it looked as if Whitney would be named interior secretary. Then the press tagged him with the sobriquet of "Coal Oil Billy" and raised the specter that Standard Oil would loot public lands. As a consolation prize, Whitney settled for an appointment as secretary of the navy. For all the baseless speculation about his links to Standard Oil, Whitney was seldom asked to perform favors for the trust and spent most of his time constructing a new steel navy. Around the time that William and Flora Whitney moved to Washington, Oliver Payne, citing the "need for a rest," resigned from Standard Oil.[28]

Despite its many shareholders, the Standard Oil trust was always controlled by a small clique of powerful families. "I think it is true that the Pratt family, the Payne-Whitney family (which were one, as all the stock came from Colonel Payne), the Harkness-Flagler family (which came into the Company together) and the Rockefeller family controlled a majority of the stock during all the history of the Company up to the present time," Rockefeller commented in 1910.[29] Because the Harkness and Payne families were sociable and intermarried with the Vanderbilts and Whitneys, they spread a great deal of Standard Oil bounty through America's social aristocracy.

While Standard Oil gadflies pounced on the political bonds between the Paynes and William Whitney, they missed a more flagrant case of political corruption: that of Johnson Newlon Camden, who served as a West Virginia senator from 1881 to 1887 but never severed his ties to Standard Oil. Approaching his 1881 election to the U.S. Senate as a straight business proposition, he favored a liberal distribution of cash to the West Virginia legislature to secure results. As he plaintively told Flagler that year, "Politics is dearer than it used to be—and my understood connection with the Standard Oil Co. don't *tend to cheapen it*—as we are all supposed to have bushels." This was prelude to an urgent request for "$10,000 in some turn—stocks or oil—Please keep an eye out and let me know."[30] Apparently, Standard Oil obliged, for in the next letter,

Camden reported victory to Flagler. "I also appreciate sincerely the substantial kindness of the Ex[ecutive] Com[mittee]—and used it without hesitation as I needed it temporarily."[31]

Even after entering the Senate, Camden continued to correspond with Rockefeller and Flagler as if he was still an active Standard Oil executive, and he discussed the trust's negotiations with the B&O Railroad on U.S. Senate stationery. He organized a railroad with Oliver Payne and urged Rockefeller, Flagler, and Harkness to join them. Throughout his term, Camden stood sentinel over Standard Oil interests, and when two pipeline bills inimical to the trust appeared in the Maryland legislature in 1882, he acted promptly, informing Flagler with satisfaction, "My dear Mr. Flagler, I have arranged to kill the two bills in Md. legislature at comparatively small expense."[32]

With Grover Cleveland's election in 1884, many businessmen braced for reform in Washington, but he turned out to be quite moderate. Nonetheless, the public revulsion against monopolies steadily gathered force, producing an Anti-Monopoly Party that condemned railroad pools and rate discrimination. Although grain elevators, meatpackers, and harvesting-machine companies were all feeding off railroad rebates, Standard Oil was thrust into the foreground of antimonopoly indictments. As the World wrote in a scorching attack against the trust in 1887, "When the 19th century shall have passed into history, the impartial eyes of the reviewers will be amazed to find that the U.S., supposed to be conservative of human liberty and human right, tolerated the presence of the most gigantic, the most cruel, impudent, pitiless and grasping monopoly that ever fastened itself upon a country."[33]

Nonetheless, it took time to establish the legal rationale for government regulation of private business. In 1876, in Munn v. Illinois, the Supreme Court had famously declared, "Property does become clothed with a public interest when used in a manner to make it of public consequence, and affect the community at large."[34] By this point, Standard Oil wasn't overly worried about an interstate-commerce bill against railroad discrimination. The trust ran its own pipeline system to the seaboard and was confident that if railroad regulation came it could still be bypassed. When Congress finally passed the Interstate Commerce Act in 1887, outlawing railroad pools and rebates and setting up the first regulatory commission, Senators Payne and Camden dutifully voted against the bill, but its defeat had not been assigned a high priority by the trust.

In public, Standard Oil pretended to welcome the equal treatment mandated by the new act and vowed to accept no more rebates. As Rockefeller and Archbold later claimed in 1907 when their subsequent behavior was questioned, "Since the enactment of the interstate commerce law in 1887, the Standard Oil Co. has most carefully observed its provisions and in no case has wilfully violated the law."[35] Rockefeller tended to portray himself as a hard-driving executive who went as far as the law allowed but not an inch further. Allan Nevins concurred in this view, noting that "following the Interstate Commerce Act of 1887, the Standard, as careful observers generally agree, came close to a general obedience of the new law, and asked no outright rebates."[36]

But there is reason to question this assertion. Right before the act's passage, Standard had to grapple with state challenges to railroad rebates, and the ubiquitous Colonel Thompson, closeted with railway officials, found ways to skirt the new regulations. In the spring of 1886, Thompson conferred with officials of the Lake Shore Railroad after the Ohio Supreme Court had outlawed freight discriminations. They came up with a way to create the illusion that all shippers paid the identical posted rates while Standard Oil was compensated secretly through an accounting gimmick. As Thompson explained this subterfuge to Rockefeller:

> Our arrangement is a very simple one: We are paying the open tariff rates to Michigan and all other points and this same is required of all other shippers. I have a distinct understanding with the proper persons that we are not required or expected to pay more than formerly and in order that we may not be out any money . . . we deduct from Chicago payments an equivalent amounting to what would have been a proper payment on all the other points, each month. You will readily see the object of this and you will observe in the situation we are in that no better or fairer arrangement could possibly have been made or one more satisfactory to us.[37]

When the Missouri railroad commissioner ordered uniform freight rates in 1888, Thompson advised Rockefeller, "We have reason to think that this order will be withdrawn. At any rate, the roads will pay no attention to it."[38]

Such oral arrangements may have helped to pacify Standard Oil in the wake of the Interstate Commerce Act. Also, no governmental body could strip it of its giant tank-car fleet and the lucrative royalties they brought in; Standard Oil wasn't compelled to supply tank cars to competitors. There were even unexpected dividends from the equality prescribed by the act. The new Interstate Commerce Commission said the railroads had to charge the same rate for oil in barrels (used by independents) and in tank cars (used by Standard Oil); as a result, the roads, for the first time, could charge for the weight of the barrels, penalizing independent shippers. For a brief period, the Interstate Commerce Act might have chilled collaboration between trusts and railroads, but they gradually figured out ways to evade the law and slip back into well-worn arrangements. The fight against the railroad rebate remained a hardy perennial of reform politics for a generation. In 1907, Standard Oil was briefly slapped with the largest fine in corporate history for a practice it had supposedly given up long before.

By the 1888 election, protests against the trusts—oil, whiskey, sugar, and a score of others—had broken out in so many places that the national platforms of both parties harshly condemned economic concentration. Agrarian reformers in the South and West agitated against the railroads as the midwives of monopoly. Protestant evangelicals deplored the moral crisis that accompanied industrialization and the lopsided distribution of wealth. There was a great upsurge of activity among organized labor as membership in the Knights of Labor soared to 700,000 in 1886. That year, policemen fired on picketers at the McCormick reaper plant in Chicago, provoking the protest at the Haymarket in which a bomb exploded, killing seven people. In 1888, Edward Bellamy published his best-selling utopian novel, *Looking Backward*, with its socialist version of the technocratic society overtaking America. The general public was of two minds and viewed the new entrepreneurs as alternately sinister and heroic. By 1888, Rockefeller began to pop up in fawning magazine features about rich Americans, but he was also singled out as a notorious trust king in Joseph Pulitzer's *World* and other papers. The press kept up an editorial drumbeat against Standard Oil, demanding vigorous state and federal antitrust action.

Amid this crescendo of criticism, Rockefeller again came under the scrutiny of government investigators. When a New York senate committee investigated Standard Oil in 1888, it learned just how elusive he could be. When a process server came to 26 Broadway, he was told that Mr. Rockefeller was out of town. When he went to 4 West Fifty-fourth Street, he was told that Mr. Rockefeller was at home but could not be seen. At this point, the process server spent the night dozing on Rockefeller's stoop, lest the mogul attempt an early-morning departure. Ringing the doorbell shortly after daybreak, he was told Mr. Rockefeller had left. Blandly denying that he had fled the process server, Rockefeller later explained that he had been in Ohio and hastened back when notified of the investigation. In fact, Rockefeller had also kept his visit to Cleveland a secret because he feared being served there with a subpoena in a suit by local refiners.

To coach Rockefeller for the New York senate hearings, Standard Oil hired an eminent lawyer, Joseph H. Choate. Choate was slow to appreciate his unusual client, who greeted him cordially then stretched out on a couch with a languid air. When Choate tried to sound him out on several company matters, his tight-lipped client revealed nothing. Choate was frustrated by this seemingly indolent man who kept quizzing *him*. "I wonder how we shall make out with Mr. Rockefeller," Choate asked Flagler in concern. "He seems so helpless. He is asking questions all the time." Flagler was amused. "Oh, you will find that he can take care of himself," he replied. "You needn't worry about him."[39]

Several years earlier, during testimony in Albany, Rockefeller had given identical replies to thirty consecutive questions, declining each time to answer on advice of counsel. This time, he knew he had to be, or at least seem, more forthcoming. On a frosty morning in February 1888, clad impeccably in frock coat and top hat, Rockefeller entered a packed hearing room of the superior court in New York City, flanked by Joseph Choate. Since he was fast becoming a mythical figure, his testimony drew extensive press coverage. Still handsome at forty-eight, with a full head of close-cropped hair and a neat reddish brown mustache, he strode in with a purposeful air. On closer inspection, however, one could detect lines around his eyes, and he seemed older and more tired than a few years earlier. He was now carrying a more onerous burden than he knew.

Choate soon discovered that he didn't need to worry about his client. Like many businessmen of his era, Rockefeller prided himself on his obfuscatory powers and excelled at fuzzy answers. Under oath, he turned into a vague and forgetful fellow, pleasant but slightly muddled, who wandered lost in the stupendous maze of Standard Oil. He was also a terrific showman, a trait he inherited from his father. When sworn in on the stand, he "kissed the Bible vehemently," according to one reporter, underscoring which party had God on its side.[40]

Rockefeller was interrogated by the committee counsel, Roger A. Pryor, a histrionic lawyer who paced back and forth, his lank black hair flying about his shoulders. He fixed Rockefeller with a penetrating eye and shook an accusatory finger at him. Rockefeller remained placid, accentuating the contrast between them in his favor. As one thunderstruck newspaper wrote of Rockefeller, "He seems the embodiment of sweetness and light. His serenity could not be disturbed. . . . In tones melodious, clear, and deliberate he gave his testimony. . . . At times his manner was mildly reproachful, at others tenderly persuasive, but never did he betray an ill temper or vexation."[41] As Choate watched in amazement, Rockefeller maintained an unruffled exterior: His client was not exactly the absent-minded rube he had pictured.

Standard Oil's strategy was to furnish as little information as possible. As Rockefeller's associate Paul Babcock advised him in emphatic language, "I think this anti-Trust fever is a craze, which we should meet in a very dignified way and *parry every question* with answers which while perfectly truthful are evasive of *bottom facts!* I would *avoid* the preparation of *any* statistics."[42] True to this advice, Rockefeller economized with the truth, yet so little was known about Standard Oil that the most meager information produced sensational headlines. In his testimony, Rockefeller supplied for the first time the Standard Oil trust agreement that had been drawn up in 1882; named the eight current trustees; revealed that the trust now had seven hundred shareholders; and, most startling of all, listed forty-one companies that belonged to the trust—many of which had never publicly disclosed this association before. To refute the notion that Standard Oil was a monopoly, Rockefeller submitted a list of 111 competing refineries and gave his own stirring account of spirited competition from Russian oil.

The most controversial exchange came when Pryor turned to the darkest episode of Rockefeller's past: the South Improvement Company. Pryor misspoke and asked if he had ever belonged to the *Southern* Improvement Company; Rockefeller, quick to spot a slip, denied being a member of such a company. With his superb memory, he remembered that an unused charter had been granted for a Southern Improvement Company. Pryor reacted with disbelief:

"There was such a company?"

"I have heard of such a company," Rockefeller conceded.

"Were you not in it?"

"I was not."[43]

Rockefeller's later gloss on this testimony reveals his craftiness:

I never undertake to instruct the man who asks me questions. I remember that incident as if it were this morning. . . . I did not stop to correct my questioner. There is the record to stand on. Of course, I knew what I was answering. . . . I did not testify like Mr. Brewster and Mr. Flagler, so hot-tempered that they would fly right into an argument with counsel. I was quiet and self-controlled. It was no part of my duty as a witness to volunteer testimony. While they thought they were leading me into a trap, I let them go into the trap themselves.[44]

The bane of interrogators, Rockefeller had an eerie gift for catching the subtle drift of a prosecutor's questions. A distinguished twentieth-century lawyer, Samuel Untermyer, called Rockefeller the ablest mind he had ever encountered on the witness stand, a man with a sixth sense for a legal trap. "He could always read my mind and guess what the next six or seven questions were going to be," said Untermyer, who cross-examined Rockefeller during litigation in the early 1900s. "I would start with questions intended to lay the foundation for questions far in the future. But I would always see a peculiar light in his eyes which showed that he divined my intention. I have never known a witness who equalled him in this clairvoyant power."[45] At the February 1888 hearing, Roger Pryor was so impressed by Rockefeller that at the close of questioning, he came to the railing, pumped his hand heartily, and asked if he could visit Standard Oil plants with Rockefeller. As for Joseph Choate, Rockefeller asked casually during the lunch break how he was doing. The chastened lawyer replied, "I could not ask for a better witness."[46] Choate said later that Rockefeller's partners "seldom knew what he was thinking but he always knew what we were thinking."[47]

However well Rockefeller handled his testimony, the committee report threw a lurid light on the workings of Standard Oil, calling it "the most active and possibly the most formidable moneyed power on the continent."[48] "This is the original trust," the report stated. "Its success has been the incentive to the formation of all other trusts and combinations. It is the type of a system which has spread like a disease through the commercial system of this country."[49] The trust floated free of legal restraints, the forty-one constituent companies having "turned their affairs over to an organization having no legal existence, independent of all authority, able to do anything it wanted anywhere, and to this point working in absolute darkness."[50] While absolving the trust of charges of rapacity, it also dissented from Rockefeller's portrait of lively competition, calling Standard Oil "almost the sole occupant of the field of oil operations, from which it had driven nearly every competitor."[51] Standard Oil stood out as the great test case in the growing national debate on antitrust legislation. When the House Committee on Manufactures issued its report on trusts that spring, it dedicated 1,000 of 1,500 pages to the oil trust, five times the space given to the sugar trust and ten times that given to the whiskey trust.

In a sense, John D. Rockefeller simplified life for the authors of antitrust legislation. His career began in the infancy of the industrial boom, when the economy was still raw and unregulated. Since the rules of the game had not yet been encoded into law, Rockefeller and his fellow industrialists had forged them in the heat of combat. With his customary thoroughness, Rockefeller had devised an encyclopedic stock of anticompetitive weapons. Since he had figured out every conceivable way to restrain trade, rig markets, and suppress competition, all reform-minded legislators had to do was study his career to draw up a comprehensive antitrust agenda.

Standard Oil had taught the American public an important but paradoxical lesson: Free markets, if left completely to their own devices, can wind up terribly *unfree*. Competitive capitalism did not exist in a state of nature but had to be defined or restrained by law. Unfettered markets tended frequently toward monopoly or, at least, toward unhealthy levels of concentration, and government sometimes needed to intervene to ensure the full benefits of competition. This was particularly true in the early stages of industrial development. This notion is now so deeply embedded in our laws that it has become all but invisible to us, replaced by secondary debates over the precise nature or extent of antitrust enforcement.

During the antitrust agitation of the late 1880s, Standard Oil consistently underestimated the ability of critics to marshal public support. Small businessmen, alleging that the great corporations thwarted individual opportunity, formed a particularly potent lobby for reform. When both Grover Cleveland and Benjamin Harrison inveighed against the trusts in the 1888 presidential campaign, Archbold wrote dismissively to Rockefeller that these strident speeches were just for show. "We do not think that much will come of the talk at Washington regarding Trusts," he reported that summer. "The demagogues are simply trying to outtalk each other for political effect."[52]

Archbold proved a poor prognosticator. In a legislative flurry, many states enacted antitrust laws in the late 1880s, while fifteen or sixteen bills circulated in Congress. From Standard Oil's viewpoint, the most threatening bill was introduced in December 1889 by Ohio senator John Sherman, brother of General William Tecumseh Sherman. A few years earlier, Rockefeller tried to buy his way into the senator's good graces. In August 1885, soliciting a campaign contribution for Sherman, Mark Hanna had told Rockefeller that "John Sherman is today our main dependence in the Senate for the protection of our business interests."[53] Dubious at first, Rockefeller finally sent a check for six hundred dollars. Before long, the protector of business interests proved a turncoat, flailing Standard Oil as a corporation so rich that it bought entire railroads. In debates over the senator's antitrust bill, Standard Oil was constantly held up as a prime example of the problem to be remedied. Flushed into the open, Rockefeller took the unusual step of publicly rebuking Sherman's legislation. "Senator Sherman's bill is of a very radical and destructive character, proposing to fine and imprison all who directly or indirectly participate in organizations over which it is even doubtful whether Congress holds any jurisdiction."[54]

The opposition of the trusts only hastened passage of the law. On July 2, 1890, President Harrison signed the Sherman Antitrust Act, which outlawed trusts and combinations in restraint of trade and subjected violators to fines of up to $5,000 or a year's imprisonment or both. President William Howard Taft later identified Standard Oil as the chief reason for the law's passage. To its proponents, the law proved a severe disappointment, a stillborn piece of legislation. It was vague in meaning and poorly enforced and so riddled with loopholes that it was popularly derided as the Swiss Cheese Act. By outlawing cooperative efforts through trade associations, it forced many companies into mergers to curb excess capacity in their industries, spurring further concentration and subverting the act's intention. As for the main target of the law, the Standard Oil juggernaut was not deflected by this nuisance. For many years, the Sherman Act was a dead letter, and big business happily went on as usual.

Rockefeller was never tempted to reconsider the issues raised by the Sherman Act. As far as he was concerned, practical, hardheaded businessmen had long ago resolved these issues to their satisfaction, and only fanciful scribblers and tendentious rabble-rousers saw the need to tamper with current practice, which had served the country well. He remained an unreconstructed believer in trusts. Never one to hold grudges in business, unfazed by the new law, Rockefeller supported the reelection of Senator Sherman in 1891.

CHAPTER 17

Captains of Erudition

B y the late 1880s, it seemed as if half the country wanted to lynch John D. Rockefeller, while the other half only wanted to cadge a loan from him. He was assailed by journalists, reform politicians, and embittered rivals but also besieged by a growing legion of flatterers and schemers with designs on his fortune. This national ambivalence must have confirmed Rockefeller's view that his critics were just envious hypocrites. The press fed this fascination with him. One 1889 newspaper article showcased Rockefeller as America's richest man, with a net worth of $150 million—an estimate he regarded as much too high, pegging forty to sixty million as the correct range. (That would translate into between $635 and $950 million in contemporary money.) Another article clocked his income pouring in at $750 an hour. Whenever such articles appeared, hordes of supplicants emerged, making bad publicity in many ways less troublesome than favorable coverage. "I have been run down by adventurers during the last few days, owing to some foolish newspaper article," Rockefeller complained after one flattering piece.[1] He mused, "Great wealth is a great burden, a great responsibility. It invariably proves to be one of two things—either a great blessing or a great curse."[2]

Wherever he went, he was now trailed by a small army of petitioners. For someone of Rockefeller's private nature, it was disconcerting to be approached in the street by strangers seeking money. "Mr. Rockefeller was constantly hunted, stalked and hounded almost like a wild animal," said Frederick T. Gates, the Baptist minister who would soon help to alleviate the problem. "Neither in the privacy of his home nor at his table, nor in the aisles of his church, nor during his business hours, nor anywhere else, was Mr. Rockefeller secure from insistent appeal."[3] Supplicants breakfasted with him, rode to and from work with him, dined with him in the evening, then retired with him to the privacy of his study. "The good people who wanted me to help them with their good work seemed to come in crowds," Rockefeller moaned. "They brought their trunks and lived with me."[4]

Rockefeller had always required rest and solitude, but by the late 1880s these petitioners had stolen from his daily schedule those all-important intervals of relaxation:

> At dinner they talked to me and, after dinner, when a little nap and a comfortable lounge, or a restful chair and a quiet family chat seemed about the most desirable occupations until bedtime, these good people would pull up their chairs and begin, "Now, Mr. Rockefeller—." Then they would tell their story. . . . There was only one of me and they were a crowd—a crowd increasing in numbers every day. I wanted to retain personal supervision of what little I did in the way of giving, but I also wanted to avoid a breakdown.[5]

Mountains of mail tumbled in from around the globe, and by 1887 Rockefeller was so oppressed by appeals that he grumbled to brother Frank, "I have been overwhelmed with this sort of thing of late and want to shut down brakes a little until I can catch breath."[6] The begging letters—many scarcely literate, often scrawled in pencil in foreign tongues—typically pleaded for money to relieve some personal misfortune. People wrote to Rockefeller the way small children pray to God for presents. In 1887, a distraught lady told him, "I wish I could see you and talk with you as I can with God but it seems harder," while another woman confessed, "Last night as I lay thinking (for I could not sleep for the anxiety) asking the Lord for deliverance you came to me in a way that I could not banish it."[7]

The volume of mail defied the imagination. One steamer alone brought five thousand begging letters from Europe. After the announcement of one large educational gift, Rockefeller received fifteen thousand letters during the first week and fifty thousand by the end of the month. He needed a staff just to sift through these appeals. His overtaxed subordinates opened each envelope and tried to identify genuine cases of need, but they could gratify only a tiny fraction of such hopefuls. Many requests were frankly selfish, as Rockefeller tartly noted. "Four-fifths of these letters are, however, requests of money for personal use, with no other title to consideration than that the writer would be gratified to have it."[8]

Although Rockefeller didn't recognize it at first, brewing here was a personal crisis more debilitating than anything he had encountered in business. As early as 1882, he lamented to the Reverend Edward Judson that he was

John D. Rockefeller striding briskly across the University
of Chicago campus with William Rainey Harper.
(Courtesy of the University of Chicago Library)

swamped by charitable appeals, many from Baptist causes. "I am about leaving Cleveland and have a regular deluge of calls from every hand. . . . I was up until eleven o'clock last night and the night before on this general character of work trying to help to devise ways and means."[9] Personal charity had long been his pleasure, his pride, his recreation, not something delegated to underlings, and he found it hard to break these honorable habits, especially in the midst of so much controversy about his business methods. As Gates noted of his early years, "He used to meet people, read letters, weigh appeals, send checks and receive grateful replies, all in his own person."[10] For such a perfectionist, giving money away was fraught with far more nervous tension than making it. He valued money too highly to dispense it lightly and wanted to investigate all requests before acting upon them. As the Lord's fiduciary, he was responsible for seeing the money well invested. As he said in 1886, "I haven't a farthing to give to this or any other interest unless I am perfectly satisfied it is the *very best* I can do with the money."[11]

Now, as the sheer magnitude of his wealth rendered his accustomed approach obsolete, he was frustrated that he couldn't give money away quickly enough to keep pace with his mounting income. It took several years before he learned to donate money in the systematic, scientific fashion that befit the scale of his fortune. He needed to forge a new set of working principles for his charity, and it was in his creation of the University of Chicago that he came to define his future style as a philanthropist.

=

Rockefeller's involvement in the university started in a roundabout fashion through his friendship with the Reverend Augustus H. Strong, an eminent Baptist theologian and exponent of the social gospel. For seven years after the Civil War, Dr. Strong had served as pastor of the First Baptist Church of Cleveland, where he officiated at the funeral of Rockefeller's second child, Alice, who died in infancy. In 1872, he headed east to assume the presidency of Rochester Theological Seminary, the citadel of Baptist orthodoxy. Awed by the erudite piety of this Yale graduate, Rockefeller supplemented his income, paid his vacation expenses, and, heeding his entreaties, gave $500,000 to his seminary over the years. A fine-looking man with a bushy mustache, Strong was grave, witty, and charming but tightly buttoned up and incapable of levity. An autocrat by nature, he didn't become convinced by an idea so much as possessed by it to an extent that other people could find insufferable.

Starting in the early 1880s, Dr. Strong began to pitch to Rockefeller a grandiose scheme for an elite Baptist university in New York City over which he would himself preside. Convinced that the Baptists were lagging in the denominational race, he feared that many young Baptists were going by default to

Harvard, Yale, or Princeton. His "university of the future," as he dubbed it, would sit on Morningside Heights and cost Rockefeller a breathtaking $20 million. Since New York was becoming America's foremost metropolis, Dr. Strong thought it a fitting home for this institution. Modeled after Johns Hopkins, it would accept only graduate students and research fellows, attracting the cream of Baptist undergraduates from around the country. Above all, the university would defend the faith against the encroaching forces of modernism, banning "infidel" teachers from the campus. This educational vision was Dr. Strong's monomania throughout the 1880s—he contended that he had a "divine mission" to promote it—and he badgered Rockefeller about it at every turn.[12] Strong knew how to couch his appeals in religious terminology and dress up self-interest as heaven-sent duty.

Hypersensitive to pressure, Rockefeller tended to stiffen up whenever he felt pushed. He feared the elaborate nature of Strong's project and grew deaf to his entreaties. Several times, he asked Strong to table the subject and finally imposed a moratorium on all further discussion of it. Rockefeller was always quick to spy the worldly ambition when men of the cloth falsely claimed to pursue godly objectives. Ordinarily, he would have made quick work of such a pushy supplicant, but he tolerated Strong out of respect for his scholarship as well as because of growing ties between their two families.

Whenever Dr. Strong returned to Cleveland, his children were among the very few who frequented Forest Hill, and the Rockefeller children were especially fond of his brilliant eldest son, Charles. Tall and handsome, with curly black hair, Charles would sit in their favorite beech tree, reading ballads to them while perched on a bough. At first, Charles was attracted to Alta, then moved on to her older sister, Bessie. The striking compatibility of the Strong and Rockefeller children must have comforted John and Cettie, who worried that less-religious children might spoil their wholesome environment. For years, John Strong corresponded with Edith and might even have proposed to her, while Junior had a schoolboy crush on Mary Strong, ten years his senior. Later, he wrote affectionate, flirtatious letters to Kate Strong—addressing her as "My dear sister Kate"—even though she, too, was many years older.

Bessie and Charles became so wildly smitten with each other that friends said they were almost foolishly in love. They might have been secretly engaged as early as 1885, when Bessie was nineteen and Charles twenty-three. Charles was a prodigious young philosopher, a perfect reasoning machine, who inhabited a cold world of abstractions. He graduated summa cum laude from Harvard in 1885, where he was both a pupil and a friend of William James. As the two star philosophers among the Harvard undergraduates, Charles and George Santayana cofounded a philosophy club and were natural rivals for the Walker Travelling Fellowship, which paid for two years of study in Germany.

Santayana was so daunted by Strong's intellect that before the winner was announced, he prevailed upon Strong to split the prize. It was awarded to these two remarkable students with the understanding that they would divide the money.

In 1886, John and Cettie were searching for a suitable college for Bessie after she graduated from the Rye Female Seminary, and Dr. Strong accompanied them on a tour of Vassar, Smith, and Wellesley. That the Rockefellers finally opted for Vassar owed much to the fact that the strong-willed Dr. Strong chaired its board of trustees. Since Bessie had eye trouble and found it difficult to read, Dr. Strong made special arrangements that allowed her to skip the entrance exams and room with a friend who read aloud to her. When Kate Strong decided to share a suite of rooms with Bessie, it seemed to seal a sacred bond between the two families—surely what the Reverend Strong coveted. He accomplished another strategic objective when Rockefeller became a trustee of Vassar and erected buildings bearing the names Strong, Davison, and Rockefeller.

The only Rockefeller daughter to attend college, Bessie must have been smart and tenacious to overcome her eye troubles. Her few surviving letters evoke a lively, appealing young woman. She was perhaps the most eloquent Rockefeller child, very fond of music and charitable to the poor. As one friend said, "Bessie was a slender rosy-cheeked girl, vivacious, pretty and charming."[13] George Santayana, who met Bessie fresh from Vassar, fondly recalled her as "the image of vigorous health and good sense, nice-looking, frank, and with manlike college airs."[14] Santayana always suspected that Reverend Strong conspired to marry off his eldest son to Bessie to snare the Rockefeller millions for his beloved university project. He also believed that Rockefeller had welcomed this match of his favorite daughter to a "good-looking, high-principled young man" who would "never separate her from her father, either in place or residence or in sound Christian sentiments."[15] If those were the hidden hopes superimposed upon this youthful romance, both fathers were cruelly disappointed.

During the interval between his graduation from Harvard and his two-year German sojourn with Santayana, Charles underwent a spiritual crisis that had profound repercussions for the Rockefeller family. For two months, he preached in Salem, Ohio, then entered the Rochester Theological Seminary, where he was to study for the Baptist ministry under his father's vigilant supervision. For the first year, he faithfully attended prayer meetings and taught Sunday school, but his rational Harvard education now corroded the spiritual verities of his youth. Later on, Charles made the terrible confession that he had lost his faith while correcting proofs of one of his father's theology books. A wholly cerebral man, fearless in exploring forbidden thoughts, Charles realized that he could no longer accept supernatural revelation. He went to his father and announced that he couldn't stay at the seminary and would openly declare himself an agnostic.

For Reverend Strong, it was a shattering moment—one that he later characterized as his life's most agonizing ordeal. As a distinguished Baptist theologian, he had groomed Charles as his successor and boasted of his intellectual prowess, confident it would be put to the service of the faith. "He depreciates insight," he said of Charles, struggling to comprehend his apostasy. "He is critical rather than constructive."[16] Once his son decided to leave the seminary, the unforgiving Dr. Strong even had him excommunicated, bidding the First Baptist Church of Rochester to withdraw the "hand of fellowship" from his son because he had "ceased to believe in the fundamentals of doctrine."[17] Only later did Dr. Strong realize that his own rigidly doctrinaire attitudes about religion had helped to drive Charles from the church.

Charles's confidential admission must have stunned his father on several levels. If this loss of faith upset his marriage to Bessie, it might also derail Dr. Strong's scheme to have Rockefeller finance a Baptist superuniversity in New York; it might even jeopardize Rockefeller's future gifts to the Rochester seminary. It is not clear when Charles confided his spiritual turmoil to Bessie, or when Rockefeller became aware that his daughter's suitor was a radical freethinker. Santayana's comment clearly suggests that during Bessie's courtship with Charles, Rockefeller was ignorant of Charles's heretical tendencies and derived comfort from his sound views. This leads one to wonder whether Augustus and Charles—the one for money and the other love—tacitly decided to draw a discreet veil across Charles's loss of faith.

The family association emboldened Dr. Strong to renew his pleas for a university in New York. While Bessie was still a freshman at Vassar, Dr. Strong dared to reopen the taboo subject. In a January 1887 letter, he began by telling Rockefeller that he had abided by his promise not to broach the forbidden subject, but time constraints now forced him to break long silence. "It has haunted me day and night for years," Strong said of his proposal, "but I have had to keep my mouth shut. Meantime, years are passing and we are hurrying on to meet God."[18] Competing plans were now afoot for a Baptist university in Chicago, and Dr. Strong panicked at the thought of others gaining ground on him.

Rockefeller rebuffed this overture, then sweetened the pill by giving another $50,000 to the seminary. Since he admired Dr. Strong and didn't wish to alienate him, he proposed that they travel through Europe that summer with Charles and Bessie. For Strong, this presented a miraculous chance to push his scheme in an intimate setting. "He accepted an invitation to tour Europe with Mr. Rockefeller for the reason chiefly, as he once told me, of using the opportunities daily association at leisure would give him of expounding his great theme and winning Mr. Rockefeller's adherence," said one theologian friendly with Strong.[19] In their travels, Dr. Strong planned to acquaint Rockefeller with the great European universities to whet his interest in founding an American school.

On the other side of the Atlantic, George Santayana was sharing the Walker Travelling Fellowship with Charles Strong in Germany and noted his friend's moody behavior. In January 1887, Santayana wrote to William James that Charles was "very reticent about all personal matters, so that I know less about what has been troubling him than you probably do."[20] A month later, Santayana told James that he had "no idea what has been the matter with [Charles] this winter except that evidently he has not been at ease."[21] Charles kept his engagement to Bessie so secret that when he went to Paris that spring he didn't tell Santayana that he was meeting the Rockefellers. Santayana caught up with the party in London, where they were enjoying the festivities of Queen Victoria's jubilee. Though Santayana met and liked Bessie, he was repelled by Rockefeller, who seemed devious and avaricious as he meditated ways to expand Standard Oil sales to Spain.

Encouraged by their travels together that summer, Dr. Strong increased the pressure on Rockefeller in the autumn. He completely misread Rockefeller's psychology. Where Rockefeller preferred a modest approach, Dr. Strong was often overbearing, as if trying to bully him into endorsing the project. He committed an unforgivable sin by suggesting that Rockefeller could sanitize his reputation by funding the university. "You have the opportunity of turning the unfavorable judgments of the world at large into favorable judgments—and not only that—of going down to history as one of the world's greatest benefactors."[22] This argument miscarried on several counts: Rockefeller resented any references to his infamy, felt no need to cleanse his reputation, and rebelled against any insinuation that his charity was selfishly motivated. Four days later, he decided to postpone consideration of Dr. Strong's project.

Meanwhile, Charles Strong's suit to win Bessie's hand prospered, and sixteen months later, on March 22, 1889, Bessie Rockefeller, twenty-three, adorned with $8,000 in pearls, married Charles, twenty-seven, in the front drawing room of 4 West Fifty-fourth Street in a marriage performed by Reverend Augustus H. Strong. With 125 guests, it was as opulent an occasion as the Rockefellers had ever staged, and Bessie's favorite teachers and classmates were brought down from Vassar in a private railroad car. The morning after the wedding, Charles and Bessie sailed for Germany so he could resume his philosophical studies, which explains why Bessie didn't finish her final year at Vassar. She was also suffering from psychological problems, the first sign of nervous symptoms that made her adult life a huge mystery to posterity. In his letters, Rockefeller urged her to avoid all unnecessary excitement and strain, old-fashioned advice that would prove increasingly inadequate in coping with her deep-rooted troubles.

Having piqued Rockefeller's interest in endowing a major Baptist university, the Reverend Augustus H. Strong had to ward off competing plans backed by no less spirited advocates. The most promising alternative, for a university in Chicago, had the advantage of building on preexisting foundations. In 1856, Stephen A. Douglas had contributed ten acres of land to start a small University of Chicago under Baptist auspices. It expired exactly thirty years later, the victim of debt and mismanagement. Many of its alumni considered this a disgrace to the Baptists and tried, at the last minute, to salvage the institution. Quite naturally, they turned to Rockefeller, who had aided the Baptist Union Theological Seminary in suburban Morgan Park, a sister institution. The seminary's secretary, Thomas W. Goodspeed, unfortunately broached his rescue plan to Rockefeller at an inopportune moment, when the latter was being hounded mercilessly by Dr. Strong; the proposal was consequently rejected. In spring 1887, on the eve of Rockefeller's European trip, Goodspeed again sounded out Rockefeller, but the titan cordially sent back fruit and flowers, not cash. Nevertheless, Goodspeed had drawn Rockefeller's attention to Chicago's merits as a home to a great Baptist university.

Goodspeed was a much better lobbyist than Dr. Strong, with a finer instinct for Rockefeller's sensibility. With snow-white beard and blue eyes, he was a dignified man who knew how to lobby a rich donor with exquisite tact as opposed to Dr. Strong's blunderbuss approach. He saw that Rockefeller flinched at anything that smacked of coercion and that patience was better than high-pressure salesmanship. From the outset, Goodspeed made practical arguments, pointing out that construction costs were cheap in Chicago and that the Baptists lacked a first-rate midwestern college, forcing their children to study at eastern schools. Goodspeed was heartened by Rockefeller's response when the most gifted member of the Morgan Park faculty, the thirty-year-old biblical scholar William Rainey Harper, was being wooed by Yale. Rockefeller knew Harper's reputation as one of the foremost Baptist scholars of the Old Testament and urged Goodspeed to retain him at all costs. Though Harper was eventually spirited off to Yale, he stayed in close touch with Goodspeed and consistently supported a Chicago university project, though without committing himself to any role beyond a consulting one. As early as January 1887, he wrote to Rockefeller, "There is no greater work to be done on this continent than the work of establishing a University in or near Chicago."[23]

Rockefeller felt comfortable with worldly theologians, people determined to find an honored place in both this life and the next, and he was absolutely enthralled by Harper, the student of sacred literature who yearned to build an academic kingdom. Born in New Concord, Ohio, in 1856, Harper gave new meaning to the term wunderkind. He had entered college at ten, took a B.A. at fourteen, and completed his Ph.D. at eighteen. When this prodigy joined the Morgan Park faculty at twenty-two, he was younger than many of his seminary students. Many Baptist leaders recognized him as a man with a special future in the denomination, a dynamo bursting with energy and ideas. While still in his thirties, he opened Bible schools in five cities, founded a correspondence school, and coaxed seventy professors to join an American Institute of Hebrew that was assisted financially by Rockefeller.

While teaching at Yale, Harper often traveled to Vassar on Sundays to teach a Bible class and stayed with the college president, Dr. James M. Taylor. Since Rockefeller often visited Bessie for the weekend, Taylor brought the two together for breakfast, and the mutual attraction was instantaneous. Rockefeller later paid tribute to Harper as "a man of exquisite personal charm" and admitted that he had "caught in some degree the contagion of his enthusiasm. . . . As a friend and companion, in daily intercourse, no one could be more delightful than he."[24] Rockefeller didn't issue such glowing testimonials lightly.

Harper was a pudgy man with a soft, jowly face behind round, thick spectacles. He exuded optimism and captivated people with his visionary ardor. As one newspaper noted, "Dr. Harper is a marvel of energy. His face shows as much eagerness and aggressiveness as that of Luther."[25] Yet he had enough tact to steer clear of the pitfalls that tripped up the more egotistical Dr. Strong. In October 1887, fresh from his transatlantic voyage with Strong, Rockefeller invited Harper to lunch at 26 Broadway. The meeting went swimmingly, and a week later the impossibly busy and resolutely private Rockefeller cleared his schedule and spent an entire day with Harper—lunching with him at noon, then driving for a few hours in Central Park, then chatting again in the evening. For Rockefeller, this was an eternity of conversation. Equally unprecedented, he gave Harper a standing invitation to speak with him at any time. As he plumbed the plans for Baptist universities in different cities, Rockefeller always regarded Harper as an emissary for the Chicago group. After his heady day in Manhattan, Harper wrote excitedly to Goodspeed, "Again and again [Rockefeller] referred to you and to his thorough appreciation of your excellence and worth."[26] On future visits to Vassar, Rockefeller and Harper were often seen cycling around the campus together.

With all the hostile publicity directed against Standard Oil during the debate over the Interstate Commerce Act of 1887, it was certainly an auspicious time for Rockefeller to consider a major philanthropic bequest. The newspapers were now puffing him as one of America's richest men, possibly *the* richest man, so he was under a certain pressure to show that he could discharge this large responsibility. Education was a safe, neutral area in which he had twenty years of experience, having contributed generously to Denison University in Granville, Ohio; Indian University in Muskogee, Oklahoma; Barnard College in New York, which appointed Cettie to its first board of trustees; and Cornell University, whose president, Andrew D. White, he had met on a European trip. Most notably, he was the godfather of Spelman Seminary in Atlanta. Yet Rockefeller was, in many ways, an improbable university founder, for he was not bookish, never attended college, and operated more in a world of facts than theories. Having skipped college, he never automatically recommended it to young people, telling one minister, "I should say in general the advantage of education is to better fit a man for life's work. I would advise young men to take a college course, as a rule, but think some are just as well off with a thorough business training."[27]

Yet precisely because Rockefeller had missed college, no school could stake a claim on him. While he had the option of distributing his educational largesse widely, such dispersed giving didn't jibe with his philosophy. In religion and education no less than in business, Rockefeller thought it a mistake to prop up weak entities that might otherwise perish in the evolutionary race. "I think mistakes are made by organizing too many feeble institutions—rather consolidate and have good, strong working church organizations," he wrote in 1886—a remark that could have applied to his educational views.[28] In the long run, Rockefeller transposed to philanthropy the same principle of consolidation that had worked so well for him in business. Worn down by masses of people clamoring for his money, Rockefeller knew that he now needed a larger and more efficient method for disposing of his fortune. Without it, he would lapse into the slipshod amateurism that he detested. Dr. Strong and Dr. Harper had planted a vision of a large project in his mind, but it would require the careful tending of a lapsed Baptist minister named Frederick T. Gates to bring this seed to glorious life.

＝

While Rockefeller was casting about for some means to spend money more liberally without compromising his scrupulous standards, a group of Baptist leaders met in Washington in May 1888 to form the American Baptist Education Society (ABES). The driving force behind this new association was Dr. Henry Morehouse, the executive officer of the American Baptist Home Mission Society who had advised Rockefeller on Spelman Seminary. Morehouse thought Baptist education was in a woeful state and urgently in need of reform. For Rockefeller, the new group was providential, promising to serve as a handy conduit for channeling large amounts of money to worthy, well-researched Baptist schools.

To serve as executive secretary of the new group, Morehouse drafted a fiery, articulate young Baptist minister, the thirty-five-year-old Frederick T. Gates, who had recently resigned a pastorate in Minnesota and now gravitated toward more worldly affairs. Soon after he assumed the post, Gates championed a Baptist university in Chicago to fill a glaring void. The eastern churches held more money, but the fastest-growing part of the membership resided in the Mississippi Valley and Great Lakes region. Before writing his report, he conducted an intensive study of Baptist education with prosecutorial zeal and ministerial fervor and he confirmed many of the arguments that Thomas W. Goodspeed had adduced. Because many Baptists schools were located in rural backwaters, midwestern congregants often attended schools of other denominations. Having tripled in size in two decades and ranking as America's second largest metropolis with 1.7 million residents, Chicago seemed the optimal site for a major college.

Gates presented his findings in a richly detailed report that exhibited the exhaustive research that would endear him to Rockefeller. At the beginning, Gates, still unfamiliar with his patron, believed that Rockefeller would respond better to a bold plan than something tentative or equivocal. Hence, he portrayed this new Baptist university as the nucleus of a national educational network, confiding to Morehouse, "A scheme so vast, so continental, so orderly, so comprehensive, so detailed, will in my view capture a mind so constituted as Mr. Rockefeller's is."[29] On October 15, 1888, he electrified a Baptist convention in Chicago with an impassioned paper entitled "The Need for a Baptist University in Chicago, as Illustrated by a Study of Baptist College Education in the West."

The Gates report has often been credited with convincing Rockefeller to opt for Chicago, yet William Rainey Harper provided timely assistance. Two weeks after Gates made his sensational address, Dr. Harper spent ten hours at Vassar with Rockefeller and then joined him on the train to New York. During this momentous day, Rockefeller first declared his intention to found a Baptist university in Chicago. As Harper informed Goodspeed, "[Rockefeller] himself made out a list of reasons why it would be better to go to Chicago than to remain in New York."[30] Rockefeller leaned toward the Midwest for several reasons. He feared the complications that might result from the bullheaded Dr. Strong's leadership of any New York school. He also worried that an eastern school might be encrusted with tradition, whereas a Chicago school could "strike out upon lines in full sympathy with the spirit of the age."[31] Then there was a political dimension that Rockefeller never dared to articulate openly. He had to convince the public that he would not meddle or convert the school into a mouthpiece for his corporate interests. As he put it three decades later, Chicago "was sufficiently removed from Wall Street to encourage the hope that it would escape suspicion of being dominated by the so-called interests."[32]

Twice during the next month, Rockefeller spent a day with Harper, first in Poughkeepsie, then in New Haven, for nonstop talks about the proposed university. Harper was astonished by his patron's unreserved passion. "I have never known him to be so interested in anything," Harper told Goodspeed, "and this promises much."[33] Growing more enthusiastic by the hour, Rockefeller advanced a three-pronged plan for a college and university in Chicago, a theological seminary in New York (doubtless to placate Dr. Strong), and an educational trust of western colleges. This last step, a brainchild of Harper, envisioned a string of colleges throughout the West sharing common management with the Chicago university. Warming to the project, Rockefeller planned to visit Cornell on an inspection tour and court three Baptist professors for Chicago. In eloquent testimony to his commitment, Rockefeller told Harper of his readiness to give three million of the first four million dollars needed by the Chicago school. On December 3, 1888, the ABES formally endorsed the plan to found a new school in Chicago; ABES would be the official channel for Rockefeller's contributions.

Then suddenly, in early 1889, Rockefeller grew aloof toward William Rainey Harper, who had committed the classic error of promoting his cause too assertively. What especially distressed Rockefeller was that Harper wanted to start with a full-blown university, whereas he preferred to begin with a college and expand incrementally. To break this impasse, Harper tactfully bowed out and allowed Gates to take charge of the lobbying campaign. A master at reading the minds of potential donors, Gates intuited that Rockefeller felt put upon by Harper's quixotic plans and, to lessen his anxieties, he sent Rockefeller a scaled-down plan for a plain Chicago college. Much relieved, Rockefeller invited Gates and Morehouse for lunch on January 21, 1889. When Gates first set eyes on the great sphinx, he found him polite and decorous, if cryptic. "In parting with me," Gates reported to Harper, "he said that his mind worked slowly in these matters, but he was glad to have had this opportunity for extended conversation, and closed by saying, 'I think we are in the way of progress.' "[34]

An important upshot of the lunch was that Rockefeller invited Gates to accompany him on a train trip to Cleveland. Gates saw that a low-key approach was the perfect antidote to Harper's rousing oratory, and he decided to let Rockefeller initiate discussion about the Chicago school aboard the train. "I think this was soon perceived by Mr. Rockefeller," Gates said in his memoirs, "that it surprised and pleased him, and that he amused himself by putting my sense of propriety to the test." Though the train left New York at 6 P.M., the two men never referred to what was uppermost in their minds. When they were joined by a phalanx of Standard Oil men, Gates noted the magnetic power Rockefeller had over them. "I observed that he spoke very little indeed, and always in a low and quiet voice."[35] At one point, when the porter making up Rockefeller's berth accidentally smacked him over the head, Rockefeller "uttered no word, made no exclamation, gave not one word of reproof to the careless porter, and reassured him when he offered profuse apologies," recalled Gates.[36]

Having failed to broach the Chicago question with Rockefeller, Gates crept into his sleeping berth that night "a miserable, disappointed man."[37] As it turned out, Rockefeller was coyly enjoying a cat-and-mouse game, and as they neared Cleveland the next morning, he began to pummel Gates with questions about the ABES. Rockefeller wanted reassurance that the ABES board was truly disinterested and devoid of unstated agendas. He also wanted Gates to make on-site inspections of schools and not rely on secondhand reports. On the strength of these assurances, Rockefeller decided to make the Baptist society his preferred vehicle for denominational gifts, an important first step on the road to wholesale philanthropy. Clearly, Rockefeller was contemplating new ways of distributing money through central agencies that could offer expert advice and buffer him from applicants.

Gates often marveled at the inexplicable ways of his new patron, who enjoyed keeping everyone in suspense. As the ABES board meeting approached on February 20, 1889, Gates awaited word of a large contribution from Rockefeller. Only as the meeting was called to order did a messenger arrive with a $100,000 pledge to the organization. Later on, when Rockefeller asked him what the society did with the money, Gates said it went into a bank account that paid no interest. This so mortified Rockefeller's sense of thrift that he borrowed back the $100,000 and paid the society 6 percent. "I can't endure to see that money idle," Rockefeller told Gates. "I feel about it as one does to come into a room, ill swept, with the corners full of cobwebs and dust. I want to clean up that room."[38]

In the spring of 1889, Gates went through another baffling period of silence. He was hoping to announce Rockefeller's decision to bankroll a Chicago university when the ABES held its general meeting in Boston on May 18. At the last minute, Rockefeller advised Gates to stop by his home en route to Boston and listened silently to the latter's appeal for a large commitment to the Chicago project. Sticking with his habitual policy of creative procrastination, Rockefeller promised nothing and invited Gates for breakfast the next morning.

After all these excruciating dilatory tactics, the campaign for a Chicago college or university reached a surprisingly swift climax on a clear spring morning in May 1889. After breakfast, the two men strolled to and fro before the Rockefeller house on Fifty-fourth Street. After months of stalling, Rockefeller said he was ready to provide $400,000—considerably short of the figure he had quoted to Harper six months before. When Gates rejected this as insufficient, Rockefeller raised the ante to $500,000. Once again, Gates spurned the offer, citing the advantages of Rockefeller contributing the majority of the money. Gates held out for a stunning $600,000 contribution—equal to $9.5 million today—which was predicated upon another $400,000 being raised from other sources. Eager to commit this historic pledge to paper, they went down to Rockefeller's office where he put his promise in writing.

The next day, clutching this paper, Gates rose before the Baptists in the Tremont Temple in Boston. Rumors had circulated about the gift, creating a tingling mood of expectation. "I hold in my hand," Gates thundered, "a letter from our great patron of education, Mr. John D. Rockefeller." A groundswell of cheers surged from the floor. "A letter in which, on the basis of the resolutions adopted by our board, he promises that he will give six hundred thousand dollars—" At this point, pandemonium erupted, with clergymen waving their handkerchiefs, whistling, and applauding. Driven to ecstasy by this earthly bounty, one minister on the podium flung his hat heavenward, while another theologian sprang to his feet and praised "the coming to the front of such a princely giver. . . . It is the Lord's day. . . . As an American, a Baptist, and a Christian I rejoice in this consummation. God has kept Chicago for us; I wonder at his patience."[39] On this note, the ecstatic holy men rose up to offer a lusty rendition of "Praise God from Whom All Blessings Flow."[40] Overnight, for all his infamy in business, Rockefeller wore a golden nimbus in the eyes of many Baptists.

This was a bruising repudiation of Dr. Augustus H. Strong, who had ridden his hobbyhorse too hard and given the victory to his enemies. At first, it was exceedingly difficult for him to renounce his dream and concede defeat. Falling into deep dejection, he went on plying Gates with letters for Rockefeller until Gates had to inform him point-blank, "There is no hope. Mr. Rockefeller returned your letter to me with the request that the subject be dropped, and that I so write you as would leave no hope of any interest on his part."[41] After a time, when Strong's name surfaced in conversation, Rockefeller would drawl sarcastically, "Well, I hope Dr. Strong finds his man!"[42] It took Strong years to recuperate.

In June 1889, a few weeks after Rockefeller's gift, Andrew Carnegie began to publish in the *North American Review* an influential essay entitled "Wealth." Carnegie saw capitalism as threatened by the widening gulf between the swelling fortunes of the great industrialists and the meager wages of downtrodden workers. To defuse tensions and spread economic benefits more widely, he argued that the rich should donate large sums to worthy causes during their lifetimes, lest their money be frittered away by idle heirs. "The man who dies thus rich dies disgraced," Carnegie declared bluntly.[43] Rockefeller was greatly influenced by Carnegie and when the Carnegie Library opened in Pittsburgh in 1896 dashed off a congratulatory note. "I would that more men of wealth were doing as you are doing with your money; but, be assured, your example will bear fruits, and the time will come when men of wealth will more generally be willing to use it for the good of others."[44] Rockefeller was especially struck by the broadly systematic nature of Carnegie's library program, which would bring some twenty-eight hundred public libraries into existence worldwide. When Rockefeller later addressed Marshall Field, Philip D. Armour, and other Chicago moguls about philanthropy, he echoed Carnegie's plea to make bequests before they died.

In private, Rockefeller and Gates sometimes faulted Carnegie for letting his vanity peep out behind his benevolence. As Gates griped to Rockefeller, "Mr. Carnegie's intimate friends tell me that it is no secret between them and him that he does these things for the sake of having his name written in stone all over the country. Have you observed that he always gives buildings while somebody else furnishes the money to keep them in repair?"[45] Rockefeller's philanthropy was relatively discreet. Another tycoon might have been tempted to plaster his name on the Chicago college, especially during a contentious period that saw the passage of both antitrust and railroad-reform legislation. Yet this only hardened Rockefeller's resolve to prove that he was not currying public favor. With the University of Chicago, his sole concession to vanity was to allow the trustees to affix his name to the school seal, official documents, and letterheads. A proposal to place a lamp on the university seal was rejected, lest anyone mistake it for a vulgar allusion to oil. Even though Rockefeller was the Prospero who single-handedly conjured the University of Chicago into being, he didn't allow any campus building to bear his name, and the Rockefeller Memorial Chapel was christened only after his death.

It was an auspicious time for such a venture. While enjoying the wealth of a nascent world power, America was still saddled with cultural institutions that seemed provincial beside their European counterparts, and many businessmen were eager to endow schools and museums. Rockefeller was not the only magnate to create a major university in the late nineteenth century: The railroad fortunes of both Johns Hopkins and Leland Stanford were similarly applied, while closer to home Rockefeller had the example of the Pratt Institute, set up by Charles Pratt in 1887. Instead of making isolated gifts, Rockefeller wanted to finance institutions whose research would have a pervasive influence. Of the University of Chicago, he later said, "Following the principle of trying to abolish evils by destroying them at the source, we felt that to aid colleges and universities, whose graduates would spread their culture far and wide, was the surest way to fight ignorance and promote the growth of useful knowledge."[46] To Rockefeller, the least imaginative use of money was to give it to people outright instead of delving into the causes of human misery. "That has been our guiding principle, to benefit as many people as possible," he affirmed. "Instead of giving alms to beggars, if anything can be done to remove the causes which lead to the existence of beggars, then something deeper and broader and more worthwhile will have been accomplished."[47]

Businessmen such as Rockefeller and Carnegie saw themselves as applying their managerial wisdom to the charity world. As at Standard Oil, Rockefeller wanted to reduce waste and duplication in the charitable sphere and deplored the lack of study behind much giving. "Today the whole machinery of benevolence is conducted upon more or less haphazard principles," he stated in his memoirs.[48] The University of Chicago was Rockefeller's signature project in which he clarified his approach and schooled Frederick T. Gates, his son, and other advisers as his future surrogates.

From the outset, Rockefeller swore that he would avoid the rich man's trap of endowing institutions that would become dependent wards. His ideal was to create organizations that would take on independent lives and outgrow him. Having pledged $600,000 for the Chicago college, he gave the ABES one year from June 1, 1890, to drum up the other $400,000 from outside sources. To accomplish this, Gates moved temporarily to Chicago and joined forces with Goodspeed in a grueling fund-raising drive that nearly drove them to distraction. They were stymied by restrictions written into the school's articles of incorporation, which stipulated that two-thirds of the trustees and the president be members of Baptist churches. If the enterprise's spirit was ecumenical (several prominent Jews contributed), the institution's charter was explicitly denominational. This confusion emanated from Rockefeller, who insisted that the new institution remain under Baptist auspices yet be "conducted in a spirit of the widest liberality," with students drawn from every class of society.[49] Unfortunately, Chicago numbered few Baptists among its high-spending citizens. Instead of being stimulated by Rockefeller's involvement, many potential donors smugly assumed that the fledgling school would never want for money. Of their excruciating year of pleading, Gates later said it "cost more brain work, anxiety, anguish, tears, prayers and shoe leather than all the millions that have since gone into the university."[50] A promising contribution came in January 1890 when Marshall Field donated a ten-acre parcel for the new school on the south side of Chicago, just north of the site of an upcoming fair that would attract worldwide attention: the World's Columbian Exposition. Delighted by this act of faith, Rockefeller agreed that he and Field would jointly review the names of proposed trustees.

Having devoted his career to eliminating risk from the petroleum business, Rockefeller was unsettled by the uncertainties that dogged the Chicago project. For a long time, the question of who would lead the college was every bit as vexing as who—besides Rockefeller—would support it. William Rainey Harper seemed the natural candidate. As the star salesman who had converted Rockefeller to the cause, he enjoyed his special trust. Whatever his occasional qualms about Harper's flamboyant rhetoric, Rockefeller was sure the young biblical scholar had unique credentials to run the school. Although Harper might not have known it, Rockefeller revealed his thoughts to him in an unprecedented fashion. Right after Christmas 1888, Harper had dropped by 26 Broadway. Since Rockefeller had been ailing, he asked after his health and Rockefeller replied:

I have made little progress, Doctor Harper. My wife has been sick and I have been anxious about her. My time has been taken up with the consideration of petitions from many sources—I have never known them so numerous. Montreal has come down upon me. Richmond, with a great reinforcement, has come down upon me. From every quarter the demands are growing more numerous, and more insistent. . . . I did not ask you to come and see me Sunday because I spent the day in bed; Christmas, too, I spent in bed—I was so tired. I have had some unusually worrying business matters in the last three weeks; still, the thing [the University of Chicago] is on my mind and I want to hear more about it.[51]

For a man who lived behind the heavy draperies of Victorian reticence, this was a remarkably candid response.

The intuitive Harper sensed that something else was preying on his mind, and Rockefeller confided that he had received a jarring letter from Dr. Strong. While masquerading as a family Christmas greeting—Charles's marriage to Bessie lay just ahead—it was a transparent attempt to sabotage Harper and the Chicago project. A self-styled inquisitor, Dr. Strong had examined the class notes of his daughter Kate, who was taking a Bible course at Vassar with Harper, and written to Rockefeller that he had unearthed heretical tendencies in Harper's teachings. Rockefeller was far more disturbed by Strong's defamatory tactics than the specific charges leveled against Harper. When Harper was next in Poughkeepsie, he was greeted by a letter from Dr. Strong, who threatened, as a Vassar trustee, to lodge an official complaint if Harper continued to teach the Sunday Bible class there. When Goodspeed found out about this mean-spirited attack, he said to Harper, "The man seems mad, daft."[52]

Harper was always Rockefeller's choice for president, and at times the venture seemed to hinge upon his acceptance. In his grandiloquent visions of this new institution, Harper was not above gently flattering Rockefeller, making the new institution sound like the collegiate equivalent of Standard Oil. "And let it be a university made up of a score of colleges with a large degree of uniformity in their management; in other words, an educational trust," Harper advised him.[53] These sublime words both inspired and petrified Rockefeller. Hounded by requests for money, he didn't know if he had the income to juggle so many commitments. In January 1889, he told Harper that they should start modestly with a college and defer the university till a later day. "So many claims have pressed upon me," he explained, "I have not really needed a University to absorb my surplus."[54]

Harper agonized over whether to take the presidential post at Chicago or stick with the biblical scholarship he loved. The question was a proxy for the larger issue of whether he sought power and status in life or the quieter rewards of scholarship. Harper was an original theorist and a charismatic teacher who hated to lose contact with his students, but he was also intensely ambitious. To pin him down, Yale offered him a generous, six-year compensation package that would allow him to hold two prestigious chairs at once. Learning of this, Rockefeller wrote Harper, "It would break my heart if I did not believe you would stay in the fold all right. For all the reasons I believe you will. Be sure you do."[55] When Harper conferred with him two weeks later, Rockefeller pleaded with him to avoid any permanent commitment to Yale.

When the University of Chicago charter was adopted in May 1890, the school still lacked a president. To force the issue, Rockefeller dispatched Gates to New Haven that July to notify Harper that he was the board's unanimous choice to head the school. Far from settling things, this only sent Harper into fresh paroxysms of indecision. In spite of Rockefeller's reiterated preference for a small college, Harper wanted nothing less than a full-fledged university and believed the one million dollars raised so far a mere pittance that fell short of his visions. As Harper wrestled with the dilemma, Rockefeller wrote to him in August, promising to add a premium to his salary. "I do not forget that the effort to establish the University grew out of your suggestion to me at Vassar and I regard you as the father of the institution, starting out under God with such great promise of future usefulness."[56] Harper must have noted Rockefeller's use of the hitherto taboo word *university.*

This letter alerted Harper to the fact that he now enjoyed considerable bargaining power in shaping the new institution, and his rhetoric only grew more sonorous. "The denomination and indeed the whole country are expecting the University of Chicago to be from the very beginning an institution of the highest rank and character," he replied to Rockefeller. "Already it is talked of in connection with Yale, Harvard, Princeton, Johns Hopkins, the University of Michigan, and Cornell."[57] Harper characterized the money raised so far as insufficient to realize such lofty aims. Among other things, he envisaged a university where he could perpetuate his own scholarly interests and act as president and professor. When Rockefeller consented to his demand for an extra million dollars to transfer the Morgan Park Theological Seminary to the new Chicago campus, the thirty-four-year-old Harper capitulated and formally accepted the presidency in February 1891. It now seemed clear that his spacious dreams would carry him beyond the small, cloistered world of a biblical scholar.

Over time, the immoderate Harper gave liberal interpretations to Rockefeller's vague promises of money, but he never misrepresented the scope of his plans. Even before accepting the presidency, he boasted to Rockefeller, "I believe that ten years will show an institution at Chicago which will amaze the multitudes."[58] Working sixteen-hour days, Harper now negotiated more than 120 faculty appointments in little more than a year. Rockefeller might think the university a plant of slow growth, but Harper wanted it to bloom overnight. The new president raided so many Ivy League faculties—the ranks of Yale and Cornell were especially depleted—that his ransacked rivals complained of foul play. Harper dangled sizable sums before reluctant prospects, enlarging the school's future financial requirements. This nationwide talent search netted nine college presidents for the first faculty. Harper signed up John Dewey and George Herbert Mead for the philosophy department and enticed novelist Robert Herrick to join the English department, while Albion Small initiated America's first graduate department in sociology. Another eminent recruit, economist Thorstein Veblen, came to regard Harper as the educational counterpart of capitalists such as Rockefeller and satirized him as a captain of erudition, one of a new species of empire builders in higher education.

However inspired he was by Harper, Rockefeller felt sorely beset by his extravagant spending, and their relations began to fray. With outside fundraising stalled, it seemed that Rockefeller's worst nightmare was coming true: He would end up sole benefactor of an institution that would bleed him dry for years. Whenever they met, they stayed away from money talk and spoke of educational policy. Financial matters were shunted off into increasingly testy private exchanges between Gates and Harper—exchanges that Rockefeller reviewed privately. By the spring of 1891, Rockefeller began to develop the queasy sense that Harper regarded his money as a blank check to cover annual deficits. To their surprise and disbelief, Rockefeller and Gates saw that the new president would not drop his busy lecture schedule (which netted him $4,000 a year) and contemplated a $3,000 offer to head the Chautauqua School of the English Bible, while also planning a fancy European trip—all the while banking a handsome $10,000 salary at the University of Chicago. As Rockefeller fumed in the summer of 1891, Gates met with Harper and urged him to shed his outside activities. "Of course he rejected these proposals," Gates informed Rockefeller, "as well as the intimation contained in it that his motives are not without their mercenary side."[59] It was an odd situation: the world's richest man chastising a biblical scholar for unseemly materialism.

To some extent, Rockefeller sent out conflicting messages and was partly to blame for Harper's profligacy. It was Rockefeller, after all, who urged Harper to pay top dollar for America's best academic minds. As Gates told Harper after one meeting with Rockefeller, "We talked *at great length* about salaries of head professors pro and con and as a result *he wished me to say to you positively that the best men must be had.*"[60] Such talk could easily inspire a cavalier attitude toward money. Gates also had an ulterior motive for wishing Harper away from the lecture circuit. Though he was not the freethinker darkly portrayed by Dr. Strong, Harper did have heterodox religious views and brooded morbidly on his own heresy. Practicing the higher criticism, he had moved away from a stress on biblical inerrancy to a scholarly search for the authorship of sacred texts. Though becoming a modernist in his own right, Gates wanted Harper to muzzle his unorthodox views in public. Potential donors were already worried about the new university's diluted Baptism and questioned Harper's doctrinal purity. To one such critic, Gates insisted, "Dr. Harper is a man of evangelistic spirit and *annually secures scores of conversions at Yale,*" implying that he would continue this practice at Chicago.[61] When Gates expressed concern to Harper about his views, the latter made a clean breast of his liberal religious views to Rockefeller so that he would never be shocked by his unorthodoxy.

The newspapers were not privy to these internal tensions and lampooned the implausible pairing of the trust king and the biblical scholar. Harper was irritated by cartoons that showed him sprinting after Rockefeller and his money bags. In one cartoon strip, Harper desperately pursued Rockefeller across a frozen Hudson River, hopping from one ice floe to the next until a weary Rockefeller dropped a thick wad of bills behind him to sate the university president. When Rockefeller later gave one million dollars to Yale, another cartoonist drew Harper astride a college building marked "University of Chicago," glaring enviously at another college building marked "Yale." Harper was often portrayed as a sycophant of the rich. In one cartoon, he was seen greeting fashionable ladies at the train station and carrying their luggage, which was marked "Proper Function of College Presidents."

There must have been moments in 1891 when John D. Rockefeller wondered how he had gotten entangled in a project so vast and headed by such a brilliantly erratic man. Had he known what lay ahead, it seems doubtful that he would have persevered. But he had now publicly staked his reputation on this hugely expensive endeavor and, in the last analysis, wherever William Rainey Harper led, John D. Rockefeller would grudgingly follow. He was not a man to abandon a project that had received his blessing.

However mingled with joy, Rockefeller's anguish over the University of Chicago came at a moment of physical vulnerability and tipped him over the edge toward a breakdown. Gates's letters to Harper are laced with references to their patron's sharply deteriorating health. In April 1891, Gates said after a tête-à-tête with Rockefeller: "He was kindness itself, but appeared very sad and depressed. . . . He even told me that anxiety and worry about the matter [i.e., university finances] had made him sick and it was this that took him from his business and drove him to Cleveland. We *must* not press him for money. Let us see to it and see if we can not cut down expenses and get through the first year with the smallest possible deficit."[62]

This was more than mere bluff or tactical posturing on Gates's part, though there was doubtless some of that. Starting in early 1889, Rockefeller had complained continually of fatigue and depression. For several decades, he had expended superhuman energy in the creation of Standard Oil, mastering myriad details; all the while, pressure had built steadily beneath the surface repose. One could now see in his face the subdued melancholy of a man who had sacrificed too much for work. In early 1890, Rockefeller stayed away from the office for several months due to an unspecified illness. Later in the year, he promised to stop working on Saturdays and take more vacations, but the symptoms harried him into the following spring.

By 1891, the top executive ranks were beginning to thin at Standard Oil. Charles Pratt died suddenly that year, and Henry Flagler was increasingly distracted by his Florida hotel and railway ventures. Having groomed John D. Archbold as his successor, Rockefeller began to shift day-to-day power to his feisty, bantam protégé. More reviled than honored for his triumphs, Rockefeller, fifty-two, felt embattled by endless subpoenas from court cases and congressional hearings. Though he brushed off his critics as minor irritants and professed faith in his own integrity, it could not have been easy to face such universal opprobrium. Keeping up the pose of indifference must have taken its own toll.

Nevertheless, Rockefeller had come through earlier assaults unscathed. What really disturbed him was not so much making money but spending it. One Cleveland society woman, a friend, told a story of sitting beside him on a streetcar when the conductor came to collect fares. When Rockefeller handed him a quarter, the conductor deducted two nickel fares, assuming he would pay for the lady, and gave him fifteen cents change. "My change is five cents short," Rockefeller declared. "Why, no. I took out two fares and gave you back fifteen cents," explained the conductor. "But I did not tell you to take out two fares," Rockefeller retorted. "Let this be a lesson to you, and never assume that a passenger is paying for two people unless he says so."[63] Rockefeller reviewed every bill that arrived at home and often patrolled the hallways, turning off gaslights. Such habits were not simply reflexive stinginess but were rooted in bedrock beliefs about the value of money. When he discovered that one railroad overcharged him $117 for carrying his family and horses, he had the Standard Oil treasurer immediately retrieve the money. "I need the $117 to build mission churches in the West," he explained, showing the association in his own mind between savings and charity.[64]

With such uncommon respect for the dollar, he couldn't cope with the psychological demands of the University of Chicago and other philanthropic commitments. As Rockefeller said, "I investigated and worked myself almost to a nervous breakdown in groping my way, without sufficient guide or chart, through the ever-widening field of philanthropic endeavor. It was forced upon me to organize and plan this department upon as distinct lines of progress as our other business affairs."[65] The figures of Rockefeller's contributions between 1889 and 1892 reflect the expanding nature of his giving. From $124,000 in 1889 (right before his big pledge to Gates), his donations soared to $304,000 in 1890, $510,000 in 1891, and then a spectacular $1.35 million in 1892 ($22 million today) as he opened the spigot for the University of Chicago. Clearly, he needed someone to help with the avalanche of appeals overwhelming him, and by late 1889 he began to forward begging letters to

Frederick T. Gates. "I am disposed more and more to give only through organized agencies," he told Gates.[66] Finally, in March 1891, suffering from broken health and all too aware of his mortal limitations, Rockefeller summoned Gates for a confidential parley:

"I am in trouble, Mr. Gates. The pressure of these appeals for gifts has become too great for endurance. I haven't the time or strength, with all my heavy business responsibilities, to deal with these demands properly. I am so constituted as to be unable to give away money with any satisfaction until I have made the most careful inquiry as to the worthiness of the cause. These investigations are now taking more of my time and energy than the Standard Oil itself. Either I must shift part of the burden, or stop giving entirely. And I cannot do the latter."

"Indeed you cannot, Mr. Rockefeller," Gates replied.

"Well, I must have a helper. I have been watching you. I think you are the man. I want you to come to New York and open an office here. You can aid me in my benefactions by taking interviews and inquiries, and reporting the results for action. What do you say?"[67]

Gates accepted and in March 1891 transplanted his family to Montclair, New Jersey, and took up offices in the Temple Court, near 26 Broadway. This action, which ended his ministerial career, made him an earthly potentate instead. At first, Gates retained his position as secretary of the ABES and funneled Rockefeller money around the country. By 1892, Gates joyously proclaimed to Rockefeller, "Our denomination has a larger, better distributed, better organized, and more efficient educational property than any other denomination in America."[68] Only after 1900 did the two men begin to branch out into the revolutionary schemes that transformed old-fashioned denominational charity into modern philanthropy. By that point, Gates had assembled a team of advisers tutored in Rockefeller's principles, trained in his methods, and fired with his evangelical zeal.

For the remainder of his life, Rockefeller's medical status provoked so much fantasy, gossip, and speculation that we should try to define it here with some precision. Rockefeller had been fit and youthful well into his fifties. He never adopted the sleek, portly look of his fellow plutocrats and seemed ten years younger than his age. What, then, ailed him in the early 1890s? Broadly speaking, the answer was overwork, brought on by the combined stress of work and charity. As his inseparable companion and homeopathic physician, Dr. Hamilton Biggar, said, "A little more of that would have killed him. Mr. Rockefeller was close to the edge of a breakdown . . . when he finally let himself be persuaded that he could no longer do the work of several men with the strength of one."[69] But if overwork weakened his immune system, he also succumbed to opportunistic diseases. In 1891, a national grippe swept the nation, and Rockefeller was laid low. Dr. Biggar also diagnosed him as having a catarrh of the upper part of the bronchial tubes. For years, Rockefeller suffered from liver trouble—at one point he bought a "liver pad" from a local drugstore, wearing it with beneficial results—and in the early 1890s, Dr. Biggar plugged him full of an unnamed brew he had concocted for this trouble.

It was Rockefeller's prolonged digestive troubles that most titillated the public, providing enduring satisfaction to moralists who believed that if Rockefeller could not be brought to justice, he could at least be tormented through his bodily afflictions. He had serious digestive problems in the early 1890s, perhaps even stress-related ulcers, and looked pale and haggard. For a time, to soothe his stomach, he lunched on milk and crackers at 26 Broadway, spartan fare that he enjoyed and sometimes even ordered by choice. He recovered from his digestive troubles, however, and they never recurred in any really threatening way. Yet he remained extremely fussy about his food, taking small, sparing bites in a manner that spawned a thousand myths about his ruined system. For years it was bruited that he had a standing million-dollar offer for any doctor who could repair his stomach.

Those who believed that Rockefeller was suffering divine retribution would have been interested to learn that in November 1888 Cettie was seriously injured in an alcohol-lamp explosion that badly burned both her hands and face. She had to be bedridden for several weeks. Only a few mystifying references to this ghastly accident appear in Rockefeller's letters. One can't help but wonder whether the lamp was actually burning Standard Oil kerosene and whether Rockefeller turned it into an alcohol lamp in his correspondence. Would the wife of John D. Rockefeller have used alcohol lamps? If Cettie was the casualty of impure Standard Oil kerosene, her husband might well have viewed her accident as celestial judgment upon him.

During 1891, under doctor's orders, Rockefeller took time off from work and spent eight months at Forest Hill, the family's sovereign cure for illness. His private secretary, George D. Rogers, was placed under strict instructions to spare him all but urgent business matters. For the first time in twenty-one years, his mind was cleansed of Standard Oil. To restore his health, he worked with his farm laborers in the field, rode his bike, ate simply, and jokingly claimed he was becoming a "great concert singer."[70] These traditional remedies worked like a charm, for by June 1891 he wrote Archbold, "I am happy to state that my health is steadily improving. I can hardly tell you how different the world begins to look to me. Yesterday was the best day I have seen for three months."[71] By the end of the summer, he had gained fifteen pounds, fresh color was restored to his face, and he resumed a more normal schedule. On February 23, 1892, he had Gates post a letter to the University of Chicago trustees, pledging another million dollars with these words: "I make this gift as a thank offering to Almighty God for returning health."[72] In fact, the offering was as much a grudging response to Harper's improvident spending as a token of Rockefeller's gratitude to the Lord.

Having always enjoyed ruddy health, Rockefeller was evidently shaken by his lengthy illness, for he dreaded rushing back to work and precipitating a relapse. He now contemplated something inconceivable for most other restless tycoons of the period: retirement. He had no psychological need to spend his life amassing money and told Gates that he had all he wanted. As he later explained, "I felt that at fifty it was due me to have freedom from absorption in active business affairs and to devote myself to a variety of interests other than money making, which had claimed a portion of my time since the beginning of my business career."[73] Though he craved retirement, several crises tethered him to business for another three or four years until he stopped going to 26 Broadway altogether in 1897. In the meantime, he reported to the office less and less, as the focus of his life shifted slowly from earning money to dispensing it as intelligently as possible.

—

Although Harper had the founder's promise that he would attend opening ceremonies, Rockefeller, eager to prove that he would not meddle with the school, later rejected the idea. One also suspects that he subtly wished to telegraph his displeasure to Harper over the handling of university finances. In early 1892, Gates visited Chicago and was "utterly appalled" at the yawning chasm between Harper's extravagant schemes and the available money. Yet with all his openhanded spending, Harper had accomplished one of the great feats in education history. True to his wishes, he opened the school on October 1, 1892, without ceremony "as if it were the continuation of a work which has been conducted for a thousand years."[74] His hastily gathered faculty was so studded with renowned scholars that the university was catapulted instantly into the front ranks of higher education. On the first day of classes, the new school boasted 750 students, one-fourth of them women, with ten Jewish students, eight Catholics, and a handful of blacks.

Architect Henry Ives Cobb had little more than a year to summon a campus into being, and five major buildings were completed in 1892, another five in 1893. Built at a moment of civic pride, the new university sprang up beside the fabled White City of the 1893 Columbian Exposition. The fairgrounds featured a spectacular Standard Oil exhibit of a miniature refinery surrounded by a strange colonnade of Ionic columns with alternating oil-filled lamps and vases. From a Ferris wheel on the midway, visitors received a superb aerial view of the new school that Standard Oil profits had produced. Since Henry Ives Cobb also helped to plan the fairgrounds, the two projects appeared to blend into a seamless whole.

Once the university was inaugurated, President Harper did not stand still. Impulsive, never satisfied, he began to advance on a hundred fronts. Heedless of costs, he broached new initiatives to create a junior college, a night school, a correspondence school, extension courses for adults, a university press, a special division for laboratories, and museums. As leader of this educational trust, he wanted to dispatch scholars to teach at affiliated colleges in other states—an expensive initiative vetoed by Rockefeller. Harper also believed a university should benefit the surrounding city, and sociologists fanned out from the campus to undertake studies at Hull House and other settlement houses.

For all his pride in the university, Rockefeller dreaded this unbridled growth, which postponed the day when the new university might survive without him. Often, when Harper bagged another famous scholar, the university had to buy equipment for the newcomer—money Harper neglected to figure into his calculations. For all their mutual attraction, Rockefeller and Harper were destined to clash. As Gates framed the contrast:

> Mr. Rockefeller, with a breadth of vision as great as Dr. Harper's, was temperamentally cool, reserved, cautious, circumspect, deliberate, amazingly patient, but in the end, inflexible, adapting means to ends with long and accurate prevision. Dr. Harper was ardent, highly imaginative, with limitless capacity and insatiable eagerness for work, an undaunted optimist, minimizing difficulties, magnifying opportunities, rapid in conception, confiding, unsuspicious, bent on immediate results, willful, and impatient of opposition or delay.[75]

As a businessman, Rockefeller believed in praying for good times while bracing for bad, and his recurring pleas for caution were vindicated in 1893 when panic seized the American economy and the university had to stall on paying salaries. To surmount the crisis, Rockefeller transferred another $500,000 to the university that October. He was now drawn in so deep that he couldn't withdraw—and Harper knew it. Having sworn he would never cover operating deficits, Rockefeller had to renounce that policy and cover the budget shortfall for the next two years.

What made it so hard to enforce discipline in Chicago was that, after the obligatory protest, Rockefeller always came through with the money. In October 1895, Gates went to Chicago armed with a letter from Rockefeller pledging another three million dollars for the school's endowment—possibly the largest such sum ever given at one time by one man for educational purposes and worth about $50 million today. Soon after, Harper and the university secretary, Thomas W. Goodspeed, attended a football game between Chicago and Wisconsin. During the first half, they told coach Amos Alonzo Stagg—who set up the first department of physical culture at an American university—about the gift. With Chicago trailing twelve to ten at halftime, Stagg suggested that the team be informed "because I felt that it would be a strong piece of psychology to do so," as he said.[76] When told by Harper of the gift in the locker room, the team's captain roared, "Three million dollars!" and gave another player a glee-ful slap on the back. "Just watch us play football."[77] With that, the born-again squad streamed back onto the field and beat Wisconsin twenty-two to twelve. Later on, students lit a huge celebratory bonfire on campus and sang hymns to Rockefeller, including one that began, "There was a man sent from God whose name was John."[78]

Despite a standing offer to tour his creation, Rockefeller declined to visit Chicago for several years, reluctant to have the university overly identified with his name. As Gates told Harper, "There are as you know advantages to the University (advantages in your canvass for funds) in the disinterested way in which Mr. Rockefeller has given his money."[79] Beyond that, Rockefeller cherished his privacy and hated public occasions. When Harper finally persuaded John and Cettie to attend the first class quinquennial celebration in July 1897, he promised that Rockefeller would not need to speak. The patron's ideal was to amble unseen through the campus for a couple of hours, an anonymous voyeur, relishing his creation.

As hundreds of students and professors, clad in caps and gowns, trooped into a huge tent in the central quadrangle on a sweltering July day, only one fig-ure wore a plain frock coat and silk hat: the university founder, who marched, as he had since boyhood, with his eyes fixed on the ground. Far from being a fire-breathing mogul, he seemed quiet and faintly embarrassed by the fuss being made over him. When he got up on stage, three thousand people gazed in fascination at this reclusive American legend who had mesmerized the public as both a sinner and saint. It was so stifling inside the tent that hundreds of palm-leaf fans undulated in the audience. When Harper rose and reviewed the future needs of the university, he turned expectantly toward Rockefeller and re-ferred to the pressing need for a hall to replace this temporary tent, eliciting an ambiguous smile from Rockefeller, who must have squirmed in his seat. Then the titan rose to address the crowd:

"I want to thank your Board of Trustees, your President and all who have shared in this most wonderful beginning. It is but a beginning"—he was in-terrupted by frenzied applause—"and you will do the rest." The audience qui-eted down. "You have the privilege to complete it, you and your sons and your daughters. I believe in the work. It is the best investment I ever made in my life. Why shouldn't people give to the University of Chicago money, time, their best efforts? Why not? It is the grandest opportunity ever presented. Where were gathered ever a better Board of Trustees, a better Faculty? I am profoundly, profoundly thankful that I had anything to do with this affair." A roar of ap-

preciative laughter. "The good Lord gave me the money, and how could I withhold it from Chicago?"[80]

Whatever his own discomfort, Rockefeller made an excellent impression. Before the day was out, he had laid cornerstones, listened to sermons, and given
two more short talks. He spent the night at Harper's house and was so unnerved by the absence of clocks—the visit made him deviate from his usual
daily schedule—that he gave Mrs. Harper a thousand-dollar check as a gift and
suggested she buy clocks. The next morning, Rockefeller mounted a bike and
set off on a campus tour with university administrators in tow. Attired in a bicycle suit, he set off at a brisk pace, waving at cheering students along the
route. The entourage flew down the midway to Jackson Park, circled the
ghostly remains of the Columbian Exposition, stopped for refreshments, then
whirled back down the midway. Rockefeller was enormously gratified and
touched by the warm, spontaneous enthusiasm of the students. Everywhere
he went they chanted, "John D. Rockefeller, wonderful man is he / Gives all his
spare change to the U. of C." Another knot of students burst into a fight song:
"Who's the feller? Who's the feller? Rah, Rah, Rah / Rockefeller, he's the feller,
Sis, Boom Bah!"[81]

As a philanthropist, Rockefeller chose to cultivate a wise detachment from
his creations and told Harper that he saw himself as a silent partner in the operation. Despite intermittent accusations to the contrary, he did not interfere
with academic appointments or free expression, though sometimes tempted to
do so. When several Chicago students denounced his monopolistic practices,
an enraged Rockefeller complained to Gates of "statements from the students,
derogatory to the founder, careless and inexcusable; but whether the report is
correct, I do not know. . . . It seemed to me if . . . [it was] correct the men
should be expelled from the Chicago University."[82] In this and other cases, as
best as one can tell, Rockefeller then countermanded the order, fearing the
threat to academic freedom or at least to his own reputation.

It took courage to start a university in the 1890s, when academe swarmed
with vocal critics of big business, and many of Rockefeller's industrialist
friends saw universities as so many breeding grounds for subversion. William
chided his brother for sponsoring the school: "You are getting together a lot of
scribblers, a crowd of Socialists who won't do any good."[83] Rockefeller wrestled
with the issue but believed, on balance, that "while scribblers of the worthless
kind brought poison with their ink to the minds of the people, yet multitudes of
others come out of these institutions of learning to strengthen the good among
us. Let us so hope."[84] The University of Chicago was scarcely immune to the
radical currents on campus. In 1899, while at Chicago, Thorstein Veblen published *The Theory of the Leisure Class*, which portrayed the new captains of in-

dustry as brutal troglodytes and exposed the primitive impulses lurking behind their gaudy consumption habits.

The best-publicized controversy about Rockefeller's role at Chicago involved the dismissal in 1895 of a young political economist, Edward Bemis, who advocated municipal gas ownership and attacked the Standard Oil–controlled United Gas Improvement Company. The official explanation for the firing was that Bemis was more an activist than a scholar and did not measure up to the university's high standards. Since Bemis had been hired by Harper himself and went on to a career of some distinction in utility regulation, one suspects a political motive behind his dismissal, yet there is no evidence that Rockefeller was the culprit. It seems more likely that Harper sacked him in anticipation of Rockefeller's wrath. A year earlier, Harper had warned Bemis about his political activities after he made an inflammatory speech criticizing the railroads' behavior during the Pullman strike. Such visible activism handicapped Harper in courting local business, as he made clear in a letter to Bemis in July 1894:

> Your speech at the First Presbyterian Church has caused me a great deal of annoyance. It is hardly safe for me to venture into any of the Chicago clubs. I am pounced upon from all sides. I propose that during the remainder of your connection with the university you exercise great care in public utterances about questions that are agitating the minds of the people.[85]

Rockefeller refrained from such pressure because he knew the political value of his nonpartisan patronage of a university at a time when he was being accused of subverting other institutions to advance his own interests.

Rockefeller did, however, request a voice in fiscal matters—the one thing that Harper denied him. Like many donors, Rockefeller wished to give freely, but Harper was constantly trying to speed up the process. In appointing Gates as his buffer with Harper, Rockefeller hoped to keep the university guessing about future gifts, but the tactic did not work. "Harper was insatiable in his appetite for money," said one Standard Oil counsel. "Gates was the guardian of the treasurer."[86] As time passed, the strains between Gates and Harper grew intolerable. Both men were idealists steeped in religion, marred by a streak of worldly ambition, and each accused the other of hypocritically exploiting Rockefeller for personal gain.

At first, Gates admired Harper as an inspirational figure who overspent out of naive enthusiasm. He later modified this sanguine view when Harper stoutly denied that a first-rate university could be run as an efficient business and declared, "A university that is properly operated always has a deficit." When this remark appeared in the press, it grated on Rockefeller and Gates as rank betrayal.

According to Gates, Harper flouted several clear understandings with Rockefeller: that the university would never be indebted; would never use endowment funds for university buildings; and would never form an alliance with any medical college in Chicago. When Gates put these points in writing and asked Harper to circulate them to board members, they mysteriously disappeared. When he remonstrated with Harper for hiring more expensive professors and launching new journals, the university president simply ignored him. Soon after Gates insisted that he forgo new buildings, Harper appealed to Chicago's citizens to support a new building campaign. Just as Rockefeller feared, Harper had rashly leaped straight from a small college to a big university.

As Harper rolled up deficits, his patron kept adding millions to the endowment, but he could only be pushed so far. As legions of business rivals had learned, he sometimes groped toward a solution then acted in a swift, decisive manner. "I warned Dr. Harper," Gates said. "I warned him many times. I warned him in words, in deed and in every possible way."[87] Sometimes, when Harper journeyed to New York, Gates thought the president had learned the error of his ways. Then Harper returned to Chicago and relapsed into free-spending habits.

After years of fruitless wrangling, the university was still struggling with a deficit of $200,000 in early 1897 when Rockefeller decided he had had enough. Bypassing Harper, he summoned two representatives from Chicago, Goodspeed and Henry Rust, to meet with Gates and Junior. Rockefeller himself did not attend these meetings, leaving these negotiations to his proxies. On this historic occasion, Gates expressed Rockefeller's disappointment at Harper's failure to raise money from outside sources to reduce the deficit. As Gates pointed out, Rockefeller believed that nonprofit institutions should be even *more* circumspect with money than business organizations:

> [Rockefeller] feels that an institution of learning should be far more conservatively managed than, for instance, a bank, or even a savings bank or a trust company. These companies need only assure the depositor or investor that his funds will be duly cared for during the limited time in which they may be deposited. But a university invests the funds of those who are seeking to make an investment of money for the good of humanity, which shall last, if possible, as long as the world stands.[88]

Like Dr. Augustus H. Strong before him, Harper had fundamentally miscalculated in approaching Rockefeller for money. Gates noted that Rockefeller had long ago planned to found a great university and had ample resources to do so. It was the cavalier, high-handed way that Harper dunned him for money that rankled. "Mr. Rockefeller comes instinctively to feel that the methods of securing his assistance are too often methods of compulsion," said Gates. "The appeals come to him in the shape almost of forced contributions."[89]

Though the meeting ended with Gates acknowledging Harper's accomplishments, he had delivered a humiliating rebuke to his leadership. After reading a stenographic transcript of the meeting, Rockefeller asked that every university board member read it and took the unusual step of having it deposited in his safe as a personal testament of his future wishes for the school. Two months later, the University of Chicago trustees instituted drastic changes. Henceforth, Rockefeller would be notified of new expenditures and given a chance to protest. Gates had joined the board the year before, and Junior followed a year later, giving John D. direct representation in the university's management.

The breach that had opened up between the university's patron saint and its charismatic president was distressing to both men, who had enjoyed an intimate, father-son relationship. Now proscribed from asking Rockefeller for more money, Harper forfeited the easy access he had long cherished. For the emotional Harper, prone to both wild elation and inconsolable gloom, it was hard to be muzzled in his patron's presence. According to legend, when prohibited from talking about money directly to Rockefeller, Harper circumvented the ban by praying aloud for money in his presence. The story, if true, suggests that he still had not absorbed the lesson that Rockefeller had reluctantly and repeatedly tried to teach him.

The powerful Eastman Johnson portrait of John D.
Rockefeller, painted in 1895.
(Courtesy of the Rockefeller Archive Center)

Nemesis

ven as Rockefeller tried to shift his attention away from business
in the 1890s, the political backlash against him gained fresh momentum, making it impossible for him to sever himself from his
brilliant but tarnished record. As he tried to move ahead, his past
loomed ever larger in the public imagination. During the next twenty years, it
kept returning to haunt him, like an inescapable shadow.

The Sherman Antitrust Act had proved an ineffectual piece of legislation.
The real threat to Standard Oil arose in an improbable spot: a small bookstore
in Columbus, Ohio. In 1889, the state's young Republican attorney general,
David K. Watson, wandered into the shop one evening and happened upon a
slim volume by William W. Cook, cheaply bound in imitation leather and bearing the title *Trusts: The Recent Combinations in Trade.* He took the book home and
perused it late into the night. In the appendix, Watson was fascinated to discover Standard Oil's trust deed, which he had never seen before. He was aghast
to learn that for the past seven years Standard Oil of Ohio had violated its state
charter by transferring control of the organization to mostly out-of-state
trustees in New York. Capitalizing on this discovery, Watson filed a quo war-
ranto petition against Ohio Standard in the state supreme court in May 1890,
seeking nothing less than the dissolution of Standard Oil.

Standard Oil executives reacted, as always, by denigrating such measures as
transparent harassment by their business enemies. Frank sent a letter to John
saying that he was "not sure as to who the instigators are but believe Cleveland
refiners have a hand in it" and conjectured that Watson was feeding off information from John Sherman.[1] In rebutting the charges, Standard's attorney,

Samuel C. T. Dodd, offered the same legal fig leaf that the combine had exploited for years: that Ohio Standard shares had been transferred by individual stockholders, not the company itself, to its New York trustees. By now, the ruse was wearing thin.

Ironically, this sortie against Standard Oil came in a conservative, industrial state where its influence was pervasive. As a rock-ribbed Republican contributor, Rockefeller felt betrayed by such ingratitude and protested to a Cleveland friend that "we have not received fair treatment from the Republican party."[2] Never one to mince words, Mark Hanna, the party kingpin, sent a strongly worded message to Watson, telling him that "the Standard Oil Company is officered and managed by some of the best and strongest men in the country. They are pretty much all Republicans and have been most liberal in their contributions to the party, as I personally know, Mr. Rockefeller always quietly doing his share."[3] Although Hanna urged him to drop the suit, Watson would not relent. While Rockefeller blandly denied knowledge of Hanna's action, his memory was conveniently faulty, for on April 7, 1891, Hanna had written to him, "I caught our distinguished Attorney General Watson here the other day and gave him a piece of my mind."[4] Watson's successor, Frank Monnett, alleged that on six occasions Watson was offered bribes to terminate the case—in one instance as much as $100,000 in cash—but Monnett never provided corroborating evidence, perhaps fearing Standard Oil reprisals against his sources.

Such intimidation, if it did occur, only stiffened Watson's resistance to pressure. On March 2, 1892, he won a famous victory when the Ohio Supreme Court ruled that Standard Oil of Ohio was indeed controlled by trustees at 26 Broadway and had to renounce the trust agreement. The trust was also accused of trying to monopolize every phase of the petroleum business. One enterprising reporter who rushed to 26 Broadway was assured that the decision would in no way affect the trust. When a reporter showed up on Samuel Dodd's doorstep, the Standard counsel was a model of urbanity: "The [trust] agreements were not really necessary," he said. "They were simply made as a matter of conscience. The only effect of the decision will be to inconvenience us a little."[5]

This insouciance was only partly studied. In responding to legal challenges, the combine had reconstituted itself many times, like some mythical, protean creature that could metamorphose into infinite shapes to elude lawmakers. For several years, Dodd and Rockefeller had studied possible responses in case the trust had to be dissolved in an antitrust suit. They had taken note of an 1889 New Jersey law that permitted corporations resident in the state to hold stock in other corporations. This revolutionary development opened the possibility of forming holding companies that could operate nationwide and provided a critical escape hatch for embattled trusts. As a result, Standard Oil calmly greeted the 1892 Ohio decision less as a mortal threat than an opportunity for a long-overdue reorganization.

For several days, Standard executives tried to figure out how best to comply with the ruling. Their minds were focused by the knowledge that if they didn't act, the New York attorney general was poised to file antitrust papers. On March 10, 1892, one week after the Ohio decision, Samuel Dodd announced that the trust would be dissolved. The next day, a mailing went out to all holders of Standard Oil trust certificates, summoning them to a March 21 meeting and inviting them to exchange their certificates for proportionate shares of twenty constituent companies. The distribution of power, money, and dividends within the Standard Oil empire would remain exactly the same, a deft maneuver that would be copied by other corporations harried by antitrust laws.

As the holder of 256,854 of 972,500 outstanding shares of the Standard Oil trust, John D. Rockefeller chaired the March 21 meeting. Even though 300 people were jammed into a room designed to hold only 200, the stage-managed event was brief and businesslike; the unanimous vote to dissolve the trust was a foregone conclusion. Though designated one of eight liquidating trustees, Rockefeller had just recuperated from the breakdown in his health and wanted to transfer the burden of reorganization to his colleagues. He was spared a terrible ordeal, since the liquidation proved highly contentious. Small shareholders balked at trading in trust certificates for fractional shares that paid no dividends and could not be redeemed in any secondary market. In the eyes of Standard's detractors, the exchange dragged on for a suspiciously long time.

Aided by changes in New Jersey's incorporation law, Standard Oil of New Jersey took on a unique status in the transformed company. Renamed Standard Oil (New Jersey), it bought in whole or in part huge blocks of stock in the other Standard companies and thus legally held stock in properties from coast to coast, functioning as both an operating and holding company. Standard of New York also attained new status in a reorganization that initiated the seven-year period of the so-called Standard Oil Interests.

The 1892 overhaul was mostly shadow play, a charade to appease the courts. The executive committee at 26 Broadway was formally dissolved, but the members lost only their titles and were soon converted, by the nicest legal cunning, into the presidents of twenty affiliated companies. In Standard parlance, these men were now the "gentlemen upstairs" or the "gentlemen in Room 1400." Nobody had to switch seats at the lunch table, and Rockefeller and his coterie ruled as absolutely as before. Seventeen individual stockholders—almost all Standard Oil executives or family members—controlled a majority of stock in the twenty companies and elected their directors. This legal legerdemain again frustrated lawmakers who felt that the combine was so vast, slippery, and elusive that it could never be tamed or held accountable.

Standard Oil executives saw the major threat to the company in 1892 as the aging of their leadership. The organization was still piloted by the same sturdy souls who had steered it since the 1870s and were now beginning to die off or retire. The alarm bells must have sounded when Rockefeller sought retirement, a decision postponed temporarily by the economic crisis of 1893. The panic showed him functioning less as a Standard Oil executive than as a sovereign power, endowed with resources rivaling those of government. He continued, however, to operate in the shadows, a spectral figure whose presence was mostly felt, not seen.

=

The depression heralded by the June 1893 stock-market crash was one of such excruciating length, such grinding and unrelieved misery, that economic historians labeled it the Great Depression until that title was usurped in the 1930s. During the troubled summer of 1893, the Erie and Northern Pacific railroads failed, followed by many others bloated with debt and riddled with fraud. Mass unemployment across the nation sharpened class tensions. During the sanguinary clash a year earlier at the Homestead, Pennsylvania, steel mill, Henry Clay Frick had ordered Pinkerton detectives to fire at workers—a step that drew a rousing congratulatory telegram from John D. Such corporate truculence provoked calls by the new Populist Party for a graduated income tax, government ownership of railroad and telegraph companies, and tougher safeguards for trade unions. Rockefeller stood high on the list of bogeymen regularly berated by Populists, and legend has it that he began to sleep with a revolver by his bed. As the country grew more polarized, many people wondered whether America had paid too dear a price for the industrialization that had so quickly propelled it from an agrarian society to a world economic power.

By early 1894, the slump had toppled six hundred shaky banks, and an almost palpable threat of insurrection hovered in the air, prompting financial writer Alexander Dana Noyes to observe that "there were periods when industrial unrest seemed to assume the proportions of anarchy."[6] In the spring of 1894, General Jacob Coxey of Ohio led his bedraggled Army of the Commonwealth of Christ in a doomed march on Washington to entreat Congress for legislative relief. Two months later, workers at the Pullman Palace Car Company struck to reverse massive layoffs and wage cuts, triggering a sympathy strike by the American Railway Union under Eugene V. Debs. When President Cleveland sent troops to Chicago, Debs was jailed, and seven strikers were gunned down. All the pent-up frustrations produced by the accelerated change of the late nineteenth century were vented in spontaneous, often violent dissent.

To the dismay of critics, Standard Oil and other trusts fared quite well during the prolonged downturn. Demand for illuminating oil and lubricants—now necessities of life—remained healthy, leading Standard Oil to prosper amid the general austerity. Meanwhile, a new source of future profits beckoned in the middle distance. In the early 1880s, Gottlieb Daimler strapped light gasoline engines onto bicycles, tricycles, and other vehicles, experiments that culminated in the motorcar, while another German inventor, Karl Benz, patented a three-wheeled automobile with a single-cylinder engine in 1886. In 1892, the Duryea brothers were tinkering with their first automobile. Recognizing a fantastic market in the offing, Standard Oil sent a representative to attend the test of a new gasoline engine for a streetcar motor. The next year, Henry Ford tested a two-cylinder auto that sped along at thirty miles an hour, resuscitating fears that existing oil supplies might fall short of needs—an anxiety somewhat assuaged by oil discoveries in Los Angeles and elsewhere in California in the 1890s. So remarkable was this West Coast boom that it soon furnished more oil than the old Pennsylvania and Ohio fields that had formed the basis of Rockefeller's wealth. The advent of the automobile was a godsend for Standard Oil, for the more lightbulbs shone across America, the more kerosene was relegated to remote rural areas without access to electric power.

Standard Oil again benefited from hard times to extend its powerful reach. For several years, the trust had watched the exploits of Pittsburgh's Mellon family with apprehension, and Archbold was under strict orders from Rockefeller to grab any of their oil properties that came on the market. As the Mellons emerged as a worrisome threat in the export market, Rockefeller feared they might strike an alliance with the French Rothschilds. In August 1895, having borrowed heavily against Pittsburgh real estate to build their budding oil empire, the Mellons were forced to sell their Crescent Pipe Line Company and other properties to Standard—a huge windfall that yielded 14,000 acres and 135 producing wells. It now seemed that Standard Oil owned the entire industry, lock, stock, and barrel. When the Geodetic Association announced plans to measure the earth, the *World* opined that the information would "enable the Standard Oil Trust and other trusts to learn the exact size of their property."[7]

Soon thereafter, to everyone's amazement, the independents, after so many hapless drubbings, rallied one last time and made a successful run at the trust. Through a new company, the Producers' and Refiners' Oil Company, a thousand well owners agreed to supply crude oil to fifteen independent refineries, linked by a new network of local pipelines. In the fall of 1892, that perennial Standard scourge, Lewis Emery, Jr., had organized United States Pipe Line, which now promised to give the rebels a vital pipeline to the seaboard. To lay the pipe, Emery's men had to ward off savage harassment from the railroads; locomotives would roar by and douse them with scalding steam, boiling water, and glowing coals. Despite these obstructive tactics, independent oil began to flow in 1893. Shifting tactics, the trust then engineered a steep decline in kerosene prices—no mean trick in a period of rising crude prices. Squeezed by dwindling profit margins, three large independent refineries finally submitted to the trust's suzerainty, but the Producers' and Refiners' Oil Company miraculously survived. In 1895, emboldened by a new sense of Rockefeller's vulnerability, thirty independent refiners coalesced into the Pure Oil Company—the first enduring domestic competitor of Standard Oil. To preserve their autonomy, they sequestered half their voting stock in the hands of five men eternally sworn to keep it free of Standard influence. Thus, several years before federal trustbusters mobilized to smash the Rockefeller monopoly, serious competition had already taken root in the marketplace.

=

Despite this setback, Rockefeller was not hurting in the 1890s. There was now a self-perpetuating quality to his wealth. Whether he was gardening, eating, or just lying in bed, his prolific savings quietly grew around the clock. He was receiving about $3 million yearly in Standard Oil dividends (more than $50 million in 1996 dollars) and redirecting that into a vast portfolio of outside investments that made him a one-man holding company. With $24 million now invested outside the oil and gas business, he held sizable stakes in 16 railroad companies, 9 real-estate firms, 6 steel companies, 6 steamship companies, 9 banks and financial houses, and even 2 orange groves.

The oil trust's resilience during the depression of the 1890s, its tested immunity from market fluctuations, cheered Rockefeller, who attributed this to Standard's large cash reserves and conservative dividend policy. The panic seemed to offer irrefutable proof to Rockefeller that cooperation was superior to the vagaries of cutthroat competition. It certainly allowed him the luxury of a benevolent paternalism at a time of labor strife in other industries. "We held things together so steady that our fortunate laboring men got their pay, though in other concerns many of them were compelled to go, and without bread," he later told William O. Inglis. "It was a matter of congratulation with us that we could look into the happy faces of our workmen in these perilous times and hand them the wages they had earned."[8]

Since the early 1880s, Standard Oil had been self-financing, very liquid at all times, and free from the thrall of Wall Street bankers. As a result, no other industrial corporation was so fearless or independent. It was one of Rockefeller's proudest boasts that unlike other trusts, he had not needed a J. P. Morgan to forge his combine. Standard Oil anticipated a major feature of the twentieth-century economy: the tendency of sophisticated, cash-rich corporations to outgrow their traditional bankers and become financial-service giants in their own rights. As journalist John Moody perceptively wrote, "The Standard Oil

Trust was really a bank of the most gigantic character—a bank within an industry, financing this industry against all competition and continually lending vast sums of money to needy borrowers on high class collateral, just as the other great banks were doing."[9]

It was Standard Oil of New York that functioned as the main banker for the affiliated companies, governing what was arguably the most stupendous cash flow ever produced in American industry. To maximize its leverage over Wall Street, it scattered its gigantic balances among many banks; a single Standard Oil entity, the National Transit Company, sometimes kept as much as $40 million on deposit. Standard Oil of New York also made large loans to banks, brokerage houses, railroads, and steel companies. So rich in cash, Standard Oil wielded a make-or-break power over Wall Street houses, which defied it at their peril. Standard directors often took out prodigious loans from the trust. On the eve of the 1893 panic, John D. had a $1.36 million loan outstanding while brother William owed $865,000.

As president of New York Standard, William Rockefeller parlayed his position into one of exceptional prominence on Wall Street. For John, the street might be a sinful haunt, but it had its own sulfurous charms for William. In 1884, while they both served as directors of the Chicago, Milwaukee, and St. Paul Railroad, William had met James Stillman, the youngest director of National City Bank. In an inspired move, Stillman recruited William as a director. By the time Stillman became the bank's president in 1891, National City had been so enriched by the Standard Oil bounty that it was nicknamed the Oil Bank.

When the 1893 panic struck, John D. was just emerging from the seclusion occasioned by his medical problems. He raced back to New York from Cleveland to orchestrate a massive salvage operation. In the course of the panic, he provided almost $6 million to fifty-eight individuals and firms who were turned down by banks and desperately needed his intervention. To bail out these borrowers, Rockefeller had to borrow almost $4 million, and nearly $3 million of that came from Standard of New York. This was a tricky balancing act, since he was borrowing on the collateral of securities then collapsing in value. In October 1893, the Standard Oil treasurer, William T. Wardwell, having decided that Rockefeller had reached the permissible limit, did the unthinkable: He shut down the lending window on the company founder. A stupefied George Rogers relayed this verdict to his boss: "He has refused to give me any more money, because he had no assurance of getting it back when he wanted."[10] After frantic negotiations, Wardwell boosted Rockefeller's credit line to $2.8 million in exchange for a lien on his quarterly dividend of $775,000 from Standard Oil stock. Some of Rockefeller's letters reflect tragicomic confusion as he struggled to collect loans from debtors in order to pay off his own debt to Standard Oil. In early September, he wrote to Cettie from New York that he had settled his debts, with $550,000 to spare. "We are steadily emerging from the panic, but I hope never to go through with another such experience."[11]

When it came to old friends, his generosity could be dazzling. When Captain Vandergrift telegraphed from Pittsburgh that a trust company he directed stood in mortal peril, Rockefeller telegraphed promptly, "How much do you want?" "One million dollars," came the response to which Rockefeller replied, "Check for one million is on the way."[12] But he was so inundated with pleas that many more people were spurned than saved, generating unavoidable bitterness. Frederick T. Gates referred to these painful quandaries in an October 1893 letter: "I have today on my desk urgent imperative appeals to save old friends [of Mr. Rockefeller's] amounting to many hundreds of thousands of dollars. I have incurred the enmity of many important business enterprises because I have had to decline to assist them in the last few days."[13] More than one person who was refused later accused Rockefeller of having ruined him.

During the panic, Rockefeller awakened to the public responsibilities attending great wealth. Having long been reflexively hostile to government, he now found himself cooperating with Washington to calm the jitters in financial markets. In 1894, the U.S. Treasury, alarmed by the outflow of gold that legally backed the gold standard, turned to J. P. Morgan for a rescue operation. After telling John G. Carlisle, the Treasury secretary, that this was impossible, Morgan conferred hastily with Stillman—a measure of Stillman's new stature on Wall Street. "He was greatly upset and overcharged," recalled Stillman, "nearly wept, put his head in his hands and cried: 'They expect the impossible!' So I calmed him down and told him to give me an hour and by that time I cabled for ten millions from Europe for the Standard Oil and ten more from other resources." When Stillman walked into Morgan's office to report the $20 million, Morgan grew giddy and triumphant. "He took the pose of savior of his country and assumed all the credit," Stillman observed archly, crediting the real success to himself and Standard Oil. "But then you see, he is a poet; Morgan is a poet."[14] Rockefeller never claimed credit for his action and preferred no publicity.

Stillman's behavior during the panic had a deleterious effect on his relationship with Rockefeller, who had given him $5 million amid multiple demands. Rockefeller believed that the crafty Stillman had not only held his money longer than necessary but employed it to buy stocks at bargain prices instead of using it to shore up his bank. Under any circumstance, Rockefeller would have been critical of an alliance between Standard Oil and a Wall Street bank, but after the 1893 panic his disenchantment with Stillman gave him extra misgivings about William's policy of placing large balances in his bank. One of Rockefeller's financial advisers, Henry E. Cooper, indignantly told him, "You ought to get after him hard!" "No, Mr. Cooper, we will do nothing," said Rockefeller evenly. "But we shall not forget it!"[15]

In November 1887, as he listened to Rockefeller testify before the new Interstate Commerce Commission, Henry Demarest Lloyd saw the witness as the prince of darkness, evil incarnate. Afterward, he furiously scribbled notes that he headed "Fanatic Standard Oil," and had this to say about Rockefeller:

> He is . . . a depredator . . . not a worshipper of liberty . . . a Czar of plutocracy, a worshipper of his own Money Power over mankind. He will never sacrifice any of his plans for the restraints of law or patriotism or philanthropy. . . . His greed, rapacity, flow as a Universal solvent wherever they can, melting down into gold for him, private enterprise, public morals, judicial honor, legislative faith, gifts of nature. He will stop when he is stopped—not before. Not a tiger but a lynx . . . a make-up like that of the "gentleman pirate" of romance, think cold ruthless.[16]

Convinced that Standard Oil was the archetypal trust, Lloyd embarked on a book-length study two years later, and by the time *Wealth Against Commonwealth* appeared in 1894, he was sure that the public was ripe for his revelations. As he wrote on the eve of publication, "the sky seems full of signs that the time for the appearance of such information has come."[17]

Known as "the Millionaire Socialist," the natty Lloyd had longish hair, wire-rimmed spectacles, and a flowing mustache, which gave him a vaguely artistic air. Among his friends he included Clarence Darrow, Jane Addams, Eugene Debs, and Booker T. Washington. He was toasted by many literary figures, and Robert Louis Stevenson called him a "very capable, clever fellow," asserting that "he writes the most workmanlike article of any man known to me in America."[18] A foppish reformer, Lloyd attended trade-union meetings wearing pince-nez on a gold chain, a gray top hat, and glossily polished boots. When he supported anarchists blamed for the Haymarket Square riot in Chicago in 1886, his outraged father-in-law, a co-owner of the *Chicago Tribune*, disinherited him and placed his estate in trust for Lloyd's children. To maintain his existence as a dapper millionaire and literary troubadour for radical causes, Lloyd relied on his wife's income.

Lloyd's politics became more radical over time. With a messianic outlook, he had promiscuous sympathy for every crusade. Starting out as a free-market liberal, he then turned to socialism, trade unions, worker cooperatives, and utopian communities. He once referred to himself as "a socialist-anarchist-communist-individualist-collectivist-cooperative-aristocratic-democrat"—and that was just for starters.[19] Scarcely a cause in the Progressive panoply—from attacking tariffs to favoring municipal ownership of utilities to combating sweatshops—escaped his wide-ranging vision. Like Karl Marx, he believed in the inevitable collapse of capitalism, which he thought corrupt and predatory. Also like

Marx, he imagined that competition led to monopoly—a welcome step since it was "a necessary and indubitable step toward national and international cooperation."[20]

Lloyd returned to Standard Oil—the subject of his 1881 story in the *Atlantic Monthly*—for several reasons. Dismayed by the failure of the Sherman law to curb monopolies, he ridiculed it as "The Anti-Trades Union Law," a mere ruse perpetrated by "a world-wide concert of action of a money power, crazy with greed, and fanatical to the hilt, to re-enslave the working people."[21] He could also now draw upon a wide body of material churned up by government investigations against Standard Oil. Drawing on a small army of Rockefeller haters, including George Rice, Lewis Emery, and Roger Sherman, he gathered court records and trial transcripts, which he stuffed into pigeonholes at his home in Winnetka, outside Chicago. When one acquaintance visited him there, Lloyd told him, "I will prove that John D. Rockefeller is the most selfish usurper that ever lived."[22] With Dostoyevskian passion, he filled notebooks with flaming diatribes against the American plutocracy, describing the Rockefellers and Vanderbilts as members of a "cruel, selfish, carnivorous, short-sighted herd."[23] The lists of sensational titles he compiled for his Standard Oil book—including *Slime in Genesis, Fountains of Pitch,* and *Barbarians of Business*—said as much about his overheated imagination as they did about the trust.[24] In fact, Lloyd spouted so much fustian that it made it easy for businessmen to dismiss him despite his often accurate insights.

Wealth Against Commonwealth had no kind words to spare for Standard Oil. Lloyd marshaled every wispy allegation made against the trust and printed it as gospel truth. Where Ida Tarbell later portrayed Rockefeller and his cohorts as superb if immoral businessmen, Lloyd presented them as brazen criminals who owed everything to diabolical deeds. Later on, speaking privately of the "criminal character" of the Standard Oil executives, he insisted that they "ought to be in the penitentiary."[25] Like his *Atlantic Monthly* piece, his book was chockablock with errors and egregious misrepresentations—for instance, he described the Rothschilds as Standard Oil's agents abroad. Accusing Rockefeller of rigging artificial shortages to drive up kerosene prices, Lloyd failed to see that the trust maintained its dominance by keeping prices low and selectively engaging in predatory pricing. He ennobled any businessman, however greedy or inept, who opposed Rockefeller.

Yet for all its weaknesses, the book had a profound and lasting impact and ranks as a classic of muckraking literature. Lloyd was a superb stylist whose mellifluous prose captivated readers. Every paragraph was a call to arms.[26] Whatever the holes in his argument, he gave a clear, intelligent shape to a complex story, especially when it came to the importance of railroad rebates in the rise of Standard Oil. When he argued that the South Improvement Company never died but became Rockefeller's master blueprint, he laid down a line of argument followed by Ida Tarbell. What also gave the book its force was Lloyd's political message: "Liberty produces wealth, and wealth destroys liberty."[27] As the trusts' power rippled through society, he said, it corrupted every corner of American life. The noble experiment of American democracy was being undermined by businessmen who had grown more powerful than the state and controlled its elected representatives. "Our system, so fair in its theory and so fertile in its happiness and prosperity in its first century, is now, following the fate of systems, becoming artificial, technical, corrupt."[28]

In *Wealth Against Commonwealth*, Lloyd omitted all names, even though Rockefeller, Flagler, and others were all too recognizable. Standard Oil was never mentioned and was usually referred to as the "oil combination" or some other euphemism. This technique protected Lloyd from libel prosecution, though he fell back upon a highfalutin explanation for it. "It seems of the highest importance that the book should retain its character of an *illustration* of the motives and results of our commercial civilization, not an attack on a particular corporation or body of men."[29]

Lloyd's manuscript found a publisher with difficulty. Mark Twain, who then had his own publishing venture, turned it down in deference to his close friendship with Henry H. Rogers. As Twain told his wife, "I wanted to say [to Lloyd] the only man I care for in the world; the only man I would give a *damn* for; the only man who is lavishing his sweat and blood to save me & mine from starvation and shame, is a Standard Oil fiend . . . but I didn't say that. I said I didn't want *any* book; I wanted to get out of the publishing business."[30] Luckily for Lloyd, he won the passionate sponsorship of another literary luminary, his former *Atlantic Monthly* editor, William Dean Howells, who was bowled over by his indictment of Rockefeller. "I think that the monstrous iniquity whose story you tell so powerfully, accomplished itself in our time, is so astounding, so infuriating, that I have to stop from chapter to chapter, and take breath."[31] Howells steered Lloyd to Harper and Brothers, who agreed to issue the book if the author substantially condensed it, paid for publication, and guaranteed a sale of fifteen hundred copies—a deal only a rich radical could afford.

Published in 1894, the book passed through four printings within a year and sold a respectable eight thousand copies in its first decade. Some sour notes were heard amid the praise. The *Nation* began its scathing review by saying, "This book is a notable example of the rhetorical blunder of overstatement," and it branded the book "five hundred pages of the wildest rant."[32] Yet the work was praised widely by many reformers, including Louis Brandeis, and Edward Everett Hale called it the most important American book since *Uncle Tom's Cabin*. Since Lloyd distributed free copies to politicians, it became the bible of Washington trustbusters.

With his penchant for melodrama, Lloyd claimed he had been tailed by Standard Oil detectives and told friends that he "expected to be *crushed* by the Standard people." He seemed half disappointed when 26 Broadway reacted to his book with stern silence. Although colleagues informed him of the book's accusations, Rockefeller did not read it and said Standard Oil "paid no more attention to all this nonsense than an elephant might be expected to pay to a tiny mosquito."[33] Rockefeller now declined almost weekly requests to sit for magazine profiles, including one from a new magazine being launched by Samuel S. McClure, who was then in Paris trying to sign up an obscure young writer from Pennsylvania, Ida Minerva Tarbell.

Even after the publication of *Wealth Against Commonwealth*, Lloyd regaled friends with scurrilous gossip about Rockefeller, telling one correspondent, with cynical relish, that the mogul had recently gone abroad, ostensibly to recuperate from the strain of his charities. Sure that Rockefeller had left the country to divide up global oil markets with the Russians, Lloyd guffawed at reports that Rockefeller's health had broken down under the crushing weight of his beneficence. "The wonder is that he expects people to believe that sort of thing, and that they do believe it!" Lloyd told a friend.[34] The irony, of course, is that Rockefeller spoke the unvarnished truth. Lloyd was always as blind to Rockefeller's virtues as he was sensitive to his glaring vices.

By 1895, Rockefeller, age fifty-six, had begun to fade by imperceptible degrees into retirement. That year, he sat for a haunting portrait by Eastman Johnson that was commissioned by the board of the University of Chicago and that shows him toward the close of his business career. Set against a dark backdrop, the titan sits on a simple wooden chair, fixing the viewer with a fiery stare. His long, tapered fingers are delicately interlaced and his legs urbanely crossed, but there is a blazing intensity, an inextinguishable fire, in his eyes. Rockefeller still looks powerful and surprisingly youthful, but there is a sadness about him, as if he were stooped under a great weight and enveloped in unfathomable gloom.

Since he dated his retirement as early as 1894 and as late as 1897, there is some uncertainty as to when Rockefeller officially left 26 Broadway, but 1895 and 1896 are the likely watershed years. Though he was still suffering from sporadic digestive problems and nervous strain, the 1893 panic had forced him to postpone his departure several times. In explaining his retirement, the Rockefeller literature has always stressed his health and the heavy burden of his charities, though another factor contributed as well: He had perfected the gleaming machinery of Standard Oil, and, his appointed task done, he felt he should pass the reins to younger men. As Gates put it, the business "had ceased to amuse him, it lacked freshness and variety and had become merely irksome and he withdrew."[35] By 1896, Rockefeller was skipping the daily lunch meetings at 26 Broadway and only occasionally exchanged memos with other executives. By June 4, 1896, he had already relinquished most of his duties, for he ended a letter to Archbold, "I shall be very pleased at any time to hear anything new that is important in the business, if it will not trouble you too much, or if you will kindly call Mr. Rogers."[36]

In September 1897, Rockefeller suffered another medical setback, apparently related to circulatory problems, and his doctors insisted that he promptly transfer more day-to-day decisions to his representatives. "I do not call myself sick," Rockefeller commented to one relative, "but this little warning I will promptly heed, as health is of the first importance."[37] So in 1897—the year his son graduated from Brown—Rockefeller walked away from the empire that had consumed his energies for more than thirty years, and during the next fifteen years he scarcely appeared at 26 Broadway. He was succeeded by John D. Archbold, his jovial, pugnacious protégé, who gave a more defiant and combative tone to the trust in its duels with government investigators, committing a public-relations blunder of no small magnitude.

In a grave misstep, Rockefeller never publicly announced his retirement and retained the titular presidency of Standard Oil of New Jersey. As a result, he remained an inviting target for critics and was personally held liable for many of the questionable judgments made by Archbold, who was nominally vice president of New Jersey Standard.

In our age of an assertive business press, when corporate secrets are readily ferreted out by reporters, it is scarcely conceivable that the world's richest man, running the world's largest business, could have drifted away from business without public knowledge. Yet much of the press—to Rockefeller's later chagrin—swallowed the cover story whole. While some reporters knew that he no longer reported to work, they doubted that he had really surrendered supervisory power. The misconception was understandable. He owned nearly 30 percent of Standard Oil stock—far more than anyone else—and did not hesitate to proffer advice as the urge seized him. Small groups of company lawyers and executives periodically briefed him, and Archbold made regular weekend pilgrimages to consult him at his Westchester estate. As trustbusters took dead aim at the company, Rockefeller was driven to develop a common defense with current executives, pulling him back into the past even as he tried to move on to new pursuits.

Rockefeller entered retirement just at the birth of the American automobile industry. As he noted, "When I retired from business . . . we had just begun to hope that some day [autos] would be practical."[38] That year, Frank and Charles Duryea produced thirteen two-cylinder runabouts in Springfield, Massachusetts—the first time a car company had produced several cars from a standardized model—and Henry Ford put the finishing touches to the quadricycle, his first horseless carriage. The automobile would make John D. Rockefeller far richer in retirement than at work. When he stepped down from

Standard Oil, he was probably worth about $200 million—$3.5 billion today—whereas, thanks to the internal-combustion engine, his fortune soared to $1 billion by 1913—surely history's most lucrative retirement, and one that must have softened the sting of press vituperation.

=

In 1897, Joseph Pulitzer's *World* showcased John D. Rockefeller and Henry M. Flagler as two of the five chief overlords of the Standard Oil trust, yet Flagler had now ranged even farther afield than Rockefeller. A man with many cronies but few close friends, Rockefeller reserved warm praise for Flagler. "You and I have been associated in business upwards of thirty-five years," Rockefeller wrote to him in 1902, "and while there have been times when we have not agreed on questions of policy I do not know that one unkind word has ever passed or unkind thought existed between us. . . . I feel that my pecuniary success is due to my association with you, if I have contributed anything to yours I am thankful."[39] Flagler repaid the compliment, telling one Baptist preacher that "if he would spend the remainder of his life in praising Mr. Rockefeller he could not say too much nor more than was actually deserved."[40]

But these high-flown, touching tributes masked a certain *froideur* that had crept into their relationship as they neared retirement. Although Rockefeller never said so outright, one senses that he thought Flagler had become a slave to fashion and ostentation, a traitor to the austere puritanical creed that had united them. Though his hair and mustache were now dusted with gray, Flagler had a lean, handsome face and was highly susceptible to female charm. He had suffered many personal misfortunes in marriage and exercised woefully bad judgment. His consumptive first wife, Mary, had become a professional invalid. When doctors recommended an extended winter stay for her in 1878, Henry joined her in Florida, but, itching to get back to Standard Oil, he bolted for New York after a few weeks. Unwilling to stay alone, Mary followed him back instead of taking time to recuperate properly. When she died in May 1881, Henry felt profoundly guilty. At that point, he took stock of his life and decided he had sacrificed too much to business, telling one reporter, "I have been giving all my days to the Lord hitherto, and now I'm taking one for myself."[41] During the winter of 1882–1883, he was hospitalized with a liver ailment and began to pore over newspaper articles about Florida land deals. In 1883, at age fifty-three, Flagler married Ida Alice Shourds, thirty-five, a former actress who had nursed Mary during her illness. A short woman with red hair, electric blue eyes, and an incendiary temper, Ida Alice seemed determined to run through Flagler's money, gathering an expensive wardrobe and trying to buy her way into New York high society.

Whatever his reservations about the match, Rockefeller visited Henry and Ida Alice on their honeymoon in Saint Augustine, Florida, during the winter of

1883–1884. No less prophetic in his business hunches than at Standard Oil, Flagler had faith that Florida would someday be converted from a pestilential, mosquito-ridden jungle into a place of wonder, recreation, and exotic beauty. The next winter, when the Rockefellers and Flaglers again traveled to Saint Augustine, Henry bought several acres of orange grove as the site for the future Ponce de Leon Hotel. To cater to a less-affluent clientele, he added the Alcazar Hotel across the street, its façade patterned after the Alcazar Palace of Seville. As the resident railroad expert of Standard Oil, Flagler saw that Florida's development had been retarded by inadequate transport, and in the late 1880s he bought two railroads that opened for settlement a coastal stretch around Ormond and Daytona beaches. Buying a large hotel on the Halifax River, he remodeled it, grafted on an eighteen-hole golf course, and renamed it the Ormond Beach Hotel. Years later, John D. Rockefeller's winter home, The Casements, stood directly across the street.

Driven by his faith in Florida's future, Flagler merged his railroads in 1892 and conceived a master plan for a railroad that would snake down the length of Florida's Atlantic coast to Key West, with Flagler resorts dotting the route—a vision he realized in 1912. Each time Flagler pushed the railway farther south, it opened more swamp to development, triggering another land boom.

As always when infected with development fever, Flagler ran up bills that taxed even his massive fortune. In 1890, he sold 2,500 shares of Standard Oil stock to Rockefeller for $375,000 and made further stock sales to him for several years—right on the verge of the auto boom that would send those shares soaring. Rockefeller followed Flagler's business adventures in Florida with sympathy but at a distance. "Henry did a great job in Florida," he said. "Think of pouring out all that money on a whim. But then Henry was always bold."[42] Yet he turned a deaf ear to his friend's repeated entreaties to visit again. "I believe this country would be a revelation to you, if you would take a week to look into it," Flagler pleaded with him in 1889.[43] Yet Rockefeller still stayed away from the state after his 1884–1885 visit. "It is marvelous what Mr. Flagler has wrought in that southern country," Rockefeller told William Rainey Harper in 1898, "and I regret not to have paid him a visit long ago."[44]

Why this sudden distance in so singular a friendship? When they did see each other, Rockefeller and Flagler were always nostalgic, yet they seldom contrived to meet. One suspects that John and Cettie were scandalized by the showy airs and sybaritic indulgence of Ida Alice Flagler. Bowing to his second wife, Henry had bought a private railroad car and a 160-foot yacht (both tellingly named the *Alicia*), and the Flaglers behaved more and more like the gaudy arrivistes the Rockefellers abhorred. Then Ida Alice began to show incipient signs of the mental illness that overtook her in later years. Out of the blue she began to chatter about her husband's adultery—a real enough situation, but one magnified in Ida Alice's fevered mind. In 1891, Henry became infatuated with Mary Lily Kenan, a beautiful, gifted twenty-four-year-old from a prominent North Carolina family who offered him respite from his moody, unstable wife, and Ida Alice became pathologically obsessed with this relationship.

During the summer of 1893, Ida Alice's manic behavior worsened when she obtained a Ouija board. Closeted in her room, she spent hours communing with astral spirits, convinced the czar of Russia had fallen madly in love with her. When she threatened to kill Flagler in October 1895 and accused him of trying to poison her, she was committed to a sanatorium in Pleasantville, New York. In the spring of 1896, after the doctors declared Ida Alice cured, she returned to live with Henry at their large estate, Satan's Toe, in Mamaroneck, New York. For a few happy weeks, they rode bikes together and read aloud to each other, suggesting a tenuous return to happier times. Then Ida Alice bribed a servant to smuggle in a Ouija board and promptly succumbed to old demons. Once back at the board, she relapsed into her paranoid dreamworld. When she flew at one doctor, wielding a pair of scissors, she was returned to the Pleasantville sanatorium in March 1897. There she renamed herself Princess Ida Alice von Schotten Tech and never saw Henry again.

After the courts ruled Ida Alice Flagler insane in 1899, Henry set up a trust fund for her, stocked with $2 million in Standard Oil shares, which would appreciate to more than $15 million by her death in July 1930. Henry, meanwhile, was in a bind: New York state law would not permit divorce on grounds other than adultery, and he could not prove adultery against a woman confined to an asylum. Never deterred by restrictive laws, Flagler switched his legal residence to Florida and applied his influence with state legislators. On April 9, 1901, a special law was enacted permitting divorce on grounds of incurable insanity—a law known as the Flagler divorce law. Within two weeks, Flagler married Mary Lily Kenan. The wedding was performed in high style, Flagler bringing friends down from New York in a private railroad car, but Rockefeller did not attend. He must have felt Flagler was making a spectacle of himself, especially when he was named correspondent in a divorce suit in Syracuse, New York, one month after his marriage. That the Rockefellers had drifted away from Flagler is suggested by a note Cettie wrote her son in August 1900. "We have the announcement of Mr. Flagler's marriage to a Miss Kenan, of N. Carolina. She is thirty-six, he, seventy-two."[45] Cettie expresses no pleasure at the marriage, but only cites, with implicit disapproval, the difference in age. Mary Kenan was actually thirty-three at the time.

CHAPTER 19

The Dauphin

hen he entered college in 1893, John D. Rockefeller, Jr., seemed like the prototype of the poor little rich boy, stuck with an overdeveloped conscience and the badge of being the son of one of the world's wealthiest men. Having had a rather solitary childhood in mansions and on estates, he did not have the social ease of other young men of his age and class. Desperately eager to please his parents, he had exhausted himself in trying to scrub sin from his soul.

Much like his father, Junior couldn't make decisions lightly and fretted over his choice of a college. Set to go to Yale, he passed its preliminary entrance exam and had even selected a room when reports reached him from one minister that a fast set dominated the Yale social scene. Others might have found this decidedly in Yale's favor, but Junior decided to look elsewhere and finally selected Brown because three close friends had chosen to attend it. As he told Dr. William Rainey Harper, whom he consulted, in a tone of excruciating humility, about the choice of schools, "Being naturally somewhat retiring (I beg you to pardon personal references), I do not make friends readily, and some of those interested in my welfare fear if I go to Yale in a class wholly strange to me, I will be 'lost in the crowd' so to speak and remain much by myself, instead of getting the social contact I so greatly need."[1] Junior tended to discuss himself clinically, as if he were a laboratory specimen wriggling under glass, his parents, especially his mother, having taught him to probe his behavior with such antiseptic detachment.

Junior entered Brown in September 1893, just as the industrial slump worsened, and his college years unfolded against a turbulent backdrop of radical rhetoric and labor unrest, much of it directed against his father. Founded in the eighteenth century, Brown was the oldest and best-endowed Baptist college, and its president, E. Benjamin Andrews, was a Baptist clergyman–cum–political economist. In those days, college presidents were often ordained ministers who had a profound impact on the student body in classroom and chapel alike. During the Civil War, Andrews had lost an eye in the Petersburg siege, and his glass eye endowed him with a visionary gaze. Junior admired his spiritual zeal and keen intelligence and was especially struck one day when Andrews told him, "Rockefeller, never be afraid to stand up for a position when you know you are right."[2]

Six months before Junior arrived at Brown, Andrews had composed a flattering letter to Henry Demarest Lloyd about *Wealth Against Commonwealth*. "It is decidedly in my line," he assured him, "although you are more radical than I am at some points."[3] Not averse to trusts, Andrews wanted to regulate them for the public good and distribute their benefits more equitably. When Junior took a course with him in practical ethics, Andrews gave him a finer appreciation for employer responsibility in big business. In one undergraduate essay, Junior already evinced the proclivity for corporate reform that would mark his adult life: "Who can look about upon the millions of laborers whose life is a treadmill, a continuous round of work to which they are driven by dire necessity . . . without being fired with a desire to revolutionize their condition by adopting the profit-sharing system?"[4] However idolized by students, Andrews was roundly condemned by many alumni when he supported William Jennings Bryan's presidential bid in 1896 and endorsed free coinage of silver, an episode that cost him his job. Henry Demarest Lloyd spied Rockefeller's fine hand in the ouster, telling a friend, "One of the reasons which actuated the trustees in crowding [Andrews] out was the statement that as long as he remained, Mr. Rockefeller would never give the university any money."[5]

The bashful young Rockefeller, quartered in Slater Hall, was much shorter than his father but broad chested and square shouldered. Both his mother and Grandma Spelman exhorted him to be vigilant against dormitory vice. In his first letter home, he reassured them by saying that he had already attended a prayer meeting, adding, "Grandmother will be interested to know that there are three colored men in the class."[6] He also had begun teaching a Sunday-school class at a Baptist church in Providence, and his relieved father wrote him that "the moral and religious tone seem of the best."[7] During his busy freshman year, Junior joined the glee club, the mandolin club, and a string quartet with some young ladies. As he ventured timidly beyond the self-contained world of his youth, he could not just enjoy spontaneous pleasure and had to justify it in terms of self-improvement. When he joined a college operetta, he wrote his mother, "Then too appearing on the platform before people as I would do and have done in the Glee Club gives me confidence in myself, and helps me to become easy in public which I always need."[8]

Abby Aldrich Rockefeller and John D. Rockefeller, Jr.,
around the time they were married.
(Courtesy of the Rockefeller Archive Center)

Doggedly earnest, tenacious in his studies, Junior was a good enough student to make Phi Beta Kappa, and he especially enjoyed economics and sociology. Unlike his father, however, his self-confidence was a fragile bloom, easily crushed. "If a person scolded me," he said, "I shut up like a clam. I wasn't much of a scholar, but I always tried hard and I didn't like to be reproached."[9] Everybody noticed his Baptist austerity: He did not drink, smoke, play cards, go to the theater, or even read Sunday papers. True to his temperance pledge, he plied students with crackers and hot chocolate when they came to his room, but he terribly upset Grandma Spelman when he let boys smoke there.

Junior's frugality was the stuff of campus legend, and everybody had a favorite anecdote: how he soaked apart two two-cent stamps that got stuck together or how he pressed his own trousers, sewed his own buttons, and mended his own dish towels. Following his father's example, he recorded every expense in his little book—sometimes to snickers from classmates—and even recorded bouquets of flowers bought for dates. Whether putting money in the plate at church or buying a pencil from a beggar, he jotted down everything to the last decimal. "He told me that his father allowed him all the money he wanted," said a friend, "but insisted on an exact account of every penny."[10] Another classmate recalled, "It used to be a great joke, particularly among the girls in Providence, and they used to laugh a good deal about being treated to a soda by John D. Rockefeller, Jr., and having him enter it into his book as he sat at the soda fountain."[11]

Despite his shy formality, Junior was generally popular at Brown or, at least, highly respected. Some students were bound to see him as a hopeless prig, and one day as he was crossing the campus, one heckled him, "Here comes Johnny Rock, reeking with virtue and without one redeeming vice!"[12] For the most part, however, he became more sociable and self-assured and slowly weaned himself from the airless morality of his upbringing. He was tolerant by nature, telling Grandma Spelman in one letter, "One sees all sorts and conditions of men here viewing life, duty, pleasure and the hereafter, so differently. My ideas and opinions change I find in many ways. I would stickle less for the letter of the law, now, more for the spirit."[13] Haltingly, he forged an identity separate from those of his forebears. He was more ecumenical, more open to the outside world, more considerate of alternate views. As president of his junior class, he got his classmates to desist from drinking alcohol at the class supper, which had traditionally been a drunken debauch. And when his class took its annual stag cruise to Newport, Junior agreed to keep kegs of beer on hand but tried to avert heavy indulgence. His parents were ecstatic. "Dear John," his mother wrote, "you have been our pride and comfort from the day of your birth but at no time have we been more grateful for such a son as at the present moment—Tears of joy filled dear father's eyes when your letter was read and he wants me to tell you how proud and happy it made him."[14]

At Brown, Junior learned to savor such illicit pleasures as theater and dancing, small triumphs for a Baptist boy bred with such unrelenting morality. After his sophomore year, he took a bicycle trip through England with Everett Colby, a classmate whose father was a railroad builder. (John D. had invested in his ventures.) In London, Junior saw his first plays: *The Two Gentlemen of Verona*, *Charley's Aunt*, and *A Midsummer Night's Dream*. As if admitting to a furtive visit to a brothel, he told his mother: "I shouldn't have done it at home on account of the example but thought it not harmful in London, where I knew no one and had an opportunity of seeing several of Shakespeare's plays."[15] Junior made it through his freshman year without dancing, then succumbed to this vice sophomore year by dancing all evening at a party thrown at the home of a university trustee. To practice for the event, he whirled his friend Lefferts Dashiell around his dormitory room. The whole evening, as he danced with a Miss Foster, he feared that he would crash to the floor. Holding on for dear life, he had the distinct impression that Miss Foster was propping him up. That evening, he met the vivacious Abby Aldrich, daughter of Rhode Island senator Nelson Aldrich, but could not muster the courage to dance with her. The love of dancing lasted, and by the time he graduated Junior indulged this sinful passion two or three times a week.

Cettie Rockefeller never entirely relaxed her militance about this pastime. During his senior year, Junior wanted to repay his classmates for their kindness to him and asked his parents to host a dance in Providence. Striking a compromise, John and Cettie agreed to have a musical evening of Mendelssohn, Bach, Chopin, and Liszt, followed by informal dancing. When they mailed out the invitations, the infernal word *dancing* appeared in small, almost apologetic lettering in the lower left-hand corner of the card. Yet when the evening arrived, Cettie developed a headache and took refuge in her hotel room. As a result, Senior, resplendent in tails and white gloves, stood alone on the receiving line, cordially greeting three hundred guests. Cettie's behavior on this and other occasions supports the thesis that she retreated to her bed as an escape from threatening realities.

Before Brown, Junior had known little about sports: The Rockefellers were more interested in exercise, which stressed health, than in sports, which stressed pleasure. When he became a manager of the football team his senior year, Junior endured endless ribbing when he referred to the center as "the middle." He was so much his thrifty father's son that when one husky lineman asked for new shoestrings, Junior retorted, "What did you do with the pair I gave you last week?"[16] Because of his son's position, Senior, who had never been to a football game, attended one in New York between Brown and the Carlisle Indians. He started out in the stands, calmly surveying the spectacle, then grew so excited that he rushed down to the field in his tall silk hat and began to race up and down the sidelines with the coaches. The captain of the team assigned a lineman to explain the fine points of the game to him, and with his exceptional mind for tactical maneuvers John D. Rockefeller gave the impression that he had mastered the game, with all its subtleties, within five minutes.

=

Junior needed somebody who would release him from the suffocating prudery of his upbringing, and that liberating figure was Abby Aldrich. She was a confident girl who did not need his money and was not awed by his name. Something about the socially maladroit Junior appealed to the maternal instincts of this sophisticated young lady with the gracious manners and erect carriage of a senator's daughter. One of eight children, she had often hosted her father's Washington receptions and had met everyone from General Ambrose Burnside to William McKinley to Custer's widow. Tall, voluptuous, and somewhat matronly in appearance, she was handsome rather than pretty. She liked to wear broad-brimmed, eccentric hats, a symbol of her outgoing personality. She seemed to give Junior the faith in himself that his parents couldn't foster. As he said of their meeting sophomore year, "She treated me as if I had all the savoir faire in the world and her confidence did me a lot of good."[17] Through Abby, Junior made a startling discovery that had been artfully concealed from him: Life could be fun.

Abby came from old New England stock on her mother's side and was descended from Elder William Brewster, a passenger on the *Mayflower*. Though the son of a mill hand, Senator Aldrich claimed Roger Williams, the founder of Rhode Island colony, as an ancestor. Tall and virile, with thick mustache and side-whiskers, the unflappable Senator Aldrich had escaped from poverty, but he never lost his dread of it. He was elected to the U.S. Senate in 1881 and held that seat for the next thirty years, winding up as chairman of the Senate Finance Committee. A confirmed protectionist and devoted servant of the trusts, he used public office to feather his own nest. Bolstered by a $5 million loan from the American Sugar Refining Company—the so-called sugar trust—he invested in four Providence street-railway companies while also representing the New Haven Railroad. Senator Aldrich turned public service into such a lucrative racket that he amassed $16 million by his death. As if he were a mogul, not a public servant, he built a 99-room château at Warwick Neck on Narragansett Bay and sailed a 200-foot yacht, equipped with 8 staterooms and a crew of 27. He bore a host of pejoratives, most notably those conferred by Lincoln Steffens, who referred to him in *McClure's Magazine* as the "political boss of the United States, the power behind the throne, the general manager of the U.S."[18] Too entrenched to be ruffled by such journalistic pinpricks, Senator Aldrich stuck by his policy of "Deny nothing, explain nothing."[19]

Abby grew up in a lively atmosphere of balls, parties, and plays. Opposed to religious severity, Aldrich spoiled his children with presents and seldom disciplined them. At the Aldrich mansion at 110 Benevolent Street in Providence, the senator liked to play bridge or even poker with Abby. (In later years, Junior would not join the game but sat quietly with a book, unable to break that taboo.) A self-taught aesthete with a highly cultivated taste for books and art, the senator had an excellent library of antique books, frequented auctions for furniture, rugs, and art, and so thoroughly schooled Abby in European museums that she knew their paintings by heart. As a teenager, she dipped into the novels of Dickens, Trollope, Hawthorne, Jane Austen, and George Eliot.

Junior's romance with Abby played itself out amid a whirl of college dances, football games, tandem-bike rides, and canoe trips, as well as church services on Sundays. When they strolled along, Junior carried graham crackers in his pocket, and Abby freely reached in and helped herself. As Junior said, "She was so gay and young and so in love with everything."[20] By the spring of junior year, Junior was a regular visitor at Benevolent Street. One Sunday, he mentioned in passing to the senator his summer plans to cruise the Norwegian fjords with his sister Alta. The senator must have warmed to the idea of Abby marrying young Rockefeller, for a few weeks later he bought tickets for himself, his wife, and two daughters on the same ship, and they dined together during the cruise. Back in Providence in the fall, Junior saw Abby so frequently that people began to speculate when they would marry. But Junior approached the matter with the same soul-searching and nervous energy that he brought to every major decision, and he vacillated through four years of tortured introspection. It was perhaps apparent to everybody in Providence except him that he would someday marry Abby.

Certainly the size of his projected inheritance made the choice of wife a momentous decision. Junior idealized his father, and yet he had to deal with a mounting drumbeat of criticism against him. Abby seemed tailor-made to help him with this predicament, for they were both the children of public pariahs. Junior must have admired her ability to be the loyal daughter of a controversial senator while clinging to her own liberal beliefs. She lived in a way that betrayed neither her father nor herself and thereby pointed a path for Junior.

As he approached graduation, Junior still engaged in hero worship of Senior. His glorified image of his father was inextricably bound up with his lowly image of himself. On his son's twenty-first birthday, Senior sent him twenty-one dollars, along with a tender note. "We are grateful beyond measure for your promise and for the confidence your life inspires in us, not only, but in all your friends and acquaintances and this is of more value than all earthly possessions." To this, Junior replied, "People talk about sons being better than their fathers, but if I can be half as generous, half as unselfish, half as kindly affectionate to my fellow men as you have been, I shall not feel that my life has been in vain."[21] As Junior contemplated the duties that awaited him after college, the prospect only magnified his sense of inadequacy. Shortly before graduation, he was invited to join the board of the American Baptist Home Mission Society. When he asked his father's advice, Junior made clear that "my first duty as well as my pleasure after this year would be to help you in whatever capacity or position you might see fit."[22] He never wavered in this decision to subordinate his life to his father's.

As graduation neared, Junior grew wistful about his years at Brown and the relaxed camaraderie it had allowed him. He would shortly emerge into the spotlight of public attention, which would burn brightly for the rest of his life. As he thought of following in his father's footsteps, his courage failed him, and he told his mother soon after graduation, "I feel but little confidence in my ability to fill the position which is before me, but know that I am not afraid to work or do whatever is required of me, and with God's help I will do my best."[23] "The future is glowing with possibilities of service for God and man," Cettie wrote back. "May the Holy Spirit take possession of your entire being, and guide you into all truth."[24] By making him view life so loftily, by encouraging him to see himself as a valiant Christian soldier, she might have inadvertently exacerbated his anxieties. This transcendent perspective seemed to allow little room for normal human failure. Junior's father, meanwhile, remained inscrutably silent about Junior's forthcoming role at 26 Broadway, which could only have deepened his dread of the unknown.

=

When John D. Rockefeller, Jr., started work on October 1, 1897, he was entering 26 Broadway not long after Senior had left it. He was installed at an oak rolltop desk on the austere and slightly shabby ninth floor, in an office suite dedicated to his father's outside investments and philanthropies. He worked cheek by jowl with Frederick T. Gates, George Rogers, and a telegrapher, Mrs. Tuttle, who had the dubious honor of opening Rockefeller's crank mail—and "there was a great deal of it," said Junior.[25] Though he worked in the Standard Oil building, Junior was uninvolved in its management, and he belonged instead to the incipient Rockefeller family office. If his $6,000 annual salary, paid by father, seemed generous, it was a disguised allowance that kept Junior in a state of childlike dependence.

Junior turned aside suggestions that he go to law school or treat himself to an around-the-world trip. "I felt that I had no time for either, that if I was going to learn to help Father in the care of his affairs, the sooner my apprenticeship under his guidance began, the better."[26] Junior was again living at 4 West Fifty-fourth Street and had ample opportunity to sound him out, yet the taciturn Senior provided no clues about what he expected of his son, leaving him in limbo. "Father never said a word to me about what I was to do in the office before I began work there, nor has he ever since. Moreover, he did not say anything on the subject to anyone else in the office, so far as I have ever learned. Apparently he intended that I should make my own way."[27] Junior never admitted to being bothered by this tight-lipped approach. Like God, father's ways were mysterious but, it was always assumed, benevolent in the end. As a stout believer in self-reliance, Senior probably wanted to test his son's aptitude for business and let him find his own way without coaching.

Rockefeller had numerous channels of intelligence, and Junior marveled at his knowledge of everything that went on at 26 Broadway. At a certain point during dinner, Rockefeller would apologize to guests for changing the subject and query Junior about his day's work, displaying seeming omniscience about affairs downtown. Rockefeller's gentle, probing questions were the closest Junior came to a business education from him. Father and son disagreed more than they publicly acknowledged, and Rockefeller was once heard to grumble, "You know, boys go to college and come back knowing everything about business and everything else."[28]

At work, Junior had no formal place in the hierarchy and had to guess at his powers. He performed some menial tasks, such as filling inkwells. Never given his father's power of attorney, he began to sign papers for him, unsure whether father would object; when he did not, Junior took this for a sign of approval and continued the practice. The first major task that Senior assigned his son was a ghoulish one: to supervise the design and transport of a soaring granite obelisk for the family burial plot in Cleveland, a shaft so huge it took up two freight cars. The young Brown graduate also picked out wallpaper for the family houses, sold worn-out buckboards and carriages, and managed Rockefeller real estate in Cleveland. One observer called it an "anxious and troubled" time for Junior, who felt that his performance was wanting, that he was not earning his keep, and that he was unequal to his appointed destiny.[29]

If Junior did not feel totally adrift in these years, the credit must go to Frederick T. Gates, who gave him the guidance he sorely missed from his father. Together, they toured iron ranges in Minnesota and timberlands in the Pacific Northwest, often playing violins together in their private railroad car. Gates invited Junior to audit business meetings, and he responded with everlasting gratitude. Under Gates's tutelage, Junior began to assume his rightful place in the Rockefeller firmament and joined the University of Chicago board just three months after starting work. While still in his twenties, he became a director of U.S. Steel, National City Bank, the Delaware, Lackawanna and Western Railroad, and, of course, Standard Oil.

Bowed by a sense of premature failure, Junior was desperate to succeed at *something* and decided to try his hand at the stock market. Since his father had professed a puritan contempt for Wall Street, Junior was surprised to learn that he had played the market for years and traded actively. To teach them the art of investing, Rockefeller allowed Junior and his sister Alta to borrow from him at 6 percent and invest in equities. During his maiden year at 26 Broadway, Junior made several thousand dollars in the market and, like all giddy novices, began to take more risks and place ever-larger bets.

Meanwhile, a Wall Street operator named David Lamar—later styled the Wolf of Wall Street—began to cultivate George Rogers, Senior's private secretary. In the fall of 1899, Rogers served as the gullible go-between for a scam. Transmitting information from Lamar, Rogers informed Junior that James R. Keene, a celebrated stock trader, had taken a big position in U.S. Leather and suggested that Junior join the buying. Led to believe that he was acting in concert with Keene, Junior took a gigantic stake in the stock. Upon learning that George Rogers was meeting secretly with Lamar at lunchtime, he had a queasy intuition of foul play. Junior summoned Lamar to his office, and he arrived with a flushed, agitated air. As Junior recalled, "One look at him was enough. I knew I had been sold out."[30] It turned out Keene knew nothing of the affair and that Lamar was liquidating leather stock as fast as Junior bid it up. The unthinkable had happened: The meek Junior had dropped nearly a million dollars—equal to more than $17 million today—of father's money in the market. He knew the situation was unforgivable: He had never asked to meet Keene, had done no research, and had thrown away a fortune on a wild tip.

One can only guess Junior's emotional turmoil when he broke this astonishing news to father, a harrowing meeting that was forever seared into his memory. "Never shall I forget my shame and humiliation as I went up to report the affair to Father. I hadn't the money to meet the loss; there was nothing else to do."[31] Senior listened quietly and conducted a calm but thorough inquiry, investigating every detail of the transaction—all without a syllable of reproach. At the end, he simply said, "All right, I'll take care of it, John."[32] Junior waited for some criticism, some outburst, some paternal homily about future behavior. But nothing further was said. It was a vintage Rockefeller performance: The true lesson lay in what he did not say and what he did not do. Rockefeller sensed that his insecure son had castigated himself so unmercifully that bitter reproaches were superfluous. By showing generosity, he enlisted his son's loyalty forever. The incident must have reinforced Junior's innate conservatism, for the one time he had entered into a rash, immoderate scheme he had been severely punished.

Working for months without a break, Junior began to carry a lot of pent-up tension. To purge this nervous energy, he went after work to the West Fifty-fifth Street stable, where his father's horses exercised in bad weather, and furiously chopped firewood from twenty-foot logs. Over lunch one day with Henry E. Cooper, a former Brown classmate, Junior brooded about his own inadequacy. Startled by the personality change, Cooper followed up with a letter of friendly advice. "You are altogether too grumpy, too morose and gloomy, John. . . . I truly think it would do you good, for instance, to take up smoking an occasional cigarette, or something of that sort. I am not joking. Just try being a shade more reckless or careless as to whether or not you reach perfection within five years, and see if you don't find more happiness."[33] Pathetically eager to please, Junior noted in his ledger a few days later, "pack of cigarettes—10 cents." It was the last time he ever smoked.

Trapped on a treadmill of work, duty, and prayer, Junior found it hard to squeeze in time for Abby Aldrich. Sometimes on weekends, he took the train to Providence after work, dined with her, then grabbed the midnight train back to New York. In Manhattan, Junior often attended dances and parties with Alta, who was also living at home. She developed such an excessive attachment to her brother that she treated Abby as a rival and tried to undermine her. Alta's adamant opposition could only have prolonged Junior's doubts about marrying Abby.

Senior saw that his son could not carry his load lightly and begged him to relax more. Cettie, however, insistently pushed him forward in his quest for moral perfection. Two days after he began at 26 Broadway, she prodded him to join the Bible class at the Fifth Avenue Baptist Church, telling him to be "mighty in the Scriptures. The most powerful Christians are *Bible Christians.*"[34] Sometimes she made it seem that humanity's salvation hinged upon his personal purity. In an astonishing letter of July 23, 1899, Cettie likened her husband to God and Junior to the Christ child. "You can never forget that you are a prince, the Son of the King of kings, and so you can never do what will dishonor your Father or be disloyal to the King."[35] Cettie's tone is especially revealing amid the rising attacks against Standard Oil. Much like her husband, she had fashioned an alternate reality in which, instead of being a corporate villain, he was converted into an American saint. There were no shades of gray permitted in the Rockefeller household.

Exhausted by work and beset by self-doubt, Junior pondered whether to marry Abby Aldrich and prayed daily for divine guidance for four years. "I always had a dread of marrying someone and finding out later that I loved someone else more. I knew a great many girls and I had so little confidence in my own judgment."[36] Things looked promising in April 1900, when Junior joined Senator Aldrich and Abby on a journey to Cuba aboard President McKinley's yacht, the *Dolphin,* a senatorial trip to study conditions there following the Spanish-American War. Still, Junior hesitated, unable to suppress his doubts. In the stuffy Rockefeller household, both parents and son balked at bringing up the subject. Finally, his sister Edith, acting as intermediary, told her brother that their parents were worried about him and felt that they were being kept in the dark, at last opening the forbidden subject to discussion.

In February 1901, Junior and Abby submitted to a six-month separation as a trial of their affections. After the time had expired, Junior was strolling by the lake at Forest Hill with Cettie when he summoned up the strength to ask her opinion of Abby Aldrich. Her hearty, laughing response was categorical. "Of course you love Miss Aldrich. Why don't you go at once and tell her so?"[37] Junior needed that maternal validation, that direct push. Soon afterward at West Fifty-fourth Street, he heard God's voice in the wee hours, blessing his choice of Abby. "After many years of doubt and uncertainty, great longing and hope, there came a supreme peace of calm."[38] Before dawn, he dashed off a letter to Abby, asking if he could visit her. Stopping off to see Senator Aldrich on his yacht in Newport, he asked for his daughter's hand and began to lay out his salary and financial prospects. Doubtless with some amusement, the senator brushed aside all money concerns and delivered the predictable bromide, "I am only interested in what will make my daughter happy."[39] An ecstatic Junior went to the Aldrich summer estate at Narragansett Bay and proposed to Abby by moonlight. "I can't believe that it is really true that all this sacred joy . . . is mine. . . . For so long, long a time it has been the one thing in life above all others that I have yearned for," Junior wrote his mother.[40] Abby then had six suitors, leading Junior to observe retrospectively, "I kept wondering why she ever consented to marry a man like me."[41] But she never regretted her decision. As she wrote to a cousin many years later, "Don't you think him quite the dearest man that ever was?"[42]

When the engagement was announced in August 1901, the press had a field day. "Croesus Captured," trumpeted one paper.[43] Many articles commented upon the odd match of the fun-loving Aldriches and the dour Rockefellers. As one paper said, "Young Mr. Rockefeller . . . is a Sunday-school teacher, and doesn't believe in cards, dancing or decollete gowns, and Miss Abbie [*sic*] has never been able to make up her mind that she can renounce these things."[44] Although Senator Aldrich and Senior came in for their usual rough treatment, Abby and Junior were applauded for their more progressive views.

The extravagant wedding at Warwick on October 9, 1901, reflected the cosmopolitan style of Senator Aldrich, who made scant concessions to his Baptist in-laws. By chartered steamer and private railway car, he transported a huge portion of the American plutocracy to the affair, which glittered with Goulds and Whitneys, McCormicks and Havemeyers. The marriage was a satirical bonanza for muckrakers. As David Graham Phillips darkly interpreted the union, "the chief exploiter of the American people is closely allied by marriage with the chief schemer in the service of their exploiters."[45]

The affair began with a small private wedding, limited to thirty-five guests and presided over by the Reverend J. G. Colby, who had married John and Cettie thirty-seven years before. Then a thousand people trooped gaily through a vast reception in the ballroom. Senator Aldrich refused to truckle to the temperance views of his in-laws and personally selected an array of vintage wines. This was too much for Cettie, who developed chills, asthma, and diarrhea the night before the wedding and took to her bed for spiritual safety, skipping the ceremony the next day—an exact replica of her performance at Junior's senior-year dance at Brown. Once the stylish guests had fled, Junior and Abby spent a glorious month in seclusion at the house Senior had purchased in the Pocantico Hills of Westchester.

For the first months of married life, the newlyweds lived with John and Cettie at 4 West Fifty-fourth Street then crossed the street to a rented four-story mansion at number 13. Junior tried, with some trepidation, to initiate his free-spirited wife into the cramped, clerical ways of the Rockefellers, suggesting she might like to keep a weekly expense account. "I won't," Abby said bluntly, ending the matter forever. To a family muzzled by taboos, she brought a refreshing candor. When a visitor asked her, "Whatever are you going to do with this great big empty house, Abby?" she looked at him in astonishment. "Why, we shall fill it up with children!"[46]

The young Frederick T. Gates.
(Courtesy of the University of Chicago Library)

The Standard Oil Crowd

utwardly at least, Frederick T. Gates was the antithesis of his famous patron, as florid and melodramatic as Rockefeller was cool and withdrawn. With close-set eyes that looked slightly crossed, head tilted to one side with a sardonic smile, the philanthropic chief often looked as if he was skeptically sizing up the world. A tall, well-built man with a restless, energetic air, he could talk with gusto for hours at a stretch, as if delivering a fiery sermon or Shakespearean soliloquy. Capable of tremendous flashes of wrath or indignation, he was colorful in both action and speech. When he pontificated, he threw his feet up on the desk, jabbing his finger through swirling cigar smoke, or jumped up from his seat, hair tousled, tie askew, to pace the floor with lawyerly deliberation. One colleague said he had "a voice that thundered out of Sinai" and he knew no middle ground in advocating a cause.[1] In a prose self-portrait, Gates described himself as "eager, impetuous, insistent, and withal exacting and irritable."[2]

Like Rockefeller himself, Gates yoked together two separate selves—one shrewd and worldly, the other noble and high-flown. Born in upstate New York in 1853, not far from the Susquehanna River that flowed through Rockefeller's boyhood, Gates was the son of a high-minded, impecunious Baptist minister, who had eked out a meager existence in small, impoverished towns. As a boy, Gates rebelled against the Puritan heritage that viewed earthly life as a melancholy sojourn. In his memoirs, he recalled that the "singing was pleasing, but otherwise Sunday school was a bore, as was church. I remember well my weekly relief when it was over and we could go home for dinner."[3] Of his twice-daily prayers, he said, "If it taught anything, it taught us thus early that prayer is a mere empty form of words."[4] The wonder was that the boy grew up to be a preacher.

When Gates was a teenager, his father went to Kansas for the American Baptist Home Mission Society, which only aggravated the family's financial woes. Gates had to quit school at fifteen to help pay off their debt. For several years, he taught school and clerked in a dry-goods store and a bank, storing up valuable business experience. After briefly attending Highland University in Kansas, he entered the University of Rochester in 1875, where his interest in religion was rekindled. A good Baptist, he would not dance, play cards, or frequent the theater. Two years later, he entered the Rochester Theological Seminary, then under the sway of its president, Dr. Augustus H. Strong. Gates was briefly entranced by Strong's theological system. "His instruction formed the foundation of our seminary course, and at that time it was almost wholly imaginary" was his later mordant judgment.[5] Gates was drawn to the ministry, not as a retreat into an otherworldly life so much as a liberation from poverty and academic drudgery.

After graduating from the seminary in 1880, Gates was assigned his first pastorate in Minnesota. When his young bride, Lucia Fowler Perkins, dropped dead from a massive internal hemorrhage after sixteen months of marriage, the novice pastor not only suffered an erosion of faith but began to question the competence of American doctors—a skepticism that later had far-reaching ramifications for Rockefeller's philanthropies. A period photo shows a handsome young man with a long, lean face, a handlebar mustache, and a somewhat wistful air. After launching into "a zealous campaign to convert sinners," Gates soon lightened up, scrapping much of the scholastic baggage he had picked up in the seminary. To succeed as a pastor, he decided that he had to study the economic, intellectual, and social forces of his time. A biblical modernist, he employed science, history, and reason to explicate sacred texts. He also worked to retire the church's debt and wrote essays for the *Minneapolis Tribune*.

After eight years in Minnesota, Gates, thin and emaciated, seemed destined for a career as theadbare as his father's. Then one day in 1888, heaven sent relief in the shape of a rich man, George A. Pillsbury, a founder of the flour fortune, the state's wealthiest Baptist, and then the mayor of Minneapolis. He told Gates in confidence that he suffered from an incurable disease and needed advice about making a $200,000 bequest to a local Baptist academy. Gates advised Pillsbury to start out by giving the academy $50,000, contingent on the Baptists raising an equal sum—what we would today call a matching grant— then leave the remaining $150,000 in his will. Gates was subsequently drafted to drum up the $50,000, which he did so superlatively well that he threw up the ministry for good and became executive secretary of the new American

Baptist Education Society. His contact with Rockefeller and involvement in the University of Chicago followed soon thereafter.

Those Baptists who thought they had slipped an advocate into Rockefeller's inner sanctum were grievously disappointed. At first, Rockefeller still gave disproportionately to Baptist causes, as missionaries from every continent descended upon Gates's office in droves. But despite his fondness for Baptist clergy, Rockefeller was also exposed to many greedy, calculating pastors and began to retreat from the sectarian spirit that had guided his giving. As Gates said, "I think his greatest trouble was with ministers because he had a natural liking for them and they were always trying to get money out of him."[6] By 1895, Rockefeller told Gates that he wanted to give to the five main Protestant denominations. This delighted the lapsed minister, who had grown so dismayed by the Baptist church in his town of Montclair, New Jersey, that he had switched to the local Congregational church. He was increasingly convinced "that Christ neither founded nor intended to found the Baptist Church, nor any church."[7]

═

For someone like Gates, torn between heaven and earth, serving as Rockefeller's chief philanthropic adviser was an ideal synthesis. When they started working together in 1891, Rockefeller was fifty-two and Gates thirty-eight. In spite of his uncommon intelligence, Gates often felt self-conscious under Rockefeller's icy scrutiny. As he grew more comfortable in his presence, he developed a powerful loyalty to him. "I will do my best to serve in any business capacity," Gates humbly told him early on, "but I beg you not to place any confidence in me (I have little in myself) and to begin with matters in which I could not possibly do much harm." He ended by saying, "No one but my father has been so kind to me."[8] Having long chafed at a minister's salary, Gates could now indulge his ripest fantasies of wealth. Where his father had made less than $400 a year, Gates started with Rockefeller at $4,000 a year, his salary rising to $32,000 by 1902.

What Gates gave to his boss was no less vital. Rockefeller desperately needed intelligent assistance in donating his money at a time when he could not draw on a profession of philanthropic experts. Painstakingly thorough, Gates combined moral passion with great intellect. He spent his evenings bent over tomes of medicine, economics, history, and sociology, trying to improve himself and find clues on how best to govern philanthropy. Skeptical by nature, Gates saw a world crawling with quacks and frauds, and he enjoyed grilling people with trenchant questions to test their sincerity. Outspoken, uncompromising, he never hesitated to speak his piece to Rockefeller and was a peerless troubleshooter.

Gates believed implicitly in Rockefeller's goodness and wisdom. "If he were placed in a group of say twenty of the greatest men of affairs of today," he once remarked in a speech, "before these giants had been with him for long, the most self-confident, self-assertive of them would be coming to him in private for his counsel."[9] Having known many rich people, Gates was impressed that Rockefeller had no private yachts or railroad cars. He was always quick to defend Rockefeller, sometimes wittily. When a man complained to him that Rockefeller in his Cleveland years cared only for money, Gates retorted, "In heaven's name, what else could he do in that city!"[10] In a typical utterance, Gates said, "The Rockefellers have done incomparably more to permanently enrich the commonwealth than any other family since the founding of the republic."[11]

Gates did not consider Rockefeller totally innocent in business, but he believed that whatever reprehensible deeds he had committed had simply reflected the business morals of his time. Yet he had no firsthand knowledge of the matter, for while he supervised Rockefeller's philanthropic and outside business investments, he was always excluded from anything pertaining to Standard Oil. As Junior said, "The oil companies didn't like him and consequently I was the person who was the liaison."[12] Since Gates entered the scene just as Rockefeller was retiring and was sequestered from his single largest holding, he had the luxury of believing in Rockefeller's innocence by assuming that he had behaved as well at Standard Oil as in his subsequent ventures.

Significantly, Rockefeller surrounded himself in the early 1890s with brand-new men who could defend his past with total sincerity—and total ignorance. By recruiting subordinates who had never worked at Standard Oil, he had a chance for a fresh start, where he could make his behavior, for the first time, as ethical as his rhetoric. Led by Gates, these subordinates guaranteed that the Rockefeller millions were donated or invested scrupulously. Once he had an ex-pastor on the payroll, Rockefeller was necessarily kept on his best behavior, locked into a new moral regimen. Junior's presence at 26 Broadway further ensured that father would behave more ethically than in the past.

As at Standard Oil, Rockefeller encouraged independence, and once he had carefully trained his philanthropic lieutenants, he gave them a wide berth. Gates found his boss patient, kind, and considerate, but realized that Rockefeller's genial midwestern manner and humor were something of a cover. "His usual attitude towards all men was one of deep reserve, concealed beneath commonplaces and humorous anecdotes. He had the art with friends and guests of chatting freely, of calling out others, but of revealing little or nothing of his own innermost thoughts."[13] When Gates went to the oracle for guidance, he sometimes left more mystified than before. As he wrote of Rockefeller, "His deliberation was sometimes extreme; his reluctance to argue and speak out his thoughts fully, his skill in not exposing the slightest surface for attack, his long silences, so that we could not locate even his objections, were some-times baffling."[14] Rockefeller never offered blame or praise and revealed his opinion of employees only by adding or subtracting to their duties. His psyche was like a set of Chinese boxes: If you penetrated the outer wall, then you faced another wall, then another, ad infinitum.

—

As Rockefeller moved into retirement, his wealth was accumulating at an as-tonishing rate. During his tenure at Standard Oil, the trust had usually paid a fixed dividend of 12 percent, reflecting his prudent leadership. With Archbold at the helm, by contrast, the dividends surged, jumping to 31 percent in 1896 and 33 percent in 1897 and 1899. Buoyed by these dividends, the price of Standard Oil shares leaped from 176 in 1896 to a high of 458 three years later. However much Rockefeller deplored this extravagant dividend policy, he was its foremost beneficiary, and it heightened the pressure on him to gear up his phil-anthropy to handle increasing amounts of money.

With hundreds of appeals pouring in daily from around the world, Rockefel-ler made Gates promise that he would never forward begging letters to him or reveal his address. While Rockefeller continued to give out hundreds, if not thousands, of individual bequests to needy friends, relatives, and strangers—he sent one upstate cousin a pair of well-worn shoes, another an old suit—he increasingly followed a policy enunciated in an 1889 letter to Gates: "I am more and more disposed to give only through organized institutions."[15] Gates executed this policy of wholesale giving faithfully, dismissing small requests for money with the fatal remark, "This is a retail business."[16]

Sometimes Rockefeller gave Gates glimpses into his inner sadness. One day, Gates remarked to Rockefeller that benevolence was its own reward, that the man who looked for gratitude would die embittered. "His only reply, uttered with deliberation and unwonted emphasis, was, 'DON'T I KNOW THAT?' "[17] Gates saw that while he was always surrounded by people, Rockefeller had few, if any, real friends and was isolated by his wealth. Visiting Rockefeller at a southern hotel around 1910, Gates found him rather lonely and forlorn and suggested he contact some cultivated local men. "Well, Mr. Gates," said Rocke-feller, "if you suppose I have not thought about the matter you are mistaken. I have made some experiments. And nearly always the result is the same—along about the ninth hole out comes some proposition, charitable or financial!"[18] Rockefeller experienced more disenchantment with people in charity than in commerce, once telling his son, "I have lent and given people money, and then seen them cross the street so that they would not have to speak to me."[19]

From the time he signed on as chief almoner, Gates knew his life had changed irrevocably. "I now saw myself largely cut off from disinterested friendships and almost of necessity a centre of intrigue and dislike," he wrote in his memoirs.[20] As he watched people scheme and grovel for Rockefeller's fortune, it was hard to preserve his faith in human nature. "If you could be here in this office," he once wrote William Rainey Harper, explaining his own caution, "and see the exhibition of human meanness, and even dishonor, among otherwise respectable men when they come to negotiate with Mr. Rockefeller's wealth, you would appreciate better than you can now how this perhaps unnatural caution has arisen."[21]

A close student of the boss's psychology, Gates was aware of Rockefeller's preferred self-image and played on it effectively. There was a manipulative side to Gates, as shown by a letter he wrote a friend in which he set forth twenty-two fund-raising tips. Tip number six read: "If you find [the prospective donor] big with gift do not rush him too eagerly to the birth. Let him take his time, with gentle management. Make him feel that *he* is *giving* it, not that it is being taken from him with violence." Number seven advised: "Appeal only to the noblest motives. His own mind will suggest to him the lower and selfish ones."[22] One suspects Gates applied some of these pointers to Rockefeller himself, posing all the while as the faithful servant.

Gates had a talent for dressing up proposals to Rockefeller with the right touch of historic drama. He made each gift seem a momentous advance in human civilization and often mimicked Rockefeller's own business rhetoric—talking about educational trusts, for instance—to sell him a program. Gates knew that Rockefeller viewed himself as an instrument of God in business and philanthropy. By striking this note, Gates could always capture his mentor's attention. Many years later, Gates sent him the following New Year's greeting:

> Certainly no man can survey your marvelous career without feeling that it bears in very high and special degree the marks of a "Plan of God." I remember well how your life has been to yourself a series of great surprises, how vistas altogether unexpected have suddenly opened before your astonished gaze, and now that you have arrived at a point when you can look back over a long course, how often and how deeply must it have impressed itself on your mind that you have been simply an instrument in the hands of the Great Power that is not ourselves. How clear must it now be to you in the retrospect that this Great Unseen Power was guiding you all the time and ever to ends unseen, vaster, more varied, more far reaching than any human wisdom could compass or conceive. If now at the beginning of this new year I may venture to offer you a toast, it would be—John D. Rockefeller, His Life, A Plan of God.[23]

While Gates would function as a never-ending source of ideas for the philanthropies, it is important to credit Rockefeller's own contribution. The same mind that created the Standard Oil empire was actively engaged in building up his charitable empire. As Gates noted, Rockefeller "came to have hardly less pleasure in the organization of his philanthropy than in the efficiency of his business."[24] In retirement, he actually gave more time to philanthropy than to investments. While Gates often generated ideas, Rockefeller never hesitated to wield his veto power or force Gates to rethink proposals. Gates had to take account of the many things that Rockefeller had ruled off-limits, such as funding social-welfare agencies. He never had infinite freedom to draw up programs and needed to conform to Rockefeller's wishes. His power, if vast, was circumscribed.

=

Rockefeller developed such a mystique of infallibility that people assumed his touch was no less unerring in his private investments than at Standard Oil. Whenever it was known that he had bought a stock, exultant investors rushed to join him. Sometimes, Rockefeller contributed to his own myth. "It has always been my rule in business to make everything count," he once told an old friend. "To make every cent something. I never go into an enterprise unless I feel sure it is coming out all right."[25]

If he ever set eyes on that windy boast, Frederick T. Gates would have grimaced, for he had found Rockefeller's personal finances in a shocking state, run haphazardly without a full-time portfolio manager. The mastermind of Standard Oil had proved to be a passive and easily hoodwinked investor. By 1890, as he banked ten million dollars in annual income, Rockefeller still deferred, with surprising credulity, to advice proffered by supposed friends. He fell particularly under the sway of two fellow congregants from the Fifth Avenue Baptist Church, Colgate Hoyt and Charles Colby. Hoyt often dropped by his house in the morning and accompanied him downtown, touting stocks all the while. Rockefeller reposed implicit faith in these two churchgoers, who induced him to pour millions into ruinous investments in a score of companies. Through their exertions, he acquired an investment empire that he knew solely from misleading figures on a statement. What reconciled Rockefeller to this setup was that he took minority stakes and imagined that his partners were investing equivalent amounts.

As members of the executive committee of the Northern Pacific Railroad when Rockefeller was its major stockholder, Colby and Hoyt avidly pushed investments in timber stands of the Pacific Northwest. They planned to build up the town of Everett, Washington, at the juncture where the Northern Pacific would supposedly establish its major terminus on Puget Sound. As the Great Northern Railroad also neared completion, the whole area was convulsed by a speculative mania. Colby and Hoyt erred, however, in one small but costly matter: The Northern Pacific terminal ended up in Tacoma, not Everett. Meanwhile, blindly following their counsel, Rockefeller had added mines, steel mills, paper mills, railroads, and even a nail factory to his holdings.

Rockefeller's unwonted lack of vigilance owed something to his fragile health during the early 1890s, when he was trying to clear his mind of cares. Sensing that some of his outside investments might not be as sound as advertised, he mentioned to Gates one day that if, on his philanthropic excursions, he happened to be near one of these investments, he might want to scout out the premises. While Rockefeller was already impressed by Gates's resourcefulness, he also knew that with Gates he risked less potential embarrassment than with a professional financial analyst who might broadcast his failures on Wall Street.

Soon after Gates moved to New York in 1891, he was about to embark on a tour of Baptist schools in Alabama when Rockefeller asked if he would inspect an iron furnace he had bought there on an old friend's advice; he said he was perplexed why it had fallen into a receiver's hands. When Gates filed his report, it was instantly clear that he was no courtier serving up syrupy lies to soothe his sovereign. The entire operation, Gates said bluntly, had nothing to do with iron but was a thinly veiled attempt to boom local real estate; many Baptist ministers had been tricked into buying nearby land that was supposed to appreciate because of its proximity to the iron operation. Rockefeller hid his amazement and contended breezily that he had taken this "little flyer" to help an old friend's son learn the iron business. By way of comparison, Rockefeller alluded to his lucrative iron business in Wisconsin, then allegedly yielding $1,000 per day. A few months later, he sent the intrepid Gates to take a look.

Gates traveled to Wisconsin and with quiet tenacity began asking questions. He found exactly the same fraud as that perpetrated in Alabama: The ironworks were being used to pump up local real estate and auction off lots at inflated prices. The supposed profits were pure moonshine: Rockefeller was actually *losing* about $1,000 per day. To anyone who knew Rockefeller, the situation seemed inconceivable: He had made large investments without independently verifying the numbers sent by his friends.

When he appeared at Forest Hill to relay the bad news, Gates knew that the boss could not dismiss $600,000 in mortgage bonds as a "little flyer," and Rockefeller was visibly upset. As Gates recounted the meeting:

> He was deeply agitated and, had I not been able to give him the most positive assurances, would have been incredulous. He kept me with him at Forest Hill until he could get the old friend to his side from Wall Street, who had been mainly instrumental in selling him the bonds. This gentleman denied every one of my allegations, but he could only meet my proofs with protestations and tears of rage and apprehension.[26]

A few days later, the contrite scoundrel—whether Colby or Hoyt is unclear—returned to Rockefeller, confirmed the truth of Gates's allegations, and agreed to have the mortgage-bond covenants rewritten.

Shaken by this duplicity, Rockefeller sent his sleuth to probe his investment in the San Miguel Consolidated Mines high in the Rocky Mountains. The scheme's promoter had entertained many previous investors who had journeyed westward to tour the site. At once, Gates scented trouble when he quizzed a mining engineer in Denver about the San Miguel properties. "What!" the man shouted. "Do you mean to tell me that John D. Rockefeller has invested money in that Damned Swindle!!"[27] When Gates journeyed to Telluride, he learned that the mines were phantoms and that the company had only abandoned claims.

At this point—it was now late 1892—Gates was still operating at one remove from Rockefeller in a nearby office in the Temple Court; after the San Miguel fiasco, Rockefeller moved him into his office at 26 Broadway. He saw that Gates had a flair for business that surpassed anything he had encountered at Standard Oil. In a stunning display of trust, Rockefeller gave him unrestricted access to his files for all investments outside of Standard Oil. As Gates poked around in this fetid swamp, he was appalled by what he found. "I unearthed some twenty of these sick and dying corporations," he recalled, "every one of which showed a balance sheet in red ink."[28]

As Gates sorted through the failed investments, George Rogers joined the chorus of those urging Rockefeller to institute new oversight procedures for his $23 million investment portfolio, including $14 million in railroad securities. Emboldened by Gates's findings, Rogers suggested creation of an executive committee. Gates would handle investments and benevolent matters; Gates's Montclair neighbor Starr Murphy would assume legal responsibilities; and Rogers would take care of office matters, each to be paid $10,000 a year. As Rogers candidly told his chastened boss, "This will seem to you at first as very high but it will be considerable [*sic*] cheaper than being robbed as you have been and even now you are without exact knowledge as to many of the investments in which you have large sums involved."[29] Pointing out the perils of passive investment, he suggested that Rockefeller assign deputies to oversee these companies.

Beyond the shocking misrepresentation of his investments, Rockefeller had another dispiriting discovery in store: Hoyt and Colby had surreptitiously bailed out of the worthless operations and left him holding the bag, often with a majority stake. Even though he terminated relations with this pair, he could not dispose of their sour investments so easily and thought the most prudent course was to buy total control of the companies and turn them around. Holding practically all the stock of thirteen foundering companies, Rockefeller made Gates president of virtually all of them. Overnight, the young minister who had dreaded poverty was running two railroads plus a far-flung group of mines, timber, and manufacturing concerns. Most of these highly speculative investments never panned out.

As if born to rule business empires instead of saving souls, Gates operated with great swagger and panache. While he jettisoned many money-losing enterprises, he developed great affection for the Everett Timber and Investment Company. Touring this terrain each year in a luxurious private railroad car, he bought up for Rockefeller all the forests in sight, a spree that finally netted 50,000 acres in Washington State and another 40,000 on Vancouver Island. Eventually, these timber tracts fetched five or six times their purchase price, compensating Rockefeller for the losses he had sustained in the Pacific Northwest debacle. Gates himself invested in several of the companies he managed for Rockefeller, and in 1902 he cashed in a tidy $500,000 profit.

In Gates, Rockefeller had found not merely an able investor but a prodigy. In 1917, asked by B. C. Forbes to name the greatest businessman he had ever encountered, Rockefeller startled readers by skipping Flagler and Archbold—not to mention Henry Ford and Andrew Carnegie—and naming Frederick T. Gates. "He combines business skill and philanthropic aptitude to a higher degree than any other man I have ever known," stated Rockefeller.[30] Enough Puritan guilt resided in Gates's soul that he always stressed his charitable work and deprecated his business exploits. When Adolph Ochs, publisher of *The New York Times*, asked for background information about him in 1912, Gates replied modestly, even evasively, "While I have had intimate relation with Mr. Rockefeller's private business, that is, his private and personal investments, my interests are and always have been rather in his benevolent work than in his business."[31] This would have been news to many on Wall Street who had experienced the temper of this hard-driving, cigar-smoking, flamboyant majordomo of the world's largest private fortune.

=

Even though he stayed in the background, the press soon detected the power held by the eccentric, shaggy-haired Gates. "In appearance Mr. Gates is not the ordinary type of financier," the *New York Daily Tribune* noted. "Everything about him, from the carelessly brushed iron gray hair and cropped moustache to his feet indicate breezy indifference to what others may think about him."[32] Investment houses trifled with him at their peril, for Gates oversaw a securities portfolio of unprecedented size for a private individual. At a time of thin capital markets, he needed to scrounge to find gilt-edged securities to absorb the Rockefeller millions. As if he were a one-man investment bank, Rockefeller participated, under Gates's supervision, in major stock-and-bond underwriting syndicates alongside the most august Wall Street houses. While it was not unusual in that era for rich individuals to complete syndicates, the sheer scope of Rockefeller's involvement was something novel.

Even in old age, Rockefeller received stock quotes twice daily and could rattle off the precise number of shares he owned in many stocks. He adhered to several hallowed investing rules. Perhaps the most sacred was that Gates not disturb his Standard Oil stock, the bulk of his fortune. As at Standard Oil, Rockefeller insisted upon keeping a cash balance that never dipped below $10 million. Since he also had a sizable stake in U.S. government bonds, he felt he could play the market with impunity. A born contrarian, Rockefeller insisted upon buying in declining markets and selling in rising ones. When accumulating a position, he bought stocks each time they declined an eighth of a point; when unwinding a position, he sold each time the stock rose an eighth of a point—a technique that gave him an average over an extended period. Having twice been sued by people for offering incorrect market advice, he refrained from offering stock tips. There was also some genuine humility at work, for Rockefeller admitted that he had no "prophetic vision as would make me try to mislead anybody else . . . by one of my miserable guesses."[33]

Since his aides superintended a royal treasury of securities, he had to implement special security precautions. He laid down an ironclad rule that no employee could invest in stocks or bonds of any company in which he held a major stake, and a minimum of two people had to be present whenever the safe housing his securities was opened. Rockefeller's subordinates seemed more jittery than their phlegmatic boss about dealing with such stupendous sums. Starr Murphy recalled an occasion when the boss asked him and a colleague to bring $60 million in securities to his Pocantico estate for his personal inspection. With no small dread, the two men drove up to Westchester, totally unguarded. Rockefeller did not show any anxiety about the absence of security and only at the end alluded to the situation by remarking, with deadpan face and humorous drawl, "I suppose that you gentlemen will return to New York together."[34]

Efforts to manipulate Rockefeller often backfired after the Colby and Hoyt affair. In 1910, for instance, Rockefeller was vacationing in Augusta, Georgia, when he received a visit in his hotel suite from Henry Clay Frick, who solemnly advised him to buy 50,000 shares of Reading Railroad stock. The moment Frick left, Rockefeller got on the phone and issued orders to liquidate his block of 47,500 shares; he had the satisfaction of selling the final 2,500 shares at the stock's peak.

Rockefeller grappled with the classic dilemma faced by all large investors: how to buy stocks without pumping them up or sell without dragging them down. As his fame spread, his market moves could set off frenzied stampedes of traders. To forestall this, Rockefeller employed a double set of brokers: a primary broker parceled out orders among dozens of secondary brokers who were ignorant of his identity, thus masking his steps behind a maze of intermediaries. For a long time, he paid double commissions, before he worked out a single-commission arrangement with a broker named Paul D. Langdon. On fin-de-siècle Wall Street, stock pools were both legal and voguish, and Rockefeller had no ethical qualms about participating in them.

Entering the autumnal phase of his life, Rockefeller preferred sure, steady gains to speculative killings. When one promoter tried to peddle some gold-mining shares, Gates cut him off short. "If you were to say that the vein was pure gold, 24 karats fine, broad, easily workable, and close to a railway, to be had for a song, I doubt if Mr. Rockefeller's attention could be attracted. . . . He has come to a time in life and circumstances in fortune when these things no longer attract his cupidity."[35] Rockefeller seldom responded to the countless inventors who trooped to his office hoping to sell patents. It was easier to lend large sums, backed by first-class securities as collateral, than to have investments dispersed among dozens of enterprises. For all his fabled rapacity, Rockefeller was a forgiving lender and, by all accounts, lenient to a fault. "Never have I known Mr. Rockefeller to call a private loan, foreclose a private mortgage, or oppress a debtor," complained Gates.[36] Another investment adviser, Henry E. Cooper, concurred: "He was never too hard on people in business; he was too easy."[37]

To finance sporadic stock-market forays, Rockefeller borrowed huge sums from banks, up to fifteen or twenty million at a time, pledging his government bonds as collateral. This was all a trifle confusing for Junior, who continued to take his father's straitlaced pronouncements against speculative investing at face value. As he moved into middle age, the son even took to lecturing his wayward father, chiding him with his own rhetoric. On the eve of World War I, when Senior's borrowings swelled to nearly $10 million, Junior reminded him of how he had "frequently given utterance to my belief, that you should never be a borrower, but always long of cash."[38]

For a long time, Rockefeller resisted efforts to professionalize his investment team, and Gates soldiered on as best he could. In 1897, Charles O. Heydt—later Rockefeller's expert on real-estate matters—joined the staff, followed a few years later by Bertram Cutler, who helped manage the family investments for the next fifty years. Even with this team in place, the investment operation was still slipshod, and in 1907 Gates told Rockefeller, "I have long thought that it would prove helpful if you could have a man in the office who had before him at all times every day the complete list of your investments and whose business it is to familiarize himself intimately with every one of them—to have his finger, so to speak, on the pulse of every one of them all the time."[39] The following year, Rockefeller finally capitulated and formed a four-member committee, including Gates and Junior, to manage his money.

As with the Rockefeller philanthropies, Gates operated tentatively at first in the wolfish world of Wall Street but was soon very much master of the situation. Before long, he confidently conveyed to Rockefeller his scathing opinions of such globe-straddling moguls as Andrew Carnegie and J. Pierpont Morgan. At the time, the world of high finance revolved around a spirited rivalry between Morgan and Jacob Schiff of Kuhn, Loeb. Convinced that Rockefeller was already controversial enough, Gates tried, whenever possible, to avoid clashes between these two financiers, and he balked at joining boardroom revolts, stock-market squeezes, and other activities that might bring Rockefeller into any further disrepute.

Famished for blue-chip securities, Gates clamored for inclusion in both J. P. Morgan and Company *and* Kuhn, Loeb syndicates, but always believed that he got superior treatment from Kuhn, Loeb. Under the aegis of this house, Rockefeller swallowed huge chunks of railroad issues, including giant stakes in the Southern Pacific, the Union Pacific, and the Pennsylvania Railroads. He also took a large share in loans floated for the Imperial Japanese government in 1904–1905 during the Russo-Japanese War and for the Chinese government in 1911. He contributed to Kuhn, Loeb's consolidation of the Chicago meat-packers, led by Armour and Swift, helping to foster another trust. Constantly on the prowl for good securities, he sometimes bought from Kuhn, Loeb just to maintain harmonious relations.

Gates and his minions smarted at the high-handed treatment they received from J. P. Morgan and Company, where they were routinely assigned small portions of mediocre issues—curious treatment for the world's richest investor. In the early 1900s, Rockefeller found himself with disconcerting frequency involved in Morgan's biggest blunders, including the Chicago Street Railway that he financed for the magnate Charles Yerkes and the International Mercantile Marine, Morgan's abortive effort to forge a North Atlantic shipping cartel. For Rockefeller, this was not happenstance but reflected Morgan's settled antipathy. Bruised by these bad investments, Rockefeller told his son in 1911, "In future, when investments are offered us by this house, we will be of one mind, I think, in accepting nothing which we do not all agree is very desirable for us to have." [10] After J. P. Morgan, Sr., died in 1913, Rockefeller told his advisers to keep up cordial relations with the Morgan bank while tartly reminding them that "we have had sufficient experience with the House of Morgan & Company in the role of 'pack horses' for their poor investments." [41]

In spite of his phalanx of able advisers, Rockefeller had a very uneven record as an investor. Among his triumphs, he extended a six-million-dollar loan to the fledgling General Motors in 1906—about $98 million today—taking notes for his cash. When the notes were paid off, Rockefeller took payment in General Motors shares, which then obligingly soared from 200 to 1,500. He also fared well as the premier investor in Consolidation Coal and the B&O Railroad. Yet Rockefeller could stumble abysmally, as evidenced by his mystifying relationship with George Gould. When Jay Gould, who had memorably looted the Erie

Railroad, died in late 1892, leaving an estate of more than $100 million, his twenty-eight-year-old spendthrift son George inherited his investments. He proved an unlikely business partner for Rockefeller. Where Rockefeller frowned upon the expense of private railroad cars, George Gould owned an entire train and savored the patrician pleasures of fencing, hunting, yachting, and polo. The New York tabloids also delighted in reporting upon his racy relations with women. Whatever his misgivings about George's philandering, Rockefeller was attracted by the Missouri Pacific and other western railroads that Gould wanted to weld into a transcontinental empire. In 1902, Rockefeller took giant portions of a Missouri Pacific stock offering, and before long he had buried $40 million in this graveyard, as much as George Gould himself had.

Troubles soon developed. In 1906, irate over Gould's profligate spending and failure to consult him, Rockefeller had his son withdraw from the Missouri Pacific board. By 1909, Rockefeller felt so abominably treated by Gould that he refused further cooperation unless his representatives controlled the board. As the price of rescuing the Missouri Pacific, Jacob Schiff of Kuhn, Loeb likewise insisted upon heavy board representation. When Gould finally resigned the presidency, he installed a crony in his stead, leading Gates to declare it high time to terminate relations with "the mad failed Gould."[42] In 1912, Rockefeller unloaded his holdings in the Missouri Pacific stock, ending the misadventure.

=

Starting in the late 1890s, newspapers published sensational accounts of a shadowy cabal known on Wall Street as the "Standard Oil Crowd." As diarist Henry Clews recorded, "A new order had come, due to the most powerful influence that had ever manifested itself in Wall Street. This influence was very largely composed of the Standard Oil combination, who introduced in their Wall Street operations the same quiet, unostentatious, but resistless measures that they had always employed in the conduct of their corporate affairs."[43] It was popularly assumed that John D. Rockefeller masterminded these diabolical exploits and was determined to digest Wall Street itself. "It has been said that I control all the banks, all the trust companies, all the insurance companies, even all the railroads in the United States," a chagrined Rockefeller told one reporter in 1906. "Will you believe me when I say that I do not own a controlling interest in any bank, trust company or insurance company?"[44]

Rockefeller dabbled in stocks more than he admitted, but he was largely a passive investor and remained as leery of Wall Street as any cracker-barrel Populist. Once pressed for investment advice, he retorted, "I suppose if I were to give advice it would be to keep out of Wall Street."[45] When he bought a seat on the New York Stock Exchange in 1883, he made an obligatory appearance before the admissions committee, then avoided the exchange for the next fifty-four years. He proudly pointed out that, during his tenure, Standard Oil was never listed on the exchange and that management's attention was "directed to the administration of the business rather than to the stock gambling."[46] Although he never issued a public refutation, Rockefeller played no part in the Standard Oil crowd and cringed at the exploits of its three mainstays: Henry H. Rogers, James Stillman, and his own brother William. Rogers and William paid for their speculations with Standard Oil checks, a practice that always riled John D.

While John always professed warm friendship for his brother, their values had radically diverged over the years as William became a typical grandee of the Gilded Age and plunged lustily into a world of fashionable clubs and resorts. Having sold much of his Standard Oil stock to his brother, William was not nearly as rich as John, but he was still one of the six major recipients of Standard Oil stock and was often listed among the ten richest Americans. A connoisseur of the good life, he loved cocktails, gambling, fast-trotting horses, hunting, fishing, opera, theater, and yachts. His Fifth Avenue mansion faced Alva Vanderbilt's French limestone château, and he frequented her costume balls. His weekend house, Rockwood Hall, a vast pile of towers and turrets with 204 rooms and gardens landscaped by Frederick Law Olmsted, loomed over the Hudson River. He also had a rugged Adirondack estate of several thousand acres. In 1888, along with such moguls as J. P. Morgan, William K. Vanderbilt, and Cyrus McCormick, William founded the Jekyll Island Club—the posh resort of the "One Hundred Millionaires"—on an island off the Georgia coast that soon boasted roads with names such as Morgan Road and Rockefeller Path. In his later years, William traded in his Baptist upbringing for a more epicurean life. "I used to be very much interested in the church," he told a friend in later years, "but I haven't attended for many a day."[47] Unlike John, William gave little to charity and turned a deaf ear to John's entreaties to contribute to the University of Chicago. At one point, when pressing William to help build a church, John needled him by saying: "Paintings are good, this would be better."[48] William was more jaundiced than John was about the motives of people who solicited his money.

It was in their stock-market operations that the two brothers differed most—so much so that John stayed aloof from enterprises in which William was involved. In declining a proposed investment, John simply told his financial staff, "No, that is William's," and that ended all discussion.[49] As a denizen of Wall Street, William was often found in his downtown office, puffing on a cigar and glancing at a stock ticker by the window. Besides being president of Standard Oil of New York, he was a director of forty companies, including railroads, banks, and copper mines, plus steamship, gas, and water companies. What irked John was that William engaged in stock promotions and market raids and other activities that he equated with gambling and manipulation. It might have been friction over this issue that caused their relationship to cool in the late 1890s. In 1897, John omitted William's name alone from a list of top Standard Oil executives slated to receive large salary increases, prompting this plaintive protest from Flagler:

> I wish you would include Will—from a purely business standpoint. I think he is worth as much as the younger of "the three others" and I doubt if you realize what a reflection upon him it would seem to be left out. The last day of this month will round out thirty years since I joined you and Will in business. Do not let us at this late day do anything that will have the appearance even of unkindness. I think I know Will's personal feeling for you better than you do—it is far more kindly than you imagine.[50]

John held back from William's stock-market deals in part because he associated them with James Stillman, who on the strength of his Standard Oil connections and his friendship with William had converted National City Bank into New York's largest bank. "I like William," said Stillman, a darkly elegant, taciturn man, "because we don't have to talk. Often we sit fifteen minutes in silence before one of us breaks it!"[51] They were an oddly matched pair, William good-natured and easygoing, Stillman an icy individual who played his cards close to the vest. One of Stillman's descendants left this description of him: "Stern, brooding, forever silent except when dropping sardonic remarks, he was known on Wall Street as 'the man with the iron mask.' "[52] At one point, Stillman feuded with his wife and banished her forever from the house, forbidding his five children from mentioning her name. The rapport between James Stillman and William Rockefeller was transferred to their children. Stillman's daughters, Elsie and Isabel, married William's sons, William G. and Percy, breeding a line of Stillman Rockefellers who would be central figures in the subsequent history of National City Bank, today's Citicorp.

Many contemporary critics assumed that John D. formed an investing triumvirate with his brother and Stillman; in fact, he had serious reservations about Stillman's character and regretted his friendship with William. Evidently, Stillman repaid the compliment. One day, he dropped by 26 Broadway to visit William, strolled over to Junior's desk, and proceeded to make derogatory comments about Senior. At once, Junior rose stiffly to his feet, spluttering, "Mr. Stillman, you can say those things to my father but you can't say them to his son. Good day."[53]

In spite of their uneasy relationship, Stillman invited Junior to become a National City Bank director in 1901. Junior was tempted to accept but feared that Stillman's rival J. P. Morgan might retaliate by excluding his father from underwriting syndicates. Senior was more concerned that the appointment might lend credence to the bothersome canard that he held a major stake in National City Bank. If Junior took the position, Senior warned him, it "might seem to indicate a closer relation in that quarter than really exists, or would be wise for us to publish to the world."[54] For once defying his father's wishes, Junior joined the National City Bank board; Senior, relenting, bought ten thousand shares of the bank's stock. As it turned out, Junior resigned from the bank board the following year, finding some of its practices questionable.

The significance of Senior's stake in National City Bank should not be overstated. A 1906 statement of his holdings shows that he had $415,000 invested in the bank as opposed to $375,000 in the First National Bank—controlled by Morgan's crony George F. Baker—while his largest bank holding was $1.4 million in New York Trust, dominated by the Harkness family. He also bought a substantial stake in Bankers Trust when it was started in 1903. In general, Rockefeller deliberately avoided National City Bank and the Standard Oil crowd, but he chose never to make that public and thought it unconscionably craven that William, Stillman, and Henry Rogers failed to disabuse the press. Once asked privately about Stillman's bank, he replied dryly, "It is called, I am told, the Rockefeller institution. But I don't control it. I have perhaps $300,000 of its stock, and its capital is $200,000,000. . . . I have never been in the building in my life. Why, I declare I don't even know where it is located."[55]

Rockefeller did acquire a major interest in one bank. After the Armstrong Investigation of 1905 exposed massive double-dealing between insurance companies and their bankers, reform legislation was enacted in 1911 that forced the Equitable Life Assurance Company to spin off its subsidiary, the Equitable Trust Company. Seizing this chance, Rockefeller, George Gould, and Kuhn, Loeb took control, with Rockefeller the principal shareholder. Rockefeller hoped to participate in the bank's lucrative financial operations and soon urged all companies within the Standard Oil universe to switch their accounts to the bank. Profiting from the Rockefeller tie, the Equitable Trust became within a decade America's eighth-largest bank. The move was fraught with significance for the Rockefellers, for the bank was to merge with the Chase Bank following the 1929 crash; the resulting institution would be the fortress of Rockefeller-family finance. If the descendants of William Rockefeller were identified with National City, the progeny of John D. were always associated with Chase.

=

Of the three principals in the Standard Oil crowd—Rogers, Stillman, and William Rockefeller—it was Henry H. Rogers who most entranced the public. In the pantheon of Standard directors, nobody save John D. himself achieved wider fame. There was something lithe and lethal, charming and fierce, about Rogers that made him a magnetic figure even to those he repelled. At Standard Oil, they affectionately dubbed him the "Savage Old Tiger," while Wall Street, taking his initials, christened him Hell Hound Rogers. He was a handsome and athletic man, with a theatrical mustache, a sharp gaze, and a swashbuckling aura.

Rogers had a chameleon personality. He could be sensitive and generous one moment, a pitiless foe the next. In Manhattan clubs and drawing rooms, he charmed companions, relating hilarious stories and playing a wicked game of poker. He was also very charitable: He helped Colonel Edwin Drake's impoverished widow and also built a school, library, church, parish house, and masonic hall in his hometown of Fairhaven, Massachusetts. "He looked at you and he owned you," said one Standard Oil colleague, fascinated by his kaleidoscopic moods. "He was affable unless you tramped on his little toe. He was a man of the fiercest likes and dislikes that I ever knew in the business."[56] "His expression could transform itself totally while he blinked his eyes," a reporter wrote in the *Evening Post*. "His voice could travel through the scale of vindictiveness, indifference, politeness, affability and friendliness in a single sentence."[57]

Rogers's journey from an impecunious boyhood to the summit of Wall Street affluence was startling. A sea captain's son, he spent his adolescence clerking in a grocery store, hawking newspapers, and working on a railroad before setting off with a friend to operate a small refinery outside Oil City. Through a mutual friend, he was introduced to Charles Pratt, who bought his operation and ushered him into the Standard Oil fold. Had he stuck to oil, Rogers would have fared far better in his relations with Rockefeller, who thought he divided both his time and loyalty. From his elegant mahogany office, decorated with small bronze bulls and bears, Rogers hatched deals by the dozen, forcing reporters to work full-time to track his machinations. At one point, he became the veritable czar of Staten Island, controlling its trolleys, railroads, ferries, and electric and gas companies. In 1884, he and William Rockefeller formed the Consolidated Gas Company to provide gas to Brooklyn, and he also vied with J. Edward Addicks for control of Boston gas.

With his executive flair, Rogers thought he was the ideal candidate to succeed Rockefeller and he was elevated to vice president of the trust in 1890. He therefore bristled when Archbold was tapped for the top spot. The decision was partly a question of style. Rockefeller was irked by Rogers's gambling and profanity, his strutting in public and mingling with high society. Rockefeller also favored Archbold because he was wedded to Standard Oil business, whereas Rogers was often distracted by other interests. Rogers sometimes bullied Standard Oil subordinates to starve his gas competitors of needed oil, even if this hurt Standard profits—a cardinal sin in Rockefeller's view.

The flash point in the feud between Rockefeller and Rogers came in 1899 when James Stillman, William Rockefeller, and Rogers acquired secret control of Anaconda Copper of Butte, Montana, a mining venture formerly owned by Senator George Hearst. They made the purchase with a $39 million loan from National City Bank. They then turned around, restyled the new holding company Amalgamated Copper, and fobbed it off on a gullible public for $75 million, retiring the $39 million loan and pocketing a $36 million profit. Rockefeller was incensed by the issuance of so much watered stock, which gave him a chance to feel self-righteous when his own virtue was under attack. The new company was floated by Stillman and National City Bank, and both William and Rogers exploited their Standard Oil connections to stoke a speculative fever.

To execute this deal, Rogers made the mistake of inviting a sharp-eyed Boston stockbroker named Thomas W. Lawson into the project. Starting in July 1904, Lawson published a tell-all account in *Everybody's* magazine that was later collected into a classic volume entitled *Frenzied Finance*. The most melodramatic potboiler in American financial history, the book opened with this histrionic dedication: "TO PENITENCE: that those whose deviltry is exposed within its pages may see in a true light the wrongs they have wrought—and repent."[58] Describing himself as a mere "neophyte in crime," Lawson gave his exposé a confessional note: "I have unwittingly been made the instrument by which thousands upon thousands of investors in America and Europe have been plundered."[59]

The gist of his indictment was that the public paid two-thirds of the purchase price for Amalgamated Copper while Rogers and his comrades took two-thirds of the stock. At the time, Lawson noted, Standard Oil was considered "the greatest power in the land," and its supposed involvement had stimulated a buying mania.[60] At the subscription deadline on May 4, 1899, mobs had formed outside National City Bank, and four burly policemen had to shut the doors against these disappointed investors. With the offering five times oversubscribed, Rogers handed out preferred allotments to favored politicians. Rogers and William Rockefeller had lured investors with the promise of their own involvement, but they dumped stock soon after it was issued. Lawson's character sketches were as memorable as his revelations about the syndicate's methods. Oddly, he expressed affection for William Rockefeller, whom he portrayed as solid, laconic, and far more trustworthy than Rogers. In Henry Rogers, he found his true protagonist, a mutable man of violent extremes, an actor of genius who got lost in the many roles he shuffled:

> Yet away from the intoxicating spell of dollar-making this remarkable man is one of the most charming and lovable human beings I have ever encountered, a man whom any man or woman would be proud to have for a brother. . . . Once he passes under the baleful influence of "The Machine," however, he becomes a relentless, ravenous creature, pitiless as a shark, knowing no law of God or man in the execution of his purpose.[61]

By liberally splashing the names *Rockefeller* and *Standard Oil* across his pages, Lawson made it seem as if John D. had formed a conspiratorial trio with Rogers and William. At one point, he said more truthfully, "It was the first venture of size these two strong wheelmen [Rogers and William] of 'Standard Oil' had undertaken without the cooperation of John D. Rockefeller, and it appeared that he was considerably worked up over the public hubbub, and so opposed to the whole Amalgamated affair that nothing short of a great success could justify his subordinates' temerity."[62] In a footnote, Lawson further conceded that Rockefeller never put a dime into the Amalgamated flotation. Nevertheless, the general public came away with the impression that John D. was pulling the strings.

At one point, Lawson quoted Rogers's views on the merits of cartels versus competition: "No man has done his business properly who has missed a single dollar he could have secured in the doing of it. . . . It is one of the first principles Mr. Rockefeller taught me; it is one he has inculcated in every 'Standard Oil' man, until today it is a religion with us all."[63] While Rogers was talking in general terms, it again left the impression that John D. lurked somewhere behind the copper trust.

Had he not been unfairly implicated, Rockefeller might have enjoyed the rebuke delivered to Rogers. When the Lawson series began, Junior rushed him a copy, declaring, "I think you will be well repaid for reading this article, although it seems to be written in a bitter, vituperative, sensational manner."[64] Any such satisfaction, however, paled before the sense that he had been unjustly slandered. "They said I owned copper stock—that Boston man said it—when as a matter of fact it belonged to my partners and I had nothing to do with it," he was still seething years later. "It was not pleasant to sit still and take all the abuse and not hear one word of explanation from them."[65] Rockefeller suffered in silence, knowing that if he spoke up he would have to repudiate his brother. After the Lawson series, John D. and Rogers saw each other only twice during the next five years.

In early 1907, Rockefeller took revenge against Rogers at a meeting of Standard Oil's board of directors. After investing millions of his own money in the Virginia Railway, a coal-carrying railroad in Virginia, Rogers could no longer carry the debt and sought relief from Standard Oil. Spying his chance to cut Rogers down to size, Rockefeller told his partners, "Gentlemen, we should not as an organization become involved in other corporations or side issues. We are making money and success as an oil corporation and we should confine our efforts to Standard alone." When a vote was taken, Rockefeller prevailed, and Rogers grew so enraged that he slammed his fist on the table, threatening to sell every share of Standard Oil stock he owned. To this, Rockefeller placidly replied, "What is your price?" When Rogers named it, Rockefeller rejoined, "I will meet you here with a certified check tomorrow at 10." The next day, in an incalculable blunder, Rogers handed over his block of Standard Oil stock to Rockefeller, surrendering in a moment of pique a vast fortune in future dividends and appreciation.[66] As we shall see shortly, Rockefeller might have had more than the Lawson series on his mind, for he thought that Rogers had played a treacherous trick on him by meeting with Ida Tarbell.

Posterity has received another portrait of Henry H. Rogers, and, given the power of the pen that drew it, it has been an imperishable one. Something of a literary man, Rogers had long admired Mark Twain and read his books aloud to his children. "If I ever meet that man," he once commented, "I'd like to do something for him."[67] He thus responded with alacrity in 1893 when Twain's friend Clarence Rice asked if Rogers would meet the author at the Murray Hill Hotel to discuss the bankruptcy of Twain's publishing house, which was staggering under heavy debts. The two men, who had met on a yacht two years before, were both legendary raconteurs and wits and developed an instant rapport. Rogers decided to mount a rescue effort and the next morning wrote out a check for eight thousand dollars. Taking Twain's finances in hand, he kept Twain's creditors at bay and rallied his spirits, inviting him along with Archbold to prizefights at the New York Athletic Club. With canny foresight, Rogers insisted that Twain retain all his copyrights, "a service which saved me and my family from want and assured us permanent comfort and prosperity," Twain said later.[68] Under Rogers's tutelage, Twain invested his royalties wisely and paid off his debts. Awash with gratitude, Twain refused to publish Henry Demarest Lloyd's *Wealth Against Commonwealth.*

A friend of infinite tact, Rogers endeared himself to Twain as much by the manner as the substance of what he did. "By no sign, no hint, no word did he ever betray any consciousness that I was under obligations to him," Twain wrote. "I have never been so great as that, and I have not known another who was."[69] Their friendship survived Twain's financial crisis, and Rogers later negotiated lucrative book contracts for Twain, who became a frequent guest aboard Rogers's steam yacht, the *Kanawha.* (During one cruise, Twain composed his sketch "The Loaves and the Fishes," in which he argued that the true miracle of the biblical story was not the multiplication of bread and fishes but that twelve disciples served five thousand people and lived to tell the tale.) When Rogers was devastated by Lawson's vitriolic portrait in *Frenzied Finance,* Twain supplied favorable anecdotes about him for a profile in *The World's Work,* a magazine published by Frank Doubleday. For Rogers, Twain reserved his highest encomium: "He is not only the best friend I have ever had, but is the best man I have known."[70]

A frequent visitor to 26 Broadway, Twain loved to smoke cigars, read, and lounge on the sofa in Rogers's office while his friend entertained a steady stream of visitors. He had no concerns about Rogers's reputation. "He's a pirate all right," Twain said, "but he owns up to it and enjoys being a pirate. That's the reason I like him."[71] For a time, Twain turned 26 Broadway into his downtown clubhouse and sometimes lunched with Junior. "I got down here to the Standard Oil in time for late luncheon with young Rockefeller—it is the best homemade table in the North," Twain once told his wife.[72] He formed a favorable opinion of Junior as "a plain, simple, earnest, sincere, honest, well-meaning, commonplace person, destitute of originality or any suggestion of it."[73] A defender to the end, Twain later blamed the muckrakers and Teddy Roosevelt for Standard Oil's infamy. That the trust had scarcely had a strike in more than four decades proved to him that "the Standard Oil chiefs cannot be altogether bad or they would oppress their sixty-five thousand employees from habit and instinct, if they are so constituted that it is instinctive with them to oppress everybody else."[74]

Another perceptive author developed intense affection for Rogers. In 1896, the sixteen-year-old Helen Keller, who was blind and deaf, met him and Twain at a gathering to raise money for her future education. Even before the meeting, Twain laid the groundwork, telling Mrs. Rogers, "It won't do for America to allow this marvelous child to retire from her studies because of poverty."[75] Rogers paid for much of Helen Keller's education at Radcliffe College, which she gratefully acknowledged. "That I haven't missed my small part of usefulness in the world, I owe to Mr. Clemens and Mr. Rogers," she wrote.[76] After graduating cum laude, Helen stayed in touch with Rogers and poignantly dedicated her book *The World I Live In* to "My Dear Friend of Many Years."[77] Before he died, Rogers established an annuity that gave her lifelong security. Helen Keller's teacher, Anne Sullivan, later revealed that "Mr. Rockefeller [Junior] and his father have been interested in Helen most of her life."[78] Unlike the help from Rogers, the Rockefeller money was given anonymously.

In the 1890s, Rockefeller stumbled, almost by accident, into owning most of the iron ore on the Mesabi Range, the last business project that he executed on a monumental scale.

This legendary investment began as another blunder bequeathed by his bumbling former advisers, Colby and Hoyt. When Gates first examined the iron-ore properties the two had bought in Cuba, Michigan, and Wisconsin, he thought they were worthless holes. Colby and Hoyt had, however, unearthed one promising entity: the Minnesota Iron Company. Gates was impressed on a westward journey by the potential of the Mesabi Range, which contained a broad band of iron ore laid across a 120-mile strip in northern Minnesota. Though it held out hope of being the richest such vein ever found in North America, its commercial utility had not been demonstrated. Unlike hard rock dug from underground mines and fed into blast furnaces, the Mesabi ore was fine, powdery stuff that either clogged furnaces or blew out their chimneys, scattering dust across the countryside. On the other hand, it lay close to the surface and in such abundance that it could be scooped out by steam shovels at a fraction of the expense of underground mines.

Among the pioneers in Mesabi ore were the backwoods Merritt family. These so-called seven men of iron—four brothers and three nephews—borrowed recklessly, snapped up tremendous tracts of land, then launched construction of a railroad to carry the ore to Lake Superior. When the 1893 panic savaged iron prices, however, they faced a severe cash squeeze. The atmosphere in Duluth grew incendiary as workers with drawn pistols forced their way into the office of the Merritts' railroad to demand payment of overdue wages.

In rescuing the Merritts, Rockefeller reenacted his old pattern of swooping down, fortified with cash, on distressed properties and seizing a commanding position. As with the malodorous Lima oil, he wagered that the Mesabi ore would someday be of value—even as Andrew Carnegie and his experts gleefully scoffed at this preposterous idea. As Carnegie's right-hand man, Charles Schwab, said of these naysayers, "They couldn't understand how [Rockefeller], without knowledge of the iron business, could invest money in ores that were useless—at least for a long time to come."[79] To which Rockefeller retorted tersely, "It was a surprise to me that the great iron and steel manufacturers did not place what seemed to be an adequate value on these mines."[80] He believed that, like the early days in oil, the steel industry was on the verge of overproduction and would soon fall prey to suicidal competition unless stabilized by strong owners. An expert in the strategic importance of transportation, he avidly eyed the extensive rail and dock facilities controlled by the Merritts.

When Rockefeller advanced money to the Merritts in the panic summer of 1893, he was one of the few people who could have saved them. Naively, he expected to disburse a modest $100,000, and he never imagined that the Mesabi project would tax his colossal resources and consume eight years of his time. In exchange for his investment, Rockefeller negotiated a deal with the Merritts to set up a holding company, the Lake Superior Consolidated Iron Mines, which would combine the Merritts' rail and mining assets and the rather mediocre mining properties cobbled together by Colby and Hoyt. The idea was that the Merritts would run the company and employ Rockefeller's cash infusion to finish the stalled railroad. At first, Rockefeller owned only a fifth of the stock, but he exercised final control through his first mortgage bonds, which enjoyed a lien on the entire company in the event of a default.

Given their intertwined fates, it seems odd that Rockefeller met the head of the Minnesota family, Leonidas Merritt, on only a single occasion and then briefly in June 1893. Gates tried to shield Rockefeller from such contacts, but Merritt warmly insisted that he wished to shake his savior's hand. When they met at 26 Broadway, the meeting lasted five minutes, and Rockefeller was the pattern of affability. He touted the virtues of the Mesabi venture then turned to the Minnesota weather. After a few more pleasantries, he politely excused himself and never saw any of the Merritts again. Afterward, Gates made it clear that his boss would now withdraw behind his customary screen. "In talking to me," he told Leonidas Merritt, "you are talking to Mr. Rockefeller."[81] Even by his own extremely reclusive standards, Rockefeller was remarkably aloof during his eight-year fling in the iron business. Though he became chief landlord of the Mesabi Range, he set foot on its slopes only once and that was long after he had disposed of his properties.

In the autumn, Rockefeller's goodwill toward the Merritts ebbed. As their notes matured, they frantically pressed Gates for cash, and Rockefeller reluctantly obliged them with loans. Gates matured as a businessman during this crisis, and Rockefeller bestowed exceptional authority on him. When Gates visited Duluth in September, Rockefeller confided to Cettie, "[Gates] reports progress daily, and has one hundred thousand dollars in his pocket to use at his discretion."[82] By October, the initial loan had burgeoned to nearly $2 million, with no guarantee that the Mesabi ore would ever demonstrate commercial value. It all seemed a gamble gone hideously wrong. Pacing the Forest Hill porches, Rockefeller later remembered the harrowing, sometimes daily emergencies forced upon him by the uncouth Merritts, who kept their securities stuffed in their pockets: "I had to loan my personal securities to raise money, and finally we were compelled to supply a great deal of actual cash, and to get it we were obliged to go into the then greatly upset money market and buy currency at a high premium and ship west by express to pay the laborers and the railroad and to keep them alive."[83]

In early 1894, still burdened by debt, the Merritts were forced to offer Rockefeller ninety thousand shares of Consolidated stock at ten dollars a share. As with Standard Oil, Rockefeller kept adding to his Consolidated holdings, the ten-dollar price being on a par with his other purchases at the time; the Merritts, though, vociferously claimed they had been swindled. A year later, they had to forfeit to Rockefeller an option on another 55,000 shares of Consolidated stock, surrendering to him complete control of the company. With fullthroated passion, Gates urged Rockefeller to expand his investment. "It is, in my opinion, the opportunity of a lifetime, one of those opportunities, the seizing or failing to seize, which marks the difference between success and failure in life."[84]

During the next few years, as steelmakers found ways to adapt their furnaces to the bargain-priced Mesabi ore, Consolidated stock rose to stratospheric heights. In a paroxysm of frustrated rage, the Merritts demonized the man they had earlier heralded as their savior. In a rancorous suit filed against Rockefeller in federal circuit court in Duluth, they portrayed themselves as innocent lumberjacks fleeced by the eastern mogul. Fearing a biased local jury, Rockefeller retained a Minnesota newspaperman to counteract local hostility toward him and even stepped up his Baptist-missionary donations in the state. As Rockefeller feared, the Duluth jury reached a verdict in favor of the Merritts, though it was overturned on appeal. The whole feud was finally settled out of court: Rockefeller paid $525,000 to the Merritts, who publicly retracted their charges. Of this settlement, Rockefeller commented sarcastically, "We settled, paid money, rather than submit to larger robbery by the twelve just and good men, as we could not get to a higher court."[85] Stung by the controversy, Gates was still defending his behavior almost twenty years later in a short polemical pamphlet, *The Truth About Mr. Rockefeller and the Merritts*, which he mailed out gratis to ten thousand people.

While Rockefeller and Gates were irked by the Merritts' ingratitude, they were not entirely blameless. The Merritts alleged that Rockefeller had inflated the value of the mining properties he contributed to Consolidated, a charge that seems substantiated by Gates's own papers. In early 1893, he had written two letters to Frank Rockefeller, expressing shock at the high prices Colby and Hoyt had paid for the mines. He summed up their value as follows: "Whatever induced Colby Hoyt & Co. to form syndicates to pay such enormous figures for those worthless properties, I cannot understand. I mean to keep pegging along at it from time to time until the whole thing comes out."[86]

⸻

Having acquired several million tons of iron ore and a railroad to cart it off, Rockefeller was now stymied by a group of Lake Superior shippers who would lease him vessels only at extortionate rates. To end the deadlock, Rockefeller again recruited a talented man from the enemy ranks, Samuel Mather of Cleveland, a son-in-law of Amasa Stone. On one of those historic occasions when the curtain parted fleetingly to reveal the wizard working the levers, Rockefeller held a cordial, ten-minute, predinner chat with Mather at West Fifty-fourth Street. The visitor left with a three-million-dollar order to build twelve ore-carrying ships, steel monsters that would surpass in size anything ever floated on the Great Lakes. After shaking hands with Rockefeller, Mather never saw him again.

Given the large number of ships that he had to build, Mather figured that the shipyards would gang up and gouge him, so he pretended that he needed only one or two. After the contractors submitted their bids, they were stunned to discover that they all had contracts. The operation of this fleet required another engineering feat: the creation of specially constructed docks on Lake Superior with long railroad trestles extending hundreds of feet into the water. As the lake's shipping cartel watched in consternation, the Rockefeller operation began to load ore at the stupefying rate of ten thousand tons every six hours.

Where the schooners had charged $4.20 a ton, Rockefeller's operators carried their mineral cargo at a cost of 80 cents a ton.

When Mather declined to manage the fleet, Rockefeller asked Gates to suggest an experienced firm to pilot the ships. "No," said Gates, increasingly showing flashes of a quirky independence, "I do not know of any firm to suggest at the moment, but why not run them ourselves?" Taken aback, Rockefeller replied, "You don't know anything about ships, do you?" Gates confessed not but nominated his uncle LaMont Montgomery Bowers as a candidate. "He lives up the state, and never was on a ship in his life. He probably wouldn't know the bow from the stern, or a sea-anchor from an umbrella, but he has good sense, he is honest, enterprising, keen, and thrifty."[87] Having often hired people based on general ability, not specific skills—Gates himself being a prime example—Rockefeller acceded to the choice.

Bald and well-tailored, Bowers had an extensive business résumé, ranging from selling soap to running a real-estate agency in Omaha to selling groceries in upstate New York. Much to Rockefeller's delight, he not only ably commanded but considerably expanded the fleet. Mostly under the aegis of the Cleveland-based Bessemer Steamship Company, Rockefeller acquired fifty-six steel vessels, the largest fleet on the Great Lakes and the world's biggest assemblage of ore carriers. His position in lake shipping was so unassailable that he could dictate rates on Lake Superior, much as they had been dictated to him a few years earlier—a situation that galvanized Andrew Carnegie into organizing the competing Pittsburgh Steamship Company.

Tutored by Gates in the eccentric ways of Mr. Rockefeller, Bowers was told that he must not, under any circumstances, communicate with the boss. Rockefeller never saw the vast majority of ships in his armada. One day, however, Rockefeller dropped by unexpectedly to consult him on a shipping matter, prompting a humorous exchange. "You are making me break the orders I have from your own office, Mr. Rockefeller," Bowers reminded him. "Oh, Mr. Bowers, I am getting along in years," Rockefeller replied in his droll, midwestern manner. "I think I may really be allowed a little liberty by my office!"[88] Bowers's success in managing the fleet was perhaps unfortunate, for it led directly to his later assignment to a Rockefeller-controlled mining venture in the Rocky Mountains called Colorado Fuel and Iron, where he would bring lasting disgrace to the Rockefeller name.

Rockefeller's success on the Mesabi Range precipitated a clash between America's two wealthiest individuals, John D. Rockefeller and Andrew Carnegie. In their approach to business, the two men had often mirrored each other, stressing attention to detail, ruthlessly slashing costs, and keeping dividends low. Both had struggled with their own unacknowledged avarice, pioneered in philanthropy, and prided themselves on being friends of the working man. Yet they never seemed to get along. Each Christmas, they perfunctorily exchanged gifts, Rockefeller giving Carnegie a paper vest, while Carnegie sent the teetotaler excellent whiskey. In letters to his colleagues, Carnegie often struck a jeering tone toward Rockefeller, refusing to concede his business acumen, and he suffered under the misapprehension that Rockefeller had conspired with Standard Oil colleagues in the Mesabi venture. Upon first hearing of his pact with the Merritts, Carnegie lectured his steel-company board, "Remember Rockafellows [sic] & Porter will own the [railroad] and that's like owning the pipe lines—Producers will not have much of a show. . . . I don't think Standard people will succeed in making ore a monopoly like oil, they have failed in every new venture and Rockefeller's reputation now is one of the poorest investors in the world."[89]

Much too patronizing toward Rockefeller, Carnegie had seriously misjudged developments in the ore business. Having moved decisively to control coke and coal supplies, he assumed that ore would always remain cheap and plentiful and flatly told colleagues that their "brilliant and talented young partners" should stay clear of that business.[90] When a colorful Pittsburgh promoter, Henry Oliver, tried to interest Carnegie in a joint venture with the Merritts, he responded with a tongue-lashing: "If there is any department of business which offers no inducement, it is ore."[91] Luckily, Carnegie's subordinates overruled him and took a stake in the Mesabi ore. As a result, Carnegie Steel was not entirely excluded from the rush to secure properties in northern Minnesota.

Having failed to move aggressively, Carnegie looked on impotently as Rockefeller applied to iron ore lessons he had learned in oil, such as controlling an industry through transportation and demoralizing competitors with prices too low for them to match. Two industry trends finally compelled Carnegie to broker a deal with Rockefeller. As mergers consolidated the steel industry, it became essential to pin down sure sources of supply. And as new furnaces were equipped to use the dirt-cheap Mesabi ore, it developed into the industry standard. By 1896, the press buzzed with speculation that Rockefeller would build a huge steel mill in Cleveland or south Chicago, forge a steel trust on the Standard Oil model, and go head-to-head with Andrew Carnegie. Meanwhile, Rockefeller poured another nineteen million dollars into the Mesabi Range to buttress his railroad and shipping operations.

It vexed Carnegie that Rockefeller, an oilman, had possessed such superior foresight in the iron-ore business. In his private correspondence, he vented his frustration in petty digs, referring to him derisively as Rockafellow and later on as Wreckafellow. In December 1896, a humbled Carnegie at last consented to a sweeping deal. He promised to consume the entire output of Rockefeller's chief mines (a minimum of 600,000 tons of ore) at the rock-bottom royalty rate of twenty-five cents a ton. In exchange for this steep discount, however, Carnegie agreed to ship the entire amount plus another 600,000 tons from his own mines over Rockefeller's railroads and on his vessels. It was the same kind of back-scratching arrangement that Rockefeller had negotiated with the railroads to monopolize the oil industry. To complete their truce, Carnegie pledged to refrain from buying new Mesabi fields or transporting iron ore, while Rockefeller renounced any ambition to construct a steel mill. A generation later, Carnegie still boasted of this deal before a Senate committee. "Don't you know, it does my heart good to think I got ahead of John D. Rockefeller on a bargain."[92] In fact, the bargain had been Carnegie's belated attempt to redress his own error.

Small competitors found it impossible to survive the union of the largest producer and largest consumer of iron ore, and Carnegie and Rockefeller profited smartly. As with oil, ore prices skidded lower, bankrupting marginal producers and bolstering the Rockefeller-Carnegie alliance. As the decade closed, ferocious competition broke out for the remaining Mesabi properties. The price of Lake Superior Consolidated stock that Rockefeller had bought for $10 in 1894 levitated to $60 in 1899, $70 in 1900, then a staggering $100 in 1901.

=

America now stood on the threshold of an era of economic consolidation that saw trusts spread to many industries. What Rockefeller had accomplished in oil a generation earlier was now being imitated in steel, copper, rubber, tobacco, leather, and other products—much to the alarm of many voters. The ideological lines were drawn sharply in the 1896 presidential election. The Democratic candidate, William Jennings Bryan, an eloquent orator adored by socialists, populists, and silverites, vied with former Ohio governor William McKinley, a staunch advocate of tariffs, trusts, and hard currency. Apprehensive about a Bryan presidency, businessmen transformed the McKinley campaign into a crusade against trustbusting infidels. Standard Oil supplied $250,000 to McKinley's coffers—equal to half of the total Democratic contributions—and Rockefeller sent another $2,500 to campaign manager Mark Hanna. For a man normally scornful of politicians, Rockefeller displayed unusual passion for McKinley, asserting, "I can see nothing else for us to do, to serve the Country and our honor."[93]

The business community reacted to the McKinley victory as if America had been blessedly spared a revolution, a mood summed up in Hanna's congratulatory telegram to McKinley: "God's in his heaven—all's right with the world."[94] During the next few years, a new faith arose in business circles about the inevitability and unrivaled efficiency of monopolies. Mark Hanna, now tagged "Dollar Mark" by the press, proclaimed loudly that the Sherman Antitrust Act would never be allowed to thwart this trend in a Republican administration.

Stimulated by the Spanish-American War, the Klondike gold strike, and McKinley's reassuring presence, the American economy surged ahead in the late 1890s, propelling the United States past all other nations in industrial capacity. In a country that still liked to picture itself as composed of small businesses, huge companies now blanketed markets from coast to coast. As satirist Finley Peter Dunne observed in 1897, "I have seen America spread out from th' Atlantic to th' Pacific, with a branch office iv th' Standard Ile Comp'ny in ivry hamlet."[95] Between 1898 and 1902, 198 trusts or giant new corporations were created in coal, sugar, and other industries, prompting a growing backlash. At a Chicago antitrust conference in 1898, William Jennings Bryan drew roars from the faithful when he shouted, "One of the great purposes of government is to put rings in the noses of hogs!"[96] The McKinley administration, true to its promises, stood guard over the new corporate giants.

The merger wave conferred a new centrality on Wall Street investment houses, for the capital needs of the new trusts dwarfed the resources of small-town banks and private individuals. Only the prestigious Wall Street firms such as J. P. Morgan and Company or Kuhn, Loeb could tap the foreign and domestic capital needed to execute these transactions. Switching their focus from railroad bonds to industrial securities, they forged the new trusts, issued their stock, tucked away shares for themselves, and handpicked their executives. However much reformers deplored the trusts, they excited many investors, who absorbed wave after wave of new issues sponsored by Wall Street. While many Americans quaked before these giant new concerns, many others were trying to figure out how to profit from them.

When J. P. Morgan decided to create a steel trust in late 1900, he knew he would have to tangle with two men who were confirmed cynics about Wall Street: Carnegie, master of the steel mills, and Rockefeller, king of the iron ore. Morgan was worried that Carnegie would diversify into finished steel products and threaten his recently launched Federal Steel Company, while Carnegie feared a reverse maneuver by Morgan. Meanwhile, Carnegie and Morgan were both alarmed by reports that Rockefeller might diversify into steel mills. To avert overbuilding and internecine price wars, Morgan decided to spearhead a new steel consolidation.

Morgan was not thrilled about catering to Rockefeller, who had flouted Wall Street by financing his trust from retained earnings and holding cash reserves equal to those of many banks. He was also well aware of William Rockefeller's intimacy with James Stillman of National City Bank. When Morgan contemplated a merger with the London house of Barings in 1904, his counterpart, Lord Revelstoke, reported afterward to a partner that Morgan "inveighed bitterly against the growing power of the Jews and of the Rockefeller crowd, and said more than once that our firm and his were the only two composed of white men in New York."[97]

In many respects, Rockefeller and Morgan were antithetical types, offering a vivid contrast between the ascetic and the sybarite, the Roundhead and the

Cavalier. As the chieftain of the Anglo-American financial establishment, the wellborn Morgan, expensively educated in America and Europe, was a consummate insider in the business world. For more than forty years, he had been the chief conduit for British capital that had financed American railroads and industry. Blustery and theatrical, Morgan was impetuous and hot-blooded, cursed with a short attention span. At his headquarters at 23 Wall Street, he often seemed harried, ruling by brilliant snap judgments. Fond of luxury, Morgan inhabited the world of the ultrarich, with their gargantuan cigars, fine port, and oversized steam yachts.

For Rockefeller, Morgan embodied all the sins of pride, luxury, and arrogance. When they first met at William Rockefeller's Hudson River mansion, they took an instant dislike to each other. "We had a few pleasant words," noted Rockefeller. "But I could see that Mr. Morgan was very much—well, like Mr. Morgan; very haughty, very inclined to look down on other men. I looked at him. For my part, I have never been able to see why any man should have such a high and mighty feeling about himself."[98] For Morgan, Rockefeller was too dry and prudish, devoid of manly charms and vices. And how could he not grumble at the effrontery of someone who had created a cartel without him?

Nevertheless, both men detested competition as a destructive force, a dangerously antiquated notion. For years, Morgan had arbitrated disputes among railroad presidents, helping them to carve up territories, and his formation of industrial trusts constituted a logical progression in his career. When Judge Elbert H. Gary informed Morgan in early 1901 that Rockefeller's Mesabi interests had to form part of any steel cartel, Morgan balked. "We have got all we can attend to," he told Gary. When Gary persisted, Morgan glumly agreed that they had to incorporate Lake Superior Consolidated Iron Mines and Bessemer Steamship into U.S. Steel.

"How are we going to get them?" he asked.

"You are going to talk to Mr. Rockefeller," said Gary.

"I would not think of it," said Morgan.

"Why?"

"I don't like him."

"Mr. Morgan," Gary retorted, "when a business proposition of so great importance to the Steel Corporation is involved, would you let a personal prejudice interfere with your success?"

"I don't know," said Morgan.[99]

In all likelihood, Morgan's attitude was a mixture of haughtiness and cowardice, for Rockefeller was one of the few people he could not intimidate. In an act of considerable self-mortification, Morgan asked Rockefeller if he could see him at 26 Broadway. Explaining that he was retired and never went to the office, Rockefeller said he would be happy to receive him at West Fifty-fourth Street. Rockefeller knew the bargaining edge of the last-minute holdout and enjoyed tweaking Wall Street's foremost banker. Soon after he arrived at Rockefeller's house, Morgan gruffly asked the price of the ore properties. Rockefeller threw up his hands in mock despair, reminded Morgan that he was retired, and told him to discuss the deal with his twenty-seven-year-old son, "who would undoubtedly be glad" to talk with him.[100] This was a blatant affront, but the banker grudgingly said that Junior should call at his office at Broad and Wall Streets.

Relishing their little game, Senior and Junior stalled in arranging the meeting and very nearly overplayed their hand. Then, on the morning of February 25, 1901, Henry Rogers stopped by Junior's desk and inquired, "Would you like to go with me to meet Mr. Morgan?"[101] Sensing that the time had come to put Morgan out of his misery, Junior accompanied Rogers that afternoon. Now it was Morgan's turn to behave in a condescending manner. When Rogers and Junior entered his office, he was consulting with his partner Charles Steele and did not look up from his desk. When Steele left, Morgan finally lifted his eyes, and Rogers introduced Junior. Morgan complained about the delay and said matters had to be wrapped up within twenty-four hours. Junior explained that it had taken time to appraise the properties. "Well," Morgan barked, glowering at Junior, "what's your price?"

If Morgan thought he was dealing with a choirboy, he was soon undeceived. Showing an unexpected pluck that nobody, not even Junior, knew was there, he shot back, "Mr. Morgan, I think there must be some mistake. I did not come here to sell. I understood you wished to buy."[102] He asked Morgan to name a price that his father might accept or decline. For Junior, it must have been a revelatory moment: He was sparring with Wall Street's potentate. When Morgan stepped out briefly, Henry Rogers, flabbergasted, advised Junior to soften his tone, but Junior said he meant every word and that he and father were "absolutely indifferent about coming into the consolidation."[103] The tense standoff ended in a compromise: Morgan and Junior agreed that Henry Clay Frick would serve as an honest broker to establish a mutually agreeable price. As Junior was leaving, he asked Morgan whether his father might take a share in the steel syndication. Taking another jab, Morgan replied that the offering was oversubscribed and that he had delayed too long in submitting his request. Since Morgan had already set aside five-million-dollar allotments for William Rockefeller and James Stillman, he must have known that John D. would be stung by this exclusion.

When Junior returned to 26 Broadway, he immediately wrote to his parents, describing Morgan's brusqueness and his response. "The whole thing suggested the final sweep-up of the room and we seemed to be the crumbs around the edge which of course must be swept up and expect to be swept up and which it was most annoying to find at this late date still on the floor."[104] His parents were overjoyed that Junior had stood up to Morgan. His father, reading the letter aloud to Cettie, paused every few sentences to exclaim, "Great Caesar, but John is a trump!" Cettie—every inch the Spartan mother—was no less amazed. "Indeed you were masterly in the conduct of the negotiation," she wrote back, "and you are so quiet and unassuming in both words and manner. Control of self wins the battle, for it means control of others."[105] The ecstatic response of Junior's parents perhaps hints at relief from unspoken doubts, as if they both had wondered whether he could meet the demands imposed by the family fortune.

After the meeting, Morgan urged Frick to visit Rockefeller at his Pocantico estate. To avoid publicity, Frick took a carriage up after dark, and the coachman waited at the front gate while Frick and Rockefeller huddled behind some shrubbery. "Wouldn't it have made quite a story for the newspapers—our skulking around in the bushes in the dark?" Rockefeller later mused.[106] As usual, he was wary and distant, not tipping his hand. "As my son told Mr. Morgan, I am not anxious to sell my own properties. But as you surmise, I never wish to stand in the way of a worthy enterprise. I do frankly object, however, to a prospective purchaser arbitrarily fixing an 'outside figure,' and I cannot deal on such a basis."[107] When Frick finally told him that Judge Gary's figure for Rockefeller's ore properties was five million dollars below its true value, Rockefeller said curtly, "Then, I will trust you to represent me."[108] With his usual minimalist art, Rockefeller had concluded this epochal meeting in about fifteen minutes. On February 28, when Gates and Junior sat down with Frick at 26 Broadway, they maintained the party line that Rockefeller was not eager to sell. Just two weeks later, Rockefeller's papers show a startling development that altered the course of the negotiations. Gates had commissioned new maps of potential ore deposits along the Mesabi Range that disclosed for the first time the likely existence of undiscovered mines. As Junior interpreted this catastrophic news to his father, "We had supposed up to date that we now controlled practically all of the ore reserve of the range. In view of this new map, the information of which is known only to ourselves, we are more inclined to make some trade."[109] After this, the Rockefellers subtly softened their negotiating posture, aided by a rapport between Junior and Frick so strong that Junior was later made an executor of Frick's estate. "I have met no one in business whom I have been more strongly drawn to and have greater confidence in than Mr. Frick," Junior told his father in mid-March.[110] The talks were also assisted by Rockefeller's declared resolve not to extract the last penny so as "to leave a favorable and friendly impression on Mr. Morgan," as Junior put it.[111]

For all that, Rockefeller reaped a fantastic profit in the creation of U.S. Steel, the first billion-dollar corporation and the first trust to overtake Standard Oil in size. The Consolidated stock originally bought for $10 a share in 1893 now fetched the equivalent of $160 in cash in 1901. Gates and Junior made an agreement with Frick that the Rockefellers would receive $80 million for the

Consolidated stock—half in the form of U.S. Steel common stock and half in preferred—and another $8.5 million for the fifty-six lake vessels of the Bessemer fleet. Gates estimated that $55 million of the $88.5 million was clear profit. The U.S. Steel deal swelled Rockefeller's net worth beyond $200 million ($3.5 billion today) and made him the second-richest man in America. On the other hand, he fell further behind Andrew Carnegie, who had received $300 million in bonds as his portion for the sale of Carnegie Steel. But this moment marked the zenith of Carnegie's wealth, whereas Rockefeller was just warming up.

Having overseen the Mesabi operation, Gates was not shy about demanding his due. When he delivered an oral report on the $55 million profit, Rockefeller saluted his effort and murmured quietly, "Thank you, Mr. Gates—thank you!" Gates fixed Rockefeller with a steady, quizzical look. For a long time, he had shown an almost filial deference toward his boss, but he was now well aware of his worth. Seizing the moment, he had the courage to say, " 'Thank you' is not enough, Mr. Rockefeller." Forced to reconsider, Rockefeller evidently came up with a large enough bonus, although Gates never revealed the exact amount.[112] Notwithstanding his veneration of his mentor, Gates griped for years about his compensation and sometimes stooped to nasty jokes about Rockefeller's avarice.

For a time, it seemed the steel trust might effect a rapprochement between Rockefeller and J. P. Morgan. As one of the largest U.S. Steel stockholders, Rockefeller demanded and won board seats for himself and his son. Yet financial differences quickly soured his relations with Morgan. Rockefeller was upset by U.S. Steel's extravagant dividends, even though he was a major recipient. In 1904, to register his protest, he resigned from the board, never having attended a meeting, and left Junior behind to represent him. By 1911, the Rockefellers liquidated the last of their U.S. Steel holdings. During the next two years, Morgan enjoyed an unspoken revenge by continuing to assign Rockefeller inferior positions in the weaker bond syndicates while excluding him from the sounder issues. Gates was always mystified by Morgan's success. "He seems to be a man incapable of calm and reasoning reflection; the victim of a succession of unreasoning impulses."[113]

—

Before leaving Rockefeller's exploits in the realm of iron ore, we should mark a prominent casualty of this adventure: his already troubled relationship with brother Frank. During the 1890s, Frank remained a vice president of Standard Oil of Ohio and took home a generous salary, despite his extended absences from Cleveland and a scornful indifference to business. As irascible as ever, he wrote testy letters to Standard Oil colleagues, forcing John and William to mediate. Frank was devoured by bitterness and often lapsed into violent, ungovernable rages that were aggravated by his alcoholism.

Frank could never curb his compulsive gambling. Wanting to emulate the big killings of his brothers, he was tempted again and again into foolhardy ventures. With the best intentions, John fed Frank's gambling addiction, even though Frank often did not realize the source of the loans. John and William continued to carry a $180,000 mortgage on his Kansas ranch and bailed him out when his crops failed in 1893. This generosity only highlighted Frank's chronic dependency and further embittered him. In extending loans to Frank, John followed his usual strict accounting rules, which he always applied in a compulsive, inflexible fashion. Nevertheless, when it suited his convenience, Frank was offended by his brother's refusal to compromise on his business principles.

Frank's best friend at the time was a bluff Irishman named James Corrigan. They hunted together, maintained adjoining estates in Ohio, and often invested together. A handsome man with a heavy jaw and bull neck, Corrigan was a popular, pugnacious Cleveland businessman. In the early 1880s, he had sold several refineries to John D., who had given him his first job and counted him as a friend. As payment for one refinery, Rockefeller gave Corrigan 2,500 shares of Standard Oil. With this money, Corrigan bought a half interest in the Franklin Iron Mining Company in the Lake Superior region of Wisconsin—the investment that first piqued Rockefeller's interest in the Mesabi Range. John loaned Frank the money to purchase the other half, keeping the mining stock as collateral. Not without reason, John D. later ruefully stated, "Neither my brother nor Corrigan had any reason to complain of my conduct. I made James Corrigan his fortune. I made my brother his fortune."[114]

When the 1893 panic struck, John D. behaved in exemplary fashion. He and William agreed to cancel their mortgage on Frank's Kansas ranch. Corrigan, meanwhile, took more loans from John D., secured by his Standard Oil stock, bringing the total to more than $400,000; Frank ran up debts to his brother in excess of $800,000, or $13 million in contemporary dollars. By these actions, John D. acquired considerable power over the two men, for he had retained as collateral their Franklin mining stock, Corrigan's Standard Oil shares, and Corrigan's share in a lake shipping fleet.

As the panic deepened, Rockefeller refused to release collateral despite Corrigan's pleas that he could use his lake vessels to raise additional money. In October 1894, Corrigan tried to borrow another $150,000 from John without posting extra collateral. George Rogers tersely informed Corrigan that "Mr. Rockefeller had advanced all he ought to on the Franklin mine property and that unless he could offer some further collateral, I felt very sure Mr. Rockefeller could not help him out."[115] When Corrigan stopped making interest payments altogether, Rockefeller carried him for another year before calling the loan. He offered to pay Corrigan $168 or $169 per share for his 2,500 shares of Standard Oil, which would yield enough to retire his $400,000 in debt.

To gauge the value of this stock, Corrigan's attorney asked Rockefeller to provide detailed information about the trust's stocks, assets, investments, and earnings during the previous five years. Rockefeller refused to publicize such sensitive information. "The securities to which you refer have a well-known market value, which is published in the newspapers every day," Rockefeller told the attorney.[116] At the time, few companies published annual reports. Yet Frank interpreted his brother's behavior in darkly conspiratorial terms. Several years later, he told Ida Tarbell that when he met with him to plead for more time for Corrigan, John said, "Frank, persuade Corrigan to sell me his Standard Oil stock. He is in a tight place. He can never get out and I might as well have the stock as anybody."[117] Frank took this to mean that John was bent upon destroying Corrigan to obtain his Standard Oil stock, and Frank advised his friend not to sell under any circumstances.

Corrigan finally sold his Standard Oil stock to John D. at $168 a share in February 1895. Rockefeller paid the market price, roughly equivalent to what he paid his Standard colleagues for their stock that month. One Standard executive, Joseph Seep, said that Rockefeller did not even keep Corrigan's stock but distributed it among his colleagues. Nevertheless, before a month had elapsed, the stock zoomed to $185 and then much higher. Instead of blaming bad luck, Corrigan decided he had been swindled and in April 1895 wrote Rockefeller to that effect. When he received the letter, Rockefeller was stunned. "Is it possible that 'Jim Corrigan' should be willing to write me such a letter," he wrote back, "after my uniform kindness to him for a lifetime?"[118] Some years later, possibly with the Corrigan affair in mind, Rockefeller lectured his son, "John, never lend money to your friends; it will spoil your friendships."[119]

Rockefeller had been neither Santa Claus nor Scrooge but simply a hard, unsentimental lender. It is true that he had more than enough collateral to cover Corrigan's $400,000 in loans, but he had exercised patience and carried Corrigan for a year after payments ceased. Gates even complained that Rockefeller was coddling him. Corrigan waited until July 1897 before filing suit, saying it had taken that long to serve a subpoena on Rockefeller. The delay was more likely due to the continuing rise in Standard Oil stock, which had jumped to nearly $350 a share because of Archbold's generous dividend policy. Corrigan issued an ultimatum: Rockefeller could either give back his Standard shares or pay him $500 a share. The court-appointed arbitrators in the case, given rare access to Standard Oil's confidential books, decided that Rockefeller's conduct had been blameless. Even though Frank hotly insisted that John had cheated his best friend, he continued to touch his brother for money and a year later borrowed another $130,000. Still unaware of the true depth of Frank's bile, John jotted down a memo for his files in February 1896, saying of Frank, "He is all very nice and pleasant and I think appreciates that I am doing things for him."[120]

After the Corrigan case, Frank began to seem deranged on the subject of his brother. He began to materialize at 26 Broadway or on the broad veranda at Forest Hill, boisterously demanding to see him. Because of the pending Corrigan suit, John would receive him only with a secretary present to record what he said. In 1898, John told William that Frank was now threatening him and asked him to intercede. John then had some long talks with a drunken Frank, who made extremely abusive remarks about him. Frank felt that his brother was so rich that he should forgive all his loans. When John differed, the breach between them widened. During their last meeting, as they walked down the street together, John said to him, "Frank, I'll always be a brother to you."[121] They never spoke to or set eyes on each other again.

Nursing an obsessive resentment, Frank decided to make a symbolic break with his brother. When John erected the towering obelisk at the family plot in Cleveland's Lake View Cemetery in 1898, Frank had the caskets of his two children who had died in childhood disinterred from the family plot and transferred to another part of the cemetery. "Not one of my blood," he declared, "will ever rest upon land controlled by that monster, John D. Rockefeller."[122] Soon thereafter, Frank, his wife, and three daughters withdrew from the Euclid Avenue Baptist Church.

Even after these unforgivable insults, John let Frank represent him on several corporate boards. While Frank's salary was reduced from $15,000 to $10,000 for his sinecure at Standard Oil of Ohio, he continued to draw this largely unearned salary until 1912. In September 1901, his finances ravaged by speculation, Frank told William that he would file for bankruptcy if he did not receive an immediate cash infusion of $86,000. When William secretly asked John to contribute half the amount, John wrote to him: "I will take half of the $86,000 if you take the other half, but Frank must not know that I am loaning the money."[123] In 1907, John and William again saved Frank from bankruptcy by guaranteeing loans that Frank had gotten from his stockbroker.

After the Corrigan business, Frank no longer felt any need to muzzle himself. Reporters soon learned that to get an inflammatory quote about John D., they simply had to contact Frank Rockefeller. Discussing the Corrigan affair, Frank told one reporter, "That treacherous act was but a detail in my brother's long record of heartless villainy. . . . He seems never to get enough. I wonder where it would end—this desire of his for more millions?"[124] John never commented publicly on these diatribes. Unfortunately for John's reputation, Frank began to spew forth this invective just as the muckraking era got under way. Coming from a brother, these highly quotable remarks made a tremendous impression upon the public, who never dreamed that John D.'s treatment of Frank was one area of his life where his record was spotless.

CHAPTER 21

The Enthusiast

hen Rockefeller receded from the business world in the mid-1890s, the average American was earning less than ten dollars per week. Rockefeller's average income—a stupefying $10 million per annum in those glory days before income taxes—defied public comprehension. Of more than $250 million in dividends distributed by Standard Oil between 1893 and 1901, over a quarter went straight into Rockefeller's coffers. As Standard Oil shares took flight in the late 1890s, one periodical computed that Rockefeller's wealth had appreciated by $55 million ($972 million today) in nine months. "Where in the history of the world did any man ever make $55,000,000 in 9 months?" the editorialist demanded.[1] Rockefeller was becoming Mister Money Bags, a byword for wealth.

One might have thought Rockefeller would relax in retirement, but he was still a prisoner to the Protestant work ethic and attacked recreational interests with the same intensity that he had brought to business. "I have not had the experience of the majority of business men," he later told William O. Inglis, "who find time hanging heavily on their hands."[2] Yet his retirement was equally remarkable for its omissions. For instance, he lacked the wanderlust that infected other rich men, such as J. P. Morgan, in their later years. He never collected art or exploited his wealth to broaden his connections or cultivate fancy people. Aside from the occasional courtesy call from other moguls, he hobnobbed with the same family members, old friends, and Baptist clergy who had always formed his social circle. He showed no interest in old-money clubs, parties, or organizations. Commenting on this, Ida Tarbell branded Rockefeller a "social cripple" and detected an inferiority complex that made him afraid to venture beyond his home turf, but his behavior actually connoted mental health.[3] When someone expressed surprise to Rockefeller that he had not gotten a big head, he replied, "Only fools get swelled up over money."[4] Comfortable with himself, he needed no outward validation of what he had accomplished. We can criticize him for lack of imagination, but not for weakness.

It is striking that Rockefeller, so grave in business, was extremely fond of games in retirement and indulged in a little skylarking. As his body aged, his mind grew younger and more buoyant. Having missed a carefree boyhood, he seemed to want to compensate in his later years and he suddenly showed a lot of his father's jollity. In the 1890s, Cleveland was seized by a bicycle craze, and the "wheel season" was opened each spring by hundreds of colorful tandem bikes gliding down Euclid Avenue. Though in his fifties, Rockefeller joined the fad with boyish élan. A firm believer in appropriate dress, he bought, in assorted shades, sporty riding costumes of corded knickerbocker suits, alpine hats, and cloth leggings. Frederick Gates was at Forest Hill when Rockefeller learned to ride, and he watched Rockefeller teach himself to turn around without alighting. "He would start in with a wide circle," Gates recalled, "and then follow it round and round each time narrowing the circuit until without dismounting he was almost circling the rear wheel."[5] As with industrial methods, Rockefeller broke down cycling into its component parts then perfected each movement. Much in the spirit of Big Bill, he liked to perform stunts on the bike, often jumping onto the seat as someone held the bike or holding open an umbrella as he rode with no hands. Through his interest in bike riding, Rockefeller came to master the fundamentals of civil engineering, a subject that had long intrigued him. When he wanted to ride his bike up the steep slope to the Forest Hill house, an engineer told him that no practicable grade could be found. "Nothing is impossible," Rockefeller replied.[6] Burying himself in civil-engineering books, he figured out a suitable angle—a 3 percent grade, in engineering lingo—and, true to his prediction, rode his bike straight up to the door.

Rockefeller proved fatally susceptible to another fad: golf. In 1899, he was staying at a hotel in Lakewood, New Jersey, and pitching horseshoes with a friend, Elias Johnson, who praised his easy style and nearly unbeatable game. Johnson tried to persuade Rockefeller that these skills would serve him well in golf. "He would look me through with those calm, gray-blue eyes but say nothing," said Johnson.[7] Finally, he convinced Rockefeller to try a few swings on a grassy, secluded spot near their hotel. After a few tips, Johnson later recalled in an interview, Rockefeller drove three balls more than one hundred yards apiece.

"Is that all there is of it?" Rockefeller asked. "Yes, that's all there is of it, but not one in one hundred would do the same thing you've done just now. They want to do too much." His competitive urges surfacing, Rockefeller said, "Do

A photo of John D. Rockefeller taken in 1904,
after alopecia had drastically altered his appearance.
(Courtesy of the Rockefeller Archive Center)

not some players send the ball farther than that?" "Yes, but long shots come only after much practice."[8]

Rockefeller decided to play a little prank on his wife. He had a golf pro, Joe Mitchell, come to the hotel and give him lessons on the sly. Every time the caddies saw Cettie approaching, Rockefeller scampered for cover in the bushes. Several weeks later, he said to her offhandedly that golf seemed like a very nice sport and that he might take a shot at it. He then stepped up to a tee and smacked the ball 160 yards straight down the fairway. After marveling for a moment, Cettie shook her head and said, "John, I might have known it. You do things better and more easily than anyone else."[9]

On April 2, 1899, right before his sixtieth birthday, Rockefeller played his first complete game of golf, finishing nine holes in sixty-four strokes. After this, he took up the sport with a vengeance. Not always a powerful player, he was nonetheless eerily accurate, his swing so exacting that time seemed suspended. "It was the slowest back-swing I ever saw," said one partner. "It seemed to last for minutes."[10] Once again, Rockefeller dissected his game like a manufacturing method. Noticing that he twisted his right foot at the end of his stroke, he had his caddy nail his foot into the ground with a wire croquet wicket—a hazardous trick that he abandoned once the fault was corrected. Since he lifted his head as he shot, he hired a boy to say "Keep your head down" whenever he teed off. Rockefeller was frustrated at one point when he kept slicing his woods. To identify the source of the problem, he commissioned a Cleveland photographer to do snapshots of his swing, a time-and-motion study that enabled him to root out the troublesome flaw. Later, he had movies made of his game, which he studied intently. As part of this studious approach, he recorded all his golf scores in thick little books, with names, dates, and places included.

Rockefeller's passion for golf was linked to his medical problems of the 1890s, which turned him into a fitness buff. "Played in moderation golf is not only a fascinating game but a valuable aid to health," he advised friends.[11] His physician and frequent golf partner Dr. Hamilton Biggar credited golf with rejuvenating Rockefeller after his near breakdown. "Since he has taken it up with such gusto there has been a marked change in his appearance," he told a reporter. "His skin, which was formerly pallid and wrinkled, is now firm and ruddy and healthy."[12] In later years, Rockefeller gave up walking and bicycled from hole to hole to conserve energy for the game. As an old man, he sat upright on the bike and had it pushed along by his caddy to economize further on his strength. Nothing could keep him from his morning game. If it rained or the sun was too strong, a caddy shielded him with a big black umbrella throughout. His retinue came equipped with rubbers for muddy weather, sweaters for chilly weather, and towels to dry the clubs in a drizzle.

Golf made Rockefeller a more gregarious person, bringing out a bonhomie that had been stifled during the Standard Oil years. For a man who shrank from intimate discussion, golf provided an ideal way to socialize in a highly structured, risk-free environment from ten-fifteen to twelve each morning. As soon as he arrived, he would clown around, setting a tone of genial banter, and people responded in kind. He hummed hymns or popular songs, told humorous anecdotes, or even read short poems of his own composition. One of his favorite gags involved an eminent minister who liked to cheat at golf; an adroit mimic, Rockefeller aped the divine giving the ball a secret little kick behind a tree stump. Golf brought out a native drollery that he had never allowed to flower before. "We should not rejoice in the downfall of others," he wrote his daughter Bessie, "but I slaughtered four men at golf on Saturday last. . . . This was very wrong, and of course I will never do it again."[13]

Rockefeller established various taboos on the course, including that no business or charitable bequests should ever be discussed. People who flouted these rules were never invited back, and Rockefeller was extremely uncompromising on the subject. He wanted to keep things on a superficial, slightly unreal level and ward off any serious discussion. In this way, he could be with people yet surrounded by his own ring of silence, an isolated figure amid the crowd, setting the terms of social intercourse.

—

Despite his unmatched place in America's urban and industrial growth, Rockefeller remained a country boy at heart and now receded further from the city. Perhaps as a legacy of his upstate boyhood, he was drawn to hilltop houses with spacious water views. Seeking an escape from Manhattan, he was especially attracted to the Hudson River, on which William had built his thousand-acre manor. John D. was moved by the river's beauty and majestic shoreline, flanked by rolling farmland and picturesque villages. When land prices plunged during the 1893 panic, he bought four hundred acres in the Pocantico Hills of North Tarrytown, just south of Rockwood Hall. Though he considered establishing a weekend house or summer hideaway, he had no exact plan. "As I stated to you before coming," he wrote to Cettie in early September 1893, "I have no scheme whatever in reference to this new property on the Hudson, further than to own it and let the future determine how [we] wish to use it."[14]

Rockefeller was drawn to the spot by natural beauty, not elegant neighbors. "He chose the site of his house on Pocantico Hills for its glorious view of the Hudson and the Catskills, one of the most magnificent landscapes in America," reported Gates, who accompanied him on the first trip.[15] The property included a jagged ridge called Kykuit Hill—pronounced *kye*-cut and derived from the Dutch word for lookout—which enjoyed splendid views of the river and distant Palisades. As at Forest Hill, Rockefeller simply took the furnished house that came with the property, a modest frame structure with wide verandas known as the Parsons-Wentworth House. As was his wont, he kept remodeling the house over the years, enlarging a room here, making one more comfortable there. It was his own Walden, a place where "fine views invest the soul and where we can live simply and quietly."[16]

By 1900, Rockefeller had acquired 1,600 acres and eventually the Pocantico Hills estate expanded to 3,000 acres, threaded by dozens of miles of winding roads and bridle paths. Rockefeller could tolerate extravagance as long as the style was understated and did not trumpet his wealth too loudly. He avoided a gaudy residence and had no desire to impress other people. If anything, he craved seclusion. At one point, Rockefeller decided that he had to purchase a small corner property owned by Thomas Birdsall. He offered an excellent purchase price and said he would buy a nearby strip of land to which Birdsall could move his house. When Birdsall refused, Rockefeller ordered his superintendent to surround the offending property with the largest cedar trees he could find, casting the house into perpetual gloom. Birdsall caved in.

Almost as soon as he caught the golf fever in 1899, Rockefeller laid out four holes at Pocantico. "Mother and Father crazy over golf," Junior told a college chum in 1900. "Father plays from four to six hours a day, and Mother several hours."[17] William Tucker, a golf pro from nearby Ardsley, coached Rockefeller regularly. By 1901, the titan hired a golf architect, William Dunn, to plot a twelve-hole course, and he also had a nine-hole course designed for Forest Hill. Gamely trying to please his father, Junior took lessons for a year, but he was not cut out for competitive games and favored the more solitary pleasure of horseback riding.

At some point, Rockefeller decided that he had to play golf daily at Pocantico. In early December 1904, after four inches of snow had fallen on Westchester County, Elias Johnson was taken aback to receive a call from Rockefeller, inviting him up for a foursome. When Johnson objected that they could not possibly play in the snow, Rockefeller said, "Just come up and see." Even as they spoke, a team of workmen with horses and snowplows were assiduously clearing snow from five fairways and putting greens; the next morning, Johnson found a shimmering green course, carved from a wintry landscape. "We never had a finer game," said Johnson.[18] Rockefeller played in all kinds of weather. "Yesterday morning I played with the thermometer at 20 in the shade," he boasted to a niece in 1904. "It was cold indeed on these Pocantico Hills, but a good thing for my health."[19] To keep his partners warm, he distributed paper vests, which became a trademark gift.

Golf was his greatest indulgence. A full-time crew at Pocantico was charged with keeping the greens clear, and they were often out in the early morning, wiping dew from the grass with special mowers, rollers, and bamboo poles. An account book from early 1906 shows that Rockefeller spent $525,211.47 on personal expenses during the previous year, devoting an astounding $27,537.80—or $450,000 in 1996 dollars—to golf.[20]

Another rich man might have turned to his estate for rest, but for Rockefeller much of the charm lay in the construction and heavy labor. At first, he had the firm of Frederick Law Olmsted, who had designed Central Park and many other parks, do the landscaping at Pocantico. Then, he took this work in hand himself, relegating outside firms to advisory roles and building a surveying tower to help him lay out the gardens. Rockefeller had a flair for landscape design and delighted in transplanting trees as tall as ninety feet. By the 1920s, he had some of the world's largest nurseries at Pocantico, where he planted as many as ten thousand young trees at a time, selling some of them at a profit.

Rockefeller belied Thorstein Veblen's generalization that rich men possessed "an instinctive repugnance for the vulgar forms of labor," for he always believed in the dignity of manual labor.[21] Along with his son, he laid out sinuous trails and framed striking vistas, leading the work gangs himself. "How many miles of roads I have laid out in my time," he reflected, "I can hardly compute, but I have often kept at it until I was exhausted. While surveying roads, I have run the lines until darkness made it impossible to see the little stakes and flags."[22] He became so skillful that he built roads without an engineer. "I am thinking of moving that hillock," he would say, quickly sizing up the volume of material involved. "Offhand, I would say there are just about 650,000 cubic feet of dirt here."[23]

As at Standard Oil, Rockefeller was a paternalistic boss at home. Among his three hundred mostly black and Italian workmen he outlawed profanity and even tried to purchase and shut down Tarrytown's lone tavern. Though he was exacting and did not pay high salaries, he never yelled at his employees and dealt with them in a patient, considerate manner, occasionally inviting them to sit by the fire for a chat.

Rockefeller's absorption in his estates might well have stemmed from his fear of the general public and preference for staying in a protected home environment. As one early biographer noted, "Universally execrated, broken physically and nervously, he was forced almost three decades ago to retreat behind stone walls, barbed wire fences, grilled iron gates."[24] He preferred to socialize on home turf, where guests had to conform to his rules and his timetable. He was also concerned about terrorist acts. In early 1892, George Rogers told Cettie that he had just gotten a letter signed "Justice or Extermination," which warned that a packaged bomb was on the way.[25] Such threats posed a dilemma for Rockefeller in fashioning his estates, for he wanted to keep his lands open to the public. He finally decided to protect himself by having a secure, private core of four to five hundred acres, including the family houses and golf course, ringed by fences and manned by watchmen. The public was allowed to wander through the rest of the estate, provided that they brought no cars. For decades,

Pocantico was a hiker's and rider's paradise, making the Rockefeller domain at once exclusive and democratic.

===

In retirement, Rockefeller subordinated many things to the overriding goal of longevity. "I hope you will take good care of your health," he once told Junior. "This is a religious duty, and you can accomplish so much for the world if you keep well and strong."[26] His Baptist avoidance of tobacco or alcohol made him a natural advocate of abstemious living, and he was convinced that virtuous habits were medicinal. "I enjoy the best of health," he said in later years. "What a compensation for the loss of the theaters, the clubs, the dinners, the dissipations which ruined the health of many of my acquaintances long, long years ago. . . . I was satisfied with cold water and skimmed milk, and enjoyed my sleep. What a pity that more men did not enjoy these simple things!"[27]

Rockefeller's boon companion was Dr. Hamilton F. Biggar. They had met in the 1870s in the early days on Euclid Avenue when Rockefeller, playing blind-man's buff with the children, was dashing madly about the parlor and ran smack into a doorway; Dr. Biggar came to stitch the wound and remained in the family bosom. Born in Canada, Biggar moved to Cleveland after the Civil War and became a leading figure in the increasingly popular field of homeopathic medicine. He rose to professor of anatomy and clinical surgery in the local Homeopathic Hospital College and counted William McKinley and Mark Hanna among his patients. Founded by the German physician Samuel Hahnemann (1755–1843) and prevalent in nineteenth-century America, homeopathy cured disease by using minute amounts of substances that in larger doses might cause the disease. At Biggar's behest, Rockefeller served as a vice president and trustee of the Homeopathic Hospital College, providing money for land, building, and instruction. It was a striking paradox that the philanthropist who would create the Rockefeller Institute for Medical Research and did more than anyone else to advance scientific medicine in the twentieth century was emotionally wedded to traditional remedies. Rockefeller sometimes smoked mullein leaves in a clay pipe to heal respiratory problems and never lost a residual suspicion of medical doctors. "The doctor came to see me today," he once reported to his son. "He wouldn't give me the medicine I wanted, and I wouldn't take the medicine he prescribed, but we had a lovely talk."[28]

Portly, tall, and round-faced, given to derby hats and watch chains, Dr. Biggar shared Rockefeller's love of yarns and dry wisecracks and they took pleasure in good-naturedly ribbing each other. Since Biggar dressed in a more dapper fashion than his rich friend, many people imagined that *he* was the titan when they traveled together. More than anybody, Dr. Biggar brought out Rockefeller's amiability, as reflected in his description of Rockefeller: "He has a keen sense of humor, is fond of jokes, sharp in repartee, an entertaining conversationalist and a gracious listener."[29]

Not everybody was enamored of Dr. Biggar. As Rockefeller's official doctor, issuing medical bulletins to the press, he struck some as pompous and self-serving. Some physicians even thought him a charlatan with a good bedside manner. One such doubter was Harvard president Charles Eliot, who told Frederick Gates that most Harvard doctors considered Biggar inept. In 1901, according to Eliot, when Biggar had a physical breakdown, Rockefeller paid his expenses for a European trip to recuperate. While he was away, Rockefeller had a renewed attack of hydrocele, an accumulation of serous fluid, which Biggar had pronounced incurable. Rockefeller summoned a doctor from the Harvard Medical School "who not only promptly relieved him of present pain but in a month effected a permanent cure, which Mr. Rockefeller had been led to believe was not possible," Eliot told Gates nine years later.[30] After that, Rockefeller consulted other doctors, especially an elderly German named Dr. Henry N. Moeller, but Biggar was often at his side and had a continuing influence on his views.

By the early 1900s, Dr. Biggar frequently prophesied in the press that Rockefeller would live to one hundred (which doubtless endeared him to his patron), and he became such a zealous spokesman for Rockefeller's health principles that it became hard to tell where Biggar ended and Rockefeller began. In 1907, Biggar stated his foolproof rules for long life: "At fifty the American businessman should cease to worry, eschew liquor and tobacco and make play in 'God's out of doors' his chief aim in life."[31] As time passed, Biggar added an admonition to rise from the table a little bit hungry, while Rockefeller laid additional stress on nine hours of daily sleep, including a long siesta after lunch.

There are hints that Rockefeller had a more than ordinary dread of death. Years later, he was playing a golf foursome at Ormond Beach, Florida, when one partner, a Mr. Harvey, thought he had a severe attack of indigestion. Rockefeller took his arm and uttered consoling words before Harvey crumpled to the ground from a heart attack. Doctors were summoned while Harvey was carried inside, where he died thirty minutes later. Rockefeller, so compassionate at first, unceremoniously fled the scene. As one golfing partner recalled, "Mr. Rockefeller turned away and walked rapidly to his car and drove off. I always felt that he did not want to witness death."[32] Nowhere in his voluminous records does he ever even remotely discuss death.

Rockefeller seemed to believe that he could keep death at bay if he adhered to his fixed rules. Extremely finicky about diet, rest, and exercise, he reduced everything to a routine and repeated the same daily schedule, forcing other people to fall in step with his timetable. In a letter to his son, Rockefeller credited his longevity to his willingness to reject social demands. "I attribute my good condition to my almost reckless independence in determining for myself what to do and the rigid adhering to regulations which give me the maximum of rest and quiet and leisure, and I am being richly paid for it every day."[33]

Part of his single-minded program for reaching one hundred was to go through life in a steady, unhurried fashion. He paced himself, husbanded his energy, and took pride in his abnormally low pulse: "That indicates a capacity for enduring and retaining one's balance."[34] In his early years, he had struggled to master his temper and clear his mind of petty annoyances; now, he had a medical rationale for purging his system of turbulent emotions, especially anger. "It produces in the blood a lot of toxins that poison the system of the angry person. That tires him out and renders him less efficient, to say nothing of causing him to grow old and wear out before his time."[35] Worry was also to be avoided. "I am certain that worry causes a greater strain upon the nerves than hard work."[36] This outlook further encouraged him to avoid spontaneous, potentially confrontational encounters with people.

Rockefeller was partial to massage and other forms of bodily manipulation. In the early 1900s, he became a passionate devotee of osteopathy, which tries to restore the body's structural integrity by manipulating the skeleton and muscles, and he talked Cettie and Lute into going for treatments. In one rapturous outburst in 1905, he told his son that he had profited from osteopathy while at Forest Hill and was "more grateful than I can tell you for the good health which I have and which enables me to do two or three times as much work, Mrs. Tuttle [his telegrapher] says, as I used to do when she was here before. Osteopathy! Osteopathy! Osteopathy!"[37] When exponents of more advanced medicine—spurred on, ironically, by Rockefeller philanthropy—tried to enact legislation to bar osteopaths, Rockefeller rushed to the osteopaths' defense. "I believe in osteopathy," he instructed his secretary, "and if any of our people at 26 Broadway can say or do anything to aid the osteopaths at this time of their struggle, I should appreciate it."[38] A visit to an osteopath occasioned one of Rockefeller's most celebrated witticisms. As the osteopath cracked his vertebrae, Rockefeller said wryly, "Listen to that, doctor. They say I control all the oil in the country and I haven't enough even to oil my own joints."[39]

In the early 1900s, the press still circulated preposterous stories of how Rockefeller could digest only milk and crackers and had a standing offer of one million dollars to anyone who could fix his stomach. The most ghoulish myth claimed that he needed mother's milk to survive and that his caddy smuggled it to him daily in a thermos on the golf course. Thousands of letters flooded into 26 Broadway, offering remedies for stomach troubles. Rockefeller was perplexed by these weird rumors. When approaching eighty, he said wearily, "There are multitudes of people in the country today who, from these false reports, believe that I am in such a sad condition that I would give all I possess on earth to be a well man. And I know of no man in better health than I am—and so it goes."[40] Biggar had, in fact, prescribed bread and milk for Rockefeller's digestive troubles in the 1890s, and he continued to drink milk and cream regularly in the early 1900s, believing that "fresh milk is an excellent food for the nerves."[41] Yet as his health returned in the late 1890s, he resumed a varied menu, which he consumed slowly and in tiny portions. He had a plain but healthy diet: green peas and string beans from his garden, rice, barley water, lettuce, fish, brown bread, and baked potatoes twice a day.

In the early 1900s, portly tycoons such as Morgan incarnated the robust prosperity of the era, while Rockefeller weighed in at a lean 165 pounds. Still the ascetic Protestant, he decried overeating, warning that it caused more sickness than did any other cause. He never ate hot food, waited for dishes to cool, and encouraged guests to start without him. Food was fuel for Rockefeller, not a source of sensual pleasure. "He could not understand why anyone would eat a piece of candy, if that piece of candy were not good for him, just because that person liked candy," Junior explained.[42] Once, in an uncharacteristic moment, he had a craving for ice cream and humbly asked Dr. Moeller for a waiver from his prohibition against eating it. "If I had a license from you to eat a very little ice cream occasionally it would be a special dispensation which I would much appreciate, but, you are the Doctor," he said meekly.[43]

Rockefeller's most distinctive piece of medical advice—and the eternal bane of his dinner guests—was that people should chew each bite ten times before swallowing. So conscientiously did he adhere to this practice that he even advised people to chew liquids, which he would swirl around in his mouth. He would still be eating a half hour after other guests had finished. To promote digestion, he also thought it important to linger at the table for an hour or so after dinner. To pass the time, he played a parlor game with guests called Numerica, a form of competitive solitaire. Since, as a Baptist, he could not play cards, he had square counters made to replace the poker decks that were ordinarily used. Any number of guests could play, and Rockefeller distributed a dime to the winner, nickels to the losers. The game required a certain agility with figures, and Rockefeller grew so proficient from incessant practice that he tended to award himself the dime.

=

For Americans of a later day, John D. Rockefeller was etched in their minds as a bald, wizened man, a desiccated fossil. Yet before his health troubles of the early 1890s, the few reporters who penetrated his inner sanctum were struck by his youthful demeanor. His correspondence does show that his problem with hair loss began earlier than previously imagined; in 1886, at age forty-seven, he was already ordering bottles of hair restorative. In 1893, Rockefeller's hair loss, or alopecia, suddenly worsened as he struggled with digestive problems and fretted over the University of Chicago finances.

Generalized alopecia, or total loss of body hair, has been attributed to many causes, ranging from genetic factors to severe stress, but remarkably little is known for certain. For Rockefeller, the onset of the disease coincided with his breakdown of the early 1890s. In 1901, the symptoms worsened markedly, with Cettie recording in a memo book that in March of that year "John's moustache began to fall out, and all the hair on his body had followed by August."[44]

The change in his appearance was startling: He suddenly looked old, puffy, stooped—all but unrecognizable. He seemed to age a generation. Without hair, his facial imperfections grew more pronounced: The skin appeared parchment dry, his lips too thin, his head large and bumpy. Soon after losing his hair, Rockefeller went to a dinner thrown by J. P. Morgan (one of the few public dinners he ever attended) and sat down next to a mystified Charles Schwab, the new president of U.S. Steel. "I see you don't know me, Charley," said Rockefeller. "I am Mr. Rockefeller."[45]

Coming on the eve of the muckraking era, Rockefeller's alopecia had a devastating effect on his image: It made him look like a hairless ogre, stripped of all youth, warmth, and attractiveness, and this played powerfully on people's imaginations. For a time, he wore a black skullcap, giving him the impressively gaunt physiognomy of a Renaissance prelate. One French writer wrote that "under his silk skull-cap he seems like an old monk of the inquisition such as one sees in the Spanish picture galleries."[46]

The alopecia dealt a blow to Rockefeller's morale—the psychological effect is crushing for most people—and he dabbled restlessly in remedies. Biggar started him on a hair-restoration regimen in which he took phosphorus six days a week and sulfur on the seventh. When such remedies failed, Rockefeller decided to buy a wig. Self-conscious at first and reluctant to wear it, he tested it one Sunday at the Euclid Avenue Baptist Church. Before the service, he stood in the pastor's office, nervously adjusting it and telling a listener what an ordeal it would be to wear it in the church. When the wig met with a good reception, he was almost boyishly elated. Soon, he grew to love this wig, telling daughter Edith, "I sleep in it and play golf, and I am surprised that I went so long without it, and think I made a great mistake in doing so."[47] He became so fond of wigs that he started to wear rotating wigs of different lengths to give the impression of his hair growing then being cut. He even had wigs styled for different occasions: golf, church, short walks, and so on. For all his wealth, however, Rockefeller could never find the ideal wig. Starting out with a fashionable wig maker on the rue Castiglione in Paris, he grew disillusioned when springs in the framework pushed up through the hair. He then switched to a Cleveland wig maker whose product had another maddening defect: The foundation fabric would shrink, making the wig suddenly slide across his bald pate. What God had taken away, it seems, could never be perfectly restored.

Before Rockefeller's hair fell out, people noted the contrast between him and his often sickly wife. Then, overnight, the alopecia seemed to equalize their ages. John and Cettie had enjoyed a happy marriage, if one constrained by formality. Whether playing with the children or golfing with cronies, John was capable of a certain hilarity—he could kick up his heels and have fun. Cettie—gentle, sweet, charming—remained immured in her cloistered world of religion and clung to her belief in John as a superman. One observer described Cettie as "a dignified, simple-minded, elderly lady, pleasant faced, soft spoken, entirely without ostentation" for whom John "was still her hero after all the years."[48] As reformers branded her hero a corporate malefactor, she found a necessary sanctuary in Christianity, her mind soaring to serene religious heights far above the din of political strife.

It is hard to date with precision Cettie's transformation from an alert, capable woman into a professional invalid. She had never had a strong constitution: As early as the 1880s, Junior had taken care of many household tasks, such as buying carpets and overseeing repairs, because his mother lacked the strength. By the early 1890s, she complained of "a general state of prostration."[49] John had always confided in her about business and in 1893 was still sending her detailed reports about Mesabi ore. Then, abruptly, in the mid-1890s, his letters to her became empty and platitudinous, stuffed with bland descriptions of weather, garden walks, or golf, and they remained so for twenty years. It is hard to avoid the impression that he was deliberately tiptoeing around unpleasant subjects out of respect for her delicate medical state.

Cettie suffered from so many strange symptoms and vague ailments as to defy precise medical diagnosis. She complained in the 1890s of asthma and colitis, as well as sporadic problems with her eyes and spine. For her intestinal troubles, doctors ordered her to cut out fruits and vegetables in favor of a diet rich in milk, cream, butter, and eggs. At first, despite her problems, she was not bedridden. She and John took long drives before lunch, and around 1900 she often sneaked in several holes of afternoon golf. Then, in April 1904, at the height of the publication of Ida Tarbell's series in *McClure's Magazine*, she had an attack, perhaps a mild stroke, that left her nearly paralyzed. As she told her diary, "Dr. Allen says it will take two years of the most quiet living to be myself again. This I accept and shall gain daily feeling thankful that it is no worse."[50] John took her to Forest Hill, where she sunned on the porch and listened to him read aloud daily portions from *With God in the World* by Bishop Brent. She never entirely recuperated.

The image of Cettie projected by her family was invariably that of the stoic mother. "Everything which came to her, she accepted," her daughter Edith once wrote, "and she bore her frailty of body with uncomplaining patience."[51] Outsiders, however, saw less of this patient nobility. Where she had always been considerate with servants, she now became finicky and demanding. "Her hot milk must be brought to her at 11 o'clock each morning," one of Rockefeller's secretaries, H. V. Sims, recalled. "The little napkin which went with it must be inserted by the maid between the 4th finger and the little finger—or all was wrong."[52] She would ask nurses to extract shawls from the middle of a tall stack without disturbing the others. Everybody crept on eggshells around her.

John learned to coax and humor her to get his way. The nurses often wilted in the stifling heat that Cettie demanded and were afraid to open the window. John would waltz in and say, "Mother, don't you think you should have the window open just so much?" He would spread his fingers slightly apart. When she replied, "Very well, John, if you think so," he signaled the nurses, when she wasn't looking, to open it far more.[53] John treated his wife tenderly, but his behavior now became largely ceremonious. If she stayed up too late with guests, he would slip his hand through her arm and announce, "This is good night, as it is Mother's bedtime."[54]

In a 1905 portrait of her by Arthur Ferraris, which shows her in a lovely black dress with her hair swept up and holding a prayer book, she seems despondent but still sensitive and wise. She clung ever more assertively to religion and wrote to her children in the elevated language of sermons, telling Junior as he was about to embark on a trip that she was "blessed of God above so many mothers, in my children, my precious jewels—loaned me for a season to be handed back when the call comes."[55] On his twenty-first birthday, she congratulated her son thus: "You can celebrate your birthday in no better way, whether at home or not, than by such earnest work as I know you are giving, for God and the saving of the souls of your fellow students."[56] It never seemed to dawn on her to encourage her children to have a good time.

Cettie's invalidism must have tormented Rockefeller. Since his boyhood, he had felt a particular affinity for women and taken special delight in their company. He would not have contemplated extramarital affairs, as other moguls might have done. He stayed loyal to Cettie and his Baptist upbringing, and he always had the specter of Big Bill before his eyes to remind him of the extreme perils of philandering. He had long lived with the knowledge of man's sinful nature. As long as Cettie was alive, so far as we can tell, he kept his amorous impulses in check and remained a model paterfamilias.

—

The Rockefellers found it difficult to confront the infirmities of both the mind and flesh. A whole world of forbidden, subversive feelings simply did not exist for them. If you averted your eyes from unpleasant things, they seemed to believe, they would lose their sting. For this reason, the story of the eldest Rockefeller daughter, Bessie, has long been an impenetrable mystery.

After Charles Strong had married Bessie in 1889, he taught briefly at Clark University and then became an associate professor of philosophy at the new University of Chicago in 1892. While Charles had ambivalent feelings toward his father-in-law, he never hesitated to exploit his connections and largesse. In 1895, the Strongs had to abandon Chicago, owing to Bessie's poor health. As Charles informed his Harvard mentor, William James, his wife's health was "still so delicate that it seems unwise to expose her to the inclemencies of the Chicago climate, and the result is that I find myself permanently settled in New York."[57] So that Charles could write his treatises and live with Bessie in New York, Rockefeller gave him a thousand-dollar subsidy for a year's work. When Bessie gave birth to a daughter, Margaret, at Pocantico in 1897, Rockefeller declared a holiday for workmen on his estate.

Since Charles had become a freethinker, Rockefeller might have feared for the immortal soul of his granddaughter. "Charles would tell Margaret, 'There is no God,' " Margaret's daughter would recall. "Both mother and father concurred and agreed not to contaminate her with uncertain belief."[58] Perhaps aware of this indoctrination, Rockefeller was eager to keep the Strongs in New York. He had Junior approach Seth Low, the president of Columbia College, about endowing a professorship in psychology for Charles, who increasingly studied both psychology and philosophy in his work. Junior suggested that it would be more gracious to endow the chair and then let the college voluntarily appoint him, rather than to demean Charles by creating a chair expressly for him. Senior followed this advice and, after making sure that Columbia would give him the chair, gave the school a $100,000 endowment, effectively buying his son-in-law's job at considerable expense.

For a time in the early 1900s, Rockefeller saw a lot of Charles and Bessie, thanks in part to his newfound passion for golf. Desperate for a place where he could extend Pocantico's limited golf season, he found it in the tony resort of Lakewood, New Jersey, where George Gould and other rich residents played polo, attended tea parties, rode to hounds, and held cotillions. Rockefeller began buying property there in May 1901, and a year later a dreamlike opportunity appeared. The Ocean County Hunt and Country Club decided to merge with another club and abandon its clubhouse, which was surrounded by a golf course set amid seventy-five acres of spruce, fir, pine, and hemlock. Only eight or nine miles from the sea, this flat, sandy country had "delicious, dry air," Rockefeller told a friend, and would permit him to golf nearly ten months a year.[59] The big, rambling, three-story wooden clubhouse—which Rockefeller always called Golf House—had striped awnings and a glass-sheltered porch that gave a view of sheep browsing on the lawn. This hideaway could be reached only by a twisting road of crushed bluestone that ran through dense woods—perfect for security purposes. Expanding the house and adding acreage, Rockefeller transplanted thousands of trees from Pocantico to this new estate. Rockefeller loved his new, relaxed place. "I believe I have recovered my health," he wrote to a friend from Lakewood in 1903. "I feel better now than I have felt in years. . . . I believe the improvement in my condition is due to my newly acquired habit of playing golf."[60]

To provide company, Rockefeller also bought the small Claflin Cottage at Lakewood, where Charles and Bessie stayed for three seasons. To hear William James, a frequent visitor, tell it, it was a gloomy place. When Strong's first major book, *Why the Mind Has a Body*, appeared in 1903, James extolled it as "a sterling work, admirable for clearness of statement & thoroughness of discussion, luminous, and likely to be much used by students of philosophy."[61] During his stays at Lakewood, James accompanied Charles on walks around the lake and the two often paused to sit on pine needles and reflect. On such a stroll, James paid them both a high compliment when he turned to Strong and said, "I am John the Baptist and you are the Messiah."[62] Yet James was more versatile than Strong and came to dread these Lakewood trips, where he felt trapped by perpetual shoptalk. Charles could convert a pleasant weekend into an interminable seminar, and James voiced his frustrations to his wife, Alice, tempering them with his great admiration for Charles. "I never knew such an unremitting, untiring, monotonous addiction as that of his mind to truth. He goes by points, pinning each one definitely, and has, I think, the very clearest mind I ever knew. . . . I suspect that he will outgrow us all, for his rate accelerates, and he never stands still."[63]

As an antidote to Charles, William James especially welcomed his Lakewood encounters with Rockefeller, who would sometimes materialize at lunch, fresh from golf. Rockefeller had only the most fleeting encounters with the intelligentsia, which makes James's descriptions of him the more valuable. The philosopher had an uncanny knack for telescoping titanic figures into thumbnail sketches. He was especially struck by Rockefeller's willpower and wrote to Alice about the primordial strength that radiated from him, telling her that Rockefeller was a "very *deep* human being" who gave him "more impression of *Urkraft* [primitive or original force] than anyone I ever met." He was also unexpectedly charmed by his genial style: "Glorious old John D. . . . [is] a most loveable person." To round out this portrait, he marveled that Rockefeller could be "so complex, subtle, oily, fierce, strongly bad and strongly good a human being."[64]

William dashed off an even more vivid description to his brother Henry:

> Rockefeller, you know, is reputed the richest man in the world, and he certainly is the most powerfully suggestive personality I have ever seen. A man 10 stories deep, and to me quite unfathomable. Physionomie de Pierrot (not a spear of hair on head or face) flexible, cunning, quakerish, superficially sug-

gestive of naught but goodness and conscientiousness, yet accused of being the greatest villain in business whom our country has produced, a hater of cities and lover of the open air (playing golf & skating all the time at Lakewood) etc.[65]

James wrote this while Ida Tarbell was inflaming popular opinion against Standard Oil. He urged Rockefeller to discard his policy of silence and combat the attacks by letting the public become better acquainted with him. When Rockefeller published his memoirs in book form in 1909, James applauded. "This is what I proposed to you many years ago!" he wrote to him. "Expansiveness wins a way where reserve fails!"[66]

In 1902, the already somber world of Charles and Bessie Strong darkened suddenly when Bessie, age thirty-six, experienced fresh medical problems. One cannot state with certainty what this ailment was, but in one letter to her brother, she refers to her "most weak and unreliable heart."[67] We do know that her condition deteriorated dramatically in the spring of 1903, for that autumn Charles wrote to William James, "Mrs. Strong is pretty well for her, thank you; but she had an attack in the spring which gave some cause for disquietude."[68] Her granddaughter later contended that Bessie had "suffered a stroke and consequent impairments."[69]

In the few brief, cryptic references to Bessie's illness in the press, it was always said that she had withdrawn from Lakewood society to lead a quiet life—a cover story that does not begin to capture the pathos of what happened. Overnight, the stroke or heart condition turned this pretty young woman into someone much older and frailer. The Rockefellers always suppressed the fact that it affected her mind. As Strong's friend George Santayana wrote, "She was always, as they put it, in delicate health, which was a euphemism for not being in her right mind."[70] Turned into a semi-invalid who spent much of the day in bed, she shuffled slowly about the cottage in a gray shawl, careworn and bent. She sometimes lapsed into morbid fears of poverty, retrenching on household expenses, reworking gowns to save money, and informing friends that she could no longer afford to entertain. During these periods, Charles supplemented her spartan grocery orders with extra purchases. Even as she wondered darkly in early 1904 how she and Charles would survive, Bessie was worth $404,489.25, with an estimated annual income of $20,030. At moments, she also threw off her imaginary cares and gaily announced that they were rich.

After a while, transported into a dreamworld, Bessie started to babble in childlike French. William James arrived in Lakewood one day and was thunderstruck by Bessie's condition. To his wife, he reported Bessie's words as follows:

"M. James, cela me fait de joie de voir votre bonne figure, vous avez un coeur généreux comme mon papa. Nous sommes tres riches maintenant. Mais Papa me donne tout ce que je lui demande pour le donner a ceux qui ont besoin. Mois aussi j'ai un bon coeur." (Translation: "Mr. James, it gives me joy to see your nice face, you have a generous heart like my papa. We are very rich now. But Papa gives me everything I ask him for, to give to those who are in need. I too have a good heart.")

A flabbergasted James said afterward, "It was just like a fairy-tale."[71] It was an indescribably sad fate for the one Rockefeller daughter who had gone to college.

It was also a bitter irony for Charles Strong, with his overpowering intellect, to become a nursemaid for the blighted, demented Bessie. Solitary and emotionally blocked, he soon grew bored with any conversation that did not revolve around philosophic disputation. His letters to William James contain few personal asides or mundane details, and they read like philosophic abstracts. For such a man to have ended up the caretaker of a wife spouting gibberish must have been an intolerable strain. In the spring of 1904, nervous and rundown, Charles took a leave of absence from Columbia and sailed for Europe with Bessie. He planned to consult with French specialists in nervous diseases and hoped that his wife might be helped by the warm climate of southern France. It might also have been for Charles a chance to escape from both his overbearing father and father-in-law.

=

Like Bessie, the Rockefeller's youngest daughter, Edith, was beset by nervous troubles throughout her life. Unlike Bessie, her maladies led her on an odyssey of sustained introspection unique in Rockefeller annals. She experimented with psychology and other spheres alien to the rest of the family, subjecting the Rockefeller verities to the cold test of modern skepticism and threatening her relationship with her father along the way.

Among the four children, Edith seemed the family changeling. Where her siblings had been submissive children, Edith was recalcitrant, headstrong, and outspoken. Once, as an adolescent, she greeted Grandma Spelman with a hug so fierce that she cracked one of her ribs. She read voraciously and by an early age entertained religious doubts. In a smart but not reflective family, Edith had intellectual aspirations. "Reading has always been more important to me than eating," she confessed to a newspaper reporter late in life. "Except in a case of dire starvation, if a bottle of milk and a book were placed on the table, I would reach for the book, because I must feed my mind more than my body."[72] Such a person might well find something antiseptic about the Rockefeller life.

In 1893, twenty-seven-year-old Bessie and twenty-one-year-old Edith went to Philadelphia for a rest cure at the Hospital for Orthopedic and Nervous Diseases, run by the patrician neurologist-cum-novelist, S. Weir Mitchell. A specialist in female nervous disorders, Mitchell separated his patients from their quotidian world, banning casual visits or even mail from relatives. Rockefeller visited his daughters only once, in February 1894, and would have heartily endorsed their program of relaxation, massage, good food, and electrical stimulation of muscles. Bessie responded better than Edith, who required an extended follow-up rest in a cottage at Saranac Lake in upstate New York.

In November 1895, hard on the heels of her recovery, Edith married Harold McCormick of Chicago, who had just graduated from Princeton. He was the son of Cyrus McCormick, the developer of the mechanical reaper and founder of what became International Harvester. Junior had befriended Harold at the Browning School and was the inadvertent matchmaker. During the World's Columbian Exposition in 1893, he, Cettie, and his three sisters traveled west to Chicago by private railroad car and stayed with Nettie Fowler McCormick, Cyrus's indomitable widow, at her Rush Street mansion. Devout Presbyterians and generous donors to missionary work, the McCormicks resembled the Rockefeller family in many respects. They had raised their children strictly, giving them small allowances and urging them to donate to the poor. There was also a streak of mental instability among the McCormick children that would be far more pernicious than that among the Rockefeller offspring.

The Rockefellers deplored the vogue among rich Americans of marrying off their daughters to titled Europeans and welcomed the McCormicks as an upright, God-fearing industrial family. As the heir to a fortune, Harold McCormick did not have to allay suspicions that might have shadowed another suitor for Edith's hand, and John and Cettie found something winning about his expansive ways. He was an athletic man with luminous blue eyes and a dreamy gaze who wore jeweled cuff links and embroidered vests. Among his tightly wound in-laws, he stood out for his free and open manner. Yet he got along well with Senior and was the only son-in-law allowed to smoke in Cettie's presence.

The only misgivings that John and Cettie had about the marriage centered on Harold's drinking. Several times before the wedding, Rockefeller tried to extract a pledge that he would abstain from liquor, but each time Harold firmly resisted. "While I believe we hold the same general views as to the ruin wrought in the world by strong drink, and as to individual responsibility with regard to it, I am convinced that for me a life pledge is not for the best," Harold told Rockefeller two months before the wedding. As a concession, he stopped drinking briefly. Senior was again receiving threats, and Harold closed his note by adding, "I am distressed to have the subject renewed, and just at a time, when you, and therefore we, have much anxiety and worry by reason of the cranks."[73]

Edith and Harold were to be married in November 1895 at the Fifth Avenue Baptist Church in Manhattan, but Harold got a cold and the ceremony was shifted to the Buckingham Hotel. Right before the wedding, Senior sent for his daughter, telling her that they needed to have one last confidential chat. Once they were alone, Edith recounted in a later interview, he said in his most portentous manner, "I have brought you here to make a request that lies very close to my heart and a request that has been very carefully considered." "Yes, father," Edith replied, "but why be so serious. . . . what is this request that stirs you so much?" "It is this daughter. I want you to promise never to serve a drink of liquor in your home. . . . Promise me that and you will never regret it." As Edith recalled, "Unthinkingly, I said, 'Why, of course, father,' and immediately set off in a peal of laughter over the solemnity of what seemed such a trivial request."[74] This agreement concluded, father and daughter proceeded to the ceremony, and Edith entered on her father's arm, wearing a tiara of diamonds and emeralds given to her by Harold. In the press coverage, Edith was labeled the "Princess of Standard Oil" and Harold the "Prince of International Harvester." Henceforth, Edith was always known as Edith Rockefeller McCormick, signaling that she planned to retain her own identity.

With his children, Rockefeller had tried to create that most elusive thing, a self-perpetuating puritanism, but he was destined to produce at least one rebellious spendthrift and that honor fell to Edith. After an Italian honeymoon, at last emancipated from her austere past, she and Harold moved into a grand stone mansion at 1000 Lake Shore Drive in Chicago. In this Gold Coast fortress, barricaded behind a high iron fence, Edith vied for social preeminence. She displayed in bold relief qualities that Rockefeller had struggled to root out of his children—vanity, ostentation, narcissism, and hedonism—but they were redeemed in part by her prolonged introspection and intellectual fearlessness. In Chicago, away from her father, Edith cultivated a separate set of interests.

All the affectations of European royal courts were displayed in Edith's mansion, and Chicago society tattled about her "imperial complex."[75] After being welcomed by footmen, guests were escorted into sumptuous rooms embellished with beautiful pictures and chandeliers. Edith decided that the Rockefellers were descended from the noble La Rochefoucaulds, and this accounted for a French motif throughout the house. Her dinner guests, sometimes numbering as many as two hundred, received menus and place cards printed in French and engraved with raised gilt letters. The guests dined off a gilded-silver service that had belonged to the Bonapartes and footmen stood stiffly behind every second chair. Edith had a majestic empire room that featured four of Napoleon Bonaparte's royal chairs—two with Ns emblazoned across the back and two with Bs. Edith slept in an ornate Louis XVI bed and kept a gold box on her dressing table that had been a gift to the Empress Marie Louise from Napoleon.

Edith was not shy about her self-presentation. She ran through clothes like a queen, renewing her wardrobe yearly, and always shimmered in jewels. A 1908 painting shows a demure, gray-eyed Edith gazing knowingly at the viewer in tiara and expensive décolleté gown, a boa draped over her shoulders. A short, slender woman, she daringly exposed her ankles and wore a gold ankle chain. On one social occasion, she appeared in a silver dress of such imposing weight that it was said she could scarcely breathe. She had one cape of 275 animal skins, laboriously stitched together, which all but smothered her. Doubtless to her father's horror, Edith assembled a jewelry collection that would have made an eastern potentate blush. She had a Cartier necklace strung with ten emeralds and 1,657 tiny diamonds. For her wedding, her parents gave her a $15,000 rope of pearls, a modest gift soon overshadowed by her $2 million string of pearls. In 1908, discovering that Edith and Harold were borrowing to support this luxury, Rockefeller scolded Harold: "Since my attention was called to this subject, I have made inquiries of Alta and John as to their expenses, and find that theirs have been less than one-third of what yours have been."[76]

Edith's temperance pledge cramped her style as a hostess. Noticing that her soirées lacked a certain sparkle, she turned to Harold for an explanation. "My dear," he said, "don't you realize that these red-blooded young Chicagoans are used to having liquor? They simply must have their cocktails, their wine, their highballs and cordials."[77] No child of John D. Rockefeller would flout a temperance oath made to him, so Edith had to contrive ways to compensate. "I invited the most brilliant men and women whom I met," she told one reporter. "I gave musicales at which I presented the greatest artists of the day."[78] She befriended artists, intellectuals, and society figures and developed into a prominent patroness of the arts, collecting antique furniture, lace, Oriental art, and fine books.

Having always loathed hymns, Edith shared Harold's affection for the opera—she paid for the translation of several librettos into English—and they frequently threw dinner parties on opera nights. In a habit that curiously parodied her father, Edith kept a small jeweled clock at the dinner table and held the guests to a precise schedule, so that everyone arrived at the opera on time. When she pressed a button for the next course, the team of waiters whisked plates away from the startled guests, whether they were finished or not. Edith ran a hierarchical household and never addressed most of the servants directly, dealing exclusively with the top two of them.

It is easy to satirize Edith's foibles and dismiss her as dilettante, yet she was fiercely devoted to her adopted causes. After she had five children—John, Fowler, Muriel, Editha, and Mathilde—Edith created a kindergarten for girls, with classes held in French. Senior doted on her eldest son, John Rockefeller McCormick, known as Jack. During the winter of 1900–1901, Jack and Fowler were staying at Pocantico when both boys contracted scarlet fever. Whatever the latent tensions between them, Edith gratefully remembered her father's behavior during Jack's illness. "As long as I live I shall never forget the great love and the untiring effort which you put forth to save dear Jack's life," she wrote to him a few years later. "Absolutely forgetful of self and showing a love much like the Christ love."[79] To confine the disease, Rockefeller constructed a special staircase that allowed the children and nurses to go from the upstairs sickroom to a glass-enclosed porch without infecting other household members. Rockefeller offered one New York physician a half-million dollars to save the two boys. Little was then known about the cause or treatment of scarlet fever, and although Fowler recovered, John Rockefeller McCormick, nearly four years old, died at Pocantico on January 2, 1901. The shock was no less profound to Rockefeller than to Edith and Harold. A scurrilous rumor later circulated that Edith had learned of Jack's death from a butler during a dinner party at her Chicago mansion, but the report was bogus. Edith happened to be at Pocantico at the time.

Jack McCormick's death strengthened Rockefeller's resolve to endow a medical-research institute. A year later, as a memorial to their son, Edith and Harold created the John McCormick Institution of Infectious Diseases in Chicago. Among the grants it gave out was one to researchers at Johns Hopkins, who isolated the bacterium that causes scarlet fever and set the stage for a treatment.

After Jack's death, Harold succumbed to depression. His charm and gaiety had always veiled a deep vein of melancholy, and he now sought psychiatric help in Switzerland. In 1908, he returned as a patient to the Burghölzli Psychiatric Clinic outside Zurich under the care of Dr. Carl Jung. Edith had also long exhibited manic-depressive mood swings that only widened after the birth of Mathilde in April 1905. Because she had been ill during the pregnancy, Edith and Harold toured Europe by automobile that summer, leaving the baby with John and Cettie. After a fleeting improvement in her health, Edith relapsed the next spring and was belatedly diagnosed as suffering from tuberculosis of the kidney. Rockefeller knew his daughter's troubles were as much psychological as physical in origin and observed to Harold's brother Cyrus that Edith would "require quiet and rest for some time, after all the severe strain through which she has passed in the last few years."[80] For both Harold and Edith, the lure of Europe deepened over the years, a magnetic attraction that the provincial Rockefellers found difficult to fathom.

—

Edith's marriage to Harold McCormick brought Rockefeller under renewed scrutiny because it attached him to the reaper trust as well as the oil trust and steel trust. In August 1902, George Perkins, a J. P. Morgan partner, amalgamated McCormick Harvesting Machine, Deering Harvester, and three smaller competitors into International Harvester, a behemoth with 85 percent of the farm-equipment market. Harold McCormick was named vice president and brother Cyrus president of the company. It was a troubled merger, and the

McCormicks feared that Perkins and the Deerings were secretly plotting to gain control of the company. To create a counterweight, they persuaded Rockefeller to take a five-million-dollar block of preferred stock. Never one to do things by halves, Rockefeller soon expanded his stake to between twenty-five and thirty million dollars. His loans to International Harvester later rose as high as $60 million, and he took stock in the trust as collateral.

This discreet collaboration did not thaw the icy relations between the Rockefeller family and the house of Morgan. On the contrary, the Rockefellers spied conspiracies everywhere. When Junior learned that control of International Harvester would be vested in a three-man voting-trust committee composed of Perkins, Cyrus McCormick, and one of the Deerings, he felt their worst fears were confirmed. "The object of so tying up these securities is that J.P. Morgan & Co. may be assured of the control of the business for a given period of years, and they have made every effort to make it difficult, yes well nigh impossible, for the securities to change hands," he wrote to Senior.[81] Though Rockefeller requested a board seat, George Perkins countered that this would tip the power balance toward the McCormicks and "engender feelings so strong that he could not hope to harmonize them," as Junior told his father.[82] Since the Rockefellers thought that J. P. Morgan and Company secretly exercised the Deering shares, they were not entirely surprised when their vigorous dissent came to nothing.

Equipped with a fine instinct for flattery, Harold professed the greatest admiration for Senior's business abilities. "I have always taken you and the Standard Oil Company as my ideals in the progress of a large company," he told him a year after the reaper trust was formed.[83] Rockefeller did not reciprocate the sentiment and grew critical of Harold's stewardship of International Harvester. He developed a lengthy list of grievances, including Harold's failure to notify him of upcoming earnings reports. Sounding an old refrain, he also chastised Harold for paying excessive dividends. In time, George Perkins grew adamant that the dividend should be boosted, even though the company was borrowing heavily. When Gates went to Morgan to protest, he came away convinced that the house of Morgan was milking the stock for short-term profit. "It is further highly probable," he told Rockefeller, "that the reason why Morgan & Co. are so insistent on increasing the dividend from 4 to 6% is to enable them to sell out their stocks at a very high figure on the basis of the increased dividend. The stock has lately been manipulated upward clearly by an insider namely Mr. Perkins who knew that it was closely held and little was to be had."[84] Senior was dismayed when Harold and Cyrus McCormick protested this only in the lamest fashion. When the voting trust expired in 1912, the McCormicks, with a majority of shares, grimly maintained control, but Rockefeller gradually sold off his position. He would not allow family sentiment to overrule his business judgment.

Unlike the nonconformist Edith, the middle daughter, Alta, was kind and obedient and always eager to please her parents. Slender and dainty, she was an anxious teenager and wrote to her brother reassuringly from the Rye Female Seminary, "Classes are not very large and I shall not be frightened."[85] Of the three daughters, she probably felt most affectionate toward father and never strayed too far from the family fold. "No, I don't change," she once confessed to a friend. "I'm still wearing cotton stockings."[86] She could exhibit a touching innocence and even when married with children radiated a girlish charm. "She seemed just like the 16 years old daughter of the home," Cettie told her diary after a visit from the forty-one-year-old Alta.[87]

As would happen to her brother, Alta suffered from terrible headaches. At age eight or nine, she had an attack of scarlet fever that left her partly deaf in one ear, an affliction that brought her closer to her parents. She later found significant relief with a Viennese physician, Dr. Isidor Muller, and for decades thereafter made annual pilgrimages to Karlsbad to renew this ear treatment. Alta was such a fine singer and pianist that many people did not detect the handicap, but close observers noted the quick, subtle way she flicked her good ear toward the speaker to catch his words.

Forever vigilant against fortune hunters with designs on his daughters, John D. worried the most about Alta, who was passionate and impressionable. Easily smitten, she was constantly falling in love with the wrong men, prompting family rescue operations. Often her crushes were mixed up with a missionary impulse to redeem her beloved from some presumed failing.

If Rockefeller had thought Alta safe in the sanctuary of the Baptist Church, he was rudely awakened in early 1891. Though the Rockefellers had moved to Manhattan, they resumed their involvement in the Euclid Avenue Baptist Church every summer when they returned to Forest Hill. As a deacon and superintendent of the Sunday school, Rockefeller still paid half the church expenses from his own pocket. While teaching in the Sunday school, Alta, nineteen, became infatuated with the forty-seven-year-old pastor, the Reverend Dr. L. A. Crandall. Despite the considerable age difference between them, Alta tried to wean him from his evil smoking habit. Though only five years younger than Rockefeller himself, Reverend Crandall was highly susceptible to Alta's adoration. His wife had died a year and a half earlier, leaving him with a son in college, a daughter in private school, and an emotional void in his life.

Persuaded that Alta genuinely loved him, Crandall began to talk to her about marriage. When Rockefeller heard rumors of this, he refused to believe them at first, then summoned people to his home, quizzed them, and was stunned to discover the truth. Rockefeller delivered a stern ultimatum to Dr. Crandall: Either he would resign or the Rockefellers would withdraw from the Euclid Avenue Baptist Church. The church would have been devastated without the Rockefeller money and torn apart by the scandal. Submitting to a superior force, Dr. Crandall left for a Chicago pastorate under the cover that he was moving there to seek a superior education for his children.

Three years later, Alta fell in love with a young minister named Robert A. Ashworth, who was in poor health. When Rockefeller got wind of his daughter's attachment, he tried to figure out how to cure her of it without showing his hand. In late December 1894, he suddenly organized a party of young people, including Junior, Alta, and Ashworth, for a festive sledding and tobogganing trip to the Adirondack Mountains. Rockefeller chose to emphasize vigorous sports that would expose Ashworth's frailty to Alta. "Most of the young men taken along were highly robust, and the minister in his physical weakness cut a sorry figure beside them," said Junior's friend Everett Colby.[88] The ploy apparently worked and the problematic relationship ended a week later.

Of all the Rockefeller children, Alta was the most affected by the plight of the poor immigrant populations crowding into American cities in the late nineteenth century. Where her father exercised his benevolence at a distance, Alta rolled up her sleeves, went into the slums, and administered self-help programs for the poor. At Tenth Avenue and Fifty-fifth Street in Manhattan, she set up a sewing school for indigent girls, drafted a corps of volunteer teachers, and enrolled 125 pupils. She also set up a small private clinic for invalid women.

Despite her managerial talents, Alta departed from her father's penchant for building large institutions and favored small-scale charities, of which the best example was Alta House in Cleveland. In the 1890s, a local minister interested Rockefeller and his daughter in a charity, the Day Nursery and Free Kindergarten Association, serving poor Italian immigrants in the Murray Hill district, the Little Italy of Cleveland. Many working couples left their children there during the day. Rockefeller agreed to construct a new settlement building, Alta House, which was dedicated in February 1900 and furnished with a family laundry and medical dispensary. Although he supplied the money and covered the budget for its first twenty years, Alta did the legwork. She enjoyed direct contact with the immigrant families and took special delight in dressing up dolls for their children.

After completion of the settlement house, Alta was desperately eager to marry. When Edith married Harold McCormick in 1895, Alta was openly envious and told her brother that "I must try to enter heartily into all her happiness."[89] Through Harold McCormick, Alta met Ezra Parmalee Prentice, then working in Chicago as general counsel for the Illinois Steel Company. Cold and smart, a rigid perfectionist, Parmalee was also an amateur scientist with a large collection of meteorological instruments. The scion of an old Albany family and a graduate of Amherst College and Harvard Law School, he underwent the same microscopic scrutiny that awaited any supplicant for Alta's hand. As she told Junior in early 1900, "[Parmalee] gave Father the names of four of his friends who would answer any questions about him that Father might want to ask and said that he would add to this list if it were desired."[90] When Parmalee passed muster, he and Alta were married the following year, but Parmalee and Senior had a remote relationship and seldom saw each other. Parmalee penned formal letters to his father-in-law that began, "Dear Mr. Rockefeller" and were signed, "E. Parmalee Prentice."

Unlike Edith, Alta wanted to live near her parents. Perhaps Parmalee erred by abandoning his Chicago job to practice law in New York and join a firm that would one day evolve into Milbank, Tweed, Hadley and McCloy. Surrendering his freedom by slow degrees, he allowed Junior to buy and furnish a new home for them at 5 West Fifty-third Street. A gift from Senior, this house stood behind his own home on West Fifty-fourth Street. "Uncle John did furnish that house," one of Alta and Parmalee's children said. "My father could not have cared less and my mother did not have the know-how. She had grown up in the same rut as Uncle John and had no one to pull her out. She was timid, spiritual like her mother, and besides, she had the idea that her brother always knew best."[91] Parmalee had a fine legal mind, authored two legal books, and argued cases before the Supreme Court. At first, Rockefeller referred legal work to him and advised other moguls to follow suit, but he never got the expected gratitude from his proud son-in-law. In 1905, when Rockefeller asked him to reorganize Colorado Fuel and Iron, he was not only outraged by the fees Parmalee charged but indignant at his high-handed treatment of the bondholder representatives. At that point, Rockefeller advised Gates to refer less business to Parmalee's firm. Unable to compromise on business principles, Rockefeller chose to jeopardize family relations instead.

Instead of distributing money to his children at maturity, Rockefeller kept them on allowances after they married and reserved the right to oversee their finances. Junior was appointed family auditor, and this turned him, perforce, into an irritating, censorious presence in the lives of his three brothers-in-law. When Junior decided in 1904 that Alta and Parmalee were spending twice as much as their income warranted, Parmalee bristled at this intrusion into their private lives. The prodigal generosity displayed by Senior after Alta's wedding now turned into its opposite, and she was placed in the demeaning position of having to beg him for money. After a point, she did not disguise her anger. "Ten years ago when we came into the house you were good enough to pay for all the lace curtains," she wrote to her father. "These curtains are now worn out and I have bought new ones. . . . Would you help me out by buying the curtains. If so, I shall be greatly pleased. If not, of course it will be all right."[92] Once he had made them feel punished for earlier extravagance, Senior would relent and disburse the money. As long as the right conditions were met, this controlling father was always happy to be generous. In 1910, he offered Alta and Parmalee $250,000 to purchase a house and land, and they bought a thousand-acre farm, which they christened Mount Hope, in the Berkshire Mountains near Williamstown, Massachusetts.

It is interesting that both Alta and Bessie married cold, remote, self-absorbed men. One can speculate that they chose these men because of their resemblance to their father, yet neither Charles Strong nor Parmalee Prentice had Rockefeller's redeeming cordiality or spontaneous interest in other people. Many observers felt that Alta had blundered in marrying the autocratic Parmalee. Priggish and straitlaced, he demanded that their three children dress formally for dinner each night, and he never allowed them to bring friends to the table. Highly cerebral, Parmalee translated *Treasure Island* into Latin and insisted that the children converse with him in Latin each evening. Each Sunday, he prepared an essay on a theme and led a family discussion. Parmalee was so fearsome a father that even Junior's children felt their own home positively wild and decadent in comparison.

Whatever her frustrations, Alta put the best face on the marriage. "Parmalee is beautiful in his thoughts for me and his consideration of me, and if he had his way nothing would ever be allowed to fret me nor disturb me for one single minute," she wrote to her father. "He makes my life one long, glad song." While Parmalee had rather cool relations with his children, Alta insisted to her father that they "love him as dearly and respect him so much that they cannot bear to see even the slightest shadow cross his face."[93] The compliment can also be read to connote a certain fear that the children had of him.

After purchasing the farm, Alta and her husband increasingly inhabited a rural world, tramping about the muddy fields and growing corn, oats, potatoes, buckwheat, and McIntosh apples. Alta's letters abound in talk of plowing, threshing, and manure. Prompted by an interest in Gregor Mendel's genetic theories, Parmalee began to experiment with scientific agriculture and studied ways to boost the output of their potato crop, dairy herd, and hens. Visitors to Mount Hope were far more likely to meet geneticists from Williams College than society figures. When Parmalee organized an experiment to cross black and white mice, Alta had to photograph a thousand mice. Where Edith had ventured out into the world, Alta—who had little contact with her sister—stuck to a simple life that revolved around her husband, children, farm, and horses.

Senior wanted all three sons-in-law, along with Junior, to be involved in the Rockefeller philanthropies; for reasons discussed later, he skipped over his three daughters. Senior and Junior made intermittent efforts to interest Parmalee, but he habitually declined their offers. At one point, Harold McCormick tried to relieve tensions between Junior and Parmalee. While admitting to Senior that Parmalee had "a proud and perhaps even haughty spirit," Harold maintained that he was a good-hearted man who suffered from a "feeling on the part of the harsh world . . . that he is discredited by his family or even viewed with indifference." Citing the hostility between Junior and Parmalee, Harold added, "Alta is torn almost in two in her love."[94] Apparently, Senior was not convinced. Soon after Harold's plea, he complained to Edith that Junior was overburdened with charitable work and explicitly blamed his sons-in-law: "I could wish that Harold and Parmalee, with their broad shoulders, were heart and soul in this work with us."[95] Yet it was never clear how they could do that without subordinating their identities to Rockefeller, who never understood their need for freedom from his domineering presence.

While Parmalee craved distance from Senior, he did not renounce the financial rewards that came with the relationship. In 1912, Rockefeller guaranteed him a $30,000 annual income from his legal work; if he failed to reach that level, Rockefeller would make up the difference. Whether Parmalee suddenly grew lazy or suffered a sharp downturn in business is unclear, but two years later Rockefeller had to pay $26,000 of his salary. Two years after that, he doubled Parmalee's annual guaranteed salary to $60,000. Meanwhile, Alta's annual allowance was boosted to $50,000 in 1914. By transferring more money to Alta and Parmalee and giving them the means to pay their own bills, Rockefeller hoped to end the constant tussles between them and Junior over money—something that he should have done in the first place.

CHAPTER 22

Avenging Angel

The relief that washed through Standard Oil after William McKinley's 1896 election had proved short-lived. Despite a sudden upsurge of prosperity, the electorate remained wary of the new monopolies and the muscular arrivistes who had created them. The crusade to curtail the trusts was very much alive, if temporarily shunted to the state level. Once again, the first salvo against Standard Oil was fired in Ohio. The state attorney general, Frank Monnett—successor to the crusading David K. Watson—was the son of a Methodist preacher, a former railroad attorney, and a hardworking public servant. In 1897, he received a visit from the maverick refiner George Rice, who persuaded him that Standard Oil had never complied with the 1892 decision to sever Ohio Standard from the trust. To check up on his adversaries, Rice had bought six shares of Standard Oil trust certificates. When he tried to redeem them for fractional shares in the twenty constituent companies spun off by the 1892 decision, the liquidating trustees—including Rockefeller—procrastinated for four years. Now, five years after the verdict, $27 million in trust certificates remained unredeemed. On November 9, 1897, Monnett charged that Standard of Ohio had never seriously planned to leave the trust and was in contempt of court. It had all been a charade to pacify trustbusters.

Rockefeller's retirement began to assume the inexorable nature of a Greek tragedy: Just as he sought to extricate himself from the trust, its legal troubles deepened. Conditioned by a long history of Standard Oil mendacity, both press and public mocked his so-called retirement as a tawdry ruse to evade testimony. It defied the common conception of villainy to think that such a man could simply walk away from his creation.

To expedite the case, Monnett had a master commissioner interrogate witnesses in New York. On October 11, 1898, Rockefeller was summoned to testify at the New Amsterdam Hotel, the prosecution hoping to prod him into an admission that he had stalled in liquidating the trust. Through more than five hours of questioning, Rockefeller, as imperturbable as ever, spoke in such a low voice that people strained to hear him, and he conceded so little that the next day's *World* ran the headline, "Rockefeller Imitates a Clam."[1] Standard lawyers spent much more time objecting to questions than Rockefeller did in answering them. Once again, he presented the past as a dense fog that he could scarcely penetrate. As the *World* dryly observed, "The virtue of forgetting, which is one of the most valuable virtues that a monopolist can have under cross-examination, is possessed by Mr. Rockefeller in its highest degree."[2]

Rockefeller, as always, refused to believe that anybody could have a legitimate objection to Standard Oil. Once again, he fell back on his all-purpose explanation that the suits filed against him were just extortion rackets posing as public service. Later on, he said that Monnett's motive was to "blackmail the Standard Oil Company" and that he was a "comrade in schemes with George Rice."[3] Rockefeller suppressed signs of irritation at the hearing, yet he seemed edgier than on earlier occasions. Reporters noted telltale nervous habits that called into question his surface composure—the way he kept shifting his weight, crossing and recrossing his legs, rubbing his nape, blowing out his cheeks, and biting his mustache.

At the end of his testimony, Rockefeller, discernibly relieved, did something very unusual for him: He bounded straight over to George Rice, extended his hand, and tried to engage him in conversation. He suddenly grew very chatty, as two newspapers reported:

"How are you, Mr. Rice? We are getting to be old men now, eh? Don't you wish you had taken my advice years ago?"

"Perhaps it would have been better for me if I had," said Rice, glaring at him. "You have ruined my business, as you said you would."

"Pshaw! Pshaw!" replied Rockefeller, moving away.

"You did, you ruined me," persisted Rice, chasing him. (Rice, a well-to-do businessman, perhaps overstated his case.)

"Pshaw! Pshaw!" said Rockefeller, donning his silk hat. "I would rather have given ten—"

"It's no use your saying 'pshaw,' " Rice interrupted. "You know damned well you did."[4]

Rockefeller flashed a funereal smile, then disappeared from the room. It was one of the few times in his mysterious career that he ever confronted one of his nemeses. If Rockefeller's style was to slip away from attacks, the Monnett in-

Ida Minerva Tarbell, seated before her
rolltop desk at McClure's Magazine in 1898.
(Courtesy of the Drake Well Museum)

vestigation displayed the two-fisted style of his successor, John D. Archbold. On the stand, Archbold accused Rice of trying to extort $500,000 from Standard Oil for his refinery, and at the lunch recess, according to one newspaper, he marched up to Rice, jabbed a finger in his face, and said, "You are nothing but wind and weight." "And you," retorted Rice, "are nothing but money stolen from the people."[5] The impetuous Archbold behaved as if public opinion were of no importance. He did not see that the day of reckoning for Standard Oil was fast approaching and that he would soon need all the friends he could get. In a preview of his brawling, arrogant style with authorities, Archbold got into a heated shouting match with a man named Flagg, one of Monnett's assistants:

"You keep still or I'll expose you right here," Archbold shouted at him.

"You couldn't if you tried," said Flagg. "I'm not afraid of your millions."

"Shut up or I will show you up," cried Archbold.

"Is any one low lived compared with a Standard Oil magnate?"

"You know what you are."

"You are a coward and a liar," shouted Flagg.

"You are a stinking liar," Archbold shot back.[6]

What prompted this vehement exchange was the burning of company records at a Standard Oil facility in Cleveland. Monnett had charged Standard of Ohio with surreptitiously paying dividends to holders of trust certificates after 1892, which Rockefeller and other officials denied. To resolve the matter, the state supreme court ordered Standard of Ohio to produce its books in December 1898. Two weeks later, reports filtered out that sixteen boxes of books had been incinerated by Standard employees. Amid a national furor, Standard attorneys denied that the boxes contained the ledgers in question—"from time to time," said Standard Oil's attorney, Virgil Kline, the company destroyed "useless material which accumulates in its business"—but he refused to produce the pertinent ledgers.[7] Monnett thought the books were torched to shield Rockefeller. As he told Henry Demarest Lloyd, "I am of the opinion that the books were burned at least in part. . . . They were obliged to either let the books contradict Mr. Rockefeller . . . or else take a defiant stand and conceal the books from the court."[8]

Among other damning accusations, Standard Oil was said to have hired the Malcolm Jennings Advertising Agency to promote its products in Ohio and Indiana newspapers in exchange for favorable news items. The most sensational charge trumpeted by Monnett involved an alleged attempt by Standard Oil to bribe him into dropping the case, much as had been alleged with David K. Watson. Monnett said that a nameless emissary had come to his Columbus office with an offer of $400,000. The money was to be left in a safety-deposit box in New York, with Monnett given the key. Standard attorneys hotly disputed this, demanding the name of their putative agent. When Monnett would not identify him, citing fears of reprisals, it cast doubt on the story. In a later statement, he named Feargus Charles Haskell and Frank Rockefeller as the culprits. Rockefeller's papers, unfortunately, shed no light on the situation.

Before Monnett could inflict lasting damage upon Standard Oil, he became persona non grata in many sections of his own Republican Party. He especially incurred the wrath of U.S. senator Joseph B. Foraker of Ohio, who was on the Standard Oil payroll. (In 1900 alone, Archbold disbursed $44,500 in lobbying fees to the senator.) At a Washington meeting, Foraker gave Monnett a brief but unforgettable education in Ohio political realities. As Monnett re-created the discussion:

> I at first discussed the impropriety and danger of [Foraker's] representing these trusts, criminal and civil violators of his own State, as long as he as well as myself should be interested in the welfare of the people of Ohio. He told me that he never allowed his law practice to interfere with politics or his politics with law practice, and added that he was a judge of ethics of our profession. He then took up the cause of action against these companies and reminded me of the great power financially and politically of the Standard Oil crowd. After talking a short time, he asked me to have the proceedings delayed in order to accommodate him. I firmly declined to concede any time whatever and told him so. He recalled the great power of the Oil Trust to anyone opposed to it.[9]

True to Foraker's warning, Monnett failed to win the Republican renomination for attorney general in 1899; disillusioned, he joined the Democratic Party two years later.

=

Even though the Ohio suit fizzled, it alerted the trust to the need for a permanent corporate structure that could weather legal challenges. Ever since 1892, Standard Oil had sustained a precarious arrangement in which seventeen leading shareholders, many of them the liquidating trustees, held a majority of the stock of twenty constituent companies. These oil-industry veterans were now graying—Archbold, in his early fifties, was among the youngest—and since they alone bound the Standard Oil units together, they feared that if they died, their heirs might squabble, sell the shares, or otherwise threaten the trust's cohesion. It was time for a less-shaky corporate framework.

The trust had long struggled with the legal straitjacket that prevented companies from holding stock in out-of-state corporations. In 1898, heeding the clamor against the trusts, Congress created the U.S. Industrial Commission to study the American economy. Testifying before that body a year later, Rockefeller bemoaned this legal anachronism. "Our Federal form of government, making every corporation created by a State foreign to every other State, ren-

ders it necessary for persons doing business through corporate agency to organize corporations in some or many of the different States in which their business is located."[10] To rectify the problem, Rockefeller endorsed a federal
incorporation law, even if a measure of government regulation came with it.

In the meantime, Standard Oil was aided by recent amendments to the New
Jersey incorporation law. In June 1899, undergoing yet another change in
form, Standard Oil became a full-fledged holding company under New Jersey
law with the legal parent, Standard Oil of New Jersey, controlling stock in nineteen large and twenty-two small companies. Though he owned more than one-
fourth of the shares, Rockefeller wanted to stay retired and avoid operational
responsibility. Loath for him to relinquish his titular leadership amid legal troubles, his colleagues insisted that he remain honorary president. "I declined to
have any official position in the Standard Oil Company of New Jersey in 1899,"
Rockefeller later told Harold McCormick, "and urged my brother [William] to
take this position, but as he declined and all the others were very urgent, I was
called the President, and have been since, although the position is and has all
the time been entirely nominal."[11] Unbeknownst to the general public, Rockefeller never attended a meeting or drew a salary, and Archbold, the new vice
president, ran the organization.

In many respects, Standard Oil attained its peak influence in the 1890s. It
now marketed 84 percent of all petroleum products sold in America and
pumped a third of its crude oil—the highest percentage it ever reached. After
years of harrowing prophecies that the industry might vanish, the business
outlook had never looked brighter, despite the growing use of electricity. Sales
boomed in everything from oil stoves to parlor lamps to varnish, soaking up oil
supplies and driving up prices. In 1903, the British navy outfitted some battleships to use fuel oil instead of coal, attracting the notice of the U.S. Navy. Paraffin wax had become a vital insulator in the burgeoning telephone and electrical
industries. Most momentous of all, the automobile promised to consume that
vile, useless by-product, gasoline, and Standard Oil cultivated the new carmak-
ers. When Henry Ford rolled out his first vehicle, Charlie Ross, a Standard Oil
salesman, stood by with a can of the trust's Atlantic Red Oil. The number of
registered automobiles in America leaped from eight hundred in 1898 to eight
thousand in 1900. When the Wright brothers took off from Kitty Hawk in
1903, their flight was powered by gasoline brought to the beach by Standard
Oil salesmen. These new petroleum applications more than offset the dwindling kerosene business.

Though it had some scrappy competition at home from Pure Oil, Standard
Oil's monopoly seemed secure in the 1890s. But developments at home and
abroad soon imperiled its power even before Teddy Roosevelt's trustbusters entered the scene. In the late 1890s, Russia temporarily surpassed the United
States to become the world's largest crude-oil producer, capturing 35 percent

of the world market. The trust's global monopoly was sharply eroding on other fronts: The new Burmah Oil sold oil actively in Indian markets, Royal Dutch expanded its drilling in Sumatra, and Shell Transport and Trading stepped up its East Asian activities. In October 1901, Sir Marcus Samuel of Shell held secret talks at 26 Broadway. Archbold reported to Rockefeller, "This company [Shell] represents by all means the most important distributing Agency for Refined Oil throughout the World, outside of our own interests. He is here undoubtedly to take up with us the question of some sort of an alliance, preferable on his part of the sale to us of a large interest in their Company."[12] Two months later, afraid of ceding too much power to Archbold, Samuel signed an agreement instead with Henri Deterding of Royal Dutch, creating a major new alliance along with the French Rothschilds. Archbold responded to this new threat with unrelenting price wars.

The home situation had grown no less treacherous. In 1900, the Waters-Pierce Company, Standard Oil's rogue marketing subsidiary, was ousted from Texas for violating the state's antitrust law. It had cornered 90 percent of the oil market, winning universal infamy for its cutthroat sales practices. This legal setback mattered greatly, for it evicted the trust from the state on the eve of a revolution. In 1901, drillers in Beaumont, Texas, made a major find in a dreary mound called Spindletop, which spouted oil with such explosive force that it spewed tens of thousands of barrels into the air for days before it was capped. The Texas oil boom, which spawned five hundred new companies during its first year alone, redrew the industry map. By 1905, Texas accounted for more than a quarter of the crude oil being pumped in America. Popular antagonism toward Standard Oil in Texas prevented the trust from moving aggressively to exterminate these new competitors, though the trust did have several refining affiliates there. When the Mellons, who had financed Spindletop, offered to sell it to Standard Oil, they were bluntly informed by one director, "We're out. After the way Mr. Rockefeller has been treated by the state of Texas, he'll never put another dime in Texas."[13] Standard had to sit back and suffer the emergence of a host of competing producers, including Gulf Oil and the Texas Company, later called Texaco.

So while reformers noisily denounced the omnipotence of Standard Oil, its monopoly was swiftly crumbling at home and overseas. With additional oil strikes in California, Indian Territory (later Oklahoma), Kansas, and Illinois in the early 1900s, the industry became too vast and far-flung for even Standard Oil to control. It might not be too much of an exaggeration to say that the antitrust cases brought against the trust in the early 1900s were not just belated but were fast becoming superfluous.

After a young anarchist assassinated William McKinley in Buffalo in September 1901, the country was swept by widespread trepidation that the shooting had formed part of a broader conspiracy. In Chicago, a traveling salesman captivated reporters with tales of a conversation that he had overheard at a local train depot where J. P. Morgan and John D. Rockefeller were mentioned as potential assassination targets. A heavily armed contingent of guards ringed Rockefeller's residence and he remained incommunicado.

As it turned out, the gravest threat to the titan's welfare emanated not from shadowy, gun-toting subversives but from the new White House occupant, forty-three-year-old Theodore Roosevelt. So long as McKinley was in the White House, Rockefeller had implicit faith that his business interests would be safeguarded. "America is truly to be congratulated upon Mr. McKinley's election," he had written in November 1900. "With financial interests on a sound basis, the next four years ought to accomplish much for the general welfare of the American people."[14] In Roosevelt, however, whom he credited as the "shrewdest of politicians," Rockefeller knew he had a formidable rival.[15]

In a political world degraded by corrupt bosses and ward heelers, Teddy Roosevelt was that rara avis: a cultivated, well-to-do man. Descended from Dutch settlers who had emigrated to New Amsterdam before 1648 and later made a fortune in Manhattan real estate, Roosevelt, like many of his social peers, was scandalized by the sordid ethics of the new industrial class. As a New York state assemblyman in 1883, this aristocratic renegade reviled Jay Gould and his ilk as members of "the wealthy criminal class," the first of many such rhetorical blasts.[16] In 1886, Rockefeller contributed one thousand dollars to Roosevelt's unsuccessful mayoral campaign only because he feared even more the single-tax policy espoused by one of his opponents, Henry George. Running for New York governor in 1898, Roosevelt accepted contributions from Henry Flagler and a number of Wall Street executives, whom he promptly double-crossed by enacting a tax on corporate franchises and supporting factory regulation. A militant preacher against class divisions, he warned that politicians ignored popular discontent about the trusts at their peril. If they stuck to laissez-faire neglect, he predicted, "then the multitudes will follow the crank who advocates an absurd policy, but who does advocate something."[17] A dyspeptic Henry Flagler spluttered: "I have no command of the English language that enables me to express my feelings regarding Mr. Roosevelt."[18] New York businessmen were so eager to get rid of Roosevelt that they eased him out of the governorship and into the vice presidential slot on the McKinley ticket in 1900. Roosevelt always believed that Standard Oil had formed part of the effort to export him from state politics.

By 1901, virtually all American industrialists were converts to the doctrine of cooperation preached by Rockefeller and feared Teddy Roosevelt's reputation as a trustbuster, even if that anxiety was somewhat overblown. Like

Rockefeller, the new president favored industrial consolidation to exploit economies of scale. Scoffing at calls by William Jennings Bryan and Robert La Follette to dismantle the trusts, he contended that any such course would thwart the economy's natural tendency. "Much of the legislation not only proposed but enacted against trusts is not one whit more intelligent than the medieval bull against the comet, and has not been one particle more effective."[19] Roosevelt distinguished between bad trusts, which gouged consumers, and good trusts, which offered fair prices and good service. Instead of indiscriminate trust-busting, he concentrated on the worst offenders, and he singled out Standard Oil as emblematic of the abusive trusts.

When Roosevelt became president, Mark Hanna urged him to reassure skittish businessmen by avoiding provocative statements. With mischievous relish, the young president threw a dinner for J. P. Morgan, telling one cabinet member, "You see, it represents an effort on my part to become a conservative man in touch with the influential class and I think I deserve encouragement."[20] He sought the advice of Senator Aldrich and stayed on his best behavior around businessmen. In November 1901, after a friendly meeting with Roosevelt, an aide to Henry Flagler suggested that he meet with the president and patch up hard feelings between them. "I don't believe there is a man in America who dreads such a thing as much as I do," Flagler responded. "I am glad you saw him, for I am sure I don't want to do it."[21] The statement captured the hubris that would soon be the downfall of Standard Oil, which treated the federal government as a meddlesome, inferior power.

Roosevelt trod a tightrope between radical reformers and trust kings. He had a clever way of delivering sharp, sudden blows against business, then following with conciliatory speeches. By nature, he was a political hybrid: Strident reformers brought out his conservatism while stand-pat businessmen brought out his crusading zeal. Much like Franklin Roosevelt in the 1930s, he introduced regulation in order to save the country from social unrest and forestall more extreme measures. He was accused of appropriating the policies of William Jennings Bryan, much as Franklin Roosevelt was later said to have undercut his left-wing critics by appropriating many of their policies.

In February 1902, as businessmen speculated about his true colors, Roosevelt showed that he had not mellowed. Without consulting Wall Street, he launched an antitrust suit against the Northern Securities Company, a holding company created by J. P. Morgan to consolidate railroads in the Pacific Northwest. Stunned businessmen sold stocks on the news. However aggrieved, J. P. Morgan did not declare open warfare on Roosevelt and later in the year helped him arbitrate an end to the anthracite coal strike. As Roosevelt turned the presidency into an honest broker between capital and labor, Morgan, unlike the more myopic Rockefeller, saw that Roosevelt stood ready to make concessions to cooperative businessmen.

In early 1903, Roosevelt supported the Elkins Act, which strengthened penalties for railroad rebates, and energetically promoted plans for a new Department of Commerce and Labor, which would include a Bureau of Corporations with broad powers to investigate the trusts. The new bureau was indispensable to his antitrust program, since the federal government was too small and thinly staffed to tackle the trusts on anything like an equal basis. In the 1890s, the entire Justice Department staff in Washington had only eighteen lawyers. To take on the industrial giants, Roosevelt needed more staff and, especially, more information.

As business interests fought the bureau, Roosevelt artfully manipulated the press to demonize his foes. In February 1903, he informed reporters that six senators had received telegrams from John D. Rockefeller urging defeat of the proposed bureau in these words: "We are opposed to the anti-trust legislation. Our counsel will see you. It must be stopped. John D. Rockefeller."[22] This mighty revelation, as Roosevelt expected, caused a terrific commotion. Rockefeller's name was now shorthand for corporate villainy so that his opposition to the bureau appeared conclusively to prove its need. As Teddy Roosevelt exclaimed jubilantly, "I got the bill through by publishing those telegrams and concentrating public attention on the bill."[23]

In truth, the telegrams were sent by Junior after prodding from Archbold. Shocked and embarrassed by the uproar, Junior resented Archbold for having dragged him into the ill-advised lobbying operation. That everybody believed his revered father had authored the telegrams only made it the more mortifying. "I came out of college something of an idealist," he later reflected, "and I was immediately thrust into the tough give and take of the business world. I really wasn't ready for it."[24] No stranger to controversy, Rockefeller told his son to ignore his critics—"Let the world wag," he said—but Junior kept brooding.[25] He desperately wanted to rehabilitate the family name and live an irreproachable life, and here he was already wading hip-deep in Standard Oil muck. It was one of several events that finally convinced him that he was too squeamish for a business career.

Fiercely self-righteous, Teddy Roosevelt never forgot Standard Oil's attempt to sabotage his new department, but he was a practical politician and recognized the value of winning Standard Oil support in his 1904 election campaign. Trying to mediate a truce between Standard Oil and the White House, Congressman Joseph C. Sibley told Archbold that the president thought the oil trust was hostile toward him, to which Archbold said facetiously, "I have always been an admirer of President Roosevelt and have read every book he ever wrote, and have them, in the best bindings, in my library." Sibley relayed this flattering news to Roosevelt—minus, of course, the sarcasm. "The 'book business' fetched down the game at the very first shot," Sibley reported back to Archbold. "You had better read, at least, the titles of those volumes to refresh your memory before you come over."[26] The rapprochement did not survive the 1904 election, for once the voting was over the president had an unpleasant surprise in store for Standard Oil.

===

In stalking Standard Oil, Teddy Roosevelt had no more potent ally than the press. In the spring of 1900, Rockefeller could still reassure a correspondent that favorable publicity about him overshadowed adverse coverage. "No man can succeed in any calling without provoking the jealousy and envy of some," he observed. "The strong level-headed man will go straight forward and do his work, and history will rightly record."[27]

Several trends gave birth to a newly assertive press. The gigantic trusts swelled the ranks of national advertisers, fattening the pages of many periodicals. Aided by new technologies, including linotype and photoengraving, glossy illustrated magazines streamed forth in such numbers that the era would be memorialized as the golden age of the American magazine. Paralleling this was the rise of mass-circulation newspapers, which catered to an expanding reading public. Competing in fierce circulation wars, Joseph Pulitzer, William Randolph Hearst, and other press barons plied readers with scandals and crusades. Nonetheless, the turn of the century marked more than the heyday of strident tabloids and yellow journalism, as sophisticated publications began to tackle complex stories, illustrating them lavishly and promoting them aggressively. For the first time in history, college graduates went to work on newspapers and magazines, bringing a new literary flair to a world once considered beneath the dignity of the educated elite.

Studded with star writers and editors, the most impressive periodical was *McClure's Magazine,* which was started by Samuel S. McClure in 1893. In September 1901, the same month that Roosevelt ascended to the presidency, the magazine's managing editor, Ida Minerva Tarbell, sailed to Europe to confer with McClure, then taking a rest from his strenuous life in Vevey, Switzerland. In her suitcase she carried an outline for a three-part series on the Standard Oil Company, though she wondered whether anyone would ever wade through a long, factual account of a business empire—a journalistic enterprise never assayed before.

The Standard Oil story was intertwined with Tarbell's early life. Born in 1857 in a log cabin thirty miles from where Drake struck oil two years later, she was a true daughter of the Oil Regions. "I had grown up with oil derricks, oil tanks, pipe lines, refineries, oil exchanges," she wrote in her memoirs.[28] Her father, Franklin Tarbell, crafted vats from hemlock bark, a trade easily converted into barrel making after Drake's discovery. The Tarbells lived beside his Rouseville barrel shop, and Ida as a child rolled luxuriously in the heaps of pine shavings. Down the hill from her house, across a ravine, lived an amiable young refiner named Henry H. Rogers, who later recalled seeing the young girl picking wildflowers on the slope.

Ida watched men with queer gleams in their eyes swarming through Rouseville en route to the miracle-turned-mirage of Pithole Creek. Franklin Tarbell set up a barrel shop there and cashed in on the boom before Pithole's oil gave out. But Franklin's prosperity was tenuous, based on an antiquated technology. Wooden barrels were soon replaced by iron tanks—the first of several times that Ida's father was hurt by progress. He then sought his fortune as an independent oil producer and refiner, just as Rockefeller was consolidating the industry and snuffing out small operators.

In 1872, as an impressionable fifteen-year-old, Ida saw her paradise torn asunder by the South Improvement Company. As her father joined vigilantes who sabotaged the conspirators' tanks, she thrilled to the talk of revolution. "On the instant the word became holy to me," she later wrote.[29] The SIC darkened her sunlit world. The father who once sang, played the Jew's harp, and told funny stories became a "silent and stern" man, breeding in his sensitive daughter a lifelong hatred of Standard Oil.[30] For her, Standard Oil symbolized the triumph of grasping men over decent folk, like her father, who played fair and square.

She remembered the Titusville of her teenage years as divided between the valiant majority who resisted the octopus and the small band of opportunists who defected to it. On the street, Franklin pointed out turncoats to his daughter. "In those days I looked with more contempt on the man who had gone over to the Standard than on the one who had been in jail," she said.[31] After a time, Franklin's family would not speak to blackguards who had sold out to Rockefeller. It revolted Ida that the trust could turn proud, independent entrepreneurs into beaten men taking orders from distant bosses.

Although Tarbell had a more genteel upbringing than Rockefeller, with more books, magazines, and small luxuries, one is struck by the similarity of the Rockefellers' Baptist and the Tarbells' Methodist households. The straitlaced Franklin Tarbell forbade cards and dancing and supported many causes, including the temperance movement. Ida attended prayer meetings on Thursday nights and taught an infant class of the Sunday school. Shy and bookish, she tended, like Rockefeller, to arrive at brilliant solutions by slow persistence.

What set Tarbell apart from Rockefeller was her intellectual daring and fearless curiosity. As a teenager, despite her family's fundamentalism, she tried to prove the truth of evolution. By the time she enrolled at Allegheny College in Meadville, Pennsylvania, in 1876—she was the sole girl in the freshman class of this Methodist school—she loved to peer through microscopes and planned to become a biologist. What distinguished her as a journalist was how she united a scientific attention to detail with homegrown moral fervor. After graduation, Tarbell taught for two years at the Poland Union Seminary in Poland,

Ohio, then got a job on the editorial staff of *The Chautauquan*, an offshoot of the summer adult-education movement, which originated as a Methodist camp meeting. The fiery, militant Christian spirit of the movement made Ida even more high-minded in her expectations.

Tall and attractive, with dark hair, large gray eyes, and high cheekbones, Tarbell had an erect carriage and innate dignity and never lacked suitors. Yet she decided never to marry and to remain self-sufficient. She steeled herself against any feelings that might compromise her ambitions or integrity, and she walked through life, perhaps a little self-consciously, in a shining moral armor.

In 1891, the thirty-four-year-old Tarbell moved to Paris with friends and set up Bohemian quarters on the Left Bank—an unusually courageous decision for a young American woman at the time. She was determined to write a biography of the Girondist Madame Roland while selling freelance articles to Pennsylvania and Ohio newspapers and attending classes at the Sorbonne. Hardworking and levelheaded, she mailed off two articles during her first week in Paris alone. Even though the prim Tarbell was taken aback when lascivious Frenchmen flirted with her, she adored her time in Paris. She interviewed eminent Parisians, ranging from Louis Pasteur to Emile Zola, for American newspapers and won many admirers for her clean, accurate reportage; she claimed that her writing had absorbed some of the beauty and clarity of the French language. Still, she struggled on the "ragged edge of bankruptcy" and was susceptible when McClure wooed her as an editor of his new magazine.

While she was still in Paris, two events occurred that would lend an emotional tinge to her Standard Oil series. One Sunday afternoon in June 1892, she found herself roaming the Paris streets, unable to shake off a sense of doom. Later that afternoon, she read in the Paris newspapers that Titusville and Oil City had been ravaged by flood and fire, with 150 people either drowned or burned to death. The next day, her brother, Will, sent a single-word cable— "Safe"—relieving her anxieties, but the event reinforced a guilty feeling that she had neglected her family. In 1893, one of her father's oil partners shot himself in despair because of poor business, forcing Franklin Tarbell to mortgage his house to settle the debts he inherited. Ida's sister was in the hospital at the time, and "here was I across the ocean writing picayune pieces at a fourth of a cent a word while they struggled there," she later recalled. "I felt guilty, and the only way I had kept myself up to what I had undertaken was the hope that I could eventually make a substantial return."[32] While in Paris, Ida Tarbell laid hands on a copy of *Wealth Against Commonwealth*, where she rediscovered the author of her father's woes: John D. Rockefeller.

Once in New York in 1894, Tarbell published two biographies in serial form that might have predisposed her to focus on a single figure at Standard Oil. Anticipating her portrait of Rockefeller, she presented Napoleon as a gifted megalomaniac, a great but flawed man lacking "that fine sense of proportion which holds the rights of others in the same solemn reverence which it demands for its own."[33] Lifted by this series, *McClure's* circulation leaped from 24,500 in late 1894 to more than 100,000 in early 1895. Then followed Tarbell's celebrated twenty-part series on Lincoln, which absorbed four years of her life (1895–1899) and boosted the magazine's circulation to 300,000. She honed her investigative skills as she excavated dusty documents and forgotten courthouse records. In 1899, after being named managing editor of *McClure's*, Tarbell took an apartment in Greenwich Village and befriended many literary notables, including Mark Twain, who would soon provide her with entrée to Henry H. "Hell Hound" Rogers. By this time, having sharpened her skills, she was set to publish one of the most influential pieces of journalism in American business history. The idea of writing about Standard Oil had fermented in her mind for many years before she worked for *McClure's*. "Years ago, when I dreamed of some day writing fiction. . . . I had planned to write the great American novel, having the Standard Oil Company as a backbone!"[34]

After receiving McClure's blessing, Ida Tarbell launched the series in November 1902, feeding the American public rich monthly servings of Rockefeller's past misdeeds. She went back to the early Cleveland days and laid out his whole career for careful inspection. All the depredations of a long career, everything Rockefeller had thought safely buried and forgotten, rose up before him in haunting and memorable detail. Before she was done, Ida Tarbell turned America's most private man into its most public and hated figure.

=

The inspiration for publishing the anatomy of a major trust came from Samuel McClure, one of the most gifted windbags ever to occupy an editorial chair, who recruited writers with marathon speeches about his magazine's greatness. High-strung, mercurial, seized by hourly brainstorms, McClure was described by Rudyard Kipling as a "cyclone in a frock coat."[35] Moving through life at breakneck speed, he seemed forever to be veering toward a nervous collapse. When McClure first materialized in Tarbell's Paris apartment in 1892, he appeared distracted and breathless. "I've just ten minutes," he told her, checking his watch, "must leave for Switzerland tonight to see [English physicist John] Tyndall."[36] Eager to sign up this startled young woman, the man with the tousled, sandy hair and electric blue eyes stayed for three hours. "Able methodical people grow on every bush but genius comes once in a generation and if you ever get in its vicinity thank the Lord & *stick*," Tarbell once told a colleague apropos of McClure.[37]

That McClure hired a young, relatively inexperienced woman as his first full-time staff writer attests to his unorthodox style. He would collar every talented young writer in America—Frank Norris, Stephen Crane, Theodore Dreiser, Willa Cather—as well as more established figures, such as Mark Twain and

Rudyard Kipling. O. Henry, Damon Runyon, and Booth Tarkington debuted in his pages. Yet it was perhaps in nonfiction that McClure left his most lasting imprint, for the best investigative reporters, from Lincoln Steffens to Ray Stannard Baker, gravitated to the magazine. Of his first office visit, Baker reminisced, "Even with S. S. McClure absent, I was in the most stimulating, yes intoxicating editorial atmosphere then existent in America—or anywhere else."[38] McClure watched over the creative chaos like a restless genie. "I can't sit still," he once told Lincoln Steffens. "That's your job. I don't see how you can do it."[39] Amid this swirling lunacy, Ida Tarbell sat in her high collar and shirtwaist dress, a model of calm sanity. As Lincoln Steffens recalled, she "would come to the office, smiling, like a tall, good-looking young mother to say, 'Hush, children.' "[40]

A man with a weakness for big, startling facts, McClure commissioned articles on new gadgets, scientific research, and futuristic technologies. This penchant for facts enabled him to spot Tarbell's talent for enlivening a dry subject when she wrote an entertaining article about the paving of Parisian streets. Instead of the scandalmongering being offered by Pulitzer or Hearst, McClure wanted to analyze complex issues and explore them with scientific precision. Aiming at a comprehensive critique of American society, McClure concluded by 1901 that two great issues confronted the country: the growth of industrial trusts and political corruption. Before long, Lincoln Steffens was digging out municipal corruption in a series entitled "The Shame of the Cities" that started to run in October 1902. (In the February 24, 1905, issue, he skewered Senator Aldrich in a piece on Rhode Island corruption.) The choice of the proper trust to expose was a trickier issue. At first, Tarbell contemplated the steel trust and the sugar trust before the discovery of oil in California turned her attention to Standard Oil as the "most perfectly developed trust."[41] Since it had been investigated by various government bodies for three decades, it had left a rich documentary trail. At first projected for three issues, the Standard Oil series eventually stretched, by popular demand, to nineteen installments. It was inaugurated in November 1902 against an especially timely backdrop: An anthracite coal strike during the winter of 1902–1903 deprived the poor of coal, forcing them to heat their homes with oil, and the subsequent sharp rise in oil prices made energy an incendiary issue.

Although Tarbell pretended to apply her scalpel to Standard Oil with surgical objectivity, she was never neutral and not only because of her father. Her brother, William Walter Tarbell, had been a leading figure in forming the Pure Oil Company, the most serious domestic challenger to Standard Oil, and his letters to her were laced with anti-Standard venom. Complaining of the trust's price manipulations in one letter, Will warned her, "Some of those fellows will get killed one of those days."[42] As Pure Oil's treasurer in 1902, Will steered legions of Rockefeller enemies to his sister and even vetted her manuscripts. Far from cherishing her neutrality, Tarbell in the end adhered to the advice she had once received from Henry James: "Cherish your contempts."[43] Amazingly enough, nobody made an issue of Tarbell's veritable partnership with her brother in exposing his chief competitor.

When Franklin Tarbell heard that his daughter was taking on the mighty Standard, he warned her that she was exposing herself to extreme danger. "Don't do it, Ida—they will ruin the magazine," he said and even broached the possibility they might maim or murder her—a far-fetched scenario but suggestive of the dread that the trust inspired.[44] As her research began, she made a sentimental trip to Titusville, which rekindled her old animosity toward Standard Oil. Her father was slowly dying of stomach cancer while she was writing her series, and this might have further embittered her toward Rockefeller, however unfairly; Franklin Tarbell would die on March 1, 1905. Contrary to her father's predictions, Ida inflicted far more damage on Standard Oil than she received in return. The closest she came to being threatened was at a Washington dinner party where Frank Vanderlip, a vice president of National City Bank, drew her into a side room to voice his strong displeasure with her project. Sensing a vague financial menace to *McClure's*, she retorted, "Well, I am sorry, but of course that makes no difference to me."[45] In fact, what was most notable about Standard Oil's response was its haughty, self-defeating silence.

Tarbell approached her work methodically, like a carpenter, but she soon reeled under the weight of documentary evidence. After a week spent combing through reports of the Industrial Commission in February 1902, she wrote despairingly, "The task confronting me is such a monstrous one that I am staggering a bit under it."[46] By June, having completed three installments, she confessed that the material had acquired an obsessive hold over her mind and even invaded her sleep. On the eve of a needed European vacation, she told her research assistant, "It has become a great bugbear to me. I dream of the octopus by night and think of nothing else by day, and I shall be glad to exchange it for the Alps."[47]

Upon her return from vacation, she met with Henry Demarest Lloyd at his seaside estate in Sakonnet, Rhode Island. He insisted that, despite the Interstate Commerce Commission, large shippers were still getting the same old freight rebates, although they carefully destroyed the evidence. He told her, barely containing his rage, that Rockefeller and his associates embodied "the most dangerous tendencies in modern life."[48] At one point, when he learned that Ida Tarbell had met with Henry H. Rogers, Lloyd thought she might be in cahoots with the company and warned his Pennsylvania contacts to watch out for her. His doubts were instantly dispelled as the series got under way. "When you get through with 'Johnnie,' " he applauded her in April 1903, "I don't think there will be very much left of him except something resembling one of his own grease spots."[49] In the end, Lloyd handed over his abundant notes to her and urged George Rice, Lewis Emery, and other independents to talk with her. Having passed the torch, Henry Demarest Lloyd died in September 1903, before the series was finished.

Shortly before Tarbell began her research, Sam McClure tried to coax Mark Twain into editing a magazine, but Henry H. Rogers persuaded Twain to resist. As early as December 1901—almost a year before the series started to run—Rogers spotted an ad announcing *McClure's* forthcoming series on Standard Oil and was startled that nobody at 26 Broadway had been contacted by the author. Concerned, he wrote to Twain, "It would naturally be supposed, that any person desiring to write a veritable history, would seek for information as near original sources as possible."[50] Fearing that Tarbell might be consorting with the enemy, Rogers suggested that Twain tell McClure that he should verify all statements with the trust before they were published. When Twain pressed for details about the series, McClure balked, saying, "You will have to ask Miss Tarbell." To which Twain replied, "Would Miss Tarbell see Mr. Rogers?"[51] Tarbell had, of course, hoped to interview the top brass at Standard Oil, and when McClure burst into her office with the invitation, she was eager to seize the chance.

A veteran charmer, Hell Hound Rogers invited Tarbell for a two-hour chat at his home on East Fifty-seventh Street. She had never met a real captain of industry before and seemed entranced by his resemblance to Twain. "His big head with its high forehead was set off by a heavy shock of beautiful gray hair; his nose was aquiline, sensitive," she wrote, still betraying admiration years later.[52] Rogers seduced her with nostalgic recollections of the days when they were Rouseville neighbors. "That reminiscence of Henry H. Rogers is only one of several reasons I have for heartily liking as fine a pirate as ever flew his flag in Wall Street."[53]

The upshot of the meeting was that Tarbell agreed to give Rogers a chance to react to any revelations she unearthed, and for two years she periodically visited him at 26 Broadway. These encounters had a quasi-clandestine aura, with the reporter whisked in one door and out another. In a spirit of guarded cooperation, Samuel Dodd assembled material for Tarbell, while Daniel O'Day passed along information on pipelines. Since Tarbell had spoken with Rogers for nearly a year before the series started, she held her breath when the first issue appeared in November 1902. "I rather expected him to cut me off when he realized that I was trying to prove that the Standard Oil Company was only an enlarged South Improvement Company."[54] To her astonishment, Rogers still received her and, while occasionally miffed by this or that article, he remained on friendly terms with her.

Rogers's complaisance has always been a huge mystery, engendering two schools of thought. Tarbell cited Rogers's self-interest. He and Archbold had been stung by accusations that they had conspired to blow up a Buffalo refinery that competed with Standard Oil. "That case is a sore point with Mr. Archbold and me," he immediately told Tarbell. "I want you to go into it thoroughly."[55] Responding to his heightened sensitivity on this matter, she agreed to let him review anything she wrote about it. (Rogers's strategy paid off as far as the Buffalo imbroglio was concerned.) In Tarbell's view, Rogers was willing to see Standard Oil's reputation sullied as long as his own was preserved.

Another school of thought hypothesized that Rogers was both deflecting attention from his own misdeeds and taking revenge against Rockefeller, who had disapproved of his stock-market speculations. This argument suggests that Rogers enjoyed Tarbell's series as a rebuke to his colleague's sanctimony. Rockefeller privately denounced Rogers as a traitor who had fed Tarbell false, garbled information to defame him.[56] Many years later, after a confidential chat with John D. Rockefeller, Jr., Allan Nevins recorded in a memo, "Junior thinks that [Rogers's] part in the publication of Ida Tarbell's book was far from unselfish; that he was secretly glad to see Rockefeller attacked, and supplied some of the material."[57] Tarbell's own notes reveal that while Rogers often defended Rockefeller, he also kept the spotlight tightly focused on the founder and away from himself. Rogers did not terminate his meetings with Tarbell until February 1904, when she published a shocking account of railway agents spying on Standard Oil competitors—a practice that Rogers had strenuously denied. When she next arrived at 26 Broadway, he demanded, "Where did you get that stuff?" That tense, brief meeting ended their relationship.[58]

While stewing about Rogers, Rockefeller would have been equally shocked and wounded had he seen the acidulous comments made to Ida Tarbell by his old pal Henry M. Flagler, who portrayed the titan as petty and miserly. After their confidential talk, Tarbell recorded in her notes, "Mr. Flagler talked to me of J.D.R. Says he is the biggest little man and the littlest big man he ever knew. That he would give $100,000 one minute to charity and turn around and haggle over the price of a ton of coal. Says emphatically: 'I have been in business with him 45 years and he would do me out of a dollar today—that is, if he could do it honestly.' "[59] Though Flagler dispensed some pious claptrap about how "the Lord had prospered him," Tarbell could not draw him into any serious, sustained discussion of Standard Oil history.[60]

From the start, sensing that Tarbell was full of malice toward Standard Oil, Archbold had refused to cooperate. As for Rockefeller, he was slow to fathom the magnitude of the gathering threat and had no notion that this magnificent journalist could wield her slingshot with such deadly accuracy. Having weathered thirty years of assaults in the courts and statehouses, he must have felt invulnerable. When associates clamored for a response to Tarbell, Rockefeller replied, "Gentlemen, we must not be entangled in controversies. If she is right we will not gain anything by answering, and if she is wrong time will vindicate us."[61] To sit through an extended grilling from Tarbell would have violated his lifelong approach to business. This was a tactical blunder, for in dodging Tarbell he inadvertently seemed to validate her portrait.

===

From the perspective of nearly a century later, Ida Tarbell's series remains the most impressive thing ever written about Standard Oil—a tour de force of reportage that dissects the trust's machinations with withering clarity. She laid down a clear chronology, provided a trenchant account of how the combine had evolved, and made the convoluted history of the oil industry comprehensible. In the dispassionate manner associated with *McClure's*, she sliced open America's most secretive business and showed all the hidden gears and wheels turning inside it. Yet however chaste and clearly reasoned her prose, it was always informed by indignation that throbbed just below the surface. It remains one of the great case studies of what a single journalist, armed with the facts, can do against seemingly invincible powers.

Tarbell is perhaps best appreciated in comparison with her predecessor, Henry Demarest Lloyd, who was sloppy with his facts, florid in his prose, and too quick to pontificate. A meticulous researcher, Tarbell wrote in a taut, spare language that conveyed a sense of precision and restraint—though she had more than her quota of strident moments. By writing in such a relatively cool style, she made her readers boil with anger. Instead of invoking political panaceas or sweeping ideological prescriptions, she appealed to the reader's sense of common decency and fair play and was most effective where she showed something small and mean-spirited about the Standard Oil style of business.

Like Teddy Roosevelt, Tarbell did not condemn Standard Oil for its size but only for its abuses and did not argue for the automatic dismantling of all trusts; she pleaded only for the preservation of free competition in the marketplace. While she was by no means evenhanded, she was quick to acknowledge the genuine achievements of Rockefeller and his cohorts and even devoted one chapter to "The Legitimate Greatness of the Standard Oil Company." "There was not a lazy bone in the organization, not an incompetent hand, nor a stupid head," she wrote.[62] It was the very fact that they could have succeeded without resorting to unethical acts that so exasperated her. As she said, "They had never played fair, and that ruined their greatness for me."[63]

If Tarbell gave an oversimplified account of Standard Oil's rise, her indictment was perhaps the more forceful for it. In the trust's collusion with the railroads, the intricate system of rebates and drawbacks, she found her smoking gun, the irrefutable proof that Rockefeller's empire was built by devious means. She was at pains to refute Rockefeller's defense that everybody did it. "Everybody did not do it," she protested indignantly. "In the nature of the offense everybody could not do it. The strong wrested from the railroads the privilege of preying upon the weak, and the railroads never dared give the privilege save under the promise of secrecy."[64] To the contention that rebates were still legal, Tarbell countered with the questionable theory that they violated the common law. She argued that Rockefeller had succeeded by imbuing subordinates with a ferocious desire to win at all costs, even if that meant trampling upon others. "Mr. Rockefeller has systematically played with loaded dice, and it is doubtful if there has ever been a time since 1872 when he has run a race with a competitor and started fair."[65] Tarbell rightly surmised that Standard Oil received secret kickbacks from the railroads on a more elaborate scale than its rivals did. This is abundantly borne out by Rockefeller's private papers, which show that the practice was even more pervasive than Tarbell realized.

Beginning with the Cleveland Massacre of 1872, Tarbell showed that Rockefeller had taken over rival refineries in an orchestrated atmosphere of intimidation. She exposed the deceit of an organization that operated through a maze of secret subsidiaries in which the Standard Oil connection was kept secret from all but the highest-ranking employees. She sketched out many abuses of power by the Standard Oil pipelines, which used their monopoly position to keep refractory producers in line while favoring Standard's own refineries. And she chronicled the terror tactics by which the trust's marketing subsidiaries got retailers to stock their product exclusively. Like Lloyd, she also decried the trust's threat to democracy and the subornation of state legislators, although she never guessed the depths of corruption revealed by Rockefeller's papers.

Nevertheless, as Allan Nevins and other defenders of Rockefeller pointed out, Tarbell committed numerous errors, and her work must be cited with caution. To begin with, the SIC was initiated by the railroads, not Rockefeller, who doubted the plan's efficacy. And for all its notoriety, the SIC did not cause the oil crisis of the early 1870s but was itself a response to the glut that forced almost everybody to operate at a loss. It is also true that, swayed by childhood memories, Tarbell ennobled the Oil Creek drillers, portraying them as exemplars of a superior morality. As she wrote: "They believed in independent effort—every man for himself and fair play for all. They wanted competition, loved open fight."[66] To support this statement, she had to overlook the baldly anticompetitive agreements proposed by the producers themselves. Far from being free-marketeers, they repeatedly tried to form their own cartel to restrict output and boost prices. And, as Rockefeller pointed out, they happily took rebates whenever they could. The world of the early oil industry was not, as Tarbell implied, a morality play of the evil Standard Oil versus the brave, noble independents of western Pennsylvania, but a harsh dog-eat-dog world.

Though billed as a history of Standard Oil, the Tarbell series presented Rockefeller as the protagonist and center of attention. Tarbell made Standard

Oil and Rockefeller interchangeable, even when covering the period after Rockefeller retired. Sometimes it is hard to tell whether Rockefeller is a real person or a personification of the trust. Significantly, Tarbell chose for her epigraph the famous line from Emerson's essay on self-reliance, "An Institution is the lengthened shadow of one man." When Henry Rogers questioned this approach, Tarbell noted the dramatic effect of focusing on one individual, writing in her notes after the meeting, "Illustrate it by Napoleon work and the effort to keep the attention centered on Napoleon, never mentioning anybody if I could help it."[67] This great-man approach to history gave a human face to the gigantic, amorphous entity known as Standard Oil but also turned the full force of public fury on Rockefeller. It did not acknowledge the bureaucratic reality of Standard Oil, with its labyrinthine committee system, and stigmatized Rockefeller to the exclusion of his associates. So Flagler came off relatively unscathed, even though he had negotiated the secret freight contracts that bulk so large in the *McClure's* exposé.

However pathbreaking in its time and richly deserving of its accolades, the Tarbell series does not, finally, stand up as an enduring piece of history. The more closely one examines it, the more it seems a superior screed masquerading as sober history. In the end, Tarbell could not conquer her nostalgia for the Titusville of her girlhood, that lost paradise of heroic friends and neighbors who went forth doughtily to do battle with the all-devouring Standard Oil dragon.

=

The most celebrated and widely quoted charge that Tarbell made against Rockefeller was the least deserved: that he had robbed Mrs. Fred M. Backus— forever known to history as "the Widow Backus"—blind when buying her Cleveland lubricating plant in 1878. If every melodrama needs a poor, lorn widow, cheated by a scheming cad, then Mrs. Backus perfectly fitted Tarbell's portrait of Rockefeller. "If it were true," Rockefeller later conceded, it "would represent a shocking instance of cruelty in crushing a defenceless woman. It is probable that its wide circulation and its acceptance as true by those who know nothing of the facts has awakened more hostility against the Standard Oil Company and against me personally than any charge which has been made."[68]

The background of the story is simple. In his early Cleveland days, Rockefeller had befriended Fred M. Backus, who worked as a bookkeeper in his office and taught in the Sunday school of their church. In time, Backus married, had three children, and started a small lubricating company. In 1874, the forty-year-old Backus died, likely from consumption, and his widow inherited an obsolete plant that consisted of little more than a primitive cluster of sheds, stills, and tanks. Its hilltop site meant that raw materials had to be hauled up the slope at great expense, and then the lubricating oils had to be carted down the same steep path—not the most efficient of venues. Before it entered the lubricating business, Standard Oil had tolerated this marginal operation. When it branched out into lubricating oils and greases in the late 1870s, it absorbed three small lubricating companies, of which Backus Oil was probably the most backward. In fact, the Backus operation was so outmoded that Standard Oil eventually shut it down. This did not prevent the Widow Backus from stirring up a rabid national controversy about Rockefeller's supposed theft of her priceless plant.

When Standard Oil first approached her about the purchase, she insisted upon dealing with Rockefeller who, for old time's sake, agreed to meet her in her house. Appealing to her status as a widow and trusting to his gentlemanly honor, she pleaded for a fair price for her property. As she recalled, "he promised, with tears in his eyes, that he would stand by me in this transaction, and that I should not be wronged. . . . I thought that his feelings were such on the subject that I could trust him and that he would deal honourably by me."[69] Backus told a friend that Rockefeller suggested that they kneel together in prayer. Up until this point, her story tallied closely with Rockefeller's, who said that he had been "moved by kindly consideration to an old employee."[70]

While Backus wanted Rockefeller to conduct the negotiations for her plant, he knew nothing about lubricants and sent his associates instead. According to Backus, Rockefeller's hirelings bilked her unmercifully. She valued her operation between $150,000 and $200,000, whereas the Standard Oil people refused to pay more than $79,000—$19,000 for the oil on hand, plus $60,000 for the factory and goodwill. (Out of regard for Backus, Rockefeller had had his appraisers bump up this last figure by $10,000.) Backus's negotiator, Charles H. Marr, later swore that his client, in an estimated inventory of her assets, had written down $71,000 for plant and goodwill—not much more than Rockefeller finally paid. Yet she grew incensed over the purchase price and drafted a savage letter to Rockefeller, accusing him of double-dealing, to which he made the following reply:

> In regard to the reference that you make as to my permitting the business of the Backus Oil Company to *be taken* from you, I say that in this, as in all else that you have written . . . you do me most grievous wrong. It was of but little moment to the interests represented by me whether the business of the Backus Oil Company was purchased or not. I believe that it was for your interest to make the sale, and am entirely candid in this statement, and beg to call your attention to the time, some two years ago, when you consulted Mr. Flagler and myself as to selling out your interests to Mr. Rose, at which time you were desirous of selling at *considerably less price*, and upon time, than you have

now received in cash, and which sale you would have been glad to have closed if you could have obtained satisfactory security for the deferred payments.

He then pointed out that the $60,000 paid for the property was two or three times the cost of constructing equal or better facilities—a statement corroborated by a Mr. Maloney, superintendent of the Backus plant. "I believe that if you would reconsider what you have written in your letter . . . you must admit having done me great injustice, and I am satisfied to await upon [your] innate sense of right for such admission."[71] In closing, Rockefeller offered to restore her business in return for the money or give her stock in the company at the same price paid by Standard Oil. It was an eminently fair offer, and yet the histrionic Backus flung the letter in the fire.

Because Ida Tarbell insisted upon reviving this hoary story—Henry Demarest Lloyd had already wrung tears from readers with it—in 1905 Rockefeller's attorneys leaked to the press a letter written by H. M. Backus, the widow's brother-in-law. Having lived with his sister-in-law during the period in question, he was present the day Rockefeller paid his visit. As he told Rockefeller, "I know of the ten thousand dollars that was added to the purchase price of the property at your request, and I know that you paid 3 times the value of the property, and I know that all that ever saved our company from ruin was the sale of its property to you, and I simply want to easy my mind by doing justice to you by saying so."[72] It was exceedingly lucky for Backus that she bowed out of business, for Standard Oil built more modern lubricating plants, marketed 150 different lubricants, and drove prices far below the price at which she could have operated profitably. Had she stayed in business, she would have been bankrupt within a few years.

By investing her proceeds in Cleveland real estate instead, Backus, far from being reduced to filth and misery, became an extremely rich woman. According to Allan Nevins, she was worth approximately $300,000 at her death.[73] Nevertheless, the supposed theft of Backus Oil became an idée fixe, and she dredged up the story for anyone who cared to listen. The notion of Rockefeller gleefully ruining a poor widow was such a good story, with so fine a Dickensian ring, that gullible reporters gave it fresh circulation for many years.

If Tarbell perpetuated one myth about Rockefeller, she also had the honesty to debunk another: that Rockefeller had blown up a competing refinery in Buffalo. It was this allegation that so upset Henry Rogers that he cooperated with Tarbell to clear his name. Swallowed whole by Lloyd and constantly brandished by the *World*, the tale was a hardy perennial of the anti–Standard Oil literature.

Like the Backus case, the incident dated back to the period when Standard Oil entered the lubricating business in the late 1870s. The trust had coveted the Vacuum Oil Works in Rochester, New York, owned by a father-and-son team, Hiram and Charles Everest. One day, John Archbold shepherded Hiram Everest into Rockefeller's office and asked him point-blank to name a price for his firm. When Everest obliged, Archbold threw back his head and roared with laughter, dismissing the figure as absurd. Taking a suaver approach, Rockefeller leaned forward, touched Everest on the knee, and said, "Mr. Everest, don't you think you would be making a mistake to go into a fight with young, active men, who mean to develop the entire petroleum industry?" When Everest shot back that he was a fighter, Rockefeller just smiled.

Everest eventually realized he was dealing with an immovable force and sold a three-fourths interest in his firm to Henry Rogers, John Archbold, and Ambrose McGregor, acting as agents for Standard Oil. Because the Everests remained the managers, the Standard executives were involved only tangentially. In 1881, a trio of Vacuum employees—J. Scott Wilson, Charles B. Matthews, and Albert Miller—defected to start a rival refinery, the Buffalo Lubricating Oil Company. They brazenly planned to re-create their old firm by transferring technology, poaching clients, and copying processes patented by Vacuum. When the Everests learned of this, they threatened legal action. Albert Miller repented and sought help from Hiram Everest. Together, they consulted a Rochester lawyer, and at this meeting Everest allegedly floated the idea of Miller sabotaging the new plant: "Suppose he should arrange the machinery so it would bust up, or smash up, what would the consequences be?"[74] A tall edifice of speculation would be erected on this query.

According to a later conspiracy charge, on June 15, 1881, Miller ordered the fireman at the Buffalo plant to heat the still to such explosive temperatures that the heavy crude oil began to stir and boil. Pretty soon, the brickwork cracked, the safety valve blew off, and a large volume of gas hissed out—without kindling a fire. A week later, Miller met in New York with Hiram Everest and Henry Rogers, who packed him off to work at a California cannery. When the Everests filed patent-infringement suits against the Buffalo refinery, Charles Matthews, ringleader of the renegades, retaliated with his own civil suit, charging a conspiracy to blow up his Buffalo works and seeking $250,000 in damages. The three Standard Oil worthies on the Vacuum board—Rogers, Archbold, and McGregor—despite the distant nature of their involvement in Rochester, were indicted along with the Everests. Only vaguely aware of the brouhaha, never having met Miller, Rockefeller was roped into the case for publicity purposes and subpoenaed as a prosecution witness. The case always struck him as a petty irritant, distracting him from more pressing matters. Nothing in Rockefeller's papers suggests that he regarded the suit as anything other than outright extortion.[75]

In May 1887, Rockefeller sat captive in a packed Buffalo courtroom for eight days. Resentful of being turned into a public spectacle, he felt he was being served up as a sideshow freak to "this curious class of wonder-worshippers, the class whom P. T. Barnum capitalized [on] and made his fortune out of."[76] When Rockefeller testified, he displayed, as always, total forgetfulness, but in this instance he really knew little about the case. At the end of eight days, the judge dropped charges against Rogers, Archbold, and McGregor. While Rogers hugged a bunch of pansies given by a well-wisher, Rockefeller, in a rare display of public fury, rose from his seat, jaw clenched, and said, "I have no congratulations to offer you, Rogers. What should be done with people who bring an action against men in this way—what?" Wheeling about, he shook his fist at Charles Matthews. Then, muttering "what an unheard-of-thing," he strode briskly from the courtroom, his retinue in tow. In later years, he fulminated against Matthews as a "scheming, trouble-making blackmailer" who offered to sell his refinery to Standard Oil for $100,000 and only initiated his nuisance suit after being rebuffed.[77]

The Buffalo suit, in truth, had scant merit. The prosecution never established that an explosion had taken place or even that a high flame was necessarily hazardous when starting up the still. Though the Everests were convicted and fined $250 apiece, this small figure mirrored the jurors' belief that the Everests did not conspire to blow up the refinery and were guilty only of luring away Albert Miller. If Henry Rogers cooperated with Ida Tarbell for the sake of vindication in the Buffalo case, he was amply rewarded. She stated categorically: "As a matter of fact, no refinery was burned in Buffalo, nor was it ever proved that Mr. Rogers knew anything of the attempts the Everests made to destroy Matthews' business."[78] Yet the notion that Rockefeller enjoyed blowing up rival plants so tickled the popular fancy that it remained enshrined as a story much too good to retire, and it was duly revived, along with the musty canard about the Widow Backus, by Matthew Josephson in his 1934 book *The Robber Barons*.

=

By the third installment in January 1903, President Roosevelt himself was voraciously reading Tarbell's articles and even sent her a flattering note. Her celebrity spread with each issue, and her level gaze stared out from countless newspaper profiles. "The way you are generally esteemed and reverenced pleases me tremendously," McClure told her. "You are today the most generally famous woman in America."[79] That she had succeeded in a traditionally masculine field only added to her mystique.

Samuel McClure would let a series run as long as the public kept snatching up copies. As Tarbell summarized this policy, "No response—no more chapters. A healthy response—as many chapters as the material justified."[80] Hence, her series was open-ended and profited from the tremendous crescendo of attention, which drew more and more Rockefeller critics from the woodwork. The circulation of *McClure's* had risen to 375,000 by the time Tarbell's series was finished. Though the series was published as a two-volume book in November 1904, she then capped it with a scathing two-part character study of Rockefeller in *McClure's* in July and August of 1905.

It does not detract from her achievement to state that she enjoyed the services of a first-rate research assistant, John M. Siddall. Short, pudgy, and bespectacled, the young Siddall was an experienced hand, having been a cub reporter at the Cleveland *Plain Dealer* and secretary to the Cleveland Board of Education during Mayor Tom Johnson's reform administration. Based in Cleveland, he not only supplied Tarbell with numberless facts but charged her imagination. "I tell you this John D. Rockefeller is the strangest, most silent, most mysterious, and most interesting figure in America," he wrote to her. "The people of this country know nothing about him. A brilliant character study of him would make a tremendous trump card for *McClure's*."[81] At first, Siddall thought Rockefeller cold and humorless but had to modify the caricature. "My informant states that John has a real delightful way of cultivating the speaking acquaintance of all sorts of people—rich and poor, black and white. That only illustrates again the marvelous complexity of Rockefeller's character."[82]

One of the first and most shocking revelations dug up by Tarbell and Siddall came from a teenage boy who had been assigned to burn records at a Standard Oil plant each month. He was about to incinerate some forms one night when he noticed the name of a former Sunday-school teacher who was an independent refiner and Standard Oil rival. Leafing through the documents sent for burning, he realized that they were secret records, obtained from the railroads, documenting the shipments of rival refiners. Tarbell knew Standard Oil was ruthless, but she was shocked by this outright criminal activity. "There was a littleness about it that seemed utterly contemptible compared to the immense genius and ability that had gone into the organization," she said.[83] At this point, she realized she was being snookered by Henry Rogers.

Tarbell and Siddall were willing to take their own moral shortcuts to expose Rockefeller. To spy on him, Siddall had a friend from the *Plain Dealer* impersonate a Sunday-school teacher to sneak into the annual church picnic at Forest Hill. At Siddall's behest, an old Rockefeller friend, Hiram Brown, pumped the mogul on several matters, including his reaction to the *McClure's* series. At the mention of Tarbell's name, Rockefeller steadied himself with a long breath. "I tell you, Hiram, things have changed since you and I were boys. The world is full of socialists and anarchists. Whenever a man succeeds remarkably in any particular line of business, they jump on him and cry him down."[84] To secure photos, Siddall had a friend pose as an agent of some distant Rockefeller relatives to obtain snapshots of the magnate from Cleveland photo studios. "Now of course these pictures were got under false pretenses," Siddall reminded Tarbell, "and we must protect our over-zealous friend."[85]

Since Rockefeller banned Tarbell from his presence, Siddall searched for a way that she could obtain a firsthand glimpse. During summers at Forest Hill, Rockefeller appeared in public only for Sunday services at the Euclid Avenue Baptist Church. By the early 1900s, this event had taken on the air of a circus spectacle as hundreds of people massed outside the church to view him. As the Tarbell series swelled the gaping throngs, Rockefeller would gingerly approach his church bodyguard before the service and ask, "Are there any of our friends, the reporters, here?"[86] Even though Pinkerton detectives mingled with the crowd, Rockefeller now felt anxious about public exposure. Sometimes, he confessed, he wanted to bolt from the service, but he feared that people would brand him a coward.[87] At one Friday-evening prayer service, when a radical agitator sat opposite him all evening, his hand stuffed menacingly in his pocket, Rockefeller grew so rattled that he put away his planned speech on socialism.

It probably hurt his image that he appeared in public only at church, for it played to the stereotype of a hypocrite cloaking himself in sanctity. In fact, his motivation for churchgoing was quite simple: Aside from the spiritual pleasure of prayer, he was loath to give up contact with ordinary people, many of them old friends. The church retained many blue-collar members, enabling Rockefeller to chat amiably with a blacksmith or mechanic. Such everyday experiences increasingly eluded him as he withdrew behind the high gates of his estates.

On Sunday, June 14, 1903, John Siddall got a windfall beyond his most feverish hopes when Rockefeller not only appeared but delivered a short "Children's Day" talk at the Sunday school. "If I had been able to foretell what happened yesterday I should have advised you to come from Titusville to spend Sunday in Cleveland," Siddall told Tarbell.[88] He described Rockefeller, in ministerial coat and silk hat, sitting before the pulpit and surveying the crowd apprehensively, as if fearful for his safety. "He bows his head and mutters his prayer, and sings the hymns, and nods his head, and claps his hands in a sort of a mechanical way. It's all work to him—a part of his business. He thinks that after he has done this for an hour or two he has warded off the devil for another week."[89] Only months later did Siddall learn of the anonymous charity Rockefeller practiced each Sunday morning, handing out money in small envelopes to needy congregants. "Doesn't this shake your belief in the theory of pure hypocrisy?" Siddall then asked Tarbell, noting the curiously compartmentalized nature of Rockefeller's mind. "In one part is legitimate business, in another corrupt business, in another political depravity, in another—somewhere in his being—religious experience and life."[90] This was a richer, more accurate appraisal of Rockefeller than that contained in his earlier, reductive gibe.

In the early fall, Siddall found out that Rockefeller, before returning to New York, would deliver a short farewell address at the Sunday school, and he begged Ida Tarbell to attend. "I will see that we have seats where we will have a full view of the man," he promised her. "You will get him in action."[91] They planned to squeeze between them an illustrator, George Varian, who would execute rapid sketches of Rockefeller. Tarbell felt "a little mean" about secretly ambushing Rockefeller in church, and she dreaded that they would be caught. To prevent this, she asked Siddall to pack the pew with three or four tall confederates who would shield Varian and his notebook.

When Tarbell and Siddall arrived at the Sunday-school room that morning, she wrinkled her nose at the shabby surroundings, "a dismal room with barbaric dark green paper with big gold designs, cheap stained-glass windows, awkward gas fixtures."[92] Suddenly, Siddall gave her a violent dig in the ribs. "There he is," he breathed. The hairless figure in the doorway did not disappoint Tarbell. As she wrote, "There was an awful age in his face—the oldest man I had ever seen, I thought, but what power!"[93] He slowly doffed his coat and hat, slid a black skullcap over his bald head, and sat flush against the wall, giving him an unobstructed view of the room—which Tarbell thought a security precaution. During his brief talk to the children, she was impressed by the clear strength of his voice. After the Sunday-school speech, the *McClure's* contingent packed a church pew in the auditorium for the service. Self-conscious about being there, Tarbell was convinced that Rockefeller would pick her out of the crowd, but he apparently did not.

In her 1905 character study, Tarbell stressed Rockefeller's fidgety behavior, the way he craned his neck and scanned the room, as if searching for assassins. "My two hours study of Mr. Rockefeller aroused a feeling I had not expected, which time has intensified. I was sorry for him. I know no companion so terrible as fear. Mr. Rockefeller, for all the conscious power written in face and voice and figure, was afraid, I told myself, afraid of his own kind."[94] It did not occur to her that she had contributed to that fear. This edgy behavior was vitally important for Tarbell because it suggested that Rockefeller had a guilt-ridden conscience, that God was torturing him, that he could not enjoy his ill-gotten wealth; the ordinary reader could find no more satisfying fantasy. "For what good this undoubted power of achievement, for what good this towering wealth, if one must be forever peering to see what is behind!"[95] It certainly never occurred to Tarbell that Rockefeller might be searching the congregation for charity recipients.

Despite her fears, Tarbell and her associates evaded detection at the Euclid Avenue Baptist Church that Sunday morning. It was the only time that Tarbell ever actually stood in Rockefeller's presence. Ironically, he never knowingly set eyes on the woman who did more than any other person to transmogrify his image.

By the end of her nineteen-part series, Tarbell had come to regard Rockefeller as the embodiment of evil. She had largely maintained a clinical tone, despite many shrill digressions, but in the poisonous two-part character study of July and August 1905, she allowed her vengeful feelings to blossom. Throwing off any pose of objectivity, she found in Rockefeller "concentration, craftiness, cruelty, and something indefinably repulsive." She described him as a "living mummy," hideous and diseased, leprous and reptilian, his physiognomy blighted by moral degeneracy. The pious, churchgoing image that Rockefeller projected was only a "hypocritical façade brilliantly created by the predatory businessman."

The disease which in the last three or four years has swept Mr. Rockefeller's head bare of hair, stripped away even eyelashes and eyebrows, has revealed all the strength of his great head. . . . The big cheeks are puffy, bulging unpleasantly under the eyes, and the skin which covers them has a curiously unhealthy pallor. It is this puffiness, this unclean flesh, which repels, as the thin slit of a mouth terrifies. . . . Mr. Rockefeller may have made himself the richest man in the world, but he has paid. Nothing but paying ever ploughs such lines in a man's face, ever sets his lips to such a melancholy angle.[96]

Rockefeller could brush off Tarbell's critique of his business methods as biased, but he was deeply pained by the character study. He was furious that Tarbell converted his alopecia, which had produced so much suffering, into a sign of moral turpitude. He was no less upset by her charge that he was ill at ease in his church, for this struck at the heart of his lifelong faith. As he said later, he was not fearful in church "because there was no place where I felt more at home in a public assembly than in this old church, where I had been since a boy of fourteen years of age and my friends were all about me."[97] The patent cruelty of the character study steeled Rockefeller against Tarbell's valid strictures about his business methods. For Rockefeller, this malice was the final proof he needed of Ida Tarbell's bias against him.

━━

As legions of Rockefeller enemies sought interviews with Tarbell, she was bound to encounter the most vituperative foe, his brother Frank. Refusing to forgive John after the Corrigan affair, Frank still popped up in the press from time to time to deliver flaming imprecations against John. During the *McClure's* series, he was quoted by a Washington paper as saying that "the fear of kidnapping [had] become a mania" with his brother and that "armed men accompany him everywhere ready to repel any effort to capture him."[98] In fact, Frank had not set eyes on his brother in years and could only parrot gossip.

Tarbell was always coy about how she met Frank Rockefeller, but her papers tell a startling tale. Although Siddall's brother had been one of Frank's attorneys, this had not helped him to line up an interview. Then a breakthrough occurred in January 1904, when Siddall learned that the Tarbell series had won two unexpected admirers: Frank's daughter and son-in-law, Helen and Walter Bowler. Using Mr. Bowler as a go-between, Frank stipulated his conditions for a tête-à-tête with Tarbell: "I want no member of my family to know of this interview. Nobody is ever to know of it. I shall see Miss Tarbell in my Garfield Building office. No one is to be present. No clerk is to know who Miss T is."[99]

Following instructions, Tarbell even donned a disguise. It would be one of the most disturbing interviews of her long career. Though Frank seemed candid, he chewed tobacco and talked incontinently, spewing forth bile against his brother. At moments, his self-pitying harangues suggested a deranged man. Afterward, Tarbell jotted down impressions, including his off-the-record statements, for her files:

> He seemed dimly conscious that it was unnatural and monstrous to talk to me, and yet to be so bitter that he could not restrain himself. He began to talk of his brother by referring to him as "that individual." "I have nothing to do with that individual," he said. "I never want to see him. I have not seen him but once for eight years, and that was by accident. He has ruined my life. Nearly drove my wife insane. Two years ago I had to put her in a sanitarium, where she stayed for nearly a year, and this entirely came of this man's vindictive feeling of me." He says, "I have read every one of your articles. Some of them I have read two or three times. I have never known of any literary subject which interested me so much, or interested the people with whom I came in contact so much."[100]

Unaware of the stormy history between the two brothers, Tarbell confessed that Frank was the last person she had expected to volunteer as a source. A brisk, businesslike journalist, she was appalled by the ugly emotions he betrayed, however much she welcomed his information. Predictably, Frank dragged out his self-serving version of the Corrigan case. He portrayed John as a sadist who took pleasure in lending people money then seizing their collateral and destroying them when they did not repay: "Cleveland could be paved with the mortgages that he has foreclosed on people who were in a tight place."[101] Though Tarbell came to believe that John D. had acted in an ethical manner with Corrigan, she quoted so freely from the original lawsuit against Rockefeller as to obscure that she was siding with him.

Aside from the Corrigan case, Frank contributed few facts and preferred to vent his spleen. He told Tarbell that John had only two ambitions, to be very rich and very old, and he even chastised Cettie, calling her a "narrow-minded, stingy and pious" woman, whose greatest goal was "to be known as a good Christian, and to impress the world with the piety and domestic harmony of the family."[102] According to Frank, Cettie was a crafty, avaricious hypocrite who ensured that John's charities were widely publicized and tinged with the proper religious coloring. Touching up this gruesome portrait, Frank later told one of Tarbell's assistants: "[John] has the delusion that God has appointed him to administer all the wealth in the world, and in his efforts to do this he has destroyed men right and left. I tell you that when you publish this story the people will arise and stone him out of the community. . . . He is a monster."[103]

Frank had two other shockers for Tarbell. First, he told her that "the real reason that I have sent for you is that I want some day to write the life of my brother. I cannot write. You can do the kind of thing I want, and I want to know if you will do it using my material."[104] Tarbell did not quite picture herself as Frank Rockefeller's ghostwriter. On the other hand, she did not wish to alienate him and mumbled something about helping him if her editorial work allowed the time. Then Frank came up with a remarkable finale to his ravings about his brother: "I know you think I am bitter and that it is unnatural, but this man has ruined my life. Why I have not killed him I do not understand. It must be that there is a God who prevented me doing such a thing, for there have been a hundred times when, if I had met him on the street, I know that I should have shot him."[105]

Tarbell did not quote these background statements and preserved Frank's anonymity. But such lunacy should have told her to exercise extreme care in dealing with the Corrigan case. Instead, in a lapse in judgment, she used Frank's material in such a slipshod, misleading manner that Rockefeller justly accused her of slanting the story.

Perhaps the main reason that Frank did not blow out his brother's brains was that he did not want to murder one of his main bankers. Unable to curb his speculative appetite, Frank took another emergency loan of $184,000 from William during the 1907 panic. What Frank did not know—but surely must have suspected—was that John had guaranteed half the loan, secured by eight hundred head of cattle and one hundred mules on Frank's Kansas ranch. In fact, John D. carried this debt until Frank died, though a moment came in early 1912 when Frank again sounded off about his brother to reporters and John dispatched a lawyer to inform his ungrateful brother about the true source of the money that had so long sustained him.

———

For nearly three years, from November 1902 to August 1905, Ida Tarbell fired projectiles at Rockefeller and Standard Oil without taking fire in return. As one newspaper wondered aloud, "Is the Pen Mightier than the Money-Bag. . . . Is Ida M. Tarbell, weak woman, more potent than John D. Rockefeller millionaire?"[106] As the Tarbell series demonstrated, the new media possessed a power that rivaled that of the business institutions they covered. Paradoxically, the more Tarbell invoked the malevolent power of Standard Oil, the more she proved the reverse. At moments, Tarbell herself was startled by the kid-glove treatment. She wrote to Siddall in February 1903, "It is very interesting to note now, that the thing is well under way, and I have not been kidnapped or sued for libel as some of my friends prophesied, people are willing to talk freely to me."[107]

From today's perspective, when corporations have teams of publicists who swing into action at the first whiff of trouble, Standard Oil's muted reaction appears to be a perplexing miscalculation. Tarbell got enough wrong that a modern public-relations expert could have dented her credibility and shaken Samuel McClure with the threat of a libel suit. Rockefeller could, for instance, have exposed the hoax of the Widow Backus story. In the spring of 1905, he contemplated a lawsuit against Tarbell for alleging that he had perjured himself by denying knowledge of a *Southern* Improvement Company when his interrogator had garbled the name of the *South* Improvement Company. After Tarbell published her character study of Rockefeller, he authorized Virgil Kline to contest her treatment of the Corrigan case. Kline pointed out that Tarbell's fallacious account was drawn largely from the original petition filed against Rockefeller, not the exculpatory testimony that followed in the case. "Mr. Kline says I used charges made in the petition instead of in the testimony," Tarbell wrote, unfazed, in an internal memo at the time. "I did, and I see no reason why I should not have done so."[108] Tough challenges from Rockefeller might have blunted Tarbell's confidence and made readers question her sources.

The *McClure's* series showed that the public-be-damned attitude that had served industrial barons well in the nineteenth century now made them easy prey for investigative journalists who fed a public famished for revelations of misconduct. The schizoid American worship of millionaires was shot through with envy and a desire to see these demigods punished and desecrated. So why did Rockefeller stick to his self-defeating silence? One side of him simply did not want to be bothered by libel suits. "Life is short," he wrote to Parmalee Prentice, "and we have not time to heed the reports of foolish and unprincipled men."[109] He was also afraid that if he sued for libel, it would dignify the charges against him and only prolong the controversy. Strolling about Forest Hill one day, a friend suggested that he respond to the Tarbell slanders. At that moment, he spotted a worm crawling across their path. "If I step on that worm I will call attention to it," he said. "If I ignore it, it will disappear."[110] In certain instances, he was muzzled from responding because of his involvement in ongoing court cases.

But the main reason for Rockefeller's silence was that he couldn't dispute just a few of Tarbell's assertions without admitting the truth of many others, and a hard core of truth did lie behind the scattered errors. When Gates urged him to rebut Tarbell on the Backus affair and the SIC perjury charge, Rockefeller agreed he could do so but that "going further than the Backus and the

South Improvement Company cases may involve the necessity of going thoroughly into the whole book"—and he did not wish to do that.[111] Two months later, Tarbell herself reached a similar conclusion in *McClure's:* "His self-control has been masterful—he knows, nobody better, that to answer is to invite discussion, to answer is to call attention to the facts in the case."[112]

Rockefeller claimed that he had not even deigned to glance at *McClure's,* a claim inadvertently refuted by Adella Prentiss Hughes, Cettie's nurse and companion, who traveled with the Rockefellers on a western train trip in the spring of 1903. "He liked to have things read to him, and during these months I read aloud Ida Tarbell's diatribes," she recalled. "He listened musingly, with keen interest and no resentment."[113] He tossed out wisecracks about "his lady friend" or "Miss Tarbarrel" but would not be drawn into serious discussion about her. "Not a word," he said. "Not a word about that misguided woman."[114] His office, however, kept him well apprised of her allegations as they appeared.

Nonetheless, it is true that Rockefeller never formally sat down and read her searing indictment. "I don't think I ever read Ida Tarbell's book: I may have skimmed it," he said a decade later. "I wonder what it amounts to, anyway, in the minds of people who have no animus?"[115] When William O. Inglis began to interview Rockefeller in 1917 and read aloud portions of Tarbell's work, it grew clear that Rockefeller had only a vague familiarity with the series. It was equally clear that beneath his pose of stoic fortitude he was still angry. His private comments about her were marked by a heavy sniggering and dry mockery that he never exhibited in public. "How clever she is, compared with poor Lloyd, who was always hysterical! She makes her picture clear and attractive, no matter how unjust she is. She really could write."[116] At the same time, he was convinced that this daughter of Oil Creek was "animated more with jealousy begotten by the inability of her father and her brother and some of her neighbors to do as well as the Standard Oil Company."[117] Far from making him repent and reconsider, the Tarbell series hardened his faith in his career. How dismayed Tarbell would have been to find Rockefeller writing to Archbold in July 1905: "I never appreciated more than at present the importance of our taking care of our business holding it and increasing it in every part of the world."[118]

Faced with Tarbell's invective, Rockefeller was too proud to give the world the satisfaction of knowing that he was wounded. The press was rife with speculation about his reaction. "Mr. Rockefeller's friends say that it is all cruel punishment for him, and that he writhes under these attacks," reported one Detroit newspaper.[119] A Philadelphia paper chimed in that "the richest man in the world sits by the hour at Forest Hill, his chin sunk on his breast. . . . He has lost interest in golf; he has become morose; never free in his conversation with his employees, he now speaks only when absolutely necessary, and then gives his directions tersely and absently."[120] These reports tell more about the popular thirst for revenge than about Rockefeller's actual response. He was never tormented by guilt and went on playing golf.

Yet he *was* more vulnerable to criticism than he admitted. During this period, he grew closer to his son, who became his confidant just as Cettie's maladies made it more difficult for her to discharge that function. Junior remembered, "He used to talk to me about the criticisms to which he was exposed, and I think it eased his mind to do so, because beneath his apparent insensitiveness, he was a sensitive man, but he always ended up by saying: 'Well, John, we have to be patient. We have been successful and these people haven't.' "[121] Even John D. Rockefeller, Sr., required cathartic chats in time of trouble.

Having been filled to the brim with morality and religion, Rockefeller's children must have been disoriented to see him exposed as a corporate criminal. How did they reconcile the rapacious Rockefeller splashed across *McClure's* pages with the reverent father that they knew? As a rule, they fell back upon an implicit belief in father's integrity, which was more a matter of religious faith than anything grounded in fact.

Senior might talk in general terms about Tarbell's criticisms but refrained from specific rebuttals, an omission that especially tormented his son, who had taken his parents' morality at face value. Junior had always been prey to tension-related symptoms, and they intensified with each new installment of *McClure's*. By late 1904, gripped by migraine headaches and insomnia, he wavered on the edge of a breakdown. Under doctor's orders, he, Abby, and their baby daughter Babs sailed to Cannes in December 1904 for what would extend into a yearlong absence from 26 Broadway. They toured the charming Languedoc country towns, drove through the maritime Alps, and ambled along the Promenade des Anglais. But Junior's troubles were so intransigent that their projected one-month stay lengthened to six. Junior's breakdown has been variously attributed to overwork, exhaustion, or an identity crisis, but he himself privately emphasized the toll of the Tarbell series, as well as two subsequent controversies: the tainted-money affair and his leadership of a Bible class.

While Tarbell's articles were running, Rockefeller, his wife, his son, and two of his three daughters were afflicted by serious medical problems or nervous strain. In 1903, Rockefeller had such severe bronchial troubles that he took a rest cure near San Diego. That spring, Bessie suffered the stroke or heart ailment that left her sadly demented, and the following April Charles Strong took his wife off to Cannes, where she and Junior may have consulted the same nervous-strain specialists. In April 1904, Cettie had the attack that left her semiparalyzed and from which she took two years to recover. Finally, plunged into depression after the birth of her daughter Mathilde in April 1905, Edith fled to Europe. Understandably, the Rockefellers did not wish to broadcast their misfortunes to the world. The price that the series exacted on them, like so much else, was scrupulously hidden from both the public and posterity.

The most stinging personal blow to Rockefeller was not Tarbell's exposé of his chicanery but her defamatory portrait of his father, published in the two-part character study. Rockefeller had never dropped the pretense that his father, like his mother, was a person of sterling virtue. Even in later years, he told one of his grandsons, "I had a rich inheritance in foundation building from both my father and mother, and I reverence them, and often long to see them even though it is so many years since they passed away."[122] Now readers across the country were introduced to the protean Doc Rockefeller, snake-oil salesman, ne'er-do-well, bigamist, and absentee father. Most mortifying of all to Rockefeller, Tarbell disinterred his oldest and deepest shame: Big Bill's rape indictment in Moravia in the late 1840s.

By this point, Rockefeller seldom had dealings with his infirm, elderly father, who was increasingly crotchety, and routed urgent queries to him via brother Frank—to whom he was not speaking either. Tarbell had stumbled upon Doc Rockefeller's existence in serendipitous fashion. One day in April 1903, J. M. Siddall was on the phone with Rockefeller's brother-in-law, the genial William Rudd, when Rudd let slip that William Avery Rockefeller was still alive. Perhaps Rudd did not at first perceive the magnitude of this admission. "Oh yes, the old gentleman is living. He travels about from place to place in the west. The last I knew of him was in Dakota. We don't know where he is now."[123]

Sitting there agape, Siddall could scarcely believe his ears: Scoops did not come any bigger than this. The second he got off the phone, he pounded out a typewritten report to Tarbell.

> I have always supposed that Mr. Rockefeller's father died years and years ago, and I am startled almost beyond expression to learn, as I have through the telephone within the last five minutes, that the old man is living. . . . I never in my life was more surprised. . . . I am under the impression that I have been told over and over that the old man died some years ago, and I am sure from W. C. Rudd's attitude toward me today that there is something secret and mysterious about the thing.[124]

In his hands Siddall now had a thread that would lead him and then other reporters into a vast investigative maze. Through his brother, Siddall sounded out Frank Rockefeller's secretary, who offered a helpful hint: Doc Rockefeller lived in either North or South Dakota. "He doesn't know where and says frankly—though confidentially—that he *doesn't dare ask Frank or any members of the family*," Siddall informed Tarbell.[125] This only added to the mystery: Why had Rockefeller so thoroughly expunged his father from his life? Siddall next prodded a reporter from the Cleveland *Plain Dealer* to ask Dr. Biggar, very casually, whether on a recent trip west with Rockefeller they had detoured to visit Doc Rockefeller. At first Biggar walked straight into the trap. "No, we didn't go through Dakota," he began to blurt out, then, seeing his error, clammed up.[126] Siddall and Tarbell scored their biggest coup with Rockefeller's old friend Hiram Brown, whom Tarbell had met while researching her Lincoln book. During a meandering chat at Forest Hill, Brown sounded out Rockefeller about his father, which produced the following exchange, as recorded in Tarbell's research files:

"Well, sir, the old gentleman is on his last legs I guess. He is absolutely senile. He is living on a farm near Cedar Valley, Cedar County, Iowa. He has lost all his powers. He is ninety-three years old, you know. They say the old gentleman is so deaf that he cannot hear a word. His nieces are taking good care of him. He is living on the farm because he owns it . . . because it is the place that is most pleasing to him."

"Well, John, what a comical, funny old fellow he is," Brown said.

"Yes," John replied. "They say the old gentleman lies on the bed and swears all day. I haven't seen him since he was here three years ago."[127] This last sentence alluded to the party that John had thrown at Forest Hill for Bill and his erstwhile cronies.

When Ida Tarbell interviewed Frank Rockefeller in 1904, he gave his own self-serving account of John and Bill's final break. At age ninety, Bill had decided to bequeath his $87,000 in property equally among his four living children. According to Frank, John had wanted his one-quarter share *plus* repayment of an outstanding $35,000 loan; Bill, irate, believed that the gift should cancel out the loan. As Tarbell paraphrased Frank's narration in a memo, "The old man was so furious that now he will not come home. He says he will not live in the same state with his son."[128] As Tarbell peeled away bits and pieces of Bill's clandestine life, she did not know how abominably Bill and Frank had behaved over the years, how much they had borrowed from John, nor how erroneous their tirades against him were. Tarbell was never able to track down Doc Rockefeller or figure out the riddle of his double life, but her revelation that he was still alive somewhere created a national sensation.

Among the intrigued was Joseph Pulitzer, publisher of the *World*, who had inveighed against Standard Oil as the most pitiless trust. Pulitzer served his readers an incongruous mix of scabrous stories and lofty crusades against corporate abuse. "Money is the great power of today," he declared. "Men sell their souls for it. Women sell their bodies for it."[129] He wished to purge capitalism of its vulgar excesses so that a more enlightened capitalism might flourish, and he evinced a special animus toward Rockefeller, whom he christened "the father of trusts, the king of monopolists, the czar of the oil business," a man who "relentlessly crushes all competitors."[130] Hence the story of Doc Rockefeller— uniting, as it did, the spice of family scandal with Standard Oil's notoriety—was a godsend. Stirring the pot, Pulitzer offered eight thousand dollars to anyone who could provide information about Rockefeller's father, a reward that set off a nationwide manhunt.

It is a credit to Bill's matchless duplicity that teams of reporters were immediately stymied in this search. There was also a fair bit of luck involved. When *McClure's* printed a picture of Rockefeller's father to accompany the character sketch, many Freeport, Illinois, residents were shocked to see Dr. William Levingston staring out at them. Many traits that Tarbell attributed to Doc Rockefeller sounded oddly reminiscent of their queer local resident. The editor of the *Freeport Daily Bulletin* contacted *McClure's* to inform them that they might have mistakenly printed a picture of Dr. William Levingston. Indignant at this insinuation—and totally oblivious of the revelation implicit in the Freeport editor's query—*McClure's* wrote back and assured the editor that the photo of Rockefeller's father was indeed authentic. Amazingly enough, the national press corps never picked up on all the rumors buzzing around Freeport, Illinois.

An impatient Pulitzer dispatched one of his star reporters, J. W. Slaght, to Cleveland, hoping for a quick solution, but two weeks later Slaght slogged back to New York, weary and dispirited. In a despairing memo to Pulitzer, he stressed the inordinate effort required to track down Rockefeller's father and hinted that it would be thankless drudgery. He hoped that the matter would end there. "In just about time enough for the report to have reached Mr. Pulitzer I was ordered to take up the search and stay on it until I found Mr. Rockefeller, regardless of time or expense," Slaght revealed to William O. Inglis a decade later. "It seems that the story fascinated Mr. Pulitzer—the disappearance of the father of the richest man in the world, a thrilling mystery that would interest people everywhere."[131]

So thoroughly had Doc Rockefeller erased his tracks that Slaght had only one tenuous clue. During the reunion a few years earlier at Forest Hill, Big Bill had slyly told his buddies that he resided somewhere out West and shot "shirt-tail swans" in a nearby lake. Slaght consulted a naturalist who said that a wild goose nicknamed the "shirt-tail swan" abounded in parts of Alaska. Setting forth with this sketchy information and a photo of Doc Rockefeller, the miserable Slaght trekked through Alaska, tramping from lake to lake. Once he had exhausted this terrain, he heard that Bill had been sighted in Indiana and was off on another wild-goose chase. For a time, he peddled razors door-to door, trying to pry information loose from suspicious German farmers. "I'll bet I shaved myself ten or fifteen times a day, till my face was sore, selling the blamed razors."[132] Even clean shaven, Slaght again came up empty-handed.

Desperate, he turned to Frank Rockefeller, the only person in direct communication with the phantom. Bribing Frank's secretary with candy and theater tickets, Slaght gained access to Frank, who was no less protective of his father than John was. He was quite upset by Slaght's quest and offered a straightforward deal: If Slaght called off the search, Frank would repay him with sensational findings about his brother. To enhance the deal's allure, Frank exhumed from his drawer an impressive manuscript, thick as a telephone directory.

After a flurry of calls to New York, the *World* editors agreed to terminate their search for Doc Rockefeller for sixty days if they could, in return, publish Frank's philippic against John. Having never dealt with Frank, Slaght naively trusted him. But when the time expired, Frank would not return his calls, and Slaght had no choice but to accost him on a Cleveland street and bluntly remind him that the *World* had fulfilled its end of the bargain; in exchange, he demanded the manuscript. "No, sir," Frank snapped, "not one word of it."[133] Aghast, Slaght said the *World* would publish the inflammatory remarks Frank had made about John in his office. "If you publish that," retorted Frank, "I'll kill you."[134] However much he detested John, Frank must have feared that any published comments would dry up the loans from his brothers.

In August 1907, still baffled in its search for Doc Rockefeller, the *World* ran the interview with Frank recorded a year and a half earlier. "My father is alive and well," a defiant Frank was quoted as saying. "He is dependent upon no man. He would scorn the proffer of financial aid from John D. and would not take it from me. He has means of his own, ample for all his needs." Then he openly taunted his brother for his estrangement. "Go ask John D. where our father is; tell him that I sent you and that I dare him to answer."[135] By this point, the Pulitzer reporters labored under insane pressure to come up with fresh leads. When William Randolph Hearst also threw reporters into the search, Pulitzer (who referred to Rockefeller as "Grasping" in internal coded messages) could not bear the thought of being beaten and offered a handsome cash bonus to any reporter who broke the story. To bolster the burned-out Slaght, he assigned another reporter, A. B. Macdonald of the *St. Louis Post-Dispatch*, to the chase.

Before turning to the finale of this cross-country quest, let us fill in a few blanks about Bill's life during these past years. Too old to travel, Bill had renounced his itinerant life and mostly remained in Freeport, Illinois. As garrulous as ever, he spent his days dabbling with his guns, telling hunting stories to whoever would listen, or boasting of his big ranch and fine horses in North Dakota. When he visited Frank's ranch, he sat on the front porch and fired at targets Frank set up for his amusement. One night in 1904, the portly, ailing Bill, then ninety-four, lowered himself into a chair but missed it. As he tried to grab something to break his fall, he broke his arm near the shoulder, an accident so severe that his survival seemed doubtful, and it became necessary to contact his next of kin. Until this time, Margaret Allen Levingston had not known that her husband was a bigamist with five children and that one of them was among the world's richest men. A proper lady, active in the First Presbyterian Church and the Women's Christian Temperance Union, she must have reeled from this revelation.

There is reason to suspect that John D. met Margaret Levingston at this time. The nurse who treated Bill, Mrs. J. B. Gingrich, told of the arrival of a mysterious visitor from the East who came by private railroad car, slipped into the house discreetly by a side door, and only entered Bill's room after she and the doctor had left. She remembered the sound of this visitor pacing up and down an adjoining room as Bill lay in pain. One suspects that John D. was the spectral figure, since William would not have asked for these special security precautions. If it was John D., it would have been the first time he ever set eyes on the wife whose legitimacy he had never acknowledged.

As he recuperated, Bill was often delirious, though still talkative. "Even as sick as he was he was jovial in his rational moments and in his delirium," said Mrs. Gingrich. "He talked of his vast business interests in the East. He sang often a ditty about a frog in a well, and he sang often a lullaby which he said his mother used to sing to him when he was a baby nearly 100 years before."[136] As if shedding all the accumulated artifice of his double life, Bill's mind frequently reverted to his early days as Doc Rockefeller in upstate New York. In the feverish mental state of his final days in early 1906, he repeatedly babbled the names of the five children from his first marriage—John, William, Frank, Lucy, and Mary Ann. And he would stare at the loyal Margaret and suddenly cry out, "You are not my wife. Where is Eliza?"[137]

It was to be a season full of bitter surprises for Margaret, who had been gulled by Bill's braggadocio into thinking they were supremely wealthy. During his illness, Bill had trouble paying his medical bills and even contemplated pawning the big, gaudy diamond he had always stuck in his shirtfront. The night that Bill died, Margaret was unsure of the Rockefellers' reaction and did not know exactly what to do. She apparently stored the body for several months at the City Cemetery, awaiting a request to have it shipped back to Cleveland. When word never came from the family, she transferred the body to the Oak Knoll section of the Oakland Cemetery. Though Bill is always said to have died on May 11, 1906, references to his estate suddenly appear in John's papers in January 1906, suggesting that the burial may have taken place on that later date, not the death itself. Only Frank and Pierson Briggs attended the belated funeral in which Bill was entombed in a plain, unvarnished box in an unmarked grave. That Margaret was worried about her future financial state is confirmed by the fact that she paid the gravediggers three dollars, but could not afford the extra dollar for a brick vault—standard procedure at the time. It would be another five years, after Margaret's own death, before a granite memorial bearing the Levingston name in raised lettering was finally erected on the site. Few—if any—Rockefeller descendants seem to know that William Avery Rockefeller is buried there under his assumed name.

The tangled skein of Bill's life finally unraveled in early 1908, two years after his death, when a druggist in Madison, Wisconsin, told A. B. Macdonald that for years a friend and fellow druggist in Freeport named George Swartz had sold medical concoctions to a Dr. William Levingston. Swartz had always wondered whether the name was a fabrication, a suspicion confirmed when he saw a picture of Dr. Levingston gazing at him from Tarbell's series. Acting on this tip, Macdonald traveled to Freeport. When he flashed a photo of Bill Rockefeller to neighbors, everybody agreed that it was Dr. Levingston. Then he rang the doorbell of a private home on West Clark Street. A refined, elderly lady in her early seventies answered, her white hair covered by a lace cap. When the reporter disclosed his mission, Margaret Allen Levingston lifted her hands and started to sob. "I have been wondering when one of you would come," she said, sniffling. "And I have been dreading it, for I knew the secret could not be kept forever, now that my husband is dead." When Macdonald asked whether William Avery Rockefeller and Dr. Levingston were the same person, she replied, "Go to the other side if you want the facts." What other side? "To John D. Rockefeller. Let him tell if he will. It is not for me to talk. I lived happily with my husband for fifty years. He was kind and true. It is all I can say or will say. I must be a true woman to the end."[138] She furnished pictures of both herself and her husband—in fact, over the mantel Macdonald saw a crayon version of the photo of Bill he held in his hand—then told her visitor in parting, "I wish it were possible for you to leave me alone with my dead."[139]

To retire any lingering doubt, Macdonald went to the local library and found an obituary notice, dated May 11, 1906, for Dr. William Levingston, who had died at age ninety-six and was listed as the oldest man in Freeport. The death notice listed his birthday as November 13, 1810—the same date as Doc Rockefeller's—settling the great mystery. Greatly relieved, Macdonald was at last liberated from Pulitzer's obsession.

On February 2, 1908, the nightmare that had haunted John D. Rockefeller his whole life suddenly burst forth in bold print. On its front page, the *World* trumpeted the headline "Secret Double Life of Rockefeller's Father Revealed by the *World*." The story received the coverage ordinarily reserved for major elections or great natural disasters, with the single column on the front page followed by an entire page inside. Nothing in the text was quite so cogent as the proof provided by two adjoining, identical photos of William Avery Rockefeller and Dr. William Levingston. The article gave a sketchy picture of his double life, his fifty-one years as a bigamist, his footloose life as a mountebank in the Dakotas, and his burial in an unmarked grave. It was a story more bizarrely implausible than anything ever invented by the tabloid press. For Big Bill, who had always wanted to be somebody important, it was a queer sort of posthumous fulfillment.

Rockefeller's archives do not reveal a single public or private reaction to the *World* article. His friends never dared to elicit his response, while his family pretended that the article did not exist. There were two noteworthy public reactions. First, Frank again decided to make mischief by publicly denying that his father had been a bigamist or even that he was dead. "Like others which have preceded it, the story is an unqualified lie. The whereabouts of my father concerns no one but his immediate family and it is precisely to protect himself from being hounded by cranks and others who would break in upon the peace and quiet of his retired life that he prefers to live in such seclusion as suits his convenience."[140]

Second, the article brought an emotional response from Dr. Charles Johnston, Bill's handsome, dark-skinned young disciple and traveling companion in the Dakota years. When he read the *World* exposé, Johnston was petrified that he would lose his license to practice medicine if it was shown that he and Bill had sold patent medicines illegally. Released from his pledge of secrecy by Bill's death, he told the *World*, "For years I have wondered why the secret was kept so safely. For twenty-five years the secret has been locked in my breast, but it was well known to others, and I have wondered when it would become known."[141] To protect his professional status, he portrayed Bill sympathetically as a "natural healer," not as a cunning mountebank. Years later, when he no longer feared legal reprisals, he gave a less sanitized history of their scams. Perhaps more than Bill's real children, Charles Johnston retained a tender spot for him, telling the *World* that he still cherished the violin that Bill had given him when he was too old and gouty to play. And he made a public plea that the Rockefeller family should posthumously forgive this fallible man. "I think it's time that John D. Rockefeller and his brother should acknowledge him as their father, because all the world knows it now."[142]

Deaf to Johnston's plea, Rockefeller probably never forgave the father whose erratic ways had likely set him off on his exaggerated quest for money, power, and respectability. Bill's body was never brought back to Cleveland and his granite tombstone was paid for from Margaret Levingston's meager estate.

Frederick T. Gates, seated, with Dr. Simon Flexner,
director of the Rockefeller Institute for Medical Research.
(Courtesy of the Rockefeller Archive Center)

Faith of Fools

ad John D. Rockefeller died in 1902, at the outset of the Tarbell series, he would be known today almost exclusively as a narrow man of swashbuckling brilliance in business, a man who personified the acquisitive spirit of late-nineteenth-century American industry. But just as the muckrakers were teaching the public that Rockefeller was the devil incarnate, he was turning increasingly to philanthropy. What makes him so problematic—and why he continues to inspire such ambivalent reactions—is that his good side was every bit as good as his bad side was bad. Seldom has history produced such a contradictory figure. We are almost forced to posit, in helpless confusion, at least two Rockefellers: the good, religious man and the renegade businessman, driven by baser motives. Complicating this puzzle is the fact that Rockefeller experienced no sense of discontinuity as he passed from being the brains of Standard Oil to being the monarch of a charitable empire. He did not see himself in retirement as atoning for his sins, and he would have agreed emphatically with Winston Churchill's later judgment: "The founder of the Standard Oil Company would not have felt the need of paying hush money to heaven."[1] He was also insistent that his massive philanthropy paled in importance beside the good he had done in creating jobs and furnishing affordable kerosene at Standard Oil.

As his fortune grew big enough to beggar the imagination, John D. retained his mystic faith that God had given him money for mankind's benefit. Obviously, God disagreed with Miss Tarbell, or else why had He lavished such bounty on him? Rockefeller regarded his fortune as a public trust, not as a private indulgence, and the pressure to dispose of it grew imperative in the early

1900s as his Standard Oil stock and other investments appreciated fantasti- cally. In the pre-Gates era, Rockefeller had found it difficult to expand his giving in proportion to his wealth—a strain that had pushed him steadily toward a psychic precipice. Tarbell stressed that Rockefeller had given away only a small fraction of his total wealth: between thirty-five and forty million dollars, or the equivalent of three years of Standard Oil dividends. (In fact, he had already given away several times that amount.) To parry the political attacks against him and mollify public opinion, he now had to disburse money on a much larger scale. For purely selfish reasons, he had to show that as a philanthropist he could act in a disinterested, public-spirited manner. Those commentators who see his charity as crudely furthering his economic interests miss a far more important goal: his need to prove that rich businessmen could honorably discharge the burden of wealth. The judicious disposal of his fortune might also blunt further inquiry into its origins.

It was thus from political necessity that Rockefeller distanced himself from his philanthropies, which would be marked by a low-profile style. The muck- rakers had fostered such distrust of Rockefeller that he needed to counter sus- picions that his charity was just another trick, a way to burnish his public image in the wake of investigations. The Rockefeller philanthropies would be constrained by a fundamental paradox: While extremely powerful, they were also inhibited in exercising that power. In explaining why members of the Rockefeller boards never gave interviews, Gates once said that if they extolled their benefactions, it would "inevitably lend color to the suspicion that [Rocke- feller's] gifts are not free from the taint of self-seeking."[2]

Gates helped Rockefeller to define his priorities so as to forestall political crit- icism. Rockefeller began to assign a lesser place to partisan or parochial con- cerns, such as the Anti-Saloon League or Anthony Comstock and his New York Society for the Suppression of Vice, in favor of programs with broad appeal and universal support—things unarguably good that helped all classes of people and lacked any tincture of self-interest. Groups that did not meet these criteria were either relegated to Rockefeller's small, private gifts or discarded altogether. In his memoirs, Rockefeller said that he had sought progress in six areas of life, and the choices are notable for their general, noncontroversial nature: "(1) material comforts (2) government and law (3) language and literature (4) sci- ence and philosophy (5) art and refinement (6) morality and religion."[3] Who could protest such emphases?

The most perplexing issue for Rockefeller was how to square philanthropy with self-reliance. His constant nightmare was that he would promote depen- dence, sapping the Protestant work ethic. "It is a great problem," he acknowl- edged, "to learn how to give without weakening the moral backbone of the beneficiary."[4] He dreaded the thought of armies of beggars addicted to his handouts. Back in the 1880s, when considering support for a veterans' organization in Cleveland, he warned brother Frank that he did "not want to encourage a horde of irresponsible, adventuresome fellows to call on me at sight for money every time fancy seizes them."[5] He constantly reminded his son that it was easier to launch a charitable commitment than to end it.

He was also wary of upsetting the existing social hierarchy. Staunchly convinced that society meted out just deserts, he believed that the rich had been recompensed for superior intelligence and enterprise. Conversely,

> the failures that a man makes in his life are due almost always to some defect in his personality, some weakness of body, mind or character, will or temperament. . . . It is my personal belief that the principal cause for the economic differences between people is their difference in personality, and that it is only as we can assist in the wider distribution of those qualities that go to make up a strong personality that we can assist in the wider distribution of wealth.[6]

He contributed to education and medical research, for they strengthened recipients and better prepared them for the evolutionary struggle—that is, he equipped them to compete but did not tamper with outcomes. For this reason, he never used his wealth to alleviate poverty directly and scorned any charity that smacked of social welfare. "Instead of giving alms to beggars," Rockefeller said, "if anything can be done to remove the causes which lead to the existence of beggars, then something deeper and broader and more worthwhile will have been accomplished."[7] Unlike Carnegie, he did not build libraries, athletic facilities, or music halls for the recreation of ordinary people but promoted pure research that would lead to more generalized benefits.

In focusing on prevention rather than relief, Rockefeller was influenced by two contemporary reform movements. By 1900, many progressives had tired of dealing with the symptoms of social ills and began to search for fundamental causes. Instead of falling back on isolated good deeds, they aspired to a systematic attack on the underpinnings of poverty. Backed by a new faith in scientific method, they drew on a burgeoning new middle class, educated by an expanding university system, and enlisted the knowledge of experts in business, labor, agriculture, and other areas. This new technical class provided a ready-made population to staff the Rockefeller philanthropies. Such "scientific reform" appealed to Rockefeller, who liked to analyze systems and probe underlying causes. After all, he himself had profited from scientific breakthroughs at Standard Oil, such as the Frasch process.

Rockefeller's work was also buttressed by the social-gospel movement, which united social reform with moral uplift and religious renewal, reaching its high point between 1900 and 1920. For both Rockefeller senior and junior, this was a perfect synthesis, a way to be politically liberal and modern while clinging to an old-fashioned aversion to gambling, prostitution, alcohol, and other vices traditionally shunned by Baptists. It also guaranteed that reform took place under the safe aegis of religious authority. The social-gospel movement provided a way that the Rockefellers could make a smooth transition from narrow denominational giving to more secular, ecumenical causes.

===

Frederick T. Gates was the tutelary spirit of the Rockefeller philanthropies. Though nearly invisible to the public at the time, he advanced large claims for his contributions in his posthumously published memoirs. Yet Gates was groomed by Rockefeller, and if he was granted a large measure of freedom, it was partly because Rockefeller had trained him as his proxy. Since he held aloof from his charitable empire, Rockefeller's role has almost invariably been underrated, but Gates allowed that it was Rockefeller himself who furnished the idea for founding a medical-research institute. Around 1894, when William Rainey Harper first proposed a medical school for the University of Chicago, Rockefeller countered with a novel proposal for a medical department devoted mainly or exclusively to research. Gates had the courtier's knack for delivering on his sovereign's wishes with unmatched energy and intelligence, so when he proposed a medical-research institute three years later, he knew his words would find a sympathetic echo in Rockefeller.

On summer vacation with his family in the Catskill Mountains in 1897, Gates tackled a book of door-stopping length: *Principles and Practice of Medicine*, a thousand-page tome by William Osler of the Johns Hopkins Medical School, the most renowned contemporary physician. (Whereas Rockefeller scarcely ever cracked a book, except for slim volumes of sermons, Gates read exhaustively and said he had scoured more than a thousand volumes in steering the Rockefeller philanthropies.) That spring, Gates had survived a serious illness, awakening his curiosity about American medicine. Osler's magnum opus was not light summer fare, but with a medical dictionary at his side Gates waded through its pages with mounting amazement. He confided to William Rainey Harper that he had "scarcely ever read anything more intensely interesting."[8] Gates was appalled by the backward state of medicine unintentionally disclosed by Osler's book: While the author delineated the symptoms of many diseases, he seldom identified the responsible germs and presented cures for only four or five diseases. How could one respect medicine that was so strong on anecdote and description but so weak on diagnosis and treatment? Gates had a sudden, vivid sense of what could be done by a medical-research institution devoted to infectious diseases. His timing was faultless, for major strides were being made in bacteriology. For the first time, specific microorganisms were being isolated as the causes of disease, removing medicine forever from the realm of patent-medicine vendors such as Doc Rockefeller.

With a rush of emotion, Gates drafted a strongly worded memo to Rockefeller, advocating the establishment of such an institute and citing European precedents, including the Pasteur Institute in Paris (founded in 1888) and the Koch Institute for Infectious Diseases in Berlin (1891), both of which greatly elevated the prestige of European medicine. At the time, the concept of a medical-research institute was still alien in America. The country's medical schools were mostly commercial operations, taught by practicing doctors who picked up spare money by lecturing on the side. Standards were so abysmal that many schools did not even require a college degree for entry. Since these medical mills had no incentive to undertake serious research, medicine hovered in a twilight area between science and guesswork. Gates got Rockefeller to hire Starr Murphy to canvass medical opinion about setting up an institute. He found that many physicians were frankly skeptical that the country contained enough scientific talent to staff such an institution, and they recommended the distribution of small grants to individual labs instead.

Rockefeller responded to Gates's memo with prolonged silence and let it marinate for a couple of years. But Rockefeller eventually realized that medical research ideally suited his needs. It would be safe, universally popular, and noncontroversial. While there was no guarantee that Rockefeller scientists would discover anything new, there was equally little chance that they would embarrass the founder. They would pick scientists associated with topflight universities and then set them to work with a free hand. Such an institution would also fill a void in the philanthropic universe. Gates told Osler, "This line of philanthropy, now almost wholly neglected in this country, is the most needed and the most promising of any field of philanthropic endeavor."[9] In fact, the promotion of medical science tallied so perfectly with Rockefeller's needs that it would end up forming the common denominator of his foundations.

The proposal encountered skepticism in the medical community. It seemed quite rash, even quixotic, to pay grown men to daydream and come up with useful discoveries. At the time, institutionalized innovation was no less novel a notion in medicine than in industry. With other Rockefeller ventures, Gates had mostly responded to entreaties, whereas he now had to sell the idea in the teeth of widespread resistance.

Gates had hoped the institute would be associated with the University of Chicago, an opportunity lost when Dr. Harper consummated a merger with the Rush Medical College. Rush was exactly the sort of proprietary medical school that Gates wanted to see abolished. American medicine was then embroiled in open warfare between two schools: the allopaths, who used remedies that produced effects different from the disease in question, and homeopaths, who tried to induce in healthy persons prophylactic symptoms similar to the disease being fought. Rush was strongly biased toward allopathy, while Rockefeller favored homeopathy; Gates dismissed both allopathic *and* homeopathic medicine as scandalous pseudo-science. In 1898, he admonished the University of Chicago, "I have no doubt that Mr. Rockefeller would favor an institution that was neither allopath or homeopath but simply scientific in its investigation of medical science."[10] Nevertheless, Harper persisted in the Rush merger and forfeited any chance to have a Rockefeller medical-research institute in Chicago. After encountering allopathic sympathizers at Harvard and Columbia, Rockefeller's advisers decided that it would be easier to set up an autonomous institution in New York.

Rockefeller was pleased by the decision to support a modest, freestanding research center. After all the bitter wrangling with Harper, he was doubtless sated with academic politics and administrative dreamers. An independent medical institute would be tightly controlled and minimize the chances of unpleasant fiscal surprises. In endowing the Rockefeller Institute for Medical Research (RIMR), he rigorously avoided the mistakes he had made with the University of Chicago, which became his cautionary tale of how *not* to build an institution. After the battle royal with Augustus Strong over the site for a Baptist university, Rockefeller must also have been glad to select his adopted town as the site of the research center.

—

If the University of Chicago seemed to emerge full-blown from the fertile brain of Dr. Harper, then the RIMR, founded in June 1901, was deliberately launched more modestly. It had no initial endowment and was lodged in temporary quarters in a Lexington Avenue loft building. This muted approach was designed to cool off any expectations that sudden miracles would emerge from this first American facility devoted solely to biomedical research. Deviating from custom, Rockefeller consented to the use of his name. The amount he pledged for this project—$200,000 over ten years—was considered spectacular at the time. To avoid a reprise of his Chicago problems, Rockefeller promised no additional gifts and deliberately kept administrators in the dark so that they would not feel overly confident of his support.

Rockefeller placed a premium on recruiting the best people for leading positions. "John, we have *money*," he told his son, "but it will have value for mankind only as we can find able *men* with ideas, imagination and courage to put it into productive use."[11] That Rockefeller placed scientists, not lay trustees, in charge of expenditures was thought revolutionary. This was the institute's secret formula: gather great minds, liberate them from petty cares, and let them chase intellectual chimeras without pressure or meddling. If the founders created an atmosphere conducive to creativity, things would, presumably, happen.

A stellar team was soon assembled. The chief adviser in this search was Dr. William H. Welch, professor of pathology and first dean of the Johns Hopkins Medical School. A bald, portly bachelor with a goatee, fondly called "Popsy" by his students, this sociable bear of a man liked everything from food to theater to Shakespeare's sonnets. Trained in Germany, he had transplanted high German medical standards to America by opening the first pathology lab at Bellevue Hospital Medical College in 1878. When Hopkins inaugurated its medical school fifteen years later, Welch oversaw a faculty trained mostly in Germany and working as full-time teachers and researchers—a milestone in American medicine. Spurred by Rockefeller money, this model would later be copied across America. When in doubt, the Rockefeller lieutenants used the Johns Hopkins Medical School as the benchmark by which they judged progress in medical education.

As president of the RIMR board, Welch wooed as its first director his protégé Simon Flexner, whom he had considered his most gifted pupil and America's best young pathologist. Of German-Jewish ancestry, raised in Louisville, Kentucky, Flexner neatly fitted into the Rockefeller mold of disciplined, self-made men.

Though highly respected in the medical world, Flexner was not a luminary when Welch approached him in early 1902. At thirty-nine, he faced an excruciating decision: whether to surrender a lifetime appointment as a pathology professor at the University of Pennsylvania to leap into the vortex of "an institution devoted exclusively to discovery of something new," as he put it.[12] When Flexner asked Gates why he was certain they would find something new, Gates smirked and replied that he had the faith of fools. The whole thing seemed so shadowy and insubstantial that Flexner hesitated for several months to accept the post. He bargained hard for the ability to offer high salaries to prospective researchers as well as for a promise that the institute would have a small, adjoining hospital in which diseases under study could be tracked in a clinical setting.

Flexner—spare, lean, ascetic, bespectacled—had features as sharp and precise as his mind. He was the sort of fair but tough-minded administrator who appealed to Rockefeller. Many people saw warmth beneath his businesslike exterior, but he was not a bluff clubman. "Flexner was competent," said H. L. Mencken, "but he was a precise and somewhat pompous fellow."[13] More than one scientist quaked at his exacting expectations and incisive criticisms. Evidently heartened by this perfectionist director, Rockefeller pledged another one million dollars to the RIMR that June. Recalling how quickly Harper had burned up money, he stipulated that Flexner should receive the payments staggered over a ten-year period, slowing the pace of development.

Simon Flexner came to symbolize the institute, and his high-minded tone of scientific rigor established its enduring character. (Sinclair Lewis patterned the character of A. DeWitt Tubbs, the worldly director of the McGurk Institute of Biology in *Arrowsmith*, after him.) He exhibited a shrewd talent for exciting the public about the RIMR's work. Soon after his appointment, a reporter tracked him down at his Philadelphia lab amid "the gruesome cans and jars of his work, busy as a hornet," and he conveyed the audacious nature of the nascent institute, which he called "an extensive scheme, embracing the whole field of study of the cause and prevention of disease."[14] He had a missionary ardor for pure research, then rare in scientific circles. "There is no such thing as useless knowledge in medical research," he said. "Ideas may come to us out of order in point of time. We may discover a detail of the facade before we know too much about the foundation. But in the end all knowledge has its place."[15]

With Flexner signed up, a search committee surveyed Manhattan for a permanent home, and in 1903 bought thirteen acres of farmland on a stony bluff overlooking the East River between Sixty-fourth and Sixty-eighth Streets. When Junior first spotted this site, it was a bleak, treeless slope with cows browsing on the grass. The district was still so poor that the steam-heat company had not run lines there, and it attracted unsavory industries, such as breweries and slaughterhouses. For this so-called Schermerhorn tract, the Rockefellers paid $660,000. After an interim period of eighteen months spent in two brownstone houses at Lexington Avenue and Fiftieth Street, the RIMR moved into its new home on York Avenue in May 1906. Photos show a solid six-story brick building standing on a bare, windswept hill, flanked by a tiny copse of trees and a few sheds, with the Queensborough Bridge being constructed in the background. It is hard to match up this picture with today's Rockefeller University, the pampered home of Nobel laureates, with its lushly landscaped grounds, screened from the city by magnificent gates and lofty trees.

=

As at Standard Oil, Rockefeller played the grand ventriloquist, operating at arm's length. In pithy notes, he transmitted his wishes to subordinates, reserving the right to approve all major commitments of money. Having learned in business to rely on experts, he could seem remote from his own philanthropies. In 1910, Charles W. Eliot, the former Harvard president, lamented to Gates, "Mr. Rockefeller's method of giving away money impersonally on the basis of investigation by others was careful and conscientious; but it must have cut him off almost completely from the real happiness which good deeds brought to the doer."[16]

Rockefeller refrained from interfering with the medical institute's autonomy and for a long time did not even visit it. While appreciating this restraint, Simon Flexner repeatedly invited him to tour the premises. "Very graciously he said that he could not take the valuable time of the workers," said Flexner, "and when I said we had many visitors he remarked that made it more important that he should not consume my time."[17] Several years after the main building's dedication, Rockefeller *père* and *fils* were in the vicinity one day when Junior suggested, "Father, you have never been at the Institute. Let us take a taxi up there and look at it."[18] Rockefeller agreed reluctantly. When they pulled up outside the institute, he just sat in the car and stared at it. "Father," Junior gently prodded, "don't you want to go in and look at it?" "No," said Rockefeller, "I can see the outside."[19] After more coaxing, he finally went inside. A staff member gave them a brief tour. Rockefeller expressed his gratitude then left, never to return. His craving for anonymity, such a controversial feature of his business career, seemed noble in his benefactions, and his respectful diffidence before scientific expertise won him praise as an exemplary donor.

However enlightened, Rockefeller's detachment was also self-protective, for he feared that face-to-face encounters would generate fresh pleas for funds. One reason he did not visit the RIMR sooner was almost certainly that he wished to keep Flexner guessing about his intentions. As late as 1911, he advised his son, "I think it better that no intimation shall reach the Institute representatives of any purpose to increase the endowment in the near future. Let us hold the Institute to the strictest administration and observe for a further time how they get along and delay committal, as long as we can, to be confirmed as to the wisdom of such additional endowment."[20] This slow development of the RIMR was a classic Rockefeller move.

In retirement, he devoted about one hour per day to philanthropy. Yet he managed to preside over this charitable universe in deed as well as name, demanding that his administrators have the exactitude of scientists, the sound economy of businessmen, and the passion of preachers. It was not the case, as Charles Eliot feared, that Rockefeller derived no pleasure from his good works, for he was engrossed in the RIMR. "If in all our giving, we had never done more than has been achieved by the fine, able, honest men of the Medical Institute," he once remarked, "it would have justified all the money and all the effort we have spent."[21] Doc Rockefeller's son took more pride in the RIMR than in any of his creations other than Standard Oil. In response to Eliot's letter, Gates explained that Rockefeller stayed abreast of developments there:

I make it my business to keep Mr. Rockefeller personally informed of every important thing done and every promising line of inquiry at the Institute. He knows the lines of experiment trembling on the verge of success and their thrilling promise for humanity. I have seen the tears of joy course down his cheeks as he contemplated the past achievement and future possibilities of the Institute. He is a man of very quick and tender sympathies just as he is a man of a keen and lively sense of humor.[22]

Allowing for a certain hyperbole, the portrait is essentially just.

While Flexner paid social calls on Rockefeller and always found him cordial, he and Welch dealt mostly with the nonmedical trustees—Gates, Junior, and Starr Murphy—on policy matters. They made presentations that evoked the high drama of their medical sleuthing, holding their auditors rapt. As president of the trustees, Gates sat at the head of the table, his tie askew, shaggy hair falling over his forehead, flaming with enthusiasm at each new discovery, while the self-contained Junior posed well-chosen questions. Both Gates and Junior brought an almost mystical intensity to these meetings, as if their spirituality was finding a new home in scientific research. Gates likened the RIMR to a "theological seminary" and described Flexner's work as a kind of prayer. He told Flexner, "To you He is whispering His secrets. To you He is opening up the mysterious depths of His Being. There have been times when, as I looked through your microscopes, I have been stricken with speechless awe. I felt that I was gazing with unhallowed eyes into the secret places of the Most High."[23] For many of the men associated with the early Rockefeller philanthropies, science seemed to beckon as a new secular religion as the old spiritual verities waned.

—

Since cynics thought the RIMR would be relegated to ivory-tower irrelevance, Gates tried to shelter Flexner from any anxiety about immediate results. Then a sudden opportunity for heroism arose during the winter of 1904–1905, when three thousand New Yorkers died in a cerebrospinal meningitis epidemic. In response, Flexner developed a serum in horses to treat the disease. During monkey trials in 1907, he found that if injected at the proper spot in the spinal canal, the serum would treat the disease effectively. Rockefeller eagerly followed developments, telling a friend on January 17, 1908, "Only two days ago I was called on the telephone to speak with a German doctor, who had given it to a patient, and he reported that in four hours after the first application, the temperature became normal and so continued, and he was very hopeful at that time of the recovery of the patient."[24] Until early 1911, when the New York City Board of Health took up the slack, the RIMR distributed the Flexner serum free as a public service. Later, the disease was treated with sulfa drugs and then antibiotics, but in the meantime Flexner's serum mercifully spared hundreds, perhaps thousands, of lives. The press lionized him as a miracle worker, redounding to the lab's benefit.

In a turbulent season of antitrust suits, Flexner's triumph generated goodwill for Rockefeller, and this loosened the master's purse strings. In early 1907, the institute directors asked Rockefeller for a $6 million endowment; eager to dampen starry-eyed hopes, he consented to $2.6 million, or less than half the desired amount. That same year, Junior advised him that the time was ripe to build the small adjoining hospital that had been promised to Flexner; the combined cost of endowment and hospital would be $8 million. As Rockefeller pondered this, the triumph of Flexner's serum tipped the scales, and in May 1908 Junior notified the board that his father, in homage to this feat, would create a sixty-bed hospital and a nine-bed isolation pavilion. As blueprints were rolled out, Rockefeller tempered his generosity with his usual pinchpenny pleas for economy. "It is easy for these institutions to ask for money," he told his son. "We have not one farthing to expend injudiciously."[25] When it opened in 1910, the hospital treated, free of charge, patients afflicted with any one of five priority diseases under study: polio, lobar pneumonia, syphilis, heart disease, and intestinal infantilism. Four rooms on the top floor were reserved for the Rockefeller family, but Senior never took advantage of this privilege, despite Gates's constant urging: "The physicians are extremely polite, gentle, and courteous, and the nurses the very paragons of their tribe," he assured him.[26] But Rockefeller stubbornly preferred his osteopaths and homeopaths, whom he could also more easily control.

Now an independent foundation established in perpetuity, the RIMR adopted bylaws creating a board of scientific directors with unlimited control over research—a declaration of faith in science unprecedented in American philanthropic annals. (A separate board of trustees saw to fiscal matters.) In the estimation of one periodical, the RIMR was now "probably the best equipped institution for the study of the causes and cure of disease to be found anywhere in the world"—high tribute for an outfit less than ten years old.[27] It was becoming the most richly endowed institute of its kind on earth, cranking out an enduring catalog of medical wonders.

More than a laboratory wizard, Flexner was a master talent scout. He collected brilliant strays, loners, and eccentrics who found the relaxed atmosphere of the institute congenial to their creative work. On his East River bluff, he marshaled an outstanding stable of scientific talent—he proudly dubbed them his prima donnas—including Paul Ehrlich and Jacques Loeb. Another inspired hire was a Japanese lab worker, Hideyo Noguchi, who would perform pathbreaking work in the study of syphilis. Flexner turned the institute into a series of autonomous departments, with each fiefdom shaped around a resident genius, while he kept close tabs on the central budget.

Flexner's most prescient decision was to recruit the French-born surgeon Dr. Alexis Carrel from Chicago. Short and thickset, with an erect, military bearing, Carrel was a Catholic mystic and diehard royalist. His future medical agenda was defined in 1894 when President Sadi Carnot of France was stabbed by an assassin and died from the hemorrhaging of a severed blood vessel. Then only twenty-one, Carrel turned to the puzzle of rejoining severed vessels and devised solutions that would facilitate blood transfusions, organ transplants, and other advanced surgical procedures. Rockefeller frequently told dinner guests the dramatic tale of how Dr. Carrel, in 1909, saved the life of a premature infant who developed *melena neonatorum,* a condition in which blood oozes from the digestive tract. In a wondrous operation, Carrel resuscitated the pallid infant by attaching a vein in its leg to the artery of its father, a New York physician; within minutes, a rosy flush suffused the baby's face. In 1912, Carrel won the Nobel Prize for medicine, the first ever awarded to a researcher in America.

Rockefeller was fortunate to have applied his money at the precise moment that medical research matured as a discipline and offered unbounded opportunities. None of the titan's other philanthropies was perhaps such an unqualified success. Bowing to a serviceable division of labor, Andrew Carnegie ceded medicine to Rockefeller. Once approached about building medical facilities, he smiled shrewdly and said, "That is Mr. Rockefeller's specialty. Go see him."[28]

After decades spent warding off abuse, Rockefeller and his entourage were delighted, perhaps even mildly surprised, by the unalloyed praise heaped upon the RIMR. Gates fairly glowed with pleasure: "The nicest ear can scarcely detect a single discordant note."[29] In pleading for money for the RIMR, Junior observed to his father that "none of the Foundations which you have established are so popular with the public generally or so free from criticism as the Institute. I feel, therefore, that large sums of money are, in a sense, safer there than in other fields."[30] Gates expanded on the theme that through medical research Rockefeller money touched everyone on earth and that "the values of medical research are the most universal values on earth, and they are the most intimate and important values to every human being that lives."[31] How could Rockefeller, long the target of almost universal obloquy, not embrace this new role of benefactor of all humanity? His gifts also reflected his own obsessive concern with longevity. When Carl Jung, the Swiss psychoanalyst, met Rockefeller in 1912, he recorded this impression: "He is almost exclusively preoccupied with his bodily health, thinking of different medicines, new diets and possibly new doctors!"[32]

In his inner circle, Rockefeller faced one boisterous critic of the RIMR: his golfing pal and crony Dr. Hamilton F. Biggar, a champion of homeopathy. A small-town doctor of the old school, Biggar was wont to pontificate: "We have too much laboratory and not enough bedside practice."[33] It was partly at Biggar's behest that Rockefeller had balked at the merger of the University of Chicago with the allopathic Rush Medical College. Under Biggar's influence, Rockefeller nearly refused to provide a $500,000 check to repair the Johns Hopkins Medical School after it was partially destroyed by fire in 1904—simply because the school refused to recognize homeopathy. Gates dismissed the work of Samuel Hahnemann, the German founder of homeopathy, as "the wild imaginings of a natural fool turned lunatic," and found it hard to endure Rockefeller's vestigial faith in what he saw as outdated medicine.[34] Although he often muzzled his strong views on the subject, Gates's real aim was to deliver a mortal blow to homeopaths—to shut their medical schools, expel them from medical societies, and strip them of hospital privileges—so as to clear the field for scientific medicine. Gates considered Biggar, if not a charlatan, at least a fossil and feared his rearguard attempts to undermine the RIMR.

At one point, antivivisection activists created an uproar about experiments at the RIMR, and Biggar leaped into the fray, complaining to Rockefeller about the cruelty inflicted on the lab animals. At this point, Gates decided to wipe out Biggar's influence forever. In several caustic memos to Rockefeller, he lashed out at the homeopaths: "Neither Dr. Biggar nor any of his Homeopathic friends have told you, so I think it in hand to tell you, this fact—that Homeopathy is rapidly dying out in this country"—ditto for allopathy. "Both are fading away as schools of medicine with the dawn of scientific inquiry. Both were wrong. The theories of both have been completely exploded in the last twenty-five years."[35] In an early version of the letter, never sent, Gates was even more outspoken. "Dr. Biggar has not kept up with the progress of medicine and is still living in the twilight of two or three generations ago."[36] In deference to his golfing partner, Rockefeller did not acknowledge these memos.

It was deeply ironic that Rockefeller retained such residual faith in homeopathy even as he financed the world's most sophisticated medical-research operation. Periodically, he had spasms of irritation, firing off letters on the need to save homeopathy, but these outbursts quickly passed. Through his philanthropies, Rockefeller did more than anyone else to destroy homeopathy in America, and in the end he seemed powerless to stop the scientific revolution that he himself had so largely set in motion.

In all, Rockefeller gave $61 million to the research institute. By the 1950s, it had bred so many imitators that it needed to change direction and was transformed from a research center into a specialized university offering only Ph.D.s and research fellowships. The name was officially changed to Rockefeller University in 1965. Its faculty roster became heavily laden with Nobel Prize winners, and by the 1970s it had housed sixteen of them. For the son of an itinerant vendor of dubious nostrums, this was a most implausible feat. The loftiest encomium to Rockefeller's impact in this field came from Winston Churchill, who wrote shortly before Rockefeller's death:

When history passes its final verdict on John D. Rockefeller, it may well be that his endowment of research will be recognized as a milestone in the progress of the race. For the first time, science was given its head; longer term experiment on a large scale has been made practicable, and those who undertake it are freed from the shadow of financial disaster. Science today owes as much to the rich men of generosity and discernment as the art of the Renaissance owes to the patronage of Popes and Princes. Of these rich men, John D. Rockefeller is the supreme type.[37]

A documentary photo used by the Rockefeller Sanitary
Commission in trying to stamp out hookworm in the South.
The small boy on the left suffered from the disease,
which had stunted his growth.
(Courtesy of the Rockefeller Archive Center)

The Millionaires' Special

I n April 1901, a specially chartered train, jammed with million-aires, pulled out of Manhattan and headed down the eastern seaboard for a ten-day tour of black colleges in the South, many of them financed with northern money, culminating in a confer-ence on southern education in Winston-Salem, North Carolina. The train car-ried so many tony members of New York, Boston, and Philadelphia high society that the press pejoratively tagged it "The Millionaires' Special." This swank excursion was the brainchild of department-store magnate Robert C. Ogden, an associate of John Wanamaker. Certain that the "betterment of hu-manity" was "demanded by Divine authority," Ogden coupled evangelical faith with a retailer's flair for publicity.[1] In calling attention to the backward state of southern schools, he hoped to seal an alliance between Yankee philanthropists and southern reformers, healing the sectional strife left over from the Civil War and bringing southern economic development up to parity with the North.

For one passenger, twenty-seven-year-old John D. Rockefeller, Jr., the trip kindled a fuse that would glow brightly for the rest of his life. Struggling with ethical quandaries at Standard Oil, he must have hungered for the purity of so-cial activism. Having led a circumscribed life, bounded by private schools, es-tates, and 26 Broadway, Junior welcomed this firsthand exposure to urgent social problems. The train rolled through a South pervaded by Jim Crow laws and riled by repeated outbreaks of racial violence. Literacy statistics conveyed a dismal story of derelict schools. While only 4.6 percent of the American pop-ulation was illiterate, the figure soared to 12 percent for southern whites and 50 percent for southern blacks. Educational reform had scarcely penetrated

the rural hinterlands and bayous of black communities, and their impoverished schools scandalized northern educators. Kentucky was the sole southern
state with compulsory school-attendance laws, which were then all but universal in the North. Yet as the rich philanthropists alighted at the celebrated
showcases of black education—Hampton Institute in Virginia, Tuskegee Normal and Industrial Institute in Alabama, the Rockefellers' own Spelman Seminary in Atlanta—the trip had its share of inspirational interludes. "The trip
has been a constant revelation to me," Junior told newspaper reporters upon
his return. "Tuskegee was especially interesting. Mr. [Booker T.] Washington is
a truly remarkable man. His school is doing a wonderful work for the race. I'm
glad I made the trip."[2] Junior described the journey to Ogden as "the most instructive experience of my life."[3] In an elated mood, he sat down and wrote an
enthusiastic report about it to his father.

Senior's interest in southern black education antedated this junket by two
decades, going back to 1882 when Spelman Seminary was still operating from
a leaky church basement. In his own travels through the South, he often attended black Baptist churches on Sunday mornings. Each of his children had
been matched to a black scholarship student whose education was paid for by
the family, and for several years Junior corresponded with his "adopted" black
student at Hampton Institute. In 1900, the Rockefeller family had virtually
made over the Spelman campus, paying for a new hospital, two dormitories, a
dining hall and kitchen, a power plant, and a residence for the school president.
During the 1901 train tour, Junior addressed students in the Spelman chapel
and was feted with gospel music. Noting the new buildings bequeathed by the
Rockefellers, the school's annual report that year rang with resounding hosannas for the family: "The Lord gives us all these wonderful blessings through the
generous hand of Hon. John D. Rockefeller."[4]

Before the 1901 trip, Senior had toyed with establishing a trust fund for
black education instead of funneling all his money through the American Baptist Education Society—part of his evolution away from the limitations of sectarian giving. That the 1901 trip might be the prelude to some big benefaction
was hinted at when Junior told Ogden, "For several years the question of colored education has been much in our minds and in our thoughts. We have en-
deavored to arrive at some plan which might help in working out this great
question."[5] For all the noble sentiments behind the Millionaires' Special, black
education remained an inflammatory issue among southern whites, who
feared it might weaken segregation. As the chartered train circled back toward
New York, the missionary spirit of the passengers suffered a jarring clash with
political realities when Henry St. George Tucker, the president of Washington
and Lee University, boarded the train in Virginia to deliver a rebuke to the prevailing euphoria:

If it is your idea to educate the Negro you must have the white of the South with you. If the poor white sees the son of a Negro neighbor enjoying through your munificence benefits denied to his boy, it raises in him a feeling that will render futile all your work. You must lift up the "poor white" and the Negro together if you would ever approach success.[6]

Perhaps because his auditors did not fully fathom the implications of this admonition, it was lustily applauded. If it tempered naive talk with a gritty touch of political realism, it also opened the way for some egregious concessions to the more bigoted southern whites.

As well-meaning, paternalistic men eager to alleviate the suffering of blacks but not wanting to threaten the established order, these rich northern reformers typified their time and were perhaps unusual only in having any concern for black welfare at all. Nevertheless, their political compromises rendered them vulnerable to charges of racism, especially among purists champing at piecemeal reform. One is frankly taken aback by the views of some of these men committed to bettering black education—views often indistinguishable from those of the southern whites they criticized. When Ogden convened a group called the Southern Education Board, its executive secretary, Edgar G. Murphy, declared that the two races "must dwell apart," "must live apart," and "must be schooled apart."[7] Even Frederick T. Gates yanked his children from the Montclair, New Jersey, public schools because "some of the colored and of the foreign-born children were ill mannered, filthy, and unsanitary."[8] He favored vocational training for blacks, not intellectual equality with whites. "Latin, Greek and metaphysics form a kind of knowledge that I fear with our colored brethren tend even more than with us to puff up rather than to build up," he had written ten years earlier. "The colored race is not ready it seems to me for high culture."[9] Such attitudes gave a foretaste of the way that the Rockefeller philanthropies would accommodate southern segregationists.

In the aftermath of the Millionaires' Special, Junior and Senior consulted many experts on southern education, including Booker T. Washington, who joined them one Sunday night for tea on West Fifty-fourth Street. Washington, too, endorsed practical, vocational training for blacks, not exposure to abstract subjects. On February 27, 1902, flanked by Abby in an oak-paneled study of their house, Junior chaired a meeting of ten men to consider southern education. Swirling brandy snifters and warmed by a blazing fire, they talked until well after midnight, hatching plans for a new philanthropy to be launched with a one-million-dollar gift from Senior. Junior hoped to name it the Negro Education Board, but it was, tellingly, given the neutral name of the General Education Board (GEB) instead. On the same colossal scale as everything else attached to Rockefeller, it would turn into the world's foremost educational foundation. It was an extension of the ABES with the Baptist trappings pared away.

With crisp efficiency, Senator Aldrich shepherded an incorporation bill through Congress in January 1903, making it the only Rockefeller philanthropy to enjoy the public endorsement of a perpetual, federal charter.[10] Banishing the former accent on black education, the elastic charter delineated the group's aim as "the promotion of education within the United States without distinction of race, sex or creed." With the Tarbell series under way, Rockefeller kept a salutary distance from his new foundation. Where he hovered over the RIMR at one remove, he delegated more power in the GEB to his son and never met with its board. As Abraham Flexner later wrote of Senior's detachment, "I recall that when in 1914 I wrote a history of the General Education Board from 1902 to 1914 we searched the files of the General Education Board in vain in order to obtain a facsimile of his signature to be placed beneath the lithograph prefaced to the text. There was not a single letter in the files of the Board which bore his signature."[11] Nevertheless, Junior and Gates reported regularly to Rockefeller, who, along with his son, reserved the right to designate the use of two-thirds of the money given. Rockefeller believed that certain universal principles of businesslike efficiency should apply to nonprofit ventures no less than to profit-making ones. In making his first million-dollar appropriation to the GEB, he stipulated that the money should be ladled out over ten years. He tried to influence the pace and scope of his philanthropies, not their contents, and ensure measured, fiscally responsible growth.

For executive secretary, Gates shrewdly chose Dr. Wallace Buttrick, a fellow graduate of the Rochester Theological Seminary and an ex-Baptist preacher. Like Gates, Buttrick renounced the pulpit for philanthropy and more worldly satisfactions. It was no accident that so many ex-ministers flocked to the sanctuary of the Rockefeller philanthropies, which advanced secular causes with an evangelical spirit. An amiable, roly-poly man, blessed with an easy laugh, Buttrick brought consuming dedication to his work. When a minister inquired, "What is your idea of Heaven?" he rejoined, "My office."[12]

As a former board member of the American Baptist Home Mission Society, Buttrick had studied black mission schools in the South exhaustively. On his office wall, he had a large map, sprinkled with colored pins, showing the major American educational facilities. Where Gates was an uncompromising, table-thumping orator, Buttrick brought a statesman's tact to the job, defusing tense situations with humor. Without offending applicants, he could deftly expose weaknesses in their projects. His intuitions were so exact that Gates said Buttrick had "cat's whiskers; he feels objects before he gets to them."[13] His greatest drawback—and a real one—was that he thought it expedient to truckle to white supremacists to maintain GEB operations in the South. He told an audience of Tennessee school superintendents, "The Negro is an inferior race—the Anglo-Saxon is superior. There cannot be any question about that."[14]

To endow the board with a safely conservative cast, Gates preferred "successful business men who would steer the ship along traditional lines and would not be carried out of their course by any temporary breeze or even by hurricanes of sentiment."[15] The first chairman was William H. Baldwin, president of the Long Island Railroad, a vocal apostle for black education—so long as white people stayed on top. Of the southern black, Baldwin observed, "He will willingly fill the more menial positions, and do the heavy work, at less wages, than the American white man or any foreign race which has yet come to our shores. This will permit the Southern white laborer to perform the more expert labor, and to leave the fields, the mines, and the simpler trades for the Negro."[16] With such men at the helm, the GEB, for all its good works, would fall considerably short of heaven. Neither Junior nor Senior held such baldly racist sentiments, but they agreed that the board had to accommodate retrograde southern views in order to function. It is interesting to note in this context that Standard Oil of Ohio did not hire its first permanent black employee until 1906.

At the beginning, the well-heeled GEB grafted its work onto that of the Southern Education Board, the shoestring operation started by Robert Ogden. Taking up its cause, the GEB campaigned in the South to improve educational standards, taking as its first major mission the creation of high schools. Before Reconstruction, no southern state except for Tennessee had tax-supported educational systems. As a legacy of this history, the four-year high school was practically nonexistent in the region, and there was not a single such school for blacks; many high schools were really extra rooms crudely tacked on to elementary schools. The GEB identified the creation of new high schools as a top priority, since their graduates would furnish teachers for lower-grade schools and also provide a bumper crop of college students, magnifying reform efforts up and down the educational ladder.

Lacking the resources to create a complete high-school system, the GEB established a pattern mimicked by future Rockefeller philanthropies. Rather than trying to accomplish everything through its own budget, it would awaken public opinion and stimulate government action. It took on a crusading spirit, borrowed from the Baptists, and sent forth circuit riders to proselytize for the cause. Ironically, as Standard Oil took a hostile attitude toward state and federal antitrust suits, Rockefeller was forging extensive public-private partnerships for social change. The GEB paid the salaries of special professors at state universities who would roam the state, pinpoint sites for high schools, then drum up political support from local taxpayers. These professors were also affiliated with state education departments, giving a necessary political camouflage at a time when Rockefeller's name was still anathema across America. So revolutionary was the impact of GEB money that by 1910 it had helped bring into being eight hundred southern high schools.

The GEB was repeatedly blocked in its original ambition to foster black education. Submitting to racism, the foundation limited its support to a "very few" counties that could yield "the largest permanent results," in Buttrick's words.[17] Only in 1914 did the organization hire rural school agents for *both* races in the South, and even then it tended to hire white agents for black schools and continued to encourage schools to teach blacks useful trades and ignore their minds. In the end, it came in for biting criticism from blacks such as W.E.B. Du Bois who did not want to see the school system slot blacks into menial jobs. Du Bois later excoriated the GEB in his autobiography for supporting the idea "that the races in the schools should be separated socially; that colored schools should be chiefly industrial; and that every effort should be made to conciliate southern white opinion."[18] While the GEB achieved remarkable things in upgrading southern education, it failed to deliver major results where it had originally wanted them most: in black education. In the end, nine-tenths of the GEB's money went to white schools or to promote medical education—a sorry sequel for a foundation that was supposed to be called the Negro Education Board.

In 1905, the GEB extended its purview to higher education with a $10 million gift from Rockefeller, followed by another $32 million in 1907—hailed by the board as "the largest sum ever given by a man in the history of the race for any social or philanthropic purposes."[19] (It would be equivalent to $500 million today.) Much of this last gift was routed to the University of Chicago. As the GEB bolstered college and university endowments, it applied the rules that Rockefeller had insisted upon, often futilely, with William Rainey Harper: that gifts should stimulate matching grants; that local communities should help to take up the financial burden of their schools; that universities should be founded in population centers with thriving economic bases; and that endowment income should not cover more than half the operating expenses.

＝

Not long after the GEB was started, it became woefully evident that the defects of southern education could not be remedied without stronger local economies. Gates was struck by this revelation as he and Buttrick took a train excursion through the South. He was staring out the window and ruminating when he suddenly exclaimed: "This is a favored section of the world. It has a superb climate, an abundance of fertile soil, and no end of labor. It must be enriched so that it can properly tax itself if it is to support education and public health. It is your job, Buttrick, to find out how."[20]

Nobody ever accused Gates of thinking small. If education depended upon healthy tax rolls, then they would lift the entire tax base of the South. And if that meant enhancing the productivity of southern agriculture, well, so be it. Such was the godlike perspective, if not the mortal hubris, made possible by great wealth. Where other philanthropic executives could only tinker, the Rockefeller proconsuls were urged to indulge more spacious fantasies.

In the spring of 1906, Gates and Buttrick traveled to Washington to meet with a pioneering scientist at the Department of Agriculture, Dr. Seaman A. Knapp, a former teacher, editor, and gospel preacher. In his experimental farmwork, Knapp had striven toward something analogous to Rockefeller's work in medicine: He tried to bring a scientific spirit to a business bogged down in ancient folklore. Three years earlier, Knapp had gained legendary status when he saved Texas from a boll-weevil infestation that threatened to destroy its cotton industry; farms were deserted and counties depopulated as panicky people despaired of ever again profiting from the crop. If this situation was duplicated in the cotton-dependent South, it would presage disaster. By establishing a demonstration farm in Terrell, Texas, Knapp showed how the boll-weevil plague could be contained through the careful selection of seeds accompanied by intensive farming. From that time, Knapp kept an eye out for private money to enlarge his project. Now, the seventy-three-year-old Knapp and Agriculture Secretary James Wilson met with Gates and Buttrick, who gratified Knapp's dreams by calling for the sort of public-private partnership that was fast becoming a GEB trademark. If the Agriculture Department drew up plans and supervised the farm-demonstration projects, the project would be greased with monthly checks from the GEB.

In the following years, Rockefeller money helped stamp out boll weevils and improve the yield of southern crops and livestock, swelling the tax base to support public schools. By 1912, more than 100,000 farms had altered the way they cultivated cotton and other crops as a direct result of demonstration work done jointly by the GEB and the U.S. Department of Agriculture.

—

Emboldened by such feats, the Rockefeller philanthropies steadily expanded their southern programs, among which the most successful was the campaign to eradicate hookworm. As had happened with Dr. Knapp, this odyssey started out with the dispiriting quest of a frustrated dreamer on the federal payroll, Dr. Charles Wardell Stiles.

When the United States acquired Puerto Rico after the Spanish-American War, an army surgeon named Dr. Ashford made a startling discovery: Many poor islanders thought to suffer from malaria were actually infected with hookworm. The son of a Methodist minister, Stiles had crisscrossed the South for years for the U.S. Public Health Service. Based on Ashford's work, he was seized by the wild surmise that the poor whites of the South—infamous in popular myth for their indolent, sluggish lives—might be suffering from hookworm. In September 1902, outfitted with just a microscope, Dr. Stiles journeyed through the South examining human feces, and, sure enough, he found hookworm eggs everywhere. It was an exhilarating discovery, since hookworm could be cured with fifty cents' worth of salts and thymol.

When Dr. Stiles reported these results at a Washington, D.C., medical convention that December, he stated that southerners long considered lazy were simply enervated by hookworm. His remarks were greeted with both profound outrage and mocking amusement. The next day, the *New York Sun* published the lecture under the whimsical headline, "Germ of Laziness Found?" Stiles was aghast: He was being turned into a figure of fun, his great finding trivialized by interminable hookworm jokes. As a zoologist—and therefore presumed ignorant of the human body—he fared no better among physicians: Dr. William Osler went so far as to deny hookworm's existence in America. Few doctors were prepared to accept that the chronic anemia or continuous malaria commonly attributed to poor whites was, in fact, caused by hookworm, contracted by barefoot people through their soles.

For several years, Dr. Stiles persevered in his crusade to locate private money to apply his theory, and he found an unexpected champion in 1908 when President Roosevelt appointed him to a commission on country life. While touring the South that November, he told another member of the commission, Walter Hines Page, a North Carolina native, that a shuffling, misshapen man on a train platform was suffering from hookworm, not laziness or congenital idiocy. "Fifty cents worth of drugs would make that man a useful citizen in a few weeks," he said flatly.[21] He explained to Page that thymol pried the hookworms loose from the intestine walls—some victims harbored up to five thousand in their systems—and then epsom salts flushed them from the body. As a board member of the Rockefeller Institute, Page was the perfect ambassador to bring Stiles to Rockefeller's attention.

At the end of their tour, Stiles and Page stopped at Cornell University for a reception, where Stiles met a round, jovial man who had already been briefed by Page: Wallace Buttrick. The two men went back to Buttrick's hotel room and "talked hookworm almost all night."[22] After years of useless speeches, Stiles was now dazed by the dreamlike speed of events. Back in Washington, he got a telegram summoning him to a New York meeting with Gates and Simon Flexner of the RIMR. After delivering a monologue and showing slides for forty minutes, Gates interrupted him to bring Starr Murphy into the meeting. "This is the biggest proposition ever put up to the Rockefeller office," Gates told Murphy. "Listen to what Dr. Stiles has to say. Now, Doctor, start from the beginning again and tell Mr. Murphy what you have told me."[23] These sessions lasted for two days, and by the end Gates and his fellows were sold on a mass-mobilization program to eradicate hookworm from the South. It was an ideal opportunity for large-scale philanthropy: Here was a condition that could be easily diagnosed and cheaply cured, with an estimated two million victims in the South. The results would be rapid and visible, giving the program more populist appeal than the rarefied work of the medical-research institute. It would, in short, simultaneously serve the overlapping objectives of science, philanthropy, and Rockefeller public relations.

Junior was deputed, as was so often the case, to sell his father on the need for a commission to fight hookworm. Although Stiles had modestly suggested a half-million dollars, Gates fixed on one million dollars as a nice round sum that would capture the South's attention. Since the region remained touchy about any assumption that it was riddled with listless imbeciles, Junior reassured his father that the board would recruit a southern contingent. On October 20, 1909, Junior implored him to act fast and stake out a leadership role in the hookworm fight. Two days later, Rockefeller replied: "Answering your letter 20th with reference to hook worm, it seems to me that $1,000,000 is a very large amount to promise, but I will consent to this sum, with the understanding that I shall be conferred with step by step and consent to whatever appropriations are made from time to time. This, however, need only be known to such as you choose to have know it."[24] Since Rockefeller had started to take winter golfing vacations at the Hotel Bon Air in Augusta, Georgia, he derived special pleasure from the gift. As he said, "It has been my pleasure of late to spend a portion of each year in the South and I have come to know and to respect greatly that part of the country and to enjoy the society and friendship of many of its warm-hearted people."[25]

As expected, many southern editors reacted to the hookworm campaign as a calculated affront to their honor and dignity. Originally, the effort was to be known as the Rockefeller Sanitary Commission for the Eradication of Hookworm in the South. To avoid stigmatizing the South, it was shortened to the Rockefeller Sanitary Commission or even the U.S. Sanitary Commission. Instead of being based in New York, like other Rockefeller programs, it opened in 1910 in Washington, D.C., diplomatically south of the Mason-Dixon line.

The executive secretary was a Tennessee native, Dr. Wickliffe Rose. Another clergyman's son, Rose, forty-seven, was a shy, immaculate man who often wore bow ties and stared primly through wire-rimmed spectacles or pince-nez. Steeped in the writings of Kant and Hegel, grounded in the Latin and Greek classics, and fond of writing poetry in French, he had been dean of Peabody College and the University of Nashville before becoming general agent of the Peabody Education Fund, where he came to the GEB's attention. The courtly Rose, modest and painstakingly thorough, supplied both the tact and determination that made the hookworm campaign a smashing success.

In mapping out his strategy, Rose adopted the GEB model of using Rockefeller money as a catalyst for government cooperation. The first order of business was a detailed survey to identify the centers of hookworm infestation. Once again, the states were urged to hire sanitation directors to educate the public about the menace. State medical boards sent young doctors into rural areas, their salaries paid by Rockefeller money. These campaigns were often carried out under the auspices of state health boards, thus providing political protection. As Gates privately explained this decision, "To put Mr. Rockefeller's name prominently forward . . . would impair the usefulness of the work."[26] This was doubly necessary since many southern communities saw the Sanitary Commission's work as a degrading new form of northern carpetbagging. Yet for all the efforts to shroud Rockefeller's involvement, many southerners knew the program's real sponsorship and devised preposterous theories to explain it. One was that Rockefeller was entering the shoe business and financed the hookworm campaign to accustom southerners to wearing shoes year-round, instead of only during the winter months.

The campaign relied on extensive publicity and showy gimmicks, and it sent out "health trains" with traveling exhibitions on modern sanitation. Perhaps the single most important factor in its success was the introduction of dispensaries for public-health work. In 1910, only two southern counties had such dispensaries. That number burgeoned to 208 counties within three years, thanks to Rockefeller money. To coax crowds into these dispensaries, the field workers (in a manner oddly reminiscent of Doc Rockefeller) distributed handbills saying, "See the hookworms and the various intestinal parasites that man is heir to."[27] In the rousing spirit of tent revival meetings, rural people formed long lines and gaped at hookworm eggs through microscopes or examined them squirming in bottles. Because infected people were cured swiftly, it seemed no less miraculous than faith healing to many people, and the throngs often erupted into singing "Onward Christian Soldiers." In a single day in 1911, 454 people were cured of the disease. One field director in Kentucky wrote, "I have never seen the people at any place so wrought up and so full of interest and enthusiasm."[28] Except for Florida, every southern state joined in the program.

Pretty soon, the gentle, decorous Wickliffe Rose ran an operation of military scope. During the first year of work, 102,000 people were examined in nine southern states, and 43,000 were identified with hookworm. At the end of five years, Gates reported to Rockefeller that nearly half a million people had been cured. While the disease had not been extirpated completely, it had been reduced drastically. "Hookworm disease has not only been recognized, bounded and limited," Gates boasted to Rockefeller, "it has been reduced to one of the minor infections of the south, perhaps the most easily and universally recognized and cured of all."[29] Most important, the states had set up machinery to perpetuate the work and avert backsliding. Lauding the campaign as "well planned and well executed," Rockefeller especially praised its deft diplomatic touch in dealing with a politically charged situation. The Rockefeller Sanitary Commission was a landmark in epidemiology and preventive medicine, as Charles W. Eliot recognized when he called it "the most effective campaign against a widespread disabling disease which medical science and philanthropy have ever combined to conduct."[30] In 1913, the newly formed Rockefeller Foundation asked Wickliffe Rose to take the hookworm campaign abroad, extending the fight to fifty-two countries on six continents and freeing millions of people from this worldwide scourge.

≡

By 1910, medicine and education had emerged as the top priorities of the Rockefeller philanthropies, and that year the two trends fruitfully dovetailed. The stimulus was a report with the deceptively bland title *Medical Education in the United States and Canada*. Its author, Abraham Flexner, was the brother of RIMR director Simon. Where Simon was precise and conciliatory, Abe was a combative iconoclast who relished a good intellectual brawl. After graduating from Johns Hopkins, he started a small, innovative private school in Louisville that won a fine reputation among Ivy League colleges. He had the maverick's talent for casting a fresh, critical eye on practices sanctified by custom, and he provoked a national debate when he proposed that students should graduate college in three years.

When the Carnegie Foundation for the Advancement of Teaching invited him to survey American and Canadian medical schools, Abe pleaded ignorance, but with typical zealousness he visited all 155 schools and came away appalled by the experience. Like his brother, he took the Johns Hopkins Medical School as his model of a competent school. "Without this pattern in the back of my head," he admitted later, "I could have accomplished little."[31] By contrast, the majority of schools he visited seemed to be dreary, haphazard affairs, run negligently by local doctors to supplement their income from private practice.

As Flexner doggedly made the rounds, nobody realized that he was the exterminating angel who would snuff out many fly-by-night institutions. The tableaux he described would have been richly satirical had they not been strictly accurate reportage. Since most medical schools relied solely upon tuition fees and could not afford modern equipment, they still languished in the dark ages of medicine. In Washington State, Flexner asked the dean of one school whether they had a physiology lab. "Surely," said the dean. "I have it upstairs. I will bring it to you." And he proudly produced a little pulse-taking device. One osteopathic school in Iowa had desks, blackboards, and chairs but could not muster any charts or scientific apparatus. Of the 155 schools, only 23 required more than a high-school education. Since some schools did not even demand that, they were not exactly bursting with brainpower.

In 1910, Flexner published his polemic, known as the Flexner Report—the most pitiless and influential indictment of medical education ever printed. Naming the most notorious diploma mills, the report sparked furious debate, and more than one hundred schools either perished in the ensuing controversy or were absorbed by universities. Among the major casualties were the quaint homeopathic schools so dear to John D. Rockefeller, Sr. Already in decline, the schools were dealt a lethal blow by the Flexner Report.

Gates devoured the report. Disgusted with medical practice, he believed that young doctors ended up either as "confirmed pessimists, disappointed and cha-grined, or else mere reckless 'pill-slingers' for money."[32] With a big pile of cash at his disposal, Gates would not let the Flexner Report gather dust. When he in-vited the author to lunch, Flexner pointed to two maps in his book—one show-ing the locations of the medical schools he visited, the other showing what the country needed. "How much would it cost to convert the first map into the sec-ond?" Gates asked, and Flexner replied, "It might cost a billion dollars." "All right," Gates announced, "we've got the money. Come down here and we'll give it to you."[33] When Gates asked Flexner how he would spend the first million to overhaul medical research, he said, "I should give it to Dr. Welch."[34] Thus, Welch's Johns Hopkins Medical School was consecrated as the prototype to be emulated by recipients of Rockefeller money. Hopkins ran its lab departments on a full-time basis, with many faculty members applying themselves solely to teaching and research, a pattern that Gates wished to see duplicated every-where. Never before had a rich benefactor spent his money in this area. As Dr. Welch said, "It marked . . . the first large public recognition of medical educa-tion and medical research as a rewarding subject of philanthropy."[35]

In 1913, Flexner formalized his ties with Rockefeller and joined the GEB staff. Flexner and his cohorts singled out well-regarded institutions—Vander-bilt University in the South, the University of Chicago in the Midwest—to serve as regional models. Medical schools that wanted Rockefeller grants had to up-grade entrance standards, institute four-year programs, and adopt the full-time teaching approach. This movement to universalize the Johns Hopkins model proceeded even though it had one highly disgruntled critic: John D. Rockefeller, Sr., who still waged a lonely battle for an alternate form of medi-cine. "I am a homeopathist," he complained to Starr Murphy in 1916. "I desire that homeopaths should have fair, courteous and liberal treatment extended to them from all medical institutions to which we contribute." To Rockefeller's credit, he did not pull rank on his advisers and often yielded to their judgments, even when they ran counter to his personal wishes. "I am glad to have the aid of experienced men who are able to sift out the applications and give to the deserving," he once said. "I am not a good one to judge such things: I am too soft-hearted."[36]

In the spring of 1919, the GEB asked its founder for fifty million dollars to extend scientific medical education across the country, the world war having exposed the poor health of many soldiers and the inadequacy of base hospitals. For months, Rockefeller retreated into one of his baffling silences. Just when his lieutenants despaired of a response, he sent a letter pledging about $20 million for the project—a bonanza soon expanded to $50 million. By the time Flexner left the GEB in 1928, it had distributed more than $78 million to propagate the scientific approach to medical education. The sum total of these developments resulted in nothing less than a revolution in medical education. Doc Rockefeller's son had banished laggards from the profession and introduced a new era of enlightenment in American medicine. In its thirty-year existence, the GEB dispensed $130 million, equal to more than $1 billion today.

=

While keeping apart from the management of the RIMR and the GEB, Rockefeller remained more involved with the University of Chicago. Paradoxically, it was the philanthropic effort that most frustrated him and most frequently violated his charitable principles. Meant as an incentive to lure money from Chicago businessmen, his initial endowment had, perversely, deterred people from giving. Reams of press coverage presented the university as Rockefeller's hobbyhorse. In 1903, *Life* magazine ran a cartoon of Ye Rich Rockefeller University, showing a lady holding aloft a lamp marked Standard Oil, her robes checkered with dollar signs. Though Rockefeller studiously avoided the campus and visited only three times (1897, 1901, and 1903), he got little credit for this self-abnegation. The public was quick to pounce on his every move as yet another ruse. As Gates wearily recalled:

> The people of Chicago had ceased to give except in driblets. A hostile press often spoke of the University as if it were Standard Oil propaganda, its policies always dictated by the Founder, its professors subject to dismissal if they were other than mouthpieces of him, the splendid architectural creation of the Midway Plaisance was a monument to the glory of John D. Rockefeller, erected and maintained in his personal interest.[37]

This myth inverted the truth, as Ida Tarbell's spy Hiram Brown reported to J. M. Siddall. "Hiram says that John D. talks about Chicago University a good deal, but that he never brags about the money that he has given it, and that he never indicates that it is his private property," Siddall reported. "He says that John D. talks about the men who teach in the University a great deal, and that he is constantly bragging about their ability and the great things they are doing."[38] In the one area in which Rockefeller *did* openly intervene—university finances—he was powerless to brake the spendthrift Dr. William Rainey Harper. Each year, Rockefeller reluctantly gave another million dollars to bolster the permanent endowment to keep pace with his free-spending president. Though Rockefeller kept complaining about the chronic deficits, Harper ignored the founder's warnings, and relations grew very strained between him and Gates. Rockefeller hated being pressured, and Gates always believed that had Harper asked for less, Rockefeller would have willingly given much more. Then, in December 1903, Harper and the trustees were called to New York for a special session in Rockefeller's private office. In a dreadful miscalculation, Harper made an appeal for *more* money, despite the previous year's shortfall. When polled in Harper's presence, not a single trustee endorsed his position— a humiliating blow. That night, Senior and Junior huddled, and the next day Junior informed the board that his father would not add a penny to the endowment until the budget gap was plugged. Harper was strictly forbidden from enlarging existing departments or adding new ones. If harrowing for Harper, the episode was also distressing for Rockefeller, who had a fatherly feeling toward him.

Harper's health, meanwhile, was being undermined by his perpetual exertions. In 1903, he kept complaining of fatigue, yet he was congenitally incapable of moderation. As his son said, "He had frequently told the family that he knew he was shortening his life by the way he was doing his work, but explained to the family that he felt the work could be done better by this method." Three months after his showdown with Rockefeller, Harper underwent an appendectomy. The doctors found evidence of cancer but were unsure of their diagnosis and delayed telling him until February 1905. By then, the malignancy had grown incurable and Harper minced no words with Gates: "It is as clearly a case of execution announced beforehand as it could possibly be."[39]

When Rockefeller heard the news, he was distraught. "He cannot bring himself yet even to attempt to express his feelings," Gates told Harper.[40] On February 16, 1905, he wrote Harper a letter whose laconic eloquence says much about the affection he felt for this flawed but deeply inspiring educator:

> You are constantly in my thoughts. The feelings which I have always cherished toward you are intensified at this time. I glory in your marvelous courage and strength, and confidently hope for the best. I have the greatest satisfaction and pleasure in our united efforts for the university and I am full of hope for its future. No man could have filled your place.
> With highest esteem and tenderest affection.[41]

A few days later, about to undergo surgery, Harper repaid the tribute: "You have stood by me loyally; I can ask nothing more. The enterprise has proven to be larger and greater than we could have anticipated, but here it is—a splendid institution, and I know that you and your family will stand by it to the end."[42]

Harper continued to write and teach, even though he was wasting away from cancer. In August 1905, he made a final visit to his patron at Forest Hill. Though Ida Tarbell had just published her acid character portrait of Rockefeller, he seemed philosophic. As Harper said, "He believes that this is all providential, and that he is to be thoroughly vindicated. It is a subject, however, which still occupies a large part of his mind. . . . I have never known him to be more genial or communicative."[43] The two men spent bittersweet hours repairing the damage done to their friendship in recent years.

In January 1906, lying on his deathbed, William Rainey Harper, who had always had one eye fixed on heaven, the other on earthly prospects, called in two close friends, Ernest D. Burton and Albion W. Small. He had courted Rockefeller and his fortune during a period of extraordinary public outrage against Standard Oil, and now he seemed haunted, restless, his mind darkened by doubt. "I have not followed Jesus Christ as closely as I ought to have done," he confessed to his friends. "I have come down from the plane on which I ought to have lived. I have justified it to myself at times as necessary because I was carrying so heavy loads. But I see now that it was all wrong."[44] On January 10, 1906, he died at age fifty.

In the following days, Rockefeller's mind returned to the exuberant period of his and Harper's early planning for the university. Harper's death perhaps affected him more than that of any colleague or friend. As he wrote the new university president, Harry Pratt Judson, "I am personally conscious of having met with an irreparable loss in his death. It seems a mysterious providence that he should have been cut off in the prime of his life and the height of his usefulness. I mourn him as though a member of my own family had been taken, and the sense of loss increases as the days go by."[45] Seldom did Rockefeller strike such a poignant note. For all his criticism of Harper's improvidence, he recognized his supreme achievement in creating a school equivalent to an Ivy League college in little more than a decade. Soon after Harper's death, he announced plans to build a campus library in Harper's memory and provided a $100,000 endowment to support his widow. In a no-less-fitting memorial, he agreed to close the budget deficit for 1906–1907. If Judson lacked Harper's vision and eloquence, he was a cautious administrator and sound budget planner—exactly the custodial figure the institution needed.

In 1907, Gates and Junior quietly began to lobby Senior to drop the requirement that the university and a majority of the trustees be Baptists. The school's fund-raising was hampered by its denominational character. Rockefeller was always of two minds on the matter, wanting the institution to remain under Baptist auspices while also arguing that it should be "conducted in a spirit of the widest liberality" with students drawn from every class of society.[46] For two years, Rockefeller deliberated before consenting to abolish the university's denominational link. Yet this bold step was easy compared to the next one contemplated by his advisers. By 1908, Rockefeller had spent $24 million on the university, but the Chicago citizenry had not lifted the burden from his shoulders. One evening in late 1908, Gates held a conference in his Montclair home with Harry Pratt Judson and Starr Murphy. "What would be the greatest service Mr. Rockefeller could now render the University?" Gates asked Judson and then promptly answered his own question: "Dr. Judson, the greatest possible service Mr. Rockefeller could now render to the University would be to separate himself from it altogether, withdraw his representatives, and turn it absolutely over to the public forever."[47] When Judson protested that the university was still incomplete and sorely in need of funds, Gates said that Rockefeller might make one final large gift before departing.

Bent upon this plan, Gates managed to convince Junior who, in turn, tried to win over his father, who was flabbergasted by the suggestion and silently tabled it. When Junior renewed the subject in early 1909, his father rejected it categorically. "I confess the thought rather staggers me. . . . The institution is so large and far reaching in its influence and we have been such a potent factor in its upbuilding that I tremble at the possibility of cutting loose from our relation and leaving it a great craft in the middle of the ocean."[48] Though the campaign started out less than promisingly, Gates and Junior knew that major decisions were often protracted with Rockefeller. In November 1909, Junior suggested that his father make a last ten-million-dollar contribution to the school then cut loose forever. "Few men have founded great institutions and have had the courage to wean them," he said.[49]

A few weeks later, Gates weighed in with a letter that must rank as a seminal document in American philanthropy. It argued that a donor's highest ideal should be to give birth to an institution that would then enjoy a life totally independent of him. Gates noted that many schools—technology, agriculture, forestry, and others—were still needed to complete the university but that the money for them would not issue from other sources so long as Rockefeller was the university's patron. During the previous seven years, he had given nearly $12 million, while the midwestern public had given only $931,000—a pittance. Rockefeller's withdrawal was imperative on political grounds as well:

> It will conclusively demonstrate the fact which the public has not been able to grasp—the fact of your entire disinterestedness. It will disclose beyond possibility of cavil that your motives in founding the institution are solely to bless and benefit your fellow men; that you have not been seeking through it to increase your personal power, to propagate your political views, to help your cause, or to glorify your name.

Noting that other rich men demanded control, Gates went on:

Mr. Carnegie is, I believe, a member of every Board which he creates, and of course, the managing member. Mr. Clark, who founded Clark University, undisguisedly and notoriously ran the institution until his death. Mr. Stanford died soon after designating his property for the Leland Stanford, Jr. University. His wife, however, took up the reins and openly conducted the University for many years, demanding openly the dismissal of professors uncongenial to her and supervising every detail of administration.

In closing, Gates urged Rockefeller to withdraw from the university and set his creation free.[50]

At first, Rockefeller did not reply or even acknowledge this letter, yet it set up far-reaching reverberations in his mind. Gates's practical arguments must have counted heavily with him, but the idea of subordinating his ego to some larger institutional end would also have appealed to his religious sense of self-denial. He also believed that the "dead hand of fixed endowments" should not trap future generations with the outmoded agenda of the original donors. Perhaps for all these reasons, Rockefeller made a final $10 million payment to the University of Chicago in December 1910, bringing his total gifts to $35 million, or $540 million in 1996 dollars, then bid it farewell forever. In a valedictory to the board, he wrote, "It is far better that the University be supported and enlarged by the gifts of many than by those of a single donor. . . . I am acting on an early and permanent conviction that this great institution being the property of the people should be controlled, conducted and supported by the people."[51] The withdrawal was not quite as total as Rockefeller implied. Between 1910 and 1932, the GEB and other Rockefeller philanthropies channeled $35 million to the university, supplemented by another $6 million from Junior. But Rockefeller, in a statesmanlike act, had established the concept of the patron as founder, not owner or overseer, of his creation. At their December 1910 meeting, the trustees of the university paid tribute to Rockefeller: "Mr. Rockefeller has never permitted the University to bear his name, and consented to be called its founder only at the urgent request of the Board of Trustees. He has never suggested the appointment or the removal of any professor. Whatever views may have been expressed by members of the faculty, he has neither indicated either assent or dissent."[52]

—

In the early 1900s, there was a well-nigh universal perception that John D. gave generously to philanthropy to fumigate his fortune. As Governor Robert M. La Follette said in 1905, "I read yesterday that Rockefeller has been to prayer meeting again; tomorrow he will be giving to some college or university. He gives with two hands, but he robs with many. If he should live a thousand years he could not expiate the crime he has committed. . . . He is the greatest criminal of the age."[53] Cartoonists stereotyped Rockefeller as a churchgoing hypocrite. One cartoon showed him as an angel with wings sprouting from his head, beneath the caption: "John the Baptist: High Finance Is Now Getting So High That Some People Expected to Get to Heaven from the Top of It."[54]

Were John D.'s donations as saintly as he claimed? Could he possibly have been insensible to the political impact of his good deeds? An internal memo written to George Rogers in 1906 sheds some light on this intriguing question. To assist Standard Oil in its political travails, Archbold asked Rockefeller in October 1906 to publish a list of the dozen or so colleges to which he had given significant endowments. Rockefeller was extremely reluctant to print such a list. "It is a thing we have never done before," he advised Rogers, "and is very distasteful to me, and would not be considered for a moment, only with the idea that it might prove of help to us in the Standard Oil Company." If a list was made up, he wanted a guarantee that it would be returned and destroyed, blotting out any trace of his complicity.[55] This letter generally vindicates Rockefeller's assertion that he did not exploit his philanthropy for selfish reasons, but it also shows that he occasionally bent his own rules. H. G. Wells was mostly right when he wrote in a 1934 book that "of all the base criticisms [Rockefeller's] career has evoked, the charge that his magnificently intelligent endowments have been planned to buy off criticism or save his soul from the slow but sure vindictiveness of his Baptist God is surely the most absurd."[56] Since his adolescence, charity had been interwoven with the fabric of his life.

Nevertheless, the press treated each Rockefeller donation as another bid to buy back his reputation. Never was this truer than during the tainted-money controversy that flared up in March 1905, when it was revealed that Rockefeller had given $100,000 to the American Board of Commissioners for Foreign Missions, a Congregational group in Boston, likely the largest gift the group had ever received. Coming at the close of the Tarbell series, this farsighted gift was bound to stir up a hornet's nest of controversy.

With the creation of the GEB, Rockefeller had begun to funnel money to nondenominational groups and transcend religious giving altogether. Gates, who regarded sectarianism as "the curse of religion at home and abroad, a blight upon religion, whether viewed from an economic, intellectual, or spiritual standpoint," eagerly encouraged this trend.[57] As this lapsed minister jettisoned the Baptist Church, his Christianity sounded increasingly like high-minded social work. "My religion became . . . simply the service of humanity in the Spirit of Jesus. It is the religion of Jesus, of science, and of evolution alike."[58] In his papers, Gates left a startling memo, "The Spirit of True Religion," which he apparently wrote to clarify his thoughts and in which he candidly stated, "There is no essential difference between religion and morality except that the one is more intense and passionate than the other."[59] In 1903, he bluntly told one applicant that while Rockefeller was a Baptist, he would no longer establish Baptist schools "for the sole purpose of propagating those views which are peculiarly and distinctively Baptist."[60]

The $100,000 gift of what came to be called tainted money was solicited by Dr. James L. Barton, who met one Sunday with Starr Murphy and Gates in the latter's Montclair home. While Gates did not initiate the meeting, he did recommend to Rockefeller that he contribute the $100,000. In a letter to Rockefeller, Gates made a secular case for this missionary money, again showing that Rockefeller was capable of responding to explicitly worldly rationales for religious giving:

> Quite apart from the question of persons converted, the mere commercial results of missionary effort to our own land is worth, I had almost said, a thousand-fold every year of what is spent on missions. Our export trade is growing by leaps and bounds. Such growth would have been utterly impossible but for the commercial conquest of foreign lands under the lead of missionary endeavor. What a boon to home industry and manufacture![61]

Setting aside his customary silence, Rockefeller praised this letter profusely and agreed to send a $100,000 check to Boston a few days later.

So as not to be branded publicity-mongers, Rockefeller and Gates allowed beneficiaries to announce the receipt of gifts. Eager for publicity in this case— which would declare Rockefeller's emancipation from sectarian giving—Gates pored over the newspapers, vainly awaiting some mention of the record Congregational gift. When he got the Boston board's monthly publication, he expected to see banner headlines. Instead, the news was tucked away in a two- or three-line item in which the secretary noted that he had received a $100,000 check from John D. Rockefeller "with surprise," implying that the money was unsolicited.[62] There was not a grudging syllable of thanks. The gift aroused a great ruckus as a chorus of Congregational ministers demanded that it be returned. Everybody had read in *McClure's* about the nefarious methods by which this money had been procured.

The most visible critic was the Reverend Washington Gladden from Columbus, Ohio, a scourge of Rockefeller's for many years. An articulate critic of the trusts, he was a leader of the social-gospel movement. Now, armed with facts supplied directly by Ida Tarbell herself, Gladden rose up in his Congregational church one Sunday morning to deliver a stinging tirade against the $100,000 gift. "The money proffered to our board of missions comes out of a colossal estate, whose foundations were laid in the most relentless rapacity known to modern commercial history," he said.[63] In this sermon, Gladden dubbed Rockefeller's check "tainted money," an expression taken up by the press and fixed permanently in the political lexicon. He filed a protest with the Congregational Church, pleading for return of the money.

Faced with this uproar, Gates waited for the Boston board to make a clean breast of the story and admit that the money had been solicited. Instead, they suppressed the truth, and Barton even reassured reporters that it had been unsought. When Gates read this, he threatened to expose the gift's genesis, and only then did the Congregational board come clean. Both Gates and Rockefeller were disappointed that Gladden never made a widespread public retraction. As Rockefeller said, he "failed to do the manly thing and correct the false impressions which his writings had occasioned."[64] Of course, Rockefeller's self-satisfaction begged the larger question of whether people should accept money gained by what they deemed unscrupulous means.

The tainted-money controversy elicited a splendid piece of satire from Mark Twain who, having befriended the Rockefellers and Henry Rogers, knew that rapacious businessmen could be kindhearted benefactors. In *Harper's Weekly*, he published an open letter from Satan in which he chastised readers, "Let us have done with this frivolous talk. The American Board accepts contributions from me every year; then why shouldn't it from Mr. Rockefeller? In all the ages, three-fourths of the support of the great charities has been conscience-money, as my books will show; then what becomes of the sting when that term is applied to Mr. Rockefeller's gift?"[65]

As always, the public preferred to picture Rockefeller as crestfallen over the tainted-money hubbub. One newspaper said that he "sits by the hour under the trees that surround his costly home, brooding over the emphatic opposition public opinion has made against him. He speaks to no one save those who call upon most urgent matters."[66] The truth was that Rockefeller did not waver or buckle under the torrent of bad publicity, though he was sobered by it. In July 1905, he turned up at the Euclid Avenue Baptist Church in an excellent mood, if slightly worn out, and chatted jovially with old friends. He even allowed himself some drollery at the end of his Sunday-school speech. Pulling out his watch, he told the crowd, his eyes twinkling mischievously, "I've talked too long, I'm afraid. There are others here who wished to talk. I don't want you to think I'm a selfish monopolist!"[67] The congregation responded with hearty applause.

CHAPTER 25

The Codger

By the close of the Tarbell series in 1905, Rockefeller's infamy as a businessman still overshadowed his budding philanthropic fame. He continued to cherish Forest Hill and Pocantico Hills as peaceful oases, sealed off from the outer world. But where he had once let the public roam the outer grounds of these estates, he could no longer sustain this policy for safety reasons. In 1906, a forbidding iron fence, eight feet tall and topped by wire netting, suddenly rose around Forest Hill, closing off sections to the public. This caution was now warranted, since Rockefeller was inundated with death threats and hired Pinkerton detectives to protect himself. After the *McClure's* series, he kept a revolver on his bedside table. He almost never attended public ceremonies, and Cettie was so rattled by a sense of menace that she advised him to stop public speaking altogether.

Yet however many would-be assassins squatted in the shadows, Rockefeller moved through his days with equanimity. He was not the icy man of myth, and his geniality grew more pronounced with age. If more subdued during the publication of the Tarbell articles, Rockefeller began to lighten up around 1906 and relish his retirement. His health was excellent, he had cast off the excruciating burden of business, and he had put together a superb management team for his charities and outside investments. Now past sixty, he saw his first play, *The Music Master*, as well as William Gillette playing Sherlock Holmes. The Rockefellers subscribed to the Philharmonic and even sampled brother William's gilded box at the opera. For this abstemious Baptist couple, such behavior came perilously close to paganism.

Cheerful and jaunty, Rockefeller cultivated the sly asides, sage apothegms, and cornball humor of a codger. As a businessman, he had preferred dark, monochromatic suits, but now his wardrobe became dapper and eccentrically bright, like that of a retired stage actor. One favorite outfit consisted of a long yellow silk coat over a Japanese paper vest, a straw hat (likened by one periodical to "the headpiece of a rickshaw man") or a pith helmet, and a pair of goggles.[1] This sartorial change started with his alopecia, which made him experiment with skullcaps and wigs and then with a funny assortment of golf and driving hats, many of them with goofy flaps dangling over his ears. With the goggles especially, they made him look like an elderly visitor from outer space. "When he went driving he also wore round black goggles," wrote his gardener, Tom Pyle. "With his thin face and thin slash of mouth, the curious costume gave him an eerily cadaverous appearance."[2] During his digestive troubles of the 1890s, Rockefeller had grown gaunt. Now, under the care of his German physician, Dr. Moeller, he put on more weight, his face grew rounder, and his tall, rangy frame again seemed muscular, if slightly bloated at the waist. Reporters who met him found him amazingly spry—his gaze keen, his step vigorous, his handshake firm.

As he carefully plotted his moves in order to live to one hundred, Rockefeller placed great store in following the same daily schedule down to the second.[3] Whether in prayer or in wholesome recreation, he still had the Puritan's need to employ every hour profitably. Rising at 6 A.M., he read the newspaper for an hour, then strolled through house and garden from 7 to 8, giving a dime to each new employee and a nickel to each veteran. He then breakfasted at 8, followed at 8:45 by a game of numerica, which gave him time to digest his food properly. From 9:15 to 10:15 he worked on his correspondence, mostly devoted to his philanthropy and investments. (As many as 2,000 letters now arrived daily at Pocantico, most of them solicitations for money.) From 10:15 to 12 he golfed, from 12:15 to 1 P.M. he bathed and then rested. Then came lunch and another round of numerica from 1 to 2:30. From 2:30 to 3 he reclined on the sofa and had mail read to him; from 3:15 to 5:15 he motored, from 5:30 to 6:30 he again rested, while 7 to 9 was given over to a formal dinner, followed by more rounds of numerica. From 9 to 10 he listened to music and chatted with guests, then slept from 10:30 P.M. to 6 A.M.—when the whole merry-go-round started up again. He did not deviate from this routine by one jot, regardless of the weather. William O. Inglis, who observed this diurnal rhythm at close range, found "something bordering on the superhuman—perhaps the inhuman—in this unbroken, mathematical perfection of schedule. It was uncanny."[4]

By the spring of 1905, Cettie had recuperated from the attacks that had leveled her a year earlier and again took daily drives with John in a two-seat buckboard. By now, she was a chronic patient, however, and her respite was

*Rockefeller, arm in arm with an unidentified
Pinkerton detective and accompanied by a favorite grandson,
eleven-year-old Fowler McCormick, marches in the
Easter Parade on April 19, 1908.*
(Courtesy of the Rockefeller Archive Center)

short-lived: In 1906, she was again confined to bed for a month with "grippe pneumonia." Oddly enough, for all his gallant devotion to his wife, Rockefeller refused to alter his seasonal house rotation, even though Cettie could no longer follow him. For health reasons and to indulge his golf mania, he began to repair each winter to the Hotel Bon Air in Augusta, Georgia. He headed north to Lakewood for the early spring, followed by Pocantico in late spring, then Forest Hill in the summer, returning to Pocantico in October and staying there till he headed south for the winter. He adhered rigidly to this routine even though Cettie was bedridden for most of 1907; for one ten-month stretch she did not attend church or even breakfast in the parlor with her family. By the following year, suffering from emphysema, she had nurses attending her around the clock. Then, in 1909, serious congestion developed in her lungs, clumps of hair fell from her head, and she could not so much as walk across the bedroom. As she remained at Forest Hill, John was away for months at a time—remarkable for a man who had been inseparable from his wife. He must have felt that his own health would be jeopardized if he varied his rituals. He was also uncomfortable around illness, which served as an unpleasant reminder of his own mortality.

Rockefeller's life struck many observers as strangely cramped, given his gargantuan wealth: He had an annual untaxed income of $58 million in 1902—several times larger than contemporary press estimates—or about a billion dollars in tax-free income per annum in today's money. One editorial writer pictured Rockefeller this way: "When that gentleman is seated in his office coin rattles down upon him at the rate of $1.90 per second. He needs a steam shovel to keep himself from suffocation."[5] Nevertheless, Rockefeller spent only $439,000 on household expenses that year.

Rockefeller engaged in strenuous rituals of austerity, and he grimly sought to simplify his life and reduce his wants. He liked to say that "a man's wealth must be determined by the relation of his desires and expenditures to his income. If he feels rich on ten dollars, and has everything else he desires, he really is rich."[6] He and Cettie took pains to show they were not squandering money and made a point of exchanging modest gifts. In 1905, for instance, John gave Cettie $500 for her birthday and $500 for Christmas, even though her personal portfolio of railroad and gas-company bonds was now worth more than $1 million. For holidays, the Rockefellers exchanged token gifts—pens, ties, handkerchiefs, gloves—then wrote elaborate thank-you notes about how beautiful they were. In the spring of 1913, Rockefeller sent vegetables to his son at his home at 13 West Fifty-fourth Street and at Abeyton Lodge, his house in Pocantico, prompting the following outpouring from the ecstatic recipient: "As I glance at the weekly vegetable report from Pocantico Hills and see that last week $11.10 worth of asparagus went to Abeyton Lodge and $5.40 worth to No. 13. . . . I am constrained to express Abby's and my warmest thanks for your kindness in allowing us to share with you the products of the garden."[7] In this manner, the Rockefellers inhabited two worlds: a real but unspoken world of unimaginable wealth and a make-believe world of modest gifts intended to show that they were not spoiled. Since money meant nothing to them, they had to stress the sentimental value of gifts. The main thing was to prove that you were not taking your good fortune for granted. In January 1905, Cettie wrote to Junior at Forest Hill: "I am looking for snow to try our new sleigh, which is on springs and has four runners so as to turn like a carriage. Is not this luxury?"[8] When one thinks of the ornate Newport "cottages" and giant steam yachts then in vogue among the rich, it is hard not to find Cettie's conception of "luxury" poignant.

Rockefeller never lost his ingrained sense of thrift. When Junior, defying custom, gave him a fur coat and cap for Christmas in 1908, it elicited the following humorous reply: "I thank you a thousand times for the fur coat and cap and mittens. I did not feel I could afford such luxuries, and am grateful for a son who is able to buy them for me."[9] As his son should have known, Rockefeller would never strut around in this plutocrat's costume, and he returned it to Junior, who wore it instead.

Breathtakingly generous in his philanthropy, Rockefeller could also be stingy—appallingly so. Whereas most other tycoons hired subordinates to oversee personal expenditures, Rockefeller supervised every detail, and in small matters he tended to be an incorrigible skinflint. The account books of his estates were all sent to 26 Broadway and audited to the last dollar. The estates were all melded together into their own internal market system, and when Pocantico "sold" trees to Lakewood, Pocantico was credited and Lakewood debited. "We are our own best customers," Rockefeller observed archly in his memoirs, "and we make a small fortune out of ourselves by selling to our New Jersey place at $1.50 or $2.00 each, trees which originally cost us only five or ten cents at Pocantico."[10] He had studies performed to compute the cost of per-capita food consumption at his various houses and chided the housekeeper at 4 West Fifty-fourth Street for "table board" that ranged as high as $13.35 per person compared to $7.80 for Pocantico and $6.62 for Forest Hill.

Rockefeller spent a ridiculous amount of time protesting bills both large and small and scrutinized the smallest bills from grocers and butchers. Somewhat paranoid to begin with, he assumed every tradesman was an extortion artist, or at least was padding the rich man's bills. Even while walking on his estate, he tried to spot shirkers. "I have noticed of late several instances of idling," he told one superintendent, "and in one or two cases have stopped my automobile and waited to see if the men would resume their work."[11] For a time, he tipped porters by holding out a handful of change and asking them to take what they deserved; when they took him at his word, he was shocked and renounced the policy, resorting to a strict 10 percent policy.

Rockefeller was notably suspicious when it came to the medical profession. In an extraordinary number of cases, he imagined that he was being gouged by physicians and threatened lawsuits. In 1909, Dr. Paul Allen treated Rockefeller at Hot Springs, West Virginia, and brought in a consulting physician, a Dr. Smith. When Rockefeller received a $3,000 bill from Dr. Smith, he complained to Dr. Allen that he could have gotten other reputable physicians for between $500 and $1,000. "I prefer to adjust this matter with Dr. Smith without litigation, but I am in no state of mind to submit to what I regard as extortion," he warned Dr. Allen.[12] After Rockefeller threatened legal action, Dr. Smith settled for $500. Then Rockefeller received a bill from Dr. Allen himself of $350 per diem for 21 days of treatment at Hot Springs, and he again flew into a rage, refusing to pay more than $160 a day—an amount he dropped to $75 after canvassing doctor friends and examining local compensation levels. Once again, he hinted at litigation. When Junior noted that Dr. Allen had sacrificed four families as patients because of this extended West Virginia stay, Senior countered that "the prestige of his going to Hot Springs for twenty-one days as our family physician . . . might be worth a great deal more to him than this loss of patients." Calling the doctor's charges "extortionate," Senior concluded, "I believe it my duty to a good many people who have been blackmailed by doctors to stand a trial."[13] For Rockefeller, it was dogma that prices should reflect true market values, not the buyer's ability to pay, and nothing upset him more than the notion that a rich man should pay a premium on his hard-earned wealth.

═

As Senior disappeared behind the gates of his estates, the public spotlight was progressively cast on his son and heir, who shrank beneath its glare. "John D. Rockefeller, the greatest organizing genius in the world, and largest individual owner of the United States and its inhabitants, is the father of a young man called John D. Rockefeller, Jr.," opined one Hearst newspaper. "John D. Rockefeller, Jr., in his own right will be richer than many entire nations. He will be worth more money than the whole of Greece was worth when the work done by the Greeks constituted the glory of the world."[14] Nobody was more daunted by this prospect than Junior himself, who felt trapped in the iron cage of dynastic expectation. Never sure of himself, Junior plodded ahead, always wondering where he was heading.

Junior was awed by his father, whom he regarded as a marble figure on a pedestal. "To his son he had always seemed of heroic proportions—brilliant in his construction of a huge industrial empire, exacting in matters of personal integrity, disciplined in the control of his own emotions, serene in the face of public abuse, and magnanimous in his contributions toward mankind," Gates wrote.[15] Taught to regard his father in this golden light, Junior felt humble in his presence. He once told the New York Chamber of Commerce that his sole desire was to help his father and, if necessary, "to black his shoes, to pack his bag."[16] "Of my ability I have always had a very poor opinion," he told his father in 1902, "but I need not assure you that such as it is, it is wholly and absolutely devoted to your interests, and that now and always you can trust me as you always have."[17] Instead of bucking up his courage, Senior often let his son wallow in self-flagellation.

If Senior tried to shut out his critics, Junior was hypersensitive to insinuations about his father. As Gates observed, Junior's "whole conduct of life is governed by the purpose, hardly at all concealed, of rehabilitating his father's public reputation."[18] Junior's need to vindicate his father stemmed partly from love but also from more self-interested reasons. As an ethical young man, how could he feel good about himself if he was spending blood money? To give away the Rockefeller fortune with a clear conscience, he had to convince himself that it had been earned fairly.

If Junior lacked the intestinal fortitude to spend his life facing down a hostile public, this feeling only grew as he and Abby began to create a large family. Their first child, Abby—known as Babs—was born at 13 West Fifty-fourth Street in 1903, followed by John D. Rockefeller III in 1906, whose birth elicited the headline, "Richest Baby in History." Nelson was born in 1908 in Seal Harbor, Maine, on Senior's birthday, which he always regarded as an omen, if not outright proof, that he was destined to lead the next generation of Rockefellers.

Desperately in need of guidance and emotional support, Junior re-created with his wife the close relationship he had had with his mother. He clung to Abby and depended upon her judgment, and sometimes he seemed scarcely able to live without her. When Abby and Babs went off to the Aldrich estate at Warwick, he was tormented by her absence. Abby enabled him to savor all the romanticism repressed during his upbringing. Two years after their marriage, Junior could still write to her breathlessly, "How happy you made me that night, darling, in the radiance of your young womanhood, so beautiful, so fascinating, so loving, and so long the one object of my passionate desires. . . . What a beautiful night that was, darling. We were oblivious of all except each other and our great love."[19]

Cool and very shrewd in sizing up situations, Abby saw something unseemly in the demeaning tasks assigned to Junior when he started at 26 Broadway. She encouraged him to claim his rightful place as heir apparent. Junior still did not know how he would divide his time between business and philanthropy. Aware of the public-relations value of a Rockefeller heir, the Standard Oil of New Jersey chieftains were eager to use him as window dressing, and in 1904, at age thirty, he was appointed a director. Two executives, A. C. Bedford and Henry H. Rogers, took him on a whirlwind tour of the Oklahoma oil fields and discovered that this likable, unassuming young man had his own shy appeal. "Bedford and Rogers found out that I got on with the public very well and that the public was interested in seeing a live Rockefeller," said Junior. "In other words, they began to think of me as something of an asset."[20] In 1909, he was elevated to a vice presidency.

A neophyte in business, the product of a sheltered upbringing, Junior was bound to be shocked by the moral squalor of Standard Oil under John D. Archbold. The quick-witted, combative Archbold knew how to use his violent temper to bully people into submission. Since Archbold lived in Tarrytown, he stopped by Pocantico each Saturday morning to present a bright red apple to Rockefeller and to consult with his largest shareholder. Commuting to work by speedboat each morning, Archbold often invited Junior along, and they had breakfast as they raced down the Hudson River. On these occasions, Junior often quizzed Archbold about a matter that greatly upset him: the secret political payoffs—legal but seamy—routinely made by Standard Oil. As Junior explained, "The party bosses would come to the back door and it seemed to the management of the company wise to favor them. . . . I gradually became sensitive to usages and actions for which as a member of the board and an officer I felt responsible but which as a single individual I had little voice in determining."[21] The money traffic was blatant: At campaign time, Mark Hanna, Cornelius N. Bliss, and other party bosses hung around, as Junior put it, "at the back door, hat in hand." Yet when Junior protested, Archbold airily dismissed it as a matter of survival and said that all big corporations did it.[22] Did Junior ever wonder why his father, whom he considered a paragon of virtue, had groomed Archbold as his protégé?

On several occasions, Junior was asked to lobby Senator Aldrich for Standard Oil. In 1903, for instance, Junior prodded his father-in-law to appoint Senator Boies Penrose to the Senate Finance Committee because he "has for some years been a friend of certain gentlemen in our company and has usually shown himself friendly toward the company."[23] In later years, Junior must have regretted these actions, one of the few times when his ethical compass failed him. Having gotten a hint of the moral atmosphere at Standard Oil, Junior began to distance himself from its management and attended only about a third of the board meetings. While he feigned affection for Archbold—"We were all very fond of him, he was so witty and jolly"—he made a point of having less contact with him.[24]

Of course, as Junior struggled with his dawning awareness of corruption at Standard Oil, Ida Tarbell was exhuming its unsavory past, and the two overlapping events probably pushed him into his nervous breakdown in late 1904. The press did not help matters. In the gauche young heir, reporters spotted a far more vulnerable target than his father, and they ridiculed him as weak, fumbling, prudish, and neurasthenic. This coverage made Junior even more self-conscious than before, and he was pilloried no matter what he did. If he did not give tips, he was mocked, but when he gave his barber a nickel, the coin was posted on the barber's wall and reproduced in the newspapers. "He rarely spends more than 50 cents for his midday lunches," the New York *Daily News* reported. "He drinks no intoxicating liquors, uses tobacco moderately, and his tailors' bill in a year is not as heavy as that of a prosperous clerk in a Wall Street office."[25] Junior fidgeted under the attention. "It was rather expected of me that having inherited money I would waste it," said Junior. "I made up my mind that I wouldn't do it."[26]

Whenever Junior spoke in public, hard-bitten journalists turned out to record and mock his words. In February 1902, he gave a talk at the Brown University YMCA in which he tried to square business ethics and Christianity. To justify the superiority of consolidation over competition, he cited the breeding of the American Beauty rose, which had only been achieved through constant, painful pruning. This figure of speech, tossed in extemporaneously, haunted Junior for years and was cited constantly as a credo of rapacious capitalism.

As Junior said of this period, "My problem was to reconcile right and conscience with the hard realities of life on a practical level," and he groped his way unaided by his father. He clung ardently to his leadership of the men's Bible class at the Fifth Avenue Baptist Church. After he took over the class from Charles Evans Hughes in 1900, the number of young men in attendance at once quadrupled from 50 to 200 and ultimately reached 500, including many bookkeepers, clerks, salesmen, and students. In the class, Junior tried to use scripture to elucidate moral dilemmas of everyday life. "We have talks along financial, educational, sociological and religious lines, as well as talks of a generally helpful nature," he explained to William Rainey Harper in 1902.[27] It was never clear how many students were there for guidance and how many were angling for Rockefeller jobs or money. Reporters infiltrated the sessions just to hurl embarrassing questions at Junior, who sat with hands tightly clasped on the table as they made sport of his replies. Mark Twain, a guest speaker, observed Junior's predicament firsthand. "Every Sunday young Rockefeller explains the Bible to his class," he wrote. "The next day the newspapers and the Associated Press distribute his explanations all over the continent and everybody laughs."[28] Twain conceded that Junior repeated platitudes preached from every pulpit, but thought he was unfairly roughed up for political reasons.

In 1905, as attacks mounted on his father and his talks were increasingly subjected to savage derision, Junior agonized over whether to relinquish the class. Still recuperating from his breakdown, he devoted three nights each week to preparing this Sunday talk. Gates in particular thought this was taking an excruciating toll. When Junior told his father in June 1905 of his wish to resign, Senior registered unequivocal opposition. "It would interfere with my pleasure to have you give up the class," he said. "It has been a source of great joy and comfort to your Mother and me."[29] John D. himself had informed one of Junior's classes, "I would rather see my son doing this work than see him a monarch on his throne."[30]

Junior's reasons for wanting to stay were illuminating. He needed a place where he could resolve the tensions between business and religion, Standard Oil and the Baptist Church, forging a synthesis that would enable him to function in an imperfect world. If he gave up the class, he also worried that the family wealth and notoriety would isolate him from society, as had so clearly happened to his father, who led an artificial existence. He received a timely warning along these lines from Dr. W.H.P. Faunce, the president of Brown University and former pastor of the Fifth Avenue Baptist Church:

> If you drop that class, you will take a step toward retirement from your fellow-men. Your father has felt obliged—often against my protest—to barricade himself in order to avoid the imposters, cranks etc. of which the world is full. This is the inevitable penalty of his position. But there is no reason why that penalty should descend to you.[31]

For three years, Junior kept the Bible class, then, at Abby's gentle urging, withdrew in 1908 at a moment when he would not seem to be retreating under fire. As she reassured him, "You have borne all the criticism and ridicule that is necessary to let the world see that you are sincere."[32] It was not the last time that she rescued him from unnecessary martyrdom.

=

Since Junior had committed himself to serving his father, the question naturally arises of why Senior, eager to slough off cares, did not commence sooner the great transfer of wealth to his son. Other moguls, such as Commodore Vanderbilt and J. P. Morgan, Sr., had waited until their deaths to convey the bulk of their wealth to their sons, but they needed their money as working capital in their businesses and did not have extended retirements like Rockefeller's. Until 1912—when Junior was thirty-eight—Senior kept him in a prolonged adolescence, paying him a salary that was really a glorified allowance. "Why, the girls in the office here have an advantage that I never had," Junior once lamented. "They can prove to themselves their commercial worth. I envy anybody who can do that."[33] By slow increments, his father ratcheted up his allowance from $10,000 a year in 1902 to $18,000 five years later, but Junior never felt he had earned it, exacerbating his sense of inadequacy. As he told his father in 1907, "I have always wished, simply as a matter of satisfaction to myself, that my salary might represent the real value of my services in the office, while as it is and has been in the past it represents rather your generosity."[34]

Before 1911, Rockefeller made only token transfers of oil stock to his son, starting with his first annual gift of one hundred shares of Standard Oil of New Jersey in 1903, but he also deeded to him parcels of valuable property in Cleveland, Buffalo, and New York. Then, in 1909, he gave him a controlling interest in the American Linseed Company, and with this sixteen-million-dollar gift Junior saw the golden floodgates start to open. Grateful but anxious, he wrote to his father, "A deep feeling of solemnity, of responsibility, almost of awe, comes over me as I contemplate these gifts, and my heart rises in silent prayer to God that he will teach me to be a good and faithful steward as my Father has been."[35] Even though he now owned a company and extensive real estate, Junior still dangled in an awkward dependency, having to account to his father for his personal expenses. In January 1910, Senior asked how much he had spent the previous year, and Junior, like an obedient schoolboy, computed the answer, in Rockefeller style, down to the decimal points: $65,918.47.

At the turn of the century, Junior and his three sisters had roughly equal wealth—several hundred thousand dollars apiece—and father kept parity among them for several years. (Much of Junior's early income came from a $500,000 "credit" John D. had given him to supplement his salary.) Then it grew steadily clearer that Junior would be the receptacle for the bulk of the fortune. Partly this was a plain case of male chauvinism. But special factors also worked against Bessie and Edith, while frigid relations with Alta's husband, Parmalee, lessened her chances. Senior had cool relations with two of his three sons-in-law and would have hesitated to give them undue influence over his money. In Junior's opinion, his sisters were also disqualified because they did not handle their finances in the scrupulous manner demanded by father.

Constantly consulting expert opinion and learning all he could, Junior was now immersed in the Rockefeller philanthropies, and nobody enjoyed finer access to the master. In casual moments at Pocantico, Junior could lightly broach a project or have Cettie read a proposal aloud. "Gates was the brilliant dreamer and orator," Junior conceded. "I was the salesman—the go-between with Father at the opportune moment."[36] Junior discharged this role perfectly, for he lacked the itch for fame, willingly laid all glory at his father's doorstep, and held views congruent with his. For Senior, exhausted from his business labors, this conscientious son was heaven-sent. Once, during a golf game, Rockefeller announced, "My greatest fortune in life has been my son."[37]

So why did Senior procrastinate in giving him his money? Since he remained tight-lipped, we can only conjecture. One plausible explanation is that he planned to reach age one hundred and had no wish to surrender power prematurely in his sixties. He must have fretted, too, about Junior's debilitating breakdown, which started in 1904 and dragged on for nearly three years, curtailing his activities. Senior must have feared that the stupendous weight of the fortune would crush his delicate son. Rockefeller might also have waited until Junior began to show more robust self-confidence. Protective of his vulnerable son, Rockefeller was irate when the press pummeled him. "They have no right to attack Mr. John," he would insist. "All my life I have been the object of assault. But they have no ground for striking at him!"[38]

Yet the overriding fear was most likely political. Since the family fortune largely took the form of Standard Oil stock, giving it to Junior would have engulfed him in controversy far uglier than anything he had ever known. With Standard Oil besieged by state and federal antitrust suits, Junior would have inherited both the controversy and the legal liability that went with the stock. Had Rockefeller unloaded the oil stock on Junior, editorialists would also have accused him of fleeing retribution and responsibility. That Junior had such grave reservations about Standard's management under Archbold would have only strengthened his father's reluctance to hand over significant blocks of shares to him.

=

While Gates initiated Junior into the rites of philanthropy, the crown prince continued to perform many mundane domestic duties foisted upon him by his father, including paying the servants and overseeing repairs. Then, on the night of September 17, 1902, the Parsons-Wentworth house at Pocantico burned down. Hundreds of people stood by helplessly in the dark as flames consumed the wooden structure. Fortunately, nobody was hurt. John and Cettie simply moved their belongings to an undistinguished dwelling on the grounds called the Kent House. Senior had long wanted to build a new house at Pocantico anyway and was not therefore especially fazed by the fire.

From 1902, Junior and Abby had occupied a lovely house on the estate known as Abeyton Lodge, a comfortable, rambling affair in Hudson Valley Dutch style, festooned with many dormer windows and awnings. They tended to look askance at Senior's patched-up residences and wanted him to occupy a grander dwelling. As a result, they reinforced his desire to erect a new house at the property's highest point, Kykuit, a five-hundred-foot elevation with a peerless vista of the Hudson River, and took charge of planning a manor house that would be a model of quiet elegance and faultless taste. It has been hypothesized that Senior saw the project as therapeutic for Junior after his breakdown, but the latter's troubles actually stalled the project. As *The New York Times* reported accurately in May 1905, "The unexpected serious crisis in the health of John D. Rockefeller, Jr., has temporarily checked his father's plans for building a fine mansion this summer on his immense estate in the Pocantico Hills."[39] Even a year later, Senior told a cousin that he was trying to stop Junior from overwork and he would never have rushed him into building the new house. He would surely have remembered the onus of supervising construction of the family home in Cleveland as an adolescent.

In the spring of 1904, Senior had given his son permission to solicit preliminary sketches from architects, and by the following summer contracts were signed with Delano and Aldrich as architects (Chester H. Aldrich was Abby's distant cousin), Thompson-Starrett as builders, Ogden Codman, Jr., as interior designer, and William Welles Bosworth as landscape architect. Presented with these plans, Rockefeller reacted as he so often did when in a quandary—he did nothing. He exercised a pocket veto, leaving Junior in the old position of trying to figure out his intentions. "After a while," Junior said, "I became convinced that the reason he did nothing was because he hesitated to build so large a house, with the additional care which its operation would involve, but on the other hand was too generous to suggest a smaller house, which would not adequately accommodate children and grandchildren."[40] Evidently, Junior guessed right, for when he presented plans for a scaled-down house—small enough to satisfy his father's craving for simplicity, roomy enough to accommodate guests—Rockefeller consented with relief. The house would be handsome but not ostentatious, previewing a new Rockefeller aesthetic of restrained grace that owed much to Abby Aldrich Rockefeller.

Before construction started, Rockefeller, an engineering buff, brought a number of demands to the table. To reinvigorate Cettie's health, he wanted Kykuit to receive maximum sunshine in the winter. He also wanted sunlight to trail him on his daily rounds, with light shining in the dining room for lunch, for instance, but with his bedroom dipped in shadow for his afternoon nap. This demand might have flummoxed the most adept architect, but for Rockefeller, who had dabbled in construction, it was child's play. He constructed a boxlike contraption mounted on a turntable at the center of the building site. Stationed in this box for several days, working the levers, he observed how the sunlight slanted down on a small model of the house. He then presented his hourly charts to the architects, who shifted the foundation lines in conformity with them.

Junior and Abby threw themselves into Kykuit's construction with a mixture of passion and nervous energy. (Mesmerized by measurement, Junior carried a collapsible four-foot ruler in his pocket for the rest of his life.) They oversaw creation of a three-story Georgian manor house, with elegant gables and dormer windows. In deference to Baptist values, the house had no ballroom, but it did have an Aeolian organ for both religious and secular music. Junior and Abby were very partial to their creation. After they had toured some pretentious "châteaux" on Long Island's north shore, Junior said that Kykuit, by comparison, was "far less elaborate than many houses we have seen" but "more perfect of its kind, more harmonious and more charming."[41]

John and Abby enlisted the services of Ogden Codman, the Boston interior designer who helped Edith Wharton refurbish her Newport home and coauthored a book with her, *The Decoration of Houses*, in 1897. In the book, Wharton rebelled against the cold, cluttered rooms of her childhood. Codman wanted to invest Kykuit with the easy tranquillity of an English country house, furnishing it with pieces that would seem like old family heirlooms. No detail of design escaped John and Abby's exacting attention. They fussed over every item with that small flutter of anxiety that Junior always felt when performing a task for his father. "We bought all the furniture, china, linen, glass, silver and works of arts, employing, of course, the best advisers obtainable," he said.[42] Before unveiling the house to his parents, Junior and Abby slept there for six weeks, testing every bedroom and taking meals there.

Sure that the house was now ready, they apprehensively invited John and Cettie to sample it in October 1908, and it seemed, at first, an unparalleled success. "The new house all furnished by John and Abby was ready for us," Cettie recorded in her diary. "It is beautiful and convenient within and without."[43] Cettie and sister Lute delighted in playing the large pipe organ, with its player-piano attachment, and Senior imported an organist from the Fifth Avenue Baptist Church for after-dinner concerts on Sunday evenings. That Thanksgiving, three generations of Rockefellers gathered in the new house, with Abby and Junior bringing their growing brood of Babs, John III, and five-month-old Nelson. They instituted a tradition of no smoking or drinking at either Kykuit or Abeyton Lodge.

Unfortunately for Junior and Abby, their ordeal had only begun. Since Cettie had been sick, they had tried to spare her concern with construction details, but she was an extremely finicky lady. For the sake of diplomacy, John and Cettie pretended to be thrilled with their new home, but they increasingly carped in private. The third floor, reserved for guest rooms, had tiny dormer windows that made them stuffy and unsuitable. They then discovered graver problems. The elevator made an awful din; the roaring plumbing in Cettie's bathroom reverberated in the public areas; the racket from the service entrance below John D.'s bedroom grated on his nerves; rainwater dripped into the dining room; the chimneys sometimes belched smoke, and so on and so on. Cettie even found indecent the charming statues of male cherubim on the porch outside their bedroom and had them chastely converted into female angels. As his parents broke silence and confided their concerns, Junior's heart sagged: He had let them down again. After a year, it was decided that the house would be completely revamped.

Yet the brouhaha over the house was minor compared to the uproar over the grounds. William Welles Bosworth had planned to surround Kykuit with a small, formal park of 250 acres, with the rest of the estate left in something close to its wild, pristine state. Since Senior fancied himself a landscape expert, he conceived an instant dislike for Bosworth, whom he regarded as a rival and a frighteningly extravagant fellow to boot. When Bosworth submitted his plans, Rockefeller harrumphed that he could do better:

"In a few days," Rockefeller recalled in his memoirs,

> I had worked out a plan so devised that the roads caught just the best views at just the angles where in driving up the hill you came upon impressive outlooks, and at the ending was the final burst of river, hill, cloud, and great sweep of country to crown the whole; and here I fixed my stakes to show where I suggested that the roads should run, and finally the exact place where the house should be.

He then told Bosworth: "Look it all over and decide which plan is best."[44] When this plan was adopted, Rockefeller attributed this decision to its patent superiority, though it is hard to see how Bosworth could have objected. Even with the terraced formal gardens close to the house, Rockefeller interjected his own ideas. He insisted upon lime trees for the garden walk just south of the house, having learned they were the fastest growing trees and would most quickly cast shade on the footpaths.

Luckily, Rockefeller did not do everything himself and allowed Bosworth to create a majestic fantasy straight out of the Italian Renaissance, complete with grottoes, fountains, pergolas, sunken gardens, temples, topiary bushes, classical statues, and running streams. Disgruntled at the cost of these ornaments, Rockefeller would stroll the grounds with guests and tell them, only half jesting, "You know, these little brooks run mighty high!"[45] Cettie was especially fond of Bosworth's rustic Japanese garden with its quaint teahouse, but every time Rockefeller looked at it, he saw plain extortion and complained to his son. "I can hardly understand how the little Japanese house, which I supposed was to be a very superficial affair, would reach $10,000. . . . Bosworth may be all right. I hope we shall feel later on, as you do, that he has not been a too expensive luxury for us."[46]

Whenever they acceded to one of Bosworth's modest ideas, Rockefeller growled, it ended up costing much more than they imagined. Senior had first been quoted a figure of $30,000 for the entire landscaping job and was horrified in 1910 when the bill swelled to $750,000—more than the cost of house and furnishings combined! (It would equal nearly $12 million in contemporary money.) Thus far, he had been restrained, but now he gave his son a good tongue-lashing. "Granted that we have a very satisfactory result, but $750,000 is very different from $30,000, and is, indeed, *25 times* that amount, and what Mr. Bosworth has received for his services is fifty percent more than the entire original estimate of cost to me. I should not want the public to know what our expenditure has been."[47] In the end, the house paled beside the stately gardens, and this must actually have pleased the outdoorsy Rockefeller. For all his complaining, he adored the grounds and planted a network of electric lights that allowed him to illuminate them theatrically at night. "If you were to visit me on the darkest night," he would boast, "I could show you vistas of trees from one part to the other of my estate by merely touching a button."[48]

Starting in 1911, the house itself underwent two more years of renovation and was transformed into a fine specimen of American Renaissance, a voguish style that bespoke the self-confidence of the burgeoning industrial class. Narrow but deep, the house had four floors above ground and two below that were gouged into the hillside. Gone was the old dormer-ridden third floor, replaced with a mansard roof. By turning the wooden veranda into a stone loggia, the forty-room house acquired new dignity and grandeur. While not exactly modest, Kykuit was decorous and understated and testified to its owner's simplicity. It fell far short of what Rockefeller could have afforded or what other preening magnates might have built.

To Senior's delight, the redesign entailed complicated problems in civil engineering. To lengthen the approach to the house, hundreds of teamsters carted in thousands of loads of topsoil, requiring the construction of a huge retaining wall. To ferry in supplies without disturbing the occupants, an underground tunnel was created for trucks, and Senior delighted in watching the steam shovels punch a hole in the hillside. This construction thrilled him, as if he were a small boy equipped with a new set of toy trucks. The remaking of Kykuit went on until October 1913, when John and Cettie finally moved back into the house after two years of work. By that point, Cettie was very sick and did not have much longer to live.

With Kykuit complete, Rockefeller turned his attention to removing disturbing elements from the grounds. One row of houses inside the Rockefeller acreage was picked up and set back down in the nearby village. As he accumulated more land, Rockefeller was also increasingly bothered by the Putnam division of the New York Central Railroad, which cut a swath across the middle of his estate. He hated the hoboes and hunters drawn by the right-of-way, not to mention the ash that fluttered down on his golf course from the coal-burning locomotives. In 1929, Rockefeller decided to have the train rerouted and paid an estimated $700,000 to buy the entire village of East View, with its forty-six homes; after buying and razing all of the houses, he donated the land for new railroad tracks five miles to the east of the original one. Removing another unwanted intruder, Junior paid $1.5 million for the three hundred acres of Saint Joseph's Normal College, underwriting the costs of relocating it and building a new campus elsewhere.

At its peak, the Pocantico estate was a self-contained world with seventy-five houses and seventy miles of private roads. Forever reworking his domain,

Rockefeller kept hundreds of men busy moving trees and hills to open up new views. The estate included a sizable working farm that supplied the family's food needs. Rockefeller developed such a taste for Pocantico's produce and springwater that they were shipped to him wherever he went.

The Pocantico Hills estate was a marvelous haven, but the cluster of newsmen clamoring for answers beyond the majestic iron gates always reminded its owner of the hostile public. Their chorus of accusations grew only louder with time. By Teddy Roosevelt's second term, Rockefeller and Standard Oil could no longer flout the federal and state governments with impunity, as they had for so long. The moment of reckoning was at hand.

*Bessie Rockefeller Strong, whose
prolonged illness has always been surrounded by mystery.*
(Courtesy of the Rockefeller Archive Center)

CHAPTER 26

The World's Richest Fugitive

s they approached the 1904 presidential election, Standard Oil executives knew that Teddy Roosevelt was still miffed at their attempt to snuff out his new Bureau of Corporations and that the oil trust stood at the top of his list of evil trusts to be reined in by federal regulators. Since the idea of backing Roosevelt's Democratic opponent, Alton B. Parker, was unthinkable to Archbold and his associates, they smothered the incumbent with money, especially a $100,000 contribution from Henry H. Rogers. Other businessmen who feared the lash of federal regulation—including Edward H. Harriman, Henry Clay Frick, and James Stillman—also paid tribute to Roosevelt, provoking Democratic charges that the president was being bribed by the very companies he vowed to control. Attorney General Philander Knox wandered into Roosevelt's office one day in October 1904 and heard the president dictating a letter ordering the return of the Standard Oil funds. "Why, Mr. President, the money has been spent," Knox objected. "They cannot pay it back—they haven't got it." "Well," Roosevelt said, "the letter will look well on the record, anyhow."[1]

When Roosevelt won by an impressive margin in November, Rockefeller sent a telegram to him: "I congratulate you most heartily on the grand result of yesterday's election."[2] In the Standard boardroom, the contribution to Roosevelt's campaign was soon acknowledged to be the worst investment they had ever made. As Archbold moaned, "Darkest Abyssinia never saw anything like the course of treatment we received at the hands of the administration following Mr. Roosevelt's election in 1904."[3] Or as Henry C. Frick phrased it more succinctly, "We bought the son of a bitch, but he wouldn't stay bought."[4] Nevertheless, the Standard Oil hierarchs remained cocksure that, in any contest for supremacy with the federal government, they would inevitably prevail.

Before the election, the Bureau of Corporations, headed by James R. Garfield, had begun to gather data on Standard Oil. The son of the former president and active in Ohio Republican politics, Garfield was friendly with some Standard Oil lawyers, and the initial inquiry went amicably enough. Then, in February 1905, by a unanimous resolution, the House of Representatives urged an antitrust investigation of Standard Oil, a result of the oil boom in Kansas. Re-enacting a drama once played out in western Pennsylvania, independent oil producers and refiners protested that Standard Oil dominated the state's pipelines, and they also accused it of conspiring with the railroads. Their passions were fanned both by Ida Tarbell's articles and by a dramatic tour she made through the oil fields. Suddenly, Commissioner Garfield was summoning Archbold and Rogers to question them about Standard's behavior in the state. When he broached the touchy subject of rebates—the flash point for so many battles in oil history—their relations deteriorated hastily. A new generation of independent oil producers in Kansas, Illinois, Oklahoma, Texas, and California would provide the motive force behind the antitrust drive against the Standard.

As the moribund Sherman Act quickened to sudden life under Teddy Roosevelt, the Tarbell series virtually guaranteed that Standard Oil would be the central target of any federal trustbusting probe. Tarbell thought it the optimal choice because it was "the mother trust and the most nearly monopolistic."[5] It furnished a well-known consumer article, affected nearly everyone, and had an abundant history of hearings and lawsuits to excavate. In the early 1900s, petroleum was being applied to an array of new uses and it no longer seemed tolerable for one organization to retain a stranglehold over it.

For years, Rockefeller and his colleagues had ignored public opinion, refusing to give interviews and behaving defiantly at hearings. In her *McClure's* series, Tarbell had justly said, "If Mr. Rockefeller had been as great a psychologist as he is a business manipulator he would have realised that he was awakening a terrible popular dread."[6] In their hubris, the oil monopolists mocked the petty efforts of politicians to obstruct them. "We will see Standard Oil in hell before we will let any set of men tell us how to run our business," an unreconstructed Henry Rogers swore.[7] Unwilling to compromise, Standard officials dealt with government officials as roughly as they did with business competitors. At this precarious moment, the trust needed a master diplomat, not the hotheaded Archbold.

In 1906, Roosevelt signed a stack of bills to curb industrial abuses. Profiting from the outcry prompted by Upton Sinclair's novel *The Jungle*, he signed the meat-inspection bill and the Pure Food and Drug Act. Identifying railroad discrimination as a major issue, he supported the Hepburn bill, which granted broader power to the Interstate Commerce Commission to set railroad rates and placed interstate pipelines under its domain. By bringing Standard Oil to heel, Roosevelt hoped to check two abuses at once: railroad collusion and industrial monopoly. When the Bureau of Corporations sent him its report on the oil trust, it highlighted Standard's collusion, both in secret rates and open discrimination, with the railroads. Seizing upon this as a potent tool to push through the Hepburn bill, Roosevelt made the five-hundred-page report public on May 2, 1906. "The report shows that the Standard Oil Company has benefited enormously up almost to the present moment by secret rates," the president declared.[8]

Seriously misreading the punitive public mood, Rockefeller remained silent. When Charles M. Pratt drafted a reply, Rockefeller objected in no uncertain terms: "Giving broadcast [to] this information at this date is unwise and is a headliner for *more* drastic treatment by the Fed. Govt."[9] Overriding Rockefeller's dissent, Standard Oil released a statement denying that it had knowingly committed any unlawful actions.

In Standard Oil, Teddy Roosevelt found a trust tailor-made for his purposes: big, rich, brutal, unpopular, and totally unrepentant. He adored grandstanding and liked to use his bully pulpit to incite a popular furor. With an ex-pugilist's flair for feints and bluffs, he kept the combine thoroughly confused about his true sentiments. At moments, he issued strong public denunciations. "Every measure for honesty in business that has been passed in the last six years has been opposed by these men."[10] Even less temperate in private, he told his attorney general that the Standard Oil directors were "the biggest criminals in the country."[11] Then, in friendly private chats at the White House, he disarmed the very Standard directors he had reviled by seeming the soul of civility. In early March 1906, Archbold and Rogers were received cordially at the White House, as Junior reported to his father in confidence:

> [The president] professed great ignorance of the affairs of the company, saying his knowledge of it was "nebulous." As to the investigation on foot through Mr. Garfield's department, he seemed to know little. . . . He exhibited no personal animosity or unkindly feeling, nor could they judge from anything said that he himself was at the bottom of this investigation.

While Archbold professed satisfaction, Junior, educated by his father-in-law in the president's mutable ways, was more skeptical. "Senator Aldrich observed at my house the other night that while the President agreed with whoever talked last with him and seemed won over entirely to that view of the matter, the following day the next man who approached him with a different view gained an equally cordial hearing and relief."[12]

Even as Roosevelt entertained the bosses of Standard Oil, he was about to unleash the government's full fury against it. He was offended by its obstructive tactics with Garfield, its refusal to concede the legitimacy of his investigation. When he sent the Garfield Report to Congress, he warned that the Justice Department might prosecute Standard Oil for the abuses revealed. This linkage of Standard Oil with railroad rebates laid down the lines for future antitrust prosecution. Like Lloyd and Tarbell, Attorney General William H. Moody decided that the Standard monopoly had been based on a pattern of secret, illegal rebates. In late June 1906, Roosevelt summoned Moody and other cabinet members for an unusual nocturnal session at the White House to discuss possible prosecution. On June 22, Moody announced a preliminary investigation, headed by Frank B. Kellogg, of an antitrust suit against Standard Oil—a move that one newspaper reported under the stark headline, "Standard Oil Officials May Go to Prison."[13]

By this time, Standard officials knew that they had been grossly deceived by the president's genial manner. "There is no doubt that the special Cabinet meeting, which the President called, and where the action was entirely dominated by him, led to the instituting of the proceedings," Archbold told Rockefeller. Trying to strike a brave note, he added, "all well, feeling first rate, and ready for the fight."[14] As always, Standard Oil reacted with bravado, and Hell Hound Rogers sent these fighting words to Rockefeller: "It is my opinion that we are all right and going to win out sure, without doubt I do not think we have anything to fear."[15]

In retrospect, it seems clear that the ambiguous signals from the White House reflected more than duplicity on Roosevelt's part, for he was genuinely reluctant to wield the big stick against Standard Oil. He preferred compromise to antitrust cases, which were slow, time-consuming, and fiendishly difficult to win. He wanted to supervise trusts, not break them up and sacrifice their efficiency, and he was searching for some conciliatory overture from his adversaries, a suggestion that they would accept government oversight and voluntarily mend their ways. But compromise was so alien to Archbold that he did not see that he might have averted an antitrust suit with a little political flexibility.

═

By the time the Roosevelt administration formulated its suit, Rockefeller had not darkened the door of 26 Broadway for years. After 1905, he even stopped drawing a token salary. But Rockefeller was still held responsible for the sins of Standard Oil and most vilified when least involved in the business. Aware of the benefits of giving a human face to the trust, Roosevelt presented Rockefeller as the active genius of the cabal, and the press dramatized the antitrust case as a cockfight between Roosevelt and Rockefeller, the White House and 26 Broadway.

McCLURE'S MAGAZINE

FROM THE PORTRAIT BY ARTHUR DE FERRARIS

JOHN D ROCKEFELLER
A CHARACTER SKETCH BY IDA M. TARBELL

The cover of *McClure's Magazine* containing the malevolent "character sketch" by Ida Tarbell that so deeply wounded Rockefeller. (Courtesy of the Drake Well Museum)

Rockefeller en route to testify in an antitrust case against Standard Oil, November 18, 1908. (Courtesy of the Rockefeller Archive Center)

Rockefeller goes to court, escorted by John G. Milburn, a Standard Oil lawyer in the federal antitrust suit. (Courtesy of the Rockefeller Archive Center)

John D. Archbold, Rockefeller's combative protégé and successor. (Courtesy of the Rockefeller Archive Center)

Rockefeller (center) pauses at Forest Hill with some favorite golf cronies. From left: Dr. Hamilton F. Biggar, Elias M. Johnson, Capt. Levi T. Scofield, and Dr. Charles A. Eaton. (Courtesy of the Rockefeller Archive Center)

An eerily hairless Rockefeller holds an unidentified grandchild, September 23, 1904. (Courtesy of the Rockefeller Archive Center)

The first version of Kykuit, completed in 1908 and found wanting by John and Cettie. (Courtesy of the Rockefeller Archive Center)

The more compact and elegant second version of Kykuit, finished in 1913 and today open to the public. (Courtesy of the Rockefeller Archive Center)

An aerial view of John D.'s golf hideaway in Lakewood, New Jersey. (Courtesy of the Rockefeller Archive Center)

Rockefeller, nattily attired, strolls among the sheep that browsed outside his Golf House residence in Lakewood. (Courtesy of the Rockefeller Archive Center)

Chief lieutenants of the Rockefeller philanthropies: (top, left) Dr. Simon Flexner, director of the Rockefeller Institute for Medical Research; (top, right) Wickliffe Rose, head of the Rockefeller Sanitary Commission; (bottom, left) Starr J. Murphy, legal adviser to the Rockefeller Family Office; and (bottom, right) Wallace Buttrick, secretary of the General Education Board. (Courtesy of the Rockefeller Archive Center)

Abby Aldrich and John D.
Rockefeller, Jr., circa 1916.
(Courtesy of the Rockefeller
Archive Center)

The Rockefellers *could* be playful on occasion. Abby Aldrich and John D. Rockefeller, Jr., costumed
for a fancy dress ball at Louis Tiffany's home, probably around 1910. (Courtesy of the Rockefeller
Archive Center)

John D. Rockefeller, Jr., leaves hearings on the Ludlow Massacre, held at New York's City Hall in January 1915. (Courtesy of the Rockefeller Archive Center)

Junior takes the stand to testify about Ludlow. (Courtesy of the Rockefeller Archive Center)

A photographer captured an impromptu encounter between Junior and labor organizer Mother Jones—a vocal critic of Colorado Fuel and Iron—at the January 27, 1915, hearings. (Courtesy of the Rockefeller Archive Center)

Publicist Ivy Lee worked to rehabilitate the tarnished Rockefeller name after the Ludlow disaster. (Courtesy of the Princeton University Library)

Rockefeller sits wedged between two ladies in the backseat of his touring car. His hands often strayed during the afternoon drives. (Courtesy of the Rockefeller Archive Center)

Jo Davidson sculpts an equally stony-faced Rockefeller in 1924. (Courtesy of the Rockefeller Archive Center)

Abby Aldrich and John D. Rockefeller, Jr., with their children in Seal Harbor, Maine, 1921. From left to right: Laurance, Babs, John 3rd, David, Winthrop, and Nelson. (Courtesy of the Rockefeller Archive Center)

Rockefeller with Bessie's grandchildren, Elizabeth and John de Cuevas, Ormond Beach, 1933. (Courtesy of the Rockefeller Archive Center)

Rockefeller's winter home in Ormond Beach, Florida, called The Casements. (Courtesy of the Rockefeller Archive Center)

Rockefeller trades one-liners with Will Rogers in Ormond Beach, February 1927. (Courtesy of the Rockefeller Archive Center)

Rockefeller and daughter Alta at Ormond Beach, 1931. (Courtesy of the Rockefeller Archive Center)

Rockefeller, in trademark goggles, smacks a ball down the fairway at Ormond Beach, December 24, 1932. (Courtesy of the Rockefeller Archive Center)

Abby and John D. Rockefeller, Jr., tour the Grand Tetons in October 1931. (Courtesy of the Rockefeller Archive Center)

Junior bashfully greets the Rockettes at Radio City Music Hall, December 30, 1937. (Courtesy of the Rockefeller Archive Center)

Junior and Senior pose with Nelson and his first son, Rodman. (Courtesy of the Rockefeller Archive Center)

The sons of Abby and John D. Rockefeller, Jr., in their Eton collars. Left to right: David, Winthrop, Laurance, Nelson, and John 3rd. (Courtesy of the Rockefeller Archive Center)

A formal family dinner party at 740 Park Avenue in Manhattan, March 1949. Standing, from left to right: Irving H. Pardee, David, Nelson, Winthrop, and Laurance Rockefeller. Seated: John 3rd and John D. Rockefeller, Jr.(Courtesy of the Rockefeller Archive Center)

The wives at the same dinner party. From left to right: Abby (Babs) Rockefeller Pardee, Peggy McGrath Rockefeller, Mary "Tod" Rockefeller, Blanchette Hooker Rockefeller, Barbara "Bobo" Sears Rockefeller, and Mary French Rockefeller. (Courtesy of the Rockefeller Archive Center)

A photo taken on December 17, 1931, that shows the seamed, leathery face of John D. Rockefeller in his final decade. (Courtesy of the Rockefeller Archive Center)

Even before the federal government filed formal charges against Standard Oil, a rash of state suits broke out, the most aggressive one being in Missouri, where Herbert S. Hadley was elected attorney general in 1905. As a reform-minded prosecuting attorney in Kansas City, he had developed a reputation for battling corruption. No sooner did he become attorney general than he set out to prove that both Waters-Pierce and Republic Oil were secret marketing subsidiaries of Standard Oil that had fixed prices and carved up the state into exclusive sales territories with Standard Oil of Indiana. In serving subpoenas upon Standard executives in Manhattan, Hadley's men proved to be agile daredevils. "The gentlemen are following their daily avocation in town here but moving cautiously," Junior reported to his father from 26 Broadway.[16] One morning, Henry Rogers strode rapidly from his Manhattan town house to his chauffeured car. As it pulled away from the curb, a process server named M. E. Palemdo sprang from a hiding spot and landed on the running board. "Is this Mr. Henry H. Rogers?" he asked. While a speechless Rogers stared at this impudent interloper, Palemdo flung the subpoena at him, flashed his court order, then leaped from the speeding vehicle.

Even with such acrobatics, Hadley's minions could not catch Rockefeller, and the press joined in the national manhunt. Tracing a welter of rumors, reporters erroneously placed the titan aboard Henry Rogers's yacht, anchored off Puerto Rico, or in a hideaway with Flagler in Key West. As he decamped from one estate to the next, Rockefeller was reduced to the degrading life of a fugitive. Then his whereabouts were betrayed by the telltale cheese. Every day at Pocantico, Rockefeller received a shipment of his favorite cheese aboard the New York Central. One day, a local hack driver, Henry Cooge, informed the press that suspicious cheeses were again entering Pocantico. "Them cheeses," he said, "I would recognize anywhere, no matter whether it is day or night. . . . Rockefeller, in my opinion, is somewhere on his estate."[17]

Cooge's nose was correct: Rockefeller had retreated to Pocantico, turning it into his fortress, flanked on every side by detectives. Waves of process servers flung themselves against the battlements to no effect. "Time and again," said one newspaper, "process servers in various disguises have succeeded in passing the pickets, but never have they penetrated beyond the inner guard of detectives. When discovered they have been handled roughly and promptly ejected by the oil king's minions."[18] Afraid that his phone was being tapped, Rockefeller advised Cettie not to telephone him. He also advised his secretary at 26 Broadway to forward letters to him in plain envelopes without return addresses.

At a convenient moment, via a backdoor route, Rockefeller fled by boat from Tarrytown to Golf House in Lakewood, where he set up conditions worthy of a maximum-security prison. Floodlights were trained on people approaching the estate at night, and delivery wagons were searched thoroughly, lest they conceal crouching servants of the law. When Abby gave birth to John D. Rockefeller III in March 1906, the newspapers gloated that because of Hadley's marauding agents Rockefeller could not visit his first male grandson bearing the Rockefeller name. The New York *World* taunted him with the headline, "Grandson Born to John D. Rockefeller And He, Mewed Up in His Lakewood Fort, Could Only Rejoice by Phone."[19] This artful dodger urged relatives to keep his location secret. He advised brother-in-law William Rudd: "Confidentially I prefer not to have it known where I am. It often saves me much annoyance. My correspondence has been cut down fifty or seventy-five per cent since the autumn. I say this because some curious people might be asking you if you heard from me or if you were writing me, etc. I do not wish to have it known now or at any time."[20] During the first round of testimony in New York, Hadley failed to get Rockefeller on the stand, but the humiliating pursuit had made an impression on him. After Hadley returned to Missouri, Rockefeller inquired of Archbold, "Would it be well for us to see how we could settle the Missouri cases without further litigation or trouble? I am not prepared to say, but suggest that we give it careful thought."[21]

No sooner had he finished evading Hadley's men than Rockefeller's testimony was sought in a Philadelphia suit against the Pennsylvania Railroad. Instructed by his lawyers not to venture within one hundred miles of the city, he had George Rogers draw a hundred-mile radius around Philadelphia on a map, and he did not penetrate that ring. Slowly, his life was being tied into knots by court cases. In March 1906, when Junior wanted him to attend his class reunion at Brown or at least to write a congratulatory note, Rockefeller declined, explaining that "if the location from which I wrote was not given it would cause comment. If the letter was dated from 26 Broadway, that would cause comment, especially in connection with the statement that I had not been in my office for many years. . . . Possibly if no reference was made to me on this occasion, it might be better."[22]

As lawsuits kept appearing, Rockefeller reacted with the indignation of a man who felt wronged, and he cynically dismissed the politicians behind them as sensation-mongers. Nevertheless, he was being held hostage to Standard Oil's legal travails and expressed frustration with his nominal title of honorary president, which made him a lightning rod for attacks against the trust. When he sounded out Gates and Junior about resigning, he recalled that when Standard Oil of New Jersey was formed, he had allowed his name to be used "at the solicitation of my associates, though I earnestly requested them to name my successor."[23] Both Gates and Junior pressed him to drop the unwanted title, which they thought a handicap to the conduct of his philanthropies.

In August 1906, amid great secrecy, Rockefeller quietly dictated a letter to George Rogers, resigning as president of Standard Oil and asking for speedy board approval—a request he renewed several times over the next few years. As he told Archbold, "I am placed in a false position and subjected to ridicule for not knowing about the affairs as one should know to be in the official relation; and I shall not be surprised to hear of stringent legislation to punish people for occupying positions in this way."[24] Every time that Rockefeller made this plea, Archbold resisted, afraid that his departure might appear to repudiate the organization at a vulnerable moment and undermine shareholder confidence. As far as Archbold was concerned, Rockefeller was now in too deep to back out. "We told him that he had to keep" the title of president, Henry Rogers had earlier told Ida Tarbell. "These cases against us were pending in the courts; and we told him that if any of us had to go to jail, he would have to go with us!"[25]

=

Rockefeller and his colleagues had been slow to grasp the power of the growing newspaper chains and mass-circulation magazines, which could now saturate the country with a story. Rockefeller's image was suddenly everywhere. One cartoonist pictured him approaching a newsstand where his face was featured on the cover of every publication and dolefully asking the vendor: "Do you have any that aren't about me?" In another cartoon, Rockefeller shoveled coins into one side of a scale, with a scrap of paper saying "A Few Kind Words" on the other side; the caption wondered: "What Would He Give for Them?" This most secretive of men saw his most obscure designs exposed everywhere. Wanting to forget the past, he now had to confront it at every turn.

In retrospect, it seems clear that Rockefeller's press critics profited from a fleeting transitional moment when corporations had not adapted to the new media and lacked any public-relations apparatus. For nearly three years, Standard Oil was assailed by Ida Tarbell and made only halfhearted responses. When editorials appeared impugning the *McClure's* series, for instance, Rockefeller had copies circulated widely. And for years, Standard Oil clandestinely paid $15,000 per annum to an English economist named George Gunton who edited a magazine that with telltale regularity disputed Lloyd and Tarbell. (For fear of the political consequences, Rockefeller and his descendants always balked at outright ownership of major news properties.) The trust also financed a sympathetic history, *The Rise and Supremacy of the Standard Oil Company* by Gilbert H. Montague, which began as his thesis as a Harvard undergraduate. Yet these were random efforts, not a coordinated counterattack.

The real publicity watershed for Standard Oil came after the tainted-money controversy. Feeling impotent in the face of misinformation, Gates badgered Rockefeller with plans for a literary bureau, and Rockefeller encouraged him to speak to Archbold. According to Gates, Archbold was "overjoyed" by Rockefeller's change of heart, and the upshot was that the trust hired its first publicist, Joseph I. C. Clarke, an editor of the *New York Herald.*[26] Although Ivy Lee was already handling publicity for the Pennsylvania Railroad, such a step was still a novelty in corporate America. Most businesses did not concede the legitimacy of journalists poking into their affairs and consequently had no full-time publicist on the payroll. A jovial, outgoing poet and playwright, Clarke would greet reporters with a quip and a cigar to warm up the trust's image. Before long, he was lining up reporters for breezy, lighthearted interviews with Rockefeller, featuring a game of golf with the mogul, who obligingly delivered pithy observations on topical subjects. Articles began to appear with titles like "The Human Side of John D. Rockefeller," as if its existence wasn't taken for granted.

At first, Junior doubted the efficacy of even favorable stories. But as early as 1903, he and Parmalee Prentice beseeched Senior to publish an authorized biography to rebut Tarbell's work before it formed the basis of future histories. Sure that history would vindicate him, Rockefeller at first temporized, then compromised to appease his son—setting a pattern for the next three decades. In 1904, he began dictating answers to biographical questions posed by Starr Murphy, yet his heart was not in it, and the project soon expired. Work on an official Standard Oil history fared only marginally better. In 1906, a special executive committee of Standard Oil of New Jersey hired the Reverend Leonard Woolsey Bacon to write a history, and Rockefeller vetted his chapter on the South Improvement Company. Then Bacon got sick and only a pamphlet appeared.

Rockefeller imagined that the press's muckraking ardor would cool shortly. He took comfort from the fact that the new mass media exemplified the big-business capitalism they deplored and so could not very well tolerate radical critiques for long. How could big newspaper barons such as Joseph Pulitzer crusade against their own interests? As Rockefeller assured Gates, "The owner of the *World* is also a large owner of property, and I presume that, in common with other newspaper owners who are possessed of wealth, his eyes are beginning to be opened to the fact that he is like Samson, taking the initiative to pull the building down upon his head."[27] By 1905, Rockefeller and his entourage were picking up hints that investigative zeal was ebbing among the editors at *McClure's*, where, Starr Murphy reported, "the thing has now gone so far that they themselves are getting disgusted and heartily wish they were out of it."[28] In March 1906, Teddy Roosevelt delivered his famous speech at Washington's Gridiron Club in which he borrowed a term from *Pilgrim's Progress* and denounced the new investigative reporters as muckrakers who kept their eyes fixed on lowly matters instead of occasionally lifting them up to heaven. The muckrakers were now on the wane, but the trustbusters were not.

—

Hounded by government and the press, Rockefeller found little solace in family affairs. In May 1906, he provided one cousin with a somber litany of problems that had beset the family since the Tarbell series. Edith had returned from her therapeutic travels in Europe, which were supposed to alleviate her depression, but she was sick and recuperating only slowly; Junior was making progress after his breakdown but was still weak; Alta had been in bed for several weeks after surgery; and Cettie was laid low with pneumonia and grippe. "So I think we will agree," Rockefeller summed up, "that no one family has a monopoly of the ills of life."[29] At sixty-six, he was the healthiest specimen in the family.

Of all the family medical problems, the most worrisome was that of Bessie. She and her husband, Charles Strong, had moved to Cannes in May 1904 to confer with neurological experts, especially a Dr. Bourcart. Now, two years later, she was also suffering from heart trouble and was too debilitated to return home. While Rockefeller applauded her for seeking rest in a warm, sunny climate, he was distressed by her two-year absence abroad. Sensitive to her delicate psychological state, he sent her gently whimsical letters. "I weigh nearly two hundred pounds, without my five wigs," he wrote in December 1905. "You should see them! They are real works of art, and most satisfactory. I sleep in one, and do not know how I got along all these years without the hair."[30]

In spring 1906, frustrated by Bessie's absence, Rockefeller and Cettie decided to spend seven weeks with the Strongs in France—an eternity abroad for these two provincials—at their summer residence in Compiègne, northeast of Paris. That May, Charles had reported that Bessie "you will be glad to hear, is in better condition at the present than at any time since we came abroad, though we shall hardly be able to cross the ocean this summer."[31] Rockefeller might have seen a sudden chance to deliver a timely plea for Bessie's return to America. In commenting on the trip, George Santayana said of the Rockefellers, "they are going to travel under an assumed name, to protect themselves from begging letters and indiscreet curiosity."[32] But Rockefeller might also have wanted to travel incognito to foil efforts to serve him with subpoenas.

In June 1906, the Rockefeller party—including Cettie, Lute, Alta, and Dr. Biggar—sailed for France aboard the *Deutschland*, with the Rockefeller name discreetly omitted from the passenger list. When it was learned that Rockefeller was aboard, the press busied itself with speculation about his motives. Some reporters stressed his desire to avoid testimony and others his supposedly broken health. Perhaps the most outrageous theory came from a *New York American* reporter, William Hoster, who conjectured luridly that Rockefeller's stomach was ruined, that he was going to consult a renowed European specialist, and that he might never return alive. Hoping to observe Rockefeller at close range, Hoster purchased a ticket for the crossing, intending to file a series entitled "How the Richest Man in the World Plays."

During the voyage, as he stalked his quarry, Hoster was amazed at how different Rockefeller was from the stereotype that he himself had foisted on readers. For one thing, Rockefeller had an excellent appetite and wolfed down three meals a day. "It was a distinct shock to me," he later wrote, "when Mr. Rockefeller strolled up the plank to find him, instead of the hopeless dyspeptic that he had been painted, a tall, broad-shouldered, robust man, with ruddy complexion, clear eyes, alert step and altogether vigorous manner."[33] Far from being aloof, Rockefeller fairly cavorted around the ship: bursting into a dance when he bested Dr. Biggar at shuffleboard; donning a harlequin's costume the night of the captain's dinner; and delighting small children with his antics. "One sturdy little fellow one afternoon produced two pennies, which he insisted upon sharing with his playmate Rockefeller," Hoster later wrote. "The man of millions gravely accepted the copper and carefully placed it in his pocket, then, with his face turned seaward impulsively took up the child and folded his arms about it."[34] This warmhearted man was a revelation to Hoster.

One part of Hoster's assignment was to land an exclusive interview with Rockefeller. When the boat docked at Cherbourg, he knew that the Rockefeller party would shortly roar off in a touring car and that he had to confront the mogul at once. While Rockefeller wandered in an arbor, Hoster accosted him and introduced himself. Though he pretended that he never read his critics, Rockefeller evidently knew Hoster's byline and expressed bitterness at the absurd treatment of his health. Hoster meekly confessed his error. Then, with a reporter's cheek, he asked, "Mr. Rockefeller, have you ever reflected that perhaps you yourself may be in a measure responsible for the way that you have been treated by the newspapers?" He recounted how, dozens of times, he had gone to Rockefeller's homes to try to interview him but had never been admitted or even allowed a glimpse, which seemed to verify the reports of ill health. Turning to another canard that Hoster had swallowed, Rockefeller noted that he had not been involved in Standard Oil management for many years. "Is it possible that is not known?" he asked. "I have made no concealment of it. All my friends know it."[35] Yet Hoster insisted that he and other reporters were genuinely ignorant of that, and he implored him to make it public.

For a time, Rockefeller gazed stonily at Hoster and dug his walking stick into the gravel path. Then his face relaxed and a faint smile crossed his lips. "So it is all my fault," Rockefeller said, with a touch of sarcasm. Then, after a pause, he added more seriously, "I suppose there may be something in what you say, though I had never thought of it in that way before."[36] Since Rockefeller had demonized reporters, much as they had demonized him, he was surprised to find that Hoster was sincere and invented stories for lack of accurate information.

Rockefeller's attitude toward the press had already begun to evolve with Standard's hiring of Joseph I. C. Clarke, which might have predisposed him to talk more freely with Hoster. When Hoster asked if he was worth a billion dollars, Rockefeller shot back, "Nothing like it—not by one-third of that amount. I want to make clear to you the injury that is done to me by these persistent stories that I am worth a billion dollars. They provoke in the minds of thousands thoughts which lead to great unhappiness."[37] Gradually opening up as they walked along, Rockefeller told Hoster how grieved he was to be transformed into a monster. "Is it not patent that I have been made into a sort of frightful ogre, to slay which has become a favorite resource of men seeking public favor?"[38] As always, Rockefeller blamed business rivals and demagogic politicians for his troubles. Yet however self-serving his remarks, he was at least now talking to a reporter. Then, to Hoster's extreme amazement, Rockefeller invited him to accompany the party to Compiègne. How could he possibly resist?

Charles and Bessie were renting the Château des Avenues at the edge of the forest of Compiègne for the summer. Once the summer home of Queen Isabella of Spain, it was now owned by the Duc de l'Aigle. Despite his wife's illness, Charles was winding up a new book called *The Origin of Consciousness*. The Rockefellers were heartened to find the forty-year-old Bessie in improved health, though her mental faculties remained gravely impaired. When George Santayana visited during the Rockefellers' stay, he wrote to a friend, apropos of Charles, "It is a terrible life he leads as his wife is like a child, hopelessly ill, yet apparently not going to die for the present."[39] Unlike Hoster, Santayana was shocked at how poorly Rockefeller looked, old and wrinkled and wearing a "pepper and salt wig decidedly too small for him."[40]

After a lifetime spent escaping reporters, Rockefeller now converted William Hoster into his bosom companion. They rambled through the forest, golfed, and dined together in local hotels. After teaching Hoster how to ride a bike, he took him cycling down the main street of Compiègne, along with his adored nine-year-old granddaughter, Margaret. Hoster was struck by Rockefeller's strong populist streak, how he was intrigued by common people but indifferent to the highborn. In discussing Napoleon, Rockefeller said, "He was a human being and virile because he came direct from the ranks of the people. There was none of the stagnant blood of nobility or royalty in his veins."[41] Rockefeller was entranced by Joan of Arc. "Where did she get her wisdom, if it was not inspired of Heaven?" he asked.[42] Sight-seeing with Hoster, Rockefeller might have begun to taste, for the first time, the pleasures of confession. "They will know me better when I am dead, Mr. Hoster," Rockefeller said one day. "There has been nothing in my life that will not bear the utmost scrutiny."[43]

Rockefeller found it impossible during this European idyll to banish thoughts of his tribulations at home. Around the time of his departure from New York, Attorney General Moody had announced the preliminary antitrust investigation of Standard Oil. Then, in early July, Rockefeller received word that a probate court in Hancock County, Ohio, had brought an antitrust action against Standard Oil and issued a warrant for Rockefeller's arrest. The local sheriff had bragged to reporters that he would be on the dock to greet Rockefeller when he sailed back from Europe. George Rogers relayed a message from Archbold, who called the Ohio suit frivolous but advised Rockefeller to extend his European stay. Rogers also reported a new suit in the works in Arkansas. "There seems to be a perfect wave of attacks all along the line," he warned from New York.[44] By late July, the Standard lawyers, reversing their earlier position, pressed Rockefeller to return, assuring him that the Ohio case was targeted against Standard Oil companies in the state, not individuals. As it turned out, Rockefeller was not arrested at the dock, since his lawyers had arranged for him to testify voluntarily in the Ohio case.

Having booked return passage on the *Amerika* for July 20, 1906, John and Cettie yearned to take Bessie with them. Rockefeller and Charles clashed repeatedly over this question. Charles later told William James, "I had an uphill fight to prevent Mr. Rockefeller from taking his daughter back with him in defiance of expert opinion."[45] Rockefeller refused to believe that Bessie was too frail to make the crossing. In the end, somewhat reluctantly, even resentfully, he acquiesced in Charles's decision to keep her in France. Charles might have performed one signal service for him, however. One Sunday afternoon, he read aloud an essay that he had drafted on the duties of rich men, arguing that when people accumulated wealth on a colossal scale, they should then convert that wealth into public trusts, administered by trustees for the commonweal. This essay might have strengthened Rockefeller's wish to create a huge philanthropic foundation.

Back in New York in August, Rockefeller tried to launch a new era in his relations with the press. In fact, reporters were so startled by his sudden, voluble friendliness that one headline declared, "Oil King Acts Like Political Candidate."[46] When Hoster published a long, flattering interview with Rockefeller, the latter applauded the "fair and square treatment" he had received.[47] Deciding to combat ghoulish stories about his patient's health, Dr. Biggar gathered reporters and said, "Mr. Rockefeller is in stronger physical health than he has been in the last fifteen years. He is as active and as light-hearted as a schoolboy. The trip has benefited him wonderfully."[48]

Though sorry to return without Bessie, the Rockefellers had been encouraged by her progress, and Rockefeller, in thanksgiving, distributed shares of stock to family members. These hopes were cruelly dashed when word came from France on November 13 that Bessie had suffered a paralytic stroke. Rockefeller wired Charles, "Love Sympathy Hope. Leave nothing undone." He took comfort in the thought that Bessie had a good doctor, an attentive husband, and a loving daughter. But the next day came the dreadful wire from Charles: "Bessie Passed Away at Two O'Clock This Morning Without Suffering."[49] Deeply shaken, Rockefeller replied: "We all send love. All is well with dear Bessie. Command us for any service. Father."[50] By a ghastly coincidence, this news arrived just as the government began to prosecute Standard Oil under the Sherman Antitrust Act.

When Bessie Strong died, so little was known about this reclusive heiress that the newspapers strained to pad out their obituaries, admitting that she was known only to a small circle of family intimates. In late November, Charles and Margaret brought the body back for burial in the Sleepy Hollow Cemetery in Tarrytown. Having lost Bessie, the Rockefellers wanted Charles to settle in America, but he was now a permanent expatriate. As he told William James, "I have never been especially proud of being an American."[51] Fluent in German, Hebrew, Latin, Greek, and French, he wanted to return to Europe, seeing it as the fountainhead of culture. For Rockefeller, American to the marrow, convinced that European society was decadent, such an attitude was incomprehensible. Around this time, when reporters asked whether he might ever retire to Europe, he replied, "The United States can't develop enough drawbacks to make me lose the feeling that there is no place like home."[52]

To Rockefeller's immense chagrin, Charles took Margaret to England, where she went to school in Sussex and then to Newnham College, Cambridge. During the next thirty years, Charles took an apartment in Paris and a villa in Fiesole near Bernard Berenson's I Tatti, living the life of a solitary, melancholy widower. Rockefeller kept renewing his earnest plea that Margaret be educated in New York City, and it became a sore point with him that Charles refused to oblige him. A year after Bessie's death, Rockefeller discontinued all further gifts to his son-in-law, though not to Margaret. He feared that Margaret would become isolated from the rest of the family and was haunted by fears that she would be seduced by a continental fortune hunter. As he bemoaned to Edith, "[Margaret] is a dear girl. How much we wish she were at school in this country, where we could see her oftener; and when she gets all through with the English school, where are the American acquaintances to come from? I am talking this to her and Charles plainly, but without any encouraging response."[53]

Rockefeller worried that Charles was exposing his granddaughter to too many radical, secular ideas. That Charles deplored capitalism, advocated trade unions, and favored taxes to rectify inequalities of income—these things Rockefeller could tolerate. But he could not condone that Charles led his daughter away from the church and deprived her of religious instruction. In 1908, Charles told Junior that he had dismissed Margaret's beloved Irish governess, a Miss Lawrenson, for introducing religion into their household. "I find that, quite without her fault, Margaret was imbibing Catholic ideas, and there was nothing for it but to make a change, greatly as I regretted letting Miss L. go."[54] Every time that Charles and Margaret visited New York, the Rockefellers tried to lure them back to church—a strategy that probably backfired and fortified their resolve to stay away. During one such visit in 1909, Junior wrote to his mother, "Charles and Margaret took supper with us again last Sunday night and went with us to church as far as the corner of Fifth Avenue and Forty-Sixth

Street. Whether we ever get any nearer or not time only will tell."[55] More than a decade after Bessie's death, Rockefeller was still jockeying to get Margaret back, asking his son-in-law Harold McCormick if he and Edith could use their "united influence to get Charles and Margaret to come over here when it is possible to do so. We want to have Margaret live with us."[56]

=

Before considering the particulars of the antitrust case against Standard Oil, it is worth pursuing for a moment Rockefeller's metamorphosis into a master of public relations. Back at Forest Hill that autumn, Rockefeller did something unexpected: He received—in a suitably jolly mood—a delegation from the American Press Humorists, who were so charmed by his wit that they elected him an honorary member and then cheerfully boasted that they now had the highest per-capita income of any such society in the world. For a long time, Starr Murphy and other aides had argued that if only reporters would meet Rockefeller and see him as a father, friend, and neighbor, he would not be so grotesquely misrepresented in the press. Joe Clarke invited more reporters to golf with the titan, and these festive outings, full of gags and banter, invariably produced favorable articles. "I have as my constant companions at golf, magazine writers and newspaper men," Rockefeller wrote to Harold McCormick in September 1906. "They say they did not know me before, and seem entirely friendly and well disposed."[57]

As he abandoned his fearful attitude toward the press, he loosened up, as if liberated by the change. It formed part of a general development away from the more severe manner of his business years. *Leslie's Weekly* reported the following year, "At the age of sixty-seven he is growing out of his chrysalis. For the first years of his life he is beginning to enjoy himself. Two years ago he dodged newspaper men. Now he courts them."[58] Virtually every reporter who profiled Rockefeller was surprised to discover a courteous, lighthearted old gentleman. "Never have I known anyone who could approach Mr. Rockefeller in thoughtful little attentions," one impressed reporter wrote. "This is the testimony of all his guests. His worst enemy would succumb to this treatment."[59] In response to this friendlier press treatment, Edith started giving her father giant scrapbooks, stuffed with the hundreds of articles about him that appeared around the world each year.

Though he had spurned many chances to respond to Ida Tarbell and declined offers to write his life, Rockefeller now decided to publish his memoirs in Tarbell-like monthly installments in *The World's Work*. The magazine was an especially safe, attractive forum since its editor, Walter H. Page, was a member of the General Education Board. In February 1908, Rockefeller began to play golf daily in Augusta, Georgia, with the publisher, Frank N. Doubleday. Their talks resulted in a string of seven articles published under the title "Random Reminiscences of Men and Events" starting in October 1908. These quaint, superficial pieces were ghostwritten by Doubleday, assisted by Starr Murphy. After Doubleday, Page published them in book form in 1909, the volume was released simultaneously in England, Germany, France, and Italy. Rockefeller thought this due penance from publishers who were trying to undo past harm "when they supposed they were serving the cause of righteousness," as he told Edith.[60]

For legal reasons, editing the series required great tact. Rockefeller knew that the attorney general would be scanning the series for his antitrust suit and Standard's lawyers rigorously combed every word. At first, Rockefeller wanted to trim the Widow Backus section, citing the petty sums at stake, but Gates rejoined that it was precisely the minute sums that had given the story its hold over the popular imagination. "I doubt if any single libel against you or the company has done more harm," Gates said bluntly. "If a man or a company could do such things to a poor and defenceless widow and for a small sum of money, how relentless must be its spirit and its methods!"[61] Bowing to Gates's reasoning, the titan devoted more pages to Backus than to any of his mighty industrial ventures.

For the most part, Rockefeller eschewed controversy in his book. Doubleday wanted to replace the image of the forbidding Rockefeller with that of the easygoing man he had come to know. In the series, Rockefeller struck an avuncular note, presenting himself as an avid gardener and sportsman, telling the reader at the outset, "On a rainy morning like this, when golf is out of the question, I am tempted to become a garrulous old man."[62] He was just plain John, the next-door neighbor. Of his current life, he said, "I live like a farmer away from active happenings in business, playing golf, planting trees; and yet I am so busy that no day is long enough."[63] As always, he tried to seem a model of Christian forbearance, turning the other cheek to unfair attacks against him. "I have had at least my full share of adverse criticism, but I can truly say that it has not embittered me, nor left me with any harsh feeling against a living soul."[64]

In *Random Reminiscences,* Rockefeller described a fair world where strong, hardworking people were rewarded, and lazy folks punished; no admixture of tragedy clouded his vision. Despite the swelling tide of antitrust suits, Rockefeller reiterated his faith that cooperation, not competition, advanced the general welfare. "Probably the greatest single obstacle to the progress and happiness of the American people," he intoned, "lies in the willingness of so many men to invest their time and money in multiplying competitive industries instead of opening up new fields, and putting their money into lines of industry and development that are needed."[65]

Though Rockefeller's memoirs received mixed reviews, they helped to humanize his image. Everyone, of course, was eager for Ida Tarbell's reaction, and she duly delivered a booming cannonade of criticism to a Chicago newspaper:

Listen: There is the Mr. Rockefeller of his autobiography, for whom I have a real, a great admiration. He is admirable—there is no other word—in his quietly wise discussions of the proper setting out of Japanese quinces and blue firs, of the arrangements of geraniums and roses. . . . And then there is the other Mr. Rockefeller. . . . Utterly and almost as impersonally ruthless as a whirlwind or a torrent, he has swept through the country a conquering Hun, regardless of all save winning for himself. No, he's not a Hun: the destructive force of him is too intelligent. He is more like Bernard Shaw's Napoleon—great, because for himself he suspended the ordinary laws of conventionality and morality while keeping them in operation for other people. He is a mastodon of mental machinery. And would you ask a steam plow for pity? Would you look for scruples in an electric dynamo?[66]

Clearly, the lady had not mellowed.

=

Besides acting as midwife for *Random Reminiscences,* Doubleday made another valuable contribution to Rockefeller's rehabilitation. As head of the Periodical Publishers' Association, he dreamed up the idea of having Rockefeller address a luncheon of New York publishers; in a splendid coup de théâtre, the mogul would be introduced by Mark Twain, the chief satirist of the Gilded Age. As it turned out, Twain was ripe for this venture. In the summer of 1907, his dear friend Henry H. Rogers had suffered a stroke, and Twain had stayed with him in Bermuda from February 24 to April 11, 1908, easing his convalescence. Twain's favorite daughter, Susy, had died of spinal meningitis a decade earlier at age twenty-four. When Frank Doubleday told Twain that Simon Flexner's antimeningitis serum, developed at the Rockefeller Institute for Medical Research, had cut the death rate from the disease from 75 to 25 percent of those afflicted, Twain was all the more eager to help.

Always on good terms with Rockefeller, Twain thought he deserved a fair hearing from the press and was sure he would make a good impression on the publishers. Beyond his affection for Rogers, Twain recoiled at the sanctimonious tone the press often adopted in attacking the trusts. He knew all about Rockefeller's business reputation, but some perverse, irreverent streak attracted him to anyone who was so deliciously notorious. For Twain, a man so universally hated by the American public had to have many redeeming features.

When Doubleday asked Rockefeller to meet with the magazine publishers, Rockefeller, now an old hand at press relations, replied, "Certainly. Why not? I am willing to meet and talk with any body of men, friends or enemies."[67] On May 20, 1908, Doubleday sat at the head of the luncheon table at the Aldine Club, surrounded by forty or fifty magazine publishers, when the rear door flew open and Mark Twain, Henry Rogers, and the two Rockefellers, junior and se-nior, marched single file into the room. As Twain noted of those present, "there was probably not one whose magazine had not had the habit for the past few years of abusing the Rockefellers, Henry Rogers, and the other chiefs of the Standard Oil."[68] Since Rockefeller had avoided contact with the literati, three-fourths of the publishers, by Twain's estimate, had never before set eyes on him.

First Rogers and then Twain gave brief introductions before Rockefeller got up to speak. His talk, illustrated with moving anecdotes, described the work of the RIMR. Rockefeller was still a tall, imposing man, yet there was now a touch of melancholy in his eyes, and it was a sadder, more reflective face that stared out at the magazine publishers. The next morning, Twain, who had no equal himself on the lecture platform, jotted down this tribute:

> Mr. Rockefeller got up and talked sweetly, sanely, simply, humanly, and with astonishing effectiveness, being interrupted by bursts of applause at the end of almost every sentence; and when he sat down all those men were his friends and he had achieved one of the completest victories I have ever had any knowledge of. Then the meeting broke up, and by a common impulse the crowd moved forward and each individual of it gave the victor a hearty hand-shake, and along with it some hearty compliments upon his performance as an orator.[69]

It was an unlikely triumph for a reclusive man who had refrained from public speaking and had fled from the press for so long. Unfortunately, he had turned this skill to advantage much too late, since the political assault against Stan-dard Oil now headed inexorably toward its finale.

*A grim John D. Rockefeller votes in November 1908, not long
after the shocking disclosure of the Archbold bribery scandal.*
(Courtesy of the Rockefeller Archive Center)

CHAPTER 27

Judgment Day

O n November 18, 1906, the federal government filed suit in Missouri to dissolve Standard Oil under the Sherman Antitrust Act, naming as defendants Standard Oil of New Jersey, sixty-five companies under its control, and a pantheon of chieftains, including John and William Rockefeller, Henry Flagler, Oliver Payne, John Archbold, and Henry Rogers. They were charged with monopolizing the oil industry and conspiring to restrain trade through a familiar litany of tactics: railroad rebates, the abuse of their pipeline monopoly, predatory pricing, industrial espionage, and the secret ownership of ostensible competitors. The proposed remedy was sweeping: to break up the massive combine into its component companies. As a government report documented in 1907, the Standard Oil leviathan still refined 87 percent of all kerosene, handled 87 percent of exported kerosene, marketed 89 percent of domestic kerosene, and was more than twenty times the size of its most serious competitor, Pure Oil. After the suit was filed, Standard officials tried to sound sanguine and could not subdue their now delusional sense of invincibility. In a letter marked "Strictly confidential," Rockefeller told Archbold of reports that the Justice Department had scant confidence in its own case and that it was just a flimsy vendetta worked up by Roosevelt. "This program is the usual topic of his present day talk with friends and he shows a disposition that is vindictive. If his suit fails, he means to urge legislation, if he can have it framed, aimed at the same target."[1]

There seems little doubt that Standard Oil seriously misplayed its cards with Roosevelt. In January 1907, the president tangled with one of his nemeses, Ohio senator Joseph B. Foraker, before a crowded dinner at the Gridiron Club in

Washington. A stout ally of Standard Oil, Senator Foraker stiffly resisted measures to regulate business. With patent indignation, Roosevelt excoriated Foraker and the "malefactors of great wealth" behind him. As he pronounced the classic phrase, some reporters thought his gaze traveled to J. P. Morgan, whereas Morgan's friends insisted that the president eyed Henry H. Rogers, then sitting next to Morgan. The latter were probably right, for Morgan and his client firms had handled relations better with the White House. If Roosevelt treated the Morgan interests (U.S. Steel, International Harvester, et al.) more leniently than he did Standard Oil, it was partly because they had submitted to guidance from the Bureau of Corporations and worked out informal arrangements to correct violations. In briefing his father on the antitrust case, Junior relayed rumors that U.S. Steel had pushed Frank Kellogg to target Standard Oil so as to deflect heat from itself. He also mentioned that several Standard Oil executives, including Charles M. Pratt and Edward T. Bedford, thought that U.S. Steel had wisely placated the government while Archbold had been foolishly antagonistic. Senior preferred to view Standard Oil as vengefully singled out for abuse and claimed that "other large corporations went scot free who were regarded by these ablest attorneys in the land as far more vulnerable than was the Standard Oil Company."[2]

By the summer of 1907, the political fight against Standard Oil had spread across a vast, bloody battlefield, with seven federal and six state suits (Texas, Minnesota, Missouri, Tennessee, Ohio, and Mississippi) in progress against the embattled trust. New legal skirmishes seemed to crop up weekly. That year, an Ohio grand jury brought in 939 indictments against Rockefeller and other Standard Oil officers; a bill was introduced in Tennessee to oust the trust on antitrust grounds; Missouri fined and expelled the Waters-Pierce Company; and so on and so forth.

Approaching his sixty-eighth birthday, Rockefeller had never imagined that his twilight years would be so eventful. His fortune had failed to purchase him even a poor man's mite of tranquillity. As nominal president of Standard Oil, he was in a bind, responsible for actions he had not approved. In a July 1907 letter that betrayed considerable anguish, Rockefeller again pleaded with Archbold to accept his resignation and release him from his torment. During the next two weeks, he repeatedly proffered his resignation, telling Archbold this would free him from several subpoenas. Though he owned 27.4 percent of Standard Oil stock—three times the amount held by Flagler, the next largest shareholder—Archbold turned him down flat, and Rockefeller bowed to his protégé's wishes. But the decision did not sit well with him.

One thing evident amid the spate of lawsuits was that railroad rebates had not faded as an issue, even though pipelines had governed the oil business for more than a generation. When rebates were again forbidden by the Elkins Act of 1903 and the Hepburn Act of 1906, the public naively assumed they had ended. Then the Interstate Commerce Commission reported in January 1907 that Standard Oil was *still* secretly accepting rebates, spying on competitors, setting up bogus subsidiaries, and engaging in predatory pricing—the same deadly sins patented by Rockefeller back in the 1870s. Roosevelt and his cabinet thirsted for a test case that would prove Standard Oil's collusion with the railroads and dramatize the twin evils of abusive trusts and scheming railroads.

The issue was duly highlighted in a 1907 case in Chicago in which Standard Oil of Indiana was accused of taking illegal rebates from the Chicago and Alton Railroad. The shipments in question had passed between Whiting, Indiana, and East Saint Louis, Illinois, *after* such rebates were outlawed by the Elkins Act. (Rockefeller, we recall, always insisted that Standard Oil took no rebates after they were banned in 1887.) The presiding figure in the Chicago courtroom was a gaunt, outspoken judge with premature white hair named Kenesaw Mountain Landis who, at forty-one, was newly appointed to the federal bench and later served as the first baseball commissioner.

Eager to levy an eye-popping fine against the trust, Landis asked its attorneys for figures on its capitalization and earnings between 1903 and 1905. The Standard lawyers, Landis knew, were in a tight spot: If they furnished the true figures, they might invite a punitive fine, if they withheld them, they would look guilty. On June 26, 1907, the federal district attorney tried to pry loose from Standard counsel John S. Miller a list of employees privy to those numbers. "I'll see you in hell first" was Miller's cordial reply. This riposte backfired: Landis assigned U.S. marshals to subpoena several Standard Oil officials, including Rockefeller. Flouting the judge's request, Rockefeller again fled and stayed with Alta and Parmalee in Pittsfield, Massachusetts. He instructed the bedridden Cettie, by now a battle-hardened veteran, to keep quiet about his whereabouts and send him mail only under the Prentice name. For several days, as the press guessed at Rockefeller's whereabouts, Landis's process server tried to track the titan through the New England countryside.

When Teddy Roosevelt and his attorney general heard that Landis wanted to haul Rockefeller into court, they were greatly dismayed, for if Rockefeller testified in the Chicago case, he might win an "immunity bath" from possible criminal prosecution in the more important federal antitrust suit. They sent an emissary to Chicago to plead with Landis. "I'd like to oblige Mr. Roosevelt," he said. "I'd do anything in reason to oblige him. But Rockefeller is making a monkey out of my process server, and I'm going to bring him before this court to vindicate its dignity."[3] Rockefeller must have discovered the legal advantages of testimony, because he suddenly contacted Judge Landis from Pittsfield and voluntarily accepted a subpoena from a deputy marshal.

On July 5, 1907, arriving by private railroad car, John and William Rockefeller and Henry Flagler conferred with lawyers at the spacious new offices of

Standard Oil of Indiana in Chicago. Instead of cooperating with Landis, Rockefeller counseled defiance and opposed revealing the balance sheets. "But, Mr. Rockefeller, times have changed," Flagler said. "The old maxim, silence is golden, doesn't work so well." "Well," Rockefeller drawled, "it did when I was at the helm."[4] Though he had agreed to travel to Chicago, Rockefeller hesitated to appear in court, and when he canvassed the lawyers present, they seemed to side with him. Then he sounded out the youngest lawyer, Robert W. Stewart, who said, "Mr. Rockefeller, in view of the opinion rendered by the distinguished legal talent present, I hesitate to express an opinion." "Young man," Rockefeller said, "I'm paying you to give me your opinion." Summoning up his courage, Stewart said, "Mr. Rockefeller, you are no different from any other citizen before the law, and if I were you, I would appear."[5] For all his tough talk, Rockefeller was smart enough to abide by the young man's advice.

On the sultry morning of July 6, 1907, John and William Rockefeller arrived at the federal building and found streets teeming with hundreds of spectators. When Rockefeller was spotted in a straw hat, grasping a slender cane, somebody shouted, "Here he comes!" The crowd surged forward in such close ranks that it took a squad of twenty club-wielding detectives to clear a path. Rockefeller grinned when a street urchin called out, "There's a man who got his picture in the paper."[6] Some zealous onlookers tore buttons from Rockefeller's coat. By the time the Rockefeller brothers reached the sixth-floor courtroom, a red-faced William, sweating profusely, muttered, "An outrage! I never heard of such treatment."[7] By contrast, John D. exhibited his usual cool demeanor before an unruly mob. When he entered the sweltering courtroom, with electric fans slicing overhead, he even imitated a reporter trying to take notes in the crush of people. Once the doors were closed, the hum of spectators outside was still so loud that policemen had to clear the corridor.

After the marshal brought down his gavel, Rockefeller began fifteen minutes of unforgettable testimony. A virtuoso of evasive testimony, he was the tranquil eye of the storm. As one reporter noted, "Mr. Rockefeller was the coolest looking man in the room. Every motion he made was slow and dignified. His step was slow. His replies to the questions of the court were even slower."[8] Judge Landis, itching to interrogate Rockefeller, had not reckoned on his incomparable mastery of prevarication and selective memory loss. Once again, in the halls of justice, Rockefeller turned himself into a confused old dotard. The most modest question seemed to pose insurmountable challenges to his mind.

To start things off, Judge Landis asked, "Mr. Rockefeller, what is the business of the so-called Standard Oil Company of New Jersey?" "I believe, your Honor . . ." Rockefeller began, then appeared to lose his way. He paused, fiddled with his cane, crossed his legs, then made a second stab at an answer. "I believe, your Honor . . ." Here again, his mind wandered as Judge Landis tapped his spectacles on his desk in frustration. Finally, Rockefeller concentrated his faculties and replied, "I believe, your Honor, they operate an oil refinery in New Jersey."[9] To all questions, Rockefeller responded in this same slow, disconnected style, making his testimony worthless. In exchange, Landis had to give Rockefeller the one thing he dearly wanted: immunity from criminal prosecution. This testimony was not only a fiasco for the judge but a public-relations victory for Rockefeller. How, people wondered, could this sweet, bumbling old man have been the evil wizard of the trust? His testimony even received plaudits from the press. As he told Archbold afterward, "My experience at Chicago and with the newspaper people generally of late has been very satisfactory."[10]

A month later, Judge Landis took his revenge. On the morning of August 3, 1907, as more than a thousand people sought entrance to his courtroom, Landis read aloud his decision in the Standard Oil case. (Possibly in anticipation, Rockefeller had just announced a $32 million gift to the General Education Board.) Once again, with difficulty, the marshals shut the great doors to keep out waves of spectators. Pale and edgy, Judge Landis called Standard Oil no better than a common thief and castigated its lawyers for their "studied insolence."[11] As spectators guffawed at these insults, the bailiffs repeatedly had to rap for order. Then, Landis delivered his bombshell: a fine against Standard Oil of Indiana that dwarfed any other in American corporate history up until that time: $29.24 million ($457 million in 1996 dollars). This was the maximum penalty: $20,000 for each of 1,462 carloads of oil cited in the indictment. Reporters struggled to convey the magnitude of this fine. That money could build five battleships; fill 177 flatcars with silver dollars; employ 48,730 city-street workers each year. It amounted to slightly more than half the money coined annually by the federal government. Since it represented nearly 30 percent of Standard Oil's $100 million capitalization, Rockefeller's theoretical share of the fine worked out to $8,011,760. Asked about the penalty, Mark Twain said it reminded him of the bride's words the next morning: "I expected it but didn't suppose it would be so big."[12]

Rockefeller used the record fine to put on a characteristic show of aplomb. He was in the middle of a golf foursome in Cleveland when a messenger came sprinting across the fairway, clutching a yellow envelope. Taking it and handing the boy a dime, Rockefeller read the verdict without even a twitch. Finally, he put the message in his pocket and said to his golf partners, "Well, shall we go on gentlemen?"[13] Then he hit an excellent drive of about 160 yards down the fairway. At first, nobody dared to ask the question on their minds, but then one person screwed up his courage: "How much is it?" "Twenty-nine million, two hundred and forty thousand, the maximum penalty, I believe," Rockefeller answered coolly. Then he gestured toward the tee and said, "It is your honor. Will you gentlemen drive?"[14] By all reports, Rockefeller was in superb form that day and completed nine holes in fifty-three shots, his best score ever. The next day, in relating the incident, one Cleveland paper said: "Not by Change of Countenance or Movement Did the Standard's Founder Betray the Fact That He Might Have Been Annoyed or Angered by the Sentence Handed Down in Chicago."[15]

Of course, Rockefeller's poker face concealed deep rage. The Landis fine supported the thesis that the Standard Oil empire was based on unethical, even illegal, rebates, not on the business acumen of its founders. Before the day was over, Rockefeller issued a statement upbraiding the court: "A great injustice has been done the company. It was from ignorance on how the great business was founded. For all these years no one has known and no one seems to have cared how it came into existence."[16] Descrying Teddy Roosevelt's influence, Gates told Rockefeller that he had lost his admiration for the man and hoped that "this amazing and reckless robbery and plunder under the forms of law, may awake the business interests of the country and thoughtful men, to the perils into which we have drifted."[17]

At one point during that famous golf game of August 3, 1907, Rockefeller had remarked, "Judge Landis will be dead a long time before this fine is paid," and his prediction proved accurate.[18] He seldom spoke so harshly in public. Many observers saw the Landis fine as more of a political statement and a publicity stunt than sound jurisprudence. In July 1908, a federal appeals court not only revoked the fine but severely reprimanded Landis for considering each carload of oil as a separate offense. Judge Peter S. Grosscup, calling Landis's act an "abuse of judicial discretion," ordered a retrial, in which Standard Oil was subsequently found not guilty.[19] Teddy Roosevelt was hopping mad at the appeals court. While he had thought the Landis fine excessive, he had thought the trial itself fair. The day after the fine was thrown out, Roosevelt announced that the government would again prosecute Standard Oil for accepting rebates, since "there is absolutely no question as to the guilt of the defendant nor of the exceptionally grave character of the offense." Dismayed, he said with a touch of bombast that the decision had "hurt the cause of civilization."[20]

=

By the early fall of 1907, many Wall Street soothsayers were predicting a savage downturn in financial markets in response to the Landis fine and the antitrust suits. "It must be that these persecutions against business interests will not always continue," Senior warned his son in late August. "If so, we must be prepared for very disastrous results to our commercial fabric. I think we better increase our reserves of money with our income."[21] In the week after the Landis fine, Standard Oil shares skidded from 500 to 421, leading a stock-market slump.

For reform-minded critics, the ensuing panic originated with the misbehavior of the business fraternity itself. For several years, the stock market had coasted on a tide of easy money, low interest rates, and manic speculation in copper, mining, and railroad shares. In this euphoric mood, stock promoters had flogged unsound companies, and investors had gorged themselves on watered stock. Among the most flagrant speculators were trust companies that exploited legal loopholes to speculate heavily in the stock market while also lending excessively against securities as collateral. Roosevelt inveighed against "an era of over-confidence and speculation" that would lead to a severe purgative reaction.[22]

As money tightened that September, Rockefeller deposited in several New York banks bonds that could be pledged as security for government loans—a rescue operation for which he reaped a handsome 2 percent commission. As panic overtook Wall Street in late October 1907, throngs of petrified depositors lined up in front of banks to empty their accounts, and J. P. Morgan rushed back to New York from an Episcopal convention in Richmond. On October 22, after his aides examined the books of the Knickerbocker Trust, Morgan decided that it was hopelessly insolvent and had to be shut. That night, in an extraordinary pledge of faith in a private citizen, Treasury Secretary George Cortelyou met with Morgan in a Manhattan hotel and placed at his disposal twenty-five million dollars in government funds to stem the panic. While Morgan was the impresario of the salvage operation, Rockefeller provided more private money than anybody else.

When Gates got wind of the Knickerbocker's collapse, he telephoned Rockefeller at Pocantico in the early morning and said a public statement from him might restore confidence. Rockefeller stood there in his bathrobe, mulling over the matter, then decided to call Melville E. Stone, general manager of the Associated Press. He told Stone, for quotation, that the country's credit was sound and that, if necessary, he would give half of all he possessed to maintain America's credit. It was an unprecedented statement: A single citizen had promised to bail out Wall Street. The next morning, as these sedative words were reprinted across America, reporters spilled onto the golf course at Pocantico. When asked if he would *really* give half his securities to stop the panic, Rockefeller replied, "Yes, and I have cords of them, gentlemen, cords of them."[23] It was a rare case of Rockefeller boasting about his wealth, but it was clearly meant to lift public morale. Because Rockefeller deposited ten million dollars there, National City Bank had the deepest gold reserves and cash resources of any bank during the panic. "They always come to Uncle John when there is trouble," Rockefeller noted with pride.[24] When J. P. Morgan decided to save the shaky Trust Company of America on October 23, he received three million dollars in rescue funds from George F. Baker of First National Bank and James Stillman of National City Bank, the latter drawing on Rockefeller money.

For the first time in several years, John D. Rockefeller, Sr., strode through the portals of 26 Broadway on October 24 and took up his command post. "I was surprised to find so many men who had come to the front since my last visit years ago. Afterward I had an opportunity to talk with old associates and many new ones, and it was a source of great gratification to me to find that the same spirit of cooperation and harmony existed unchecked."[25] Rockefeller offered his services to J. P. Morgan, and his millions formed part of the twenty-five-million-dollar fund that Morgan marshaled that day to keep the stock market open, averting the bankruptcy of at least fifty brokerage houses. Whatever his personal distaste for Morgan, Rockefeller generously praised his leadership during the 1907 panic. "His commanding personality served a most valuable end," he wrote in his memoirs. "He acted quickly and resolutely when quickness and decision were the things most needed to regain confidence."[26]

Several family members sought Rockefeller's help to withstand the storm. He bought $4.5 million of International Harvester stock from the cash-strapped McCormicks and extended a huge $7 million loan to his brother William, who was hip-deep in stock-market maneuvers. Even with a brother, Rockefeller could not suspend standard business practices—Frank had already learned that—and he asked William to furnish a list of securities as collateral. But when Rockefeller's adviser Henry E. Cooper demanded more, it prompted an ironic reminder from Rockefeller: "Well, Mr. Cooper, don't be too rigorous. Remember, William is a very rich man."[27]

With full-blown panic raging around him, Rockefeller refused to depart from his daily schedule for long and, after his one day at the office, he returned to Pocantico to play golf. During his morning game, he was interrupted repeatedly by urgent messages, and each time he pedaled his bike back to the carriage house and made another enormous pledge to stave off trouble. He then resumed his game with his usual sangfroid and air of unconcern.

During the 1907 panic, Rockefeller, for the first time, appeared civic-minded to the general public and garnered lavish praise. As he told a relative, the newspapers had "spoken very kindly and favorably, and all have shown great appreciation of what we have tried to do to save the ship."[28] For a time, it seemed this goodwill might moderate the antitrust zeal against Standard Oil, but this hope soon evaporated when Rockefeller told a reporter, "The runaway policy of the past administration can have but one result. It means disaster to the country, financial depression, and chaos."[29] According to Rockefeller, he made this statement off-the-record and professed pity for the errant reporter who published it in violation of his solemn oath. The comment aggravated the hostility that President Roosevelt already felt toward Rockefeller, especially since Rockefeller kept pleading ill health as his reason for not coming to the White House to discuss Standard Oil. Privately, Roosevelt said that Rockefeller felt wounded because the government had published the plain truth about Standard Oil.

═══

After the Landis fine was announced, Standard Oil tried to alter its strategy and negotiate a government compromise. That September, it held out a tempting deal to investigators: It would open its books and abide by any recommendations to guarantee compliance with the antitrust laws if the government withdrew its suit. Government officials were caught off guard by this peace offering. "A really astonishing proposal," James R. Garfield wrote in his diary.[30] But Roosevelt was no longer in the mood for a truce. "If we have a criminal case against these men," he told Attorney General Charles Bonaparte, "I should be very reluctant to surrender it."[31]

Archbold should have persisted in his conciliatory approach, but he was too accustomed to heavy-handed politics. He was openly contemptuous of all political attacks against the combine. During the spring and summer of 1908, he held several confidential meetings wih President Roosevelt arranged by Senator Jonathan Bourne of Oregon. The president expressed an earnest wish to see the Standard Oil case settled out of court. While Archbold believed in his sincerity, he also knew that Roosevelt had vacillated on this issue. Archbold then resorted to a typically tactless maneuver. In late October 1907, he had Senator Bourne suggest to the president that if the government struck a deal, Standard Oil would help Roosevelt win renomination in 1908. A horrified Garfield called this brazen offer "stupidly corrupt."[32]

Because of Rockefeller's helpful intervention in the Panic, Roosevelt observed a brief moratorium in attacking Standard Oil then made up for lost time in January 1908. In a special message to Congress, he complained that "the speculative folly and flagrant dishonesty of a few great men of wealth" had engendered the loss of fiscal confidence, and he condemned the "bitter and unscrupulous craft" of the Standard Oil leadership in fighting reform measures.[33] The antitrust suit would proceed as planned.

Since Rockefeller had created the largest business empire of the late nineteenth century, it was only fitting that he should face the most massive antitrust suit of his day. Some 444 witnesses delivered 11 million words of testimony; swollen by 1,374 exhibits, the proceedings filled 12,000 pages in 21 thick volumes. Before it was over, Standard Oil also contested some 21 state antitrust suits from Texas to Connecticut, leading one historian to comment, "Never before in the history of the United States had there been so far-reaching a struggle between industry and government."[34] To supplement its legal staff, Standard Oil retained John G. Milburn and M. F. Elliott of Wall Street, D. T. Watson of Pittsburgh, Moritz Rosenthal of Chicago, and John G. Johnson of Philadelphia. For its part, the Justice Department brought in Charles B. Morrison, a federal district attorney from northern Illinois, and Frank B. Kellogg, a Saint Paul attorney whose success in the case catapulted him to the post of secretary of state in the late 1920s.

Throughout the case, the public fancied Rockefeller to be the all-powerful wire-puller who manipulated Archbold and the other pliant marionettes. If this was sheer fantasy, what then was his actual influence? He did exert limited influence on Standard Oil strategy through the medium of Henry Clay Folger, a Standard Oil director. A thin, bearded man, Folger was diplomatic and extremely diligent in his duties. Unlike the rugged Standard Oil businessmen of an earlier day, Folger had graduated Phi Beta Kappa from Amherst and then attended Columbia Law School. A cultured man, he left to posterity America's foremost collection of Shakespeare First Folios as well as a splendid library. Far more important to Rockefeller was that Folger played excellent golf and joined him on the links every Wednesday morning.

In memos to Folger about the suit, Rockefeller never touched on political or legal tactics but mostly addressed arcane calculations of profitability. Rockefeller wanted to prove that Standard Oil's profits had never been excessive or extortionate. Many other companies watered their stock—that is, issued them at inflated capitalization—so that their dividends appeared deceptively modest. To save on taxes and conform to Ohio law, Standard Oil had kept its capitalization low, which produced misleadingly high dividends of 40 or 50 percent per year. Rockefeller pegged the real dividend rate at something closer to 6 or 8 percent.

Folger performed statistical analyses showing that with its capitalization more accurately stated to reflect retained earnings, Standard Oil had paid average dividends twice as high as Rockefeller had surmised. "I am surprised to find the average dividends for twenty-five years 13.86%," the company founder confessed sheepishly to Folger. Rockefeller now had to rationalize the higher figure and suddenly found it within an acceptable range, noting the larger profits of "many other large businesses with less risk, including the *United States Steel Company.*"[35] "Business men will not regard the earnings . . . which you present as excessive," he told Folger.[36] Afraid that militant trustbusters might see things differently, he promised to destroy this incriminating data. He also reminded Folger that Standard Oil had not kept prices low out of altruism but to deter competition and "keep our profits on such a basis that others would not be stimulated to enter the field of competition with us."[37] This belied his frequent claim that his motive was to bequeath cheap oil to the working people.

During his Standard Oil tenure, Rockefeller had mollified the public by generally keeping kerosene prices low. But when Archbold took control in the mid-1890s, he kept domestic prices high while depressing foreign prices to diminish overseas competition. During the dozen years before Rockefeller's retirement, the trust's return on assets ranged from 11 to 17 percent. With Archbold at the helm, returns soared from 21 to 27 percent between 1900 and 1906. This might have been smart business but it was very poor politics: The trust was booking record profits just when it could least afford to enrage public opinion. It is no coincidence that Ida Tarbell's series and Teddy Roosevelt's trust-busting coincided with Archbold's more grasping regime. He was a much less clever monopolist than his mentor.

When Frank Kellogg grilled Rockefeller in November 1908 at the customs house in New York, much of the testimony concerned Standard Oil's pricing policy. Standing by maps showing the operational areas of Standard marketing units, Kellogg tried to entrap Rockefeller into admitting that the cartel had divided America into exclusive sales territories. "Does the Standard Oil of Ohio have a limited territory?" he asked. "It has not," said Rockefeller calmly. "Has it not in the last five years?" asked Kellogg. "Not to my knowledge," Rockefeller replied. "Its field is the world. That is its mission, to light the world with the cheapest and best."[38] Smiling and imperturbable, Rockefeller kept glancing for guidance to his lawyers, who continually raised objections to Kellogg's questions.

Kellogg tried to show that Standard Oil routinely engaged in predatory pricing, eliminating competitors and then hoisting prices to exorbitant levels. He estimated that true competition prevailed in fewer than 10 percent of all petroleum markets and noted that kerosene prices had risen unreasonably from 1895 (when Archbold took charge) to 1906, creating widespread consumer discontent. To justify Standard's plush earnings, Rockefeller cited everything from fire hazards to the vagaries of drilling to the need to invest in new fields. To which Kellogg responded with sarcasm: "But Standard Oil has been paying enormous dividends right along." Lifting his eyes heavenward, Rockefeller replied, "And we were grateful for it."[39]

Once again, the press found it hard to believe that this amiable old gent with his sudden memory lapses and fuzzy logic was the fearsome raptor of Standard Oil. "Now that Mr. Rockefeller has emerged from his seclusion and is seen in the fierce light of a public inquiry, he appears no such monster as the public fancy has painted," observed one paper. "He is affable to the point of cordiality."[40] Said another: "If Rockefeller has been playing a part, he has done so in a way that would do credit to Uriah Heep. If not, it is barely possible that the curious old man has been misrepresented . . . and that the world owes him an apology."[41] Perhaps if Rockefeller had made himself available at the beginning of his career as he now did at the end, he might not have been sitting in the witness stand.

=

In anointing Archbold as his successor, Rockefeller had made him the chief potentate in the world oil industry for the next twenty years. Round-faced, bright-eyed, and peppery, with a tiny body and big head, Archbold, the son of a poor Baptist minister, often bounded down the corridor whistling "Onward Christian Soldiers." But a violent temper lurked beneath the vivacity. Nevertheless, he and Rockefeller always traded compliments about each other. "You know, when John Rockefeller dies," Archbold said, "the world is going to be surprised to learn what a very great man he has been in every way."[42] Rockefeller responded in kind: "[Archbold] was a man of imagination, of courage, of great persuasiveness, with a genius for reading men and dealing with them."[43]

Yet as chief executive of Standard Oil, Archbold stooped to a far rougher style of combat than Rockefeller had, and he freely bribed elected officials. Rockefeller, of course, was no stranger to such skulduggery, but he engaged in payoffs more reluctantly, if only because he so disliked politicians. Archbold had fewer scruples, and as government regulation intruded deeper into business, he decided that the trust needed permanent representation in the U.S. House and Senate.

The first documented instance of Archbold suborning an official occurred in 1898, during Frank Monnett's suit against Standard of Ohio, when Archbold placed Senator Joseph B. Foraker of Ohio on the payroll. He started with a payment of $15,000, then made another of $14,500 three weeks later, winding up with a total of $44,000 in a six-month period. A corporate lawyer from Cincinnati and former Ohio governor, Foraker was a formidable speaker who earned the nickname of "Fire Alarm Joe" for his rousing oratory. Archbold got excellent value for his money. In February 1900, he wrote to the senator, apropos of a proposed bill hostile to Standard Oil: "It is so outrageous as to be ridiculous, but it needs to be looked after and I hope there will be no difficulty in killing it."[44] When Foraker helped to dispatch the bill, Archbold sent congratulations: "I enclose you a certificate of deposit to your favor for $15,000. . . . I need scarcely express our great gratification over the favorable outcome of affairs."[45] The certificate of deposit was more difficult to trace than a check and was the instrument of choice for political bribery.

Another favorite recipient of Standard Oil largesse was Senator Matthew Quay of Pennsylvania, who received $42,500 between 1898 and 1902. In one lighthearted note, Archbold told Quay that he was enclosing a $10,000 certificate of deposit as a reward for the senator's "enticing ways."[46] Evidently, Archbold felt more at ease with small, scattered payments, for he advised Quay on another occasion, "Please ask for payments as needed from time to time, not all at once."[47] Another true friend of the trust from western Pennsylvania was Representative Joseph C. Sibley, later called "a political procurer for Archbold, an agent for the seduction and corruption of public men by the Standard Oil."[48] In official Washington, Sibley acted as a conduit for Standard Oil money, once writing to Archbold, "A Republican United States Senator came to me today to make a loan of $1,000. I told him I did not have it but would try and get it for him in a day or two. Do you want to make the investment?"[49]

The trust's Washington operations might never have surfaced had it not been for a kind act by Archbold. At his Tarrytown mansion, he employed a valued black butler, James Wilkins, who had a twenty-four-year-old ne'er-do-well son named Willie. Out of sympathy for Wilkins, Archbold hired Willie as an office boy at Standard Oil at a time when few if any blacks were employed there. Willie liked to play the ponies and was chronically short of cash. Hoping to take advantage of the political backlash against Standard Oil, he teamed up with Charles Stump, a nineteen-year-old white office boy, to scout out incriminating evidence on Archbold's desk. In December 1904, the two young men pinched a couple of telegrams and contacted Fred Eldridge, an editor at William Randolph Hearst's *New York American,* who studied the loot and said it was worthless. But he expressed a special interest in letters from Archbold to senators or congressmen and gave the two enterprising young men two hundred names that might interest readers. Armed with Eldridge's wish list, Stump and Wilkins began to scour Archbold's correspondence after hours, and when they spotted letters to Sibley and Foraker, they took them to Eldridge and haggled over prices. On several occasions, when they reached an impasse, the editor would say he had to "see Mr. Hearst."[50] This espionage lasted from December 1904 until February 1905, when Archbold discovered the missing political documents, accused Stump and Wilkins of theft, then fired them. With the $20,500 that they had received from Hearst, the two young entrepreneurs were able to open their own saloon in Harlem.

For months, Archbold dreaded publication of the purloined letters and must have been puzzled when they did not appear. Hearst had stored the incriminating documents in his safe and awaited a propitious moment to unveil them. By attacking the trusts, Hearst had created a hybrid role for himself as the people's tribune, who would advance his own imperial ambitions by exposing those of his fellow empire builders. By the 1930s, Hearst became fiercely reactionary, yet in the early 1900s he was still a populist champion. Showing exceptional self-control, Hearst did not publish the letters when he ran against Charles Evans Hughes, a friend of Rockefeller's, for the New York governorship in 1906. "Charles, I do hope you beat that man Hearst!" Rockefeller told Hughes that year.[51]

But in the election of 1908, Hearst backed the Independence League Party, which nominated Massachusetts's Thomas L. Hisgen, a manufacturer of axle grease, as its presidential candidate. Hisgen had once spurned a bid from Standard Oil to buy him out for $600,000, and when the trust retaliated by slashing prices and trying to ruin him, Hisgen became an implacable foe. Hearst picked him as the party's candidate with the Archbold letters in mind. On September 17, 1908, Hearst gave a pro-Hisgen speech in Columbus, Ohio, in which he claimed that just before the talk a stranger had appeared in his hotel room and handed him copies of correspondence between Archbold and several politicians. "I am now going to read copies of letters written by Mr. John Archbold, chief agent of the Standard Oil, an intimate personal acquaintance of Mr. Rockefeller and Mr. Rogers," Hearst announced with great fanfare.[52] He then created a national sensation by reading aloud letters written by Archbold to

Senator Foraker and Congressman Sibley. Later, in a Saint Louis speech, he recited two more specimens, with the correspondence prominently reproduced in Hearst papers.

Realizing that he could not deny the authenticity of the letters, Archbold tried to finesse the charges by claiming that the correspondence was "entirely proper."[53] At first, Foraker pretended that the payments were strictly lawful and aboveboard. "That I was employed as counsel for the Standard Oil Company at the time and presumably compensated for my services was common knowledge," he insisted. "At least I never made any effort to conceal it."[54] When the public refused to buy this, Foraker and Sibley were hounded from public life. Archbold survived as head of Standard Oil, however, and the following year, perhaps to mend his increasingly tattered image, he gave one million dollars to Syracuse University.

=

The Archbold scandal convinced Junior that the doubts he had entertained about Standard Oil had not been the product of an overactive imagination. Many years later, he admitted to having been "sickened" by the Hearst exposé. "It was the political contributions that focussed the whole thing" as to whether or not he should resign from Standard Oil.[55] For more than a decade, ever since leaving Brown, Junior had been poised uneasily between business and philanthropy. He had never warmed to commerce, and the Archbold scandal pushed him toward his proper career: that of a full-time philanthropist.

The decision to leave Standard Oil was so sensitive that Junior discussed it only with his wife and father. He had to figure out how to extricate himself without hurting his father or the organization. To live with his own conscience, he told his father, he had to resign from the trust and devote his life to philanthropy. He also advocated Archbold's ouster, but Senior thought it impossible to fire Archbold in the midst of the antitrust suit. As for his son's departure, he reacted with surprising equanimity: "I want you to do what you think is right."[56] That his father honored his wish to leave Standard Oil only deepened the bond between them.

Whether as a concession to his father or to Archbold, Junior waited more than a year to depart from the company. At the January 11, 1910, board meeting, he quietly retired as a director of Standard Oil: thus, the active, daily involvement of the Rockefeller dynasty with the trust had lasted only slightly more than one generation. Two months later, when a bill was introduced in Washington to incorporate the Rockefeller Foundation, Junior's resignation was first revealed to the public, helping to separate the family's charitable efforts from Standard Oil. To purify himself of all business ties, Junior also retired at the same time from U.S. Steel. He had ended his relations with every company except for American Linseed and the one company, ironically, that would defile his name: the Colorado Fuel and Iron Company.

It seems odd that Junior's disenchantment with Archbold did not diminish his reverence for his father. We know that Archbold had studied corruption at the master's feet, but Senior made no effort to disabuse his son. Clearly, he did not want to forfeit the love of this young man whose goodness validated his own life. Perhaps he did not think Junior could live with the moral ambiguities of a fortune extracted by dubious methods. Perhaps he felt he was sparing his son disturbing knowledge. Or perhaps he had so thoroughly rationalized his own behavior that he saw himself in the same glowing, virtuous light as his son did. This last theory would seem to be the one most consistent with the rest of his career.

In the last analysis, it took a stupendous leap of faith for Junior to believe that his father was blameless and that Archbold had inaugurated corruption at Standard Oil. It is almost inconceivable that he did not suspect at moments that Archbold had learned some of his tricks from Senior. And how did Junior know that his father was innocent? By instinct, by blind faith, by knowledge of his father's private character—by everything but detailed knowledge of his business career, which Senior did not care to discuss. If Junior harbored any unspoken doubts about his father's ethics—doubts only whispered to Abby in the dead of night—the Archbold scandal gave him a convenient cover to slip away from Standard Oil without blaming his father's past.

The scandal coincided with a formative phase in Junior's life, as he caught the bracing spirit of Progressive reform. Soon after graduating from college, Junior had joined the movement to clean up tenements, making contact with reformers such as Jacob Riis and Lillian Wald and proposing to Gates an attack on tuberculosis in the slums. The Progressive movement favored peaceful, incremental change and was infused with unimpeachable ideals: that people should be healthier and better educated and that government should operate in a businesslike manner. The Progressives conjured up an antiseptic world of public administration in which decisions would be made rationally by scholars, scientists, and experts. For someone like Junior, who shrank from venomous words and violent confrontation, such clean government promised to transcend the bruising partisan politics that had sullied his father's reputation. Best of all, Progressives were well-bred, educated, upstanding types whom you could invite home to dinner without embarrassment.

In the early 1900s, the movement latched on to an ideal issue: the New York brothels then flourishing under Tammany Hall protection. During the 1909 mayoral campaign, a debate arose over something called white slavery—the traffic in young women forcibly drafted into a life of sin. After the election, a special grand jury was impaneled to weigh the matter, and in January 1910

Judge Thomas C. O'Sullivan picked Junior as its foreman. Protesting that he had never patronized the ladies and was achingly ignorant of the subject, Junior tried to beg off, only to have the judge snap: "You owe it as a duty to the city to do your part in crushing out the vile practices that are said to exist."[57]

The choice of Junior was a setup. Tammany bosses figured that he would be weak and spineless, too prudish to explore the demimonde, and that his grand jury would sit for a month and issue harmless recommendations. Instead, Junior plunged into his work with fanatic energy. "I never worked harder in my life," he said. "I was on the job morning, noon, and night."[58] The cause enlisted his deepest sympathies, for he yearned to overcome a crippling sense of amateurism and become an expert in *something.* The white-slavery jury gave him a chance to graduate from being his father's factotum and to acquire a separate identity. Emerging from Senior's shadow, Junior re-created himself as a reformer, placing himself alongside the Ida Tarbells and Henry Demarest Lloyds of the world.

Junior explored the murky realm of Manhattan bordellos at arm's length, as if afraid to expose himself to their forbidden allure. He later made an astonishing confession: "When I was investigating vice in New York I never talked to a single prostitute."[59] But behind the protective shield of scientific inquiry, he questioned countless experts and became extremely knowledgeable. Because he refused to settle for superficial answers, his grand jury extended its work from one to six months. When he handed up a presentment with fifty-four indictments, Judge O'Sullivan, aghast, quarreled hotly with him. "When O'Sullivan found out what I intended to do he was thoroughly frightened because it meant that the plans of Tammany Hall had miscarried," Junior recalled.[60] The grand jury's work was, sadly, nullified when Mayor William Gaynor—himself now at war with Tammany Hall—failed to act on the findings, and most of the indictments ended in acquittal. Despite this denouement, Junior emerged as something brand-new in Rockefeller annals: a civic hero. Not some rich patsy to be pushed around by party bosses, he now stood forth as a formidable personage in his own right.

The white-slavery jury had a lasting impact on him. When the city did not follow up on the jury recommendations, Junior consulted one hundred experts on how to solve the problem. (Among those who most impressed him was the young Raymond B. Fosdick, who had rooted out municipal corruption under two mayors; Fosdick later became president of the Rockefeller Foundation and Junior's official biographer.) In May 1913, Junior set up and personally financed the Bureau of Social Hygiene, which for twenty-five years studied urban ills ranging from venereal disease to lack of birth control to drug addiction. Cettie proudly sent him $25,000 to promote instruction in sexual hygiene for female students around the country. Junior also worked with Jacob Schiff and Paul Warburg to protect young Jewish women on the Lower East Side from procurers. The young Rockefeller heir, so long kept in limbo, was now showing a new willingness to tackle controversial social issues and place his money behind it. The more evil that people attributed to his father, the harder he worked to achieve an impossible purity.

As he awaited the verdict in the antitrust case against Standard Oil, John D. Rockefeller, Sr., gave way to uncharacteristic melancholy. While working on *Random Reminiscences,* he toted up the names of more than sixty former colleagues who had died. Henry Rogers died in May 1909, following a stroke, leaving an estate appraised at $41 million, and his memorial service was probably the last occasion that lured Rockefeller back to 26 Broadway. The titan was now one of the last veterans of the early days on Oil Creek and had to contemplate the fact that the government was about to undo his decades of work.

In trying to predict the verdict, Rockefeller, usually a tough-minded realist, fell back on the most feathery hopes. After the 1908 election, he was relieved to be free of Teddy Roosevelt, who handed over the Republican nomination to his corpulent secretary of war, William Howard Taft. On October 29, 1908, in a cameo appearance at 26 Broadway, Rockefeller endorsed Taft for president. "He is not a man, I judge, to venture with rash experiments or to impede the return of prosperity by advocating measures subversive of industrial progress." Annoyed by this implicit dig at him, Teddy Roosevelt mocked Rockefeller's endorsement: "It is a perfectly palpable and obvious trick on the part of the Standard Oil people to damage Taft."[61]

After Taft's election victory over William Jennings Bryan—who had said that Rockefeller should be sent to prison—Rockefeller understandably wired his congratulations to the president-elect. When the press hinted that Taft might be hostile toward Standard Oil, Rockefeller demurred, telling Henry Folger that "I cannot believe this is anything more than an idle rumor."[62] Actually, Taft liked Rockefeller personally but loathed the trust. He later wrote, "It was indeed an octopus that held the trade in its tentacles, and the few actual independent concerns that kept alive were allowed to exist by sufferance to maintain the appearance of competition."[63] While many industrialists hoped that antitrust prosecutions would slacken under Taft, he in fact initiated sixty-five antitrust actions, even more than the forty-four brought by Roosevelt. Throughout the antitrust case, Rockefeller woefully underestimated public animosity against Standard Oil, and as late as August 1909 he told Harold McCormick that he had stopped granting interviews for a while because "the sentiment has greatly changed in our favor."[64]

Three months later, a federal circuit court in Saint Louis ruled unanimously that Standard Oil of New Jersey and thirty-seven affiliates had violated the Sherman Antitrust Act; the holding company was given thirty days to divest itself of its subsidiaries. Taft praised Frank Kellogg for his "complete victory," while Teddy Roosevelt, on safari in Africa, where he was butchering a small zoo's worth of animals, conveyed his elation, terming the verdict "one of the most signal triumphs for decency which has been won in our country."[65]

Although the trust appealed instantly to the Supreme Court, a deep sense of gloom settled over 26 Broadway as the final verdict approached. Meanwhile, one government decision after another went against the stigmatized monopoly. In 1909, Congress largely repealed the duty that had protected the trust from foreign competition; the secretary of war halted purchase of petroleum products from it; and the president set aside petroleum-rich territory for conservation purposes. When Rockefeller crossed paths with Taft in 1910 during his stay at the Hotel Bon Air in Augusta, Georgia, they agreed to golf together, but Mrs. Taft, fearing bad publicity, got the president to cancel his game. On another occasion—doubtless when the first lady was not looking—Rockefeller asked the president to greet his five-year-old granddaughter, Mathilde McCormick. To Rockefeller's delight, the huge Taft hoisted the lovely little girl with the long curls high into the air.

By the spring of 1911, the wait for the Supreme Court's decision began to seem interminable, and even the president grumbled about the court's glacial pace. Because the court's composition changed after the death of one justice, the arguments had to be heard twice. On April 25, 1911, Junior passed along to his father Senator Aldrich's wily prediction: "He was disposed to believe that the decision will be adverse to the company, but thinks the Court will clearly define the law and hopes that it will point out a legal way for the conduct of large corporations."[66] The senator must have had excellent sources.

When the end came for Standard Oil after forty-one years of existence, it was swift, sudden, and irrevocable. At 4 P.M. on May 15, 1911, Chief Justice Edward White told a sleepy courtroom, "I have also to announce the opinion of the Court in No. 398, the United States against the Standard Oil Company."[67] At once, the room quivered with expectation as senators and congressmen streamed in to hear the verdict. For the next forty-nine minutes, White read aloud the twenty-thousand-word opinion, speaking in such a low, monotonous voice that other justices had to lean over and ask him to speak louder. In his mumbled, momentous words, White upheld the decision to dismantle Standard Oil, which was given six months to spin off its subsidiaries, with its officers forbidden from reestablishing the monopoly. Thus ended the longest running morality play in American business history.

Rockefeller reacted with studied nonchalance. He was golfing at Pocantico with Father J. P. Lennon from the Tarrytown Catholic church when he learned of the decision, and he did not seem particularly perturbed. "Father Lennon," he asked, "have you some money?" The priest said no, then asked why. "Buy Standard Oil," Rockefeller said—which turned out to be sound advice.[68] To his former partners, he sent a sad, whimsical obituary that began, "Dearly beloved, we must obey the Supreme Court. Our splendid, happy family must scatter."[69] Intent as always on ignoring bad news, Rockefeller refused to read the celebrated opinion that broke up his empire—exactly what one would have expected.

The antitrust suit against Standard tested whether the American legal system could cope with the new agglomerations of wealth and curb their excesses. The paradoxical lesson learned was that government intervention was sometimes necessary to ensure unfettered competition. Regulation did not inevitably harm business but could also aid it. The 1911 decision was not an undiluted triumph for reformers by any means, and many of them considered it a shameful betrayal. Senator Robert La Follette, who stood in the courtroom as Judge White read the verdict, told reporters afterward, "I fear that the court has done what the trusts wanted it to do, and what Congress has steadily refused to do."[70] Echoing this, William Jennings Bryan asserted that Chief Justice White had "waited 15 years to throw his protecting arms around the trusts and tell them how to escape."[71]

For fifteen years, White had vainly advanced a doctrine called the "rule of reason," which would not outlaw every combination in restraint of trade but only those that were unreasonable and violated the public interest. This doctrine vastly expanded judicial discretion and opened a loophole large enough to tolerate many trusts. In the lone dissent, Associate Justice John Harlan angrily protested this new principle, banging the bench and accusing his fellow justices of having put "words into the antitrust act which Congress did not put there."[72] He added mockingly, "You may now restrain commerce, provided you are reasonable about it; only take care that the restraint is not undue."[73] The decision tallied in many ways with Teddy Roosevelt's belief that the government should rein in irresponsible trusts but not meddle with good ones. The more militant reformers were right to consider it, at best, a partial victory.

＝

As so often happens with politics and markets, by the time of the Supreme Court's 1911 decision, evolutionary changes in the marketplace had already eroded the trust's dominance. With the final amalgamation of Royal Dutch and Shell in 1907, Standard Oil at last faced a worthy competitor abroad, while the Anglo-Persian Oil Company was tapping rich new fields in the Middle East. At home, more oil poured forth from Texas, Oklahoma, California, Kansas, and Illinois, providing an opening wedge for assertive newcomers. Where the trust had pumped 32 percent of American crude oil in 1899, its share had slumped to 14 percent by 1911. Even Standard's historic strength in refining dipped from an 86 percent market share to 70 percent in the five years before the breakup.

The automobile was also radically recasting the industry: In 1910, for the first time, gasoline sales surpassed those of kerosene and other illuminating oils. In 1908, William C. Durant launched the General Motors Corporation, and that year Henry Ford brought out his first Model T. Auto ownership soon exploded, reaching 2.5 million cars by 1915 and then 9.2 million by 1920. Though Standard Oil of California introduced the first filling station in 1907, the trust was not a pioneer in this area, and the national network of gas stations would be too extensive to be monopolized by any one company.

Those who had seen the Standard Oil dissolution as condign punishment for Rockefeller were in for a sad surprise: It proved to be the luckiest stroke of his career. Precisely because he lost the antitrust suit, Rockefeller was converted from a mere millionaire, with an estimated net worth of $300 million in 1911, into something just short of history's first billionaire. In December 1911, he was finally able to jettison the presidency of Standard Oil, but he continued to hold on to his immense shareholdings. As the owner of about one quarter of the shares of the old trust, Rockefeller now got a one-quarter share of the new Standard Oil of New Jersey, plus one quarter of the thirty-three independent subsidiary companies created by the decision. And that did not include the oil shares he had given to the GEB, the University of Chicago, and other recipients of his largesse.

At first, investors did not know how to value the shares of these Standard Oil components, since Rockefeller had resisted a New York Stock Exchange listing and the old trust never issued reports to shareholders. As one Wall Street publication warned on the eve of trading, the value of the new companies was "the merest guesswork."[74] What quickly grew apparent, however, was that Rockefeller had been extremely conservative in capitalizing Standard Oil and that the split-off companies were chock-full of hidden assets. Two other factors encouraged a veritable feeding frenzy in the stocks. For years, the shares of Standard Oil of New Jersey had been depressed by the antitrust litigation, but with the litigation ended, they bounced back to a more normal level. And the explosion of the automobile industry created euphoria about the endless growth prospects of the petroleum industry, which had been shadowed for fifty years by warnings of doom.

When trading started on December 1, 1911, the public exhibited an insatiable appetite for the new companies, especially after they declared dividends averaging 53 percent of the old capital value of Standard Oil stock. As if rejoicing in the chance to tweak trustbusters, investors bid up the shares to insane levels. Between January and October 1912, Standard Oil of New Jersey zoomed from 360 to 595; Standard of New York went from 260 to 580; and Standard of Indiana from 3,500 to 9,500. Thanks to this staggering appreciation, Rockefeller's net worth reached a lifetime peak of $900 million in 1913—more than $13 billion in 1996 dollars. (To put that $900 million in perspective, the total accumulated national debt of the United States stood at $1.2 billion that year, equivalent to 3 percent of the gross national product; federal spending was a mere $715 million.) As Junior later explained, his father never had a billion dollars at any one moment, although much more than that passed through his hands. During the ten years after Standard Oil's 1911 dismantling, the assets of its constituent companies quintupled in value. Beyond his talents as a businessman, Rockefeller benefited from a large dollop of luck in his life, making more money in retirement than on the job.

The soaring fortunes of the Standard companies made it seem as if the cagey Rockefeller had outwitted the country again. Newspapers began running daily box scores of his wealth—not exactly the chastening sequel Washington had envisioned. As former J. P. Morgan partner George Perkins told a friend, Wall Street was "laughing in its sleeve at what has been going on."[75] Nobody felt more frustrated than Teddy Roosevelt, who returned to the presidential fray with his third-party Bull Moose candidacy in 1912. Lashing out at Standard Oil again, he roared, "The price of stock has gone up over one hundred percent, so that Mr. Rockefeller and his associates have actually seen their fortunes doubled. No wonder that Wall Street's prayer now is: 'Oh Merciful Providence, give us another dissolution.' "[76]

In the eternal race for the title of the world's richest man, Rockefeller now left Andrew Carnegie far behind and probably had at least twice as much money as Carnegie did. (Exact comparisons are difficult since both men had given away so much.) Nonetheless, Rockefeller and Carnegie still enjoyed cordial if rather distant relations. In 1912, en route to Washington to give testimony, Carnegie dropped by Kykuit and found Rockefeller "tall and spare and smiling, beaming." Carnegie still savored his belief that he had outfoxed Rockefeller on their old Mesabi ore deal, for he afterward wrote a friend, "Positively it is a delight to meet the old gentleman. But I did not refer to the ore purchase I made from him."[77]

It was hard to convince a skeptical public that the thirty-four new companies, with their seventy thousand employees, would not reconstitute a new conspiracy. J. P. Morgan, upon hearing of the 1911 decision, asked, "How the hell is any court going to compel a man to compete with himself?"[78] Many of the newly independent companies were powerful enough to inspire fear as free-standing entities. Standard Oil of New Jersey remained the world's largest oil company, second only to U.S. Steel in size among American enterprises and retaining 43 percent of the value of the old trust. Five of the newly divested companies stood among the country's two hundred largest industrial firms. Since all the companies had identical owners, it was hard to foresee vigorous competition. As Roosevelt complained, "All the companies are still under the same control, or at least working in such close alliance that the effect is precisely the same."[79]

Rockefeller made all the right noises about obeying the 1911 decision. As he told Archbold on September 8, 1911, "We will do the best we can to comply with every requirement of the government, and if as much is required of others it does seem as though it must bring about a reform."[80] Yet he quietly worked to undermine the dissolution, suggesting that officials of the Standard Oil companies meet at 26 Broadway at ten-thirty each morning to maintain amicable relations and swap information. (For legal reasons, everyone was cautioned not to exchange thoughts on paper.) That both Standard Oil of New Jersey, headed by Archbold, and Standard Oil of New York, headed by Folger, kept their headquarters in the same old building said much about their relationship.

For the next decade, the divestiture often seemed a sham. The Standard companies continued to divide the country into eleven marketing territories, selling the same brand names and not competing on prices. It took a long time for former colleagues to view each other as competitors and raid each other's territories. Many critics thought that, to avert this complicity, the government should have done one of three things: keep the trust intact and regulate it; force shareholders to take stock in only one of the thirty-four companies; or create fully integrated companies that did not need to rely on other Standard companies. Standard of New Jersey, for instance, inherited a vast refining system without the crude oil to service it, forcing it into close collaboration to remedy the imbalance.

While the old guard at 26 Broadway mourned the trust's passage, some Young Turks at the operating companies were overjoyed. Many Standard Oil directors had been over sixty. This had given the organization a geriatric tone, stifling young, imaginative men at a time that demanded rapid adaptation to the auto age. One of these extraordinary mavericks, Dr. William M. Burton of Standard Oil of Indiana, thought that Roosevelt and Taft had performed an inestimable service. After the 1911 dismemberment, he said, "It was felt all along the line—younger men were given a chance."[81] Free of top-heavy bureacracy, Burton patented an exceptionally valuable process in 1913 for "cracking" crude oil—that is, for refining it so as to yield a far higher percentage of gasoline. This discovery permitted Standard of Indiana to reap windfall royalties from other oil companies. Maintaining full control of this technology until 1921, Standard of Indiana required its cousin companies to restrict sales of "cracked" gasoline to their pre-1911 marketing territories, helping to extend the trust structure for another decade.

It is an enduring tribute to Rockefeller that so many Standard Oil companies prospered during the remainder of the century, controlling a significant fraction of both the American and world oil industry. Rockefeller's stepchildren would be everywhere: Standard Oil of New Jersey (Exxon), Standard Oil of New York (Mobil), Standard Oil of Indiana (Amoco), Standard Oil of California

(Chevron), Atlantic Refining (ARCO and eventually Sun), Continental Oil (Conoco), today a unit of DuPont, and Chesebrough-Ponds, which had begun by processing petroleum jelly. Three offspring—Exxon, Mobil, and Chevron—would belong to the Seven Sisters group that would dominate the world oil industry in the twentieth century; a fourth sister, British Petroleum, later took over Standard Oil of Ohio, then known as Sohio. It was certainly not their intention, but the trustbusters helped to preserve Rockefeller's legacy for posterity and unquestionably made him the world's richest man.

*Henry H. Rogers and Mark Twain sailing together
in Bermuda in 1908.*
(Courtesy of the Mark Twain Project, the Bancroft Library)

CHAPTER 28

Benevolent Trust

s the national thirst for gasoline caused his stock in the Standard Oil companies to appreciate wildly, it was only proper that the oil king should develop a passion for automobiles. He kept a Peerless auto at Pocantico as early as 1904. In the 1910s, cars began to fill his stone coach barn alongside the old-fashioned buckboards and coaches. Even as a young man, Rockefeller had been exhilarated by speed and motion, racing his trotting horses down Euclid Avenue, and he now took daily auto drives of fifty miles or more. It was the powerful, gleaming Crane-Simplex touring car of 1918 that truly captured his fancy. Big as a cruise ship, smoothly navigating bumpy back roads, this elaborate maroon vehicle with semi-open sides had wide running boards and a glamorous interior of black leather upholstery.

Since the Crane-Simplex comfortably seated seven, Rockefeller turned the afternoon drives into carefully orchestrated social affairs, telling each person where to sit and specifying the exact itinerary to the chauffeur. Like a king enthroned in his movable court, Rockefeller always sat in the middle of the backseat. As with his golf games, the afternoon drives permitted no intimate or serious conversation, only obligatory jollity. As the huge car swept down country roads, trailing whorls of dust and ventilating the passengers with fresh air, Rockefeller hummed, sang spirituals, whistled, or joked. Social director of these excursions, he was relaxed and jovial, often sitting back and daydreaming— but without ever abandoning his competitive instincts. If a young hotshot sped by, Rockefeller would absorb the affront in silence, then bend forward and calmly instruct the chauffeur, "Phillips!" "Yes, sir." "How fast are we going?"

"Thirty-three, sir." "Could we go a little faster?" Slowly but inexorably the speedometer would climb until the young motorist was overtaken—at which point Rockefeller would stare resolutely ahead, his face impassive, betraying no sign of his joyful triumph.[1] Rockefeller clocked these drives and liked to set new speed records. "Phillips," he would say, "we got to town Monday in one hour and seventeen minutes. Let's see what we can do today."[2] Phillips would smile, touch his cap, and go for the record.

On many drives, the touring car stopped by a meadow so that Rockefeller and his guests could recline on the grass. Rockefeller chatted happily with farmers who happened by, quizzing them about their seed or fertilizer and passing along tips to the superintendents of his estates. It was one of many signs in Rockefeller's later years that he yearned for the innocent pleasures of his bucolic boyhood. "I am very sorry to see this tendency of crowding into the cities, very sorry," he once told a Bible class. "It is not like fifty years ago, when I was a boy. It seems to me that as the cities grow larger the country in general becomes weaker."[3] Carrying a cane, chatting casually with neighbors, he loved to wander around the Pocantico village in his golf knickers. Each year for his birthday, he invited the local children to Kykuit and offered them huge mounds of ice cream while a brass band boomed and flags fluttered overhead. Shedding his straitlaced image, he even stooped on all fours and played with the town children. His comfort with children was one of the conspicuous features of his later years.

For all the holiday ease of his retired life, Rockefeller could never escape a sense of danger off in the shadows. In 1912, he received threats from the Black Hand, a Sicilian and Italian American secret society engaged in blackmail and terrorism. As a precaution, Junior, Abby, and the children were packed off to Lakewood for the autumn while security was tightened at Pocantico. Senior was sufficiently spooked that he installed a special alarm system at Kykuit, with a button under his pillow. If he heard prowlers or unexplained noises, he pressed the button, which made small, inconspicuous lights twinkle in the trees at three or four spots; the night watchman would then ring Rockefeller to verify his safety.

Rockefeller devoted a great deal of his spare time to religion. Before breakfast, he reverently recited a blessing then read aloud a page from *My Daily Meditation for the Circling Year* by the Reverend John Henry Jowett, who championed a severe, uncompromising Christianity and counseled readers against pride, lust, and avarice. Jowett preached stoic calm in the face of hatred and warned against bearing grudges against enemies—advice that Rockefeller must have taken to heart. At breakfast, guests were invited to read poems or selections from the New Testament. Rockefeller turned for bedtime solace to another volume of sermons called *The Optimist's Good Night*, so that his days were bracketed with the consolations of religion.

While Rockefeller felt that his retirement years were steeped in righteousness, the American public never quite believed it. For all the good work performed by the Rockefeller Institute for Medical Research and the General Education Board, the founder was still accused of hoarding his wealth. The newspapers applied their own grinding pressure, showing that his gifts had neither matched Andrew Carnegie's nor kept pace with his own growing fortune. One statistician projected in 1906 that if he let his wealth collect compound interest for the next thirty years, he would end up sitting on a pile of ninety billion dollars.

As early as 1901, Rockefeller had realized that he needed to create a foundation on a scale that dwarfed anything he had done so far, and he toyed with the idea of establishing a benevolent trust: "Let us erect a foundation, a trust, and engage directors who will make it a life work to manage, with our personal cooperation, this business of benevolence properly and effectively."[4] Frederick Gates revived the idea in June 1906 when he wrote to Rockefeller, "I have lived with this great fortune of yours daily for fifteen years. To it, its increase and its uses, I have given every thought, until it has become a part of myself, almost as if it were my own."[5] Mustering all his rhetorical resources, Gates thundered, "Your fortune is rolling up, rolling up like an avalanche! You must keep up with it! You must distribute it faster than it grows! If you do not, it will crush you and your children and your children's children."[6] If Rockefeller did not act soon, Gates predicted, his heirs would dissipate their inheritances or become intoxicated with power. The solution he advanced was to set up "permanent corporate philanthropies for the good of mankind" that would give money to education, science, the arts, agriculture, religion, and even civic virtue.[7] These trusts would constitute something novel in American society: private money administered by competent trustees for the public weal. "These funds should be so large that to become a trustee of one of them would make a man at once a public character," Gates explained. "They should be so large that their administration would be a matter of public concern, public inquiry, and public criticism."[8]

The concept of charitable trusts was not invented by Rockefeller; Benjamin Franklin, Stephen Girard, and Peter Cooper had set up such trusts. What he brought to the concept was unprecedented scale and scope. As he contemplated the formation of a giant foundation in 1906, Margaret Olivia Sage, widow of financier Russell Sage, was about to establish a foundation to investigate the plight of working women and the social ills bred by modern life. Junior touted such philanthropies as the best way to advance the family's favorite causes. To his father, he suggested that he create one trust to promote Christian civilization abroad, a second to do the like at home, and a third to supply money to the University of Chicago, the GEB, and the RIMR. These boards would be small by design and staffed by about five family members and Rockefeller insiders. However limited the vision behind this blueprint, it began to sketch the outlines of a new approach to philanthropy. Not surprisingly, the architect of Standard Oil favored the creation of a single mammoth foundation in which he would retain veto power. Once again, the scale of the Rockefeller fortune demanded that new forms be devised to administer it.

Afraid that a state charter for a Rockefeller Foundation could be repealed at the whim of an unfriendly state legislature, Junior and Gates aimed for a more prestigious federal charter for the new foundation, such as that received by the GEB in 1903. The Rockefellers waited until early 1908 to make their pitch in Washington, possibly hoping to capitalize upon the goodwill generated by Senior's assistance in quelling the 1907 panic. By chance, on a train trip to golf in Augusta, Georgia, Rockefeller had encountered Senator "Pitchfork Ben" Tillman of South Carolina and unexpectedly charmed this critic. Junior was cheered by this serendipitous encounter: "Senator Tillman would formerly have been one of the leaders in antagonizing the bill. If he is favorable to it he could do more with the radicals than anyone else."[9]

On June 29, 1909, Rockefeller signed over 73,000 shares of Standard Oil of New Jersey, valued at $50 million, to three trustees: Junior, Gates, and Harold McCormick. This was supposed to be the first installment of an initial $100 million endowment for the projected Rockefeller Foundation. Getting the U.S. Senate to grant a charter for a tax-exempt foundation amid the tumult of the federal antitrust suit against Standard Oil proved a tricky proposition. Exactly how did legislators explain to their perplexed constituents that the ill-gotten gains now being exposed in court should be honored by a federal charter? Introduced in the Senate in March 1910, the charter bill threatened to stir up more public animosity against the Rockefellers than it assuaged. Only a week later, Standard Oil attorneys filed briefs with the Supreme Court in the antitrust appeal, mingling the two events in the public mind and putting the patently bad Rockefeller and the patently good Rockefeller on display side by side.

The charter traveled a rocky road in Congress. Following the pattern of Johns Hopkins, Rockefeller advocated a broad, unrestricted charter that would allow great flexibility. "Perpetuity is a long time," he was fond of saying, and he did not wish to saddle future foundation executives with outmoded mandates.[10] Gates thus enunciated a purposely vague mission for the Rockefeller Foundation: "to promote the well being of mankind throughout the world."[11] Critics were quick to allege that this nebulous charter gave the Rockefellers carte blanche to manipulate the foundation for their own ends. In fact, this open-ended quality was meant to free the proposed foundation from the influence of its founder. That it would be huge, global, and general—that its money could go anywhere and do anything—was the essence of its novelty. Many newspapers saw the vagueness, however, as a gauzy curtain behind which the evil wizard of Standard Oil could work his mischief. Others deplored the foundation as an elaborate publicity stunt to deodorize the Rockefeller name. In denouncing the charter, one paper called the projected organization a "gigantic philanthropy by which old Rockefeller expects to squeeze himself, his son, his stall-fed collegians and their camels, laden with tainted money, through the eye of the needle."[12]

The charter scandalized Attorney General George W. Wickersham, who was entrusted with prosecuting Standard Oil. He protested to President Taft in February 1911.

> The power which, under such bill, would be vested in and exercised by a small body of men, in absolute control of the income of $100,000,000 or more, to be expended for the general indefinite objects described in the bill, might be in the highest degree corrupt in its influence. . . . Is it, then, appropriate that, at the moment when the United States through its courts is seeking in a measure to destroy the great combination of wealth which has been built up by Mr. Rockefeller . . . the Congress of the United States should assist in the enactment of a law to create and perpetuate in his name an institution to hold and administer a large portion of this vast wealth?[13]

Taft granted the point. "I agree with your . . . characterization of the proposed act to incorporate John D. Rockefeller."[14]

Yet Taft saved these barbs for internal consumption and struck a more conciliatory tone with the Rockefellers in person. On April 25, 1911, Senator Aldrich shepherded Junior and Abby to the White House for a top secret lunch with the president. While this meeting was later interpreted as a gauche effort to sway the Standard Oil case, it was concerned exclusively with the Rockefeller Foundation charter. Petrified that the press might get wind of this lunch, Taft insisted that his guests bypass the main door and enter through a side door of the east entrance. The visitors' names were never recorded in guest books or mentioned by White House staff. Taft's trusted aide, Archie Butt, was amused by the president's discomfiture. "It is strange how men in public office shudder at the names of Aldrich and Rockefeller," he reflected.[15] Over lunch, Taft speculated that the foundation charter would pass only if held in abeyance until after settlement of the antitrust suit. Junior, heartened, left the luncheon feeling that the president had been "most agreeable and kindly."[16]

To appease the public, the Rockefeller camp volunteered some extraordinary concessions, including offering to base the new foundation in the nation's capital. When Gates ran into Taft at a Bryn Mawr College luncheon, the president suggested that he send along ideas about how to install safeguards in the plan. In a follow-up memo, Gates said that Congress could, at any time, limit how the foundation money was spent. As to fears that the Rockefellers would wield undue power, Gates said that Rockefeller intimates would make up only five or more members of a board of up to twenty-five people. Gates then made an extraordinary proposal: that all, or a majority, of the following people would have the power to veto board appointments: the president of the United States; the chief justice of the Supreme Court; the president of the Senate; the speaker of the House; and the presidents of Harvard, Yale, Columbia, Johns Hopkins, and the University of Chicago.

Despite this almost unseemly eagerness to accommodate the government, the bill had a checkered career in Congress, even with Senator Aldrich's high-powered patronage. It passed in the House then stalled in the Senate and kicked around, in various forms, for three years. After a point, legislators started to haggle with the Rockefellers, promising support only if certain foundation grants flowed to their districts. Aghast at this blackmail, Rockefeller asked his son in November 1911 whether it might not be better to seek a state charter. A federal charter, Junior rejoined, would be preferable, since states might require board members to live there, weakening the Rockefeller ties and holding them hostage to statehouse politics.

Nevertheless, the Rockefellers soon despaired of Washington and turned to New York State for a charter in 1913. Two years earlier, the state legislature had chartered the Carnegie Corporation, with a $125 million endowment. Now the Rockefeller charter was quickly approved with scarcely a whisper of protest. Between 1856 and 1909, Rockefeller had given $157.5 million for charitable purposes. Mindful of Gates's admonition that his gifts must keep pace with his exploding wealth, Rockefeller gave $100 million to the Rockefeller Foundation in its first year, bolstered by another $82.8 million by 1919. In current dollars, that would translate into a $2 billion gift during the foundation's inaugural decade. It also meant that by 1919 Rockefeller had already given away an amount roughly equal to the $350 million that Andrew Carnegie gave away in his entire lifetime; the titan would donate another $180 million before he died. Since his son gave away an additional $537 million directly and another $540 million through the Rockefeller philanthropies, Rockefeller far surpassed his great rival's benefactions and must rank as the greatest philanthropist in American history.

By securing the Rockefeller Foundation charter in 1913, Rockefeller insulated a large portion of his wealth from inheritance taxes. That year also saw the ratification of the Sixteenth Amendment, which provided for the first federal income tax. Even though the top rate was only 6 percent to begin with, Rockefeller categorically denounced this innovation. "When a man has accumulated a sum of money, accumulated it within the law, the Government has no right to share in its earnings," he complained to a reporter in 1914.[17] As taxes became steeper and more progressive in the coming decades, it became a daunting task for any businessman to amass the money that Rockefeller had earned in a laissez-faire world devoid of antitrust laws. His own wealth, in fact, was the text for many sermons in favor of using taxation as a way to check the acquisition of huge fortunes, to redistribute wealth, and to reduce social tensions.

=

The birth of the Rockefeller Foundation coincided with the gradual retreat of Frederick T. Gates from Rockefeller's business affairs after twenty years of tenacious attention. During the summer of 1909, the fifty-six-year-old Gates was suffering from nervous strain, likely from overwork, and wanted to spend more time with his wife and seven children. Around 1912, the once threadbare Minnesota preacher picked up at bargain prices twenty thousand acres of land near Hoffman, North Carolina, and set about growing cotton, corn, and oats and raising livestock on a thousand-acre farm with a peach orchard of seventeen thousand trees.

In August 1912, Gates tendered his resignation from the business side of the family office to devote himself solely to the philanthropies. Long reliant upon Gates's sound judgment, Rockefeller tried to sweet-talk him into staying: "Shall we not, dear friend, continue along life's pathway together, both of us recognizing the propriety for ourselves of increasing freedom from care, but, nevertheless, both continuing to give what time we wisely and appropriately can, to the large and important questions, old as well as new, which we find ourselves in a position to help to solve?"[18] By November, Rockefeller had capitulated and accepted his resignation. For the next five years, Gates chaired the GEB but ceased to draw a regular salary and performed only sporadic business missions for Rockefeller. For all his panegyrics about Rockefeller's wisdom, Gates had some private grievances and was irked by what he saw as his skimpy compensation; the value of his services had been a sore point with him ever since the 1901 Mesabi-ore sale to U.S. Steel. In 1915, Gates undertook a long, tortuous negotiation for Rockefeller with the Consolidation Coal Company; afterward, he rejected as too meager Rockefeller's $25,000 in compensation and held out for $60,000.

Although Gates had been the visionary behind the Rockefeller Foundation, he now became just one of nine trustees. When the foundation held its first meeting at 26 Broadway on May 19, 1913, Junior was elected president. He invited his father to attend but knew he would decline. Nominally a trustee for ten years, Rockefeller followed his usual practice and never sat in on a single meeting. He was now receding to a more distant supervisory role with his philanthropies and yielding more power to his son, although he never surrendered his veto power. Perhaps the congressional donnybrook over the foundation charter reminded him of the value of keeping a salutary distance from his foundations. Or perhaps it was just age.

Several features of the new foundation mocked the idea that it was a public trust and suggested instead a closely guarded Rockefeller preserve. Its governing structure conjured up a holding company for existing Rockefeller philanthropies instead of the autonomous operation once promised so fervently to Congress. Of the nine trustees, two were family members (Senior and Junior), three were staffers (Gates, Starr Murphy, and Charles O. Heydt, Junior's secretary), and four came from Rockefeller philanthropies (Simon Flexner and Jerome Greene from the RIMR, Harry Pratt Judson from the University of Chicago, and Wickliffe Rose from the Rockefeller Sanitary Commission). The Rockefeller philanthropies remained a self-contained universe, with the same faces rotated among the various boards.

The Rockefeller Foundation's claim to autonomy was also undercut by Rockefeller's retention of the right to allocate $2 million of its income yearly. Until this practice was abolished in 1917, these founder's designations constituted up to a third of all grants and financed several of Senior's pet projects, from Baptist missionary work to the Eugenics Record Office of Charles B. Davenport. In retrospect, Congress, by denying a charter to the foundation, had forfeited a chance to restrict Rockefeller's influence over his money.

As for the recipients of grants, buffeted by the uproar over the federal charter, the Rockefeller Foundation refrained from anything that smacked of controversy. Having had more than enough public criticism, the Rockefellers wanted everything to be simon-pure. Like the family's other philanthropies, the Rockefeller Foundation was attuned to the optimistic, rational spirit of the Progressive era and drew on its new class of technocrats. (Woodrow Wilson, a political scientist, had been elected to the White House in 1912.) Science would be the magic wand waved over any project to show that it was sound and objective, free of favoritism or self-interest. For a long time, the Rockefeller Foundation shunned the humanities, social sciences, and the arts as areas too subjective or fraught with political peril. In 1917, when advising his father to pump another fifty million dollars into the RIMR, Junior explained his preference for medicine: "This is a field in which there can be no controversy, so that I think the possibility of criticism as regards the use of the fund or its potential dangers would be almost nothing. There is no limit to the development of medical work."[19]

In its first decade, the Rockefeller Foundation focused on public health and medical education both at home and abroad. As founder of one of the first multinational corporations, Rockefeller applauded the unique global range of his new philanthropy, a feature that would always distinguish it. In its maiden action in June 1913, the new board decided to take the superb work of the

Rockefeller Sanitary Commission's antihookworm campaign and apply it around the globe. To accomplish this, it created a new International Health Commission under the leadership of Wickliffe Rose, who exported his campaign to fifty-two countries on six continents, treating millions of people.

In the future, Rose would engage in battles to subdue malaria, tuberculosis, typhus, scarlet fever, and other scourges, but he registered his most spectacular success with yellow fever, once tagged "the terror of the Western Hemisphere." During the Spanish-American War, Major Walter Reed had shown that mosquitoes transmitted yellow fever, knowledge used by Colonel W. C. Gorgas to control the disease in Panama during the building of the canal through mosquito-infested jungles. Touring the Far East in 1914, Rose heard fears from public-health officials that a fresh outbreak of yellow fever could result from ships passing through the new canal. Back in the United States, Rose consulted Colonel Gorgas, who asserted that yellow fever could be "eradicated within a reasonable time and at a reasonable cost" if a systematic campaign was mounted to stamp out seedbeds in the Western Hemisphere.[20] Hired by Rose to accomplish just that, Gorgas achieved such triumphant results that the disease was nearly wiped out in South and Central America by the late 1920s. When it flared up again, the Rockefeller Foundation sponsored a team of scientists to develop and manufacture a vaccine to fight it, a dramatic effort that yielded a vaccine by 1937 but also claimed the lives of six researchers, who contracted the disease. Millions of doses of the vaccine were distributed worldwide and saved innumerable American soldiers during World War II.

These moving crusades to eliminate infectious diseases generated one troubling afterthought: What if these diseases returned for lack of trained government personnel in the affected areas? It soon became evident that the best way to safeguard Rose's work was to assist governments in establishing public-health machinery. It was an auspicious moment for such an approach, for pure science had now begun to outstrip applied medicine, which meant that enormous gains could be made simply by implementing existing knowledge. With this in mind, the Rockefeller Foundation gave six million dollars to Johns Hopkins for a new school of hygiene and public health that opened in 1918, a new-fangled institution to train public-health professionals in such emerging disciplines as sanitary engineering, epidemiology, and biostatistics. In 1921, the foundation made a similar gift to Harvard to start a public-health school and finally spent twenty-five million dollars to create such schools from Calcutta to Copenhagen, along with numerous fellowship programs. Through its catalytic role, the Rockefeller Foundation played an integral part in the rise of American medicine to the pinnacle of world leadership.

While Rockefeller Foundation largesse was distributed across many continents, China was a special beneficiary, receiving more money than any country except the United States. As Rockefeller scaled back involvement with the

University of Chicago in 1909, Gates fancied that they might replicate this feat with a great Chinese university. Like many Baptists of his era, Rockefeller was interested in China because of the extensive missionary efforts there. Though the political unrest in China gave him pause, Gates sent a study mission there to investigate. Two groups stoutly opposed the project: local Christian missionaries, who feared the heathenish secularism of the proposed university, and government officials, who feared foreign subversion. So the interest in China turned to that old Rockefeller standby: medicine. In 1915, the Rockefeller Foundation set up the China Medical Board, which constructed the Peking Union Medical College and opened it in 1921. One of Rockefeller's most ambitious projects, the medical complex contained fifty-nine buildings, roofed with jade-green tiles (it would be dubbed the Green City) scattered across a twenty-nine-acre site. Later nationalized by the Communists, the school introduced a generation of Chinese doctors to modern medicine.

By the 1920s, the Rockefeller Foundation was the largest grant-making foundation on earth and America's leading sponsor of medical science, medical education, and public health. John D. Rockefeller, Sr., had established himself as the greatest lay benefactor of medicine in history. Of the $530 million he gave away during his lifetime, $450 million went directly or indirectly into medicine. He had dealt a mortal blow to the primitive world of nineteenth-century medicine in which patent-medicine vendors such as Doc Rockefeller had flourished. He had also effected a revolution in philanthropy perhaps no less far-reaching than his business innovations. Before Rockefeller came along, rich benefactors had tended to promote pet institutions (symphony orchestras, art museums, or schools) or to bequeath buildings (hospitals, dormitories, orphanages) that bore their names and attested to their magnanimity. Rockefeller's philanthropy was more oriented toward the creation of knowledge, and if it seemed more impersonal, it was also far more pervasive in its effect.

CHAPTER 29

Massacre

In his philanthropies, John D. Rockefeller had ascended into the pure air of good works, high above the clash of partisan politics and industrial strife. With the advent of the Rockefeller Foundation, the Rockefeller name, so besmirched by association with Standard Oil, took another long step toward redemption. And by serving on the white-slavery jury, Junior had tested a brand-new image as a social reformer. It was at this happy juncture that news reached New York of terrible bloodshed in the southern Colorado coalfields and the worst nightmare in Rockefeller history—surpassing anything ever related to Standard Oil—descended upon the family with terrible swiftness.

The Rockefellers' ill-fated involvement in Colorado dated back to 1902, when Senior was flush with windfall profits from the spectacular sale of Mesabi iron ore to U.S. Steel. At George Gould's urging, Frederick Gates visited the properties of Colorado Fuel and Iron (CFI), the state's largest employer, which owned twenty-four coal mines that provided coke for its own steel mills. If the Rockefellers controlled the company, Gould fancied, his railroads might receive lucrative coal-carrying contracts. Inspired by his Mesabi triumph, Gates had a hunch that a CFI investment might be a bonanza on an equivalent scale. In November 1902, Rockefeller paid $6 million for 40 percent of its stock and 43 percent of its bonds, gaining uncontested supremacy over the Colorado company. Only later did Gates learn that Gould had been tipped off by a trusted aide that the company management was "rotten" and that its top executives were a pack of "liars," "swindlers," and "thieves."[1]

To strengthen CFI, Gates convinced Rockefeller in 1907 to import a new management team, and he had an ideal candidate in mind: his sixty-year-old uncle, LaMont Montgomery Bowers, whose consumptive wife might benefit from the Colorado mountain air. Because of Bowers's demonstrated proficiency in running the Great Lakes ore fleet, the Rockefellers reposed extraordinary—and ultimately misplaced—trust in the abilities of this former wholesale grocer from upstate New York who became vice president of the Colorado company and the Rockefellers' chief liaison with it.

Despite this fresh leadership, the Colorado investment seemed as misbegotten as the Mesabi investment had been charmed, and for years CFI did not pay a penny on its stocks or bonds. Hobbled with a money loser, the Rockefellers took an intransigent tone with union organizers. As early as October 1903, Junior sent fighting words to CFI's president on the subject: "We are prepared to stand by in this fight and see the thing out, not yielding an inch. Recognition of any kind of either the labor leaders or union, much more a conference such as they request, would be a sign of evident weakness on our part."[2] In his decades in business, Senior had learned never to budge on the prerogatives of capital, especially when it came to unions. In 1903, Standard of New Jersey had truculently broken a strike for union recognition at its Bayonne, New Jersey, refinery. So when Bowers came on board, he had an understanding with the Rockefellers that he would be assertive in blocking unionization.

When dealing with CFI, Junior reflexively abided by his father's faith in absentee ownership and delegated wide authority to managers, monitoring their performance by ledger statistics. This approach had made sense where the Rockefellers were minority stockholders and did not wish to get in deeper but proved sadly deficient here. At CFI, the Rockefellers found themselves in the indefensible position of being all-powerful yet passive amid a spiraling crisis.

When Junior resigned from Standard Oil and other corporate boards in 1910, he stayed on at CFI because the family retained a controlling interest. The second-largest steel company and seventeenth-largest industrial firm in America, CFI still operated in the red, and Junior felt it his duty to engineer a turnaround, showing his father that he could solve a difficult situation. Prior to 1914, his papers reveal considerable correspondence about CFI matters—dreary, soulless letters filled with sterile talk about preferred stock, debentures, and dividends and far from the dismal reality of the miners. On January 31, 1910, when an explosion at a CFI mine killed seventy-nine men, Bowers blamed careless miners, even though the Colorado Bureau of Labor Statistics charged the company with "cold-blooded barbarism."[3] When Junior wrote Bowers on February 7, he did not even allude to this atrocity and merely noted that CFI's growth had stagnated in recent years. The Rockefellers had no long-term commitment to the company, which Senior planned to sell to U.S. Steel as

*William Lyon Mackenzie King (left) and John D. Rockefeller, Jr.,
don denim overalls at the Colorado Fuel and Iron Company,
September 1915, after the Ludlow Massacre.*
(Courtesy of the Rockefeller Archive Center)

soon as he could wangle a fair price. Right on the eve of the Colorado disaster, Gates urged Rockefeller to slim down his investment, but he would not hear of it.

Under Rockefeller rule, it was heretical for anyone in CFI management to concede any legitimacy to unions. To scare off union organizers, Bowers and CFI president Jesse Welborn resorted to terror, fielding spies and detectives and firing union sympathizers. At the same time, they tried to inoculate workers against unions through paternalistic measures, raising their wages 10 percent and introducing an eight-hour day. As a chastened Junior later said of Bowers, "He had the kindness-of-heart theory, i.e. that he was glad to treat the men well, not that they had any necessary claim to it, but because it was the proper attitude of a Christian gentleman. For example, he always argued in favor of company stores. He would say that the company owned the towns, why shouldn't they own the stores."[4]

If Senior's philanthropies showed his broad-mindedness, his unrelenting opposition to organized labor brought out his more antediluvian side. He could never see unions as anything other than frauds perpetrated by feckless workers. "It is all beautiful at the beginning; they give their organization a fine name and they declare a set of righteous principles," he said. "But soon the real object of their organizing shows itself—to do as little as possible for the greatest possible pay." Workers were incorrigible spendthrifts who squandered surplus earnings. "They spend their money on picture shows, and whiskey and cigarettes."[5] At Pocantico, he did not allow employees to take Labor Day as a vacation and fired one group that tried to unionize. Right before the Colorado troubles, he even tried to halt contributions to YMCA building projects that employed closed-shop union labor, but he was talked out of it by his staff. Gates, if anything, was even more obdurate about unions, warning that "it is clear that if they get the power, they have the spirit to rob, to confiscate, to absorb remorselessly, cruelly, voraciously, if they can, the whole wealth of society."[6] When union organizers targeted CFI, Rockefeller, Junior, Gates, and Bowers treated it as the industrial equivalent of Armageddon.

For years, the Colorado coalfields had been scarred by labor warfare. This was raw capitalism such as Karl Marx pictured it: dangerous mines run by harsh bosses and policed by armed guards in a desolate, hellish place. During 1913 alone, 464 men were killed or maimed in local mining accidents. Blackened by soot from coke ovens, workers lived in filth, shopped in company stores, and were ripe for unionism. Nevertheless, in May 1913, Bowers reassured the Rockefellers that CFI workers were happy souls, prompting Junior's naive response that it was "most gratifying . . . that a large industrial concern can treat all people alike, be open and above-board in all its dealings, and at the same time increasingly successful."[7]

The United Mine Workers of America (UMW) spotted fertile soil in this arid country. In the polyglot mining communities, workers came from thirty-two countries and spoke twenty-seven languages; some of them were so ignorant of American ways that they imagined Rockefeller was president of the United States. As union organizers tramped the dusty foothills, they appealed to workers in English, Spanish, Italian, Greek, and Slavic languages. By late July 1913, a showdown appeared imminent as John Lawson of the UMW announced plans to unionize local miners, making a strike all but certain. In response, the three major coal companies, CFI among them, brought in gunmen from the Baldwin-Felts Detective Agency and had them deputized by county sheriffs. Albert C. Felts took credit for designing a ghastly vehicle dubbed the Death Special, an early version of an armored car, topped with two machine guns that could be trained against strikers.

In September 1913, with a grisly confrontation imminent, the federal government tried to head off a strike. The Rockefellers' unsympathetic response was colored by a belief that President Wilson was biased toward labor. Rockefeller lamented after Wilson's election, "I wish some day that we might have a real businessman as President."[8] When Wilson appointed a former UMW official, William B. Wilson, as the first secretary of labor, he implicitly committed his administration to the concept of collective bargaining. Wilson sent a deputy, Ethelbert Stewart, to New York to confer with Junior about averting the strike. Even with arsenals being stockpiled on both sides, Junior refused to see the emissary and shunted him off to Starr Murphy, who warned that "we here in the east know nothing about the conditions [in Colorado] and would be unwilling to make any suggestions to the executive officers."[9] Junior hid cravenly behind L. M. Bowers, deferring to his judgment.

On September 26, 1913, nine thousand workers at CFI struck to demand union recognition, as well as better hours, wages, and housing conditions. In a bellicose letter to Junior, Bowers promised to resist until "our bones were bleached as white as chalk in these Rocky Mountains." From 26 Broadway, Junior cheered this combative stance. "We feel that what you have done is right and fair and that the position you have taken in regard to the unionizing of the mines is in the interest of the employees of the company." Then, in words that would resound with an eerie retrospective ring, he added, "Whatever the outcome, we will stand by you to the end."[10]

In a move that served only to polarize the situation, the coal companies evicted strikers from company homes, forcing them and their families into a massive exodus. The outcasts pitched tent colonies beyond company grounds, with the largest concentration at a spot called Ludlow. By the end of September, more than 11,000 of the nearly 14,000 workers were on strike, bringing Colorado coal mining to a virtual halt. As both sides hoarded weapons, an air of violence hung over the tent colonies. Deputy sheriffs, supplied with guns and paid $3.50 a day, cordoned off the grounds of CFI.

Afraid that the unions would trumpet any meeting as a concession, the mine owners refused even to talk with organizers. Back in New York, the Rockefellers received highly distorted pictures of events as Bowers fed them sanitized reports that made union organizers sound like common hoodlums. "When such men as these, together with the cheap college professors and still cheaper writers in muck-raking magazines, supplemented by a lot of milk and water preachers . . . are permitted to assault the businessmen who have built up the great industries . . . it is time that vigorous measures are taken," Bowers fulminated in one letter.[11] Junior held aloof from these events, not wanting to second-guess management or perhaps reluctant to soil his hands with such filthy business.

On October 17, the situation veered toward open warfare as gunfire was exchanged between strikers and deputy sheriffs at a tent colony. By the time the battle ended, sheriffs had hurtled through the colony in a Death Special, spraying machine-gun fire and killing several strikers. To intimidate workers, CFI also strafed the colony with blinding searchlights. While Bowers kept Junior well informed about the Winchester rifles and revolvers being smuggled in by strikers, he remained mute about the company's own ample cache of weaponry, including machine guns.

As the violence intensified, the well-meaning but indecisive Governor Elias Ammons sent in the Colorado National Guard to restore order. Instead of acting in an evenhanded fashion, the guard primarily protected company property from the miners. On October 30, President Wilson intervened, asking Jesse Welborn of CFI to "submit a full and frank statement of the reasons which had led them to reject counsels of peace and accommodation in a matter now grown so critical."[12] Instead of a temperate response, Bowers sent Wilson a shocking, six-page diatribe, dismissing union recognition as unthinkable: "We shall never consent, if every mine is closed, the equipment destroyed, and the investment made worthless."[13] Since the UMW had now enlisted the legendary organizer Mary Harris Jones—better known as Mother Jones—Welborn retailed vicious scuttlebutt to the president about her alleged early career in a brothel. After reviewing this response, Junior, who was sure the trouble sprang from the strikers, extolled the "energetic, fair and firm way" that CFI had conducted itself. When Labor Secretary Wilson asked Junior for his cooperation, he ducked responsibility and expressed confidence in CFI executives who "have always been quite as solicitous for the well-being of employees as for the interest of stockholders."[14] Workers had struck, he argued, only because they were terrorized by union organizers: "The failure of our men to remain at work is due simply to their fear of assault and assassination."[15] Senior shared this grievous misperception. Junior informed Bowers, "I know that Father has followed the events of the past few months in connection with the Fuel Company with unusual interest and satisfaction."[16]

That December, a terrible blizzard blanketed Colorado. Twenty thousand men, women, and children shivered in their tents, but Junior's position only hardened. While egged on by his father, he was clearly the point man during the strike. For the first time, Junior was the target of a Rockefeller political controversy. Summoned to give testimony before the House Subcommittee on Mines and Mining in March 1914, Junior saw himself perpetuating his father's noble legacy. "Father was the greatest business witness ever on the stand," he said. "No one could ever ruffle him or corner him and he never lost his temper. I had this great example before me and I felt I couldn't let him down."[17]

On April 6, 1914, Representative Martin D. Foster of Illinois questioned Junior before the subcommittee. Cool and poised, Junior made several admissions that critics thought damaging but that he submitted with pride: He had done nothing personally to end the strike; had not visited Colorado in ten years; had not attended a CFI board meeting since the strike; did not know of any valid worker grievances; and did not know the company had hired Baldwin-Felts detectives. For Foster, this seemed a damning self-indictment:

FOSTER: "Now, do you not think that your duty as a director goes further than that?"

JUNIOR: "We spent ten years testing out . . . one of the men in charge."

FOSTER: "Do you think your duty goes further than that? . . . Don't you believe that you, looking after the welfare of other civilians of the United States, that somewhat closer relations between officers and . . . these six thousand coal diggers who work underground, many of them foreigners, ignorant and unacquainted with the ways of the country, would be an uplift to them to make them better citizens?"

JUNIOR: "It is because I have such a profound interest in these men and all workers that I expect to stand by the policy which has been outlined by the officers, and which seems to me to be first, last and always, in the greatest interest of the employees of the country."[18]

At a climactic moment, when Foster posed the question of whether Junior would willingly lose all his property and see all his employees killed to uphold the open shop—that is, the principle that every employee had the right not to join a union, even if it bargained collectively for other workers—Junior replied, "It is a great principle," and then compared it to the sacred ideals of freedom for which the Revolutionary War had been fought.[19]

Thrilled by Junior's defense of their privileges, businessmen swamped him with congratulatory telegrams. Almost tearful with joy at her boy's performance, Cettie wired him that his testimony "was a bugle note . . . struck for principle."[20] A no-less-exultant Senior told a friend apropos of Junior's testimony, "He expressed the views which I entertain, and which have been drilled into him from his earliest childhood."[21] Until this point, Junior had not owned any shares in the Colorado company and acted only as his father's proxy. Now, Senior gave him ten thousand shares of CFI as a reward for his testimony. Before the month was out, the stock certificates would seem like a curse that he had myopically visited upon his son.

=

Two weeks after Junior testified in Washington, the inadequacy of his position became evident at the tent colony in Ludlow. Some thirty-five militiamen from the national guard—many of them, said the union, company gunmen sworn in as soldiers—were stationed on a ridge overlooking the camp when a shot was fired at dawn. Who fired it was never ascertained, and perhaps it does not matter, for both sides were heavily armed and ready to fight. After the shot, the militiamen pelted the gray and white tents with machine guns, the staccato fire tearing many tents to shreds, and by day's end they had killed several strikers. Then the drunken guardsmen swooped down into the colony and, by some reports, spread a blaze from tent to tent with oil-drenched torches. The arsonists did not know that two women and eleven children were huddling for safety in a dirt bunker that had been scooped out by hand under one tent. As the canvas above them caught fire, they were overcome by smoke and promptly asphyxiated—a slaughter that was not discovered until the next morning.

When Bowers informed Junior of the so-called Ludlow Massacre, he gave it his usual self-serving gloss, describing it as an act of self-defense committed by outnumbered militiamen. Echoing the party line, Junior sent back regrets over "this further outbreak of lawlessness."[22] Junior and Abby were doing landscaping at Kykuit at the time—Abby objected to the "rather cramped" proliferation of gardens, balconies, and terraces—so that the horrific news from Colorado seemed to arrive from some infernal, faraway world.[23] Having pledged his ardor in the wrong cause, Junior could not accept blame. Two months later, he wrote a strange memo for his files in which he seemed to lambaste the strikers for the deaths of their own wives and children:

> There was no Ludlow massacre. The engagement started as a desperate fight for life between two small squads of militia, numbering twelve and twenty-two respectively, against the entire tent colony which attacked them with over three hundred armed men. There were no women or children shot by the authorities of the State or representatives of the operators in connection with the Ludlow engagement. Not one. . . . The two women and eleven children who met their death in a pit underneath the floor of one of the tents, where they had been placed by the men, apparently for safety, were smothered. That

such an outcome was inevitable as a result of placing this number of human beings in a pit 8×6 and 4½ feet, the aperture of which was concealed, without any possible ventilation is evident. . . . While this loss of life is profoundly to be regretted, it is unjust in the extreme to lay it at the door of the defenders of law and property, who were in no slightest way responsible for it.[24]

However he might rationalize it, it was a nightmare for Junior, a huge stain on what he had hoped would be an immaculate life, and a reversion to the Rockefeller past. As one Cleveland paper said, "The charred bodies of two dozen women and children show that *Rockefeller knows how to win.*"[25] John Lawson castigated Junior for these "hellish acts" and sneered that he "may ease his conscience by attending Sunday school regularly in New York but he will never be acquitted of committing the horrible atrocities."[26] Others regarded Junior as an errand boy for his father, and even Helen Keller, once helped so generously by Henry Rogers and Rockefeller, now told the press, "Mr. Rockefeller is the monster of capitalism. He gives charity and in the same breath he permits the helpless workmen, their wives and children to be shot down."[27]

A show of penitence on Junior's part might have placated the public, but his defensive moralizing invited a severe backlash. In late April, Upton Sinclair sent a "solemn warning" to Junior: "I intend this night to indict you upon a charge of murder before the people of this country. . . . But before I take this step, I wish to give you every opportunity of fair play."[28] When Junior did not respond to his requested interview, Sinclair spearheaded a demonstration outside 26 Broadway, a "mourning parade" of pickets dressed in black armbands, their ranks swollen, at one point, by a delegation from Ludlow. "The harder we pound Rockefeller, the surer we are of winning," Sinclair told his associates.[29] In this threatening environment, a woman with a loaded pistol was forcibly removed from Junior's office. Senior had been unflappable in crises, but his son was shaken to the core. He now kept a Smith & Wesson .38 pistol in his office drawer and posted watchmen at Fifty-fourth Street, where another chanting contingent besieged his home.

As Emma Goldman, Alexander Berkman, and other prominent anarchists and Wobblies flocked to Kykuit to protest, guards tried to seal off the estate against these interlopers, some of whom penetrated the grounds, smashed windows, and set fire to the dairy barn. Foolishly confident of his persuasive powers, Senior marched toward the wrought-iron gates, hoping to calm the protesters, but the Burns detectives urged him to go back into the house. The local fire department was summoned to train water cannons on demonstrators who were trying to clamber over the gates. So many journalists converged on the scene that Rockefeller was distracted at golf by the incessant glare of the photographers' lights and had to alter his daily schedule. Before the summer was over, he had installed barbed-wire fences at Pocantico and strung out potentially lethal razor wire across the tops of walls. Dismayed by the fortresslike atmosphere of their compound, Junior told his father, "I am wondering whether so obvious an effort to make entrance to the place difficult at this time may not challenge attention and suggest a fear and apprehension on our part which might induce, rather than help, to keep out intruders."[30]

All the Rockefeller wealth suddenly seemed insufficient beside the magnitude of the threat. During one rally outside 26 Broadway, a speaker denounced Junior and exhorted the crowd to "shoot him down like a dog."[31] Such inflammatory rhetoric was not just political bombast. In May, several Wobblies were killed or injured when a bomb they were assembling blew up on the top floor of a Lexington Avenue tenement; it was widely thought that the explosive had been destined for Junior's town house.

After the massacre, the coalfields witnessed a fresh upsurge in violence as southern Colorado degenerated into a lawless no-man's-land, and President Wilson faced vociferous demands to dispatch federal cavalry troops to the area. To avert this, he wrote to Rockefeller and implored him to meet with Martin Foster before Foster left to tour the coalfields. Playing his sly old game, Rockefeller said he had not been to work in twenty years, but that his son would meet Foster in New York.

At this April 27 meeting, Junior was completely inflexible, telling Foster that CFI controlled a mere third of Colorado coal output and shouldn't be singled out for criticism. Afterward, Junior informed the president,

> Dr. Foster was unable to make any suggestions which did not involve the unionizing of the mines or the submission of that question to arbitration. We stated to him that if the employees of the Colorado Fuel and Iron had any grievances, we felt sure that the officers of the Company would be willing now, as they had always been, to make every effort to adjust them satisfactorily, but that the question of the open shop . . . could not be arbitrated.[32]

Wilson was stunned by this brazen indifference to a presidential request, telling Junior, "It seemed to me a great opportunity for some large action which would show the way not only in this case but in many others."[33] A few days later, Wilson sent federal troops to Colorado.

It was all a regrettable throwback to the days of Standard Oil, with Junior now cast as the villain of the piece. His inability to escape from this debacle stemmed from his own rigidity plus an unbending intolerance toward unions that was also exhibited by his father and Gates. "We are trying to move quietly, and patiently, under the trying ordeal," Rockefeller told Harold McCormick, "but I repeat it is a matter for all of us to give earnest heed to, and we must all cooperate throughout the land for the maintenance of our rights."[34] Supporting his uncle, Gates also refused to give an inch to save lives. "The officers of the

Colorado Fuel and Iron Company are standing between the country and chaos, anarchy, proscription and confiscation and in so doing are worthy of the support of every man who loves his country."[35]

Surrounded by these retrograde views, this refusal to entertain new ideas, Junior was locked in an untenable position. The Ludlow disaster threatened to undo all his efforts to cleanse the family name. His father—so long his cynosure, guide, sage, and mentor—could not graduate to new wisdom in this area. The Ludlow Massacre forced Junior to admit that his father held some antiquated views and that he must take spiritual leave of him. To do so, he needed a confidant from outside his immediate circle, someone who shared his sense of ethics and could devise a practicable, honorable way out of the impasse. He found this providential personage in William Lyon Mackenzie King.

Mackenzie King exerted a tremendous influence upon Junior in part because they had similar styles and tastes but radically different knowledge of the world. The offspring of a renowned Canadian family, King had been a wunderkind of Canadian politics. After studying economics at Toronto, Chicago, and Harvard, he was named Canada's first deputy minister of labor at age twenty-five and then minister of labor nine years later. A gently persuasive man, he had arbitrated many acrimonious labor disputes and espoused new government mechanisms for settling such disputes. In 1911, his luck expired when the Liberal government fell, depriving him of his ministerial post and throwing him into a state of acute anxiety about money. For three years, a rich British woman named Violet Markham helped him financially. King always claimed to find fault with high society, which he dismissed as petty, false, and vain, but when he needed the money, he could be obsequious toward the rich.

In early June 1914, still fretting about his finances, he received a cryptic telegram from the Rockefeller Foundation, inviting him to New York to discuss a special labor project for its new economic-research unit. On June 6, he found himself closeted in a four-hour marathon session at 10 West Fifty-fourth Street with Junior, Jerome Greene, and Starr Murphy. By the close, Junior had asked him to head the foundation's new Department of Industrial Relations—which, in essence, meant serving as his personal adviser on Ludlow. Even though Junior publicly denied it, he was smart enough to see that he needed to grope toward some new innovation in labor-management relations. An ambitious, liberal politician, King was initially petrified by the potential repercussions of this association. As he confessed to his diary, "Once associated in any way with the Rockefeller concern, my future in politics would be jeopardized."[36] For two months, King wavered about accepting the job. But since it was being offered by the Rockefeller Foundation, not Standard Oil, he was emboldened to take the risk, especially when former Harvard president Charles Eliot strongly endorsed the move. At a second meeting with Junior at Pocantico, in Senior's presence, King accepted the job.

Just about the same age, King and Junior were both short and stocky, prudish and proper, and dressed in dark, old-fashioned suits. Something about King's platitudinous moralizing was highly reminiscent of the Rockefellers'. A fervent Presbyterian, King devotedly read the Bible and abstained from cards and tobacco, and these two reserved, rather solitary young men enjoyed an immediate rapport. Many observers saw in King the very strengths and weaknesses—a messianic nature combined with a lack of social ease—often attributed to Junior. Both young men idealized their mothers, and when King later drifted into spiritualism, he claimed that he had communicated with his dead mother's spirit in séances. According to Junior, King was "quite silly about women," yet some inhibition always kept him a bachelor.[37]

Junior considered King's arrival "heaven-sent deliverance" and later said, "Seldom have I been so impressed by a man at first appearance."[38] Normally surrounded by elders, Junior found in King a peer who had known firsthand the hurly-burly of the world. Within a year of their meeting, Junior told him, "I feel I have found in you the brother I have never had and have always wished to have."[39] Despite that, Junior called him "Mr. King" for the next forty years. An idealist with a wide streak of ambition, King saw in Junior a way to carry out social reform and be well compensated in the bargain. Despite his liberal politics and initial prejudice against the Rockefellers, King liked Junior instantly and thought him a kindred spirit. "Whatever his father may have done or is," King told a friend, "that man I have found to be almost without exception the truest follower of Christ."[40]

Except to his uninhibited wife, Junior never talked as candidly to anybody as he did to King. King bluntly warned him that the Rockefellers' philanthropic work could be destroyed by Ludlow and that it would be a "Herculean task" to overcome unfair public prejudice against the family. Only King could broach the dreaded topic of Senior's business ethics without seeming disloyal. He recorded in his diary that he told Junior

> that he must recognize that we were living together in a different generation than the one in which his father had lived, and that it was possible, in building up an industry such as Standard Oil, to maintain a comparative secrecy as to methods of work, etc. and to keep business pretty much to those who were engaged in it. Today, there was a social spirit abroad, and it was absolutely necessary to take the public into one's confidence, to give publicity to many things, and especially to stand out for certain principles very broadly.[41]

He made Junior see the need to depart from his father's legacy and chart an independent course.

By this point, Junior was touchingly frank in his need for advice about Ludlow. "He had vast experience in industrial relations and I had none," Junior said of King's influence. "I needed guidance."[42] Though supporting unions, King favored compromise, opposed strikes purely for union recognition, and insisted upon gradual reform. He thought that fair-minded investigations of the facts would suggest a common ground for capital and labor. Appealing to Junior's conscience, King argued that Christian brotherhood could be brought to the bloodstained fields of Colorado through greater worker-management cooperation. Under the Rockefeller Foundation aegis, King devised a plan in which CFI employees would elect representatives to boards for dealing with worker grievances. At best a halfway house on the road to true labor reform, the plan was a cosmetic modification rather than a sharp break with the past, and organized labor scoffed at it as another paternalistic trick. But it was a courageous departure from the prevailing business ethos, however timid it might seem by later lights. As proof of this, CFI management resisted it, fearing it would deliver the company into the union's hands. In the end, Senior looked on benignly and let these changes occur. It was a road that he could not have traversed himself, but his son found the way to do so.

King led Junior away from his father's orthodoxy while simultaneously charming the old man. When King pleaded for greater public openness, Rockefeller seemed deeply moved. "I wish I had had you the thirty or forty years I was in business to advise me on policies," he said.[43] King found Rockefeller far nicer than he had expected. As he told a friend:

> In appearance, [Rockefeller] is not unlike pictures one sees of the old popes. In manner he is singularly simple and natural and genuinely kindly. . . . I had the feeling I was talking with a man of exceptionally alert mind and great discernment of character. He is a good deal of a mimic, and in telling of people and his own feelings is apt to imitate the expression of the person or the attitude he is representing. He is full of humor, particularly in conveying a shrewd knowledge of situations and men. His whole nature is a gentle one and a sweet one.[44]

═

By December 1914—eight months after the Ludlow Massacre—striking miners, their strike fund depleted, voted to end the long walkout, allowing federal troops to leave the area. With the end of the strike, Junior pressed his blueprint for labor-management cooperation upon CFI leadership with renewed vigor. Bowers and Welborn still worried that the plan might lend credence to union grievances, but Junior persisted despite their hostility. Far from fleeing criticism, he exposed himself to it. His old college classmate Everett Colby gave a dinner at the Union Club in Manhattan so that Junior could meet people who had pummeled him, including Lincoln Steffens and the socialist lawyer Morris Hillquit. During postprandial cigars, speaker after speaker reviled Junior's initial refusal to become involved in the strike. Then Colby said, "Do you want to say anything, Mr. Rockefeller?" "I certainly do," said Junior, slowly rising to his feet. Everyone expected a withering counterblast, but Junior confounded them by saying, "I want you gentlemen to realize how deeply grateful I am for this. I shan't forget any of it. My difficulty is that I can't find out the truth. A chap in my position is so used to being made a target for unjust accusations that his tendency is to disbelieve even those which may perhaps be justified."[45] It was a polite way of saying that his press critics had some truth on their side and was thus a major step forward from his earlier denials.

Unlike Senior, whose hide was thickened by abuse, Junior was traumatized by press invective. "I never read the papers when there's apt to be any trouble," he reflected years later. "I learned that in the old days during the strike out west."[46] In May 1914, while still reeling from the Ludlow Massacre, Junior asked Arthur Brisbane to recommend someone who might burnish the family image, and Brisbane suggested thirty-six-year-old Ivy Ledbetter Lee, executive assistant to the president of the Pennsylvania Railroad. The son of a Georgia Methodist preacher, the slim, blue-eyed Lee had a southern drawl and willowy southern charm that would subtly seduce a generation of newsmen. After working his way through Princeton, he traced a career route that became commonplace in the news business: After stints at two New York papers, Hearst's *Journal* and Pulitzer's *World*, he went into corporate public relations, a budding field fostered by the dual impact of investigative journalism and government regulation of business. At their first encounter at 26 Broadway, Junior told Lee, "I feel that my father and I are much misunderstood by the press and the people of this country. I should like to know what your advice would be on how to make our position clear."[47] Instead of buying press coverage, Lee expounded his belief that businessmen should present their views fully and frankly—then trust to the truth. Said a relieved Junior: "This is the first advice I have had that does not involve deviousness of one kind or another."[48]

Still committed to an unfinished project at the Pennsylvania Railroad, Lee started out by working on a $1,000-a-month retainer for Rockefeller, which was shortly increased to a handsome full-time salary of $15,000 a year. Though he soon defected to set up his own consulting firm, he faithfully served the Rockefellers and Standard Oil of New Jersey from this outpost. So pervasive and trusted was his counsel that Junior later told a head of Standard of New Jersey: "Mr. Lee is very much more than a publicity agent. He is one of our advisers in regard to various matters of policy."[49]

It is difficult to assess whether Ivy Lee had a beneficial effect upon the Rockefellers. His instructions to Junior sounded commendable enough: "Tell the truth, because sooner or later the public will find out anyway. And if the public doesn't like what you are doing, change your policies and bring them into line with what people want."[50] Excellent advice, to be sure, but did it reflect Lee's own behavior? For several months in mid-1914, he issued a series of bulletins called "Facts Concerning the Struggle in Colorado for Industrial Freedom" that were broadly disseminated to opinion makers, giving the Rockefeller version of events. Many critics faulted Lee for playing fast and loose with the facts when he grossly overstated the pay given to strike leaders by the union, dished out scabrous stories about Mother Jones's supposed early career as a brothel madam, and blamed the Ludlow Massacre on an overturned tent stove instead of militia gunfire. The literary fraternity skewered him: Carl Sandburg published an article called "Ivy Lee—Paid Liar"; Upton Sinclair memorably branded him "Poison Ivy"; and Robert Benchley later mocked him for suggesting that "the present capitalist system is really a branch of the Quaker Church, carrying on the work begun by St. Francis of Assisi."[51]

Initially, Lee repeated the error that had landed the Rockefellers in trouble in the first place: He relied upon slanted reports from CFI executives. After some embarrassing gaffes, he traveled out West in August 1914 and returned with a more balanced picture. Lee discovered that Bowers and Welborn had issued distorted information and that CFI employees were too cowed to voice complaints. "It is of the greatest importance," he advised Junior, "that as early as possible some comprehensive plan be devised to provide machinery to redress grievances."[52] Whatever his truth-shading tendencies, Lee probably helped to bring about more humane policies at CFI.

Under the joint tutelage of King and Lee, Junior regained his equanimity and even launched a publicity offensive for improved labor relations, a transformation evident when he testified in January 1915 before the U.S. Commission on Industrial Relations at New York's City Hall. Assembled by President Wilson, the commission was composed of representatives of employers, employees, and the public. The hearing was chaired by Senator Frank P. Walsh, a reformist Missouri lawyer who had won his spurs defending Jesse James. With an impressive mane of hair and a histrionic manner, Walsh was gunning for Rockefeller. To coach Junior for this event, King gave him a brief reading list on trade-union history and issued a delphic warning: "I reported . . . to him, that there appeared no alternative so far as he was concerned, to his being either the storm centre of a great revolution in this country or the man who by his fearless stand and position would transfuse a new spirit into industry."[53] For his part, Lee insisted that Junior not skulk around and behave guiltily. When the question arose of which door Junior would enter upon arriving at City Hall, Jerome Greene said, "Oh, the rear door of course." At once, Lee jumped to his feet. "The days of the rear door philosophy are over. Mr. Rockefeller will have to enter through the same door as everyone else."[54] When Junior, clad in derby and chesterfield coat, arrived at City Hall, looking pale and tense, he strode down the center aisle, pausing to shake hands with Mother Jones and other Colorado union organizers.

The next three days of arduous testimony provided a catharsis for John D. Rockefeller, Jr. During the first day's testimony, he still professed ignorance of the CFI situation. He endorsed the right of labor to organize but also the right of capital to resist. At day's end, when he strolled down Broadway to his office, he was trailed by masses of jeering demonstrators. Even though Police Commissioner Arthur Woods assigned special details to 26 Broadway and West Fifty-fourth Street, Junior declined this special protection. "Father never was afraid of anybody," he explained. "He was the most completely fearless man I ever met, and I don't want the public to think that I had to have police around me to protect me."[55]

The second day held surprises for Junior's detractors. He buttonholed Mother Jones—who had been jailed in Colorado for nine weeks and escorted from the state at bayonet point—and invited her to visit his office. Responding in a friendly manner, she told Junior that she had never believed he knew what "those hirelings out there were doing. I can see how easy it is to misguide you." Junior kidded her about throwing compliments his way. To the delighted roar of press and spectators, Mother Jones retorted, "I am more inclined to throw bricks."[56] On the stand that day, Junior delivered the mea culpa so long awaited by the public when he admitted that he had taken too narrow a view of a director's responsibilities. "I should hope that I could never reach the point where I would not be constantly progressing to something higher, better— both with reference to my own acts and . . . to the general situation in the company. My hope is that I am progressing. It is my desire to."[57] Mackenzie King later identified this testimony as the turning point in Junior's life.

Such public confessions of error were alien to Senior, who interpreted criticism as the martyrdom of the just. In Junior's place, he would have reacted with cool defiance or expedient forgetfulness. Yet he saw that his son was following King's advice, exhibiting uncommon courage, and accomplishing a critical shift in the family's public posture. Moved by his son's strength, Senior bequeathed to Junior another eighty thousand shares of CFI stock, which gave him effective control of the company. If he had been scanning the heavens for a sign that his son was strong enough to carry the burden of a colossal fortune, this was it. He said later of his son's testimony:

> They tried so hard to badger my son, to harrow him into saying something that they could use against him, against us. It was like the trial of Joan of Arc. I don't know where he got the answers, his language, so quick, so instant to every question. . . . He surprised us all. He seemed to answer like one inspired. Indeed, I believe that his sainted mother must have inspired him; he was so kindly, so right in his attitude and all his statements.[58]

For most reporters, Junior came across as frank and sincere, if a trifle stuffy. Walter Lippmann, however, accused him of mouthing commonplaces.

Those who listened to him would have forgiven him much if they had felt that they were watching a great figure, a real master of men, a person of some magnificence. But in John D. Rockefeller, Jr., there seemed to be nothing but a young man having a lot of trouble, very much harassed and very well-meaning. No sign of the statesman, no quality of leadership in large affairs, just a careful, plodding, essentially uninteresting person who justifies himself with simple moralities and small-scale virtues.[59]

It was a savage indictment and one repeated frequently over the years. But it failed to appreciate how bravely this pedestrian young man at age forty had managed to appease both a venomous public and an all-powerful father. He had repudiated his father's principles without seeming to repudiate the man, an ingenious strategy that opened up fresh possibilities for the family. To see how far Junior had traveled beyond his reactionary mentors, one need only cite a hysterical memo that Gates wrote after the Walsh testimony, deploring Junior's leniency:

I do not so understand Christ that he adopted any spirit of conciliation toward those who came to him in the spirit of these Unionists. . . . I would have engaged an array of the most brilliant and able counsel to be gotten in New York—men not afraid, if necessary, to make a scene in court. . . . If necessary I would have carried the matter so far as to invite arrest, and I would have resisted arrest, and been carried struggling—shrieking from the court room for the purpose of getting my case vividly, powerfully, before the people of the United States.[60]

How much Junior had evolved beyond such die-hard opposition was also made clear when Mother Jones visited him at 26 Broadway. The eighty-four-year-old, cheerfully vulgar, Cork-born rabble-rouser liked to rally striking miners while outfitted in boots and bonnets and peering at them humorously through granny glasses. Now, having helped to turn the Colorado strike into an anti-Rockefeller vendetta, she stood face-to-face with Junior. She teased him that she had pictured him with a hard jaw and firm-set mouth, clutching for money. Mimicking this, she added, "When I saw you going on the stand, and listened to the evidence, and saw the kind of man you are, I was filled with remorse. I felt I had done you a great injustice."[61] Having paid tribute to Junior's sincerity, Mother Jones did not mince words about his employee-representation plan, which she called "a sham and fraud."[62] But after the bitter stalemate of past years, this meeting represented a major advance in mutual confidence.

After the chat, Ivy Lee invited in reporters, and Junior, his face reddening shyly, said, "Gentlemen, I know it is my duty as a director to know more about actual conditions in the mines. I told Mother Jones that, of course, there should be free speech, free assembly, and independent, not company-owned, schools, stores and churches in the mine field. I am going to Colorado as soon as I can to learn for myself."[63] The promised two-week trip was made in September 1915, an overdue rite of passage that would complete the partial conversion begun in New York.

When Junior journeyed to southern Colorado, he betrayed the feverish urgency of a man on a spiritual quest. In a second round of hearings in May, Frank Walsh had released subpoenaed copies of correspondence that had passed between Junior and CFI executives during the strike. They showed Junior in his most militantly antiunion mood, implicating him more deeply in management than he had admitted and making the expiatory trip to Colorado even more essential. Having always shrunk from contact with his anonymous foes, Senior confided to a friend that he would give a million dollars to spare his boy exposure to peril in Colorado. He tried to prevail upon Charles O. Heydt to carry a gun, but Junior, determined to prove his courage, refused either weapons or bodyguards. The eight reporters who tagged along were requested, as a security precaution, to keep his itinerary a secret.

The trip pointed up critical differences between Senior and Junior. For Senior, vast wealth had permitted a retreat to his estates, whereas for Junior it underscored the need for greater openness. Instinctively, he behaved like a head of state, always cordial and generous in public—a style he transmitted to his children. Unlike his father, he did not wish to be eternally at war with the American public and had the courage to make the necessary midcourse corrections; in this last respect, he was a stronger person than his indomitable father, who had always dug in his heels and become intransigent when attacked.

Throughout his life, Junior had shadowboxed with unseen enemies who suddenly became three-dimensional human beings in the Colorado mining camps. Now, he would mingle with workers whose fate he had governed from afar. First, the caravan stopped at Ludlow itself, a haunted, windblown spot, now denuded of its tents. Emerging from their cars, Junior, King, and the reporters solemnly approached two railroad ties, nailed together in a black cross, marking the spot where the two women and eleven children had been suffocated in the pit. Afterward, they rode to the first of eighteen CFI coal towns, where they lunched on beefsteak, beans, and mashed potatoes. Entering into the spirit of the place, Junior and King responded to Ivy Lee's suggestion and bought two-dollar suits of denim overalls from a company store before descending a coal shaft.

At one coal-mining camp, Junior delivered a short talk to workers in the local schoolhouse then suggested, with uncharacteristic spontaneity, that they clear the floor and hold an impromptu dance. As a little four-piece band struck up "The Hesitation Waltz," he grabbed a miner's wife and gaily stepped onto the floor. Too well-bred for tokenism, Junior spent the evening dancing with each of the twenty or so women in attendance—an ironic sequel for a young man once so bashful at Brown that he hesitated to dance at all. Nobody was more flabbergasted than Abby, who tracked his progress in the press. "From the papers I gather that your dancing has been one of your greatest assets," she wrote to him. "I will never demur again."[64]

On October 2, 1915, in the town of Pueblo, Junior addressed two hundred CFI workers and managers. "This is a red-letter day in my life," he began. "It is the first time I have ever had the good fortune to meet the representatives of the employees of this great company, its officers and mine superintendents, together, and I can assure you that I am proud to be here, and that I shall remember this gathering as long as I live."[65] Preaching his gospel of cooperation, he laid out his plans for a joint labor-management grievance panel along with new committees for health, sanitation, mine safety, recreation, and education. Significantly, nobody would be fired for joining a union, and there were promises of new housing, schools, and recreation centers. Taking a down-home approach, Junior laid three heaps of coins on a table to represent workers, managers, and directors then tried to show how each group siphoned off coins, leaving nothing for dividends on the $34 million Rockefeller investment. In the end, Junior must have been fairly persuasive, for 2,404 of 2,846 miners voted for his plan in a secret ballot. On the other hand, possibly from disdain for this paternalism, 2,000 miners boycotted the vote.

Selling the plan to management was no easier. After initial resistance, Welborn accepted the grievance mechanism and introduced other innovations, but L. M. Bowers opposed this reform, and Junior realized he had to cashier Gates's uncle. "One of the most unpleasant tasks I ever performed was to get his resignation," he said. "I shall never forget the three or four hours I spent with him in my house here trying to get him to retire amicably—for he could be a nasty enemy."[66] At this point, Junior's relations with Gates began to cool forever. The tradition-minded Junior never formally deposed the old gods—his father and Gates—but instead staked out new directions with new advisers. When E. H. Weitzel, CFI's fuel manager, complained about his clemency toward unions, Junior shot back: "Your attitude in this respect is definitely paternalistic, an attitude which on general principles I am sure you will agree it is unwise for any corporation to maintain. . . . Paternalism is antagonistic to democracy."[67] Junior had defected, at least halfway, to the enemy camp. But his representation plan was, at best, only a middling success. In the following years, the company weathered four more strikes before the UMW finally won recognition in 1933. Junior's species of "company union" was outlawed by the Wagner Act in 1935.

For Junior, the Colorado trip was a trial by fire from which he emerged triumphant, converting the worst moment in the family history into something more promising. As King told Abby during the tour, "From now on he will be able to devote his time to advancing the vast projects . . . [relating] to human beings, without being thwarted at every step by . . . the voice . . . of popular prejudice."[68] Although much of what Junior had done was likely anathema to him, Senior cheered his son's journey of reconciliation. "Yes, it was excellent," he told an old friend. "I could not have managed it better myself."[69]

After the Colorado trip, Junior became a prophet for improved labor relations throughout American industry, an evangelical role he enjoyed more than browbeating unions. Seizing the high ground, he sold his stock in U.S. Steel during a 1920 strike when management would not annul its policy of twelve-hour days, seven days a week. Junior and King introduced employee-representation plans at both Standard Oil of New Jersey and Standard Oil of Indiana. Abby even contributed to trade unions and to funds for striking workers—which her husband thought was going a bit far. As a nationwide drive to retain the open shop swept American business in the 1920s, many industrialists looked upon Junior as a dangerous liberal, even though many trade unionists saw his company unions as traps for unsuspecting workers.

In one respect, Junior's work with Mackenzie King proved a setback for the family: It fueled popular suspicion of the Rockefeller Foundation. From the outset, the family had insisted that it would be a public trust, not a vehicle to promote Rockefeller causes. Because King's work was underwritten by the foundation, though, it looked as if the Rockefellers had exploited their philanthropy to lend a veneer of legitimacy to their business activities. After public hearings into the matter, the foundation decided to avoid economic issues and concentrate on public health, medicine, and other safe areas. To boost faith in the foundation's autonomy, in July 1917 Rockefeller waived his future right to make founder's designations.

If the Ludlow Massacre was a turning point in Rockefeller family history, much of the credit must go to Mackenzie King, who emancipated Junior from strict obedience to his father. He strengthened Junior's tenuous faith in his own judgment, making him feel that he was strong enough and fit enough to manage the family fortune. King probably did not exaggerate when he said of Junior in his diary: "I really think he feels closer to myself than to any other man he knows."[70] Politically, Mackenzie King emerged both well paid and unscathed from his detour into the Rockefeller universe. In 1919, he was elected leader of the Liberal Party in Canada and two years later became prime minister, serving in that post off and on for a record twenty-two years and forging much of the modern Canadian welfare state. Like many counselors to the Rockefellers, he had enjoyed the satisfaction of serving both his conscience and his bank account.

CHAPTER 30

Introvert and Extrovert

T he Ludlow saga was intertwined with the final, troubled phase of Cettie's life. When demonstrators stormed the Pocantico gates, Rockefeller grew alarmed because, among other reasons, his wife lay terminally ill inside. Junior was about to make his trek of atonement to Colorado when his mother died on March 12, 1915, forcing him to postpone it until September. One of the first sympathy notes came from Mother Jones: "The sympathy of one whom thousands of men have called 'Mother' is with you at this time when your heart is filled with sorrow for her who called you 'Son.' "[1] A month later, Senator Aldrich, who had retired from the Senate in 1911, died of a stroke, steeping Junior and Abby in the thick gloom of double mourning.

Cettie had been withering away for many years. When she took up winter residence at 4 West Fifty-fourth Street in late 1909, she was already restricted to a wheelchair, so that Junior and Harold McCormick had to hoist her up the front steps. Largely bedridden, requiring round-the-clock nursing, she was inexplicably reluctant, like her husband, to consult the eminent physicians at the Rockefeller Institute. As her diaries show, she suffered from a gruesome host of afflictions, including pneumonia, shingles, pernicious anemia, and sciatica. She was pestered by so many ailments that it is impossible to come up with a single, clear diagnosis.

Senior's response to her chronic troubles was ambivalent. He was often loving and infinitely patient. At dinner parties, he would pluck a flower, excuse himself, tiptoe up the stairs, and present it to her, along with some amusing tidbit of table talk. "He was the most affectionate and thoughtful man in illness and sorrow I have ever known," said his son. "No woman could have been more tender."[2] During Cettie's siege, they remained an old-fashioned couple, sweet and unfailingly courtly with each other.

Yet for all his devotion, Rockefeller was often away, refusing to modify his seasonal rotation of houses. During the winter of 1909–1910 at West Fifty-fourth Street, for instance, Cettie inscribed in her diary: "John Sr. is at Pocantico coming down Sundays."[3] Though he stayed away for long patches—sometimes weeks at a stretch—Cettie expressed no bitterness.

During the summer of 1913 at Forest Hill, with Dr. Biggar in constant attendance, Cettie's condition deteriorated as lumbago, pleurisy, congestive heart failure, and bladder and rectal problems were superadded to her already long list of maladies. In this cheerless season, sister Lute grew ill and took to a wheelchair, though she recovered by the spring. When doctors warned Rockefeller that Cettie was too frail to leave Cleveland, he was caught in an excruciating predicament, for his seasonal rotation demanded his presence at Pocantico in October. If he stayed through February, he could be listed as a Cleveland resident and face severe tax penalties. Nonetheless, he repeatedly postponed the trip due to Cettie's frailty. Making the best of things, he drove Cettie around the grounds each day in an old-fashioned open phaeton or new-fangled automobile. "John so very cheerful and comforting and glad I am slowly improving," Cettie told her diary.[4] During one visit to the Euclid Avenue Baptist Church, Rockefeller was addressing the congregation when his gaze alighted upon Cettie's pale, upturned face, and he was moved to a personal utterance. "People tell me I have done much in my life," he said. "I know I have worked hard. But the best thing I ever accomplished and the thing that has given me the greatest happiness was to win Cettie Spelman. I have had but one sweetheart and am thankful to say I still have her."[5]

In February 1914, John preceded Cettie to Kykuit to ensure that the remodeled house would accommodate her comfortably. Perhaps with a premonition that she would never see Cleveland again, Cettie postponed her departure for New York. When one employee softly prodded her, she balked. "I don't want to go yet," she said. "This is where the children used to be, and Mr. John's little rocking chair is upon the attic floor."[6] The journey east in February proved an unspeakable ordeal. When the train stopped at Philipse Manor in North Tarrytown, Cettie, attended by doctors and nurses, was lifted to a waiting automobile. Once she was settled in at Pocantico, Senior promptly resumed his self-imposed routine and rushed off to his Lakewood haunt for his usual spring retreat. Without reproach, Junior wrote him, "Mother misses you, but is glad to feel that you are having a good rest, and while she will welcome you home, realizes that you should have this change."[7]

Dismayed by his wife's sickness and perhaps feeling faintly guilty, Rockefeller tried to offset his absences with extravagant romantic gestures. On their golden

John D. Rockefeller attends the ailing Cettie,
who was confined to a wheelchair in her final years.
(Courtesy of the Rockefeller Archive Center)

wedding anniversary in September 1914, he brought a brass band to Kykuit, placed them on the lawn, and had Cettie carried from the house to Mendelssohn's "Wedding March."

During her last Pocantico winter, strengthened by a brew of barley, oatmeal, and milk, Cettie seemed to rally, so that Junior and Abby felt confident enough to join Senior at his new winter retreat in Ormond Beach, Florida. As workmen painted the master bedroom for John D.'s return, Cettie was in better spirits than she had been in for a long time. On March 11, 1915, she asked for a wheelchair, wanting to tour the garden and smell the flowers. During this fleeting reverie, she downed a glass of milk, pronounced it good, then wearily sank back on her pillow, feeling faint and weak. Lute and Dr. Paul Allen maintained an overnight vigil at her bedside, and the two sisters were clasping hands at 10:20 A.M. the next morning when Cettie expired. At Ormond Beach, Rockefeller received two telegrams in rapid succession: the first announcing that she was dying, the second her death. Though he had gotten accustomed, by degrees, to the possible imminence of her death, he was still stunned by the finality of the news. When he shuffled back to the breakfast table with the news, John and Abby saw something they had never seen before: Senior was openly weeping.

Returning by train from Florida with his son and daughter-in-law, Rockefeller was amazed by the many expressions of sympathy he received from railway officials and conductors along the route. As Abby said, "He was wonderfully calm and brave but it was a great shock to him."[8] At Pocantico, Rockefeller found Cettie laid out peacefully where she had died and for a long time stared pensively at the woman who had shared the unprecedented achievements and tumult of his life. Alta came to Pocantico but not Edith, who was studying with Carl Jung in Switzerland. Seven years later, Rockefeller reconstructed for her his impressions of Cettie's death, saying that "she triumphed gloriously when the end came, and to the last view we took of her, her face bore that angelic radiance."[9]

Rockefeller was always sentimental about his wife, and as he reminisced about their early married days on Cheshire Street in Cleveland, he would take out and lovingly handle the first dishes they had purchased. While grappling with both grief and wistful memory, he had to endure an infuriating tax battle with the city of Cleveland. He had been a legal resident of New York since the 1880s and paid all his taxes there. During the winter of 1913–1914, Cettie's illness had forced him to prolong his stay at Forest Hill beyond February 3—the tax-listing day that determined taxable residence in Ohio. Rockefeller's extended sojourn had been dictated solely by the medical emergency.

Nonetheless, his political enemies welcomed this chance to vex him. Declaring Rockefeller a legal resident for 1913, the Cuyahoga County tax office assessed him $1.5 million in taxes. Having already paid taxes in New York, he refused to submit to this extortion, even after Ohio governor James M. Cox threatened to subpoena him if he crossed the state line. While Rockefeller stalled, the Cuyahoga commissioners threatened to slap on a 50 percent penalty. Later on, the courts declared that Rockefeller had been assessed wrongfully, but meanwhile he had no choice but to boycott the state.

The way Cleveland dealt with him had long been a sore point with Rockefeller, who believed that no other town so regularly abused him. He thought the city ungrateful for Standard Oil's economic contribution and railed against "low politicians" who tried to extract taxes from him. "Cleveland ought to be ashamed to look herself in the face when she thinks of how she treated us," he stated.[10] It irked him that local groups badgered him for money while he was being so mercilessly berated by local reporters and politicians. During his lifetime, he donated more than three million dollars to several local institutions— including the Euclid Avenue Baptist Church, Alta House, Western Reserve University, the Case School of Applied Sciences, and the Cleveland Orchestra— and gave the land for two spacious parks, Rockefeller Park and Forest Hill Park. Yet these gifts were extremely modest compared to what Cleveland would have received had it not antagonized him. Rankled, Rockefeller transferred his love and loyalty to his adopted town. "New York has always treated me more fairly than Cleveland, much more."[11] How many New York hospitals, museums, and churches would be enriched by Cleveland's blunder!

Because of the virulent tax dispute, Rockefeller could not bury Cettie in the family plot in Cleveland without facing a subpoena and had to postpone the burial. To the press, he contrived a saccharine story that he could not bear to part with her remains. "I want to keep her with me as long as I can," he told reporters.[12] For four and a half months, he stored her casket in the green granite mausoleum of the Archbold family at Sleepy Hollow Cemetery in Tarrytown, which was patrolled at all hours by two armed guards.

The casket was finally moved to Cleveland under top secret conditions. During a pelting rain and hailstorm, two guards were sent down to the cemetery gate to pick up some decorative plants for the vault—a diversionary tactic that distracted them for twenty-five minutes. While they were away, a local undertaker named Vanderbilt drove up to the vault, peeled away the flower-covered pall, removed Cettie's casket from its container, substituted a new empty casket, then replaced the pall and flowers. Once he had executed this switch, Vanderbilt drove out the front gate with Cettie's coffin hidden inside a rough, plain, unmarked box. Driving to the Harmon station of the Lake Shore Railroad, the undertaker loaded the box into a baggage car amid the intermittent flashes of an electrical storm. Nobody associated with the railroad knew the identity of the cadaver, which was accompanied to Cleveland by Vanderbilt and two men from 26 Broadway. One conspirator recalled Rockefeller's peculiarly boyish pleasure at this intrigue: "To plan and carry out the removal of the body without the papers and the public discovering a thing until all was over, was a source of satisfaction to him."[13]

Perpetuating this intrigue at Lake View cemetery, only Senior, Alta, Parmalee, and Aunt Lute stood by when Cettie's coffin was lowered into the earth beside Eliza—with a gap left in between them so that Rockefeller could spend eternity flanked by his two favorite women. Rockefeller selected Christian verse to be read aloud at the gravesite, and this clandestine sunset burial filled him with emotion. "That was all so beautiful, so lovely," he said. "It was just as mama would have wished."[14] It also ended Rockefeller's association with Cleveland, since two years later the old Forest Hill house mysteriously burned down on a frosty December night. After a failed attempt to create a residential development with houses designed in Norman-château style, Junior transferred the remaining land to Cleveland for Forest Hill Park.

As part of the probate of her will, Cettie's wardrobe was inventoried and revealed her nunlike simplicity. The most costly item of clothing was a seal coat and muff, appraised at $150. She had a dowdy collection of garments, with 15 suits valued at $300 and 10 hats at $50. Cettie had never replaced the thin gold wedding ring of 1864, which was now valued at $3. As one dumbfounded reporter commented: "Able to have a wardrobe as extensive as Queen Elizabeth's, she was content with a supply which in quantity and quality could be duplicated by the wife of an ordinarily successful business man."[15]

Cettie's death elicited Rockefeller's last major philanthropic commitment: In 1918, he gave $74 million to endow the Laura Spelman Rockefeller Memorial. To commemorate his wife, he stipulated that this foundation should promote various causes that she had championed, such as Baptist missions, churches, and homes for the aged. But the Laura Spelman Rockefeller Memorial moved beyond the denominational giving she had favored. In 1922, under the direction of Beardsley Ruml, it began to pour nearly fifty million dollars into research in the social sciences. A husky, loquacious young man, always twinkling with ideas, the cigar-smoking Ruml stimulated the growth of many university research centers in social science and was a moving force behind the creation of the Social Science Research Council. By the time the memorial was folded into the Rockefeller Foundation in 1929, it had left an enduring imprint on the academic world in only a decade of existence. As Robert M. Hutchins of the University of Chicago said, "The Laura Spelman Rockefeller Memorial in its brief but brilliant career did more than any other agency to promote the social sciences in the United States."[16]

＝

By the time her mother died, Edith had already spent two years in self-imposed exile in Switzerland and was increasingly alienated from her father and siblings. Aside from a single meeting with Junior, she seemed to have no contact with the other Rockefellers during her years abroad. She kept up a sporadic, stilted correspondence with her father that was both warm and distant, loving and subtly hostile, as she tried to sort out her confused feelings toward him.

Edith and Harold McCormick had a close but tumultuous marriage. It was, in many ways, a classic mismatch: Harold was free and expansive, while Edith was aloof, imperious, and cerebral, very much the mistress of her emotions. Sometimes she found her husband too exuberant, while he criticized her for being standoffish. Their marital tensions were likely aggravated by the death of two of their children: four-year-old Jack in 1901 and one-year-old Editha in 1904, events that cast a shadow across Edith's life. To worsen matters, between 1905 and 1907 she suffered from tuberculosis of the kidney, which fortunately went into remission. Edith became more rigid, a stickler for a frosty sort of protocol, even forcing her children to make appointments to see her. When she went out driving, she planned the exact itinerary for the coachman then refused to speak to him again during the drive. She and Harold constructed a forty-four-room mansion in Lake Forest, Illinois, called the Villa Turicum, which they never occupied, and the unpacked crates of china and chairs lingered dustily in the storerooms. Once a brilliant society hostess, Edith became increasingly immured in their mansion at 1000 Lake Shore Drive, incapacitated by a terrifying agoraphobia.

In 1910, to investigate new sites for an International Harvester factory, Harold spent two summer months motoring through Hungary with Edith, a trip that sorely debilitated her. The following year, at the last minute, she canceled a cotillion ball for two hundred people without any explanation, fostering rumors that she had had a nervous breakdown. Around this time, she also suffered a crisis of religious faith, producing a breach with her father. For a long time, she had suspected that preachers dressed up their personal beliefs as gospel truth. "I never heard a Baptist minister say anything from a pulpit that convinced me he was Divinely inspired," she once remarked.[17] The upshot, she recalled, was that "as the minister finished his sermon one Sunday I walked from my pew and out into the air vowing never to return and I kept that vow."[18] For Edith, it was a bracing moment that allowed her to map her own route to salvation, yet it also estranged her from a family spoon-fed on simple Baptist pieties.

During the summer of 1912, in a ten-week stay at a Catskill Mountains clinic run by a Dr. Foord, she rebelled against the conventional regimen of fresh air and exercise being prescribed for her depression. She was ripe for some daring approach—"My object in the world is to think new thoughts," she once stated—ideally one with quasi-mystical ingredients that might substitute for her shattered religious faith.[19] She was primed, in short, for her first encounter with Carl Jung, the Swiss clinical and experimental psychiatrist who had treated Harold several years earlier.

While Jung was in New York in September 1912, Harold's cousin Medill McCormick—an editor and co-owner of the *Chicago Tribune* who had been treated by Jung for alcoholism—introduced Edith to him. As he began to analyze her, Jung liked her mental sparkle but thought her emotional state extremely precarious. Jung diagnosed Edith as suffering from "latent schizophrenia," a hypothesis confirmed for him when she told him about a dream she had of a tree struck by lightning and split in two.[20] Edith responded to analysis like a frustrated searcher who had at last found her destination. According to one version of the story, the bossy Edith urged Jung to move with his family to America, where she would buy him a house and help him to establish his practice. This grandiosity only strengthened Jung's misgivings about Edith as a woman who thought "she could buy everything."[21] Regarding American life as sterile and deracinated, Jung recommended that Edith come to study with him in Zurich instead.

Since Edith spent years under Jung's spell, it is worth noting his intense dislike of Rockefeller. On October 20, 1912, Jung spent the day with Edith at Kykuit, doubtless savoring the chance to study an archetypal figure such as Rockefeller up close. He glibly dismissed the titan as narrow, empty, and sanctimonious. "Rockefeller is really just a mountain of gold, and it has been dearly bought," he said.[22] He thought Rockefeller lonely, obsessed with his own health, and tortured by a bad conscience. At one point, Rockefeller told Jung that the Austrians were bad people. "You know, Doctor, perhaps, of my idea for a standardized price in favor of the Standard Oil Trust; you see what a great advantage it is to pay the same price for oil all over the world—it is for the good of the people—but the Austrians have made a separate contract with Rumania. Those people are very bad."[23] For Jung, who viewed Standard Oil as a monstrous operation, such talk corroborated his worst suspicions. As he later wrote, "We had three great organizations before the war, the famous trinity— the Germany army, the Standard Oil Company, and the Catholic Church. Each considers itself a perfectly moral institution . . . [yet] thousands of decent human beings have been destroyed by the Standard Oil Trust."[24]

Having failed to woo Jung to American shores, Edith consented to sail with him to Switzerland in April 1913. For weeks before sailing, Jung met with her daily, and he continued the analytic sessions on board. Sigmund Freud, who had grown increasingly disenchanted with his onetime disciple, believed that Jung was scheming for the Rockefeller money and told Sándor Ferenczi that March that "Jung has gone to America again for five weeks, to see a Rockefeller woman, so they say."[25] For the crossing, the Rockefeller-McCormick retinue included Edith's son Fowler and his tutor, daughter Muriel and her governess, plus a clutch of servants; Harold and their other daughter, Mathilde, stayed behind in Chicago. In Zurich, the group settled into a suite at the fancy Hotel Baur-au-Lac, where Edith spent the next eight years. At first, nobody, least of all Edith, thought in terms of such an extended stay. For Fowler, the Zurich summer proved intolerable. "This is a very queer place," he wrote to Rockefeller. "It has rained here this summer almost incessantly and some very peculiar weather phenomenons happen."[26] When autumn came, he returned to America to attend Groton, but Edith tarried in Zurich, consulting Jung daily. In October, Harold and Mathilde went to Europe, hoping to bring Edith back in November, but given her growing attachment to analysis, Harold knew this was impossible. Hence, their two daughters stayed in Switzerland: Muriel was placed in a strict German school, while Mathilde, who suffered from weak health, stayed in a sanatorium.

By late December, lingering in Zurich with Edith, Harold saw the need to defend her protracted absence to her father. In a long letter to Rockefeller, he tried to explain some of Jung's methods, though he was often reticent about the substance of Edith's analysis. "Edith is becoming very *real*, and *true to herself* and is seeking and I am sure will succeed to find *her path*. . . . At any rate, she is in absolutely safe and trustworthy hands for no finer man ever breathed than Dr. Jung. He has an intense admiration for Edith and yet recognizes that she is the toughest problem he ever had to deal with." To head off family criticism, Harold added, "It was a God-send that she met Dr. Jung and that *her family stood back of her in her resolve* and that she felt this assurance."[27]

Served with this warning to be tolerant, Rockefeller tried to be forbearing, but for a nineteenth-century man, Jung's modern approach to nervous jitters sounded like so much mumbo jumbo. In detailed, informative letters, Harold gamely outlined Jung's theory of the unconscious and how he investigated that realm through dreams, reveries, and free association. Rockefeller was diplomatic but obviously befuddled. "I have not been able up to date to get down satisfactorily to all the underlying principles," he apologized to Harold. "But so long as they exercise a beautiful, helpful, continuing influence for good over the lives, that is the thing."[28]

On December 20, Harold sailed back to America without Edith. Beyond her veneration of Jung, she was immobilized by a travel phobia that made even brief train trips unbearable torments. The severity of her fears can be gleaned from a gossipy account written by her Zurich chauffeur, Emile Ammann, who was driven to distraction by her antics. He portrayed Edith as a vain, haughty, narcissistic woman with a slender waist and bright, piercing eyes. He said she was known for her eccentric behavior, her furs and diamonds, and her beautiful fashions straight from Paris and Wiesbaden. According to Ammann, she was indifferent to her family, brutal with servants, and preoccupied with punctuality in a way that mirrored her father. On his first morning, she ordered him to pick her up at 9:14. After he arrived, she checked her diamond-studded wristwatch. "Ammann," she said, "I ordered you to be here at 9:14. You were here at 9:13. Naturally, that's not the same thing."[29]

Ammann claimed that Edith had been able to sail to Switzerland because Jung had effectively sedated her by putting her in a hypnotic trance. The chauffeur played a pivotal role in the therapy to cure her travel phobia. Jung recommended that Edith board a train and travel as far as she could; sometimes, however, she sprang from the train in terror before it even left the station. But if she could stave off the terror and stay aboard, Ammann would speed ahead in the Rolls-Royce and meet her at the next station; if she felt secure enough to go on, she waved from the train window and he raced to the next station. Sometimes these grueling exercises lasted three hours, leaving both Edith and Ammann exhausted. Jung evidently thought Edith had to conquer her haughtiness as well, for he had her kneel down in her luxurious hotel suite and scrub the floors. Like some self-flagellating penitent, she also walked hatless and dripping through the rain while Ammann trailed alongside her in the car.

If Rockefeller had hoped that Harold would rescue Edith from this life, he was soon disabused as his son-in-law was sucked into the vortex of the Zurich group with its quasi-religious intensity. Returning to Switzerland in September 1914, Harold grew so entranced by Jung that he decided to stay and resigned as treasurer of International Harvester, ceding control to brother Cyrus while remaining a board member. He knew that such an abrupt change required some explaining. "I am trying to learn to *think*, for I have always had a superabundance of 'feelings'—With Edith it's just exactly the other way," he reported to Rockefeller.[30] Having grown up with both a mentally ill brother and sister, Harold was quick to brood about any deviant behavior in his children, especially the impetuous, twelve-year-old Muriel, who had started analysis with Jung that summer. The following year, Edith announced to her son, "Fowler, this question of analytical psychology is a very important one," and he, too, was herded into analysis with a Jung associate.[31]

By October 1914, Edith had graduated from straight analysis with Jung and started a course of supplementary study. As Harold reported to his now-restive father-in-law, "She studies astronomy, biology and history, and music. She does not go to see Dr. Jung anymore."[32] Whatever patience Rockefeller had shown began to evaporate in early 1915 when Edith failed to attend the wedding of Harold's brother Cyrus in February and did not come to Cettie's funeral service in March—despite Harold's talk about all the progress she had made. Rockefeller began to grumble that Edith and Harold were "banqueting" in Switzerland, forcing Harold into extended self-defense: "This is not a tabernacle of joy," he told Rockefeller, "but a shrine to which seekers only address themselves, and it is in this spirit that I have postponed again my sailing and that Edith still finds herself held."[33] By this point, Harold had adopted Jung as his guru as well, accompanying him on mountain walks and idealizing him as being "as nearly perfect to my mind as a man can be."[34] This all sounds rather starry-eyed given Jung's limited success with Edith. In a letter to his mother,

Harold admitted that Edith was still prey to agoraphobia, had not left the hotel grounds for almost a year, and could not travel on a train for more than twenty minutes—hardly a glowing testimonial to Jung's method.

What complicated relations between Rockefeller and Edith was that in working with Jung, she was trying to extirpate the cool, controlling nature she had internalized from her father. Jung classified Harold as too extroverted and Edith, like her father, as too introverted. As Harold told Rockefeller, "In Edith, Father, I see the near counterpart of your personality. I think she is more like you than any other of your children all attributes considered. . . . She has your purpose and tenacity without one little diminution."[35] Precisely for that reason, Edith knew the little devices by which her father cunningly walled himself off from people. As she wrote to her father after Cettie's death, "There is warmth and love in your heart when we can get through all the outside barriers which you have thrown up to protect yourself—your own self—from the world."[36] On another occasion, she repeated this leitmotif. "I wish sometimes that you would let me get near to you . . . so that your heart would feel the warmth of a simple human sort."[37]

Such straight talk probably made Rockefeller squirm. The human psyche was a boggy, fetid terrain that he never cared to explore, and he had spent a lifetime trying to conceal his motives and emotions. He had been largely insulated from criticism within his own family, and Edith was the first child to press him, however gingerly, on taboo topics. It is testimony to his fatherly love that, despite his complete bafflement about her exile, he tried to respond to Edith with patient sympathy. To her plea for greater closeness, he replied, "I can think of nothing which I would more devoutly desire than that we should be constantly drawn closer and closer together, to the end that we may be of the greatest assistance to each other, not only, but to the dear ones so near and so dear to us."[38] For the most part, he was too shrewd to try to induce outright guilt in Edith about her stay overseas and simply said how much he missed her and that he knew her absence must be for the best.

In 1915, Jung recommended that his followers read Friedrich Nietzsche, especially *The Will to Power,* and Edith and Harold sent a copy to Rockefeller to promote self-awareness. "It cites the theory," Harold explained excitedly, "you exemplify the practice."[39] One can only picture Rockefeller's puzzlement as he thumbed these pages. "I'm sure the book will prove very interesting reading, though it may be far beyond me," Rockefeller replied. "I keep to a simple philosophy and almost primitive ideas of living."[40] In a later letter to Rockefeller—having clearly forgotten the earlier one—Harold explained that Nietzsche was attempting to show how some people need to impose their wills on others. Yet for all their efforts to enlighten him, Harold and Edith never made much progress with Rockefeller, who was comfortable with himself and lived quite nicely with his own repressions.

Increasingly, Edith saw in Jungian psychology a mystic path as well as a therapeutic method. "You on your path have your philosophy and your religion which guide you," she wrote to Rockefeller in words that would have sounded blasphemous to him. "I on my path have my philosophy and my religion which guide me."[41] Edith wanted to use the Rockefeller fortune to proselytize for Jung, and she bristled that her father demoted her and Alta to a subordinate status behind Junior. With a protofeminist consciousness, she resented the flagrant inequality in the treatment of the son and daughters. In September 1915, she told Rockefeller of her wish to help with his philanthropies. "It is beautiful and enveloping work and John is privileged in a way which Alta and I as yet have not had the opportunity of being. I am sure that as women we are serious minded and earnest and deeply interested in mankind."[42] When this produced no effect, Edith upped the pressure in January 1916. "As a woman of forty-three I should like to have more money to help with. . . . I am worthy of more confidence on your part."[43] Rockefeller was not exactly punishing his daughter—he was sending her $2,500 monthly and had already given her and Harold more than $2 million in gifts—but his favoritism toward his son was clear.

What Edith could not admit was that she argued from a weak position. She had cut herself off from her family, skipped her mother's funeral, often showed little interest in her children, had crippling phobias, and had no immediate plans to return to the United States. She was a spendthrift with a habit of running up debt, which would have only deepened her father's doubts about her ability to manage money. As Rockefeller said, citing her stay abroad, he regretted that he could not be "more familiar with your benevolences as I have been with John and Alta in respect to their contributions to good causes. This contact and the more intimate knowledge of all that they are doing in this regard has afforded me much pleasure."[44] Eventually, he doubled Edith's monthly allowance to $5,000 but went no further for the moment.

That Edith wanted additional money to advance the cause of Jungian analysis became clear in 1916 when she put up $120,000—$80,000 of it borrowed—to rent and renovate a posh Zurich mansion for a new Psychological Club, complete with a library, restaurant, recreation rooms, and guest rooms. The intention was to have a place where analysts and patients could socialize and listen to lectures. When the setting proved too costly, the club moved to more modest quarters on the Gemeindestrasse. Edith also sponsored translations of Jung's work into English that significantly expanded his influence. Disturbed by this largesse, Rockefeller demanded that Edith send him a list of her chief charitable benefactions. In her reply, she showed that her gift to Jung far surpassed her donations to her two other main causes: the John McCormick Institution of Infectious Diseases and the Chicago Opera Company.

Upon learning of Edith's contribution for the Psychological Club, Freud, who had since broken with his heretical disciple, greeted the news with a sneer. "So

Swiss ethics have finally made their sought-after contact with American money."[45] It is easy to understand Freud's cynicism. After her gift for the Psychological Club, Edith was suddenly allowed by Jung to graduate from an analysand with unusually intractable problems to the role of analyst. That Jung had allowed the phobic Edith to function as an analyst raises some profound questions about Jung's judgment. By the following year, Edith wrote to her father, "I am teaching six hours a day besides my own studies."[46]

Edith was also subsidizing writers and musicians. Her most important patronage was of James Joyce, who had found sanctuary in neutral Zurich during the war. In February 1918, Edith set up a bank account for the financially beleaguered Joyce that allowed him to withdraw a thousand francs monthly. Eager to thank his anonymous patron, Joyce managed to ascertain her identity. When Joyce met Edith, she said to him, "I know you are a great artist" then bubbled over with talk about Jungian analysis.[47] In her typical domineering fashion, Edith decided that Joyce should undergo analysis with Jung and she would pay for it. Possibly because he spurned this offer, Joyce found his credit line abruptly terminated after eighteen months. The author did not welcome the volte-face. As Joyce's biographer Richard Ellmann observed, "It is unlikely that Joyce would allow [Edith] to escape scot-free from artistic punishment; and in the *Circe* episode of *Ulysses*, Mrs. Mervyn Talboys, the society woman with a riding crop and a sadistic bent, may owe something to Edith Rockefeller McCormick, a noted horsewoman."[48] Even Joyce's wife, Nora, made Edith the butt of ribald jokes, wondering what kind of sumptuous underwear the rich American woman wore.

Edith certainly had her ridiculous aspects. She was an unlikely cross between the *grande bourgeoise* and the impractical bohemian, a dreamer caught up in the cultlike atmosphere of Jung's practice. Yet in the Rockefeller family, she was a pioneer, the first to peer into the mysteries of human nature and confront social inhibitions and moral restraints that had long been held sacrosanct by the family.

———

It seemed at first that the mutual interest in psychoanalysis might bridge the temperamental divide between Edith and Harold. He was patient, compassionate, and eager to see his wife freed from the demons that beset her. "I must tell you in a word how lovely Edith is developing," a rhapsodic Harold wrote to his mother in September 1917. "*You would not know her.*"[49] Indeed, Edith seemed to be thriving in Zurich, her caseload of patients growing. "New patients are coming to me all the time and I have had some fifty cases now," she told her father in 1919. "I hear in a year twelve thousand dreams."[50] This pleasant interlude might have lasted forever if Harold had not been named president of International Harvester in 1918, pulling him back into the workaday world of Chicago.

Psychoanalysis had stimulated both Edith and Harold to experiment freely with their lives. Like other novices, Edith converted Jungian analysis into a license for wildly uninhibited behavior. Jung himself did not believe in or practice monogamy. "Ammann," Edith told her chauffeur, "if your unconscious causes you to love several women, you need not feel any guilt. . . . Psychoanalysis will conquer all."[51] She posted Emma, her private secretary, at the threshold of her hotel suite to safeguard her trysts. One day, Harold showed up without warning and brushed past Emma before she could stop him. A startled Edith began to shout, "Harold, I . . . shan't have it. You're not to come to my rooms without first having Emma announce you."[52] Now that Harold and Edith lived far apart, each had numerous opportunities for escapades.

Edith's liaisons managed to skirt scandal until a young Austrian named Edwin Krenn came onto the scene. A man of shadowy antecedents—Edith described him as the son of a famous European painter—he was short, blond, chubby, and always foppishly attired. When he arrived in Switzerland and entered analysis with Edith, he did not have any apparent means of support. Edith not only financed him but helped him to obtain Swiss citizenship. She was convinced that he was an architect of genius, and they became constant companions, driving together in the afternoons, attending theater in the evening, then retiring to her hotel suite for private dinners. According to Emile Ammann, Jung warned her of the scandal that might erupt from this love affair. "This is my problem," Edith replied curtly, "and I can do what I please."[53]

Alone in Chicago, Harold was highly susceptible to alluring women. Since he and Edith had recently made a five-year commitment to support the Chicago Opera Company, many pretty, aspiring singers passed his way. In September 1919, when the Chicago Opera performed in New York, a Polish singer named Ganna Walska tracked him down at the Plaza Hotel. Even though he was now balding and pudgy, Walska claimed that she swooned over his "wonderful boyish blue eyes."[54] A voluptuous woman with a hypnotic gaze, Walska wore ponderous jewelry and oversized hats and fancied herself a femme fatale; much like Edwin Krenn, she was a gold digger who wrapped herself in a cloud of exotic mystery.

In 1920, the two McCormick daughters, alarmed by their mother's affair with Edwin Krenn, pleaded with Harold to come to Zurich at once. By this point, Harold was already smitten with Walska and had little incentive to terminate the match, but he perhaps went to Switzerland, in part, because of Rockefeller's concern about the perilous state of Edith's finances. Bent upon showing that she possessed her father's business flair, she had blundered into one catastrophic deal after another. In late 1919, a German scientist had come to Switzerland peddling a secret process for hardening wood, which was supposed to make it usable for everything from railroad ties to telegraph poles.

Even Jung initially encouraged Edith in the venture. She set up a company, appointed herself board chairman, and invested $100,000, promising to boost that amount to $1 million. Rockefeller pleaded with Harold to stop her. "I am opposed to Edith having anything to do with the project at all. I fear that it will result in great loss and trouble. I most earnestly entreat her to discontinue this not only but not to engage in any business schemes."[55] There was a touch of the willful adolescent about Edith, chafing at daddy's authority, and Rockefeller's intervention probably backfired. He quickly proved to be prescient: After the German scientist left Switzerland, Edith could not reproduce his results, and eventually she had to write off a $340,000 investment. Edith also piled up staggering debts to support the Chicago Opera and gave a $300,000 piece of property to Cook County for a zoo; Harold, Rockefeller, and Junior first learned of this last act of munificence in the morning papers. By early 1920, Edith's debts had ballooned to $812,000, and her father was obliged to tide her over with a transfer of Standard Oil of New Jersey stock.

However sharp Rockefeller was in criticizing her finances, he was even more concerned about his daughter's negligence as a mother, especially toward his favorite grandson, Fowler. As lovingly as he could, he prodded Edith to devote more time to her children. As he told her in April 1921:

Edith dear, the financial question, while important, is not important when compared to the other question—the great question of your being present with your children. And how sadly they need your presence, and how very solicitous we are all for them! In this connection I may add that you could have been a great comfort and help to your mother and me. But this sinks into insignificance also, when we consider the dear children. . . . I am not lecturing. I am not scolding. I love you, Edith dear; and I am still hoping.[56]

By late August 1921, Edith had sufficiently overcome her travel phobia that she was able to book passage for America, where she planned to visit her father upon arrival. She had not set eyes on him for eight years, yet when she docked in New York, she told him that she wanted to bring along two companions: Edwin Krenn and his old boarding-school chum, Edward Dato. Properly offended—and possibly privy to rumors about Edith's affair—Rockefeller insisted upon seeing Edith alone. She grudgingly agreed to venture to Lakewood alone to see him. It took ten years for Edith to explain to her father why she never arrived on the agreed day. "When I got to the ferry, a terrific thunder storm broke the terrible heat and my nerves which had been sorely tried by the difficult divorce conditions of my arrival in New York added to the treatment of my children, broke down and I was forced to turn back instead of going to you."[57] This was as close as father and daughter came to seeing each other during the last nineteen years of Edith's life. Despite eight years of intensive study with Jung, Edith still could not fully conquer her travel phobia, at least when it came to seeing her father.

A month after Edith returned to Chicago, Harold filed for divorce. Like her father, Edith harbored hopes for a reconciliation, but Harold had the stronger legal case: His lawyer, Paul Cravath, had brought over from Europe a witness who had apparently observed Edith's infidelities. This unidentified witness was convincing enough that Alta suggested that her sister make an early settlement. By Christmas, Edith was forced to sign a harsh divorce settlement, stipulating that she would receive no alimony and would pay Harold $2.7 million for their homes, plunging her further into debt. (In 1922, Edith still owed $726,000 to the banks, despite having received more than $14 million from her father over the years.) As if to register sympathy for his son-in-law, Rockefeller sent Harold a $1,000 Christmas check even as his daughter was signing the punitive papers. Though Edith pressed him to cut off communications, Rockefeller stayed in touch with Harold, but they saw each other less frequently as time passed.

Upon returning to Chicago, Edith planned to establish a center for Jungian psychology, possibly housed in the Villa Turicum. Not particularly modest about her aspirations, she explained, "It was pointed out to me that, psychologically, Chicago will be the greatest center in the world. That is why I have come back to live."[58] Before long, Edith attracted one hundred patients to her private practice, many of them socialites enticed by the Rockefeller and McCormick names. Perpetuating her interests in astrology and the occult, she paid fantastic sums for horoscopes and hosted occasional séances; at one session, she swooned into a trance then announced that she was the reincarnated spirit of Tutankhamen's child bride. Also feeding the curiosity of prospective patients was Edith's rumored liaison with Krenn. As in Zurich, they made daily rounds together: They lunched together, then shared language tutors, followed by late-afternoon tea and evening movies. Some observers thought Krenn might be involved in a homosexual affair with Dato, although it is impossible to verify the truth of these assertions.

Still persuaded of her business acumen, Edith started a real-estate venture in late 1923, headed by her European companions and called Krenn and Dato. Once again, she proved as gullible and impulsive as Rockefeller had feared. To float the venture, Edith deposited $5.23 million ($45 million in today's money) in an entity called the Edith Rockefeller McCormick Trust, naming Krenn and Dato as cotrustees. Seeing Edith about to step off another cliff, Rockefeller wrote to her, "I shall expect later on that you will have great disappointment in connection with these real estate transactions, and it would give us all great humiliation to find a duplication of the experience which you have already had in your business adventures with foreigners."[59] The warning was not heeded.

Though Edith planned to build affordable housing for the poor near Highland Park, Krenn and Dato's flagship venture was to be a 1,500-acre haven for millionaires on Lake Michigan called Edithon, complete with a marina for owners' yachts. For the town's design, Krenn ransacked the styles of Atlantic City and Palm Beach. Trapped in Chicago by her travel phobia, Edith could not visit the building site or inspect the books or even stop by the Krenn and Dato offices. When Edith proudly mailed her father the firm's prospectus, he must have groaned inwardly, and he issued yet another jeremiad. "While you are a brilliant and mature woman of great mental capacity, I cannot forget you are my own flesh and blood. Therefore, it seems my duty to warn you of the pitfalls and vagaries of life."[60] Rockefeller had already heard reports that Edith was again borrowing heavily and that midwestern creditors were in New York, inquiring about her net worth. Yet Edith took umbrage at her father's well-meant concern: "I cannot refrain from telling you that I have been pained by your expressions of doubt as to the way my business Trust is managed and as to my two partners. Both Mr. Krenn and Mr. Dato are men of the highest integrity."[61] By 1927, as they lurched toward disaster, Krenn and Dato waded deeper into debt. The firm was not strong enough to withstand the 1929 crash, which left Edith with piles of unsold real estate. She never recouped her huge losses.

Throughout the 1920s, Edith kept reassuring her father that she would visit him but never made the trip. One is finally left to wonder whether her travel phobia provided her with a handy excuse to avoid a problematic relationship. Father and daughter often exchanged brief, loving letters and never lost touch, but they continued to disappoint each other. Edith wanted a modern father, not the antique figure she got. She tended to approach him as an oracle but then was hurt and baffled by the advice she received. Edith never expressed any remorse for having deserted her father during the last twenty years of her life. She had long been liberated from such outmoded concepts.

John D. Rockefeller with his adored grandson David in the 1910s.

(Courtesy of the Rockefeller Archive Center)

CHAPTER 31

Confessional

I f Rockefeller gave way to many lonely moments after Cettie's death, he was also liberated from the marathon ordeal of her illness. In the coming years, even as his shrunken frame grew spindly, he seemed lighter and more ebullient, more Bill's son than Eliza's. Though he lived a solitary life in many ways—Cettie and Bessie were dead, Edith was in Switzerland or Chicago, Alta was often at her Mount Hope farm, and Junior was busy disposing of his fortune—he assembled a substitute family around him.

Until her death in 1920, his prim, precise sister-in-law Lute pitched in as his hostess. But the most enduring presence after Cettie's death was the buxom Fanny Evans, Rockefeller's cousin from Strongsville, Ohio, who served as his housekeeper and companion. Rockefeller engaged in wry banter with Evans, who was thirty years his junior. As they sat at opposite ends of the dinner table, Rockefeller took a wicked old man's delight in both ribbing and flattering her. "I am constantly calling her an angel to her face," he told his son, "which causes her to throw up both hands and register somewhat of incredulity."[1] They saluted each other as "Mr. Rockefeller" and "Mrs. Evans," though he sometimes called her Aunt Fanny. They conspired in the fiction that he had to submit to her tyranny because she governed his social calendar—a useful device for getting rid of people who stayed too long. Among the supporting actors was the smartly attired Swiss valet, John Yordi, who did everything from overseeing his master's diet to entertaining him on the organ. (He specialized in hymns, of course.) Invested with dictatorial powers, Yordi was authorized to stop Rockefeller from engaging in anything too strenuous.

After all the agonizing effort expended by Junior and Abby on Kykuit, John and Cettie spent little time there. Cettie died soon after the renovation was complete, while he preferred his Lakewood hideout in the spring and Florida in the winter. His romance with the southern latitudes blossomed during his February golf vacations in Augusta, Georgia, where he could hop a trolley car or wander the streets without bodyguards. For all of Pocantico's magnificence, he felt caged and cut off from the outer world there, held hostage by his wealth. Had he not gotten too chilly on the golf course each morning, he might have selected Augusta for his winter home. When a friend then sent euphoric letters extolling the climate of Seabreeze, Florida, Rockefeller contacted the U.S. Weather Bureau and ascertained that Seabreeze regularly soaked up more winter sunshine than Augusta. Since this would extend his golf season, he made an exploratory trip there with Dr. Biggar in 1913 and found the weather just splendid. Rockefeller spent several winters at the nearby Ormond Beach Hotel, created by Henry Flagler, taking up a whole floor with his entourage, and then finally bought a house in Ormond Beach in September 1918. One must note a small irony. For years, Flagler had begged him to come to Florida, but only after Flagler's death in 1913 did Rockefeller regularly visit the state, again suggesting his tacit disapproval of his friend's divorce and ostentation in later years.

As he aged, Rockefeller felt the tug of his Puritan roots and made a fetish of simplicity. "I am convinced that we want to study more and more not to enslave ourselves to *things* and get down more nearly to the Benjamin Franklin idea of living, and take our bowl of porridge on a table without any table cloth," he wrote.[2] At Ormond Beach, a popular resort sprinkled with hotels, Rockefeller tried to return to comparatively humble living. He settled on a three-story, gray-shingled house across from the Ormond Beach Hotel that was called The Casements in tribute to its awning-covered windows. Afraid that the price would soar exorbitantly if his interest was known, he had an associate purchase it, and he took up winter residence there starting in early 1919. Simply furnished, the house was shaded by towering palms and had well-tended terraces sloping down to the Halifax River, an ocean inlet that paralleled the beach. Unassuming by Rockefeller standards, the house had eleven guest bedrooms to handle his growing brood of descendants, though it never teemed with as many family members as Rockefeller had hoped. Showing his old love of tinkering with houses, he would grab a walking stick and outline additions to the house in the wet sand or make quick sketches with a stubby pencil. A veteran sun worshiper, he installed an enclosed sunporch, which enabled tourists to view him, like some American waxwork, sitting inside. Most of all, he wanted to flood the place with music and furnished the house with a Steinway piano, a Victrola, and a lovely church organ. "I reverence a man who composes music," he once exclaimed after listening to the music of Richard Wagner. "It is a marvelous gift."[3]

Rockefeller liked to welcome visitors while sitting in Eliza's old rocking chair. The Casements had no guards or gatehouse, just a protective hedge, and reporters constantly marveled at its apparent lack of security. "It would have been the easiest thing possible for a Corsican to slip a stiletto into [Rockefeller's] side any minute," said one local reporter.[4] Though the house was not quite as unguarded as it looked—two watchmen stayed inside and another two patrolled the grounds, while Yordi also acted as a bodyguard—Rockefeller strolled around the town unattended, a geezer wrapped in a scarf and tweed cap on cool days. One day, a small boy called out to him, "Hello John D.," and Rockefeller commented, "It would have been nicer if he had said, 'Hello Neighbor John.' "[5] The townspeople thereafter catered to him by calling him Neighbor John, an honorary title that he cherished. As one reporter wrote, "At Ormond he is looked upon somewhat in the aspect of an idolized old mayor, or school teacher, or even minister."[6] He often motored the six miles to Daytona Beach, where he sat in a hooded white wicker chair, curtained from sun and breeze, watching racing cars speed over hard-packed sand.

Rockefeller indulged his two consuming pastimes: God and golf. Each Sunday morning, he donned a black derby and cutaway coat and attended the nondenominational Ormond Union Church, where he sat erect in a pew midway up the aisle, belting out hymns with gusto. Afterward, he lingered ouside the church, courteously greeting fellow worshipers and passersby. He always trusted the citizens of Ormond Beach and mingled freely with them. Once a year, he deftly slipped into the pastor's hands an envelope that contained a check covering both his salary and church operations for the year.

At Ormond Beach, Rockefeller for the first time developed true friends, not just golf cronies or acquaintances. He was belatedly learning to live more fully, more freely, than ever before. His most frequent companion was the ancient Civil War general Adelbert Ames, a ramrod-stiff West Pointer who had been wounded at Bull Run, served as a Mississippi governor during Reconstruction, and returned to battle as a volunteer brigadier general during the Spanish-American War. On the golf course, Ames, who was four years older than Rockefeller, was amused by the petty economies practiced by his thrifty friend. Around water holes, Rockefeller insisted that they switch to old golf balls and marveled at profligate players who used *new* balls in these treacherous places. "They must be very rich!" he told Ames.[7]

Often in a lighthearted mood at Ormond Beach, Rockefeller did not mind mugging for newsreel cameras when celebrities made courtesy calls. Henry Ford dropped by without an appointment and was informed that Rockefeller appeared at the public golf course at exactly twelve minutes past twelve each day. The two men met and clasped hands at that precise instant. Ford was struck by Rockefeller's calm, leathery face and keenly observant eyes. "As soon as I saw his face I knew what had made the Standard Oil Company," he said.[8]

Rockefeller was also visited by humorist Will Rogers, whose dry, folksy quips were not unlike Rockefeller's own. Rogers had breakfast at The Casements twice, followed by golf. When Rockefeller gave him a souvenir dime, Rogers replied, "You know, after the company this little dime has been keepin', I'm afraid it's gonna be plumb lonesome in my pocket."[9] And when Rockefeller beat him at golf, Rogers said, "I'm glad you beat me, John. The last time you were beaten, I noticed the price of gasoline went up two cents a gallon."[10] That Rogers dared to joke about such matters—and that Rockefeller dared to throw back his head with laughter—says much about his growing relaxation. The fearsome corporate outlaw was fast becoming a beloved old storybook figure, a certified American character, and his more cheerful mood reflected that.

On Sunday evenings, resplendent in a well-tailored tuxedo, Rockefeller attended the weekly concerts at the Ormond Beach Hotel and often invited visiting divas such as Mary Garden to join him for golf the next morning. With Cettie gone, he could play the gallant openly and liked to disappear with his new lady friends for long afternoon drives.

=

Benjamin Franklin once observed, "I believe long habits of virtue have a sensible effect on the countenance," and Rockefeller's nature became engraved in his aging face. The finely wrinkled, papery flesh told of frugality, the steady gaze of resolute purpose, the masklike face of cunning and craft. He was an ideal subject for a portrait artist, but for a long time he betrayed an ascetic distaste for personal representation. Junior and Abby admired portraits of the Widener family executed by John Singer Sargent, and in 1916 they suggested to Rockefeller that they hire Sargent for five portraits—three of John senior, one of Junior, and one of Abby. The bookkeeper in Rockefeller promptly asserted itself. "What about Kohlbach?" he asked. "The price seems very, very high, but I am willing to consider this question further with you."[11] Junior noted that Sargent, who had studied in Florence and Paris and was the son of expatriate American painters, was possibly the greatest living portrait painter and that Kohlbach, a minor figure, was not in his league. For his part, Sargent was reluctant to do the great man—he was tired of portraits and wanted to devote more time to watercolors—and consented at first only as a favor to Junior.

When the sixty-one-year-old Sargent began to paint Rockefeller at Ormond Beach in March 1917, he discarded the stereotypical images. Instead of painting him in somber business black, he captured him in a casually elegant mood, wearing a blue serge jacket with a white vest and slacks. The face was thin but not yet gaunt, the eyes pensive, and the pose softer and more relaxed than in Eastman Johnson's 1895 painting. By setting Rockefeller against an unadorned backdrop, Sargent stressed his simplicity rather than his royal wealth. Rockefeller was so pleased that he sat for a second portrait at Pocantico. Sargent found Rockefeller highly evocative and reminiscent of strong-willed figures in ecclesiastical history: "He seemed to me most like an old medieval saint with a great deal of intellect. . . . I was struck first of all by his thoroughbred appearance, the fineness of his type, the fine, keen ascetic type, one might say, and his expression of benevolence."[12] The two men talked about the brickbats flung at Rockefeller over the years, and Sargent said that while Rockefeller felt their injustice keenly, he had attained a state of philosophic resignation.

Sargent recommended that Rockefeller hire the sculptor Paul Manship, and they, too, developed an easy working relationship. At Lakewood and Pocantico, while Manship chipped away, Rockefeller diverted him with tales of his career and explained the heavenly sanction behind his wealth. "He would repeat to me several times how he considered the fortune that he had acquired as having been given to him as a responsibility, that he must not do with it except for the good of man."[13] Drawn to the busts of Roman emperors and Renaissance potentates, Manship also saw in Rockefeller the simple but august power of old Vatican prelates. "He struck me as being an extraordinary man, and I would say to myself, 'If he'd lived in the Middle Ages, he'd have been Pope at Rome.' You know, he had that kind of intensity and concentration and with his Baptist upbringing and intensity of belief and his genius, his power, I felt sure that would have been the case." Manship executed two busts of Rockefeller. In one, the titan seems a saintly figure, thin face upturned, eyes lifted meekly heavenward—a highly unusual bust for a magnate. And in the second bust, Manship sculpted Rockefeller's harder look, face stern and lips tightly compressed. The two sculptures side by side form a composite portrait of Rockefeller, forever torn between heaven and earth, earthly gain and eternal salvation.

As he loosened up in his later years, Rockefeller showed a real aptitude for image-making. His great brainstorm was undoubtedly his decision to dispense shiny souvenir dimes to adults and nickels to children as he moved about. On his morning rounds, Rockefeller dispensed dimes to household employees or caddies on the golf course. Contrary to myth, it was Rockefeller, not Ivy Lee, who dreamed up this gimmick. Lee's signal contribution was to get him to make this private practice a public trademark.

Rockefeller added his own symbolism to the coin distribution. He delivered brief sermons along with the coins, exhorting small children to work hard and be frugal if they wanted a fortune; the coins were for savings, not indulgence. "I think it is easier to remember a lesson when we have some token to recall it by, something we can look at which reminds us of the idea," he remarked.[14] He informed children that the nickel represented a year's interest on a dollar. For someone of Rockefeller's sententious nature, this was a very comfortable persona to adopt.

When he ventured forth in public, Rockefeller often had one pocket bulging with nickels, the other with dimes, while the faithful Yordi carried a backup mint. It has been estimated that Rockefeller distributed between 20,000 and 30,000 coins, and many recipients cherished these mementos, wove them into amulets, or displayed them at home. Because he hated signing autographs, which he thought a stupid custom, and was often ill at ease in public, the dimes gave him a handy ritual to smooth his dealings with strangers and enabled him to hide behind banalities. His grandson David noted, "Here was a means of quickly establishing a basis of conversation and rapport with people he saw, which he enjoyed."[15]

Rockefeller devised myriad uses for the dimes. Whenever somebody excelled at golf, out popped a dime. When Harvey Firestone slipped in a long, tricky putt, Rockefeller stepped over merrily, coin in hand. "Beautiful! Beautiful! That's worth a dime."[16] Dimes were given for well-told tales at dinner. If somebody spilled something, Rockefeller poured dimes over the stains as a tip for the person who mopped it up. Sometimes, he teased people by holding back the dime or dropping a horse chestnut into their palms instead, telling them it was good for rheumatism. Old newsreels capture Rockefeller handing out dimes in papal fashion, saying in a reedy voice, "Bless you! Bless you!" as if dispensing communion wafers.

By the time Ivy Lee appeared, Rockefeller had become, implausibly, the darling of feature writers, who found him colorful and easy to dramatize. Lee ensured that the coverage remained understated and devoid of unseemly self-promotion. He perpetuated the policy of letting recipients announce large gifts from Rockefeller and was scrupulous that the titan not play favorites or grant an exclusive interview to one paper that might antagonize another. Such trust did Lee develop with the press corps that many reporters let him vet their stories for accuracy, permitting a more controlled portrait of Rockefeller. Nevertheless, Rockefeller retained a healthy skepticism about the press, and his new openness was largely a cosmetic adaptation of a basically suspicious nature. As one newspaper observed, "So averse is Mr. Rockefeller to being quoted, even indirectly, on public questions that he does not discuss such subjects even with friends, and it is an unwritten rule that guests content themselves with anecdotes and small talk."[17]

If Ivy Lee enjoyed excellent rapport with Rockefeller, it was because he understood his operating style. He saw Rockefeller as a man of superior judgment who was far more adept in reacting to ideas than in initiating them. Whenever Lee laid any proposal before Rockefeller, he was required to list all opposing arguments. Faced with two sides of any question, according to Lee, Rockefeller had an unerring ability to make the right choice.

=

Encouraged by their ability to shape public opinion after Ludlow, Junior and Lee dusted off the long-dormant idea of an authorized biography of Senior. For Junior, refurbishing the family image was complicated by the fact that he did not know what had happened at Standard Oil and took his father's integrity as an article of faith. When talking about the infamous South Improvement Company, Rockefeller made this startling confession in the 1910s: "Most of what my son knows of this situation is his memory of what he has read in [Ida Tarbell's] book, with only here and there a statement of fact by me."[18] That Junior had been kept ignorant of such critical matters might have been one reason that Rockefeller agreed to undertake the three-year interview with William O. Inglis. As Rockefeller told Inglis, "I have gone into it because my son, very conscientious, has heard all this talk and cannot answer it himself and wants to have all the facts at hand."[19] The Rockefeller family had long been riddled by strange silences, especially about Standard Oil. Among other things, Inglis asked Rockefeller all the sensitive questions that Junior had never dared to pose himself.

With Rockefeller serenely confident about his place in history, Junior and Lee knew they would have to ease him by imperceptible degrees into any biographical project. In early 1915, Lee approached his old friend Inglis, a genial New York *World* editor who often golfed with celebrities and then published appreciative profiles about them. The Brooklyn-born Inglis wrote sports and feature stories, had an agile style, and was sufficiently malleable to toe the Rockefeller line. At first, Rockefeller refused to golf with him, even though Lee assured him that "you can be sure that anything he writes will be absolutely friendly."[20] When this gambit did not work, Lee wrote to Rockefeller later in the year, "He would print nothing at all that he did not let us see in advance of publication."[21] Rockefeller at last acquiesced, and Inglis produced, as expected, an admiring story.

In May 1917, a month after the U.S. entry into World War I, Rockefeller invited the newsman to golf at Forest Hill but did not commit himself to a biography. Inglis found him a bit more stooped and wrinkled but sunburned and radiating an air of command. He was amazed when Rockefeller announced out of the blue, "We shall not take up anything controversial. A great deal of mud has been thrown at me in the past. Much of it has dried and fallen off since then. To take up those questions now would only revive bitter controversy."[22] For the next six weeks, Rockefeller golfed with Inglis and recounted innocent boyhood memories in a noncommittal fashion. At the end of this probationary period, Rockefeller agreed to sit for an unprecedented, open-ended private interview. "You have won the old gentleman's confidence by keeping quiet," Lee told Inglis, "and now you can go down to Lakewood and ask him any questions you like."[23] If Flagler had not died in 1913 and Archbold in December 1916, Rockefeller might well have declined this chance to talk, for the proposed biography would violate their policy of never responding to critics. As Rockefeller told Inglis, "If my old associates, Mr. Flagler and others, were here, they'd say, 'Why, John, what's come over you?—wasting your time like this!' "[24]

Between November 1, 1917, and December 13, 1920, under conditions of the utmost secrecy, Inglis interviewed Rockefeller for approximately an hour each day, usually before breakfast or golf. (At one point, Rockefeller cooled on the project, which lapsed from July 1919 to November 1920.) Trailing Rockefeller from estate to estate, Inglis extracted a verbatim transcript of 480,000 words from his taciturn subject. His method was quite unusual. He would read aloud portions from Lloyd and Tarbell—both of whom Rockefeller professed never to have read—then record Rockefeller's responses. With his usual conservation of energy, Rockefeller often reclined on a lounge, shut his eyes, and seemed inert as Inglis read a passage; just when Inglis thought he was fast asleep, his eyes would pop open and he would deliver an exact response to the selection. Inglis also roamed about upstate New York and Cleveland, gathering anecdotes about Rockefeller from his boyhood haunts of Richford, Moravia, Owego, Strongsville, and Cleveland.

At first, Rockefeller regarded the interview as a private record for the family archive, but he was galvanized as he articulated, for the first time, his own defense. By March 1918, Inglis reported this change to Lee: "He says that he now feels it his duty, no less to his family than to himself, to put on record the truth about so many incidents which have been falsely reported."[25] The daily exploration transported Rockefeller back to his glory days. One morning, he told Inglis of a dream he had had: "I was back again in the harness, desperately in earnest and hard at work in the endeavor to meet embarrassing situations, to overcome the difficulties."[26]

Junior was relieved by his father's enthusiasm. "I had never even dreamed of your pursuing the matter with the persistence and continuity of which Mr. Inglis writes," Junior told his father. "I thank you a thousand times for what you are doing."[27] It tells much about Junior's underlying motivation and insecurity that he specifically asked Inglis to quiz Senior about Ida Tarbell. "To be able to take the words out of her own mouth and prove the case against her is of the utmost value," Junior instructed him.[28] In responding to Tarbell, Rockefeller alternated between biting criticism and his express desire to avoid unpleasantness. "But let us avoid anything controversial," he told Inglis. "We don't want to start another set of Tarbells and such people with their slanders."[29]

The Rockefeller that emerges from this transcript is alternately wry and genial, fiery and sardonic. An articulate man, he had worked out elaborate justifications for his actions that he had never shared with anyone, the vital inner reflections in which he reconciled his business and religious beliefs. The interview shows the extraordinary energy he invested in rationalizing those actions and forging exculpatory positions. If he felt no need to explain himself to the public, he had a powerful need to justify his behavior to himself. With Inglis, Rockefeller delivered an extended defense of trusts probably unique among those who created them. Yet even in this confession-box setting, Rockefeller was often voluble rather than candid; the habit of secrecy was too deeply ingrained. He voiced no regrets about his anticompetitive practices and seemed incapable of true self-criticism. To hear Rockefeller tell it, Standard Oil was now a beloved organization, worshiped by the masses for bringing them cheap oil. "It is conceded today that the whole performance from beginning to end was one of the most remarkable, if not indeed the most remarkable, in the annals of commercial undertakings of all times."[30] Never once in the three-year interview did Rockefeller refer to the 1911 dismemberment, and he bizarrely talked of Standard Oil as if the trust still existed. When Inglis volunteered to read aloud the 1911 Supreme Court opinion, Rockefeller declined. "No; I have never heard the decision read. I shirked it; left it to the lawyers."[31]

Throughout the interview, Rockefeller contended that cooperation had triumphed over competition in American life—which might sound odd coming so soon after both the 1914 passage of the Clayton Antitrust Act—which outlawed unfair trade practices, such as interlocking directorates—and the 1915 creation of the Federal Trade Commission, which policed anticompetitive measures and enshrined competition as the central tenet of American economic life. But lest it seem that Rockefeller had succumbed entirely to self-delusion, we must recall that the Inglis interview commenced shortly after the United States entered World War I. In a reversal of past antitrust policy, the government urged the Standard Oil companies to pool their efforts, leading Rockefeller to gloat that "the Government itself has adopted the views [that the Standard Oil leaders] have held all these years, and notwithstanding the Sherman law and all the talk on the other side, the Government itself has gone further than any of these organizations dreamt of going."[32] In February 1918, an Inter-Allied Petroleum Conference was created to coordinate oil supplies, and Standard Oil of New Jersey, which provided one-fourth of all Allied oil needs, worked closely with its bitter rival, Royal Dutch/Shell. Oil's strategic importance was now universally recognized, and 80 percent of that oil came from American companies. When Lord Curzon, a member of the British war cabinet, rose at a postwar dinner in London and stated, "The Allied cause had floated to victory upon a wave of oil," Rockefeller was elated, certain that his own pioneering work in the field had contributed materially to the victory.[33] In all, Rockefeller gave $70 million to the war cause, including $22 million from the Rockefeller Foundation to rescue Belgium from famine after the German invasion, and his generosity elicited loud hosannas from a once wary public. For Rockefeller, Germany's defeat signified nothing less than God's final blessing on Standard Oil. "There must have been a Providence ruling over these aggregations of great funds which have been used with such conspicuous benefit in helping to liberate the world from the bondage of the arbitrary military power which was threatening to crush out the liberties of mankind everywhere."[34]

So the general backdrop to the Inglis interview must have strengthened Rockefeller's confidence in his own rectitude. As Inglis waded through Lloyd and Tarbell, Rockefeller pounced on many errors but also listened to many long passages in silence, tacitly acknowledging their truth. As if unable to mouth the names Lloyd and Tarbell, he would refer mockingly to "the distinguished historian" or some other scornful description. He saw Lloyd as reckless, hysterical, and inaccurate. "Tarbell is much more dangerous," he said. "She makes a pretence of fairness, of the judicial attitude, and beneath that pretence she slips into her 'history' all sorts of evil and prejudicial stuff."[35] He largely responded to her charges with ad hominem attacks, dripping with a fair amount of male chauvinism. "Like some women, she distorts facts, states as facts what she must know is untrue, and utterly disregards reason."[36] At first, Rockefeller noted how Tarbell would praise him to establish the credibility of her subsequent criticism, yet as the interview progressed, he had to concede that her impartiality was not just a pose. "Say, I'm amazed at her writing, all the time!" he exclaimed at one point. "There's so much in it favorable to the Standard Oil Company. What with all her prejudices . . . it is really surprising that she would be willing to speak so favorably and give so much credit to the Standard Oil Company and its leaders."[37] Without citing a shred of evidence, he manufactured a cockeyed fantasy that Ida Tarbell was now tortured by guilt for having defamed him. "And if she could only cause the general public to forget what she said and the venomous way she said it, would she not live a more peaceful life, and wouldn't she die a more peaceful death? Peace to her ashes!"[38]

Though Rockefeller tried to sound statesmanlike, his anger leaked out around the edges. Even though the Lloyd and Tarbell exposés had led to the breakup of Standard Oil, he insisted of these critics that "their writing fell flat and proved a boomerang to them."[39] The more he talked, the more bottled venom surfaced, until he was spewing hatred at "socialists and anarchists" who dared to attack him. "They are a stench today in the nostrils of all honest men and women. They are a poison; and I would have them go and colonize and live out their theories and eat one another up; for they produce nothing, and they subsist as suckers on what honest men, frugal and industrious, produce."[40] This was a voice that Rockefeller's family and closest confidants never heard—the raw, uncensored Rockefeller who had been so carefully muzzled by the Christian Rockefeller. In the last analysis, the Inglis interview was a talking cure as the titan dredged up buried pain whose existence he had long denied. He was not a Christian martyr but a man with a very human vulnerability and an understandable need for catharsis.

Inglis was taken in by Rockefeller's charade of candor. Instead of engaging in extemporaneous discussion, Inglis stuck to the safe, prescribed format of reading from Lloyd and Tarbell then recording the responses verbatim. He expressed no discernible desire to examine Standard Oil files or Rockefeller papers and lazily received most of the history through the filter of Rockefeller's memory. Though he interviewed many relatives and business associates, they knew that he had been sent by Rockefeller, and, not surprisingly, they tended to remember him in a rosy glow.

Junior soon saw that Inglis was being seduced by the easy life on the Rockefeller estates and would be tempted to prolong his work. Inglis later admitted that he had been lulled by the narcotic power of his boss's monotonous but pleasant daily routine. Finally, in early 1924, after seven years of work, Inglis finished his biography, which presented a sanitized, adulatory version of Rockefeller's life. Junior had the good sense to circulate it to reliable judges, including William Allen White, the Kansas newspaper editor, and George Vincent, president of the Rockefeller Foundation, both of whom delivered a damning verdict. White said it was "too toadying and reverential" and advised the Rockefellers not to publish it.[41]

Following a suggestion from Ivy Lee, Junior naively rushed the manuscript over to Ida Tarbell in her apartment on Gramercy Park in Manhattan. They had worked together at an industrial conference arranged by President Wilson in 1919 and developed a cordial relationship. "Personally I liked her very much," Junior said, "although I was never much of an admirer of her book."[42] Tarbell reciprocated this fondness, telling a friend, "I believe there is no man in public life or in business in our country who holds more closely to his ideals than does John D. Rockefeller, Jr. In fact, I will go so far as to say I do not know of any father who had given better guidance to a son than has John D. Rockefeller."[43] Over the years, Tarbell had become more conservative and sympathetic to business—in 1925, she published a laudatory biography of Judge Elbert H. Gary of U.S. Steel—yet she found the Inglis biography evasive and one-sided and recommended that it be shelved. With immense disappointment, Junior consigned the manuscript to the Rockefeller archives forever.

*An unusually ebullient John D. Rockefeller, Jr., returns
from Europe aboard the S. S. Mauretania, December 1925.*
(Courtesy of the Rockefeller Archive Center)

CHAPTER 32

Dynastic Succession

hough heir to the throne, Junior had now waited many years to assume his rightful place, and this had made it only more difficult for him to win the respect of others. H. L. Mencken, among other skeptics, was fond of pointing out that Junior's eminence was purely derivative. "He is attended to simply because he happens to be the son of old John, and hence heir to a large fortune. So far as the records show, he has never said anything in his life that was beyond the talents of a Rotary Club orator or a newspaper editorial writer, or done anything that would have strained an intelligent bookkeeper."[1]

Despite their mutual devotion and intertwined lives, father and son were separated by a reticence that neither could overcome. They corresponded frequently, embraced warmly when they met, and enjoyed a solid rapport; when his boy was to come for dinner, John senior evinced a visible eagerness for him to arrive. Yet their relationship was also hobbled by an old-fashioned reserve, with neither of them capable of any real ease or spontaneity. "Neither Father nor I had the temperament which gives itself freely," said Junior. "We talked about whatever we had to talk over—never discursively."[2]

One day at Ormond Beach, Inglis happened to mention to Rockefeller how much Ida Tarbell's account supported his own version of events, and it prompted this melancholic remark: "I wish you would tell that to my son. . . . I must say that I have never had time to become really acquainted with my son. He has been very busy always."[3] When Inglis transmitted this to Junior, Junior was touched but blamed his father for their constrained relationship. "There is no subject that I have not always been happy to discuss with Father," he explained to Inglis, "but as you yourself have observed, he is inclined less and less to discuss subjects which he does not himself initiate; hence our serious interchange of view is perhaps more limited than might otherwise be the case."[4] Rockefeller could not suppress his controlling nature even with the son he so dearly loved.

The tension latent in their relationship flared up when Junior displayed a serious interest in art. Enough of a Calvinist to consider artworks idolatrous, Rockefeller saw collecting as both wasteful and egotistical. Despite Abby's prodding, Junior could not stop feeling guilty about his new hobby. "When I first began buying art objects," he conceded, "I had a feeling that perhaps it was a little selfish. I was buying for myself instead of giving to public need."[5] Then he grew enthralled by the exquisite Chinese porcelains owned by J. P. Morgan that were being exhibited at the Metropolitan Museum of Art. For Junior, they represented an ideal art form, for they were expertly crafted and devoid of any subversive themes or sensuality. After Morgan died in 1913, Joseph Duveen, the art dealer, bought the collection, put it up for sale, and offered Junior the first pick of any pieces. Junior coveted so many pieces that the total cost to buy them would have exceeded one million dollars. Like a trembling, sweaty schoolboy, he wrote to his father in January 1915 and asked to borrow the money. He tried to show that he had proceeded in the most painstaking Rockefeller style. "I have made many visits to the Museum and have studied carefully the most important pieces. I have also sought expert advice regarding them. Such an opportunity to secure the finest examples of Chinese porcelains can never occur again, and I want to avail myself of it."[6]

Instead of honoring or even gratifying this unusual request, Rockefeller played the proud philistine and turned it down cold. But Junior was now past forty and would not simply let the matter drop, as he would have in the past. In an anguished letter, he vented his frustrations:

> I have never squandered money on horses, yachts, automobiles or other foolish extravagances. A fondness for these porcelains is my only hobby—the only thing on which I have cared to spend money. I have found their study a great recreation and diversion, and I have become very fond of them. This hobby, while a costly one, is quiet and unostentatious and not sensational.[7]

Faced with this unprecedented revolt against his judgment, Rockefeller not only had the good sense to relent but gave his son the money outright. Deeply touched, Junior responded with profuse, breast-beating gratitude. "I am fully conscious of the fact that I am in no sense worthy of such munificence on your part," he wrote his father. "Nothing that I have ever done or could do will make me worthy."[8] When Junior received the porcelains at West Fifty-fourth Street, he sat down on the floor and rolled them about, fondly studying them and searching for cracks or marks of repair. Had Junior not established at this point his right to collect art, free of parental interference, he might never have been emboldened to create The Cloisters or Colonial Williamsburg. To demonstrate that his new interest was not frivolous, Junior developed great expertise on Chinese porcelains and put together one of the outstanding collections in private hands.

The friction over the Chinese porcelains highlighted Rockefeller's pressing need to make some final disposition of his fortune. Even though Junior had a net worth of about $20 million in early 1917, it was not generating much income. He had received large blocks of stock in American Linseed and Colorado Fuel and Iron, but the latter paid little or nothing in dividends and had only ensnared him in controversy. He also owned real estate in Cleveland and New York plus railroad and gas bonds. Junior's combined salary and allowance provided him with several hundred thousand dollars a year—which was a fantastic sum for any ordinary mortal but small beer for the son of the world's richest man.

It was likely the Ludlow Massacre that convinced Rockefeller that his son had the fortitude to manage the family affairs. "There was reason for Grandfather to feel uncertain in terms of how much Father could handle until Ludlow came along," David Rockefeller later observed. "I think it was a searing but very much of a learning experience for him as well as one that toughened him."[9] Rockefeller's decision to transfer the money was probably clinched in 1916 and 1917 when the federal government twice boosted inheritance taxes. Characteristically, Rockefeller had waited a long time to decide to transfer his money to his son, but once he began to strip himself of wealth, he acted with electrifying speed, as if pleased by this act of renunciation. On March 13, 1917, he gave his son 20,000 shares of Standard Oil of Indiana, inaugurating the biggest intrafamily transfer of money in history. On July 10, 1918, he gave 166,072 shares of Standard Oil of California; two weeks later came large blocks of stock in Atlantic Refining and Vacuum Oil. On February 6, 1919, Junior received 50,000 shares of Standard Oil of New Jersey, followed by another 50,000 shares on November 20. In 1920, Rockefeller bequeathed thick heaps of New York City and Liberty Bonds. These transfers occurred without poetry or preamble, accompanied only by terse, businesslike notes. For example, on February 17, 1920, Rockefeller wrote: "Dear Son: I am this day giving you $65,000,000 par value of United States Government First Liberty Loan 3½% bonds. Affectionately, Father."[10]

In possession of these miraculous gifts, Junior was left staggered, dazed, speechless. Before 1917, Rockefeller had given $275 million to charity and $35 million to his children. (In November 1917, he estimated that if he had kept and invested all his money until that time, he would have been worth $3 billion, or well in excess of $30 billion today. That would have put Rockefeller second only to William Henry Gates III, with $40 billion, among the billionaires listed by *Forbes* magazine in its 1997 ranking of the richest Americans.[11]) Between 1917 and 1922, he gave away another $200 million to charity and $475 million to his children, with almost all of the latter going to Junior. A profound dichotomy now opened in the Rockefeller family between the dutiful son and the wayward daughters and sons-in-law—a dichotomy so deep that the world would think of Junior's descendants alone as the real Rockefellers. (Of course, they also had the Rockefeller name.) By keeping the fortune in one compact mass, Rockefeller enabled his son to magnify its impact. The poor little rich boy was now the planet's foremost heir. Within the space of five years, Junior's net worth soared from $20 million to about $500 million—more than the $447 million that his father had given to the Rockefeller Institute, the General Education Board, the Rockefeller Foundation, and the Laura Spelman Rockefeller Memorial combined—and equivalent to $4.4 billion today. Thus, for all their public-spirited generosity, the Rockefellers still retained control over a great deal of the fortune, though much of it would be distributed to deserving parties over time. After disbursing so much, Rockefeller left himself with pocket change—somewhere in the neighborhood of twenty to twenty-five million dollars—for playing the stock market.

In 1917, Rockefeller formed special trusts at the Equitable Trust for Alta and Edith, depositing twelve million dollars apiece in their accounts ($140 million apiece today) and terminating their allowances. This money, if more than enough to make them comfortable for life, seemed a bagatelle beside Junior's cache. In defending this blatant imbalance, Junior later argued that his father had favored him because he could "carry on his philanthropic and charitable work in the same spirit which had activated him, and . . . anything he gave me would be administered with the same sense of duty and stewardship which impelled his giving."[12] In a way that would have been impossible for Alta and Edith, Junior adopted his father's principles and functioned as his surrogate. Rockefeller told his son, "What a providence that your life should have been spared to take up the responsibilities as I lay them down!"[13] Rockefeller was increasingly buoyed by the admiration of this son who viewed him as a heroic figure in business and philanthropy. As he told Inglis, "I really think I could not have had so good and true a son as he is if I had been half so bad as the prejudiced and interested 'historian' [Tarbell] would seek to make me out."[14] For Rockefeller, only a good tree brought forth good fruit, and Junior's virtue was therefore incontrovertible proof of his own.

—

By the time that Junior inherited his golden treasury, he and Abby had brought forth a large, energetic family of six children, having added Laurance (1910), Winthrop (1912), and David (1915). After Laurance's birth, Junior and Abby decided that 13 West Fifty-fourth Street could not accommodate this growing tribe, and in 1911 they bought the property at 10 West Fifty-fourth Street. Having finished with Kykuit, William Welles Bosworth—the landscape architect whom John senior found so infuriatingly extravagant—constructed a nine-story mansion for the younger Rockefellers that resembled a miniature city. Lavishly appointed with a rooftop squash court and playground, an art gallery, a music room, two drawing rooms, and an infirmary, it was one of New York's largest private residences. The family occupied the new domicile beginning in September 1913.

To escape the sultry Manhattan summers, Junior and Abby began to spend summers on Mount Desert Island in Maine in 1908. A favorite getaway of the rich since the 1880s, it was now colonized by several Rockefeller intimates, including Charles Eliot, Simon Flexner, and Christian Herter. John and Abby were so enchanted by the island's rocky, rugged beauty that in 1910 they bought a hilltop house called the Eyrie in Seal Harbor on the quieter southern side of the island. Set on a granite bluff overlooking the harbor, the Eyrie was a heavily gabled, Tudor-style cottage in the same sense that Newport mansions were cottages—that is, it was a colossal affair. Starting with the original 65 rooms, Junior expanded the place to palatial scope until it contained 107 rooms, 44 fireplaces, 22 bathrooms, and 2,280 windows.

When Junior and Abby first visited Mount Desert Island, it was a pristine place that still banned autos, and they could explore any number of wild, unspoiled places on foot or horseback. Junior took special delight in constructing carriage roads on his property. During these Maine summers, he developed a special feeling for wilderness, which inspired in him feelings of religious awe and perhaps memories of the lakes and ravines of his Forest Hill boyhood. For a man sorely taxed by responsibility, these solitary haunts refreshed an overburdened mind.

In 1916, President Wilson created the Sieur de Monts National Monument on the island, which became Lafayette National Park in 1919—the first national park created in the East—and then was renamed Acadia National Park in 1929. To serve the cause of conservation, Junior not only donated thousands of wilderness acres to the park but personally charted fifty-seven miles of auto-free carriage roads (engineers calculated the grades), studded with charming stone bridges and gatehouses that blended seamlessly into the scenery. From his father, he had learned the art of opening vistas and making the roads as unobtrusive as possible. While some environmental purists faulted Junior for tampering with nature, he had a democratic vision of how the parks might be of use to ordinary people. Whereas he often seemed wearily dutiful at philanthropic board meetings, he showed an undisguised zest for scenic preservation. It was an early sign of what became a continuing interest: preserving ancient beauty from the encroachments of modern life. At the same time, he tried, whenever possible, to retreat from the chaos of modern urban life into the peace and dignity of an uncorrupted rural past.

‗

Abby Aldrich Rockefeller, unlike her husband, was attuned to the modern, the daring, and the spontaneous. "Mother would love to have an idea and say, 'Let's go do it,' " said her son David. "She enjoyed the unexpected very much."[15] She could be satirical or flippant and admired the saucy young flappers of the 1920s. "I love to see the old hypocrisies being shattered," she said.[16] Never fearful or inhibited, she was pleased by impulsive behavior and once said of her grandchildren, "I love even their naughtiness, their funny wants and their plots to get them, which I can see lurking in their minds."[17] Such an attitude perplexed Junior, who was irritated by the high jinks of small children.

Though she adhered to her father's economic conservatism, Abby helped to broaden the political spectrum for the Rockefeller family. She was a liberal Republican who supported Planned Parenthood, the United Jewish Appeal, and the League of Nations. After the Ludlow Massacre, to improve labor relations, she contributed up to a third of the annual budget of the National Women's Trade Union League. In the 1920s, she also teamed up with Standard Oil of New Jersey to create a community center, the Bayway Community Cottage, for refinery workers in Elizabeth, New Jersey, and frequently stopped by its baby clinic. After one trip, she told her daughter Babs, "I held twenty-five naked, squirming babies today in our new baby clinic at Bayway, some of them took the occasion to drench me thoroughly. Most of them were fat, rosy, and cheerful, but once in a while they all began to howl at once. I had a wonderful time."[18] She was the major benefactor of the Grace Dodge Hotel in Washington, D.C., a 350-room hotel for professional women operated by the YWCA and staffed entirely by women, down to the bellhops and elevator operators.

Abby was vocal in her passion for social justice, and this had a lasting influence on her descendants. While staying with Senior at Ormond Beach in 1923, she wrote a letter to her three oldest sons that throbbed with outrage at discrimination. "It is to the everlasting disgrace of the United States that horrible lynchings and brutal race riots frequently occur in our midst. The social ostracism of the Jews is less barbaric, but . . . causes cruel injustice. . . . I long to have our family stand firmly for what is *best* and *highest* in life."[19] Though Junior subscribed to many of Abby's views, he was guided more by abstract codes of conduct than visceral sympathy with the oppressed.

Abby made sure that her children did not flaunt their wealth, and she turned down one son who wanted extra travel money in college by telling him, "The boys who cannot afford to go away will feel restless and envious."[20] Constantly vigilant against the disfiguring effects of wealth, she lectured Laurance when he was only thirteen on the perils of having too much money: "It makes life too easy; people become self-indulgent and selfish and cruel."[21] Abby once told Nelson, "I am sure that too much money makes people stupid, dull, unseeing and uninteresting. Be careful."[22] During World War I, Abby directed five hundred workers of the Red Cross auxiliary that operated out of 4 West Fifty-fourth Street, which Senior had obligingly vacated to aid the war effort. She stationed her white-uniformed children in the basement to roll bandages and had them tend victory gardens at Pocantico.

In running their various households, Abby often chafed at Junior's niggardly style but submitted for the sake of marital harmony. She waited until the January white sales to buy new linen, and when the children went off to school, she had to telephone them clandestinely from the bathroom, since her husband considered these calls superfluous luxuries. One son observed pointedly, "His calls were business and therefore justifiable, hers were personal, and possibly frivolous."[23]

If John junior and Abby had a marriage of passionate intensity, it was because his buttoned-down life required one great release. He beamed in her presence, could not take his eyes off her. "I never knew a man more completely attached to the woman he married," said Tom Pyle, the game warden at Pocantico. "When they were grandparents, in the latter quarter of their lives, he still treated her with the adoration and devotion of a young lover."[24] Many people found something unhealthy about his constant need for her, which one daughter-in-law later said "seemed almost primitive and uncontrollable."[25] Even when traveling, Junior hovered over her with a proprietary air, refusing to share her company with others. Once when they were away, Abby wrote to a son, "Your father is afraid that I shall become intimate with too many people and will want to talk to them, so generally we eat in what I call the old people's dining room where he feels I am safer."[26]

Even at home, Junior tried to monopolize Abby, and he cast a jealous eye on his six children as potential competitors for her time. Always warm and natural with the children, Abby did not abandon their upbringing to servants and governesses. She played cards with them, read to them, took afternoon tea with them, and tucked them into bed at night. A convivial lady married to a professional homebody, she followed the example of countless other women in her position and tried to shape her sons into model husbands, devoid of the faults of her own husband. Junior, perhaps subconsciously, saw her attention to the children as time stolen from him, and this could make him seem to be a grouchy, schoolmasterish father. "We grew up realizing that we had to compete with Father for her time and attention," his son David said. "He expected her to be available when he needed her and his needs seemed insatiable."[27]

Whatever its drawbacks, it was generally a happy marriage. While they would have bruising quarrels over modern art, they were devoted to each other and shared many pleasures, including theater, concerts, and film as well as walking, riding, and driving. After evenings out, they loved to return home and sip hot chocolate in the intimacy of Junior's dressing room. During these cozy moments before bed, they practiced the latest dance steps learned from their Arthur Murray teachers, read aloud from a Victorian novel, or sat back and listened to music on the Victrola. Whatever her frustrations with her husband, Abby thought him a man of sterling probity whom she respected as well as loved. As she once wrote, "I feel sorry for all the women in the world who haven't as good husbands as I have."[28] And for Junior, Abby added many brilliant colors to the palette of what might otherwise have been a monochromatic life.

—

For the six Rockefeller children, their grandfather was a boon companion whom they remembered in various guises: as a wit, a clown, an ace raconteur, a frisky codger on the golf course, a cracker-barrel philosopher. Already in his eighties when some of them entered their teens, he seemed a spry fellow who joined readily in their games, whether playing hide-and-seek in the shrubbery or bounding across the room in blindman's buff. He was probably no less colorful a specimen for his descendants than Devil Bill had been to his grandchildren. Like his siblings, John III remembered grandfather's playfulness: "A very wonderful person with a sense of humor; he loved to tell jokes, starting out with something serious. He was warm, friendly, and accessible, and he never preached."[29]

Junior taught his children to venerate their grandfather, and as they grew up they were slightly astounded to discover that this jolly old eccentric had pulled off one of the biggest feats in business history. From an early age, they were aware that unusual controversy attached to the family name, since reporters and photographers were constantly caught vaulting the Pocantico fences. On May Day 1919, during a reign of anarchist terror, Rockefeller, J. P. Morgan, Jr., and other prominent Americans were sent letter bombs that were intercepted by the post office, yet no special guards were posted at Kykuit. "We always had to live with the fear that something would happen to the children," Junior said, and he adopted a policy of never permitting them to have their pictures taken by strangers, lest it give ideas to terrorists or criminals.[30] He kept them out of the papers so assiduously that they remained faceless to the general public until they entered college. Sometimes, after receiving menacing calls, the children were shadowed by guards.

On Sundays, the six grandchildren often strode from Abeyton Lodge over to Kykuit to dine with grandfather, the five boys wearing mandatory uniforms of stiff Eton collars, dark coats, and pin-striped pants. Like a pastor receiving his flock, Rockefeller greeted each grandson as "Brother." Seated at the head of the table, he spouted tales from his past and mimicked people, gesturing with a spotless white napkin. The grandchildren whooped at his deadpan humor. The contrast between the lighthearted Senior, who seemed so relaxed, and his intense, edgy son probably did not help Junior with his children.

Yet Rockefeller's insouciance also masked deeper concerns. Breakfasting with his grandchildren, he dispensed a nickel and a kiss to each, accompanied by a little pep talk. "Do you know," he would ask, "what would hurt grandfather a great deal? To know that any of you boys should become wasteful, extravagant, careless with his money. . . . Be careful, boys, and then you'll always be able to help unfortunate people. That is your duty, and you must never forget it."[31] The grandchildren credited their conceptions of philanthropic stewardship as much to their grandfather as to their father.

Despite his rigidity, Senior had derived real pleasure from being a father, while Junior took it all too seriously. A number of factors made Junior an inflexible parent. The controversies around his father had molded him into a man of granite respectability who found it hard to lighten up with his own family. He was overly tense and disapproving when faced with unruly impulses in his offspring. Since they were to spend their lives in the public spotlight, he wanted his children to mirror his own starchy sense of rectitude. This mattered to him so desperately that he ruled his family with a quiet tyranny, inspiring more fear than affection. Sometimes, he lashed out unexpectedly, showing flashes of anger or ridicule that he screened from the world. He tried to imitate his father's style as a parent, but he could not do it with John D.'s good humor. "I was always so afraid that money would spoil my children and I wanted them to know its value and not waste it or throw it away on things that weren't worthwhile," Junior said. "That was why I insisted that my children keep accounts just the way I did and I think the effect has been good."[32]

On Saturday mornings, stomachs aflutter, the children filed one by one into Junior's study and had their account books scrutinized. Although they received only a thirty-cent allowance—much less than their friends—they had to account for every penny. They were fined a nickel for omissions and awarded a nickel for scrupulous record keeping. They were expected to spend a third of their money, save a third, and donate a third to charity. Bound by these rules, the Rockefeller children acted like destitute waifs and constantly scrounged small change from friends. As Nelson lamented, "I can honestly say that none of us has ever had a feeling of actually being rich—that is, of having a lot of money."[33] Like Junior as a boy, they often dressed in old clothes and were denied ordinary trips to theaters or the movies until they were well into their teens.

In a repetition of his own upbringing, Junior gave the children opportunities to earn pocket change at Pocantico or Seal Harbor. They made money by killing flies (ten cents per hundred), buffing shoes, working in the garden, or trapping attic mice (five cents per mouse). The six children were taught to garden, sew, and cook—once a week, they had to prepare dinner together—and were encouraged to master hand tools. Each studied a different musical instrument, with one evening per week given over to hymn singing. Even family vacations became tutorials in personal responsibility, with one son assigned to buy railroad tickets, another to run errands, a third to handle the luggage, a fourth to book hotel rooms, a fifth to shine the shoes, and so on.

Junior naively imagined that he had a fine, open relationship with his children, but they saw him as a forbidding figure, and Abby had to defuse tensions festering below the surface. She ended up serving as interpreter for them, saving the day with straight talk, common sense, and wisecracking humor. She also helped the children to please Junior in practical ways. When he wished them to memorize biblical verse, she printed out extracts on flash cards for them, and she also tidied up their account books before the weekly paternal audit.

Junior wanted to saturate the children with sermons and religious tracts. Each morning at seven forty-five, even with guests present, the butler circulated a stack of Bibles on a silver tray. Junior read a portion of scripture and asked others to read aloud before they touched breakfast. Trying to keep alive the Sabbath tradition, he led his children, single file, on Sunday nature walks around Pocantico, lecturing them on trees and wildflowers and meting out fines for those who fell out of line. One Sunday in the 1920s, he deliberated long and hard about whether to allow his children to play tennis on the Sabbath. He consented only under pressure from Abby. The children were baptized, but they never turned into such regular churchgoers as their parents or grandparents, and the Baptist Church never formed the focal point of their lives.

Past, Present, Future

Blessed with his father's longevity, Rockefeller outlasted all his siblings. Though Frank was vice president of two Cleveland steel companies in his later years, he never got over his antipathy to John and raged against him till his dying day. In 1916, John gave a thousand dollars apiece to Frank's three daughters and contemplated forming trust funds to provide each of them with a lifetime income. Nevertheless, even on his deathbed, following a stroke in early 1917, Frank still ranted against his oldest brother. "I was with him constantly and was there when he died," said one of Frank's friends. "You can understand the depth of his feeling when I say that his greatest fear during those last days was that John might try to come and see him."[1] After Frank died in April 1917, John and William attended the Cleveland funeral at Lake View Cemetery, where Frank was lowered into the plot he had chosen apart from the rest of the Rockefellers. Frank's wife, Helen, and his three daughters had no plans to perpetuate his crazy vendetta and after the funeral cordially received John, who canceled his dead brother's outstanding loans.

In his last twenty years, Rockefeller felt the subterranean pull of tender boyhood memories. In June 1919, right before his eightieth birthday, he and William loaded up three Crane-Simplex touring cars and set out for the verdant Finger Lakes region of their boyhood. They returned to Richford, Moravia, and Owego and so cherished the memories that they reenacted the trip every year until William's death in 1922. The Moravia house, with its splendid view of Owasco Lake, now lodged convicts from the Auburn prison who were working, by a bizarre coincidence, on the nearby Rockefeller Highway. On Rockefeller's last visit, gazing at the old frame house, he doffed his cap, bowed his head, and declaimed with an actor's panache, "Farewell old home!"[2] Several days later came news reports that the house had burned to the ground, probably from a faulty chimney. Affected by the news, Rockefeller jotted down in a short-lived diary that he kept, "That was the scene of our first business venture, when we engaged in the raising of a flock of turkeys."[3] He had traveled so unimaginably far beyond his rustic boyhood world that his life seemed unreal to him at times.

In June 1922, following one of these upstate jaunts, William Rockefeller consulted doctors about his problems with a raspy throat and was diagnosed as having throat cancer. In this weakened state, he decided to canter briskly through Central Park one day, contracted pneumonia, and died shortly afterward. In a letter to Henry Clay Folger, Rockefeller eulogized his brother as a "strong, resourceful, kindly man."[4] Though always overshadowed by John, William left a sizable fortune of about $200 million ($1.8 billion today), eclipsing the estates of Payne Whitney and Thomas Fortune Ryan. Yet aside from a million-dollar gift for war relief, William had shown no charitable impulses, even though John had pleaded with him to endow educational or medical projects. Virtually all of William's estate went to his four children: Emma Rockefeller McAlpin, William Goodsell Rockefeller, Percy Avery Rockefeller, and Ethel Geraldine Rockefeller Dodge.

By 1922, Rockefeller had lost his parents, his four brothers and sisters, his wife, his eldest daughter, two grandchildren, and the vast majority of his old business partners. As he wistfully told Henry Clay Folger, "The ranks of the older associates are thinning out and we of the Old Guard naturally draw closer together."[5] He understandably dwelled on his own mortality. In July 1919, on his eightieth birthday, Junior wanted to give him a Rolls-Royce, but he asked how much it would cost and took the $14,000 check instead. As part of the festivities, Rockefeller told the press that he devoutly wished to live to one hundred and credited his good health to golf and a daily tablespoon of olive oil. The white-haired Dr. Biggar repeated his long-standing prophecy: "Mr. Rockefeller will live to be 100 years old."[6] Rockefeller and Dr. Biggar shook hands on a pact that they would play a round of golf on July 8, 1939. Dr. Biggar, alas, canceled the appointment: He expired in the 1920s while his celebrated patient, touting the Biggar gospel of fresh air and five daily periods of rest, soldiered on. Because of Rockefeller's abstemious eating style, along with a substantial loss of bone mass, his weight dipped below one hundred pounds. Once tall and rangy, he was now a wizened little man, no taller than his son.

Despite his rather eerie, cadaverous look, Rockefeller still gazed shrewdly at the world, his eyes alert as he sized up newcomers. He tried to banish gloomy thoughts and admit only joy and pious gratitude for God's bounty. Though somewhat lonely and susceptible to occasional bouts of depression, he would rally and emerge more ebullient than before. Typically surrounded by six or

Four generations of Rockefellers in 1928.
From left to right: John D. Rockefeller, Sr., John D. Rockefeller, Jr.,
Abby (Babs) Rockefeller Milton, and Abby Milton.
(Courtesy of the Rockefeller Archive Center)

eight people at golf or meals, he cultivated the company of younger people, especially younger women. On his eighty-sixth birthday, he wrote the following sugary verse:

> *I was early taught to work as well as play,*
> *My life has been one long, happy holiday;*
> *Full of work and full of play—*
> *I dropped the worry on the way—*
> *And God was good to me every day.*[7]

Throughout his life, the mutable Rockefeller had continually re-created himself while adhering to certain core principles. As H. G. Wells wrote, "Manifestly he has grown and broadened at every stage of his career."[8] Perhaps the most startling transformation came in his behavior toward women as he sloughed off the old Victorian inhibitions. Free from Cettie's restraining influence, Rockefeller became positively ribald. When an old colleague, William T. Sheppard, introduced him to a Mrs. Lester one day, Rockefeller said suggestively, "Mr. Sheppard, your friend, Mrs. Lester, is very easy to look at." Junior stood there aghast. "I beg your pardon," he apologized to Mrs. Lester, "but my father has picked up some slang phrases without understanding their meaning." Evidently no prude, Mrs. Lester shot back, "Oh, Mr. Rockefeller, you do not need to apologize for *your father.*"[9]

It was a rare golf party that did not include a lady golfer for Rockefeller's delectation, and when he got off a good shot he erupted into a little mock Charleston, telling the lady, "You ought to kiss my hand for that."[10] When crowds clustered about him in public, Rockefeller conspicuously waved at the pretty young women. "He was like a little boy in his playtime," noted one photographer.[11] Rockefeller, for the first time, had an identifiable lady friend: Mrs. Ira Warner of Bridgeport, Connecticut, the stout wife, then widow, of an optical-instruments manufacturer and a constant visitor at both Kykuit and Ormond Beach.

Rockefeller increasingly used the afternoon drives as opportunities for hanky-panky. Wearing thick black or amber goggles to screen out the sun, he sometimes borrowed a veil from one of the lady passengers and laced it dramatically across his face and wound it around his ears. He sat tightly wedged in the backseat between two buxom women, usually neighbors or visitors, with their laps covered by a blanket, and he became notorious for his hot schoolboy hands roving under the blanket. The man who had been a model of self-mastery now seemed, on occasion, an itchy-fingered old satyr. Tom Pyle, the head gardener and gamekeeper at Pocantico, steered the second car in the daily motorcade and was often astonished at his employer's outrageous behavior. When Rockefeller's car stopped one afternoon at a traffic light, a young woman riding in the backseat with him suddenly burst forth and scrambled back to Pyle's car. "That old rooster!" she said. "He ought to be handcuffed." Pyle noted that some local matrons enjoyed the hot seat and frequently returned for more. "I never decided whether different women received different treatment or whether some found it acceptable to be pinched by a ninety-year-old multimillionaire."[12]

As if he were living his life backward, Rockefeller belatedly entered adolescence in his ninth and tenth decades. It was as if, after all his preternatural exertions, he had attained the one thing denied him: a carefree childhood. Growing younger in spirit, he became something of a clotheshorse with an extensive wardrobe of dandyish costumes. He now owned sixty stylish suits and several hundred ties and sometimes changed outfits three times a day. To Junior's astonishment, he squired ladies to concerts and dances at the Ormond Beach Hotel. "What a gay person you are becoming: An opera one night and the Governor's ball another," he wrote his father. "I do hope things will quiet down before Abby and I arrive."[13] Around this time, Rockefeller also developed a strange fondness for antic behavior. One evening, when the dinner talk turned to corns, Rockefeller said, "I never had one and to prove it I will show you my foot"—then he peeled off his shoe and stocking and placed a bare foot on the table.[14]

As he and his guests drove through the Florida countryside one afternoon, they nearly ran out of gas but found a rural filling station nearby. When a husky country woman appeared, the chauffeur asked for five gallons—which struck her as too small for this mammoth vehicle. Where were they going? she asked. Leaning forward in the backseat, Rockefeller piped up, "My dear woman, we are on our way to heaven. And we'll get there sooner or later." She peered at him dubiously. "Yer may be on yer way to heaven, whoever you are," she told Rockefeller, "but I warn yer you'll never get there on five gallons o' gas!"[15] It became one of Rockefeller's favorite tales. Often, if there were empty seats in the car, he picked up hitchhikers or pedestrians to keep the stream of conversation flowing.

Each year, Rockefeller threw an annual Christmas party at Ormond Beach for his neighbors. The Casements was illuminated with a radiant star of Bethlehem over the door and glowing candles twinkled in each window. Rockefeller appeared in a tuxedo, bowed, pronounced seasonal greetings, and distributed gifts. He then led the group in Christmas carols and tooted party horns along with the children. Rockefeller increasingly warmed to strangers. One day, George N. Rigby, the local newspaper editor, wrote an article titled "Ormond the Different," a panegyric to the town's friendliness. When Rockefeller went to congratulate him, they chatted outside the newspaper office, beside a railway siding. As people on the train recognized Rockefeller, they pressed their faces to the windows and started taking pictures. Far from minding this attention,

Rockefeller seemed to bask in it. Back in the car, Mrs. Evans reproachfully asked whether he had not made a spectacle of himself. "Of course," he said. "But I wanted to prove that the article Mr. Rigby wrote, 'Ormond the Different,' was true."[16]

After a life spent fleeing the press, Rockefeller proved an instinctive master of the new cinematic medium. Curt Engelbrecht, a photographer for the Hearst newsreel company, Movietone News, pursued Rockefeller until he agreed to pose for the cameras. On his ninetieth birthday in 1929, Rockefeller donned a foppish light-gray cutaway suit, white vest, and boutonniere and spent two hours slicing an oversize cake and ad-libbing before the cameras. As Engelbrecht recalled, "He had a lot of fun playing the star of the production, and he was not ready to stop until the last foot of film had been used."[17] In movie theaters across America, audiences saw John D. Rockefeller on the screen, walloping golf balls with a fierce but clumsy stroke and leading cronies in a rousing medley of hymns. People suddenly found something endearing about this anachronistic old gentleman who had graduated to the status of an American legend.

Why the sudden change in Rockefeller's image? The titan was always a touchstone for American attitudes toward money, and the nation worshiped it in the 1920s. The passage of time had also spread a mellow glow over his depredations, which seemed to belong to an earlier, half-forgotten era. He also represented an increasingly honored American type: the practical, thrifty, laconic men who had established the country's industrial base. Now succeeded by salaried managers and corporate bureaucrats, these first-generation industrialists retrospectively took on a new heroic sheen. Perhaps the most obvious reason for Rockefeller's enhanced stature was that the public now associated him far more with philanthropy than with Standard Oil. The press, once hostile to him, formed his biggest cheering section. "It is doubtful whether any private individual has ever spent a great fortune more wisely than Mr. Rockefeller," Pulitzer's *World* editorialized in 1923, while the Hearst press, not to be outdone, stated, "The Rockefellers have given away more money and to better advantage than anybody else in the world's history since the ark stranded on Ararat."[18]

═

Even as Rockefeller became sporty and dapper in the Roaring Twenties, keeping up with the times, his son clung to dark business suits and starched white shirts. Now in his fifties, graying and bespectacled, Junior began to look like a museum piece. In 1923, as if taking refuge in a more comforting past, Junior had his office at 26 Broadway renovated by Charles of London, who installed oak paneling from an English Tudor mansion, bookcases with leaded glass panes, an Elizabethan conference table, and a Jacobean refectory table. While the Standard Oil companies raked in money from the auto boom, Junior preferred horse-drawn carriages and balked at setting foot inside an airplane.

Nothing made both father and son seem so old hat or controversial in certain quarters as their emphatic support of Prohibition. Not only had they never tasted liquor in their lives, but they had steadily supported the Anti-Saloon League and given it $350,000 since its founding in 1895. Before enactment of the Eighteenth Amendment in 1920, Rockefeller had doubted that prohibition would work. "It is a vile agent of destruction," he said of drink, "yet men will go on making it and selling it. It is the right hand of the devil."[19] Yet whatever their private skepticism, the Rockefellers were strongly associated with temperance. To connoisseurs of bathtub gin, Junior seemed a rich, stuffy prig who denied the worker a glass of beer. "One glass of beer may lead to another," he declared. "Therefore, I say one glass is one glass too many."[20] By 1926, Junior had sufficient doubts about the course of Prohibition that he withdrew his support from the Anti-Saloon League, but it was several years before he entirely retracted it.

Saddled with the burden of managing half a billion dollars, Junior had little time left over for diversion. An unexceptional man thrust into exceptional circumstances, he accepted his fate with reluctance. As Frederick Gates said, "He would have preferred . . . to cut loose from his father's fortune and make for himself like other men a wholly independent career. But he was an only son, the heir of colossal wealth, dedicated from his birth to overwhelming burdens, not to be evaded."[21] The constant pressure of the Rockefeller philanthropies was a responsibility from which he could never escape, and he continued to be plagued by stress symptoms, including migraine headaches, stomach ailments, and sinus infections. Very often, he came home from work with dreadful headaches and had to lie down in his bedroom for an hour, his brow covered by a soothing compress. As his father had feared, the weight of the Rockefeller fortune often seemed to overwhelm him.

In late 1922, tormented by headaches, nervous exhaustion, and even temporary deafness, Junior checked into the Battle Creek Sanitarium of Dr. John H. Kellogg, an eccentric visionary who prescribed a vegetarian diet and spartan regimen for patients. Junior heard the inevitable: He worked too hard, suffered from strain, and should set aside more time for recreation. Upon leaving the sanitarium, he was still too weak to return to work and contracted a severe flu; to recuperate fully, he went down to Ormond Beach and spent several months with his father. For the next twelve years, unable to release the nervous tension inside him, Junior seldom went for more than two days without an excruciating headache.

The demands of spending his father's fortune were never-ending. During the 1920s, Junior's annual income fluctuated between $35 million and $57 million. Since he diverted 30 to 40 percent for charitable purposes, he was dispensing, on average, $11.5 million per year—or more than the Rockefeller Foundation's annual grants.[22] Junior had to grapple with the increasingly unwieldy structure of the overlapping Rockefeller philanthropies. This fragmentation had partly come about in order to head off the political criticism that would have greeted a single, all-encompassing foundation. In a sweeping and long-overdue reorganization in 1929, Junior supervised the absorption of the Laura Spelman Rockefeller Memorial and the science and humanities programs of the General Education Board into the Rockefeller Foundation.

Just when he needed advisers most, Junior was abruptly deprived of them. By 1923, Frederick T. Gates was taking insulin treatment for diabetes at the Rockefeller Institute and had to resign from the foundation; he died of pneumonia in Phoenix in February 1929 after acute appendicitis. He had given the Rockefeller philanthropies much of their fervent vision as well as their tenacious attention to detail. After Starr Murphy died in 1921, Junior needed a new general counsel and three years later drafted his old fraternity brother Thomas M. Debevoise, a man of such daunting formality that Junior's sons christened him "the Prime Minister." But Junior still needed a strategic thinker of the stature of Gates or of Mackenzie King, whom he still saw periodically but who was now too busy for frequent consultations. Junior found his ideal theoretician in Raymond B. Fosdick, who served as his trusted friend, lawyer, adviser, and finally biographer. The two had met in May 1913 when Junior was forming the Bureau of Social Hygiene and Fosdick was a crusading mayoral aide who had worked with Lillian Wald at the Henry Street Settlement. After World War I, Fosdick sailed to France with Woodrow Wilson and served as a civilian aide to General Pershing before being appointed Under Secretary General of the League of Nations by Wilson. After the Senate vetoed U.S. participation, an embittered Fosdick resigned and lobbied for the global body, advocating a "planetary consciousness" and "collective intelligence."[23]

As a good Republican, Junior had initially refrained from endorsing the League, but under Fosdick's tutelage, he shed his isolationism and gave two million dollars for its new library and liberally endowed its health organization. To foster international harmony, he undertook projects ranging from support for the new Council on Foreign Relations, which was founded in 1921, to creating International Houses at four universities. (Each Christmas, he and Abby hosted a reception for one hundred students from the International House at Columbia University.) Junior's largest single donation of the decade was a twenty-eight-million-dollar gift to create an International Education Board that would grant fellowships in the natural sciences and transpose the work of the GEB to a global plane.

During a trip to France in June 1923, Junior and Abby were startled by the deteriorating state of the Versailles palace: Iron fences rusted, water dripped from the ceiling, statues were crumbling in the garden. Junior offered the

French prime minister, Raymond Poincaré, a million dollars to refurbish the Versailles roof and gardens; make emergency repairs at Fontainebleau; and restore the splendid Reims cathedral, scarred by wartime bombing—an offer the French could not very well refuse. Though shocked by his preference for Perrier over champagne, the French adored Junior's self-effacing manner, so at odds with their cartoon image of the humptious American millionaire. When he drove to Versailles from Paris late one afternoon, the guards at the visitors' entrance told him that the palace was closed. Refusing special treatment, he got back in his car and returned to Paris—a modest act that won him plaudits across France and helped to offset some controversy over his purchase of the famous Unicorn tapestries. Junior spent millions more in France and contributed to a new building for the American Church overlooking the Seine. Suddenly an omnipresent philanthropist, he restored the library of the Imperial University of Tokyo after the 1924 earthquake; paid for the excavation of the Agora, the ancient Athenian marketplace; set up an oriental institute at the University of Chicago; and financed the Palestine Museum in Jerusalem to conserve biblical artifacts.

=

After his mother's death in 1915, Junior also widened his sights in the religious arena and adopted a more experimental, open-minded approach. As early as the tainted-money controversy, the Rockefellers had tried to shed their exclusively Baptist orientation. After seven religious-service organizations pooled their resources to aid American troops during World War I, the atmosphere seemed auspicious for interdenominational work. Senior believed that denominations had value but should all report, on the Standard Oil model, to one centralized governing body, whereas Junior believed that churches could operate more efficiently if they were not broken up into denominations. He sponsored studies that showed surplus churches in rural communities and proposed consolidation to trim excess capacity. Starting in 1920, he spearheaded the Interchurch World Movement, which encouraged unity among the various Christian denominations. Like an electioneering politician, he went on an exhausting fund-raising tour of twelve cities. This ecumenical effort turned into a fiasco when he raised only three million dollars—one-third of that coming from the Rockefellers; most of the denominations cynically exploited the movement to siphon off money for their own sectarian purposes.

In December 1917, Junior delivered a speech at the Baptist Social Union that struck orthodox folk as rank heresy. Sketching out a new, unified church, he said, "It would pronounce ordinance, ritual, creed, all non-essential for admission into the Kingdom of God or His Church. A life, not a creed, would be its test; what a man does, not what he professes; what he is, not what he has."[24] Adopting a position that would have sounded blasphemous to his mother—

and that he would never have voiced while she was alive—Junior now believed that people who manifested Jesus' moral spirit were religious, whether or not they practiced Christian rituals.

In the early 1920s, the Baptist Church was rent by vitriolic clashes between southern fundamentalists and northern liberals over the proper interpretation of the Bible, a heated debate that culminated in the 1925 Scopes monkey trial. Throwing off his diffidence, Junior inveighed against the "narrow and medieval creed" of the fundamentalists, whom he accused of breeding enmity and division. This was sharper, more self-confident criticism than Junior had ever expressed and by the mid-1920s he openly doubted the literal interpretation of the Bible, regarding it as incompatible with modern science. By this point, even Senior was coming around to figurative interpretation. For fundamentalists, such heretical views diluted religion to a watery form of social work, and in 1926, in a mounting reaction, the Southern Baptist Convention reaffirmed the Genesis account of creation and unequivocally rejected the theory of evolution.

Junior was backed up in his views by a new influence: Harry Emerson Fosdick, the older brother of Raymond B. Fosdick. In 1924, when Cornelius Woelfkin retired as pastor of the Fifth Avenue Baptist Church (which had moved to Park Avenue two years earlier), Junior saw an opening for a charismatic leader who would courageously lead the congregation toward interdenominationalism. As a young pastor, Fosdick had championed the Social Gospel and preached to the dispossessed in lower Manhattan slums and Appalachian shantytowns. Even something of a muckraker in his early days, he had admired the work of Lincoln Steffens, Ray Stannard Baker, and other colleagues of Ida Tarbell. In 1922, he delivered a controversial sermon, "Shall the Fundamentalists Win?" that was such a strong, unadulterated statement of modernist beliefs that he was nearly tried for heresy by the Presbyterian Synod. Sometimes tagged a socialist and once branded "the Jesse James of the theological world," Fosdick denied the virgin birth, the inerrant Bible, and the conventional version of the Second Coming.[25]

In 1925, Fosdick, who was actually a Baptist, left the First Presbyterian Church because of his iconoclastic views. Junior wooed him at the height of this controversy. It was very rare for Junior to court trouble, and Fosdick was thunderstruck by his invitation to him to head the Park Avenue Baptist Church. During their meeting, the left-leaning Fosdick confessed to misgivings about becoming the pastor of such a swank church. To entice him, Junior floated the idea of creating a new church to serve a more heterogeneous community. Still, Fosdick demurred. When Junior pressed him for a reason, Fosdick blurted out, "Because you are too wealthy, and I do not want to be known as the pastor of the richest man in the country." Embarrassed silence ensued. Then Junior replied, "I like your frankness, but do you think that more people will criticize you on account of my wealth, than will criticize me on account of your theology?"[26] Both men laughed, and a close relationship was started.

Even before the ground breaking for a new church began, Fosdick threw open the Park Avenue Baptist Church to new members, including those not baptized by immersion. A year after his arrival, Junior initiated a project that had long tantalized him: building a great interdenominational church in New York City. With Junior himself chairing the building committee and donating ten million dollars to the project, a site was selected in Morningside Heights for what would become the Riverside Church. The Gothic building, designed by Charles Collens and Henry C. Pelton, was inspired by the cathedrals of Chartres and Laon.

Formally dedicated in 1931, the church was an ecumenical shrine that seemed to bridge both the spiritual and temporal worlds. Instead of saintly statues lining the chancel screen, one found scientists, doctors, educators, social reformers, and political leaders, including Louis Pasteur, Hippocrates, Florence Nightingale, and Abraham Lincoln. Statues of Confucius, Buddha, Mohammed, and Moses stared down from archivolts above the main portal, while Darwin and Einstein occupied honored niches. After a few years, the congregation was both interdenominational and interracial, with fewer than a third of the members coming from Baptist backgrounds. Once exponents of the old-time religion, the Rockefellers had now advanced into the vanguard of liberal Protestantism and were loudly denounced by conservative theologians for desecrating the true church. The Baptist Bible Union said of Riverside Church that it was "obviously part of a plan to extend to the whole Baptist denominational life the influence of the Rockefeller Foundation, which already had succeeded in converting nearly all our educational institutions into hotbeds of modernism."[27] Thirty years after left-wing social reformers had vilified the Rockefellers, the family, under Junior's influence, was now being excoriated from the right. In 1935, John D. Rockefeller, Jr., who had been the principal lay donor to the Northern Baptist Church, made his last annual gift. "What gives me pause," he said in his valedictory letter, "is the tendency inherent in denominations to emphasize the form instead of the substance, the denominational peculiarity instead of the oneness of Christian purpose."[28]

＝

In 1924, John Jr., Abby, and their three oldest boys made a swing through the American West in a private railroad car, stopping to camp along the way. Outside the Northeast, Junior was seldom recognized, and he thrived on the anonymity of the open road. When they arrived at Yellowstone National Park, the family was greeted by park superintendent Horace Albright, who was startled to see the Rockefeller boys pitching in to assist the porter with the luggage. As Albright escorted them around the park, Junior and Abby were chagrined by tree stumps and fallen timber that littered the roadside. Later, in a letter to Albright, Junior offered money to clean up and beautify these thoroughfares. On their second day, Albright drove the Rockefellers to see the craggy, snow-capped Grand Tetons. Struck as with the sudden force of an epiphany, Junior decided to preserve this exquisite view for posterity.

On a subsequent visit to the Grand Tetons in 1926, Junior and Abby recoiled at the creeping blight of hot-dog stands, gas stations, and gaudy billboards that were beginning to clutter the countryside around Jackson Hole. As Albright recorded in his journal, "I believe Mr. Rockefeller had a genuine distaste for the garish advances of civilization—and what's more he feared them. So he took every opportunity he felt possible to step in and save his fellow humans from the onslaught of the crippling effects of industrial society."[29] The son of America's foremost industrialist now worked assiduously to save nature's monuments and preserve the spirit of America's preindustrial past. It was a propitious time to do so: The National Park Service had been created by Congress in 1916 with a large mandate to promote and regulate national parks and monuments but without an adequate budget to accomplish this. The first two directors, Stephen Mather and Albright, cultivated philanthropists as a way to rectify this.

Lacking his father's hostility toward government and imbued with a Wilsonian sense of public service, Junior, under Albright's tutelage, formed a unique partnership with Washington to save wilderness areas. Upon returning home, Junior began to buy thousands of acres in the Jackson Hole Valley with an eye to creating a new park—an idea anathema to many local cattlemen, hunters, and dude-ranch operators who saw this as meddling in their businesses. To minimize political opposition and keep land prices down, Junior made the land purchases through a front group, the Snake River Land Company. Though he accumulated 33,562 acres and yearned to hand them over to the National Park Service, his bountiful gift was consistently spurned due to fierce, short-sighted local opposition. Only in 1943 did President Roosevelt create the Jackson Hole National Monument and accept the Rockefeller land, which was merged into an expanded Grand Teton National Park in 1950. Once infected with preservation fever, Junior gave money to buy vast acreage for the Shenandoah National Park in Virginia and the Great Smoky Mountains National Park in North Carolina and Tennessee, plus a major tract to connect them via the Skyline Drive threaded through the Blue Ridge Mountains.

If Horace Albright was one of Junior's environmental gurus, the other was Henry Fairfield Osborn, president of the American Museum of Natural History. As founder of a group called the Save-the-Redwoods League, Osborn sounded the alarm about the impending destruction of redwood forests in northern California, which were being felled rapidly by lumber companies. When one company started to chop down redwoods on Bull Creek Flat, an especially fine stand, Junior supplied one million dollars to stop the logging and save the virgin woods. He later gave money to save other redwood forests, along with $1.5 million to preserve thousands of pristine acres of sugar pines in Yosemite Valley. Closer to home, he assembled seven hundred acres of land along the New Jersey shore of the Hudson River that he donated to the Palisades Park Commission. What makes these conservation efforts notable is that Junior was putting his own stamp on Rockefeller philanthropy and having a striking national, even global, impact. His conservationist impulse was quite different from the forward-looking, scientific spirit that his father had exhibited in medical research and education.

Junior's veneration of the past and implicit discomfort with the modern era were exemplified by several restoration projects in his later years that again marked a break with his father's legacy. He seemed at times not so much to want to study the past as to inhabit it, taking on its recaptured dignity. His most celebrated exercise in time travel came through the Reverend Dr. William Goodwin, a professor of sacred literature at William and Mary College, who met Junior at a Phi Beta Kappa banquet in 1924. Goodwin tried to pique Junior's interest in his personal obsession: restoring the old colonial capital of Williamsburg, Virginia. A monomaniac on the subject, Goodwin often ambled about the town in a moonlit reverie, communing with eighteenth-century ghosts. Though Junior turned him down, the Episcopal clergyman sensed that he had stumbled upon the one man in America willing and able to implement his fantasy. For the next two years, Junior had to steel himself against Goodwin's maddeningly persistent entreaties.

In the spring of 1926, when Junior decided to speak at the Hampton Institute, Goodwin saw a chance to waylay him to Williamsburg. When John Jr. and Abby arrived, he took them about town, a clinging, heavy-breathing cicerone. At one point Junior asked innocently whether plans existed to preserve the old buildings; at this, the minister must have seen a ray of divine sunlight. As he sheepishly said, "I found it exceedingly hard at the time not to burst forth in the presence of Mr. Rockefeller into unfolding my cherished dream."[30] He soon swamped Junior with artistic renderings of how the restored town might look.

When Junior consented to underwrite the project the following year, he estimated it would cost five million dollars and he faced the familiar dilemma of buying up land without triggering a real-estate boom. With the Rockefeller involvement concealed, Goodwin referred to his patron by the code name "Mr. David." As lawyers, real-estate agents, and property owners flocked to Goodwin's office in suspicious numbers, the rumor mill churned with guesses about the project's rich backer: Henry Ford, George Eastman, J. P. Morgan, Jr., and Otto Kahn were all mentioned. When this speculation grew counterproductive, Goodwin gathered the local citizenry and announced, "It is now my very great privilege and pleasure to announce that the donors of the money to restore Williamsburg are Mr. and Mrs. John D. Rockefeller, Jr., of New York."[31]

As always, the Rockefeller method was to start slowly, test the concept, and then expand. True to this approach, Junior planned to redo one building at a time. He never dreamed he would resurrect the whole town, but the idea of meticulously restoring the past cast a potent spell over his mind, and he became fantastically engrossed in the most minuscule details. As he told his subordinates, "No scholar must ever be able to come to us and say we have made a mistake."[32] At one point, the resident architect reminded Junior that everything wasn't spotless in the eighteenth century. "But Mr. Rockefeller did not like that at all," he recalled. "He wanted everything to be perfect."[33] Junior had a special affinity with this lovingly retrieved world. "I really belong in Williamsburg," he once said. He and Abby bought an elm-shaded manor house, Bassett Hall, where they spent two months each year and where Abby created a first-rate collection of American folk art.[34]

As a form of recreation rich in social value, Colonial Williamsburg captivated Junior and grew into such a passion that he eventually spent fifty-five million dollars on it. "I gave more time, thought, and attention to Williamsburg than I did to any other project I ever undertook—far more than I gave to Rockefeller Center. . . . The more I did the more complete the project became and the greater my interest became."[35] Senior never discussed Colonial Williamsburg with his son and, in solipsistic fashion, tended to edit out of his mind what he himself had not originated, even though Junior's projects were perpetuating his legacy and enormously enhancing the Rockefeller image. Nevertheless, when Junior was later honored by the Virginia legislature, he became choked up and departed from his prepared text to say, "How I wish my father were here! I am only the son."[36] Such self-abnegation had become a habit—never mind that John D. had ignored the project. In 1934, President Roosevelt opened Colonial Williamsburg to the public.

Another project conceived in an analogous spirit was The Cloisters museum, which reflected Junior's long-standing interest in medieval art, with its hierarchy, exacting craftsmanship, and strong spiritual content. His West Fifty-fourth Street home was decorated with gorgeous medieval tapestries, including the Hunt of the Unicorn, and his collection expanded after William Welles Bosworth introduced him to a highly romantic sculptor named George Grey Barnard. Barnard traveled through France and Italy each summer, scooping up Gothic statues and other medieval treasures and bearing his trophies back to New York. The Cluny Museum in Paris gave Barnard the idea for a medieval museum in upper Manhattan which came to be known as The Cloisters (later the Barnard Cloisters). In 1914, this one-man museum opened on Fort Washington Avenue in a small brick building. Barnard created for visitors a full-blown medieval fantasy: Robed figures would lead visitors through a shadowy, churchlike interior perfumed with incense and echoing with medieval chants. By the time Barnard put up his entire collection for sale in the 1920s, Junior had already purchased one hundred Gothic pieces from him, storing most of them in delivery tunnels at Pocantico.[37] The Metropolitan Museum of Art took the entire collection, with money provided by Rockefeller.

As a boy, Junior had frequently taken horseback rides along the Hudson to a high, wooded point that enthralled him. Even then he had vowed that he would someday buy the land and give it to the city. Now such an opportunity presented itself. Having bought the Cornelius Billings estate and other parcels near Barnard's museum, he offered them to the city for a park. Five years later, the city accepted this gift for a new Fort Tryon Park and honored Junior's proviso that four elevated acres be set aside for a new museum, The Cloisters, to house the medieval art collection of the Metropolitan Museum.

As with Colonial Williamsburg, Junior loved the demanding scholarship that went along with the creation of the medieval museum. He paid for a building that ingeniously blended cloisters from five French monasteries as well as many pieces that he had previously bought from Barnard. As he was reviewing plans for The Cloisters one day, he noticed a room marked "Tapestries" and asked James Rorimer, the curator, what he had in mind. "Oh, something like the Unicorn Tapestries," Rorimer said airily. Junior grimaced. But, in an act of supreme sacrifice, he eventually parted with his precious tapestries. By the time the Cloisters opened in 1938, Junior had donated or underwritten the cost of more than 90 percent of the art displayed.

———

The greatest friction between Junior and Abby arose over the subject of modern art, which exposed fundamental differences in their personalities. Junior seemed to be unnerved by the outlaw, bohemian side of modern art, its free experimentation with form and content. While he was stubbornly mired in the past, as if escaping the strife associated with his father's career and the Ludlow Massacre, Abby embraced change and responded to the freedom and spontaneity of the new European art. She was enamored of German Expressionist paintings, with their bold colors, grotesque themes, and nightmarish sensuality. When she began to collect such works, Junior found them raw and harshly unappealing. Banishing the forbidden art to an upper-floor gallery at 10 West Fifty-fourth Street, he often struck a patronizing tone when talking about Abby's picture collection. "These were strange, irresponsible objects that she was bringing into his home," said their son Laurance. "He did not approve of them."[38]

Many things about modern art—including the sometimes garish colors, dreamlike imagery, and violent or distorted forms—disconcerted this inhibited man. "I am interested in beauty and by and large I do not find beauty in modern art," Junior said, preferring the classic beauty of, say, Chinese porcelains. "I find instead a desire for self-expression, as if the artist were saying, 'I'm free, bound by no forms, and art is what flows out of me.' "[39] Junior must have identified the freedom inherent in modern pictures with Abby's emancipation in collecting them, for otherwise it is hard to account for his vehement resistance to her avocation. Frustrated by her husband's hopelessly blinkered vision, Abby found compensation in her sons, especially Nelson, who shared her love of these threatening objects.

For once heedless of her husband's wishes, Abby joined with Lillie P. Bliss and Mary Sullivan in 1929 to found the Museum of Modern Art (MoMA), which provided an outlet for the talents of many wealthy New York women. It was a brave act at a time when most Americans still sneered at such artistic innovation. At first, the museum rented gallery space in the Heckscher Building before moving to a West Fifty-third Street house owned by the Rockefellers. Even as the museum grew in popularity, Junior kept up his deprecating tone. "I showed Papa the pictures and the gallery today," Abby wrote to Nelson, "and he thinks that they are terrible beyond words, so I am somewhat depressed tonight."[40] Filling the breach left by his father, Nelson was named chairman of the museum's Junior Advisory Committee in 1930—he was only twenty-two and still in his last semester at Dartmouth—and ended up as its president.

Notwithstanding his hatred of modern art, Junior became the museum's chief benefactor, donating a total of six million dollars in endowment grants and land. So considerable was the Rockefeller largesse behind MoMA that one historian has written that "since the beginning" it has "been a Rockefeller responsibility, a protectorate, one might almost say."[41] Modern art nevertheless remained contentious at home. Distressed that her budget allowed her to buy just one small Matisse painting and drawing, Abby instructed an intermediary, "Please tell him [Matisse] the only reason I have no more is my inability to acquire them."[42] To remedy this, Abby invited Matisse to dinner in December 1930 and the French master grew impatient that someone of Junior's cultural attainments could be so insensitive to the beauty of Cézanne, van Gogh, Picasso, and Braque. One editor present, Frank Crowninshield of *Vanity Fair,* registered Junior's tactful response, saying that "the philanthropist, who had listened very politely, regretted quite as politely, and in the most polished French, that he must still appear adamant. Then, with an engaging burst of confidence, he added that Mr. Matisse must not altogether despair, because, though he might still seem to be stone, he suspected that Mrs. Rockefeller, thanks to her very special gifts of persuasion, would eventually wear him down to the consistency of jelly."[43] Unfortunately, this charm was strictly for public consumption and Junior kept up his stony obduracy.

Overriding Junior's objections, Abby served as MoMA's first treasurer and gave the museum its first fund for acquiring art. She was a blithe, energetic, ubiquitous figure in the museum's maiden years. All this prodigious work only alienated Junior further, a disapproval so noticeable to the young director, Alfred H. Barr, Jr., that he once told Abby, "Remember me cordially to Mr. Rockefeller (who I find hard to forgive his granite indifference to what interests you so much)."[44] Philip Johnson was no less scornful: "He was a bulldog, a very strong man, one who would say, 'As my wife you can do this and not that.' "[45] Since Abby's involvement with MoMA coincided with the years in which her children graduated from college, married, and started jobs, it grated on Junior that he could not now have his wife all to himself. "We children, who had been his competition, were on our own now—presumably our needs were no longer a threat to him," said David. "But here was the museum, more complex than ever, demanding her energy, and it rankled."[46] Having bequeathed a stunning 181 artworks to MoMA in 1935 alone, Abby attained a new celebrity status and was featured on the January 1936 cover of *Time* magazine, which named her "the outstanding individual patron of living artists in the U.S."[47]

Abby's work gave the family an important presence in art patronage that it had largely lacked to date because of Senior's conspicuous indifference to painting, inherited by his son. However much he inwardly writhed with displeasure, Junior kept the money spigot open. After Lillie Bliss died in 1931, her collection came up for sale—brimming with twenty-four Cézannes, nine Seurats, eight Degases, and so on. She had left it to the museum with the proviso that it have an endowment fund sufficient to ensure its permanence; Junior gave $200,000 and Nelson $100,000. In 1935, to encompass this swelling collection, the trustees voted for a new building to be fashioned by Philip L. Goodwin and Edward Durell Stone in the International Style. For the site, the Rockefellers provided land on both West Fifty-third Street and West Fifty-fourth Street and contributed 60 percent of the building-fund money. The homes of Senior and Junior were razed to make way for the museum and the adjoining Abby Aldrich Rockefeller Sculpture Garden. In early 1938, Junior and Abby moved into a new apartment at 740 Park Avenue. For Junior, it must have been the ultimate affront that his nine-story mansion had been demolished to make way for modern art.

A soaring nocturnal vision of Rockefeller Center.
(Courtesy of the Rockefeller Archive Center)

CHAPTER 34

Heirs

enior's worst forebodings about the fates of his grandchildren seemed to materialize during the 1920s, especially with the McCormicks. He had long doted on his grandson Fowler, who had become a friend, acolyte, and traveling companion of Carl Jung, whom he lauded as a "God figure" in his life.[1] Having weaned Fowler away from conventional mores, Jung might have inadvertently prepared the ground for Fowler's unorthodox marriage. In 1921, the tabloid press feasted on the racy divorce of James Stillman, Jr., and Anne "Fifi" Stillman. Fifi—a striking redhead with a flirtatious manner and volatile temper—was a siren to young men, and Fowler became smitten with her when he roomed with her son Bud at Princeton. Scenting danger, Edith warned her father in 1922, "There is always a pitfall for a rich young man in a much older, designing and fascinating woman."[2] To Rockefeller's horror, Fowler later married Fifi, a divorcee who was eighteen years his senior and had four children. Although he occasionally received the couple (who remained childless), Rockefeller was heartsick over the match and doubtless blamed Edith's self-absorption for her children's troubles.

Beautiful and temperamental, Edith's daughter Muriel had her mother's headstrong nature. When Rockefeller sent her a birthday check in 1922, she mailed it right back, professing outrage that he would express his "loving feeling in such a materialistical manner."[3] Since her parents were leading patrons of the opera, Muriel decided to become a diva and appeared with her mother at a fund-raising luncheon. "Following the luncheon," reported one Chicago paper, "after the coffee had been drunk and the men guests were lighting up

their cigars, Miss McCormick drew a slender ebony cigarette holder and cigarette from her gold mesh bag and joined the smokes."[4] Adopting the stage
name of Nawanna Micor, Muriel studied opera with Ganna Walska, acted
briefly on the New York stage, and even tried her luck in Hollywood before
turning to interior decorating and marrying Elisha D. Hubbard, the son of a
former bank president.

Rockefeller received more warmth from her sister, Mathilde, a bright, winning young woman and the only McCormick child exempted from analysis
with Jung. Fearful that Mathilde would fall prey to some scoundrel in Switzerland, Rockefeller told her: "We want you all to be true Americans and to love
your own country and not to be enamored with the allurements that come especially to our American girls sometimes by the fortune hunters of the world."[5]
Rockefeller had the talents of a sibyl in these matters. In 1922, Mathilde, seventeen, decided to marry her Swiss riding master, a forty-five-year-old widower
named Max Oser. Having paid for Mathilde's expensive riding lessons, Edith felt
betrayed and was sure the treacherous Oser was out to bilk them. As she told
her father, Oser had only taken an interest in Mathilde because she was "the
daughter of wealthy parents and the granddaughter of the wealthiest man in
the world. As we unfortunately all too well know, all of the children are flattered and toadied to by people of none too worthy characters, who hope
thereby to get money from them."[6]

Forgetting her own recent escapades, Edith mounted her high horse and
sounded like a conservative, self-righteous mother, suggesting that Rockefeller
withhold money from his grandchildren to make it "less possible for them to be
taken in by swindlers and by evil minded people."[7] "We have our sorrows,"
Rockefeller replied to Edith. "How thankful I am that dear mother is spared
them."[8] He was sufficiently swayed by Edith's argument that he discontinued
many of the annual gifts he had routinely been making to his grandchildren.

Refusing to accept the match with Oser, Edith attempted to scare the daylights out of Mathilde, telling her that the twenty-six-year age difference between her McCormick grandparents had yielded a terrible legacy of mental
illness among their seven children. "Two died young and two are insane," she
pleaded with her daughter. "Do you not see how unjust it is to bring children
into the world doomed to insanity?"[9] Not relenting after Mathilde's marriage in
1923, Edith refused to see Max Oser or even her own grandchildren for many
years. When the couple visited America in 1929 in an attempt to close this
breach, Edith told Mathilde that she still had no desire to see her grandchildren.
"Children really aren't at all important," she informed her daughter, "they're
just necessary for procreation."[10] Edith grew so spiteful that when Mathilde
and Max planned to visit Senior, Edith telegrammed ahead to her father: "I
would appreciate very much if you did not receive the fortune hunter Mr. Oser
in your home."[11] About to celebrate his ninetieth birthday, Rockefeller was in

no mood to snub a beloved granddaughter, so he graciously received Max, Mathilde, and their children at Lakewood. Rockefeller even slipped into a confidant's role with Mathilde, who poured out her troubles about Edith. After being reviled as a robber baron for so many decades, he enjoyed playing the sage, soft-shoe grandfather.

Rockefeller continued to feel highly protective toward his granddaughter Margaret, who reminded everybody of Bessie as she grew up, making her an object of special concern. She had grown up in a lonely, bookish atmosphere with her father, Charles Strong, who kept Margaret away from America—to Rockefeller's everlasting dismay. Paralyzed from the waist down by a tumor on his spine, Charles was confined to a wheelchair cushioned with a rubber pillow, and this made his life only more cerebral. While staying in his Paris apartment or his villa at Fiesole, Charles and his close friend George Santayana shared a paternal solicitude toward Margaret, who was always encircled by suitors. Her marital plans provided grist for speculation between these two weighty philosophers.

It was Santayana, not Strong, who gave away the bride when Margaret married the fashionable George de Cuevas in a Paris church in 1927; Margaret thought that her father would disapprove and got married while he was out of town. After her solitary, repressed home environment, Margaret was swept up in de Cuevas's warmth, spontaneity, and charm. Almost invariably labeled a Spanish nobleman, de Cuevas was neither Spanish nor noble but the scion of a Chilean banking family that was richer in land than cash, and he was clever in plotting ways to remedy that deficiency.

In January 1929, Margaret gave birth to a baby girl named Elizabeth (followed by a son, John), and later in the year she and George headed off to America "to see the old man Rockefeller, now 90 years old," as Santayana described their plans. "He has already treated Margaret generously—she has $75,000 a year—but gratitude is the hope of favors to come, and no doubt they will do their best in Florida to make a good impression, to be passed on from the old gentleman to John D. Jr. who now holds the purse-strings."[12] Later on, George de Cuevas jested that he had trekked off to the Florida jungles to play golf to provide for his children. He knew the proper line to take with Rockefeller and portrayed Margaret as a poor waif who needed protection. Margaret and George moved to America with their two children in the 1930s, a stay punctuated by return trips to Paris and Florence, and for several years they lived near Rockefeller in Lakewood, much as Charles and Bessie had done three decades earlier. In his will, Rockefeller offered striking proof of his concern for the welfare of Bessie's daughter. Since he had already distributed almost all of his money to his philanthropies and children, he left an estate of only $26.4 million, with $16.6 million of that skimmed off by state and federal taxes. In a decision that took many people by surprise, the chief recipient of the remaining money was Margaret Strong de Cuevas—a tribute both to Margaret and to her now sainted mother.

=

With Junior's six children, Rockefeller suffered much less anguish, for they were brought up under their father's unswerving discipline. In his desire to have a shining, spotless family and cleanse the Rockefeller name, Junior became a hard and often unforgiving parent. Of the children, Babs, the sole daughter, was most often at loggerheads with her parents. She felt that Abby doted on her sons and that Junior singled her out for a disproportionate share of pent-up rage. Junior was poorly equipped to fathom youthful revolt, especially when it came from an emancipated daughter. Tall, lithe, and slender, a true child of the Jazz Age, Babs looked terrific in flapper outfits and cloche hats, enjoyed high-speed chases in her sports car, adored tennis, and patronized Harlem jazz clubs. She also adroitly managed to evade her chaperons, and on the night Uncle William died in 1922 it took time to track her down at a Long Island party. She hated churchgoing and mockingly recalled "the fannies waving" during morning prayer.[13] In keeping her accounts, she settled for a slapdash job and refused to follow tradition and hustle for pocket change. "I can always get a dollar from Grandpa," she boasted to her brothers, knowing her grandfather's weakness for the ladies.[14] At Brearley and Chapin Schools, she showed little initiative and resented her father's caustic comments about her report cards, not to mention his meddlesome calls to school to check up on her progress.

Junior offered his children a $2,500 reward if they did not smoke before age twenty-one, and for Babs he tossed in a car as well, yet she started to sneak cigarettes at fifteen. After inhaling a single cigarette in October 1922, Babs, nineteen, sat down and wrote to her father as if confessing to some monstrous crime: "This is going to be the hardest letter I have ever had to write. . . . I've smoked, thereby losing my car. Mama told me to take it up to Tarrytown tomorrow and put it away." When Babs brazenly continued to smoke, Junior volunteered to double her allowance if she abstained in the future. Even after she set her bed ablaze while smoking in bed, she still was not cured of the habit, and Junior was horrified when she added a taste for bootleg liquor.

Babs saw her father as a tense man who converted everything into a test of morality and his personal authority. Like her brothers, she found redeeming qualities in her grandfather, including good-humored sympathy, that were sorely missing in her father. Twice during the winter of 1923–1924, Babs was dragged into traffic court for speeding, and twice she pleaded guilty. While Junior would not countenance this, Senior dropped her a comforting note, admitting that he was partial to fast cars himself. The clashes with her father scarred Babs. As Laurance's daughter later said of a talk with Babs about her upbringing,

> I cannot convey the tone of bitterness that crept into her speech. . . . She constantly said that [her father] meant well and expressed her admiration for [him], and yet it is clear that she feared and hated him. He never got angry in the sense of raising his voice or losing his temper. When he got angry, he would get very sarcastic as she recalled. She viewed him as a man who was incapable of enjoying himself.[15]

On May 14, 1925, Babs married a young lawyer and childhood friend: the handsome, easygoing David Milton. Twelve hundred people, including Governor Al Smith, attended the wedding at 10 West Fifty-fourth Street, with Ivy Lee hovering in the background, making sure photographers did not snap pictures of Babs in her wedding gown, lest anyone accuse the Rockefellers of ostentation. In the press, the story was predictably served up in hackneyed prose as a fairy-tale union of the "world's richest bride" and a "penniless law clerk."[16] Later, with more truth than diplomacy, Babs pronounced the day after the wedding "her first day of freedom." As a vast, expectant throng craned their necks outside, Babs and David slipped out a back door. When Junior saw the crowd standing outside, he asked if they would like to come in and see where the wedding had taken place. Pretty soon, he and his sons were squiring curiosity seekers, twenty at a time, to tour the flower-filled rooms. Eighteen years later, following in Edith's footsteps, Babs divorced her lawyer husband. She then married Dr. Irving Pardee, a neurologist, and, after he died, Jean Mauzé, a senior vice president of the United States Trust Company. In her later years, she was a substantial contributor to the Memorial Sloan-Kettering Cancer Center and other New York City institutions.

From his first breath, John D. Rockefeller III had grown up in the long shadow of dynastic expectation. When he was born, one New York paper joked that Wall Street brokers were debating whether the event would "buoy the market or merely hold it steady."[17] Tall and lean, with a long, craggy face, John had a tightly wound personality, which he inherited from his father. Shy and introspective, he was severely self-critical. Like his father, he aspired to be a paragon of virtue and, also like his father, paid a terrible emotional price for it. For all their similarities—or perhaps because of them—Junior and his eldest son had a relationship fraught with tension. John III felt overshadowed by his father and dejected by a sense that he could never measure up to his lofty standards. Babs claimed that John III was the most keenly injured by Junior's "primly correcting supervisory stance."[18] John chafed at his father's limitations, noting once in his diary, "F[ather] always has own way. He is . . . broad in business relations, but so narrow in some of his family details."[19] Unlike Babs, John showed no flashes of rebellion and swallowed his anger.

John went through several private schools, including the Roger Ascham School, the Browning School, and the Loomis Institute, but, unlike his younger brothers, he was not allowed to attend the progressive Lincoln School, which had been started in 1917 with a grant from the General Education Board. Embarrassed by his large jaw and convinced that the right side of his face was deformed, he began to manifest in adolescence the same litany of psychosomatic ailments (headaches, stomach pains, and so forth) that afflicted his father. In early 1922, he developed such torturous earaches that he had to spend the winter with his grandfather in Florida, where he enjoyed the old man's waggishness on the golf course. Senior added a bright touch of eccentricity to his dour world. He filled up his diary with dreary self-deprecation: "I have no personal attraction. Nobody wants to sit next to me at the table or anything." "I have no real friends here at school." "Wish I was more popular." "I wish I was different in many ways than I am." "Am much too self-conscious at all times."[20] He had inherited Eliza's puritan conscience without Big Bill's saving levity.

As an adolescent, John saved or donated half his income to charity and had little inkling of the magnitude of the Rockefeller fortune. According to legend, he was steering a decrepit rowboat at Seal Harbor one day when a neighbor's son said, "Why don't you get a motor boat?" Taken aback, John replied, "A motor boat! Gee whiz! Who do you think we are—Vanderbilts!"[21] At Princeton, he was not among the few hundred students who owned a car. One tale, perhaps apocryphal, claims that John was derided when he tried to cash a check at an Italian restaurant on Nassau Street in Princeton; he had accepted checks signed by George Washington and Julius Caesar, the owner explained, but he was not such a dunce as to take one signed by John D. Rockefeller. Although the 1920 appearance of F. Scott Fitzgerald's first novel, *This Side of Paradise,* had certified Princeton's reputation for fast living, John III did not drink, smoke, curse, or study on Sunday. During receptions at his eating club, he would only brush the silver loving cup against his lips when it was passed around in order to avoid contaminating contact with liquor. While his classmates drank themselves into oblivion, John taught English to immigrants at a local settlement house or volunteered at the YMCA. Even at Princeton, he was already serving on the board of the Dunbar National Bank, a black-managed bank in Harlem supported by his father and other businessmen. Probably more popular at Princeton than he realized, John nonetheless portrayed his undergraduate years as a lonely purgatory. Crippled by his conscience, he dwelled morbidly on his own imperfections in his diary. "Am afraid I have an inferiority complex— really know I have. Never feel as if people—both boys and girls—wanted to be with me."[22] "Can't keep smile on my face which is most embarrassing. Muscles tremble. Give anything to be over it."[23] In his final bleak college entry, John recorded, "Guess the reason I am glad to get through college is because I have made rather a mess of it; also haven't really made hardly any friends."[24]

After graduating, John traveled around the world before taking up his duties at 26 Broadway, where he placed himself at his father's disposal. The family office was now an enormous bureaucracy staffed by more than one hundred people, including lawyers, accountants, money managers, and real-estate experts. If Rockefeller had let Junior wander confusedly during his early years at 26 Broadway, Junior handled his son in a much more direct and stifling manner. During John's first day at work on December 2, 1929, Junior held a press conference to introduce his son then proceeded to dominate the discussion. Each time the reporters posed a question for the lanky, fidgety young man, Junior answered for him. Though Junior had soon placed his son on fifteen boards, including the Rockefeller Foundation and the Rockefeller Institute, and given him a small, adjoining office, John seldom saw his father. Obsessive and driven, John III worked around the clock, six days a week, delving into everything from juvenile delinquency to population control. Like his father in his early years, John III was often the token Rockefeller on charity boards, and all the responsibilities took their toll.

This high-strung young man needed a woman who could save him from his nervous system, as Abby had with Junior, and he found an ideal partner in Blanchette Ferry Hooker. The Vassar-educated Blanchette was a beautiful heiress, sweet and charming, who behaved with a dignified but unaffected manner. Her father had founded the Hooker Electrochemical Company while her mother had inherited money from the Ferry retail seed business. John III was such a bashful wooer that to speed things up, Junior gave him the key to a private cottage at Seal Harbor and encouraged him to take Blanchette there. The couple were finally married on November 11, 1932, before 2,500 guests at the Riverside Church.

During their courtship at Seal Harbor, Blanchette learned just how guilt-ridden John was when he handed her a comprehensive list of his faults then asked her to reciprocate. She saw that her future husband was bowed beneath the weight of the family name and fortune, and she helped him to strike out on his own. It was not easy. Like his aunt Edith, John III had suffered from intermittent bouts of agoraphobia in school, a condition that worsened after his marriage. When he and Blanchette went into society, he occasionally submitted to dizzy spells that nearly sent him into a dead swoon. Though the condition eventually subsided, as long as it lasted John and Blanchette seldom ventured out to public functions.

The least-known of the brothers, John was the most conscientious philanthropist. Besides the Rockefeller Foundation, he chaired Lincoln Center and the Population Council and become the most significant force behind the Asia Society. Avoiding limousines and luxury hotels whenever possible and often traveling under the fictitious name John Davison, he refrained from any self-aggrandizement. Oddly, like his father, John could not abide his wife's fondness for modern art and, taking a leaf from Abby, Blanchette firmly defied him and became president of the Museum of Modern Art. Also like his father, John reacted to the controversial Rockefeller legacy by acquiring a conscience that was a punishing taskmaster. His daughter said, "He was someone who suffered from never doing things just for enjoyment."[25]

If John III seemed imprisoned by the abundant family rules, Nelson seemed heedless of the inhibitions that ruled their father's life. Nelson's brash exuberance only sapped John's confidence further. As the latter recorded in his diary, "Nelson dances very well. I am rotten." "Nelson always makes a big hit."[26] While his brothers were rangy, the young Nelson had Junior's short, square frame. Named after Senator Aldrich, he inherited the Aldrich charm and extroversion, and alone of the six children he exhibited a flamboyant craving for publicity, a cheerful egotism in a family that frowned on self-assertion. A naturally commanding figure, Nelson behaved less like a student at the Lincoln School, where he zipped about in a flashy Ford roadster, than a principal. He accosted one startled new teacher with an invitation to call on him if she needed any information because "you're new here and I've been around for quite a while."[27] Not since Big Bill had there been such a fun-loving, narcissistic Rockefeller. Junior often winced at Nelson's cocky antics, while Abby strongly identified with his "frank and outspoken" nature and clearly favored him over the other children.[28]

A popular student at Dartmouth, Nelson made the soccer team and was elected vice president of his junior class. Even then, he was ingratiating himself with people, sharpening his political skills. With his worn corduroy pants and sagging sweaters, he tried to blend into the crowd, but he was a star in sackcloth and converted the Dartmouth president, Ernest Hopkins, into a pal. He did not drink, taught a Sunday-school class, got high enough grades to make Phi Beta Kappa, and humbly rode a bike instead of a car.

After his parents scotched his dream of becoming an architect, Nelson majored in economics. For his honors thesis, he wanted to write an essay that would vindicate his grandfather and Standard Oil and was eager to hear the story from the patriarch's own lips. A wonderful raconteur about so many events, Rockefeller carefully avoided serious discussion of his business history. "I was thinking the other day that Grandfather has never mentioned the Company to us," Nelson wrote to his father, "nor has he ever told us anything about his stupendous work in organizing the Company and leading it for so many years."[29] To remedy this omission, Nelson asked if his father could set up a talk, saying it "would be an outstanding and unforgettable experience in our lives."[30]

While Rockefeller mulled this over, Junior mailed his son the hagiographic Inglis manuscript, which Nelson found engrossing. "It was thrilling!" he told Junior. "For the first time I felt that I really knew Grandfather a little—got a glimpse into the power and grandeur of his life."[31] Nelson did not realize that he was only reading a pretty family fiction; the Rockefeller children were being duped, inadvertently, by family public relations. As for Rockefeller, though flattered by the request, he declined to speak to his grandson, leaving Nelson—like Junior and the other Rockefellers—no better informed about Standard Oil than any well-read stranger. Senior's behavior guaranteed that anxiety over the fortune's legitimacy would spread to his descendants, strengthening their guilty consciences. In his thesis, Nelson, coached by Inglis, flatly denied that Standard Oil ever drove competitors from business unfairly. "These companies were treated with extreme fairness and in many cases with generosity," he wrote, dismissing as mythical that Standard Oil had amassed power "through local price discrimination, bogus independents and espionage."[32]

In 1929, Nelson turned twenty-one on the same day that Rockefeller reached ninety. "The 90 makes my 21 seem mighty small and insignificant," he wrote his parents, "just like a little sapling standing by a mighty fir. But the sapling still has time to grow and develop and someday it might itself turn into a tree of some merit. Who knows?"[33] Nelson leaped at any chance to golf with Rockefeller in Florida and was an attentive audience for his yarns and witticisms. After one 1932 visit, Nelson told Junior that Rockefeller "certainly is an extraordinary man, about the finest I know. There are few people that I really admire as being all-round success, but he leads the list. His point of view and outlook on life are so perfectly grand. And what a sense of humor!"[34]

In the autumn of 1929, in his can-do, take-charge style, Nelson declared that he would marry a childhood friend, Mary Todhunter Clark, known as Tod. Thin and aristocratic in manner, she was a granddaughter of George Roberts, a former president of the Pennsylvania Railroad. Junior was irate that Nelson had not consulted him and consented only after Abby lobbied him. Nelson and Tod went to Ormond Beach to see Rockefeller, who gave his blessing after golfing with this young lady from the Main Line suburbs of Philadelphia. Tod struck observers as witty and intelligent, an excellent mimic and fine sportswoman, if rather cool and self-contained. On June 23, 1930, Nelson married her in Bala Cynwyd, Pennsylvania, while police restrained a thousand spectators outside. At the last minute, Rockefeller could not come and sent $20,000 in securities instead. More and more, he refrained from trips that might threaten his health.

For their honeymoon, Nelson and Tod spent two weeks in Seal Harbor, where they were attended by twenty-four servants. As a wedding gift, Junior treated them to a nine-month around-the-world trip that took on the trappings of a state visit. At each port of call, they were escorted by Standard Oil officials who introduced them to prime ministers and other dignitaries. For Nelson, the meeting with Mahatma Gandhi in India had one severe shortcoming: "He showed no interest in me whatever," he complained.[35]

During the summer of 1931, Nelson started work at 26 Broadway, where he felt crowded out by Junior's phalanx of advisers. In an abortive venture, he launched a company for marketing merchandise and discussed the project at length with Rockefeller in Florida. "Every morning we'd take turns reading Psalms before breakfast, which consisted of floods of orange juice," said Nelson. He made his mark by hustling tenants for Rockefeller Center and ended up as the project's chief panjandrum. During his eventful career, he served as an assistant secretary of state for Latin America under Roosevelt and undersecretary of health, education, and welfare under Eisenhower. When sworn in as governor of New York in 1959, he took the oath of office on the Bible of his great-grandmother Eliza. After thirty years and five children, the marriage to Tod ended in divorce in 1962. When he married Margaretta "Happy" Murphy the following year, many people thought his marital history had irreparably harmed his presidential ambitions, and he had to settle for the vice presidency under Gerald Ford.

When Laurance was born in 1910, the family chose this strange spelling of his name to honor the ailing Cettie. "This we do so as to make it as much like Laura as possible," Junior told his mother.[36] Everybody said the thin, sharp-featured Laurance looked more like Senior than any of the other children did. Bright and laconic, with an incisive wit, he also had his grandfather's enigmatic detachment. However, he lacked the "power to concentrate on difficult and routine tasks," as Junior said when Laurance was at the Lincoln School.[37] The boy took up photography, built a wooden auto powered by a motorcycle engine, and showed a flair for gadgetry. As a philosophy major at Princeton, Laurance shed many of his boyhood religious beliefs in the face of rational scrutiny. While studying at Harvard Law School, he developed pneumonia during his first semester and had to spend the winter with Senior at Ormond Beach. Because he had qualms about the social philosophy of the law and had to struggle to get through his finals, he decided to drop out without taking his degree.

In 1934, Laurance married Mary French in Woodstock, Vermont. A charming Vassar graduate of quiet strength, Mary was the granddaughter of Frederick Billings, a president of the Northern Pacific Railroad. Mary's brother had roomed with Nelson at Dartmouth. Laurance had his grandfather's sound instinct for business opportunities and the same unwavering confidence in his own judgment. When he inherited Rockefeller's New York Stock Exchange seat, he became the youngest member of the exchange. At twenty-eight, with his friend Captain Eddie Rickenbacker, Laurance joined a syndicate to buy Eastern Airlines, eventually becoming its largest shareholder. He also took a sizable stake in the McDonnell Aircraft Corporation, which surged ahead on the strength of aviation contracts during World War II. He was later involved in the Viking rocket and other aerospace projects, and enjoyed flying his own plane. After the family made its first trip to the Grand Tetons in the early 1920s, he became entranced by conservation no less than his father had been. "I was the youngest one there, and therefore the most impressionable," he said. He later created vacation resorts in places of unspoiled scenery, managing them through a company called Rockresorts that eventually owned some of the world's most gorgeous vacation spots.

Winthrop's life nearly started out with an embarrassing blunder. Junior and Abby were about to christen him Winthrop Aldrich Rockefeller (after Abby's brother) when they realized what his initials would spell and scrapped the middle name. He was a chubby, maladroit boy who bore the brunt of Nelson and Laurance's sadistic urges. When he developed kidney trouble, his two older brothers considerately reminded him that another young cousin named Winthrop had died of kidney disease.[38] Abby felt protective toward her vulnerable son and once said of him, "Abuse only makes him angry and much worse, while for love and kind treatment he will do anything."[39]

There was something ineffably sad about Winthrop's youth. Squirming under his father's stern rigor, he longed for escape to a less-taxing world. Easily distracted, he did poorly at Lincoln and Loomis, where he enjoyed playing practical jokes and chasing girls. A big, handsome, hulking boy—at sixteen he was six-foot-one and weighed 185 pounds—he lacked the energy and drive that came so effortlessly to his more dynamic brothers. Winthrop later admitted that as a Yale undergraduate, he had mastered only two subjects: how to smoke and how to drink. At first, he could not keep down more than three drinks without getting sick: "Unfortunately, I later got over that."[40] At Yale, he played cards and—committing one of the cardinal Rockefeller sins—began to neglect his account book. In the middle of his freshman year, Winthrop realized that his prodigality might cost him his allowance, and he negotiated a large rescue loan from Babs.

During the 1933 summer vacation, he toiled as a roustabout in the Texas oil fields for Humble Oil, which was now owned by Jersey Standard, and he felt more at home doing manual work among these rough, simple men than he had among his Yale classmates: "That was what I had been looking for! . . . men working with their hands, producing something real. . . . I was fascinated by everything I saw—I wanted to become part of it, to do what they were doing, to prove to myself that I was as good a man as any of them."[41] If a tonic for his morale, the Texas adventure did not enhance his school performance, and he continued to favor booze and cards. At one point while Winthrop was in Texas, a New Haven publican named Curly Levine made the mistake of sending him a telegram at West Fifty-fourth Street. Junior read the message and secretly contacted Yale president James R. Angell, who informed him that Curly was mixed up with gambling and shady elements. When confronted, Winthrop broke down and confessed to his horrified parents, "Curly is a Jewish bartender in a speakeasy in New Haven where I have gotten liquor while I was at college."[42] In his junior year, Winthrop was expelled from college after being discovered in the shower with a young lady.

After Yale, Winthrop resumed work for Humble Oil in the Texas fields. When he announced the news, Rockefeller, whatever his reservations, expressed pleasure at a family member being back on the Standard Oil payroll. When Winthrop visited Lakewood to tell him about Humble's advanced production methods in Texas, the old man listened patiently, then said, "Well, brother . . . I appreciate that—but I must remind you that the important thing is the figures."[43] In his amiability, Winthrop reminded people of Rockefeller, and perhaps for that reason he was very sensitive to the contradictions of the old man's personality: "There was always an indefinable aloofness, a detachment that I cannot describe. He was warm, human and real—his every act was an act of warmth—and yet this other quality was there."[44] The other brothers did not see this subtle discrepancy between the inner and outer man.

For three years, Winthrop enjoyed the camaraderie of the Texas roustabouts and smoked, drank, and philandered. Winthrop was "big and broad-shouldered, like a friendly young Koala," said one contemporary magazine writer.[45] In this schizoid existence, he worked and ate with other workers during the week and lived on seventy-five cents an hour, then dined on weekends at a country club with the company president. Winthrop welcomed his transient experience of ordinariness in Texas. As he once noted with regret, if your name is Rockefeller, "you can almost feel the prices rise when you walk into a store."[46]

Returning to New York, Winthrop trained at the Chase National Bank, worked for the Socony–Vacuum Oil Company—the former Standard Oil of New York—and served as a vice chairman of the Greater New York Fund. These jobs drew less press attention than his evening prowls through café society. As one reporter remarked, Winthrop "handled all the night life" for the Rockefellers.[47] As his drinking and womanizing crept into gossip columns, Junior scolded him, but Winthrop resented his father's autocratic manner and attempt to perpetuate what seemed an obsolete way of life. After one quarrel, Winthrop said bitterly, "By God, if I ever have children, I'm going to *talk* to them, not just make an appointment to see them and then get up after five minutes to go get a haircut."[48]

In 1948, after dating actress Mary Martin, Winthrop married a voluptuous blonde named Barbara "Bobo" Sears—née Jievute Paulekiute, the daughter of Lithuanian immigrants. Junior and Abby boycotted the Florida wedding, and the marriage scarcely lasted the year. When Winthrop later bought a large spread, Winrock Farm, in Arkansas, Junior found one excuse after another not to visit. Much to the surprise of his family, Winthrop was elected Arkansas governor in 1966, the first Republican to manage that feat in ninety-four years.

Like Winthrop, David was pudgy as a child but was spared the rough attention of his older brothers. Like a miniature banker, he moved with serene self-confidence and punctiliously kept his account books. Smart, docile, and cherubically round-faced, he was adored by Rockefeller, who loved to croon carols with him at The Casements. As Rockefeller told his son after one of David's holiday visits, "He is a worthy son of worthy parents, and his grandfather dotes on him."[49] David reciprocated the affection, calling his grandfather "the least dour man I've ever known, constantly smiling, joking, and telling shaggy dog stories."[50] Senior once told John Yordi that David was the grandchild who most resembled him.

As the youngest son, David was solitary, yet he compensated for this by creating a self-contained world, collecting butterflies, moths, beetles, and grasshoppers. (Eventually, he developed a world-famous trove of forty thousand beetles.) By the time he graduated from the Lincoln School, he was, like Rockefeller, outwardly genial and inwardly reserved. Steady and methodical, he experienced no scandals or crises at Harvard, graduating cum laude in 1936 after having written his senior thesis on Fabian socialism. After a postgraduate year at Harvard and another at the London School of Economics, he completed a doctorate in economics at the University of Chicago. Though his thesis, "Unused Resources and Economic Waste," dealt with issues of corporate concentration that had preoccupied his grandfather, David arrived at free-market conclusions and criticized monopolies as counterproductive. While paying tribute to Standard Oil for imposing order on an anarchic industry, he agreed with the court's 1911 decision to break up the trust. As he later argued, "Some units [of Standard Oil] are now bigger and better than grandfather could ever have imagined even the whole company would be."[51] This preference for neoclassical economics reflected changes both in the Rockefeller family and in the American business community.

Upon leaving Chicago, David worked for eighteen months as an unpaid secretary to Mayor Fiorello La Guardia of New York. He had the wisdom to marry a feisty, red-blooded woman, Margaret "Peggy" McGrath, who complemented his more detached personality. She came from a comfortable but not blue-ribbon family and had little tolerance for grandiosity like Nelson's. With a sometimes fiery temper and activist bent, she donated her time to worthwhile causes, including saving the Maine shoreline, raising cattle, and working on behalf of farmland conservation. David dedicated his career to the Chase Manhattan Bank, rising to the chairman's post and becoming an eminent, peripatetic international banker. As he told an interviewer, he was "the first member of the family since Grandfather who has had a regular job in a company and has devoted a major part of his time to being in business."[52]

CHAPTER 35

See You in Heaven

The world's richest man never lost the thrifty boyhood habits that had made him the nonpareil of American business. One day at Ormond Beach, he was studying the blazing hearth when he turned to Michael, the butler, and asked, "How long are those sticks of wood?" Fourteen inches, Michael replied. "Do you think they would do just as well if they were cut twelve inches in length?" Michael conceded this was possible. "Then the next time the wood is being sawed have it made twelve inches in length."[1] Since twelve inches gave sufficient light and heat at less expense, it became the new household standard. His frugality was deeply rooted. One Christmas, he was delighted when his son gave him two dozen golf balls and some fountain pens—his idea of wonderfully practical gifts.

Rockefeller had now lived so long and grown so famous that a number of promoters sought to cash in on his fame. In 1930, Sarah S. Dennen, secretary of the Coney Island Chamber of Commerce in Brooklyn, New York, tracked down the Richford house in which the titan had been born. Wind now blew through the chinks of this tottering clapboard dwelling. She had a vision of sudden riches: She would dismantle the house and ship it to Coney Island, where an estimated five million annual paying customers would tour this new shrine of American capitalism. Cringing at the thought, Rockefeller took legal steps to stop the commercialization of his name. After Dennen had bought and dismembered the structure, Rockefeller's lawyers marshaled state and local authorities to prevent the house from moving over public highways; the heap of numbered planks made it only as far as Binghamton.

During the Wall Street boom of the 1920s, Rockefeller took a guilty thrill in playing the stock market, despite Junior's reproaches. If his son was present when somebody alluded to his trading, Rockefeller, like a naughty child, would shift the subject. As the market surged, he jovially passed out dollar bills as bull-market dividends to companions. After breakfast, he often announced, "Well, I guess I'll see what I can do to keep the wolf away from the door," then scurried over to his office to get fresh quotes by telephone or telegraph.[2] When the market either swooped or soared, a messenger tracked Rockefeller down on the golf course to deliver a folded sheet with share prices. Aside from cash, railroad securities, U.S. bonds, and Wall Street loans, Rockefeller retained most of his money in Standard Oil companies and could quote the precise number of shares he held in each of his stocks, even when they ran to five digits.

Partial to old habits, Rockefeller continued to trade by buying each time a stock declined an eighth of a point or selling on each eighth-point rise. Having relinquished most of his money to Junior, he often borrowed up to twenty million dollars to execute these transactions and occasionally cadged loans from his son. "John," he said to him one day, "I've been following the stock market carefully. I think that if I had a little money, I could use it to make some more. Do you believe you could lend me several hundred thousand dollars?" "Well father," said Junior wryly, "do you think you are old enough to use it wisely?"[3]

The Rockefellers fared handsomely in the effervescent market of the Roaring Twenties. As the market soared, Junior more than doubled the $450 million he had received, and his assets approached the billion-dollar mark. When the market crashed in October 1929, the Rockefellers were caught by surprise. Ivy Lee convinced Junior of the publicity value of a calming statement from his father. After buying a million shares of Standard of New Jersey, Rockefeller issued a press release that had been scripted by Lee: "These are days when many are discouraged. In the ninety years of my life, depressions have come and gone. Prosperity has always returned, and will again." In his peroration, he said, "Believing that the fundamental conditions of the country are sound, my son and I have been purchasing sound common stocks for some days."[4] When the comedian Eddie Cantor was informed that the Rockefellers had resumed buying stocks, he responded with the wisecrack, "Sure, who else had any money left?"[5]

After the crash, Junior and Tom Debevoise worried about the financial health of the Equitable Trust, which had operated under Rockefeller control since 1911. They plucked Abby's brother, Winthrop Aldrich, from the law firm of Murray, Aldrich, and Webb and placed him in charge of the Equitable. A few months later, Aldrich orchestrated a merger with Chase National, creating the world's largest bank and one henceforth referred to as "the Rockefeller Bank"—even though the descendants of James Stillman and William Rockefeller steered the rival National City Bank. Some years later, Aldrich also ef-

A poetic picture of John D. Rockefeller taken on his ninety-first birthday at Pocantico Hills, July 8, 1930.
(Courtesy of the Rockefeller Archive Center)

fected a merger of his old law firm with that of Bert Milbank (Junior's old friend from the Browning School) to form the firm known today as Milbank, Tweed, Hadley and McCloy, which would be closely associated with the Rockefellers.

Junior was dispatched to Chicago to salvage what he could from the wreckage of Edith's business affairs—which did not endear him to Edith, who saw this as more high-handed meddling. At Junior's behest, she moved from her Lake Shore mansion into a suite at the Drake Hotel, where she was provided with a family allowance. Then, in early 1930, she was diagnosed with cancer in her right breast and underwent a mastectomy and radiation therapy. While convalescing, she tried to stave off bankruptcy by selling her pearls and emeralds to Cartier for nearly one million dollars, begging Junior for a million-dollar loan for her real-estate business, and asking her father to buy the Villa Turicum for more than two million dollars. Having had more than enough, Rockefeller declined to advance her additional money.

In 1932, after she developed a chronic cough, doctors found a dark spot on Edith's lower ribs; she tried, to no avail, to cure this cancer through psychological techniques. Until the end, she promised that she would try to see her father, but these ritual assertions had become a polite fiction between them. Her children and even her ex-husband, Harold, made repeated visits to her bedside. On August 25, 1932, Edith died in her suite at the Drake Hotel. For all her unconventional ideas, Edith had never renounced the possibility that Harold would leave Ganna Walska and return; like an old-fashioned wife, she had long kept his room at 1000 Lake Shore Drive untouched, with the furniture unchanged and his clothes hanging in the closet. It was a strange clutch of pallbearers who carried her coffin to the grave: Harold, Fowler, Junior, and Edwin Krenn. When Junior tried to exclude Krenn from the funeral, Harold, in deference to Edith, overrode his objections. In her will, Edith left more money to Krenn— five-twelfths of her estate—than to any of her three children. The Rockefeller lawyers furiously battled the bequest to Krenn until he capitulated and settled for a $24,000 annuity for life. At the news of her death, James Joyce struck a belated note of forgiveness. "I'm sorry to learn of the death of Mrs. McCormick," he told a friend. "She was very kind to me at a difficult moment and was a woman of considerable distinction."[6]

=

For all his financial savvy, Senior was democratically dragged down in the crash along with lesser mortals and saw his rump fortune of $25 million dwindle to a mere $7 million, prompting grandson Winthrop to exclaim, "For grandfather, that was being practically broke!"[7] In 1932, in a passing, persnickety moment, Rockefeller told Debevoise that Junior should give him $3.5 million as an "equitable adjustment" for all the money he had spent on the Rockefeller family office during the previous ten years. Rockefeller soon retracted his request, but his momentary pique showed that he was unnerved by his thin cushion of cash.

Junior also had unaccustomed money worries after the crash, as his net worth was slashed from almost $1 billion in 1929 to less than $500 million in 1934. The damage to his annual income was still more savage: From a peak of $56.7 million in the 1920s, it dropped to $16.5 million by the second year of the New Deal. Because he had made so many charitable pledges during the 1920s boom, his expenditures began to outpace his income by the early 1930s. Right before Roosevelt's inauguration, Junior had to liquidate large positions in Standard of New Jersey and Indiana and borrow almost eight million dollars to meet prior commitments.

Throughout the Roosevelt years, the Rockefellers struggled with an ideological dilemma. As longtime donors to Republican causes, they found much of the New Deal abominable and feared, like many other rich Americans, that Roosevelt was giving away the country. At the same time, they had a patrician sense of obligation toward the poor. While Hoover was still president, Senior and Junior gave two million dollars to the Emergency Unemployment Relief, a private charity. When Roosevelt became president in 1933, Rockefeller was nudged by his son into issuing a patriotic statement in praise of "the courage and progressive leadership of President Roosevelt."[8] (Setting an amusing example of austerity for the masses, he started to give out nickels instead of dimes.) In 1933, Junior even broadcast a radio appeal for the ultraliberal National Industrial Recovery Act. Yet despite the lip service paid to Roosevelt's policies, the Rockefellers continued to prefer private charity to public-works programs. At Pocantico, Junior charted fifty miles of new carriage trails to create extra jobs and gave generously to the American Red Cross and other relief agencies. Senior quickly cooled on the New Deal, and when the Social Security Act was enacted in 1935 he was sure it would destroy America's moral fiber.

As Junior's net worth tumbled after the crash, he began to feel the financial strain of Colonial Williamsburg and a new real-estate project in midtown Manhattan that was at first known as Metropolitan Square. With this last project, Junior became entangled in the sort of high-stakes maneuvering that had distinguished his father's career but had played no part in his own. The genesis of the project dated back to 1928 when the Metropolitan Opera Company decided to abandon its old quarters and create a new opera house on a site owned by Columbia University between Forty-eighth and Fifty-first Streets and Fifth and Sixth Avenues. Flanked by the Sixth Avenue elevated train and studded with speakeasies, pawnshops, bars, and other such sleazy haunts, the area was an unlikely choice for an opulent new opera house. Otto Kahn, a Kuhn, Loeb partner and chairman of the Metropolitan Opera Company, convinced Junior that he could render a community service and turn a tidy profit (an irresistible combination for a Rockefeller) by leasing the surrounding parcels from Columbia and building a showcase setting for the opera. After Charles O. Heydt canvassed five real-estate experts, Junior, seized by an impulse and without consulting a lawyer, authorized Heydt to close the deal with Columbia for a lease that would cost more than three million dollars per year.

The Metropolitan Opera could not fetch a high-enough price for its old building to construct a new one and suggested to Junior that he pay for half the cost of its new eight-million-dollar home. Feeling used and blackmailed, Junior turned them down, and when the Metropolitan Opera withdrew from the project, he was suddenly saddled with 229 shabby old brownstones amid the worsening economic environment. Without the opera, the development seemed to lose both its centerpiece and raison d'être, yet bills kept pouring in, and by the spring of 1930 Junior had paid out ten million dollars. Each year he was liable for another four million dollars in leases and taxes, and the rentals scarcely covered a tenth of that amount. One option was simply to scuttle the development. But Junior had always had a nagging sense of being patronized by the business community, and perhaps he now saw a chance for vindication, a chance to prove that he was really his father's son. In his most audacious career decision, he decided that he would personally finance a new complex of office buildings and round up the corporate tenants himself. As he persevered, he endured gales of ridicule and was even mocked in a Broadway play, *As Thousands Cheer,* where the hapless Junior was depicted as trying to palm off Rockefeller Center as a birthday gift on his unsuspecting father.

As might be expected, Junior suffered dreadful tension and insomnia over the midtown project. "I walk the floor nights," he told architect Wallace Harrison, "wondering where I'm going to get the money to build these buildings."[9] A novel situation for a Rockefeller, indeed. In the spring of 1931, recognizing the telltale symptoms, doctors advised him to take a vacation with Abby in Arizona. At the Arizona Inn in Tucson, a lady sitting at a nearby table in the restaurant waved to Junior, and only later did he discover that it was Ida Tarbell. By the 1920s, her famous history of the Standard Oil Company could be found only in secondhand bookstores, and when reissued in 1925 it failed to sell.

Returning to New York, Junior endured a debilitating case of shingles, which the doctors blamed on nervous exhaustion. He was also suffering such frequent colds that tests were performed at the Rockefeller Institute to see whether a serum could be developed from his germs that might prevent future colds. Despite his medical problems, Junior displayed a new toughness in dealing with the midtown complex. First, he had to settle the vexed question of a name to supersede the now obsolete Metropolitan Square. Like his father, Junior hesitated to employ the Rockefeller name, but a team of advisers, from Ivy Lee to son Nelson to managing agent John Todd, convinced him that "Rockefeller Center" would be the most potent marketing tool—an indication of how far the family image had advanced since the dark days of the muckrakers. To lend the complex a forward-looking image, the managers decided to create a "radio city" as its linchpin. In July 1931, after RCA, NBC, and Radio-Keith-Orpheum (RKO) agreed to lease one million square feet of office space for $3 million a year, Junior broke ground on the first of fourteen projected buildings.

Junior supervised Rockefeller Center with a command he had never shown before in any moneymaking venture. Each morning, he arrived at work by eight o'clock, a golden five-foot ruler wedged into his back pocket. Taking huge blueprints off the table, he would unroll them on the floor and crawl about, taking measurements with his ruler. Construction during the Depression had distinct advantages, most notably in lower costs for labor and building materials, and Rockefeller Center provided work for 75,000 unionized building workers.

From the outset, Junior told John Todd that the cluster of buildings had to be architecturally distinguished and harmonious. Wallace Harrison, who had studied at the Ecole des Beaux-Arts in Paris, and his colleagues turned to European modernism to endow Rockefeller Center with a sleek, futuristic look. Junior's one—and quite major—concession to contemporary taste had a canny commercial rationale behind it. Had the design of the complex been stodgy and old-fashioned, it would have undercut the Radio City marketing approach and the technologically advanced aura of the project. Ornamented with Art Deco motifs, the tapered towers of Indiana limestone, steel, glass, and masonry shot 850 feet into the air yet were spaced widely enough to create an airy sensation at plaza level. Though critics eventually labeled Rockefeller Center the world's finest skyscraper ensemble, they almost universally carped at it at its inception.

To lend added artistic distinction to the project, Diego Rivera was commissioned to paint a mural for the prestige spot in the RCA Building lobby. Despite his left-wing politics, Abby had bought Rivera's watercolors, exhibited his frescoes at MoMA, and invited him and his wife, Frida Kahlo, to 10 West Fifty-fourth Street. Nelson negotiated the coveted commission, and the Rockefeller Center overseers chose a suitably momentous and ostensibly noncontroversial theme: "Man at the Crossroads Looking with Hope and High Vision to the Choosing of a New and Better Future."[10] In the spring of 1933, Rivera began to sketch his vision of capitalist society as a diseased world of brutalized workers and scrofulous, card-playing capitalists, contrasting it with a hopeful, revolutionary world, symbolized by red flags and crowned by Lenin's saintly visage. His wife and assistants begged him to delete the head of the Bolshevik leader, but Rivera was determined to *épater les bourgeois*, and the press gloated over the Rockefeller predicament. "Rivera Perpetrates Scenes of Communist Activity for R.C.A. Walls—and Rockefeller Foots the Bill," one paper said.[11] After Rivera refused to delete Lenin's head, he was paid in full and dismissed from the job. He had told Nelson that he preferred the destruction of his piece to any tampering with it, and his mural was in fact reluctantly dismantled. "The picture was obscene and, in the judgment of Rockefeller Center, an offense to good taste," Junior hastily explained to his father. "It was for this reason primarily that Rockefeller Center decided to destroy it."[12]

With the completion of the RCA Building in 1933, Junior moved the Rockefeller family offices from 26 Broadway to the fifty-sixth floor of the new skyscraper. Henceforth, room 5600 would be the seat of the Rockefeller empire, with several hundred employees. Nelson, who was still in his twenties, got a real-estate license and soon became a frenetic salesman for empty office space at Rockefeller Center. To woo tenants, he offered attractive rents and agreed to assume their old leases. Several companies in the Rockefeller fold—including Standard Oil of New Jersey, Socony–Vacuum, Standard Oil of California, and Chase National Bank—took space in the new midtown complex. In 1938, the first year it turned a profit, Nelson was named president of Rockefeller Center. By the time Junior hammered in the last of some ten million rivets in 1939, he had transformed the project from the butt of malicious jokes into one of the Depression's outstanding business triumphs.

Even as his son created one city in midtown Manhattan and re-created another in Williamsburg, Virginia, Rockefeller remained curiously indifferent toward the urban complex that would so lastingly perpetuate his name. Amazingly enough, he probably never set foot in Rockefeller Center. "He wasn't interested in things of that sort," said Junior, "and I don't think we ever discussed Williamsburg and seldom discussed Rockefeller Center. . . . He was broadminded and tolerant but this kind of thing didn't enter his life. He might conceivably have asked about questions of financing or labor troubles at Rockefeller Center or Williamsburg, but that would be the only type of question that he would be interested in."[13] Senior might have followed its progress more closely than Junior realized, for Nelson remembered him waking from a nap, motioning him over to his Morris chair, and firing penetrating, detailed questions about the midtown project. Nevertheless, absorbed with his own creations, Rockefeller tended to screen out his son's accomplishments and overlook what he himself had not initiated. For all that, Junior remained slavishly devoted to his father. A wire that he sent on the eve of a visit seems to sum up this reverence: "Am not coming because I think you need me but because I know I need you."[14]

=

In his nineties, Rockefeller radiated the cheer of an elder statesman. The spindly little man weighed less than one hundred pounds and looked as if he had been shrunk by a witch doctor. He was scarcely affected by the recrudescence of Rockefeller-baiting books that appeared in the left-wing atmosphere of the Depression. In such polemics as *The Robber Barons* by Matthew Josephson, critics returned to the view popularized by Henry Demarest Lloyd and Ida Tarbell that Rockefeller had been the greatest corporate brigand of his day and owed his success to his ruthlessness and dishonesty, not to his business acumen. Yet this resurgence of old resentments was short-lived. The surge of patriotic feeling that accompanied World War II led to a renewed appreciation of the iron men of American industry who had bequeathed such military might to the country—a view very much in evidence in the authorized two-volume biography of Rockefeller that was published by Columbia University historian Allan Nevins in 1940 and in revised form in 1953. Rockefeller was always either lionized or vandalized according to the temper of the times.

Still vigorous, Rockefeller could send a golf ball sailing 165 yards down the fairway. In 1930, he marched through six holes in twenty-five shots. Then, his strength began to wane, and he gradually had to curtail his game. With typical precision, he reduced his number of daily holes from six to four to two; after contracting a severe cold in 1932, he had to abandon golf altogether. The ninety-three-year-old Rockefeller bounced back from this ill health with renewed good humor. One paper reported, "He was so delighted to be out in the warm sunshine again that once he stopped and sang a hymn as he gazed with twinkling eyes at the myriad of brilliant flowers and shrubs."[15] He reiterated his wish to live to one hundred, viewing it as God's final verdict on his life. "Many folks believe I've done much harm in the world," he told Ormond Beach's mayor, George N. Rigby, "but on the other hand I've tried to do what good I could and I really would like to live to be a hundred."[16] As Rigby described it, Rockefeller grew even more detached from material things as he approached the end of life:

> I recall one day we were sitting on his front porch at Ormond watching a most elaborate yacht winding its way down the Halifax River toward Palm Beach. He expressed his wonder at the possible pleasure a man could get out of such show and pretension. Then, after a moment or two, the whole expression of his face changed and he asked enthusiastically, "Wasn't that a beautiful rain we had last night?"[17]

Rockefeller's improbable love affair with the movie camera flourished. In 1930, he was invited to attend festivities in Cleveland to celebrate the sixtieth anniversary of Standard Oil of Ohio. Too frail to go, he agreed to shoot a newsreel that would be shown at the celebration. Sitting on his sunlit porch as the cameras rolled, Rockefeller delivered a congratulatory message in a thin voice. "And the gesture of his removing his glasses when he finished reading and turned to regard me where I stood behind the camera revealed a natural actor," said his handpicked cameraman, Curt Engelbrecht. Two weeks later, when a Standard of Ohio executive flew down to Ormond Beach, Rockefeller was shot playing golf and greeting the executive as his plane alighted on the green.

Showing surprising spunk, the ninety-one-year-old Rockefeller boarded the airplane and was eager to fly off, cameras rolling, when his vigilant valet, John Yordi, called off the flight as subjecting him to too much excitement. In a compromise, the monoplane taxied up and down the runway, with Rockefeller inside waving to the cameras. "You make me feel like a movie actor," Rockefeller told Engelbrecht.

Though free of self-pity, Rockefeller often seemed forlorn in the 1930s. Too proud to plead for visits from descendants, he dropped hints and tactful suggestions that he would like to see them more, but this did not seem to work. He craved some human warmth that he never fully got from his own family or perhaps had never really allowed to flower. Engelbrecht noted Rockefeller's strange fascination with a little girl named Lucille, who was the daughter of his chauffeur, Vincent Frasca.

> She somehow filled a tremendous gap for him, and it may be safely asserted that he demonstrated an affection for her that he was never known to manifest for one of his own blood. Never a day passed but she paid a visit to him or he came looking for her. In her presence everything else was forgotten. She was a charm for him. He talked with her and told her stories. His face brightened to her responses, and his eyes warmed in his glances in her direction.[18]

As the Depression progressed, Junior found himself in the same uncomfortable position that his father had been in a generation before: His children were restive and wanted him to make some final disposition of his money. It infuriated them that they were now married grown-ups still living on allowances who had to go hat in hand to father for a new car or trip abroad. In May 1933, Junior heard the first murmurs of outright rebellion when his children complained in a collective letter that too much of their time with him was taken up with money squabbles that jeopardized family relations, and they petitioned him for larger allowances. To mollify his mutinous offspring, Junior gave his three oldest children—Babs, John III, and Nelson—200,000 shares of Socony–Vacuum apiece, providing each with about $3.2 million.

The following year, Congress sharply boosted tax schedules. Rates jumped for the top income bracket from 55 to 63 percent, while the estate tax soared from 45 to 60 percent for estates valued beyond $50 million and the gift tax rose from 33 to 45 percent for sums beyond $10 million. Junior decided to set up trusts for his wife and children before the steeper gift tax took effect at year's end. To safeguard this money, which would be managed by the trust department of the Chase National Bank, he stipulated that the children could draw income, but that principal withdrawals had to be approved by trustees.

(Junior made an invidious exception for Abby and Babs, who could not touch principal under any circumstances.) Since the trustees included such intimates of Junior as Raymond Fosdick, Tom Debevoise, and Winthrop Aldrich, he did not forfeit total control. The largest single trust went to Abby, who received $18.3 million and the full freedom to purchase modern art with her income. Babs, John III, and Nelson got $12 million apiece and Laurance, Winthrop, and David smaller amounts. The following year, Junior added money to these last three accounts to equalize the trusts.

In all, Junior transmitted $102 million—or more than $1 billion in 1996 dollars—to his wife and children through the trusts. As he explained the operating philosophy behind them to Laurance:

> They have been created in accordance with the policy which your Grandfather Rockefeller adopted with his children and which I hope your children will ultimately follow. . . . As you know, Grandfather and I have always been keenly alive to the responsibilities inherent in the possession of wealth. He believes, as I do, that these responsibilities and the opportunities which they bring for useful living and unselfish service to mankind should be shared with those of the next generation when and as soon as they have reached such an age and attained such a maturity as justifies their being entrusted with them.[19]

The $102 million that Junior bequeathed to his heirs was a stupendous sum, yet it represented only a fraction of the money he had inherited. Between 1917 and 1960, Junior gave away $537 million directly, plus another $540 million indirectly through organized Rockefeller philanthropies. (Junior did not leave himself a pauper. He was left with about $200 million in the 1950s, while his descendants, wisely investing their inheritances, were worth more than $6.2 billion in 1996.) He also paid $317 million in taxes to federal, state, and local governments. So whatever Rockefeller's plunder, the great bulk of the gain was ultimately plowed back into worthwhile projects and the public purse. Such was the indignation aroused by Standard Oil, however, that perhaps only generosity on this extraordinary scale could have softened memories of the ravening monopolist.

⸺

Rockefeller inspired many premature reports of his demise, and his habitual secrecy about his medical condition kept the press on high alert. In 1934, at ninety-five, he suffered a bout of bronchial pneumonia that threatened to thwart his goal of reaching one hundred, but he managed to recover. His weight dropped below ninety pounds, and he decided to abandon Kykuit for good. He loaded up a private railroad car with fruits, vegetables, cultured milk, and oxygen canisters and traveled to The Casements, where he settled permanently. Determined to eke out five more years, he drastically restricted his routine to conserve energy. No more golf, no more afternoon larks in the car, no more garden walks. He took off his expensive silver wigs, never to don them again. As his pace slackened, the servants marched to his slower tempo, and a twilight hush seemed to descend over the Ormond Beach house. Watchful and alert, the wizened little man sat for hours on the sunporch. To maintain muscle tone in his legs, he mounted a stationary bicycle in his room every day and slowly cycled. When he reached ninety-six on July 8, 1935, his insurance company, abiding by an old custom, had to pay him five million dollars, the face value of his policy. According to contemporary actuarial tables, only one person in 100,000 lived that long.

Always ready to embrace change, the old man liked to watch Hollywood movies at home, especially those with shapely blondes, such as Jean Harlow. His life, however, still revolved around religion, and when he was too weak to go to church, he listened to sermons on a bedside radio. His thoughts turned toward eternity. When Henry Ford was leaving one day, Rockefeller said to him, "Good bye, I'll see you in heaven," and Ford replied, "You will if you get in."[20] Yet Rockefeller seemed to know for certain that the Lord was not a radical critic of society and would reward him in the hereafter. He started a new routine, singing hymns accompanied by a violinist who came to the house. For all his religious certitude, however, death remained the one unmentionable subject for Rockefeller. "Never did he speak of death in relation to himself; rather did he speak always of life, of activity, of accomplishment," said Junior.[21]

In early 1937, as Rockefeller approached ninety-eight, his body was feeble, but his mind was lucid. "Father is very well," Junior wrote an old friend in March 1937, "better even than for the past year or two. We are having a delightful time here with him, and the weather is beautiful."[22] He still gambled in stocks and enjoyed his unvarying comedy routine with Mrs. Evans. On Saturday, May 22, he was taking the sunlight when Evans said to him, "Mr. Rockefeller, the sun has given you some color. You look so much better." When he just flashed a wordless smile, she added, "Mr. Rockefeller, you haven't said anything about how I look." In his chair, he made a chivalric bow and said, "Mrs. Evans, that is because I am never able to do the subject justice."[23] That same day, he paid off the mortgage of the institution that had so profoundly affected him: the Euclid Avenue Baptist Church.

Before the day was over, Rockefeller had a heart attack. At 4:05 A.M. on the morning of May 23, he lapsed into a coma and died in his sleep. The official cause of death was sclerotic myocarditis, a hardening and inflammation of the heart wall, although it is probably more accurate to say that he died of old age. Rockefeller drifted off peacefully, six weeks short of his ninety-eighth birthday.

His placid end disappointed critics who were still hoping for some earthly retribution.

As news of Rockefeller's death spread, crowds gathered outside his compound and the sexton of the Union Baptist Church tolled the steeple bell. After a private funeral at Ormond Beach for staff and friends, a motorcycle guard accompanied the casket to the railroad station, where it was placed on a private car for the northward journey to Pocantico. When the train arrived at Tarrytown, Junior and his five sons were waiting on the platform in identical homburgs. On May 25, the Reverend Harry Emerson Fosdick delivered a brief, touching eulogy at the Pocantico funeral while Dr. Archer Gibson played the Kykuit pipe organ. As a reminder that the deceased had never lacked detractors, state troopers scoured Pocantico Hills for trespassers as the service progressed. Around the world, employees in the offices of all Standard Oil successor firms observed five minutes of silence. On May 27, Rockefeller's body returned to Cleveland and was lowered into the earth between the two Baptist women who had so devotedly believed in him, Eliza and Cettie. Because of fears that vandals might desecrate the grave, Rockefeller's casket was placed in a bombproof tomb, sealed by heavy slabs of stone.

Having given away most of his money, Rockefeller left behind an estate of $26.4 million, showing that he had recouped his stock-market losses after the 1929 crash. Most of his estate took the form of U.S. Treasury notes, though he had retained, for sentimental reasons, one share of Standard Oil of California marked "Certificate No. 1." The fabulous oil wealth of Saudi Arabia and Kuwait would be tapped within a year of Rockefeller's death, ensuring the preeminent place of petroleum in the twentieth-century economy. Sixty years after their founder's death, four of the Standard Oil successor firms—Exxon, Mobil, Amoco, and Chevron—numbered among the fifty largest companies on earth.

To an extent that would have seemed inconceivable in Ida Tarbell's heyday, the newspaper obituaries dwelled on Rockefeller the benign philanthropist, not Rockefeller the ferocious trust king. He was "the world's greatest philanthropist and organizer in the science of giving," said one editorial.[24] Most striking was that the laudatory comments emanated from across the political spectrum and included those who had jousted with him in the past. Attorney Samuel Untermyer issued this paean to the elusive witness he had interrogated: "Next to our beloved President, he was our country's biggest citizen. It was he who visualized as did no other man the use to which great wealth could wisely be put. Because of him the world is a better place in which to live. Blessed be the memory of World Citizen No. 1."[25]

In truth, John D. Rockefeller, Sr., had left behind a contradictory legacy. An amalgam of godliness and greed, compassion and fiendish cunning, he personified the ambiguous heritage of America's Puritan ancestors, who had encouraged thrift and enterprise but had also spurred overly acquisitive instincts.

He had extracted mixed messages from his religious training as well as from his incongruously matched parents. Not surprisingly, he had served as an emblem of both corporate greed and philanthropic enlightenment.

Starting in the 1870s, Rockefeller's stewardship of Standard Oil had signaled a new era in American life that had both inspired and alarmed the populace. His unequaled brilliance and rapacity as a businessman had squarely confronted the country with troubling questions about the shape of the economy, the distribution of wealth, and the proper relationship between business and government. Rockefeller perfected a monopoly that indisputably demonstrated the efficiency of large-scale business. In creating new corporate forms, he charted the way for the modern multinational corporations that came to dominate economic life in the twentieth century. But in so doing he also exposed the manifold abuses that could accompany untrammeled economic power, especially in the threat to elected government. As architect of the first great industrial trust, he proved the ultimately fragile nature of free markets, forcing the government to specify the rules that would ensure competition and fair play in the future.

The fiercest robber baron had turned out to be the foremost philanthropist. Rockefeller accelerated the shift from the personal, ad hoc charity that had traditionally been the province of the rich to something both more powerful and more impersonal. He established the promotion of knowledge, especially scientific knowledge, as a task no less important than giving alms to the poor or building schools, hospitals, and museums. He showed the value of expert opinion, thorough planning, and competent administration in nonprofit work, setting a benchmark for professionalism in the emerging foundation field. By the time Rockefeller died, in fact, so much good had unexpectedly flowered from so much evil that God might even have greeted him on the other side, as the titan had so confidently expected all along.

Although Junior moved into Kykuit after Rockefeller's death, he knew that his father was inimitable, and so he decided to retain the *Jr.* after his name. As he was often heard to say in later years, "There was only one John D. Rockefeller."[26]

ACKNOWLEDGMENTS

It has taken the kindness of many strangers to explore the labyrinth of materials now available on John D. Rockefeller, Sr.

Because Rockefeller died in 1937, there are few people today who can provide information from either firsthand experience or hearsay, which made me especially grateful to the family members who spoke with me. David Rockefeller not only sat for an interview but graciously offered a sneak preview of the chapter on his grandfather in his forthcoming memoir. Other descendants of figures discussed in this book—including Nelson Aldrich, Jr., Elizabeth de Cuevas, John de Cuevas, James T. Flexner, Abby O'Neill, Spelman Prentice, Ann Rockefeller Roberts, J. Stillman Rockefeller, and O. Stillman Rockefeller—added shading and nuance to many events. Peter Johnson, the resident historian at the Rockefeller family office, reacted to all of my requests for information in a fine, collegial spirit.

My foremost debt is to the staff of the Rockefeller Archive Center, which is situated on the family estate in Sleepy Hollow (formerly North Tarrytown) but is operated by a team of professional archivists under the very able direction of Darwin Stapleton. The center, first opened to researchers in 1975, is a division of the Rockefeller University. I am especially grateful to Tom Rosenbaum, who expertly guided me through the vast trove of documents and had stimulating things to say about so many of them. His help was invaluable and always graciously rendered. Ken Rose was especially adept when it came to Cleveland history, while Valerie Komor was indispensable in elucidating the mystery of Charles and Bessie Strong. Michele Hiltzik and Robert Battaly did yeoman's work in helping me with the photos. I salute the professionalism of the entire staff and the exemplary work it performs each year for so many scholars.

Among other Samaritans who supplied aid and comfort, I would like to single out Jean Ashton and the staff of the Rare Book and Manuscript Library at Columbia University, which houses the voluminous collection of Rockefeller material in the Allan Nevins papers; Meredith Nevins Mayer, who permitted me to quote from her father's papers; Ronald Grele and the Columbia University Oral History Project; Barbara T. Zolli, Beth Davidson, and the staff of the Drake Well Museum in Titusville, Pennsylvania, which contains Ida Tarbell's extensive files on Standard Oil; Caroline Tarbell Tupper, who gave permission to quote from the papers of her grandaunt Ida Tarbell; Harold Miller and the staff of the State Historical Society of Wisconsin, which made available the papers of Henry Demarest Lloyd by interlibrary loan; John Grabowski and the staff of the Western Reserve Historical Society in Cleveland; William Massa, Jr., of the Manuscripts and Archives Collection at the Yale University Library, who tracked down some critical letters; Daniel Meyer and the Department of Special Collections at the University of Chicago Library; and Letitia Yeandle and Theresa Helein of the Folger Shakespeare Library in Washington, D.C., who provided Rockefeller's correspondence with Henry Clay Folger.

Sir David Simon, the former chairman of British Petroleum, took a special interest in this project and arranged for me to examine the original minute books of Standard Oil of Ohio, which was absorbed by British Petroleum in the 1970s. Dorothy Jankowski, Barbara Rutigliano, and George Dunn served as gracious hosts during my Cleveland visit. Robert Craig Brown, the chairman of the University of Toronto history department, went beyond the call of duty in showering me with information about William Lyon Mackenzie King. I enjoyed the cheerful, efficient help of two delightful people at Spelman College—Tanya Sharpe, the interim director of the archives, and undergraduate Darsheika Giles—who sifted through many unexplored files pertaining to early Rockefeller history. Dr. Deborah Dependahl Waters kindly escorted me on a tour of the Rockefeller rooms at the Museum of the City of New York. Richard Warshauer, George Picon, and John Nesimi allowed me a glimpse of the old Standard Oil offices at 26 Broadway. Cynthia Altman, Carol Moberg, and David Lyons were knowledgeable guides on a stroll around Rockefeller University, while Vicki Manning filled in blanks about the Judson Memorial Church. Peter Kraus of the New York Public Library provided statistical tables for converting figures into contemporary dollars. Jennifer Shaw extracted many interesting articles for me from local libraries. Susan Sacharski, archivist of the Northwestern Memorial Hospital in Chicago, and William Beatty, professor of medical bibliography emeritus at Northwestern University, counseled me in tracking down that phantom, Dr. Charles Johnston. Dr. Josef Jelinek and Alice DeLury provided some needed guidance on Rockefeller's alopecia.

Three people in Lakewood—Deborah Kern, chairwoman of the Lakewood Heritage, her husband, Jerome Kern, and Judith Robinson of the Lakewood Public Library—helped to re-create that colorful phase of Rockefeller's life. Laurel Auchampaugh and Ann Townsend of the Cayuga-Owasco Lakes Historical Society in Moravia, New York, passed along some piquant folklore about Rockefeller's childhood and secretly initiated me, in a back room, into the mysteries of *Joshua: A Man of the Finger Lakes Region.* I was delighted to receive unsolicited aid from George Plimpton, a descendant of General Adelbert Ames, who rounded up background materials on a trip to Ormond Beach. Leslie Bottarelli of the Ormond Beach Community Enrichment Center sent additional information. Jean S. Hoefer of the Stephenson County Genealogical Society and Michael Cline of the Oakland Cemetery in Freeport, Illinois, helped to unravel the mystery of Dr. William Levingston's last days in that town.

The generous Deirdre Bair, now working on a biography of Carl Jung, gave me a road map of Jung scholars who might be of assistance in unearthing the story of Edith and Harold McCormick in Switzerland. William McGuire of Princeton University, the editor of Jung's Collected Works, dipped into his formidable database on several occasions and came up with splendid discoveries. James Hillman, formerly the director of the Jung Center in Zurich, introduced me to the hilarious memoir of Edith's chauffeur, Emile Ammann.

James A. Smith and Kathleen McCarthy helped to locate Rockefeller in the broad stream of philanthropic history. Alan Brinkley provided a timely perspective on the often-tangled question of business corruption in American political history. Judith Goldstein deepened my understanding of John D. Rockefeller, Jr.'s conservation work on Mount Desert Island. Other friends who offered welcome advice, referrals, stories, and suggestions include Robert Caro, Jonathan Coss, Andrew Delbanco, Paula Giddings, Robert C. Kochersberger, Jr., the late J. Anthony Lukas, Vincent McGee, John Rousmaniere, Willie Ruff, Tom Ryley, and Scott Sandage.

Both the research and writing stages of this book proved unexpectedly rich in medical emergencies, and I would like to express special thanks to some superb physicians. Dr. Eric Rackow, chief of medicine at Saint Vincent's Hospital, and Dr. Jay Weinstein helped to rescue me from a nasty brush with a blood clot. They consulted closely with my brother, Dr. Bart Chernow, now a vice dean at the Johns Hopkins Medical School. I would also like to thank Dr. Dennis Fabian of Saint Vincent's for operating on my knee and Dr. Jonathan Deland of the Hospital for Special Surgery for operating on my foot.

Alberto Vitale, Harold Evans, and the other Random House executives generously supported this project from the outset. I would like to extend special thanks to S. I. Newhouse, Jr., for his early encouragement. My editor, Ann Godoff, found time in her busy schedule to combine fine, tough, old-fashioned editing with her usual bountiful enthusiasm. I am grateful to her assistant, Enrica Gadler, for many small favors performed over the years. Gaby Bordwin created the outstanding cover for the book, while Jim Lambert did his usual fine work on the interior design. Benjamin Dreyer was the soul of patience in supervising the copyediting process, and Timothy Mennel did an outstanding job copyediting the manuscript. Melanie Jackson continues to define my notion of the ideal agent. Each year, she improves just when I thought that she had already attained perfection. My parents were, as usual, unstinting in both their love and support. The single most important figure in the creation of this book was my wife, Valerie, who again endured the prolonged periods of insanity that overtook her obsessed husband. More than just a lovely martyr, she was my dinner-table muse, bedtime confidante, and most perceptive critic. Her editorial contribution to this biography cannot be overstated, for she enabled me to find that often elusive voice—neither too sympathetic nor too sharp—that would best capture the complexities of Rockefeller's character. *Chapeau,* my dear.

NOTES

ABBREVIATIONS

AN—Allan Nevins Papers, Butler Library, Columbia University, New York, New York

CUOH–ABF—Columbia University Oral History Collection, Abraham B. Flexner interview

CUOH–PM—Columbia University Oral History Collection, Paul Manship interview

FSL—Folger Shakespeare Library, Washington, D.C.

HDL—Henry Demarest Lloyd Papers, State Historical Society of Wisconsin, Madison, Wisconsin

IMT—Ida Minerva Tarbell Papers, Pennsylvania Historical & Museum Commission, Drake Well Museum Collection, Titusville, Pennsylvania

RAC—Rockefeller Archive Center, Sleepy Hollow, New York. Papers of John D. Rockefeller, Sr., John D. Rockefeller, Jr., and other family members

RAC–CAS—Rockefeller Archive Center, Charles A. Strong Papers

RAC–FTG—Rockefeller Archive Center, Frederick T. Gates Papers

SOCMB—Standard Oil Company Minute Books, BP America, Cleveland, Ohio

UC–JDR—University of Chicago, John D. Rockefeller Papers

UC–UPP—University of Chicago, University Presidents' Papers

B = Box

F = File

FOREWORD

1. Wells, *The Work, Wealth and Happiness of Mankind,* p. 454.

PRELUDE: POISON TONGUE

1. RAC, Inglis interview, p. 1062.
2. Ibid., p. 916.
3. Ibid., p. 375.

4. Ibid., p. 962.
5. Ibid., p. 601.
6. Ibid., p. 493.
7. Ibid., p. 891.
8. Ibid., p. 1309.
9. RAC, III 2.H B30 F17.
10. RAC, III 2.H B9 F37.
11. *McClure's Magazine,* July 1905.
12. RAC, Inglis interview, p. 1648.
13. Ibid., p. 1650.

CHAPTER 1: THE FLIMFLAM MAN

1. RAC, Inglis notes, 4.12, "Hoster Manuscript."
2. Nevins, *John D. Rockefeller: The Heroic Age of American Enterprise,* vol. I, p. 141.
3. Rugoff, *America's Gilded Age,* p. 97.
4. *The World,* November 1, 1903.
5. Ibid.
6. Ibid.
7. Nevins, *John D. Rockefeller,* vol. I, p. 151.
8. RAC, Inglis notes, 4.8, "Richford."
9. RAC, Inglis interview, p. 1665.
10. *The World,* November 3, 1903.
11. RAC, Inglis notes, 4.8, "Interview with Mrs. John Wilcox."
12. Ibid.
13. Ibid., "Interview with S. H. Steele."
14. IMT, B 4/14 T-293, "Report on Rockefeller Family."
15. RAC, Inglis notes, 4.8, "Richford."
16. Ibid.
17. Ibid., "S. H. Steele."
18. *The World,* November 1, 1903.
19. *Cosmopolitan,* November 1908.
20. *The World,* November 1, 1903.
21. William H. Allen, *Rockefeller: Giant, Dwarf, Symbol,* p. 233.
22. *The World,* November 1, 1903.
23. RAC, III 2.H B3 F15, letter from William O. Inglis to Ivy Lee, June 24, 1922.
24. *The World,* November 1, 1903.
25. Nevins, *John D. Rockefeller,* vol. I, p. 30.

CHAPTER 2: FIRES OF REVIVAL

1. RAC, Inglis notes, 4.8, "Moravia."
2. Nevins, *John D. Rockefeller: The Heroic Age of American Enterprise,* vol. I, p. 48.

3. RAC, Inglis notes, 4.10, "Tours to Owego and Moravia."
4. Nevins, *John D. Rockefeller,* vol. I, pp. 34–35.
5. RAC, Inglis notes, 4.8, "Interview with Peter Brown."
6. Nevins, *John D. Rockefeller,* vol. I, p. 39.
7. *The World,* February 2, 1908.
8. RAC, Inglis notes, 4.9, "Early Training."
9. John D. Rockefeller, *Random Reminiscences,* p. 42.
10. Nevins, *John D. Rockefeller,* vol. I, p. 40.
11. RAC, Inglis notes, 4.13, "Interview Conversations—1929."
12. Nevins, *John D. Rockefeller,* vol. I, p. 46.
13. RAC, III 2.Z B21, "Miss Spelman's Recollections."
14. RAC, Inglis notes, 4.11, "Mrs. William C. Rudd."
15. RAC, Inglis interview, p. 1665.
16. William H. Allen, *Rockefeller: Giant, Dwarf, Symbol,* p. 47.
17. RAC, Inglis notes, 4.11, "Mrs. William C. Rudd."
18. Nevins, *John D. Rockefeller,* vol. I, p. 41.
19. RAC, Inglis notes, 4.9, "On Mother's Discipline."
20. John D. Rockefeller, *Random Reminiscences,* p. 42.
21. Winkler, *John D.: A Portrait in Oils,* p. 139.
22. RAC, Inglis interview, p. 503.
23. RAC, Inglis notes, 4.9, "Mr. Rockefeller and the Indigestion Myth."
24. Nevins, *John D. Rockefeller,* vol. I, p. 92.
25. RAC, III 2.2 B21, "Antecedents and Childhood."
26. Nevins, *Study in Power,* vol. I, p. 31.
27. RAC, Inglis notes, 4.9, "Early Training."
28. RAC, Inglis notes, 4.12, "Hoster Manuscript," p. 20.
29. *The World,* March 1, 1908.
30. RAC, Inglis notes, 4.8, "David Dennis."
31. Nevins, *John D. Rockefeller,* vol. I, p. 37.
32. Tarbell, *The History of the Standard Oil Company,* vol. I, p. 40.
33. RAC, Inglis interview, p. 124.
34. Ibid., p. 390.
35. Ibid., p. 1651.
36. Russell, *Freedom Versus Organization,* p. 316.
37. Brutcher, *Joshua,* p. 10.
38. Ibid., p. 95.
39. Ibid., p. 138.
40. IMT, B 4/14 T-293, "Report on Rockefeller Family."
41. Nevins, *John D. Rockefeller,* vol. I, p. 50.
42. IMT, B 4/14 T-293, "Report on Rockefeller Family."
43. RAC, Inglis interview, p. 1649.
44. RAC, Inglis notes, 4.8, 3.1.1, "William Avery Rockefeller Court Records."
45. Stasz, *The Rockefeller Women,* p. 19.
46. IMT, B 4/14 T-293, "Report on Rockefeller Family."
47. RAC, Inglis notes, 4.8, 3.1.1, "William Avery Rockefeller Court Records."

48. RAC, Inglis interview, pp. 1648–49.
49. Lundberg, *The Rockefeller Syndrome*, p. 104.
50. William H. Allen, *Rockefeller*, p. 238.
51. Nevins, *Study in Power*, vol. I, p. 9.
52. RAC, Inglis notes, 4.8, "Owego."
53. Ibid.
54. William H. Allen, *Rockefeller*, p. 44.
55. AN, B110 F15, letter to Eliza Rockefeller, July 18, 1885.
56. RAC, Inglis notes, 4.8, "William A. Smyth."
57. Nevins, *John D. Rockefeller*, vol. I, p. 78.
58. RAC, Inglis notes, 4.8, "C. M. La Monte."
59. RAC, Inglis notes, 4.8, "Mrs. S. J. Life."
60. Nevins, *John D. Rockefeller*, vol. I, p. 65.
61. RAC, Inglis notes, 4.9, "Childish Customs."
62. *McClure's Magazine*, July 1905.
63. Tarbell, *History of the Standard Oil Company*, vol. I, p. 40.
64. *Human Life*, April 1905.
65. RAC, Inglis notes, 4.8, "Owego."
66. AN, B126, letter to J. O. Lacey, January 9, 1899.
67. Nevins, *John D. Rockefeller*, vol. I, p. 73.
68. Nevins, *Study in Power*, vol. I, p. 71.
69. RAC, Inglis notes, 4.8, "Mrs. S. J. Life."
70. Ibid.

CHAPTER 3: BOUND TO BE RICH

1. IMT, B 1/14, letter from J. M. Siddall to Ida Tarbell, November 3, 1903.
2. Ibid.
3. AN, B126, letter to Mr. Spalding, August 16, 1923.
4. William H. Allen, *Rockefeller: Giant, Dwarf, Symbol*, p. 104.
5. Ibid., p. 102.
6. Flynn, *God's Gold*, p. 52.
7. RAC, III 2.Z B21, "Miss Spelman's Recollections."
8. *The Atlanta Georgia*, February 12, 1922.
9. Winkler, *John D.: A Portrait in Oils*, p. 131.
10. IMT, B II, letter from J. M. Siddall to Ida Tarbell, December 10, 1903.
11. Nevins, *Study in Power*, vol. I, p. 51.
12. Ibid., p. 61.
13. RAC, III 2.Z B21, "Miss Spelman's Recollections."
14. John D. Rockefeller, *Random Reminiscences*, p. 51.
15. William H. Allen, *Rockefeller*, p. 74.
16. Goulder, *John D. Rockefeller*, p. 10.
17. Ibid.
18. Nevins, *John D. Rockefeller: The Heroic Age of American Enterprise*, vol. I, p. 83.

19. Winkler, *John D.*, p. 45.
20. *The World*, March 1, 1908.
21. Ibid.
22. William H. Allen, *Rockefeller*, p. 82.
23. RAC, Inglis notes, 4.8, "Cleveland—First Employment."
24. RAC, III 2.H B2 F11.
25. Nevins, *Study in Power*, vol. I, p. 10.
26. RAC, III 2.H B3 F14.
27. Hawke, *John D.*, p. 18.
28. Nevins, *John D. Rockefeller*, vol. I, p. 96.
29. John D. Rockefeller, *Random Reminiscences*, p. 43.
30. RAC, III 2.H B3 F16, letter from William O. Inglis to Ivy Lee, September 25, 1926.
31. Hawke, *John D.*, p. 18.
32. Nevins, *Study in Power*, vol. I, p. 11.
33. Nevins, *John D. Rockefeller*, vol. I, p. 104.
34. Winkler, *John D.*, p. 25.
35. John D. Rockefeller, *Random Reminiscences*, p. 34.
36. Weber, *The Protestant Ethic and the Spirit of Capitalism*, p. 22.
37. Schumpeter, *Capitalism, Socialism and Democracy*, p. 123.
38. Nevins, *Study in Power*, vol. I, p. 18
39. John D. Rockefeller, *Random Reminiscences*, p. 44.
40. Winkler, *John D.*, p. 39.
41. Nevins, *John D. Rockefeller*, vol. I, p. 103,
42. Nevins, *Study in Power*, vol. I, p. 11.
43. John D. Rockefeller, *Random Reminiscences*, p. 46.
44. Nevins, *John D. Rockefeller*, vol. I, p. 107.
45. IMT, B 2/14, memo from J. M. Siddall to Ida Tarbell, n.d.
46. Nevins, *John D. Rockefeller*, vol. I, p. 105.
47. Ibid., p. 111.
48. John D. Rockefeller, *Random Reminiscences*, p. 14.
49. Hawke, *John D.*, p. 22.
50. *New York Herald*, n.d. [1897].
51. Flynn, *God's Gold*, p. 65.
52. *The New Yorker*, January 22, 1927.
53. AN, B126.
54. Nevins, *Study in Power*, vol. I, p. 16.
55. Nevins, *John D. Rockefeller*, vol. I, p. 124.
56. Hawke, *John D.*, p. 43.
57. William H. Allen, *Rockefeller*, p. 249.
58. Stasz, *The Rockefeller Women*, p. 232.
59. Nevins, *John D. Rockefeller*, vol. I, pp. 119–20.
60. IMT, B 1/14, letter from J. M. Siddall to Ida Tarbell, October 26, 1903.
61. RAC, Inglis notes, 4.12.
62. RAC, Inglis notes, 4.8, "Cleveland."

63. RAC, Inglis notes, 4.12, "Hoster Manuscript," p. 71.
64. IMT, B 1/14, letter from J. M. Siddall to Ida Tarbell, October 26, 1903.
65. RAC, Inglis notes, 4.8, "Cleveland."
66. William H. Allen, *Rockefeller,* p. 249.
67. John D. Rockefeller, *Random Reminiscences,* p. 52.
68. Ibid., p. 55.
69. Nevins, *John D. Rockefeller,* vol. I, p. 121.
70. Flynn, *God's Gold,* p. 395.
71. Innes, *Creating the Commonwealth,* p. 114.
72. Swanberg, *Whitney Father, Whitney Heiress,* p. 71.
73. RAC, Inglis notes, 4.9, "Early Giving."
74. *The New York Times,* October 20, 1907.
75. Schenkel, *The Rich Man and the Kingdom,* p. 14.
76. Weber, *Protestant Ethic,* p. 53.
77. Ibid., p. 17.
78. Innes, *Creating the Commonwealth,* p. 26.
79. Stampp, *America in 1857,* p. 231.
80. Ibid., p. 232.
81. Ibid., p. 235.
82. RAC, Inglis interview, p. 390.
83. RAC, Inglis notes, 4.8, "Self-Reliance."
84. Hawke, *John D.,* p. 25.
85. Winkler, *John D.,* p. 16.
86. Dreiser, *The Financier,* p. 29.
87. RAC, Inglis notes, 4.9, "Getting His First Job."
88. *Los Angeles Tribune,* March 25, 1917.
89. John D. Rockefeller, *Random Reminiscences,* p. 46.
90. Ibid.

CHAPTER 4: BAPTISM IN BUSINESS

1. Goulder, *John D. Rockefeller,* p. 44.
2. William H. Allen, *Rockefeller: Giant, Dwarf, Symbol,* p. 113.
3. RAC, Inglis interview, p. 125.
4. Hawke, *John D.,* p. 28.
5. Nevins, *Study in Power,* vol. I, p. 10.
6. John D. Rockefeller, *Random Reminiscences,* p. 40.
7. Ibid., p. 50.
8. Ibid.
9. RAC, Inglis notes, 4.9, "Early Training."
10. AN, B126.
11. RAC, III 2.H B2 F11.
12. Nevins, *John D. Rockefeller: The Heroic Age of American Enterprise,* vol. I, p. 131.

13. RAC, Inglis notes, 4.12, "First Years in Cleveland."
14. *The World,* June 7, 1925.
15. Winkler, *John D.: A Portrait in Oils,* p. 54.
16. *The World,* June 14, 1925.
17. Ibid.
18. Ibid.
19. *New York Herald,* November 29, 1908.
20. *The World,* June 7, 1925.
21. Nevins, *Study in Power,* vol. I, p. 18.
22. RAC, Inglis notes, 4.10, "On Arrogance."
23. John D. Rockefeller, *Random Reminiscences,* p. 50.
24. RAC, III 2.II B2 F11.
25. Nevins, *John D. Rockefeller,* vol. I, p. 135.
26. RAC, Inglis interview, p. 463.
27. John D. Rockefeller, *Random Reminiscences,* p. 49.
28. *Yakima* (Wash.) *Herald,* January 14, 1920.
29. Winkler, *John D.,* p. 51.
30. Ibid., p. 52.
31. Flynn, *God's Gold,* p. 101.
32. Nevins, *Study in Power,* vol. I, p. 271.
33. *Woman's Home Companion,* January 1907.
34. William H. Allen, *Rockefeller,* p. 20.
35. AN, B133, "Interview with Frank Rockefeller's Daughters."
36. Collier and Horowitz, *The Rockefellers,* p. 14.

CHAPTER 5: THE AUCTION

1. RAC, Inglis interview, p. 1264.
2. *New York Herald,* November 29, 1908.
3. Ibid.
4. *The World Mirror,* January 1909.
5. RAC, Inglis notes, 4.12, "Comments on T J Gallagher."
6. RAC, Inglis interview, p. 389.
7. Ibid., p. 1300.
8. Tarbell, *The History of the Standard Oil Company,* vol. I, p. 42.
9. RAC, Inglis notes, 4.9, "On Early Economies."
10. RAC, Inglis notes, 4.11, "Interview with Mrs. William C. Rudd."
11. Nevins, *Study in Power,* vol. I, p. 33.
12. Ibid.
13. *New York Herald,* November 29, 1908.
14. Tarbell, *History of the Standard Oil Company,* vol. I, p. 43.
15. AN, B130, letter from John D. Rockefeller, Jr., to Allan Nevins, April 9, 1937.
16. RAC, Inglis interview, p. 900.
17. Ibid., p. 96.

18. Weber, *The Protestant Ethic and the Spirit of Capitalism*, p. 69.
19. Dolson, *The Great Oildorado*, p. 43.
20. Cleveland *Plain Dealer*, October 5, 1902.
21. RAC, Inglis interview, p. 1472.
22. Winkelman, *John D. Rockefeller*, p. 42.
23. Dolson, *The Great Oildorado*, p. 31.
24. Ibid., p. 132.
25. Ibid.
26. Winkler, *John D.: A Portrait in Oils*, p. 62.
27. Dolson, *The Great Oildorado*, p. 60.
28. Hawke, *John D.*, p. 27.
29. RAC, III 2.H B2 F11.
30. RAC, Inglis notes, III 2.H B4 F20, p. 5.
31. Nevins, *John D. Rockefeller: The Heroic Age of American Enterprise*, vol. I, p. 133.
32. RAC, Inglis interview, p. 251.
33. RAC, III 2.H B2 F11.
34. Nevins, *John D. Rockefeller*, vol. I, p. 183.
35. RAC, Inglis interview, p. 261.
36. IMT, "Documents to Be Catalogued," letter from J. M. Siddall to Ida Tarbell, October 8, 1903; and B 14/15, "Interview with James Clark."
37. RAC, Inglis notes, III 2.H B4 F20, p. 4.
38. RAC, III 2.H B2 F11.
39. Dolson, *The Great Oildorado*, p. 177.
40. Ibid., pp. 180–81.
41. Nevins, *Study in Power*, vol. I, pp. 34–35.
42. Nevins, *John D. Rockefeller*, vol. I, p. 187.
43. Ibid.
44. Ibid., p. 188.
45. Ibid., p. 189.
46. Ibid.
47. John D. Rockefeller, *Random Reminiscences*, p. 59.
48. Nevins, *John D. Rockefeller*, vol. I, p. 190.
49. Nevins, *Study in Power*, vol. I, p. 36.
50. RAC, Inglis interview, p. 260.
51. Ibid., p. 367.
52. *The New York Times*, March 13, 1915.
53. Ibid.
54. RAC, III 1S B1 F56, letter from Harvey B. Spelman to "Esteemed Cousin," April 6, 1879.
55. *In Memoriam: Mrs. Lucy Henry Spelman*, p. 71.
56. Stasz, *The Rockefeller Women*, p. 46.
57. Collier and Horowitz, *The Rockefellers*, p. 79.
58. Ibid., p. 17.

59. RAC, III 2.Z B21, "Miss Spelman's Recollections."
60. *The New York Times,* March 13, 1915.
61. RAC, III 1. SL B2 F11, "1855 Valedictory Address."
62. Ibid.
63. RAC, III 1.SL B1 F8, letter from Laura Spelman to Mrs. Hawley, May 16, 1858.
64. RAC, III 1.SL B2 F11, unidentified article, March 18, 1859.
65. RAC, III 2.Z B20.
66. RAC, Inglis notes, 4.11.
67. RAC, III 1.SL B1 F8, letter from Laura Spelman to Mrs. Hawley, April 30, 1860.
68. Winkler, *John D.,* p. 68.
69. *The World,* March 1, 1908.
70. Goulder, *John D. Rockefeller,* p. 67.
71. Flynn, *God's Gold,* p. 115.
72. IMT, uncataloged material. Letter from J. M. Siddall to Ida Tarbell, August 6, 1903.

CHAPTER 6: THE POETRY OF THE AGE

1. Mellon, *Thomas Mellon and His Times,* p. 238.
2. Twain and Warner, *The Gilded Age,* p. 87.
3. Rugoff, *America's Gilded Age,* p. 42.
4. Grant, *Personal Memoirs of U.S. Grant,* p. 589.
5. Tarbell, *The History of the Standard Oil Company,* vol. I, p. 131.
6. Dolson, *The Great Oildorado,* p. 138.
7. RAC, Inglis notes, 4.9, "Bad Temper."
8. AN, B120, "Interview with John T. Sencabaugh."
9. RAC, Inglis notes, 4.10, "On Training Executives."
10. Nevins, *Study in Power,* vol. I, pp. 156–57.
11. Dolson, *The Great Oildorado,* p. 99.
12. RAC, Inglis interview, p. 1086.
13. RAC, Inglis notes, 4.10, "H. C. Folger vs. Tarbell."
14. RAC, Inglis notes, 4.9, "Early Standard Oil History."
15. RAC, Inglis interview, p. 1477.
16. Nevins, *John D. Rockefeller: The Heroic Age of American Enterprise,* vol. I, p. 208.
17. RAC, III 1.2 B36 F270.
18. Brady, *Ida Tarbell,* p. 11.
19. Nevins, *John D. Rockefeller,* vol. I, p. 272.
20. John D. Rockefeller, *Random Reminiscences,* p. 59.
21. RAC, Inglis interview, p. 1.
22. AN, B130.
23. Inglis, "Impressions of John D. Rockefeller," p. 22.

24. RAC, III 2.H B2 F11.
25. RAC, Inglis interview, p. 528.
26. Ibid., p. 406.
27. John D. Rockefeller, *Random Reminiscences*, p. 52.
28. RAC, Inglis interview, p. 10.
29. *Boston Herald*, July 3, 1927.
30. Flynn, *Men of Wealth*, p. 73.
31. RAC, Inglis notes, 4.10, "Interview with P. S. Trainor."
32. John D. Rockefeller, *Random Reminiscences*, p. 32.
33. Ibid., p. 52.
34. RAC, Inglis notes, 4.12, "Charles M. Higgins Interview."
35. David Leon Chandler, *Henry Flagler*, p. 18.
36. Ibid.
37. John D. Rockefeller, *Random Reminiscences*, p. 22.
38. David Leon Chandler, *Henry Flagler*, p. 43.
39. Ibid., p. 44.
40. Winkler, *John D.: A Portrait in Oils*, p. 77.
41. *The Cleveland Leader*, March 4 and 5, 1867.
42. *The New York Daily Tribune*, December 23, 1906.
43. John D. Rockefeller, *Random Reminiscences*, p. 22.
44. Ibid., pp. 23–25.
45. RAC, Inglis notes, 4.12, "Charles M. Higgins Interview."
46. David Leon Chandler, *Henry Flagler*, p. 260.
47. RAC, Inglis interview, p. 211.
48. David Leon Chandler, *Henry Flagler*, p. 82.
49. RAC, Inglis interview, pp. 176–77.
50. RAC, III 2.H B2 F11.
51. Hawke, *John D.*, p. 189.
52. *Philadelphia Press*, February 2, 1896.
53. AN, vol. 4, no. 26, B118, letter from Henry M. Flagler to Mr. Rutter, April 30, 1878.
54. RAC, vol. 220, no. 227, letter to Mr. Barstow, April 3, 1907.
55. *McClure's Magazine*, July 1905.
56. Nevins, *John D. Rockefeller*, vol. I, p. 256.
57. AN, B113 F 28, letter to W. H. Thompson, May 2, 1885.
58. RAC, III 1.2 B36 F270, letter to Laura S. Rockefeller, August 19, 1868.
59. *McClure's Magazine*, July 1905.
60. RAC, Inglis interview, p. 3.
61. Nevins, *Study in Power*, vol. I, pp. 93–94.
62. RAC, Inglis interview, p. 1446.
63. *McClure's Magazine*, July 1905.
64. RAC, Inglis interview, p. 1657.
65. Ibid., p. 973.
66. Nevins, *John D. Rockefeller*, vol. I, p. 264.

CHAPTER 7: MILLIONAIRES' ROW

1. Weber, *The Protestant Ethic and the Spirit of Capitalism*, p. 71.
2. RAC, Inglis notes, 4.8, "Mr. Rockefeller's Humor."
3. Goulder, *John D. Rockefeller*, p. 87.
4. RAC, Inglis notes, 4.9, "Cleveland."
5. RAC, Inglis notes, 4.12, "Joe Davidson."
6. RAC, Inglis notes, 4.9, "Rockefeller on Aloofness."
7. John D. Rockefeller, *Random Reminiscences*, p. 32.
8. RAC, Inglis interview, p. 838.
9. RAC, Inglis notes, 4.13, "Golf with Rockefeller."
10. RAC, Inglis notes, 4.12, "Hoster Manuscript," p. 32.
11. AN, B131, "Interview with Aunt Lute."
12. Fosdick, *John D. Rockefeller, Jr.*, p. 9.
13. *Chicago Sunday Tribune*, October 6, 1907.
14. AN, B131, letter from John D. Rockefeller, Jr., to Allan Nevins, January 9, 1937.
15. Collier and Horowitz, *The Rockefellers*, p. 80.
16. *The* Cleveland *Plain Dealer*, February 12, 1922.
17. IMT, unmarked box, "Conversation with Mr. Southard."
18. Flynn, *God's Gold*, p. 232.
19. RAC, III 2.Z B46.
20. *The* Cleveland *Plain Dealer*, February 12, 1922.
21. Ibid.
22. Schenkel, *The Rich Man and the Kingdom*, p. 10.
23. Ibid., p. 11.
24. Manchester, *A Rockefeller Family Portrait*, p. 101.
25. Jones, *The Correspondence of Mother Jones*, p. 138.
26. Manchester, *A Rockefeller Family Portrait*, p. 32.
27. Winkler, *John D.: A Portrait in Oils*, p. 70.
28. Collier and Horowitz, *The Rockefellers*, p. 80.
29. Fosdick, *John D. Rockefeller, Jr.*, p. 14.
30. Stasz, *The Rockefeller Women*, p. 195.

CHAPTER 8: CONSPIRATORS

1. RAC, Inglis interview, pp. 97–98.
2. Ibid., p. 1063.
3. Ibid., p. 96.
4. William H. Allen, *Rockefeller: Giant, Dwarf, Symbol*, p. 230.
5. RAC, Inglis interview, p. 2.
6. Ibid., p. 1647.
7. Nevins, *Study in Power*, vol. I, p. 82.
8. RAC, Inglis interview, p. 1399.
9. IMT, "Documents to Be Catalogued," "Interview with John Prindle."

10. *Columbus* (Ohio) *Dispatch,* November 3, 1918.
11. RAC, Inglis interview, p. 1557.
12. Ibid., p. 460.
13. Tarbell, *The History of the Standard Oil Company,* vol. I, p. 51.
14. Hawke, *John D.,* p. 68.
15. Hidy and Hidy, *History of Standard Oil Company (New Jersey),* p. 27.
16. SOCMB, 1870–1885.
17. Nevins, *John D. Rockefeller: The Heroic Age of American Enterprise,* vol. I, p. 100.
18. Ibid.
19. RAC, Inglis interview, p. 1306.
20. AN, B128.
21. RAC, Inglis interview, p. 15.
22. Flynn, *Men of Wealth,* p. 444.
23. RAC, Inglis interview, p. 19.
24. Nevins, *John D. Rockefeller,* vol. I, p. 321.
25. Ibid., p. 115.
26. RAC, III 1.2 B36 F270, letter to Laura S. Rockefeller, November 30, 1871.
27. Ibid., December 1, 1871.
28. Ibid., January 25, 1872.
29. Ibid., December 1, 1871.
30. Ibid., January 20, 1872.
31. RAC, III 1.2 B36 F270.
32. Hawke, *John D.,* p. 86.
33. Flynn, *God's Gold,* p. 164.
34. RAC, Inglis interview, p. 47.
35. Tarbell, *The History of the Standard Oil Company,* vol. I, p. 71.
36. *The Courier,* February 28, 1872.
37. *Pittsburgh Commercial,* March 1, 1872.
38. Dolson, *The Great Oildorado,* p. 265.
39. Hawke, *John D.,* p. 85.
40. AN, B120, "Interview with Joseph Seep."
41. William H. Allen, *Rockefeller,* p. 30.
42. Tarbell, *All in the Day's Work,* pp. 23–24.
43. RAC, Inglis interview, p. 1369.
44. Ibid., p. 115.
45. *American Magazine,* November 1910.
46. Nevins, *John D. Rockefeller,* vol. I, p. 339.
47. RAC, III 1.2 B36 F270, letter to Laura S. Rockefeller, March 15, 1872.
48. Ibid., March 21, 1872.
49. Ibid., March 22, 1872.
50. Winkler, *John D.: A Portrait in Oils,* p. 98.
51. Tarbell, *The History of the Standard Oil Company,* vol. I, p. 94.
52. Ibid., p. 96.
53. RAC, Inglis interview, p. 203.

54. Nevins, *Study in Power*, vol. I, p. 130.
55. Tarbell, *The History of the Standard Oil Company*, vol. I, p. 65.
56. Nevins, *John D. Rockefeller*, vol. I, p. 384.
57. Goulder, *John D. Rockefeller*, pp. 112, 114.
58. Flynn, *God's Gold*, p. 157.
59. Nevins, *John D. Rockefeller*, vol. I, p. 364.
60. IMT, uncataloged material, letter from J. M. Siddall to Ida Tarbell, October 20, 1902.
61. Tarbell, *The History of the Standard Oil Company*, vol. I, p. 63.
62. IMT, B AB-1, "Interview with J. W. Fawcett."
63. Ibid.
64. IMT, B 1/14 T-082, "J. W. Fawcett interview."
65. RAC, Inglis interview, p. 21.
66. IMT, B AB-1, "Interview with J. W. Fawcett."
67. Tarbell, *The History of the Standard Oil Company*, vol. II, p. 330.
68. Ibid., p. 1037.
69. Nevins, *Study in Power*, vol. I, p. 135.
70. RAC, III 2.H B3 F17.
71. Russell, *Freedom Versus Organization*, p. 317.
72. RAC, III 2.H B2 F11
73. RAC, Inglis interview, p. 30.
74. Nevins, *Study in Power*, vol. I, p. 141.
75. RAC, Inglis interview, p. 319.
76. *The New Yorker*, January 29, 1927.
77. Flynn, *God's Gold*, p. 159.
78. RAC, Inglis interview, p. 1215.
79. Flynn, *God's Gold*, pp. 159–60.
80. IMT, uncataloged material, "Affidavit of John D. Rockefeller," in *Standard Oil v. William S. Scofield et al.*
81. Wilson, *Famous Old Euclid Avenue*, p. 149.
82. RAC, Inglis notes, 4.9, "Genesis of Standard Oil."
83. *The New York Sun*, March 6, 1872.
84. RAC, Inglis interview, p. 559.
85. Ibid., p. 1383.
86. Ibid., p. 50.
87. *The New York Herald*, November 29, 1908.
88. RAC, Inglis interview, p. 1582.
89. Ibid., p. 1210.
90. Ibid., p. 200.
91. Schumpeter, *Capitalism, Socialism and Democracy*, pp. 95, 91.
92. Ibid., p. 88.
93. RAC, III 2.H B9 F37.
94. Flynn, *God's Gold*, p. 401.
95. RAC, Inglis interview, p. 555.
96. Nevins, *John D. Rockefeller*, vol. I, p. 373.

97. RAC, Inglis interview, p. 601.
98. Ibid., p. 299.
99. Ibid., p. 1589.
100. RAC, Inglis notes, 4.12, "Hoster Manuscript," p. 34.
101. RAC, Inglis interview, p. 195.
102. Ibid., p. 274.
103. Ibid., p. 257.
104. Ibid., p. 1217.
105. Ibid., p. 244.

CHAPTER 9: THE NEW MONARCH

1. Tarbell, *The History of the Standard Oil Company*, pp. 104–5.
2. Ibid., pp. 105–6.
3. RAC, Inglis interview, p. 575.
4. Ibid., p. 134.
5. Ibid., pp. 526, 757.
6. Tarbell, *The History of the Standard Oil Company*, p. 125.
7. Nevins, *Study in Power*, vol. I, p. 175.
8. Ibid., p. 99.
9. Flynn, *God's Gold*, p. 174.
10. Winkler, *John D.*, p. 117.
11. Nevins, *Study in Power*, vol. II, p. 16.
12. RAC, 1.2 B71 F528, letter from William G. Warden, November 22, 1884.
13. Nevins, *Study in Power*, vol. I, p. 271.
14. RAC, Inglis interview, p. 388.
15. RAC, 1.2 B63 F468, letter from Charles Pratt, October 4, 1881.
16. RAC, Inglis interview, p. 1611.
17. AN, B130, "Interview with Mr. Ellis."
18. RAC, Inglis interview, p. 1589.
19. Nevins, *Study in Power*, vol. I, p. 118.
20. *The World*, March 31, 1890.
21. Moore, *John D. Archbold*, p. 98.
22. *The Saturday Evening Post*, October 21, 1911.
23. RAC, Inglis interview, p. 348.
24. RAC, 1.2 B51 F377, letter from John D. Archbold, January 23, 1878.
25. Ibid., January 31, 1878.
26. Lloyd, *Wealth Against Commonwealth*, p. 74.
27. Summers, *Johnson Newlon Camden*, p. 174.
28. Ibid., p. 175.
29. RAC, 1.2 B54 F401, letter from J. N. Camden, March 20, 1878.
30. *Forbes*, September 29, 1917.
31. RAC, Inglis notes, 4.12, "Hoster Manuscript," p. 33.
32. RAC, Inglis interview, p. 1031.
33. Ibid., p. 802.

34. *The Atlantic Monthly*, March 1881.
35. RAC, III 2.4 B3 F14.
36. Manning, *The Standard Oil Company*, p. 21.

CHAPTER 10: SPHINX

1. Nevins, *Study in Power*, vol. I, p. 153.
2. *Middletown* (Connecticut) *Press*, April 23, 1922.
3. *The Saturday Evening Post*, October 21, 1911.
4. Ibid., May 23, 1925.
5. Hawke, *John D.*, p. 158.
6. Fosdick, *John D. Rockefeller, Jr.*, p. 190.
7. William H. Allen, *Rockefeller: Giant, Dwarf, Symbol*, p. 201, and Manchester, *A Rockefeller Family Portrait*, p. 70.
8. Manchester, *A Rockefeller Family Portrait*, p. 91.
9. RAC, Inglis notes, 4.8, "Mr. Rockefeller on Concentration."
10. Nevins, *Study in Power*, vol. I, p. 328.
11. *The Saturday Evening Post*, October 21, 1911.
12. Nevins, *Study in Power*, vol. I, p. 154.
13. RAC, III 2.H B9 F37, "Inglis impressions."
14. IMT, "Documents to Be Catalogued," "Interview with John Prindle."
15. AN, B120, "Interview with John T. Sencabaugh."
16. Hawke, *John D.*, p. 44.
17. Lundberg, *The Rockefeller Syndrome*, p. 115.
18. *The Saturday Evening Post*, October 21, 1911.
19. Flynn, *Men of Wealth*, p. 448.
20. AN, B11 F19, letter from John D. Archbold, September 25, 1881.
21. Ibid.
22. AN, B113 F32, letter from F. T. Barstow, September 13, 1886.
23. Nevins, *Study in Power*, vol. I, p. 328.
24. RAC, Inglis notes, 4.9, "How to Develop Executives."
25. Nevins, *Study in Power*, vol. I, p. 327.
26. AN, B126, letter from Frederick T. Gates to William O. Inglis, April 7, 1920.
27. Winkler, *John D.: A Portrait in Oils*, p. 67.
28. Beer, *Hanna*, p. 249.
29. Flynn, *God's Gold*, p. 290.
30. Nevins, *John D. Rockefeller: The Heroic Age of American Enterprise*, vol. I, p. 74.
31. RAC, Inglis notes, 4.8, "Owego."
32. Winkler, *John D.*, p. 67.
33. RAC, Inglis notes, 4.10, "The Red Notebook."
34. Nevins, *Study in Power*, vol. I, p. 281.
35. AN, B129.
36. Moore, *John D. Archbold*, p. 118.
37. Flynn, *God's Gold*, p. 237.

38. *The New York Sun,* November 30, 1878.
39. *Nation's Business,* April 1931.
40. RAC, Inglis interview, p. 1300.
41. Packard, "Informal History of the Standard Oil Company (Ohio)," p. 65.
42. *The New York Herald,* November 29, 1908.

CHAPTER 11: THE HOLY FAMILY

1. *McClure's Magazine,* August 1905.
2. Nevins, *John D. Rockefeller: The Heroic Age of American Enterprise,* vol. II, p. 164.
3. AN, B108 F6, letter to H. M. Sinclair, November 5, 1877.
4. RAC, III 2.Z B20 F3, letter from Laura Spelman Rockefeller to John D. Rockefeller, Jr., August 10, 1909.
5. RAC, III 2.Z B46.
6. RAC, III 2.Z B20, letter from Laura Spelman Rockefeller to John D. Rockefeller, Jr., January 29, 1896.
7. Fosdick, *John D. Rockefeller, Jr.,* p. 30.
8. Ibid., p. 8.
9. RAC, III 2.Z B44, letter from Kate Strong Sewall to John D. Rockefeller, Jr., December 21, 1925.
10. Fosdick, *John D. Rockefeller, Jr.,* pp. 8–9.
11. Manchester, *A Rockefeller Family Portrait,* p. 13.
12. *Middletown* (Connecticut) *Press,* April 23, 1922.
13. AN, B131, "Interview with Dr. Biggar."
14. The Cleveland *Plain Dealer,* February 12, 1922.
15. Reich, *The Life of Nelson A. Rockefeller,* p. 10.
16. Fosdick, *John D. Rockefeller, Jr.,* p. 81.
17. Harr and Johnson, *The Rockefeller Century,* p. 39.
18. The Cleveland *Plain Dealer,* February 12, 1922.
19. RAC, III 2.Z B44.
20. RAC, III 2.Z B46.
21. Nevins, *Study in Power,* vol. I, p. 343.
22. AN, B110 F15, letter to the Reverend J. E. Clough, June 13, 1885.
23. RAC, Inglis notes, 4.12.
24. Russell, *Freedom Versus Organization,* p. 314.
25. Nevins, *John D. Rockefeller,* vol. I, p. 642.
26. *The Dunbar News,* April 23, 1930.
27. The Cleveland *Plain Dealer,* February 12, 1922.
28. Goulder, *John D. Rockefeller,* pp. 104–5.
29. RAC, III 1.S B1 F6, letter from Harvey B. Spelman to Mr. F. Spelman, May 26, 1878.
30. RAC, III 2.Z B21, "Recollections of Father."
31. AN, B110 F15, letter to Eliza Rockefeller, June 8, 1885.

32. Fosdick, *John D. Rockefeller, Jr.*, p. 26.
33. Goulder, *John D. Rockefeller*, p. 21.
34. AN, B128, "Interview with Mr. Murray."
35. RAC, III 1.2 B36 F273, letter from John D. Rockefeller, Jr., to Bessie Otis, October 18, 1890.
36. Nevins, *Study in Power*, vol. I, p. 337.
37. AN, B128, "Interview with James C. Jones."
38. Flynn, *God's Gold*, p. 160.
39. HDL, reel 27, "Frank Rockefeller testimony, 1876, before a House of Commerce Committee."
40. Hawke, *John D.*, p. 201.
41. RAC, Inglis notes, 4.9, "Washington Gladden."
42. Nevins, *John D. Rockefeller*, vol. I, p. 377.
43. IMT, B 1/14 T-082, "Fawcett Interview."
44. Nevins, *Study in Power*, vol. II, p. 71.
45. Tarbell, *The History of the Standard Oil Company*, p. 166.

CHAPTER 12: INSURRECTION IN THE OIL FIELDS

1. RAC, 1.2 B62 F458, letter from Daniel O'Day, October 24, 1879.
2. AN, B127.
3. AN, B133, memo by S.C.T. Dodd.
4. RAC, Inglis notes, 4.11, "Theodore M. Towl."
5. *The New York Sun*, November 30, 1878.
6. Nevins, *Study in Power*, vol. I, p. 297.
7. RAC, Inglis interview, p. 741; Nevins, *Study in Power*, vol. I, p. 235.
8. Winkler, *John D.: A Portrait in Oils*, p. 116.
9. Ibid., pp. 119–20.
10. *The New York Sun*, November 4, 1878.
11. Hawke, *John D.*, p. 111.
12. RAC, Inglis interview, p. 1303.
13. Manchester, *A Rockefeller Family Portrait*, p. 82.
14. AN, B132, "Interview with William M. Potts."
15. Tarbell, *The History of the Standard Oil Company*, p. 194.
16. AN, B108 F3, letter from J. N. Camden to A. C. McGregor, February 17, 1876.
17. AN, B108 F6, letter to J. N. Camden, February 4, 1878.
18. AN, B108 F3, letter from J. N. Camden, July 18, 1876.
19. Ibid., letter from J. N. Camden to A. McDonald, November 28, 1876; Summers, *Johnson Newlon Camden*, p. 181.
20. AN, B128, letter to J. N. Camden, March 11, 1878.
21. RAC, 1.2 B54 F401, letter from J. N. Camden, December 21, 1877.
22. AN, B113 F52, letter from Daniel O'Day to John D. Archbold, August 7, 1886.
23. RAC, 1.2 B62 F459, letter from Daniel O'Day, May 29, 1880.

24. Hawke, *John D.*, p. 128.
25. RAC, 1.2 B54 F461, letter from J. N. Camden to H. M. Flagler, July 17, 1878.
26. RAC, 1.2 B51 F377, letter from John D. Archbold, December 28, 1877.
27. Hawke, *John D.*, p. 129.
28. RAC, 1.2 B62 F458, letter from Daniel O'Day, January 14, 1878.
29. Ibid., letter from Daniel O'Day, March 23, 1878.
30. Beer, *Hanna*, p. 70.
31. AN, B108 F6, letter from H. M. Flagler to J. H. Devereux, December 31, 1877.
32. Akin, *Flagler*, p. 81.
33. AN, B109 F8, letter from H. M. Flagler to H. J. Hewett, April 25, 1878.
34. Ibid., letters from A. N. Cole, March 4 and May 14, 1878.
35. Flynn, *God's Gold*, p. 205.
36. Martin, *Florida's Flagler*, p. 74.
37. Smith, *The Life and Letters of James Abram Garfield*, p. 1025.
38. RAC, 1.2 B62 F458, letter from Daniel O'Day, October 25, 1879.
39. RAC, 1.2 B56 F414, letter from H. M. Flagler, May 10, 1879.
40. Winkler, *John D.*, p. 124.
41. AN, B110 F13, letter to Captain J. J. Vandergrift, December 2, 1879.
42. Nevins, *Study in Power*, vol. I, p. 319.
43. Ibid., vol. I, p. 331.
44. AN, B131, letter from O. H. Payne, March 1, 1879.
45. Ibid., letter to O. H. Payne, March 5, 1879.
46. Wall and Gibb, *Teagle of Jersey Standard*, p. 20.
47. AN, B110 F11, letter to Captain J. J. Vandergrift, May 19, 1879.
48. William H. Allen, *Rockefeller: Giant, Dwarf, Symbol*, p. 141; Nevins, *Study in Power*, vol. I, p. 141.
49. Flynn, *God's Gold*, p. 219.
50. *American Heritage*, December 1964.
51. Flynn, *God's Gold*, p. 218.
52. Winkler, *John D.*, p. 125.
53. Hawke, *John D.*, p. 150.
54. RAC, 1.2 B62 F459, letter from Daniel O'Day, March 11, 1880.

CHAPTER 13: SEAT OF EMPIRE

1. Beer, *Hanna*, p. 124.
2. Hawke, *John D.*, p. 99.
3. Nevins, *Study in Power*, vol. I, p. 323.
4. *The New York Sun*, November 30, 1878.
5. Ibid.
6. *The Boston Herald*, July 3, 1927.
7. RAC, III 2.Z B46.
8. Fosdick, *John D. Rockefeller, Jr.*, p. 34.

9. RAC, III 1.2 B36 F273, letter to John D. Rockefeller, Jr., January 20, 1888.
10. Nevins, *Study in Power,* vol. II, p. 83.
11. *Truth,* July 1891.
12. Collier and Horowitz, *The Rockefellers,* p. 37.
13. *The New York Daily Tribune,* December 23, 1906.
14. Lawson, *Frenzied Finance,* p. 5
15. Nevins, *Study in Power,* vol. II, p. 229.
16. Schreiner, *Henry Clay Frick,* p. 135.
17. *The Saturday Evening Post,* October 21, 1911.
18. Fosdick, *John D. Rockefeller, Jr.,* p. 413; Hawke, *John D.,* p. 171.
19. *Nation's Business,* April 1931.
20. RAC, Inglis notes, 4.10, "Joseph Seep."
21. Nevins, *Study in Power,* vol. II, pp. 30–31.
22. RAC, Inglis interview, p. 1581.
23. John D. Rockefeller, *Random Reminiscences,* p. 13.
24. Nevins, *Study in Power,* vol. I, p. 191.
25. Ibid., p. 388.
26. Carr, *John D. Rockefeller's Secret Weapon,* p. 48.
27. RAC, Inglis interview, pp. 66–67.
28. Nevins, *Study in Power,* vol. I, p. 392.
29. RAC, Inglis interview, p. 1290.
30. Nevins, *John D. Rockefeller: The Heroic Age of American Enterprise,* vol. I, p. 505.
31. Amory, *The Last Resorts,* p. 335.
32. RAC, Inglis notes, 4.13, "Interview Questions 1929."
33. Flynn, *Men of Wealth,* p. 451.
34. Yergin, *The Prize,* p. 36.
35. RAC, Inglis interview, p. 1107.
36. RAC, III 2.H B1 F8, "Taylor History."
37. Nevins, *John D. Rockefeller,* vol. I, pp. 502–3.
38. Cleveland *Plain Dealer,* October 4, 1906.
39. *Leslie's Weekly,* February 2, 1905.
40. Manchester, *A Rockefeller Family Portrait,* p. 84.
41. *Reader's Digest,* April 1927.
42. *The New York Tribune,* n.d. [1906].
43. Schenkel, *The Rich Man and the Kingdom,* p. 14.
44. Innes, *Creating the Commonwealth,* p. 26.
45. Nevins, *Study in Power,* vol. II, p. 91.
46. Fosdick, *John D. Rockefeller, Jr.,* p. 19.
47. Collier and Horowitz, *The Rockefellers,* p. 37.
48. IMT, B 1/14 T-020, letter from Vinnie C. Hicks to Ida Tarbell, June 29, 1905.
49. Nevins, *Study in Power,* vol. II, p. 87.
50. RAC, III 2.Z B46.
51. Fosdick, *John D. Rockefeller, Jr.,* p. 39.

52. RAC, III 2.Z B44, letter from John D. Rockefeller, Jr., to Kate Strong, January 18, 1888.
53. AN, B131, letter from John D. Rockefeller, Jr., to Allan Nevins, January 8, 1937.
54. *The Metropolitan Magazine*, December 1904.
55. AN, B113 F32, letter to Benjamin Brewster, August 3, 1886.
56. AN, B114 F34, letter to George Rogers, June 8, 1887.
57. Ibid.
58. Nevins, *Study in Power*, vol. II, p. 194.
59. Ibid., p. 95.
60. AN, B112 F24, letter to Mr. Dowling, December 1, 1883.
61. AN, B110 F15, letter to Rev. Edward W. Oakes, April 27, 1885.
62. Brumberg, *Mission for Life*, p. 187.
63. Rose, "Why Chicago and Not Cleveland?"
64. AN, B112 F26, letter to Mr. Reynolds, March 8, 1884.
65. Read, *The Story of Spelman College*, p. 64.
66. Fosdick, *John D. Rockefeller, Jr.*, pp. 373–74.
67. AN, B115 F37, letter to Dr. Morehouse, August 25, 1888.
68. RAC, III 1.CO B30 F233, letter from Sophia Packard and Harriet Giles, December 29, 1883.
69. Read, *The Story of Spelman College*, p. 82.
70. Ibid.
71. AN, B110 F15, letter to Dr. Morehouse, April 25, 1885.
72. Rose, "Why Chicago and Not Cleveland?"
73. RAC, III 2.Z B30 F233, letter from S. B. Packard and H. E. Giles, November 7, 1888.

CHAPTER 14: THE PUPPETEER

1. AN, B112 F26, letter to Mr. Barstow, July 12, 1884.
2. Hidy and Hidy, *History of Standard Oil Company (New Jersey)*, pp. 122–23.
3. John D. Rockefeller, *Random Reminiscences*, p. 10.
4. *Business Week*, July 17, 1995.
5. Hidy and Hidy, *History of Standard Oil Company (New Jersey)*, p. 135.
6. John D. Rockefeller, *Random Reminiscences*, p. 10.
7. Nevins, *John D. Rockefeller: The Heroic Age of American Enterprise*, vol. II, p. 184.
8. Hidy and Hidy, *History of Standard Oil Company (New Jersey)*, p. 147.
9. Nevins, *Study in Power*, vol. II, p. 115.
10. RAC, 1.2 B51, letter from John D. Archbold, July 13, 1892.
11. Yergin, *The Prize*, p. 66.
12. RAC, Inglis interview, p. 627.
13. Ibid., p. 582.
14. AN, B117 F68, letter to President Charles Eliot, December 31, 1914.
15. RAC, Inglis interview, p. 992.

16. Ibid., p. 727.
17. AN, B110 F15, letter to A. J. Cassatt, March 29, 1881.
18. RAC, 1.2 B69 F513, letter from W. P. Thompson, February 15, 1886.
19. RAC, 1.2 B69 F570, letter from W. P. Thompson, January 31, 1885.
20. John D. Rockefeller, *Random Reminiscences*, p. 6.
21. AN, B112 F23, letter to Oliver H. Payne, May 3, 1883.
22. *The New York Herald*, December 31, 1906.
23. Yergin, *The Prize*, p. 50.
24. AN, B110 F16, letter to Oliver H. Payne, March 18, 1881.
25. Carr, *John D. Rockefeller's Secret Weapon*, p. 69.
26. Flynn, *God's Gold*, p. 259.
27. RAC, 1.2 B69 F508, letter from W. P. Thompson, May 23, 1881.
28. AN, B128, "Charles M. Higgins interview."
29. RAC, Inglis interview, p. 1409.
30. RAC, 1.2 B69 F508.
31. Ibid., letters from W. P. Thompson, May 23, 1881, and May 15, 1882.
32. RAC, 1.2 B69 F508.
33. AN, B112 F23, letter to O. H. Payne, January 30, 1883.
34. RAC, 1.2 B51 F379, letter from John D. Archbold, December 9, 1891.
35. *The Saturday Evening Post*, October 21, 1911.
36. RAC, Inglis interview, p. 1402.
37. *The Saturday Evening Post*, October 21, 1911.
38. Ibid.
39. AN, B120, "Interview with Joseph Seep."
40. AN, B131, letter to H. C. Folger, September 21, 1885.
41. RAC, Inglis interview, p. 224.
42. Hidy and Hidy, *History of Standard Oil Company (New Jersey)*, p. 194.
43. AN, B133, letter from Henry Demarest Lloyd to George Rice, November 20, 1891.
44. *The Saturday Evening Post*, December 7, 1907.
45. RAC, Inglis interview, p. 1407.
46. RAC, 1.2 B69 F513, letter from W. P. Thompson, February 3, 1886.
47. RAC, Inglis interview, p. 1555.
48. Ibid., p. 531.
49. AN, B110 F15, letter to Colgate Hoyt, July 17, 1882.
50. *The Tribune*, February 28, 1888.
51. Baldwin, *Edison*, p. 137.
52. AN, B115 F37, letter from G. A. Shelby, October 17, 1888.
53. RAC, 1.2 B62 F461, letter from Daniel O'Day, October 16, 1886.
54. AN, B113 F32, letter from Daniel O'Day to Henry M. Flagler, July 7, 1886.
55. AN, B114 F35, letter from Charles Foster, January 4, 1888.
56. Hidy and Hidy, *History of Standard Oil Company (New Jersey)*, p. 213.
57. Tarbell, *The History of the Standard Oil Company*, vol. II, p. 63.
58. RAC, 1.2 B66 F487, letter from anonymous Bradford producer, May 12, 1887.

59. AN, B114 F33, letter from anonymous oil producer, May 12, 1887.
60. AN, B115 F38, letter from P. O. Laughner, June 10, 1888.
61. RAC, Inglis interview, pp. 1210–11.
62. Ibid., p. 181.
63. Fosdick, *John D. Rockefeller, Jr.*, p. 194.
64. AN, B130.
65. RAC, Inglis interview, p. 527.
66. RAC, Inglis notes, 4.8, "Lewis Emery, Jr."
67. Ibid.
68. RAC, 1.2 B51 F379, letter from John D. Archbold, July 13, 1892.
69. Nevins, *John D. Rockefeller*, vol. II, pp. 70–71.
70. RAC, 1.2 B68 F507, letter from W. P. Thompson, November 21, 1879.
71. RAC, Inglis interview, p. 1059.
72. RAC, 1.2 B54 F404, letter from W. H. Tilford, October 15, 1885.
73. Ibid., letter from L. T. Rosengarten to W. H. Tilford, October 10, 1885.
74. *The Atlantic Monthly*, March 1881.
75. Ibid.
76. Ibid.
77. Ibid.
78. Nevins, *Study in Power*, vol. I, p. 333.
79. RAC, Inglis interview, p. 1302.
80. AN, B114 F35, letter to Rev. H. S. Lloyd, March 9, 1888.
81. RAC, Inglis notes, 4.11, "William W. Clark."
82. *The World*, March 29, 1890.
83. *Truth*, July 1891.
84. Packard, "Informal History of the Standard Oil Company (Ohio)," pp. 107, 144.
85. AN, B114 F34, letter from William G. Warden, May 24, 1887.
86. Ibid.
87. RAC, vol. 13, p. 356, letter to William G. Warden, May 31, 1887.

CHAPTER 15: WIDOW'S FUNERAL

1. *The World*, March 1, 1908.
2. Ibid.
3. Ibid.
4. Ibid.
5. Ibid.
6. *The St. Louis Post-Dispatch*, May 30, 1937.
7. *The World*, February 2, 1908.
8. *The World*, March 1, 1908.
9. Ibid.
10. Ibid.
11. Ibid.
12. Ibid.

13. RAC, vol. 19, no. 191, letter to an unnamed cousin, March 28, 1889.
14. RAC, vol. 3, no. 244, letter to Frank Rockefeller, March 30, 1882.
15. RAC, vol. 19, no. 168, letter to Frank Rockefeller, February 10, 1889.
16. RAC, Inglis notes, 4.11, "J. W. Slaght Interview."
17. AN, B115 F38, letter to Uncle Egbert Rockefeller, April 18, 1889.
18. *The St. Louis Post-Dispatch,* May 30, 1937.
19. RAC, III 1.2 B36 F273, letter from John D. Rockefeller, Jr., to Bessie Otis, October 18, 1890.
20. Ibid.
21. RAC, III 2.C B59 F466, letter to Frank Rockefeller, September 28, 1898.
22. RAC, Inglis notes, 4.11, "J. W. Slaght Interview."
23. IMT, T-057, letter from J. M. Siddall to Ida Tarbell, August 6, 1903.
24. IMT, T-054, B1/14, letter from J. M. Siddall to Ida Tarbell, May 2, 1903.
25. RAC, Inglis notes, 4.11, "J. W. Slaght Interview."
26. RAC, Inglis interview, p. 23.
27. AN, B111 F21, letter from Oliver H. Payne, March 15, 1882.
28. AN, B110 F15, letter from Frank Rockefeller, April 3, 1884.
29. AN, B112 F23, letter from Frank Rockefeller, April 8, 1883.
30. AN, B110 F15, letter to Frank Rockefeller, November 18, 1884.
31. RAC, Inglis interview, p. 23.
32. AN, B115 F38, letter from Frank Rockefeller, May 17, 1887.
33. RAC, 1.2 B64 F471, letter from Frank Rockefeller, September 3, 1886.
34. RAC, 1.2 B64 F472, letter from Frank Rockefeller, December 10, 1886.
35. Ibid., letter from Frank Rockefeller, February 19, 1887.
36. Packard, "Informal History of the Standard Oil Company (Ohio)," p. 126.

CHAPTER 16: A MATTER OF TRUST

1. Nevins, *Study in Power,* vol. II, p. 97.
2. RAC, 1.2 B51 F378, letter from John D. Archbold, September 24, 1885.
3. *The New York Herald,* October 15, 1922.
4. RAC, 1.2 B51 F377, letter from John D. Archbold, September 25, 1884.
5. RAC, vol. 191, no. 134, letter to Charles Pratt, September 17, 1888.
6. Packard, "Informal History of the Standard Oil Company (Ohio)," p. 131.
7. RAC, Inglis interview, p. 557.
8. RAC, III 2.H B1 F8, "Taylor History."
9. RAC, Inglis interview, p. 557.
10. *The New York Herald,* May 5, 1891.
11. Nevins, *Study in Power,* vol. II, p. 29.
12. *Collier's,* July 2, 1927.
13. John D. Rockefeller, *Random Reminiscences,* p. 21.
14. AN, B113 F32, letter from Daniel O'Day, July 17, 1886.
15. Hidy and Hidy, *History of Standard Oil Company (New Jersey),* p. 163.
16. Baldwin, *Edison,* p. 48.
17. *The World,* June 6, 1890.

18. Nevins, *Study in Power*, vol. II, p. 100.
19. Ibid., p. 101.
20. Hidy and Hidy, *History of Standard Oil Company (New Jersey)*, p. 165.
21. RAC, 1.2 B51 F379, letter from John D. Archbold, December 9, 1881.
22. Swanberg, *Whitney Father, Whitney Heiress*, p. 79.
23. Ibid., p. 53.
24. Nevins, *John D. Rockefeller: The Heroic Age of American Enterprise*, vol. II, p. 103.
25. Swanberg, *Whitney Father, Whitney Heiress*, p. 39.
26. Swanberg, *Pulitzer*, p. 89.
27. AN, B110 F15.
28. Swanberg, *Whitney Father, Whitney Heiress*, p. 79.
29. RAC, vol. 232, no. 166, letter to H. C. Folger, October 24, 1910.
30. RAC, 1.2 B54 F403, letter from J. N. Camden to H. M. Flagler, January 17, 1881.
31. Ibid., January 29, 1881.
32. Ibid., March 16, 1882.
33. *The World*, May 19, 1887.
34. Moore, *John D. Archbold*, p. 109.
35. Cleveland *Plain Dealer*, July 7, 1907.
36. Nevins, *Study in Power*, vol. II, p. 61.
37. RAC, 1.2 B69 F513, letter from W. P. Thompson, April 27, 1886.
38. RAC, 1.2 B69 F570, letter from W. P. Thompson, January 26, 1888.
39. RAC, Inglis interview, p. 861.
40. William H. Allen, *Rockefeller: Giant, Dwarf, Symbol*, p. 144.
41. Flynn, *God's Gold*, pp. 283–84.
42. Hidy and Hidy, *History of Standard Oil Company (New Jersey)*, p. 214.
43. Lloyd, *Wealth Against Commonwealth*, p. 28.
44. RAC, Inglis interview, pp. 69–70.
45. *The New York Herald Tribune*, March 17, 1940.
46. RAC, Inglis interview, p. 861.
47. William H. Allen, *Rockefeller*, p. 224.
48. Nevins, *John D. Rockefeller*, vol. II, p. 123.
49. Tarbell, *The History of the Standard Oil Company*, vol. II, p. 131.
50. Nevins, *Study in Power*, vol. II, p. 223.
51. Hidy and Hidy, *History of Standard Oil Company (New Jersey)*, pp. 206–7.
52. RAC, 1.2 B51 F378, letter from John D. Archbold, August 15, 1888.
53. AN, B113 F28, letter from M. A. Hanna, August 31, 1885.
54. *The New York Weekly World*, April 2, 1890.

CHAPTER 17: CAPTAINS OF ERUDITION

1. AN, B115 F38, letter to Mr. Potter, n.d.
2. *The Philadelphia Press*, December 22, 1906.
3. Gates, *Chapters in My Life*, p. 161.

4. Nevins, *Study in Power,* vol. II, p. 156.
5. Cleveland *Plain Dealer,* October 7, 1906.
6. RAC, vol. 13, no. 347.
7. Sandage, "I Do So Long to Save My Husband," p. 2.
8. John D. Rockefeller, *Random Reminiscences,* p. 109.
9. AN, B111 F21, letter to Mr. Edward Judson, November 29, 1892.
10. Gates, *Chapters in My Life,* p, 312.
11. Nevins, *Study in Power,* vol. I, p. 342.
12. UC–JDR, B1 F2, letter from Dr. Augustus H. Strong, November 26, 1887.
13. IMT, B 1/14, letter from V. C. Hicks to Ida Tarbell, June 29, 1905.
14. McCormick, *George Santayana,* p. 283.
15. Ibid.
16. Wacker, *Augustus H. Strong,* p. 84.
17. Ibid., p. 101.
18. AN, B130, letter from Dr. Augustus Strong, January 4, 1887.
19. Ibid., editorial note from T. W. Goodspeed.
20. McCormick, *George Santayana,* p. 282.
21. Santayana, *The Letters of George Santayana,* p. 22.
22. UC–JDR, B1 F2, letter from Dr. Augustus H. Strong, November 26, 1887.
23. Ibid., letter from W. R. Harper, January 11, 1887.
24. John D. Rockefeller, *Random Reminiscences,* pp. 112, 116.
25. *The New York Tribune,* September 21, 1890.
26. AN, B130, letter from William Rainey Harper to T.W. Goodspeed, November 7, 1887.
27. AN, B115, letter to Rev. D. W. Hulburt, July 30, 1888.
28. AN, B113 F31, letter to W. H. Doan, March 12, 1886.
29. RAC–FTG, B4 F80, letter from Frederick T. Gates to H. L. Morehouse, October 9, 1888.
30. Nevins, *Study in Power,* vol. II, p. 170.
31. RAC, Inglis notes, "Hoster Manuscript," p. 54.
32. Ibid.
33. AN, B130, letter from W. R. Harper to T. W. Goodspeed, November 5, 1888.
34. Storr, *Harper's University,* p. 28.
35. Gates, *Chapters in My Life,* p. 107.
36. Ibid.
37. Ibid., p. 106.
38. RAC–FTG, B3 F57.
39. Lloyd, *Wealth Against Commonwealth,* p. 123.
40. Nevins, *John D. Rockefeller: The Heroic Age of American Enterprise,* vol. II, p. 228.
41. RAC–FTG, B4 F80, letter from F. T. Gates to Dr. Augustus Strong, November 18, 1890.
42. AN, B125, Frederick T. Gates, autobiography manuscript, p. 211.
43. Jonas, *The Circuit Riders,* p. 17.
44. Nevins, *Study in Power,* vol. II, pp. 92–93.

45. AN, B117 F59, letter from F. T. Gates, April 24, 1905.
46. RAC, Inglis notes, 4.13, "Interview Questions 1929."
47. *Forbes*, September 29, 1917.
48. John D. Rockefeller, *Random Reminiscences*, p. 119.
49. Nevins, *Study in Power*, vol. II, p. 181.
50. AN, B130, letter from F. T. Gates to T. W. Goodspeed, January 9, 1915.
51. Nevins, *John D. Rockefeller*, vol. II, p. 220.
52. AN, B130, letter from T. W. Goodspeed to W. R. Harper, January 22, 1889.
53. Storr, *Harper's University*, p. 24.
54. AN, B115 F37, letter to W. R. Harper, January 15, 1889.
55. AN, B130, letter to W. R. Harper, January 11, 1889.
56. UC–JDR, B1 F11, letter of August 6, 1890.
57. Storr, *Harper's University*, p. 47.
58. UC–JDR, B1 F10, letter from W. R. Harper, June 13, 1890.
59. Ibid., letter from F. T. Gates, July 29, 1891.
60. RAC–FTG, B4 F80, letter from F. T. Gates to W. R. Harper, April 27, 1891.
61. Ibid., letter from F. T. Gates to Dr. Stephens, January 10, 1891.
62. RAC–FTG, B4 F80, letter from F. T. Gates to W. R. Harper, April 27, 1891.
63. *The World*, June 14, 1925.
64. AN, B115 F38, letter to Mr. Severance, June 14, 1889.
65. *The New York Times*, May 24, 1937.
66. Storr, *Harper's University*, p. 31.
67. Brown, *Rockefeller Medicine Men*, p. 35.
68. RAC–FTG, B4 F80, letter from F. T. Gates, June 30, 1892.
69. Cleveland *Plain Dealer*, October 7, 1906.
70. RAC, III 2.Z B21, letter to John D. Rockefeller, Jr., June 11, 1891.
71. AN, B132, letter to J. D. Archbold, June 17, 1891.
72. AN, B130, letter from F. T. Gates to T. W. Goodspeed, February 23, 1892.
73. John D. Rockefeller, *Random Reminiscences*, p. 88.
74. UC–JDR, B11 F6, letter from W. R. Harper, May 7, 1892.
75. Gates, *Chapters in My Life*, p. 193.
76. *The Chicago Times Herald*, November 3, 1895.
77. Ibid.
78. Destler, *Henry Demarest Lloyd*, p. 370.
79. AN, B130, letter from F. T. Gates to W. R. Harper, May 29, 1893.
80. RAC, III 2.Z B21, and *The Dial*, July 16, 1896.
81. Collier and Horowitz, *The Rockefellers*, p. 50.
82. RAC, vol. 217, no. 423, letter to Frederick T. Gates, April 14, 1905.
83. RAC, Inglis interview, p. 1664.
84. Ibid., p. 1259.
85. Flynn, *God's Gold*, p. 308.
86. AN, B128, "Interview with Mr. Murray."
87. RAC–FTG, B2 F30, letter from F. T. Gates to Dr. Harry Pratt Judson, April 6, 1908.

88. Storr, *Harper's University*, p. 268.
89. Gates, *Chapters in My Life*, p. 265.

CHAPTER 18: NEMESIS

1. AN, B115 F41, letter from Frank Rockefeller, May 8, 1890.
2. Carr, *John D. Rockefeller's Secret Weapon*, p. 82.
3. Nevins, *Study in Power*, vol. II, p. 230.
4. AN, B116 F43, letter from M. A. Hanna, April 7, 1891.
5. Flynn, *God's Gold*, p. 301.
6. Burr, *The Portrait of a Banker*, p. 119.
7. Hidy and Hidy, *History of Standard Oil Company (New Jersey)*, p. 648.
8. RAC, Inglis interview, p. 121.
9. Moody, *The Masters of Capital*, p. 58.
10. Hawke, *John D.*, p. 200.
11. AN, B126, letter to Laura S. Rockefeller, September 2, 1893.
12. RAC, Inglis notes, 4.9, "Help to End Panics."
13. Flynn, *God's Gold*, p. 326.
14. Ibid., and Burr, *The Portrait of a Banker*, p. 117.
15. Nevins, *John D. Rockefeller: The Heroic Age of American Enterprise*, vol. II,
    p. 586.
16. Destler, *Henry Demarest Lloyd*, p. 292.
17. Ibid., p. 295.
18. HDL, reel 8, letter from Robert Louis Stevenson to Mr. Iles, December 14,
    1887.
19. Wiebe, *The Search for Order*, p. 64.
20. AN, B133, letter from H. D. Lloyd to H. M. Hyndman, January 14, 1895.
21. Destler, *Henry Demarest Lloyd*, p. 238.
22. RAC, Inglis notes, 4.10, "Interview with Dr. H. A. Cuppy."
23. Destler, *Henry Demarest Lloyd*, p. 248.
24. HDL, reel 27.
25. AN, B131, letter from H. D. Lloyd to Samuel Jones, August 7, 1899.
26. Destler, *Henry Demarest Lloyd*, p. 454.
27. Ibid., p. 9.
28. Ibid., p. 170.
29. HDL, reel 8, letter from H. D. Lloyd to Mrs. Ford, September 8, 1896.
30. Yergin, *The Prize*, p. 103.
31. AN, B130, letter from W. D. Howells to H. D. Lloyd, November 2, 1894.
32. *The American Historical Review*, April 1945.
33. RAC, Inglis interview, p. 1237.
34. HDL, reel 8, letter from H. D. Lloyd to Mrs. Ford, September 8, 1896.
35. RAC–FTG, B3 F57, "The Secret of Mr. Rockefeller's Character and Success."
36. AN, B116 F50, letter to J. D. Archbold, June 4, 1896.
37. AN, B126, letter to Cyrus McCormick, September 20, 1897.

38. William H. Allen, *Rockefeller: Giant, Dwarf, Symbol*, p. 44.
39. Akin, *Flagler*, p. 255.
40. *The New York Daily Tribune*, December 23, 1906.
41. Chandler, *Henry Flagler*, p. 99.
42. Winkler, *John D.: A Portrait in Oils*, p. 241.
43. RAC, 1.2 B56 F416, letter from H. M. Flagler, March 8, 1889.
44. AN, B130, letter to W. R. Harper, February 28, 1898.
45. RAC, III 2.Z B20, letter from Laura S. Rockefeller to John D. Rockefeller, Jr., August 28, 1900.

CHAPTER 19: THE DAUPHIN

1. Fosdick, *John D. Rockefeller, Jr.*, p. 45.
2. Harr and Johnson, *The Rockefeller Century*, p. 47, and RAC, III 2.Z B46.
3. AN, B133.
4. RAC, III 2.Z B49 F24, "Profit Sharing as a Remedy for Industrial Ills," by John D. Rockefeller, Jr.
5. HDL, reel 10, letter from Henry Demarest Lloyd to Morley Roberts, August 23, 1899.
6. Ernst, *"Dear Father"/"Dear Son,"* p. 11.
7. RAC, III 1.2 B36 F273, letter to John D. Rockefeller, Jr., September 27, 1893.
8. Fosdick, *John D. Rockefeller, Jr.*, p. 51.
9. Ibid., p. 41.
10. RAC, III 2.Z B44, letter from William B. Peck to Charles Towne, April 9, 1953.
11. RAC, III 2.Z B49 F25.
12. RAC, III 2.Z B44, "The College Career of Johnny Rock," by Charles Towne.
13. Fosdick, *John D. Rockefeller, Jr.*, p. 75.
14. Ibid., p. 64.
15. Ibid., p. 61.
16. Collier and Horowitz, *The Rockefellers*, p. 85.
17. RAC, III 2.Z B46.
18. *McClure's Magazine*, February 24, 1905.
19. Reich, *The Life of Nelson A. Rockefeller*, p. 4.
20. *Time*, September 24, 1956.
21. Ernst, *"Dear Father"/"Dear Son,"* pp. 14–15.
22. Ibid., p. 16.
23. Ibid., p. 81.
24. RAC, III 2.Z B20, letter from Laura S. Rockefeller to John D. Rockefeller, Jr., June 28, 1897.
25. RAC, III 2.Z B46.
26. Nevins, *Study in Power*, vol. II, p. 214.
27. Fosdick, *John D. Rockefeller, Jr.*, p. 83.
28. RAC, III 2.Z B49 F25, "Interview with Charles O. Heydt."

29. Manchester, *A Rockefeller Family Portrait*, p. 107.
30. Fosdick, *John D. Rockefeller, Jr.*, p. 90.
31. Nevins, *Study in Power*, vol. II, p. 215.
32. Ibid.
33. Ibid., p. 89.
34. RAC, III 2.Z B20, letter from Laura S. Rockefeller to John D. Rockefeller, Jr., October 3, 1897.
35. Ibid., letter from Laura S. Rockefeller to John D. Rockefeller, Jr., July 23, 1899.
36. RAC, III 2.Z B46.
37. Fosdick, *John D. Rockefeller, Jr.*, p. 100.
38. Kert, *Abby Aldrich Rockefeller*, p. 77.
39. Fosdick, *John D. Rockefeller, Jr.*, p. 100.
40. Kert, *Abby Aldrich Rockefeller*, p. 79.
41. Ibid., p. 3.
42. RAC, 2.Z B49 F23, letter from Abby Aldrich Rockefeller to Lucy Green, March 24, 1915.
43. *The Oakland Enquirer*, August 27, 1901.
44. *Town Topics*, August 24, 1901.
45. Aldrich, *Old Money*, p. 24.
46. AN, B130.

CHAPTER 20: THE STANDARD OIL CROWD

1. Harr and Johnson, *The Rockefeller Century*, p. 164.
2. Fosdick, *The Story of the Rockefeller Foundation*, p. 1.
3. Gates, *Chapters in My Life*, p. 15.
4. Ibid., p. 16.
5. Ibid., p. 74.
6. RAC, III 2.Z B46.
7. Jonas, *The Circuit Riders*, pp. 24–25.
8. RAC–FTG, B3 F57, letter from F. T. Gates, January 18, 1892.
9. RAC–FTG, B3 F62, speech given at the tenth anniversary of the RIMR.
10. Goulder, *John D. Rockefeller*, p. 174.
11. RAC–FTG, B3 F57, F. T. Gates memo of December 31, 1926.
12. RAC, III 2.Z B46.
13. Gates, *Chapters in My Life*, p. 240.
14. Ibid., p. 241.
15. AN, B130, quoted in a letter from F. T. Gates to W. R. Harper, November 30, 1889.
16. Manchester, *A Rockefeller Family Portrait*, p. 109.
17. Gates, *Chapters in My Life*, p. 210.
18. Nevins, *Study in Power*, vol. II, p. 293.
19. AN, B122, "Everett Colby interview."
20. Gates, *Chapters in My Life*, p. 160.

21. Storr, *Harper's University,* p. 135.
22. RAC–FTG, B4 F80, letter from F. T. Gates to Brother Sunderland, April 20, 1891.
23. RAC–FTG, B1 F14, letter from F. T. Gates, January 2, 1924.
24. Gates, *Chapters in My Life,* p. 163.
25. Flynn, *God's Gold,* p. 131.
26. Gates, *Chapters in My Life,* p. 168.
27. Ibid., p. 169.
28. Ibid., p. 173.
29. AN, B116 F46A, letter from George Rogers, July 25, 1893.
30. Gates, *Chapters in My Life,* p. 240.
31. AN, B117 F66, letter from F. T. Gates to A. S. Ochs, January 18, 1912.
32. *The New York Daily Tribune,* February 17, 1907.
33. RAC, vol. 215, no. 266.
34. AN, B128, "Interview with Starr Murphy."
35. AN, B116 F50, letter from F. T. Gates to W. W. Huntington, June 6, 1896.
36. Gates, *The Truth About Mr. Rockefeller and the Merritts,* p. 16.
37. AN, B130, "Interview with Henry Cooper."
38. AN, B117 F67, letter from John D. Rockefeller, Jr., October 23, 1913.
39. RAC–FTG, B3 F57, letter from F. T. Gates, May 6, 1907.
40. AN, B117 F65, letter to John D. Rockefeller, Jr., January 31, 1911.
41. AN, B117 F67, letter to Bertram Cutler, December 31, 1913.
42. RAC–FTG, B3 F49, "Frederick T. Gates Speech in 1911 to the Missouri Pacific Board."
43. Henry Clews, *50 Years on Wall Street,* pp. 745–46.
44. RAC, Inglis notes, 4.12, "Hoster Manuscript," p. 46.
45. Fosdick, *John D. Rockefeller, Jr.,* p. 90.
46. RAC, Inglis interview, p. 993.
47. AN, B126, "Interview with William T. Sheppard."
48. RAC, B114 F33, letter to William Rockefeller, March 26, 1887.
49. AN, B130.
50. RAC, 1.2 B56 F416, letter from H. M. Flagler, February 7, 1897.
51. Nevins, *Study in Power,* vol. II, pp. 285–86.
52. Elmer, *Cinderella Rockefeller,* p. 4.
53. Ibid.
54. AN, B116 F55, letter to John D. Rockefeller, Jr., August 26, 1901.
55. RAC, Inglis notes, 4.12, "Hoster Manuscript," p. 47.
56. AN, B128, "Interview with C. M. Higgins."
57. *The Evening Post,* May 19, 1909.
58. Lawson, *Frenzied Finance,* dedication.
59. Ibid., pp. 294, vi.
60. Ibid., p. 35.
61. Ibid.
62. Ibid., p. 347.

63. Ibid., p. 291.
64. AN, B116 F58, letter from John D. Rockefeller, Jr., July 26, 1904.
65. RAC, Inglis notes, 4.8, "Miss Tarbell, etc."
66. AN, B126, "Interview with William T. Sheppard."
67. Flynn, God's Gold, p. 335.
68. Twain, The Autobiography of Mark Twain, p. 258.
69. Ibid., p. 257.
70. Twain, Mark Twain's Correspondence with Henry Huttleston Rogers, p. 5.
71. Kaplan, Mr. Clemens and Mark Twain, p. 323.
72. Twain, Mark Twain's Correspondence with Henry Huttleston Rogers, p. 466.
73. Twain, Mark Twain in Eruption, p. 83.
74. Ibid., p. 99.
75. Lash, Helen and Teacher, p. 209.
76. Ibid., p. 210.
77. Ibid., p. 355.
78. Ibid., p. 588.
79. AN, B130, "Interview with Charles Schwab."
80. John D. Rockefeller, Random Reminiscences, p. 80.
81. HDL, reel 27, "Opening Statement of Henry E. Harris in Alfred Merritt vs. John D. Rockefeller."
82. AN, B126, letter to Laura S. Rockefeller, September 2, 1893.
83. John D. Rockefeller, Random Reminiscences, p. 80.
84. AN, B116 F49.
85. Ibid.
86. AN, B116 F46a, letter from Frederick T. Gates to Frank Rockefeller, April 7, 1893.
87. John D. Rockefeller, Random Reminiscences, p. 85.
88. Nevins, Study in Power, vol. II, p. 262.
89. Wall, Andrew Carnegie, p. 600.
90. William H. Allen, Rockefeller: Giant, Dwarf, Symbol, p. 274.
91. Wall, Andrew Carnegie, p. 170.
92. Schreiner, Henry Clay Frick, p. 134.
93. AN, B132, letter to F. Barstow, July 21, 1896.
94. Schreiner, Henry Clay Frick, p. 146.
95. Lyon, Success Story, p. 175.
96. Ibid., p. 176.
97. Chernow, The House of Morgan, pp. 103–4.
98. Nevins, Study in Power, vol. II, pp. 268–69.
99. Allen, The Great Pierpont Morgan, p. 143.
100. Flynn, God's Gold, p. 350.
101. Nevins, Study in Power, vol. II, p. 269.
102. Fosdick, John D. Rockefeller, Jr., p. 105.
103. Nevins, Study in Power, vol. II, p. 270.
104. Ibid.

105. RAC, III 2.Z B20, letter from Laura S. Rockefeller to John D. Rockefeller, Jr., March 5, 1901.
106. AN, B126, "Interview with William Sheppard."
107. Nevins, *Study in Power,* vol. II, p. 271.
108. Schreiner, *Henry Clay Frick,* p. 188.
109. AN, B116 F55, letter from John D. Rockefeller, Jr., March 12, 1901.
110. Ibid., March 16, 1901.
111. Ibid., March 15, 1901.
112. Nevins, *Study in Power,* vol. II, p. 274.
113. AN, B117 F60.
114. AN, B120.
115. RAC, 2.C B60 F470, memo of George Rogers, October 20, 1894.
116. Ibid., letter to Stevenson Burke, November 19, 1894.
117. IMT, B 4/14 T-298, "Notes on Interview with Frank Rockefeller."
118. AN, B116 F49, letter to James Corrigan, April 24, 1895.
119. Nevins, *Study in Power,* vol. II, p. 416.
120. RAC, III 2.C B59 F464, "Memo of February 29, 1896."
121. RAC, Inglis interview, p. 24.
122. Winkler, *John D.: A Portrait in Oils,* p. 66.
123. RAC, III 2.C B60 F468, letter to William Rockefeller, September 20, 1901.
124. Hawke, *John D.,* p. 204.

CHAPTER 21: THE ENTHUSIAST

1. *The New Era,* June 11, 1897.
2. RAC, Inglis interview, p. 1615.
3. *McClure's Magazine,* August 1905.
4. *Middletown* (Connecticut) *Press,* April 3, 1922.
5. RAC–FTG, B3 F57, "The Secret of Mr. Rockefeller's Character and Success."
6. *Middletown* (Connecticut) *Press,* April 3, 1922.
7. RAC, III 2.H B3 F15, "Interview with Elias M. Johnson."
8. Ibid.
9. Manchester, *A Rockefeller Family Portrait,* p. 133.
10. RAC, III 2.H F18, "Golf with John D. Rockefeller."
11. RAC, Inglis notes, 4.13, "Golf with Rockefeller."
12. *Memphis* (Tennessee) *Commercial Appeal,* October 21, 1918.
13. RAC, vol. 214, no. 98.
14. AN, B126, letter to Laura S. Rockefeller, September 2, 1893.
15. RAC–FTG, B3 F57, "The Secret of Mr. Rockefeller's Character and Success."
16. John D. Rockefeller, *Random Reminiscences,* p. 34.
17. AN, B126, letter from John D. Rockefeller, Jr., to Everett Colby, September 24, 1900.
18. Nevins, *Study in Power,* vol. II, p. 293.
19. RAC, vol. 212, no. 472, letter to Laura Rudd, November 29, 1904.
20. AN, B117 F60, expense account, January–February 1906.

21. Veblen, *The Theory of the Leisure Class*, p. 37.
22. John D. Rockefeller, *Random Reminiscences*, p. 37.
23. Nevins, *Study in Power*, vol. II, p. 291.
24. Winkler, *John D.: A Portrait in Oils*, p. 228.
25. AN, B132, letter from George D. Rogers to Laura S. Rockefeller, March 11, 1892.
26. Ernst, *"Dear Father"/"Dear Son,"* pp. 86–87.
27. RAC, Inglis interview, p. 1414.
28. Fosdick, *John D. Rockefeller, Jr.*, p. 116.
29. Biggar, *Compiègne and Personal Reminiscences*, p. 97.
30. RAC–FTG, B1 F21, letter from Charles Eliot to Frederick T. Gates, December 23, 1910.
31. *The New York Herald*, October 3, 1907.
32. RAC, Inglis notes, 4.14, "Ira Warner Memo."
33. Ernst, *"Dear Father"/"Dear Son,"* p. 139.
34. RAC, Inglis notes, 4.8, "Miss Tarbell, etc."
35. RAC, Inglis notes, 4.9, "Bad Temper."
36. RAC, vol. 213, no. 307, letter to Watson Van Duyne, March 27, 1905.
37. Ernst, *"Dear Father"/"Dear Son,"* p. 23.
38. RAC, vol. 217, no. 355, letter to George Rogers, March 31, 1906.
39. Winkler, *John D.: A Portrait in Oils*, p. 23.
40. RAC, Inglis interview, p. 1267.
41. RAC, vol. 213, no. 307, letter to Watson Van Duyne, March 27, 1905.
42. RAC, III 2.Z B22, John D. Rockefeller, Jr., quoted in an Associated Press article, attached to a letter from John D. Rockefeller, Jr., May 15, 1935.
43. RAC, vol. 235, no. 464, letter to Dr. Henry Moeller, November 15, 1911.
44. RAC, III 1 SL B2 F10, Laura S. Rockefeller diary, March 1901.
45. AN, B133.
46. *McClure's Magazine*, August 1905.
47. RAC, vol. 216, letter to Edith Rockefeller McCormick, November 1, 1905.
48. RAC, Inglis notes, 4.12, "Hoster Manuscript," pp. 31–32.
49. AN, B130, letter from Laura S. Rockefeller to W. R. Harper, September 24, 1892.
50. RAC, III 1 3L B2 F10, Laura S. Rockefeller diary, April 1904.
51. RAC, III 2.A B32 F250, letter from Edith Rockefeller McCormick, March 14, 1915.
52. AN, B128, "Interview with H. V. Sims."
53. Ibid.
54. Ibid., letter from John D. Rockefeller, Jr., to Allan Nevins, February 8, 1940.
55. RAC, III 2.Z B20, letter from Laura S. Rockefeller to John D. Rockefeller, Jr., June 17, 1895.
56. Fosdick, *John D. Rockefeller, Jr.*, p. 58.
57. RAC–CAS, II, letter from Charles A. Strong to William James, December 6, 1895.
58. Elizabeth de Cuevas, interview with author.

59. RAC, vol. 219, no. 6, letter to Reverend Charles Aked, February 18, 1907.
60. Flynn, *God's Gold*, p. 450.
61. William James, *Selected Unpublished Correspondence*, p. 382, letter from William James to Macmillan Company, October 22, 1901.
62. RAC–CAS.
63. William James, *The Letters of William James*, vol. II, p. 229, letter from William James to his wife, May 13, 1905.
64. Lewis, *The Jameses*, p. 545.
65. William James, *The Correspondence of William James*, vol. III, p. 225, letter from William to Henry James, January 29, 1904.
66. AN, B131, letter from William James, June 1, 1909.
67. RAC, III 2.2 B49 F23, letter from Bessie Strong to John D. Rockefeller, Jr., March 12, 1904.
68. RAC–CAS, II, letter from Charles A. Strong to William James, October 1903.
69. McCormick, *George Santayana*, p. 553.
70. Ibid.
71. Lewis, *The Jameses*, p. 546.
72. *The Chicago Daily News*, March 12, 1931.
73. RAC, III 2.Z B49 F23, letter from Harold McCormick, September 28, 1895.
74. *The New York Evening Journal*, August 31, 1932.
75. Stasz, *The Rockefeller Women*, p. 137.
76. RAC, vol. 223, no. 102, letter to Harold McCormick, April 20, 1908.
77. *The New York Evening Journal*, August 31, 1932.
78. Ibid.
79. RAC, III 2.Z B49 F23, letter from Edith Rockefeller McCormick, October 11, 1905.
80. RAC, vol. 215, no. 462, letter to Cyrus McCormick, October 17, 1905.
81. AN, B116 F56, letter from John D. Rockefeller, Jr., November 19, 1902.
82. AN, B116 F57, letter from John D. Rockefeller, Jr., January 26, 1903.
83. RAC, III 2.A B33 F253, letter from Harold McCormick, January 10, 1919.
84. AN, B117 F64, letter from Frederick T. Gates, November 11, 1910.
85. RAC, III 2.Z B49 F23, letter from Alta Rockefeller to John D. Rockefeller, Jr., November 2, 1889.
86. RAC, III 2.Z B49 F25.
87. RAC, III 1 SL B2 F10, Laura S. Rockefeller diary, July 1912.
88. AN, B122, "Talk with Everett Colby."
89. RAC, III 2.Z B20, quoted in letter from John D. Rockefeller, Jr., to Laura S. Rockefeller, June 25, 1895.
90. RAC, III 2.Z B49 F23, letter from Alta Rockefeller to John D. Rockefeller, Jr., March 31, 1900.
91. Kert, *Abby Aldrich Rockefeller*, pp. 76–77.
92. Stasz, *The Rockefeller Women*, p. 156.
93. RAC, R62 B31 F237, letter from Alta Rockefeller, February 4, 1915.

94. RAC, III 2.Z B49 F23, letter from Harold McCormick, April 25, 1915.

95. RAC, III 2.A B32 F250.

CHAPTER 22: AVENGING ANGEL

1. *The World,* October 12, 1898.

2. Ibid.

3. RAC, Inglis interview, pp. 1463, 1624.

4. *The World,* October 13, 1898, and *The New York Herald,* October 13, 1898.

5. *The New York Herald,* March 18, 1899.

6. Ibid.

7. Bringhurst, *Antitrust and the Oil Monopoly,* p. 26.

8. AN, B132, letter from Frank Monnett to Henry Demarest Lloyd, January 19, 1899.

9. Bringhurst, *Antitrust and the Oil Monopoly,* p. 27.

10. Manning, *The Standard Oil Company,* p. 20.

11. AN, B117 F61, letter to Harold McCormick, June 29, 1907.

12. Yergin, *The Prize,* p. 121.

13. Ibid., p. 89.

14. AN, B126, letter to Andrew White, November 28, 1900.

15. RAC, Inglis interview, p. 1115.

16. Miller, *Theodore Roosevelt,* p. 147.

17. Bringhurst, *Antitrust and the Oil Monopoly,* p. 121.

18. Chandler, *Henry Flagler,* p. 236.

19. Bringhurst, *Antitrust and the Oil Monopoly,* p. 123.

20. Pringle, *Theodore Roosevelt,* p. 227.

21. Chandler, *Henry Flagler,* p. 236.

22. Flynn, *God's Gold,* p. 381.

23. Bringhurst, *Antitrust and the Oil Monopoly,* p. 129.

24. RAC, III 2.Z B46, "Interview with John D. Rockefeller, Jr."

25. Fosdick, *John D. Rockefeller, Jr.,* p. 415.

26. Pringle, *Theodore Roosevelt,* p. 350.

27. AN, B126, letter to Mr. Baer, May 14, 1900.

28. Tarbell, *All in the Day's Work,* p. 203.

29. Ibid.

30. Ibid., p. 24.

31. Ibid., p. 83.

32. Ibid., p. 99.

33. Brady, *Ida Tarbell,* p. 91.

34. *The World,* n.d. [1905].

35. Lyon, *Success Story,* p. 146.

36. Ibid., p. 117.

37. Ibid., p. 199.

38. Ibid., p. 152.

39. Steffens, *The Autobiography of Lincoln Steffens*, p. 361.
40. Ibid., pp. 392–93.
41. Tarbell, *The History of the Standard Oil Company*, p. ix.
42. IMT, "Documents to Be Catalogued," letter from W. W. Tarbell to Ida Tarbell, April 14, 1893.
43. Tarbell, *All in the Day's Work*, p. 45.
44. Ibid., p. 207.
45. Brady, *Ida Tarbell*, p. 123.
46. Ibid., p. 129.
47. Ibid., p. 130.
48. Destler, *Henry Demarest Lloyd*, p. 353.
49. Brady, *Ida Tarbell*, p. 132.
50. Twain, *Mark Twain's Correspondence with Henry Huttleston Rogers*, p. 478.
51. Tarbell, *All in the Day's Work*, p. 211.
52. Ibid., p. 212.
53. Ibid., p. 10.
54. Ibid., p. 220.
55. Ibid.
56. RAC, III 2.H B14 F87, letter from William T. Sheppard to John D. Rockefeller, Jr., June 16, 1937.
57. AN, B131, "Interview with John D. Rockefeller, Jr."
58. Tarbell, *All in the Day's Work*, p. 227.
59. IMT, "Documents to Be Catalogued," "Memo of a conversation with Mr. Flagler."
60. Tarbell, *All in the Day's Work*, p. 219.
61. AN, B126, "Interview with William T. Sheppard."
62. Tarbell, *History of the Standard Oil Company*, vol. II, p. 126.
63. Tarbell, *All in the Day's Work*, p. 230.
64. Ibid., p. 26.
65. Tarbell, *History of the Standard Oil Company*, vol. II, p. 287.
66. Ibid., p. 101.
67. IMT, B 1/14, "Interview with Henry H. Rogers."
68. John D. Rockefeller, *Random Reminiscences*, p. 68.
69. Tarbell, *History of the Standard Oil Company*, vol. I, p. 204.
70. Nevins, *John D. Rockefeller: The Heroic Age of American Enterprise*, vol. II, p. 50.
71. Tarbell, *The History of the Standard Oil Company*, vol. I, p. 206.
72. John D. Rockefeller, *Random Reminiscences*, pp. 71–72.
73. Nevins, *John D. Rockefeller*, vol. II, p. 51.
74. Tarbell, *The History of the Standard Oil Company*, vol. II, p. 94.
75. AN, B114 F36, letter from J. D. Archbold, May 2, 1888.
76. RAC, Inglis interview, p. 1091.
77. Nevins, *John D. Rockefeller*, vol. II, p. 85.
78. Tarbell, *The History of the Standard Oil Company*, vol. II, p. 110.
79. Lyon, *Success Story*, p. 213.

80. Tarbell, *All in the Day's Work*, p. 202.
81. Yergin, *The Prize*, p. 102.
82. IMT, B 1/14 T-057, letter from J. M. Siddall to Ida Tarbell, August 6, 1903.
83. Brady, *Ida Tarbell*, p. 145.
84. Ibid., p. 143.
85. IMT, B 1/14, letter from J. M. Siddall to Ida Tarbell, n.d.
86. *The American Magazine*, November 1910.
87. RAC, Inglis notes, 4.12, "Reminiscences."
88. IMT, B 1/14, letter from J. M. Siddall to Ida Tarbell, June 15, 1903.
89. Ibid.
90. Ibid., letter from J. M. Siddall to Ida Tarbell, October 26, 1903.
91. Tarbell, *All in the Day's Work*, p. 234.
92. Ibid., p. 235.
93. Ibid.
94. Ibid., p. 236.
95. *McClure's Magazine*, August 1905.
96. Ibid.
97. RAC, Inglis notes, 4.10, "Myths as to Rockefeller's Boyhood."
98. Nevins, *Study in Power*, vol. II, p. 403.
99. IMT, B 1/14, letter from J. M. Siddall to Ida Tarbell, January 8, 1904.
100. IMT, "Documents to Be Catalogued," T-066, "Memo of Interview with Frank Rockefeller, January 22, 1904."
101. IMT, B 4/14 T-298, "Notes on Interview with Frank Rockefeller."
102. IMT, "Documents to Be Catalogued," T-066, "Memo of Interview with Frank Rockefeller, January 22, 1904."
103. RAC, Inglis notes, 4.11, "J. W. Slaght."
104. Ibid.
105. Ibid.
106. *The Cleveland Press*, n.d. [ca. 1905].
107. Brady, *Ida Tarbell*, p. 137.
108. IMT, B 4/14 T-288, "Memo on Corrigan case."
109. RAC, vol. 214, no. 347.
110. Winkler, *John D.: A Portrait in Oils*, p. 28.
111. RAC, vol. 213, no. 348, letter to F. T. Gates, April 3, 1905.
112. *McClure's Magazine*, July 1905.
113. Hughes, *Music Is My Life*, p. 71.
114. Tarbell, *All in the Day's Work*, p. 239.
115. RAC, Inglis interview, p. 13.
116. Ibid., p. 1457.
117. Ibid., p. 1430.
118. RAC, vol. 215, no. 49, letter to J. D. Archbold, July 29, 1905.
119. *The Detroit Tribune*, July 24, 1905.
120. *The Philadelphia Ledger*, July 21, 1905.
121. RAC, III 2.Z B46, "Interview with John D. Rockefeller, Jr."

122. Stasz, *The Rockefeller Women*, p. 232.
123. IMT, B 1/14 T-053, letter from J. M. Siddall to Ida Tarbell, April 28, 1903.
124. Ibid.
125. IMT, "Documents to Be Catalogued," letter from J. M. Siddall to Ida Tarbell, April 30, 1903.
126. IMT, B 2/14, letter from J. M. Siddall to Ida Tarbell, n.d.
127. IMT, B 1/14, letter from J. M. Siddall to Ida Tarbell, September 22, 1903.
128. IMT, "Documents to Be Catalogued," T-066, "Memo of Interview with Frank Rockefeller, January 22, 1904."
129. Rugoff, *America's Gilded Age*, p. 162.
130. Swanberg, *Pulitzer*, p. 187.
131. RAC, Inglis notes, 4.11, "Interview with J. W. Slaght."
132. Ibid.
133. Ibid.
134. Ibid.
135. *The World*, August 11, 1907.
136. Ibid., February 2, 1908.
137. *The St. Louis Post-Dispatch*, May 30, 1937.
138. Ibid.
139. Ibid.
140. *The New York Times*, February 3, 1908.
141. *The World*, March 1, 1908.
142. Ibid.

CHAPTER 23: FAITH OF FOOLS

1. *The St. Louis Post-Dispatch*, July 8, 1936.
2. AN, B122, letter from F. T. Gates to George B. Atwood, April 4, 1921.
3. John D. Rockefeller, *Random Reminiscences*, p. 104.
4. RAC, Inglis notes, 4.8, "On Gratitude and Giving."
5. AN, B114 F33, letter to Frank Rockefeller, December 24, 1886.
6. *Farm and Fireside*, January 6, 1917.
7. *Forbes*, September 29, 1917.
8. Storr, *Harper's University*, p. 143.
9. AN, B116 F58, letter from F. T. Gates to Dr. Osler, April 13, 1904.
10. Storr, *Harper's University*, p. 144.
11. Fosdick, *John D. Rockefeller, Jr.*, p. 421.
12. John D. Rockefeller, Jr., et al., "Addresses to Honor the Memory of Frederick Taylor Gates," privately printed, RAC, p. 15.
13. Mencken, *My Life as Author and Editor*, p. 276.
14. Flexner, *An American Saga*, p. 403.
15. Fosdick, *Chronicle of a Generation*, p. 218.
16. RAC–FTG, B1 F21, letter from Charles W. Eliot to F. T. Gates, December 23, 1910.
17. AN, B128, "Simon Flexner Interview."

18. Nevins, *John D. Rockefeller: The Heroic Age of American Enterprise*, vol. II, p. 479.
19. CUOH–ABF, p. 36.
20. RAC, vol. 233, letter to John D. Rockefeller, Jr., January 14, 1911.
21. *Forbes*, September 29, 1917.
22. RAC–FTG, B1 F21, letter from F. T. Gates to Charles W. Eliot, December 30, 1910.
23. Schenkel, *The Rich Man and the Kingdom*, p. 85.
24. RAC, vol. 223, no. 47, letter to Lucy Fuller, January 17, 1908.
25. RAC, vol. 226, no. 41, letter to John D. Rockefeller, Jr., February 19, 1909.
26. Corner, *A History of the Rockefeller Institute*, p. 105.
27. *The Outlook*, December 17, 1910.
28. Wall, *Andrew Carnegie*, p. 832.
29. RAC–FTG, B1 F21, letter from F. T. Gates to Charles W. Eliot, December 30, 1910.
30. AN, B119, letter from John D. Rockefeller, Jr., March 11, 1919.
31. Brown, *Rockefeller Medicine Men*, p. 122.
32. Jung, *Modern Psychology*, p. 71. Lectures given by Jung at the Eidgenössische Technische Hochschule in Zurich.
33. Cleveland *Plain Dealer*, December 7, 1919.
34. Gates, *Chapters in My Life*, p. 180.
35. Fosdick, *John D. Rockefeller, Jr.*, p. 116.
36. RAC–FTG, B2 F33, letter from F. T. Gates, January 26, 1911.
37. *The St. Louis Post-Dispatch*, July 8, 1936.

CHAPTER 24: THE MILLIONAIRES' SPECIAL

1. Link, *The Paradox of Southern Progressivism*, p. 129.
2. *The World*, April 28, 1901.
3. Lewis, *W.E.B. Du Bois*, p. 271.
4. Read, *The Story of Spelman College*, p. 139.
5. AN, B132, letter from John D. Rockefeller, Jr., to Robert C. Ogden, April 25, 1901.
6. Fosdick, *John D. Rockefeller, Jr.*, p. 117.
7. Link, *The Paradox of Southern Progressivism*, p. 27.
8. Gates, *Chapters in My Life*, p. 134.
9. RAC–FTG, B4 F80, letter from F. T. Gates to Dr. Augustus Strong, May 14, 1891.
10. Fosdick, *John D. Rockefeller, Jr.*, p. 118.
11. RAC, III 2.Z B21, letter from Abraham Flexner to John D. Rockefeller, Jr., October 23, 1940.
12. AN, B126, letter from A. Flexner to Allan Nevins, August 25, 1950.
13. Abraham Flexner, *Autobiography*, p. 141.
14. Schenkel, *The Rich Man and the Kingdom*, p. 75.

15. Brown, *Rockefeller Medicine Men*, p. 55.
16. Schenkel, *The Rich Man and the Kingdom*, p. 75.
17. Link, *The Paradox of Southern Progressivism*, p. 241.
18. Du Bois, *Autobiography*, p. 223.
19. The General Education Board, *The General Education Board: An Account of Its Activities*, p. 220.
20. Abraham Flexner, *Autobiography*, p. 131.
21. Morris, *Those Rockefeller Brothers*, p. 140.
22. Ettling, *The Germ of Laziness*, p. 102.
23. Sullivan, *Our Times*, vol. III, p. 324.
24. RAC, vol. 228, no. 230, letter to John D. Rockefeller, Jr., October 22, 1909.
25. Ettling, *The Germ of Laziness*, p. 107.
26. RAC–FTG, B1 F21, letter from F. T. Gates to Charles W. Eliot, December 30, 1910.
27. Link, *The Paradox of Southern Progressivism*, p. 153.
28. Ibid., pp. 151–52.
29. RAC–FTG, B2 F34, letter from F. T. Gates, August 10, 1914.
30. AN, B117 F65, letter from F. T. Gates, October 23, 1911.
31. Brown, *Rockefeller Medicine Men*, pp. 144–45.
32. Fosdick, *The Story of the Rockefeller Foundation*, p. 93.
33. CUOH–ABF, p. 19.
34. Abraham Flexner, *Autobiography*, pp. 109–10.
35. "Addresses to Honor the Memory of Frederick Taylor Gates," RAC, p. 8.
36. RAC, Inglis notes, 4.10, "On Stewardship."
37. RAC–FTG, B3 F72, "The Ten Million Gift."
38. IMT, B 1/14, T-056, letter from J. M. Siddall to Ida Tarbell, June 24, 1903.
39. Storr, *Harper's University*, p. 359.
40. AN, B131, letter from F. T. Gates to W. R. Harper, February 11, 1905.
41. AN, B117 F59, letter to W. R. Harper, February 16, 1905.
42. UC–UPP, 1889–1925, B56 F1, letter from W. R. Harper, February 22, 1905.
43. Nevins, *John D. Rockefeller: The Heroic Age of American Enterprise*, vol. II, p. 625.
44. Storr, *Harper's University*, p. 366.
45. RAC, vol. 217, no. 76, letter to Harry Pratt Judson, January 26, 1906.
46. Nevins, *John D. Rockefeller*, vol. II, p. 181.
47. RAC–FTG, B3 F72, "The Ten Million Gift."
48. RAC, vol. 225, no. 459, letter to John D. Rockefeller, Jr., February 3, 1909.
49. AN, B117 F63, letter from John D. Rockefeller, Jr., November 5, 1909.
50. RAC–FTG, B3 F72, letter from F. T. Gates, November 24, 1909.
51. RAC, vol. 232, no. 374, letter to University of Chicago, December 13, 1910.
52. Fosdick, *The Story of the Rockefeller Foundation*, p. 7.
53. *The World*, August 20, 1905.
54. Steffens, *The Autobiography of Lincoln Steffens*, p. 528.

55. RAC, vol. 218, no. 460, letter to George Rogers, October 6, 1906.
56. Wells, *The Work, Wealth and Happiness of Mankind*, p. 461.
57. RAC–FTG, B3 F58, letter from F. T. Gates to John D. Rockefeller, Jr., October 19, 1911.
58. Gates, *Chapters in My Life*, p. 205.
59. RAC–FTG, B3 F67.
60. AN, B116 F57, letter from F. T. Gates to T. W. Todd, n.d. [October–November, 1903].
61. RAC–FTG, B2 F48, letter from F. T. Gates, n.d.
62. Gates, *Chapters in My Life*, p. 201.
63. *The New York Herald*, March 29, 1905.
64. RAC, Inglis interview, p. 1048.
65. *Harper's Weekly*, April 8, 1905.
66. New York *Daily News*, n.d., IMT.
67. Nevins, *John D. Rockefeller*, vol. II, p. 546.

CHAPTER 25: THE CODGER

1. *The American*, November 1910.
2. Pyle, *Pocantico*, p. 103.
3. Fosdick, *John D. Rockefeller, Jr.*, p. 198.
4. Inglis, "Impressions of John D. Rockefeller," typescript in AN, p. 24.
5. Chicago *Record-Herald*, December 12, 1906.
6. *Cosmopolitan*, May 1902.
7. RAC, 2.Z B21, letter from John D. Rockefeller, Jr., May 12, 1913.
8. RAC, III 2.Z B20.
9. Ernst, *"Dear Father"/"Dear Son,"* p. 30.
10. John D. Rockefeller, *Random Reminiscences*, p. 37.
11. RAC, vol. 230, no. 238, letter to Mr. Ailes, May 9, 1910.
12. RAC, vol. 227, no. 65, letter to Dr. Paul Allen, June 5, 1909.
13. RAC, vol. 228, no. 266, letter to John D. Rockefeller, Jr., October 30, 1909.
14. *The New York Evening World*, April 27, 1901.
15. Fosdick, *John D. Rockefeller, Jr.*, p. 192.
16. Manchester, *A Rockefeller Family Portrait*, p. 60.
17. Ernst, *"Dear Father"/"Dear Son,"* p. 22.
18. Fosdick, *John D. Rockefeller, Jr.*, p. 193.
19. Reich, *The Life of Nelson A. Rockefeller*, p. 6.
20. RAC, III 2.Z B46.
21. Ibid.
22. Ibid.
23. AN, B133, letter from John D. Rockefeller, Jr., to Senator Aldrich, August 14, 1903.
24. Nevins, *Study in Power*, vol. II, p. 281.
25. New York *Daily News*, August 27, 1901.
26. RAC, III 2.Z B46.

27. UC–UPP, 1889–1925, letter from John D. Rockefeller, Jr., to W. R. Harper, October 7, 1902.
28. Twain, *Mark Twain in Eruption*, p. 83.
29. RAC, vol. 214, no. 296, letter to John D. Rockefeller, Jr., June 27, 1905.
30. Winkler, *John D.: A Portrait in Oils*, p. 197.
31. RAC, III 2.Z B44, letter from Dr. W.H.P. Faunce to John D. Rockefeller, Jr., September 12, 1905.
32. Kert, *Abby Aldrich Rockefeller*, p. 115.
33. RAC, III 2.Z B46.
34. RAC, III 2.Z B21, letter from John D. Rockefeller, Jr., January 4, 1907.
35. Ernst, *"Dear Father"/"Dear Son."* pp. 35–36.
36. Fosdick, *John D. Rockefeller, Jr.*, p. 111.
37. Fosdick, *The Story of the Rockefeller Foundation*, p. 4.
38. Nevins, *Study in Power*, vol. II, p. 407.
39. *The New York Times*, May 21, 1905.
40. Nevins, *Study in Power*, vol. II, p. 289.
41. RAC, III 2.Z B20 F4.
42. AN, B132, "Interview with John D. Rockefeller, Jr., January 1940."
43. RAC, III 1.SL B2 F10, Laura S. Rockefeller diary, October 1908.
44. Ibid., p. 37.
45. Kert, *Abby Aldrich Rockefeller*, p. 121.
46. RAC, vol. 226, no. 308, letter to John D. Rockefeller, Jr., April 17, 1909.
47. RAC, vol. 229, no. 194, letter to John D. Rockefeller, Jr., January 11, 1910.
48. William H. Allen, *Rockefeller: Giant, Dwarf, Symbol*, p. 45.

CHAPTER 26: THE WORLD'S RICHEST FUGITIVE

1. Yergin, *The Prize*, p. 107.
2. RAC, vol. 212, p. 400, letter to President Theodore Roosevelt, November 9, 1904.
3. Ibid.
4. Carr, *John D. Rockefeller's Secret Weapon*, p. 134.
5. IMT, 14/15, "Interview with Mr. Wickersham, May 7, 1924."
6. Tarbell, *The History of the Standard Oil Company*, p. 66.
7. Flynn, *God's Gold*, p. 335.
8. Pringle, *Theodore Roosevelt*, p. 421.
9. Nevins, *Study in Power*, vol. II, p. 359.
10. Yergin, *The Prize*, p. 108.
11. Ibid.
12. AN, B117 F60, letter from John D. Rockefeller, Jr., March 13, 1906.
13. *The New York Herald*, June 23, 1906.
14. AN, B117 F60, letter from John D. Archbold, July 5, 1906.
15. Ibid., quoted in a letter from George Rogers, June 25, 1906.
16. AN, B117 F59, letter from John D. Rockefeller, Jr., December 5, 1905.
17. *The New York Herald*, February 13, 1906.

18. Bringhurst, *Antitrust and the Oil Monopoly*, p. 92.
19. Ibid., p. 244.
20. RAC, vol. 217, no. 44, letter to William Rudd, January 18, 1906.
21. AN, B117 F60, letter to John D. Archbold, April 24, 1906.
22. RAC, vol. 217, no. 262, letter to John D. Rockefeller, Jr., March 15, 1906.
23. RAC, vol. 217, no. 285, letter to John D. Rockefeller, Jr., March 19, 1906.
24. Hidy and Hidy, *History of Standard Oil Company (New Jersey)*, p. 322.
25. Yergin, *The Prize*, p. 100.
26. AN, B128, letter from F. T. Gates to W. O. Inglis, January 12, 1922.
27. RAC, vol. 214, no. 79, letter to F. T. Gates, May 12, 1905.
28. AN, B117 F59, letter from S. Murphy, August 16, 1905.
29. RAC, vol. 217, no. 480, letter to Mrs. Watson Van Duyne, May 1, 1906.
30. AN, B117 F59, letter to Bessie Strong, December 20, 1905.
31. RAC–CAS, III, "Letters 1906–1907."
32. Santayana, *The Letters of George Santayana*, p. 86.
33. RAC, Inglis notes, 4.12, "Hoster Manuscript," p. 4.
34. Ibid., p. 5.
35. Ibid., p. 19.
36. Ibid., p. 8.
37. Flynn, *God's Gold*, p. 424.
38. Ibid., p. 423.
39. McCormick, *George Santayana*, p. 284.
40. Ibid.
41. RAC, Inglis notes, 4.12, "Hoster Manuscript."
42. AN, B131.
43. RAC, Inglis notes, 4.12, "Hoster Manuscript," p. 27.
44. AN, B117 F60, letter from George Rogers, July 9, 1906.
45. RAC–CAS, III, "Letters 1906–1907," letter from Charles A. Strong to William James, July 23, 1906.
46. Nevins, *John D. Rockefeller: The Heroic Age of American Enterprise*, vol. II, p. 567.
47. RAC, Inglis notes, 4.12, "Hoster Manuscript," p. 72.
48. *The New York Herald*, July 30, 1906.
49. RAC, III 2.II D112 F846, telegram from Charles A. Strong, November 14, 1906.
50. Ibid., telegram to Charles A. Strong, November 14, 1906.
51. RAC–CAS, III, "Letters 1902–1905," letter from Charles A. Strong to William James, October 19, 1902.
52. William H. Allen, *Rockefeller: Giant, Dwarf, Symbol*, p. 232.
53. RAC, III 2.Z B20 F3, letter to Edith Rockefeller McCormick, April 15, 1910.
54. RAC, III 2.H B112 F846, letter from Charles A. Strong to John D. Rockefeller, Jr., April 16, 1908.
55. RAC, III 2.Z B20 F3, letter from John D. Rockefeller, Jr., to Laura S. Rockefeller, March 11, 1909.
56. RAC, III 2.A B33 F252, letter to Harold McCormick, May 25, 1917.

57. RAC, vol. 218, no. 332, letter to Harold McCormick, September 1, 1906.
58. *Leslie's Weekly*, May 16, 1907.
59. *The Woman's Home Companion*, January 1907.
60. AN, B117 F62, letter to Edith McCormick, June 11, 1908.
61. RAC, III 2.H B1 F2.
62. John D. Rockefeller, *Random Reminiscences*, p. 1.
63. Ibid., p. 19.
64. Ibid., p. 118.
65. Ibid., p. 94.
66. Chicago *Record-Herald*, April 25, 1909.
67. Twain, *Mark Twain in Eruption*, p. 101.
68. Twain, *Mark Twain's Correspondence with Henry Huttleston Rogers*, p. 577.
69. Twain, *Mark Twain in Eruption*, p. 102.

CHAPTER 27: JUDGMENT DAY

1. AN, B117 F60, letter to John D. Archbold, November 13, 1906.
2. RAC, III 2.H B1 F8, "Taylor History."
3. AN, B131, "Interview with Mr. Brown."
4. AN, B130, "Interview with Charles T. White."
5. Giddens, *Standard Oil Company (Indiana)*, p. 110.
6. *The Sun*, July 7, 1907.
7. Ibid.
8. Ibid.
9. AN, B128.
10. Hidy and Hidy, *History of Standard Oil Company (New Jersey)*, p. 703.
11. Winkler, *John D.: A Portrait in Oils*, p. 147.
12. Kaplan, *Mr. Clemens and Mark Twain*, p. 323.
13. Cleveland *Plain Dealer*, August 4, 1907.
14. Ibid.
15. Ibid.
16. Flynn, *God's Gold*, p. 426.
17. RAC–FTG, B2 F39, letter from F. T. Gates, August 9, 1907.
18. Collier and Horowitz, *The Rockefellers*, p. 58.
19. Flynn, *God's Gold*, p. 432.
20. Pringle, *Theodore Roosevelt*, p. 481.
21. RAC, vol. 221, p. 374, letter to John D. Rockefeller, Jr., August 31, 1907.
22. Pringle, *Theodore Roosevelt*, p. 367.
23. RAC, Inglis notes, 4.9, "Help to End Panics."
24. Flynn, *God's Gold*, p. 429.
25. John D. Rockefeller, *Random Reminiscences*, p. 5.
26. Ibid., p. 88.
27. AN, B130.
28. AN, B117 F61, letter to George Rudd, October 26, 1907.
29. Flynn, *God's Gold*, p. 428.

30. Kolko, *The Triumph of Conservatism*, p. 124.
31. Bringhurst, *Antitrust and the Oil Monopoly*, p. 135.
32. Ibid., p. 136.
33. Ibid., p. 140.
34. Carr, *John D. Rockefeller's Secret Weapon*, p. 147.
35. Hidy and Hidy, *History of Standard Oil Company* (New Jersey), p. 635.
36. Ibid., p. 634.
37. RAC, vol. 230, p. 7, letter to H. C. Folger, March 14, 1910.
38. Flynn, *God's Gold*, p. 414.
39. Ibid.
40. *The Morning Telegraph*, November 20, 1908.
41. Cincinnati *Times-Star*, November 20, 1908.
42. Nevins, *Study in Power*, vol. II, p. 277.
43. RAC, Inglis notes, 4.10, "John D. Archbold."
44. Collier and Horowitz, *The Rockefellers*, p. 56.
45. Ibid., p. 57.
46. Flynn, *God's Gold*, p. 355.
47. Ibid.
48. *Hearst's Magazine*, June 1912.
49. Flynn, *God's Gold*, p. 353.
50. Swanberg, *Citizen Hearst*, p. 228.
51. Goulder, *John D. Rockefeller*, p. 215.
52. Swanberg, *Citizen Hearst*, p. 260.
53. Ibid., p. 261.
54. Flynn, *God's Gold*, p. 435.
55. RAC, III 2.Z B46.
56. Ibid.
57. Fosdick, *John D. Rockefeller, Jr.*, p. 137.
58. Collier and Horowitz, *The Rockefellers*, p. 105.
59. McGovern and Guttridge, *The Great Coalfield War*, p. 197.
60. RAC, III 2.Z B46.
61. Flynn, *God's Gold*, p. 436.
62. RAC, vol. 226, p. 488, letter to H. C. Folger, May 20, 1909.
63. Pringle, *The Life and Times of William Howard Taft*, p. 660.
64. RAC, vol. 228, p. 23, letter to Harold McCormick, August 27, 1909.
65. Nevins, *Study in Power*, vol. II, p. 378, and Yergin, *The Prize*, p. 109.
66. Ernst, *"Dear Father"/"Dear Son,"* p. 46.
67. Yergin, *The Prize*, p. 109.
68. AN, B126.
69. Collier and Horowitz, *The Rockefellers*, p. 59.
70. Bringhurst, *Antitrust and the Oil Monopoly*, p. 173.
71. Ibid.
72. Pringle, *The Life and Times of William Howard Taft*, p. 665.
73. Flynn, *God's Gold*, p. 445.
74. *Bradstreet's*, September 2, 1911.

75. Kolko, *The Triumph of Conservatism*, p. 194.
76. Yergin, *The Prize*, p. 113.
77. Schreiner, *Henry Clay Frick*, p. 135.
78. Winkler, *John D.: A Portrait in Oils*, p. 157.
79. Nevins, *Study in Power*, vol. II, p. 383.
80. RAC, vol. 235, p. 107.
81. AN, B126, "Interview with Dr. W. M. Burton."

CHAPTER 28: BENEVOLENT TRUST

1. RAC, III 2.H B9 F37, "Inglis Impressions."
2. *The New Yorker*, January 29, 1921.
3. *The New York Herald*, January 6, 1905.
4. Harr and Johnson, *The Rockefeller Century*, p. 65.
5. Brown, *Rockefeller Medicine Men*, p. 48.
6. Harr and Johnson, *The Rockefeller Century*, p. 82.
7. Gates, *Chapters in My Life*, p. 20.
8. Ibid., p. 209.
9. AN, B117, letters from John D. Rockefeller, Jr., February 10 and 12, 1908.
10. Harr and Johnson, *The Rockefeller Century*, p. 9.
11. Ibid., p. 121.
12. Brown, *Rockefeller Medicine Men*, p. 169.
13. Pringle, *The Life and Times of William Howard Taft*, pp. 661–62.
14. Ibid., p. 663.
15. Butt, *Taft and Roosevelt*, p. 615.
16. RAC, III 2.Z B20 F24, letter from John D. Rockefeller, Jr., to Laura S. Rockefeller, April 25, 1911.
17. *The Sun*, January 11, 1914.
18. RAC–FTG, B4 F78, letter to F. T. Gates, August 19, 1912.
19. RAC, III 2.Z B21, letter from John D. Rockefeller, Jr., April 17, 1917.
20. Fosdick, *The Story of the Rockefeller Foundation*, p. 59.

CHAPTER 29: MASSACRE

1. AN, B117 F59, letter from Frederick T. Gates, December 2, 1905.
2. AN, B116 F57, letter from John D. Rockefeller, Jr., to F. J. Hearne, October 27, 1903.
3. McGovern and Guttridge, *The Great Coalfield War*, p. 53.
4. RAC, III 2.Z B46.
5. RAC, Inglis notes, 4.8, "On Profit-Sharing and Unionism."
6. RAC–FTG, B1 F9, "Capital and Labor."
7. AN, B117 F66, letter from John D. Rockefeller, Jr., to L. M. Bowers, May 21, 1913.
8. Nevins, *Study in Power*, vol. II, p. 419.
9. McGovern and Guttridge, *The Great Coalfield War*, p. 98.

10. Ibid., p. 111.
11. Collier and Horowitz, *The Rockefellers*, p. 110.
12. McGovern and Guttridge, *The Great Coalfield War*, p. 135.
13. Ibid., p. 136.
14. AN, B117 F67, letter from John D. Rockefeller, Jr., to W. B. Wilson, November 19, 1913.
15. Ibid.
16. Ibid., letter from John D. Rockefeller, Jr., to L. M. Bowers, December 26, 1913.
17. RAC, III 2.Z B46.
18. McGovern and Guttridge, *The Great Coalfield War*, pp. 198–99.
19. Ibid., p. 201.
20. Collier and Horowitz, *The Rockefellers*, p. 115.
21. AN, B117 F68, letter to E. B. Thomas, April 11, 1914.
22. McGovern and Guttridge, *The Great Coalfield War*, p. 232.
23. Ibid.
24. Gitelman, *Legacy of the Ludlow Massacre*, p. 23.
25. Hiebert, *Courtier to the Crowd*, p. 99.
26. McGovern and Guttridge, *The Great Coalfield War*, p. 239.
27. Lash, *Helen and Teacher*, p. 428.
28. Pickersgill and Forster, *The Mackenzie King Record*, vol. III, p. 144.
29. McGovern and Guttridge, *The Great Coalfield War*, p. 278.
30. RAC, III 2.Z B21, letter from John D. Rockefeller, Jr., August 7, 1914.
31. Fosdick, *John D. Rockefeller, Jr.*, p. 152.
32. Gitelman, *Legacy of the Ludlow Massacre*, p. 20.
33. McGovern and Guttridge, *The Great Coalfield War*, p. 257.
34. AN, B117 F68, letter to Harold McCormick, May 11, 1914.
35. Fosdick, *John D. Rockefeller, Jr.*, p. 144.
36. Dawson, *William Lyon Mackenzie King*, p. 229.
37. RAC, III 2.Z B46.
38. Dawson, *William Lyon Mackenzie King*, p. 229, and Harr and Johnson, *The Rockefeller Century*, p. 132.
39. Ibid.
40. Harr and Johnson, *The Rockefeller Century*, p. 133.
41. Gitelman, *Legacy of the Ludlow Massacre*, p. 64.
42. RAC, III 2.Z B46.
43. Harr and Johnson, *The Rockefeller Century*, p. 133.
44. Ibid.
45. *Hearst's International*, July 1923.
46. Collier and Horowitz, *The Rockefellers*, p. 116.
47. Hiebert, *Courtier to the Crowd*, p. 97.
48. Ibid., p. 100.
49. RAC, III 2.H B1 F3, letter from John D. Rockefeller, Jr., to Walter C. Teagle, June 25, 1918.
50. Hiebert, *Courtier to the Crowd*, pp. 4–5.

51. Gitelman, *Legacy of the Ludlow Massacre*, p. 59.
52. Harr and Johnson, *The Rockefeller Century*, p. 130.
53. Dawson, *William Lyon Mackenzie King*, p. 237.
54. Hiebert, *Courtier to the Crowd*, p. 104.
55. RAC, III 2.Z B46.
56. McGovern and Guttridge, *The Great Coalfield War*, p. 318.
57. Ibid.
58. RAC, Inglis interview, pp. 332–33.
59. *The New Republic*, January 30, 1915.
60. Fosdick, *John D. Rockefeller, Jr.*, p. 158.
61. Harr and Johnson, *The Rockefeller Century*, pp. 138–39.
62. Jones, *Autobiography of Mother Jones*, p. 201.
63. Winkler, *John D.: A Portrait in Oils*, p. 201.
64. Kert, *Abby Aldrich Rockefeller*, p. 151.
65. Fosdick, *John D. Rockefeller, Jr.*, p. 162.
66. AN, B128, letter from John D. Rockefeller, Jr., to Allan Nevins, April 3, 1939.
67. Fosdick, *John D. Rockefeller, Jr.*, p. 165.
68. Kert, *Abby Aldrich Rockefeller*, p. 151.
69. RAC, Inglis notes, 4.8, "Mrs. S. J. Life."
70. Pickersgill and Forster, *The Mackenzie King Record*, vol. III, p. 360.

CHAPTER 30: INTROVERT AND EXTROVERT

1. Jones, *The Correspondence of Mother Jones*, p. 134.
2. Nevins, *John D. Rockefeller: The Heroic Age of American Enterprise*, vol. II, p. 676.
3. RAC, III 1 SL B2 F10, Laura S. Rockefeller diary, December 1909.
4. Ibid., September 25, 1913.
5. Flynn, *God's Gold*, p. 463.
6. RAC, III 2.Z B49 F25.
7. Ernst, *"Dear Father"/"Dear Son,"* p. 49.
8. Fosdick, *John D. Rockefeller, Jr.*, p. 426.
9. RAC, III 2.A B33 F257, letter to Edith Rockefeller McCormick, September 12, 1922.
10. RAC, Inglis interview, p. 233, and Inglis notes, 4.9, "Rockefeller and Cleveland."
11. RAC, Inglis notes, 4.9, "Rockefeller and Cleveland."
12. *The New York Tribune*, March 15, 1915.
13. RAC, III 1 SL B2 F13, letter from M. S. Richardson to John D. Rockefeller, Jr., August 12, 1915.
14. Ibid.
15. *The Detroit Free Press*, January 3, 1916.
16. Harr and Johnson, *The Rockefeller Century*, p. 190.
17. *The New York Evening Journal*, August 30, 1932.

18. Ibid.
19. Dedmon, *Fabulous Chicago*, p. 315.
20. Burnham, *Jelliffe*, p. 247.
21. Ibid., p. 245.
22. Jung, *Modern Psychology*, p. 71.
23. Jung, *Nietzsche's Zarathustra*, p. 583.
24. Ibid.
25. Noll, *The Aryan Christ*, p. 207.
26. Ibid.
27. RAC, III 2.A B32 F249, letter from Harold McCormick, December 28, 1913.
28. RAC, III 2.A B32 F250, letter to Harold McCormick, December 30, 1915.
29. *Spring* 52, 1992.
30. RAC, III 2.A B32 F250, letter from Harold McCormick, September 1, 1915.
31. Noll, *The Aryan Christ*, p. 215.
32. Stasz, *The Rockefeller Women*, p. 192.
33. RAC, III 2.A B32 F250, letter from Harold McCormick, June 18, 1915.
34. Noll, *The Aryan Christ*, p. 216.
35. RAC, III 2.A B33 F252, letter from Harold McCormick, August 25, 1917.
36. RAC, III 2.A B32 F250, letter from Edith Rockefeller McCormick, October 22, 1915.
37. RAC, III 2.A B33 F252, letter from Edith Rockefeller McCormick, June 22, 1917.
38. Ibid., letter to Edith Rockefeller McCormick, July 27, 1917.
39. RAC, III 2.A B32 F251, letter from Harold McCormick, February 16, 1916.
40. RAC, III 2.A B32 F259, letter to Harold and Edith McCormick, January 26, 1916.
41. Noll, *The Aryan Christ*, pp. 230–31.
42. RAC, III 2.A B32 F250, letter from Edith Rockefeller McCormick, September 4, 1915.
43. Stasz, *The Rockefeller Women*, p. 201.
44. Ibid.
45. Noll, *The Aryan Christ*, pp. 225–26.
46. Ibid., p. 232.
47. Ellmann, *James Joyce*, p. 422.
48. Ibid., p. 469.
49. Noll, *The Aryan Christ*, p. 231.
50. RAC, III 2.A B33 F233, letter from Edith Rockefeller McCormick, March 24, 1919.
51. *Spring* 52, 1992.
52. Ibid.
53. Ibid.
54. Walska, *Always Room at the Top*, p. 24.
55. RAC, III 2.A B33 F254, letter to Harold McCormick, January 27, 1920.
56. RAC, III 2.Z B22, letter to Edith Rockefeller McCormick, April 9, 1921.

57. RAC, RG2 B34 F262, letter from Edith Rockefeller McCormick, April 17, 1931.
58. *The Chicago Daily News*, March 12, 1931.
59. RAC, RG2 B34 F259, letter to Edith Rockefeller McCormick, December 27, 1923.
60. Birmingham, *The Grandes Dames*, p. 140.
61. RAC, RG2 B34 F259, letter from Edith Rockefeller McCormick, January 14, 1924.

CHAPTER 31: CONFESSIONAL

1. RAC, III 2.Z B22, letter to John D. Rockefeller, Jr., October 11, 1926.
2. Fosdick, *John D. Rockefeller, Jr.*, p. 196.
3. RAC, III 2.H B9 F37, "Inglis Impressions."
4. William H. Allen, *Rockefeller: Giant, Dwarf, Symbol*, p. 250.
5. AN, B128, letter from George N. Rigby to John D. Rockefeller, Jr., April 27, 1940.
6. *The Salt Lake City Tribune*, April 27, 1919.
7. Strickland, *Ormond's Historic Homes*, p. 57.
8. *The New York American*, February 5, 1927.
9. Engelbrecht, *Neighbor John*, p. 98.
10. Chandler, *Henry Flagler*, p. 301.
11. RAC, III 2.Z B21, letter to John D. Rockefeller, Jr., March 15, 1916.
12. RAC, Inglis notes, 4.11, "John S. Sargent Interview, November 27, 1922."
13. CUOH–PM, p. 23.
14. RAC, III 2.H B9 F37, "Inglis Impressions."
15. David Rockefeller, interview with author.
16. Engelbrecht, *Neighbor John*, p. 148.
17. *The Brooklyn Citizen*, March 4, 1923.
18. RAC, Inglis interview, pp. 363–64.
19. Ibid., p. 1061.
20. RAC, Inglis notes, 4.7, 3.1.1, letter from Ivy Lee, February 11, 1915.
21. RAC, III 2.H B3 F17, letter from Ivy Lee, October 14, 1915.
22. RAC, III 2.H B3 F18, "Meeting Mr. Rockefeller."
23. Ibid.
24. RAC, Inglis interview, p. 237.
25. RAC, III 2.H B3 F14, letter from W. O. Inglis to Ivy Lee, March 25, 1918.
26. RAC, Inglis interview, p. 343.
27. RAC, III 2.Z B21, letter from John D. Rockefeller, Jr., September 28, 1917.
28. Brady, *Ida Tarbell*, p. 231.
29. RAC, Inglis interview, p. 23.
30. Ibid., p. 1313.
31. RAC, III 2.H B1 F8, "Taylor History."
32. RAC, Inglis interview, p. 1280.
33. Yergin, *The Prize*, p. 183.

34. RAC, Inglis interview, p. 1252.
35. Ibid., p. 105.
36. Ibid., p. 1647.
37. Ibid., p. 149.
38. Ibid., p. 1396.
39. Ibid., p. 1264.
40. Ibid., p. 1291.
41. RAC, Inglis notes, "John D. Rockefeller Biography," letter from William Allen White to John D. Rockefeller, Jr., May 21, 1925.
42. RAC, III 2.Z B46, "Interview with John D. Rockefeller, Jr."
43. RAC, III 2.Z B44, "Memo of William G. Rose, March 10, 1953."

CHAPTER 32: DYNASTIC SUCCESSION

1. Mencken, *Prejudices: Fifth Series*, p. 287.
2. Collier and Horowitz, *The Rockefellers*, p. 136.
3. RAC, Inglis interview, p. 177.
4. RAC, III 2.H B3 F14, letter from John D. Rockefeller, Jr., to W. O. Inglis, February 19, 1918.
5. RAC, III 2.Z B46.
6. Foodick, *John D. Rockefeller, Jr.*, p. 334.
7. Ibid.
8. RAC, III 2.Z B21, letter from John D. Rockefeller, Jr., May 25, 1915.
9. David Rockefeller, interview with author.
10. Harr and Johnson, *The Rockefeller Century*, p. 158.
11. RAC, Inglis notes, 4.9, "What Mr. Rockefeller Gave to Win the War."
12. RAC, III 2.Z B21.
13. Nevins, *Study in Power*, vol. II, p. 411.
14. RAC, Inglis interview, p. 239.
15. David Rockefeller, interview with author.
16. Chase, *Abby Aldrich Rockefeller*, p. 47.
17. Ibid., p. 85.
18. Ibid., p. 120.
19. Kert, *Abby Aldrich Rockefeller*, p. 208.
20. Chase, *Abby Aldrich Rockefeller*, p. 59.
21. Kert, *Abby Aldrich Rockefeller*, p. 208.
22. Reich, *The Life of Nelson A. Rockefeller*, p. 116.
23. Kert, *Abby Aldrich Rockefeller*, p. 228.
24. Pyle, *Pocantico*, p. 180.
25. Kert, *Abby Aldrich Rockefeller*, p. 419.
26. Chase, *Abby Aldrich Rockefeller*, p. 32.
27. Kert, *Abby Aldrich Rockefeller*, pp. 172–73.
28. Chase, *Abby Aldrich Rockefeller*, p. 46.
29. *The New Yorker*, November 4, 1972.
30. RAC, III 2.Z B64.

31. RAC, III 2.H B9 F37, "Inglis Impressions."
32. RAC, III 2.Z B46.
33. *The Saturday Evening Post,* July 16, 1938.

CHAPTER 33: PAST, PRESENT, FUTURE

1. AN, B128, "Interview with James C. Jones."
2. AN, B131.
3. Nevins, *Study in Power,* vol. II, p. 419.
4. FSL, JDR, B23, letter to Henry Clay Folger, June 28, 1922.
5. Ibid., letter to Henry Clay Folger, January 1, 1923.
6. *The Evening World,* November 30, 1926.
7. Winkler, *John D.: A Portrait in Oils,* p. 254.
8. Wells, *The Work, Wealth and Happiness of Mankind,* p. 462.
9. AN, B126, "William T. Sheppard Interview."
10. Winkler, *John D.,* p. 47.
11. Engelbrecht, *Neighbor John,* p. 42.
12. Pyle, *Pocantico,* p. 111.
13. AN, B119, letter from John D. Rockefeller, Jr., February 28, 1928.
14. AN, B126.
15. Engelbrecht, *Neighbor John,* p. 102.
16. AN, B128, letter from George N. Rigby to John D. Rockefeller, Jr., April 27, 1940.
17. Engelbrecht, *Neighbor John,* p. 107.
18. *The World,* May 20, 1923, and *Hearst's International,* July 1923.
19. RAC, Inglis notes, 4.9, "Mr. Rockefeller and Alcohol."
20. Winkler, *John D.,* p. 189.
21. RAC, III B36 F273.
22. Harr and Johnson, *The Rockefeller Century,* p. 355.
23. Fosdick, *Chronicle of a Generation,* p. 223.
24. Fosdick, *John D. Rockefeller, Jr.,* p. 206.
25. Fosdick, *The Living of These Days,* p. 146.
26. Ibid., p. 178.
27. Schenkel, *The Rich Man and the Kingdom,* p. 222.
28. *The Jacksonville Times-Union,* November 15, 1935.
29. Roberts, *Mr. Rockefeller's Roads,* p. 6.
30. Fosdick, *John D. Rockefeller, Jr.,* p. 278.
31. Ibid., p. 292.
32. Ibid., p. 297.
33. Kert, *Abby Aldrich Rockefeller,* p. 389.
34. Manchester, *A Rockefeller Family Portrait,* p. 172.
35. RAC, III 2.Z B46.
36. Manchester, *A Rockefeller Family Portrait,* p. 110.
37. RAC, III 2.Z B46.
38. Kert, *Abby Aldrich Rockefeller,* p. 283.

39. RAC, III 2.Z B46.
40. Reich, *The Life of Nelson A. Rockefeller,* p. 102.
41. Harr and Johnson, *The Rockefeller Century,* p. 219.
42. Kert, *Abby Aldrich Rockefeller,* p. 262.
43. Ibid., p. 304.
44. Ibid., p. 283.
45. Ibid., p. 284.
46. Ibid., pp. 418–19.
47. Ibid., p. 377.

CHAPTER 34: HEIRS

1. Noll, *The Aryan Christ,* p. 208.
2. RAC, III 2.A B33 F257, letter from Edith Rockefeller McCormick, October 20, 1922.
3. Stasz, *The Rockefeller Women,* p. 236.
4. *The Chicago Journal,* October 25, 1921.
5. RAC, III 2.A B33 F252, letter to Mathilde McCormick, January 28, 1922.
6. RAC, III 2.A B33 F256, letter from Edith Rockefeller McCormick, January 28, 1922.
7. Ibid.
8. RAC, III 2.A B33 F258, letter to Edith Rockefeller McCormick, April 19, 1923.
9. RAC, III 2.A B33 F256, letter from Edith Rockefeller McCormick, October 23, 1922.
10. RAC, RG2 B34 F261, letter from Mathilde Oser, July 3, 1929.
11. Ibid., telegram from Edith Rockefeller McCormick, May 27, 1929.
12. McCormick, *George Santayana,* p. 288.
13. Reich, *The Life of Nelson A. Rockefeller,* p. 16.
14. Stasz, *The Rockefeller Women,* p. 244.
15. Harr and Johnson, *The Rockefeller Century,* p. 102.
16. Ibid., p. 254.
17. Ibid., p. 90.
18. Kert, *Abby Aldrich Rockefeller,* p. 227.
19. Ibid., p. 228.
20. Harr and Johnson, *The Rockefeller Century,* pp. 246, 248.
21. Winkler, *John D.: A Portrait in Oils,* p. 207.
22. Harr and Johnson, *The Rockefeller Century,* p. 261.
23. Ibid., pp. 258, 261.
24. Ibid., p. 274.
25. Collier and Horowitz, *The Rockefellers,* p. 366.
26. Harr and Johnson, *The Rockefeller Century,* p. 246.
27. Morris, *Those Rockefeller Brothers,* p. 56.
28. Reich, *The Life of Nelson A. Rockefeller,* p. 247.
29. Ibid., p. 59.

30. Ibid.
31. Ibid.
32. Ibid., p. 60.
33. Collier and Horowitz, *The Rockefellers*, p. 199.
34. RAC, III 2.Z B22, letter from John D. Rockefeller, Jr., August 1, 1932.
35. *Newsweek*, April 28, 1958.
36. RAC, III 2.Z B20 F4, letter from John D. Rockefeller, Jr., to Laura S. Rockefeller, July 30, 1910.
37. RAC, III 2.Z B22, letter from John D. Rockefeller, Jr., February 28, 1934.
38. Reich, *The Life of Nelson A. Rockefeller*, p. 29.
39. Manchester, *A Rockefeller Family Portrait*, p. 52.
40. Collier and Horowitz, *The Rockefellers*, p. 220.
41. Kert, *Abby Aldrich Rockefeller*, p. 366.
42. RAC, III 2.Z B21, letter from Winthrop Rockefeller to John D. Rockefeller, Jr., and Abby Aldrich Rockefeller.
43. Winthrop Rockefeller, *A Letter to My Son*, pp. 83–84.
44. Ibid., p. 85.
45. *The Saturday Evening Post*, July 16, 1938.
46. Manchester, *A Rockefeller Family Portrait*, p. 9.
47. Harr and Johnson, *The Rockefeller Century*, p. 391.
48. Collier and Horowitz, *The Rockefellers*, p. 256.
49. AN, B119, letter to John D. Rockefeller, Jr., December 28, 1927.
50. David Rockefeller, interview with author.
51. Morris, *Those Rockefeller Brothers*, p. 30.
52. Collier and Horowitz, *The Rockefellers*, p. 430.

CHAPTER 35: SEE YOU IN HEAVEN

1. AN, B126.
2. Collier and Horowitz, *The Rockefellers*, p. 71.
3. AN, B128.
4. Collier and Horowitz, *The Rockefellers*, p. 172.
5. Chernow, *The House of Morgan*, p. 319.
6. Ellmann, *James Joyce*, p. 469.
7. Winthrop Rockefeller, "A Letter to My Son," p. 88.
8. RAC, III 2.Z B22, letter from John D. Rockefeller, Jr., June 28, 1933.
9. Manchester, *A Rockefeller Family Portrait*, p. 118.
10. Kert, *Abby Aldrich Rockefeller*, p. 357.
11. Ibid., p. 360.
12. Reich, *The Life of Nelson A. Rockefeller*, p. 111.
13. RAC, III 2.Z B46.
14. *Time*, September 24, 1956.
15. *The New York Evening Post*, February 9, 1932.
16. AN, B128, letter from George N. Rigby to John D. Rockefeller, Jr., April 27, 1940.

17. Ibid.
18. Ibid., p. 71.
19. Collier and Horowitz, *The Rockefellers,* p. 204.
20. RAC, Inglis notes, 4.14, "Ira Warner Memo."
21. AN, B129.
22. RAC, III 2.Z B44, letter from John D. Rockefeller, Jr., to Kate Sewall, March 20, 1937.
23. Winthrop Rockefeller, "A Letter to My Son," p. 86.
24. *The Argonaut,* June 16, 1937.
25. Winkelman, *John D. Rockefeller,* p. 4.
26. Pyle, *Pocantico,* p. 189.

BIBLIOGRAPHY

Ahlstrom, Sydney E. *A Religious History of the American People.* New Haven: Yale University Press, 1972.

Akin, Edward N. *Flagler: Rockefeller Partner & Florida Baron.* Kent, Ohio: Kent State University Press, 1988.

Aldrich, Nelson W., Jr. *Old Money: The Mythology of America's Upper Class.* New York: Alfred A. Knopf, 1988.

Allen, Frederick Lewis. *The Great Pierpont Morgan.* Reprint. New York: Harper and Row, 1949 [1948].

Allen, William H. *Rockefeller: Giant, Dwarf, Symbol.* New York: New York Institute for Public Service, 1930.

Amory, Cleveland. *The Last Resorts.* New York: Harper and Brothers, 1948.

Axel-Lute, Paul. *Lakewood-in-the-Pines: A History of Lakewood, New Jersey.* Self-published. South Orange, N.J. Copy in Lakewood Public Library.

Baldwin, Neil. *Edison: Inventing the Century.* New York: Hyperion, 1995.

Beer, Thomas. *Hanna.* New York: Alfred A. Knopf, 1929.

Biggar, Hamilton F. *Compiègne and Personal Reminiscences: A Souvenir of a Very Pleasant Trip to France with Mr. and Mrs. John D. Rockefeller and Party Summer 1906.* Privately printed copy in RAC.

Birmingham, Stephen. *The Grandes Dames.* New York: Simon and Schuster, 1982.

Brady, Kathleen. *Ida Tarbell: Portrait of a Muckraker.* New York: Seaview/Putnam, 1984.

Branch, Taylor. *Parting the Waters: America in the King Years, 1954–63.* New York: Simon and Schuster, 1988.

Bringhurst, Bruce. *Antitrust and the Oil Monopoly: The Standard Oil Cases, 1890–1911.* Westport, Conn.: Greenwood Press, 1979.

Brown, E. Richard. *Rockefeller Medicine Men: Medicine & Capitalism in America.* Berkeley and Los Angeles: University of California Press, 1979.

Brumberg, Joan Jacobs. *Mission for Life.* New York: The Free Press, 1980.

Brutcher, Charles. *Joshua: A Man of the Finger Lakes Region: A True Story Taken from Life.* Privately printed. Syracuse, N.Y., 1927. Copy in Cayuga-Owasco Lakes Historical Society (Moravia, N.Y.).

Burnham, John C. *Jelliffe: American Psychoanalyst and Physician.* Chicago: University of Chicago Press, 1983.

Burr, Anna Robeson. *The Portrait of a Banker: James Stillman, 1850–1918.* New York: Duffield and Co., 1927.

Butt, Archie. *Taft and Roosevelt: The Intimate Letters of Archie Butt, Military Aide.* Vol. 2. Garden City, N.Y.: Doubleday, Doran and Co., 1930.

Carr, Albert Z. *John D. Rockefeller's Secret Weapon.* New York: McGraw-Hill, 1962.

Chandler, Alfred D., Jr. *Scale and Scope: The Dynamics of Industrial Capitalism.* Cambridge, Mass.: Harvard University Press, Belknap Press, 1990.

————. *Strategy and Structure: Chapters in the History of the Industrial Empire.* Cambridge, Mass.: MIT Press, 1969.

Chandler, Alfred D., Jr., and Richard S. Tedlow. *The Coming of Managerial Capitalism: A Casebook in the History of American Economic Institutions.* Homewood, Ill.: Richard D. Irwin, 1985.

Chandler, David Leon. *Henry Flagler: The Astonishing Life and Times of the Visionary Robber Baron Who Founded Florida.* New York: Macmillan, 1986.

Chase, Mary Ellen. *Abby Aldrich Rockefeller.* New York: Macmillan, 1950.

Chernow, Ron. *The House of Morgan: An American Banking Dynasty and the Rise of Modern Finance.* New York: Atlantic Monthly Press, 1990.

Cigliano, Jan E. *The Euclid Avenue Elite.* Master's thesis, Oberlin College, May 1978. Copy in Western Reserve Historical Society.

Collier, Peter, and David Horowitz. *The Rockefellers: An American Dynasty.* New York: Holt, Rinehart and Winston, 1976.

Corner, George W. *A History of the Rockefeller Institute 1901–1953: Origins and Growth.* New York: Rockefeller Institute Press, 1964.

Dawson, R. MacGregor. *William Lyon Mackenzie King: A Political Biography, 1879–1923.* Toronto: University of Toronto Press, 1958.

Dedmon, Emmett. *Fabulous Chicago.* New York: Random House, 1953.

Delbanco, Andrew. *The Death of Satan: How Americans Have Lost the Sense of Evil.* New York: Farrar, Straus and Giroux, 1995.

Destler, Chester McArthur. *Henry Demarest Lloyd and the Empire of Reform.* Philadelphia: University of Pennsylvania Press, 1963.

————. *Roger Sherman and the Independent Oil Men.* Ithaca, N.Y.: Cornell University Press, 1967.

Diggins, John Patrick. *Max Weber: Politics and the Spirit of Tragedy.* New York: Basic Books, 1996.

Dolson, Hildegarde. *The Great Oildorado: The Gaudy and Turbulent Years of the First Oil Rush: Pennsylvania, 1859–1880.* New York: Random House, 1959.

Dreiser, Theodore. *The Financier.* Reprint. New York: Penguin, 1981 [1912].

Du Bois, W.E.B. *The Autobiography of W.E.B. Du Bois: A Soliloquy on Viewing My Life from the Last Decade of Its First Century.* New York: International Publishers, 1968.

Ellmann, Richard. *James Joyce.* New and revised edition. New York: Oxford University Press, 1982.

Elmer, Isabel Lincoln. *Cinderella Rockefeller.* New York: Freundlich Books, 1987.

Ely, Richard T. *Monopolies and Trusts.* London: Macmillan, 1912.

Engelbrecht, Curt E. *Neighbor John: Intimate Glimpses of John D. Rockefeller.* New York: Telegraph Press, 1936.

Ernst, Joseph W., ed. *"Dear Father"/"Dear Son": Correspondence of John D. Rockefeller and John D. Rockefeller, Jr.* New York: Fordham University Press, 1994.

———. *Worthwhile Places: Correspondence of John D. Rockefeller, Jr., and Horace M. Albright.* New York: Fordham University Press, 1991.

Ettling, John. *The Germ of Laziness: Rockefeller Philanthropy and Public Health in the New South.* Cambridge, Mass.: Harvard University Press, 1981.

Finke, Roger, and Rodney Stark. *The Churching of America, 1776–1990: Winners and Losers in Our Religious Economy.* New Brunswick, N.J.: Rutgers University Press, 1992.

Flexner, Abraham. *An Autobiography.* New York: Simon and Schuster, 1960.

Flexner, James Thomas. *An American Saga: The Story of Helen Thomas and Simon Flexner.* Boston: Little, Brown, 1984.

———. *Maverick's Progress: An Autobiography.* New York: Fordham University Press, 1996.

Flynn, John T. *Men of Wealth: The Story of Twelve Significant Fortunes from the Renaissance to the Present Day.* New York: Simon and Schuster, 1941.

———. *God's Gold: The Story of Rockefeller and His Times.* Westport, Conn.: Greenwood Press, 1932.

Fosdick, Harry Emerson. *The Living of These Days: An Autobiography.* New York: Harper and Brothers, 1956.

Fosdick, Raymond B. *Chronicle of a Generation: An Autobiography.* New York. Harper and Brothers, 1958.

———. *John D. Rockefeller, Jr.: A Portrait.* New York: Harper and Brothers, 1956.

———. *The Story of the Rockefeller Foundation.* New Brunswick, N.J.: Transaction Publishers, 1989.

Franklin, Benjamin. *The Autobiography of Benjamin Franklin.* Reprint. Roslyn, N.Y.: Walter J. Black, 1941 [1818].

Garden, Mary, and Louis Biancolli. *Mary Garden's Story.* New York: Simon and Schuster, 1951.

Gates, Frederick Taylor. *Chapters in My Life.* New York: The Free Press, 1977.

———. *The Truth About Mr. Rockefeller and the Merritts.* Privately printed. Copy in RAC.

Gay, Peter. *Freud: A Life for Our Time.* Reprint. New York: Anchor Books, 1989 [1988].

The General Education Board: An Account of Its Activities, 1902–1914. New York: GEB, 1930.

Gibb, George Sweet, and Evelyn H. Knowlton. *The Resurgent Years, 1911–1927.* New York: Harper and Brothers, 1956.

Giddens, Paul H. *Standard Oil Company (Indiana): Oil Pioneer of the Middle West.* New York: Appleton-Century-Crofts, 1955.

Gitelman, H. M. Legacy of the Ludlow Massacre: A Chapter in American Industrial Relations. Philadelphia: University of Pennsylvania Press, 1988.

Gladden, Washington. Recollections. Boston: Houghton Mifflin, 1909.

Goldstein, Judith S. Crossing Lines: Histories of Jews and Gentiles in Three Communities. New York: William Morrow and Co., 1992.

Goodspeed, Thomas Wakefield. A History of the University of Chicago: The First Quarter Century. Reprint. Chicago: University of Chicago Press, 1972 [1916].

Goulder, Grace. John D. Rockefeller: The Cleveland Years. Cleveland: Western Reserve Historical Society, 1972.

Grant, Ulysses S. Personal Memoirs of U. S. Grant. Ed. E. B. Long. New York: Da Capo, 1982 [1885].

Hannah, Barbara. Jung: His Life and Work. New York: G. P. Putnam's Sons, 1976.

Harr, John Ensor, and Peter J. Johnson. The Rockefeller Century. New York: Charles Scribner's Sons, 1988.

———. The Rockefeller Conscience: An American Family in Public and in Private. New York: Charles Scribner's Sons, 1991.

Harris, Leon. Upton Sinclair: American Rebel. New York: Thomas Y. Crowell, 1975.

Hawke, David Freeman. John D.: The Founding Father of the Rockefellers. New York: Harper and Row, 1980.

Hays, Samuel P. The Response to Industrialism: 1885–1914. Chicago: University of Chicago Press, 1957.

Hidy, Ralph W., and Muriel E. Hidy. History of Standard Oil Company (New Jersey): Pioneering in Big Business, 1882–1911. New York: Harper and Brothers, 1955.

Hiebert, Ray Eldon. Courtier to the Crowd: The Story of Ivy Lee and the Development of Public Relations. Ames, Iowa: Iowa State University Press, 1966.

"A History of the Rise and Fall of the South Improvement Company." Report of the Executive Committee of the Petroleum Producers' Union. Lancaster, Pa., 1872. Typescript in HDL.

Howells, William Dean. The Rise of Silas Lapham. Reprint. New York: W. W. Norton and Co., 1982 [1885].

Hoyt, Edwin P. The Whitneys: An Informal Portrait, 1635–1975. New York: Weybright and Talley, 1976.

Hughes, Adella Prentiss. Music Is My Life. Cleveland: World Publishing Co., 1947.

Inglis, William O. "Impressions of John D. Rockefeller." Typescript in AN.

In Memoriam: Mrs. Lucy Henry Spelman—1810–1897. Funeral Services at Forest Hill, September 9, 1897. New York: Knickerbocker Press, 1898.

Innes, Stephen. Creating the Commonwealth: The Economic Culture of Puritan New England. New York: W. W. Norton and Co., 1995.

James, Henry. The American Scene. New York: Charles Scribner's Sons, 1946 [1907].

James, William. The Correspondence of William James. Vol. 3, William and Henry, 1897–1910. Ed. Ignas K. Skrupskelis and Elizabeth M. Berkeley. Charlottesville: University Press of Virginia, 1994.

———. The Letters of William James. Vol. 2. Ed. Henry James. Boston: Atlantic Monthly Press, 1920.

————. *Selected Unpublished Correspondence, 1885–1910.* Ed. Frederick J. Down Scott. Columbus: Ohio State University Press, 1986.

Johnson, Arthur M. *Winthrop W. Aldrich: Lawyer, Banker, Diplomat.* Boston: Graduate School of Business Administration, Harvard University, 1968.

Johnson, Paul E. *A Shopkeeper's Millennium: Society and Revivals in Rochester, New York, 1815–1837.* New York: Hill and Wang, 1978.

Jonas, Gerald. *The Circuit Riders: Rockefeller Money and the Rise of Modern Science.* New York: W. W. Norton and Co., 1989.

Jones, Mary Harris. *Autobiography of Mother Jones.* Ed. Mary Field Parton. Chicago: Charles H. Kerr and Co., 1925.

————. *The Correspondence of Mother Jones.* Ed. Edward M. Steel. Pittsburgh: University of Pittsburgh Press, 1985.

Jowett, John Henry. *My Daily Meditation for the Circling Year.* New York: Fleming H. Revell Co., 1914.

Joyce, Henry. *Tour of Kykuit: The House and Gardens of the Rockefeller Family and a Property of the National Trust for Historic Preservation.* Blauvelt, N.Y.: Historic Hudson Valley Press, 1994.

Jung, C. G. *Letters.* Selected and ed. Gerhard Adler and Anieda Jaffé. Trans. R.F.C. Hull. Vol. 2, *1951–1961.* Princeton: Princeton University Press, 1976.

————. *Modern Psychology.* Notes on Lectures Given at the Eidgenössische Technische Hochschule, Zurich, October 1933–February 1934. Comp. and trans. from shorthand notes by Elizabeth Welsh and Barbara Hannah. Multigraphed typescript. Zurich, 1934–1942.

————. *Nietzsche's "Zarathustra": Notes of the Seminar Given in 1934–1939,* Vol. 1. Princeton: Princeton University Press, 1988.

Kaplan, Justin. *Mr. Clemens and Mark Twain: A Biography.* New York: Simon and Schuster, 1966.

Kert, Bernice. *Abby Aldrich Rockefeller: The Woman in the Family.* New York: Random House, 1993.

Kolko, Gabriel. *The Triumph of Conservatism: A Reinterpretation of American History, 1900–1916.* Reprint. Chicago: Quadrangle Paperbacks, 1967 [1963].

Lash, Joseph P. *Helen and Teacher: The Story of Helen Keller and Anne Sullivan Macy.* New York: Delacorte Press, 1980.

Lawson, Thomas W. *Frenzied Finance.* New York: Ridgway-Thayer, 1906.

Lewis, David Levering. *W.E.B. DuBois: Biography of a Race.* New York: Henry Holt and Co., 1993.

Lewis, R.W.B. *Edith Wharton: A Biography.* Reprint. New York: Fromm International, 1985 [1975].

————. *The Jameses: A Family Narrative.* New York: Anchor Books, 1991.

Link, William A. *The Paradox of Southern Progressivism, 1880–1930.* Chapel Hill: University of North Carolina Press, 1992.

Lloyd, Henry Demarest. *Wealth Against Commonwealth.* Reprint. Englewood Cliffs, N.J.: Prentice, Hall, 1963 [1894].

Lottman, Herbert R. *The French Rothschilds: The Great Banking Dynasty Through Two Turbulent Centuries.* New York: Crown, 1995.

Lundberg, Ferdinand. *The Rockefeller Syndrome.* Secaucus, N.J.: Lyle Stuart, 1975.

Lyon, Peter. *Success Story: The Life and Times of S. S. McClure.* New York: Charles Scribner's Sons, 1963.

Manchester, William. *A Rockefeller Family Portrait: From John D. to Nelson.* Boston: Little, Brown, 1958.

Manning, Thomas G. *The Standard Oil Company: The Rise of a National Monopoly.* Revised by E. David Cronon and Howard R. Lamar. New York: Holt, Rinehart and Winston, 1962.

Marcus, George E., with Peter Dobkin Hall. *Lives in Trust: The Fortunes of Dynastic Families in Late Twentieth-Century America.* Boulder, Colo.: Westview Press, 1992.

Marten, Hans-Georg. *Rockefeller: L'Homme le Plus Riche du Monde.* Trans. Max Roth. Paris: Buchet/Chastel, 1964.

Martin, Sidney Walter. *Florida's Flagler.* Athens, Ga.: University of Georgia Press, 1949.

Marty, Martin. *Pilgrims in Their Own Land: 500 Years of Religion in America.* Boston: Little, Brown, 1984.

McCarthy, Kathleen. *Noblesse Oblige: Charity & Cultural Philanthropy in Chicago, 1849–1929.* Chicago: University of Chicago Press, 1982.

McCormick, John. *George Santayana: A Biography.* New York: Alfred A. Knopf, 1987.

McCormick, Richard L. *The Party Period and Public Policy: American Politics from the Age of Jackson to the Progressive Era.* New York: Oxford University Press, 1986.

McFeely, William S. *Grant: A Biography.* Reprint. New York: W. W. Norton and Co., 1982 [1981].

McGovern, George S., and Leonard F. Guttridge. *The Great Coalfield War.* Boston: Houghton Mifflin, 1972.

McPherson, James M. *Battle Cry of Freedom: The Civil War Era.* Reprint. New York: Ballantine Books, 1989 [1988].

Mellon, Thomas. *Thomas Mellon and His Times.* Pittsburgh: University of Pittsburgh Press, 1994.

Mencken, H. L. *My Life as Author and Editor.* Reprint. New York: Vintage, 1995 [1992].

———. *Prejudices: Fifth Series.* New York: Alfred A. Knopf, 1926.

Miller, Nathan. *Theodore Roosevelt: A Life.* Reprint. New York: William Morrow, Quill, 1992.

Moody, John. *The Masters of Capital: A Chronicle of Wall Street.* New Haven: Yale University Press, 1919.

Moore, Austin L. "John D. Archbold and the Standard Oil Company." Typescript. AN.

Morris, Joe Alex. *Those Rockefeller Brothers: An Informal Biography of Five Extraordinary Young Men.* New York: Harper and Brothers, 1953.

Neatby, H. Blair. *William Lyon Mackenzie King: 1924–1932: The Lonely Heights.* Toronto: University of Toronto Press, 1963.

————. *William Lyon Mackenzie King: 1932–1939. The Prism of Unity.* Toronto: University of Toronto Press, 1976.

Nevins, Allan. *John D. Rockefeller: The Heroic Age of American Enterprise.* 2 vols. New York: Charles Scribner's Sons, 1940.

————. *Study in Power: John D. Rockefeller, Industrialist and Philanthropist.* 2 vols. New York: Charles Scribner's Sons, 1953.

Noll, Richard. *The Aryan Christ: The Secret Life of Carl Jung.* New York: Random House, 1997.

Packard, Roy D. "Informal History of the Standard Oil Company (Ohio) (1870–1911)." 2 vols. Typescript in archives of British Petroleum (Cleveland). July 1958.

Parker, Elizabeth C., ed. *The Cloisters: Studies in Honor of the Fiftieth Anniversary.* New York: Metropolitan Museum of Art, 1992.

Penrose, Edith T. *The International Petroleum Industry.* London: George Allen and Unwin, 1968.

Pickersgill, J. W. *The Mackenzie King Record: Volume 1, 1939–1944.* Toronto: University of Toronto Press, 1960.

Pickersgill, J. W., and D. F. Forster. *The Mackenzie King Record: Volume 3, 1945–1946.* Toronto: University of Toronto Press, 1970.

————. *The Mackenzie King Record: Volume 4, 1947–1948.* Toronto: University of Toronto Press, 1970.

Popp, Richard L. *The Presidents of the University of Chicago. A Centennial View.* Chicago: University of Chicago Library, 1992.

Pringle, Henry F. *The Life and Times of William Howard Taft.* 2 vols. New York: Farrar and Rinehart, 1939.

————. *Theodore Roosevelt: A Biography.* New York: Harcourt, Brace and Co., 1931.

Pyle, Tom, as told to Beth Day. *Pocantico: Fifty Years on the Rockefeller Domain.* New York: Duell, Sloan and Pierce, 1964.

Read, Florence Matilda. *The Story of Spelman College.* Atlanta. Printed by Princeton University Press, Princeton, N.J., 1961.

Reed, Henry Hope. *Rockefeller New York: A Tour.* New York: Greensward Foundation, 1988.

Reich, Cary. *The Life of Nelson A. Rockefeller: Worlds to Conquer, 1908–1958.* New York: Doubleday, 1996.

Roberts, Ann Rockefeller. *Mr. Rockefeller's Roads: The Untold Story of Acadia's Carriage Roads & Their Creator.* Camden, Me.: Down East Books, 1990.

Rockefeller, John D. *Random Reminiscences of Men and Events.* Tarrytown, N.Y.: Sleepy Hollow Press and RAC, 1984 [1909].

Rockefeller, John D., Jr., et al. "Addresses to Honor the Memory of Frederick Taylor Gates." Delivered at a meeting of the Rockefeller Institute for Medical Research, May 15, 1929. Privately printed. Copy in RAC.

Rockefeller, Winthrop. "A Letter to My Son." Typescript. RAC.

Rose, William Ganson. *Cleveland: The Making of a City.* Kent, Ohio: Kent State University Press, 1990.

Rousmaniere, John. *The Life and Times of the Equitable*. New York: Equitable Companies, 1995.

Rugoff, Milton. *America's Gilded Age: Intimate Portraits from an Era of Extravagance and Change, 1850–1890*. New York: Henry Holt and Co., 1989.

Russell, Bertrand. *Freedom Versus Organization, 1814 to 1914*. New York: W. W. Norton and Co., 1934.

Sampson, Anthony. *The Seven Sisters: The Great Oil Companies and the World They Shaped*. Reprint. New York: Bantam Books, 1975 [1973].

Santayana, George. *The Letters of George Santayana*. Ed. Daniel Cory. New York: Charles Scribner's Sons, 1955.

———. *Persons and Places: The Background of My Life*. New York: Charles Scribner's Sons, 1944.

Schenkel, Albert F. *The Rich Man and the Kingdom: John D. Rockefeller, Jr., and the Protestant Establishment*. Minneapolis: Fortress Press, 1995.

Schreiner, Samuel A., Jr. *Henry Clay Frick: The Gospel of Greed*. New York: St. Martin's Press, 1995.

Schumpeter, Joseph A. *Capitalism, Socialism and Democracy*. Reprint. New York: Harper Torchbooks, 1950 [1942].

Smith, James Allen. *The Idea Brokers: Think Tanks and the Rise of the New Policy Elite*. New York: The Free Press, 1991.

Smith, Theodore Clarke. *The Life and Letters of James Abram Garfield. Vol. 2, 1877–1882*. New Haven: Yale University Press, 1925.

Stampp, Kenneth M. *America in 1857: A Nation on the Brink*. New York: Oxford University Press, 1990.

Stasz, Clarice. *The Rockefeller Women: Dynasty of Piety, Privacy, and Service*. New York: St. Martin's Press, 1995.

Steffens, Lincoln. *The Autobiography of Lincoln Steffens*. New York: Harcourt, Brace and Co., 1931.

Storr, Richard J. *Harper's University: The Beginnings*. Chicago: University of Chicago Press, 1966.

Strickland, Alice. *Ormond's Historic Homes: From Palmetto-Thatched Shacks to Millionaire's Mansions*. Ormond Beach, Fla.: Ormond Beach Historical Trust, 1992.

Sullivan, Mark. *Our Times: The United States, 1900–1925. Vol. 3, Pre-War America*. New York: Charles Scribner's Sons, 1930.

Summers, Festus P. *Johnson Newlon Camden: A Study in Individualism*. New York: G. P. Putnam's Sons, 1937.

Swanberg, W. A. *Citizen Hearst: A Biography of William Randolph Hearst*. New York: Charles Scribner's Sons, 1961.

———. *Pulitzer*. New York: Charles Scribner's Sons, 1967.

———. *Whitney Father, Whitney Heiress*. New York: Charles Scribner's Sons, 1980.

Tarbell, Ida M. *All in the Day's Work: An Autobiography*. New York: Macmillan, 1939.

———. *The History of the Standard Oil Company*. 2 vols. Gloucester, Mass.: Peter Smith, 1963 [1904].

Tolf, Robert W. *The Russian Rockefellers: The Saga of the Nobel Family and the Russian Oil Industry.* Stanford, Calif.: Hoover Institution Press, 1976.

Twain, Mark. *The Autobiography of Mark Twain.* With an introduction by Albert Bigelow Paine. Vol. 1. New York: Harper and Brothers, 1924.

————. *Mark Twain in Eruption.* Ed. Bernard De Voto. New York: Harper and Brothers, 1922.

————. *Mark Twain's Correspondence with Henry Huttleston Rogers, 1893–1909.* Ed. Lewis Leary. Berkeley: University of California Press, 1969.

Twain, Mark, and Charles Dudley Warner. *The Gilded Age: A Tale of Today.* Garden City, N.Y.: Nelson Doubleday, n.d. [1873].

Veblen, Thorstein. *The Instinct of Workmanship and the State of the Industrial Arts.* Reprint. New York: Augustus M. Kelley, 1964 [1914].

————. *The Theory of the Leisure Class: An Economic Study of Institutions.* Reprint. London: George Allen and Unwin, 1924 [1899].

Wacker, Grant. *Augustus H. Strong and the Dilemma of Historical Consciousness.* Macon, Ga.: Mercer University Press, 1985.

Wall, Bennett H., and George S. Gibb. *Teagle of Jersey Standard.* New Orleans: Tulane University Press, 1974.

Wall, Joseph Frazier. *Andrew Carnegie.* New York: Oxford University Press, 1970.

Walska, Ganna. *Always Room at the Top.* New York: Richard R. Smith, 1943.

Weber, Max. *The Protestant Ethic and the Spirit of Capitalism.* Trans. Talcott Parsons. Reprint. New York: Charles Scribner's Sons, 1958 [1920].

Wells, H. G. *The Work, Wealth and Happiness of Mankind.* London: William Heinemann, 1934.

White, William Allen. *The Autobiography of William Allen White.* New York: Macmillan, 1946.

Wiebe, Robert H. *The Search for Order: 1877–1920.* New York: Hill and Wang, 1967.

Wilson, Ella Grant. *Famous Old Euclid Avenue of Cleveland.* Privately printed, 1937. Copy in Western Reserve Historical Society.

Winkelman, B. F. *John D. Rockefeller: The Authentic and Dramatic Story of the World's Greatest Money Maker and Money Giver.* Philadelphia: Universal Book and Bible House, 1937.

Winkler, John K. *John D.: A Portrait in Oils.* New York: Blue Ribbon Books, 1929.

Yergin, Daniel. *The Prize: The Epic Quest for Oil, Money, and Power.* Reprint. New York: Simon and Schuster, Touchstone, 1993 [1991].

Zweig, Phillip L. *Wriston: Walter Wriston, Citibank, and the Rise and Fall of American Financial Supremacy.* New York: Crown, 1995.

SELECTED ARTICLES

Ammann, Emile. "Driving Miss Edith." *Spring 52: A Journal of Archetype and Culture,* (1992).

Archbold, John D. "The Standard Oil Company: Some Facts and Figures." *Saturday Evening Post,* December 7, 1907.

Atwood, Albert W. "The Rockefeller Fortune." Saturday Evening Post, June 11, 1921.

Ballinger, Willis J. "The Man Who Saved an Industry." Nation's Business, April 1931.

Bedford, Edward T. "Human Side of John D. in Early Days of Standard Oil." Boston Herald, July 3, 1927.

———. "My Partner, John D." Reader's Digest. April 1927.

Briggs, H. M. "An Intimate View of John D. Rockefeller." The American Magazine, November 1910.

Chenoweth, Austin K. "Rockefeller." Middletown (Conn.) Press, April 23, 1922.

Churchill, Winston. "An Appraisal of John D. Rockefeller." St. Louis Post-Dispatch, July 8, 1936.

"Circular Letter Regarding Freight Rates on Oil, and Past and Present Discriminations in Favor of the Standard Oil Trust." Privately printed in Cleveland, Ohio, by Scofield, Shurmer, and Teagle, August 23, 1888.

Couch, W. S. "Rockefeller Urges National Development." Cleveland Plain Dealer, October 4 and 7, 1906.

Davis, Aaron. "The Responsibility of Wealth." Saturday Evening Post, May 23, 1925.

"Death of Mr. Rockefeller Recalls His Many Benefactions to Spelman." Spelman Messenger, May 1937.

Decker, Norman. "Neighbor Recalls Rockefeller's Boyhood in the Hill Country." New York Herald Tribune, June 3, 1928.

"Father and Five." Newsweek, April 28, 1958.

"First Ledger of a Successful Man of Affairs." Dunbar News, April 23, 1930.

Fistere, John Cushman. "The Rockefeller Boys." Saturday Evening Post, July 16, 1938.

"Follow the Ball and Don't Talk Too Much—John D." Salt Lake City Tribune, April 27, 1919.

Forbes, B. C. "John D. Rockefeller Tells How to Succeed." Forbes, September 29, 1917.

Fox, J. Dewitt. "How John D. Rockefeller Lived to Be 97!" These Times, December 1956.

Giddens, Paul H. "The Search for a New Illuminant and Lubricant." Titusville (Pa.) Herald, August 27, 1980.

———. "True Significance of the Drake Well." Titusville (Pa.) Herald, August 27, 1980.

———. "Why Ida M. Tarbell Wrote History of Standard Oil Company." Titusville (Pa.) Herald, August 27, 1980.

Gilcreest, Edgar Lorrington. "Rockefeller, Osler and Welch." The Argonaut, June 16, 1937.

"The Good Man." Time, September 24, 1956.

Gordon, John. "John D. Rockefeller's Right Hand: H. H. Rogers of Standard Oil." Chicago Tribune, October 23, 1904.

Heilbroner, Robert. "The Grand Acquisitor." American Heritage, December 1964.

Hellman, Geoffrey T. "Out of the Cocoon on the Fifty-sixth Floor." *The New Yorker*, November 4, 1972.

"History of Spelman Seminary." *The Home Mission Monthly*, October 1895.

"History of Spelman Seminary." *Spelman Messenger Supplement*, April 1891.

"The Human Side of John D. Rockefeller." *Woman's Home Companion*, January 1907.

"John D. Rockefeller." *New York Weekly World*, April 2, 1890.

"John D. Rockefeller Discusses Big Questions." *New York Sun*, January 11, 1914.

"John D. Rockefeller's Pocantico Estate." *The Country Calendar*, November 1905.

Jones, Roger M. "The Rockefeller Fleet." *Inland Seas—Quarterly Bulletin of the Great Lakes Historical Society*, July 1947.

Kelly, Fred C. "Tales of Rockefeller." *The World*, May 31, June 7, 14, 21, and 28, and July 5, 1925.

"The King of the Oil Trade." *New York Sun*, November 30, 1878.

Lewis, Alfred Henry. "Owners of America: John D. Rockefeller." *Cosmopolitan*, November 1908.

Lippmann, Walter. "Mr. Rockefeller on the Stand." *The New Republic*, January 30, 1915.

Lloyd, Henry Demarest. "Story of a Great Monopoly." *Atlantic Monthly*, March 1881.

Macdonald, A. B. "How I Found the Lost Father of John D. Rockefeller." *Kansas City (Mo.) Star*, May 30, 1937.

March, F. O. "The Human Side of John D. Rockefeller." *Leslie's Weekly*, May 16, 1907.

Mayo, Earl. "John D. Rockefeller—The World's First Billionaire." *Human Life*, April 1905.

McCormick, Edith, as told to Mary Dougherty. "Life as It Seemed to Me." *New York Evening Journal*, August 30–31, 1932.

McGuire, William. "Firm Affinities: Jung's Relations with Britain and the United States." *Journal of Analytical Psychology* 40 (1995).

Miller, Ernest C. "Ida Tarbell's Second Look at Standard Oil." *Western Pennsylvania Historical Magazine* 39 (Winter 1956).

"Millions to Spend and the Brains to Spend Well." *New York Daily Tribune*, February 17, 1907.

Montague, Gilbert Holland. "History of the Standard Oil Company." *North American Review*, September 1905.

Morrow, James B. "Standard Oil's First Rebate: Henry M. Flagler Tells How He Got It from President Scott." *New York Daily Tribune*, December 23, 1906.

Nevins, Allan. "Letter to the Editor About Henry Demarest Lloyd." *American Historical Review* 50 (April 1945).

"New Facts About Oil King's Father Told by Partner." *The World*, March 1, 1908.

Norden, Van. "Rockefeller: Man or Monster?" *The World Mirror*, January 1909.

Patteson, Suzanne Louise. "At Home with the Rockefellers in the Seventies." Cleveland *Plain Dealer*, February 12, 1922.

Paulson, F. M. "The House by the Side of the Road." *The Sohioan,* October 1947.

Ralph, Julian. "John Davison Rockefeller." *Cosmopolitan,* May 1902.

Randall, S. E. "A Square Deal for John D. Rockefeller." *Leslie's Weekly,* September 20, 1906.

Roan, Leonard. "Atlanta Knows the Real John D." *The Atlanta Georgia,* February 12, 1922.

Rockefeller, John D. "Giving Away Money." *Farm and Fireside,* January 6, 1917.

"Rockefeller Sees No Portent of Disaster." *The New York Times,* October 20, 1907.

"The Rockefeller Story." New York *Daily News,* August 23, 1959.

Rose, Kenneth W. "Why Chicago and Not Cleveland? The Religious Imperative Behind John D. Rockefeller's Early Philanthropy, 1855–1900." Typescript. RAC.

Sandage, Scott. " 'I do so long to save my husband': Ruined Men and Desperate Wives in Nineteenth-Century America," presented at the annual meeting of the Organization of American Historians Conference, Washington, D.C., March 1995.

Schmitt, J. P. "John D. Rockefeller as He Is and the Lesson His Life Teaches." *New Yorker Echo,* May 30, 1908.

"Secret Double Life of Rockefeller's Father Revealed by *The World.*" *The World,* February 2, 1908.

"Standard Oil Company (N.J.) Passes Half-Century Mark." *Oil, Paint and Drug Reporter,* January 19, 1920.

"The Standard Oil Melons." *The Literary Digest,* October 28, 1922.

Stapleton, Darwin H. "Religion, Reform, Race and Rockefeller: Cleveland History Viewed Through the Lens of Philanthropy." Typescript. RAC.

Steffens, Lincoln. "Rhode Island: A State for Sale." *McClure's Magazine,* February 24, 1905.

Tarbell, Ida M. "John D. Rockefeller: A Character Study." *McClure's Magazine,* July and August 1905.

———. "The Oil Age." *McClure's Magazine,* November 1924.

Train, Arthur. "Rockefeller Challenges Capital." *Hearst's International,* July 1923.

Vandegrift, Josephine. "*Brooklyn Citizen* Writer Spends a Week with John D. Rockefeller on Vacation." *Brooklyn Citizen,* March 4, 1923.

Wallis, Louis. "Mr. Rockefeller's Dilemma." *Harper's Weekly,* November 8, 1913.

Ware, Louise. "The Rockefeller Benefactions." *Seminar Report,* May 20, 1937.

Waters, Deborah Dependahl. "Guide to the Rockefeller Rooms." Typescript. The Museum of the City of New York, April 1993.

"What Rockefeller Thinks of Rockefeller." *The World,* March 7, 1915.

"What the Town That Makes Him Shudder Thinks of John D. Rockefeller." *The World,* November 1, 1903.

White, Clarice F. "Over Fifty Years a Cleveland Doctor." Cleveland *Plain Dealer,* December 7, 1919.

Williamson, Samuel T. "The Rockefeller Boys." *The New York Times Magazine,* April 9, 1939.

Wills, Garry. "Sons and Daughters of Chicago." *New York Review of Books,* June 9, 1994.

Wilson, George, and N. W. Winkelman. "Generalized Alopecia." *Journal of the American Medical Association,* May 8, 1926.

Winkler, John K. "Notes on a Well-Known Citizen." *The New Yorker,* January 22 and 29, 1927.

Woodbury, Charles J. "Rockefeller and His Standard: Some of the Unwritten Rules He Enforced." *Saturday Evening Post,* October 21, 1911.

INDEX